THE PACIFIC RIM ALMANAC

THE PACIFIC RIM ALMANAC

❖

Edited and Written by
ALEXANDER BESHER

Associate Editor, John Wilcock

HarperPerennial
A Division of HarperCollinsPublishers

For permissions information, see p. 825.

Library of Congress Cataloging-in-Publication Data

Besher, Alexander.
   The Pacific Rim almanac/edited and written by Alexander Besher; associate editor, John Wilcock.
      p.   cm.
   Includes index.
   ISBN 0-06-271524-0—ISBN 0-06-273065-7 (pbk.)
   1. Pacific Area—Commerce—Handbooks, manuals, etc.   2. Investments—Pacific Area—Handbooks, manuals, etc. 3. Marketing—Pacific Area—Handbooks, manuals, etc. 4. Finance—Pacific Area—Handbooks, manuals, etc.   5. Pacific Area—Economic conditions —Handbooks, etc.   I. Wilcock, John.   II. Title.
   HF4030.7.Z6B47   1991
   382′.099—dc20   90-55996

91   92   93   94   95   DT/RRD   10   9   8   7   6   5   4   3   2   1

For Françoise
and
For Nicholas
and for the rest of the Family
everywhere

CONTENTS

FOREWORD

Ten years ago, the term Pacific Rim and Pacific Basin were familiar mostly to oceanographers and geographers. Where the average American thought of Europe and "Atlantic" as somehow "close," because of traditional and emotional (as much as geographic) ties, "Pacific" suggested something more romantic—and far more remote. As far as the Asian nations on the Pacific's western banks, the attitude was all too often one of suspicion and hostility. The very word "Pacific" symbolized for many, ironically, a theater of war.

Over the past decade, our sense of the Pacific has changed rapidly. More people started thinking of the ocean as an avenue to peaceful trade and travel rather than war, as a huge neighborhood of related peoples rather than remote or hostile ones, as something to work in rather than visit. The catalyst for change was the continuing revolution in transportation and communications which, almost without our realizing it, was turning an old geographical barrier into a new economic and social highway.

In 1981, The Pacific Basin Institute edited and produced the *Whole Pacific Catalog,* a new kind of publication designed to interest readers in some of the people, places, contrivances, movements, situations and events which make the new Pacific world an exciting community. Just ten years later, Alexander Besher has far exceeded our original effort with this comprehensive, absorbing, and highly imaginative *Pacific Rim Almanac.* I

know of few people who have been able to acquire so much information about the Pacific Rim and its cultures and peoples and describe them so interestingly as Mr. Besher. We have here not only an awesome amount of factual information on the entire Pacific area, with the accent on business and economics, but Mr. Besher and his fellow editor have also assembled a fascinating collection of odd and interesting facts which will repay the browser's attention.

For the past ten years, a good bit of my own activity has focused on the objective of making Americans aware of not merely how much American culture, economics and policy affects peoples on the other side of the Pacific, but how much and in how many diverse ways their cultures, economics and activities affect us. What used to be thought of as an impassible ocean barrier has become in every sense of the word a huge two-way street.

Knowing from experience the difficulties of juggling unities and diversities in this way, I can doubly appreciate Mr. Besher's achievement. I would recommend this book unhesitatingly for anyone with an interest in this area. And if a reader doesn't already have some interest in the area, a look at this book will impel him to acquire one.

Frank B. Gibney
President
Pacific Basin Institute

ACKNOWLEDGMENTS

The Pacific Rim Almanac could never have been completed without the support and assistance of numerous individuals and organizations.

Assisting with an initial sponsorship grant which made possible some of the editorial research were the Walden Group of Venture Capital Funds, the Momenta Corporation, Microscience International Corp., and Io Publishing. Lip-Bu Tan and Robert Chou of Walden and Kamran Elahian all shared in the vision of the Pacific Rim as a catalyst for global change. David Bunnell of Io is himself a living catalyst.

On the technology side, I would like to thank Apple Computer Corp. and Ricoh Corp. for supporting the project with a loan of their state-of-the-art computing, scanning, fax, and office equipment. At Apple, I would like to thank Pam Miracle, Keri Walker, and Doedy Hunter. At Ricoh, I would like to thank Tomoko Kikuchi, director of the Ricoh Software Research Center. Caere Corp. provided their OmniPage scanning software that worked with Apple's scanner.

On the editorial side, I would like to thank Jack Maisano, publisher and editor-in-chief of the Hong Kong-published Asian Business magazine for his tremendous vote of confidence and support—and for generously sharing material, including the Asian Investment Guide and the Asia 2000 report. Similarly, I would like to extend my deepest appreciation to the following people and organizations:

Business International Asia/Pacific Ltd. and Bill Henderson for generous use of Marcel Toussaint's marvelous charts from BI's The New Asian Market Atlas, 1988 Edition (the 1991 edition will be appearing this year); the Washington-D.C. published magazine Export Today, for sharing their special report on Pacific Rim trade in the 1990s; Herb Berkowitz of The Heritage Foundation and Thomas J. Timmons, research associate at the foundation's Asian Studies Center, for their special version of U.S. and Asia: Statistical Handbook; Roy Howard, publisher of Asian Advertising & Marketing Magazine in Hong Kong for his support and use of annual Asian marketing review; Charles T. Whipple, publisher of the Tokyo-based Japan Free Press, for sharing his newsletter, which is one of the finest sources on Japanese culture and society; Lewis H. Young, president and editorial director of the Hong Kong-published Far East Business; Berton Woodward, senior editor of Asiaweek, for all his support; Amitabha Chowdhury, chief executive editor of the Hong Kong-published Asian Finance magazine, for use of their Top 50 Asian companies list; the East–West Center in Honolulu for their consistent support and use of their South Pacific resource materials; the Asia Foundation and Pacific Basin Economic Conference; Gordon Feller of Integrated Strategies for his Soviet Rim expertise; William Grindley of Pacific Strategies for his Latin American know-how; Phillip Ruthven of Melbourne, Australia's IBIS Group for his visionary input; Max Wyman in Vancouver for his grasp on the new Rim art fusion; Walden Bello of Food First in San Francisco; Sanjoy Chowdhury, the Asian economic analyst at Merrill Lynch Pierce, Fenner & Smith in Singapore; to Bernie Krisher of Tokyo for his wonderful help and access to *Focus* magazine; Jimmy Yapp, an early supporter and now retired editor of the *Sing Tao International* newspaper in Hong Kong; to Robert Yahng of Baker & McKenzie, who helped move the Rim for me; John Chan for being a liaison to the Asian-American electronics industry; Chin-Ning Chu and Curt Paulson; and Leonard Koren for his compassionate expertise and insight and support.

I would like to thank my dear friends Joachim and Jenny Burger, Hans and Ellen Stettler, as well as Ernie Beyl for his years of forbearance and support, Freuda Bartlett, George Csicsery, Joe Holzer and Margaret Hoshimi, Pat Bertrand, Alex Caceres of Dynamic EverChange for faithfully delivering laserprinter cartridges in times of need, Suzanne Head of the Rainforest Action Network, plus special thanks to Renee Wildman and Cynthia Maslanik for being such good friends. If I've forgotten anyone, please forgive me.

To John Wilcock, old soul and veteran writer and video producer of Asia, Europe, Latin America, the Middle East, and all points between, eternal gratitude for invaluable help on the book.

The author acknowledges the kind permission of Chronicle Features to reprint from my recent syndicated "Pacific Rim" columns. I am personally grateful to Stuart Dodds, a gentleman and a scholar, for his support over the years.

Lastly, I could not have prevailed without the support of my patient and loving family, who made sure I had both feet on the Rim at all times—and who tolerated my lapses when I didn't.

Alexander Besher
San Francisco

INTRODUCTION

ON THE RIM OF FIRE

Before the Pacific Rim became an economic buzzword in the 1980s, it was a term used by geologists to describe the "ring of fire"—that chain of ruptures, earthquake faults, and volcanoes, which encircles the Pacific Ocean.

These days, the energy that gives the Rim its dynamism springs not from molten rock and steam, but from the presence of a vast, powerful, and interconnected economic and cultural community.

"Pacific Rim" has now become a term that is more commonly used to describe a sweeping circle—a "rim of the wheel" which encompasses Southeast Asia, northeast Asia including the Soviet Far East, Australasia and the South Pacific, New Zealand, Papua New Guinea, Latin America, and the West Coast of North America right up to Canada. It represents a $3 trillion market, which is growing at the rate of an estimated $3 billion a week.

Not only is it the fastest growing region of the world—in terms of GNP growth, population, resource endowment, trade share, and industrial capacity—but its growth continues to accelerate dramatically. Here are some amazing facts:

Today, Japan controls more than 41% of the world's financial assets, while the region as a whole accounts for an estimated 65% of the world's total wealth. The combined Asia-Pacific economies are projected to grow to about twice the size of a post-1992 "unified Europe," reaching an estimated $13 trillion by the beginning of the next millennium. Furthermore, interregional Asian trade, which has been growing by about 12% a year, is expected to surpass the region's $250 billion in two-way trade with the United States by 1991.

Yet most Americans—even those who are engaged in doing business with Pacific Rim countries—remain woefully uninformed about the region as a whole or even in terms of individual countries. For example, many Americans can't tell the difference between Hong Kong and Singapore, Indonesia and Malaysia, Australia and New Zealand, or between Taiwan and Thailand.

Basic facts of history, culture, and social customs—essential to the success of any business transactions or for the cultivation of interpersonal relations—elude them. If anything, they see the region as a sort of amorphous, homogeneous entity—perhaps highlighted by a few higher-profile nations, such as Japan, South Korea, and China.

In a survey conucted by the National Geographic Society in 1989, less than 33% of Americans surveyed could even identify Japan on the world map. "Have you heard of the lost generation?" asked Gilbert Grosvenor, president of the society. "We have found them. They are lost. They haven't the faintest idea where they are."

The Pacific Rim Almanac will fill that information vacuum. It is the first popular compendium of informative, useful, and entertaining facts about the entire Asia-Pacific region. It is designed to be used as an essential reference source for the general reader as well as for the international business and financial community.

The basic structure of the *Almanac* is that it can be assimilated randomly, starting at the back or in the middle, or even at the beginning of the book, as the need arises. It contains over 2,000 items of information, including comprehensive overviews, analyses, articles, interviews, quotes, lists, and a smattering of insightful Asian proverbs, as well as mini-excerpts from historical travelogs written by early Rim travelers.

The purpose of all this organized data is to provide nuggets of information—sort of the "minitrends" of the Pacific Rim—which will enable readers to more easily grasp the "megatrends" of the overall picture on their own. Hopefully, as a result, they will come away with a deeper and more personal understanding of the "living context" of the region.

Because the Pacific Rim is essentially a "trade-driven" phenomenon, the nine sections of the *Almanac* have been arranged in the following sequence: Marketing, Trade, Money, Work, Life on the Rim, Ecology & Environment, The South Pacific Rim, Information (Technology & Communications), Infrastructure (Cities, Transportation, & Travel), and The Future.

The appendices in the back of the book feature indispensible reference material, including country-by-country statistical background information, lists of private and semigovernmental trade and research organizations, a ranking of the "PacRim Top 500 Companies," as well as a complete "Asian Investment Guide," covering finance and investment throughout the entire region, among other things.

FROM THE SILK ROAD TO THE SILICON ROAD

There is yet another dimension to the Pacific Rim besides business and trade which the *Almanac* seeks to address—and that is a vision of the Rim in a global context as a technocultural phenomenon, as a catalyst for global change.

To gain a perspective on what global role the region will play in the future, it may be useful to draw upon some historical parallels.

More than 2,500 years ago, caravans carrying silks, teas, and spices plied the ancient Silk Road from India to China. Those early exports made their way from the Middle Kingdom to the rest of Asia, Eurasia, and to Europe. That was the original Pacific Rim trade of its day. It flourished, with intermittent political disruptions, from about 3 B.C. to about 1600 A.D., when the sea routes finally displaced the traffic on the well-worn camel tracks of Central Asia.

Those nascent commercial links between East and West resulted in much more than the mere distribution of consumer goods or state-of-the-art technologies, such as printing and gunpowder.

Equally important, but perhaps less visible, the seeds of culture and of religion—exemplified by the teachings of Buddhism—also traveled along the same route from India to China before becoming diffused throughout the region.

Later, China's own unique sociopolitical system of Confucianism was exported abroad and became adopted as a state cult by Asian societies such as Japan and Korea. Indeed, the Confucian model has been cited as a major factor behind the success of the modern Pacific Rim trading dynamos, including Japan and the so-called "Four Tigers" (the NIEs, or "newly industrializing economies" of Taiwan, Singapore, Hong Kong, and South Korea).

Today, a similar diffusion of cultures is taking place—this time not on the Silk Road of days gone by, but along the new "Silicon Road." The difference is that the caravans of the 1990s travel the "on-line," and not the overland route, via optic fiber cables and satellite transmissions. The treasures which they bear include "real time" data and electronic fund transfers, along with subtle cultural and philosophical inputs.

Moreover, this Silicon Road traffic is definitely traveling *both* ways—from East to West and vice versa. These transcultural influences are unmistakably synergistic. They embrace everything from Japanese finance to Burmese cuisine; from Korean martial arts to Balinese music; from Malay systems of dream analysis to holistic Chinese medicine; and from Confucian group-think to American-style democracy, which is held in particularly high esteem by the NIEs as they evolve from state-run economies into distinctly Asian-style democracies during this pivotal decade of the 1990s.

Slowly, but surely, we are witnessing the emergence of a "Pacific Matrix"—a cross-cultural template that is developing from this fusion of East–West cultures. It is as much a new mindset as it is a new way of doing business.

The Pacific Matrix person may have been born in Taipei, but raises their venture capital in Singapore, has a manufacturing business in Hong Kong or in South China's special economic zones, while maintaining a residence in Southern California or in Vancouver, British Columbia. Or they may be Anglo-Saxon Rim dwellers who commute on business between Manila and Seoul, but who choose to reside in Tokyo or in Bangkok.

As we enter the twenty-first century, this new Pacific Matrix promises to impact not only regional trade, but is also likely to have

profound implications for the way that people live, think, commute interregionally, raise their children, deal with the environment, and view the world.

FROM THE PACIFIC RIM TO THE GLOBAL RIM

However, we don't need to look too far into the future to see what global changes have been spawned by the burgeoning Pacific Rim trade of the past decade.

Perhaps one of the most crucial changes of the twentieth century may be directly attributed to what the Rim has wrought in terms of its economic miracles. This has been the shift from the old Cold War era of geopolitical confrontation to an evolving world order based on new geoeconomic paradigms. The most dramatic symbol of the shedding of the old geopolitical skin of the world, of course, is the dismantling of the Communist system in the East bloc.

The Soviet Union, historically a Euro-Asian nation if there ever was one, has been drawn resolutely into the trade melee sparked by the Pacific Rim-driven trade revolution of the 1980s. Strategically, the USSR sees a viable solution to its dire economic woes in the development of its incredibly rich Pacific coastal regions—lands which can only be developed through the investment participation of its cash-rich Asian neighbors and former foes, including South Korea, Taiwan, and Japan.

With the lessening of tensions in the region, the area surrounding the Sea of Japan, which borders North and South Korea, the Soviet Union, China, and Japan, promises to become transformed from a one-time military hot spot into an oasis of North Asian trade.

Following the footsteps of the Soviet

Union, the Communist nations of the Indochina Rim are being gradually propelled onto the economic globalization path, although monolithic China remains temporarily stuck in a totalitarian time-warp, as the Chinese people wait for their geriatric rulers to succumb to the call of their ancestors. Meanwhile, Latin America strives to emulate the economic models of Japan and the Four Tigers.

Even the European Community, in its quest for economic unification in 1992, has been in no small part influenced in its drive by its response to the perceived economic threat from Asia's trade dynamos. As Australian futurist Phillip Ruthven put it, "It is an acknowledgement that Europe has lost its economic and technological dynamism and that leadership in these areas has passed elsewhere."

Essentially, thanks largely to the enduring economic and technological changes brought about by the Pacific Rim, the world is now entering into a new era in which all ideologies are disappearing—including socialism and raw capitalism. It is too simplistic to describe what is happening in the world as the triumph of the Western capitalist system over Communism. In fact, the drastic changes in Eastern Europe more than likely presage the sweeping changes that will inevitably be felt in the West as well.

It is, of course, too early to tell exactly what form these changes will assume. With all the pitfalls of shedding the old order for the new, it may not be a perfectly smooth transition into the much vaunted "Pacific Century," at least not initially.

Protectionism, threats of regional trade blocs, environmental concerns, and the growing gap between the rich, the developing, and the hopelessly third-world nations will probably dominate the attention of the global media.

Other expressions of economic confrontation may seem as ominous and threatening in their own way as the missile-packed silos of the Cold War. Economic hawks on opposing sides of the Pacific—or the Atlantic—may declaim threats to their nations' economic security; and new doomsday scenarios may feature the specter of Trade Wars, including devastating Pearl Harbor-style economic strikes and monetary battle rivaling in intensity those of Guadalacanal or Corregidor during the First Pacific War of 1941–1945.

Add a few natural catastrophes, like a super-earthquake which devastates Tokyo or the West Coast, and the world's interrelated global markets will cause further economic havoc in addition to untold human suffering.

Not that any of these grim events are likely to occur. They are simply the ever-present negative static that define the parameters of the Silicon Road. As the Chinese proverb notes, "Make ready the coffin and the patient is certain to live."

It is all part of the journey on the Silicon Road as we seek to reach the Global Rim on the other side of the next century.

Alexander Besher
San Francisco, 1990

SOURCES: For statistics about interregional Asian trade and growth of Asian economies, the article "What 1992 Europe Means to the Pacific Rim," by Phillip Ruthven, executive director, The IBIS Group, Melbourne, Australia, 1989.

For description of the Ring of Fire, "PacRim 2010," report by Hank Koehn, Los Angeles, 1986.

For history of the Silk Road, *Encyclopedia of Asian History,* prepared under the auspices of The Asia Society, Ainslie T. Embree, editor-in-chief, Charles Scribner's Sons, Macmillan Publishing Co., New York, 1988.

1

◆

MARKETING

DOWN UNDER DEMAND

What are the goods and the brands that Australians buy most? According to *The Australian Magazine,* here's what they went for the most in 1988:

During a typical day, many of Australia's 16.8 million population will sit down to a breakfast of Sanitarium Weet-Bix, Tip Top white bread, and a cup of Lipton's tea and then head off for lunch to Australian's favorite takeaway, McDonald's, which served 84 million customers. They also love Heinz baked beans for breakfast, with more than 58 million cans sold.

The national campaign to "buy Australian" has not caused much guilt. They still buy French perfume, Japanese cars, Taiwanese shoes, and Korean microwaves. It seems that as long as something works, Australians don't care where it comes from.

More than $25 million worth of Vegemite (which some non-Australian food critics have described as tasting like organic axle-grease) was bought, accounting for 90% of Australia's yeast-extract market.

More than 900,000 Australians were loyal to Speedo's Great Aussie Cossie swimbriefs, but the men were the best customers, buying 600,000 of the total figure.

Outside the United States, the Aussies were Garfield's top fans in 1988. The sticky "Stuck On You" Garfield doll won more than 250,000 Australians. Student Travel Australia's top destination for young travelers—more than 3,500—was Bali.

Ken Done products range from bed linen to fashion accessories. Almost 30,000 "Digger Koala" T-shirts were sold. Of the 22 million condoms sold in Australia in 1988, the Checkmate brand accounted for more than half the sales. Moet et Chandon Champagne was the most popular French champagne. And Levi Strauss would be happy to know his 1850 brainchild ranks No. 1 in Australia. Red Tab Levis are the nation's best-sellers.

While each State remains loyal to its own local brew—XXXX in Queensland, Toohey's in New South Wales, and VB in Victoria—Foster's was Australia's No. 1 amber fluid with a grip on 16% (13.2 million liters) of the total beer market. The best-selling drill was

Black and Decker's, which sold more than 17,500 at $75 each.

Swatch watches were an instant best-seller when they came on the market and have already sold more than one million in Australia. Peter Carey's "Oscar and Lucinda" was the most popular Australian novel that year—95,000 copies were sold.

SAO biscuits—the name is popularly thought to be an acronym for Salvation Army Officer—have been around for 82 years. The Aussies bought 572 million of them in 1988.

Launched in 1959, OMO has been the No. 1 laundry detergent since 1972. About 40% of households in Australia own at least one pair of Reebok running and sport shoes.

Australians are the highest consumers of shampoo in the world and Pears was the No. 1 brand. Aussies each eat an average 4.8 kg of chocolate each year. They munched their way through 110 million Kit Kats in 1988.

KOREANS FOR CARDIN

After years of austerity and workaholic habits, South Koreans are turning to consumerism, taking long-delayed vacations, wearing fancy, imported clothes, and buying more cars at home than they export. But, writes *Washington Post* columnist Peter Maas, this "relatively sudden release of affluence in a country that could not feed or clothe itself a generation ago is causing remarkable behavior shifts . . . creating self-doubts and turmoil."

With an annual average income of about $4,000, there is still enormous disparity in lifestyles between chauffeur-driven businessmen and farmers lacking indoor plumbing, and it is doubtful how much the economy gains by investment in high-priced designer goods.

"The consumption level is higher than reasonable—we need national wealth for investment instead of purchasing $3000 clothes," says Shin Byung II. "It's good for my business but, frankly, it's not good for the Korean economy." The disparity in lifestyles is part of the reason many people have misgivings about the 30% jump in imports of consumer goods, Maas writes. "There is also a feeling that the champagne corks are popping a bit too soon."

JAPAN'S NEW CONSUMERS

A study of Japan's young singles by *American Demographics,* a publishing subsidiary of the Dow Jones Co., concluded that "wrapping the minimum amount of work around their play schedule" is a generational preoccupation: Roughly double the number of young adults over middle-aged adults supported such attitudes as "heart-over-head" in decision-making. Being noticed is all important and Life is to be enjoyed, according to figures compiled by the Hakuhodo Institute of Life and Living Study concerning young adults in Japan.

Young people seeking an "individual" lifestyle seem to predominate, although cynical market analysts see them as the prototype of the future Japanese consumer. "Being different takes on different proportions in Japan than in the U.S. Young Japanese, for the most part, are not prepared to go out on a limb,"

4-20 Sales of Japan's Nine Sogo Shosha (FY 1989)
(¥ billion)

	Total	In Japan	Exports from Japan	Imports into Japan	Offshore Trade
C. Itoh	20,533	9,867	2,937	3,386	4,343
Mitsui	20,300	7,000	3,553	4,524	5,222
Sumitomo	21,404	8,175	4,591	5,298	3,340
Marubeni	18,248	6,965	3,014	3,463	4,806
Mitsubishi	16,614	7,267	2,495	3,152	3,701
Nissho Iwai	15,047	4,404	2,003	4,346	4,295
Tomen	6,324	3,185	712	1,162	1,265
Nichimen	5,893	1,850	670	984	2,389
Kanematsu-Gosho	5,502	1,430	863	2,420	789
Total	**129,866**	**50,142**	**20,836**	**28,736**	**30,151**
Share (%)	100.0	38.6	16.1	22.1	23.2

Source: Japan Foreign Trade Council, Inc.

comments the report on Japanese consumers, which points to specific popular magazines as being the determinant of behavior.

Popeye boys, for example, see themselves as kooky individualists; *An-an* boys and girls are stylishly elegant; *Non-no* girls project innocence and feminity; and *JJ* boys and girls are preppies.

Japanese youth create a network of friends in separate, non-overlapping groups, so they can express different aspects of their personality within each group, playing tennis with some, shopping or traveling with others. The previous generation's penchant for radical thought and student activism has been replaced by a quest for novelty and an interest in fashion and other superficialities.

Socializing is done in large, mixed groups, with dating relationships taking place later than in the U.S. An unusual amount of attention is devoted to doing things exactly right, from wearing the appropriate skiing or scuba-diving equipment to which hotels to stay in.

"The time is ripe for American manufacturers to market in Japan," declared "Japan's New Consumers," a special report published by *American Demographics* in 1985 as part of a series about foreign consumer markets.

"Buying U.S. products makes Japanese youths feel American and that's just what they want right now." Whereas their parents preferred prestigious, brand-name exports representing tradition and elegance, their children go for American novelty and sportiness. Nevertheless, purchases are rarely made spontaneously but only after careful advance study and research.

Most young singles live in one room and this contains all their possessions resulting in a preference among youth for things "smaller, lighter and thinner." According to the Hakuhodo survey quoted in the consumer report, young men tended to spend more on personal enjoyment, young women more on self-improvement.

One of the strongest consumer groups, young working women who live at home with their parents, have good incomes with as much as $500 discretionary spending each month. (As for young men, the *Japan Times* estimated recently that the average 20-year-old who worked only part-time spent an average of $312 monthly on clothes; and a new line of male cosmetics by the Shiseido Company made $25 million in its first four months.)

Travel, both domestically, to the mountains for skiing and hiking, and abroad is commonplace, with at least 20% of Japanese overseas tourists being women in their twenties. Over 50% of all young Japanese men owned cars by 1980, and the 68,000 cars imported from abroad in 1986 was a 36% increase over the previous year. These young singles (aged 20 to 29) together with the empty-nesters (aged 45 to 59) are the major consumer groups to watch for in the 1990s, forecasts "Japan's New Consumers"

"The new young Japanese would rather work to live than live to work," editor Denise Rusoff commented. "The new crop of workers are markedly less ready to submerge their personal ambitions and private lives to the success of the company . . . Practical, easygoing and disturbingly money-minded . . . a surprising (number) said they wanted to start up their own businesses at some time in their careers."

From observations so far, young people getting married today tend to become as frugal as their parents, many abandoning their earlier leisure-oriented lifestyles and instead saving for a home despite the fact that skyrocketing land prices have placed this beyond the reach of the average salary worker in Tokyo. Young, urban professional couples without children often indulge themselves, however, in gourmet dining, overseas jaunts, imported cars, and concerts. Typical young executives of large corporations earn about $2000 monthly, some much more, and many are delaying parenthood to sustain spendthrift lifestyles.

Japan's married couples between the ages of 45 and 59 whose children have left home—"empty-nesters"—are increasing constantly as members of the postwar baby boom enter middle age, and this category is expected to account for 44% of consumption expenditures by 1990.

They are prime candidates for luxury imports despite the fact they see themselves as poor because of their grueling workdays, long commutes, and scant family life. Some Japanese analysts feel they have a psychological aversion to spending because of their deep roots in the work and saving ethic. This older generation of Japanese worker is accustomed to clocking in 454 hours more per year than a German (285 more hours than an American) and is content with 10 days annual vacation.

Whatever change in habits that might occur will likely be spearheaded by the women, who have turned increasingly to self-improvement courses and cultural activities. As for their aimless, retired husbands who never established a household niche during their working years, they are now "the bane of middle-aged Japanese women's existence," suggests "Japan's New Consumers." There is even a name for them: *sodai gomi* or "giant garbage husbands."

CANNED CHEWING GUM

A new packing method enabling canned betel nuts to be exported around the world is bringing prosperity to a Taiwanese manufacturer. Sometimes called "the chewing gum of China," betel nuts have hitherto been packed in unwieldy casks with preservatives.

RICH BLEND OF TAIWANESE COFFEE

In "rich Taiwan," coffee is now selling for $7 a cup at many large hotels in Taipei, according to a Tourism Bureau survey.

TEA TIME IN PAKISTAN

Pakistan is one of the world's biggest tea consumers, with imports exceeding 87,000 tons per year. Per capita consumption of tea in the country is about 1 kg per person a year. Its neighbors, India and Bangladesh, two significant producers of tea, consume much less than Pakistan on a per capita basis, according to tea industry analysts in Islamabad. Tea is used as part of food in northern Pakistan, especially in its hilly areas, where it is consumed along with bread.

SOFT DRINKS OF INDIA

But is it the real thing? In the hot Indian subcontinent, giants of the soft drinks industry—Parle, Duke's, Pure Drinks, and Indo Lowenbrau—spend millions marketing Thums Up, Mangola, Limca, Gold Spot, Campa Cola, and Thril sodas. But soft drink pirates are stealing the fizz from their bottom lines by tapping into about 50% of the market with counterfeit soft drinks. An estimated 1,000 or more illicit companies share an approximate Rs *crore* (about U.S. $3.6 million) between them annually. The trouble is, they use cheap and sometimes dangerous ingredients, including unpurified tap water or even well water. With an investment as little as Rs 7,000 (about U.S. $420) and second-hand bottling equipment, they're in business.

BEATING THE HEAT IN BANGKOK

In Bangkok, there are said to be only three seasons a year—hot, hotter, and hottest—which makes Thailand a prime market for soft drinks. Pepsi and Coca Cola are the leaders in the soft drinks market, with Pepsi holding a 60% share of the market with sales of 2.34 billion *baht*. The total soft drink market is estimated to be worth about 7.5 billion *baht*. Freshly squeezed orange juice sold by street vendors is another favorite Thai drink—served Thai-style with the addition of salt to replenish the body's supplies. Thais are also partial to *kafe oleang,* coffee with sweetened condensed milk and served with ice, or *kafe yen,* plain black coffee with sugar and ice.

Gatorade, an American electrolyte drink marketed by Quaker Oats, has been launched onto the Thai market with an extra-sweet taste to suit Thai preferences.

Also popular cooling agents in Thailand's hot and humid climate are talcum powders. Thais smother themselves with the fine white powder both to cool down and to prevent the blazing sun from darkening their skin. There are three distinct talcum powder markets—baby powder, mentholated powder, and cosmetic powder. Mentholated candies are also popular for their cooling properties.

THE SUDS OF PHNOM PENH

One of the hottest selling commodities in Phnom Penh, capital of war-ravaged Cambodia, is imported beer. It is said you can get beer from anywhere in the world in the city's restaurants and hotel bars. An estimated one million cans of foreign beer are consumed here each month, according to *Asian Advertising & Marketing* magazine. In a city where the average monthly income is about $5, consumers apparently think little of paying as much as $1.50 for a single can of their favorite brand, which just happens to be Heineken.

News about the unexplained popularity of Heineken (there has never been any organized marketing campaign of the beer in Cambodia) has only recently reached the Dutch brewer's Asian headquarters in Singapore. The firm is now said to be negotiating to set up a brewery either in Phnom Penh or in the southern Cambodian port of Kompong Som. Most of the Heineken beer reaching Cambodia is smuggled in across the border from Thailand. But the Cambodian government has also been engaged in importing the beer from Singapore, via the Vietnamese capital and port city of Ho Chi Minh, and up the Mekong River to Phnom Penh. The Cambodians prefer to drink their beer with ice, at any hour of the day or night, including breakfast.

IT'S THE REAL TIANGFU

Brand-consciousness is on the rise in the People's Republic of China. The Xingfu is Chin-

a's most popular motorcycle, with sales of 90,000 units of its 250cc model in 1988. The Shanghai company entered into a technical agreement with Honda to produce a line of 125cc motorcycles. They're looking for export markets, and are test-marketing in Nigeria and South America. Now China's biggest cola maker, Tiangfu Cola, is aiming to beat Coca Cola in the Chinese market. Production of Tiangfu has increased 60-fold since 1982. Chinese authorities also busted a ring of counterfeit brewers who have been producing a fake Tsingtao beer, China's internationally acclaimed brew.

COMPARISON OF WORLD-FAMOUS AND JAPAN-FAMOUS BRANDS

Landor Associates, the San Francisco-headquartered design firm, announced the results of an international brand awareness survey among 3,000 respondents in Europe, Japan, and the United States in 1988. Here are the top 10:

Worldwide	*Japan*
1. Coca-Cola	Takashimaya department store
2. IBM	Coca-Cola
3. SONY	National electronics products
4. Porsche	SONY
5. McDonald's	Toyota
6. Disney	NTT (Nippon Telegraph & Telephone)
7. Honda	JAL (Japan Air Lines)
8. Toyota	ANA (All Nippon Airways)
9. Seiko	Hattori Seiko watches
10. BMW	Shiseido cosmetics

ASIAN BRANDS STRUGGLE FOR RECOGNITION
by Brian Caplen

Trying hard—but Daewoo was still number 668 out of a list of 672 in a U.S. survey.

"Who? Daewoo that's who." This snatch from the advertising campaign of one of Korea's top companies sums up how far many Asian firms have gone when it comes to recognition overseas. Nowhere.

In a recent survey, Daewoo came a miserable fourth from bottom in a list of 672 brand names tested for U.S. consumer awareness. Its close neighbors in obscurity were Blue Mountain pet food and Ricola cough drops.

Daewoo made about U.S. $24 billion in 1987. It may, as its ads say, "have gone from mini technology to micro technology in just 20 years"—a reference to its humble origins as a small textile company—but the fact remains that in downtown Los Angeles, it's a complete unknown.

Things aren't much better for Asian companies in Europe. While Germany's major personal computer magazine *Chip* is crammed with Taiwanese product ads, their status, apart from Acer, remains strictly as "no-name clones."

Korea's Samsung may have spent U.S. $600,000 sponsoring Cologne's soccer team and have its image cast, literally, in stone at London's Heathrow airport. But still, to the British housewife, Samsung does not *mean* microwave ovens in the same way that Hoover means vacuum cleaners.

In fact, as far as Western consumers are concerned, Asian goods from anywhere except Japan continue to be regarded as cheap copies. Homes are crammed full of "Made in Taiwans" and "Made in Koreas," but because so many of the products are sold under international names, few realize they are there.

In one sense, the Asian manufacturers that supply mass merchandisers such as Sears and K-Mart, or original equipment manufacturers (OEM), such as Philips and IBM, are laughing all the way to the bank. They get their profits without any of the enormous marketing costs.

But there are dangers for the Asians who are stuck in the OEM role. Buyers are notoriously fickle. They will switch suppliers at the drop of a currency or the adjustment of a quota. Taiwan's footwear and toy manufacturers have already seen this happen.

A brand name equals power. If the market knows a manufacturer's product and asks for it by name, the supplier, not the buyer, is calling the shots.

Further, an established name sells not only the line it is associated with, but also shifts a whole range of items. This is the niche Hyundai is trying to exploit through its opening into the U.S. market with its Pony, Excel, and Stellar cars.

"Hyundai motor cars now have a good reputation in the U.S. market. If we can build a quality image through Hyundai cars, that image will be helpful in marketing Hyundai personal computers and other products," explains company PR manager Park Il-kwon.

By contrast, Daewoo's LeMans car is sold through a 50/50 joint venture with General

Motors' Pontiac division. Under the contract, GM takes care of the advertising.

FROM BRAND X TO PRO-KENNEX

Making the jump from workshop to Madison Avenue isn't easy. The cost is enormous and for Asian family businesses it means leaving decisions in the hands of the professionals, to an extent they feel unhappy with.

The elderly chairman of a Korean *chaebol* doesn't like to be told by a zany creative director that his advertising ideas are bunk. And he may interfere with designs, even though his alterations disagree with the results of extensive market research.

"Koreans have got to stop thinking of designers as being at the bottom of the totem pole," says one frustrated advertising executive in Seoul. "They concentrate too hard on what management is going to think and not enough on what the readers are going to think."

Manufacturers must also beware, when entering the big time, that they do not upset their existing OEM customers who fear the emergence of a new competitor.

Yet a handful of Asian companies are deciding what brand awareness is worth the price, and some have been successful in achieving it.

Take Taiwan's Kunnan Enterprise, which has pushed its Pro-Kennex tennis rackets at a top-three ranking in the midrange to high-quality market segment. Today, 56% of its U.S. $80 million revenues comes from sales of its own brand products.

Back in the mid-1970s, even though the company was the world's largest tennis-racket manufacturer, producing under OEM contracts for most of the leading companies, it was completely unknown.

"What gave us our big chance was when Prince shook up the market by bringing out its oversize racket," recalls Kunnan president Kunnan Lo. "Very quickly we followed suit by introducing a mid-size racket. That gave us something special. Before long, every brand joined in with mid-size products, but we had already shown ourselves to be a leader."

But even with a superior product, the Pro-Kennex marketing effort in the U.S. floundered for the first few years.

"When we started out, we sent people from Taiwan to take charge of the marketing, but we learned the hard way that that was the wrong approach," said Kunnan Lo. "You need to have local people who understand the market and the local customs. Now the heads of all our sales organizations around the world are locals."

Several other problems plagued the company in the early stages. One was pressure from its big OEM customers, who didn't like the idea of Kunnan setting itself up as a competitor. Kunnan's response was to ensure that it provided such good quality and service that the OEMs would not want to take their business elsewhere.

A second challenge was market acceptance for a Made-in-Taiwan brand. Though it didn't disguise the product's origin, Kunnan refrained from calling unnecessary attention to it, and many consumers simply assumed the company was American or British. The name Pro-Kennex, in fact, was chosen for its American sound, inspired by the resemblance to Kennedy.

Most users of Pro-Kennex rackets know the company is from Taiwan. They also know from favorable reviews in magazines, and from their own experience, that they have a high-quality product.

Finally, Kunnan solved the problem of matching the huge advertising expenditures of the big sporting producers by going for a "grass roots approach." It formed close relationships with the pros at local tennis clubs, often giving them free rackets for trials, and relying on them to spread the word.

THE GRASSROOTS APPROACH

That tactic is still the core of the company's marketing effort. It also spends some U.S. $5 million a year on advertising, mainly in specialized tennis publications, and U.S. $800,000 for player endorsements. Among those under contract to Pro-Kennex are Joakim Nystrom, Amos Mansdorf, Henrik Sundstrom, Robert Seguso, and Kathy Jordan.

Now that Pro-Kennex has become well known, the next step is for Kunnan to put the label on other products. These include sportswear, sporting shoes, billiard cues, and golf clubs. Sales of golf equipment alone hit about U.S. $20 million in 1988.

Manufacturers in Singapore claim that their strategy for brand recognition has been to pitch themselves upmarket, cashing in on Singapore's reputation as the high-quality producer among NICs ("newly industrializing countries," including Taiwan, South Korea, Singapore, and Hong Kong).

It's a bold assertion but one that does seem to have some foundation. Tiger Beer, for example, is marketed as a premium, expensive beer in 45 countries. As well as gaining the attention of a *New York Times* editorial, and winning countless international awards, Tiger Beer seems to have found favor with a most unlikely market segment—Japan's rebelling yuppies, whose status is wholly dependent on the acquisition of foreign goods.

In Thailand the first stirrings of brand recognition are accompanying that nation's ride into industrialization. Ocean Glassware, for example, made by Ocean Glass Co. Ltd., is exported to 60 countries, and the trading house involved, Asoke International Co. Ltd., also sells frozen chicken and canned pineapple to Saudi Arabia under its own name.

But the trend in foodstuffs is still to use foreign names. In the U.S., brands such as Dole, Del Monte, and Bumblebee sail past the inspectors more easily and are better accepted by supermarket consumers.

Even CP Intertrade, the trading arm of agrobusiness giant, the Charoen Phokphand Group, which has a registered American brand name, "Castle Pride," only uses it for selling to institutional buyers, such as hospitals, schools, and restaurants.

And, on the frozen chicken side, 80% of CP's exports to its main market, Japan, are sold under the importer's label. The CP brand name is only used in less brand-conscious markets.

On this evidence, it is likely to be years before Thai manufacturers reach the stage the Taiwanese or the Koreans have now reached in the brand-awareness stakes. And those firms are still light years behind the Japanese.

But it is a nut that Asian companies will eventually have to crack if they want to earn the full rewards of their efforts.

Written by Brian Caplen, reported by Don Shapiro in Taiwan, Caroline Dewhurst in Korea, Linda Chan in Singapore, Peter Janssen in Thailand, David Hart in West Germany, and Gary Gimson in the U.K. © *Asian Business* magazine, Far East Trade Press, Ltd., *1988.*

"Peddle salt and it rains; peddle flour and the wind starts up."

Korean proverb

MALAYSIAN CONSUMER STUDY
by Brian Caplen

While Malaysian politics are becoming ever more factionalized and splintered, there are signs that the country's consumers are beginning to unite. The cause of TVs, cars, and refrigerators—or Walkmans and compact disc players in the case of young Malaysians—is gathering different races together, in a way previously unimaginable.

What the nation's New Economic Policy couldn't achieve (see "Malaysia Eases Into the Lead," p. 161), in the sharing of wealth between communities, the supermarket impetus may yet reconcile. At least, that's the impression given by a new marketing study which abandons the conventional groupings of race, age, sex, and location, in favor of lifestyle tags.

Seven categories have been identified, from the ubiquitous yuppies (the latest Asian barometer in determining whether a country is approaching NIC status) through to such innovative modern tribes as the "chameleons," the "sleepwalkers," and the "kampung (village) trendsetters."

All this will come as a great surprise to marketing executives, used to thinking of Malaysia in strictly racial terms. The complex ethnic mix—roughly 60% Malay or Bumiputra, 30% Chinese, and 10% Indian—has brought difficulties in politics and business, but made gauging where to aim a product somewhat simpler.

The only required knowledge was that the Chinese were the city slickers, going after fashionable imports; the Malays, apart from the elite, were the rural "sons of the soil," buying basic goods; and the Indians with spending power were the professionals looking for books and learning.

If such stereotyping ever was true, it certainly isn't now. Survey Research Malaysia, in its Malaysian Lifestyle Study, found a plethora of young, well-educated citizens, with above-average incomes, who come from a variety of backgrounds.

As well as the yuppies, who are mainly young Chinese, there are the "new breed" and the "kampung trendsetters," both combining a belief in traditional moral and religious values with a fondness for modern consumer products. Both are described as family, and community-oriented, seeing themselves as leaders, with above-average incomes and education. The main difference between the groupings is that the "new breed" live in towns, while the "kampung trendsetters" occupy the countryside.

Altogether, these three groups constitute 47% of the population, according to the survey. That is some 8 million people eager to get their hands on a slice of the action and, barring a major economic crisis, a significant percentage are bound to make it.

It is interesting to compare this predominantly youthful sector with the percentage of the population under 25—about 60%. This indicates that a major proportion of the young population are falling into the new categories, promising an even stronger consumer market tomorrow. With a government policy that assumes Malaysia is underpopulated, and is aimed at reaching a total of 70 million by the year 2100, only the sky is the limit.

But what is happening to the other 53% of the Malaysian community, either not attracted by the acquisition rush, or unable to join it because of material circumstances?

Again, Survey Research Malaysia finds they come from across the board. The "yesterday people," the "chameleons," the "loners," and the "sleepwalkers" are characterized by their introversion and lack of confidence. But while the "yesterday people" are disproportionately older, female, and Malay, the "sleepwalkers" are more likely to be Chinese and female.

This survey must be only the start. Based on the answers of 2,067 randomly selected adults, it promises to shake up staid and complacent marketers. That task probably needs doing twice a year, if companies are really to keep in touch with changing trends and keep tabs on their customers.

Political scientists, on the other hand, will not be convinced. They maintain that the racial divisions which erupted in 1969 have yet to be exorcised. They are always lurking in the background and could reappear in a crisis.

Almost certainly, under such conditions they would be right. But if the country can keep up its current 5% growth rate, the machinations in the political arena may never reach their devastating potential, and Malaysians can play the Asian NIC game of "never mind the politics, feel the money."

FOR YOUR THAIS ONLY

Thailand, unlike most of its neighbors in Southeast Asia and Indochina, has never been colonized. During World War II, the government banned centuries-old Thai traditions, such as betel-nut chewing and the wearing of sarongs for men, in the belief that these customs were backward, forcing Thais to adopt Western habits. In recent years, in an attempt to end the Thais' love affair with the West, the government has imposed hefty import duties of up to 300% for some luxury goods and 600% on expensive cars.

Regardless, Thailand's long-time infatuation with foreign goods is fading as wealthier and better educated Thais go for locally made products. This is good news for the govern-ment-sponsored Niyom Thai (Buy Thai) Association, which had been fighting what seemed to be a losing battle. In 1979, the association even lodged a strong protest to then Prime Minister Kriangsak Chomanan when he presented British silverware to a foreign visitor.

BLACK CARICATURE PRODUCTS IN JAPAN

Sanrio Co., which controls about 70 percent of Japan's toy market, took a Y1.5 billion loss (about $115.3 million) in 1989 when it abandoned its lucrative line of black caricature Sambo products after drawing charges of racism from the United States' Afro-American

RIM VOICES

WHAT'S WRONG WITH HOME-GROWN, HOME-MADE?

"I was surprised that the new Garuda logo was not designed by an Indonesian. There are many Indonesians capable of doing the job."
 —From Sudarsono Asmara of Tanjungpinang, Bintan in *Kompas*, Indonesia.

"The Hercules bicycle which my father bought 30 years ago served him all through his service career and also us, his offspring, who used it until our adulthood and then sold it at double its original price. Can one imagine such durability in any Pakistani-manufactured goods? No doubt our patriotic duty demands that we be Pakistani and buy Pakistani, but are the manufacturers being patriotic by fleecing people?"
 —From Hamid Briggi of Islamabad in *The Muslim,* Pakistan

"It's been almost half a year that five private radio stations in Bandung have been repeatedly broadcasting advertisements for Minakjinggo cigarettes. Listening to the ad slogans we learn that the cloves are from Zanzibar, the tobacco from America, the aroma from France and the machines for making the cigarettes from Britain. Yet home-grown cloves and tobaccos are plentiful."
 —From W. O. Ondang of Bandung, Java in *Kompas,* Indonesia

"In our country, cars are bought to show off and impress rather than as a means of transportation. Do these crazy people understand how much foreign exchange is wasted?"
 —From Khalid Khan of Rawalpindi Punjab in *The Muslim,* Pakistan

community. While a number of other major Japanese firms have also been dropping black caricature products—giant beverage company Calpis Food Industry Co. dropped its 65-year-old trademark of a black person—other smaller Japanese firms are still selling Uncle Tom and Mammy design products.

DESIGNER CONDOMS

A Malaysian-Japanese joint venture, Salami Industries Sdn. Bhd. conducted an unusual feasibility study to determine if there is a market for condoms with designer labels such as Pierre Cardin, Gucci and Yves St. Laurent.

ASIA'S CONSUMER INTERPOL: FIGHTING EVERYTHING FROM JR. ASPIRIN TO BIOTECH COLONIALISM

The consumer movement, so entrenched and well-developed in the West, has begun to flex its muscles in Asia. One of its chief watchdogs is Consumer Interpol, which is headquartered on the Malaysian island of Penang. This group monitors the entire spectrum of consumer affairs in the Pacific Rim, from identifying potential Bhopal disasters to exposing cases of "dumping" by unscrupulous Western pharmaceutical companies of products judged unfit for home consumption.

"We can't rely on governments to impose restrictions because of the trade implications involved, and we can't expect industry to apply self-discipline—so this is the citizens' response to the problem," says Dr. Martin Abraham, coordinator of the program, which operates under the auspices of the Asia-Pacific regional division of the International Organization of Consumer Unions (IOCU).

"Just like the police Interpol goes after crooks, we've established a consumer Interpol to go after corporate criminals who kill or injure consumers."

Among its most notable campaigns, IOCU successfully lobbied to have the "Hatch Bill" blocked in the U.S. Congress. The bill sought to permit the export of drugs not yet approved by the FDA. IOCU has also been actively fighting against the sale of so-called "junior aspirin" which has been associated with Reyes syndrome in children. So far both Malaysia and Singapore have banned the product.

Pesticides used to be the main headache for IOCU in its agricultural watchdog program. Now, with the advent of biotech developments in agribusiness, a whole new Pandora's box has been opened on the seed level. "It's a new form of colonialism," says Dr. Abraham, referring to biotech companies that patent the genes which go into the creation of new varieties of plants and grains. These companies end up in control of the final product, with farmers unable to grow their own seeds beyond a single planting because their hybrid nature has rendered them sterile.

"They have to keep buying seeds from the same supplier in order to stay in business," he notes. "This form of agriculture is more suited to plantation-type growing than to subsistence farming which is the predominant form of farming in the Third World."

U.S.–JAPAN HOUSEHOLD APPLIANCES

Japanese households have more electrical appliances than American homes in certain categories. Ninety-nine percent of Japanese homes have electric washing machines, compared to only 73% of American homes. Ninety-nine percent of Japanese have color televisions; 98% of U.S. homes have televisions, color or black-and-white. Eighty-eight percent of American homes have at least one color set, but in Japan there are now 187.7 color sets for every 100 households, which means that most Japanese families have two color televisions per family. Almost 53% of Japanese homes are equipped with VCRs, while America only had 48.7 percent VCRs at the end of 1987. But Americans have more clothes dryers. Only 12.7 percent of Japanese have dryers in their homes, compared with 61.5% of Americans.

SOURCES: The Statistical Abstract of the United States and a survey of 2,015 Japanese households done by Japan's Economic Planning Agency.

ATTENTION JAMES BOND

China is emerging as a major global arms dealer with its missiles and tanks, but one of the most interesting new Chinese products unveiled at a 1988 arms show in Singapore was a tiny dagger with a special magazine in its handle capable of firing three bullets. Price tag for this deadly collectible—about $75. (For a report on Asian arms dealers, see "An Explosion in the Making," p. 215.)

KOREAN VCRs

South Korean electronics, once considered shoddy and out of date, are earning a reputation for quality and are gaining an increasing share of the world market. The Koreans produced more than $17 billion worth of electronics in 1987, 44% more than in 1986, and trail only Japan as a supplier of VCRs and color televisions. Although trailing the Japanese in most technologies by 2 to 10 years, Korean consumer electronics have become good enough to address the lower end of the mass market. South Korea sold 2.3 million VCRs in the United States in 1987, capturing 17% of the market, according to the Electronic Industries Association of Korea.

WATERBEDS OF TAIWAN

Taiwan is the world's largest producer of waterbeds, accounting for an estimated 80% of world production.

NO FANS OF MAO

The electric fan is the first item that a Chinese peasant will buy if he has money to spare, a 1988 survey conducted by the State Statistics Bureau on the consumption behavior of the peasants revealed. Next on the list: a television set, combined radio and cassette player, washing machine, refrigerator, camera, bicycle, sewing machine, and watch. The Mao suit is also still prevalent among peasants, while its popularity in urban areas is dwindling rapidly.

THROWAWAY HIT

The first Japanese throwaway camera, which hit the market in 1986, sold a million units the first year. In 1989, sales reached 20 to 30 million units. That's a gain of 2,000% in only three years. They come in all kinds—ones that take panoramic shots, one that can get as close up as 40 cm, waterproof versions, telephoto versions, and versions with built-in flash. Priced at between $7.50 and $15, they are available anywhere in Japan where film is sold.

FASHIONABLE POLICIES

Japanese insurance companies in search of new prospects have been branching into the fashion business, opening clothes boutiques in which brochures and contract papers are casually mixed in with piles of shirts on display. "The clothes are the bait that attract women in their thirties who are good potential customers for us," admits a spokesman for the Sumitomo Life Insurance Co., whose boutique in Tokyo's affluent Omotesando district is the sixth opened recently by various companies including Nippon Life, Dai-Ichi Mutual Life, and Meiji Mutual Life. Most such stores also offer free lectures and fashion shows and have a salesroom at the rear in which customers can discuss policy details and sign up for insurance.

THE CREATIVITY REVOLUTION

In recent years, there has been a great deal of concern about how the West appears to be losing its creative edge to Japan. The Japanese now appear to be mastering "creativity techniques" in much the same way that they mastered quality control 25 years ago. As a result, they are now rolling out original new products and virtually pushing them through creativity assembly lines.

Here are two views of the phenomenon. The first is a global view of Japan's creativity revolution by Japan analyst Sheridan Tatsuno, and the second is by Julian Gresser, an American creativity training expert, who has an opposite perspective.

THE FUTURE OF CREATIVITY

Sheridan Tatsuno, author of *The Technopolis Strategy* and *Created in Japan: From Imitators to World Class Innovators,* is a seminal Japan-watcher and global visionary. Formerly an analyst with Dataquest, he now has his own high-tech consulting company, Neo-Concepts, in Fremont, California, and publishes a newsletter called *NeoTrends.*

Tatsuno believes there is "global creativity revolution" underway which will lead to the next stage of the information revolution. He sees a "new paradigm" of creativity emerging —one that will reshape the world's consciousness.

Another way to describe it, he says, is as a "global neural network." This network will have as its framework the minds of people all over the world who are connected by real-time global communications. The final result will be a total "creative fusion," incorporating all the various ideas and philosophies and cultures of the world.

Before this new creativity revolution can occur, however, old paradigms of creativity must become transformed. The Western approach of Cartesian, linear, individualistic thinking—which dominates product development in America, and which currently represents the global standard—must be merged with the more holistic Buddhistic approach of unified, group thinking which is prevalent in Japan today.

In the meantime, America is losing its position as "creative director" of the world, and the Japanese are slowly beginning to assume that role just as they have taken their lead in international finance, marketing, distribution, and manufacturing. It's part of the necessary process of changing paradigms. Just as the world has shifted from geopolitical concerns to geoeconomic priorities, the pendulum is now swinging to a geocultural age.

CROSSROADS OF CREATIVITY

"The Japanese are at the stage in creativity where they were in quality by 1955 or 1956," Tatsuno says. "They've conquered quality, they know how to do that, it's just a matter of execution . . . Now they're trying to figure out how to do that with creativity."

"Most Westerners don't think it can be done," he notes. "They believe you can't quantify or systematize creativity . . . but they were saying the same thing about quality 20 year ago."

Tatsuno's thesis is something he calls the *"yin and yang"* of creativity. (According to Chinese philosophy, *yin* and *yang* represent the principles of duality in the universe, the eternal opposites: male and female, positive and negative, right brain and left brain).

"We Americans have the *yin,* the Japanese have the *yang,*" he says. "We're good at breakthrough technology, we're good at basic research. That's half the circle. They're good at cultivating technology . . . at refining and recycling technology. They have half, we have half," he says.

The problem arises because "the Japanese realize they only have half, while the Americans are convinced they have the whole pie," according to Tatsuno.

"Most American companies are asleep at the wheel. They think they know it all. They don't. Because they don't realize there are other forms of creativity."

"[Since] the Japanese realize they only have half the pie, right now they're putting all their efforts into basic research in 'breakthrough thinking' . . . If they figure that out, and they can adapt it to Japanese culture, watch out!"

CREATIVITY TECHNIQUES

In their search to discover a methodology of creativity, the Japanese have been experimenting with some 100 creativity techniques, Tatsuno says. About half of those are derived from the West, while the other half are unique to Japan.

Among them are the Buddhist (Indian) "lotus blossom" technique based on the mandala design. "You put (out) a seed idea and have nine or eight petals around it. Then you think of all the different applications—say, for superconductors—and that petal becomes the core for the next flower out."

As an example of this graphic approach, Tatsuno cites a beautiful "HDTV" (High-Definition TV) mandala poster designed by the Japanese ad agency Dentsu, depicting 50 or 60 different applications of HDTV.

Then there is a whole series of Japanese "karuta" card games in which "you try to match 300 different poems with 300 different endings." This creativity technique translates into the Japanese turning out "a lot of process spin-offs . . . where you actually take processes and spin off a lot of products. Oftentimes, it's the spin-off product like the VCR which makes more money than the main system."

The Japanese also love to create "technology roadmaps" which extend 20 to 30 years, or sometimes as far as 40 to 50 years into the future, as in the case of Matsushita and Mitsubishi, which have developed half-century technology projections of various spin-off products. "They have some 200 technologies in their ISDN (Integrated Services Digital Network) roadmap to show where they're headed."

FUTUROPOLIS

Assuming Tatsuno's thesis is correct—that the Japanese will manage to crack the nut of creativity and develop a world-class blueprint for new product development, thus cornering the world marketplace (since they have already mastered manufacturing and distribution, and control international finance as well)—where will that leave the rest of the world?

Tatsuno believes that the future lies in joint alliances based on mutual trust and technology-sharing. "The real players, the Sonys of the world, the Toshibas, the IBMs, and the DECs—all the really big players are going to have global alliances."

Mazda and Toyota are now building overseas R&D centers in order to tap into local talent. Mazda has already reaped the benefits of a new global creative approach in the case of its runaway hit car, the Miata. "Half of this car was designed in Irvine, California, [the other] half in Yokohama—and it took off screaming," Tatsuno notes.

"It's what I call combining 'creative fusion' [the Japanese approach] and 'creative fission' [the American approach]," he says. "Anybody who can put these (two approaches) together has a really good chance of doing well in the world markets [in the 1990s]. . . . [But anyone] who [denies these trends] and is culturally arrogant will get left behind."

Yankee Ingenuity Tackles U.S.–Japan "Creativity Gap"

In case you're worried about a "creativity gap" developing between the U.S. and Japan, don't despair. There already is an American antidote.

American experts hold that you can dabble with different techniques all you want, but if you can access the original source of creative ideas, and have a hot line to innovation—that's all you really need anyway.

"The Japanese may understand . . . the competitive implications of these new techniques for creativity," concedes Julian Gresser, president of the Sausalito, California-based creativity training company Discovery Engineering International (DEI). "They are taking them seriously, whereas we Americans are, as usual, being different, ignorant, and arrogant . . . but there is a difference between *techniques* and *technologies* which enhance consciousness."

Gresser's company has developed a biofeedback program which is aimed at American corporations and industry and is designed to help them tap into the source of creative consciousness. This is the "theta" state—located in between wakefulness and sleep—which has traditionally been linked with many historical breakthroughs in science, business, music, literature, and the arts.

His goal is nothing short of establishing a new "science of consciousness." He believes that "this whole new quite straightforward science will become the basis for the next industrial revolution."

This may sound too New Age to be taken seriously. But Gresser can't be easily dismissed as a quack. An internationally known expert on U.S.–Japan trade, he is an attorney at Crosby, Heafey, Roach & May, a leading California law firm with a reputation for being staunchly conservative. He developed his ideas about creativity after his experience in Washington, D.C., during the Carter presidency, when he organized a group in the State Department called the Japan Industrial Policy Group.

"The key idea was that certain industries—in particular, the semiconductor industry in Japan—were viewed as sort of levers for the whole economy . . . [Their concepts] would diffuse rapidly to many other industries . . . and be used there to increase productivity."

After studying the history of strategic industries of the past in order to develop guidelines for American strategic industries in the future, Gresser discovered that most breakthrough ideas occurred during a state of "creative reverie," identified as theta (a low-frequency brainwave, between 4 to 8 hertz).

This evolved into his theory of using "consciousness" as a lever to develop insights into creative problems, to generate new ideas for business, to develop new products and services, and to engineer strategic market breakthroughs.

From there, Gresser developed his Discovery Engineering Theta Training Program in conjunction with the Topeka-based Menninger Foundation, a pioneering psychiatric insti-

tute. Their combination hardware–software system can be integrated with any computer workstation, and future interfaces will eventually include 3D computer graphics, holographic sound, and virtual-reality systems, according to Gresser.

In effect, what Gresser has come up with is the twenty-first century equivalent of word processing programs—except that his are "consciousness processors." His modest goal is to become "the Genentech" of the consciousness industry.

Of course, the Japanese aren't far behind. One of his partners and investors in DEI is Shigeo Ihori, a Japanese entrepreneur and president of Taiyo Kikaki Co., Ltd., one of Japan's leading computer graphics and media companies, who has set up a DEI-based "creativity center" in Tokyo.

STIR-FRY QUOTE

Creativity is like a fish. You can steam it, fry it, or boil it, but if it's not fresh it won't taste good.

KUO CHENG-FONG, *president of Taipei-based Taiwanese agency Hwa Wei & Grey Advertising*

CREATIVE TIPS FROM JAPANESE ENTREPRENEURS

The Japanese magazine *Shukan Post* surveyed some of Japan's most innovative entrepreneurs about their "secrets" of creativity. They came up with a working list of creative tips:

1. The blocks to success are more likely to be mental than external. Hiwada Toshiyuki (age 46) developed a straw that changes colors as you drink. It went on

the market in April 1987 and sold an estimated 200 million the first year. Said Toshiyuki, "The biggest block to ideas is that thing you have inside yourself that tells you 'It can't be done.' "
2. Keep records of every interesting fact or incident you hear.
3. When you have a good idea, tell 10 people about it. If their reaction is favorable, then you should go with it because you'll have done a minimarket research.
4. Always take notes. Even when you're out drinking.
5. Don't forget that the buyer likes to be "involved."
6. When you've hit a block, get advice from the broadest selection of people possible.
7. Live life to the hilt. Sasanuma Ki-ika (age 73) invented a filter that strains the lint from the water in automatic washers. Since the product was introduced,

500,000 have been sold, and annual sales top Y900 million (about $6.9 million). She commented, "I never forgot that I was a housewife with four children. I was always wondering, 'What can I do that's interesting? What can I do that's more convenient?' "

8. Don't be afraid to spend time and money testing. Murakami Hideyasu (age 35) sells drip coffee at Y50 (about 38 cents) a cup, and he delivers it to your door. Since he started business in September 1986, he's sold more than 100,000 cups of coffee for sales of Y120 million (about $923,000) the first year. Hideyasu said, "I must have tested more than 500 vacuum jugs to find one that would keep the coffee hot until it reached its destination. And I sampled blends from at least 30,000 tons of beans."

9. Make friends with experts. Inoue Tetsu-hiko (age 49) invented a dry paint, a film that can be stuck on any wall, and can be easily removed. The product should sell more than Y100 million (about $769,000). . . . Tetsuhiko remarked, "The idea 'Why does it always have to be paint?' could only come from an amateur in the business. Still, I'd never have been able to perfect the product without the help of a lot of expert friends."

10. "Practicality and "Fun" are the two key words. In a world overflowing with similar products, the HITs always have one thing in common: They are absolutely practical . . . yet they let you have fun while you're using them. In other words, the basic concept should be "Convenience, with fun built in."

Translated from *Shukan Post* by *Japan Free Press*

JAPAN'S DESIGNER GENIUS

Here's a sampling of some of Japan's products, gizmos, and neo-services born from their creative brainstorming methods. A few of them may strike us as being a bit far-fetched perhaps, while others are extraordinarily practical. But they all reflect an intensely visionary attitude towards product development.

VEGETARIAN BALLPOINT PEN

Sailor, Japan's leading penmaker, has introduced a vegetarian ballpoint pen called "My Plantation." The gimmick: It grows three different kinds of herbs on the end, with pens retailing for about $7.50. It also comes in red, black and blue colors.

DIALYSIS TRAVEL TOURS

JTB, the nation's biggest travel agency, is now marketing "dialysis tours" for Japanese travelers who have kidney ailments. They're offering tour packages to Hawaii, Singapore, and Hong Kong which include visits to dialysis centers so their clients can combine sightseeing with their regular treatment. The packages are priced about the same as regular tours.

DRIVE-IN BOOKSTORE

The world's first drive-in bookstore opened in a Tokyo suburb. It's designed like a fast food joint featuring an outdoor menu of daily book and magazine "specials," and driver-browsers can order their selections over the Hisamido Bookstore's intercom system, then drive over to the checkout counter to pick up their order. About 2,700 people visit the store each day.

E.T., FLUSH HOME

"Etiquette Tone" is an electronic water-conservation gadget that emulates the sound of a flushing toilet. The manufacturer's market research revealed that self-conscious Japanese women use at least 100 liters of water a day to "cover up" the sound of urination. Fuji Bank installed ninety E.T.s in their women's restrooms and calculates it is saving about $46,000 a year in water bills.

SPRAY-ON HAIR

"Wigless" is a spray-on hair product. The spray can is filled with tiny artificial fibers about the same thickness as natural hair. Just spray them on the part that's starting to thin and comb your natural hair over the spot. It's supposedly good for people who haven't progressed to the point where they need a hair piece. It costs about $75 a can.

OXYGEN ON THE ROCKS

A pub in Tokyo's Shibuya section has a pure oxygen room where you can burn off the al-

cohol before heading home after a night out drinking. It costs about 75 cents for five minutes.

AEROSOL COFFEE

While it looks like a can of mousse for the hair, this product from Honen is really a condensed coffee aerosol that uses CO_2 as a propellant (not freon). A two-second burst in a cup, add water (hot or cold)—and you get a delicious cup of coffee. Up to 40 cups per aerosol container, costs about $7. Just don't put it in your hair by mistake.

SHAKE N' CHIC

"Traveling Laundry" is really just a bag. You put your dirty laundry in it and submerse in 40° or 60° C water. Slush it up and down a few times and let it sit for 20 minutes. Rinse and your laundry is done. "Great for those who have had to extend their stay a few days without extra underwear," notes *Bungei Shunju* magazine. It costs about $3.00 per bag.

WASH 'N DRY 2001

Sanyo Electric and Kyushu Electric Power Company joined to create a combination clothes washer/drier that automatically takes clothes from the wash cycle through the dry circle with no input from the user. Put in ten white shirts, punch a button, wait two hours and 15 minutes—then remove clean, dry shirts from the unit. Costs about $1,550. Sanyo has also put out a clothes dryer that adds fragrances to the clothes it dries. It offers a choice of three or four fragrances that last for about two days, and costs about $507.

Smelling Good

Japan's annual fragrance market is about Y36 billion (about $276 million). Now where once people complained about smelly feet, Kanebo has marketed panty hose in three fragrances, from about $1.15 to about $4.00.

Monden Hifuku Kohgyo has developed fragrant cloth for trousers and jeans. It's 100 percent cotton and contains tiny capsules of five fragrances including jasmine, floral bouquet, lavender, freesia, and rose. As the wearer moves, the tiny capsules break and fragrances are emitted. What fragrance issues forth depends on how the wearer moves.

INAX has developed disposable cartridges of fragrances for your shower: two for morning use, one for daytime use, and two for nighttime use—five fragrances in all, costs about $7.50 for a package of five cartridges.

Fragrant Conversation

Hitachi's "Populene" features a plastic mouthpiece capsule containing dried flowers. Smelling of roses and lavender, the push-button phone comes with five tunes to serenade callers on hold, plus a 20-number memory storage. It costs about $170.

Sound-sensitive camera

Konica's *"Kanpai!"* ("Cheers!") compact camera is the first in the world to react to sound. Set it up at a party, and when the laughter goes over a certain decibel level, the flash goes off, the shutter clicks, and the moment is captured on film. The camera moves after every shot, so once it's been set upon the tripod, you get lots of pictures from different angles. Costs about $215 with the tripod.

Speed Listening

Sony's TSC-2000 does what they call a "sound scan" on audio cassette tape. Press the sound scan button, and the machine gives you the first eight seconds, zooms forward for 40 seconds, then gives you another eight seconds, etc., to give you the "drift" of what's going on. Costs about $269.

Super Noodles

Nisshin Foods, Japan's giant food company which launched instant noodles, has introduced "Super Boil." You just add water and wait. In minutes you have a piping hot bowl of ramen noodles. The product comes in a self-heating can, and it costs about $3.85.

Electric Persian Rugs

Electric heated carpets are popular in Japan. In 1989, Matsushita Electric featured a 2 meter by 3.16 meter carpet for $7,697—made to order, with only 500 made. Sanyo Electric's carpet, also 2 m x 3 in size, is made of fine Belgian silk. Toshiba entered the fray with a heated *tatami* mat topped with real *igusa* rushes, $1,538 for each mat.

Timeless Pieces

"Chikateru-Kun" ("Subway Kid") is a watch with a difference. It will tell you all the shortcuts in the Tokyo metropolitan area—and it costs only about $100.

The "Bar Graph Watch" shows the time in bar graphs. Hours are in purple, minutes in pink. Although some people mistake it for a thermometer, its novelty is driving up sales. From Twin Bird, for about $30. "Harmony," a watch from Seiko, plays a tune when you lift the lid. What's more, the second hand starts to dance in time to the music. Tunes available include "Bibbity, Boppity, Boo" and the "Turkish March."

On "Challenging Time," the little hand and the big hand are backwards. The face is upside down. The stem is on the wrong side. And the hands move counterclockwise. You really have to concentrate to tell the time . . . which lets you escape reality for an instant. From Hankyu Department Store in Osaka for Y15,500 (about $120).

Seiko's "Vib Travel," which costs under $27, is a battery-powered, bean-shaped alarm clock that awakens the sleeper by vibrating under the pillow. "Alarm Nighty" are pajamas that come with an alarm clock that's attached by a string to the shoulder. From Japanese lingerie giant Wacoal, it's priced at about $65.

Swell Pen

Use the "Mokorin Pen" to write or draw a picture on ordinary paper. Then heat it up with a hair dryer. The heated ink swells up and makes the whole piece a work of art. A three-color set sells for about $5.80, six colors for about $11.50.

Cotton Tea Bags

Asahi Kasei has developed cotton cloth bags to replace paper tea bags. There are fewer stray fibers, no starch to seep into your tea, and it works even when the water is not boiling hot.

Magazine (The Snack Food)

The front of the package features an illustration by a popular illustrator. On the back side

is a very funny cartoon (which has nothing to do with the product inside). The consumer is attracted by the illustration, laughs at the cartoon, buys the product, and finds that it's not half bad. From Nissin Foods at most Japanese convenience stores.

Family-style Saloon

A Japanese-style bar in Osaka named Maruchu Suikoden has become a family affair. Bring the kids and drink up. While the parents are drinking, the kids get to play in their own special play room. According to *Shukan Post* magazine, there are up to 50 kids in that room on busy days.

Aerobix Faxes

The growth of all-night facilities in Tokyo has taken a curious turn with the onset of Cerium, a fitness center that features not only the gym, aerobics room and jacuzzis in which young executives relax away from the strains of the office, but a top floor Business Intelligence Center is equipped with all the panoply of office machines, stock tickers and newswires they're trying to get away from.

Musical Toilet Paper

Melody Holder is a toilet paper holder with a musical integrated circuit (IC) in its core. When you pull off the paper, you get serenaded with 30 seconds of melody. The IC is good for about 10,000 tunes.

Anti-Pigeon Device

Osaka Winston, a company whose business is the cleaning of air conditioning ducts, has come up with a product, Hatocon, which uses magnetics to get rid of pigeons. In 1981, a researcher at MIT theorized that pigeons have a living magnet in their bodies that reacts to the earth's magnetic field and tells them which way to fly. The Hatocon product was developed based on this theory. It is a two-meter rope with eight 1.5 centimeter-diameter permanent magnets attached to it. These magnets cause a disturbance in the earth's field so that when a pigeon flies into the disturbed area, its instinct is to turn around to fly the opposite direction.

WHAT A YARN

Japan's Yamanashi Knitwear Manufacturers Association has developed the world's first temperature-sensitive sweater. The yarn changes color when you come in from the cold. One type of yarn changes colors at 28° C, another at 16° C. Supposedly, the colors keep changing even after many washings. But the cost is about five times the price of a regular sweater.

THE SMART BRA

They've already done it to automobiles by putting the smarts into car fenders so they can "undent" themselves after a collision, reverting to their natural shape. Now the Japanese are applying the same technology to brassieres. Wacoal America, Inc., the U.S. division of the leading Japanese lingerie maker, Kyoto-based Wacoal Corp., introduced the "Memorywire" bra which uses a super elastic metal alloy combination of nickel and titanium with a shape memory function. The so-called "NT" alloy has been programmed in such a way that it always "remembers" the

wearer's original form. The technology for this bra is derived from the U.S. space program.

Undercover:

RECYCLING PANTIES

Ropé, a chic Japanese boutique, markets *futon* (Japanese bedding) covers with a difference. They are made of 50 used panties (that have been sterilized, they say) and cost Y30,000 each (about $230). The store also has pillow slips (covered with 20 pairs of panties) at Y20,000 (about $153). Or you can buy a mask to cover your face when you've caught cold (made of old panties, of course).

Risque Briefs: Melody Shorts are a women's briefs with a light-sensitive microchip that plays "The Wedding March" or "My Way" when exposed to light. The chip is not triggered by the mere lifting of a lady's skirts. The legs must be spread wide in order for enough light to strike the sensor to trigger the melody. They cost about $23 a pair. Who's buying them? Mostly "dirty old men," according to the *Shukan Sankei* weekly magazine.

SILKY ROAD

Silk Road is a new towel that's 100% silk on one side, 100% cotton on the other. Rubbing your skin with silk after a bath is supposed to make it silky smooth. It costs about $27.

HOT SPRINGS-TO-GO

Hot springs resorts in Niigata, Japan, have come up with the ultimate service for hedonistic couch potatoes. They will ship their famous hot springs water anywhere in Japan via a specially outfitted van. The rubberbooted, uniformed delivery man will fill their tubs with a hose. *Sake* and a *geisha* may also be ordered for local delivery, but they cost extra. Either way, you get soaked. "What a marvelous gift in a culture that's so preoccupied with bathing," notes author Leonard Koren, author of the classic study of Japanese creative zaniness, "283 Useful Ideas from Japan."

CLOSE SHAVE

Among the legion of disposable products in Japan, here's one that stands out: An electric razor that works for only 15 minutes.

NEW AGE BATH SALTS

"*Onsen* (Hot Springs) Ball" is a bioceramics polyethylene ball that releases infrared rays when placed in the bath. These rays gradually warm your body. The ball also turns the water alkaline, which is supposed to be good for you. Showa Package Industries makes the product, three balls for Y15,000 (about $115).

FOR FAMILIES WITH TEENAGERS

Enjoy Telephone is a phone with a large built-in liquid crystal display. Ordinarily the display shows the time. When the phone is in use, a small dog appears on the screen. If a conversation goes on too long, it starts to fidget. And when two minutes have passed, it turns its back on the caller. This device will supposedly shorten your teenager's telephone calls. It costs Y17,800 (about $136).

TALKING PLANTER

The Kagawa prefecture development group has come up with a planter that talks. If the planter is knocked over, or if there is a sudden change in light levels, the sensor triggers a tape recorder which plays the appropriate message. It costs about $20.

FLAMELESS LIGHTER

The flame is entirely within the framework of the lighter, so it will light your cigarette in winds of up to 10 meters per second. It costs about $77.

GOLFER'S INSURANCE

A major department store, Tokyu, is selling golfer's insurance in partnership with a casualty insurance firm. A one-time $40 premium will cover you against unusual disbursements such as hole-in-costs (up to $1,500) and in case you bonk someone on the head accidentally.

CARD BUSINESS

The high-tech business card dispenser holds up to eight cards and lets you slip them out like a Las Vegas blackjack dealer. You just have to get your timing right. It costs about $22.

Other new cards are soaked in perfume, others turn colors when the recipient touches them, some have musical ICs embedded and play tunes, while some are pure gold (costing about $46 each). According to business card analysts in Japan, an unusual business card is good for at least ten minutes of conversation.

NEO-LOCKERS

Cold storage lockers keep their contents at 0° C. They also contain a deodorizer. Y100 (about 75 cents) lets you in. When you come back to get your goods, the Y100 is refunded. Forty-eight of these lockers are located in the Tokyu Plaza in Shibuya and twelve each in the Seibu stores in Kinshincho and Hikari-gaoka in Tokyo.

Parcel delivery lockers can be found at Tokyo, Ueno, and Shinjuku Japan Railway stations in Tokyo. They provide wrapping paper, string, and gummed tape so you can properly wrap your package. All you have to do is weigh in, punch in the destination and weight on the panel on the locker, and it will tell you the price of delivery. Put in the proper amount and the locker opens. Leave package and shut door. The postal service promises next-day delivery if you get the package in before 6:00 p.m. It's a great way to get your skis to the slopes.

WIRELESS DEPTHFINDER

Let the sensor down in the water on a string, and this wristwatch-size depth finder will tell you where the fish are. The $369 gizmo is effective up to 96 meters deep.

QUEEN-SIZE CEILING

For tiny studio apartments, Sanwa Shutter has devised a bed that hides away in the ceiling. $1,097 for a single, $2,604 for a queen, and about $230 for the installation.

INFRARED CUDDLES

A Japanese bedding company, Nishikawa Sangyo, has developed a stuffed animal that stores infrared rays—and radiates them. The toy dog, called Danpei, is covered with a polyester cloth which is coated with a ceramic and aluminum compound. The idea is that when a child hugs Danpei, its body heat is absorbed by the toy which then radiates a warm hug back to the child. It comes in two sizes, priced from $37 to $52.

LOFTY 'LOONS

Kurray Co. Ltd. has developed a balloon that will stay inflated for more than a month. This super long-lasting balloon is called "Evaloon" and costs about $6.15.

HELIUM DUCK

A popular children's novelty item is "Duck's Voice" (about $2.50). It's actually a hit of helium inside a balloon that makes your voice sound like the popular cartoon character "Donardo Duckoo." The inventor, Komaba Kunio, can't keep up with demand.

WISH YOU WERE HERE

Novelty postcards are big in Tokyo. Here's an amazing one—"Chijime-ru"—which is made from shape-memory plastic that shrinks when heated. Recipients collect favorite cards from favorite people, shrink them, and wear them like jewelry around the neck. The handwriting shrinks, too, but remains legible.

Private Postcard: Adhesive aluminum foil on this 10 cent postcard keeps prying eyes from reading personal messages.

FLY BY NIGHT?

The Battery Industry Association of Japan held a contest for new ideas for products powered by battery. The cost of materials had to be less than Y10,000 (about $77), but that was the only rule. One was a device that pets the cat even when the master is not at home. Another was a powered cutting board that wiggles the fish to make them look alive. Then there was one that lets you ring the phone for an excuse to send unwelcome guests home. But the Gran Prix (Y300,000 or about $2,300 in prize money) went to a device that starts beeping if you've left your fly open more than 50 seconds. Saves embarrassment. Invented by a 62-year-old man, too.

IDEA OLYMPICS

To promote innovation and entrepreneurship in Japan, Toyota Corp. sponsors an annual Idea Olympics in Toyota City. The event is produced by the Toyota Engineering Society, an organization comprised of 28,300 of Toyota's 60,000 employees. Among the leading entries from the 1989 competition: a "Rack-and-Pinion Car" which is started, stopped and turned by a steering-wheel which is completely detached from the rest of the car. The wheel can be carried away with a shoulder-strap as a fashion accessory.

JAPAN, INC. CHANGES ITS TUNE

Japanese corporate anthems have traditionally sounded like martial riffs with a *banzai* beat. Now the emphasis is on New Age lyrics, with buzzwords like Tomorrow, Breeze, Love and Hope. A Tokyo ad agency, Dentsu PR Center, has jumped into this booming new market for corporate ditties with packages ranging from $35,000 to $70,000 for lyrics, music, arrangements, and recording.

TROLLY BILLBOARDS

Hong Kong advertisers have rediscovered the city's 163 lumbering trams as a prime medium to promote such upmarket products as airlines, hotels, and photographic equipment. Advertising revenue from the fleet now tops about $115,000 monthly. The major change, inaugurated by British Caledonian's Scottish tartan tram, has been from small sectional ads to covering the vehicle's entire surface with one ad which gets high visibility during the tram's sluggish 13-kilometer journey from Shau Kei Wan to the city's Western district.

PACIFIC IMAGES FOR SALE

With the Pacific Rim becoming more of a marketing concept, multimedia images of the region are increasingly in demand by international marketing, advertising, and communications agencies. One agency that is pioneering the field is Pacific Stock, a Honolulu-based company that represents some 50 still photographers and motion picture producers scattered throughout the region. Categories of photographs stocked by PS include color transparencies of travel, scenic, ocean sport, underwater, marine science, and industrial representations. It maintains a computerized filing system with a bar code application that can call up an image of a specific Micronesian atoll faster than you can say "sunscreen." Turnaround time on orders is 48 hours.

VALET MARKETING

In a fiendishly clever marketing ploy, Thai automobile marketers have been selling low-end economy models of foreign cars as luxury

ASIAN CHRONICLES:

THE FADS OF JAPAN

After more than four centuries of isolation from the rest of the world, the Japanese opened to the West during the Meiji Restoration period (1868 to 1912). They quickly demonstrated their intense faddishness as they adopted one Western notion after another. Early Japan-watcher Basil Hall Chamberlain was an Englishman who became a distinguished scholar of Japanese and philology at Tokyo's Imperial University in the late 1800s. In his book, Japanese Things: Being Notes on Various Subjects Connected with Japan *(reissued by Charles E. Tuttle Co. of Tokyo in 1971), he describes the voracious consumerism of the Japanese which still remains their cultural hallmark today in the 1990s.*

Japan stood still so long that she has now to move quickly and often to make up for lost time. Every few years there is a new craze, over which the nation, or at least that part of the nation which resides in Tokyo, goes wild for a season. Eighteen seventy-three was the rabbit year. There had been none of these little rodents in Japan. Hence, when imported as curiosities, they fetched incredible prices, as much as $1,000 being sometimes paid for a single specimen. Speculations in $400 and $500 rabbits were of daily occurrence. In the following year, 1874, the government put a capitation tax on rabbits, the price fell in consequence from dollars to cents, and the luckless rabbit-gamblers were ruined in a moment. Eighteen seventy four to 1875 were the cockfighting years.

In 1882 to 1883, printing dictionaries and other works by subscription was the order of the day. Many of these literary enterprises turned out to be fraudulent, and had to be dealt with by the courts. About 1883, it was also the great time for founding societies, learned and otherwise. Next came athletics in 1884 to 1885. A rage for waltzing and for gigantic funerals marked 1887 to 1888. During these years there was also, in official circles, an epidemic of what was locally known as "the German measles"—a mania for imitating all things German, doubtless because "safer," more genuinely monarchical, than free Anglo Saxondom. Eighteen eighty-nine saw the sudden rise of joint-stock companies, together with a general revival of all native Japanese amusements, Japanese costume, antiforeign agitation, etc.

[In] 1893, the whole nation went mad over Col. Fukushima's successful ride across Siberia; a perusal of the newspapers of the time can alone give any idea of the popular frenzy. [In] 1898 to 1900, garden-parties. One of them lasted five days; others were held even in the snow, with bonfires lit in the vain hope of warming the shivering guests. Certain merchants of Yokohama, failing a real garden, went so far as to hold their garden party (so-called) on board some lighters moored together and covered with an awning!

Another craze of the closing years of the century was for busts and statues—even silver statues of oneself. [In] 1901, monster outings for children and workmen. One of the leading newspapers organized an excursion to Tokyo for 120,000 operatives. But when this vast multitude neared the spot, only 5,000 were allowed by the police to proceed, and rioting ensued. A picnic of more manageable proportions was attended by 380 blind shampooers, who went out to see (?) the plum-blossoms at Sugita, and were made safe by means of a long rope after the fashion of Alpine climbers.

models. Because the tax rate for imported cars is so incredibly high—as much as seven times the original sticker price—Thai car manufacturers import components of low-end foreign cars which are then assembled locally. Still, with taxes and the cost of required local content (45%) and problems linked to quality control, the Thai consumer ends up paying a luxury car price for a little Peugeot. One Thai company, Yontrakit, assembles the low-end Series 3 BMW compact, retailing it for about $40,000. But the advertising and marketing deliberately position the roadster on a par with a Mercedes SL. Meanwhile, Nissan's four-cylinder Sentra (marketed elsewhere as the Sunny) is touted in commercials as the next spiffiest thing to a Lamborghini.

THE GLASNOST WATCH

The Soviets are pushing their reverse-chic paratrooper's watch all around the world, but apparently they've thrown up some marketing flack in Singapore in a row over a distributor's ad for the product. The Soviet embassy in Singapore is said to have disliked the ad's copy, which was held to be insulting to the memory of the October Revolution. Dickson Trading, the offending company, had been running a campaign featuring the slogan: "Watch a Russian Revolution Every Minute."

ELECTRONIC SCRATCH 'N' SNIFF

One of the fastest growing and most innovative marketing companies on the Rim is a young Aussie entrepreneurial firm named Creata Promotions. Their revolutionary "Speak 'n' Win" electronic promotion system enables advertisers to encode products or promotional game pieces with messages played back at the point of purchase.

Here is how it works: The customer brings back his barcoded card or direct mail flyer to the participating retailer who runs it through the scanning unit. The scanner reads the barcode and activates a voice-synthesized chip which tells the customer whether he has won or lost the contest.

The gimmick is now catching on in North America. K-Mart and Pizza Hut have both used the promotion in Canada, while Midwest Savings and Loan Bank has used Speak 'n' Win to attract new depositors in the United States.

The company also lauched a "Sing and Win" campaign Down Under. In that promotion, consumers removed the barcode label from a shampoo bottle and trekked on down to the nearest participating movie theater. There a winning—or losing—musical jingle was played to them. And reportedly, Creata Promotions is close to announcing a brand-new system that combines scanning barcodes with video. "The results are so fantastic that it makes Speak 'n' Win almost obsolete," says company spokesperson Norma Rosenhain.

NICOTINE NICHE-MARKETING

Increased taxes and high-pressure tactics of the antismoking lobby are forcing Hong Kong tobacco marketers into a search for small, well-defined groups of consumers to whom they can pitch their product. Women and upwardly mobile social snobs appear to be their majors targets. Tobacco consumption in the colony peaked at around 9,000 million sticks in 1981 and was already declining steadily when the local government mandated in late 1987 that television advertising must carry a health warning. A total ban on broadcast advertising by tobacco products went into effect in 1990. Some idea of this opposition faced by the tobacco companies is indicated by the attempt to promote upmarket Cartier Vendome cigarettes as sponsor of the Hong Kong ballet's production of The Nutcracker. Antismoking campaigners responded with a vociferous outcry, demanding a ban on sponsorship by tobacco companies of not only cultural but also sporting events.

HERBAL SMOKES

A Chinese marketing success story was touted at the Advertising Congress meeting in Beijing. Jiang Tianfu, a representative of Beijing Cigarette Factory, revealed that BCF was exporting only $250,000 worth of cigarettes in 1985. But by 1987 that figure jumped to $1.8 million. Noted Jiang, "Our cigarette mixed with traditional Chinese herbs is especially appealing to the Japanese, though we are not pinning our hopes on that market alone."

Japanese smokers are beginning to develop a taste for offbeat cigarettes (i.e., the expensive "Dajarum" brand clove cigarettes from Indonesia). They're attracted by the exotic fragrance and by the occasional snap, crackle, and pop sound the cigarette makes when it burns. Djarums first caught the fancy of Japan's surfer crowd but are now gaining wider appeal among less athletic smokers. Sales are averaging at 250,000 cigarettes a month, with 12 in a pack selling for about $2.40.

ZAPPING COMMERCIALS IN CHINA

That old bugbear of American advertisers, zapping commercials, has already taken root in China where bargain rates of $5,000 per 30-second spot turn out to be not so much of a bargain if the commercial isn't seen. The difference is, however, that sometimes it is the local station tht preempts the commercial—substituting its own local one—without bothering to inform Beijing. All types of media are expanding dramatically in China but television is making the greatest strides with about 40% of the population within its range. Penetration varies from about 90% in the cities to as low as 10% in the countryside where, nevertheless, there may be as many as 10 viewers per set.

Nine out of 10 Chinese television viewers do not like commercials, according to a 1988 survey published by the *Youth Daily* newspaper. Viewers surveyed described commercials on television as being boring, badly produced, uninformative, and often misleading. The survey was based on interviews with 634 viewers in Kunming, capital of Yunnan province in southwestern China. The newspaper said some consumers had bought products after seeing them advertised on television, only to discover they were misled. "Now the more often a commercial appears, the less viewers believe it," the newspaper said.

CRAZY ABOUT CONTESTS

Contests are very big in Japan—especially corporate-sponsored contests which can offer cash prizes of up to $80,000. There were more than 3,500 contests held in 1988, up 11% from 1986, according to a new publication which tracks such phenomena. The magazine is naturally named *Contest Guide*. It's a publishing phenomenon in itself. Subscriptions are now up to 100,000 copies a month compared to when the magazine premiered as a quarterly in 1986 with a print run of only 5,000.

THE COCKROACH OF THE YEAR AWARD

In a highly unusual marketing ploy, Japan's Cynamid company which sells cockroach killer launched a "cockroach contest." Contestants were invited to mail their best looking specimens of cockroaches (dead, not alive) to be judged by a distinguished panel of experts. First prize was Y100,000 (about $760), and other prizes were offered in various categories. The 1989 contest was deemed a huge success by the company. There were a total of 774 entries of 13 kinds of cockroaches, according to a company spokesman. Declared one of the judges, Mihara Minoru, a researcher at the National Institute of Health: "Not only were they big, but their color and shape were magnificent. Truly beautiful."

CONFUCIAN CONSUMER SYMBOLS

To sell goods in Taiwan, it is necessary to have a thorough understanding of Confucian principles, according to local market research experts. These include frugality, sobriety, and "a finely graded system of status symbols that embraces everything from one's home, clothes and car to how one eats or drinks." The frugality of previous decades, brought about by government propaganda that conspicuous consumption was unpatriotic, has of course led to high personal incomes and expenditures in the current decade, say Mark Van Roo and Pedro Reyes of International Research Associates (HK) Ltd., Taiwan, but the contemporary Taiwan consumer "is searching for the equivalents of the traditional Confucian symbols" in the modern goods he buys and even in the way he spends his leisure hours.

VALENTINES DAY'S DUTY

Only one out of every six male recipients of chocolates on Valentine's Day gets the gift out of love rather than obligation according to a survey by Tobu, the Japanese department store, of its female employees. Most of the women agreed that they make the gifts—an average of six each to friends and colleagues—from a sense of duty. When the store polled male employees the previous year, respondents expected an average of 2.4 gifts. The period around Valentine's Day accounts for about one sixth of annual chocolate sales, and imported chocolate now totals about 13% of the Japanese market, a figure that has tripled in the last couple of years.

MATCHING THE WEATHER TO THE COMMERCIALS

FM Tokyo fits advertisers' commercials to the weather. Their new computerized systems hold up to 16 commercials in memory. Then two hours before on-air time, they check with the weather bureau, find out what the weather's going to be, and feed that information to the computer so it can choose the proper spot.

NIC SHOPS

It may be the Pacific Century—but maybe we should call this the "Decade of the NICs." In Hozumi, Japan, the first shop to feature products exclusively from Hong Kong, South Korea, Taiwan, and Singapore opened its doors recently. Called "The NICs Super Shop," it sells NICs-made electronic appliances, clothes, leatherwear, furniture, bicycles, and food products. One Tokyo entrepreneur launched another NICs-oriented enterprise. Dubbed "Korean Express," the venture consists of two refrigerated trucks that make neighborhood rounds selling fresh Korean foodstuffs—*ramen* noodles, hot *kimchi* pickles, and barbecued meats. The drivers also carry catalogs featuring inexpensive appliances and products that can be ordered from Korea. In its first three months of operation, the business was grossing about $1,500 a day.

PacRim Toll-Free 800 Service

The era of toll-free 800 telephone service arrived in Asia when Worldwide 800 Services, a Hong-Kong-headquartered telecom firm, launched an 800 line telephone service in Singapore, Taiwan, Hong Kong, Malaysia, Indonesia, and the Philippines. AT&T also offers toll-free 800 service from Japan and ASEAN (Association of Southeast Asian Nations including Brunei, Indonesia, Malaysia, Philippines, Singapore, and Thailand.)

Rating "X"

The letter X is currently in favor with new Japanese companies (among them, Inax, Orix, Injex, KX), and Dentsu's Sawa Shigeki explains why, with such reasons as: it's a nice sound and, easy to remember; it has no Japanese equivalent, making trademarks easy to protect; it has a high-tech image because of its mathematical connotations; it represents "an unidentified variable," implying growth possibilities; and it is interesting from a design point of view.

Billboard Heaven

In Bombay, the ad Mecca of India, Indian advertisers have taken to the great outdoors. Bombay has about 40,000 billboard sites, with rents ranging from about $750 a month for sites in low traffic or remote locations to about $450 a day for prime sites. There are 40 ad companies alone in Bombay that specialize in billboards.

The Big Wet Screen

Ishikawajima-Harima Heavy Industries has created a unique visual display: A pipe sprays out a screen of water (ranging in size from 3 meters to 30 meters high), and a perfectly clear image is projected on it. The effect is one of "cool tech."

Talking Posters

Talking posters are getting big in Japan. These are poster panels with a small infrared sensor hidden in a hole in the center. If anyone comes within 10 feet of the poster, it plays a recorded message. Each poster costs about $100, but it's extremely cost-effective in areas where there is high foot traffic. The posters made their debut in Japan's 1989 elections.

Soft Soap

"Ad Clear Soap" allows advertisers to put their message in the middle of a transparent soap bar on a strip of film. This can be words, pictures, or anything. The user can even put their loved one's picture in the bar. From a Tokyo company called M & M.

Cheesecake Boards

One of the hottest advertising gimmicks in Japan is a revival of the U.S. depression years classic, the sandwich board. Business is booming for one Tokyo company, Gendai Kokokusha. They have 3,000 young girls on call, and whenever they run a help-wanted ad, a thousand girls apply, according to vice president Matsuzawa Dai. "The era of mass-produced everything, mass-consumed everything is over," says Dentsu marketing analyst Yoshino Takasaburo. "Thus, new advertising methods must naturally evolve." The kids earn between $346 to $769 for a four-hour shift.

MARKETING TO MALAYSIA'S MUSLIMS

With the worldwide Islamic resurgence that began in the early 1970s, Malaysian marketers have started to look specifically at Malaysia's predominantly Muslim market as a separate and potentially lucrative niche. Muslims number about 54% of Malaysia's 16 million population.

On television, the number of hours allotted for religious Muslim programs has increased dramatically over the last few years, especially over Networks One and Two, the government-owned channels.

Practically every government department is equipped with a *surau,* or prayer room. Most multinational corporations and local private companies have followed suit, and banks, hotels, and factories also cater to the spiritual needs of the Muslim community. Hotels are required by Islamic authorities to provide a *kib'lah* (the arrow that points the direction of Mecca for prayer purposes) in each room.

Maternity clinics are run according to Islamic codes. Prayer is recited before, during, and after each delivery, and women are briefed on proper ways of bringing up children according to Islam.

Pork is *haram* (forbidden according to Muslim code), as is eating any meat that is not slaughtered according to Islamic rites. Companies involved in the business of food, whether in food processing and preparation or fast food and restaurant outlets, routinely promote their products as being *halal* (manufactured according to Islamic rites).

Malaysia's Kentucky Fried Chicken franchise—once the victim of a boycott in 1984 because of a rumor its chicken was *haram*—now features the words *Di-tanngung Halal* on all its marketing materials and in the outlets, at the entrance, on the take-away box, and on the menu.

An entire range of Muslim products has sprung up without alcohol and animal fats. Now *halal* marketing is applied to shampoo, toothpaste, soap, and talc. One Malaysian company, Al-Murni (*murni* is Malay for "peaceful") had a successful promotion, giving away 30,000 free samples of its minaret-shaped toiletries to Malaysian pilgrims on their way to Mecca.

THE SUBTLE ART OF SELLING TO ASIA'S SUPER-RICH

By Brian Caplen

Fabulously wealthy Asians have displaced oil-rich Arabs as the world's fattest cats when it comes to looking for ways to show off their money.

Booming industries, property prices, and—in the case of Japan, Korea, and Taiwan—stockmarkets have created a crop of overnight millionaires and billionnaires from Bangkok to Yokohama.

Eager to flaunt their riches, the new Asian "emperors" are snapping up the most expensive and extravagant cars, jewellery, and liquor. But not all marketing executives for luxury products are rushing out to exploit this sales dream. The purveyors of the most sought-after status symbols say they deliberately limit sales to maintain exclusivity. The customer can and will wait.

This is just one example of the soft sell—some might call it a whisper—that is intrinsic to the subtle art of high-class marketing. An *Asian Business* investigation revealed that in the creme-de-la-creme market:

- Prices must not be set too low.
- Personal service and confidentiality are at a premium.
- Marketers worry about the overcommercialization of their brand.
- Customers are rejected if it is feared they might bring the product into disrepute.

Being able to choose one's customers may sound like paradise. But staying exclusive is no easy task. One false move can wipe out a reputation that has taken years to establish. And pampering existing clients—and consoling frustrated ones on the waiting list—takes as much time and energy as cold-calling does for a vacuum cleaner salesman.

Terry Tan, the marketing genius behind Ferrari cars in Singapore, estimates that 90% of his work is attending to clients. A call came in from a leading banker, trying to jump the queue for a Ferrari Testarossa.

"Even kings have to wait their turn," croons Tan, whose dress and charm are as immaculate as the sleek machines he sells.

Right now, the Singapore waiting list for the U.S. $350,000 Testarossa is more than a year, slightly longer than the queue time for a Jaguar, and about four months longer than for a Rolls Royce.

Satisfying appetites for Rolls Royces and mink coats is not as easy as it sounds. The customers are there but the service quality has to match the product. And, above all, image must be preserved.

Small wonder then that Ferrari seldom advertises, rarely has to prospect for customers, does product launches once in a blue moon, and has absolutely no need for a sales team.

In fact, Tan's problem is getting enough Ferraris to meet the burgeoning demand. He is only allocated 20 a year out of a worldwide production of 3,000.

Rolls Royce's global output is the same—which explains why sales in Hong Kong of just 40 cars amounted to a bumper year in 1987. They brought up to 800 the number jockeying for space in the colony's congested streets, the highest density of Rolls Royces anywhere.

Chris Blake, managing director of MD Motors, the Rolls Royce distributor in Hong Kong, says that with such relatively small sales volumes, TV advertising is a waste of money.

Instead, the cars are sold in a low-key manner. Whenever new models or improvements to old models are made, prospective customers who are assumed to have large bank balances are sent letters inviting them to private showings. One such showing to introduce a Rolls Royce relative, the Bentley Turbo R, resulted in the immediate sale of two cars, one of them the car on show.

A similar technique is used by Liebermann Overseas Trading, Ltd., which sells expensive fashion garments in Hong Kong, such as Leonard dresses, Porsche Design accessories, and Fogal lingerie through exclusive boutiques. A select client list is drawn up, based on the names of past buyers and wealthy potential clients. Those on the list are sent catalogues and are invited to private fashion shows to whet their appetite.

Sometimes the selling of the catalogue can be a profitable business in its own right. Sotheby's, the world's largest and oldest fine-art auctioneer, charges U.S. $9,460 for a year's subscription to its catalogues. But since Sotheby's holds an auction nearly every day in one of 16 world capitals, the task of putting the catalogues together is formidable. The end result is super glossy books, illustrating and describing in meticulous detail every item or collection.

With Sotheby's, again, finding the customers is not difficult. Keeping them informed and happy is.

"Weeks before a famous collection or item is auctioned, our offices around the world are flooded with enquiries from collectors and dealers," says the company's Singapore branch manager Quek Chin Yeow. "These people know the market and hear about sales through the grapevine. They don't need us to tell them."

But they do look for other kinds of service. If you want to bid for a Ming vase in a Hong Kong auction while on business in Zurich, Sotheby's will arrange a telephone bid—at its expense. It also takes care of the shipping, insurance, and export licensing and gives free valuations within hours for regular clients.

This formula is a huge success. Last year, Sotheby's did U.S. $1.4 billion in sales, taking 10% to 15% commission from sellers and 10% from buyers. The recent auction of Hong Kong tycoon T. Y. Chao's collection of Chinese ceramics and jade carvings raised U.S. $20 million.

High prices are no deterrent to the new Asian millionaires. In fact, the greatest mistake could be to pitch them too low.

Japanese sports cars, which have gained in price due to the strength of the yen, have made great strides in image power, it is claimed. Conversely, a sports car, such as the Italian Alfa Romeo, which has become relatively cheaper, may no longer be perceived as a luxury car, according to Henry Lee, managing director of the Hong Kong importer Sime Darby Motors Group.

But the biggest debate of all is about advertising. The purists maintain that if your product is really exclusive, advertising is not necessary. It may even be harmful, they say, if it overcommercializes the brand.

Yet watchmaker Patek Philippe spends large sums on advertising, even though production is limited to 12,000 watches a year. "Patek Philippe could easily sell more than this. But for the sake of quality and exclusivity, we have to sacrifice volume," says Daisy Chia, managing director of Singapore distributor Geneva Master Time.

She points out that it takes nine months to make a Patek Philippe. Each is hand-finished and undergoes 600 hours of testing. And, if the wait for a Ferrari Testarossa seems long, consider that in the case of one particular Patek Philippe pocket watch, the waiting time is now five years.

So why advertise? Apparently, in 1985, the company discovered that while most people could picture what the world's best car looked like, they had no inkling about the finest watch. Every watch, without its label, looks more or less the same.

Patek Philippe embarked on a U.S.$10 million annual campaign to give the product the right image. It also spends U.S.$250,000 a year sponsoring tournaments, exhibitions, and charitable events in Singapore, Malaysia, and Indonesia alone.

There is clearly another reason why a company such as Patek Philippe advertises extensively, whereas Rolls Royce doesn't. The smaller high-class products, such as watches, fashion goods, and liquor, while expensive in their own terms, can nevertheless be afforded by a large number of people who are prepared to spend a hefty percentage of their income on a single item, just to tell their friends they have "arrived."

While anyone can buy a Patek Philippe watch, Rolls Royce claims to choose its customers carefully to preserve its image, and was reported to be incensed that an Asian royal had converted one into a patrol vehicle for his bodyguard. His chances of getting another are not thought to be good. The company was also not pleased when a Kuwaiti buyer turned his Rolls into a taxi.

Expensive goods sell well in Hong Kong because image is so important to the Chinese psyche, says Dr. Yang Chungfang, a psychology lecturer at the University of Hong Kong.

The Chinese develop a sense of their own worth by comparison with others, she says, and parents drum in the message that, to be successful, a person must be more successful than his neighbors.

"Brand names are a way to demonstrate that status, to show they are important," says Yang, adding that the success of fake products shows it is image more than function that attracts.

But another psychology lecturer, Leung Kwok, of the Chinese University of Hong Kong, says that brand name products do carry a practical value—they get the owner better service in restaurants, stores, and other service places.

"It's a social reality. Brand name products get you more respect," says Leung. The rich, and the aspiring rich, of Asia undoubtedly agree with him.

Excerpted from an article written by Brian Caplen, reported by John Keating in Hong Kong, Linda Chan in Singapore, and Ron Sternberg in Tokyo. © *Asian Business* magazine, Far East Trade Press, Ltd., 1988.

VENI, VIDI, VENDING MACHINES

There are 5.2 million vending machines in Japan—one for every 23 people, which is double the per capita count in America. This leads to the Japanese saying that if it's the right size for a chute, it must have come out of a machine. Last year, the Japanese bought an estimated $41.3 billion worth of products and services from vending machines, according to the newspaper *Yomiuri Shimbun*.

THAT'S ZENTERTAINMENT

In Tokyo, thousands of adults and children regularly queue up in front of electronics shops to buy hot new videogames when they're released. That's literally thousands of buyers—3,000 lined up in front of one store; 1,500 at another to buy Dragon Quest III. The game's maker, Tokyo-based Enix, sold an estimated 5 million copies for a total of $230 million. The game retails for about $46.

THERE'S NO PLACE LIKE HOME

The Hong Kong Chinese Bank Group plans to develop a "Hong Kong Village" luxury residential complex in Manila, which will cater to Hong Kong residents who plan to emigrate to the Philippines before Hong Kong is taken over by China in 1997.

HONG KONG CREATIVES IN CANADA

Ad agency emigres from Hong Kong have established a high-powered Toronto agency, Lotus International, to introduce Asian products to the North American market. One of their initial campaigns was to introduce Ching Chun Bao (CCB), an all-natural premium Chinese ginseng drink in Canada. CCB contains ginseng, natural Chinese herbs, with white grape juice added for the Western palate. It's supposedly based on a formula that dates back 600 years to the Ming dynasty.

HINDI HEADLINES

Because the Indian government gives official recognition to 15 major languages in that country, the plight of the advertising copywriter is not an enviable one. Oddly enough, English is the only language that is understood throughout the entire country—but only by the educated upperclass, a minor percentage of the population, albeit the target of 50% of the print advertising expenditure. Advertising for such categories as industrial products, automobiles, and office equipment is almost always in English, even when it appears in other-language magazines. There has been an attempt to impose Hindi as the official national language but almost all the Hindi-speaking population is in the north, which means that national ads appearing in Hindi are not understood by approximately half of India's population, an enormous group divided by 13 other languages—not to mention several thousand dialects. Apart from English, there is no language that is understood by more than 10% of India's 802 million population.

RETAILING ON THE RIM

STORE WARS USE NEW WEAPONS
by Ron Sternberg

Computers and free customer services are changing the face of retailing as Japan's convenience stores battle for business.

Walking into your average neighborhood convenience store in Japan these days means walking into an unprecedented revolution in retailing.

Not only are there hundreds more convenience stores every year to walk into, but all are being transformed into ever more perfect selling machines. To accomplish this task, convenience stores use the technologies and innovation that have made Japan the world's most successful production machine.

As these selling machines expand into the rest of Asia, they stand ready to revolutionize each nation's retail trade in ways that one can only begin to imagine.

Japan's first convenience store, a 7-Eleven, opened 15 years ago in Koto-ku, Tokyo. Today, there are over 3,700 7-Elevens, and each day a new one opens up. 7-Eleven is not only the largest convenience store company in Japan, it is also the nation's number-one food retailer. Last year, it had more than one billion customer visits.

But 7-Eleven faces tough competition, particularly from Lawsons (3,100 stores) and Family Mart (1,700 stores). Apart from opening more stores, all three chains are seeking to increase efficiency and potential profits of each store through the use of point-of-sale (POS) systems. In this, 7-Eleven is the pi-

oneer and leader, having installed its first system in 1982.

Walk into a 7-Eleven, and as your order is rung up, the complex system does more than just add up the tally. A row of pink and blue keys to the right of the keypad carry the numbers 12, 18, 29, 49, and 50. These are discreetly punched to denote the sex and approximate age of each buyer.

This is added to the information taken from the bar code on each package to record who bought what, when, and in what quantity. A color graphic readout in the backroom computer lets each store know what is selling and allows it to place new orders efficiently.

Computers in the main office allow the company to do large-scale ordering and tracking to refine operations further.

Such an exact tracking system is necessary, given the small size of each store (about 100 square meters), the small number of people operating each one (no more than two to three at any time), and the lack of storage space. Convenience stores carry an average of 3,000 to 3,500 items, each compared to 15,000 or 20,000 for a typical supermarket, making multiple daily deliveries a must.

"Each of these items has to be a best-seller or we remove it," says Hidetoshi Akiyama, public relations manager for 7-Eleven Japan

Co. "Our shelves are our stock, and we can't afford to waste any space." 7-Eleven says it replaces about half of the 8,000 products that appear in its stores every year.

Using its point-of-sale system, 7-Eleven has begun to expand its services to customers in ways that bring in profits with a minimum of cost.

For example, the chain accepts payment of Tokyo Gas, Tokyo Electric Power (TEPCO), and Daiichi Seimei (insurance) bills. For this it receives Y30 per transaction. Pure profit. This is a major coup for the company, as there are an estimated 2.88 million TEPCO customers in the Tokyo area alone, who do not have their monthly bills automatically deducted from their bank accounts (checks are almost unheard of in Japan).

Paying at the local 7-Eleven means that bills can be paid not only during banking hours or TEPCO office hours, but at any hour of the day, a convenience 7-Eleven is counting on. Of course, 7-Eleven also expects many of those paying bills will also decide to buy a loaf of bread or a pack of cigarettes when they stop by.

7-Eleven also provides a small parcel service in conjunction with Yamato Transportation Co., next-day film developing, and advanced order services for gift-packaged flowers, Christmas cakes, Valentine's Day chocolates, and *bento* (Japanese-style prepared lunch box) for the New Year celebrations.

Family Mart offers JR Tokai Train tickets (for which it receives Y200 per ticket), film development, parcel delivery, and copy machine services (as does Lawsons) in addition to telephone cards and Seibu Saison ticketing for movies, concerts, and other events.

It is also working on selling tickets for All Nippon Airlines, says a spokesman. Family Mart lags behind 7-Eleven in its POS systems, and this has somewhat delayed expan-

sion of its services, but the company is working to move itself up to date by spending Y3 billion to bring all its stores in line by 1991.

Ironically, it has laws designed to protect small retailers from large ones that prompted 7-Eleven's parent in Japan, general department store and supermarket chain company Ito Yokada, to obtain the exclusive franchise for the chain from America's Southland Corp. (which Ito Yokada later acquired in 1990).

The Large Store Retail Law has long been a barrier to the establishment of large retailers. It regulates store hours, product mix, and general retail operations as well as requiring companies to obtain the consent of local retailers before opening a store of more than 1,500 square meters.

"Japanese law allows small neighborhood retailers the right to refuse entry of large department stores or supermarkets into established neighborhoods," explains 7-Eleven's Akiyama. "We saw the potential to expand our business through small shops."

The law is now under fire as a barrier to foreign trade, because large retail outlets are seen as one of the best ways for foreign goods to be brought into Japan on a large scale.

In recent years, pressure from within Japan and from abroad has grown to change the law. Its almost certain demise and coming rationalization of the retail sector has made the nation's 1.7 million small retail shops, 161,000 of which are of the "mom and pop" variety, prime candidates for 7-Eleven and other franchise operations.

7-Eleven is not the only one looking for expansion. Lawsons and Family Mart are also looking to expand their bases.

As if all the domestic action were not enough to keep things busy, Family Mart is expanding its operations overseas. The only Japanese convenience store company with an overseas strategy, Family Mart began its first joint ventures in Taiwan with the island's largest auto dealer, Kokusan Kisha, and C Itoh, the Japanese trading house.

The move overseas should help Family Mart keep its position as the fastest-growing convenience store. Last year sales were up 27.5% over 1987, to Y230.3 billion (U.S$1.6 billion).

THE STORE THAT CAN SAY NO

Japanese stores are famous for their super-service and total dedication to the customer. All, it would appear, except for a Chiba prefecture store named STEP which is bucking the trend. There, if any of the employees so much as strike up a conversation with a customer, they risk getting their salary docked by 5%, according to the *Shukan AERA* weekly.

STEP is an electronics warehouse outlet that offers discounts ranging from 20% to 40% off the manufacturer's suggested retail price. The owner, Terada Yoshio, explains that it's all a question of cost: "Every time an employee bows and intones *irasshaimase* (welcome), it costs the company 150 yen (about $1.15)."

IT'S CONVENIENT

Convenience stores are taking off in Taiwan. So far the biggest success story is the 7-Eleven chain, according to the Taipei-based financial newspaper *Economic News*. Taipei-headquartered President Chain Store Corp. brought the American franchise to Taiwan in 1979 with an initial investment of $69,000. Now 200 stores later, the chain has revenues of $90 million and is projecting 1,000 stores by 1998.

ASIAN TV IN EUROPE

The first Chinese-language satellite TV station in Europe began operating from London in 1990. Financed by a wealthy Hong Kong travel agent and two London-based Chinese businessmen, the station beams programs 12 hours a day to some 500,000 residents on the European Continent. The largest European Chinese communities are in the United Kingdom and Ireland with 170,000 people, and in France with 125,000 people. Most of the broadcast materials will be acquired in Hong Kong, Taiwan, or Mainland China, according to a company spokesman. Japan's Marubeni Corp. began transmitting Japanese-language programs across Europe from London on the Astra Satellite in 1989.

TAIWANESE SOAPS

Between eight and nine o'clock every night if you're tuned in to television on Taiwan you'll be watching the latest episode of a "drama" (otherwise known as a soap opera) one or another of which has dominated that time slot on all three networks as far back as anyone can remember. Akin to American night-time serials, these Chinese versions tend to drag on for so long that each is now limited to 40 episodes, a number set by the Government

Information Office which regulates media in the Republic of China. Production costs are relatively low, about $14,800, but even that is expensive compared with the cost of a good American film which might run to as much as $10,000. The dubbing of foreign films and TV programs began only about two years ago but have achieved much higher ratings than subtitled versions, because dubbing uses Chinese names and familiar Chinese colloquialisms instead of flat translations from the script. Reruns are not popular, so seasons tend to be continuous. About 85% of programming on TTV is produced by the network itself, but competition for viewers is heating up since last year's decision to legalize small satellite dishes which can pick up programs from Japan.

CNN in Vietnam

Vietnam acquired the rights to use Turner Broadcasting System's Cable News Network's 24-hour a day television programming. The Atlanta-headquartered broadcaster was bounced out of China after its coverage of the Tiananmen Square massacre and plans to install a satellite dish receiver in Hanoi.

Quick Reads

New-style "commuting" magazines with nontaxing content and big pictures have grown immensely in popularity among the vast number of Japanese workers who spend as much as four hours on trains every day. Many of the magazines are designed to be read in 15 or 20 minutes and have greatly encouraged the rise of papparazzi-style reporting which, says one media commentator, offer "hazy telephoto glimpses into the private lives of the stars."

Chinese *Elle*

The glossy French fashion magazine *Elle,* which at $2 costs more than the average Chinese worker earns in a day, is selling well in Beijing bookstores. The Chinese edition is printed quarterly in Shanghai.

Rim Review

The Medium Is the *Manga*

The "*manga*-ization" of America's info-media continues. The publication in English of *Japan, Inc.* (University of California Press), a comic book presenting Japan's view of world economics, gave the West its first taste of Japan's serious *mangas* (comics). Now we've got an original American *manga* in the form of Leonard Koren's compendium, *283 Useful Ideas From Japan: For Entrepreneurs and Everyone Else* (Chronicle Books). Koren's *manga*-style book is a primer on Japanese creativity in four major areas: products, services, marketing and communications. From rental restaurants (where customers pay to cook their own meals) to video billboards on wheels, we are treated to glimpses of Japanese ingenuity in action. Western entrepreneurs will especially benefit from a useful appendix which lists contact addresses and phone numbers of Japanese companies whose products and services are featured in the book.

Unease in Indonesia

Because the official policy in Indonesia is to discourage the concept of national newspapers in favor of provincial ones, the country—from a marketing point of view—is a collection of separate and widely different enclaves

RIM VOICES

IDEA FOR NEW TV SHOW: "INDONESIA'S MOST CORRUPT"

Many corruption cases involving government officials are being tried these days. We know this from reports by the print media. But for various reasons people don't read newspapers with the same (interest) as they watch TV. So why not televise court sessions, so that the people will not be lulled by reports on development, inaugurations, and comedy show songs and suchlike? Of course, not all corruption trials could be televised as corruption is already so prevalent. It would suffice to transmit the most spectacular cases. I do not believe the presentation of the faces of government officials who are suckers of the people's blood rather than public servants will disturb national stability.

From Djuhari of Lamongan, East Java in *Panji Masyarakat,* Indonesia

which must be targeted individually. There are at least 31 semi-rural/semi-urban areas with populations over one million with, according to one Jakarta businessman, "strong regional variations."

"What sells for one reason or another in one province won't sell in another," he says. Nevertheless, the provincial press has a long way to go to catch up with Jakarta-based *Kompas,* which usually receives more than half of Indonesia's total print advertising budget. The paper's recent bid to print simultaneously in both Jakarta and Surabaya was turned down by the country's Ministry of Information.

WANTED: MALAYSIAN MODELS ONLY

Scantily clad women and other ingredients of Western lifestyles depicted in commercials have been banned from Malaysian television on the grounds that they are an attempt to change the country's identity. Information Minister Datuk Mohamed Rahmat said such advertisements did not reflect the image of the majority of Malaysians and projected the superiority of Western lifestyles to attract customers. In the future it would be mandatory for ads to depict "the actual picture" in the country. Up to now advertisers have had to submit story boards for broadcasting approval but it had been discovered that the actual ad often differed from what had been approved, so that in the future advertisers would have to submit a videotape of the proposed ad. The minister added that he hoped the ban would be extended to the print media.

"Wash a crow with rose-water, its feathers will still remain black."

Malaysian proverb

BULLETIN FROM MANILA

Although Manila's eager newspaper readers are sometimes confronted with as many as 27 papers from which to choose (most in English but others in Chinese and Filipino), the *Manila Bulletin* is clearly the market leader, economically if not editorially. Its daily circulation is a disputed 250,000—some of its rivals say it's less than half that figure—but its advertising

CHINESE NEWSPAPERS TOO EXPENSIVE

Even though a price increase has increased the cost of some Chinese newspapers to the equivalent of only five U.S. cents per copy, this is still four times the previous price, and much too expensive for many buyers. As a result, the number of newspaper subscriptions has dropped by one third in recent years. Despite enormous government subsidies, most newspapers are losing money.

IRATE INDONESIAN JOURNALISTS

Indonesian journalists are up in arms about the recent anticommunist campaign which required them to fill in elaborately detailed questionnaires about their families' past associations. A handful of journalists with distant relatives who had communist associations have been fired although even some ministers had condemned such actions as overzealous. "One chooses one's wife but not one's parents or grandparents," one editor commented, "so why hold us responsible for what they might have done in the past? It's totally ridiculous." The crackdown came after the former head of the pro-government Federation of Indonesian Journalists was replaced with hardliner Sug-
eng Wijaya, a former general who headed the army daily *Berita Yudha* ("War News").

WORLD'S MOST EXPENSIVE AD SPACE

The world's most expensive page of advertising is undoubtedly one in Japan's *Yomiuri Shimbun,* top national paper in two thirds of the country's 47 prefectures, with a total morning circulation of 9.6 million copies. Even in black and white, that page will cost $319,615, and the addition of color and choice of placement brings the cost to $417,746. All Japan's national papers have colossal circulations—the total exceeds 50 million in a population of 102 million—but *Yomiuri,* with its editorial staff of 1,000, is part of a group that also turns out 120 books each year, magazines, operates the national NTV network, and owns Japan's leading ball club, the Yomiuri Giants. With the world's highest literacy rate and a home delivery of 99%, Japanese are voracious newspaper readers, partly because of the time most of them spend commuting to work. Men spend an average of 50 minutes daily reading newspapers, women 35 minutes.

MULTIPLEX THEATERS IN THAILAND

Mini-movie theaters are on the rise in Thailand. They're springing up in crowded areas such as department stores and shopping centers. One reason for creation of mini-theaters like the McKenna cinema group's Major 1 and 2 theaters in Bangkok's gigantic Mah Boon Krong Shopping Complex is changing Thai law, implementing copyright and censorship regulations on the video industry. Not only is the quality of video movies declining due to multiple copying, but rentals are increasing as

THE PEOPLE'S DAILY (QING DYNASTY EDITION)

C. F. Gordon Cummings was an intrepid Scotswoman who traveled throughout China in the 1870s. In her two-volume chronicle of her experience, entitled Wanderings in China, *she covers the subject of newspapers in the Middle Kingdom.*

Business-like Britons, who look to their daily paper for tidings of fluctuations in the money-market, may well wonder that a great mercantile nation such as this can exist virtually without newspapers, but so it is. While the native press of little, ultraprogressive Japan already produces no less than 250 newspapers (all of which circulate freely among eager purchasers, thirsting for the latest news of all sorts), the vast Chinese empire produces only 22 periodicals, and of these only 12 are in the vernacular; nine are in English, and one is in French. Even of these, the circulation is so extraordinarily small that newspapers may fairly be considered unknown to the 400 million inhabitants of the Celestial Empire. Liberty of the press is altogether a thing not realized.

The sole newspaper of the whole vast extent of northern China is the *Peking Gazette,* which is beyond doubt the oldest newspaper in the world and claims to have existed long before the Western barbarians invented printing for themselves. There seems no reason to doubt that it was in circulation in the twelfth century.

Though said to be not positively official, it is under the strictest government control, and beyond imperial edicts and petitions, contains only such Morsels of information as the paternal government sees fit to impart to its babes. It is in the form of a pamphlet, seven inches in length by four in breadth, and stitched into a yellow paper cover.

There are, however, three editions, one of which has a red cover, and another a white cover, and I am not sure which is which. I understand, however, that the red one (which is only published every other day) contains only official information, while the white one, which appears daily, contains information on police reports and other matters of local interest. The third edition contains the cream of the other two, in a cheaper form.

The news thus disseminated is sometimes extraordinarily puerile, and that which relates to intercourse with foreigners is apt to be amazingly mendacious. But true or false, this metro-politan oracle is republished under strict official supervision; and woe betide the luckless publisher or printer who ventures to alter one jot or one title, even when he is aware of the utter falsity of the information he may be called upon to print!

well. Video distributors by law have to pay about 100 *baht* per tape to have their videos censored and licensed, a cost which is passed on to renters. So a new and improved cinema environment in the minis, which feature advanced sound systems, is attracting movie-goers.

MTV IN TAIWAN

To the Taiwanese teenager, MTV doesn't mean what it does to an American viewer of cable. The term stands for "Movies on TV," and the type of clubs in which they are shown. Proliferating all over Taipei, the MTV clubs have survived early criticism that they were a threat to traditional Chinese values (by allowing privacy in comfortably furnished rooms) and allegations that they were thriving on "pirated" foreign films. Many young Taiwanese complain that at home the VCR is usually devoted to screening the old-fashioned Chinese movies favored by their conservative parents, whereas the MTV is not only a refuge from noisy, crowded street and coffee shops, but entertainment more to their taste. Potential operators of MTV clubs, of which there are now about 1,000 on the island, must apply for a license and prove they have capital of at least $34,700. The clubs, however, are gold mines, often operating 24 hours per day and charging up to $8 for the rental of videotapes, which can be watched by up to four or five people at a time.

HOT AND COLD CDs

More than 1.5 billion records have been sold over the last decade in Japan, according to the Japan Phonograph Record Association. But Japan's record industry is rapidly transforming into the "music software" industry as records are being phased out in a shift to compact discs. According to Sony Corp. research, the Japanese market is nearly 40% saturated with compact disc players compared to 25% to 30% in the United States. Sony expects that figure to reach 60% soon—the same level of saturation of VTR (video tape recorder) machines. Total sales in Japan of compact disc players by all makers were 5 million in 1988, up from 3.8 million in 1987. World sales were estimated at 20 million in 1988.

FORBIDDEN DITTY?

Defrocked American television evangelist Jimmy Swaggart sold 15 half-hour music programs to China's state-run national television network. But the programs have no religious content, according to China Central Television's International Department. The programs consist entirely of classical piano music, with no singing, no preaching, and not even a greeting from Swaggart. According to Swaggart, his company, Starcom, sold the programming to China for $250,000.

VIDEO VIGILANCE

A Kaohsiung, Taiwan videotape vendor was sentenced to 7½ years imprisonment under Taiwan's subversion act for publicly showing a tape of a Communist Chinese military parade. The same tape had been shown on the Chinese Television System (CTS) news that night. But CTS claimed it aired the tape to stir up vigilance among Taiwanese against a possible military invasion, whereas the videotape vendor was using the tape to promote business.

HIGH-YEN MEDIA WEDDING

Japanese pop singer Hiroshi Itsuki and his bride Yuko had a televised wedding which aired as a two-hour program. The event cost $3.5 million, of which $285,000 was spent on flowers alone. Sponsors spent about $4.5 million for the eight minutes of advertising.

TUNING IN TO THE ZOO

For more than a year now, Singapore's young radio listeners have been forsaking their local stations in favor of The Amazing FM Zoo broadcast from atop a hill on Indonesia's Batam Island, a half hour's ferry ride away. Officially known as Radio Ramako Batam, the station is one of four owned by Bambang Rachmadi, the 38-year-old son-in-law of Indonesia's vice president, who says the station's high-energy, fast-swinging, and cool-talking mix, combined with fewer commercials, wooed customers away from the more staid, blander fare of Singapore stations with their constant interruptions and excessive chatter. "The market was ready, provided there was the right product," he says, "and we came in with the right product."

ASIAN MARKETING IN REVIEW

The following is an overview of Pacific Rim marketing by Asian Advertising & Marketing, *a Hong Kong-based regional industry publication.*

With a recession overseas and the specter of war in the Persian Gulf, advertising expenditure in an otherwise buoyant 1990 was visibly dampened by the end of the year. With the outbreak of hostilities, the first quarter of 1991 saw already conservative plans put on hold or cancelled as businesses headed into an uncertain future.

Despite the problems, Malaysia, Thailand, Indonesia and China all saw substantial increases in ad billings in 1990. Leading the region in economic growth, Malaysia's advertising industry had a similarly good year, with prospects for new business in the hot property development and financial services sectors. Adspend again surged with Thailand's dynamic economy, while the bloodless coup in late February is not expected to unsettle business or advertising activities. Indonesia saw the shift from print to TV advertising becoming more pronounced, following the government decision to allow TV commercials from March 1990. Although Beijing's Asian Games in September 1990 were a flop as an advertising event, China's ad business grew perceptibly.

The good times were no longer with Hong Kong, Taiwan and the Philippines. Along with a slowing economy, Hong Kong's brain drain continues to sap the territory of its talent, although new media options may enliven adspend. Consumer spending in Taiwan fell with the collapse of the stock market and cooled real estate speculation, and competition is intense between agencies for shares of a smaller pie. Although the Philippines was rocked by calamities both political and natural, its agencies had a surprisingly good year until oil prices skyrocketed in late 1990. Most plans are on hold, while agencies anticipate an increase in business preceding presidential elections in 1992.

CHINA

1990 was a watershed for advertising in China, a year in which international advertising became a business, says J Walter Thompson's Ron Cromie. "We are forecasting growth in our China business of over 50 percent in 1991," he says. "We recognize this is very high growth on a very small base, but you don't get 50 percent growth in very many markets very often." It comes on top of growth of about 20 percent in 1990 with total adspend of 3.32 billion yuan (US$637 million).

Certainly such a change is welcome news for the faithful few international agencies who have stuck to China in the decade since the country reopened its doors to the outside world, and comes after considerable uncertainty following the political and economic crises of 1989.

Like all companies that have chosen to operate in China, advertising agencies have had to adopt a long-term view. They have struggled to serve their foreign clients operating in China, accepting meager returns at best in the hope that one day they would reap a rich harvest. They faced myriad difficulties, especially in the early days, from all-pervasive red tape to general ignorance of the advertising business. These problems are ones associated with doing business in the mainland, while working with a small client base and often tiny budgets compared with those in more mature markets. But now this is changing as the level of advertising spending by multinational companies grows rapidly to match their expanding operations in China.

The development is only partially the result of the recent marginal improvement in the Chinese economy from the disastrous slump which occurred after Beijing's imposition of austerity measures in late 1988. The recovery has seen increase in industrial output, reduction of inflation and a sharp improvement in the country's trade performance. But it is unclear how far improvements will go and how they will last. "There are some factors which nobody can predict and nobody dares to predict, and these relate to the political scenario," says Chinalink's Joseph Tong. Predicting economic trends is also difficult. "I hope that 1991 will be better, but there are conflicting views. Some local people in China expect 1991 to be even tougher than 1990 for the domestic economy. It depends on the industry," he says.

But the main reason behind the rapid increase in advertising expenditure has been the start-up of many major Sino-foreign joint ventures producing for the domestic market, ventures that were negotiated during the high tide of Western enthusiasm for investment in China during the mid-1980s. "As those joint ventures come on-stream, the parent companies greatly increase their advertising spend in China," says Cromie. "They may have had some spending before to support import sales, and suddenly they have got much larger production and they have to build market share, and build demand for those new products and new brands."

The bulk of the products, and the advertising spend to support them, comes from major consumer-product multinationals. Statistics from China indicate that in general, consumer spending has not yet recovered from the slump following the imposition of austerity measures and many locally produced goods are still piling up unsold in warehouses. But demand for products turned out by the multinationals in their joint ventures has been powering ahead, fulfilling the hopes of their foreign backers, which was to get into the highly protected Chinese market. Before, when the multinationals relied on importation to get their consumer products into the mainland for their sales, they faced many obstacles, not the least [of which were] Beijing's efforts to restrict tightly the amount of hard currency spent on goods considered to be luxuries unnecessary to China's development.

"China is a hard market to get into and very hard to sell into in terms of import sales, but once you do get in, the demand for your products can be enormous," says Cromie. "Some of these joint ventures are seeing incredible volume of production. Even though the domestic pricing is low, the volume is tremendous. From an advertising point of view you support that volume and keep it growing."

The reason is that many products' sales are not driven by demand, he says, but by supply. The key is being able to get your product to the market. Demand is not the problem, concurs Tse, nor is creating effective advertising campaigns. "There are obstacles like distribution," he says. "That is a difficult job—getting the product to the market at the right time and the right place. It is much more difficult than creating good advertising."

For this reason China is not suddenly being blanketed with ads selling soap and shampoo. Advertising campaigns in the main are still directed towards specific regional markets which can be supplied by established joint ventures. These are usually sited in areas with the highest living standards like Shanghai and the Yangtze Delta or Guangdong province, both of which enjoyed dynamic growth in the years of reform, and have managed the fastest recovery from the slump of 1989. It is in these dynamic regional markets that consumer spending is strongest.

Some companies, with a presence already established in these primary markets are, however, moving into other secondary areas in major cities like Beijing, Tianjin and Chengdu, again increasing advertising spend to support their expansion.

Despite this optimism and growth, there were still difficulties and disappointments in 1990. One of the greatest disappointments was Beijing's Asian Games, which, although a great sporting and propaganda success for China, failed to live up to its potential as an advertising event. This was largely due to poor promotion of the event as an advertising venue by the Chinese organisers, indicating that much still has to be learned by the domestic industry.

The advertising industry in China is huge. There are 11,000 to 12,000 "advertising agencies" in China, although only 1,100 are specialized agencies, the rest mostly being advertising departments in various media companies. In 1989 total advertising revenue was about 2 billion yuan (US$384 million). Foreign advertising is estimated to account for about 10 percent of the total. While standards in the domestic industry are improving, especially on the creative side, gaps still exist. "Advertising professionals, outstanding ones, good ones, are still a rare species," notes Tong.

Advertisers are also facing increased costs, although the exact amount is still unclear. According to some, cost inflation last year was about 10–15 percent, but increases for 1991 may be significantly greater. China still operates with a complex rate system, with differing rates for domestic Chinese, joint venture and overseas advertisers. In a typical example, Shanghai TV has a rate of 1,100 yuan (US$211) for a 30-second floating spot for domestic advertisers, 1,500 yuan (US$288) for joint ventures and US$1,100 for foreign companies selling imported goods in China.

Television stations have been asking for rate increases of up to 100 percent, says Cromie, but it is unclear whether they will actually get them. Greater premiums are also being asked for fixed spots. Rates for joint ventures, with their hugely expanded demand, are likely to rise the most, he believes, but despite the increases, television advertising remains remarkably cheap.

Rate increases may have their benefits, says Tse. Previously the domestic media have earned so little from the low rates that they frequently prefer to bypass the agencies and deal directly with the clients, cutting out the agency commission. Higher rates may help reduce this practice, enhancing the role of the agencies.

The effects of greater adspend in the mainland will not simply be confined to those in the industry serving clients in China. It will spill over to the industry in Hong Kong, as many of the biggest players begin to spend more on advertising in the mainland than in Hong Kong. "The implications for the industry in Hong Kong are quite significant if suddenly some of your biggest clients are spending more in China than in Hong Kong," says Cromie.

In Hong Kong, China advertising has generally been viewed as a poor, and unglamorous, relation. But this is changing. In 1990 the Hong Kong 4As established a China committee, with expectations of a limited response from the member agencies. However, virtually all of the 19 members of the association joined the committee, indicating a very high level of interest and recognition of China's growing importance, even though only a few of the agencies have a significant presence in the country.

One of the purposes of the 4As' China committee will be to develop the industry as a whole. "One of the challenges for us is to bring people into China advertising. There is real need now for talent, to convince people working in Hong Kong that it is where the real opportunities are. But it's a hard sell," says Cromie. "It will change as soon as people recognise the opportunities. If you do a good TV commercial for China it's going to be seen by anywhere from 50 to 200 million consumers. You can create a whole new brand. There's nowhere else in the world where you can do that right now."

by Duncan Freeman

HONG KONG

Hong Kong's advertising and media people had a steady year in 1990. "It was the same as always. We pedalled the bike fast but it didn't go very far," says executive director of Lintas: Hong Kong, Robert Wilson, in exasperation. As the shadow cast by events in Beijing's Tiananmen Square in 1989 lightened somewhat, the Gulf crisis and recession took their toll. Clients held back on spending, budgets fell or remained at 1989 levels, and the industry resigned itself to consolidation, careful spending and cautious optimism for the future.

Adspend figures for the year tell a revealing story. Expenditure in measurable media at rate-card level reached HK$6.72 billion (US$863 million), a growth of 21.3 percent, four percent higher than 1989's growth, according to Hong Kong Adex 1990. When inflation (nine percent) and rate-card increases are taken into account, however, the real growth rate is likely to be nearer six percent, say industry observers.

The economy had a large part to play in the ad industry's performance. With the slowing of global export trade, on which Hong Kong is so dependent, the industry was forced to look inwards. As recession benefited the sectors that could display measured results for investment—market research, sales promotion and direct marketing—advertising agencies had to take stock of budget cuts and increasing competition for business.

Hong Kong experienced some economic recovery, boosted partly by the growth of tourism and also by China's improving economy. Hong Kong's exports to the PRC totalled HK$112 billion (US$14.3 billion) for

Top 10 Hong Kong Ad Agencies (capitalized billings in U.S.$ millions[a])

	(US$ millions) 990	(HK$ millions) 1990	1989
1. Leo Burnett	68.2	532.0★	453.0★
2. J. Walter Thompson	48.5	378.3	299.6
3. Ogilvy & Mather	48.5	378.1	352.2
4. The Ball Partnership	46.4	361.4	282.2
5. HDM	44.5	347.1	328.7
6. BBDO	41.6	324.0	241.0
7. Backer Spielvogel Bates	39.3	306.2	303.8
8. McCann Erickson	35.7	278.0	226.0
9. Bozell	33.9	264.5	183.6
10. DDB Needham	32.6	254.5	213.4

★Includes DM and China billings
Source: Individual agencies.

the first nine months of 1990, two percent up on the 1989 figure, and China is still the territory's biggest export market, according to Hong Kong's Trade Development Council (TDC). Meanwhile, an influx of short-haul visitors led to 10.7 percent growth over the 1989 arrivals figure and a 6.3 percent rise in visitor spending (which actually represented a drop in per capita spend from 1989). Tourists from Southeast Asia, Japan, Taiwan and South Korea represented 62.6 percent of the total visitors for the year. The increase in tourists visiting the territory, however, did not improve, disappointing retail sales for the last few months of 1990.

Unfortunately, developments in the Middle East reduced the strength of the post-Tiananmen Square recovery and high oil prices increased inflation so the territory's overall growth estimates for 1990 dropped. Estimated figures from the government Census and Statistics Office revised GDP and inflation to 2.3 percent and nine percent, respectively.

Confidence in Hong Kong's future experienced yet another period of uncertainty.

While the UK parliament passed the Hong Kong Passport Bill, giving passports to 50,000 Hong Kong professionals and their families, Hong Kong people reacted with skepticism, saying the number was inadequate for the territory's 5.6 million population. And the parade of companies incorporating offshore was joined by the Hongkong Bank when it announced its intention to establish a holding company in London.

A total of 62,000 people left Hong Kong in 1990, contributing to the co-called "brain drain" of professional and qualified personnel.

Perhaps the most significant change in 1990 was that marketers started to look beyond TV and print media and seriously consider promotional activity and direct mail as a cost-effective method of advertising. Companies like sales promotion agency Triangle Pacific did reasonably well, taking on over 20 new clients, all of them blue-chip companies. "Most companies demanded that advertising work harder for them so they turned to direct marketing and below-the-line because of its immediacy and response," says Deb Coulson.

Direct marketers, flushed with the success of increasing business, are forecasting over 20 percent growth for 1990 and the next five years, barring unforeseen circumstances.

In the case of tobacco companies, the broadcast advertising ban which came into effect from December 1, 1990 forced their budgets below-the-line and impacted not only ad agencies with tobacco accounts—Leo Burnett (Philip Morris) and J. Walter Thompson (R J Reynolds)—but also Hong Kong's Commercial Radio station and two television stations, Asia Television (ATV) and Television Broadcasts (TVB). Estimates are that the TV stations will lose around 10 percent of their revenue which will be put into print media and below-the-line marketing activities. As radio braved the loss of tobacco advertising, notching up a very satisfying 42.5 percent growth in adspend last year (HK$295 million or US$37 million), television emerged the loser, bringing in HK$3.3 billion (US$422 million) which represented an adspend increase of only 17.5 percent over 1989. Narrowcast station ATV trounced mass appeal station TVB into second place with an adspend increase of 40 percent compared to TVB's nine percent, though TVB's total adspend was HK$2.7 billion (US$344 million) compared to ATV's HK$605 million (US$78 million).

For the print media, the year was both good and bad. Print continued to snap at television's heels, increasing its share of the media cake and registering 48 percent growth over 1989 figures, HK$1.9 billion (US$247 million) in the press and HK$904 million (US$116 million) in magazines. While panic reigned as budgets were squeezed, a more deal-oriented mentality emerged among clients as they haggled over rates. "People were looking for more value for money and so they should," says the publisher of a Chinese-language regional news weekly *Ya-zhou Zhoukan,* Winnie Wong. "If publishers can come up with more creative ideas to sell a page, it forces everyone to think harder and that's got to be good for business."

The year was tough for English-language publications which followed one another in quick succession into decline and fall. First the Sing Tao Group's *China Review* ceased publication, then *Billion,* Sing Tao's joint venture with Swiss publishing house Ringier. *Asia Technology* folded amidst cries that parent company Dow Jones was cutting back at a time of low investor morale. Ambitious niche title *All Asia Review of Books* folded and even the Chinese-language *Sing Tao Business Magazine* admitted defeat in an increasingly competitive market and closed its doors shortly before year-end.

Failures and cries of "saturated market" did nothing to deter new launches, which simply added paper to the already over-burdened newsstands. Advertisers continued to support the market leaders as well as some of the newcomers—several new titles which had entered the market and, at press time, still remained. Witness the franchised Hachette women's monthly *Marie Claire* and the handful of women's titles including *Domina, Lady First,*

Advertising Expenditure in Hong Kong by Medium (U.S.$ millions)

	(US$ millions) 1990	(HK$ millions) 1990	1989
Television	422.1	3291.0	2804.3
Radio	37.9	295.8	207.6
Newspapers	247.3	1927.6	1587.0
Magazines	116.0	904.0	714.9
MTR	25.2	196.7	140.4
Cinema	11.2	87.2	75.2
Other	2.1	16.5	11.2
Total	861.8	6718.8	5540.6

Source: HK Adex.

Top 10 Hong Kong Advertisers by Brand
(U.S.$ millions)

| | (US$ millions) | (HK$ millions) | |
	1990	1990	1989
1. Marlboro cigarettes	10.6	82.3	69.0
2. Sharp products	9.4	73.5	40.1
3. Kao products	9.3	72.7	47.9
4. Hong Thai Travel	8.3	64.9	54.2
5. McDonald's	7.8	60.7	45.8
6. Mild Seven cigarettes	6.3	49.1	50.9
7. Sunflower Travel	6.3	49.0	36.9
8. Kent cigarettes	6.2	48.0	38.8
9. Salem cigarettes	6.0	46.9	35.1
10. National products	5.8	44.4	42.8

Source: HK Adex.

Top 10 Hong Kong Advertisers by Category
(U.S.$ millions)

| | (US$ millions) | (HK$ millions) | |
	1990	1990	1989
1. Leisure	138.4	1079.0	905.8
2. Retail	78.9	614.8	526.7
3. Foodstuffs	61.2	477.0	428.7
4. Personal Items	59.9	467.2	372.0
5. Real estate	59.3	462.4	312.3
6. Toiletries	57.6	449.0	366.8
7. Electrical appliances	48.9	381.1	310.7
8. Smoking and accessories	43.6	339.7	282.7
9. Clothing	40.9	318.5	271.5
10. Finance/investment/ banking	37.1	289.1	235.7

Source: HK Adex.

Working Woman and *Mary*. Far East Trade Press' monthly travel title *Arrival* published its first issue in October, and entrepreneur-turned-publisher Jimmy Lai is said to have filled a gap in the market with a Chinese consumer weekly magazine, *Next*. Another publisher, Albert Cheng, riding on the success of Chinese-language business weekly, *Capital,* launched a sister English-language magazine, *HongKong,inc,* and announced plans for launching a Chinese version of Forbes magazine—*Forbes Zibenjia* (Capitalist)—in 1991.

Though pessimism prevailed in the short-term view of Hong Kong in 1990, optimism was evident for the long term with the expansion of television and radio options. Following months of deliberation, the government finally deregulated satellite television and paved the way for HutchVision's regional English-language satellite service. The satellite ruling sounded the death knell for cable plans and the five-member cable consortium de-

cided to abort the project in the face of rising costs and competition from satellite. Shortly after the satellite decision, the government awarded the licence for a new commercial radio station to Metro Broadcast, a group consisting of Hong Kong filmmakers Golden Harvest, D & B Films, trading and communications giant Hutchison and the US-based Indev Group. Metro plans to have one of its three channels on air this month and is vying directly with the territory's existing advertising station, Commercial Radio and Radio Television Hong Kong, for advertisers and audience.

Radio's progress during 1990 was steady following three years of growth in adspend and listenership, but fears are that a recent slight overall decline in listenership indicates the market cannot take another station. But, if Metro can promote more competition and attract new advertisers to radio, then anything is possible.

by Karen Winton

INDONESIA

A new force was unleashed on Indonesia's media market in late 1990 as television commercials began broadcasting nearly nationwide for the first time since 1981. For new educational TV station, Televisi Pendidikan (Educational) Indonesia (TPI), ad income will be a significant source of revenue, and the station is aiming to gobble up nine million rupiah (US$4,775) every 30 seconds, 24 times an hour, during each of its four-hour broadcast days. The expanded scope of TV advertising will affect the entire media industry in Indonesia—radio stations and magazines are already planning to reposition themselves to sidestep an expected drain of dollars away from lackluster performers. "TV has awakened the media scene," observes Philip Rich of Survey Research Indonesia (SRI).

As the educational TV channel geared up for its launch in early 1990, Jakarta's established commercial station, Rajawali Citra Tel-

evisi Indonesia (RCTI), set up sister stations in Surabaya and Bandung, with another planned to open in Denpasar by the end of 1991. Altogether, the private stations are expected to pull in 105 billion–140 billion rupiah (US$55.7 million–74.3 million) more in advertising revenues than the 45 billion–60 billion rupiah (US$23.8 million–31.8 million) TV earned in 1990. All the stations now operate without decoders, even Jakarta-based RCTI, which began as a cable station but abandoned decoders last September. RCTI was given permission to run commercials in March 1989, and the switch from decoders boosted potential viewership from 125,000 subscriber households to four million individuals thought to have UHF antennas.

Those figures pale in comparison with the estimated 70 million Indonesians thought to live within TPI's footprint. Of those people, 24 million are students who will soon be required to watch the channel's math and science programs in school—the government has committed itself to equipping all schools with TV sets by July, 1991. But besides the upcoming junior and senior high-school student viewers, no one is sure who else is tuning into TPI's morning broadcasts, especially to

Top 10 Indonesian Advertising Agencies (media billings in U.S.$ millions)[a]

	(US$ million) 1989	(Rupiah millions) 1990*	1989*
1. Citra: Lintas Indonesia	19.1	36,000	30,000
2. Matari, Inc.	15.4	29,000	20,200
3. Indo Ad	12.7	24,000	13,000
4. Fortune	11.9	22,500	9,000
5. Ad Force JWT	9.0	17,000	8,800
6. Interadmark	6.4	12,000	11,000
7. Grafik	5.0	9,500	4,900
8. Rama Perwira	4.5	8,500	7,300
9. Binamark	4.4	8,200	NR
10. Perwanal DMB&B	3.7	7,000	4,100

*Estimated
Note: Billings based on net media expenditure on TV, magazine, newspaper, and radio only.
Source: Citra: Lintas Indonesia Media Monitoring Dept.

Advertising Expenditure by Medium— Indonesia (U.S.$ millions)

	(US$ millions) 1990	(Rupiah millions) 1990*	1989*
Television	23.9	45,000	15,835
Radio	31.8	60,000	50,500
Newspapers	132.6	250,000	176,335
Magazines	30.8	58,000	42,430
Outdoor	32.4	61,000	55,000
Cinema	3.2	6,000	5,300
Total	254.7	480,000	345,400

Source: PT Citra: Lintas Indonesia Media Monitoring Dept.

Top 10 Indonesian Advertisers by Brand
(U.S.$ millions)

		(US$ millions) 1990	(Rupiah millions) 1990	1989
1.	Sampoerna	2.7	5000	2600
2.	Djarum	2.4	4500	3400
3.	Bank Danamon	2.3	4300	NR
4.	Toyota	2.1	3900	4000
5.	Daihatsu (car)	1.9	3600	NR
6.	Bank Duta	1.9	3500	NR
7.	Bendera/ Bendira 123	1.8	3300	2500
8.	Lippobank	1.6	3100	2500
9.	Marlboro	1.6	3000	NR
10.	Bank Central Asia	1.4	2600	NR

Note: Figures are based on media expenditure on TV, magazine, newspaper, and radio only.
Source: PT Citra: Lintas Indonesia.

Top 10 Advertisers by Category—Indonesia
(U.S.$ millions)

		(US$ millions) 1990	(Rupiah millions) 1990	1989
1.	Banks and insurance	30.4	57,300	21,000
2.	Vehicles and spare parts	15.5	29,200	22,450
3.	Body care products	14.7	27,800	26,650
4.	Cigarettes	10.5	19,800	15,000
5.	Beverages	9.9	18,700	14,300
6.	Retail	8.1	15,300	NR
7.	Tours and travel	7.6	14,300	NR
8.	Media	7.3	13,700	7,200
9.	Real estate	6.0	11,400	6,800
10.	Food	6.0	11,300	11,900

Note: Figures are based on media expenditure on TV, magazine, newspaper and radio only.
Source: PT Citra: Lintas Indonesia.

the station's prime-time 6AM-to-7AM news and callisthenics. (That hour is prime time because Indonesians try to tackle the most onerous chores before the heat of the day sets in.)

But "it's all a big guess at the moment," says SRI's Rich. "Maybe people will go to the market early, then come home to watch other shows later."

TPI is confident that 6AM viewing will prove a hit, so it is charging 14.4 million rupiah (US$7,600) for 46-to-60-second commercials before 7:01AM. The station's broadcast day ends at 11AM, but it is slated to expand gradually to 11 hours a day by year's end. As the largest segment of the viewing audience is expected to be housewives, potential advertisers are thought to include marketers of fast-moving consumer goods such as detergents, toiletries, food and beverages. TPI hopes to sell 60 percent of its commercial slots in 1991, says advertising columnist and TPI consultant Ernst Katoppo. By the end of December 1990, some advertisers had already reserved space for the year ahead.

State-run channel TVRI plans to continue to broadcast without commercials until further notice. The government banned advertising on TVRI in 1981 out of concern it would instill unrealistic expectations among the populace, but there has been recent talk of ads returning to the station. "So much is happening in TV that anything could happen in the coming year," notes Rich.

Jakarta's RCTI gives advertisers more choice in its 1991 rates, creating a cheaper category (725,000 rupiah for 10 seconds) on weekend mornings and post-midnight weekdays. But prime time became more expensive through RCTI's new "packaging," whereby advertisers must buy fringe time along with prime time. For example, to buy 60 seconds (10.2 million rupiah or US$5,400) during one of six "gold programs" requires also buying a slot in the third- and fourth-ranked time zones.

Overall advertising budgets are expected to increase to 800 billion rupiah from 1990's 640 billion rupiah (US$424.4 million, from

US$339.5 million), says Katoppo. Unfocused magazines and radio stations will suffer the most. Newspapers are expected to continue buoyant. In predicting casualties, industry sources note that TV remains too expensive for most clients, while radio is increasingly recognized as good value, and top city radio stations and regional stations broadcasting in local dialects should do well. Advertisers are likely to increase their use of radio to reinforce and echo their TV campaigns. "Radio is the only effective way to reach beyond the cities," says SRI's Rich. "People out there don't read newspapers or magazines."

Yet advertisers will continue to line up for space in the best-read journals. An example is the general news weekly, *Tempo,* which grows thicker with ads as its chief rival, *Editor,* limps along. According to an SRI study, *Tempo* was read by 18 percent of ABC males over age 25 in 1990, up from 11 percent in 1988, while *Editor* has garnered a flat one percent of the males in that group since 1988. The magazine is considering a revamp to reposition itself, says SRI's Rita Dumais.

A vacuum was left by the government shutdown of *Monitor,* an entertainment weekly, in October, 1990, after Muslim protests over a poll that ranked the prophet Mohammed as the 11th most-admired person in Indonesia after singers, politicians and a journalist. At press time, the former editor, Arswendo Admowiloto, was on trial for blasphemy. A successor clone was rumored to be waiting in the wings at the beginning of the year. The sports tabloid, *Bola,* did very well during World Cup year, attracting 21 percent of male ABC readers over age 25, the highest male readership of any magazine, according to SRI.

Advertising in Indonesia's magazines and newspapers is limited by law to 35 percent of total content. Sponsored supplements can be inserted in magazines with alphabetical subnumbers (such as 35a through 35h). Newspapers do not have that option, and to make it even more difficult, they are limited to 16 pages a day. Indonesia's most influential newspapers are expensive buys. The national leader, *Kompas,* was charging 93 million rupiah (US$49,300) for a full page in December, yet advertisers were queuing up for space, demand spurred on largely by the burgeoning Jakarta Stock Exchange. Companies about to go public are required to publish full-page prospectuses, followed by half-page quarterly earnings reports. The main beneficiaries of the demand for space were *Kompas, Bisnis Indonesia* and *Tempo.*

Advertisers hope the migration of budgets into TV will deflate the price of newspaper and magazine space, among the most expensive in the world. "The print media has been enjoying a very privileged situation," says Katoppo.

Billboards, both expensive and hard to monitor, are expected to decline as TV dilutes their value as a visual medium, but there is continuing interest in outdoor, and novel media are being launched. Tethered hot-air balloons, often lit at night, have become an increasingly common attention-getter in Jakarta. Cinema, an expensive medium, could increase its share of budgets because companies will be making more TV commercials and can adapt footage for screening in movie theaters.

A Lintas survey shows that in the first nine months of 1990, banking and insurance advertising placements accounted for 39 billion rupiah (US$20.6 million) or nearly 15 percent of total adspend in TV, print and radio. They were followed by vehicles, cigarettes, beverages, supermarkets and department stores, toiletries, tours and travel, medicine and real estate.

A survey of publications, compiled by PT Surindo Utama, ranked banks and insurance as top spenders (23 percent), followed by vehicles and spare parts (10 percent), food and drinks (6.3 percent), cigarettes (6 percent), toiletries (4.8 percent), real estate (4.6 percent), medicines (3.5 percent), and hotels and restaurants (3.4 percent). Lintas' survey showed that, of the top nine spenders by brand, four were cigarette manufacturers, three were Japanese automakers and two were banks.

The government's tightening of the money supply continued to pressure banks into luring deposits through full-page announcements of new savings instruments and lotteries. Citibank used direct mail to pitch its credit cards. Several banks launched "golf cards" for men. For women, there is the new Lady Card, Carte I and Beauty Card. These and other developments acknowledge women's spending power and the raised expectations of working women, says president and director of Grafik Advertising, Lotte Mohamad. "Fifteen years ago, women didn't go to banks," she says.

Mohamad, the new head of the Indonesian Association of Advertising Agencies' Jakarta chapter, has watched the emergence of a middle class in the past five to seven years. For a sense of the Indonesian meaning of middle class, consider the RCTI surveyed its subscribers in April 1989, while still on decoders, and found that 16 percent spent more than US$340 a month per household. The remaining 84 percent spent less, with 40 percent spending below US$242 a month per household. RCTI's present audience is far less affluent now without decoders and TPI's audience has even less discretionary income per capita.

Competition between brands vying for ad dollars intensified in 1990. The previous year's tug-of-war between two-in-one shampoos Dimension and Rejoice was joined by me-too products from other manufacturers, including Kao. Coffee brands, such as Kapal Api and Tora Bika, appeared on the market with sophisticated gimmicks as launch promotions and widespread sampling programs. "Suddenly coffee is moving from a commodity weighed from a barrel in the market to a brand name," says Modesto.

Restrictions on advertising stimulated some creative treatments. Cigarette and liquor advertising, for example, is allowed on the Rajawali group stations, provided none of the actors is seen smoking or drinking on film. The most spectacular solution to this caveat was the corporate image Sampoerna shot in the volcanic crater on top of Mount Bromo near Surabaya. Featuring 200 members of the Sampoerna marching band, other characters, daring helicopter film work and an original musical score, the two-and-a-half day shoot yielded the highest-quality ad ever produced in Indonesia, payment for which was still outstanding at the time of writing.

In the absence of studio facilities, post-production work is still done mostly in Singapore, or in Bangkok, Sydney and Hong Kong. But a sign of the maturing Indonesian advertising scene was the launch of a public service advertising clearinghouse, patterned on the Ad Council of the United States. In Asia, only Japan has an agency like this one, which will coordinate volunteer creative efforts, marshall donated space and prioritize campaigns, making sure important social concerns are addressed. Before the founding of the Yayasan Pariwara Social (YPS), public service advertising was an ad hoc affair, handled individually by agencies and organizations. The group plans to use radio, especially broadcasts in local dialects, and to a lesser extent television. Print is less effective in reaching semiliterate rural dwellers.

Indonesia's media scene is cluttered, with more than 600 radio stations, more than 160 newspapers, some 100 magazines and five new or about-to-be-born private TV stations. TV will further complicate an already complicated situation, says SRI's Rich.

by Sally Gelston

JAPAN

Some of the luster began to fade from Japan's "economic miracle" in 1990, although economic fundamentals remained strong as Japan entered its fifth consecutive year of growth. The government estimates GNP growth to have been 5.2 percent for the year ending March 31 1990, and projects a rise in GNP of 3.8 percent in 1991.

The economy received a severe shock in early 1990 as the yen, stocks and bonds all fell in value in what was termed the "triple decline." The yen gradually recovered to around 130 yen to the US dollar after dropping to almost 160 yen, but financial markets have yet to bounce back.

The 225-issue Nikkei Stock Average plunged 48 percent from its high of 38,915 yen at the end of 1989 to the year's low of 20,221 yen on October 1, 1990. By the end of the year the Nikkei had climbed back up to above the 24,000 yen mark, but there is still concern that the market may not have bottomed out.

Other worrying factors on the Japanese economic front in 1990 were rising interest rates and a small but steady increase in inflation. Land prices continued stabilizing after the excessive growth of the past few years, but analysts warn of the effects a crash in land prices would have on both the Japanese and world economies, due to the widespread practice of using overvalued land as collateral for loans.

The government introduced legislation to raise the country's relatively low property taxes, but it's doubtful the ruling Liberal Democratic Party (LDP), especially under politically weak Prime Minister Toshiki Kaifu, can muster the will to address the land-price problem seriously. The business community was heartened by the LDP's resounding victory in last year's February 18 lower-house parliamentary election, but the upper house remains under the control of opposition parties, which has slowed the legislative process at times.

Meanwhile Emperor Akihito was formally enthroned November 12, 1990 under tight security as representatives from more than 150 countries converged in Tokyo for the ceremony.

The cutoff in oil supplies from Iraq and Kuwait as a result of the Mideast crisis and war had little effect on Japan, which is much less dependent on oil from that region than it was during the "oil shocks" of 1973–1974 and 1979.

Another problem is a serious labor shortage in the industrial sector. There was cutthroat competition among companies for university graduates during the annual recruitment season. Firms favored by this year's crop of grads were those in "glamourous" fields like media and finance, while more traditional manufacturing firms and trading houses had a

**Top 10 Japanese Advertising Agencies
(Billings in U.S.$ millions[a])**

	(US$ millions) 1990	(Yen billions) 1990★	1989
1. Dentsu Inc.	7077.4	937.8	1180.3
2. Hakuhodo Inc.	3140.6	416.1	527.7
3. Tokyu Agency Inc.	1069.6	141.7	169.0
4. Daiko Ad. Inc.	1004.1	133.0	161.6
5. Asatsu Inc.	716.3	94.9	112.4
6. I&S Corp.	653.0	86.5	103.4
7. Yomiko Ad. Inc.	643.5	85.3	101.1
8. Dai-ichi Kikaku Co. Ltd.	593.2	78.6	98.1
9. ME Hakuhodo Inc.	461.1	61.1	81.1
10. Asahi Ad. Inc.	404.4	53.6	68.4

★ Jan. to Sept. 1990.
Source: HDM/Koukoku Keizai Kenkyuujo.

tougher time attracting talent.

Consumer and capital spending remained steady during the year as Japan's economy steadily became more driven by domestic demand.

High land prices mean many Japanese have given up on the idea of ever owning a home and are instead spending their money in other ways. For example, more Japanese traveled overseas in 1990 than ever before, with over 11 million venturing beyond Japan's shores. Luxury goods continued to sell well and new car registrations set records each month through July. One market analyst expects luxury cars to account for five percent of the Japanese car market in the next few years. Meanwhile, Japanese businessman Ryoei Saito proved there's still lots of spare cash lying around Japan by buying Van Gogh's painting "Dr. Gachet" for US$82.5 million in May, 1990.

While there were signs that Japanese financial institutions were cutting back on lending overseas due to the government's tight-money policy, other Japanese firms continued to make headlines with purchases of foreign companies.

The biggest single example of this was Matsushita Electrical Industrial's purchase of American entertainment conglomerate MCA in November, 1990 for US$6.13 billion—the largest buyout ever of a foreign company by a Japanese firm. Like Sony's 1989 buyout of Columbia Pictures, the move is part of Japanese electronics firms' efforts to combine their hardware skills with American know-how in the "software" side of the business.

The advertising business had a good year, with billings at the country's top 10 advertising agencies in the first 10 months of 1990 totalling 2.34 trillion yen (US$18.72 billion), up 10.5 percent from the same period in 1989. Spending on newspaper advertising was 452 billion yen (US$3.62 billion), only 5.9 percent more than the first 10 months of 1989. Re-

**Top 10 Advertisers by Category—Japan
(U.S.$ millions)**

	(US$ millions) 1990	(Yen billions) 1990	1989
1. Food/beverages/ tobacco	4,236.8	561,380	561,138
2. Service/leisure	3,494.6	463,040	399,850
3. Real estate/ Housing facilities	1,811.9	240,080	201,280
4. Cosmetics/ Toiletries	1,794.3	237,740	224,540
5. Automobiles/ Related goods	1,742.6	230,890	203,750
6. Publications	1,611.5	213,530	199,790
7. Distributors/ Retailers	1,561.1	206,840	196,410
8. Banking/ Insurance	1,433.7	189,970	176,400
9. Pharmaceuticals	1,323.8	175,410	173,920
10. Home electronics/ Audiovisual equipment	1,205.3	159,700	147,900

Advertising Expenditure by Medium—Japan
(U.S.$ millions)

	(US$ millions) 1990	(Yen billions) 1990	1989
Television	12,110	1,604,600	1,462,700
Radio	1,762	233,500	208,400
Newspapers	10,258	1,359,200	1,272,500
Magazines	2,823	374,100	335,400
Sales Promotions	14,955	1,981,500	1,783,000
New Electronics Media	90	11,900	9,500
Total	41,998	5,564,800	5,071,500

flecting the vibrant periodicals market, magazine ad expenditures totaled 116 billion yen (US$928 million) for the period ending October 31, up 9.9 percent over the previous year's figure.

While television and spending grew at a moderate 9.6 percent to 887 billion yen (US$7.1 billion) at end October, radio bounced back. Spending on radio ads rose 13.6 percent in the first 10 months of 1990 to 78 billion yen (US$624 million), partly because of FM radio's increasing popularity. Advertising expenditure on other media rose a healthy 14.2 percent to 814 billion yen (US$6.51 billion), as of the end of October, 1990.

The stock market crash and the yen's ups and downs had little effect on the industry, as Japan's economic fundamentals remained strong. "The advertising industry did really well in Japan compared with other industries," says general manager of McCann Direct in Tokyo, Tom Ainlay. "You can't say advertising is recession-proof but it's about as close as you can get."

But the prospect of recession in North America and Europe could put a damper on the Japanese advertising business, since between 15 and 20 percent of ad spending in Japan is by foreign firms, according to managing director of HDM in Tokyo, Derek Hall.

Foreign brand names have begun to lose some of their automatic allure as Japanese consumers become more sophisticated. Celebrities from overseas are also becoming a less common sight in Japanese ads, although All Nippon Airways launched a major campaign in the fall in which Frank Sinatra extolled the virtues of ANA's new Paris service.

At the same time, a fascination with things European led to increased use of French and Italian in commercials (one instant curry company even uses French in its TV spots), and meanwhile Italian restaurants, along with Italian luxury goods, became popular among fashion-conscious Japanese.

Japanese agencies, following the lead of other Japanese firms, began to make their presence felt in Europe in 1990. Dentsu bought 40 percent of Collett Dickenson Pearce (CDP) in October after the failure of an earlier joint effort with Berkett Weinrich & Bryant to land Mazda's pan-European ac-

Top 10 Advertisers by Brand—Japan
(U.S.$ millions)

	(US$ millions) 1990	(Yen billions) 1990*	1989**
1. Matsushita Electric Industrial	341.1	45,190	43,486
2. Kao	318.0	42,130	43,925
3. Suntory	315.5	41,810	36,509
4. Hitachi	298.9	39,610	33,411
5. Mazda	295.6	39,170	NR
6. Nissan	263.7	34,940	32,302
7. Toshiba	263.1	34,860	NR
8. NEC	260.4	34,500	30,043
9. Mitsubishi Motors	251.2	33,280	32,345
10. Toyota	239.4	31,720	28,635

* April 1989 to March 1990.
** April 1988 to March 1989.
Source: Nikkei Advertising Research Institute.

count. "A lot of Western agencies are looking at Japanese agencies as 'sugar daddies,'" says HDM's Hall. The Japanese, however, may gain more from such link-ups because of their need for creative staff, he adds.

In December, 1990, France's Eurocom announced it was pulling out of HDM, which was formed in 1987 by Young and Rubicam, Dentsu and Eurocom. Dentsu meanwhile bought Eurocom's stake in Alice, a French agency which is part of the CDP European network. Japanese agencies also expanded their activities in Southeast Asia in 1990, in the wake of increased activity in the region by Japanese firms.

Japan's nascent DM (direct marketing) industry continued to grow in 1990 to where it now represents 1.2 percent of retail sales, roughly twice the level of five years ago. Further growth in the DM field is expected as Japan moves towards "niche" markets and the percentage of working women increases. In general, traditional above-the-line advertising is still very predominant in Japan, accounting for roughly two-thirds of all advertising-related expenditure.

Japan's first daily paper for women, *Lady Kong,* hit the newsstands in 1990. The paper has to surmount one big obstacle: Japanese women rarely read newspapers, preferring magazines or novels as they commute to work. While the men's fashion magazines introduced a few years ago remained popular in 1990, three new magazines, *Gainer, Crocodile,* and *Cadet,* started up, all aimed at "macho" men in their 20s. And three magazines aimed at people in "late middle age" made their debut in 1990, in anticipation of the greying of Japanese society.

The world's first digital radio station went on the air in December 1990 in Japan. The station, beamed via satellite, will be joined by as many as 18 others later this year when Japan's second direct-broadcast satellite is scheduled to be launched. TV satellite broadcasting is also expanding rapidly. The first private station to broadcast by satellite went on air in December, joining the two channels operated by government-affiliated NHK.

Two women dominated the Japanese popular consciousness in 1990: cartoon character Chibi Maruko-chan (Little Maruko) and real-life Princess Kiko. Since making her TV debut in January, Chibi Maruko-chan's image has been used to sell everything from soup to telephones. A lazy but amiable eight-year-old girl, Chibi Maruko-chan offers Japanese women in their 20s and 30s a cutesy, idealized version of their childhoods. The June 29 marriage of commoner Kiko Kawashima to Prince Aya, second son of Emperor Akihito, resulted in a "Kiko boom" of products such as pearls and hats of the type favored by the new princess.

The environment was a popular theme in 1990. Major department stores featured special displays of "eco-friendly" products such as washing powder and stationery made from recycled paper, while Suntory introduced its "The Earth" beer using the slogan, "Suntory is thinking about the Earth." "Sensitivity to such kinds of issues is very important in establishing a good reputation with consumers," says manager of Dentsu's overseas communications department, Tetsuji Shimizu.

Other trends in the beer industry were the popularity of "luxury" beers such as Kirin's Ichibanshibori beer, which outsold Asahi Breweries' Super Dry and helped Kirin regain the market share it had lost to Asahi. Other "hit" beers included Suntory's imaginatively named Beer Nouveau.

Banks began advertising on TV for the first time in 1990, as liberalization of the Japanese banking industry continued. "Most banks are pursuing soft-sell strategies," says Shimizu, adding that he expects the volume of banking ads to increase in 1991. One of the most visible banks in terms of ad activity was Citibank, which is making aggressive moves into retail banking, until now the preserve of Japanese institutions.

Hit products in 1990 included electric appliances using "fuzzy logic," which mimics human thought processes in choosing, for example, what temperature of water to use with different types of clothes in a washing machine. Matsushita was one of the companies to lead the way in introducing fuzzy logic into Japanese daily life.

Other big-selling products were compact video cameras, book-type personal computers, portable telephones, satellite tuner-equipped TVs, nutrition-fortified drinks and recreational vehicles.

by Steve McClure

MALAYSIA

Malaysia's advertising industry is projecting another prosperous year in 1991. As well they might—the economy is tipped to become Asia Pacific's star performer, with GDP growth reaching nine percent. The industry's total billings, last year around M$750 million (US$27.6 million), should increase by almost 25 percent.

Great news? Not really. Friends of the industry are unanimous that a third straight year of easy pickings will give agencies all the excuses they need to postpone reforms. Plots to wrest the TV-audience rating system from monopoly control will not be hatched. Individual agencies will put on hold all those grandiose programs to turn themselves into producers of totally integrated marketing packages—and will just churn out ads instead.

Inauspicious they may be, but the good times certainly are here again. Some of the bigger agencies are turning away potential clients because they don't have the staff to handle the accounts. Advertising is a people business and it is people—good, experienced people—that are in short supply. Bemoaning the 4As' inability to tackle the people problem, general manager of Frank Small, Michel Akavi, comments: "Agencies are not only competing with each other for staff, they are competing with other industries. Keeping good staff will be a big challenge in 1991." Lucky Malaysia. Elsewhere in the world, industry leaders like Akavi are worrying more about how to get rid of staff.

Sadly perhaps, the big issue of 1991 will be how to cope with growth, which Akavi reckons to be between 20 and 25 percent. The same old sectors—tobacco, food and beverage, upscale designer merchandise—will bring in the most cash. New business will come from property developers and the financial services industry. The property people will increase outlays because, like financial services, there is intense competition and a downturn in the offing.

Newcomers? While the privatization program is on everyone's lips, the advertising accounts are in few pockets. So far the government has taken to market three outfits: a port services company, and the telecoms and electricity monopolies. Seventy percent of Malaysia's adspend is still on direct consumer advertising. Among total advertising expenditure, M$800 million (US$294 million) in 1990, TV is still top, with a 46 percent slice against 40 percent for print. The balance is

Top 10 Advertisers by Brand—Malaysia
(U.S.$ millions)

	(US$ millions) 1990	(M$ billions) 1990	1989
1. Peter Stuyvesant Travel	3.4	9.2	4.0
2. Marlboro World of Sports	2.9	8.0	NR
3. Perilly's Black & Gold Collection	2.1	5.6	4.1
4. Salem High Country	2.1	5.6	5.2
5. Telekom Malaysia	2.0	5.3	NR
6. Shell Petrol Promotion	1.5	4.0	NR
7. McDonald's Hamburger Restaurant	1.5	4.0	3.8
8. Roth Int'l Executive Travel	1.4	3.9	5.3
9. Sabah Indera Permai Borneo	1.4	3.9	3.3
10. Kentucky Fried Chicken	1.4	3.7	3.9

Source: SRM Adex.

Top 10 Malaysian Advertising Agencies
(advertising billings in U.S.$ millions)

	(US$ millions) 1990	(M$ billions) 1990	1989
1. AMC—Melewar Zecha Communications Sdn Bhd	28.0	76.3★	65.4
2. Ogilvy & Mather	27.1	73.8	58.1
3. McCann-Erickson	24.9	67.8	58.8
4. HDM	23.5	64.0	42.0
5. Leo Burnett	21.3	58.0★	49.0
6. BSB Malaysia	20.3	55.3	45.5
7. Lintas	18.4	50.0	42.0
8. J. Walter Thompson	16.5	45.0	40.0
9. AP: Foote Cone & Belding	13.6	37.0	32.0
10. Wings/BBDO	12.9	35.0	25.0

★ Estimated.
Source: Individual agencies.

unlikely to change, despite all the complaints about commercials saturating the three channels. "With breaks having 12 and 13 commercials, it will really be pointless to advertise," says Ding. "The only problem with TV is the sheer lack of airtime—peak-time slots are jam packed," notes Grey's Craighead.

Saturated or not, TV is set to pull further ahead of print. Wai Hong of SRM foresees a move to fringe time to beat the clutter at peak hours. And there is the prospect of a fourth channel, and even of 24-hour programming.

The industry unanimously agrees that the quality of Malaysian TV has improved immensely, thanks largely to intense competition between RTM and upstart TV3. And the industry has responded in kind. Saatchi's Pat-

rick Bret points to the blossoming of local production houses and their experiments with sophisticated techniques learned abroad. Now that the two TV companies happily accept video and do not insist on film, the cost of producing little gems has actually declined.

If King TV is unlikely to be dethroned, neither is his consort, print, which is increasingly the preferred medium for tactical campaigns, especially for luxury goods, says media director at Leo Burnett, HK Seetho. Also bolstering the position of print in Malaysia's racial mix. To reach the 30 percent of the 18 million Malaysians who are Chinese, print makes better sense than TV; by the same measure, print works better for the nine percent or so who are Indian.

Outdoor, that medium so loved by Japanese companies, is riding high. Utusan Pearl & Dean, which used to have this sector to itself, recently won back ground lost to nim-

Advertising Expenditure by Medium—Malaysia (U.S.$ millions)

	(US$ millions) 1990	(M$ billions) 1990	1989
Television★	129.9	353.6	303.8
Video	2.1	5.8	6.6
Radio★★	2.9	7.8	★★★★
Sound Ads (in supermarkets and shopping centers)	0.9	2.5	2.5
Cinema	1.1	3.1	0.7
Newspapers	132.5	360.8	263.9
Periodicals	20.0	54.4	50.0
Rediffusion	1.5	4.2	3.4
Taxi Top	★★★	★★★	0.6
Outdoor	9.5	25.9	13.7
Total	300.4	818.1	645.2

NB ★   includes Sponsorship Cost
  ★★   July–Dec. only
  ★★★   not measured in 1990
  ★★★★ not measured in 1989
Source: SRM Adex.

Top 10 Advertisers by Category—Malaysia (U.S.$ millions)

	(US$ millions) 1990	(M$ billions) 1990	1989
1. Entertainment/ Franchise	23.7	64.6	42.7
2. Travel & Tour Agencies	15.2	41.4	35.4
3. Communication, Publishing & Media/ Exhibitions	12.8	34.7	16.4
4. Banks/Credit Cards	10.6	28.9	18.7
5. Department Stores, Emporiums/ Pharmacies	10.1	27.6	23.7
6. Accessories (Range)	10.1	27.5	20.1
7. Petroleum Products/ Petroleum Cos.	9.3	25.3	17.0
8. Entertainment, Hotel, Bar, Restaurants, MTE	8.9	24.2	23.5
9. Watches/Clocks	8.0	21.8	NR
10. Real Estate	7.9	21.4	NR

Source: SRM Adex.

bler competitors by sealing a contract for signage on the massive north-south highway project. But, as ever, outdoor has its detractors. The mayor of Kuala Lumpur has said he has had enough of billboards, which have multiplied at strategic sites over the past months. Growth, then, will be a stately affair rather than a stampede.

In contrast, radio looks set for a second golden age. Last year, SRM won access to the state-owned radio network and now monitors what ad people say is a greatly improved service. The figures are impressive. Advertising revenue, M$12 million (US$4.5 million) in 1989, clocked in at M$16 million (US$5.9 million) last year. "Radio could revamp itself next year and cause quite a shift in Adex," says Wai Hong of SRM, with a smile. But everything is not so rosy, according to Craighead. "Radio is not cheap and notoriously difficult to monitor," he says.

And so to cinema, another likely winner. The increase in audiences, up another 10 percent last year, is set to continue. The reason is better programming and the emergence of multiplex cinemas. Gaining ground against home video and hit by more responsible attitudes to copyright, the cinema is making a comeback.

Overall, then, a very buoyant year in prospect and a prosperous one too. "Malaysia has always been considered something of a backwater. But now it is one of the markets to be in," says Saatchi's Patrick Brett.

by Sid Astbury

PHILIPPINES

Crisis and the Philippines may be old-time companions, but never before has the country experienced anything like 1990. The year brought a string of calamities that wound like a noose around the economy's neck. And while the rest of the world fretted about the impact of war in the Gulf, the Philippines girded itself for more problems.

Even before the Middle East situation developed, the 1990 advertising market in the Philippines was going soft, say analysts. The previous year had seen record levels of ad spending in print and real growth for the industry of around eight percent. But 1990 was worrisome politically and economically and advertisers moved ahead frugally.

Though estimates vary, adspend increased by upwards of 20 percent, says Antonio de Joya, whose Advertising and Marketing Associates Consolidated (AMA) surveys the industry. Discounting inflation of about 15 percent, the real growth in 1990 was around five percent—much lower than the expected growth of 20 percent.

"It was a mediocre year," says de Joya, adding that if the downturn continues, "there is little prospect of growth in 1991." At best the outlook for 1991 is uncertain, and those in the Philippines still tied up by the string of bad luck are moving cautiously forward.

The Philippines' recent troubles began in December 1989 when rightist rebel soldiers opened fire on the government and fellow comrades-in-arms—and shot a promising economic picture full of holes. The unsuccessful December coup attempt and continuous

rumors about subsequent uprisings, combined with threats from communist rebels, a rash of bombings, kidnappings and assassinations scared off new foreign investment. Then nature pummelled the country first with a severe drought, then with power blackouts, a killer earthquake, massive flooding and a devastating "super-typhoon" that ravaged the country's only prosperous region.

Before August 1990, the advertising industry looked as if it was weathering the storm well, but then Iraq invaded Kuwait and the price of oil skyrocketed. As prices rose (the

Top 10 Philippine Advertising Agencies (advertising billings in U.S.$ millions)

	(US$ millions) 1990	(Peso millions) 1990	1989
1. McCann-Erickson	23.0	635.0	544.0
2. Basic/Foote, Cone & Belding, Inc.	18.8	520.0	356.0
3. JWT	16.5	456.0	457.3
4. ACE/Saatchi & Saatchi	15.6	430.6	389.2
5. Lintas	10.9	301.5	232.2
6. PAC/BBDO Worldwide	10.3	285.2*	195.9
7. AMA Consolidated	9.9	273.8	271.5
8. Hemisphere—Leo Burnett	9.7	267.0	229.7
9. HDM—Alcantara	9.1	252.0*	248.0
10. J. Romero & Associates	5.8	160.0	143.8
OlbCs, Ogilvy & Mather	5.8	159.7	108.8

* estimated
** net, excluding fee
Source: Individual agencies for 1990 and 1989

premium fuel cost per litre doubled in November in the Philippines), so did food costs. And to prop up its budget, the government increased taxes on imports and the sale of "sinful" commodities like liquor and cigarettes.

Workers' demands for wage increases kept pace with these hikes. A 17-peso increase took effect in November, 1990 and another of 12 peso was approved for workers in metro Manila. Officially the inflation rate is 13.5 to 15 percent, but de Joya estimates it is closer to 20 percent. Interest rates went from 22 percent in January to more than 30 percent by the end of the year.

The Philippines' advertising industry is slow in gathering figures, but analysts and agency heads say the miserable fourth-quarter activity was like a sandbag that pulled down overall growth rates. Despite modest real growth in the industry for the year, agencies were cutting budgets in the fourth quarter by as much as 20 percent, estimates president of Admakers, Frankie Roman, referring to a 4As survey of the country's 35 top agencies. "The boom didn't quite hit," says de Joya. "Belt-tightening was evident in the flow of traffic and decline of people in shopping centers." Retail trade, except food and clothes, suffered heavily during December, and Christmas sales were 12 to 13 percent below expectancy, he says.

Food advertising maintained its level, as did expenditure for white goods such as refrigerators and air conditioners that are not usually pushed during the fourth quarter. The AMA, which studied first-semester print advertising in 27 newspapers, 30 magazines and 46 comic books, reported that banks, department stores and personal care products registered the highest increases in print ad spending.

Adspend gained ground not only from banks, but beverages and pharmaceuticals as well, says president of Jimenez and Partners,

Top 10 Advertisers by Category—Philippines (U.S.$ millions)

	(US$ millions) 1990	(Peso millions) 1990	1989
1. Airlines, shipping lines, and travel agencies	10.9	300.5	272.3
2. Beers	9.0	248.5	214.2
3. Miscellaneous institutional ads	8.8	242.6	168.2
4. Cigarettes	7.9	218.4	191.9
5. Hotels, restaurants, resorts, and clubs	7.5	206.2	186.5
6. Banks, finance companies	7.4	203.4	139.6
7. Government agencies and public utilities	7.1	195.0	156.4
8. Department stores, supermarkets, jewelry, beauty salons, boutiques	7.0	193.1	NR
9. Softdrinks	5.5	151.6	158.3
10. Business machines and office equipment	5.4	149.2	129.1

* estimates
Source: Philippine Monitoring Services, Inc. (PMS)

Mon Jimenez. A recently passed generics law created competition for over-the-counter products and companies saw better margins from cold preparations, vitamins, eye drops and mouth fresheners, he says.

A portion of adspend shifted from TV to print or even radio. According to de Joya's AMA, display print advertising hit a record one billion pesos (US$33 million) in 1989, representing 44 percent growth over 1988. After a mid-year survey, AMA discovered that half of the country's top 40 advertisers had actually reduced their print advertising expenditures from January to July 1990 by between 10 percent and 95 percent as a precau-

Advertising Expenditure by Medium—Philippines (U.S.$ millions)			
	(US$ millions) 1990	(Peso millions) 1990	1989
Television	89.7	2481.0	1966.9
Radio	47.2	1305.5	1069.0
Print	68.4	1890.7	1602.8
Total	205.3	5677.2	4638.7

* estimates
Source: Philippine Monitoring Services, Inc. (PMS)

Top 10 Advertisers by Brand—Philippines (U.S.$ thousands)[a]		
	1989	1988
1. Philippine National Bank	377.5	271.3
2. Philippine Long Distance Tel. (PLDT)	361.1	295.4
3. Citibank	278.8	NR
4. National Panasonic	277.1	NR
5. Development Bank of the Philippines	273.7	160.5
6. Philippine Airlines	272.8	276.8
7. Shoemart	262.4	224.78
8. Philippine Nissan Inc.	235.6	NR
9. Coca-Cola	218.9	NR
10. National Power Corporation	210.4	NR

[a] note that figures for print expenditure only.
Source: AMA Consolidated.

tion against negative trends. However, of those reducing their adspend, only two were among the top 10 companies, the AMA reported.

On the creative front, there were no breakthroughs during 1990, just a refinement of computerized techniques, Jimenez says. For the coming year, he is unsure how creative heads will perform while strapped by tight budgets. Print is being rediscovered, he believes. "We're seeing more innovation there than in TV—more white space, powerful cut-throughs, better writing."

Dennis Cabalfin, marketing director for one of the five big TV networks in Manila, doesn't expect much drop in TV spending by the big 10 advertisers for the coming year. "They have a lot to protect," he says. Most agency heads see the situation as highly uncertain, while Cabalfin is more upbeat. He believes "business is going forward with blinders, not minding the political situation." Those who've been through crises before in the Philippines remain undaunted, but "those less than experienced might not advertise at all," he says.

Cabalfin's station changed strategy during 1990 and he predicts the network may see a 70–72 percent increase in business. The change in strategy was made by increasing the amount of foreign programming at the expense of local shows. For the most part, foreign programming means American movies, sit-coms and animation specials, he says.

This year may see 18 percent nominal growth in media expenditures over 1990, but media inflation will register about 23 percent to 25 percent, says de Joya. "It doesn't look too good," he says. But below-the-line advertising should grow encouragingly. De Joya expects this segment to increase by as much as 30 percent. The run of bad luck afflicting the Philippines' economy in 1990 does not appear to be slackening. In addition to the uncertainty brought by the war, the Philippines was bracing for another drought as rainfall was down by 40 percent as of December, mostly in rural areas (which accounts for 40 percent of consumer-spending). Foreign currency is getting scarce, and labor costs, oil prices and interest rates are expected. Further depreciation of the peso is expected.

One hope for an otherwise-bleak 1991 is the general elections in May 1992, which could trigger a spurt in the two final quarters' growth rates. Media spokespeople predict 10 billion peso (US$330 million) adspend in 1991 through the first quarter of 1992.

by Karen Emmons

SINGAPORE

While numbers don't lie, they can sometimes exaggerate. This appears to be the case in Singapore, where 1990's bullish advertising figures looked great on paper but did not translate quite as well into real life. Total ad spending in 1990 hit S$580 million (US$336.4 million), a whopping 25 percent increase over 1989's S$464 million (US$269 million) mark. The Lion City's economy also finished the year with a roar, achieving an unexpectedly high growth rate of 8.5 percent (compared to 9.2 percent growth in 1989).

Despite these indicators, however, there was very little dancing in the streets—unless it was in conjunction with Singapore's 25th-anniversary celebrations, which climaxed in 1990. It was partly the anniversary-related ad spending, in fact, that contributed to the mirage. In reality, celebratory promotions were "one-off" affairs, with advertisers abruptly closing their pocketbooks as soon as the confetti had been swept off the streets.

In assessing the health of the ad industry, many warn not to pay too much heed to Singapore's robust economic figures. "Growth in GDP is not really filtering down to the advertising system," says director and general manager of HDM, James Ng. "I think the investments coming through pertain more to the infrastructural, niche areas of Singapore's economic growth, such as petrochemicals— infrastructural things that are not consumer-oriented."

As advertising years go, 1990 was fairly placid, a good but unspectacular year that wit-

Top 10 Singapore Advertising Agencies (advertising billings in U.S.$ millions)

	(US$ millions) 1990	(S$ millions) 1990	1989
1. Batey Ads	48.7	85.0	68.0
2. McCann-Erickson	28.7	50.0	51.0
3. Saatchi & Saatchi	26.9	47.0	40.0
4. Ogilvy & Mather	25.9	45.2	39.0
5. HDM	25.9	45.2	37.4
6. Leo Burnett	22.1	38.5	37.5
7. J. Walter Thompson	19.2	33.4	27.3
8. Spenser/BBDO	16.8	29.2	15.6
9. The Ball Partnership	16.1	28.0	12.0
10. DNC	15.5	27.0	27.0

Source: Individual agencies.

Advertising Expenditure by Medium— Singapore (U.S.$ millions)

	(US$ millions) 1990	(S$ millions) 1990	1989
Television	99.5	173.6	140.8
Radio	6.8	11.9	11.7
Rediffusion	2.2	3.8	3.1
Newspapers	171.8	299.7	243.0
Magazines	36.1	63.0	41.9
Cinema	2.1	3.7	2.7
Busback/Taxi Top	8.1	14.2	10.7
Poster	6.9	12.1	10.6
Total	333.5	582.0	464.5

Source: SRS Adex.

Top 10 Advertisers by Brand—Singapore (U.S.$ millions)

	(US$ millions) 1990	(S$ millions) 1990	1989
1. McDonald's Fast Food	3.2	5.6	5.0
2. Yaohan	3.0	5.2	4.9
3. Singapore Airlines	2.2	3.8	3.0
4. American Express Card	2.1	3.6	4.0
5. Kentucky Fried Chicken	2.0	3.5	3.1
6. Telecom	1.8	3.1	1.5
7. Courts	1.7	3.0	2.6
8. Metro	1.7	2.9	2.4
9. Min of Communications & Information	1.6	2.8	0.8
10. Tiger Beer	1.6	2.8	2.8

Source: SRS Adex

Top 10 Advertisers by Category—Singapore (U.S.$ millions)

	(US$ millions) 1990	(S$ millions) 1990	1989
1. Department Stores/ Retail	23.1	40.2	35.3
2. Entertainment	22.4	39.1	30.4
3. Watches/Clocks	20.8	36.2	28.0
4. Leisure, Travel	13.8	24.0	10.5
5. Transportation	11.1	19.4	13.4
6. Banking, Finance	10.2	17.9	14.2
7. Corporation	9.3	16.3	13.1
8. Fast Food Outlets	9.3	16.2	13.0
9. Govt/Social orgs	9.2	16.1	9.7
10. Office Equipment/ Services	9.2	16.0	11.7

Source: SRS Adex.

nessed no shocking account movements, personnel changes or dramatic new arrivals on the media scene. "For the ad industry, it was simply a year of solid progress and some further belt-tightening," says Burnett's Copus. "Singapore agencies have never been known for mega-profits. It's a small marketplace."

"Generally, everybody's had a pretty stable year," adds Ng.

Profits continue to be the bane of agency chiefs. Escalating office rents, coupled with the republic's well-documented labor shortage (which translates into spiralling salaries) are facts of life here. "Salary costs are going up by 15 to 25 percent a year," says managing director of J. Walter Thompson, Ted Nation. "It's harder to make money here than I thought it was going to be," says managing director of Backer Spielvogel Bates, Chris Jacques, who moved from Hong Kong in October 1988. "Far and away the majority (of multinational agencies here) are either losing

money, or still maintain accumulated losses that they're paying off."

With more and more agencies joining the fray, and with the big boys—under increasing pressure from New York headquarters to beef up profits—grappling for even the relatively small local accounts, Singapore agencies will have to look beyond the country's borders in order to flourish. "For our survival, we must be able to merchandise our services on a regional basis," says HDM's James Ng. "What seems to be the way to go is networking, trying to put together packages for clients that could be merchandised across the region, because we can't really look to Singapore's internal growth as a major engine to sustain advertising as an industry per se. Not that I don't want local clients, but local clients have that limitation; the marketplace is [only] 2.7 million people." Ng is pleased that HDM is increasingly managing some client's regional businesses from Singapore. The trend will deepen, he hopes, as other Asian economies begin to take off in the 1990s. "We see dramatic growth in our neighbors—they need toothbrushes, toothpastes, condoms, televisions, soap—the basics," he says. "Singapore is a small environment and too competitive.

The task for us is really to echo that of the nation's task: to become the regional hub."

by Matthew Lewis

SOUTH KOREA

The only "Singapore girl" in South Korea is a cardboard cutout which greets visitors to the airlines' office in Seoul's Chosun Hotel. The famous air hostess with the seductive smile in Singapore Airline's worldwide TV commercial fell victim to a government austerity campaign and was banned before her debut last year for being a "foreigner."

The government campaign, which specifically targeted high-quality foreign imports, also grounded a Cathay Pacific "new horizons" advertisement made for Korean TV and other items which featured non-Korean models. Industry sources say that while market opening continues on track, "trip wires" such as the rulings against the airline ads are being set up. Since May, 1990, foreign models have no longer been permitted to star in television commercials and cannot receive more than US$5,000 for "assisting" in other ads. The guidelines also barred commercials filmed overseas.

In enforcing the ban, the government claimed the public was becoming alarmed at the number of highly paid foreign models appearing on the two state-run television stations. While pointing out there are no regulations forbidding the screening of foreign television commercials, the Korea Broadcasting Advertising Corporation (Kobaco), a government-run exclusive sales agency for all three TV networks, has effectively kept any new foreign-made commercials off the air.

Fearing a new round of trade wars with the U.S. and Europe if it is seen to be backing down on liberalizing the advertising market this year, there have been no direct rejections of overseas commercials. The storyboard goes like this: Kobaco sighs deeply and says a particular commercial being submitted for screening is not acceptable. But if such and such a change is made it can be aired. However, when the change is made, there seems to be some other tinkering needed. "They keep changing the goalposts," says one airline official.

The broader anti-import drive, launched to counter a rising trade deficit, was met with a howl of protest from the country's trading partners, notably the U.S. Toward the end of last year, the government tried to repair the damage by claiming that the local media and low-level bureaucrats had distorted what was intended as a campaign to discourage conspicuous consumption and boost savings.

Despite the passions roused, advertising industry watchers played down the significance. "It's a question of having taken two steps forward and now taking one step back," says managing director of the Korea Audit Bureau of Circulations Shin In-sup.

Few foreign account executives see immediate changes in a difficult market environment. One predicted more "trip wires" designed to minimize profits by foreign agencies. Pointing to a ruling last year by Kobaco that companies cold have only two advertising agencies on their books, the source said: "This was obviously a decision to ensure the *chaebols* (conglomerates) stay in-house and keep out of the foreign agencies."

Generally, foreign advertisers are upbeat. "This is the second largest ad market in Asia after Japan. Every magazine here has hundreds of ads," says J. Walter Thompson's Julie Smith. "It's still in the early stages but [advertising] will continue to develop." Foreign participation in the industry is increasing and three advertising firms bought equity shares in Korean agencies in 1990. DMB&B bought up 20 percent of Seoul Advertising, McCann-Erickson owns 51 percent of a joint venture with businessmen affiliated with the Doosan Group and J. Walter Thompson holds 93 percent of a partnership with Business World. The new arrival brought the number of such joint ventures to seven since liberalization in 1988. In addition, last year Saatchi & Saatchi and Leo Burnett signed association agreements with Korean agencies. Leo Burnett and DDB Needham plan to buy equity shares this year.

For the Korean industry, by far the most significant development of the year was the launching of new broadcast media. Three new FM stations started up, one Buddhist, one Roman Catholic and the third a traffic station, popular with drivers seeking to avoid the increasing traffic snarls in Seoul. In August the government started two experimental cable services in two residential areas of the capital. This year the government will announce the expansion of the system nationwide and private participation will be allowed.

In October, 1990, the Information Ministry announced that a construction company, Taeyong Corporation, had won the bid to operate Korea's first private TV channel. The new channel is expected to start broadcasting in 1992 and will cover Seoul and some parts of Kyonggi and Chungchong provinces, reaching an estimated 43 percent of Korean homes.

The decision came after months of wrangling over a new broadcasting law between the government and opposition. Although the new legislation allowed for the establishment of a private TV station, the opposition charged that it tightened the government's grip on the media. Government officials contend the law expedited competition, leading to better programming and more choice of channels in the monopolized broadcast industry. At the height of the furor, unions at Munhwa Broadcasting Company (MBC) and Korea Broadcasting System (KBS), the two existing state-run TV stations, walked out and staged anti-government protest rallies.

One of the most unusual events of 1990 was a major gamble by Korea Survey Poll, the Gallup associate in Korea, which in June launched a TV ratings service covering the

Top 10 South Korean Advertising Agencies
(billings in U.S.$ millions)

	(US$ millions) 1990	(Won millions) 1990	1989
1. Cheil Communications	257.1	184,800	166,647
2. Daehong	179.2	128,800	105,190
3. LG Ad	178.8	128,500	108,197
4. Oricom	146.5	105,300	106,403
5. Korad Ogilvy & Mather	120.8	86,800	80,200
6. Samhee Communications	94.9	68,200	42,006
7. Diamond	92.5	66,500	46,937
8. Dong Bang Advertising	90.6	65,100	59,730
9. Union Advertising	87.2	62,700	55,984
10. Seoul Advertising	62.3	44,800	35,704

★ Total capitalized billings includes subsidiaries.
Source: 1989—National Advertising Council of Korea (NACK)

1990—Korea Federation of Advertising Associations (KFAA)

Advertising Expenditure by Medium—South Korea (U.S.$ millions)

	(US$ millions) 1990	(Won millions) 1990	1989
Television	832.2	598,191	525,991
Radio	132.6	95,318	62,682
Newspapers	1,186.2	852,663	613,792
Magazines	162.6	116,879	82,860
Other	469.0	337,082	279,590
Total	2,782.6	2,000,133	1,564,915

Source: Cheil Communications.

Top 10 Advertisers by Brand—South Korea (U.S.$ millions)

	(US$ millions) 1990	(Won millions) 1990	1989 *
1. Samsung Electronics	44.4	31,899	26,200
2. Goldstar (electronics)	35.0	25,144	19,100
3. Lucky (detergent, cosmetics)	33.3	23,911	23,900
4. Pacific Chemical (cosmetics)	31.8	22,839	22,800
5. Dongsuh Foods	23.6	16,938	11,900
6. Lotte Confectionary	20.5	14,744	11,700
7. Lotte Chilsung (soft drinks)	18.4	13,211	10,700
8. Daewoong Pharmaceutical	17.7	12,738	10,400
9. Daewoong Electronics	16.7	11,983	10,200
10. Chiel Sugar	16.4	11,812	NR

* Four media only
Source: Cheil Communications.

Seoul area. This was met with some skepticism. "People asked: Gallup doing TV ratings? It was totally unrelated, rather like Unilever producing tanks or GM producing shampoo," says Shin In-sup. The start-up of the service was a departure from the usual practice in which a committee of broadcasters and advertisers invited a firm to do the research. In the Korean case, there was no prior consultation with the industry.

Gallup's move was seen as a pre-emptive strike against rivals AC Nielsen, which has a branch doing retail index work, and Audit of Great Britain, which has a 30 percent share of Hankook Research. At present neither Kobaco nor the TV networks are buying the daily ratings report. With a three-month wait to buy TV time, few experts last year were predicting a rush to subscribe.

The number of advertising agencies recognized by Kobaco surged from 36 to 64 over the year, due largely to a relaxation in Kobaco regulations. The corporation stipulated that it would recognize agencies with paid-in capital of 50 million won (US$70,000) and at least three clients. The Korea Publishers' Association, a private group which is more selective in according recognition, added seven new firms to its list of recognized agencies, bringing the total to 32. Industry sources expect several of the small Kobaco-recognized firms to fold this year.

Thirty-four small and medium-sized agencies formed the Association of Independent Advertising Agencies in 1990, setting themselves apart from the more powerful Korea Association of Advertising Agencies, formed in 1986 by the leading firms, all of which are affiliated with conglomerates.

The explosion of new print media, which followed democratization in 1987, continued through 1990 with 10 new dailies bringing the total to 80. Among them was the *Korea Daily,* the country's third English-language morning newspaper. As of the end of November, the number of weeklies had risen by 194 to 1,013, monthlies by 299 to 2,436 and other publications by 227 to 1,601.

**Top 10 Advertisers by Category—
South Korea (U.S.$ millions)**

	(US$ millions) 1990	(Won millions) 1990	1989
1. Foods, beverages	363.7	261,444	217,300
2. Pharmaceuticals	259.2	186,316	142,100
3. Garment, textile	189.0	135,881	78,600
4. Service, entertainment	187.4	134,676	105,100
5. Household products	169.0	121,500	97,200
6. Cosmetic, detergent	168.8	121,369	107,900
7. Government, associations	142.2	102,231	83,800
8. Precision office equipment	138.3	99,422	70,600
9. Electric, electronic appliances	119.3	85,723	63,900
10. Retail	118.2	84,946	NR

Four media only (newspaper, magazine, TV and radio)
Source: Cheil Communications

The Daewoo Group brought the ailing *Hungdo Ilbo* and the Lotte Group took over the *Kukje Shinmun*. Both are dailies in Pusan, Korea's second largest city. The Korea Explosives Group took over the *Kyunghyang Shinmun,* a pro-government evening paper in Seoul which has been struggling since the end of the regime of former President Chun Doohwan which used to buy up half of its print run.

Of more political than business interest, Korean firms in 1990 invested so heavily in the Beijing Asian Games that local wags were referring to the sports fest as a second Korean Asiad (Seoul hosted the last Games in 1986). Korean Air, Goldstar, Samsung, Hyundai and Daewoo all loomed large in Beijing. What initially began as business initiative received strong support from the Seoul government eager to pursue ties with its former Korean War foe and eclipse arch-rival North Korea.

by Michael Breen

TAIWAN

High hopes for Taiwan's advertising industry were dashed in 1990, as the stock market plummeted, real estate speculation cooled, and consumption of white goods and luxury items faltered.

With the market doubling between 1986 and 1989, a slowdown was not accepted easily. Two miltinational agencies sacked and replaced their chief executives, while other agencies dropped clients that were a drain on the bottom line. Others looked to below-the-line activities like sales promotion and public relations to bolster shrinking profits.

Operating costs for agencies rose at least 50 percent between 1988 and 1989. And costs continued upward in 1990, with figures showing high-cost expenses like personnel at 55 to 73 percent of total costs versus to 50 to 65 percent in 1989 and rent at 8 to 15 percent up from 5 to 12 percent, notes general manager of Eastern Advertising and current president of the Association of Accredited Advertising Agents (Taiwan 4As), Clark Huang.

"In mass media, newspapers were hit most," says Miro Oshima, president of McAnn-Erickson. "TV slowed down, but there was still growth over 1989. TV people

Top 10 Taiwanese Advertising Agencies (advertising billings in U.S.$ millions)

		1989	1988	1987
1.	United Advertising	44.2	45.3	32.9
2.	Ogilvy & Mather	34.2	26.1	20.8
3.	McCann-Erickson	35.0	25.4	17.0
4.	Kuo Hwa Advertising	25.2	22.8	12.3
5.	Hwa Wei & Grey	29.0	21.4	12.0
6.	Bozell CCAA[a]	24.2	20.6	14.5
7.	DIK-Ocean Advertising	23.8	19.6	14.7
8.	Regal International	25.1	18.1	13.2
9.	Leo Burnett	23.0	NR[b]	NR
10.	Eastern Advertising	22.5	17.7	12.6

[a] Listed as China Commercial in 1988.
[b] NR, Not ranked.
Source: Brain Magazine.

Advertising Expenditure by Medium— Taiwan (U.S.$ millions)

	1989	1988	1987
Television	517.9	411.2	249.1
Radio	83.4	69.3	49.8
Newspapers	763.4	577.2	357.1
Magazines	112.5	95.7	66.4
Other	281.4	203.5	NA[a]
Total	1758.6	1356.9	830.5

[a] NA, Not applicable.
Source: Taipei Advertising Agencies' Association.

agree that newspapers advertising has been shifting to TV, and some advertisers have cut spending on TV, so recently there has been more room for people who had been using papers," he adds.

Although since 1988 Taiwan has allowed newspapers to carry more pages and for new papers to be launched, prime space continues to be dominated by a mighty few. Major advertisers sometimes use small newspapers in local markets, but buyers generally find that, even for regional cities, the big national dailies are more efficient. Unfortunately, the two majors, the *United Daily News* and *China Times,* persist in producing split runs. Their A and B editions are run on two printing presses, with the same editorial on the same day, randomly distributed, but with different ads. Therefore, two copies of the same paper bought at the same place could actually contain different advertising. This is an ongoing nightmare for marketers, who can't pinpoint who saw their ad where.

Frustrated, many media buyers have turned to *Ming Sheng Pao,* which doesn't split its runs

and delivers an affluent urban audience. *Ming Sheng Pao* claims 800,000 circulation, while the *United Daily* and the *Times* each have about one million readers. Of all print media, only the circulations of the *China Times* and *Reader's Digest* (by far the leading magazine at 200,000-plus) are ABC-audited. With the unaudited publications, in most cases, "circulation figures are based on very rough estimates including machine printing speed, how many hours the machines are run, the number of copies printed, and so forth," says media buyer for Saatchi & Saatchi, Michael Yao.

A drive by the 4As to develop an auditing foundation is being spearheaded by vice chairman of United Advertising, Tomming Lai, but the effort continues to be thwarted by media opposition. Lai argues that establishing a Chinese ABC would benefit print media. "In the past there were only 31 newspapers allowed, there are now over 160. There is a crucial need for this type of organization, so the media understand what circulation really is," he says. "Also, newspapers will face a very strong challenge in the next couple of years in the form of cable TV."

Raymond So, managing director of J. Walter Thompson, views the language barrier as one of the biggest handicaps to development. "International agencies face a big problem in recruiting here because the standard of English is not as high as in Hong Kong, Singapore or Malaysia, and they must communicate a lot with other markets in English," he says. But he concedes that language problems work both ways. It is also a problem for most multinational advertising agencies to access local business, he has found. "You must have people who know the culture and can get along with and speak to locals. Local agencies tell clients and media that international agencies don't know the Taiwan market," he says.

An indication that style is coming into its own came at Cannes, where Leo Burnett won Taiwan's first National Award for its TV spot for the Black & Decker electric iron. Production was by Bin-Mone Company.

The standard of public relations in Taiwan continued to improve "a little," says the president of Compass Public Relations, Pauline Leung. Her company is two years old and has so far achieved nearly 100 percent growth. Leung estimates it will be a couple more years before the industry matures.

Public relations has suffered far less from the economy's problems than has advertising.

"We see traditional advertising money going into public relations, so the PR industry as a whole will continue to grow," notes Daniel Teh-yen Tu, president of Taiwan's largest agency, United Pacific International.

PR isn't the only marketing tool that has gained attention from anxious, budget-conscious clients. More and more clients are looking at what HDM-Taiwan's managing director Richard Hsiung calls "the whole egg:" advertising, public relations, direct marketing, promotional marketing and marketing-related design.

The big story coming up is the advent of

Top 10 Advertisers by Brand—Taiwan (U.S.$ millions)

		(US$ millions) 1990	(NT$ millions) 1990	1989
1.	President	21.7	580.3	435.2
2.	Ford	9.9	265.0	NR
3.	Toyota	9.8	263.4	NR
4.	Kao	8.9	237.1	164.4
5.	FUIC	8.6	229.0	NR
6.	Nan Yang	8.1	217.2	NR
7.	King Car	7.6	204.1	169.0
8.	San Yang	6.8	183.4	NR
9.	Sampo	6.8	180.9	217.0
10.	Kolin	6.7	180.6	165.4

Source: Taipei Advertising Agencies Association.

Top 10 Advertisers by Category—Taiwan (U.S.$ millions)

		(US$ millions) 1990	(NT$ millions) 1990	1989
1.	Entertainment, Stock and commodities commercial services	456.4	12,223	12,002
2.	Transportation/ Travel	177.8	4,762	4,207
3.	Food	153.8	4,118	3,485
4.	Real Estate	140.1	3,753	4,890
5.	Personal care products	133.9	3,585	3,627
6.	Medicine/ Pharmaceuticals	103.4	2,769	2,471
7.	Publishing/ Stationery	82.6	2,213	2,288
8.	Consumer electronics	81.0	2,168	2,284
9.	Beverages/Dairy products	80.8	2,165	1,790
10.	Watches, eyeglasses, photography	25.7	689	603

* Figures based on TV, newspaper and magazine expenditures only.
Source: Taipei Advertising Agencies Association.

cable television, which will be a rough-and-tumble event. Anticipated for 1993, planning is already underway. One industry veteran says, "A lot of local news and radio stations are expected to disappear" when cable comes in.

Many industry people believe that several advertising agencies will disappear in 1991 by folding or pulling out, because the year will be tough. "Most people are saying now that things won't be good until at least the third quarter. Not only is economic growth slow, but there are not many new products coming out in the near future," says United Advertising's Lai.

Japanese agencies have intensified competition by moving into Taiwan in a big way, led by Hakuhodo and Tokyu, which has established a joint venture with Eastern, the oldest local agency. Most major Taiwan agencies now have at least informal relationships with agencies abroad.

Signs augur a period of warlike competition. "For the next two or three years it will be survival of the fittest," says general manager of Leo Burnett, Andy Lai. McCann's Oshima puts it more bluntly: "Instead of expecting trees to grow, we'll have to pull them out from another yard and plant them in our own."

by Gisela Moriarty

THAILAND

1990 was another terrific year for Thailand's advertising industry, with total adspend topping 12 billion baht (US$480 million), an increase of about 20 percent over 1989. The main difficulties were the problems of success: gearing up to handle new business without over-extension and retaining experienced staff while coping with spiraling media costs.

Bangkok's new satellite city development of Muang Thong Thani was Thailand's largest advertiser, spending 88 million baht (US$3.52 million) in the first three quarters alone.

The losers' prize for timing goes to BSB, whose managing director David Bell announced, "This is a very important development for BSB," with their signing of the Kuwait Oil account in July 1990.

Real estate and housing spending grew strongly due to the continuing boom in that industry and was the largest category by far in 1990, recording some 1.18 billion baht (US$47.2 million) up to the end of Novem-

Top 10 Thai Advertising Agencies
(billings in U.S.$ millions)

		(US$ millions) 1990	(Baht millions) 1990	1989
1.	Lintas	57.6	1457.0	1236.0
2.	Ogilvy & Mather	35.6	899.9	698.4
3.	Far East	27.7	700.0	565.0
4.	Leo Burnett	25.5	645.0	470.0
5.	Spa	25.3	640.0	432.0
6.	McCann-Erickson	19.9	504.2	360.2
7.	Prakit/FCB	19.8	500.0	467.0
8.	HDM	18.6	470.0	360.0
9.	J. Walter Thompson	15.0	380.0	320.0
10.	The Ball Partnership	10.7	271.9	123.2

Source: individual co.

Media Focus, as reported in the Bangkok Post.★

Advertising Expenditure by Medium—Thailand (U.S.$ millions)

	(US$ millions) 1990	(Baht millions) 1990	1989
Television	256.9	6,502.1	4,957.9
Radio (est.)	61.6	1,560.0	1,300.0
Newspapers	143.1	3,620.9	2,650.1
Magazines	47.9	1,211.8	1,016.4
Cinema	0.5	11.9	8.2
Outdoor	24.0	607.0	482.2
Total	534.0	13,513.7	10,414.8

Source: Media Focus, Bangkok.

Top 10 Advertisers by Brand—Thailand (U.S.$ millions)

	(US$ millions) 1990	(Baht millions) 1990	1989
1. Muang Thoug Thani (industrial estate)	3.6	91.7	N/R+
2. Kratingdaeng (energy drink)	3.3	82.5	45.8
3. Bank of Ayudhya (corp. ad)	2.3	57.6	N/R+
4. Colgate (toothpaste)	1.9	49.3	57.5
5. Nissan (passenger car)	1.9	48.6	39.9
6. Shark & White Shark (energy drink)	1.9	48.0	N/R+
7. Fuji (color films)	1.8	46.5	N/R+
8. Nescafe (coffee)	1.7	43.2	N/R+
9. Toyota (passenger car)	1.7	42.7	N/R+
10. Sony (stereo set)	1.7	42.1	N/R+

N/R+ = not ranked
Source: Media Focus, Bangkok.

Top 10 Advertisers by Category—Thailand (U.S.$ millions)

	(US$ millions) 1990	(Baht millions) 1990	1989
1. Housing projects/ Real estate	49.8	1259.2	649.6
2. Pharmaceutical products	19.0	480.1	375.1
3. Department Stores/ Trade Centers	17.4	439.2	355.6
4. Alcoholic beverages	14.5	367.8	273.1
5. Energy drinks	13.1	332.0	259.3
6. Shampoo and Hair conditioners	12.6	319.1	261.0
7. Cosmetics—Skin Care	11.7	297.1	249.7
8. Milk & dairy products	11.5	290.0	235.8
9. Office machines & equipment	11.0	278.8	N/R+
10. Petroleum products	10.1	254.5	N/R+

N/R+ = not ranked
Source: Media Focus, Bangkok.

★ For a listing of Asian advertising, marketing, and public relations firms, see Appendix H.

ber, 1990. This was more than double the next category—pharmaceutical products—which registered a total of 4.35 billion baht (US$174 million) at the end of November.

As the real estate market in Thailand weakened, there was a distinct lowering of profiles by condominium developers. The financial ramifications of this development were spread fairly evenly throughout the industry. The reason for this fragmentation is not difficult to understand. Major agencies shy away from the real estate and housing category for several reasons. Credit risk in some projects is too high, for example, while in other cases, the return spent on getting to know the client and his product is often not worthwhile as the campaigns are often "one-offs" lasting only about six months. Finally, real estate companies' demands on agency resources have often been unrealistic for established agencies who prefer to service better-known, long-term clients. Some agencies have been reluctant to take on too much new business for fear of expanding their cost base. Thus the impact of growth in the real estate/property development sector has been less than might have been expected for the major agencies.

One new-product category which turned profits in Thailand was two-in-on shampoo/conditioner such as Procter & Gamble's Rejoice, which was handled by Leo Burnett, and Unilever's Dimension, handled by Lintas. This category generated 2.82 billion baht (US$113 million) during the first 11 months of 1990.

The two biggest challenges for agencies were the lack of experienced staff—an inevitable result of the industry doubling in size over the past three years—and the changeover from a buyer's to a seller's market in the media. This has indeed been a remarkable about-turn, but with TV advertising time restricted by the government and demand growing, it suddenly became difficult to book TV time in 1990. This created more than a little competition among the various agencies' media departments, and the TV channels predictably reacted with major rate hikes.

The two major stations, channels 3 and 7, which are operated, respectively, by the Mass Communications Organisation of Thailand and the army, announced prime-time rate increases of between 20 and 27 percent. A minute of prime viewing time in Thailand now costs around 120,000 baht (US$4,800). This was a particularly important change in Thailand where TV accounts for approximately 50 to 57 percent of all advertising expenditure.

Print media also had a good year and there was substantial growth in space availability. *Bangkok Post*'s year was extremely successful primarily due to growth in real estate advertising, says the newspaper's advertising manager, Ladaval. An unusually high proportion of property ad spending (around 80 percent) went to newspapers and the *Bangkok Post* added a new special weekly section called "Investment and Real Estate" to help soak up excess adspend. There have also been several new business magazines produced this year.

The local industry produced some first-class ads in 1990. The technical quality of local production houses has always been extraordinarily high, and the best production of 1990 shows that Thailand can produce world-class results, even though the average quality of creative ads can often be depressingly low.

As 1990 ended, there was growing optimism that the law prohibiting the use of foreign languages in television and radio broadcasting would be lifted in line with Thailand's growing liberalization, while the Food and Drug Administration was beginning an inquiry into the possible prohibition of alcoholic beverage advertisements to protect public health.

President of the Advertising Association of Thailand, Yupon Thammasri, expects growth to be in the region of 15 percent. He also suggests the industry will not be too badly affected by the economic downturn, which appears to be the consensus view—advertising expenditure in Thailand is still among the lowest as a proportion of GNP in the region, and international advertisers are still eager to capture their share of this growing consumer market.

by Mathew Welch and Patricia Bjaaland

2

❖

TRADE

PACIFIC RIM TRADE IN
THE 1990s

The 1990s will see a powerful boom for U.S. companies in the already emerging market named for the area along the Pacific Rim, according to Export Today Inc., *a Washington, D.C.-based trade publication. Here a number of trade experts present their analysis of these markets.*

In the 1990s the Pacific Rim will exceed the rest of the world in economic growth—as it has for the past several years. Over the next two years, analysts at the Bank of America predict that the Rim will average 4.8% annual growth, compared with 2.7% growth for Western Europe, and 2% for North America. The overall growth figure for the Rim is skewed since Japan accounts for the lion's share of the Rim's economic activity. Japan is expected to grow at a "modest" 4% per year rate over the next few years. The majority of other Rim markets will grow at a far greater pace than 4.8%.

In the past most Pacific Rim growth was export-driven. U.S. exporters will see a Rim in the 1990s that is more dependent on domestic growth, and this trend will not only increase but will alter demand for U.S. goods. Domestic import demand and consumer spending will outpace exports from the Rim. There are several major trends in the region that will affect U.S. exporters.

First, structural adjustments among all the

countries in the Rim are creating a region whose dynamics will be drastically different in the years ahead.

Second, as the more industrialized countries enjoy the affluence they have worked so hard for, domestic spending will gradually replace export activities as the primary contributor to economic growth.

And third, the developing nations in Southeast Asia will assume the roles previously held by their northern neighbors as the major beneficiaries of foreign investment.

American companies interested in exploiting the plentiful business opportunities that exist and are emerging in the region should be aware of the differences between the various subregions of the Rim.

There are five primary subregions in the Pacific Rim—each with their own unique economic characteristics, levels of development, trade flows, and commercial and consumer needs.

Japan and China are subregions of their own: Japan—because it accounts for over 70% of present economic activity in the Rim and is an extremely homogeneous society; China—because it represents the world's largest potential consumer market and because the recent turmoil there will have profound effects not only on its own economic future but on the entire Pacific Rim as well.

The "Four Tigers" or the newly industrialized countries (NICs)—Singapore, Hong Kong, Taiwan, and South Korea—are the next major subregion, as they are rapidly approaching the industrial levels of Japan and the industrialized countries of the West.

The lesser developed countries (LDCs) of Southeast Asia—Indonesia, Malaysia, the Philippines, and Thailand—constitute another subregion. They will grow the most rapidly throughout the 1990s. The last subregion consists of Australia and New Zealand,

the only non-Asian countries among the major economies of the Pacific Rim.

JAPAN

Little has to be said concerning Japan's ascension to economic superiority. It is among the most vibrant and diverse markets in the world and will play an increasingly important role in the U.S. economy in the coming decade.

One could say "As Japan goes, so goes the Rim." Japan is the number-one foreign supplier to most of the countries in the Rim, as well as the primary source of investment and development funds. Along with the U.S., Japan is the principal market for exports from the other Pacific Rim countries. As long as Japan's economy remains healthy, the Rim should prosper. If Japan's economy should stumble, the rest of the Rim will feel damaging repercussions.

Despite the emergence of Japan-bashing as a popular diversion among U.S. politicians and business groups in recent years, Japan is really no more protectionist in many ways than Western Europe. This is not to suggest that the U.S. doesn't have legitimate concerns with various Japanese trade practices and structural barriers to trade. Japan is in fact—in terms of both tariff and nontarrif barriers—more hospitable to U.S. imports than most of the other Pacific Rim nations (Hong Kong and Singapore being the principal exceptions). While Japan accounts for 33% of total Pacific Rim imports, it is responsible for 41% of the region's imports from the U.S.

CHINA

The tragic suppression of political protest in China has cast a shadow on what would have been a very exciting era for U.S. exporters.

Gross Domestic Product, Regional Shares

(% of world total)

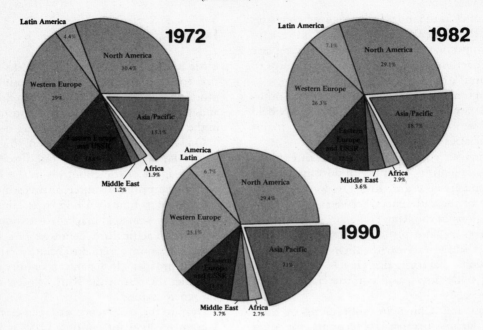

Gross Domestic Product

(US$ billions)

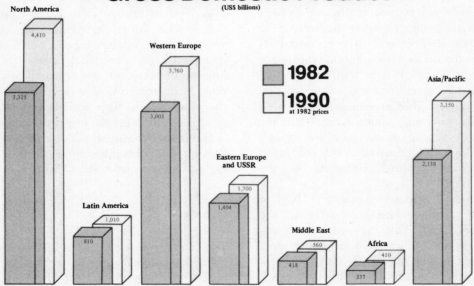

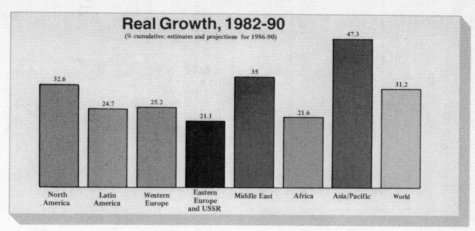

Real Growth, 1982-90
(% cumulative; estimates and projections for 1986-90)

- North America — 32.6
- Latin America — 24.7
- Western Europe — 25.2
- Eastern Europe and USSR — 21.1
- Middle East — 35
- Africa — 21.6
- Asia/Pacific — 47.3
- World — 31.2

Consumer Price Increases
(annual % rise over previous year)

15.0
13.2
11.8
10.7

World 13.7
Australia
Developing Asia 6.8
Japan 2.0

1975 1976 1977 1978 1979 1980 1981 1982 1983 1984 1985

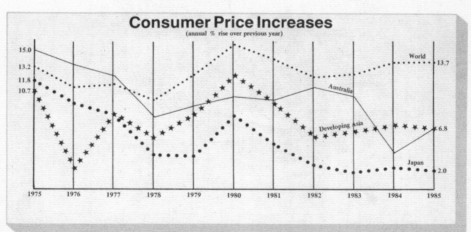

Index of Market Size

The index of market size, as presented below, is a convenient tool that may be used to assess priorities quickly and roughly. It has been constructed by combining various indicators to arrive at a common figure that expresses the relative size of a market. The nine indicators used are population size (given double weight), urbanization, private consumption spending, electricity consumption, steel consumption, newsprint consumption, telephones in use, automobiles registered, and TV sets in use. The figures shown express each country's percentage of the total of all countries covered.

China, India, and Japan — in that order — emerge as the region's largest markets by far. One reason is that the double weight for population size works in favor of populous nations.

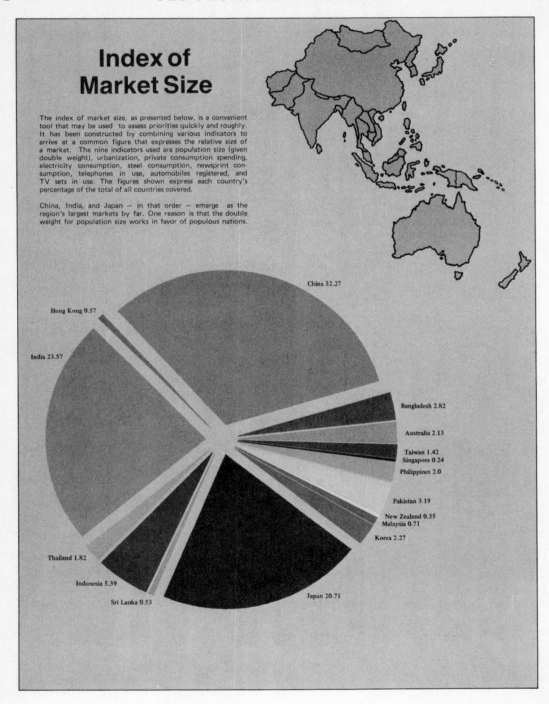

China 32.27
Hong Kong 0.57
India 23.57
Bangladesh 2.82
Australia 2.13
Taiwan 1.42
Singapore 0.24
Philippines 2.0
Pakistan 3.19
New Zealand 0.35
Malaysia 0.71
Korea 2.27
Thailand 1.82
Indonesia 5.39
Sri Lanka 0.53
Japan 20.71

Index of Market Intensity

The index of market intensity below is another tool for assessing markets — but rather than stressing size, it puts more emphasis on wealth. It is based on the same indicators as the index of market size (see preceding page), but double weight is given not to population size, but rather to private consumption expenditure, urbanization, and passenger car ownership.

On that basis, Japan — as is to be expected — ranks highest, with the rest of the region far behind. Nevertheless, the huge populations of China and India secure second and third place for these two countries.

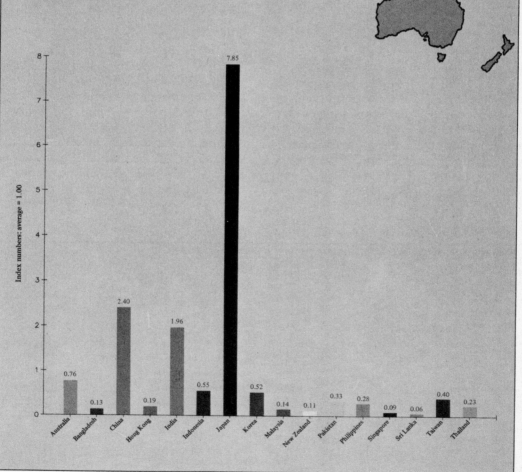

Index numbers: average = 1.00

Australia	0.76
Bangladesh	0.13
China	2.40
Hong Kong	0.19
India	1.96
Indonesia	0.55
Japan	7.85
Korea	0.52
Malaysia	0.14
New Zealand	0.11
Pakistan	0.33
Philippines	0.28
Singapore	0.09
Sri Lanka	0.06
Taiwan	0.40
Thailand	0.23

1-14 Demographic and Economic Statistics for ASEAN and Other Asian Countries (1989)

	Estimates of Mid-year Population (millions)	Area 1987 (1,000 km²)	Density[b] (population per km²)	GNP (1988) (at current prices)		Average Annual Growth Rate (Real) 1985—1989	Inter-national Reserves[d] (US$ million)	Foreign Trade (US$ million)	
				(US$ billion)	Per Capita (US$)			Exports (f.o.b.)	Imports (c.i.f.)
Japan	**123.12**	**378**	**322**	**2,866.9**	**23,382**	**4.5%**	**85,071**	**275,173**	**210,840**
China	1,119.70	9,597	112	376.5	341	9.3[c]	18,547	51,631	58,561
Korea, Rep. of	42.38	99	420	171.3	4,082	9.8	15,513	62,375	61,448
Hong Kong	5.77	1.05[b]	5,294	54.7	9,637	7.1	—	73,140	72,153
ASEAN[a]	**314.24**	**3,048.6**	**103**	**238.3**	**758**	**—**	**47,619**	**—**	**—**
Indonesia	179.14	1,905	88	82.7	471	4.8	6,498	19,218[f]	13,249[f]
Philippines	60.01	300	185	39.1	667	3.1	2,376	7,747	10,732
Thailand	55.45	513	102	57.9	1,062	7.5	10,508	15,952[f]	20,285[f]
Malaysia	16.96	330	49	34.6	2,047	4.2	7,892	25,080	22,558
Singapore	2.68	0.6	4,185	23.9	9,009	5.7	20,345	44,678	49,676

a) Association of Southeast Asian Nations. Excludes Brunei. b) 1986. c) 1984—1987. d) End of 1988 and Total Reserves minus Gold plus Gold (National Valuation). e) Total Reserves. f) 1988.
Source: Bank of Japan, *Comparative International Statistics*, 1990; IMF, *International Financial Statistics*, June 1990; U.N., *Monthly Bulletin of Statistics*, July 1990.

With over a billion people, China presented international traders around the world with a virtually untapped market with almost unlimited opportunities. While the optimism that accompanied U.S. business prospects in China may not be completely dead, the short-term outlook is not good, especially for companies not already active in the market. The current moratorium on foreign exchange from the U.S., European Community (EC), and multilateral lending organizations severely limits the funding essential for increased U.S. exports. And the doors that China was gradually opening to the world community are now closing once again.

As a result of the turmoil, China's primary effect on Rim dynamics will be passive. Billions of dollars in development funding and

3-7 The *Fortune* Ranking of 25 Japanese Manufacturing Companies (1989)

Rank[a]		Sales (US$ million)	Net Income (US$ million)	Employees (1,000)	Rank[a]		Sales (US$ million)	Net Income (US$ million)	Employees (1,000)
6	Toyota Motor	60,444	2,631	91.8	104	NKK	10,926	715	30.1
9	Hitachi	50,894	1,447	274.5	107	Sanyo Electric	10,487	124	55.5
12	Matsushita Electric Ind.	43,086	1,664	193.1	118	Canon	10,024	278	44.4
17	Nissan Motor	36,078	890	117.3	121	Sharp	9,928	226	32.3
24	Toshiba	29,469	931	125.0	123	Kobe Steel	9,886	198	24.5
30	Honda Motor	26,484	759	71.2	124	Isuzu Motors	9,868	122	24.3
32	NEC	24,595	503	104.0	126	Nippondenso	9,663	348	49.3
42	Mitsubishi Electric	21,213	415	85.7	127	Sumitomo Metal Ind.	9,643	452	26.8
44	Nippon Steel	20,767	608	64.5	138	Kawasaki Steel	9,081	378	24.5
49	Fujitsu	18,734	541	104.5	149	Mitsubishi Kasei	8,650	157	19.1
56	Mitsubishi Motors	16,840	147	37.9	**Ref.**				
57	Sony	16,680	564	78.9	—	General Motors	126,974	4,224	775.1
62	Mazda Motor	15,573	99	28.3	—	Ford Motor	96,933	3,835	366.6
67	Mitsubishi Heavy Ind.	15,007	482	55.5	—	IBM	63,438	3,758	383.2
84	Bridgestone	12,379	68	93.1	—	General Electric	55,264	3,939	292.0

a) Rank outside U.S. and excludes three oil and mining related companies.
Source: Time Inc., *Fortune*, April 23 and July 30, 1990.

4-1 Value of Foreign Trade Per Capita and Degree of Dependency on Foreign Trade

	Value of Foreign Trade Per Capita (1989)[a]		Degree of Dependency on Foreign Trade (1989)[c]	
	Exports (f.o.b., US$)	Imports (c.i.f., US$)	Exports	Imports
U.S.A.	1,478[b]	2,001	7.0%	9.4%
Canada	4,677	4,669	25.0[d]	23.8[d]
Germany, F.R.	5,578	4,408	28.4	22.4
U.K.	2,669	3,464	18.3	23.7
France	3,211	3,455	17.7[d]	18.8[d]
Italy	2,450	2,664	16.4	17.8
Netherlands	7,310	7,063	45.6[d]	43.7[d]
Switzerland	7,915	6,939	26.2[d]	29.1[d]
Japan	**2,244**	**1,720**	**9.7**	**7.4**
Korea, Rep. of	1,485	1,461	35.9[d]	30.7[d]
Hong Kong	12,854	12,681	114.2[d]	115.6[d]
Singapore	16,855	18,742	158.5[d]	176.9[d]

a) Trade values divided by 1988 estimated population. b) f.a.s. basis. c) Calculated by dividing trade values by GNP. Hong Kong by GDP. d) 1988.
Source: Bank of Japan, *Comparative International Statistics*, 1990.

foreign investment originally slated for China is and will be diverted to the LDCs in the region.

THE NICs

These nations—which have made remarkable strides in the past 20 years—will probably see their roles change the most dramatically in the 1990s. Once considered vendor nations to Japan and the U.S. (remember the stigma of a "Made in Hong Kong" label)—they are themselves becoming consumer nations.

Rather than import raw materials and low-end capital goods to produce consumer goods for industrialized nations, these nations are becoming sophisticated industrial economies

4-4 Balance of Trade for Selected Countries (1980—1990)
(US$ million)

	Japan[a]	U.S.A.[b]	Germany, F.R.	France	U.K.	Italy	Canada	Australia	Mexico	Korea, Rep. of
1980	**2,125**	−25,500	8,720	−13,419	3,362	−16,943	8,001	1,369	−2,830	−4,384
1981	**19,967**	−27,970	16,180	−9,970	7,155	−12,141	6,578	−2,324	−4,099	−3,628
1982	**18,079**	−36,450	24,730	−15,785	3,710	−8,911	14,991	−2,612	6,795	−2,594
1983	**31,454**	−67,080	21,420	−8,754	−1,676	−2,508	14,972	30	13,762	−1,763
1984	**44,257**	−112,510	22,290	−4,651	−6,109	−5,818	15,967	−884	12,941	−1,036
1985	**55,986**	−122,160	28,510	−5,276	−2,653	−6,083	12,574	−1,317	8,451	−19
1986	**92,827**	−145,050	55,740	−2,081	−12,801	4,525	7,565	−2,076	4,599	4,206
1987	**96,386**	−159,490	69,880	−8,667	−17,962	−73	9,063	−480	8,433	7,659
1988	**95,012**	−127,210	79,410	−8,089	−36,994	−768	8,881	−1,128	1,752	11,445
1989	**76,917**	−113,240	76,710	−10,338	−37,958	—	5,047	−3,647	—	—
1989 III	**19,770**	−31,540	19,260	−1,998	−11,057	—	904	−1,571	—	1,098
IV	**16,042**	−29,730	17,960	−2,903	−5,458	—	1,788	−513	—	—
1990 I	**14,393**	—	23,090	—	—	—	—	—	—	—

a) Based on *Balance of Payments Monthly*. b) Excludes military grants. Based on *Economic Indicators*. c) Seasonally adjusted.
Source: IMF, *International Financial Statistics*, August 1990.

4-9 U.S. Merchandise Trade by Area (1978—1989)

(US$ million, adjusted to balance-of-payments basis, excluding military)

	Total U.S. Merchandise Trade			with Japan			with EC[a]			with Latin America[b]	with Asian NIEs[c]	with OPEC
	Exports	Imports	**Balance**	Exports	Imports	**Balance**	Exports	Imports	**Balance**	**Balance**	**Balance**	**Balance**
1978	142,054	176,001	**−33,947**	12,960	24,540	**−11,580**	31,778	29,049	**2,729**	**869**	**−5,293**	**−18,440**
1979	184,473	212,009	**−27,536**	17,629	26,260	**−8,631**	42,474	33,219	**9,255**	**−154**	**−4,168**	**−30,483**
1980	224,269	249,750	**−25,481**	20,806	31,216	**−10,410**	53,466	36,077	**17,389**	**2,476**	**−3,556**	**−38.234**
1981	237,085	265,063	**−27,978**	21,796	37,597	**−15,801**	51,366	41,416	**9,950**	**3,627**	**−6,095**	**−28,837**
1982	211,198	247,642	**−36,444**	20,694	37,683	**−16,989**	46,905	42,342	**4,563**	**−4,751**	**−7,335**	**−10,866**
1983	200,745	262,757	**−62,013**	21,677	41,306	**−19,629**	43,251	43,733	**−482**	**−12,330**	**−11,434**	**−10,035**
1984	217,888	325,726	**−107,838**	23,575	57,135	**−33,560**	46,379	57,774	**−11,395**	**−14,175**	**−20,144**	**−13,081**
1985	213,146	345,276	**−132,130**	22,631	68,783	**−46,152**	48,994	67,822	**−18,828**	**−13,021**	**−22,148**	**−10,321**
1986	217,304	369,961	**−152,657**	26,882	81,911	**−55,029**	53,154	75,736	**−22,582**	**−9,793**	**−27,846**	**−8,906**
1987	252,866	405,901	**−153,035**	28,249	84,575	**−56,326**	60,575	81,188	**−20,613**	**−11,507**	**−34,117**	**−12,895**
1988	320,385	441,282	**−120,897**	37,732	89,802	**−52,070**	75,926	84,991	**−9,065**	**−8,286**	**−28,350**	**−9,042**
1989(P)	364,350	472,926	**−108,576**	44,584	93,586	**−49,002**	86,592	85,129	**1,467**	**−5,797**	**−24,298**	**−17,367**

a) 1976—1980 Nine countries, 1981—1985 Ten countries, 1986—Twelve countries. See P. 5. b) 1978—Brazil, Mexico and Venezuela. 1989—Mexico and Brazil. c) Hong Kong, Korea, Republic of, Singapore and Taiwan.
Source: U.S. Department of Commerce, *Survey of Current Business; Highlights of U.S. Export and Import Trade.*

and are increasingly looking to the LDCs to invest in labor-intensive industries. As their industrialization accelerates, they are having to deal with the loss of developing-nation status—and the breaks that come with such designation.

In a sense, this subregion needs to be broken into two additional sub-subregions. Hong Kong and Singapore—as former British colonies—were natural crossroads for Asian–Occidental trade and, as such, were and are the world's best examples of truly free trade. And because of their relatively small populations and land area, they more resemble cities than full-scale nations.

Taiwan and South Korea, on the other hand, are now major industrial nations. The world trading community, especially the

4-10 Leading Trading Partners of Selected Asian Countries (1989)

		Total[a] (US$ million)	Top Four Partners (%)							
			No. 1		No. 2		No. 3		No. 4	
China	Exports	51,626	Hong Kong	42.6	**Japan**	**15.8**	U.S.A.	7.7	U.S.S.R.	3.3
	Imports	58,282	Hong Kong	23.7	**Japan**	**17.3**	U.S.A.	11.9	Germany, F.R.	5.6
Korea, Rep. of	Exports	62,331	U.S.A.	33.7	**Japan**	**21.6**	Hong Kong	5.5	Germany, F.R.	3.5
	Imports	61,300	**Japan**	**28.7**	U.S.A.	25.8	Germany, F.R.	4.3	Australia	3.7
Hong Kong	Exports	73,140	China	25.7	U.S.A.	25.3	**Japan**	**6.2**	Germany, F.R.	5.0
	Imports	72,155	China	34.9	**Japan**	**16.6**	Taiwan	9.2	U.S.A.	8.2
Singapore	Exports	44,665	U.S.A.	23.4	Malaysia	13.7	**Japan**	**8.6**	Hong Kong	6.3
	Imports	49,667	**Japan**	**21.4**	U.S.A.	17.2	Malaysia	13.1	Saudi Arabia	4.8
Malaysia	Exports	25,053	Singapore	19.8	U.S.A.	18.7	**Japan**	**16.0**	Korea, Rep. of	5.0
	Imports	22,496	**Japan**	**24.2**	U.S.A.	16.9	Singapore	13.6	U.K.	5.4
Indonesia	Exports	21,936	**Japan**	**42.2**	U.S.A.	15.8	Singapore	8.2	Korea, Rep. of	4.1
	Imports	16,467	**Japan**	**23.3**	U.S.A.	13.5	Taiwan	6.3	Singapore	6.3
Philippines	Exports	7,766	U.S.A.	37.8	**Japan**	**20.4**	Germany, F.R.	4.3	Netherland	4.2
	Imports	11,171	**Japan**	**19.5**	U.S.A.	19.1	Taiwan	6.5	Singapore	4.7

a) U.S. dollar figures are calculated according to the annual average exchange rates of the IMF, *International Financial Statistics.*
Source: IMF, *Direction of Trade Statistics,* 1990.

4-21 Volume Shipments of Japan's Imports and Exports (1989)

	Volume (million tons)	Share Carried by Japanese Vessels (P)
Imports, total	**683.2**	**32.7%**
Crude Oil	178.0	50.9
Iron Ore	127.6	44.2
Coal	105.0	42.2
Wood	28.3	9.9
Maize	15.8	2.6
Salt	7.6	3.8
Wheat	5.6	2.8
Exports, total	**70.7**	**8.4**
Iron & Steel Products	19.9	5.7
Cement	6.6	3.4
Passenger Cars	5.5	32.9
Electrical Goods	2.1	9.9

Source: Ministry of Transport, Japan.

U.S., is pressuring these countries to reflect their increased economic status in their policies toward international trade. Massive liberalization, the most ambitious in the Rim, is taking place for both imports and investment.

THE LDCs

As the primary recipients of foreign investment, the LDCs will see the most rapid growth in the 1990s. U.S. companies will have many new export opportunities, especially in industrial equipment, machinery, and technology, as the LDCs strive to develop export industries and wean their economies away from dependence on oil and agriculture. This trend will accelerate as development funds and foreign investment are diverted from China.

These will become the new vendor nations of the region, providing low-tech consumer goods and equipment to the more industrialized countries in the Rim as well as the West. They will be particularly attractive targets for U.S. companies interested in establishing a base in the Rim. The LDCs are currently in heated competition, trying to outdo one another in providing investment incentives to foreign companies. Substantial liberalizations are taking place for foreign investment—especially for export-related industries.

AUSTRALIA AND NEW ZEALAND

Australia and New Zealand are often overlooked when U.S. exporters think about the exciting opportunities in the Rim. But these

5-1 Current Account Balance for Selected Countries (1981—1990)
(US$ million)

	Japan[a]	U.S.A.	Germany, F.R.	France	U.K.	Italy	Canada	Australia	Mexico	Korea, Rep. of
1981	**4,770**	6,870	−3,310	−4,811	14,112	−9,705	−5,110	−8,507	−13,899	−4,646
1982	**6,850**	−8,640	4,980	−12,082	8,041	−6,391	2,231	−8,459	−6,307	−2,650
1983	**20,799**	−44,310	5,410	−5,166	5,831	1,381	2,487	−5,868	5,403	−1,606
1984	**35,003**	−104,210	9,750	−876	2,608	−2,501	1,995	−8,577	4,194	−1,372
1985	**49,169**	−112,750	17,000	−35	4,765	−3,540	−1,470	−8,913	1,130	−887
1986	**85,845**	−133,230	40,090	2,426	158	2,912	−7,600	−9,731	−1,673	4,617
1987	**87,015**	−143,700	46,120	−4,436	−7,373	−1,663	−7,060	−8,397	3,968	9,854
1988	**79,631**	−126,580	50,470	−3,549	−26,733	−5,446	−8,330	−10,093	−2,905	14,161
1989	**57,157**	−105,900	55,480	−4,299	−34,065	—	−16,593	−15,677	—	—
1989 II	**14,283**	−31,920	14,000	−955	−8,626	—	−4,617	−3,915	—	1,197
III	**14,957**	−27,860	11,120	−467	−10,822	—	−2,706	−4,558	—	1,099
IV	**11,853**	−20,130	13,560	−2,425	−6,816	—	−4,109	−3,471	—	—
1990 I	**12,305**	—	—	—	—	—	—	—	—	—

a) Based on *Balance of Payments Monthly*.
Source: IMF, *International Financial Statistics*, August 1990.

6-5 Japan's Direct Overseas Investment by Region and Country (As of March 31, 1990)
(US$ million)

	FY 1989 Amount	FY 1951—1989 total		FY 1989 Amount	FY 1951—1989 total
U.S.A.	32,540	104,400	Malaysia	673	2,507
Canada	1,362	4,593	Taiwan	494	2,285
North America, total	**33,902**	**108,993**	Thailand	1,276	2,088
U.K.	5,239	15,793	Philippines	202	1,322
Luxembourg	654	5,383	**Asia, total**	**8,238**	**40,465**
Netherlands	4,547	10,072	Australia	4,256	12,394
Germany, F.R.	1,083	3,448	**Oceania, total**	**4,618**	**13,933**
France	1,136	2,899	Saudi Arabia/Kuwait	32	1,415
Switzerland	397	1,829	**Middle East, total**	**66**	**3,404**
Spain	501	1,546	Panama	2,044	14,902
Europe, total	**14,808**	**44,972**	Brazil	349	5,946
Indonesia	631	10,435	Cayman	1,658	6,743
Hong Kong	1,898	8,066	**South America, total**	**5,238**	**36,855**
Singapore	1,902	5,715	Liberia	643	4.301
Korea, Rep. of	606	3,854	**Africa, total**	**671**	**5,275**
China	438	2,474	**Total**	**67,540**	**253,896**

a) Figures are the accumulated value of approvals and notification.
Source: Ministry of Finance, Japan.

two countries offer U.S. firms some excellent export opportunities.

The business practices in Australia and New Zealand are the most familiar to U.S. exporters since these nations share a similar Anglo-Saxon background. As the only non-Asian countries among the major Rim economies, U.S. exporters won't encounter the problems inherent in doing business with an extremely different culture. Although the Oceanic nations will not experience the explosive growth and change that the Asian countries will undergo, they present U.S. exporters with stable, developed markets familiar with and fond of U.S. products.

JAPAN

- The second-largest export market for U.S. goods and services, accounting for 41% of U.S. exports to the Pacific Rim.
- American firms permeate several key Japanese industries, making inroads for additional U.S. companies easier. For example,

more than 350 U.S. electronic firms operate in Japan with over 37,000 workers. Several major U.S. industry trade associations form trade partnerships with Japanese counterparts to facilitate greater bilateral cooperation and increase trade.
- Rising incomes and increasing Westernization, a new generation of Japanese more willing to spend larger shares of their considerable affluence on leisure activities, consumer goods, recreation, travel, and other areas where U.S. goods are quite popular.
- The present value of the dollar against the yen, making U.S. goods among the most price-competitive in the Japanese market. Trade conflicts between the U.S. and Japan slowly abating; U.S. exporters finding previously restrictive areas more hospitable.

POLITICAL AND ECONOMIC TRENDS

GENERAL OUTLOOK

Japan is still recovering from the Recruit scandal, its biggest political scandal since World

War II. In its wake there's been a revolving door for its Prime Ministers, the current Prime Minister having no experience in trade or economic matters. However, the well-entrenched business and bureaucratic communities—which work quite independently of the political leadership—have kept business operating as usual. But bilateral trade negotiations have been slowed.

When Japan was branded a "Super 301" offender (as per the provisions of the 1988 Omnibus Trade Act) by the U.S. Trade Office, Tokyo spoke of swift and harsh reprisals. However, once the rhetorical smoke cleared, it became evident that the Japanese are willing to negotiate. For the long run, anti-American feelings aren't expected to be greatly inflated.

The Japanese economy continues its vibrant growth. The only major problem is that prices in the major metropolitan areas, especially Tokyo, are so high that they are pushing the population into far lower standards of living than they would like. Much of this has to do with the extreme complexity of Japan's distribution system, which guarantees full employment, but also high prices.

One interesting trend that may help bring U.S.–Japan trade into balance in the 1990s is that Japanese economic growth seems to be driven more by increased domestic spending than by exports.

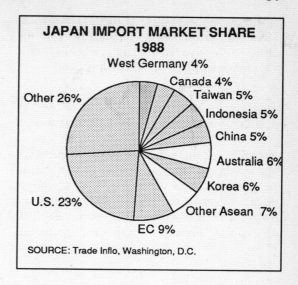

sions—such as on U.S. beef and citrus products and telecommunications equipment. Japan also agreed to hold discussions on the issues leading to its Super 301 designation—namely, unfair government procurement policies and discriminatory technical standards—as well as some of the structural barriers to trade, such as its distribution system, high savings rate, and dependence on exports rather than domestic growth.

BEST-SELLING PRODUCTS FOR THE YEARS AHEAD

IMPORT AND INVESTMENT LIBERALIZATION

Japan's tariffs are relatively low—in many instances lower than in the United States. But American exporters find nontariff barriers to be the primary impediments to increased sales to Japan. Those barriers are slowly coming down. In recent months, the Japanese have made considerable market-opening conces-

COMPUTER SOFTWARE

This is the major U.S. export market in Japan for the 1990s. With an estimated demand of $3.3 billion in 1988, it's among the most dynamic and sophisticated high-tech markets in the world. Growth is projected at an average annual rate of 25% for well into the next decade. Software development is one area where

Japanese industry lags far behind America. Domestic competition—especially for the more advanced systems and programs—is at a minimum, at least for the time being.

TELECOMMUNICATIONS EQUIPMENT

Recent concessions by the government have opened up the Japanese market to U.S.-made cellular telephones and two-way radio equipment. Although the United States only controls 5% of the market, it accounts for 90% of imports. Import growth throughout the 1990s is estimated at 6% a year.

PROJECT DESIGN AND CONSTRUCTION

After much pressure from the U.S. government, the Japanese are finally opening major construction projects to U.S. firms. This offers many new opportunities for U.S. subcontractors and suppliers of construction equipment and supplies.

CONSUMER GOODS

U.S. fads and fashions are extremely popular in Japan, as are American consumer products. Increased leisure time and rising incomes are producing a consumer-goods market approximating the vibrancy of the U.S. market. Especially popular items include: sporting goods, gourmet foods, pet care products, jewelry, furniture, and apparel. Japanese women are increasingly entering the workforce, creating a booming market for processed foods, especially fish—one of the staples of the Japanese diet.

MEDICAL TECHNOLOGY

Spending on medical-related fields exceeded $130 billion in 1989. While imports account for roughly only 12% of the market, the United States provided the lion's share of 60%. Japanese firms are fiercely competitive and on the same field technologically with U.S. companies. Several recent regulatory improvements in standards and certification processes will bode well for U.S. suppliers.

OTHER PRIME EXPORT OPPORTUNITIES

Wood products, pulp and paper, chemicals, foodstuffs.

WHEN DOING BUSINESS IN JAPAN KEEP IN MIND:

- Japan is an extremely homogeneous society, wary of both Westerners and other Asians. Establishing relationships with Japanese partners takes time. By stressing goodwill, reliability, and a commitment to the transaction—before, during, and especially after completion—you can overcome cultural differences.
- Never approach any potential Japanese business venture unprepared. More often than not, you will be working with people put in that position because they are the best at what they do—and they do their homework. They expect no less from you. A serious gaffe can cost you honor and respect—qualities harder to regain than in the United States.
- Japanese employers are more concerned with the company's well-being than with personal accomplishment or profit—they're often considered one and the same. Remember to stress benefits at the group level.

CHINA

NEGATIVE TURNAROUND FOR A HOT U.S. EXPORT MARKET

The unfortunate events in Tienanmen Square in May 1989 not only affected the people of China, but the whole world. When the first shots were fired on June 6, the economic reforms of several years came to an abrupt halt. What made this tragedy all the more disappointing—especially from an American point of view—was that China had made such astonishing progress in opening its economy to the world.

In addition, U.S. companies were taking advantage of the market reforms in droves. U.S. exports to China in 1988 grew 44% over 1987 and for the first time exceeded $5 billion. In the first five months of 1989, U.S. exports increased 30% over the 1988 levels.

Although it's not possible to determine what direction U.S.–China trade will move, the only thing that is certain is that U.S. export prospects won't improve in the short term. Depending on future world reaction and the severity of China's contraction back into a closed society, experts are rating short-term U.S. export prospects anywhere from lukewarm to stagnant.

It's now unwise to approach China's import markets as you would the other Pacific Rim economies, as too much uncertainty exists for any meaningful future-oriented analysis. Many of the factors that made China such an attractive market for U.S. exports are no longer relevant—or simply no longer true. Unlike the rest of the region, short-term economic performance does not look promising. Other dissimilarities with its Pacific Rim neighbors are that import and investment liberalizations, once quite elaborate, have ceased —at least for the time being.

CAUSES OF THE TURMOIL

Ironically, China was ultimately a victim of the very reforms that made it such a promising future market. By opening up its economy to the world and embarking on an ambitious journey of unprecedented economic reform, China experienced explosive growth of 11% in 1988—the highest growth among the world's major economies. In fact, over the past couple of years the Chinese government was concerned that the economy was growing too quickly and had actually taken steps to decelerate growth.

Industrial output surged 21% in 1988, intensifying the existing chronic energy and raw materials shortages. In addition, inflation soared to close to 40% in many urban areas, as China relaxed credit controls to stimulate export industries and meet credit demands of foreign investors.

FOREIGN EXCHANGE THE KEY

Having a nonconvertible currency, a steady flow of foreign exchange from the West is essential to continued increases in trade between China and the West. For now, foreign exchange in the form of developmental lending has been cut off by the U.S., EC, and Japan—this includes multilateral lending organizations, such as the International Monetary Fund. Tourism, another principal source of China's foreign exchange, has plummeted since the violence. And many foreign investors seeking low-coat production sites in the Pacific Rim are looking to other lesser-developed nations in the region, nations with more predictable political stability.

Hong Kong companies, which account for two thirds of China's foreign investment income, have been divesting from existing projects and putting planned projects on hold. The fears associated with being ceded back into China in 1997 have intensified investment concerns. Despite PR efforts on the Chinese bureaucracy's part, foreign investors just don't believe China is as safe to do business in as before the turmoil.

Should foreign exchange dry up, the chances for additional increases in U.S. exports will disappear as well, at least in the form of direct sales. Any American firms having business in China would increasingly have to depend on other types of transactions, such as counter-trade and joint ventures.

IMPORT RESTRICTIONS

Chinese officials have acknowledged that they plan no further progress on foreign trade reform for at least the next few years. Indeed, we've seen many of the improvements in the system start to move backward.

Most overt is the imposition of import restrictions on several product categories as Beijing struggles to conserve precious foreign exchange reserves. Exporting entities, which had recently been allowed a small portion of foreign exchange earnings to use as they saw fit, have seen that small bit of autonomy disappear.

The extensive controls the government uses to guide Chinese trade—such as quotas and licenses—will be tightened. And the few factories that had the authority to sign trade contracts with foreign firms will be restricted.

Grain and agricultural imports will likely stay at present levels. However, imports of raw materials may be channeled away from Western sources to conserve foreign exchange. Barter with the Soviet Union and Eastern Europe would likely become the replacement source.

If the foreign exchange crunch becomes especially tight, further restrictions might be placed on imports of industrial equipment and technology. This would likely lower industrial output and exports, creating more severe foreign exchange shortages—a vicious circle from which China will find it hard to escape.

NO CONSENSUS

Neither China experts nor exporters who are doing business in China can reach a consensus on the short-, medium-, and—to a lesser extent—long-term effects of the China situation on future U.S.–China trade. Some feel that

---

SELECTED U.S. EXPORTS TO CHINA: 1987–1988

Unfortunately, the trouble in China came just as U.S. exports to China were booming. Listed below are some of the product sectors that saw particularly vibrant growth between 1987 and 1988.

Growth 1987–1988	
Grains	199%
Wood products	167%
Plastics and resins	134%
Organic chemicals	71%
Specialized machinery	42%
Fertilizers	40%
Scientific equipment	20%
ADP equipment	6%

SOURCE: U.S. Commerce Dept.

after an initial cooling-off period of a year or so, U.S. firms may be able to return to business as usual. Others feel business prospects have been irreparably damaged—at least as long as the current regime is in power.

Still others point out that once the Chinese people have had this chance, however limited, to move forward, they will not stand repression for long. While the Chinese government may succeed in suppressing further dissident action, the pressure may build to the point where the demonstrations of April–June 1989 pale in comparison.

SINGAPORE

- The highest per capita destination of U.S. exports in the world, $2,071 for every resident of the island city-state. America's 13th-largest export market . . . and growing.
- Affluent, with a highly skilled workforce, and a consumer-oriented market.
- A complete business center, with outstanding telecommunications and shipping facilities. Future improvements, such as a 100% local fiber optic network to be completed in the coming decade. Second-busiest cargo-handling port facility in the world, with a new state-of-the-art container port due to be completed in 1992.
- Hub for regional trade and investment involving other Pacific Rim countries, such as Thailand, Malaysia, and Indonesia. Regional leader for joint ventures, distribution, and reexport trade.
- Major financial center for Southeast Asia. Important adjunct to development regional trade and home to full-service foreign departments and branch offices of many of the largest U.S. banks.

POLITICAL AND ECONOMIC TRENDS

GENERAL OUTLOOK

The government of Singapore is often considered to be the most stable in the region. It enjoys close relations with the U.S., and the U.S. remains its most important trading partner. Recent bilateral trade figures show continued strong growth for imports from the United States.

The Singapore economy continues on an upswing that has lasted for three years, with GDP growing nearly 10% annually. While GDP will slow down from the rapid pace set since 1986, real GDP is forecasted to grow by 7.5% in 1989 and by 6.5% in 1990. These forecasts represent rates that are among the highest in the Pacific Rim for those two years.

Consumer spending will continue to grow as well. The people of Singapore enjoy the second-largest per capita income in Asia, behind only Japan. As the city-state is a developed industrial nation with a rising standard of living, its consumers desire the most ad-

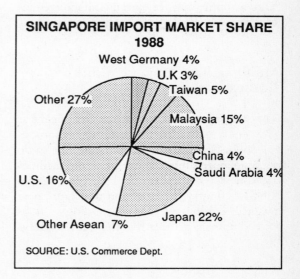

SINGAPORE IMPORT MARKET SHARE
1988

West Germany 4%
U.K 3%
Taiwan 5%
Malaysia 15%
China 4%
Saudi Arabia 4%
Japan 22%
Other Asean 7%
U.S. 16%
Other 27%

SOURCE: U.S. Commerce Dept.

vanced high-tech consumer goods available. And industry seeks to buy the best and latest in high-tech capital goods. The inflation rate remains extremely stable; hovering between 0% and 1%.

IMPORT AND INVESTMENT LIBERALIZATION

Singapore is one of the world's bastions of free trade and investment. Few restrictions exist.

BEST-SELLING PRODUCTS FOR THE YEARS AHEAD

INFORMATION TECHNOLOGY

The U.S. leads foreign suppliers in sales that are projected to grow by 120% from 1988 to 1991. The fastest-growing market in Singapore, this sector continues to boom, due primarily to a combination of the use and support of the government and Singapore's large banking, finance, and manufacturing industries.

MEDICAL AND HEALTH CARE EQUIPMENT

The United States dominates this field, as U.S. equipment is preferred for its technological sophistication, and should continue to do so. Singapore's medical expertise and facilities are considered the best in the region. Often the first country in the region to acquire new medical equipment and technology, it is looked upon as a leader by other regional buyers.

TELECOMMUNICATIONS EQUIPMENT

One of the principal U.S. exports to Singapore in 1988, this sector should continue to grow for the next several years. With the highest telephone density in Asia, Singapore is always seeking the latest technological advances in the field. Our main competitor is Japan.

TEXTILES (NONGARMENT)

Though the United States is the number-one supplier of a related product, carpeting, it accounts for only 2.5% of the overall textiles market at this time. Textile imports from the U.S. are growing at an annual rate of 20%. Domestic production of nonapparel textiles is limited and demand is increasing, especially in the home furnishings market. This fast-growing market includes finished draperies, bed clothes, upholstery, as well as fabrics used in the production of these products.

OTHER PRIME EXPORT OPPORTUNITIES

Printing and packaging equipment, office and data machines, consumer specialty and luxury items, applications software.

WHEN DOING BUSINESS IN SINGAPORE KEEP IN MIND:

- U.S. products enjoy a cost advantage over their Japanese competitors as a result of the appreciation of the Singapore dollar vis-à-vis the U.S. dollar and its concurrent depreciation against the yen.

- English is the language of business and an official language in Singapore—an interpreter is unnecessary; other official languages include Malay, Mandarin Chinese, and Tamil.
- All methods of advertising familiar to U.S. exporters—newspapers, billboards, television, radio—are well-developed in Singapore. The most effective medium is the daily newspapers. U.S. companies interested in doing business in Singapore should consider a media campaign.

HONG KONG

- No nontariff import barriers—and so few duties—that more than half of U.S. exports to Hong Kong enter tariff-free.
- The center for all types of business—from banking to manufacturing to shipping—for most of Asia, facilitating access to the entire Asian market, not just to Hong Kong alone.
- Almost no restrictions of any kind imposed on direct foreign investment.

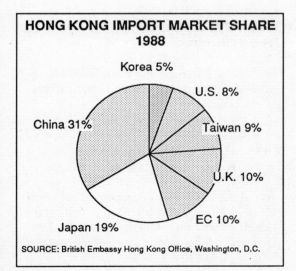

HONG KONG IMPORT MARKET SHARE 1988

Korea 5%
U.S. 8%
Taiwan 9%
China 31%
U.K. 10%
EC 10%
Japan 19%

SOURCE: British Embassy Hong Kong Office, Washington, D.C.

- Home of the largest container port facilities in the world, with plans to build two more terminals to handle the expected increase in the next decade.
- U.S. exports during the first five months of 1989 up over 23%, even though some slowdown predicted.

POLITICAL AND ECONOMIC TRENDS

GENERAL OUTLOOK

Clearly, U.S. exporters need only to read a newspaper on any given day since June 1989 to wonder if the Hong Kong of laissez-faire capitalism fame will exist after July 1997, when the British surrender control of the territory to the Chinese. This concern is well placed, requiring any businessman with long-term interests in Hong Kong to remain vigilant. If the outlook for the post-1997 period looks bleak as time goes on, many of the significant banking, manufacturing, and shipping interests may begin to shift away from Hong Kong. Despite this, several reasons allow a strong amount of guarded optimism when considering Hong Kong's economic future.

The agreement signed by London and Beijing in 1984 to return Hong Kong to Chinese control provided for a number of guarantees to continue the current system for 50 years after 1997.

Economic reasons, in combination with political reasons, seem to offer the best hope for Hong Kong's future. China has a vital interest in seeing Hong Kong remain the way it is. Beijing receives most of its foreign exchange through Hong Kong.

Hong Kong is China's primary export and import outlet to the rest of the world. China is the largest outside investor in Hong Kong, owning banks, factories, warehouses, and a large real estate portfolio. And although the political reform movement in China has received a severe setback, the leadership in Beijing has given strong indications that it wishes to continue the economic direction of the last decade.

However, it's impossible to accurately predict precisely how Beijing will act in the coming months and years, both internally and with relation to Hong Kong. While Hong Kong's future remains uncertain, one should remember it is coming off of several boom years, with a great deal of potential business to be done in the future. U.S. exporters should approach Hong Kong with some concern for the future but an expectation of profit at least for the short-term.

IMPORT AND INVESTMENT LIBERALIZATION

Hong Kong's import and investment laws are the most liberal in the world. The United States is the leading overseas source of investment in the manufacturing sector, accounting for over $1 billion in assets. Over 800 U.S. companies operate in Hong Kong.

BEST-SELLING PRODUCTS FOR THE YEARS AHEAD

INDUSTRIAL PACKAGING EQUIPMENT AND MATERIALS

Beset by an acute labor shortage, Hong Kong needs more capital intensive, labor-saving packaging methods. This trend can be expected to generate increased sales for U.S. exporters.

COMPUTER EQUIPMENT AND SOFTWARE

Sales to the banking and financial service sectors will offer increased opportunities for U.S. companies in one of the world's major financial centers.

PLASTIC RAW MATERIALS

Hong Kong's manufacturing emphasizes light industry. Plastic products are a perfect fit and will be a steadily growing market for the foreseeable future.

OFFICE EQUIPMENT, FURNITURE, AND SUPPLIES

This is another sector that has seen development generated by Hong Kong's growing service industries. Many corporations demand offices furnished with U.S.-built equipment and supplies.

OTHER PRIME EXPORT OPPORTUNITIES

Textile fabrics, carpets and rugs, food and agricultural products, hospital and physical therapy equipment.

WHEN DOING BUSINESS IN HONG KONG KEEP IN MIND:

- Avoid the high costs of setting up an actual office in Hong Kong by using a well-established distributor. Distributors encounter far fewer problems and can lower costs and limit legal liability.

- A sales agency is an alternative often used by smaller U.S. exporters, which provides local contacts, negotiating support, and an arrangement that is more easily terminated. While this entails more legal responsibility than with a distributorship, it could be a good first step.
- The Hong Kong dollar is pegged to the U.S. dollar at a ratio of 7.8 to 1, making long-term cost and revenue determinations straightforward.
- Hong Kong business practices more closely emulate those of the West than in any other Asian country. Less emphasis is placed on friendships, social interaction, and long-established personal ties than with most of Hong Kong's neighbors. The profit motive is most often the bottom line.

TAIWAN

- U.S. products in great demand, to lessen dependence on imports from Japan and improve the heavily out-of-balance bilateral trade relationship.
- Imports planned to rise 20% per year over the next three years; consumer spending in

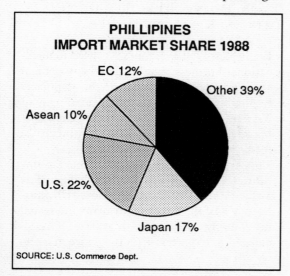

**PHILLIPINES
IMPORT MARKET SHARE 1988**

EC 12%
Other 39%
Asean 10%
U.S. 22%
Japan 17%

SOURCE: U.S. Commerce Dept.

an increasingly affluent market to rise 12.5% per year.
- 1988 imports grew at a faster pace than exports for the first time since 1980—a trend that should continue into the 1990s.
- Taiwan maintains high growth, conservatively targeted for 6.5% to 7.5% during the 1990s, while the rest of the world slows down.
- U.S. imports given preference over other foreign imports in all major government procurement.

POLITICAL AND ECONOMIC TRENDS

GENERAL OUTLOOK

U.S. exports to Taiwan were up over $2 billion in 1989, 29% over 1987. This doesn't include Taiwan's purchase of $2.5 billion of U.S. commodity gold. Early indications for 1989 show strong growth again, slowing somewhat to 19% during the January–May period.

Friction between Washington and Taipei has developed over the last several years as a result of Taiwan's enormous trade surpluses with the United States. One positive development for U.S. exporters has been the adoption by Taipei of a four-year Trade Action Plan designed to stimulate domestic demand and increase government spending. Government purchases present the best opportunities for increased U.S. exports as Taiwan favors U.S. contractors for government purchasing as part of the plan.

IMPORT AND INVESTMENT LIBERALIZATION

High tariffs, Taiwan's primary import barrier, have been falling in recent years. And they will continue to fall, expanding opportunities for U.S. exporters. An extensive import licensing system makes trade difficult and more costly for first-time exporters. At present, more than 50% of tariff schedule items require some licensing. Proposed plans to streamline this system will provide a boon for new-to-market U.S. exporters. Many barriers to the service sector have fallen in the past few years, but markets are not fully open for U.S. insurance firms.

Infringement of intellectual property rights is a serious ongoing problem. Some effort has been made by the Taiwanese in the copyright area, where a bilateral agreement has been reached by Taipei and Washington. But the agreement does not cover key U.S. exports, such as videotapes, and property rights enforcement has been arbitrary and ineffective at best. This is an area of continual bilateral negotiations.

Foreign investment is prohibited in about 28% of Taiwan industries, such as most agricultural activities, real estate services, and national defense industries.

BEST-SELLING PRODUCTS FOR THE YEARS AHEAD

POLLUTION CONTROL AND WASTE DISPOSAL

Heavy pollution has prompted the need for environmental protection. Sector investment is expected to total $33.3 billion by the year 2000. In the next five years over $10 billion will be spent on air and water pollution controls.

TELECOMMUNICATIONS

Favorable procurement for U.S. suppliers should result in strong sales as Taiwan spends over $2 billion into the early 1990s on digital network systems.

COMPUTER EQUIPMENT

U.S. sales are forecasted to grow 20% annually to $1.4 billion in 1991—50% of the Taiwanese market.

POWER PLANTS

Over $750 million dollars over the next eight years in designated foreign procurement for projects slated to cost in excess of $3.5 billion for transmission control systems and four thermal plants.

OTHER PRIME EXPORT OPPORTUNITIES

Scientific instruments, transportation—rapid transit—home furnishings and appliances, medical and hospital equipment.

WHEN DOING BUSINESS IN TAIWAN KEEP IN MIND:

- English, as well as Japanese, is used in international business. English is widely spoken at various levels by most of the populace, facilitating all aspects of a business trip to Taiwan. An English-language telephone book and telephone assistance number are readily available when visiting Taiwan.
- The American Institute in Taiwan, the unofficial U.S. presence on the island, offers Value-Added Business Sponsored Promotion (VABSP), a service to firms interested in entering Taiwanese markets. VABSP aides U.S. exporters with the entire market-

ing effort from market-entry research and trade shows to collecting follow-up information and catering cocktail parties.

- Personal contact and relationships are traditionally the cornerstones of conducting business in Taiwan. U.S. exporters are advised to send representatives on frequent trips to visit buyers to cultivate friendly relationships.

SOUTH KOREA

- Diversification away from Japanese imports leaves U.S. exporters with a golden opportunity for market penetration.
- Wages have risen 20% annually for the last three years, fostering a consumer-oriented mood. Has the largest percentage increase in disposable income of any country in the Pacific Rim.
- Government policy strongly encourages Korean firms to buy American whenever possible.
- A shift from export-led growth to domestic

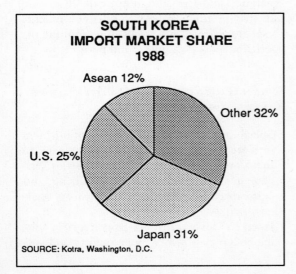

**SOUTH KOREA
IMPORT MARKET SHARE
1988**

Asean 12%

Other 32%

U.S. 25%

Japan 31%

SOURCE: Kotra, Washington, D.C.

development translates into increased spending throughout Korean society.

- Overall imports projected to grow 400% by the year 2000, importing $200 billion by 2000.

POLITICAL AND ECONOMIC TRENDS

GENERAL OUTLOOK

The rate of growth for Korean imports of U.S. goods has been dramatic, with 1988 sales rising almost 40% over 1987. Korea is America's seventh largest export market—and still growing. While an economic slowdown is occurring in Korea, it comes on the heels of phenomenal double-digit growth during the last three years, and should still amount to over 7% in 1989. Growth of U.S. sales has slowed somewhat as might be expected, but still grew 22% during the first five months of 1989 over the same period in 1988.

Rising wage levels will result in increased consumer goods sales, a market that should provide U.S. exporters with strong returns. The Government of Korea's (GOK) directed policy to ease its trade deficit with Japan while narrowing its trade surplus with the U.S. has prompted many sectors of business and industry in Korea, along with the GOK, to "Buy American" whenever possible.

Politically, Korea is a country in transition. The recent concerted effort to turn the country toward democracy has not been easy and has brought out a strong undercurrent of anti-American sentiment. But so far this has not directly affected Seoul–Washington ties, nor has it hurt U.S. sales in Korea.

IMPORT AND INVESTMENT LIBERALIZATION

Korea, while having relatively high tariff rates averaging 12.7%, has made great strides in lowering duties among nonagricultural items. Tariffs are scheduled to be lowered further to an average of 7.9% by 1993, while agricultural duties will average 16.6%.

Ongoing U.S. efforts to lower duties and remove import quotas have proved successful. Barriers to many service sectors, such as insurance, have been eased or removed as well. Investment barriers are gradually being opened. It remains difficult to gain approval for 100% foreign ownership, however.

While Korea began to adopt laws protecting intellectual property several years ago, enforcement of these laws has generally been lax until recently. Piracy of items such as software and textbooks is common. Recent formation by the GOK of a task force to aggressively enforce intellectual property laws, along with assurance that enforcement will improve dramatically, could promise a safer future market for U.S. producers of intellectual property.

BEST-SELLING PRODUCTS FOR THE YEARS AHEAD

INDUSTRIAL PROCESS EQUIPMENT

A total market of $1.46 billion in 1988, real growth is projected at 17.5% annually through 1991. Imports dominate this sector, the Japanese capturing the majority of import sales. However, nearly 25% of sales were accounted for by U.S. firms, and future demand for U.S. goods should outpace overall demand.

ENGINEERING SERVICES AND EQUIPMENT SALES

Major infrastructure projects may offer U.S. firms opportunities in three projects that will cost in excess of $10 billion. A new international airport and two high-speed railway lines are to be built. Other projects to watch for include expansion of container-handling facilities at two major ports.

INDUSTRIAL RAW MATERIALS

One of the major markets for which the Koreans look to the United States to provide products—sales in this diverse sector should give U.S. exporters outstanding opportunities.

MACHINERY

A sector already 100% import-liberalized— U.S. sales for machinery such as pumps, filters and purifiers, spray equipment, valves, and office machines should jump dramatically in the next few years.

OTHER PRIME EXPORT OPPORTUNITIES

Analytical and scientific equipment, electronic industry production and testing equipment, food processing and packaging equipment, special purpose computers and peripherals.

WHEN DOING BUSINESS IN SOUTH KOREA KEEP IN MIND

• Social interaction is a major part of business in Korea. If U.S. exporters expect to sell to the Koreans, they must attend parties, engage in after-business-hours socializing, and enjoy friendly relations with Korean businessmen.

• Japan has several distinct advantages in selling to Korea—primarily proximity and cultural understanding. U.S. exporters must use aggressive marketing and strong after-sales service to counteract the Japanese advantages.

- English usage in Korea is somewhat limited. It is used more extensively in international business, especially among top government officials and business executives. If they aren't fluent in English, they usually have a translator available. But be prepared to have Korean-language translator resources as well.

INDONESIA

- Changing industrial base creating virgin markets practically nonexistent just a few years ago. In 1987 alone, U.S. companies sold products under 228 tariff classifications that had never been exported from the U.S. to Indonesia.
- One of the primary recipients of foreign capitalization among LDCs in the region. Import and consumer spending growth expected to remain high throughout the 1990s.

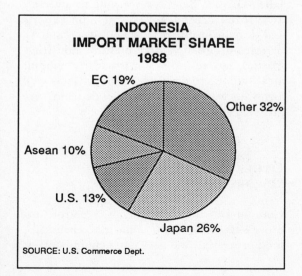

INDONESIA IMPORT MARKET SHARE 1988

EC 19%
Other 32%
Asean 10%
U.S. 13%
Japan 26%

SOURCE: U.S. Commerce Dept.

- Appreciation of the yen against the dollar, giving U.S. firms increased market share in almost all import sectors.
- A labor wage rate of approximately $0.23 per hour, making Indonesia attractive for low-cost assembly and other business operations in the Rim.
- A trade promotion schedule unmatched by any other developing nation in the region. A prime target for U.S. exporters to introduce their products to the region.

POLITICAL AND ECONOMIC TRENDS

GENERAL OUTLOOK

Since the overthrow of President Sukarno 20 years ago, Indonesia has enjoyed two decades of political stability. To lessen its dependence on oil exports, the Indonesian government has prioritized the modernization of nonpetroleum-related export industries, offering U.S. exporters a varied and vibrant industrial market.

Following a recession in the mid-1980s, Indonesia's economy is back on track, growing at a rate of over 5% annually.

Austerity measures instituted during the recession are being eased, freeing money for commercial expansion and increased consumer spending. Indonesia is one of the few Pacific Rim markets where consumer-spending growth is predicted to continue accelerating.

An ambitious privatization program is in effect, revitalizing the industrial markets, and providing foreign investors with opportunities in previously closed areas. However, those industries losing the most money will likely be the first to become available to foreign interests. Inflation has been on the rise—not unusual for a developing economy in such a high state of flux—but has not yet become a major impediment to business. The rate actually fell from 9.1% in 1987 to 8% in 1988, but continued upward pressures are likely to prevent any further declines.

IMPORT AND INVESTMENT LIBERALIZATION

A pact between Indonesia and the U.S. regarding intellectual property protection took effect in mid-1989 that should help U.S. exporters of software, books, audio recordings, and film. In November 1988, nontariff barriers were removed on over 300 product categories, including plastics, iron and steel products, and a variety of agricultural goods. Watch for additional import liberalization in the 1990s, especially for export industries. Tariffs are currently high, but should follow the regional trend and come down. Easing of limits on foreign ownership and joint-venture export requirements are attracting manufacturers from around the world.

BEST-SELLING PRODUCTS FOR THE YEARS AHEAD

INDUSTRIAL MACHINERY

As Indonesia diversifies its industrial base, this will be the most active import sector, especially in government-targeted export industries, such as textiles, wood products, consumer-goods production, chemicals, steel, pulp and paper, and chemical processing.

TELECOMMUNICATIONS

Over the past two years, demand in Indonesia's telecommunications market has boomed —from a $200 million market in 1986 to a market of over $300 million in 1988. Imports account for 95% of domestic consumption. The import market is diverse, with several countries supplying significant exports. The U.S. accounts for about 12% of imports. Primary competition comes from Japan, West Germany, and France. However, U.S. sales are expected to grow at a 10% annual rate well into the 1990s.

INSTRUMENTATION

With no domestic production to speak of, the U.S. is head-to-head with Japan as the leading supplier to this $125-million-a-year market. Import growth is expected to continue at 5% annually for the next few years. Especially popular are engineering, radiation, physical analysis, meteorological, and drafting instruments.

PLASTICS AND RESINS

Like Malaysia, Indonesia is trying to diversify away from dependence on crude oil exports and develop viable petrochemical, secondary petroleum product, and plastics industries. Plastics and resins is a particularly vibrant area. Imports to develop the industry, as well as to meet present domestic demand, are growing at a rapid pace.

OTHER PRIME EXPORT OPPORTUNITIES

Computers and peripherals, petroleum-processing equipment, industrial chemicals, food processing and packaging equipment.

WHEN DOING BUSINESS IN
INDONESIA KEEP IN MIND:

- Indonesia is second only to China in population in the Rim, with a population of more than 173 million. Though a far smaller market than China, it presents U.S. exporters with a mammoth market for low-end consumer goods. Indonesia has the second-lowest per capita GDP of any major market in the region—only China is lower.
- Indonesia is largely Moslem, so U.S. exporters should use similar business approaches as when marketing to Middle Eastern markets. Otherwise, Indonesians are more typically Asian—status conscious, low key, and more leisurely paced than in the West.
- Indonesia was once among the most active import markets in the region. Following the mid-1980's recession, imports plummeted. Today they are not yet near their prerecession levels. Moderate growth will continue, as the government prudently rations growth. Imports should exceed prerecession levels sometime during the 1990s.

MALAYSIA

- Set in a region of rapidly expanding economies, Malaysia predicted to be among the five fastest-growing economies in the world over the next two years. U.S. exports up 24% in 1988 to $2.3 billion. The trend continues.
- A well-educated younger generation with a rising disposable income and high savings rate that looks to invest the increasing wages. Expresses their higher standard of living with the consumption of specialty and luxury consumer goods.
- An economy driven by trade, raising the

living standard of its people—relying on two-way trade, not simply exports.
- A government that recognizes the importance of the free market, and is committed to maintaining open trade policies.
- Dollar depreciation of recent years—making U.S. goods more competitive—expected to continue over the next two years.

POLITICAL AND ECONOMIC TRENDS

GENERAL OUTLOOK

The Government of Malaysia continues on its ambitious economic plan, refocusing the country from an agrarian base to manufacturing. The inflation rate remains low, only about 3%. It recently reduced the corporate tax rate from 40% to 35%. Privatization of key industries should continue, opening up new sectors for U.S. companies in areas such as television, radio, electric power production, railways, and shipping. As a result of the government's refocus, Malaysia's debt service has been significantly reduced—freeing up more foreign exchange.

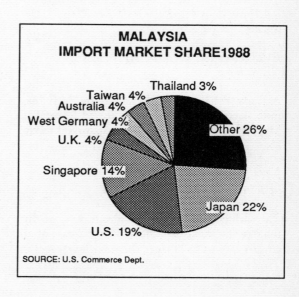

MALAYSIA IMPORT MARKET SHARE 1988

- Thailand 3%
- Taiwan 4%
- Australia 4%
- West Germany 4%
- U.K. 4%
- Singapore 14%
- U.S. 19%
- Japan 22%
- Other 26%

SOURCE: U.S. Commerce Dept.

Malaysian imports rose 39% in value during the first five months of 1989 over the same period in 1988. While U.S. exports rose 15%, they dropped in total market share of this fast-paced growth market.

Negotiations continue between the United States and Malaysia on intellectual property rights issues. Malaysia has tightened laws concerning patents and copyrights, including software, and diminishing piracy, though all U.S. works are not yet accorded full protection. Should this change, entire new areas will open up to U.S. exporters, such as a promising market for the video entertainment industrys. This is an area to watch closely.

IMPORT AND INVESTMENT LIBERALIZATION

Current tariffs average 25%, but a gradual reduction is taking place. Foreign investors that apply for new projects through 1990 will be able to retain 100% of the equity in the enterprises if they either export at least half of their output or employ 350 Malaysians.

BEST-SELLING PRODUCTS FOR THE YEARS AHEAD

ELECTRONIC COMPONENTS

Already by far the overwhelming U.S. export, accounting for 62% of the U.S. total to Malaysia. Much of this sector is linked to the assembly of finished products for re-export.

OIL AND GAS EQUIPMENT

The United States controls about 50% of this market. Demand is expected to increase at an annual rate of 15% over the next few years as Malaysia upgrades the equipment for increased petroleum production, a major source of foreign exchange. Products particularly in demand include oil exploration, gas processing, and transmission equipment.

TELECOMMUNICATIONS

As a result of modernization efforts, the telecommunications market is forecast to grow at 10% a year. Recent structural changes in certain sectors of the industry allow U.S. companies unprecedented market opportunities.

EDUCATIONAL AND TRAINING AIDS

Imports must fill almost all of the growth. The Malaysian government, conservative in its spending patterns, has demonstrated the importance of this area, slating it for increased funding.

OTHER PRIME EXPORT OPPORTUNITIES

Computers and peripherals, American-style food processing and packaging equipment, insurance services, water resources equipment.

WHEN DOING BUSINESS IN MALAYSIA KEEP IN MIND

- With a plentiful amount of export and investment opportunities exist, the Malaysian market is wide open. In many cases, U.S. companies are not as aggressive as their competitors from Japan and Singapore.
- In addition to the national language, Bahasa Malaysia, about half of all Malaysians speak

and write English. This greatly facilitates business opportunities for U.S. exporters.

• Imported goods in Malaysia are marketed primarily by large trading companies that operate sales outlets in the principal cities. Most of the large trading firms are foreign-owned, many by British interests, several by U.S. concerns.

THE PHILIPPINES

• Has the closest ties with the U.S. of any Pacific Rim nation—especially after the U.S. assisted in the toppling of the Marcos regime. U.S. companies, long established in the Philippines, importing much of their needed raw materials, machinery, and components from the United States.

• Among the biggest recipients of development aid—both U.S. and multilateral—in the region, providing exporters with scores of project-related opportunities.

• One of the top targets for foreign investment, producing greater demand for raw materials and machinery and equipment imports.

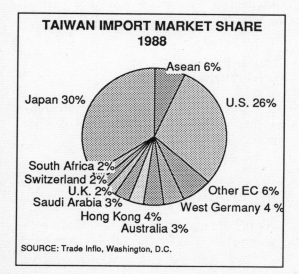

TAIWAN IMPORT MARKET SHARE 1988

Asean 6%
Japan 30%
U.S. 26%
South Africa 2%
Switzerland 2%
U.K. 2%
Saudi Arabia 3%
Other EC 6%
Hong Kong 4%
West Germany 4%
Australia 3%

SOURCE: Trade Inflo, Washington, D.C.

• One of the most well-educated countries in the Rim, and the best educated among the LDCs. Despite its poverty, offers a highly skilled workforce.

• Expected to experience the greatest growth and improvement in the region through the 1990s, after being the most crippled economy, reaching its post-crisis level by the end of 1992.

POLITICAL AND ECONOMIC TRENDS

GENERAL OUTLOOK

The 1990s look especially promising. With inflation remaining in single digits, unemployment gradually coming down, labor tensions easing, and more money available for economic development rather than debt service, the Philippine market will become increasingly attractive for U.S. exports. Although the Philippines has posted three consecutive years of moderate to high growth, the country's economic recovery is far from complete. The capital drain on the Philippines treasury by Ferdinand Marcos and his cronies, rampant poverty, and serious labor unrest left the economy in shambles. Many of those problems are still being felt.

One positive sign for both the economy and the political savvy of its government is the "Mini Marshall Plan." In July 1989, officials of all the multilateral lending organizations, the United States, Japan, several EC countries, and several Asian nations agreed to a $3.5 billion aid package for the Philippines. World Bank officials said that the package's total was about double the expected commitment levels. Part of the reason for this was a unified satisfaction with the series of market-oriented reforms being established. The infusion of development funds will help the country address some of its pressing economic problems and also provide funding for additional imports.

Another international financial boost came in August 1989 when the Philippines and its commercial lenders reached an agreement under the Brandy debt-reduction plan. It avoids the aspect most painful to the banking community—writing off loans. Instead, the Philippines will issue bonds on the world markets and work with its creditors to reestablish its creditworthiness. Of all the third-world debt reductions thus far, this might be the most successful.

IMPORT AND INVESTMENT LIBERALIZATION

Throughout the 1980s the Philippines has lowered its tariffs from an average of 42% at the beginning of the decade to approximately 29% now. About 80% of quantitative barriers to imports have been removed. The primary interest in further import liberalization for U.S. suppliers is in the agricultural sectors. In addition, the Philippines is competing with the other LDCs to attract foreign capital to assist in further industrial development. Foreign investors will find an abundance of recently instituted incentives to invest.

BEST-SELLING PRODUCTS FOR THE YEARS AHEAD

TELECOMMUNICATIONS

Probably the country's fastest-growing import sector. Several recent major telecommunications projects have opened up the market for U.S. subcontractors and producers of value-added services. Because the prevalence of major projects can skew growth rates, it's difficult to give realistic growth projections.

But growth has been robust and will remain so throughout the 1990s.

FOOD PROCESSING EQUIPMENT

Like its neighbors, the Philippines needs to produce more processed foodstuffs to meet the demand of an improving consumer base, as well as build a viable export market.

CHEMICALS

Given the levels of expected industrial growth in the coming years, the demand for industrial chemicals will rise sharply. Agricultural chemicals are among the most popular imports from the U.S. and should also see healthy sales increases.

ENERGY GENERATION EQUIPMENT

As a result of accelerated industrial investment and development, this is another basic area where demand will increase. U.S. suppliers will see significant potential for increased sales, especially in the less-developed areas of the country.

OTHER PRIME EXPORT OPPORTUNITIES

Metal-working equipment, textile machinery, medical equipment, computers and peripherals.

WHEN DOING BUSINESS IN THE PHILIPPINES KEEP IN MIND:

• As the Philippines is a former U.S. commonwealth, English is still the dominant language in government and business, making communication somewhat less difficult for Americans. In fact, English usage is more frequent in the Philippines than in any other Asian country in the Rim.

- The Philippines is also the only Asian country in the Rim that is predominantly Christian, reducing many cultural differences U.S. exporters face in other Asian countries.

- The primary impediment to further business involvement in the Philippines is the country's relatively undeveloped infrastructure. However, improvements in the infrastructure are taking place rapidly and are among the government's top priorities. U.S. companies that endure this inconvenience in the short run will benefit over firms that wait.

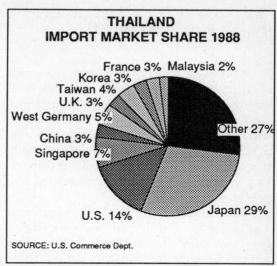

THAILAND
IMPORT MARKET SHARE 1988

France 3% Malaysia 2%
Korea 3%
Taiwan 4%
U.K. 3%
West Germany 5%
China 3%
Singapore 7%
Other 27%
Japan 29%
U.S. 14%

SOURCE: U.S. Commerce Dept.

petitive markets wide open to other exporters —including foreign competitors.

THAILAND

- Often called the "Fifth Tiger" of the Pacific Rim. A dynamic, rapidly developing country—the type of market in which aggressive U.S. exporters prosper.

- U.S. products more affordable than ever in Thailand, as a result of dollar depreciation vis-à-vis the yen.

- Two new deep-water ports to be completed in the next three years will facilitate trade by relieving some of the considerable overcrowding at Bangkok's river port as well as providing for direct unloading off container ships.

- An economy with an ever-expanding base. Significant industries range from computer components to tourism, to farm products and natural gas.

- Major U.S. exporters thus far concentrating efforts on a few areas, leaving many com-

POLITICAL AND ECONOMIC TRENDS

GENERAL OUTLOOK

Economic performance in 1988 was the best in more than 20 years, and strong growth is taking place in all economic sectors. U.S. exporters rode this wave with great skill in 1987, improving sales to Thailand by 27%. While 1989 was not the banner year that 1988 was in terms of percentage increase in sales for U.S. exporters, figures for the January–May period of this year showed a 19% increase over the same period in 1988.

Bangkok and Washington have traditionally had a close relationship, primarily security-oriented. As Thailand's commercial position has changed, so has the focus of the bilateral relationship. Currently, disputes exist over intellectual property rights for software and pharmaceuticals. This has placed Thailand on the "watch" list of the most significant violators.

IMPORT AND INVESTMENT LIBERALIZATION

Thailand has a series of policies that restrict many imports—in some cases effectively banning them all together. The U.S. government is actively pursuing both bilateral and multilateral efforts to reduce or eliminate these barriers. If and when these barriers are lowered, significant new opportunities will develop for U.S. exporters in an already burgeoning import market.

Of the utmost concern to U.S. exporters is Thailand's lax intellectual property rights laws and enforcement. This requires close scrutiny by U.S. exporters considering sending potentially affected products to Thailand. The Thai and U.S. governments are involved in continuous talks designed to reach a satisfactory agreement in this area.

Foreign investment in Thailand is strong and has been rising at a rate of 65% a year for the last two years. Much of this investment has been in large-scale electronics industry projects. Thai officials welcome U.S. investment proposals to reduce the risk of becoming too dependent on a limited circle of companies for technological and capital inputs.

BEST-SELLING PRODUCTS FOR THE YEARS AHEAD

FOOD PROCESSING AND PACKAGING EQUIPMENT

These will be needed to assist in Thailand's effort to become a leading producer and exporter of processed food. Projections for growth in this sector are at 10% per year through 1991.

MEDICAL EQUIPMENT AND SUPPLIES

The forecast is for continuous growth of at least 10% a year well into the future to meet the demand of Thailand's expanding medical facilities. Overall sales reached $88 million in 1988.

TELECOMMUNICATIONS EQUIPMENT

In light of the government's recognition of the necessity to upgrade existing facilities as well as implement new ones, such as a paging system and phone card service, sales could total several hundred million dollars. Another telecommunications area slated for expansion, the mobile cellular telephone system, should go nationwide in its coverage.

COMPUTERS AND PERIPHERALS

A $100 million market in 1988, growth is projected to be at a phenomenal 30% or more annually to accommodate upgrading and automation by government agencies, universities, and the private sector. The U.S. government's Trade and Development Program is assisting in this effort. But the uncertainty of effective copyright protection clouds this otherwise bright sector.

OTHER PRIME EXPORT OPPORTUNITIES

Agricultural and high-value grocery products—cotton, tobacco, wheat, apples, organic chemicals and related products, synthetic resins, rubber and plastic, plastic production machinery.

WHEN DOING BUSINESS IN THAILAND KEEP IN MIND

- English is the language of commerce in Thailand. Thai-speaking representatives, however, are necessary for wide-spread marketing of consumer goods. Although Western culture has had strong and positive influences on Thailand, it's imperative to learn and utilize the many distinct business and social customs of the country.
- Quality counts in Thailand. Despite the disadvantages that U.S. exporters may have due to the distance their products must travel as compared to closer Asian suppliers, Thais recognize U.S. products as being superior and prefer them. Pricing is not necessarily the bottom line.
- Careful selection of local representation is crucial to achieve the greatest market impact. Some importers and distributors may not devote the time and attention a medium- or smaller-size exporter needs. Look for a smaller importer specializing in one line of business, who will have the valuable contacts essential to introducing a new product. A sound alternative for mid-size exporters is a firm with a more technical background that stresses modern marketing techniques.

AUSTRALIA

- The Pacific Rim's third-largest economy, behind Japan and China, and the region's second-largest per capita income, only Japan being greater.
- U.S. products account for the largest share of this $30 billion import market—almost 22%—from 10,000 U.S. companies. More than 750 U.S. companies with local subsidiaries.
- Political and economic focus shifting from Europe to the Pacific Rim. Maintains close relations with Washington. Pushing Pacific Rim market compact to rival EC.
- An even larger market in the South Pacific in 1992, when Australia and New Zealand will join markets in a Free Trade Agreement, eliminating all trade barriers between the two countries.

POLITICAL AND ECONOMIC TRENDS

GENERAL OUTLOOK

Australia has moved from a highly regulated economy to a market economy during the 1980s that has benefited U.S. exporters and investors. But current U.S. subsidies to agricultural products have put a damper on recent bilateral economic relations. On the verge of national economic collapse in 1983, Australia has rebounded through macroeconomic measures, such as sizeable tax cuts, tariff reductions, limitations on government spending, and removal of exchange controls. One example of this can be seen in the recent corporate tax cut that reduced the top tax rate from 49% to 39%.

The inflation rate crested at 9.3% in 1987, and is dropping at a steady rate—7.3% in 1988 and a projected 5.5% in 1989. This should help U.S. exporters.

IMPORT AND INVESTMENT LIBERALIZATION

Tariff rates in Australia average about 15%—among the highest of industrialized nations. Significant tariff "peaks" protect sensitive domestic industries. The positive news for U.S. exporters is that these rates are falling. All duties will be down to 15% or less by 1992 and are scheduled to average 5.5% by the mid-1990s. Other barriers concerned with standards, testing, labeling, and certification exist and can prove to be cumbersome for U.S. exporters.

Despite some limits to foreign investment, U.S. direct investment in Australia has grown by more than 20% since 1987, reflecting economic deregulation.

BEST-SELLING PRODUCTS FOR THE YEARS AHEAD

COMPUTER SOFTWARE/HARDWARE

Imports of ADP machines and peripherals are among the lead prospects, with U.S. products accounting for over 43% of a $490 million market in FY87/88. Desktop publishing systems and hardware adaptable to Australia's Integrated Services Digital Network (ISDN), industrial process controls, and software offer competitive opportunities.

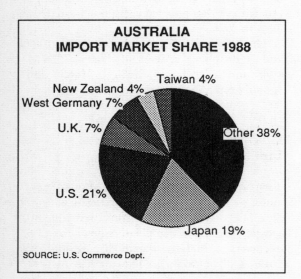

AUSTRALIA IMPORT MARKET SHARE 1988

New Zealand 4%
Taiwan 4%
West Germany 7%
U.K. 7%
Other 38%
U.S. 21%
Japan 19%

SOURCE: U.S. Commerce Dept.

MEDICAL INSTRUMENTS AND EQUIPMENT

Growth should reach $330 million by 1992 in a market where the U.S. controls 40%. Competition with the Japanese in a number of sectors is strong, but aggressive marketing can serve U.S. exporters well.

INDUSTRIAL MACHINERY

The U.S. took only 17% of this competitive, half-a-billion dollar import market. Many key Australian industries are seeking to modernize machinery and improve manufacturing techniques.

AEROSPACE

As scheduled regulatory controls are liberalized, export opportunities are expanding for smaller firms marketing avionics, particularly those suited for small aircraft. The total aerospace market is growing 25% annually, totaling nearly $400 million in sales.

OTHER PRIME EXPORT OPPORTUNITIES

Hospitality services, organic and inorganic chemicals, civil engineering and contractor's equipment, electrical apparatus—circuits.

WHEN DOING BUSINESS IN AUSTRALIA KEEP IN MIND:

• Sales agents offer many advantages to the novice in the Australian market, including ability to access buyers and arrange appointments for visiting exporters, availability for follow-up visits and negotiations, continuous monitoring of sales and knowledge of the local market. They can more readily address the often different Australian markets and their local customs.

- Because of Australia's immense geographical size, and the long distances between major population centers, U.S. exporters may find it cheaper and easier to ship to several final destinations in Australia, rather than breaking up shipments and transhipping across the continent.

- The business and economic environment is continually changing in Australia, much as it is in the rest of the Pacific Rim. The Australian government has seen the need to adapt, has done so, and is expected to continue those efforts. The status quo cannot be assumed here any more than it can anywhere else in the Pacific Rim.

NEW ZEALAND

- An affluent, well-educated, English-speaking country where U.S. products and marketing adapt easily.
- After several years of economic restructuring, opportunities abound in a growing, newly deregulated market place.
- U.S. dollar appreciation vis-à-vis the New Zealand dollar of 40% since 1985, substantially increasing U.S. price competitiveness.
- Well-established U.S. market; U.S. ranks third for imports, accounting for approximately 17% of New Zealand imports.
- With a population of only 3.3 million, offers an outstanding consumer market for medium- to smaller-sized exporters.

POLITICAL AND ECONOMIC TRENDS

GENERAL OUTLOOK

U.S. exports have shown strong gains recently, rising 15% in 1988 from 1987, and 20% during the first five months of 1989 over 1988. The strong showing early in 1989 on the heels of a recession in 1987 reflects a reinvigorated New Zealand economy buying more American goods and services.

In recent years, New Zealand has undergone dramatic and often quite painful changes in its economic structure. Like its cousin down under, Australia, a highly regulated economy existed into the 1980s. Reorientation to a market-focused economy has raised unemployment somewhat and tightened the money supply.

The plus side is a dramatically reduced inflation rate and significant tax cuts. Corporate taxes for foreign investors have been reduced from 53% to 33%.

The change in prime ministers in 1989 (but within the same political party) may have been related to the acrimony over the economic hardships. Little change is expected to take place in the current economic direction of the country.

IMPORT AND INVESTMENT LIBERALIZATION

The deregulation of the economy has led to liberalization of the import-licensing system and lowering of tariffs in areas where no domestically produced equivalent product exists. Further substantial reductions are to take place by 1992.

New Zealand has for the most part dismantled its import-licensing controls. These requirements now apply to less than 5% of total

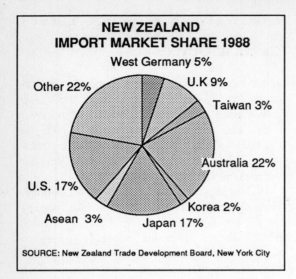

NEW ZEALAND IMPORT MARKET SHARE 1988

West Germany 5%
U.K 9%
Taiwan 3%
Other 22%
Australia 22%
U.S. 17%
Korea 2%
Asean 3%
Japan 17%

SOURCE: New Zealand Trade Development Board, New York City

exporters. The New Zealand national telecommunications provider, Telecom Corporation, welcomes bids from U.S. firms to fill equipment needs on such items as electronic PABXs and novelty telephones.

SERVICES SECTOR

As New Zealand shifts from a highly regulated economy to one led by market structures, a demand for computer and management consulting services has developed to assist with the adjustment process.

TOURISM SERVICES AND EQUIPMENT

A revitalized sector promises increased sales of automated food preparation and processing equipment for hotels and restaurants. Additionally, tourism-related services should grow substantially.

OTHER PRIME EXPORT OPPORTUNITIES

Mini- and microcomputers, data processing machinery, computer software, sporting goods and recreation equipment.

WHEN DOING BUSINESS IN NEW ZEALAND KEEP IN MIND:

- A great many similarities exist between the "Kiwis" and their "Aussie" cousins, especially to an American. While the markets are also quite similar, a wise U.S. exporter will recognize New Zealanders' pride in their own country and not brusquely lump them together with current popular American perceptions of Australians.

imports. Investment laws are fairly liberal, allowing 100% foreign ownership and full repatriation of profits.

BEST-SELLING PRODUCTS FOR THE YEARS AHEAD

TEXTILE ITEMS

U.S. prospects appear to be particularly good in the specialty apparel area. Products such as women's stretch swimwear and casual wear and men's wool-like synthetic trousers should be among the best-sellers. Tariffs were recently removed on items where no equivalent locally made product exists. These items now account for over $200 million in imports overall.

TELECOMMUNICATIONS AND DATA COMMUNICATIONS

New Zealand's high level of computer literacy makes this an excellent market for U.S.

- New Zealand is emerging from a difficult economic period. The market shows definite potential for continued improvement, but should be closely monitored during all phases of the export process in order to adjust or fine tune export strategies to the realities of the changing situation.
- The people of New Zealand are justifiably proud and protective of their environment and culture. Environmental concern has led to disputes between Wellington and other governments in recent years. Products exported to New Zealand can profit by demonstrating a sensitivity to these two concerns.

THE BEST OF THE REST

There are several smaller countries in the Pacific Rim whose individual market size may preclude an exporter from solely targeting them. However, if targeted in conjunction with neighboring markets, these smaller countries can offer opportunities for a boost in sales for the savvy exporter.

MACAO

The most prominent of these smaller export markets, Macao is a Chinese territory under Portuguese administration just across the Pearl River delta from Hong Kong. Macao's economy is intricately linked with that of Hong Kong's and the surrounding region in China. Well-educated and increasingly affluent, Macao's 500,000 residents have created a booming economy. Although English is spoken in the business community, a Cantonese-speaking interpreter may be useful at times.

A new international airport and a deep-water shipping facility are currently under construction in Macao, both scheduled to be completed in the early 1990s. Air and shipping traffic must now move through facilities in Hong Kong. The new facilities, designed to serve the bordering special economic zone in China as well, are expected to have a strong positive effect on Macao's economic future—and to stimulate imports from the United States. An exact accounting of U.S. exports is difficult to arrive at, as all Macao's imports move through Hong Kong. But according to Macao government figures, U.S. imports rose 7% last year, while overall imports grew 15%.

U.S. firms will find that best-selling products for the years ahead will include data processing equipment, electronics machinery, and textile industry machinery.

After the recent turmoil in China, Macao finds itself questioning its future. An agreement similar to Hong Kong's will return Macao to Chinese control in 1999, two years after the British colony. At that time Macao will become a special administrative region of China, maintaining its free-market system. For the long-term, exporters will have to wait and see what happens in both Macao and Hong Kong. But in the short term, exporters and investors will find a booming domestic market.

BRUNEI

This oil-rich sultanate lies on the northern coast of the island of Borneo and is the smallest market in ASEAN. Brunei has many of the needs of a lesser-developed country, yet at the same time has the resources available to pay for those needs. While the capital, Bandar Seri Begawan, is modern, much of the countryside is less developed.

While exports to Brunei grew by about 175% during the first five months of 1989, this figure is somewhat misleading as U.S. exports for that period only totaled $35 million. U.S. products, such as telecommunications equipment, oil and gas equipment, and educational materials, will find a receptive market. Exporters find that in some respects that the Brunei market is easier to sell to than other countries in the region.

PAPUA NEW GUINEA

The small island nation directly north of Australia, Papua New Guinea accounts for a greater amount of U.S. exports than either Macao or Brunei. During 1988, the United States exported over $113 million in goods to PNG, a 120% increase over 1987. Growth for 1989 appears to be following the same pattern, rising 97% during the January–May period. Papua New Guinea, a parliamentary democracy and member of the British Commonwealth, encourages U.S. imports and private investment. There now exists direct air freight and shipping links between the United States and PNG.

U.S. exports relate primarily to PNG's mining and petroleum sectors, the mainstays of the domestic economy. Consumer items for both the home and private sectors could be excellent new markets for U.S. exporters to consider. Currently, however, the majority of goods for these sectors are supplied by Asian nations.

EXPORTING TO THE PACIFIC RIM

A MARKETING GUIDE FOR THE 1990s
by Michael S. Tomczyk

Less than a generation ago, Japan was recovering from the war and the lesser developed countries of East Asia were struggling to gain a foothold in the world economy. Today Japan and the "Four Tigers" of East Asia—Taiwan, South Korea, Hong Kong, and Singapore—are dominant forces in the world manufacturing economy. Michael Tomczyk, formerly of Commodore International and now CEO of his own international marketing company, the Aranda Corporation, lays out how American firms need to shape their thinking and approach to these highly lucrative markets.

Spurred by a knack for cost-cutting and technology adaptation, Japan and the Four Tigers have achieved a level of industrial dominance that has created some of the world's strongest economies. And most importantly for U.S. exporters, this new industrial status provides a dynamic, growing consumer and industrial marketplace now in the Pacific Rim. Today, East Asians have greater disposable income, a growing middle class, and a yen for the same status symbols—car, home, TV—that Americans are famous for. Now that our Pacific Rim allies have achieved economic success—and deservedly so—it's time to stop carping about how our former proteges turned the tables on their "mentor" the

United States. We need to consider these Tigers not just as vendors and contractors but as consumers to be targeted and pursued.

As marketing pioneers, it would seem appropriate that U.S. industry should be flooding Asia with American products. Why aren't we?

WHEN VENDORS BECOME TIGERS

To begin with, we don't have a realistic view of the problems—and opportunities—of the Pacific Rim marketplace. Americans still consider Pacific Rim countries as "vendor states" rather than partners and potential customers.

Mentors never like to be surpassed by their former proteges, which probably explains why many Americans are so resentful that our Pacific Rim proteges have evolved from vendors to competitors. It's time to become realistic.

There is a distinct progression at work in the Pacific Rim, a "tigering process," whereby small, poor, overpopulated nations start out as weak vendor states providing contract goods and services to the industrialized western markets and their more industrialized Pacific Rim neighbors. As they achieve success, these vendor states are themselves required to industrialize to meet the needs of their industrialized customers.

It started with Japan in the 1950s and 1960s, spread to the Four Tigers in the 1970s and 1980s, and during the 1990s will grow to include a new group of lesser-developed countries in the Pacific Rim.

Many nations such as China and the Philippines have not yet participated in the tigering process because of the internal social and political strife. However, these nations are poised to become the region's new vendor states. As they stabilize, they will eventually occupy the "low-end" niche formerly held by

Japan and the Four Tigers—and will in turn industrialize, prosper, and become consumer and industrial markets in their own right.

The Oceanic countries—Australia and New Zealand—have not followed the Asian template, and for several reasons: They have relatively low population densities, well-developed economies, and their Western cultures are not as well suited to international vending as their Asian neighbors. However, as consumer nations, Australia and New Zealand represent established markets that offer excellent potential for success for U.S. exporters.

KEYS TO THEIR SUCCESS

The leading Asian vendor states have all followed the same prescription for success: They used their best and cheapest resource—labor—to become primary suppliers of manufactured products to the world; they learned to live and work in close quarters by creating societies based on order, cooperation, and conformity; and they took great pains to study American language, culture, and technology.

SPEAKING THE RIGHT LANGUAGE

Language is one of the reasons why Pacific Rim–U.S. trade is so one-sided. They speak our language, but we don't speak theirs! Most Asian students are required to become bilingual. Japanese students are required to learn English. Taiwanese students learn either English or Japanese in addition to their native Chinese. Korea has tens of thousands of American troops who exert an English-speaking influence. As former British colonies, Hong Kong and Singapore had a linguistic head start.

Yet consider this: How many American college students do you know who speak Japanese or Chinese?

Language is only one of several barriers to market entry by American firms. Other obstacles often mentioned range from closed distribution channels to government protectionism. The greatest barrier, however, to market entry by American firms is not knowing how to effectively deal with the homogeneity of the tiger states, which is as much an accident of geography as anything else.

ACCIDENTS OF GEOGRAPHY

It's no coincidence that the most successful tiger states are also the most crowded. Japan is an overpopulated chain of islands. South Korea is a peninsula. Hong Kong is a house of matches with homes and offices staked vertically on an island and a tiny piece of mainland China. Singapore occupies an island and shares a strip of coast with Malaysia. All have high population densities.

Geography has forced the peoples of the Pacific Rim to live together in close quarters, forced them to learn to work together, to trust each other—to mistrust outsiders—and to conform, accommodate, and cooperate in ways which are extremely advantageous when applied to a targeted or global business effort.

UNDERSTAND FIRST, EXPORT SECOND

The best thing any American exporter can do to gain a foothold in the Pacific Rim consumer or industrial marketplace is to gain an understanding of what it means to live and work in an overpopulated, homogeneous culture. We go to great pains in the U.S. to study a market before entering it, but in Asia and the Pacific Rim, we seem inclined to skip this step because market research requires that we go back to school to learn what we think are "exotic" cultures and languages—which is frankly difficult. But to export to the Pacific Rim, it's also very necessary.

Since Japan is responsible for the bulk of economic activity in the Pacific Rim, and is the market that most often immediately comes to mind when considering the Pacific Rim, it's best we begin our discussion of export strategies with Japan. The Japanese market is a good example of the unusual types of problems you'll encounter exporting to the Asian nations of the Pacific Rim. Many of the lessons apply to the other markets. Here are a few things would-be American exporters should know about Japanese society and business.

Business cooperation viewed as unfair competition here is seen as good business sense in Japan.

ACCOMMODATION COUNTS

Americans are taught to be individualistic, independent, and self-starting. But Japanese are encouraged to be homogeneous, interdependent, and group-oriented. Japanese live, work, and travel in a crowded environment where everyone is expected to understand everyone else's role. Business people, especially, are expected to know their place in the organization. The importance of fitting in is described by a Japanese saying: "The nail that sticks up gets hammered down."

Much of Japan's business success comes from their ability to organize cohesive work groups to analyze, understand, and accommodate to the needs of a market or industry. In this sense, Japanese business acumen—and dominance—derives from a sophisticated form of fitting in or at least finding the right fit.

BUSINESS BY COMMITTEE

Asian business is like a tea ceremony or a dance. It involves a certain peace and orderliness and requires consensus-building. This means you need to talk to many people at many levels if you want to gain a decision from a top manager. Japanese decisions are researched, discussed, and endorsed by a committee in almost all cases. If you're asked to present your business proposition to a committee, you're probably being taken seriously. If you present it to an individual, you're more than likely at an entry level.

Because important decisions must be reviewed and endorsed by a group, don't expect a quick decision on a complex or high-priced business deal. Japanese firms favor 12- to 18-month planning cycles, and like to be thoroughly satisfied they'll benefit before they enter a business deal.

DISTRIBUTION

The Japanese ethic of cooperation expresses itself in a very complex and orderly product distribution system which can effectively freeze out entry by U.S. exporters. To begin with, there are more middlemen and intermediaries in the Japanese distribution system than in ours. Many products are regulated more vigorously than in the United States, due in part to the Japanese need to conserve, recycle, and protect their fragile, overcrowded environment. Again, it is the homogeneity that marks the difference between our two markets.

Distribution requirements vary from industry to industry. For example, a craft product might be imported directly, but a medical system requires extensive government testing and approval.

Consequently, you need a local Japanese distributor or agent with existing contacts to guide you through the maze of regulations and protectionist barriers and plug you into the distribution system. When choosing an agent, be sure the agent believes in your product or service; has something to gain by supporting you; and has established distribution channels.

TRUST AND ANTITRUST

One of the major differences among U.S. and Japanese firms is that Japanese firms cooperate in many ways which would spark an antitrust action in the United States. Business cooperation viewed as unfair competition here is seen as good business sense in Japan.

They see nothing wrong with two or more business entities sharing information and technology or pooling their collective resources to dominate a market. This works well when technical standards need to be consolidated, such as VHS videotape formats or high-definition television. It works poorly (from our view) when U.S. companies are trying to penetrate a market where most of the major players work together and with the government to share and protect their market from outsiders. The important thing to remember is that in the Japanese view, it's not malicious but good business and good economics. And it works.

STATUS CONSUMERS

Because of their homogeneous nature, the Japanese create status based on academic performance, occupation, companies, and organizations. They seek the same status items we enjoy in the United States—homes, cars, and so on—except these large items take on a greater status dimension in Japan. For example, in a country where high-speed public transportation makes cars virtually unnecessary, you've got real status if you can afford a car, a license (hard to get), a parking place (ever harder to get), and the high cost of insurance, inspections, and maintenance.

PUTTING THEIR STAMP ON YOUR PRODUCT

Your product, packaging, literature, and advertising must be in Japanese, although American fad items may be in both Japanese and English. Good translation is essential, since there are four alphabets in Japan—*Kanji* (pictographs), *Katakana* (phonetic sound-characters for foreign words), *Hiragana* (phonetic sound-characters for standard Japanese words), and *Romaji* (romanized or "English" alphabet). Japanese expect sophisticated marketing, including the proper use of their alphabets.

SMALLER IS BETTER

You'll also need to take into account differences in the environment. For example, living in crowded conditions means many common items tend to be smaller and more compact. Houses are smaller and streets are narrower, which means prefabricated structures and cars must be smaller than American models. Refrigerators must be smaller to fit in compact apartments. Also, electrical standards are different, and standards for items such as medical equipment and foodstuffs are more rigorous.

ENLISTING TRANSLATORS' HELP

Last, but not least, when doing business in Japan, don't assume your Japanese contacts speak English—although they probably do. Bring along a translator, as expensive as that may be, and be sure to have your business cards printed in Japanese on the reverse side. It's only courteous, and in Japan, that may be more important than product quality.

OBSERVE THE LOCAL BUSINESS ETIQUETTE

This refers to Japan, but applies as well to many of the other Pacific Rim countries.

THE PROPER LEVEL OF FORMALITY

Japanese business people are more formal during the day than American business people are used to at home, yet they're congenial within the context of the meeting. However, after hours it's not unusual for an executive or group to go out and indulge themselves with an expensive night of entertainment which may involve drinking and even a degree of rowdiness. But don't mistake this informality for friendship or familiarity. You will be expected to maintain the proper amount of decorum the next day.

BODY LANGUAGE

Japanese live in close quarters, so they avoid a lot of body contact. Don't clap them on the back or wave your hands around. Many Americans who are tall or large-bodied in comparison to Asian colleagues have an annoying tendency to wave their arms around while talking—which in Asia is seen as violating the space of the people in the vicinity. I've seen Asian business people wince and physically duck an arm-waving American whose extravagant gestures disturbed them.

BOWING

It doesn't take long to pick up the Japanese habit of making a slight bow, either when meeting, leaving, or during a conversation. A bow is like nodding your head or waving your hand. The one who bows the lowest is showing the most deference. So, if the chief executive of a company bows relatively low to you, as a gesture of humility and respect, you will compliment him by bowing the same or slightly lower. But don't exaggerate the bow, or you'll look foolish.

LAW

If you can't do a deal with the Japanese on a handshake basis, you won't do a deal based on a contract. Business in Asia in general is based on trust and a mutual understanding of each other's needs.

The advantage of this system is that a deal can be altered if the advantage shifts too far on one side or the other. The exception to this philosophy is when one side loses its balance because of stupidity or oversight.

The Traditions of Legal Systems in Pacific Rim Countries

BY ROBERT T. YAHNG

In 1980, Dr. Wulf Döser, a prominent German attorney, visited Taiwan. Although he was a legal scholar, he spoke no Chinese and had never studied Taiwanese laws. Yet when he attended a civil trial proceeding at the Taipei District court as a spectator, he not only found the court procedures similar to those he was familiar with in Germany, but he was also able to predict the judge's decision in the trial. Even the robes of the judges and opposing lawyers were similar to those worn by judges and lawyers in a German court. Further, the commentaries of German legal scholars were admissible in court as persuasive force in interpreting provisions of the Taiwan Civil Code.

If this story seems surprising, then the revelation that most countries of Asia have legal systems and laws actually based on or greatly influenced by western jurisprudence may be even more startling.

Considering their histories, it really is not all that strange that Hong Kong and Macau have British and Portuguese legal systems, respectively. After all, they are still colonies. The fact that Singapore, Malaysia, and India have systems of law anchored in the British legal traditions or that Indonesia would have a Dutch-inspired system is explained by their former status as colonies. Similarly, the Philippines, having a system based on both European Civil Law and U.S. common law, reflects its history as a former colony of Spain and the United States.

Certainly, New Zealand and Australia having British systems only makes sense, considering their predominantly British origins. As for Taiwan, Japan, and Korea, and to some extent, China, their story begins with Japan.

During the latter half of the nineteenth century, the Meiji reformers actively sought to modernize Japan by adopting western science and technology. These activities extended to western legal concepts. From the early years of the Meiji period (1868 to 1912), the Japanese Ministry of Justice had its own law school, where French Law was taught. Since 1874, British and U.S. laws were taught at Tokyo Imperial University.

The Dajokan Decree No. 103, issued in the Eighth year of the Meiji, set forth the principle that civil cases, in the absence of customs, were to be decided by a rule of reason, a position strongly reflective of French influence.

The renowned legal scholar, Professor Kenzo Takayanagi of Tokyo University, stated that as early as 1870, the interest in "the unification of law" was a political exigency of the first order. He reported that "the reformer, Shimpei Eto, was said to have ordered Rinsho Mitsukuri to translate the French Civil Code with all possible speed . . . never minding mistakes," with a view to promulgating it by replacing the word "French" with the word "Japanese." However, 28 years would pass before a civil code was adopted, and then it was the German code that prevailed.

In the Civil Code of 1898, Takanyanagi wrote, "the influence of the first (1887) and second (1896) drafts of the German Civil Code is clearly dominant." Further, he wrote, "The predominance of German legal science continued down to the end of World War II. Subsequent legislation and other fields of law followed German models. Stu-

dents of law went mostly to German Universities, as German textbooks, commentaries, and court decisions can most conveniently be utilized for the interpretation and application of the codes and statutes and court decisions in Japan."

Even today, despite the influence of the United States on such areas as constitutional laws, criminal procedures, and corporate laws, the Japanese legal system still retains much of its German origins.

Korea became a protectorate and colony of Japan shortly after the Russo–Japanese War of 1904 to 1905. The Japanese legal system was imposed on Korea until the end of World War II. In 1946, South Korea basically adopted the Japanese civil code and system of law for itself. Although greatly influenced by the U.S., much of the tradition of Korean law today can still be traced to the Germanic codes via Japan.

After the downfall of the Qing Dynasty in 1911, China made serious efforts to modernize. She greatly respected Japanese achievements in the area of military science and industrialization. After all, Japan had been the only Asian nation to have defeated a western power (i.e., Russia in the Russo–Japanese War of 1904 to 1905). Thus, it seemed logical that the

Chinese legal systems in the early part of this century emulated the Japanese model.

In 1949, the Communist party proved victorious in the civil war against the nationalist government. Chiang Kai Shek's administration and government moved to the island of Taiwan. Meanwhile, on the China mainland, the laws of China as promulgated by the Nationalists were not surprisingly replaced by new laws and rules which served Maoist principles and doctrine, and the needs of a new society. However, many drafters of the new rules were trained and educated in the jurisprudence of the civil code. Even in the bleakest days of the people's courts, these traditions emerged to influence court procedures.

Since 1979, in the spirit of the "open door policy," a great number of laws have been promulgated to welcome foreign investment. Much of this work has been done by the Legislative Affairs Committee, a subcommittee of the Standing Committee of the National People's Congress. Its administrators were versed in the old Chinese civil code and influenced by teachers whose education was received in the pre-1949 tradition. The legislative affairs committee consists of a number of departments whose task is to study the laws of other jurisdictions including Japan, Taiwan, Korea, various European nations, as well as the United States, with a view to adopting laws that would advance China's economic development.

In the aftermath of the Sino–Japanese War (1894 to 1895), Taiwan was ceded to Japan as one of the prizes of war. The Japanese legal system was forced upon Taiwan and remained in effect until Taiwan's liberation in 1945, when she was repatriated to China. Upon restoration to China, the Chinese legal system was instituted, but this was in fact a Japanese-inspired system, which in turn had strong German roots. Thus, it was not surprising that Dr. Döser found the Taiwan courts to be so familiar.

Although Thailand was one of the few Asian countries to have maintained its independence in the eighteenth and nineteenth centuries, it was not insulated from western influence. Led by a reform-minded monarch,

King Chulalongkorn (1868 to 1910), Thailand adopted a codified system of law, based on the French and German codes, and influenced by the common law of England and Australia.

In surveying the laws of the Pacific Rim countries, one, of course, recognizes that they are very different and derived from separate judiciaries, law-making bodies, and institutions. Any generalization about them would be dangerous to make. However, two general patterns are arguably discernable. First, that most countries in which Western entrepreneurs would have interests in doing business have legal systems which are greatly influenced by western legal traditions. And secondly, those traditions stem from the European continental civil code or the Anglo-American common law—and, in some cases, a combination of the two.

Significant differences exist between systems of laws originating from civil law and

common law countries. These approaches color the attitudes of officials, administrators, and those whose occupations are closely linked with their respective legal systems. For example, government officials in civil-code countries tend to abstractly apply the rules rather than rely on precedents; whereas officials in common-law countries are greatly affected by what other officials and tribunals have decided. Civil-law lawyers are generally more apt to draft shorter contracts than common-law lawyers. They are also more likely than common-law lawyers to render a legal opinion quickly.

The laws of the Pacific Rim countries continue to evolve. Different political, cultural and economic faces shape their evolution. However, the Western legal traditions are still influential and will undoubtedly guide the evolutionary process into the twenty-first century.

For a list of Pacific Rim law firms, please refer to Appendix B "Asian Investment Guide."

Robert T. Yahng is a partner in the San Francisco office of Baker & McKenzie, a law firm with strong Pacific Rim connections and offices in 11

Asian countries. He founded the Baker & McKenzie office in Taipei and assisted in the establishment of his firm's office in Shanghai. In his day-to-day practice, Robert Yahng advises his U.S. clients on matters relating to the laws of Asian countries, while he guides clients from Asia on matters relating to U.S. laws.

Legal Checklist

BY ROBERT YAHNG

Here are some issues to explore before investing or doing business in the Asia-Pacific region:

TAXATION

Different arrangements (i.e., joint venture, corporate forms, branch and liaison offices, and technology transfers) may result in different tax rates. Investments in industries considered beneficial to the host country are often given preferential tax treatment. But ultimately any tax planning must look to the laws of the investors' home country to ensure that the ultimate repatriation of overseas profits does not become a casualty of domestic tax application.

PROTECTION OF TECHNOLOGY, TRADEMARKS, COPYRIGHTS AND PATENTS

Generally, "first use" protects trademarks in jurisdictions based on the common-law heritage, but generally not in jurisdictions founded on the European Civil Code, where the "first to register" has considerable claim.

Registration of trademarks, patents, and copyrights does provide some protection, and in most countries of the Pacific Rim governmental agencies (i.e., bureaus of standards) have been established in accordance with relevant laws to implement and maintain systems of registration.

In countries where technology, copyrights, and patents are unregisterable, one could consider whether contract laws may be of help. If so, one must then ask whether the protection under contract law is sufficient.

FOREIGN EXCHANGE

A few countries have no restrictions (i.e., Hong Kong and Singapore). Many others have restrictions of varying limitations ranging from light (i.e., Japan, Taiwan, Indonesia) to severe (i.e., Philippines, South Korea, and China).

In restrictive jurisdictions, foreign exchange barriers act almost like semipermeable membranes. Foreign exchange flows in easily but not easily out again.

GOVERNMENT APPLICATIONS, APPROVALS, LICENSES, AND TAX RULINGS

In many Asian countries, industries can be categorized into those barred to foreign investors, those in which foreign investors may partially invest with majority ownership of the venture to be placed in the hands of indigenous citizens, and those in which foreign investors may freely invest. The last category usually involves technically sophisticated and/or capital-intensive industries, which local business lacks the resources to invest in and manage. Often, Asian countries generate lists outlining these categories and provide candid responses as to which industries welcome foreign investment.

MEETINGS

In the United States, whoever sits at the head of the table is in charge. In Japan, whoever sits farthest from the door is usually in charge, a tradition which probably dates back to the rule of the Shoguns.

In ancient times, the Shogun would sit on a raised platform surrounded by young samurai princes on a lower platform, and below them on the floor, older samurai. If one of the older samurai rose to attack, the young princes could run interference and buy time for the Shogun to slip away. On the other hand, if one of the young princes attacked him, the Shogun was experienced and strong enough to defend himself against the adolescent until other samurai aided him.

UNDERSTANDING THE CULTURE CAN HELP YOU MAKE SALES

For example, one export item which is finding favor in the Orient is wood. Japanese buyers are very sophisticated when it comes to the quality of workmanship and materials. It's not unusual for Japanese buyers to request wood that comes from "trees that grow at a high altitude, on the north face of the mountain." This wood grows more slowly and has tighter grain and is more durable, but the expressed reason why the Japanese like this wood is because "these trees must be very strong to survive in this harsh environment."

OTHER PACIFIC RIM EXPORT STRATEGIES

- **Keep current on what's happening and avoid old stereotypes.** Pacific Rim markets are changing, just like every other market. Be alert—and receptive—to what you see and hear.
- **Choose a local partner/representative.** It's easier and faster to enter a market through an established representative who knows the industry, than trying to do everything from scratch. Your partner can be a dealer/distributor, vendor, manufacturer, or technology firm.
- **Don't make a one-way deal.** As an exporter, your objective is never to simply sell products overseas. Your objective should be to establish a mutual business relationship which presents advantages to both sides.
- **Learn to appeal to the market you're targeting.** Find out what's important to your distributors, dealers, and end-users, and appeal to those concerns just as you would in the United States. Don't chintz on translation costs. Use reliable translators and interpreters.
- **Think global and be flexible.** Asian logic is based as much on intuition and emotion as logic. Keep this in mind. Also, be flexible. You may go out to Asia thinking to export to Japan or Korea—but come back with a deal which includes a joint venture to sell products in Europe.
- **Test market your products.** Get competitive and industry information through a research firm. Attend trade conventions to see if dealers are interested, and run trial ads to help gauge the interest of end-users. Almost any export product can be test marketed.
- **Focus on markets of opportunity.** Some markets are closed to U.S. firms, period. But even among these a few markets such as citrus are just beginning to open up as a result of U.S. trade negotiations and well-publicized pressures. You still need to enter them through a local distributor or partner. Some American fads, fashions, sports equipment, and high-ticket luxury items—

such as premium/quality chocolates—are currently hot in the Pacific Rim.

- **Take advantage of symposiums and other events.** Trade fairs, symposiums, seminars, sponsored trips, and other special programs are invaluable events for U.S. exporters interested in Pacific Rim markets. The U.S. Commerce Department as well as many state governments and universities and other groups, such as World Trade Centers, offer such useful programs.

- **Most importantly, get started now.** The markets are there and waiting if you take time to understand the basic differences in marketing to the Pacific Rim.

HIGH-TECH, HIGH-GROWTH

DISTRIBUTION—THE KEY TO MARKET SUCCESS

by Jon M. Stout

Profitability and success in the high-tech markets of the Pacific Rim require strong commitment, quality products, and a concerted effort to learn often complex distribution channels. Jon Stout details how even the smallest suppliers can avoid potential pitfalls in getting exports to the Pacific Rim. Stout is president of the Tag Corporation in Washington, D.C., and specializes in marketing high-tech products to the Pacific Rim.

Success in the Pacific Rim, while clearly possible, is not a given, especially in the highly competitive high-technology markets. Like any other area of the world, business affairs must be conducted on an informed and professional basis, and more often than not, by the buyer's rules. A high level of commitment, quality products, and a concerted effort to learn often complex distribution channels can help even the smallest suppliers avoid potential pitfalls and achieve a level of success. It is not easy, but those who have worked at it will agree that it can be very profitable.

There are significant opportunities for American suppliers to sell high-tech products —primarily data-processing products and medical instruments—in the Pacific Rim. In many cases, the economies in the region are undergoing double-digit growth rates and generally lag behind the level of technology found in the United States and Western Europe. In addition, with the notable exception of the recent events in China, this area of the world is enjoying extended peace and prosperity.

U.S. manufactured exports are in demand, particularly those products where the United States enjoys a technological advantage, such as computer hardware, software, telecommunications, and medical instrumentation. As in marketing to almost any region of the world, there is a basic, three-pronged prescription for success: commitment, product, and experience in establishing distribution channels.

COMMITMENT

Selling to the Pacific Rim requires a strong commitment of management and financial resources. Long-term success depends on understanding how your customer wishes to do business rather than imposing your style on the customer. This is particularly true for sales of high-tech items, requiring a much more concentrated and sophisticated sales effort than, say, certain consumer items. Each country in the Rim has distinct and different cultural, legal, and business requirements, and the exporter must understand the rules for conducting business.

EACH LEGAL SYSTEM DIFFERS

These differences are important, especially in the high-tech area where patent/intellectual property rights and contracting issues are essential aspects of doing business. It is vital to understand the legal requirements for doing business in a given country. (See Robert Yahng's "Legal Checklist" on p. 122.)

COMMUNICATIONS IS OFTEN A BARRIER

Japan, Hong Kong, Singapore, and Australia have excellent communications networks. But other areas—particularly China—are variously less effective in providing communications services.

Rules for negotiations must be scrutinized. Each country has its own set of rules developed as a by-product of its culture. Japan's rules are markedly different than those of China. Australia, although in many respects similar to the United States, has its own style of negotiation.

TIME PERCEPTION VARIATIONS FROM COUNTRY TO COUNTRY IS ANOTHER FACTOR

Hong Kong, for instance, has a very short time perspective—much like the United States—while its neighbors in China have a very long time perspective.

PRODUCT

The product offering must be very high quality in order to compete with area suppliers and other international competitors. Only in the areas of software and integrated systems does the United States enjoy such a tremendous advantage that quality is not a competitive concern. And this advantage is disappearing as local players become more comfortable with software development and systems integration techniques.

CUSTOMER SERVICE IS KEY

The high-tech product offering should be viewed as a total concept, and very importantly include pre- and post-sales support that allows the purchaser/end-user the right to enjoy the benefits of the product quickly and for a prolonged time. Hardware that does not provide full satisfaction is unacceptable.

The concept of *functionality* is important to keep in mind when marketing to Pacific Rim customers. The market is looking for complete solutions to problems, rather than components that even when combined may or may not do the job. Any hardware manufacturer must develop a distribution network that is solution-oriented and adds value to solutions throughout the network.

Quality is an issue throughout the Pacific Rim in varying degrees. For example, it is most crucial in Japan, where quality requirements are probably the strictest. Exporters hoping to get rid of substandard products, even to the less-sophisticated markets, will be in for a nasty surprise.

DISTRIBUTION EXPERIENCE

Channel decisions are critical and difficult. Proper marketing and sales research is essential to success. Preparation usually involves researching the market to determine whether the perceived opportunities are real and the development of data that will support the decision to appoint distributors, agents, or other participants in the channel.

EACH COUNTRY IS DIFFERENT

After researching the market and making the final decision to attempt entry, the first trap to avoid is establishing a channel that treats the area as a monolithic unit. Each country in the Rim has specific requirements that are reflected in distribution activities. You should never attempt to sell from one country to another because they are "the same."

Australia cannot be serviced from Hong Kong or Singapore, and attempting to service the rest of the area from Australia is not cost-effective because of the distances involved. It is a nine-hour flight from Hong Kong to Sydney—about the same as from Tokyo to Seattle.

The next common pitfall to avoid is *exclusivity*. This is a problem issue because most aggressive distributors will demand exclusivity for a country—or the entire region—and dominate the relationship with the principle under the protection of local laws.

DISTRIBUTION CHANNELS WILL VARY

In order to avoid problems with exclusivity, the channels must be subject to initial and continuing value analysis with the requirement that each player in the channel add perceived value. This is particularly true for multilayered distribution channels that are prevalent in the computer industry. Exclusivity should only be granted to proven channel players or to those willing to make a large, funded sales commitment.

Channels should also be subjected to close legal analysis not only to avoid exclusivity problems, but also to protect vulnerable patent and intellectual property rights that can be jeopardized under multilevel distribution networks.

Successful *channel management* also requires an understanding of the respective cultures as well as consistent negotiating skills. Negotiation is required to properly establish the channel and to maintain effective performance from all parties—even your own internal legal, finance, and production departments.

EXPORT LICENSES

In addition to the management of local channels, certain high-tech products require export approval from the U.S. government regulatory authorities.

Certain exports to China require a validated license from the Commerce Department, and since the recent turmoil, several types of technology have been restricted—both from the U.S. and China sides.

PACIFIC RIM HIGH-TECH MARKETS

Each country in the Pacific Rim has somewhat different high-tech needs and market characteristics, but it is useful to segment the market as follows.

JAPAN

Japan is a highly industrialized, sophisticated economy and its data-processing requirements lie in the high-speed data-processing area.

There is a distinct market niche for 32-bit super-mini and mini-super computers with sophisticated application software. In the scientific marketplace, English software can be used, but in the commercial marketplace Hansa (Korean) conversion is required.

Because Japan has standardized on the NEC microcomputer operating system, the market for PCs is limited to very specialized applications.

Networking or distributed processing is accomplished by the use of powerful CPUs (central processing units) and "dumb" or asynchronous terminals as opposed to the Local Area Network approach found throughout the rest of the world.

CHINA AND THE LDCs

Potentially the largest market is for high-technology products capable of making other high-tech products. These markets involve semiconductor manufacturing equipment or computers used for production. The best way to access these markets is usually for the foreign supplier to arrange to buy back a portion of the production.

The second-largest market is high-performance 32-bit computers used for scientific or R&D purposes. Products especially in demand in this area involve the scientific processing in the areas of natural resource development, CAD/CAM design, shipbuilding, and software development.

The market with the most potential is the commercial market for Local Area Network products. This includes the financial, factory automation, and government sectors. Sales to the commercial market, however, require Hansa conversion and local support, thus requiring local representation.

The demand for PCs—especially in China which has its own microcomputer industry—is often limited to high performance units with specialized application software.

THE FOUR TIGERS

The Four Tigers—Hong Kong, Singapore, Taiwan, and South Korea—are characterized by the rapid development of a high technology manufacturing base, particularly in the microcomputer industry. As a result of this concentration, the market for microcomputer-related development and production machinery is large. The market for Local Area

Networks is also developing rapidly, particularly for financial institutions, and CAD/CAM and software design.

AUSTRALIA AND NEW ZEALAND

These countries are excellent markets for scientific and commercial computer applications. Both have developed sophisticated financial industries, particularly in the commercial banking and insurance sectors. In addition, Australia and New Zealand also have significant research and development efforts that require scientific workstations. The Local Area Network market is undergoing rapid growth with distributed processing solutions using state-of-the-art operating systems, and peripherals are selling extremely well.

Reprinted from *Export Today's* Special Supplement—"The Pacific Rim: Export Outlook for the 1990s," October 1989, by permission of the publisher, Trade Communications, Inc., 733 15th St., N.W. Suite 1100, Washington, D.C. 20005, (202) 737-1060.

RIM RESOURCE

Published in Minneapolis, Minnesota, Export USA Publications' *Export Sales & Marketing Guide* is a 330-page procedural manual with in-depth chapters on locating foreign markets and sales representatives, pricing and budgeting for export, writing international marketing agreements, securing export licenses, shipping overseas, and receiving payment. For more information, call (612) 854-8118.

TRADE WINDS

FROM NOBLE HOUSE TO GLOBAL HOUSE

by Brian Caplen

The great trading houses are learning new lessons from Japan.

Back in the last century when tea was Taiwan's major export, the fortunes of British trading house, Tait and Co., were tied to tea leaves.

By the late 1960s when the island's export boom got underway, the canny Tait had switched to shipping. Now as the economy opens up to imports, the company is playing a leading role in the consumer revolution.

In between these major economic shifts, the trading house survived aborigine raids on its coffee plantations, the effects of Japanese occupation, and the Chinese revolution.

The experiences of Tait, and the other European trading houses which helped map out Asia commercially, explain a great deal about the fickle import–export business.

Trading houses must continually adapt to far-reaching changes or die. They must always be looking into the future and preparing strategies for what lies ahead.

While the prosperous Asia on the horizon may seem less formidable than the powder keg of the past, the challenges it presents to trading houses are no less great.

Smart trading houses are already gearing up for the coming era of Asian economic dominance. They must be ready for the unleashing of mass consumer markets in combination with continuing export success. They must find a niche in a region that relies less on Western technology and investment than it used to.

A major concern is the rise of manufacturers with the clout to do their own marketing and distribution. This has long been a threat posed by Western multinationals. Now, with Asian companies becoming more international, the dangers are compounded. The pressures to offer a sophisticated, comprehensive, yet low-cost service are greater than ever.

The European trading houses have changed, too. While some, such as Hong Kong's Jardine Matheson, are still largely controlled by the founding families, many others, such as Malaysia's Mulpha International Trading Corp., have become so Asian as to be completely cut off from their roots. Even those that have remained foreign-owned are now extensively locally managed.

NOBLE HOUSE STRATEGY IN THE 1990s

Freed from the stigma of their colonial history, the trading houses could play a part in tomorrow's Asia as dynamic as their early pioneering role. The trick is to find the right strategy.

Among the courses being taken by the houses are:

- Increasing joint ventures with principles to manufacture products that were formerly traded. The trend in Southeast Asia will be toward export projects, although import substitutions will remain important. For a trading house, this strategy cuts out the risk of being short-circuited, and is well received in host countries as a step toward building up industry.
- Provision of a total package service including finance, insurance, shipping, customer service, intelligence-gathering, marketing, and distribution. This will make it less attractive for big exporters to do their own thing and make the trading houses indispensable to smaller companies.
- Diversification of the product range so that a house does not become over-dependent on the trading of a few items.
- Use of advanced techniques such as futures and countertrading that give them advantages not available to the nonspecialist trader.
- Building up of a worldwide network that manufacturers doing their own distribution will find too expensive to match. As wide-ranging as they may seem, these strategies are in fact highly focused. Gone are the days when trading houses would merrily diversify into any business that seemed attractive. Too many, like Inchcape and Jardine Matheson, have in the past expanded into

new areas with disastrous results. Both these companies were forced to sell off unprofitable ventures and revert to their core activities.

Trading has always depended on filling the gap between geographical areas, languages, cultures, and administrations. Even in today's shrinking world, a gap still exists for the trading specialist who knows how to countertrade and gain export credits. These more sophisticated ways of crossing the basic trading bridge are where the modern company should concentrate its efforts.

THE JAPANESE MODEL

A favored model is that of the Japanese trading house, the *sogo shosha,* such as C Itoh, Mitsubishi, Mitsui, and Marubeni. These incorporate many of the characteristics now being pursued by the old European trading houses. They trade a huge range of products —between 20,000 and 25,000—using economies of scale to offset margins of 1.5%. They are masters of financial wizardry and market intelligence.

Sogo shosha will lend money for a manufacturer's export projects in return for the agency rights. They also provide loans for importers. In this way, they assume a great deal of financial risk. One management expert has described them as "finance companies, not trading companies."

For information-gathering, a *sogo shosha* such as Marubeni has more than 150 overseas offices around the world, linked by leased channels to three independent switching centers in Tokyo, New York, and Brussels.

An UNCTAD/GATT report on export houses comments: "This type of capability probably exists only in the *sogo shosha* and explains a good part of their success in recent decades.

"Worldwide sourcing has become a daily reality for them. Competitive bids for large public tenders can be submitted in a matter of hours. Exchange rate variations can be accommodated almost as soon as they occur."

Sogo shosha emerged under very special conditions in Japan. When the country was coming out of isolation and ordinary companies did not know how to deal with overseas trading partners, the *sogo shosha* stepped in as intermediaries. Restrictions on bank lending contributed to their large financial role. Despite a change in conditions in Japan, and widespread predictions of their demise, the *sogo shosha* have survived. They have done this by increasing control over their own destiny and sewing up places where they could be bypassed.

Only a few countries, such as Korea with its *chonghap sangsas,* have successfully imitated the *sogo shosha.* The European trading houses in Southeast Asia have played quite a different role—or at least they have up to now.

In his book, *Sogo Shosha: The Vanguard of the Japanese Economy,* Yoshihara Kunio describes the contrast. "Although *sogo shosha* have undertaken many such activities outside trading, they differ from Jardine Matheson and East Asiatic in one important respect: That is, trading is still the center of their activities.

"Many investments in industry, shipping, warehousing and resource development were undertaken (by *sogo shosha*) either to protect the trade channels already established or to create new ones."

Kunio, writing in 1980, went on to suggest that the *sogo shosha* might take a leaf out of the European book in diversifying further. In fact, the reverse seems to be happening with European houses following the *sogo shosha* path.

The houses which diversified too widely, such as Jardine and Inchcape, have pulled back, and those that have invested in manufacturing have done it on a very selective basis to dovetail with their trading.

Still others have been strengthening their links with sister firms and other national companies in exporting, finance, and shipping. They have been trying to create the *sogo shosha* effect without building it up from scratch.

THE MALAYSIAN MODEL

One place where the *sogo shosha* idea has caught fire is Malaysia. Prime minister Dr. Mahathir Mohamad is known to be a keen advocate, feeling that *sogo shosha* involvement in shipping and insurance would help reduce the country's invisible trade deficit and boost export performance.

Pursuing this course is Mulpha International Trading Corp., which was originally part of the old Guthrie empire founded by Alexander Guthrie in 1820.

Mulpha's latest experience of the fickle nature of trading came as recently as 1985 to 1986, during the Malaysian recession, when it lost several agencies.

This is the perennial curse for trading houses, and it doesn't only happen in recessions. Jim Cumming, the general manager of Tait, notes that success can lose a contract just as much as failure, because a principle is likely to open his own office if sales soar. All the more reason, then, to find new ways of keeping customers satisfied and getting involved in deals that tie agency rights in.

In Mulpha's case, its problems were compounded by the management and financial problems facing the Multi-Purpose Holdings group to which it belongs. But following the restructuring of Multi-Purpose—which saw a

new board headed by respected names like Robert Kuok Hock Nien and Lee Loy Seng— Mulpha may find that its group connections are the key, rather than the barrier, to success.

The point is that Multi-Purpose has extensive interests in plantations, property development, banking, manufacturing, shipping and general trading. By strengthening links with its sister companies, Mulpha could turn itself into a *sogo shosha* with minimum capital outlay.

A first step, already in hand, is to increase the number of agencies it holds to achieve diversification of trading lines. A second step, currently at the planning stage, is to go into shipping.

"Last year (in 1988), Mulpha's trading division added 14 new agency lines to the 40 or so existing ones," says executive director Tan Leong Piak.

In the foreword of Mulpha's latest annual report, the company declares that it will join forces with other Malaysian corporations to move into international shipping.

"Mulpha vessels will proudly carry forth Malaysian goods and bring back Malaysian imports while helping to restore trade balances in Malaysia's favor," it says.

Another trading house which may follow the *sogo shosha* path is Malaysia's largest quoted concern, Sime Darby. With its wide range of interests in plantations, manufacturing, property, and leasing, Sime Darby has been described by stockbroker Merrill Lynch as "a proxy of the Malaysian economy."

But while Sime Darby's general investment has aped the economy's move away from plantations to manufacturing, its trading division has lagged behind. The division deals mainly in commodities and will have to diversify to keep up. Recent indications are that it plans to do just that.

In comments on the group's restructuring, a company spokesman said: "The restructuring and revamp of PSDH (PSDH is a trading joint venture between Sime Darby and state trading concern Pernas) and the Malaysian regional activities will also see a trading arm set up to tap public sector business, while staff and management will be given further training to upgrade skills and expertise."

But not all trading houses are part of a wide-ranging business group that makes *sogo shosha* dreams easier to realize. Even those that are may prefer to go about it in a piecemeal rather than a broad-brush manner. Here, the option of vertical integration in selected areas seems very attractive.

Quite simply, a trading house takes a look at the products it trades and decides if it should be manufacturing them. Or, with a resource, whether it should be looking for new deposits.

Achieving this by working together with existing principles, rather than competing against them, avoids destroying long-standing relationships. In fact, sound principal agency ties are really the springboard for this kind of expansion.

THE THAI STYLE

In Thailand, for instance, the 100% Swiss-owned trading house Diethelm has long had a tight relationship with Nestle, a major player in the dairy industry. While Diethelm executives declined to comment, an industry source speculated that Diethelm's distribution and marketing network for Nestle accounted for at least half its turnover. Therefore, it made sense to move into local production of Nestle brands.

Other trading houses have invested in a similar way, but with less reliance on a single principle. Bangkok-based Berli Jucker Co., which is of Swiss origin, has two major joint ventures in local industry, one with glass producer Australian Consolidated Industries. "I pointed out to the Australians that sooner or later there would be an indigenous glass industry, so we ought to start it," recalls Berli Jucker chairman Walter Meyer. "So we started as an import substitution industry to replace the imported glassware."

Somchai Chaisuparakul, managing director of The Borneo Co. (Thailand), assesses the current situation—described as the marketing and import substitution era—like this: "Most of the products we are selling today are coming from local manufacturers. We feel that very shortly a high majority of our consumer products will be made in Thailand.

"So we seek distribution rights for local brands, or else we invite our international partners to come to Thailand and invest in a joint venture manufacturing operation with us. They, in turn, will entrust the marketing and distribution to us."

The next logical step is joint ventures in export projects. But so far trading houses such as Berli Jucker and East Asiatic Co. Thailand (EACT) report that their European principles have responded half-heartedly to the idea. Initial start-ups have not produced encouraging results.

"The only place where they [the European companies] are all cooperating is China," complains Berli Jucker's Meyer. "China to them is someplace everybody rushes to, tries to make a joint venture and even transfer technology. This is because it's such a big market and the 'in-thing' in Switzerland. Thailand is of very little interest by comparison."

EACT has a two-year-old company called EAC Export Corp. (Thailand), Ltd., which has been trying to export frozen shrimp and fruit to Europe.

"It's a very complicated exercise and we have learned some lessons along the way. We feel that with our local know-how, and with the shipping, we can offer a package, but I wouldn't call it a 100% success so far," says EACT's managing director Henrik de Jonquieres.

In this respect, the European houses are diverging widely from the *sogo shosha* strategy. The Japanese trading houses have been in the forefront in taking Japanese manufacturing offshore to low-cost centers such as Thailand.

But European trading house involvement in export projects is bound to come. This is a key area where they can work in tandem with the emerging economies of Thailand and Malaysia, and governments are sure to push for it. Even houses with their command lines in Europe are certain to respond eventually. The alternative will be gradual but certain decline.

THE EXPORT AGE BECKONS

When they do get into export, the trading houses will have come full circle in the economic life of Asia. They started out, after all, by exporting from the region—at that time it was commodities such as rice, teak, rubber, and tea. After World War II, the golden age of imports got underway, later leading to the current marketing and import substitution phase.

Now the export age beckons and the trading houses must take the initiative.

"The future of the trading houses is bleak if they do not adapt to the new situation," says Khalid Dahlan, managing director of Boustead Holdings Berhad.

That they will respond—indeed *are* responding—is reflected in a comment from Somchai Chaisuparakul, managing director of The Borneo Company (Thailand), Ltd., the oldest trading house in the country.

"A trading company cannot live on its past glory," he says. "A trading mentality is a survival mentality." That statement, in a nutshell, sums up what trading houses are all about.

Written by Brian Caplen, reported by Ooi Guat Tin in Kuala Lumpur, Peter Janssen in Bangkok, John Keating in Hong Kong, Mike Boydell in Taipei, and Joyce Quek, in Singapore. ©*Asian Business* magazine, Far East Trade Press, Ltd., 1989.

JAPAN'S GOLDEN DECADE

Japanese economists are predicting a "Golden '90s" decade for Japan, which will be comparable to America's era of prosperity back in the 1960s. According to a Nomura Research Institute forecast, Japan's economy will grow by almost 4% a year, doubling the nation's nominal GNP to $7.6 trillion by the year 2000, while the U.S. economy will reach only $10.4 trillion. By the twenty-first century, Japan's per capita GNP is expected to more than double to $59,200—53% larger than that of the United States.

Many Japanese economists now believe that the classic theory of business cycles no longer applies to Japan. They claim that Japan has learned over the years to minimize instability factors in the world economy, such as the two "oil shocks" of the 1970s as well as the rapid appreciation of the yen in the mid-1980s. But realistic fears still remain. These include the rise of North American and European trade blocs—and, of course, the specter of a devastating earthquake which is expected to hit Tokyo within the next few decades.

WHERE'S THE KOBE BEEF?

After being forced to liberalize their beef imports policy and promising to open the market completely to foreign beef imports in 1991, the Japanese are planning a countermeasure. They intend to export Japanese beef to foreign markets. Beef in Japan costs twice what it does in the United States, but the Japanese marketing pitch is that the quality of their beef is "twice as good." Japan already exports internationally famous Kobe beef to various Pac Rim markets including Hong Kong and Singapore.

PACKING IT UP

Inadequate packaging of Chinese export products cost the country $2 billion in lost foreign trade, the *China Daily* reported. China's packaging industry needed $400 million worth of imported material in 1988 but was only able to buy half that amount because of a shortage of foreign currency.

SINO-FOREIGN JOINT VENTURES

The China Association of Enterprises with Foreign Investment was formed in 1987 for the specific purpose of coordinating foreign trade activities of an estimated 15,000 Sino-foreign joint ventures, cooperative undertakings, and solely funded enterprises. The association has about 3,000 members in 26 branches.

TAIWAN'S OFFER TO THE PRC

In 1988, 34 senior officials of Taiwan's leading Kuomintang (KMT) party made China an offer that so far it hasn't taken up. The KMT would provide China with $10 billion to help get its mainland economy on its feet—provided that Beijing leaders renounced Communism.

BOOSTING ENGINEERING IN HONG KONG

There is a growing awareness among industrialized nations in Southeast Asia that automating the design and manufacturing of engineered products is a vital priority if they hope to retain their competitiveness in world markets. "If Hong Kong does not invest in, and master the use of, computers in engineering products within about 15 years, this sector of manufacturing will disappear," warned Dr. Donald Taylor, the technical director of the Hong Kong Productivity Council.

TURKEY: THE *MAQUILADORA* OF EUROPE?

Taiwan, like other Asian economic powers, is contemplating the riddle of a super-unified and protectionist Europe in 1992. Taking the long view—and betting on Turkey's eventual admission to the European Community—Taiwan is in the process of strengthening its economic ties with Turkey. The plan is to use Turkey as Taiwan's bridgehead into the European market.

If Turkey is eventually admitted to the European Community (it applied in 1987 and is hoping to become a member in the near future), then it might play the role of a "maquiladora" nation. Turkish factories would serve European industry, much in the same way that Mexico's "maquiladoras" (twin plant facilities) now assemble Asian-made high-tech equipment and consumer electronics products

ASIAN CHRONICLES

ON THE OLD SILK ROAD

In his action-packed book, Visits to High Tartary, Yarkand and Kashgar *(originally published in 1871, and reprinted by Oxford University Press in 1984), English adventurer Robert Shaw described his attempt to become the first Englishman to map parts of Chinese Turkistan (now Xinjiang province) in Central Asia. Here is a description of one of his experiences on the old Silk Road, the route of the original Pacific Rim traders.*

I shall never forget that night's bivouac on the snow. As soon as the horse carrying the brushwood fuel came up (it was past 12 o'clock at night), we two Englishmen made shift to light a fire against a rock, clearing away the snow for the purpose. Attracted by this, a Sikh merchant who was crossing the pass the same day came and sat down with us. His long black beard and moustache were covered with pendant icicles which dragged down the hair by their weight. His face was haggard, and his only thought seemed to be of the fire. I presently found a bottle of rum, and was proceeding to uncork it, when he looked round, laid his hand on my shoulder, and said earnestly: "I am partner in that." I laughed, and gave him some, and it seemed to revive him, for he began to bewail his fate.

He was traveling quickly with all his wealth in a portable form, carried on five lightly laden horses. One, the most valuable, he was in the habit of leading himself as he rode. He now told me that, finding his hand getting frozen by holding the leading rope, he had cast this treasure-laden animal adrift in the pass, and did not know what had become of him. On his own horse he had carried a parcel of valuable silks. This had slipped off a few hundred yards back, but he had not had the energy to dismount and pick it up. To those who know the nature of Indian merchants, such neglect will speak volumes of the state to which he must have been reduced.

I advised him for the future to take our example, and walk instead of riding when the cold was so great, assuring him that we had been comfortably warm all the time (although) our style of clothing had contributed to this. We wore each of the usual articles of dress about fourfold. I may add that our friend, Tara Sing the Sikh, recovered his treasures. One of my servants, a hillman who was coming behind, finding a stray horse in the pass, caught him and brought him on.

---

for duty-free shipment into the North American market.

WHAT WOULD HAPPEN IF U.S.– JAPAN TRADE STOPPED?

Japan's Minister of International Trade and Industry (MITI) has analyzed U.S./Japan trade. Their report says that if all trade stopped between the two countries, the U.S. economy would shrink by a paltry 0.6% while Japan's would take a 5% loss. The huge difference in dependency points up the low level of U.S. exports to Japan and it shows Japan's weakness toward the United States.

Industry foreign-market dependency ratios:

	Japan (to the U.S.)		*U.S.* (to Japan)	
1. Automobiles	28.4%	Forestry	7.0%
2. Appliances	23.4%	Fisheries	3.1%
3. Electronic parts	18.5%	Farming	31%
4. Machinery and Equipment	17.6%	Electronic parts	2.6%
5. Electronic/communications		Other transportation	
equipment	15.5%	equipment	2.4%
All industries	5.0%	*All industries*	0.6%

TOWARD ASIAN TRADE BLOCS
by Jack Maisano

There are two ways that Asian countries can be hurt—or helped—by the growing trend toward regional economic blocs:

- The overseas blocs will force economic reciprocity on Asian countries that have long denied it. That will open up certain industries, services in particular, to international competition.
- The existence of overseas blocs will force Asian countries to form their own economic bloc or blocs. That will open up other kinds of industries to greater regional competition. Since the level of merchandise trade between Asian countries is relatively low (compared with trade to North America and Europe), other kinds of exchanges would have to be encouraged to make a trading bloc meaningful.

These might include education, communications, distribution, aviation, retail, and small-scale industry.

For Asia's nationalistic, politically volatile, developing states, that would be unacceptable. Or would it? To the extent that Asia's emerging economies can internationalize—or at least regionalize—their industries, they will establish the foundations for long-term prosperity and steady growth. If they shrink from this formidable challenge, they risk being passed by. The choice is theirs.

THE ASIAN "10"

The world's most powerful economic bloc will be Asian, according to a recent report by the Republic of China on Taiwan's Central News Agency. After surveying regional economists, the Taiwanese news agency is predicting that the so-called "Asian 10" will combine to form a new trade bloc to rival any trade bloc in the West, including the post-1992 unified European Community. The 10 PacRim heavyweights cited are Japan, Taiwan, Hong Kong, South Korea, Singapore, Thailand, the Philippines, Malaysia, Indonesia, and the People's Republic of China.

Looser trade policies, improved cooperation, and new trade agreements are helping to integrate regional activities, according to the report, which also notes that Taiwan has already passed South Korea as a major semiconductor manufacturer; and South Korean and Hong Kong investments are becoming much more regional than before, while Singapore's investors tend to stay at home more than their Asian counterparts.

IT'S A GAMBLE

Macau casino tycoon Stanley Ho has a novel solution for calming jitters in Hong Kong and Macau over the scheduled return of the two territories to the PRC in 1997 and 1999, respectively. Ho proposed that the two colonies be leased to the United Nations as the UN's official headquarters for 100 years, starting July 1, 1997. According to this scenario, Hong Kong and Macau would become the "Switzerland of Asia"—purely commercial and financial centers and symbols of peace.

JAPAN-BASHING BASHED

Japan-bashing may be a popular sport among U.S. congressmen, but it does little to solve America's economic problems, notes an American scholar of Japanese government and foreign policy. "Japan isn't a major source of our trade and economic problems, and it's counterproductive to our interests to act as

though it is," insists Martin Weinstein, a University of Illinois political science professor, after he stepped down from his post as the Japan Chair at the Center for Strategic and International Studies in Washington, D.C.

Weinstein suggested that Japan-bashing is merely a symptom of American politicians' "post–Cold War psychosis about Japan."

"They need an enemy—a bad guy to be against," he said. "Now that Gorbachev is so agreeable, some people in Washington are looking around for someone to replace the Soviets. Japan is the country they've come up with."

He refuses to believe that there are fundamental conflicts of interest between Japan and the United States, or that Japan's "unfairness and political and economic defects" are the primary causes for these conflicts.

Weinstein's harsh but realistic appraisal is that "our problems are rooted in our lagging productivity and growth rates, our low savings and capital investments, and our excessive consumption and borrowing."

"Unless we take the relatively modest steps necessary to increase our productivity and improve our competitiveness, the American economic and political position will continue to decline, not just vis-à-vis Japan, but relative to Western Europe as well."

He warned, "The central issue before us is not trade policy, the U.S. trade deficit with Japan, or even the U.S.–Japan relationship. . . . It is the future of the United States, our place in the world, and what we are going to make of it."

CHINA'S HIGH-TECH EXPORTS

China earned $286 million in 1988 from exports of technology, an increase of 80% over 1987.

TAIWANESE SNAP UP CAMERA EXPORTS

Taiwan is the world's biggest exporter of cameras, having overtaken Japan. Two other Asian Tigers—South Korea and Hong Kong—are in third and fourth place, respectively, according to statistics compiled by a Japanese camera association. A total of 32 million Taiwan-made cameras were sold overseas in 1987, more than double that of the year before. But the Taiwanese cameras are unsophisticated mini-cameras which sell for about $10, compared to more sophisticated Japanese cameras which average about $102 each.

BIG ON BONSAIS

Flowers, dwarf *bonsai* trees, birds, pet animals, fancy goldfish, seeds, and foodstuffs earned China a record $32 million in 1988, according to *China Daily*.

FRAGRANT HARBORS

China became one of the world's biggest perfume and essence producers in 1986, with an annual output of 34 million liters. The country exported $180 million worth of perfume to 120 countries and regions, including Britain, France, Japan, and the United States.

PRC PRAWNS

China made about $300 million in 1988 by exporting prawns. Eels are the nation's second largest foreign currency earners after prawns, with an output of about 12,000 tons in 1988.

SILK BAZAAR

China's largest silk market—the Donfang Silk Bazaar—was built in Shengze, a border town of Jiangsu and Zhejiang provinces, near Shanghai. Two hundred fifty silk enterprises from all over China have shops there, in addition to 166 private stands. More than 2,000 varieties of garment silk fabrics as well as raw materials, machinery, and techniques are sold in the market. Shengze produces 5,500 tons of silk cocoons and 150 million meters of fabrics annually. Its exports make up one fifth of China's total.

MONGOLIAN TV SETS

Inner Mongolia now produces some of China's best color TV sets, according to the Xinhua News Agency. Some 50 electronic products produced in the autonomous region have won national recognition including an 18-inch color TV and a 14-inch black-and-white TV. The "Swan Brand" TV sets sell well at home and in 20 countries and territories, according to the regional government. Output of Inner Mongolia's electronics industry reached $67.5 million in 1987.

INDIA FISHES FOR NEW MARKETS

India is seeking joint ventures with foreign firms to triple the size of its deep-sea fishing fleet and thus enhance its seafood exports. About 85% of its foreign exchange earnings from fishing comes from exporting shrimp, with Japan as the major customer, but deep-sea fishing for tuna, lobsters, and squid awaits development. A marine exports official estimated that at least 1,500 efficient vessels were needed to fully exploit the country's 2.5 million km² deep-sea fishing zone and raise the catch from its present 4.5 million tons.

TAIWAN'S PRC TEXTILE INVESTMENTS

Mainland China has become Taiwan's third biggest textile market (after the U.S. and Hong Kong) and more than 30 small firms in Xiamen, the economic zone across from Taiwan, has some form of investment from the island, 20 of them being joint ventures. Officially, the nationalist government still bans direct trade and investment in China, so Taiwanese firms have been proceeding cautiously. "Their mainland efforts are still experimental and limited," a Xiamen official observed. The investments have been brought about largely because of the need for Taiwanese firms to find cheaper labor and raw materials if they are to compete successfully with other Asian manufacturers.

SHREWD SHANGHAI TRADERS

Shanghai, China's leading industrial center, is proving to be a shrewd and flexible operator on world trading markets, having set up more than 200 industrial and agricultural trade organizations to deal with foreign import and export companies. The city has been quick to shift from exporting raw materials to finished products such as the fashionable silk clothes now shipped by the Shanghai Silk Import and Export company after consulting with noted designers in Japan, France, and the United States.

Shanghai's exports in the field of software have earned more than $1 million in recent years, and to this can be added the $1 million

profit from laboratory findings by the Shanghai Research Institute of Pharmacy and $5 million worth of technical exports in 1987. Barter trade between Shanghai and Yugoslavia, Poland, West Germany, and Eastern Europe is also growing by leaps and bounds.

CHINA'S TOY TRADE

China's toy industry hoped to increase its exports by about 20% in 1990 to earn the country $350 million, but it has a long way to go to be a world market force. At present its trade volume accounts for about 3% of the world's total and it has only about 10,000 varieties to offer, compared with the 12,000 new toys that Japan pours onto the market each year.

UNZIPPING CHINA

The Taiwan Zipper Manufacturers Association reports that Hong Kong had become its major customer with most of the low-priced zippers being re-exported from the colony to service China's fast-growing handbag and garment industries.

BOOMERANG TRANSFERS

Many of the big Japanese companies have started to shy away from lending technology to South Korea, so Korean electronics firms have turned to small foreign companies abroad for technology transfers. "The Japanese are unwilling to assist in developing high technology because they fear a boomerang effect," said an official responsible for high-tech research at the Korean Institute for Economics and Technology, a government think-tank.

THAI TECH CITY

More than 30 Hong Kong companies announced plans to set up a $29 million "electronics city" in Thailand, according to the Hong Kong Electronics Association. It is envisaged that the city will span eight million square feet in the Bangkok region and act as a springboard to the markets of member countries of the Association of Southeast Asian nations, as well as Laos and Vietnam.

SOUTH KOREA HEADS FOR TOP

South Korea, among the world's poorest economies in the mid-1950s, could rank among the world's top 10 economies by the end of this decade, says Korean Air Lines chairman Cho Choong Hoon, who also heads the giant Hanjin industrial group. Its economic development, enhanced by open markets made available by Japan and the United States, had helped the country become "a truly advanced industrial nation," with an expected per capita income of $10,000 he said.

THE *ZAIBATSU* ARE ALIVE AND WELL IN JAPAN

On the surface it looks like Japan's corporations are engaged in free competition as independent entities in the best tradition of capitalistic enterprise. In fact, they swarm around the banks, creating *keiretsu* groups (families of companies) that work to each other's economic advantage.

Now Japanese groups of companies will be attempting to exert worldwide economic leverage as they form policies dedicated to the furthering of their own member companies, according to Japan's men's magazine *Brutus*.

Activities will center on six groups gathered around major banks. Those that are the progeny of the pre-war *zaibatsu* (monopolies) are Mitsui, Mitsubishi, and Sumitomo. The newly born *zaibatsu* are the Fuyoh group (centered around the Fuji Bank), the Sanwa group, and the Daichi Kangyo group. These six groups embrace some 188 companies, and accounted for 15% of Japan's GNP in 1986.

The web extends as many of the members of the above *zaibatsu* groups have very strong families of their own, a gathering of subsidiaries and subcontractors whose economic well-being hinges on the whims of the parent company. In all, there are 28 such corporate groups, some of which belong to the *zaibatsu* families, along with some that don't.

"Organizations are living entities, but they get the breath of life not from the power of politics, or the power of socialism, or the power of the peace constitution," noted *Brutus*. "They get their breath of life from the power of cold, hard cash."

THE 28 INDIVIDUAL COMPANY GROUPS

NTT (Nippon Telegraph & Telephone), Mitsubishi Corp., Hitachi, Mitsui & Co., Toyota

THE SIX MODERN ZAIBATSU GROUPS	Mitsui Group	Mitsubishi Group	Sumitomo Group	Fuyoh Group	Sanwa Group	Ichi-kan Group
Banks	Mitsui Bank	Mitsubishi Bank	Sumitomo Bank	Fuji Bank	Sanwa Bank	Daiichi Kangyo Bank
Insurance Co.s	Mitsui Life	Meiji Life	Sumitomo Life	Yasuda Life	Nihon Life	Asahi Life
Sogo Shosha	Mitsui & Co.	Mitsubishi Corp.	Sumitomo Corp	Marubeni	Nichimen	C.Itoh
Construction Co.s	Mitsui Constr.	Mitsubishi Constr.	Sumitomo Constr.	Taisei Constr.	Ohbayashi Corp.	Shimizu Construction
Food & Beverage	Nippon Flour	Kirin Beer	–	Nisshin Flour	Itoh Ham	–
				Sapporo Beer	Suntory	
Textile Co.s	Toray	Mitsubishi Rayon	–	Nisshinbo Textile	Unitika/Teijin	Asahi Chemical
Chemicals Co.s	Mitsui Toatsu	Mitsubishi Chem.	Sumitomo Chem.	Showa Electric	Sekisui Chemicals	Kyowa Hakko
Chemicals (con't)	Mitsui PetrChem	Mitsubishi Gas	Sumitomo Bakelite	Kureha Chemicals	Tanabe Pharm.	Shiseido/Lion
Electric Equipment	Toshiba	Mitsubishi Electric	NEC	Hitachi	Hitachi	Hitachi/Fujitsu
					Sharp / Kyocera	
Transportation	Mitsui Shipbldg	Mitsubishi Hvy Ind.	–	–	Hitachi Shipbuilding	Kawasaki Heavy Ind.
Transport (cont)	Toyota	Mitsubishi Motors	–	Nissan	Daihatsu	Isuzu
Precision machinery	–	Nikon	–	Canon	HOYA	Asahi Optical
Dept Stores	Mitsukoshi	–	–	–	Takashimaya	Seibu Saison
Distrib. /com.	MOL Shipping	NYK Shipping	Sumitomo Wrhsng	Tobu RR	Hankyu RR	Nittsu Express
				Keihin Kyuko RR	Nittsu Express	Kawasaki Shipping

Motors, Matsushita Electric, Nomura Securities, Nissan Motors, Nippon Steel, Toshiba, Mitsubishi Heavy Industries, NEC, Nippon Kokan, Sumitomo Metals, Kobe Steel, Fujitsu, Honda, Sony, Mitsubishi Chemicals, Asahi Chemicals Industry, Sumitomo Chemicals, Daiei, Tokyu Corp., Toray, Itoh Yokado, Ajinomoto, Seibu RR, and Shinetsu Chemicals. (Listed in descending order of total paid-in capital according to consolidated financial statements for the first semester of fiscal 1987.)

ZAPPING THE RIM

Nintendo Co., Japan's leading exporter of family computers and video games, reported record net profits of $227.6 million in 1989, up 11% from the previous year, thanks to the enduring market for video games in the world.

GREATER CHINA

A "China Economic Circle," encompassing the mainland, Hong Kong, Macao, and Taiwan, was proposed by noted Chinese economist, Xue Jingxiao, director of the department of international economy in Beijing's Nankai University. This "circle" would help to give free rein to the comparative advantages of labor, capital, resources, and high-tech in the region, according to Xue's blueprint. During the first phase, which would last until the end of the century, the major task would be to straighten out China's economy, to improve the investment environment, and to attract more foreign capital. During the second and final phase, which would last a further 20 years, China would become fully integrated in the world markets.

MALAYSIA'S ELECTRONICS BOOM

With ample resources and a low-cost labor force, Malaysia is seeing a boom in its electronics industry which is growing by up to 12% per year. American semiconductor firms as well as Taiwanese and Japanese entrepreneurs have been investing heavily in the country. The boom began with the country's establishment of a free trade zone in the island state of Penang two decades ago, and now seven out of the 10 largest U.S. integrated circuit producers have a stake in the country.

JAPANESE RICHER THAN AMERICANS

Citing the average per capita income of the 121 million Japanese in 1986 as $17,000 compared to the $16,000 for 242 million Americans, Britain's *Economist* claimed that Japanese were now richer than Americans. But the statistics are misleading suggests *American Demographics* because the Japanese standard of living lagged far behind their American counterparts "especially in the areas of housing, open spaces and social security programs, not to mention the toll taken by long working hours and little time for family life." Japanese costs are high, with the average family spending almost 30% of its income on food—as much as 35% in lower income households. Savings, however, were also high, with the average Japanese family accumulating $53,000.

BRIDGING CULTURES

Much as he obviously deplores "Japan-bashing," Sony's board chairman Akio Morita thinks that the fault is not all on one side, and that for relations between the two countries to really improve it is necessary for the Japanese to be less inward-looking and culturally separate. "The responsibility," he says, "is on our side. We should change; we should not be strangers." Morita leads an organization formed by the Japan Federation of Economic Organizations (Keidanren), called the Council for Better Investment in the United States, whose aim is to persuade both Japanese and Americans to be more flexible, adjustable, and tolerant enough to understand each other. Such changes, he admits, usually need a generation to mature because people's conceptions are too slow and never seem to catch up with the fast-changing world; however, there

was no time to waste and people must take it upon themselves "to loose the cultural bonds that hold them to limited perspectives."

New Rim Buzzword: "Global localization," coined by Akio Morita, describes a new strategy Japanese companies are using in their bid to internationalize their overseas operations. "GL" means local people should manage the operation, produce the products —and even do the R&D, says Morita.

CHINA'S "WRONGFUL" EXPORTS

Impractical, or "wrongful exports," have plagued China's economy in recent years. Among cases cited by the Chinese publication *Economic Information,* a company in Guizhou in South China bought 200 tons of scarce aluminum at about $1,837 a ton, and exported it to a Hong Kong businessman who resold it to a Tianjin factory in North China at $2,400 a ton. With its domestic raw material prices so much lower than world prices, localities have a great incentive to export, according to the publication. But overall management and controls have been so lax that China has been losing heavily in raw materials trade. The raw materials shortage has affected the country's industrialization program.

JAPAN'S EXTRAVAGANT EXPENSE ACCOUNTS

Japan's Mitsui group spends about $115,000 a day on company entertainment according to *Shukan Diamond* magazine which ranked Japan's biggest business entertainment spenders for 1987:

1. Mitsui & Co.   Y5.6 billion
                          ($43 million)

2. Mitsubishi Corp.   Y5.03 billion
                              ($39 million)
3. Nomura Securities   Y5.01 billion
                              ($38 million)
4. Nikko Securities   Y4.00 billion
                              ($30 million)
5. C. Itoh Co.   Y3.74 billion
                              ($29 million)

The *sogo shosha* conglomerates and securities companies topped the list. Commented Mitsui spokesman Shimada Seiichi, Planning Department Manager: "If you divide Y5.76 billion by 250 working days, and figure that one out of 10 of our 4,000 domestic employees uses entertainment funds, you can see that it's only a paltry Y50,000 (about $385) a day.

"For example, if I had dinner at a hotel for Y20,000 ($153) and there were three others with me that's already Y80,000 ($615). Four times a week would bring the total to Y320,000 ($2,461), which extrapolates to Y1.3 million ($10,000) a month. Of course I wouldn't be using this much for my own purposes, but it costs about this much. Japanese rarely say what they really feel, you know, so after dinner, you have to go for drinks. To us, it seems that entertainment money should be put in the sales.

"Entertainment costs are high because prices are high. Prices are high because land costs so much. They say that Japanese companies spend Y4 trillion ($30.7 billion) on entertainment. Well, two thirds of that is paying for the land. So the cost of entertainment won't go down until land prices go down."

That may be a while, as *Shukan Shincho* magazine observed.

LIGHTING UP THE RIM

Foreign cigarettes gained a 12% share of the Japanese market for the first time in 1988, according to the Tobacco Institute of Japan. Sales of imported cigarettes in fiscal 1987 reached $3.4 billion, up 121% from the previous year.

JAPANESE BODYGUARDS

After a wave of urban terror in Japan and kidnappings of Japanese executives in the Philippines, Japan's first bodyguard business was launched in 1988. Named Japan Secret Service Company, it is staffed by 10 ex-Japan secret service men who protect clients for retainers ranging from $7,600 to $15,000 per month.

LHASA LAMAS LINE-UP LUMBER

Tibetan management theory is enjoying a heyday of sorts. One local firm, the Tibetan Gangjian Development Corp., was formed by a group of 700 lamas from the Zhaxi Lhunbo Temple. After raising $1 million in cash, the monks set up a lumber mill, a transportation network that has lamas driving trucks and acting as tour guides, and also opened a chain of tea and silk trading stores. One store in Lhasa netted $100,000 during its first year on sales of $800,000. Lamas are now being trained in the tantric arts of accounting, cooking, and computer technology.

SPENDERS CUTTING TRADE SURPLUSES

Japan's catch phrase of "export or die" has changed to "import and buy," according to one Tokyo broker, and the consumer boom that began in Japan has spread to other countries in the region spurred by U.S. pressure on these countries to cut their trade surpluses. Militant workers and more generous employers have resulted in much more disposable income; and although the frugal Taiwanese are still saving roughly one third of their earnings, they are also buying more consumer goods. "They are getting richer and becoming big spenders," says the manager of a Taipei department store.

NESTLE-*SAN*

Giving the lie to the argument that foreign firms have a difficult time in the Japanese market is Nestle, the multinational which has operated in the country since 1913 and whose president, Alexander F. O. Yost, says they operate in the Japanese way, "so as not to cause the employees to worry too much." The company has lifetime employment and promotion by seniority—"in short, everything an ordinary Japanese firm has."

HELPING HAND

All the little problems that foreigners in Japan find so difficult—such as getting an apartment, doing market research, and hiring translators and interpreters—can now be dropped into the lap of Culture Shock, a Tokyo-based company founded by Iwatsuki Kazuko, who experienced similar frustrations while living in the U.S. as an exchange student.

THE SOUTH KOREAN THAT SAYS "WAY TO GO!"

South Korea has its own equivalent of American industrialist and book author Lee Iacocca. His name is Kim Woo Choong, and he's the chairman and founder of the giant Korean conglomerate, the Daewoo group. One of the richest men in Korea, he is now a best-selling author with his book, "It's a Big World and There's Lots to Be Done."

His collection of Confucian-style essays about the work ethic has sold over a million copies since it was published. Among his revelations, as quoted in *Asiaweek* magazine: "Sweating at work is better than sweating at the health club and it's a shortcut to good health." Kim's day is said to begin just after dawn and, always saving time, he usually shaves in his car on his way to work.

LABOR MOBILITY—PACRIM'S ACHILLES HEEL

Despite the rapid growth in recent years of intraregional Pacific Rim trade and investment, Asian economic integration is still missing a key third ingredient—namely, a steady and rising flow of human capital within Asia. This lack of labor mobility will be one of the biggest challenges for the Asian economies through the 1990s, predicted a study by Merrill Lynch Capital Market's Singapore-based research group.

"Alongside merchandise and financial capital, labor is the other important factor of production to sustaining long-term economic growth," the report noted. "Yet, despite severe labor shortages in several countries around the region—in particular, the four

Asian NIEs (the newly industrialized economies, including Singapore, Hong Kong, Taiwan, and South Korea) and, more selectively, in Malaysia, and Thailand—there is no coordinated effort being made to ease this constraint in concert with Asia's labor-surplus economies which would mainly be China, India, Indonesia and . . . the Philippines."

Among the reasons cited for the seemingly insurmountable labor barriers are the region's diverse "social, cultural, racial, religious, linguistic, historical, political, and economic" differences.

ROLLING ALONG IN INDIA

Jagraj Singh Sahney, president of New Delhi-based Sahney Skate Company, operates the nation's first and only roller skate and skateboard manufacturing enterprise. He has even begun exporting skateboards to Bangladesh and Pakistan. Sahney, the national rollerskating champion of India, estimates there are about 800 practicing roller skaters in the entire subcontinent. He doesn't know why, he says, but 90% of them are Sikhs.

LITTLE TRAMP BACK IN STYLE

At least 28 Japanese companies are making Charlie Chaplin brand goods—neckties, dolls, etc.—according to Douglas Kenrick (Far East), Ltd., which owns the rights to the late comedian's name and image.

CHINA SHOWS ENTERPRISE

There were more than 5,000 joint ventures, cooperative ventures, and wholly foreign-owned enterprises operating in China by 1989. In the five special economic zones of Shenzhen, Zhuhai, Shantou, Xiamen, and Hainan, output of these enterprises in the first three quarters of 1988 reached about $1.26 billion, accounting for about one third of the total, according to the State Statistical Bureau.

DEMONSTRATING THEIR INDEPENDENCE

Independent businesses failed to report $5.17 billion in income in fiscal 1987, according to Japan's National Tax Administration Agency.

TOURISM TO PRIME TRADE

In 1989, South Korean business tycoon Chung Ju-Yung, founder and honorary chairman of the giant Hyundai Group, made the first business trip to North Korea since the Korean Peninsula was divided in 1945. The plan is to develop tourist facilities on North Korea's scenic Kumngang Mountains as an initial step toward warming trade relations with the north.

HEAVY METAL

Most of China's large enterprises belong to basic industries, according to the results of a study of 1987's top 100 industrial enterprises in the country. Of the top 100 industries, 63 were mining and metallurgical factories. Of the top 10, eight were oil enterprises and iron and steel works.

ASIAN CHRONICLES

THE EMPEROR OF CHINA WONDERS ABOUT THE BARBARIANS

The following is a translated transcript of a conversation held in 1851 between the Qing Dynasty Chinese Emperor Xian Feng and an official from South China's Guangdong province concerning the activities of the foreign barbarians in the region. The original transcript fell into the hands of British statesman Lord Elgin (1811–1863), who headed a special mission to China to negotiate an end of the second Opium War. That settlement resulted in the Tientsin Treaty of 1858, which gave further territorial privileges to foreign powers in China. This excerpt was incorporated in the chronicles of Lord Elgin's private secretary, Laurence Oliphant.

Emperor: *Are the English barbarians quiet at the present time?*

Official: They are so far quiet.

Q: *Will no trouble be caused by their trade at some future period?*

A: In the nature of barbarians there is much to suspect. A communication received from them two or three months ago raised several questions in language of a menacing character. Seu and Yeh [Guangdong officials] perfectly understand their trickiness, and as it is only by being resolute and positive that they can deal with them. They employ no word in their replies either more or less than is sufficient fully to meet what is said by the barbarians.

Q: *How are you informed of what passes in their countries?*

A: In foreign parts [literally, in the "outer seas"] there are newspapers. In these everything that concerns any nation is minutely recorded, and these we have it in our power to procure. And as the barbarians cannot dispense with our people in the work of interpretation, Seu and Yeh manage to make their employees furnish them privately every month with all particulars.

Q: *Have you seen any barbarians or barbarian ships?*

A: Your servant has seen a Flowery Flag (American) steamer on the Canton River. There were barbarians on board the vessel, all dressed in white, both men and women. But she was too far off your servant's vessel for him to see them well.

Q: *What nation is the Flowery Flag?*

A: The American. The trade of the nation is very great; it is very rich and powerful, and yet not troublesome.

Q: *How is it that America is rich and powerful, and yet not troublesome?*

A: As a general rule, the outer barbarians trade because their nature is so covetous. If one of them breaks the peace, the prosperity of the other's trade is marred. Thus the English are at this moment beggared (and so not likely to go to war); but if they were to break the peace, it is not on their own trade alone that injury would be inflicted: other nations are therefore certain to object to any outrageous proceeding on their part.

MAKING CHEAPER TOYS

Hong Kong toymakers have been shifting their operations to Indonesia and Malaysia in addition to China, the Philippines, and Thailand. Indonesia and Malaysia attract Hong Kong toymakers with their GSP (Generalized System of Preferences) exports benefits to the United States. Macau is also a GSP beneficiary and is allowed to import Chinese labor. China remains the biggest area of concentration for production by the Hong Kong toymaking industry, which is the territory's fifth-largest export earner. The United States bought 54% of combined Hong Kong domestic toy exports and China-made exports in 1988.

CHINA'S TRASHY DIAMONDS

Outdated and inappropriate machinery are being blamed for the unsatisfactory state of China's diamond industry, now largely restricted to producing lowgrade industrial diamonds for which there is little demand. The higher strength diamonds needed for drill bits, blades, and cutting machines account for only 25% of the country's output, and at present large batches of these are having to be imported.

WOULD YOU INSURE YOUR CAR WITH THIS COUNTRY?

The People's Insurance Company of China is touting for business with foreign countries, particularly in the satellite launching industry, and claims that it can offer the best rates in the international insurance market. The company's vice president. Cheng Wanzhu, says that it was encouraged to offer insurance for the launching of a U.S. Westar-6s telecommunications satellite because of the highly successful launch rate of the Long March-3 carrier rocket by which it was to be projected.

THE BEST 100 FEMALE-RUN COMPANIES IN JAPAN

Tokyo Shoko Research did a survey in 1989 of the 100 best female-run companies according to revenues. First of all, the number of companies with female presidents grew by some 4,000 companies in 1988, to 17,155 in all—3.8% of all corporations. Still, most of these female presidents came into their jobs at the death of their husband or father. Of the best 100 female-run companies:

Inherited from husband—60
Inherited from father—18
Inherited from brother—2
Entrepreneur—15
Hired president—5

Who are leaders among the 100 companies?

	Name	Age	Industry	Revenues (Y million)
1.	Noma Sawako	45	Publishing	152,275
2.	Akiyama Kiyo	71	Pharmaceuticals	75,013
3.	Yano Keiko	58	Petroleum	69,277
4.	Iida Yuko	49	Spirits	64,978
5.	Koizuml Kiyoko	70	Clothing	61,710

TAIWAN PLANS PR CAMPAIGN TO IMPROVE ITS IMAGE

Officials of Taiwan's Trade and Economic Affairs ministries are planning a campaign to upgrade the image of the island's products after being told that they are less well-regarded in the public mind than other Asian producers. A Gallup poll in the United States found that 53% of Americans believe Taiwan-made products are inferior to those from mainland China, according to a report in the *United Daily News*. Taiwan's trade office noted that South Korea, whose economy was largely dominated by large enterprises, found it easier to promote itself on a mass scale than Taiwan with its smaller companies.

BUILDING SHIPS FOR LESS

By 1997, China may become the world's biggest shipbuilding center, according to American shipbuilding industry analysts. In the past decade, China has become a major contender in the international shipbuilding industry. The price of ships built in China is about 10% less than in leading rival South Korea, mainly because of lower labor costs. Nearly four fifths of all ship tonnage made in China in 1988, amounting to 410,000 deadweight tons, were built for export, according to the Xinhua News Service.

TAIWAN ON THAILAND
by Jack Maisano

Taiwan's new breed of senior officials are finding a lot of good reasons for dumping hard-line anticommunist ideology for economic reality. The result: More contacts with Eastern Bloc countries, Vietnam, and mainland China—all taboo not too long ago. Three of those reasons are as follows.

First, while Thailand is the "hot spot" for Taiwanese money (U.S.$1 billion invested in 1988), many manufacturers prefer mainland China for linguistic, cultural, and patriotic reasons. Direct investment is still a capital offence, but the government turns a blind eye to the estimated U.S.$200 million (but probably higher) invested in shoe, textile, toy, and other industries.

A marriage of Taiwanese management, technology, and capital with mainland resources, land, and labor would be an unbeatable combination. Even senior Taiwan

officials are coming to the conclusion that it might be desirable (read, economically necessary) to cooperate with the PRC. A bilateral trade commission is reportedly on the verge of being established, as normally "traditional" manufacturers' associations put pressure on the government to allow direct investment (which would imply direct communications, trade agreements, legal agreements, and so forth).

Second, the U.S. export market is drying up as the Taiwan dollar soars in value and export prices rise. As a result, government and business leaders are ready to jump into bed with just about anybody, including the once hated communists. In the struggle between old hardliners and the Chiang Kai-Shek era and younger pragmatic types, the latter seem to have the upper hand.

Third, in the race to gain advantage in socialist bloc markets, Taiwan is in fierce competition with South Korea. In the case of Seoul's budding relationship with China, it's also a question of face. The Taiwanese can't afford to let the Koreans get their feet in the door to the motherland first.

AUSTRALIA

DOWN UNDER PREJUDICE

Australia's potential income from Japanese tourists could reach $800 million by 1992 and both this and Japan's billion-dollar trade deficit with the country could be jeopardized by the growing anti-Japanese sentiment, consular spokesmen have warned. Conspicuous Japanese investment in hotels, golf courses, homes, and shops along Queensland's Gold Coast has led to public protests by residents "bordering on racism," but the New Zealand-born chairman of an anti-Japanese investment body seems ironically unaware that New Zealanders were still the biggest foreign investors in that area. Warren Bird, and economist with Lloyds Bank, says that Australians ought to regard the investments as a sign of confidence and "should not lose sight of the fact that [Australia] is running a current account deficit and substantial external debt," which it needed investment funds to finance.

Meanwhile in Hong Kong, immigrations consultants were bemoaning what they saw as Australia's "anti-Asian stance," which they attributed to narrow thinking. "If Australia sees itself as part of Asia-Pacific," one observed, "it has to show much greater tolerance toward immigrants from Asia. Countries everywhere which had been largely homogeneous are becoming multi-cultural and it is very important that Australia comes to grips with this reality."

AUSTRALIA AT THE CROSSROADS
by Jack Lowenstein

Two hundred years after the arrival of the first Europeans in Australia, the country is turning from the West and toward its booming neighbors to the north. But there are still problems to overcome.

In many ways they remain the odd couple: East Asia, populous, good at manufacturing and forming a huge regional market, and Australia, a sparsely populated, still mainly European country, superbly endowed with a wide range of raw materials and commodities.

They share a time zone and—for Australia at least—trade between the two is increasingly important. More than 40% of all Australia's exports now go to Asia, half of that to

Japan alone, and in the short term most economists believe the strength of the Australian economy depends directly on the dramatic increase in Japanese demand which in turn is firing up the rest of Asia.

But how close are East Asia and Australia to forming a true regional partnership? How substantial are the links? Despite more than a decade of expanded diplomatic relations, easier immigration flows and, most recently, vigorous two-way tourism, the cultural gap remains enormous.

At the same time long-standing Australian suspicion of Japanese good faith in investment and trade matters has if anything grown as a result of bitter negotiations (in 1988) over cooking coal and frustration over import restrictions on beef and other food products.

It is a frequent lament of Australians that the country fails to take full advantage of the growth to its north. Because of this, ANZ Bank economist Andrew Mohl believes Australia's integration into the wider Asian economy remains a dream. "We haven't capitalized on the growth in the Asian region all that well," he says. "It remains a potential for us, but we are still riding on the sheep's back."

Others believe progress has been greater.

Mark Fulton, strategist at the Sydney investment bank, County Natwest Australia, sees Japan, Australia, and Asia's newly industrialized countries, as a single economic entity. But he warns of tensions ahead: "If one part of that equation screws the other, in the end the system becomes unstable," he says.

Comparing the relationship with that of North and South America, he claims it is in Asia's interest to help Australia, its commodities and recreation base, to get itself back into good economic health. In particular, he worries that Japan will miss its long-term objectives by taking too much advantage of Australia.

Interestingly, it is a fear shared by many Japanese who know Australia well. In particular, warns Itaru Suzuki, chairman of the giant trading company Mitsui and Co. (Australia), Japan must be careful not to offend already fraying sensitivities Down Under through its investment activities.

For all the excitement of their newfound wealth and the low prices of Australian real estate and tourism assets, he says, the Japanese must ask themselves how they would feel if Australians with big check books started buying up large chunks of central Tokyo.

Excerpted from article by Jack Lowenstein. © *Asian Business* magazine, Far East Trade Press, Ltd., 1988.

SOLD ON THE GOLD COAST

Japanese investors have been buying up hotels and real estate in Australia's Gold Coast, a 40-kilometer stretch of tropical sun and surf in Queensland. Japanese tourism to Queensland increased 125% to over 82,000 in 1988, and is expected to increase five times by the year 2000, according to a major study. Japanese honeymooning couples typically spend about $1,740 a day during an average three-day stay. More than half of the Gold Coast's 5-star hotels are Japanese-owned.

But Warner Brothers has opened the first international film theme park in Queensland. The $50 million Warner Film World features such Warner-owned characters as Superman, Bugs Bunny, and the Roadrunner.

BUT THE BACKLASH COMETH . . .

Tous Haus, a Tokyo-based developer, pulled out of Queensland's biggest tourism project, the 1,100-hectare Villa Cairns condominium development in North Queensland, allegedly because of growing anti-Japanese sentiment in Australia. Yukihiro Handa, a Japanese property investor, reported this decision in a speech he gave at a Property Management Institute seminar in Auckland. Japan has overtaken the United Kingdom and the United States as the leading source of foreign investment Down Under. Now, the Japanese are taking a serious look at shifting some of their investments to New Zealand.

Overseas demand for Australian residential property has been so strong that one Japanese investor reportedly bought 42 houses in New South Wales without even bothering to leave his car to inspect the properties.

NICS ON THE LINE

WHAT'S IN AN NIC?

The term NIC (for "newly industrialized country") should be changed to NIE ("newly industrialized economy"), complained China, pointing out that neither Taiwan nor Hong Kong are actually "countries."

ASIA'S MIRACLE ECONOMIES: *ARE THEY A DYING BREED?*

by Walden Bello

Today, the darlings of development economists and development agencies are the so-called "Newly Industrializing Countries" (NICs) of East Asia. On the surface, it is not difficult to understand why. In 1987, while other economies were either stagnating or growing marginally, Singapore, Hong Kong, Taiwan, and South Korea registered an 11% average rise in Gross Domestic Product (GDP). Most impressive of all was South Korea, whose economy grew 12% despite a severe political crisis.

As with every new fashion in the volatile world of international economics, many myths about the NICs have been casually passed off as truths. For example, former

President Ronald Reagan noted in his 1985 State of the Union address that, "America's economic success . . . can be repeated a hundred times in a hundred nations. Many countries in East Asia and the Pacific have few resources other than the enterprise of their own people. But through . . . free markets, they've soared ahead of centralized economies."

Reagan's interpretation of the NICs' success relied on two prominent fallacies: that the NICs are classic free-market economies and that they offer an ideal model of development for other third-world countries. The opposite is closer to the truth. The NICs have achieved a high rate of growth precisely because they eschewed a *laissez-faire* approach to development in favor of active state planning and intervention in the economy. Moreover, the NICs' surge was facilitated by a unique set of historical circumstances, including massive U.S. economic aid in the 1950s, the stimulus provided by the Vietnam war, and the relatively open world trading system that existed in the 1960s and 1970s. These conditions have disappeared.

In fact, the NICs' very success in exporting to the United States and other first world markets has made it difficult for other third-world countries to base their development on export-led growth. Indeed, even as Reagan and others held them up as models, the NICs themselves are now profoundly threatened by the disappearance of the liberal international economic order and the internal conditions that made their rapid growth possible.

TRADE FAIRY TALES

Mainstream interpretations of the NIC model convey an image of economies that have successfully harnessed the two engines of capitalist development: free markets and free trade. In fact, Taiwan and South Korea—the NICs most often cited as models of industrial development for the rest of the third world—built up highly protected domestic markets at the same time that they were mounting a massive export drive to take advantage of the relatively open U.S. market in the 1960s and 1970s.

While both countries made textiles and garments the cutting edge of their export drive in the late 1960s, high tariffs and other import restrictions made it difficult for foreign imports of those same products to penetrate their domestic markets.

Moreover, both the Taiwanese and South Korean governments are interventionist states

par excellence. In South Korea, an authoritarian state, working closely with huge monopolistic conglomerates called *chaebol,* targeted promising manufacturing industries like steel, electronics, and cars for development, and supported them with a variety of direct and indirect subsidies.

The Economic Planning Board evolved into a super-ministry whose power to determine the direction of the South Korean economy rivaled that of its model, the Japanese Ministry for International Trade and Industry (MITI). The board channeled local and foreign capital into favored industries by using a variety of mechanisms, including preferential financing, protectionist barriers against competing imports, and tax incentives. But most attractive were the prospects of monopoly profits that awaited the conglomerates should they pioneer production in the industries favored by government planners.

The NICs' rise to economic prominence is also intimately related to unique international conditions that prevailed in the last two decades. First, when the NICs started their export drive in the mid-1960s, following the lead of Japan, the U.S. market was relatively open to foreign goods. Despite early attempts by the United States to impose trade barriers in textiles, the NICs had relatively easy access to the most prosperous market in the world.

Precisely because of the export success of Japan and the NICs, other third-world countries seeking to imitate their strategy now confront markets in the United States and Europe that are fortified by close to 160 nontariff barriers to trade. Euphemistically termed "orderly marketing agreements" or "voluntary export restraints," these trade restrictions apply to a range of products, including textiles, clothing, electronics, footwear, autos, and steel. The United States and the European Economic Community have imposed 14 voluntary export restraints on South Korea, four on Brazil, and 21 on other developing countries.

The status of South Korea and Taiwan as "frontline" allies in the struggle against communism also provided a crucial boost to their economies. The countries were the beneficiaries of an Asian version of the Marshall Plan. Between 1951 and 1965, the United States pumped about $1.5 billion of economic aid into Taiwan (in addition to billions of dollars in military aid). During this time, U.S. aid financed the equivalent of 95% of Taiwan's trade deficit. Economic aid to South Korea was even larger, coming to about $6 billion between 1945 and 1978—almost as much as the total aid provided to the entire African continent during the same period. More than 80% of South Korea's imports in the 1950s were financed by U.S. economic assistance.

Their strategic importance to the United States allowed the Asian NICs to implement economic policies that were frowned upon elsewhere by the managers of the international economy. The United States intentionally overlooked the strong economic interventionist policies of the Taiwanese and South Korean governments and their highly protected internal markets. At the same time, the International Monetary Fund and the World Bank—institutions dominated by the United States—were telling the rest of the third world to drastically scale down the economic role of the state and lower protective barriers to imports.

Finally, the Vietnam War was to the Taiwanese and the Korean economies what the Korean War was a decade earlier to the Japanese economy: a vital stimulus to economic take-off. Vietnam provided what University of California at Berkeley sociologist Thomas Gold described as an "incalculable boost" to the Taiwanese economy in the form of U.S. purchases of agricultural and industrial commodities, spending for "rest and recreation,"

and contract work for local firms in Vietnam.

The South Korean economy also benefited from U.S. purchases and recreational spending. But most significant were the big Vietnam-related construction contracts that firms like Hyundai were awarded as part of "offset" arrangements under which the United States paid for the services of Korean troops. By the end of the war in 1975, overseas work contracts had reached a total of $850 million annually—accounting for almost 20% of the value of Korean exports.

These external conditions were vital components of the NICs' formula for "success." Yet the NICs' basic strategy of export-oriented industrialization using cheap labor also depended heavily on repressive labor policies. In both Taiwan and South Korea, labor was kept cheap by authoritarian regimes that deployed police and military power at the first signs of workers' organizing. For example, when the Park government came to power in South Korea in 1961, one of its first acts was to ban all strikes and decertify unions.

In South Korea, such policies produced a 58-hour work-week—the longest of any country surveyed by the International Labor Organization; the world's highest industrial accident rate; and a working class that remains relatively impoverished. In 1985, 60% of South Korean workers earned less than $110 per month, far below the government's estimated minimum monthly income of $335 needed to support a family of five.

Academic apologists imply, however, that today's glittering statistics make up for a repressive past. Per capita gross domestic product (GDP) now stands at $2,900 for South Korea and about $4,100 for Taiwan, compared to $600 for the Philippines. The economic profile of Taiwan and South Korea is no longer typically third-world, where 80% to 90% of the labor force is in agriculture or services. Industry's share of GDP now comes to 40% in South Korea and 45% in Taiwan; agriculture's share has dropped to 15% in South Korea and 8% in Taiwan; and services contribute about 45% in both economies.

MIRACLES UNDONE?

Recent developments have revealed that the NICs' "economic miracle" is being challenged on several fronts. First of all, the international economic climate conducive to the NICs' continued growth is quickly disappearing, as the United States abandons the liberal free-trade regime that it set up in the 1940s and 1950s.

Ironically, Reagan's paragons of economic virtue became the prime targets of Washington's trade warfare. In what amounted to a declaration of war, David Mulford of the Treasury Department warned the Asian "tigers": "Although the NICs may be regarded as tigers because they are strong, ferocious traders, the analogy has a darker side. Tigers live in the jungle, and by the law of the jungle. They are a shrinking population."

The multipronged U.S. assault has included ending tariff-free entry of NIC goods into this country. Washington has also been prying open NIC markets to imports from the United States such as cigarettes, whose domestic market is being eroded by anti-smoking initiatives.

NIC exports are also being hurt by U.S. insistence that the countries revalue their currencies upward relative to the dollar. The New Taiwan Dollar has appreciated by about 40% against the dollar since 1986, while the Korean *won* more than 20% against the dollar in 1988.

"We can absorb wage increases," one Korean textile manager noted, "but we can't take any more appreciation."

In short, if in the 1960s and 1970s the forces of the world market favored the NICs, by the mid-1980s these very forces were turning against them.

In the short term, currency appreciation is a major concern of the NICs. But of all the changes occurring in the international economy in the 1980s, most worrisome to them over the long term is their loss of "comparative advantage" in cheap labor. Even without pressures from unions, rising real wages have been making the NICs' labor-intensive industries less competitive, encouraging manufacturers to search for cheap labor elsewhere. Thus, Uniden, a Japanese telecommunications equipment manufacturer, shifted its major factories from Taiwan and Hong Kong to the Philippines and China to take advantage of the wage differentials.

This has provoked increasing criticism by NIC economists, business people, and politicians of "footloose" multinationals interested only in profits. But the emigration of capital is not limited to Japanese and U.S. multinationals. An estimated $1.5 billion of capital from Taiwan and Hong Kong has moved to China, where labor is 10 times cheaper than in those countries. Even as Taiwan's Kuomimtang government continues to emit anticommunist propaganda, Taiwanese capitalists now view the workers of a socialist society as the key to their continued profitability.

Currently, South Korean capital is considering moving to China and following Taiwanese and Hong Kong capital to other cheap labor havens like the Caribbean and Southeast Asia. Explaining his move to open a branch in Indonesia, the president of one of South Korea's most successful timber-processing firms commented, "We have no choice if we are to survive."

To try to slow the erosion of the competitiveness of their labor-intensive industries, small- and medium-sized entrepreneurs in some of the NICs have resorted to importing cheap labor. Around Taipei, some factories are now run largely with illegal foreign labor from the Philippines, Indonesia, and Thailand, while the government looks the other way.

This trend has spawned its own set of problems. A labor system similar to that which developed in Europe in the 1960s and 1970s is quickly emerging in Taiwan and Singapore: a two-tier labor force composed of poorly paid, unorganized "guest workers" and better paid, organized indigenous workers. The presence of foreign workers dampens the wage demands of the local labor force, while chauvinism is encouraged to keep foreign workers in their place. This is a proven recipe for intense frictions between the two groups, and such conflict could further destabilize those economies.

Despite attempts to delay the inevitable, economic planners in the NICs view their labor-intensive industries, especially footwear, textiles, and apparel, as "sunset industries." They have staked the future of their economies on their ability to move up to "high-tech" or "skill-intensive" industries like computers, advanced consumer electronics, automobiles, and high fashion.

This, however, is easier said than done. In South Korea, the traditionally militant workers in the textile and apparel industries are likely to resist the technocrats' plan to "structural transformation." Indeed, the labor movements in both Taiwan and South Korea, which are now rapidly organizing after decades of repression, do not share the goal of "national development," traditionally formulated by big government and big business.

"We, the workers, will set our own agenda," a young Korean metalworker noted. Their agenda appears to consist of the following points: belt-tightening for workers is over, wages will be raised, profits will be cut. South Korean workers have also become in-creasingly aware of the ways in which employers pit them against workers in the Philippines and other Asian countries.

An equally formidable problem in the high-tech strategy is the NICs' still minimal capability to develop the technologies of capital-intensive and skill-intensive industries. As one of South Korea's leading economists put it, "We still turn out cars with Mitsubishi engines and, let's face it, our electronics industry still largely consists of assembling Japanese components."

The statistics are eloquent on this point. In 1987, while the focus of attention was on its trade surplus with the United States, South Korea had a deficit of $5.2 billion in its trade with Japan—mainly due to the importation of sophisticated electronic components, automobile parts, and machinery. Japanese components account for an incredible 85% of the value of a Korean-made color television set. Despite their joint ventures with Korean *chaebol* like Hyundai, the Japanese corporate giants are very tightfisted when it comes to transferring technology.

Two developments in the past few years, in fact, have exposed the illusion of the "Korean" car. What U.S. and Japanese capital has had a key role in creating, it can easily take away. Mitsubishi decided to market the best-selling Hyundai Excel in the United States as a Japanese car under its own name—the Mitsubishi Precis. And GM, which owns 50% of Daewoo Motor Company, vetoed Daewoo's attempt to market its Lemans model in Eastern Europe. GM decided that the Lemans, which is just the Korean version of GM's "World Car," could only be marketed by GM's European affiliates.

In their strategy to ward off the stagnation that threatens the Asian NIC economies, government planners also emphasize diversifying export markets and increasing reliance on their long-neglected domestic markets. but like the move to high-tech, these transitions will not be easy.

Exports to Japan are up these days, but NIC entrepreneurs know that Japan's watchful protectionist bureaucrats will eventually limit their market share. Already, Japanese knit-wear producers are pushing for strict quotas on rising Korean imports—a move that is seen as a test case for broader protectionist moves by the Japanese textile and garment industry.

This leaves the domestic market—and here the obstacles to further growth are not insignificant. Although absolute income levels in the NICs have been rising, they have been accompanied by an increasingly unequal distribution of income. That could spell problems ahead if growth tapers off. Government planners will also have to convince Taiwanese and Korean manufacturers to desist from moving to the cheap labor Mecca that is China, and to become good Keynesians instead—that is, pay their workers higher wages to create more purchasing power and boost demand for their goods.

Finally, the technocrats will somehow have to find a way to resolve a serious contradiction between plans to enlarge the domestic market and efforts to move up to high-tech industries. Making the transition from labor-intensive to capital and skill-intensive industries will involve shifting to technologies that absorb much less labor, creating the specter of growing structural unemployment and stagnant markets.

The current troubles of the NICs will not translate into more than a superficial boom for others. For example, Thailand, now touted as the next NIC, will eventually run up against the barriers of protectionism and extreme capital mobility—once its wage rates rise relative to its third-world neighbors.

In short, the NIC model of development increasingly appears to be one whose time has passed. While the U.S. Central Intelligence Agency is often wrong in its predictions, an assessment it made in 1984 when the NICs were at the pinnacle of their success is right on the money: "The change in the composition of NICs . . . will more likely be a result of a country falling from their ranks than advancing to the status of an industrial country."

© Walden Bello, executive director of the San Francisco-based Institute for Food and Development Policy, is author of *Dragons in Distress: Asia's miracle Economies in Crisis* (1990).

SOUTH KOREA

SOUTH KOREA—"COMING OF AGE"

by Jack Maisano

South Korea is flirting with the idea of joining the Paris-based rich man's club of OECD (Organization for Economic Cooperation and Development) countries. But there are constraints.

The main one is that to achieve the status of

a mature economy, Seoul would have to internationalize—in other words, liberalize and open up—its economy. That, it is not ready to do. But the idea of Seoul joining the club is causing officials sleepless nights in Tokyo. The Japanese have put together a team to look into the implications of South Korea's so-called "coming of age."

Other OECD members are more encouraging. Said one observer: "By being one of us, South Korea has no option but to act like us—meaning, open its markets and buy more OECD goods."

KOREA'S INVESTMENT IMMIGRATION
by Jack Maisano

Times have changed in South Korea. Not only has the government liberalized overseas travel for South Korean citizens. Now investment emigration is being encouraged.

In 1987, a total of 34,798 South Koreans emigrated, of whom 4,269 went for reasons of investment. The number for last year may be double that. (In 1988, the government increased the ceiling on funds each household may take out of the country from U.S.$300,000 to U.S.$500,000)

Overseas investments by nonemigrant Koreans are increasing, too, following liberalization measures. In the United States, Canada, and Australia, Koreans are following the Japanese lead and buying property. It was only three years ago that Seoul's current account went into surplus. But judging by the Korean obsession with grandeur and "face," overseas investment may soon become the country's Number One status symbol.

© *Asian Business* magazine, Far East Trade Press, Ltd., 1989.

SOUTH KOREAN EXPORTS

South Korea's exports hit a record high of more than $60 billion in 1988, despite the appreciation of the Korean *won* and chronic friction with its main trading partners, according to the Ministry of Trade.

EXCEL EXCELS

Exports of Hyundai Motor Co.'s Pony Excel subcompact topped the one million mark in 1989 when 3,000 cars were shipped from the eastern South Korean port of Ulsan to the United States, according to company officials. Annual shipments of Pony Excels totaled 13,101 in 1985, 239,656 in 1986, 365,347 in 1987, and 377,521 in 1988.

KOREAN CONDOMS

Korean cars are one thing. But condoms? South Korea's leading condom-maker, Hankook Latex Company, is doing a land-office business with its condom exports, according to company official Kwak Ho Woong. In 1986, South Korea exported about 360 million condoms, a third more than the year before.

1987 exports exceeded 580 million. Kwak believes the condom boom is due to fear of AIDS rather than for purposes of contraception. Korean condom-makers are also anticipating a rise in condom use domestically as well.

CONFUSION ABOUT THE HERMIT KINGDOM

Most American firms haven't the vaguest notion about how to do business with South Korea. Those are the startling findings of a study released by the Korea Trade Promotion Corp. (KOTRA), an official trade promotion agency of the Republic of Korea government.

In a survey of 261 major U.S. firms either currently engaged in exports to Korea or planning to enter the Korean market, 49% acknowledged they have no understanding whatsoever of Korean market conditions. They also admitted they have no coherent strategy for penetrating the Korean marketplace. Only 29% said they were familiar with Korean trade laws and business practices.

"I think the percentage of people who are in the dark about Korea is even higher," commented Ken Hild, president of San Francisco-based Trade Pacific International, a Pacific Rim-oriented export management and consulting firm.

"Some of the people who are somewhat sophisticated, who already feel they have a start in that market, may be assuming that it's simply an extension of the Japanese market, but they would be completely mistaken in believing that," added Hild.

He noted that South Korea's market is substantially smaller than Japan's, that Korean consumers have a much lower per capita income than the Japanese ($3,300 for Korean in 1988 vs. $19,500 in 1987 for Japan), and that there is not as much free access to local mar-

kets despite the recent gradual liberalization of Korean trade laws.

Despite the KOTRA survey's gloomy assessment, a total of 129 American firms said they believe their products have a competitive edge in the South Korean market, thanks to the falling U.S. dollar's value against the Korean *won*.

> "When there's rice to be pounded, you miss even a dead mother-in-law."
>
> *Korean proverb*

RUIN MAN

Even Indiana Jones would think twice about easing into his seat in a Seoul movie theater these days. Despite South Korea's opening of its film market, members of the Korean Motion Picture Association have been resorting to intimidating tricks to block direct distribution of American films in the country. Movie-goers who attended "Rain Man" shortly after its Seoul opening in 1989 found the premises occupied by 19 snakes (including three deadly Korean vipers), along with four containers of hydrochloric acid.

U.S. film distributor United International Pictures, which handles overseas distribution of MGM/United Artists, Universal, and Paramount films, claimed to be undeterred and went ahead with plans to release the latest James Bond film, "License to Kill," that summer.

RIM REVIEWS

TRADING WITH THE SOUTH KOREANS

One of the most thorough, complete, and most useful guides for penetrating the South Korean market is the 320-page *International Business Handbook: Republic of Korea,* published by Global Quest, Inc., 2101 Crystal Plaza Arcade, Suite 238, Arlington, Virginia 22202. The $135 book lists over a thousand information sources, and provides inside intelligence on the corporate strategies of Korea's leading *chaebols,* including Hyundai, Daewoo, Lucky Goldstar, and others.

All aspects of marketing, manufacturing, and investing in the region are also covered in Mike Van Horn's comprehensive *Pacific Rim Trade: The Definitive Guide to Exporting and Investment* (American Management Association, 1989, $29.95). Everything from the ins and outs of exporting to various markets to the initial decision of whether your product or service is suited to a particular market is explored. A must for the exporter's reference shelf.

SINGAPORE

SINGAPORE LURES MULTINATIONALS
by Joyce Quek

Short of land and natural resources, Singapore is concentrating on attracting multinational firms to set up their headquarters on the island.

Singapore is working toward being a total business center "and that is why we want more multinational corporations to set their operational headquarters here to service their regional network of companies," says Tan Chin Nam, general manager of the Economic Development Board.

With other countries, particularly the other Asian NICs, harboring similar ambitions, Singapore has had to come up with something extra to pull in the customers.

The bait, granting operational headquarters (OHQ) status with tax breaks, is attractive. Together with Singapore's other advantages, it is helping the republic keep its competitive edge.

One hurdle that stood in the way of the OHQ scheme was Singapore's long-standing shortage of technical, clerical, and administrative staff.

The republic has an answer for this: The multinational corporations (MNCs) should take advantage of Singapore's competitive business environment and advanced infrastructure for their headquarters but locate the other parts of their operations in other countries that have bigger, cheaper labor pools.

"Labor-intensive parts of a product can be done in neighboring countries, and exported to Singapore for the more capital-intensive or skill-intensive work," suggested former prime minister Lee Kuan Yew, so that they can make the most of what the various Asian countries have to offer.

The incentives in the OHQ scheme reduce corporate tax rates from 33% to 10% on Singapore-derived income and grant effective tax relief on foreign-source income for services rendered by MNCs, such as dividends from subsidiaries.

It is a powerful incentive, enough to lure the Asia-Pacific office and training center of West Germany's Deutsche Bank from Hamburg to Singapore.

So far, 16 firms have followed Deutsche Bank, including Sony, ANZ Bank, Polysar, Foxboro, and Fukijura. Kajima Corporation, Japan's largest construction firm, is a likely seventeenth.

To qualify, firms must establish either a regional HQ, a distribution base, a manufacturing base, a technical service center, a gateway to Southeast Asia and China, a product development center, a training and education center, or a market base for gathering or exchanging information. International purchasing offices (IPOs) are also encouraged.

Singapore, lacking land and natural resources, has had to tie its future to the growth of the Asia-Pacific region as a whole, especially in the finance and manufacturing sectors, which offer scope for upgrading workers' skills and salaries. Its starting point was being "home" to about 600 MNCs.

Foreign direct investment may still be important, but the emphasis has now shifted from manufacturing to services, making possible the introduction of the OHQ incentive in 1986 to attract MNCs.

Japan has wooed with great success. In 1986, it displaced the U.S. as the biggest foreign investor. And the famed herd instinct of Japanese companies, together with the search for cheaper locations in the face of the high yen, are likely to prompt more Japanese firms to follow.

Lee Kuan Yew suggested that Japanese MNCs, which used Singapore as a "total business location," serve not only their home market but regional and world markets as well.

The Mitsubishi Research Institute agreed. It reasoned: "The republic should not be used as a base for the production of unsophisticated goods in future . . . but for the production of high-technology or value-added goods, or as a regional headquarters for the operations of Japanese firms in Asia."

Company headquarters in Singapore should handle operations and remain complementary to the head offices in Japan, while regional offices could be responsible for framing marketing and export policies and support operations in Thailand and Malaysia, it added.

Infrastructure—or the lack of it—can be a problem for businessmen in Thailand, currently the darling of the Japanese investors because of its plentiful cheap labor.

Singapore's other rival, Hong Kong, suffers from political and economic uncertainty as the 1997 takeover by mainland China approaches. One important side effect of this uncertainty has been the flight of technicians and other professionals. High rents have also affected businessmen's ratings of the colony.

All other factors being equal, political and economic stability rank alongside wage costs in picking a base.

With its stability and the measures it has taken to lower employers' mandatory provident fund contributions and to tie pay rises to profits, Singapore looks increasingly attractive.

© *Asian Business* magazine, Far East Trade Press, Ltd., 1988.

"The essence of a city is its people, not its walls."

Chinese proverb

MALAYSIA

MALAYSIA EASES INTO THE LEAD

Money is pouring into Malaysia. But how long will it stay?

Forget Thailand, Malaysia is the place to be. Foreign investors have got a bull on Malaysia and are pouring money into everything from manufacturing to stocks to property.

New equity guidelines, allowing majority foreign ownership, together with a probusiness budget, have made Malaysia the investor's favorite Asian choice, especially now that Thailand's honeymoon period is over. That country is said to be increasingly congested, expensive, and xenophobic.

The factors pointing to the boom–bust theory are that the Malaysian economy is riding the back of a commodity surge that could soon fizzle out; Kuala Lumpur property is attractive only for its cheapness; and, most importantly, the liberal equity climate may not last.

In 1991 a replacement for the controversial New Economic Policy (NEP) will have to be found. The NEP, which has boosted Malay equity ownership at the expense of Chinese and foreign holdings, is currently on pause. But its total abandonment is unthinkable and a successor could put everything back to square one.

This is fueling investment activity. Projects put in place now on favorable terms will remain untouched, and the thinking is: "There may never be another chance like this. Get into Malaysia today."

Highly favorable economic conditions serve to heighten the optimism and are the basis for thinking that Malaysia is on the verge of NICdom. Interest rates are at a 20-year low of 7% compared with 12% in Thailand. The *ringgit,* which has depreciated against the dollar since 1985 while the Thai *baht* has increased, makes buying assets cheap and exporting competitive. Inflation is about 4% as opposed to Thailand's 8%.

The Malaysian labor pool offers one of the best combinations of skills at low wages in the region, and the economy is expanding fast —7.5% in 1988 and about 6% to 7% in 1989.

To top it off, as well as the troubles in Thailand, all other investment sites are facing problems: Hong Kong has a critical labor shortage, Singapore is too expensive, Korea has political problems. No wonder Malaysia is everyone's darling of the moment.

"Compared with neighboring economies, Malaysia looks particularly attractive to investors now," says Alan Hargreaves, director of Asia-Pacific Research at Hoare Govett in Singapore. "It's on the early part of its recovery path and there's still abundant excess capacity. Malaysia has abundant untapped capacity. By contrast, Thailand is facing congestion of its infrastructure, its banks are fully lent and interest rates are high. South Korea has a political problem and workers there are demanding higher wages, while Singapore and Hong Kong are burdened by labor shortages."

One company which has reached similar conclusions is Japan's Toshiba Corp. It has located its only semiconductor manufacturing plant in Southeast Asia on the outskirts of Kuala Lumpur.

To date, M$120 million (U.S.$45 million at a rate of M$2.67 to U.S.$1.00) has been sunk into the factory at Telok Panglima Garang, with further plans to invest another M$30 million in equipment and new technology. Business grew by 50% in 1987 and a further 10% to 20% in 1989, says managing director Michio Otsuka.

Further astronomic growth came from Taiwanese investors whose equity commitments soared 438% to M$238 million over the same period. An example is the formation of a joint venture company to produce polypropylene, involving Titan Plastic Industries, a Singapore-based marketing company belonging to Taiwan's China General Plastics Corp.

On the property side it has been Hong Kong buyers who have been snapping up the bargains. With prices in their home territory at an all-time high (U.S.$650 per square foot in the Central business district, compared with U.S.$300 per square foot in Singapore and U.S.$75 in Malaysia), Kuala Lumpur seems very undervalued. Among the buildings they have bought are the Kuala Lumpur Plaza for M$85 million, the Prince Hotel for M$60 million, and the Amoda Building for M$55 million.

The number of property transactions rose 22% to 54,302 during the first half of 1988 from the same period a year earlier, while the value rose slightly to M$3.6 billion from M$3.2 billion.

"Because of the depreciation of the *ringgit,* commercial buildings in Malaysia are now some of the cheapest in the region in terms of rental and selling price," says Jordan Lee, managing director of Malaysian property consultants Colliers Jordan Lee and Jaafar.

But will the boom last? Or will Malaysia's dreams, of becoming the kind of tiger that leaves American and European businessmen sleepless nights, fade away as fast as they began? This is what seems to have happened to Thailand—at least temporarily—and projections about when it will make the NIC grade are moving further into the future.

The two major unknowns in the Malaysian equation are the NEP—or rather, what replaces it—and the element of unsustainable speculation in the current upturn. The wrong outcome on either of these and Malaysia's new backers could be off to the Philippines and Indonesia as quickly as they left Thailand.

The NEP has been the critical element in Malaysia's business scene since it first came into existence in 1970. The 20-year program was designed to give Malays or *bumiputras* (sons of the soil) a 30% stake in corporate equity through a takeover and restructuring process. Foreigners would be limited to 30% and other Malaysians, such as Chinese and Indian investors, to 40%.

While the target has no chance of being achieved *bumiputra* ownership has risen dramatically, from 1% in 1970 to 22% by 1985. But the cost has been an acute wariness among foreign and Chinese investors. In the last recession of 1985 to 1986, just when they were most needed, the foreigners pulled the plug on investments and caused a decline of 18.3%, the first in a decade.

Alarmed, the government laid out its most attractive welcome mat ever and paved the way for the current boom. Apart from lifting ownership restrictions on export-oriented projects, the government has recently waived a ban on total foreign equity ownership and control for ventures aimed at the local market. Permits are granted for five years only—foreign investors must find a suitable local partner after that—but it's still a considerable attraction.

The results have been stunning. In the first

eight months of 1988, projects approved by the Malaysian Industrial Development Authority (MIDA) jumped 251% to M$1.3 billion from a year earlier. But since the new equity guidelines apply only to investors whose applications are received between October 1986 and December 1990, there may be a strong element of rushing to beat the deadline.

"Many foreign investors are taking advantage of this period when the government says, 'come in, you can keep your equity share, we won't change it;' " says John Ip, former director of Business International Asia/Pacific Forecasting Services.

"Many want to get in now rather than wait and miss out on it because they don't know what's going to happen after 1990," he adds.

Some signs pointing to what will happen after 1990 are extremely positive. Gone are the days when *bumiputra* ownership was being sought at all costs, and a strong sense of business realism has crept into present calculations.

In response to criticisms of lack of consultation on the issue, prime minister Dr. Mahathir Mohamad announced the setting up of a National Economic Council, consisting of the various interest groups, whose major focus will be the NEP.

Other comments and actions by prime minister Dr. Mahathir Mohamad have indicated a willingness to be flexible. In a major speech given in October 1988, Mahathir said: "The granting of opportunities, facilities, cap-

ital, and other forms of aid is insufficient for *bumiputras* to succeed in business. For their success, efficient management—a rare commodity among *bumiputras*—is important.

"The giving of a project to a 100% *bumiputra* concern just because it is a 100% *bumiputra* concern, even though it is incapable of handling the project, will be against the objective of helping *bumiputras*."

The prime minister's thinking has thus clicked with what earlier studies, in particular, the World Bank, had said of the NEP: While wealth redistribution through the state machinery might be easy, the building of individual entrepreneurs to create and maintain wealth was another matter.

"We have no intention of making Malay businessmen and entrepreneurs bankrupt so that they are dependent on the U.S.," says Mahathir. "We want to make Malays efficient industrialists and businessmen, capable of standing on their own feet and capable of competing successfully with anyone."

The NEP cannot be swept aside because it is too crucial for *bumiputra* political support. But it's unlikely that it will come back in a more stringent form than its original 30% ownership stipulation, and it may be a good deal more pragmatic.

The astute Dr. Mahathir is in fact playing a clever political game with the NEP. By putting it on pause under special circumstances, he has managed to cut out the negative effects on foreign investment without incurring *bumiputra* wrath.

"It is the fate of the coconut husk to float, of the stone to sink."

Malaysian proverb

INDONESIA

INDONESIA OPENS NEW BUSINESS HORIZONS
by Ooi Guat Tin

Indonesia Aims for NIC Status by 1994.

Sitting at his sewing machine by the side of the Jatinegara market compound road in east Jakarta, a tailor stitches *sarongs* at a furious pace, oblivious to the cacophony around him.

Children are screaming, women haggling with vegetable vendors, and men pushing out their stalls yell at others blocking the narrow red dirt path that leads to the front of the main market compound.

But the tailor, Pak To, stitches on, unperturbed. After three years of poor business, life suddenly looks very bright. Orders for his *sarongs* have doubled over the past year, and he is only too happy to work more than 20 hours a day, selling the *sarongs* to a local trader, Pak Tiko, who in turn sells them on to retail shops in central Jakarta. Pak To earns good money, about 5,000 *rupiahs*—just under U.S.$3.00— a day, and such an opportunity, he says, may not last.

But like most low-income people in Jatinegara, Pak To also reserves praise for the government of President Suharto whose objective, based on the state ideology, or *Pancasila,* has been to ensure that the poorest have enough shelter, food, and other basic necessities, including health and education.

"Twenty years ago," says Pak To, "there was no market, few people, and no business. Today, we're lucky. We have houses, water, electricity, and more people are moving in.

But our roads are bad. They say they will build roads. We are hopeful."

Indeed, confidence is rising as the government ushers the country into a new phase of development that promises a better quality of life for Indonesia's 172 million people.

The objective of the next five years, President Suharto has declared, "is to raise production and quality, to raise the income and living standards of farmers, stock-raisers and fishermen, to expand employment and business opportunities, to support the development of industry and to boost exports."

These are the goals the president envisages under the fifth five-year plan or *Repelita V,* which began in April 1989.

But to achieve these goals, the economy must grow by 5% a year for the next five years. Can this rate of growth be sustained, and where will the money come from to finance development?

After getting a pat on the back from the world's most reform-minded institution, the International Monetary Fund, for its prudent management of the economy, Indonesia can be assured of continued cheap loans to finance development.

And foreign banks, taking the cue from the IMF, will rush in to provide new capital to aid Indonesia's economic recovery—in contrast to the Philippines, which they have shunned since it failed to impress the IMF in November 1988.

But the Indonesian government knows the dangers of unrestrained deficit financing, even if the terms are good. The country already owes foreign creditors more than U.S.$48 billion dollars, and its debt service payments are equivalent to around 40% of export earnings.

In a speech on the eve of the forty-third anniversary of the country's independence (in August 1988), president Suharto acknowledged "the heavy pressures" caused by repayment schedules, especially with respect to the strengthening yen.

"But we have shown our ability to manage foreign loans in a responsible way," he said, and the debts "will be paid off by the gains of development financed by them."

Indonesia's debt service ratio, the president declared, will be reduced to less than 25% of export revenues by April 1994.

The target is not easy to achieve, especially when conditions for debt repayment could become more difficult. All it takes to upset Indonesia's calculations is a soaring yen or a slowdown in the U.S. economy, or another oil price crash.

"Moreover, the Minister of Finance is talking about cutting expenditures and subsidies. That will reduce income and constrain domestic demand. The belt-tightening strategy will further dampen growth," he added.

But what really give the government the confidence to set ambitious goals for the fifth plan is its commitment to press ahead with economic restructuring, no matter how pain-

---

ASIAN CHRONICLES

THE DUTCH EAST INDIA CO. IN BATAVIA

Christopher Frick was a German surgeon who signed on in 1680 with the Dutch East India Company to work in its colonial outpost of Batavia, a Dutch fortress city built on the site of the Javanese town Jacatra, which is the Indonesian capital Jakarta today. This excerpt, a description of Batavia in the year 1682—is from Frick's memoirs, A Relation of a Voyage Made to the East Indies, *which was first published in English in 1700.*

As for *Batavia,* the City and Castle are as well worth a description, as they are a Man's sight: And truly mine was ravisht with it; for I must confess, that I think them yet finer even than *Amsterdam* itself. It is five or six Miles in compass. The River *Jacatra* runs thro' most Streets of the Town, and almost encompasses it. Upon these Canals the Inhabitants have the conveniency of going in Boats to their Gardens and Pleasure-houses: The sides of them is wall'd up with good square Stone, and all along each side of it, there goes a Row or two of fine Cedar, Coco, or Figg-trees, where the Free-men use to walk at night under a most pleasant Shade.

The Castle stands toward the Sea. It hath four Bastions; two of them to the Sea, called the *Ruby* and the *Pearl,* the other two to the City, which go by the name of the *Saphir* and the *Diamon.*

It is in the whole exact square, and from top to bottom built up with excellent good square Stone. On each of these Bastions are sixteen half-Culverins [canon] planted: Besides this, they are full of fine Trees, such as Lemons, and Mangos, which makes them look most sweetly. While I was there, there was a third Gate built to the Castle, which before had but two.

ful that may be for a country used to being spoonfed with oil revenues.

"The low oil prices are going to create a lot of problems for economic growth but one positive effect is that they will put a lot of pressure on the government to deregulate," says Manggi Habir, vice president of Citibank.

When Indonesia embarked on its first five-year plan in 1969, Suharto said the 25-year goal was to elevate the country to NIC status by the end of the fifth consecutive plan.

Now on the threshold of that fifth plan, Indonesia still lags behind its Asian neighbors, notably Singapore, Thailand, and Malaysia, in industrial competitiveness.

Conservative elements of the Indonesian bureaucracy, who still hold many posts, even though they are not subordinate to the technocrats, reject such comparisons as unfair.

They say the Singapore economy is small and thrives on industrial efficiency because it has no natural resources to speak of. Thailand has never been colonized and, therefore, feels secure opening its market to foreigners. And while Indonesia's social and cultural values are similar to those of Malaysia, its vastness in area and population mean greater effort is needed to develop the country.

They continue to promote the idea of an isolated Indonesia, protected from foreign investment and influences.

Reflecting the government's determination to bite the bullet, several reform measures were unveiled in the last quarter of 1988 that are more sweeping than any since 1985.

Foreign businessmen in Jakarta see the latest reform package as an indication of pragmatism prevailing over dogma in government economic policy. But still further deregulation is necessary, they say, if Indonesia is to keep up with the brisk pace set by its Asian neighbors.

For some time Jakarta's reform-minded economists—the so-called technocrats, many of them trained in the West—have favored accelerated deregulation, but have met with fierce resistance from entrenched bureaucrats who fear that the inefficiency of local industries will show up if tariff barriers are lowered.

With the release of the November 1988 reform package, it appears that the technocrats have won the day, and will now have a bigger say in the running of the country's economic policies.

"While the government is stressing the desire to quicken the pace of industrial development, it will continue to promote agricultural growth."

"Twenty-five years ago, the country was poor, overpopulated, unstable, and predominantly agricultural," says Sjamsoe Soegito, executive director of the National Development Information Office. "Today, it has become a more dynamic industrial country . . . So long as the world economy does not deteriorate and deal unexpected blows to Indonesia, the goal of bringing the nation to the point of entering the ranks of the NICs in 1994 is achieveable."

"Duck eggs are sometimes hatched by hens."

Indonesian proverb

INDONESIAN UNEMPLOYMENT

Unemployment in Indonesia, the largest country in Southeast Asia, could become a social time-bomb by the mid-1990s unless the government takes drastic steps, noted Bohmer Pasaribu, chairman of the Indonesian Workers Federation. He said the work force of almost 73 million was expected to grow to 86 million by 1995; and while the government officially estimated unemployment at 2.2% in 1987, what he called "disguised unemployment" stood much higher at 11 million. He made his remarks after the World Bank's annual report on Indonesia, which warned that unemployment in the cities could reach threatening proportions if job creation does not keep pace with population growth.

SWISS CUSTOMS OFFICIALS FOR INDONESIA

Indonesia's national customs agency is operated under contract by the Geneva-based security form Société Générale de Surveillance (SGS). The Swiss surveyor took over the tasks of Indonesian customs in 1985. Prior to that, customs was notorious for red tape and corruption, and was cited by businessmen as contributing to high production costs in Indonesia.

TEAK-TO-GO

Indonesia's latest exports are custom-made, prefabricated, traditional-style, teakwood houses. Balinese housebuilder Dana's Company sells a 100 square-meter house (which comes complete with stone columns and Balinese statues, modern kitchens, four bedrooms, dining room, bathroom, porch and patio) for $60,000—not including shipping and assembly. Javanese firm P.T. Saran Alam has a two-story, 240-square-meter teakwood house going for $450,000. It fits in six shipping containers. The firm has already sold several houses to Japanese customers—and has orders for 20 more for next year. A traditional Javanese-style house with carved figures reminiscent of old style homes in central Java sells for $148,000—not including the airfare for eight master craftsmen who must reassemble the house when it reaches its destination. Teak forests in central Java are the main source for this wood—which doesn't bode well for the forests, although P.T. Saran Alam president Surandai claims that the business is providing thousands of jobs for local craftsmen. It takes a hundred workers about eight months to finish carving and building a two-story house. Orders are coming in from Japan, Australia, and the United States.

ON THE INDOCHINA RIM

THAILAND

THE GOLDEN PENINSULA

The Thai military is fond of citing the old Thai myth of *Suwannaphum* (The Golden Peninsula), which describes a Southeast Asian utopia in which all the people in the region live in peace and prosperity. That was their way of calling for peace in occupied Cambodia and strife-ridden Burma. Little did they know that the term would become an economic buzzword when former Thai Prime Minister Chatichai Choonhavan seized the idea to embody his vision of transforming Indochina into a single market.

Indochinese-style *perestroika* has been responsible for a slew of Thailand joint ventures and investments in neighboring Vietnam, Laos, Cambodia, and even Burma. The Tourism Authority of Thailand is even planning to position Thailand the gateway to destinations like Cambodia's Angkor Wat and resort areas in Vietnam, including organizing hunting tours in Vietnam's four national parks.

"Thai capitalism and Thai technology are at a stage when a little foreign adventure would do them good," editorialized Thai member of parliament, Surin Pittsuwan, in a newspaper column.

THE RISING PRICE OF SUCCESS
by Ooi Guat Tin

Thailand's race toward NIC status has brought rising inflation and an overtaxed infrastructure. But even these are unlikely to halt its healthy growth.

Each morning, as many as 50 Thai youngsters gather in a street across from Paak Klong Talaad—Bangkok's famous wholesale vegetable market—waiting impatiently for the clock to strike nine. At nine sharp, they rush forward, dragging round bamboo crates known as *kheng,* containing vegetables for the vendors in the market area.

The "veggy-runners" are restricted to certain hours and areas to avoid traffic congestion, and the day's earnings depend on the number of rounds they can make. Throughout the day, hundreds of tons of vegetables arrive in the vicinity of Paak Klong Talaad from all over the country, coming by truck or boat. There the vegetables are unloaded into bamboo crates and delivered to the vendors.

Chaoprai was 15 when he started out as a part-time veggy-runner, earning less than 20 *baht* (U.S. $8.00) a month; that was five years ago. Now, as a regular runner, he earns between 1,000 and 1,500 *baht* a week, heaving loads that may weigh as much as 150 kilograms.

"We do honest work," says Chaoprai, who left school to work to help support his family, "and if we work very hard we can earn as much as 6,000 *baht* a month. That is good money. We need it. Things here are getting expensive."

Earning nearly three times the monthly minimum wage of 2,200 *baht*—the official rate stipulated for Bangkok and the five surrounding provinces—Chaoprai may consider himself better off than most low-income wage earners. But like many of Bangkok's working class, he is paying a heavy price for the country's economic success.

Rapid economic growth has caught Thailand in an inflationary wage-price spiral, and the lowest paid are seeing their earnings drastically eroded in real terms. At 8% and rising, inflation is more than three times the average 2.3% annual rate of the past five years.

Even with the recent revision in minimum wage rates, some say the increase is not enough to match the rapid rise in the cost of living. The situation is likely to get worse since the spending spree of the middle and higher income groups is far from over. Bangkok's 33 department stores reported brisk sales, and despite hefty tariffs ranging up to 600%, the car industry sold a record 39,000 new cars in the first nine months of 1988 compared with 27,000 in the same period of 1987.

Thais are now, it seems, caught in a classic wages and prices spiral. A cut in petrol prices and a reduction in personal income tax scheduled for 1989 will further increase Thais' spending power—and further fuel inflation.

Says a Hong Kong analyst with the Political and Economic Risk Consultancy group: "The 13% increase in civil servants' salaries, together with an average 6.8% increase in the minimum wage, will inevitably lead to increases in the price of consumer goods."

The problem for business is lack of saving for necessary investment. Thais are not known for their frugal habits, although an official with the National Economic and Social Development Board (NESDB) rejects the view that Thais are compulsive consumers.

"Compared with Japan, South Korea, and the NICs, which have an average 33% savings rate, Thailand has 20%. That's still considerable," says Phisit Pakkasem, NESDB deputy secretary-general.

Considerable, maybe, but not enough. The director of the Bank of Thailand's governor's office, Dr. Siri Ganjarenrudee says one of Thailand's immediate problems is a growing investment/savings gap caused by the surge in both private and public investments.

While foreign investment is pouring into Thailand, the bill for the government's plans for coping with the growing demands of infrastructure and heavy industrial projects will require an estimated 280 billion *baht* investment between 1989 and 1994, with most of it invested in the next three years.

"In 1988, investment as a proportion of GDP was more than 26.9%, whereas savings were equivalent to 23.7%, so you have a large savings/investment gap in which the rate of savings cannot keep up with the rate of investment," says Siri.

Excerpted from article by Ooi Guat Tin, reported by Peter Janssen. © *Asian Business* magazine, Far East Trade Press, Ltd., 1989.

"Do not borrow another nose to breathe."

Thai proverb

RICE FROM THAILAND

Thailand exported 4.7 million tons of rice in 1988, up 9.3% from the previous year. The value of 1988's exports was estimated at about $1.2 billion, according to a government official.

STILL WAITING FOR THE AIR TO CLEAR
by Peter Janssen

Thailand is in a perfect position to exploit the markets of Indochina, but suspicion has put a damper on progress.

When the U.S.-backed Saigon regime finally collapsed in 1975, swiftly followed by Communist takeovers in Vientiane and Phnom Penh, the believers in the domino principle began a countdown for Bangkok.

For years Thailand bore the label of a "front line" state against the military and ideological threat across its borders—a stigma that once scared away foreign investment and, in the late 1970s, even caused local entrepreneurs to think twice about their country's future.

In 1989 a new countdown began, this time for the resolution of the Kampuchea issue, and Thailand is hoping to transform its front-line status from a disadvantage into a benefit.

The potential advantages are substantial. Across its borders Thailand faces a potential market of some 100 million people in Burma, Kampuchea, Laos, and Vietnam. It is well situated to become a major supply center to its neighbors, selling both its own consumer goods—textiles, garments, shoes, and canned food—and becoming a distribution outlet for the multinationals already based in the country.

Coca Cola is already eyeing the less controversial market of Laos. In the short-term, at least, opening up the Laotian market would be like adding a new province to the Coca Cola (Thailand) distribution network.

The Board of Investment sees the foreign policy initiative as a new selling point in attracting investment to Thailand, particularly from Europe and the United States.

BOI secretary general Chira Panupong explains: "Foreign investors will use Thailand as a gateway to the region. They will come to Thailand to enjoy the local markets, the ASEAN market, and now the Indochina and Burmese markets.

The new markets could also draw more tourists to Thailand, as the obvious springboard into neighboring countries. Says Luzi Matzig, a manager at Diethelm Travel in Bangkok: "If Kampuchea opens up in the next two years, we could sell a lot of package tours to Indochina via Bangkok. The big draw would be Angkor Wat."

For the Thai tax man the legitimization of trade between Thailand and its immediate neighbors will be a dream come true.

Not too long ago an estimated 20% of Thailand's textile production was finding its way into Burma, most of it tax-free. The illicit trade between Thailand and its neighbors add up to billions of *baht* each year, stocking the barren markets of Rangoon and Phnom Penh with Thai cigarettes, imitation Lacoste shirts, Japanese motorcycles, and spare parts for cars—all of it untaxed on either side of the porous borders.

But more important than tax revenue, and even the potential export markets, is the opportunity to be the first to exploit the still untapped raw materials of Indochina and Burma.

Certainly, a battle for the marketplace has already been launched. "I think [the Indochina initiative] has more to do with securing raw materials, such as timber," says Bank of Thailand spokesman Dr. Siri Ganjarerndee.

In the wake of the devastating flooding in the south of Thailand in late 1988, which was blamed in part on deforestation, the government announced a ban on all further logging in Thailand, a move which may save forests but will endanger a booming furniture industry unless the government can speed up timber imports.

Timber was a top priority for discussion when the Thai minister of commerce, Subin Pinkhayan, visited Vientiane in January 1989, especially as the Laotian government had decided to enforce a ban on all log exports.

Thailand has long been the largest importer of timber from Burma, whose teak wood is world famous. On December 17, 1988, a little-known Thai firm, the Thip Thorn Thong Co. signed two contracts with the Burmese Timber and Fishery Ministry for a 400 square-kilometer logging concession, and a fishing concession in Burmese waters. [See "Tropical Dossier," p. 407]

THE INDOCHINA INTERFACE

These were the first such concessions to be inked and local reports speculated that the firm, which has also signed a contract to renovate Rangoon's Strand Hotel, may have intimate connections with Thai army commander-in-chief Gen. Chavalit Yongchaiyudh. Chavalit visited the unpopular Saw Maung regime on December 17, 1988, the same day the contracts with Tip Thorn Thong were signed.

As long as political problems remain in Burma and Indochina, the pioneers of trade and investment in those countries are likely to be small, relatively obscure Thai companies, which may be fronts for more substantial backers.

Thailand's leading business conglomerates, such as the Siam Cement Group, the Saha Union Group, and the Charoen Pokphand Group (CP), have taken more of a "wait and see" attitude.

A certain amount of caution on the part of the big companies is understandable. While Chatichai cultivated an "identity" for himself with his Indochina initiative, he also sowed confusion. Some of his off-the-cuff remarks, such as his public invitation for Kampuchean prime minister Hun Sen to visit Thailand, flew in the face of the Foreign Ministry's well-defined policies.

But one thing the Foreign Ministry and the former prime minister agreed upon was the time is right to allow the Thai private sector to exploit opportunities in Laos and Vietnam before the floodgates open.

A certain degree of political uncertainty will

remain as long as the Kampuchea issue lingers on, and despite all the recent hoopla about a solution being on the horizon.

In the meantime, Laos is likely to be the place where Thailand will make the most progress. Already, Thai banks are looking into the possibility of setting up offices in Vientiane, and the Thai Farmers Bank plans to set up a new foreign trade center in Bangkok to facilitate trade and investment between the two countries. The Bangkok Bank is reportedly considering reopening its Vientiane and Ho Chi Minh City branches.

One tremendous economic benefit that Thailand and the entire region can look forward to, as a result of the changing political scene, is the realization of the Interim Mekong Committee (IMC) program.

"The Mekong Committee was established in 1957, and since then there has been no peace in this region," says Caspar Van Kamp, executive agent for the IMC.

The IMC has worn its "interim" status since 1975, when the infamous Khmer Rouge decided officially to drop out of the regional development program. The civil war in Kampuchea interrupted a Mekong Committee irrigation project at Prek Thnot, not far from Phnom Penh, which would have transformed the area into a rice bowl and hydroelectric power source for the capital.

Kampuchea's lack of representation (or the international community's reluctance to recognize the current Phnom Penh regime) has put a damper on many of the potential Mekong mainstream projects, which inevitably effect Laos, Kampuchea, Thailand, and Vietnam—the four countries through which the Mekong river flows.

Even without Kampuchea's active partici-

pation, the IMC is optimistic about recent developments, particularly the improved relationship evolving between Thailand and Laos. "This opens the way for a project like the Pa Mong dam, which is a mainstream project, but only between Thailand and Laos," says Van Kamp.

Thailand already buys electricity from the Nam Ngum power plant in Laos, another IMC project. The electricity exports account for approximately 80% of Laos's total foreign exchange earnings.

LOOKING TO LAOS

Laos, which is one of the world's poorest countries, is also one of the richest in water resources. Another dam/reservoir site is under study at Nam Theun, near the Laotian–Vietnamese border. "The electricity that can be generated there will be the cheapest in the world," says Van Kamp. "It's one of the best hydroelectricity projects left in the world."

Both Pa Mong and Nam Theum, besides generating electricity for Thailand and Laos, would also benefit Kampuchea and Vietnam by regulating the flow of the river to the Mekong delta region.

Of course, whether Vietnam and Kampuchea would like to have the water supply to the important delta region controlled by a dam upstream gets into the political, nationalistic, and perhaps even environmental questions that have kept IMC projects on the back burner for three decades. And although peace may be on the horizon for the region, it does not necessarily mean that old national rivalries and suspicions will disappear altogether.

BURMA

BURMA'S BEDRAGGLED ECONOMY
by Jack Maisano

If there's one thing the Burmese economy is good at, it's subsistence. One thing the turmoil in Rangoon in 1988 demonstrated is that Burma, with or without its political troubles, is about as self-sufficient as Burmese strongmen Ne Win could hope for.

"This country will never starve," a seasoned Burma watcher once said, and his words have been proven by those tumultuous events. Despite the riots, the bloodshed, the near anarchy of the political scene, there were few reports of starvation out of Rangoon.

One reason: The blackmarket, which has dominated retail sales for the past decade, kept up a steady stream of supplies throughout the turmoil. The only time there were real privations was in July 1988, when the government foolishly slapped a dusk-to-dawn curfew on Rangoon. The curfew prevented traders from bringing their goods to the market in the wee hours.

Another reason: Abundance. When a food shortage was looming that September, the military junta then in command mustered the provincial resources (maybe at gunpoint) and rice was brought down to the capital by river.

Third, and most sadly: The Burmese have become so used to tightening their belts over the past 26 years, that another notch probably went unnoticed.

© *Asian Business* magazine, Far East Trade Press, Ltd., 1988.

"The centipede doesn't stop for one bad leg."

Burmese proverb

LAND OF WASTED OPPORTUNITY

by Peter Jansen

Despite the landslide victory of Burma's National League for Democracy party in the May 1990 election, it remains to be seen whether the pro-military National Unity Party, which seized power in September 1988 after brutally crushing the opposition, will relinquish control to the pro-democracy party—especially since political opponents remain jailed or under house arrest.

Burma's recent economic history reads more like a tragic tale of opportunities lost, both by the Burmese people and foreign businessmen who are forever keen to exploit the nation's riches.

Burma (or Myanmar, to use its new official title) offers tremendous prospects because of its largely untapped treasure troves of oil, minerals, timber, fisheries, and agricultural products but few countries have managed to do so poorly with so much natural abundance as this largest country in Southeast Asia.

Although the current military regime in Rangoon has introduced several much-needed economic reforms, it is still far from clear if Burma is heading toward economic recovery, or basket-case status.

A NE WIN SITUATION

The one positive piece of news circulating in the troubled land is that socialism is definitely dead. The bad news may be that the father of Burmese-brand socialism, General Ne Win, now over 80 years old, is alive and well, as are his clique, and probably as powerful as ever.

Ne Win and his supposedly Marxist minded cohorts launched Burma on its disastrous route to socialism, intense nationalism, and xenophobic isolationism in 1962 with a bloodless coup d'etat. The so-called Burmese Way to Socialism, in the long run, ended up being Ne Win's way to national pauperism.

The demonetization of 1987 was a classic example of his idiosyncratic, unpredictable rule, which totally disregards the desires and basic rights of the Burmese people.

Ne Win simply decided to take the 25, 35, and 75 *kyat* notes out of circulation, a measure which, overnight, wiped out some 60% of the country's currency and, with it, the life savings of millions of Burmese. The riots followed by Ne Win's resignation that this brought about resulted in two months of chaos which were ended by General Saw Maung's bloody coup.

The regime legalized the border trade with Burma's neighbors: China, India, and Bangladesh (the border crossings into Thailand are still under negotiation), setting up customs checkpoints to collect tariffs on the once illicit trade.

But despite this and other reforms, few believe that the government system or the economy have been significantly improved. The crux of the problem is that while Burmese socialism is no more, the powerful military clique, with Ne Win at its center, continues to control—and restrict—the economy.

For instance, the State Law and Order Restoration Committee (SLORC), a military run tribunal, has granted some 40 timber concessions along the Thai–Burmese border to Thai companies. These concessions will earn the government an estimated U.S.$50 million in 1989, even though the land on which the concessions stand is controlled by insurgents fighting the Rangoon regime.

Of the 40 concessions, only a handful have been put into operation; and in these it has been necessary to enlist the support of the insurgents. In essence, the Thai companies have

---

ASIAN CHRONICLES

THE BURMESE KING: ARBITER OF ALL EXISTENCE

In 1875, an English schoolteacher, James George Scott, went to Burma where he became a writer and government official. In this excerpt from his book, The Burman: His Life and Notions, *Scott (later Sir James) describes how foreign visitors were subjected to all manner of indignities by the Burmese monarchs in the years before Britain annexed the kingdom to its colonial possessions in India in 1886.*

Most envoys sent to the Arbiter of Existence [the king] were treated very cavalierly in the ways of interviews; not a few in the old days waited long months without ever seeing the king at all. All, down to Sir Douglas Forsyth in 1874, had to go in shoeless and sit cross-legged on the floor, an unaccustomed attitude which did not tend to render the position less ridiculous.

In other ways they were treated with every indignity. When King Mintayagyi heard that Colonel Symes was coming, he went away to Mingon to contemplate his gigantic failure at a pagoda there. Thither the colonel had to follow him, congratulating himself on the circumstance that as the king was away from the palace, there would be the less trouble in seeing him. But he found himself vastly mistaken. On arriving in Mingon he was told to take up his quarters on an island in the middle of the river. On this barren place, shunned by all Burmese as a polluted spot where bodies were burnt and criminals executed, he had to remain 40 days, and during all that time not the slightest notice of him was taken by the court. Finally he admitted on a kadaw, or "Beg-Pardon Day," one of those set apart for all inferiors and vassals to come and do homage and worship at the Golden Feet.

Another favorite method of showing contempt for foreigners and exalting the national dignity was rather curious in its elaborate ingenuity. Foreign missions were provided for by a tax levied on outcasts. The money was only collected when an embassy was expected, and was applied to no other purpose than providing accommodation and food for the members of the mission. The coin was considered too vile to be put to any other use. Delaying the envoy at the gates was an invariable device. Just as he came up to the entrance a band of princes, with their followers, would turn in from a side street, and the luckless representative of England would have to stop and bite his nails till they had all passed in. Arrived at the palace, all the earlier envoys were made to fall on their knees, and shikho to the central spire of the royal residence.

had to pay twice for their valuable logs—once to the Burmese government and then again to the insurgents.

A similar situation applies to the ocean fishing concessions SLORC is selling. The government will collect about U.S.$17 million in revenue from 217 trawlers operated by companies from Thailand, Malaysia, Hong Kong, Singapore, and South Korea in return for the right to fish in waters which have for years been fished illegally by Thai vessels.

These measures may seem to demonstrate a new pragmatism on the part of the "interim" Burmese government. But it is a pragmatism that stems from the acknowledgment that they can no longer control their own economy, rather than from a full-blown commitment to the market.

The decision to legitimize the border trade between Burma and its neighbors is another example of accepting reality and making the most of it. Burma's state enterprises have never been able to satisfy demand for consumer goods, in terms either of quantity or quality. Goods have therefore spilled in illegally from neighboring Thailand, China, India, and Bangladesh.

By 1985, Thailand alone accounted for two thirds of the country's consumer goods supply, according to a survey conducted by Bangkok's Chulalongkorn University. By legalizing the trade, at least in items which are not under government monopoly, SLORC is collecting tariff revenue where there was previously none.

BARTER ON THE BORDER

Although most of the border trade is in the form of barter handled by the private sector, there are signs that SLORC intends eventually to monopolize these transactions. Most of SLORC's internal economic reforms amount

to carving out a share of the black market, the traditional preserve of Burma's silent private sector.

For instance, by allowing Burmese nationals with foreign earnings to open foreign exchange accounts, the government has been able to create a legitimate market to compete with the predominant black market, which accounts for between 60% and 80% of all retail sales in the country.

Previously, only certain government officials and seamen were permitted to keep their foreign exchange to make purchases, such as automobiles, from abroad. All other foreign exchange earners, such as embassy staffers, representatives of foreign firms, and Burmese with relatives abroad, were forced to transform their checks into *kyat,* a painful experience for any businessman. In July, while the official exchange rate was 6.6 *kyat* to U.S.$1.00, the black market was offering 55 to 57 *kyat*.

Under the new banking regulations, Burmese with foreign exchange accounts must transform 25% of their earnings into *kyat,* but may keep the remainder in foreign denominations. There are now more than 5,000 foreign exchange accounts holding in total more than U.S.$5 million.

"I can't pretend it's my impression that SLORC is serious about improving the trade picture," says one Asian diplomat in Rangoon. "As it is, the military may be getting a lot of profits off black-market trading, maybe even off opium exports."

Meanwhile, the Burmese people must suffer rising inflation, especially for food items. The price of rice, the food staple, has shot up from *kyat* 5 per *pyi* (2.14 kilos) in 1988, to *kyat* 22 per *pyi* in August 1989. The price of eggs skyrocketed 150% from *kyat* 1 per egg in May 1989 this year to *kyat* 2.5 in July of the same year.

The hyperinflation has been fueled by

SLORC's decision to double civil service salaries in April, and the consequent need to print massive quantities of *kyat* to meet the greater demand for currency.

Should a "freely elected" government ever come into existence, it will not only have to cope with inflation but also with Burma's debt burden of close to U.S.$5 billion, with more than U.S.$150 million already in arrears.

Burma gave up all pretence of making debt repayments after most Western donors, such as West Germany, the U.S., Britain, and France, froze their aid programs in response to the atrocities committed by the Burmese military.

Geologists who have studied Burma's mineral reserves are convinced that the country has "world class" reserves of oil, zinc, tin, gold, and even diamonds that could be generating between U.S.$25 million and U.S.$100 million in exports per month, per mine.

The proper exploitation of one of two such mines would swiftly solve Burma's foreign debt problems, but the xenophobia that has characterized Burma's rulers for the past four decades is unlikely to disappear soon.

Excerpted from an article by Peter Janssen. © *Asian Business* magazine, Far East Trade Press, Ltd., 1989.

VIETNAM

A New Kind of Battle

by Brian Caplen

Asia's commercial shock troops wait for the order to advance.

The second Vietnam War is about to begin. Reconnaissance units have already landed, troop ships are ready for dispatch, and the message back from the front is strikingly clear: Prepare for a slow invasion.

But in this latest Indochina campaign, U.S. forces are not expected to be first into the firing line. Nor is the resistance going to come from a Vietnamese jungle army.

The battle to do business in Vietnam is being led by the Japanese, and the hostilities are going to come from Asian and other commercial rivals. Koreans, Taiwanese, Singaporeans, Indonesians, and Hong Kong Chinese —all are poised to parachute in on new opportunities.

French companies with their historical connections with Vietnam are also well placed for the onslaught, as are overseas Vietnamese— the *Vietkieu*—who are starting to look more favorably on investment prospects in their homeland.

All these battalions will slug it out as Vietnam's door creaks open to free trade and enterprise.

But U.S. companies are in a weak position. They can't Do Business With The Enemy, as American law proscribes it, and must wait until their commander—the U.S. government—sounds the all clear.

While the trade embargo stands, the most American companies can do is send out reconnaissance missions. The more cautious aren't even prepared to do that.

"We are definitely at a disadvantage," says an executive with a top U.S. multinational. "No one wants to do anything that could be interpreted as unpatriotic, but we really should be doing the groundwork on Vietnam like many of our rivals."

Other governments maintain an official boycott of Vietnam because of its 1979 invasion of Kampuchea, but they don't insist that business toes the line. "While we advise caution, private sector companies are free to do business with whoever they like," says a spokesman for Japan's Ministry of International Trade and Industry (MITI).

AMERICA'S TRADE EMBARGO

This means that if the U.S. lifts its embargo, paving the way for other nations to follow suit, Asian rather than American companies will be quickest into the fray. With Vietnam indicating a full withdrawal of troops from Kampuchea, some U.S. diplomatic sources expect the sanctions to be lifted in the forseeable future.

"My understanding from the people in Washington is that the policy toward Vietnam, which is essentially a Reagan administration policy, will now change regardless of whether all the troops are removed from Kampuchea," says a U.S. consulate source in Hong Kong who did not wish to be named.

"Most other countries are trading with Vietnam anyway. Only the United States is sticking to the embargo, which means we are just hurting ourselves."

This official considers the U.S.–Vietnam relations will follow the same pattern as U.S.–China relations did in the last decade, with new institutions being created for dialogue in the absence of full diplomatic ties.

Not all U.S. diplomats are as optimistic. Bangkok's U.S. Embassy spokesman Ross Petzing, reiterating the official line, says: "Our policy toward Vietnam remains basically unchanged. As long as it continues to occupy Kampuchea illegally, it will remain ineligible for government-to-government aid and we will continue the trade embargo."

Similarly, some sources say the Missing in Action issue—the United States wants more information on servicemen still missing from the Vietnam war—remains a stumbling block. Others think Vietnam is making the right kind of noises.

But the overall impression, gained by both American and Asian businessmen, is that the ice is thawing, improving the climate for new opportunities. And the thaw comes at the same time as Vietnam's communist rulers are warming to foreign investment as part of their efforts to solve crippling economic problems.

TRADE MOVES

Success in surmounting these problems is essential if Asia's capitalist supremos are to rebuild Vietnam. They can hardly do a good job while inflation continues at 700% and the official and black-market exchange rates remain so wildly different.

Lack of management expertise in government remains a huge hurdle. But clearly, Asian entrepreneurs do feel there are grounds for optimism and have, over the past year, been priming themselves for Vietnam's resurgence.

Trade missions have been sent. Joint venture companies with Vietnamese government interests have been established to funnel goods in from around the region. Complex countertrading deals have been put in place to cope with Vietnam's chronic foreign exchange shortage.

The Japanese, as usual, are out ahead. Their great skill has been the use of front companies to escape the stigma of Vietnam deals.

A major trading house like C Itoh, for example, which collaborated in 1987 with Nissho Iwai in importing Vietnamese crude oil to Japan, conducts business with Hanoi through a subsidiary called Shinetsu Tsusho.

Mitsubishi uses a company called Meiwa Sangyo, and Mitsui—which set up a representative office in Hanoi—uses a company called Shinwa Bussan. Shinwa Bussan was one of the leading Japanese partners with the Vietnam Ship Charter Corp. (Vietfracht) in the setting up of a regular freighter service between the two countries.

Some of these companies belong to the Tokyo-based Japan Vietnam Trade Association which, with its 90 members, is a firm indication of the scale of interest.

JAPAN–VIETNAM TRADE

As a result, a flourishing Japan–Vietnam trade has developed with some U.S.$200 million of goods moving in each direction, according to Japanese Tariff Association figures. Because of the trade's clandestine nature, this is almost certain to be an understatement.

According to IMF figures, Japanese goods accounted for 33.3%—the lion's share—of IMF-reported imports in 1986 and Japan took 23.7% of exports, the second-largest destination after Hong Kong. The IMF figures exclude much of the trade with socialist countries such as the Soviet Union.

The U.S. has tried to put pressure on Japan to stop its Vietnam dealings, and Honda pulled out of a project to assemble—and later start producing—motorcycles, after it came under attack in the American Congress. Other big-name manufacturers are almost certainly holding back because of this and (equally important) the aid that would make such ventures profitable.

At present, Japanese activity is confined to trading, and smaller projects such as a U.S.$10 million rice mill project for the Foodstuffs Company of Ho Chi Minh City, involving Satake Seisakusho and Nissho Iwai. The point is that when the green light goes on, the Japanese can quickly turn their grassroots bartering into big league pump priming.

"The Japanese never left Vietnam," comments a Vietnamese banker based in Hong Kong. "They have been trading throughout the troubles using front companies. All the motorcycles in Vietnam are Japanese, so are all the household appliances."

"Gradually, the U.S. influence is going to be secondary. Japan is taking the front seat on this one," says Mark Mobius, president of Templeton Emerging Markets Fund, who is looking at investment possibilities in Vietnam. "In the coming years, the attitude and actions of the U.S. government will have less bearing, not only on Vietnam, but in the region as a whole. The diplomatic pressure will not be a restraining factor over the longer term."

What perplexes the Japanese is that while they get all the flak for trading with Vietnam, other Asian nations are just as guilty—or enterprising—depending on how you look at it.

DRAGONS ON THE TRAIL

Singapore comes first to mind. According to Tran Huan Phoi, general director of Vietnam's Ministry of Foreign Economic Relations: "Singapore has shown great political hostility toward our country but, despite this, trade is well developed."

A considerable amount of this—and the Hong Kong trade, is in goods that originate from other places, including the U.S. which, unwittingly, supplies 5% of IMF-reported imports. But there are also glaring examples of direct Singapore trade, such as a U.S.$50 million oil rig built by Far East-Levingston Shipbuilding, Ltd. in Singapore.

Inchcape Pacific, one of the largest Hong Kong-based trading companies, openly declares its Vietnam dealings. "We are very bullish on the trading prospects," a company chief has been quoted as saying.

Overseas Vietnamese are playing a key role in establishing links between Vietnam and other Asian countries.

One example is the formation of a joint venture between Indonesia's PT Astra-International and the Ho Chi Minh City government to import building materials and pesticides into Vietnam and export agricultural products. The deal was arranged by Vietnamese in Hong Kong.

Even the staunchest of the anticommunist nations, Taiwan, is interested in Vietnam trade. Six delegates from the semi-official China External Trade Development Council visited Ho Chi Minh City and Dong Nai province to promote trade in 1988. It was the first semi-official visit to a communist nation ever authorized by Taipei, and as a result the 13-year ban on Taiwanese ships visiting the country was lifted.

HAMSTRUNG IN HANOI

"They [the Vietnamese] need everything—capital, equipment, even used equipment, and know-how," says mission leader J. S. Pan. "They need many things that Taiwan can supply, but since they are also lacking in foreign exchange, it's essential to take a long-term approach."

Based on the team's findings and on a second trip by representatives of the Kuomingtang-owned China Trade and Development Corp., a full-fledged trade mission visited Vietnam in late 1988. Among the companies in the mission were China Rebar and the Pan Overseas Corp., two of Taiwan's larger enterprises which have great experience in countertrade.

Koreans, too, have been feeling their way. The Korea Trade Promotion Corp. (KOTRA) is trying to open a representative office, and dispatched an official from its Bangkok branch for negotiations.

A number of Korean companies already trade with Vietnam—Samsumg, Hyosung Corp., Daedong Industrial Co., and Tong-yang Moolsan Co.—and the first two have expressed interest in building joint venture factories. Samsung TV sets are already being assembled from knock-down kits, and Samsung has been described as "a household name in Vietnam."

But Asian businessmen do not have a monopoly on Vietnam dealings.

"Every kind of businessman is in Vietnam. Not just Asians but Americans, West Germans, Swiss. You name it, they are there," says an executive who has visited the country for French electronics company Alcatel. Negotiations between Alcatel and the Vietnamese authorities on the supply of a new telephone system are at an advanced stage.

While historical ties should give French companies some advantages in Vietnam, the

Alcatel executive stresses that "there is no room for sentiment." The dire economic situation precludes that.

One French company with a strong presence in Vietnam is chemical manufacturer Rhone-Poulenc. It started operations there in 1950, got nationalized in 1975 when the communist government came to power, and then in 1979 became one of the first joint ventures. Besides manufacturing in Ho Chi Minh City, the company also deals in agrochemicals and acts as a representative for other European firms.

OVERSEAS VIETNAMESE

Strong, too, are the opportunities for overseas Vietnamese, who will almost certainly graduate from middlemen and deal-fixers to direct investors. Serepeco, an overseas Vietnamese company based in France, supplied equipment and expertise for the new Saigon Petro oil refinery. But there is some opposition from overseas Vietnamese who feel it inappropriate to cooperate with a regime that pushed many of them out of the country.

Finally, American companies do not want to be left out of the action. Three companies —Pepsico, Sheraton, and Caterpillar—all noted pioneers in doing business in unfamiliar terrain, expressed interest in Vietnam. They said the only thing stopping them exploring the situation further was the U.S. embargo.

"We are waiting to jump in as soon as the restrictions are lifted,'" says Lai Kim Yin, Pepsico's director of operations and marketing for China.

The company has a strong track record in socialist countries and is an expert in countertrade. In China, the company uses revenues from its domestic soft drinks factory to pay the costs of export projects—mushrooms, toys, spices, and soft drinks—that generate profits in foreign exchange.

Says John Ip, forecasting services director for research group Business International Asia/Pacific, Ltd.: "A lot of U.S. companies are itching to get back in and a number of our regular customers have asked us to monitor the situation."

REBUILDING VIETNAM

But the rebuilding of Vietnam, whoever does it, requires more than just U.S. approval to make it a success. Vietnam's economy is in an appalling mess and anything but conducive to investment from overseas. Even the new foreign investment law enacted at the end of 1987 will cut no ice unless basic economic ills are healed.

Inflation, or "price fever" as the Vietnamese call it, is completely out of control at between 700% and 1,000%, depending presumably on how you measure it and whether you believe measuring that kind of hyperinflation is even a scientifically valid exercise.

Even though the government devalued the *dong* massively (in late 1988), from 368 to U.S.$1 to 2,600 to U.S.$1, this still compares feebly with the black-market rate of 4,500, and is not even a starting point for negotiations. Major transactions are now based on gold or U.S. dollars and workers' salaries are often paid according to the going price for rice.

Both problems were exacerbated in 1988 when, to avert near-famine conditions in the north, the government started printing large amounts of money. The IMF's anti-inflationary advice to officials was not to issue new denomination notes above 500 *dong*. All went by the board as 1,000, 2,000 and 5,000 *dong* notes were required to persuade southern farmers to part with their surplus rice.

The buck stops with the sorry sprawling Vietnamese bureaucracy that doesn't have either the tools or the management expertise to sort the situation out. "The Vietnam government's three main problems are management, management, and management," comments a cynical Western observer.

Fast becoming Vietnam's most famous PR man, Harvard-educated economic adviser Nguyen Xuan Oanh says he has promised the IMF he will bring back some stability to the economy.

Failure to do this prompted the IMF to delay additional financial assistance to the country at the beginning of 1988, says Oanh, who held a variety of top jobs including that of finance minister under the former South Vietnamese government. After the North Vietnamese stormed into Ho Chi Minh City in 1975, Oanh spent a year under house arrest.

The chief obstacles to stability, he says, are the state bank and inflation. Vietnam, he says, has "a state bank that doesn't stick to its role. It is managed very badly, and in terms of monetary policy it has been so weak that the reverse (of stability) has happened."

"We have three-digit inflation and a state bank that doesn't know what to do about it. I have been pushing them all along and I hope to succeed some time in the future. We need many reforms—monetary reforms, financial reforms, foreign exchange reforms—but our government seems to play footsy."

NEEDED: MANAGEMENT MEDICINE

A dose of IMF management medicine is almost certainly what's needed if it can stop short of causing street riots. The Catch-22 is that the IMF won't come in until the economy is stable, and the economy won't be stable until the IMF comes in.

Despite these problems, it is still more likely that Vietnam will develop this way, rather than retreating into the arms of its Soviet allies. The simple reason is that the Russians are tired of pouring aid—some U.S.$5 million a day—into the place.

Mikhail Gorbachev has hinted at his dissatisfaction, and more recently an unnamed Soviet economist was quoted by the *Far Eastern Economic Review* as saying: "We've always pulled these countries toward the Soviet Union. But they're in Southeast Asia—they have to develop in that context, by trading and cooperating with other Southeast Asian countries, and eventually with China."

This conforms with the basic truth that Vietnam never had a great deal in common with Moscow anyway, and the alliance was forged mainly out of a shared dislike for China. The heavy industrial development model favored by the Soviet Union is clearly inappropriate to an impoverished nation where 85% of the population live in the countryside. Indeed, it was peasant dissent—caused by the transfer of scarce capital to industry at the expense of agricultural product prices—which led to the first batch of reforms as long ago as 1980.

DOI MOI FEVER

Even if Vietnam does stick close by the Soviet Union, all may not be lost. With *perestroika* (restructuring) still in ascendency in Moscow, the Vietnamese equivalent *doi moi* (new thought) should remain on the boil.

There is always the possibility of relapse, and economics guru Nguyen Xuan Oanh says that under a cultural revolution he would be the first to go.

But, says a Vietnamese banker in Hong Kong, "We have reached the level of hope." He points out that the time between Vietnam's communist revolution and the current liberalization is relatively short, just 12 years, compared with the 30 years it took China to open up and the even longer time in the Soviet Union.

While Vietnam's government has taken the rap for a great deal—it has been compared to an old style Confucian bureaucracy where nepotism ruled—the frequently heard excuse that the country has suffered 30 years of war does have substance. Moreover, the level of development was pitifully low even before the batterings started.

A parasitic brand of French colonialism bled the place dry for a century and failed to foster a middle class strong enough to lead a national capitalist revolution. This paved the way for peasant communism and U.S. forces spent more than a decade trying to defend a middle class that didn't really exist.

According to the authors of *In Search of Southeast Asia:* "When it began its industrialization in 1954, North Vietnam had far fewer modern industrial assets than China or North Korea. The early political and military triumphs of the Vietnamese revolution, however, favored the exaltation of the imagined capacities of the Vietnamese economy in the minds of its leaders."

No one is feeling exalted these days. Vietnam's leaders know that dreams and ideology are not what progress is made of and they realize Western aid and technology would considerably speed their task.

Infrastructure is a top priority, and the familiar list of telecommunications, ports, roads, and power supplies are the things an aid package would need to get its teeth into. This would accelerate the use of Vietnam as an export processing center.

According to Vu Quang Duong, the country's trade representative in Hong Kong, the new investment code encourages firms to engage in export processing and take advantage of Vietnam's cheap labor.

The average factory worker in Ho Chi Minh City earns between 40,000 and 50,000 *dong* a month (about U.S.$9 to U.S.$11 at black-market rates and U.S.$15 to U.S.$19 at the official exchange rate). In Hanoi, rates are 50% lower.

Some Hong Kong businessmen are already sending fabric to Vietnam and receiving back garments, claims Vu, although he says he can't name them because they may also be working in China.

CLUB HO

Another main interest of foreign investors is in hotels and tourism, and French resort chain Club Mediterranee has talked about both tours and a resort—a prospect that staggers many observers. Turning a country where recent historical experiences are mainly of war and famine, into a center for fun and frolics does seem bizarre. But it is not without precedent and could provide useful foreign exchange.

Finally, there are unexploited natural recourses, especially oil. The signing of an exploration contract (in 1988) with Royal Dutch Shell and Belgium's Petrofina was a major step forward on this front.

No one thinks that building the new Vietnam will be an overnight victory. As U.S. forces discovered in the first Vietnam War, the most advanced technology and strategy can be scuppered by "the local factor."

Vietnamese bureaucrats who imagine they're still a guerrilla movement could sabotage things very quickly. If their economy resembles a jungle, modern Asian armies whose aims are profits rather than politics will leave much faster than the U.S. did. Their crack regiments can be withdrawn and redeployed in weeks, should the odds prove overwhelming.

But still this "rich land with poor people," as government adviser Le Dang Doang expressed it, ought to come through. Vietnam has shown it can win military wars, the next step is to prove it can win economic ones—by letting others do the fighting.

Written by Brian Caplen, reported by Peter Janssen in Ho Chi Minh City, Hanoi, and Bangkok, Kevin Sullivan in Tokyo, Jung Nam Chi in Seoul, Don Shapiro in Taipei. © *Asian Business* magazine, Far East Trade Press, Ltd., 1989.

"Force binds for a time; education binds forever."

Vietnamese proverb

JEANS FROM VIETNAM

South Pacific Textiles Industry, Malaysia's leading garment company, entered into a $1 million joint venture to produce jeans in Vietnam. The mill in Nha Trang, north of Ho Chi Minh City, with 100,000 spindles, is the biggest in Vietnam.

SOUTH KOREA'S VIET EXPORTS

South Korea exported $49 million worth of textile and electronic products to Vietnam in 1988.

ON THE WESTERN RIM

"There is a $3 trillion market out there in the Pacific Rim countries, and it is growing at a rate of three billion dollars a week. So I think that there are tremendous opportunities for all the people in our states to take advantage of that type of growth and expansion."
—Former Governor George Deukmajian of California

The western U.S. region has a vibrant and growing connection with the nations of the Pacific Rim region. Five western states, one commonwealth, and two Pacific territories border on the Pacific Ocean, and several western states share common borders with Canada and Mexico.

These western states—all of them members of the independent and nonpartisan Western Governors' Association—include Alaska, Arizona, California, Colorado, Hawaii, Idaho, Kansas, Minnesota, Montana, Nebraska, Nevada, New Mexico, North Dakota, Oregon, South Dakota, Utah, Washington, and Wyoming.

In 1988, as a group, they exported $44 billion dollars worth of merchandise to the Pacific Rim region, out of a total of $69 billion dollars exported world wide during that year. About 38% of these exports were shipped by air transport. Thus, these exports to the Pacific Rim constituted about 63% of total western state exports.

Between 1987 and 1988, western state exports to the Pacific Rim expanded by 33%. Nevada was the only western state which did not export over half of its exports to the Pacific Rim in 1988.

THE JAPANESE CONNECTION

Almost one third of western state exports to the Pacific Rim were destined for Japan, which is the number-one export market worldwide for western state exports, followed by Canada, the United Kingdom, Mexico, and West Germany. However, exports to Japan far exceed exports to Canada, the next largest export market, by a margin of almost two to one. Between 1987 and 1988, western state exports to Japan increased by about $4 billion.

Exports to Japan are strongest in the Pacific Coast states of California, Oregon, Washington, Alaska, and Hawaii. For example, 16% of California exports were destined for Japan in 1987, 55% of which were machinery, transportation, and instruments, and 45% of which were crops and other products. In 1987, 27% of Washington's exports were sent to Japan, of which 37% were transportation equipment products, and 28% were lumber and wood products.

Washington state is in the process of setting-up a "Washington Village" project in the Hyogo prefecture of Japan, which will promote Washington's forest products and wooden housing technology industries. It has been built with the assistance of Washington state construction workers, carpenters, and building technicians, and will be used to market the entire Washington Village project to the Japanese buying public.

DIALOGUE WITH THE DRAGONS

South Korea and Taiwan are the third and fourth largest western state export markets in the Pacific Rim. In 1988, exports to South Korea equaled $3.9 billion, and exports to Taiwan equaled $2.8 billion. This amounted to a 56% increase over 1987 for exports to Korea, and a 47% increase over 1987 for exports to Taiwan.

THE U.S.–CANADA FREE-TRADE AGREEMENT

Canada is the second largest Pacific Rim export market for the western states, and it is either the first or second most important trading partner for 16 western states. In 1988 the western states exported $8 billion worth of merchandise to Canada. This represented a $2 billion increase over 1987. In 1987, Canada was the largest export market for Minnesota, Nebraska, Nevada, North Dakota, South Dakota, Utah, and Wyoming.

The U.S.–Canada Free-Trade Agreement (FTA), which was implemented on January 1, 1989, opens the door for higher levels of economic activity. The FTA provides for the elimination of tariff and nontariff barriers over a 10-year period. The FTA also calls for continuing negotiations to enhance free trade in areas such as government procurement, services, standards, subsidies, and tariff removal. As the FTA entered its second year of implementation, trade data comparing the first half of 1988 with 1989 showed that total U.S. exports to Canada grew over 20% to

$41 billion. On the other side of the coin, imports from Canada were up by 12% to a total of $46 billion.

The U.S.–Canada FTA created some unexpected side effects, such as grass roots business and civic partnerships. Provincial and state governments have started several new joint economic development programs, ranging from setting-up compatible automatic-teller machine systems on either side of the border to designing a snowmobile trail that wanders back and forth across the border.

For example, the Canadian province of Manitoba has exchanged two provincial trade officials with the state of Kansas which is over 600 miles south of the border. And government officials in Minnesota and Montana are working in coordinating their health care services and manufacturing industries. In fact, it is quite apparent that the border between Canada and the U.S. is becoming progressively more blurred as the benefits of bilateral economic and cultural cooperation continue to grow.

SOUTH OF THE BOARDROOM: MEXICO'S *MAQUILADORAS*

Grass-roots cooperative efforts are also growing along the Southwest border between the U.S. and Mexico. Mexico is the third largest Pacific Rim export market for the West.

In 1988, western states exported $4 billion to Mexico, an increase of 38% over 1987. Mexico is the number-one export market for Arizona. In 1987, 39% of Arizona's exports to Mexico were electronic products, and 25% were other machinery products. It is believed that a large percentage of these products are exported for use by *maquiladora* industries. (For a discussion of the *maquiladora* industry, see "Mexico's High-Tech El Dorado" on p. 193.)

To facilitate transborder trade, the governors of the Southwest border of the United States joined with the governors of the Mexican border states to form the *U.S.–Mexico Border Governors' Conference.*

The Conference meets periodically to improve relations among the border governors, and to implement policies to improve the region in the areas of commerce and investment, industrial development, tourism, agriculture, and health. The border governors support the development of the *maquiladora* industries because they foster job and business growth in the border region. About 70% of the *maquiladoras* are American companies. However, Japanese and European companies are also setting up *maquiladora* operations. Companies with *maquiladoras* can take advantage of wage rates in Mexico, which are lower than Korean wage rates.

WESTERN EXPORTS TO THE PACIFIC RIM

Compared to other regions of the world, the East Asian countries in the Pacific Rim import relatively more natural resource products from the western states than manufactured products.

In 1988, $8 billion worth of food, crops, lumber, chemicals, minerals, and oil and gas products were exported from the western states to East Asia (including China, Hong Kong, Japan, Mongolia, South Korea, and Taiwan). By comparison, only $1 billion worth of similar products were exported to the European Community. The amount of manufactured products exported from the western states to East Asia and the European Community is more equivalent. Between 1987 and 1988 western state exports to East Asia increased by $7 billion.

The western states primarily export manu-

TABLE III: WHAT THE WEST EXPORTS, 1988
(Billions of Dollars)

	NTH. AMERICA	EEC	SOUTHEAST ASIA	EAST ASIA	OTHER	TOTAL
FOOD	$1	$0	$0	$2	$0	$4
CROP	$1	$0	$0	$2	$1	$4
LUMBER	$1	$0	$0	$2	$0	$3
CHEMICALS	$0	$0	$0	$1	$0	$2
MINERALS, OIL & GAS	$0	$0	$0	$0	$0	$0
SUBTOTAL	$3	$1	$1	$8	$2	$13
MACHINERY (EXCEPT ELECTRICAL)	$3	$4	$1	$3	$4	$14
TRANSPORTATION EQUIPMENT	$2	$3	$1	$4	$5	$14
ELECTRICAL, ELECTRONIC	$2	$2	$2	$3	$2	$11
INSTRUMENTS	$1	$1	$0	$1	$1	$5
SUBTOTAL	$6	$10	$4	$12	$11	$44
ALL OTHER PRODUCTS	$3	$1	$0	$5	$2	$11
TOTAL WEST	$13	$13	$5	$24	$15	$68

(Numbers may not add to totals due to rounding)

factured products to Canada and Mexico, with exports of machinery, transportation equipment, electronic products, and instruments equaling $6 billion in 1988 to both nations. Between 1987 and 1988 western state exports to Canada and Mexico increased by about $3 billion.

The countries of Southeast Asia predominantly import manufactured products from the western states. In 1988, the Southeast Asian countries imported $4 billion worth of machinery, transportation equipment, electrical products, and instruments, and $1 billion worth of food, crops, lumber, chemicals, minerals, and oil and gas products. Between 1987 and 1988, western state exports to Southeast Asia increased by $1 billion.

Interestingly, a large and growing export from the West to Pacific Rim countries is in the category of waste and scrap. With recy-

cling currently in vogue in the United States, over $1 billion dollars of waste paper, cardboard, and metal is exported from the West for reprocessing overseas. Japan and Taiwan are the leaders in purchasing used paper for reprocessing.

FOREIGN DIRECT INVESTMENT

Despite the "Pacific Rimization" of the region, the bulk of foreign direct investment (FDI) in the western U.S. states is still derived from European companies. European firms contributed about 56% of total employment generated by foreign direct investment in the West in 1987. By contrast, Japanese companies accounted for 18% of total FDI employment in the West, and Canadian companies provided 16%.

Destination of Western State Exports to the Pacific Rim

Almost one-third of western state exports to the Pacific Rim were destined for Japan in 1988. See Table I: Top Five Pacific Rim Markets for Western Exports: 1987/1988:

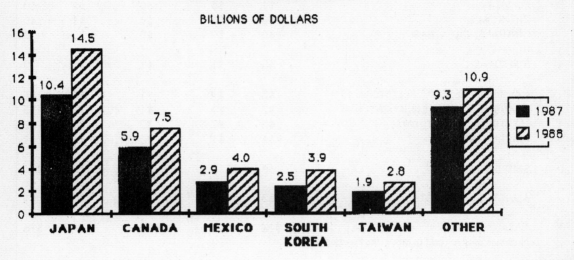

TABLE I: TOP FIVE PACIFIC RIM MARKETS FOR WESTERN
EXPORTS: 1987/1988

BILLIONS OF DOLLARS

Also see Table II: Top Five Pacific Rim Markets for Western States By Percentages, 1988:

TABLE II: TOP FIVE PACIFIC RIM MARKETS FOR
WESTERN EXPORTS: 1988, BY PERCENTAGES

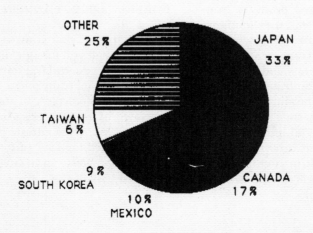

HAWAIIAN REPORT:

HAWAII'S FINANCIAL ASPIRATIONS

Positioned roughly midway between the United States and Asia, Hawaii sees itself as being in the right spot at the right time—ready to assume its obviously preordained role as a leading Pacific Rim player. The state's political and business leaders are united in their efforts to lure large brokerage houses and create financial exchanges for the trading of stocks and other commodities.

Such facilities could neatly fill the four-hour gap between the closing of the New York Stock Exchange and the opening of its counterpart in Tokyo, thus allowing for what amounts to round-the-clock trading.

"What we could make it easier for American exchanges to do," says Galen Fox, executive assistant to Honolulu mayor Frank Fasi, "is to trade with Asia on Asian time. If you want to expand business with Asia, which in some ways is already the center of the financial world, then you should be catering to their markets and interests rather than asking them to get up early in the morning or [stay up to] midnight to trade with your markets. It's a breakthrough in thinking in terms of how important it is to reach Asia. The breakthrough occurs in part because you can do it in Honolulu."

The fact that Hawaii's population is already very mixed could be a persuasive enticement to brokerage firms from both sides of the Pacific. "You have a number of people here who are very knowledgeable about both markets. I think a knowledge base exists here that few other cities would have," says the dean of Hawaii's School of Business Administration, David Bess. And another important factor to allay any lingering fears is that all trades would be regulated by U.S. security laws.

Hawaii boosters are well aware of the importance of diversifying the Hawaiian economy, 39% of whose $22 billion revenues (in 1988) came from the tourist industry. The creation of a financial center, officials feel, would bring in its wake a wide range of industries and supporting services providing hundreds of jobs.

The whole subject of international activity in fact is coming under increasing scrutiny as publicity about the Pacific Rim concept induces the island community to look more and more outward. Once tourism is excluded, international activity accounts for a mere 3% of the economy, indicating that the state "has barely tested its potential as an Asia-Pacific bridge," according to a recent survey by the East–West Center.

The Honolulu-based, nonprofit research institute reached its totals by adding such jobs as the 400 in the pineapple industry unconnected to U.S. markets, 1,700 people involved in agricultural research, and about 5,500 out-of-state persons involved there year-round in international studies. Also included in the nontourist international sphere were overseas government and consular staff and employees in the film, garment, petroleum, and coral products industries.

The survey's author, A. A. Smyser, suggested that Hawaii's international involvement had

(continued)

growth potential in such areas as Pacific transportation and communication; training and production for export; diplomatic and government activities; business, administrative, marketing and consulting services; sports and health fitness; and international arts and culture.

U.S. Navy Jumps on the Pacific Rim Bandwagon

Alarmed by possible cutbacks in national defense spending, which would sharply reduce its forces in the Pacific, the U.S. Navy has been turning to economics to make its argument for maintaining a large regional presence on the Rim.

In an interview in *Navy Times* magazine, Admiral David Jeremiah, commander of the U.S. Pacific Fleet, warned that Soviet spy ships off Hawaii may be intercepting commercial financial data as well as military information. "There is an enormous amount of financial data that filters through Honolulu because Honolulu is a time zone that can work New York and Tokyo simultaneously," he noted.

Soviet spy ships are now allegedly spending 260 days a year snooping around Hawaiian waters as opposed to 60 days a year prior to 1987.

Even as the Cold War between the U.S. and the Soviet Union succumbs to *perestroika* and *glasnost,* a new confrontation may be rising on the economic front, Jeremiah suggested. Consequently, one of the Pacific Fleet's main missions in patrolling the 100 million square miles of Pacific Ocean is safeguarding the stability of crucial trans-Pacific trade routes.

"[The Pacific Ocean] is where our technology is today, where our export markets are and where our import providers are . . . the Pacific Fleet would like to take a great deal of credit for that economic activity," he said.

"[Admiral Jeremiah's argument] is simply a way to justify the continuing existence of a bloated Pacific Fleet at a time when the Cold War is on the wane and the U.S. is being forced to confront and bring under control a huge military-driven budget deficit," remarked Jerry Sanders, professor of Peace and Conflict Studies at the University of California at Berkeley. "It's the same old geo-political argument dressed up for a geo-economic era.

"What would the Moscow intelligentsia do with its (insider information), call their traders in Hong Kong—or sell it to [former Drexel Burnham Lambert junk bond king] Michael Milken?" Sanders asked.

Although European companies hold the majority of FDI in the West, Japanese companies show the highest rate of growth in FDI during the past few years. Between 1986 and 1987, Japanese firms accounted for a 17% increase in employment generated by FDI in the West. In contrast, the employment created by European FDI declined by 2.5% during the same two years, and Canadian FDI employment declined by 5.4%.

Protectionist Fears

As in the rest of the United States, foreign investment stirs mixed emotions in the West.

Attitudes about foreign investment range from enthusiasm to fear of the "buying of America." Nobel Laureate and economist Milton Friedman argues that foreign investment is a very good thing, and that protectionism is bad for world consumers. According to Friedman, the growth of foreign investment in the United States is a sign of the strength of the nation's economy. "The U.S. has been a desirable place in which to invest. Foreigners have wanted to invest in the U.S., and U.S. investors have found the U.S. a better place to invest their funds than abroad . . . It's always been a puzzle to me why that is [seen as] a sign of weakness . . . Is it really a sign of weakness that Japan would rather invest in the U.S. than in Japan? Surely it's a sign that Japan doesn't offer attractive investment opportunities, otherwise they'd leave their money at home."

In general, most western states work on promoting foreign investment because of the economic benefits which are derived from increased employment and business activity. Nevertheless, western governors and other political leaders are mindful of the potential problems which are isolated with foreign investment, such as the potential displacement of competing domestic companies and the impact of foreign investment upon domestic real estate markets.

For example, the issue of foreign investment has generated a great deal of controversy in Hawaii, particularly as it applies to real estate property values. Currently, the Hawaii state government administrative policy toward foreign investment takes the posture that investment needs to be directed and managed, and that all investors should pay their fair share and act in a responsible manner for the benefit of the entire Hawaiian community. To enforce such actions, the government needs a variety of tools. There are several bills under consideration in the Hawaii state legislature which deal with the issue of foreign investment.

SOURCE: The Western Governors' Association. By Elizabeth J. Santillanez with the assistance of Christopher McKinnon and Derek Liston.

ON THE CANADIAN RIM

"Canadians should recognize the Pacific Region not as the Far East but as the New West."

Since former Canadian Prime Minister Pierre Trudeau made that statement over 20 years ago, Canadians have been casting an expectant eye at the Far West. Today, the Asia-Pacific region accounts for some 43% of Canada's non-U.S. trade, compared with just 34% of its European trade.

As far back as 1972, its exports to Japan surpassed those to Britain. In 1982, the Pacific sea lanes became more important than the Atlantic lanes. Today, even the province of Newfoundland depends more on Japan for its exports than any other offshore nation.

But for all the Rim optimism, Canada's

trade relations with Asia remain relatively small. Asia represents only about 10% of its exports, of which Japan makes up half. So Rim "trade fever" is still more prospect than it is bonanza.

If trade with the region is still modest, so is investment. The Asian countries account for an estimated $6 billion of $110 billion in total direct foreign investment in Canada. Portfolio investment—stocks, bonds, and direct loans —is several times that amount.

While the flow of money from Asia is comparatively small, it is going to highly publicized areas. Here is a list of Canada–Rim deals, according to a report by Andrew Cohen of the Toronto-published *Financial Post*.

In the automobile sector, South Korea's Hyundai Auto Co. invested about $450 million in Quebec; Toyota Canada, Inc., Honda Motor Co., Ltd., and Suzuki Motor Co. poured about $1 billion into Ontario.

In pulp and paper, Japan's Daishowa Paper Manufacturing Co., Ltd., committed $500 million to a plant in Alberta. In tourism, Asian interests are buying hotels in Banff, Alberta, and Whistler, British Columbia. In technology, Sumitomo Heavy Industries, Ltd. of Japan acquired Lumonics, Inc., one of the world's largest laser equipment manufacturers, which is headquartered in Kanata, Ontario.

Taiwan has been snapping up real estate and resources, as exemplified by the joint venture of Westcoast Energy, Inc. and five Taiwanese companies. China, led by Celgar Pulp Co. in British Columbia, is involved in about 40 joint ventures worth about $500 million. South Korea invested $400 million in pulp and paper, steel, and manufacturing in 1989 alone.

Then there are the faces of Asian wealth, particularly from Hong Kong: tycoon Li-Kai-shing, who controls Husky Oil, Ltd. and Vancouver's former Expo '87 lands; Stanley Ho, who has made his International Semi-Tech Microelectronics, Inc. a global player; and Cheng Yu-tung, another mogul from Hong Kong, who is a leading investor in Toronto property.

By far the biggest Asian investor in Canada is Japan. Its total foreign direct investment in 1986 was $2.3 billion. It is now said to be over $4 billion. Total two-way trade between Canada and Japan is $18 billion—twice as large as Canada's trade with Britain and three times as large as its trade with West Germany. The figure is expected to rise to $40 billion by the year 2000.

During the next decade, Canada is likely to remain attractive to Japan—and especially to Hong Kong, where political uncertainty over 1997 has caused not only a flight of capital, but of emigrants as well.

CANADA'S PACIFIC 2000 PROGRAM

In recent years, Canada has expanded its export development programs, opened new trade offices in the Asia-Pacific, and strengthened its investment promoting activities. In the fall of 1989, Canada's Cabinet approved a package of initiatives called "Pacific 2000."

The program involves a commitment of $65 million through 1994. Here are some of its components:

"Pacific Business Strategy" ($14 million) entails such activities as sustained promotional initiatives in key sectors, encouragement of the formation of business linkages, and general expansion of Canada's trade representation in Asia.

"Japan Science and Technology Fund" ($25.1 million) is aimed at improving awareness of and access to Japan's advanced technologies, as well as industry-to-industry cooperative projects.

"Asian Languages and Awareness Fund"

($14.7 million) mounts programs to develop language-training facilities, to assist with curriculum development, to provide incentives for Asian languages training, and to encourage teacher training in Canada.

"Pacific 2000 Projects Fund" ($11.4 million) includes strategic exchange programs, such as among parliamentarians and journalists, and provides for Canada's full involvement in emerging Pacific institutions.

SOURCE: External Affairs and International Trade Canada.

ON THE LATIN AMERICAN RIM

MEXICO'S HIGH-TECH EL DORADO

Tijuana is shedding its former image as "sin city," a south-of-the-border Sodom and Gomorrah. This teeming Mexican metropolis of 1.6 million people is now more commonly referred to as the gateway to the "new Hong Kong." The city has become the center of a booming industrial corridor which spans the 1,000-mile U.S.–Mexican border from Tijuana–San Diego to Matamoros–Brownsville, Texas.

From sleazy bordertown bars and raunchy strip joints to strict "clean room" environments where high-tech products like semiconductors and medical equipment are assembled by skilled, and cheap, Mexican labor, the economic transformation of Tijuana has been truly remarkable.

The key to Tijuana's, and indeed to Mexico's, economic development, are the so-called *maquiladoras,* or twin-plant facilities, located along the Mexican border.

A *maquiladora* is a factory in Mexico usually associated with labor-intensive assembly. It shares production with twin-plants in the U.S. or abroad. One special advantage is that they're exempt from limitations on foreign ownership, so they can be 100% foreign-owned and operated.

Another benefit of operating a *maquiladora* plant in Mexico is that, under a special law, raw or semiprocessed materials used to produce finished goods are exempt from import duty. More to the point, *maquiladora* products are exempt from export duties and can enter the U.S. market duty-free.

"It's cheaper to produce or manufacture in Mexico than in Hong Kong," noted Armando Ledesma, director of Phillips Ledesma Asociados, S.A. de C.V., a Tijuana-based firm which specializes in insurance bonding for the *maquiladora* industry. "The minimum wage here starts at 5,049 pesos a day (about $2.30) compared to about $15 a day in Hong Kong or Taiwan. When you figure in the costs of transportation, that takes a lot more out of the profit margin."

In 1987, the *maquiladoras* contributed an estimated $2 billion to Mexico's beleaguered economy. "It's now second to oil in terms of bringing in foreign capital to Mexico," noted

Ron Jensen, a *maquiladora* analyst. "In just five years, it's outdistanced tourism as a major revenue earner."

There are currently more than 500 *maquiladora* operations in Tijuana. One major *maquiladora* subcontractor, the San Diego-headquartered Imec, Inc., represents some of the biggest names in U.S. high-tech, including TRW, Loral, Sperry, 3M, ITT, and Hughes, to name a few. The U.S. firms are not alone. The Japanese, the South Koreans, and the Taiwanese have also discovered this El Dorado of electronics.

THE MAGNIFICENT SHOGUN

The advantages of using Mexico as a manufacturing springboard for the U.S. market have not been lost on Japan. Driven by the devalued peso, the revalued yen, and the proximity of the world's largest consumer market just across the border, major Japanese corporations have opened dozens of factories since 1988. The big guns include Mitsubishi, Sanyo, Matsushita, Hitachi, Sony, and Casio.

As the San Diego Economic Development Corp. described Japan's rationale for using *maquiladoras:* "If a firm is to be successful, it must respond to consumer demand. When Sears tells Sanyo their customers want quality refrigerators and they can get them from Korea, Sanyo has to close their U.S. operations or take part of it to Mexico to compete."

The Japanese have added a new wrinkle to their *maquiladora* operations. It is worrying U.S. firms, and it's also prompting protectionists in Congress to call for a repeal of the existing tariff law which permits duty-free *maquiladora* imports into the U.S.

Previously, the Japanese bought most of their source materials from U.S. companies.

For example, Matsushita's U.S. content is about 20%, while Sanyo uses close to 70%. (By contrast, Mexican content is less than 2%.) Now that Japanese are launching "second tier" production facilities to supply *maquiladoras* with their own components and raw materials and are eliminating their U.S. sources.

"The Japanese will drag along all their suppliers . . . and then the suppliers of the suppliers," predicted Lee Hill, a *maquiladora* industry pioneer and a founder of Imec, Inc.

Midway down the Baja California peninsula, about 500 miles south of Tijuana, Japanese, South Korean, and Hong Kong investors are building a *maquiladora* city on the site of Guerrero Negro, a former salt-mining town. "They're just buying up all the land there," said Jensen. "The project is code-named "The Zen."

SUDS FLOW SOUTH; STEEL, NORTH

In a deal that increases Mexico's steel exports to the United States, American beer and liquor manufacturers may market their products more freely in Mexico. The 1988 agreement eliminates a quota system Mexico had placed on imports of foreign liquor. Under the quota, a million dollars worth of beer, $19 million in wine, and $24 million in distilled spirits were allowed into the country. The U.S. share of that amounted to $2.5 million during the first three quarters of 1987. By contrast, Mexico shipped about $182.5 million worth of liquor—mostly beer—into the U.S. in 1987. U.S. winemakers will be exporting up to $20 million worth of wines and coolers to Mexico by 1993, predicted James Clawson, an American wine industry analyst.

LATIN AMERICA'S NEW COMPETITIVENESS
by William C. Grindley

In Latin America, as in the rest of the world, Asia's vibrant economies are making people look, buy—and think hard. Mexican businessman Armando Herrera Delgado stocks up on Toshiba batteries, Casio watches, Hong Kong-made dolls, and Samsung television sets. "Asian countries strode past the U.S.," he shrugs, "and that's why we sell their goods." As Latin Americans ponder a decade in which the collapse of Eastern Europe's "command economy" governments contrasted so starkly with the ascendancy of Asia's export-driven economies, it became clear which was the more promising model to emulate.

While the circumstances were different, Eastern Europeans had been led in the same direction—away from the rigors of global competition. Thirty years of import substitution, state industry, and central planning masked protected ruling classes and business oligarchies as well as a host of ill-conceived, central-government-financed and perpetuated schemes.

The financial consequences were the international debt crisis, with little or negative economic growth, while much of the rest of the world enjoyed an unprecedented boom. The result in Eastern Europe has been radical political change; and in Latin America the realization that the price of continuing present policies is far too high.

Some governments have done more than ponder. They have gone ahead and adopted economic policies that have worked well in Asia. The emphasis in Mexico, Chile, and Brazil, for example, is exports. Devaluation, abolition of protectionist measures, elimination of import licenses, and other such unpopular steps have been recognized as necessary, if bitter, medicine.

Latin American leaders have seen that not only is double-digit economic and trade growth Asia's norm, but that borders open to foreign investment attract capital from neighbors as well as richer nations. Simultaneously, weary Latin Americans searching the world for investment capital for their risky, protected economies have seen monies flow rapidly into Southeast Asia's freewheeling economies.

Latin Americans have historically feared that if their economies were open to foreign investment, they would be dominated by the United States, but as the world's economy became multipolar in the 1980s, with the United States becoming a less dominant economic force, the threat of reprisal from the "Yanquis," an abiding fear in Latin America, diminished. In fact, by the late 1980s, Japan had displaced the United States as the main investor in Latin America.

With the yen's value in an upward spiral, the Latin Americans have visions of an investment windfall from Japan. South America already accounts for 19.2% of the estimated $150 billion in assets Japanese investors have parked abroad since 1952. Brazil was the favorite haven in the 1970s but it has since tumbled to fifth place because of concerns about its huge foreign debt. But Brasilia is mounting a determined effort to lure Japanese money, stressing the country's low labor costs, skilled manpower, relative proximity to the United States' potentially huge domestic market—and the 800,000 Japanese Brazilians in the country, reckoned an advantage in cultivating Japan's goodwill.

A generation ago Asians were apprehensive about their dependence on the United States to absorb their exports, and the global dominance of American investment. A decade ago about two thirds of all Asian exports were U.S.-bound, with the exception of Singapore, which has always maintained strong relations with Europe. However, they largely welcomed U.S. investments, controlled them, and built relations with the United States as their principal investor and trading partner.

Today, however, the United States is no longer such a dominant trade partner for Asia's economies. As recently as 1985 over half of Taiwan's and a third of Hong Kong's goods were shipped to the United States. By 1989 those shares had decreased to a third and a fifth, respectively. Korea has halved its U.S.-bound exports, and Japan's dependency on U.S. markets for its exports has decreased 10 percentage points to about 30% over the last five years.

Share of Corporate Direct Investment Placed in Latin America

	1950	1988
U.S.	38%	13%
Japan	0%	18%

CHILI PEPPERS IMITATE DRAGONS

In the 1980s, two Latin American nations, Chile and Mexico, set out to replicate what they saw happening in Asia. With opening borders, few exchange controls, inflation-fighting monetary policies, minimal restrictions on foreign investment, and fiscal policies designed to make their economies export-driven, these two nations have been able to gain a foothold in the world economy. Other Latin American nations, notably Brazil and Venezuela, seem to be moving toward the Asia model of success.

Of the success stories being emulated, the four Little Dragons are especially admired. "Mexico's economic strategy of the past 10 years," notes Maria Antonieta Benejam of that country's Economic Research and Study Center, "has been modeled particularly on Taiwan, Singapore, Hong Kong, and South Korea." Mexico has decided to become a member of the Pacific Basin Economic Cooperation Conference. In Brazil, meanwhile, Asia as a trading partner is bidding to catch up with such well-established predecessors as the United States and the European Economic Community. Analysts say the two markets are natural complements, since most Asian nations do not produce oil and minerals, the mainstay of many Latin American economies.

During the 1980s, two Latin American economies developed open economies and practiced export-orientation policies. The smaller, Chile, was by historical necessity an exporter. Its 13 million inhabitants could not sustain an import-substitution policy with much, if any, success, and its mining, forest products, and fisheries resources would be wasted if the Chileans tried. The larger, Mexico, with 85 million inhabitants and the classic example of a protected, import-substitution economy, came very near economic collapse after the precipitous drop in oil prices of the early 1980s.

Since then Mexico has had the fortune of leadership which understood its only realistic choice was to pursue an open economy. Only then did Mexico begin to create a political economy whose painful change may be a harbinger of the Latin American nations' future.

Today Mexico leads the discussions on a hemisphere-wide free trade zone.

Importantly, both economies have laws which protect their extractive resource bases, oil and minerals in Mexico and copper in Chile. This is part of the legacy of fear about foreign domination. Mexico even celebrates the 1939 seizure of Standard Oil's assets on a coin. In times past, the extractive industries were both vertically integrated and totally government-owned. While both countries still preserve extraction of oil or minerals for domestic investors, by the end of the 1980s both invited majority foreign holdings to invest in the processing and distribution of those extractive resources.

CHILE CHARGES AHEAD

There is Australian and Finnish investment in copper and gold processing in Chile, and Japanese investment in refining in Mexico. Likewise, both economies have adopted aggressive privatization programs outside the minerals sector, with not only both national airlines now under private control, but in the case of Chile, a majority of the telephone company now being held by Spain's Telefonica. Private telephone exchanges and toll roads are in progress in Mexico.

In 1985 and 1986, Chile's GDP growth actually exceeded Singapore, Thailand, and other Southeast Asian nations' growth rates for that year. That growth was led by strong domestic and foreign investment; with opportunities strong enough to stem capital flight.

High copper prices and foreign participation in developing the country's base and precious metals have helped maintain Chile's economic momentum. But Chile has not depended on its extractive resources alone.

The country also exports out-of-season fresh fruits and vegetables to North America, Japan, and Europe. Its fishing industry now has both Asian and New Zealand participation, and sends frozen seafood products around the world. Its pulp and paper industry, which includes owners from Australia and Finland, sends products to countries as diverse as China and Germany. Its timber industry includes New Zealand owners and ships around the world. These and other exports have kept Chile's trade balance positive since the first quarter of 1982.

Since 1983 over 90 government-owned companies have been wholly or partially privatized. This included the national steel company, the telephone company whose Australian investor was replaced in early 1990 by Telefonica de Espana, the national air carrier (through a consortium of Scandinavian Airlines System and a Chilean investment group), the electrical generation company, and even the social security system.

THE MEXICAN FACTOR

At the beginning of the 1980s, Mexico was the world's fifteenth largest economy and host to nearly 7,000 international companies. In addition to its reserved mining and petroleum-extraction activities, Mexican majority-owned steel and auto production supplied the durables and white goods industries, while a host of local and minority-owned foreign enterprises fed low-end consumer goods into a demographically exploding and highly concentrated urban market.

The economy had to change almost imperceptibly within the context of a politico-economic state which protected itself from competition. The alliance of labor organizations, wealthy, protected industrialists, and bloated state companies would not have let change happen by any other means than "salami tactics": a little at a time and they would never notice where their protection went.

The OPEC-led boom of the 1970s caught Mexico somewhat unready to profit from its export-earnings capability, and Petroleos de Mexico (PEMEX) only began export expansion toward the latter part of the decade, when prices exceeded $25U.S./barrel. The government, PEMEX, and private industry borrowed large sums at variable, LIBOR plus rates. Because Mexico's wealth was largely and legally invested outside the nation, the lack of domestic savings encouraged the state-owned companies to borrow from international banks for expansion, while the overvalued peso and negative real interest rates encouraged private borrowers to do the same thing cheaply.

When oil revenues did flow and domestic consumption followed in 1977 to 1981, there was no end in sight to the extravagance of corporate jets, condominiums in Colorado, and private debt secured by apparently guaranteed growth markets. In August 1982, the party ended. With OPEC prices in a free-fall, Mexico's government organizations and many private businesses could not meet their financial obligations; and the first of a series of endless debt reschedulings began.

Outgoing President Luis Echevarria nationalized the banks in late 1982 in an almost comical ideological move. Foreign investment went negative, and will likely remain so until at least the end of the century. Money and talent emigrated to dollars and jobs abroad, and the currency dropped in value.

Under the policy direction of Miguel de la Madrid and operational guidance of now-President Carlos Salinas de Gortari, Mexico began in 1983 to open its economy to foreign ideas, investment capital, and competition. Since this had to be done on a patronage political system fossilized by 60 years of inbreeding, the two leaders had to move a careful step at a time to slice away at the fat

inherent in the static economy in such a way that no one noticed it was disappearing.

Foreign Debt as a Percentage of 1988 GNP

Argentina	65%	Indonesia	66%
Brazil	33%	Mexico	69%
Colombia	45%	Thailand	44%

Starting in 1983 Mexico began to shed some of its 1200 state-owned or majority-controlled industries. Steel companies as well as both international airlines went on the block. Less than 200 parastatal organizations now exist, largely in "reserved" industries, such as petroleum and uranium mining, railways, telegraph, retail banking, and electricity supply.

In August 1989, the Government reduced from 34 to 19 the number of petrochemicals reserved for PEMEX. That same month Mexicana de Aviacion was sold to a Mexican-led consortium (Xabre) with Sir James Goldsmith in a 16% participation, and a consortium of buyers bid for Diesel Nacional, Sociedad Anonima (DINSA), Mexico's gargantuan bus and heavy truck manufacturer.

The country has also strengthened the infrastructure for its *maquila* system. This form of goods brought "in-bond" from the United States for value-added manufacture or assembly has grown threefold in the past seven years. In 1988, exports from *maquiladoras* earned Mexico $U.S.682 million. Not only do U.S.-dollar-measured manufactured exports now exceed petroleum exports, there are now over 1,800 *maquiladoras* along the borders and throughout Mexico, with owners from Canada, Germany, Japan, Korea, Hong Kong, and the United States.

Mexico has become the "Model" debtor nation. While making the currency worth about one hundredth its 1976 value has brought enormous hardship to the nation's ability to repay foreign debt, Mexico's leadership has never spoken of a debt moratorium, nor joined Peru, Brazil, or Argentina in discussing a "debtor's club." In their own different ways, Chilean and Mexican policymakers have set the stage for economic success.

William Grindley is the managing director of Pacific Strategies, an Atherton, California-based member of the Hong Kong-headquartered Pacific Rim Consulting Group, which assists U.S. and European firms to compete in Asia and Latin America.

ON THE SOVIET RIM

THE SOVIET FAR EAST: FACTS AND FIGURES

The Far East is the biggest economic area of the USSR. From the north to the south it stretches over 4,500 kilometers from the Arctic and the permafrost belt to the warm valleys of the Amur and Ussuri rivers. From the west to the east, its expanses cover 2,500 to 3,500 kilometers from the steppes of the trans-Baikal area to the Pacific Coast.

The Far Eastern Economic Area incorporates the Maritime and Khabarovsk Territories, the Amur, Kamchatka, Magadan, and Sakhalin Regions, and the Yakut Autonomous Republic. It covers a total area of more than six million square kilometers.

The population of more than seven million is composed mostly of Russians, Ukrainians, and Yakuts. More than a dozen northern ethnic minorities reside in administrative divisions called *okrugs* and districts. They include the Chukchis, Koryaks, Itelmens, Aleuts, Orochis, Nivkhis, Evenkis, Nanays, and Udegeys, among others.

The Far Eastern Economic Area is the easternmost part of the Soviet Union washed by the Laptev, East Siberian, Chukchi, Bering Seas, and the Seas of Okhotsk and Japan and also by the Pacific Ocean. The southern edge borders on China and the People's Democratic Republic of Korea. Over three quarters of the area is covered by mountains.

The area is rich in minerals, including gold, diamonds, tin, zinc, lead, tungsten, fluorite, mercury, mica, coal, oil, and natural gas. The climate is of the monsoon type in the south and continental in the north. Permafrost lies under much of the territory of the Far East.

Forests cover over 40% of the territory (250.3 million hectares), and timber resources are estimated at 22,600 million cubic meters (almost 30% of the national timber reserves). The timber varieties include larch, white spruce, pine, and birch. The water and energy resources amount to 29.4% of the potential hydroenergy resources of the USSR. Coal reserves are concentrated in the poorly developed parts of the area. The south Yakut Basin may be of paramount importance, as its coal is good for coking.

There are vast hard and brown coal deposits. Coal reserves are estimated at 13 billion

THE PATH OF EMPIRE

George Lynch, a globetrotting English journalist and travel writer, traveled at the turn of the century by rail and steamer through the "East"—Korea, China, Manchuria, Mongolia, and Siberia. Here in this excerpt from his book, The Path of Empire *(Duckworth and Co., London, 1903), he describes his arrival via the Trans-Siberian Railway, in Irkutsk, a major Russian city in Siberia. Curiously, he found American goods in ample supply in this remote metropolis.*

Close on half-past seven [the train] steamed into Irkutsk. As we approached, the first view of it as seen across the broad-sweeping flood of the river was very striking. Above the level of the housetops rose the towers, spires and cupolas of many churches with green roofs and gilt crosses; great masses of brick and stone buildings of the administration, hospitals and a few good-sized factories give the impression of a more stately city than one was prepared to see in the middle of Siberia.

. . . The main street [of Irkutsk], a broad thoroughfare lined with solidly built stone houses on each side, runs right through the town and contains a succession of fine shops, well stocked with every variety of goods, at one of which I was able to get fresh films, as it contained all the latest photographic supplies. Alongside it was a store full of American machinery, and the city was particularly strong in excellent confectionery shops. There was a noticeable absence throughout the town of goods for sale bearing English labels, whereas American goods were plentifully in evidence; this applies not only to Irkutsk but to the whole of Siberia and Manchuria. Particularly in the sale of agricultural machinery is this the case. I met several representatives of American firms who were doing a roaring trade, and now, having been first in the field and got hold of the market, it will be all the more difficult for other manufacturers to oust them. The phonograph is a machine which has greatly taken the fancy of Russians; they are to be seen for sale in every town, and large ones take the place of a band at the chief restaurants all the way from Manchuria to Moscow.

. . . In a certain sense Irkutsk is one of the worst towns in Siberia. It is a center which attracts numbers of that large army of criminal vagabonds who roam the country living, by thieving, and highway robbery, all who are capable of committing almost any crime. The number of murders in Irkutsk in a year is simply appalling, and the police force of the town is entirely inadequate to deal with the floating population of humans who constantly infest it. In consequence it is unsafe to go about the streets at night, and I have never seen any city with such an absolutely deserted appearance after dark. Its dreary solitude after nightfall is disturbed only by watchmen who walk along the middle of the road sounding a wooden clapper somewhat after the style of those in Chinese cities with their gongs. Two murders were committed in the streets the week before I was there; garrotting is of most frequent occurrence, the assailant stealing up quietly behind his victim throws a noose of catgut over his head with which he strangles him.

tons; hypothetical reserves are 15 times higher. Geologists say oil and gas reserves are not limited to the modest deposits discovered so far. Great hopes are pinned on oil and gas prospecting on the Far Eastern shelf.

The Far Eastern *taiga* is rich not only in timber but also in nuts, berries, mushrooms, fern, ramson, and some rare medicinal herbs, such as ginseng and eleutherococcus, which are in high demand on the world market.

Over a third of Soviet furs are produced in the Far Eastern forests. Sable, mink, squirrel, and bear are but some of the species well-known to international fur dealers. Hunting in the Far East is a profitable business, since local forests are far richer in plants and animals than forests in other parts of the country.

Of special value are the biological resources of the seas washing the Far Eastern Coast. These include some commercial fishes, such as salmon, cod, navaga, herring, and pollock, and also mollusks and algae. The Kamchatka area is especially productive. According to some estimates, the value of salmon caught here during the past 50 years is roughly equal to the value of gold produced in Alaska during the same period.

Vast natural resources have made the Far East a major supplier of precious and nonferrous metals, fish products (nearly 40% of national output), timber, and fur. The mining and quarrying industry accounts for over a third of the region's industrial output.

The engineering industry consists of enterprises turning out energy-generating, hoisting, and transport equipment, ships, agricultural machinery, and equipment for the fishing and food industries. Although many of these products can compete well on the world markets, the Far Eastern engineering cannot be seen as well-developed, according to specialists. This inadequacy bears a strong impact on raw-material utilization. In the tim-

ber and wood-working industry, only 18% of timber is subject to deep processing. Losses are still high in tin and other nonferrous metal-producing industries.

The previous programs for the Far East's development elaborated by sectoral ministries often pursued short-term interests, laying stress on mineral-production expansion at whatever cost. This led to stagnation of the 1970s and 1980s, manifest disastrously in the Far East whose economic development rates declined sharply.

When Mikhail Gorbachev toured the Far East in 1986, he stressed the role of the social factors in the region's development. He said that the Far East's greater contribution to the country's economic potential required a faster growth of living standards, better work conditions and housing, improved food and industrial supplies, and increasing development of the entire social sphere. This prevented labor migration and in the final count contributed to higher rates of economic development in the Far East.

As part of the drive to achieve a thrifty use of resources and increase production efficiency in the Far East, the Soviet government adopted a comprehensive program for the development of productive resources of the Far East, the Buryat Autonomous Soviet Socialist Republic and the Chita Region for the period ending in the year 2000. By that time, the output of commodities in the Far East is to increase by 2.4 to 2.5 times, electric energy by 2.6 times, oil and gas condensate by 3.1 to 3.8 times, and gas by 7.2 to 9.3 times. The production of fish and other marine products will amount to 45% of the national output.

Relying on different financial sources, the Far East by the end of the century is to get 130 million square meters of dwelling space (close to 2.5 million apartments), schools for 1.4 million students, and creches and kindergartens for 624,000 children.

The principal objective of the program is to turn the Far East by the year 2000 into a highly developed economic zone incorporating powerful mineral production, research and manufacturing facilities, an optimum economic structure, and a well-developed social sphere, so that the region could be involved deeply in the national and international systems for division of labor.

As part of the effort to accomplish the program, plans have been laid to update the local engineering enterprises with new technologies and equipment based on production mechanization and automation. The industry will also have to update its production policies and lay greater stress on machinery and equipment required for the development of the Far East's natural resources.

Greater stress is to be laid on the construction and building materials industries as part of the effort to improve the region's economic performance. Other priorities include transport, communications, and the Far Eastern merchant marine and fishing fleet.

The program also envisages the development of agricultural and related industries in order to develop the region's food supplies.

The Far East's requirements for agricultural products are largely satisfied due to imports of milk, dairy products, meat, potatoes, etc., from other parts of the country.

With the Far Eastern population likely to increase by 20% by the end of the century, per capita production of agricultural products is to increase substantially, including potatoes by 1.5 times, vegetables by 1.7 times, meat by 1.6 times, milk by 1.4 times, and eggs by 1.3 times.

The Far Eastern farms have 212.4 million hectares of farmland. Of these only 6.9 million hectares are cultivated, including 3.2 million hectares of ploughland.

The output of fish and marine products is to increase by 28%, with the range and quality of fish products likely to improve substantially. The output of salmon of light and medium salting is to be doubled, that of herring of light and medium salting is to increase by 1.8 times, of special can salting by 1.4 times, and of edible and medicinal agar by 2.6 times.

Timber, fish, and fuels at the present time account for more than 80% of the Far East's exports. Experts believe raw materials are likely to continue to make the bulk of the region's exports in the short-term future, the fact expected to bear a strong impact on the guidelines of international cooperation in the region.

The Far East contributes tangibly to the USSR's external economic links with Asian and Pacific countries. The region accounts for 21% of the national exports of round timber, about 30% of fish, a substantial amount of pulp, etc.

The Far East's minerals are mostly imported by the developed capitalist nations, which consume close to two thirds of the region's exports. Japan is the prime importer, consuming the bulk of Far Eastern coal, wood chips, fish products, chemical raw materials, and timber.

The long-term program for the development of the Soviet Far East envisages promotion of traditional forms of partnership, such as buy-back deals, along with the quest for new opportunities offered by joint ventures and other collaborative projects. In Vladivostok, the heart of the Maritime Territory, there are at the present time seven such concerns set up with Vietnam, the United States, Japan, and Sweden, with 50 other proposals by different foreign companies still under consideration.

Soviet specialists seem to have been tempted by the proposal of some Japanese insurance companies to set up a special business zone in the Maritime territory to be leased for 50 to 60 years by a Soviet–Japanese consortium.

SOURCE: Novosti Press Agency. For more information about trade in the Soviet Far East, contact V. K. Lozovoi, General Director, The Association for Business cooperation with the Countries of the Asia-Pacific Region, 690010, Vladivostok, Okeanski Prospekt, 30. Telephones: 2-00-08. 2-00-05, 2-53-11. Telex: 213221.

ROLLING OUT THE RED CARPET FOR INVESTORS

by Michael Selwyn and Lori Valigra

Special economic zones in the USSR's Far East might melt the investment ice in the Sea of Japan.

The Sea of Japan—bordered by North and South Korea, the USSR, China, and Japan—has traditionally been a center of military rivalry. But the improved climate of East–West relations may turn it into one of North Asia's most dynamic growth regions.

By 2000 the USSR expects to triple its Asia-Pacific trade, which now accounts for only 8% of its total trade. It is proposing to open up its Pacific coastal regions to private investment, and wants to bring in Asian capital and technology to tap these regions's huge reserves of coal, timber, oil, natural gas, precious metals, and fish.

Despite the Soviet Far East's proximity to Japan and Korea, investors have been deterred by its poor infrastructure, harsh climate, and distance from decision-makers in Moscow. U.S. consultants PlanEcon says 69% of Soviet joint ventures with foreign companies are in western Russia, but only 18.3% are east of the Urals.

Now foreign firms are being wooed with a battery of incentives, including reduced customs duties on imported raw materials and three-year tax holidays.

A special economic zone is to be created at Nakhodka, where the trans-Siberian railway ends.

The island of Sakhalin and the port of Vladivostok, home of the USSR's Pacific naval fleet, are being opened to outsiders. Local officials have more leeway to negotiate directly with foreign companies.

The big Asian corporations are starting to make their moves. Hyundai, Mitsui, and Nissho Iwai have, or are planning, representative offices in Khabarovsk, Nakhodka, and Vladivostok.

Says Mitsuru Ikeya, manager of Nissho Iwai's USSR trading section: "Soviet trade is now trending toward localization. We are following this and making an effort to build new business relationships with Soviet Far East companies."

Hyundai, having capitalized on the Middle East construction boom of the early 1980s, hopes to get involved in infrastructure projects.

Hyundai is building a 200-room hotel in Nakhodka and has signed a letter of intent for a timber-processing joint venture (see table).

The USSR plans to create special economic zones along its Pacific coastline similar to China's

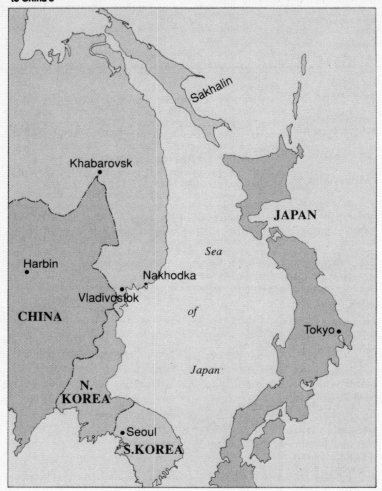

Ship repair facilities, an aluminum smelter, a hydroelectric power station, natural gas production facilities, and housing are also on Hyundai's list.

Among the most ambitious projects in the region is the exploitation of crude oil deposits of Sakhalin island. The project, which would meet 15% of Japan's demand for oil, is masterminded by Sakhalin Oil Development Company (Sodeco)—a consortium including Japan National Oil Corporation and 12 Japanese refiners and trading houses.

But the U.S.$2 billion scheme is uneconomic at current oil price levels, and would require production facilities to be built in waters that are ice-bound for seven months a year.

For now Asian investors are likely to take a

more cautious approach, focusing on small-scale projects, such as those aimed at niche consumer markets. Joint ventures on Sakhalin island, for example, cater for Japenese demand for *surimi,* the minced fish made from pollock.

Meanwhile the exposure of the USSR's Pacific seaboard to market forces is having in-triguing consequences. During a recent visit to Japan, the Bolshoi Circus acquired some unusually hefty souvenirs—used automobiles. Cars worth less than 50,000 rubles (U.S.$350) pass customs inspection as hand luggage, and the troupe took more than 50 back to Nakhodka.

Major deals between South Korea and the Soviet bloc					
Project	**Joint venture name**	**Parties**	**Ownership shares**	**Agreement & approval dates**	**Project details**
Fur retail and manufacture in the Soviet Union	Jindo-Rus	Jindo Corp (Korea), Interlink Co-operative (USSR)	50:50, with each side providing US$400,000 in initial capital	JV agreement signed in Mar 1989; Korean govt approval granted in September 1989	JV will open 10 fur shops in the USSR by 1992. First shop now open in Moscow's Intourist hotel. Goal is to sell US$20m of garments in first year
Colour TV production, Hungary	Samsung Electronics Hungarian Co	Samsung Electronics Co and Samsung Co (Korea); Orion (Hungary)	Samsung Electronics 45%, Samsung Co 5%, Orion 50%, with initial capital of US$3.2m	Initial JV agreement Dec. 1988, finalised May 1989; Korean govt approval early 1989	Initial output of 100,000 sets/yr. Plant will assemble components supplied from Korea. Primary market is domestic, though exports being considered. Full operation begins April
Financial and international services for Hungarian firms	Investrade Corp	Daewoo (Korea); Hungarian Credit Bank	50:50, with each side supplying initial capital, plus another US$25m in 1992	JV agreement signed Nov 1988; Korean govt approval granted in Nov 1989	Activities will include leasing, loans and direct investment
Hotel building and ownership, Hungary	Saint Stephan Hotel Corp	Daewoo (Korea); Hungarian Credit Bank	50:50, with each side supplying US$45m in paid-in capital	JV agreement signed Nov 1988; Korean govt approval granted in Nov 1989	JV will acquire existing 320-room Hilton hotel in Budapest and build a second 300-room Hilton. Licences to be sought for projects elsewhere in Europe
Logging and wood processing in Soviet Far East	Not determined	Hyundai Corp and Hyundai Wood Industries Co (Korea); Primorsklesprom (USSR)	Hyundai Corp 25%, Hyundai Wood Industries Co 25%, Primorsklesprom 50%; investment will be at least US$10m	Preliminary JV announced Oct 1989; Korean approval pending	JV will develop and log 10,000 sq kms of forest in USSR's Far East maritime province near the city of Svetlaya. JV will produce fibre wood and pulp. Hyundai will be able to buy US$50-100m/yr of lumber for next 30 years

Source: Asian Business

RUNNING THROUGH THE COUNTERTRADE MAZE

by Michael Selwyn

So far, Soviet currency is not convertible, so trade can be a bit tricky. One way around it is countertrade.

Free markets may be all the fashion in the Soviet Union and Eastern Europe, but Rim companies will have to learn the tricks of countertrade if they are to win business there. Accounting for at least 25% of East–West trade, countertrade is expected to grow. The main instruments of countertrade follow.

COUNTERPURCHASE

A supplier commits to compensate for his sale by purchasing qualifying goods or services of a designated value over a specified time period. There are two parallel but separate contracts, one for the principal order—paid for on normal cash or credit terms—and another for the counterpurchase.

BARTER

The direct exchange of goods for goods, without the use of money. This is a popular method of Sino–Soviet cross-border trade. One recent deal worth U.S.$94 million involves the USSR supplying China with three Tupolev-154 and three Yak-42 passenger aircraft, in return for Chinese garments, electrical goods, and basic consumer items.

SWITCH TRADING

Imbalances in long-term bilateral trading arrangements, usually between the USSR and developing countries, sometimes leads to the accumulation of uncleared credit surpluses in one country or the other. These surpluses can be tapped by third countries. For example, Hong Kong exports to the USSR might be financed by the sale of Chinese goods to Hong Kong or elsewhere.

BUYBACK

A supplier of a plant or equipment is paid in the form of future output from the investment concerned. It is used in connection with exports of capital goods, such as process plant and mining equipment. Buyback arrangements are usually long-term and are favored by the USSR as a method of industrial cooperation.

OFFSET

A supplier of high-technology equipment—usually aircraft—is commited to promote the industry of the purchasing country through co-production, licensing, subcontracting, technology transfer or investment. The concept of countertrade appears simple enough. But in practice, "there are massive risks and I would advise extreme caution," says Daniel Spitzer, managing director of MG Services, a countertrade agent in Hong Kong. Differences in pricing philosophy and product quality are two of the biggest stumbling blocks, he says.

Finding goods that will sell outside East Europe is also difficult. Traders, offered oil or other commodities in payment, risk seeing the prices plummet before they can sell them. Korean traders say their Soviet counterparts want to sell value-added products based on military technology, but that—given the size and sophistication of the Korean economy—there's little demand for them.

Getting goods out is another headache, because of frequent transport bottlenecks. "To the Soviets a frozen railroad represents force majeure; for us it doesn't," says Pak Kyungwoo, manager of Samsung Co.'s overseas marketing department.

Then there are the costs. As well as paying a commission to middlemen, most exporters using countertrade include an extra margin in the prices they quote, to allow for the fact that they may need to slash the price of inferior quality East European goods.

Countertrade can be costly and inefficient, but several specialist companies in Europe have made a success of it. MG Services, for example, is part of West German industrial commodities group Metallgesellschaft, which underwrites more than U.S.$10 billion a year in trade business.

The growing popularity of countertrade in Asia has prompted several middlemen to set up offices in the region. In Hong Kong, for example, Austria's two biggest banks, Creditanstalt and Landerbank, now have represenattion.

According to Jan Vanous, research director at U.S. consultancy PlanEcon, one alternative to countertrade is to invest in sectors like tourism and hotels, which promise guaranteed hard currency return and thus avoid problems with profit repatriation.

"With second- and third-rate hotel rooms (in the USSR) going for U.S.$150-plus per night and guaranteed near 100% occupancy rates, hotel investments offer huge cash flows strictly in hard currency and complete return on initial investment in as little as three years time," he says.

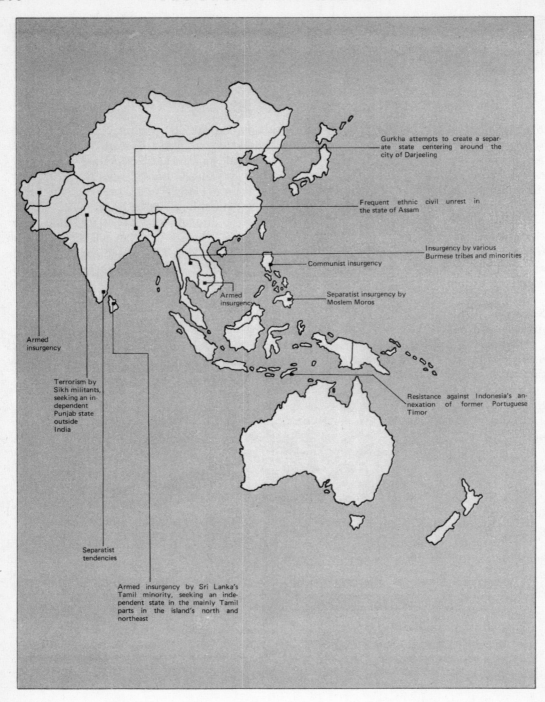

Gurkha attempts to create a separate state centering around the city of Darjeeling

Frequent ethnic civil unrest in the state of Assam

Insurgency by various Burmese tribes and minorities

Communist insurgency

Armed insurgency

Separatist insurgency by Moslem Moros

Armed insurgency

Terrorism by Sikh militants, seeking an independent Punjab state outside India

Resistance against Indonesia's annexation of former Portuguese Timor

Separatist tendencies

Armed insurgency by Sri Lanka's Tamil minority, seeking an independent state in the mainly Tamil parts in the island's north and northeast

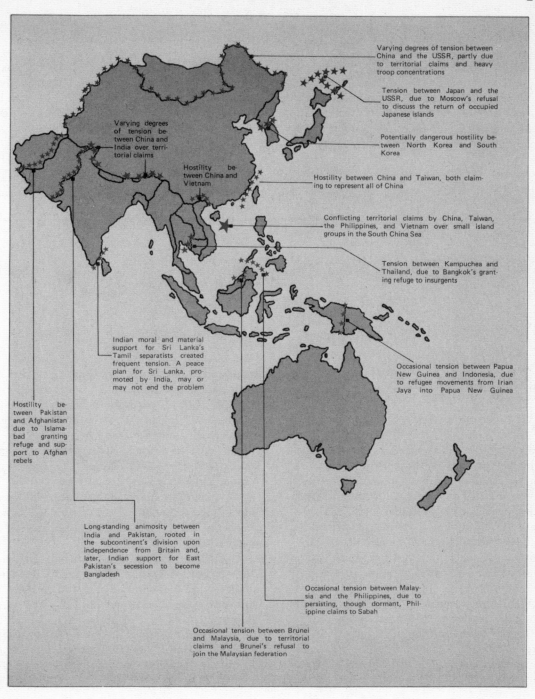

Varying degrees of tension between China and the USSR, partly due to territorial claims and heavy troop concentrations

Tension between Japan and the USSR, due to Moscow's refusal to discuss the return of occupied Japanese islands

Potentially dangerous hostility between North Korea and South Korea

Varying degrees of tension between China and India over territorial claims

Hostility between China and Vietnam

Hostility between China and Taiwan, both claiming to represent all of China

Conflicting territorial claims by China, Taiwan, the Philippines, and Vietnam over small island groups in the South China Sea

Tension between Kampuchea and Thailand, due to Bangkok's granting refuge to insurgents

Indian moral and material support for Sri Lanka's Tamil separatists created frequent tension. A peace plan for Sri Lanka, promoted by India, may or may not end the problem

Occasional tension between Papua New Guinea and Indonesia, due to refugee movements from Irian Jaya into Papua New Guinea

Hostility between Pakistan and Afghanistan due to Islamabad granting refuge and support to Afghan rebels

Long-standing animosity between India and Pakistan, rooted in the subcontinent's division upon independence from Britain and, later, Indian support for East Pakistan's secession to become Bangladesh

Occasional tension between Malaysia and the Philippines, due to persisting, though dormant, Philippine claims to Sabah

Occasional tension between Brunei and Malaysia, due to territorial claims and Brunei's refusal to join the Malaysian federation

The East West Report

The East West Report is a new monthly international newsletter "for business leaders and policy-makers," which covers new economic opportunities in the post-*perestroika* Soviet Union, including the Soviet Far East and East Europe. For more information, contact the publisher: Pergamon Press, Inc., Maxwell House, Fairview Park, Elmsford, New York 10523.

CHANGING ERAS

FROM GEO-POLITICS TO GEO-ECONOMICS

In the Wake of a Post-Persian Gulf War World

AMERICA'S ROLE IN THE PACIFIC CENTURY

In a seminal article concerning "America in the Pacific Century," the World Policy Institute's Jerry W. Sanders defines this country's major priority as abandoning the 40-year-old policy of containment which has necessitated playing the role of military protector and economic underwriter of Asian and Pacific nations. Massive cuts in the $300 billion Pentagon budget, coupled with all the long-term investments in education, health care, housing, infrastructure, technology, "and all the other neglected areas that make for a productive nation," are necessary to bring American grand strategy into line "with today's dynamic polycentric order."

Speculating on what course America's policies toward Asia might take in the next few years, Sanders, who is director of Peace and Conflict Studies at the University of California, at Berkeley, points out that trade and finance "have increasingly become the new currency of diplomacy" as could be seen by the way that trading patterns had emerged between such traditional adversaries as South Korea and the Soviet Union, Taiwan and China, and South Korea and China.

To escape "a future of economic decline and enforced austerity," he writes in *World Policy Journal,* the U.S. must rethink its world role in the 1990s.

It could not expect that Japan would continue to bear an increasing burden of responsibility without a comparable shift in power and status. To avert a decline that many saw as imminent, it would be necessary for the Bush administration to invest seriously in the nation's economic and social future; there was no precedent for a country being simultaneously both a great power and a major debtor. Costlier strategic commitments combined with its share of world production dropping by 50% had put the United States "in the untenable position of having to borrow from those it is pledged to protect."

But by the turn of the century, the gross regional product of Japan and East Asia could be expected to equal that of North America and exceed that of Western Europe, with Japan on the verge of becoming the world's largest economy. These prospects have been considerably enhanced by the increasing likelihood of normalized trade and political relations between Japan and the Soviet Union, for which opinion polls now show a consensus.

Gorbachev's peace initiatives in the region have resonated louder than America's continuing military presence, and the Soviet leader's ambitious plans for joint ventures with other Asian countries within its sphere must be taken seriously. The increasingly friendly, if guarded, relationship between the Soviet Union and China—who share similar priorities of economic reconstruction and modernization—will bring additional pressure on America's leadership role, already being tested "by the increasing gap between its commitments and resources." These emerging patterns, Sanders summarizes, could be read either as threats to America's national interests or opportunities not only to enhance the security and prosperity of the region but also to undertake economic adjustment.

Analyzing what appears to be the Bush administration's long-range policy toward Asia, Sanders sees little change in America's assumption that it will remain the leader with the U.S. locked into "a permanent military role while enhancing Japan's economic ascendancy," a policy ensuring that the American economy will become even less competitive and the nation pushed still deeper into debt. "Meanwhile, Japan, the world's banker, would lengthen its economic lead under the protective guise of a junior partnership."

Moreover, the pressure exerted by America on Japan to dismantle its trade barriers had served to open up the Japanese market to Korean rather than American products, which had not proved particularly popular with the Japanese consumer.

Sanders also warns that additional pressure by America to exploit what it sees as a "special relationship" with Japan could cause alarm in the NICs (newly industrializing countries)—South Korea, Taiwan, Hong Kong, and Singarpore—who might fear their exclusion from these markets. This growing anger, peaking on the eve of military base negotiations between Washington and Manila in 1991, could trigger demands by South Korea for the ouster of American troops from their country—the subsequent scenario calling for the U.S. once again invoking the Soviet threat.

Secretary of State Baker's evidence, in such a case, could be the Soviets' increasing economic and diplomatic ties in the region and the modernization of the Soviet Pacific fleet.

In short, if America does not act more warily it will end up appearing to be more responsible than the Soviets for the continuation of the Cold War. Trouble may also be brewing, Sanders suggests, in America's continuing attempts to keep Japan in a subordinate role in both the International Monetary Fund (IMF), where it has a fifth-place voting role inconsistent with its number-two status in the world economy, and in the Asian Development Bank, where it has the same one-eighth voting power as the U.S., despite providing one third of the capital.

"Thus far it is the United States that has withheld from Japan the political status and respect it seeks," notes Sanders. "At what point and under what circumstances will Japan exert its own veto power and withhold economic support from the United States?"

The old assumptions that Japan is dependent on U.S. protection and the strength of the U.S. economy may no longer be relevant. Will we eventually see an escalating contest to see just "who is more dependent on whom"?

This, suggests Sanders, could trigger a panicky slide of the dollar, which could be stopped only by a steep rise in interest rates, possibly plunging the world into recession—all due to a "failure of vision that misses opportunities plainly marked on the horizon."

Despite their addiction to "Cold War verities," the article warns, critics must be made to see that military-strategic postures must be discouraged and that forms of production that increase overcapacity and encourage protectionist practices must be avoided.

Simultaneously, unless the U.S. is still committed to fighting a two-front war in Europe and Asia, it should respond positively to Gorbachev's initiatives in reducing military tensions—including its "imperial outposts"—and aim for a more balanced and mature partnership with Japan in which the latter is not subservient.

One by-product of such a realignment could be a joint U.S.–Soviet/Chinese–Japanese development of Siberia's abundant natural resources to the benefit of all. Such a four-power initiative "could not help but have a ripple effect on other economic and strategic relations." On the other hand, trying to enlist Japan into a grand strategy of military containment and, with South Korea, aiming at an Asian NATO risks cutting the U.S. out of expanding East–West economic relations.

WHY DENG DID IT

This has got to be one of the most intriguing analyses of why Chinese leader Deng Xiaoping deliberately and ruthlessly ordered the tanks to crush the pro-democracy students in Tiananmen Square in May 1989. He may have done it in order to save China's economic reform program from being set back by as much as 20 to 50 years, according to Hong Kong-published *Asian Business* magazine. First of all, to really understand Deng, one must realize that he is utterly committed to one-party rule and to economic reform. The model which he follows is economic liberalism combined with draconian political control.

Prior to the Tiananmen Square incident, Deng's greatest fear was that the likely effects of more "democracy"—which is an unclear concept in today's China, at best—would have resulted in total chaos if rival political parties were suddenly permitted to be formed. As history has shown, the act of thrusting a country from a peasant economy to an urban one—and from relative equality to highly structured inequality—involves a tremendous potential for instability. Therefore, in his view, granting democratic rights would have probably set the nation's economic reform program back by several decades. Unwilling to take that risk—and in order to avert that perceived historical calamity—the determined Deng was quite willing to sacrifice the students.

ASIAN CHRONICLES

WHERE DID JAPAN INC. GET ITS LEADERS?

The year was 1938. The Imperial Navy was faced with a dearth of officers. The young elite who had just graduated from the University of Tokyo and other top schools were plucked from their jobs with government and industry, and quickly turned into Officers and Gentlemen of the navy. The method was called *Tangen,* a contraction of the Japanese term meaning Short-Term Active-Duty Naval Officer. From the first batch of *Tangen* candidates in December 1938, through the last increment in April 1945, 3,381 young men were trained in the *Tangen* school. The navy went to great lengths to search out these young men, who were then thoroughly examined by the dreaded *Kempeitai,* secret police, and cleared of all taint—no skeletons or familial embarrassments existed that could one day cause them shame. They were the creme of the elite, the sanctified.

The young men were glad for the system. The rumor soon got around that *Tangen* was the place to go if you wanted to survive the war. (And the elite actively pursued ways to survive the conflict.)

The navy's attitude was: "We can't let these fine young men go to the army to be mowed down like stalks of rice. They are far too valuable a human resource." So *Tangen* became a marriage of convenience: an unspoken contract between those who "don't want to die" and those who "don't want them killed."

After these fine young men had passed the rigorous weeding process, they spent four months at the Navy General Accounting School. Then, at the age of 23 or 24, they were commissioned as sublieutenants and sent to the quartermaster corps where they were put in charge of food and clothing, accounting, records, etc. If you were to compare their navy jobs with corporate organizations, they would have been in the general affairs section, or the personnel section, or the office of the president. Their positions were secure (and safe) and they often managed as many as 150 people.

The war ended. Walking the tightrope between life and death had honed them into a truly elite cadre. And they blossomed in the free society that followed. In other words, while it was unintentional, *Tangen* was Japan's version of an elite business school. The influence of Imperial Navy *Tangen* graduates on modern day Japan is tremendous.

Politics: More than 20 people, starting with former Prime Minister Nakasone.
Bureaucrats: Almost too many to count. Since 1967, eight vice ministers of the Ministry of Finance have been *Tangen* graduates, for example.
Academics: At least 80 professors of elite universities are from *Tangen.*
Business: 78 presidents of companies listed on Tokyo, Osaka, Nagoya stock exchanges are ex-*Tangen,* as are 185 managing directors. *Tangen* formed the core of Japan Inc. *Tangen* moves Japan. Understand *Tangen,* and you understand Japan, perhaps. Balanced. Smart. But not prone to burning themselves out. Looking after their own ego and building up
(continued)

their own organization against all odds. Good at moving men and material but lack charisma. These are the men of *Tangen*. These are the men who built Japan, the industrial giant.

SOURCE: *Sunday Mainichi,* translated by *Japan Free Press.*

WHERE JAPANESE YOUTH LEARN FROM THE IMPERIAL ARMY

There's a new organization called *Kusamoekai* whose members are the sons and grandsons of owners of large companies and former Prime ministers. Some of the business brats are from firms like Marui, Tokyo Gas, Nissin Foods, Taisho Pharmaceuticals, Ohbayashi Corporation, Suntory, Daiei, and Matsushita Electric. Thoroughbreds, all.

And the leader of this pack of silver-spoon elite is none other than Sejima Ryuzo (age 76), Special Advisor to C. Itoh & Co. Sejima is a former member of the general staff of the Imperial Army. After 11 years in prison camps in Siberia after World War II, he returned to Japan to climb to the pinnacles of power in C. Itoh, Japan's largest *sogo shosha* trading company. He successfully hurdled postwar obstacles and turned himself from an elite army officer into an elite businessman.

The young business elite of the *Kusamoekai* trust Sejima explicitly. Said one of the organizers: "The responsibility of today's businessman is very different from what it was in the past. So we have asked Sejima *Sensei* ("Master") to instruct us from his broad knowledge, experience, and theory of business autocracy."

Apparently one of the most interesting features of the *Kusamoekai* is that Sejima provides the members with the latest international military information.

Japanese news commentator Hosaka Masayasu says of the *Kusamoekai:* "The very fact that the younger generation of silver-spooners is doting on Sejima's every word indicates their lack of confidence in themselves. One has to wonder just how valid Sejima's experiences are. After all, history only happens once and people only live one life. But Sejima seems to have a plethora of lives; he's been dry-cleaned and sold for new a number of times now. Every talented person has a place in history. Sejima doesn't realize that his place has come and gone."

Still, the answer to whether or not Sejima's instruction was apropos will come after these silver-spooners take their positions in the *Keidanren* (Japan's Trade Union) and offices of state.

SOURCE: *Shukan Bunshun,* translated by *Japan Free Press.*

The Asian Arms Trade:
An Explosion in the Making

by Brian Caplen

Asia's arms-makers have a huge, hungry market on their doorstep.

The year is 1998 and U.S.–Japan relations are at a post-war low.

American engineers working on the Fraternity submarine project in Japan have just been ordered out of the country.

The decision is causing consternation around the world. The Fraternity has been hailed as a new era submarine that will ensure Western naval superiority in the Pacific, so the rupture is being seen by commentators as a disastrous goal. More setbacks like this and the Soviet Union will be steaming ahead.

But as far as Japan's number-one defense contractor and partner on the project, Yokohama Heavy Technologies, is concerned, the engineers' removal has come as a welcome relief.

The corporation didn't want American involvement in the first place. It was equal or superior to the U.S. partner in all major aspects of submarine construction and badly wanted to go it alone.

Japanese politicians felt the same. They only agreed to a joint venture to pacify American calls for balanced trade and further defense cooperation. At heart, they also wanted to see Japanese companies forging ahead in military technology unassisted. So when the opportunity arose to get back the Fraternity project for Japan, they seized it. Their chance came through another U.S.–Japan conflict, also connected with the defense business.

A row had erupted over the sale of 250 Nissan main battle tanks to the Philippines armed forces by Japan's weapons marketing agency SEA (Security Enhancement Assistance).

U.S. senators complained that American companies had not been allowed to bid for the deal. The Japanese government took the view that since the sales were made under a Japanese aid program, there was no requirement for an open tender. Angry exchanges escalated into diplomatic retaliations, the latest and most severe episode being the expulsion of the Fraternity project engineers.

As the Americans board their plane at Narita, they have time to reflect that here is another blow to U.S. military might, in terms of both technology and sales.

Don't believe it? In Asia in 1989 there were a host of signs that the above scenario will come true, either in full or in part. A key indicator was the wrangling between the U.S. and Japan over the joint development of the FS-X fighter aircraft.

U.S. politicians have made so much noise about "giving away" technology to Japan that it is almost certain Japan will conduct future R&D projects on its own.

The country's industrialists believe they have the technological capability to make the FS-X and that the joint venture, like the one in our imaginary story, was only pursued for political reasons.

Since the politics appears to be backfiring, there can be no point in repeating the exercise. Clues as to the effect this may have are already emerging.

"Japan is considering independent development of its next-generation surface-to-air missile," reported the authoritative Jane's Defense Weekly earlier (in 1989), noting that the country's current system, the Nike Hercules, and its replacement, the Patriot, are both from the United States.

Japanese exports will be felt first in vehicles and above all in materials technology.

"Going ahead with the missile project, estimated to cost Y1 trillion (U.S.$7.5 billion) would be a radical departure from [Japan's] present approach of buying off-the-shelf U.S. systems," said Jane's.

Even if Japan hasn't actually taken the lead in military technology by the late 1990s, many experts agree that the country by then will be emerging as a mass exporter of weapons.

Despite Japanese aversion to the arms business because of the country's militaristic past, pressures from the U.S. for Japan to shoulder a greater share of the Pacific defense burden are bound to provoke the Japanese response that they must recoup the costs by exploiting the commercial opportunities.

Since defense is the world's largest industry, it is unlikely that the world's most successful industrial nation is going to be locked out of it forever, especially since the most promising markets as well as the major competitors are developing right on Japan's doorstep.

Overall global military spending may be stagnating due to arms control agreements and the increasing strain of defense on government budgets, but expenditure in Asia shows no sign of slowing.

Expanding economies combined with regional insecurities give Asian nations both the means and the motive to spend on defense. The major Far East countries—Japan, Indonesia, South Korea, Malaysia, the Philippines, Singapore, Taiwan, and Thailand—currently spend a total of around U.S.$40 billion.

Add in China, India, and Australia and the figure tops U.S.$60 billion. By the end of the 1990s it is likely to be around U.S.$130 billion.

A report by the Stockholm International Peace Research Institute (SIPRI) notes: "In terms of economic performance as well as security perceptions (the Asia-Pacific area) will continue to increase in prominence.

"Its problems and characteristics—high growth, increasing international integration, flashpoints of armed conflicts, intertwined domestic and external security factors, the co-existence of opposing social systems, and superpower involvement—are not dissimilar to Europe in the 1950s and 1960s."

"I don't think that we are facing any wars in the next three years, but there will definitely be a war between Taiwan and China in the period 2000 to 2005," predicts a counter-terrorism expert based in Hong Kong.

This observer says a further demand for military supplies will come from poorly equipped national armies tackling insurgency. "The Philippine army is a disaster," he says. "There is a lack of equipment and ammunition and what they do have is obsolete. Some of the soldiers don't even have shoes."

Many Western defense companies are cranking up their regional operations in Asia, knowing that only a strong local presence can get them a share of the most politically sensitive contracts of all. They also need to offer sweeteners, and have mastered the language of licensing agreements, joint ventures, co-production, and offset deals.

Even this may not be enough. As well as

developing an insatiable appetite for killing machines, Asia has learned how to make them. Past military governments in Taiwan, South Korea, and China have concentrated their efforts on weapons production, and all three have appeared in what experts demeaningly describe as "the league of third-world arms exporters."

But Taiwan and South Korea are no longer third-world countries, and their defense expertise is growing fast. Both have fighter aircraft projects on the boil and several decades' experience in producing a wide range of military hardware. While Taiwan is limited because of its diplomatic isolation, South Korea seems certain to break into the ranks of the major exporters.

As with Japan, the link between defense strategy and business should work in South Korea's favor. Over time the United States will want to reduce its hefty military involvement in South Korea.

South Korea may emerge as a major arms supplier before Japan.

In return, Seoul will ask for greater freedom to export weapons made with technology from the United States. At present, such sales are restricted.

With Japan excelling at the high-tech end of the industry, South Korea can concentrate on tanks and frigates, leaving China to supply basic, low-cost, easy-to-use equipment. This it already does in abundance.

Indeed, if China still deserves the third-world tag given it, this is only due to quality of arms, not quantity. China's arms sales run at about U.S.$2 billion a year, making it the fourth largest defense exporter in the world.

Observers say the Chinese are very aggressive in marketing weapons and providing good after-sales service and back-up—everything that they don't do in most other areas of commerce.

So it is Japan, the most advanced nation in Asia, and not China, one of the most backward, that is the "caged tiger" of defense.

Those doubting that Japan can swiftly break out of its cage point first to Japan's well-publicized pacifism as a stumbling block. Secondly, they point out the shortcomings of the Japanese defense industry itself, such as a lack of R&D, inadequate testing of equipment, no economies of scale, no competitive bidding for contracts, and a military establishment that has variously been described as bureaucratic, senile, overpaid, and hopelessly inefficient.

But the industry is only inefficient because it is smothered by the ban on exports. Defense is an industry above all others that depends on economies of scale. Exporting is the only way to achieve them.

The industrialists know this all too well and are engaged in behind-the-scenes lobbying, and initial preparations, for an "all systems go" defense business. Since what Japanese business wants it generally gets (scandals like the notorious Recruit Cosmos affair notwithstanding), a turnaround is in the cards.

The pressure for change is not going to ease up. Apart from the six giants of Japanese defense ["metalbashers" MHI, IHHI, and Kawasaki Heavy Industries (KHI) and electronics firms Mitsubishi Electric, Toshiba, and NEC], there are 2,500 companies jockeying for contracts with the country's defense agency. To all these firms, defense means money.

But the Japanese won't have it all their own way. Right behind them, and even sometimes ahead of them, will be the South Koreans.

South Korea's defense policy is starkly different from Japan's. The threat from North Korea means it can never afford the luxury of pacifism. But the factors pushing South Korea deeper into the export business bear a remarkable resemblance to the Japanese case.

In fact, South Korea's emergence as a major arms supplier may well precede Japan's even if, due to superior technology and production capability, Japan eventually comes out on top. This is because South Korea doesn't have any scruples about arms exporting, and its relationship with the U.S. is even more fraught.

Insecurities about U.S. commitment to South Korea were what prompted the initial founding of the country's defense industry, following the American retreat from Vietnam in the 1970s. Periodic calls for U.S. troop reductions have compounded these fears. And, as in Japan, a huge number of businesses have an interest in defense.

Some 90 South Korean organizations ranging from small family firms to big companies and *chaebols* like Hyundai, Daewoo, Samsung, and Korean Air are engaged in military production. Their products range from planes and helicopters to warships and artillery.

The irony of a late appearance by Taiwan in the league of major arms exporters is that its enemy across the water, mainland China, has already taken the market by storm. "In the past, few people would even have dreamed that Taiwan could build its own aerospace industry," says W. S. Lin, president of Tatung Co., one of Taiwan's largest electronics manufacturers.

(Editorial note: In the wake of the U.S.-led Coalition forces' overwhelming victory over Iraq in the 1991 Gulf War, Taiwan has been speeding up development of its high-tech defenses against China, including local manufacture of Sky Arrow missiles which belong to the same class as the Scud-killing American Patriot missiles.)

"But the Chung Shan Institute (the fountainhead of Taiwan's defense R&D) has shown what can be done. Our steel, auto, TV, and computer manufacturing industries have given us a good foundation from which to move," says Lin. The progress being made with Taiwan's Ching-kuo fighter aircraft has clearly boosted industrialists' confidence in their defense capabilities.

Taiwan may not have many friends but it does have cash. Latest reports are that it will use its money, in the form of economic aid, to foster political links. Arms sales could figure either as an incentive or as a condition of these new ties.

"Other developing countries like Thailand, Malaysia, and even mainland China, are coming up, and they will give us a lot of competition in the production of basic consumer goods," Lin notes.

The export value of China's weapons industry is put at about U.S.$2 billion a year, making it a crucial source of foreign exchange for buying advanced military technology from the West. Key selling items are J-7 jet fighters, T-59 tanks, and Silkworm anti-ship missiles. Among the customers for Chinese arms have been Pakistan, Thailand, Iran, and Iraq.

The great attraction is, of course, their price. A T-69 tank sells for around U.S.$250,000, about a quarter the cost of its U.S. equivalent. As a U.S. diplomat in Hong Kong puts it: "For every Western widget you buy, you can have four Chinese widgets. This means that for the same price as you could put together a battalion with Western equipment, you can put together an entire armored division with Chinese equipment."

In addition to low prices, China offers value for money. "They provide basic equipment that is easy to manage and service," says the U.S. diplomat. "They're very good at standing behind their equipment. They will send technical teams, spare parts, and whatever is needed to keep things going.

"That is where they used to go wrong in the 1970s. Now they figure that if you want to sell [weapons] you have to back them up."

China has also shown marketing prowess.

"They attend arms shows, they have representatives from the arms industry out on the streets, and they offer financing that competitors just can't match," says the U.S. diplomat.

©*Asian Business* magazine, Far East Trade Press, Ltd., 1989.

FORTRESS EUROPE
NOT A REAL THREAT

Despite the apparent menace of a unified European Community in 1992—with the growing complication of Eastern Europe, and of East Germany's reunification with West Germany—the Rim nations are not overly intimidated.

As Australian futurist Phillip Ruthven, chairman of Melbourne-based think tank IBIS International, puts it: the very idea of a Fortress Europe is "an acknowledgment that Europe has lost its economic and technological dynamism and that leadership in these areas has passed elsewhere."

Although the PacRim nations feel that Fortress Europe may indeed raise its drawbridge to ward off Asian exports, the Asia-Pacific region will actually be about twice the size of Europe economically in the early part of the 21st century. "Between now and 1995, the European economy is projected to grow by about $650 billion," Ruthven says. "During this same period, Asia alone will grow by about $1.4 trillion."

Even if American protectionists should prevail, the critical mass of the region is such that if trade between the United States and Asia dropped by 5% in the next couple of years, as is currently being forecast, it could be more than compensated for by the projected 12% growth in trade within Asia itself. By 1991, intraregional Asian trade will surpass the region's $250 billion in two-way trade with the United States.

THE NEW PACIFIC WAR?

A major Japanese newspaper, the *Sankei Shimbun,* featured a column which drew a cutting analogy between America's defeat of Japan in World War II and the sharp appreciation of the yen against the dollar in the late 1980s.

"Japan and the United States are replaying the Pacific War," financial columnist Daizo Kusayanagi pointed out. "This time instead of naval power and B-29s, the weapon is currency values. At stake today is Japan's survival as an industrial economy. The outcome is uncertain as the Americans prepare for a final assault on the beleaguered yen."

The columnist's conclusion was ominous: "Japan must take defensive measures. If the U.S. government refuses to issue yen-denominated bonds, we will have to take other steps. We must not lose the Pacific War twice."

3

❖

MONEY

RIM FINANCE

ASIAN FINANCIAL MARKETS
By Kent Price

Today the financial strength of Asia is apparent to everyone. Yet less than 10 years ago, American and European banks dominated the intermediation of international capital. The New York Stock Exchange represented a large part of the capitalization of the world's stock markets. While Japan had been a quiet net exporter of capital since the early 1970s, not many had noticed.

In the mid 1960s, the principal function of international banks in Asia was to provide working and investment capital inflows for trade and infrastructural projects and plant equipment development in the Asian region.

By the mid 1980s, world-class investment banks, insurance companies, and investment managers had established a major presence throughout Asia. Local financial institutions had developed a level of sophistication that has allowed them to meet international com-

Country risk rankings 1989

Top ten in Asia/Pacific

Rank	Country	Rating
1	Japan	95
2	Singapore	84
3	New Zealand	83
4	Australia	82
5	South Korea	79
6	Taiwan	72
6	Thailand	72
8	Hongkong	70
9	Brunei	68
9	Malaysia	68

Maximum score:100   Minimum: 0
Source: Euromoney, September 1989

petition in their home markets and lessened the need and demand for local market protection.

Today, Asia can be divided into the following three broad financial service markets:

Developed Financial Market:
  Japan
  Australia
  New Zealand

Emerging Financial Market:
  Korea
  Taiwan
  Hong Kong
  Singapore

Developing Financial Market:
  Philippines
  Indonesia
  Malaysia
  Thailand
  China

In each area, the importance of international commercial banking is diminishing. Many of

the American regional and smaller European banks have been scaling down, withdrawing, or forming strategic links with major Asian financial institutions. At the same time, major investment banks and investment managers are increasing their presence in major markets —Tokyo, Hong Kong, Singapore, Sydney— and are actively traveling to and doing deals in Seoul, Taipei, Manila, Jakarta, Bangkok, and Kuala Lumpur. This reflects the changing capital needs of the Asian countries.

THE DEVELOPED FINANCIAL MARKET

Japan, Australia, and New Zealand are industrially developed economies with an outwardly thrusting business community. This has come about because of the limited size of their local market. The manpower skills are on par or better than international competitors.

Japan

Japan overshadows all other Asian markets. Japanese financial institutions are among the largest and most profitable in the world. The Tokyo Stock Exchange is the world's largest by market capitalization. Of the top 10 banks in the world in 1987, seven were Japanese:

Banks	Total Assets ($B)
Dai–Ichi Kangyo Bank	315
Sumitomo Bank	286
Fuji Bank	282
Mitsubishi Bank	277
Sanwa Bank	254
Industrial Bank of Japan	223
Credit Agricole	215
Citicorp	206
Norinchukin Bank	182
Banque Nationale de Paris	180

There are good reasons for the dominance of the Japanese banks. Among them are: the strong foreign reserve position and trade balance of Japan; the capital requirements of Japanese banks is less than many of their foreign competitors; not to mention the fact that they have much less foreign exposure to the third world.

There are 211 Japanese securities firms, but the top four account for more than two thirds of the Japanese securities market. Like the United States, Japan has separate commercial and investment banking. While this division is breaking down, the securities firms have strong retail brokerage and mutual fund positions, and underwrite and distribute corporate and government securities.

With both the government and corporations borrowing heavily, those firms are the most profitable and best capitalized in the world. They are aggressively investing in financial firms in North America and Europe, and are forming joint ventures with major investment managers by using their massive placement power through their distribution systems. The top four firms are more profitable than most of the western commercial and investment banks:

Company	1987–1988 Estimated Profit ($B)
Nomura Securities	3.2
Daiwa Securities	2.1
Nikko Securities	1.6
Yamaichi Securities	1.3

The Japanese insurance industry is well-developed in life and property and casualty. These companies are major investors in North American and European equities and are major buyers of commercial real estate in the United States.

Until recently, foreign financial institutions played a correspondent relationship to the domestic Japanese institutions, which did not have much of a foreign presence. The Ministry of Finance has allowed the Japanese companies to play an increasingly larger international role, while, at the same time, reluctantly letting foreign companies into the Japanese market. With pressure from the United States and United Kingdom, the market is slowly opening.

Foreign commercial banks play a limited and shrinking role in the domestic Japanese market, except those with a capital markets business. No major acquisition of a Japanese bank has taken place; whereas most of the middle size banks in California are Japanese-owned. The Japanese stock market is the world's largest but only 16 foreign firms are members. In all, there are only 114 members of the Tokyo Stock Exchange compared with 1366 on the New York Stock Exchange. The 16 foreign firms are:

Merrill Lynch (U.S.)
Vickers da Costa (U.S.–Citicorp)
Jardine Fleming (Hong Kong)
Morgan Stanley (U.S.)
Goldman Sachs U.S.)
S.G. Warburg (U.K.)
First Boston (U.S.)
Salomon Bros (U.S.)
Kidder Peabody (U.S.–GE Capital Corp.)
Prudential Bache (U.S.–Prudential Insurance Corp)
Shearson Lehman Hutton (U.S.–American Express)
Smith, Barney (U.S.–Primerica)
Baring Bros. (U.K.)
County NatWest (U.K.–NatWest Bank)
Kleinwort Benson (U.K.)
J. Henry Schroder (U.K.)

It is interesting to note that there are no German, Swiss, French, or Australian members. There is no coincidence that the British and American governments have been the most vociferous in the efforts to open the Japanese markets.

The Japanese market has much of the structural rigidity of the American market as much of it was copied or imposed by the MacArthur government in the 1945 to 1950 period. Like the United States, the Japanese are discovering that the separation of the financial market into neat boxes is increasingly difficult and, more importantly, is inefficient.

As many of the developing Asian markets have used Japan as their model, there has been a knock-on effect throughout Asia. Like in Tokyo, policy-makers in Taipei, Jakarta, Seoul, and other Asian cities are discovering that a highly segmented, regulated, and directed financial market is causing structural inefficiencies in the entire economy.

Australia/New Zealand

Outside of Japan, the next largest grouping of financial institutions is in the Australia/New Zealand area. In 1988, the total assets of this grouping of commercial banks totaled over $235B (note that this is smaller than the smallest of the top five Japanese banks.) Like all of the Asian banking markets, the A/NZ markets were highly controlled and closed to competitors.

In the mid-1980s, deregulation opened the market and allowed Australian financial institutions to expand abroad. The Stock Market was unified, and negotiated commissions replaced fixed ones. The entry of foreign banks into areas which had been traditionally closed to local banks forced them to enhance their products, services, and technologies.

Similar deregulation took place in New Zealand. A/NZ businessmen have been very aggressive investors in North America, Europe, and increasingly in Asia. International

banks and investment houses are focusing on this market by opening offices and backing the aggressive overseas investment of Australian and New Zealand businessmen.

Major Commercial Banks in Australia/New Zealand

Bank	Assets in 1988 ($B)
Westpac (Sydney)	60
ANZ (Melbourne)	45
Nat Australia (Melbourne)	40
Commonwealth Banking (Sydney)	−34
Bank of New Zealand (Wellington)	11

With the deregulation, growth, and increasing sophistication of the Australian banks, and the development of currency and securities futures and options, Sydney is aiming to supplant Singapore and Hong Kong as the second most important international financial market in Asia.

EMERGING FINANCIAL MARKETS

With the exception of Hong Kong, these markets have been highly regulated and largely closed to foreign competition. Even in Hong Kong, an interest-rate cartel and the prohibition of most foreign banks from having more than one branch sully Hong Kong's *laissez faire* market reputation.

The Asian markets have been characterized by tight control of the domestic financial markets, with foreign banks providing trade finance and the needed foreign exchange for the massive export-driven economies. With prolonged export success, foreign banks are having a hard time finding a profitable niche. At the same time, the domestic markets are being opened slowly to foreign competitors. Ironically, many international banks are pulling back from their foreign businesses to concentrate their capital resources in their home countries.

South Korea

In less than 30 years, South Korea has become a major industrial exporting economy. The large industrial companies work closely with government planners and coordinators in promoting the export-driven economy. Foreign banks played a key role in financing trade and providing term capital for capital projects. Beyond that, there was no role that foreign banks were allowed to play.

South Korea has recognized that the financial structure of the country was primitive and would constrain growth. Several scandals in the grey market, the inability of small companies to get loans from banks, and the growing internationalization of the Korean market, made the government focus on financial reform. At the same time, there has been pressure from foreign governments, especially the United States, to open the domestic markets.

Starting in the early 1980s, the market has slowly been opened. Joint venture banks and specialized financial companies (merchant banks, leasing companies) have been formed with varying degrees of success. The securities and insurance markets are still effectively closed, although Nikko Securities has acquired a small and insignificant stake in a Korean security firm. Deregulation efforts call for the privatization of Korean commercial banks, the elimination of exchange and interest rate controls, and the encouragement of two-way capital flows. By the mid-1990s, Korea should be exporting capital and will start to play a major role in world financial centers.

Major Commercial Banks in Korea

Bank	Assets in 1988 ($B)
Bank of Seoul (Seoul)	39
Korea Exchange Bank (Seoul)	24
Korea Development Bank (Seoul)	21
Commercial Bank (Seoul)	19
Korea First Bank (Seoul)	17
Cho Hung Bank (Seoul)	17

In 1984, closed-end mutual funds, which held a broad range of Korean equities, were floated in New York and London. Large Korean companies have issued convertible bonds on international exchanges. Over time, this and other actions will open the Korean equity market. Like the Japanese model, financial institutions are closely watched and guided to assist in the export efforts. To allow significant control outside of Korea, market forces will be a function of the growing confidence of the government in the ability of the economy to compete on a global scale.

Taiwan

By 1987, the success of Taiwan's export-driven economy resulted in the second largest foreign reserve position in the world with over $70B. This has caused an overheating of the domestic market, which has resulted, for a time, in the Taiwan stock market being the third largest in the world in market capitalization terms after Tokyo and New York.

The Taiwanese government tightly controlled the domestic financial market and limited the role that foreign companies could play. With domestic liquidity that has come from the export success, the backwardness of the financial market has become apparent. The government has taken steps to upgrade it by allowing foreign banks to be more active in domestic business. It has allowed foreign participation in investment trust businesses, has allowed Taiwanese to invest off-shore, and has announced that new private banks will be chartered. Long closed to foreign companies, the insurance industry has been opened since 1987, when seven U.S. insurance companies were granted licenses:

Life Insurance Company of Georgia
Aetna International
American Family Life
Metropolitan Insurance and Annuity Company
Chubb Corp.
Cigna corp.
American International Underwriters.

It is interesting to note that no European or Japanese companies are on this list. This reflects as much an effort to placate American trade imbalance concerns as it does an interest in upgrading a backward industry.

Major Commercial Banks in Taiwan

Bank	Assets in 1988 ($B)
Coop Bank Taiwan (Taipei)	25
Bank of Taiwan (Taipei)	23
Hua Nan Commercial Bank (Taipei)	16
Chang Hwa Commercial Bank (Taipei)	15
Land Bank of Taiwan (Taipei)	15
City Bank of Taipei (Taipei)	10
Medium Business Bank (Taipei)	10
Bank of Communications (Taipei)	8

Due to the unique position that Taiwan has with the People's Republic of China, factors that would ordinarily be present in the maturation process of the financial markets have special considerations. The government has linked economic policy to national security. It is believed that it had learned lessons from the "loss of the Mainland" and put control of inflation as a high national priority.

Financial institutions have been viewed as one of the main instruments in meeting this objective, and have had tight controls. With the continuing export success, political maturity, and an openness to and within the People's Republic of China, Taiwan could play an important role in the development of the PRC. Ties between China and Taiwan are growing. There is a strong bond between these two Chinese areas. The economic role which Taiwan could play for China could be very significant and also be a key factor in bringing the two countries much closer together.

Hong Kong

For the past 30 years, Hong Kong has been building an international financial center based upon:

- little regulation
- the need of the Japanese to finance trade and take profit outside of Japan
- the development of the Eurodollar market
- the increasing role of Hong Kong as an entrepot for China and China trade from Taiwan and Korea
- a center for foreign exchange, funding, and international merchant banking for international banks doing business in Asia

From time to time, Singapore has been a rival but the interventionist policies of that government have impeded that effort. On the domestic side, the market has been almost as protected as the other Asian economies. With an interest-rate cartel, controlled by Hong Kong Bank, a limitation on what all but a handful of foreign banks can do and the collective power of the PRC banks (the 13 sister banks), Hong Kong has had periodic banking runs and crises which come as regularly as the rise and crash of the stock market. Besides the major local and foreign banks, there are almost 400 deposit-taking companies, most of which are very small and serve special purposes.

An effort is being made by the British Administration to strengthen regulations before the 1997 hand-over to the Chinese of Hong Kong. The Hong Kong securities market has always been very active with nineteenth-century-like rises and panics.

With the rapid expansion of the Taipei stock market and the crash of the Hong Kong market following the repression of the democracy movement in China in June 1989, the Hong Kong market is the third largest in Asia.

Increasingly, local security firms have been losing out to international firms which are using Hong Kong as their non-Japanese Asian base.

In 1986, a unified stock exchange was established and efforts have been made to bring its governance to international standards. Since the mid-1980s, Hong Kong has become the center for investment managers specializing in Asian funds. In 1987, assets of over $25B were being managed in Hong Kong. The British investment and merchant banks have the leaders, but a major corporate finance and investment effort from companies like Prudential Insurance of America is developing.

With the approach of 1997, large numbers of educated middle management Chinese are looking for a safe haven. This could have a profound impact upon Hong Kong's leading position. Almost all of the major commercial and investment banks have a presence in Hong Kong and, for many, the area of interest is regional. Should manpower or political uncertainty become a problem, these companies could move to Taipei, Singapore, or Sydney —all of which have the capacity and talent to fill the role of Hong Kong.

Major Commercial Banks in Hong Kong

Bank	Assets in 1988 ($B)
Hong Kong Bank	113
Nanyang Commercial	4
Bank of East Asia	3.7
Shanghai Commercial	2.6
Wing Lung Bank	1.7

Hong Kong has lived on wits and hard work for over a 150 years. Since 1949, it has been vulnerable to the events in China. In spite of the Korean War, the cultural revolution, and constant political turmoil in China, Hong Kong has played an important niche role. As long as Hong Kong contributes to the economic progress in China, it will continue to be an important center in southeast Asia. Regardless of what happens in China, this dominant role will be challenged by others as they develop their human and financial skills.

Singapore

Singapore and Hong Kong have been rivals for the lead in the evolving international capital market activities in Asia. Singapore developed an early lead in the "Asian dollar" market, but the heavy-handedness of the government has allowed Hong Kong to surpass it as an international financial center.

Singapore has kept a very tight division between the international and local markets. The domestic market is closely controlled and regulated by the Monetary Authority of Singapore. The stock market is controlled, and foreign firms are limited in number and as to what they can do.

No foreign firm can be a member of the stock exchange, and all trades on the market have to go through Singapore brokers. The Central Provident Fund makes the Singapore government an indirect and large money manager. Most money managers prefer Hong Kong. There are plans to deregulate the exchange and to privatize many of the government companies, such as Singapore Airlines.

Singapore is encouraging regional Asian companies to list and be floated on the Singapore Exchange. Nevertheless, the often repressive policies of the government (like press censorship and periodically expelling employees of major financial institutions) send signals which make Singapore less attractive as a regional center.

Major Commercial Banks in Singapore

Bank	Assets in 1988 ($B)
DBS	11
United Overseas Bank	10
Overseas Chinese Banking Corp.	7
Overseas Union Bank	4
Tak Lee Bank	1.2

Singapore has the potential to be a major financial center and to act as a replacement to Hong Kong should that be necessary. Whether the current government can allow the types of freedom and a regulatory environment conducive to international financial management is an open issue.

THE DEVELOPING FINANCIAL MARKET

The countries in the developing financial market area are characterized by being commodity based and/or being in the first stages of industrial development.

China has had 40 years of political instability and economic turmoil. The Philippines, Indonesia, Malaysia, and to a lesser extent Thailand have had commodity-centered economies, which have been dependent upon the world prices of their products. In an effort to lessen this dependence, the governments of these countries, until very recently, have controlled the domestic financial markets very closely in order to direct investment toward industrial projects, to help the farmers when necessary, or—in certain countries—to help the indigenous population develop at the expense of the local Chinese.

Foreign banks have had branches, but their primary functions were to finance trade and to provide term capital for industrial and infrastructure development. In China, the government owns all the financial institutions. With the exception of several hold-over branches of foreign banks in Shanghai, it has been only in the last 10 years that foreign banks have started to open again in China. The extent of their business and their profits has been very limited.

Philippines

In the 1960s, the Philippines was one of the most economically advanced of the countries in Asia. The economic mismanagement of the Marcos government has made the Philippines go backward in relation to all the other countries in Asia, except China.

A few American banks have dominated the foreign banking sector of the Philippines and, as such, had very large exposure when the political crisis started by the death of Benito Aquino caused the economic mismanagement to become apparent. In 1987, the Aquino government began to privatize banks that had been nationalized under Marcos.

The Bank of Boston and American Express took equity positions in several banks which required additional capital. The process of restructuring of the economy has attracted a lot of interest from international investment bankers and insurance companies. A new economic liberalism may allow for rapid economic expansion and opportunities for foreign investment.

Major Commercial Banks in the Philippines

Bank	Assets in 1988 ($B)
Philippine National Bank (Manila)	1.8
Bank of the Philippine Islands (M)	1.5
Metro Bank & Trust (Manila)	1.2
Far East Bank & Trust (Manila)	0.9
Land Bank of the Philippines (M)	0.6

In many ways, the Philippines has the same economic and political mismanagement which China has had and has suffered the same fate. Unlike China, the Philippines has a relatively free and open economy, which gives real hope for the future.

Indonesia

With over 150 million people and a land mass spread over 10,000 plus islands, Indonesia is one of the largest countries in the world. In the past few years, the government has decided that state-directed economic growth has not worked and has shifted toward a relatively open market system. As a result, significant changes have taken place in the financial area.

The stock market was transformed in 1989, and turnover rose ninefold. New share listings should exceed 200 by 1991, up from nine in 1988. Restrictions on foreign ownership of equities will be loosened. Several Indonesian funds have been organized. These funds have been more constrained by the availability of script than by demand. Investment has been rising quickly. Direct foreign investment tripled in 1988 to $4.4 billion, while local investment increased by almost 40% to $6.5 billion.

Foreign exchange earnings from non-oil exports now exceed oil exports. Indonesia may have reached a take-off point which will attract more investors, banks, and insurance companies. Corruption still exists and remains a structural problem. It is recognized as such, and efforts are being made to reduce it. Imports into the country are now being handled by an international Swiss-run agency, rather than many levels of customs officials. Accounting rules are being tightened as companies list shares on the Jakarta Exchange.

Major Commercial Banks in Indonesia

Bank	Assets in 1988 ($B)
Bank Negara Indonesia (Jakarta)	8.7
Bank Bumi Daya (Jakarta)	6.4
Bank Rakyat Indonesia (Jakarta)	6.2
Bank Dagang Negara (Jakarta)	5.9
Bank Ekspor Impor Indonesia (J)	4.0

After years of economic stagnation and numerous debt crises, Indonesia appears to be heading toward a continued level of economic growth which is not oil-based. Many foreign financial institutions can be expected to take an active interest in the country.

Malaysia

The multiracial nature of Malaysia and the dominance of the Chinese in the economy has caused economic and social tensions. This has been reflected in economic policies directed toward the advancement of the Bumiputra (native population) at the expense of the Chinese.

Although the economy has always been broadly opened to foreign participation in financial markets, the New Economic Policy has tried to direct economic activity toward redistribution of wealth from the Chinese and British toward the Malay community.

Financial service companies have had to keep one eye on the aims of the NEP and the level of Bumiputra investment in various industries, and the other on the still-developing nature of the financial sector. Two financial scandals—the so-called Carrian affair in 1983 in Hong Kong (with heavy involvement of Malaysian banks) and the Pan-Electric crisis in 1985—resulted in major losses to banks and securities firms. Subsequent reforms should strengthen the local institutions.

After years of integration, the Kuala Lumpur and Singapore stock exchanges are being split. This should benefit the development of financial services in Malaysia as Singapore has dominated to this point. Foreign firms will be welcomed to underpin the poorly capitalized local firms. Malaysia is a commodity-oriented economy, which is moving toward industrialization. It will require capital inflows for years. If the aims of the NEP can be moderated to allow for active Chinese participation, Malaysia will be a major growth economy in Asia.

Major Commercial Banks in Malaysia

Bank	Assets in 1988 ($B)
Malayan Banking (KL)	8.6
Bank Bumiputra (KL)	7.9
Public Bank (KL)	2.7
United Malaya (KL)	2.6
Development & Commercial (KL)	1.6
Arab-Malaysian (KL)	1.5

Malaysia has been dominated by the financial markets in Singapore since Federation times. It is now trying to establish the basis for operating an independent and strong financial sector. The preoccupation with Bumiputra advancement may complicate the process; however, the chances for success are good.

Thailand

Over the past few years, the growth of the economy in Thailand has been the most impressive in Asia. The surge of economic development has put strong pressure on the financial system to open, broaden, and adapt to credit and capital formation needs. Sixteen private banks dominate the financial sector. Foreign banks have been constrained to one branch and to the types of business which can be done. The domestic accumulation and allocation of capital has proved to be inadequate. The Thai stock exchange is still underdeveloped. A little over 100 companies have been listed since 1974.

This has led to a bank-financed and -dominated economy. Banks act as bankers, underwriters, and investors. Because of this, the Central Bank plays a key role in setting interest rates and providing moral persuasion as to types and amounts that should be lent. The government plans to privatize many public enterprises which currently operate at a loss. While this will move slowly, it will put additional pressure on the developing financial sector.

Major Commercial Banks in Thailand

Bank	Assets in 1988 ($B)
Bangkok Bank (B)	14.0
Krung Thai Bank (B)	7.0
Thai Farmers Bank (B)	6.2
Siam Commercial Bank (B)	4.0
Thai Military Bank (B)	2.8
Bank of Ayudhya (B)	2.7
First Bangkok Bank (B)	1.9
Siam City Bank (Siam)	1.8

Thailand has had dramatic growth over the past few years. This should continue. The stock market continues to expand in volume, with many international fund managers arranging "Thai Funds." The domestic financial institutions, which have been protected, are now trying to cope with and service the financial needs of this expansion. There could be some major problems as Thailand moves through this phase. The country will be a major economic force and a major attraction for many years.

China

Since 1949, China has had a centralized economy. Political instability has caused great economic dislocations. Periods of introspection have impeded progress. With the gradual reopening of the country, which started in 1978, the economic fabric of the country has proven to be weak and backward. State financial institutions were manned by people with no modern experiences. It was as if there were a 40-year time gap. International bankers found themselves meeting with men in their late sixties and seventies who had been bankers prior to the revolution and whose experiences were based upon financial practices of the late 1930s. Legal and accounting practices had broken down or did not exist. For American financial institutions, outstanding issues and problems had been on hold since the Korean War (i.e., all financial transactions were frozen at that time and were not reopened until the normalization of relations between the U.S./PRC in 1978). In spite of this, an excitement has developed over the opening of the billion-people-plus market and the opportunities for investments and financial services.

The state controls all of the Chinese financial institutions. Like most centralized economies, the purpose of Chinese banks, insurance companies, and other financial institutions is to assist in the implementation of the economic plans of the state. Market-force operations are not part of the plan. Rational capital allocation is a function of central planning not risk/return calculations.

As China reenters the commercial world, modern financing and capital allocation techniques need to be developed. In order to modernize, joint ventures have been formed with leading American, European, Japanese, and other Asian financial institutions. These joint ventures tend to be specialized, like leasing, trade, investment banking, insurance, etc. Chinese institutions hope to learn modern techniques, and the international companies hope to gain access to the Chinese market.

Since the late 1970s, international financial companies have been opening representative offices and branches in Beijing. To date, more money has been spent than made. China has borrowed a large amount of "soft" money from governments and organizations like the World Bank.

In the mid-1980s, China began to borrow from commercial and investment banks. What is lacking in China is the mobilization of domestic savings and market mechanisms to allocate those funds into productive programs. Capital bottlenecks continue with this centralized approach to capital allocation. The events of the summer of 1989 will only complicate China's financial problems.

Major Commercial Banks in China

Bank	Assets in 1988 ($B)
Bank of China (Beijing)	150.0
Bank of Communications (B)	10.4
Kwangtung Provincial (B)	5.4
Sin Hua Trust & Savings (B)	4.8
Kincheng Banking	3.7

Outside of Japan, the Bank of China is the largest bank in Asia. While this is not surprising, it is interesting to note that the next largest bank is many times smaller and that all the major banks in China are headquartered in Beijing. This reflects the political reality of the financial process in China. China has a very long way to go to bring the financial elements of the economy to modern standards. There is an entrepreneurial spirit and tradition in China that does not exist in the Soviet Union. Given free reign, progress could be rapid. The largest question is the one of political stability. Without it, the future is not bright.

Kent Price is the chief financial officer of the Bank of New England Corp. in Boston and a director of Hong Kong-based Sun Hung Kai Securities Co., the largest Chinese securities firm in Asia. His career in international banking spans over 15 years, including five years based in Asia.

ASIA 2000 REPORT

ASIAN FINANCE OVERTAKES THE WEST
by Matthew Montagu-Pollock

Asian economies are growing so fast that by the year 2000 the region will dominate many aspects of world finance.

To be rich is glorious. On reasonable assumptions, the year 2000 will see the average citizen of Asia's newly industrializing countries (NICs) becoming as rich as the average citizen of Western Europe.

All areas of finance—stock markets, consultancy services, banking—will see explosive growth.

STOCK MARKETS

By 2000, Asia will account for 65% to 70% of the world's stock-market capitalization.

The Asian proportion of world stock-market capitalization will be roughly where the British Empire was 100 years ago, or where U.S. capital markets were 20 years ago.

Let us just flip a switch on our Reuter's screen, to see what the stock-market indices might possibly look like on January 1, 2000:

The most dramatic stock-market performance will probably come from South Korea, which is likely to emulate the behavior of Japan in the 1980s. Its stock market will grow from a small, closed market into a huge stock market. Anyone who invests U.S.$10,000 in South Korea now, will, if some reasonable assumptions come true, hold around U.S.$113,616 by the year 2000.

The reason? Korea is entering a high-savings period, and the government is allowing that money to enter the stock market.

Another force pushing Korea's market upward is less palpable, but nevertheless real: The echoes of Japan. Korean companies have all the key features of the Japanese "system" —extensive cross-holdings, conservative accounting systems, high debt ratios, low dividend payouts.

We have learned that this Japanese and Korean "system" behaves in a peculiar way.

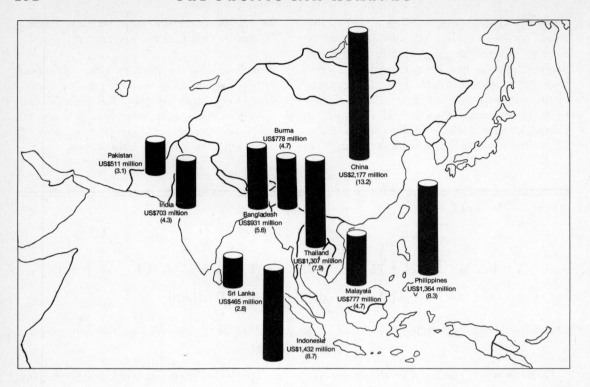

Everything seems to work together to push stock market valuations up.

First, Korean law (like Japanese law) requires that the annual report should state earngings exactly as they are submitted to the tax authorities. The rest of the world more leniently permits two sets of figures, allowing accelerated depreciation for tax purposes, while straightline depreciation is used for shareholders' reports. The general effect in Korea is for companies greatly to understate earnings.

"The accounting rules allow faster depreciation than any other country I've seen— they depreciate four or five times faster than in the U.S.," says George Long, managing director of fund managers Gartmore (HK). Companies can also underreport earnings by making certain categories of approved investment.

"The picture is not entirely straightforward because in some contexts Korean companies may not disclose losses. But the general trend is very clear," says Long.

Second, the prevalence of cross-holdings sharply reduces the number of available shares —which by supply and demand pushes up share prices.

Third, Korean companies are highly leveraged, which increases the level of risk, but also increases the return on equity (ROE), a key measure of corporate returns.

Fourth, dividend payouts are low. In a high-growth company this makes sense, and raises the long-term rate of growth, a crucial element in share valuations.

"The Koreans are perfectly aware of what is going to happen. The implications are fairly dramatic," says George Long. "By the year

2000, the Korean stock exchange will be the fourth largest in the world.

"You will see Korea's five securities firms develop into huge companies, as they have in Japan. There will be a shift in the relative hierarchies in Korean society. Brokers, who used to be considered low-down, will become the new elite," says Long.

"By the year 2000, Korea will be a large-scale capital exporter," he adds. "The Koreans are already doing loans tied to trade credits, for instance, lending to Hungary. Korean merchant banks, originally set up to borrow abroad, will become originators of debt, and will arrange syndications. You will see them in the Eurobond markets."

And in 1992, when the government plans to open up South Korea so that foreigners can buy shares freely, there will be a large inrush of money from the expatriate financial community.

The other stock markets of East Asia can be expected to follow the same broad pattern of development.

"I expect this revaluation to happen in all Asian countries over the next decade," says Peter Everington, a fund manager at Thornton Management (Hong Kong).

"There may be political accidents, of course—and we can probably expect [at least] one of the region's countries to have a political accident."

Keiichi Miki, fund manager for Hambro-Pacific (Hong Kong), says: "If we compare the countries with [the progress of] Japan, South Korea and Taiwan are in the early 1970s; Malaysia is in the mid-1960s; and China and Indonesia are in the early 1950s."

The most difficult market to predict is Taiwan's. Universally shunned by foreign fund managers who find its high price/earnings ratios (P/Es) absurd, it may be less overvalued than is thought.

This point of view is put by Francis Yuen,

chief executive of the Hong Kong Stock Exchange, who points out that most shares in Taiwan are rated at 30 or 40 times earnings—not excessive, given the country's growth rate.

The "sky-high" prices which give Taiwan a bad reputation as the world's most speculative market are, he points out, concentrated in the banks, because of their huge investments in land, and in the fringe investment companies, with their almost cult-like following.

The government is making serious efforts to deal with the second of these two problems. The most likely pattern will be a brief and controlled "crash," followed by a slow and steady upward movement.

The "younger" stock markets around the region are likely to do particularly well as beneficiaries of inward foreign investment. With populations of 170 million and 59 million, respectively, Indonesia and the Philippines are almost untapped sources of cheap labor, and should grow rapidly.

JAPAN

The stock market in Japan will probably grow much more slowly. By the year 2000, it will probably no longer amaze us with its high P/Es.

One reason is a decline in available cash. There will soon be less liquidity flowing through the system:

- Japanese savings are falling by 0.5% of GNP each year as the welfare system begins to provide sickness, unemployment, and old-age benefits.
- Japan is getting older. By the year 2000, insurance companies will be paying out more in benefits than they take in premiums.
- The birth of a competitive labor market in Japan is forcing companies to pay higher

wages to their salaried workers, which will reduce company profits. Lower profitability should mean lower share prices.

Another reason why Japanese shares are likely to fall is the beginning of the end of Japan's famous cross-holdings system. Here we find the exact reverse of Korea's situation.

The origin of the extensive network of cross-holdings between companies in Japan is partly defensive (a safeguard against take-overs) and partly positive (it cements links between companies which do business to-gether). At present, 70% of shares on the Tokyo Stock Market are cross-held. But the system is coming under intense strain. Commercial reality is increasingly at odds with it.

Now that Japanese companies are sourcing more supplies offshore, the links are coming under pressure. For example, members of a *zaibatsu* are committed to buying steel from Japanese companies with which they have traditional links. This is clearly irrational when cheaper steel can be had from South America. Most companies might find it advantageous to liquidate their cross-holding links.

The effects of such an "unwinding of the cross-holdings" could be dramatic. "If the proportion of cross-holdings falls from the present 70% of the market to a more modest 40% of capitalization, the volume of Japanese shares in circulation will double," says Hambro-Pacific's Miki. "Logically, Japanese P/E ratios should halve."

CURRENCIES

The most widely predicted scenario is that the Yen will continue to rise. The theory is that it will behave as it has been doing recently, gradually gaining value against the dollar and the other currencies.

For instance, the research organization

Business International predicted the yen, which averaged Y140 to U.S.$1 would rise to Y130 to the dollar in 1990 and Y115 in 1991, before leveling off at Y110 in 1992 and 1993.

Similar predictions have been produced by economists at UBS/Phillips and Drew, James Capel, and other brokerage houses.

But while most economists agree, there is a strong case for believing the opposite. "On the surface, the majority opinion is dead right," says economist Tim Lee of GT Brokerage (Hong Kong). "But we argue the opposite. We think the market will be wrong." The key, he says, is the relative credibility of the central banks.

"Monetary policy in the United States has been very tight. The Federal Reserve is doing the best job of any major central bank. Meanwhile money supply in Japan has been growing much more rapidly than one's accustomed to. So it's not clear that the inflation differential will be in Japan's favor.

"If U.S. inflation is lower, and trade imbalances are correcting themselves (as we believe they are), then logically, the yen should *not* rise."

A couple of other events commonly predicted for the yen probably *won't* have happened by the year 2000:

• By 2000, the yen *won't* yet be the world's principal trading currency. That will almost certainly still be the province of the greenback. Even Japan's trade continues to be overwhelmingly denominated in U.S. dollars. In 1986 only 36% of exports from Japan and only 11% of imports were denominated in yen. Only 4% of all trade between non-Japanese partners was yen-denominated—compared with 14% denominated, for example, in deutsche marks.

The reason? There is, first, little *immediate* relation between the volume of a country's trade and the position of its currency in the world's capital markets. It seems that the world has a tendency to trade with the currency of the power which *used to be* No 1. The reason is surely partly habit. It was not until 1945 that the U.S. dollar became the world's dominant trading currency—historically speaking, the second half of the "American era." Now established as the leading trading currency, the dollar is traded disproportionately in the foreign-exchange markets. It is accepted as the key reserve currency. It is an indicator for all sorts of other events. It will take a long time to dislodge.

• The yen won't be the world's principal reserve currency either. What's been happening to the world's central banks' foreign exchange holdings looks more like a flight from the dollar (mainly to the deutsch mark) than a rush to the yen. This is largely due to the restrictions on short-term money markets in Japan.

BANKING

In 2000, the world's leading banking center will not be Tokyo. It will still be London. Which is a paradox, because Japanese banks are already, in 1990, the biggest in the world: Japan has 16 of the world's 20 largest banks. There is a huge size gap between the top four Japanese banks and others. Japanese banks are expanding rapidly.

Yet Tokyo is likely to remain the most restrictive of financial centers—and banks hate regulation. That's why the volume of Japanese bank business in London is today approximately equal to the *combined* volume of U.S. and U.K. banks.

But wherever banking business is done, Japanese banks will do it.

"I would say that 90% of Asia's banking business will be controlled by Japanese banks by the year 2000," says Robert Zielinski, a securities analyst at the Japan office of Jardine Fleming.

Japanese dominance is likely to become more, not less, pronounced—because of the advantages the Japanese enjoy. The trend is so clear that William Purves, chairman of the Hong Kong and Shanghai Bank, has warned that Japanese banking dominance is reaching dangerous proportions.

In a speech in November 1989, Purves warned that one mistake by the Japanese banks could plunge the world's financial system into crisis.

What are the advantages of Japanese banks?

• The appreciation of the yen. Much of the "global dominance" of the Japanese banks is a matter of chance—they hold the right (i.e., the most valuable) currency.
• A captive market. The Japanese banking market is almost entirely closed to foreigners. "There is terrible service in banks in Japan and you definitely pay higher prices," says Jardine Fleming's Zielinski.
• Size. A great contrast: In the United States there are 14,000 different banks, some worth as little as U.S.$500,000, kept alive by government guarantees and antitrust legislation. By contrast, the Japanese banks are few in number, concentrated in focus, and huge.
• The problems of the U.S. banks, namely, third-world debt. Having expanded abroad optimistically in the 1970s, the U.S. banks are visibly retreating into the United States from everywhere in the world.

"The U.S. banks have not recovered from the debt crisis," says Phil Harris, chief corporate relations officer for the Hong Kong and Shanghai Bank.

TRENDS IN MERCHANT BANKING UP TO THE YEAR 2000

Placing equities will be a key growth area for merchant banks, because of the expected privatization bonanza in Thailand, Malaysia, Indonesia, and the Philippines. Local merchant banks will get the business.

Convertible bonds and warrants will be issued in great numbers by Taiwanese and Korean companies.

Mergers and acquisitions will multiply, but there won't be much money in them. Companies established by families whose children are unable to take over will change hands, but these businesses will be small by global standards. "Advisers are compensated in relation to the size of transaction—not time and energy," says Prudential Asia's managing director William Flanz.

Consultancy services will multiply in the financial field as the barriers of protection come down, and as banks and other financial institutions strive to become more efficient.

"The cost-bases of banks can be reduced by around 5%, and bank transaction times can frequently be halved, which means you can significantly expand the amount of time people spend marketing," says Michael Coorey, chief executive of consultancy firm Balance Corp.

Offshore markets will mushroom, assisting Japanese and Taiwanese companies to evade tax.

©*Asian Business* magazine, Far East Trade Press, Ltd.

"The prospects are that the U.S. banks will remain weak, with the exception of Citibank. It is common knowledge that Bank of America, Chase, and Manufacturers Hanover have all pulled out of retail operations in Asia."

The Hong Kong and Shanghai Bank is quietly calling for a concentration of Western banks. "We will be aiming to be a counterweight to the Japanese banks, as part of a move to consolidation by a number of big banks," says Hong Kong Bank's Harris. Says William Flanz, managing director of Prudential Asia: "It matters less how big a bank is in aggregate, than how big it is in any given city. With modern banking technology, you can no longer justify the expense structure of small banks."

Others more skeptically draw a parallel with American banks after World War II. They were expected to dominate international banking. It simply never happened.

In Asia the barrier to all banks is protectionism. In South Korea, "foreign banks will always be second-class citizens," says David O'Rear, researcher with Business International, Hong Kong. "They make good money, but not nearly as good as the Korean banks."

That's also the situation in Taiwan, though things may change there. Last year, the government put into effect legislation allowing the creation of private banks, which seems likely to usher in a banking free-for-all. New banks will be started, which will probably be more aggressive than the state banks.

"It will revolutionize the financial system here," says John Crossman, managing director of Jardine Fleming, Taiwan. "I think the new banks are going to beat the pants off the government-owned banks. The banking system is fantastically inefficient. There is tremendous demand."

Many see a future for Taiwan as an offshore banking center, with radical deregulation, doors open freely to international banks—the whole Hong Kong scene.

Stock Markets: Projections to January 1, 2000

	Index (Jan. 1, 1990)	Index (Jan. 1, 2000)	% Annual gain	U.S. $10,000 invested on Jan. 1, 1990
South Korea: KSE (CPSI)	900	10,000	31	113,616
Philippines: Manila composite	1,250	7,000	24.5	71,866
Indonesia: JKSE Index	400	2,500	24	69,309
Hong Kong: Hang Seng Index	2,600	15,000	21	55,599
Thailand: SET Index	700	3,000	18	44,254
Singapore: STI	1,400	6,000	18	44,254
Taiwan: TSE Index	10,000	30,000	14	32,519
Japan: Nikkei Index	34,000	100,000	13	30,049

Source: Asian Business.

"It could work," says Crossman. "They have the cash. They are willing to take a bet. They are willing to be 'quiet investors.' If you have three Taiwanese investors on your company's board, they come up with three different answers—very unlike the Japanese, and very reassuring.

"Taiwan could be a major, rip-roaring financial center. It could be the entrepot center for central China."

PREDICTIONS FOR THE 1990s
by Roger Suyama

Roger Suyama works in investment banking for a major investment bank in New York City.

JAPAN

Japan will experience a slow-down in corporate earnings and profitability in the period from 1990 to 1992. The effects will be devastating to the industries and countries that are heavily dependent on Japanese investment for much of their growth (i.e., Thailand, Malaysia, and Indonesia).

The Japanese Nikkei average will achieve new lows of 16,000, far below the closing of March 16, 1990 of 31,000. The sharp decline in the Tokyo stock market indicates the fundamental change in Japan's economy. The decline in the stock market was almost predicted with the rise in late 1989, of interest rates from 4% to 7%. During the 1980s, the Tokyo stock market was driven up to such a high P/E ratio (as much as 50 to 60 times earnings), by such factors as the high level of liquidity in the economy, a lack of investment alternatives (government bonds were yielding 4 or 5%), inflated real estate assets values, an easy lending policy by the major Japanese, and the lack of major decline in the Japanese stock market. Japanese investors came to believe that it was the stock market's duty to provide positive returns. The investor psychology was so perverse that one investor wanted the government to buy back his NTT shares because the shares had declined below their offering price.

The rising stock market and real estate market became a "virtuous business cycle," where the rapidly rising land values pumped up the stock market by: (1) allowing companies and individuals to cheaply borrow off their land holdings to buy more stocks; and (2) increasing the net asset value of the companies which had substantial Tokyo and other land holdings.

Because of the extensive cross-shareholdings of Japanese corporations, the rising stock market, like the real estate market, also had the effect of further increasing the net asset value of companies. Investors began to justify the 70 or 100 times earnings ratios by arguing that the value of a company's holdings of land and shares held of other companies were far higher than their reported historical costs.

While there was validity to this argument, at 100 times earnings, the company no longer trades on the fundamental business prospects of the company (i.e., earnings) but on the market value of the land and stock holdings which can fluctuate day to day. Even with the high valuation of these assets, the stock market valuations were still rising beyond reasonable "market valuations" of companies' assets. Japanese stock markets were going up, for no other reason than the faith investors had that the stock market would always go up.

With the decline in the Japanese stock market, this "tulip-bulb" market psychology is slowly being changed. This decline, however,

has been on relatively light volume. The real selling panic has not yet occurred. The virtuous business cycle has turned into a vicious business cycle. Land prices have fallen since the end of 1989 by as much as 20% in some areas. An inflation psychology is beginning to become embedded in the Japanese economy. Wholesale prices rose on annual basis by almost 4% in the first quarter of 1990. The money supply grew to 11% in 1989. Oil prices and wage rates have shot up also.

These inflationary pressures have driven interest rates up almost 60% since November 1989. With Japanese government bonds yielding almost 7%, the so-called "Tokkin" funds (insurance companies and other institutional investors) realize they can get a guaranteed rate of return instead of investing in an uncertain Japanese market. These institutions have invested an unprecedented amount of money in the Tokyo stock exchange in the 1980s. If they reduced their exposure by as little as 10% of their invested assets, some $100 billion could flow out of their market.

The vicious cycle also applies to the declining markets in both land and stocks. As the value of land and stock holdings fall, the net asset values of companies will drop, thus taking away one more pillar of support in their high valuations. The earnings of many companies will be hammered, too, not only because of the expected slow-down in the Japanese economy, but also because of the widespread practice of Zaitech. Zaitech or financial engineering includes the practice of Japanese companies playing the stock market to pump up earnings. For example, Toyota made more money from the stock market than from selling cars in 1989.

The Japanese banks will play a major role in the slow-down and liquidity crunch, which the Japanese will experience in the 1990 to 1992 period. Analogous to the leverage boom in the United States in the 1980s, the quadrupling of Japanese bank assets has helped to inflate all Japanese assets.

By providing cheap money on loans backed by Japanese real estate, the Japanese banks injected a significant amount of liquidity into the economy. In the early part of the 1990s, the Japanese banks will have tighter lending policies as their wholesale funding costs and their cost of raising equity capital rise dramatically. Earnings of banks will come under extreme pressure, because much of their funding costs are short-term in nature, while the yield on their long-term assets will remain relatively constant—not too dissimilar to the disintermediation which occurred in the early 1980s to the savings and loan institutions. The banks will also be under pressure to either significantly slow down lending or even reduce their assets because of the new Basel Capital guidelines, which were implemented one and a half years ago. Previously, the Japanese banks were in full compliance. Much of their capital, however, was composed of off-balance-sheet gains in their land and stock holdings. With a decline in prices of both assets, additional capital pressures may be put on the banks.

IMPACT ON THE RIM

The effect of this liquidity crunch in the Japanese economy will have a short-term deleterious effect over most of the Pacific Rim. The effects will be widespread. New investments in Thailand, Malaysia, and Indonesia will slow down. Real estate investment and the financing of real estate investment in the United States will slow during the early part of the 1990s. Much of the miracle growth of the Pacific Rim will be put on "hold" in many countries until Japan's economy becomes

healthy again. Individual countries, such as Singapore, Taiwan, and Korea, will continue to see good growth rates for their relatively large economies. Second-tier Pacific Rim countries, such as Thailand, Indonesia, and Malaysia, will see relatively lower growth rates of 4% to 6% (compared to the last few years). Third-tier Pacific Rim countries, such as the Philippines, may see low or even negative growth rates.

Ultimately, the miracle of the Pacific Rim countries growth rates will continue strongly upward after the Japanese economy turns around in 1992. The business fundamentals of Japan are strong once the speculative excesses are taken out of the system. The 1990s will also see Japan receive a steady stream of repatriated cash flow from their overseas investments, which now totals over $700 billion. This stream of income will lessen the business cycles in Japan, and provide a steady flow of capital for future growth. From 1993 onward, Japan will continue to have good growth for a fully industrialized country with GNP growing in the 3% to 4% range annually. The Nikkei average will fully recover and reach its previous high of 37,000 in the mid-1990s and will be at around the 45,000 level by the year 2000.

HONG KONG

Hong Kong's stock market will experience a euphoric rise after Deng dies, and a new reformist communist guard takes over China in the mid-1990s. They promise liberalization and more market and political reforms. The Hang Seng index will increase to 5,000 by 1996, some 80% more than the March 19, 1990 closing of 2,130. China's economy will also experience a mini-boom in the years leading up to 1997, as they once again begin the process of liberalization. Growth rates from 1995 to 1997 will peak at 8% annually for the Chinese economy, particularly the special economic zone in Southern China. The Hong Kong economy will also experience growth rates in excess of 6%. Although many local companies will reduce their operations in the territory, Japanese, American and European companies will continue to move to and expand their operations in Hong Kong. Hong Kong's low tax rate, unobtrusive government, well-developed infrastructure and central location in Asia will make Hong Kong a longterm good investment despite the volatility and uncertainty caused by a Chinese takeover. The Hong Kong/China economy will end the millennium on a downturn, as China and Britain complete the final terms and process for the political takeover of Hong Kong in 1997. The realization of the lack of guaranteed freedom for Hong Kong citizens generates a great outflow of capital and talented workers. This outflow forces China to restrict both capital and immigration outflows shortly after taking over Hong Kong, and international investors begin to realize that this is a very different Hong Kong.

THAILAND

Thailand will go into a "recession," or period of slow growth, in the early 1990s. This will be as a result of the accelerated growth of Thailand's economy over the last few years, which has caused numerous bottlenecks, infrastructure problems, and rapidly rising wages and land prices. Japanese investment will invest more heavily in Malaysia and Indonesia over Thailand in the early 1990s because of Thailand's infrastructure problems and the lower business costs of other Pacific Rim countries.

AIDS will also become a major problem in Thailand—as it will in other newly developing Pacific Rim countries, including the Philippines, Indonesia, Malaysia, and India.

Currently, there are no formal and complete statistics on prostitutes, drug-users, and other high-risk groups concerning the penetration of the HIV virus in Thailand, but informal surveys have shown that between 15% and 40% of Bangkok and Chiang Mai prostitutes tested HIV-positive. With the Thai tourist industry generating over $5 billion, much of it the packaged "sex tour" variety, the implications for an epidemic of AIDS will be devastating to the economy.

However, the rapid growth of the Thai economy after 1993 and the industrious nature of the Thai people, will mitigate many of these problems. By the year 2000, the Thai stock market (SET) will have increased from 653 to 2,612 for an increase of 400%.

THE PHILIPPINES

By contrast, the Philippines will continued to have a troubled economy and a major AIDs problem to deal with. Japan will begin the enforcement of an informal policy of denying entrance to potential visitors to the country who may carry the HIV virus. These will include gays from the United States and women from the Philippines.

MALAYSIA

Malaysia will be the country of choice for foreign investors in the 1990s. Inexpensive land, low wages, and an economy increasingly directed toward free-market growth will greatly expand the economy. The continued growth of Singapore in the 1990s as the stable financial and service center for Southeast Asia will positively impact Malaysia.

Malaysia's stock market composite will increase from 468 to 1,200 by the year 2340 for an increase of 500%.

NORTH KOREA

North Korea's economy will collapse in the 1990s as the rigidities of that planned economy cause the economy to freeze up like the Soviet economy. A reformist, democratic leadership takes over. South Korea will offer aid and other investments to North Korea. Unification, if it takes place at all, will be at a much slower pace than the German reunification. Confusion will reign as the South Koreans have a hard time determining not only how the unification process will work, and in what time frame, but whether they even want to be unified with such a poor and backward country.

VIETNAM

Vietnam will be one of the only countries to remain hard-line communists throughout the 1990s. Despite a liberalization of foreign investment and some markets, the international investment community will continue to shun Vietnam. The totalitarian regime will be seen as hypocritical, and a new name will be created for their market liberalization moves, "superficial capitalism." By the year 2000, Vietnam will have the lowest per capita income of all the Pacific Rim nations with an average income as low as many countries in Africa.

THE ADB'S ROLE IN THE 1990S

The Asian Development Bank (ADB) has been doing some soul-searching on its role in the 1990s and has come up with a list of recommendations from an outside panel headed by former Japanese foreign minister Saburo Okita.

Two key ones: Redirect lending to combat poverty. Do more to finance private-sector business.

One practical suggestion is for the establishment of an "Asian Financial Corp" (like the World Bank's International Finance Corp) to issue soft loans within the region. This is necessary if the war on malnutrition and homelessness is to be won. Environmental protection will also be emphasized. The key point is that the ADB will be trying to enlist more private-sector support than it has in the past. That's important news for specialized companies ready to work with the ADB and for the development effort itself.

©*Asian Business* magazine,
Far East Trade Press, Ltd., 1989.

LIST OF UNTOUCHABLE COMPANIES

Which companies would Japanese *not* want the Americans to buy? Japan's popular *Dime* magazine did a survey asking what companies would cause Japanese businessmen to claim the "soul of Japan" had been bought if an American company were to buy them?

People in their
twenties:	Toyota, Matsushita, Mitsui
thirties:	Toyota, NTT (Nippon Telephone & Telegraph), Matsushita
forties:	Japan Steel, NTT, Mitsubishi
fifties:	Japan Steel, Matsushita, NTT

Americans who know Japan well answered the question with: Mitsubishi, Sony, Fuji Sankei (the media communications company).

BANKS UNPOPULAR IN CHINA

People in China's Sichuan province have so little faith in banks that it is estimated that one quarter of all the currency in circulation, the equivalent of $700 million, remains in private hands rather than in savings accounts. This has become a problem elsewhere, too, so much so that in Guangxi province depositors have been prohibited from withdrawing their savings, and the government has instructed banks nationally to increase interest rates to encourage new deposits. (The so-called People's Bank now offers 9% for six months, and 11.34% for one year on fixed deposits.) Some banks have also turned to distinctly capitalist-style incentives—offering new depositors such gifts as refrigerators and television sets.

TAIWAN IS TOPS

Despite its heavy reliance on exports, Taiwan will remain among the world's most credit-worthy of nations, according to Business Environment Risk Information. Only four countries—including Taiwan, Singapore, Norway, and Belgium—belong to the American firm's best-risk category.

"A child does not mind its mother's ugliness; a dog does not mind its master's poverty."

Chinese proverb

MOONIES INVEST IN THE PRC AND SOVIET UNION

Businessmen linked to the South Korean-based Unification Church (a.k.a. the "Moonies") were behind a $250 million car project, which is described as being the single largest American investment in China. The plan is for the Moonie-backed Panda Motor Corp. to manufacture 300,000 cars in Guangdong (Canton), South China, according to Hong Kong's *Sing Tao* newspaper. Pak Bo-hi, the director of the firm who is the right-hand man of Rev. Sunmyung Moon, founder of the controversial Unification Church, estimates that Panda Motors will begin exporting cars in 1995.

Moon's organization has also been active in making business inroads in the Soviet Union. Moon, a fervent anti-communist, met with Soviet President Mikhail Gorbachev in Moscow in May 1990, and pledged a $1 billion investment. Moon's meeting with Gorbachev reportedly paved the way for the historic summit in San Francisco in June 1990 between the Soviet leader and South Korean President Roh Tae Woo, as first noted by Alexander Besher, the syndicated "Pacific Rim" columnist and author of this *Almanac,* and later by the *Far Eastern Economic Review*. That summit led to the restoration of diplomatic relations between the two nations much to the chagrin of the Cold War regime of North Korean strongman Kim Il-Sung.

TRANS-PACIFIC REAL ESTATE DEALS

The number of Japanese real estate agents offering joint ownership schemes for U.S. buildings and land has burgeoned since 1988. The investors who decide to participate in the scheme form an owners' union in America. The union then buys and manages the property, building, or condominium. Profits from the operation are distributed to the owners. If prices go up significantly, the union sells the property and distributes the capital gain among the owners.

Hasegawa Komuten company offers a unique system that combines real estate in Japan and the United States. This popular system offers high profits from U.S. operations, and high capital gain from Japanese investments.

First offering: L.A. office building and Minato-ku, Tokyo condominium; 80 shares (1 share = Y80 million, about $615,385); sold out in two months.

Second offering: Small L.A. building and Shibuya-ku, Tokyo condominium; 70 shares (1 share = Y70 million, about $538,461); sold out in less than two months.

Third offering: L.A. office building and Meguro-ku, Tokyo condominium; 45 shares (1 share = Y89 million, or $684,615); sold out in one month.

Of the three offerings, corporations accounted for less than 20% of the shares sold; the rest went to individuals, according to an *Asahi Shimbun* report.

GOLDBRICKING IN TAIWAN

Despite attempts by the Taiwanese government to clamp down on real estate speculation, a group of $3.6 million houses have gone up in eastern Taipei—so expensive, say critics, that a single brick in the condo-like units cost more than the average worker's salary for a month.

STOP N' SHOP REAL ESTATE DOWN UNDER

Overseas demand for Australian residential property is so strong that one Japanese investor reportedly bought 42 houses in New South Wales without even bothering to leave his car to inspect the properties.

JAPAN'S OVERSEAS INVESTMENTS

Japanese firms' overseas direct investment grew to $33.36 billion in the fiscal year which ended March 1989, up from 49.5% from 1988, according to the Japan External Trade Organization.

NOUVELLE ACQUISITION

Japan's giant Asahi Brewery purchased a top Paris restaurant, the 3-star Lucas-Carton.

RIM RUMBLINGS

WHEN TOKYO SHAKES, THE WORLD COLLAPSES

If you think Black Monday was bad, just wait and see what Black Friday has in store for the world markets. Writing in *Manhattan, Inc.*, former Salomon Brothers broker Michael Lewis presented a devastating scenario of how a Tokyo mega-quake could destroy Wall Street and the world economy.

His article was based largely on a study by Japan's Tokai Bank on the global economic consequences of the next great Tokyo earthquake, one projected to cause an estimated $1.3 trillion in damage. (The last catastrophic quake, which occurred in 1923, wiped out the Japanese capital; it also put an end to Japan's first so-called "Economic Miracle," which started when that feudal island-nation opened its doors to the West and began to industrialize.)

For starters, Lewis made the amazing revelation that the central computer of the Tokyo Stock Exchange, an antiquated Hitachi, which

ASIAN CHRONICLES

EARLY SAVINGS & LOANS OF SINGAPORE

Dr. Yap Pheng Geck was a pioneer of the banking and finance industry in Singapore in the early part of the century. In this passage from his memoirs, Scholar, Banker, Gentleman Soldier: The Reminiscences of Dr. Yap Pheng Geck *(Times Books International, 1981), he describes the structure of emerging Chinese banks in the British colony.*

The prevalent impression of banking in pre-war days was that it was a business only for the "moneyed" people. The public at large generally believed that anybody associated with a bank must be sitting on money bags, and that anybody holding a position of importance in a Chinese bank had to be rich in his own right or related to one of the directors or big shareholders. There was some justification for the view because in many cases the manager was a son of the chief director, the cashier the son-in-law, the assistant manager the nephew, and so on. As a rule, one had to belong to a rich family to work in the bank. On the other hand, however, the Chinese elite, which dominated Chinese banking at that time, was also on the lookout for promising young clansmen whom they could attract into their business and in time to come, perhaps, into their families as sons-in-law. . . .

Local Chinese banking, like most Chinese businesses, started off largely as family concerns, and bank deposits were mostly from directors themselves or their friends and business associates. Savings in banks, apart from fixed deposits of substantial sums and from selected persons only, were ironically not encouraged because of the tedious clerical work involved in the calculation and payment of petty sums of interest.

Chinese people of those days mostly invested in land and buildings, in plantations or in stock-in-trade. They had a knack of making a profit out of every cent of their surplus funds. If they should be in a liquidity squeeze, they would have no hesitation in resorting to reckless borrowing from banks or any other moneylenders. Rate of interest presented no problem. Availability of loan was more important. They had an instinctive craving for capital gains but hardly any awareness of liquidity and were most reluctant to dispose of their cherished investments. The Chinese concept of *crisis* is opportunity in difficulty, and it is their classic belief that turbulent times beget golden opportunities. Chinese banker Yap Twee once said, "In Chinese business, if you can win people's trust and amass your first $10,000, you should be on the road to prosperity."

is the sole repository of Japan's official records of stock ownership, is housed in a neighborhood that was completely destroyed in 1923. Apparently, there is a backup system. But incredibly, it stands right next to the main computer. Hence, all records of share ownership are likely to be destroyed together, sowing total confusion in the world marketplace.

Apart from the overwhelming human tragedy (in this scenario, an estimated 152,000 people in Tokyo are expected to perish), what would happen when what is now the financial capital of the world is destroyed by the quake? Two thirds of Japan's businesses, worth more than $40 million, are headquartered there. One third of everything sold in Japan is sold in Tokyo. If Tokyo were a nation, its GNP of $730 billion would exceed that of the entire nation of Britain.

Here's a look at the economic aftershocks of the hypothetical Great Tokyo Earthquake:

• As international speculators dump fantastic volumes of yen and Japanese shares, the yen collapses. Shares of Western insurance companies are next to go under. (Japanese bureaucrats had shrewdly seen to it that most Japanese fire-and-earthquake insurance migrated overseas, and Western firms had been only too delighted to suck up as much Japanese risk as they could.)

   Within a few days of the Tokyo quake, the world's stock markets collectively crash as Western insurance companies are forced to liquidate their holdings of American, British, French, German, Italian, and Australian stocks and bonds in order to cover their liabilities. Panicky investors and strapped arbitrageurs rush into selling as well. The Dow Jones Industrial Average nosedives 200 points even before the general stampede begins.

• For two shaky weeks after the quake, the silence from Japan, Inc. is deafening. Telecommunications have been totally cut. No one knows anything. ("Had Sony's headquarters survived? How about its famous chairman? What is Sony's new value?") More important, what is Japan's plan to rebuild Tokyo? Suddenly, as calls and faxes start pouring into Wall Street brokerage firms from Japanese companies, the answer becomes painfully clear: The Japanese want back all their money which they have been investing abroad so aggressively for the past decade.

• From a surplus of $85 billion in 1987, Japan is expected to fall into an annual deficit of as much as $11 billion, leaving no spare funds to invest in U.S. treasury bonds. As Japan begins to sell off all her U.S. bonds, the bond market crashes. Then Japanese banks begin calling in their estimated $1.02 trillion dollars in loans to foreign countries, and the international real estate market crumbles.

• As U.S. interest rates skyrocket by as much as 5%, American consumers, already saddled in debt, no longer can afford to repay existing loans, much less to purchase new automobiles or homes. Foreclosures are rife. America becomes a poor nation.

• As far into the future as 1994, the United States will continue to suffer from a yearly decline of 2.7% in the growth rate of its real GNP; the European Community's annual decline will be 3%; Latin America's will be a whopping 13.6%.

• Out of all this chaos, Japan turns into a nation of consumers almost overnight. They have no choice but to buy imports. In line with that, Japanese exports fizzle out—as automobile and VCR factories (the few that are still in operation)—must now exclusively service the millions of Tokyoites who survived the quake. General Motors, Phillips, and other companies once again begin to dominate their home markets.

Perhaps the greatest irony of Lewis' "doomsquake" scenario is how Japan almost effortlessly rebounds into high economic gear. Only one month after the disaster, the Tokyo Stock Exchange is reopened. It surges, thanks to the Ministry of Finance "ramping" the entire stock market. In effect, Japan has privatized the entire nation, as companies, following MOF's orders, buy up volumes of undervalued stock.

Japan's post-earthquake growth rate, according to the Tokai Bank's forecast, will be a bullish 12% in 1990 and 10% in 1991. As it did following the devastation of its defeat during World War II, Japan recovers magnificently, exceeding all expectations.

"The broader lesson (of the coming Tokyo quake) is that the imbalances in the world's financial markets are a disaster waiting to happen," Lewis warned.

On an ominous note, he pointed out that whenever foreign journalists ask Japan's Ministry of International Trade and Industry what can be done about the nation's huge trade surpluses, they usually get a cryptic reply: "When the earthquake comes, the trade surplus will go away."

MINI-TAIWAN

At an economic history conference in Hong Kong, Taiwanese academic Wei Wou, from Taiwan's National Sun Yat-sen University, proposed that China set up a "mini-Taiwan" in its southeastern Fujian province to accommodate the overflow of Taiwanese investments in the PRC.

SEXIST SECURITIES

Japan's Securities Dealers Association issued a directive in 1988 to major Japanese securities firms, advising them not to sell "risky investments" to women. In the confidential memo, women investors were classified, along with the elderly and nonprofit organizations, as among those who "should not be accommodated" by brokers. The implication being, of course, that women are too emotional and panicky to invest in bond futures. After Tokyo brokers protested the directive, the association backed down and recommended, instead, that brokers exercise their own personal judgment in dealing with female clients.

BURGER SHOGUN

Forget the piddling sums earned by Japan's headline-making inside traders. Ko Morita, who was forced to step down in 1988 as president of *Nihon Keizai Shimbun,* made only about $625,000 after trading shares on the Japanese real estate company, Recruit Cosmos. More recently, the Nippon Steel Corp. exec who inside-traded shares of music-box-maker Sankyo Seiki Mfg. Co. realized only a measly $38,000 in the process. Largely unknown to the West, one of the major delinquents of the Tokyo Stock Exchange is Den Fujita, president of Japan McDonald's, who made about $3.1 million dabbling in the Japanese stock market in 1987. The only problem is he forgot to report the money on his income tax return. Japan's IRS nailed him, and the Japanese burger shogun had to pay about $2.3 million in back taxes, according to *Shukan Yomiuri* newspaper.

HERO OF THE EXCHANGE

Manila's Makati Stock Exchange appointed its first woman president, 38-year-old stockbroker Vivian Locsin, in 1989. One of her first acts was to declare war on insider trading. She received so many death threats that she was forced to hire several bodyguards.

VENTURE-CAPITAL IN ASIA
by Tracey Chin

Venture capital is an American innovation, normally associated with start-ups of companies or the financing of high-risk situations that commercial or merchant banks will not touch. But while the concept of venture capital as it is known in the West is new in Asia, the idea is rapidly gaining acceptance in financial centers in the region as the clamor for capital from rapidly expanding enterprises and new businesses crowds out more traditional forms of financing.

The venture-capital industry is in various stages of development in Asia. But Hong Kong, with its tradition of freewheeling capitalism, has been a natural magnet for many different kinds of projects and is quickly becoming a management and service center for venture-capital companies from abroad.

Venture-capital funds have flocked to Hong Kong recently in search of both local and regional opportunities as growth rates in most countries throughout Asia continue their brisk rise. The territory is also viewed as a gateway to the vast investment opportunities in China, which although remaining problematic in many areas, pose an enormous challenge to potential trailblazers.

Industry analysts in Hong Kong say there has been a surge in venture-capital activities in Asia in the last year. Hundreds of millions of U.S. dollars are estimated to have moved into venture-capital funds in various cities in the region.

Much of the new money coming in is from the United States, where the industry is in the doldrums following a period of overinvestment and scanty returns, says Leslie Burt, editor and general manager of the *Asian Venture Capital Journal*.

"Venture capital had been tremendously successful in the United States for many years," she says, "but a recent study there shows that the average return is just over 1% a year. The market there is a bit saturated, and there are probably too many people chasing after too few deals."

Burt also says there is an increasing perception that plenty of venture-capital opportunities exist in Asia. "The returns are also much higher in Asia," she says, "and that's why the funds are coming in such a surge."

About two dozen companies are involved in full-time venture-capital investing in Hong Kong, but their level of risk-taking in investments vary. One or two companies specialize in capital for new businesses, but the majority favor financing companies that have some successful operating history.

Because many of the venture capitalists in Hong Kong used to work for commercial banks, they tend to think like bankers rather than investors. They apply the same lending criteria bankers do, but want venture capital-size returns. And the attitude of seeking a quick profit and a short-term orientation by Hong Kong entrepreneurs also affects many of the venture-capital companies in the territory.

So far, the favorite projects for venture-capital financing have been light-industrial manufacturing, consumer goods and services, and technology transfer projects. But there is also an emerging trend in computer-related, agricultural, and biomedical projects.

Several companies have set themselves up in Hong Kong as China specialists, concentrating on joint ventures in China or companies deriving most of their business income from activities in China.

While the investment climate in China is still far from conducive to the development of a proper venture-capital industry, these specialists believe that changes are in store in the near future and want to have a foothold there when the time comes.

Most venture capitalists agree that the rising appeal of Hong Kong as a regional venture-capital center has much to do with its unique business environment. Besides the well-known entrepreneurial drive of its people, the territory has low tax rates and a thriving stock market that allows investors easy exits from their investments.

"Hong Kong has a very unique and special environment for entrepreneurs," says Lewis Rutherfurd, managing director of Royal Trust Enterprise Capital, Ltd. "It has a special willingness to allow the capitalistic process to occur. It is a great place for enterprises to build capital."

Reprinted by permission from *Far East Business*. © 1989.

RIM RESOURCE

VENTURE JAPAN

This new San Francisco-published quarterly journal monitors the emerging Pacific Rim venture capital marketplace, covering merger and acquisitions activity, capital sources, franchising. ASEAN funds, transPacific recruitment, partnering trends, and licensing agreements, among other topics. For more information, contact; VJ, 110 Sutter Street, Suite 708, San Francisco, California 94104.

FOREIGN INVESTMENT IN TAIWAN

Foreign investment in Taiwan has been growing steadily and is now around the $1.5 billion mark annually, reports Wang Chih-kang, executive secretary of the country's Investment Commission who attributed part of the rise to the growing uncertainty about the future of Hong Kong. Additional factors have been Taiwan's lifting of martial law and stringent foreign exchange controls, coupled with simplifying investment procedures. Although the Taiwan dollar has surged about 30% against the U.S. dollar in recent years, "an abundant supply of skilled labor in Taiwan has offset this disadvantage," Wang explained. More than 10 American states have set up trade offices in the Taipei World Trade Center.

ROK's OVERSEAS INDUSTRIAL PARKS

The Republic of South Korea is planning to establish industrial parks in Southeast Asian countries, such as Malaysia, Indonesia, and Thailand, for exclusive use of South Korean manufacturers, according to the Trade and Industry Ministry. The proposed project fits into South Korea's plans to restructure its industries by relocating them in less-developed countries where labor costs are cheaper. South

Asian Venture Connections in the West

Firm	Location	Affiliation
Hambrecht & Quist Venture Partners	San Francisco	H&Q Philippines; H&Q Taiwan; Orient Capital Co., Ltd. (Japan)
InterPacific Group, Inc.	San Francisco	InterPacific Resources, Ltd. (Hong Kong)
JAFCO Amenca Ventures, Inc.	San Francisco	Japan Associated Finance Co. (JAFCO)
LF International, Inc.	San Francisco	Li & Fung, Ltd. (Hong Kong)
Singapore Economic Development Board	Redwood City	The Government of Singapore
Singapore Technology Corp.	Redwood City	Singapore Technology Corp. (Singapore)
Transtech Venture Management PTE, Ltd. (Singapore)	Mountain View	Transtech Venture Management PTE, Ltd. (Singapore)
Venca International Partners (Japan)	San Francisco	(Japan)
Ventana Growth Fund	Irvine	Ventana Pacific Mgmt. Co. PTE, Ltd. (Singapore)
Walden Group	San Francisco	FP Special Assets, Ltd. (Hong Kong); International Venture Capital Investment Corp. (Taiwan); PacVen Investment, Ltd. (Singapore)
Wearnes Technology Corp.	Santa Clara	Wearnes Technology (Private Ltd.) (Singapore)
Yamaichi International Amenca, Inc.	Los Angeles (branch), New York (headquarters)	Yamaichi Security Co., Ltd. (Japan)
VMA North Amenca	Portola Valley	Venture Management Associates (Australia)
OCL Technology Center, Inc.	San Jose	Consortium of companies (Japan)

Source: *Upside* magazine.

Korea's overseas investments totaled $1.11 billion for 668 projects as of the end of 1988, according to official statistics.

HAPPY JAPANESE BROKERS

Japanese brokerage houses now represent the largest foreign contingent in Hong Kong's brokerage community. Over 30 Japanese investment houses now sell Japanese equities to Hong Kong's super-rich. "The Asian econo-mies are getting better and better so we expect a very successful future," said Yoshio Ishi-kawa, director of leading Japanese brokerage house Daiwa Securities.

INDIA PACIFIC TRUST FUND

In 1989, Hong Kong investment house Jar-dine Fleming launched the first equity invest-ment fund linking the Indian stock market and the Pacific Rim markets. Due to India's foreign exchange regulations, the so-called Jardine Fleming India Pacific Trust fund is aimed exclusively at non-resident Indians.

BONDS AWAY

Taiwan has been pondering different ways to deal with its embarrassment of riches—its staggering $70 billion in foreign exchange, which ranks as one of the highest forex reserves in the world. But there is one solution Taiwan is not inclined to consider seriously. Recent Taiwanese visitors to the PRC have been returning home loaded with old Kuomingtang bonds issued by the Generalissimo Chiang Kaishek to raise funds during the final years of his Nationalist rule in China before the Communists took over. Some of these bonds are in private hands, others were confiscated by the PRC government. According to Taiwanese economists, if these bonds were all cashed in today, Taiwan would go bankrupt. It has opted to put the matter on hold, saying the government would deal with the question after the KMT is returned to power in China.

MONEYBAGS

CHINA'S MARXIST MILLIONAIRES

China's richest man, Rong Yiren, allegedly has an estimated private fortune of more than U.S. $1 billion. As managing director of CITIC, the PRC's largest private company, he controls 200 firms around the world, including the only private bank in China. He has offices in Hong Kong, Tokyo, Paris, and Frankfurt, as well as forests in the U.S. and factories in Australia and Canada. He is vice-president of the Popular Assembly and a close friend of Chinese leader Deng Xiaoping.

As heir of the wealthy Rong family of Shanghai, this "socialist capitalist" was born with a silver chopstick in his mouth. But his possessions were confiscated in the 1950s after the Communist takeover, and not restored until his subsequent rehabilitation and rise to power as head of CITIC in 1978. He has two villas, eight servants, and three cars at his disposal. His official take-home pay is U.S.$120 per month.

A list of China's Marxist millionaires featured in a recent issue of *The Australian Magazine* provides a fascinating glimpse of the new wave of moguls and tycoons who are leading PRC enterprise into the next century. Although their salaries don't always match the paychecks of their Western counterparts, perks and privileges go a long way in making up the difference.

Here's a sampling of the PRC's nouveau-powerful: Wang Defang (nickname: "Mr. 500,000 Volts") is the president of the Huaneng International Power Development Corp., a private company worth $325 million. He recently concluded a joint venture with France to build the biggest power station in the PRC. His official take-home pay—U.S. $175 per month.

Ger Fei represents "luxury" in China. He is general manager of the state-owned Dong Hu Group, which controls five complexes of luxury private villas in Shanghai that were confiscated from the pre-1949 bourgeoisie and turned into deluxe guest houses. Average room rate is U.S. $1,325 a night. The group also looks after blocks of flats, markets and restaurants. Ger's official take-home pay—$70 a month.

Wang Guang Ying (nickname: "Big Boss Wang") is reportedly personally worth about $550 million. He is president of Beijing Ever-

Bright Industrial Co., which controls 50 Chinese firms, and also serves as president of the Ever-Bright Industrial Co., a private multinational set up in 1983 with state capital, which is headquartered in Hong Kong.

Wang's private tastes: He drives a Mercedes, belongs to the Rotary Club, plays golf, drinks champagne in the finest restaurants, wears only tailormade clothes, owns a luxury apartment in Hong Kong, and maintains a villa in Beijing. In the past two years, he has brought about $45 billion into China in the form of either direct investments or technological contributions. His official take-home pay—$140 per month.

Song Huai Kuei is the Queen of the PRC. She is the exclusive representative of Pierre Cardin in China, and runs the Chinese branch of Maxim's restaurant in Beijing. She controls the interests of the Pierre Cardin China Company and recently signed a contract to design the staff uniforms of the recently renamed national airline, Air China. She plans to open a chain of Pierre Cardin boutiques throughout China.

In the New China, socialism obviously is not synonymous with poverty. As Rong Yiren likes to point out, "Nobody wants poor socialism."

SNAPSHOT OF A CHINESE MILLIONAIRE

Liang Yifeng, the owner of a photo-developing service in the southeast coastal city of Fuzhou and one of China's youngest *renminbi* millionaires, estimates his wealth at around U.S.$540,000 but says because he pays hefty taxes and "has brought prosperity to society" he does not consider himself a capitalist. Liang, 31, who heads the city's Private Entrepreneurs Association, started work at 14 with only two years of formal education and built a small photo shop into a business with 15 employees, to most of whom he gives free room and board.

HONG KONG'S "YACHT PEOPLE"

If you're looking for the richest Chinatown in North America, forget New York or San Francisco or Los Angeles; try Toronto instead.

Since 1985, wealthy Hong Kong Chinese immigrants have invested more than $1.5 billion in Canada, according to a recent consumer report published by American Demographics, Inc., a wholly-owned subsidiary of Dow Jones & Co., Inc.

These well-heeled Hong Kong immigrants —dubbed the "yacht people"—are eager to find a second home and a safe haven abroad in face of the imminent takeover of Hong Kong by the PRC in 1997. They are drawn to Canadian soil by the nation's lenient—yet expensive—immigration policy. Canada's price to "rush" a visa: $200,000 worth of investments in special funds stipulated by the Canadian government.

Canada is not the only one to tap into this lucrative new immigration market. Australia recently upped the ante for Hong Kong entrepreneurs who are seeking to resettle Down Under. Emigres must now have net assets worth about $367,647 in order to qualify for permanent residence in Australia in the "entrepreneur category"—up from about $110,294.

"The friendship of officials is as thin as paper."

Chinese proverb

THE PET SET

Now there's the "pet set"—that is, the pets of those rich Hong Kong emigrants, who travel in "kennel class" to their new homes in Vancouver, Toronto, and Sydney. Ten cats and dogs are leaving the territory each month, according to a report by the London-based Royal Society for the Prevention of Cruelty to Animals. But with stringent quarantine laws in the West, it's not cheap for these pets to emigrate with their masters. The fare for a Yorkshire Terrier that traveled to Canada recently came to over $2,500 (three times the ticket price for its owner), while a German Shepherd emigrating to the U.S. cost his owner about $6,000, in-flight kibble not included.

PHILIPPINE CONGRESS' WEALTHIEST MEMBERS

Two of Philippine President Corazon Aquino's relatives were listed among the five wealthiest members of the Philippine congress, according to statements filed with the government. Aquino's younger brother, Jose Cojuanco, listed assets of 30.075 million pesos (about $1.47 million), making him the third richest congressman in 1987. Her sister-in-law, Teresa Aquino Ortega, declared 27.027 million (about $1.32 million) to rank fifth in the list.

VIETNAM'S COMMUNIST MILLIONAIRE
by Peter Janssen

Ten years ago Madame Nguyen Thi Thi's business acumen attracted an irate mob outside the gates of her Ho Chi Minh City Food Co., (HFC) whose network of retail outlets and accumulating profits had won her a reputation as a capitalist. Sixty-two guards were dispatched by the city authorities to protect the food factory and its general director.

Today the great matriarch of Ho Chi Minh City's (formerly Saigon) food distribution business is the heroine of *doi moi*—"new thinking." Instead of angry mobs, long lines of foreign businessmen and official visitors are now banging on her doors to talk business and joint ventures.

"Some people call me the communist billionaire," says Madame Thi, her strong face breaking into a wide smile. The accusations (or compliments) stem from her successful operation of HFC since July 1980. The company now has retail outlets in 18 districts of the city, employs 1,700 people, and has 7,000 agents and an annual turnover of approximately 300 to 400 billion *dong* (U.S.$816 million to U.S.$1.1 billion at the official exchange rate of 370 *dong* to U.S.$1.00).

What makes her operation unique in Vietnam has been her use of cost accounting, or the simple business practice of matching costs with profits.

"Under the state-subsidized management system one company like ours would require 4,000 people to run it, but in our factory we need only 1,700. We follow the cost-accounting system so some people have accused me of being a capitalist, but I think if it works we can follow this system. And they can continue to call me a capitalist," says 71-year-old Thi.

Madame Thi's business theory enjoys the support of Vietnam's current leaders, including party general secretary Nguyen Van Linh, interior minister My Chi Tho, and deputy premier/economic czar Vo Van Kiet, all of whom backed her food factory plans eight years ago when they were the leading administrators of Ho Chi Minh City.

Despite her "capitalist" reputation, Madame Thi's's credentials as a communist are impeccable. She took up the struggle against the French in the early 1940s. Her husband, a high ranking communist party member, was killed by the Diem regime in 1959, but Madame Thi continued fighting until the end of the war in 1975.

Her war-time participation in the Women's Association won her faithful managers and staunch backers in the communist hierarchy. The years of leadership and espionage also taught her some valuable business lessons.

Madame Thi helped solve the urban food shortages in 1980-81 with good management, and by buying produce directly from the farmers in the rich Mekong delta. The key to her success, apart from her use of cost accounting, has been barter. She has learned to pay the farmers in the commodities that they need most—cement, fertilizers, pesticides, farm tools, processed foods, and, most recently, petrol, in exchange for their rice.

In December 1988, Thi and her management launched Saigon Petro, a small refinery, in collaboration with Serepco, an overseas Vietnamese firm based in France, and a French company, Proser. The refinery will process 40,000 tons of crude oil a year into petrol, diesel oil, fuel oil, and other oils.

"We will supply the oil to farmers in the Mekong Delta in exchange for their rice, and this in turn will also improve their production by powering their pumps and machines," says Thi.

The barter also allows her to provide the 4.2 million citizens of Ho Chi Minh City with 46,000 tons of food per month and still export large amounts of rice. With her huge profits from domestic sales and exports, Madame Thi is fast becoming one of the most influential business forces in the country.

© *Asian Business* magazine, Far East Trade Press, Ltd., 1989.

JAPAN'S BIG SAVERS

The Japanese are the world's top savers, according to a report released in Geneva by the International Savings Bank Institute. At the end of 1986, there was an average $27,303 in Japanese savings institutions for each resident. Switzerland, which was previously the number-one saving nation, had an average $23,728 per member of the population, Belgium $14,555, West Germany $12,288, Austria $10,200. Denmark, $10,164, and the United States $9,733.

SINGAPOREAN LOTTERY

Singaporeans spent an average of $145 each on lottery tickets annually, putting them in fourth place on the world table behind Norwegians, Panamanians, and Australians. Tickets for the monthly Singapore Sweep, which has a $1 million top prize, cost $2. Americans spend the largest total amount—almost $31 billion—on lottery tickets each year, but this averages out to only $126 per person.

TAIWANESE TYCOON SEEKS TO SPREAD THE WEALTH

Taiwan's richest man, billionaire Tsai Wan-lin, who has been ranked by *Forbes* magazine as the world's eighth richest tycoon, rarely discusses his immense wealth and has never been interviewed. Son of a poor rice farmer, who as a teenager ran a fruit and vegetable stand with his older brother, Tsai tripled his already substantial assets when share prices of his Cathay Life Insurance Co. shot through the roof early in 1989. He and his family own 90% of the company's stock and Tsai's personal wealth is said to be $5.6 billion. Cathay owns, among other assets, 120 office buildings, mostly in downtown Taipei, where land is more valuable than anywhere in the world except Tokyo.

Although Tsai sometimes plays golf, usually alone, he mostly lives quietly at home in a Taipei suburb with his wife of 40 years. His conglomerate boosts employee morale with a profit-sharing plan and generous bonuses, and Tsai has been heard to observe: "Being a billionaire does not mean very much to me and I would be pleased if I could make those who work for me millionaires."

ALL THAT GLITTERS

RIM OF FIRE: THE GOLD RUSH IS ON
by Mike Levin

The fevered search for gold has spread throughout the Asia-Pacific region. From China to New Zealand, the end of the rainbow has become the Rim of Fire for big-time mining companies as well as impoverished prospectors.

Gold mining has always offered a relatively stable source of income throughout the region from China to New Zealand. But new technology and the epithermal gold model—where minerals are forced to the earth's surface by volcanic action—have pushed exploration and production to a fever pitch.

Oil and gold booms of the 1960s and 1970s have given way to a new rush that promises to make the region the world's leading gold producer by the mid-1990s.

In the past few years, deposit reevaluation along the Pacific chain of volcanic islands, dubbed the Rim of Fire, has revealed mineral reserves that could hold as much as 20 percent of the world's gold. The veins lie on or near the earth's surface, making most exploration easy. Applications for development from hundreds of foreign-based companies have swamped local governments.

Mines are popping up in each country along the Pacific Rim, although one industry observer has called Papua New Guinea "the flavor of the year," because of its U.S.$2 billion-a-year revenue in proven reserves—at current prices that are hovering around U.S.$400 an ounce. The Porgera find alone, in northeastern Papua New Guinea, will produce 25 tons of gold annually.

Since relaxing the ban on gold exports in

1986, Indonesia has increased its yearly output to 15 tons, while the archipelago north of Australia, which includes the Solomon Islands, Fiji, and Vanuatu, has a geological makeup consistent with vast epithermal resources. Malaysia is just starting to reacquaint itself with gold mining, and many believe the Philippines could have the best potential of all.

Stories of children finding baseball-sized nuggets and of individual prospectors unearthing rich finds in mountain rivers pour from these countries. Thousands of local miners have flooded gold rush sites, bringing with them the excitement of instant riches and the despair of boom towns.

A slide in oil prices and the potential of huge royalties and taxes make local governments more flexible in their acceptance of foreign partnerships.

The rush is drawing many of the world's major mining corporations. In the vanguard are Australian companies, conducting about 80% of active exploration and production.

"Before, everyone considered them [Asia-Pacific mines] to be just isolated gold deposits, but now that people are beginning to understand that this epithermal system extends right around the Rim of Fire, they want in," says Frank Gardiner, general manager of City Resources (Asia), Ltd. in Hong Kong, part of the Australian City Resources Group that holds the largest exploration rights in the Pacific Rim—eight million acres.

"Man has searched for gold for thousands of years, but only in the past decade has science played a major role in tracing the precious metal. Able to predict to the minute when geothermal faults will send up a geyser of hot water, geologists have only recently understood the relationship between this volcanic action and the formation of earth's minerals. The information has led to an epithermal (formed near the surface) gold model that predicts the occurrence of gold on top of and within volcanic faults.

The Asia-Pacific region sits in the middle of some of the earth's most active tectonic plates. In fact, most islands in the area were formed through the constant collision of the Australasian and Pacific plates. As the slabs shift, molten rock, often containing gold, is forced to the surface through faults. As the rock cools, minerals are deposited. Today's miners use satellite photography and geological technology to pinpoint potential deposits.

One of the newest gold finds in Papua New Guinea, Misima, produces 400,000 ounces of gold a year, as well as 2.6 million ounces of silver. Copper reserves under that country's OK Tedi gold fields are potentially more valuable than the surface metal. Antimony, molybdenum, tungsten, and mercury are other targets.

Excerpted from an article by Mike Levin, reprinted by permission of *Far East Business,* © 1988.

CHINA'S "GOLDEN" TRIANGLES

China has become one of the world's major gold producers after South Africa, the Soviet Union, the United States, Canada, Australia, and Brazil, according to China's State Gold Administration Bureau. The nation discovered more than 400 gold deposits since 1986, and developed over 100 gold mines and placer operations. Jiaodong in Shangdong province is the biggest gold producer in China. The recent discovery of two "golden triangles"—

Gansu-Shaanxi-Sichuan and Yunnan-Guizhu-Guangxi—have led to a number of verified gold deposits. Western experts estimate that it mines an annual 50 tons of gold, and employed 88,000 goldminers in 1988.

TAIWAN'S 24K FEVER

Taiwan overtook Japan as the world's largest importer of gold in 1988. Its imports of gold soared from 87 tons in 1987 to 351 million tons worth $5.08 billion in 1988, accounting for 23.4% of the annual yearly output of non-communist countries. Taiwan's appetite for gold has been growing since the removal of restrictions on private imports in November 1986 and the cancellation of a 5% value-added tax in July 1987. But one of the driving forces has been the central bank, which launched a gold-buying spree in September 1987 to help reduce the country's trade surplus with the United States, which reached a record of $16 billion that year.

PANNING FOR GOLD BY SATELLITE

The Japanese are panning for gold—by satellite. Using advanced LADSAT satellite technology called remote sensing, Japanese scientist-prospectors discovered a major gold deposit on the remote Indonesian island of Lomblen, north of Timor. It was the first publicized case of a mineral deposit being found by satellite alone. "We are sweating in the lab in search of a jackpot, just as our predecessors did in jungles or canyons." Reuters quoted Toru Kawakami, a senior geologist at Tokyo's Earth Resources Satellite Data Analysis Center. Satellite panning is the wave of the future because most of the world's re-maining undiscovered deposits of mineral ores, oil, and precious metals are believed to be in remote locations where the cost of exploration is often prohibitive.

GOLD MINING IN THE PHILIPPINES

If there's one sector of the Philippine economy that's humming, it's mining. The busiest hive of activity is in gold exploration and extraction.

In 1987, the Philippines produced 34,081 kilos of gold, worth P9.9 billion or almost U.S.$500 million. With the price of gold set to rise (as investment money looks for havens from inflation), the value of future discoveries could be even greater.

All this activity has attracted the attention of Australian companies, which boast an "unparalleled expertise in gold mining." Fifteen companies from Australia are known to be mining in the Philippines (there may be more), and virtually all of them are in gold—through joint ventures with Philippine entities.

© *Asian Business* magazine,
Far East Trade Press, Ltd., 1989.

RIM DIAMOND FEVER

The diamond industry is booming on the Rim, with 10% of the world's diamonds now sold in Southeast Asia, according to figures released at the World Diamond Congress in Singapore.

The strength of the yen has been a boon for world diamond producers whose sales to Japan rose 50% in 1988 over the previous year, helped no doubt by an advertising campaign pushing the romantic appeal of the precious stones. But the diamond's popularity is also growing in other east Asian countries, especially in South Korea, ranked by South Africa's De Beers Consolidated Mines, Ltd. (which controls 80% of the world's diamond trade) as the fifth largest diamond market.

"You might say there is a fad among young people to own a piece of diamond jewelry," says a Japanese importer, who explained that many young workers lived at home with their parents and had money to spare for luxuries.

ASIA'S NEW ENTREPRENEURS

There is a new breed of aggressive, though not always hostile, Asian dealmaker stalking the region, who has made the business world an even better spectator sport than in the past. Here are six snapshots of the new breed of Asian wheeler-dealer by Eric Stone.

10 TRAITS OF THE NEW RIM TYCOON

While rugged individualism is vital to the job, the new dealmakers also seem to be possessed of 10 common traits.

- They are relatively young. The average age is about 44.
- They are bold, willing to take risks.
- They are opportunistic. Bad economic times for others are the stuff of which their deals are made.
- They trust their instincts. That said, while they often rely on gut feelings, they keep a cool head and don't get overly emotional about decision-making.
- They are secretive, or shy, generally shunning personal publicity despite the headlines that their big deals often make.
- They are good salesmen. They have to be to get all the diverse elements of their deals to work together and to persuade the other parties that the deal is in everyone's best interests.
- They are not afraid of debt. Indeed, they sometimes appear to revel in it and often build surprisingly strong business foundations on their borrowing.

(continued)

- They weave highly complex financial structures. Often no more than minority shareholders, they use interlocking holdings to gain control of a network of companies, somehow adding two and two to make five.
- They are hungry for land. Property, either as a means or an end, often provides the backbone of their holdings.
- They are creative. They are idea men. More often than not they hire someone else to take care of the mundane day-to-day tasks of operating the empire.

There have always been dealmakers like these, but they have recently gained new prominence, taking advantage of ever more complex economies, bending the seeming limits of finance to their own will. In the more traditional business communities, people aren't quite sure of what to make of them. The new dealmaker is viewed in some quarters as some kind of pirate.

While the old rules aren't exactly changing, there does seem to be an increasing number of dealmakers willing to step around them from time to time.

Following are three face-to-face encounters with three dealmakers—Alfredo Ramos of the Philippines, Malaysia's Loy Hean Heong, and Hong Kong's Henry Cheng. For three others—Singapore's Ong Beng Seng, Malaysia's Vincent Tan, and Sura Chansrishawala of Thailand—we talked to close associates and business observers.

PHILIPPINES

Alfredo Ramos

Said to be a pious man, Alfredo Ramos is often quiet at social gatherings—until the subject of business comes up. Then his obsession shows, "My eyes light up," he says. "I am in my element."

"Putting together a deal—the people, the timing—for me, that's what makes the world go round," said the 45-year-old, who has acquired the nickname "Pacman" in his native Philippines because of his habit of gobbling up companies.

At ease and articulate during interviews, he describes himself as more "New Yorkish" than typically Filipino-Chinese. He is a man who trusts his instincts, but then allows his mind to take over the job of putting them to work.

The risk-taking Ramos recalls how, in early 1986, he proposed that Philodrill, an oil company in which he is a minority shareholder and board member, pay 70 million *pesos* (U.S.$3.3 million) for 4.4 hectares of raw land in an unfashionable Manila suburb. His fellow board members' faces turned pale.

Today the property, acquired for P1,600 (U.S.$75.20) a square meter, is considered prime land with a market value between P30,000 and P45,000 (U.S.$1,410 to U.S.$2,115) per square meter.

Foreign investment, which has a tendency to raise land values in Manila, came from Hong

(continued)

Kong-based Robert Kuok's Shangri-La hotel chain. The aim was to bring Kuok in with cash and a commitment to build a hotel on the site.

Shangri-La Properties, Inc. was formed. Philodrill put in the 4.4 hectares of land (held by property arm Philrealty) in return for 30% share of the new company. Another 4.3 hectares of adjacent land were contributed by National Bookstore (Ramos' private family business) for which National got a 30% share. Kuok got the remaining 40%.

The end result is that Philodrill's initial investment of P70 million (U.S.$3.3 million) in 1986 has given it control of P.2.5 billion (U.S.$117.5 million) worth of land assets of Shangri-La Properties, and another P2 billion (U.S.$94 million) worth of separate Philrealty property.

Ramos is known for his complex and successful financial structures, carefully tying together minority shareholdings to gain control of what has become the Ramos Group.

By his own analogy, he ties together many publicly traded companies like sticks in a broom; they "tend to move together"—but only because of his influence, not because of the size of his financial stakes.

That broom is said by many to be the prime sweeping force on the Philippine stock market, something Ramos denies. But, says one broker, judging from the size of Ramos' transactions, "it's institution building, using different things which he puts together. Some people build cathedrals. . . ."

Whether monument-building or not, Ramos has a knack for disconcerting others. Once he was locked in negotiations with a businessmen to whom one of his companies owed money. They went around and around for hours, until both men were exhausted. Finally, Ramos asked the man, point blank, "What do you want?"

The man suggested P40 million (U.S.$1.88 million), which Ramos' company had received for the sale of another company.

"This is my offer," Ramos told the man. "If you don't accept it now I will withdraw it." He picked up a biscuit the size of a saucer and took a large bite. "I take half," he said, chewing, "you take half."

"If you don't," he added, cramming the remaining half into his mouth, "I take all of it."

The deal was done.

The Best: 1987—Forms Shangri-La Properties with 4.4 hectares of land bought by Philodrill in 1986 for P70 million (U.S.$3.3 million); 4.3 hectares of adjoining land owned by a family business, National Bookstore; and cash and hotel construction commitment from Robert Kuok's Shangri-La hotel chain. Because of property appreciation and interlocking relationships, Philodrill (Ramos) comes out with control (60%) of P4.5 billion (U.S.$211.5 million) in assets.

The Worst: No really big failures, but this year has less success in a deal than was planned when he initiates hostile takeover bid for New York-listed Atlas Consolidated Mining and Development Corp. Battles A Soriano group (Anscor) for control of management of Atlas' Philippines interests. Fails in bid to take over Atlas, but strikes a compromise whereby the newly adopted five-year management contract will be the last awarded automatically to Anscor. The Ramos group also gets U.S.$3.2 million in unexplained "further consideration of the deal."   (continued)

SINGAPORE

Ong Beng Seng

Back in 1986, Singapore's property market was slow—terrible as a matter of fact. Prices were depressed and activity was at a standstill.

But Ong Beng Seng sensed an opportunity. So he went on a buying spree. He snapped up hotels and other properties, and today some have appreciated by as much as 300%.

Ong is a man whose instincts often pay off handsomely. "He's a brilliant dealmaker," says a close associate. "He buys assets when nobody wants them and because he happens to be the only bidder, he gets to name his own price."

Ong is elusive and shuns publicity. He prefers making deals to talking about them. Whenever others have been mired in economic doldrums, he has been at his busiest, gobbling up luxury property from cash-strapped developers.

1988 was a ripe one for other people's problems. In July of that year, Ong took the Glass Hotel off the financially troubled hands of Indonesian businessman Hendra Rahardja, and in November he added Rahardja's Hotel Meridian to his take. In September he picked up the Riverwalk Galleria, a prime shopping and residential complex belonging to debt-ridden Premier Realty.

Now, with the Singapore property market recovering, he is busy developing the unfinished projects or quickly trading them at a premium.

The Glass Hotel was sold in mid-1989 for a neat S$25 million (U.S.$12.7 million) profit, while Ong disposed of a 50% stake in the Meridien, netting a gain of S$20m (U.S.$10.16 million).

He has been quick to seize upon opportunities across the border as well, having recently forked out M$33.9 million (U.S.$12.6 million) for 30% of the Kuala Lumpur Merlin Hotel, flagship of the financially rocky Faber Merlin Group.

To foster ties with the Canadian Four Seasons group, Ong sold them his 50% stake in London's Inn on the Park for C$37 million (U.S.$31.5 million) and one million subordinated voting shares in the group. He netted a small cash profit and moved a step closer to being an international hotelier in the process.

Initially, Ong's string of multimillion dollar deals and acquisitions gave the Singapore banking community a severe case of the jitters. Debt apparently doesn't frighten him. He has a reputation for buying first and worrying about finance later.

But early in 1989, with development projects totaling more than S$70 million (U.S.$355 million) in the pipeline, he announced that he was bringing in Japanese partners Kowa Real Estate and C Itoh. That quickly established his financial muscle.

Still in his early forties, Ong, who got started with money from his father-in-law, Peter Fu, now controls Hotel Properties, a listed holding company which in turn controls a web of companies in Singapore, Hong Kong, and the Cayman Islands, with interests in oil and commodities trading, stockbroking, hotels, and other property development.

(continued)

In 1989, Ong acquired the first Asian franchise for the American thematic restaurant group Hard Rock Cafe. He opened his first HRC in Singapore in 1990, and an outlet in Bangkok in 1991. Other locations planned include Hong Kong, Kuala Lumpur, Bali, Seoul, Taipei, Jakarta and the Philippines. With an eye towards the Europe 1992 market, he also acquired the Hard Rock Cafe franchise for Germany and Italy.

He doe not enjoy good relations with the local press, who regard him as too opportunistic. And while there is nothing wrong with putting together deals with the products of other's financial misfortunes, it is not a good way to win friends.

The Best: April, 1989—Sells Glass Hotel and 50% of holding in Meridien Hotel, Singapore (five and nine months after purchase, respectively) for total profit of S$45 million (U.S.$23 million).

The Worst: Early 1980s—Develops Balmoral Park, an exclusive residential development in Singapore at excessively high cost, resulting in loss, so far, of several million Singapore dollars. Holding on to several units in hope of recouping losses.

MALAYSIA

Loyheang Heong

In Malaysia, even though dealmaking is viewed with a certain amount of distaste, Loy Hean Heong boasts of having been involved in more than 100,000 deals in his 54 years.

When criticized for his activities he exclaims, "Rubbish! What is buying, selling, or lending if it's not a deal?"

Now head of the MBF group, which has assets in excess of M$3 billion (U.S.$1.1 billion) Loy is unperturbed by criticism, which has included allegations that he has edged out partners by upping the equity in joint ventures, knowing that the partner cannot come up with fresh capital.

"You're in business to make money for yourself and your company, not for your competitor," he says. "As a businessman, you look for the best deal. Of course, if you're bigger you can exercise some muscle. What's wrong with that? These days you can't afford to be complacent. Not only have you got to keep abreast of what's going on, but you have to get the sweeter deals to stay ahead."

Says an admiring associate, "Not only is he sharp and very calculating, he has incredible stamina to take a setback and still bounce back."

Other's aren't so complimentary. An ex-associate says, "He is ruthless, and if you get into bed with him you have to watch him all the time."

Loy is regarded as having good instincts and acting on them quickly. After Malaysian independence, when the large rubber estates were broken up, he lost no time grabbing several large parcels of land and several listed companies.

He later sold two of the companies to raise the M$18 million (U.S.$7.5 million) he needed to buy Island Hotels & Properties from Khoo Teck Puat.

When Loy made his offer, Khoo, a wily dealmaker in his own right, gave no quarter. "KTP

(continued)

drove a hard deal," says an unsmiling Loy. "I needed the vehicle and he knew it. He wouldn't reduce his price by 1%.

Loy reckons that about two thirds of his successful deals have been based on instinct and a good feel from the start. "Cold deals can work but if you don't have much enthusiasm for a proposition, even if it looks good on paper, chances are it will sour."

As the oldest of our profiled dealmakers, Loy's responsibilities to an established major group have put the brakes on some of his dealmaking impulses. It seems that a certain level of success breeds a certain degree of caution. "When you represent the interest of a group like MBF you cannot think just of yourself," he said.

These days, most offers are vetted by a team of professionals before Loy moves in to do the deal. Still, a large number of MBF's acquisitions, from fast-food chains, to printing and carpet-cleaning companies, have come about because Loy has been able to sell them to the board. And it doesn't hurt that he controls a third of the group. But, he reluctantly concedes, "The so-called experts are necessary in today's business environment."

The Best: Late 1970s—bought Island Hotels & Properties from Khoo Teck Puat for M$18 million (U.S.$7.5 million) for use as listed vehicle. Financed largely by sale of two other companies he had bought for their listing status shortly after Malaysian independence. Island Hotels was renamed Pacific Development Credit and was the forerunner of the MBF Group.

The Worst: A partner in Loy's early listed company, San Holdings, pulled out without repaying major loans from the company. Expensive and lengthy litigation was required to recover the money. Later, the finance license which has been vested in San Holdings was salvaged and used to establish MBF Finance.

HONG KONG

Henry Cheng

In his first eight months as managing director of New World Development, Henry Cheng entered into more than half a dozen major deals. That turned heads even in Hong Kong, where dealmaking is a kind of national sport. He seems like a man who is taking bold steps to prove something in a hurry.

Cheng does have a lot to live up to. His father, Cheng Yu-tung, founder of New World Holdings, is one of the five richest men in Hong Kong.

But the younger Cheng, who doesn't often grant interviews, is quick to deny any competition with his father. "I have no intention of doing deals simply to prove myself."

What he does must fit into company policy, but it is also based on instinct and his own ideas.

At times it is unclear just what the 42-year-old Cheng's thinking is. For example, a hostile HK$3.1 billion (U.S.$396.8 million) cash bid in 1989, for department store chain Wing On, seemed more the action of a brash young man who didn't do his homework. The Kwok family owns more than 50% of Wing On's shares and a rift in the family was highly unlikely. The bid failed.

But Cheng has crafted what could be the largest acquisition of its kind—New World Hotels' takeover of Ramada, Inc. The deal is temporarily on hold while Ramada attempts to iron out some financing problems on its end.

In the deal, New World paid U.S.$355 million for Ramada, which owns or leases more than 500 hotels in the U.S. and manages a further 255 outside America. The entire deal, as originally structured, cost about U.S.$540 million, so Cheng turned on his salesmanship and persuaded an American chain called Prime Motor Inns to put up U.S.$185 million for part of Ramada's U.S. franchise.

Despite the size of the deal and the fact that New World was originally in hot competition with at least six other suitors, Cheng seemed to treat the whole thing as a rather cool exercise in accounting.

"Ramada was on the market a long time," he says. The experts made their recommendations and Cheng made the final approval. No drama, no close calls, no late-night nail-biting in Cheng's private office.

This almost antiseptic approach to dealing is one that Cheng says he has purposely cultivated. "You can't handle the whole deal yourself," he explains.

But while he has reaped praise as an aggressive risk-taker, he has also been scorned as arrogant and uncommunicative. One analyst who has dealt with him says, "One doesn't know if he's got a complex [about his father] or if he's a cocky guy who feels he can do anything."

Perhaps some of what drives Henry Cheng can be found in an October, 1986 interview with his father, in which Cheng Yutung said, "Traditionally, many Chinese businessmen like to keep their companies for their sons and grandsons. I don't think that is the right way to do business."

The Best: Ongoing—Beats six other bidders to come to an agreement to buy Ramada, Inc. (over 750 hotels worldwide) for a total of U.S.$540 million. Brings U.S. hotel chain, Prime Motor Inns, into the deal to put up U.S.$185 million for part of Ramada's U.S. franchise.

The Worst: Makes a hostile HK$3.1 billion (U.S.$396.8 million) cash bid for Wing On holdings. Apparently thought the controlling Kwok family held 44%. The actual figure was over 50%. Now stuck with a nonvoting 27% minority shareholding.

MALAYSIA

Vincent Tan

The aggressive style of Vincent Tan still makes some Malaysians nervous. But to the surprise of many in the business community, the brash, 36-year-old "wildman" of Malaysian dealmaking is proving himself to be more than a flash in the pan.

The Inter-Pacific Industrial Group, the offspring of Tan's wheeling and dealing, posted pre-tax profits of M$42 million (U.S.$16 million) for the year ending April 1989, an extraordinary turnaround from the previous year's loss of M$500,000 (U.S.$1,850,000).

(continued)

A natural salesman, Tan started out selling insurance before winning the Malaysian franchise of McDonald's and then crowning this with the deal that set him on his present course—obtaining Sports Toto from the government.

In 1985, the Malaysian government embarked on a privatization program and Tan made an offer on the fledgling national lottery—Sports Toto. He wound up with a 51% share.

Needing a listed vehicle to further his ambitions, he quickly turned around and swapped his Sports Toto holdings for a controlling interest in investment holding company Berjaya Kawat.

Hungry for more, he went on a buying spree, increasing Berjaya's paid-up capital almost M$200 million (U.S.$74.2 million) in less than three years. That put him M$150 million (U.S.$58 million) in debt. But Tan's approach to business is daring and his solution to most problems seems to be to continue expanding.

In 1988, he initiated a reverse takeover of Raleigh Bhd, which makes bicycles and develops property. He injected his 51% of Berjaya into the deal for a total cash consideration of M$181 million (U.S.$69 million). B&B, Tan's holding company, already held a 32% chunk of Raleigh. Tan emerged with 82% of the equity.

Raleigh, renamed Inter-Pacific, was restructured to become Berjaya's holding company, and a rights issue, which analysts anticipated was going to be a disaster, paid off, putting Inter-Pacific into the black.

Adding to the coffers in 1988 was IGB, a blue-chip property developer, which bought 20% of Inter-Pacific and 12% of Berjaya. This helped provide financial backing for Tan's takeover bid for U.S.-based SSMC, Inc., the manufacturer of Singer products.

In a hard-fought battle, Tan lost to Hong Kong-based Semi-Tech Microelectronics, but not before extracting a compromise: Berjaya, at a highly favorable price, bought SSMC's 49% share of Regnis, which holds the Singer franchise for Malaysia. Berjaya, which already held 35.5% of Regnis, gained control. Regnis is likely to go public sometime soon, which should generate tremendous profits for Tan.

Tan has the ideas and the daring, but he also has the ideal partner in Patrick Low, a respected merchant banker. While Tan shakes things up and gets them motoring, it is Low who fine-tunes the engine, who carries out the restructurings that make sense of the deals and takeovers.

Low doesn't draw much attention. Tan does. He travels about in a heavily armored limousine with tinted windows and bodyguards, all of which he is said to abhor.

The low-profile Low remarks, "It's part and parcel of being wealthy, particularly if you are in the gambling business."

The Best: 1988—Accomplishes reverse takeover of Raleigh Bhd by injecting his 51% of Berjaya into the new company for a cash consideration of M$181 million (U.S.$69 million). With the 32% of Raleigh that B&B, his holding company, already owns, he comes out with 82% of Raleigh. With a subsequent rights issue and restructuring, Raleigh, renamed Inter-Pacific, becomes Berjaya's holding company. In the process he clears most of his debt.

The Worst: Like Ramos, Tan has yet to fail badly. Least successful deal in 1988 when he makes takeover bid for SSMC, Inc., Wall Street-listed manufacturer of Singer consumer durables. Loses to Hong Kong-based Semi-Tech, but achieves compromise whereby Berjaya

(continued)

buys 49% of Regnis from SSMC at a very favorable price and Regnis cuts its royalty payments to Singer from 3% to 1.75%.

THAILAND

Sura Chansrishawala

Location and cash flow are the two things property tycoon Sura Chansrishawala thinks of first when making a deal. Over the past 20 years the Thai Sikh has amassed a fortune in land, a cluster of companies, and a whopping debt that would make lesser mortals weep.

There's no false modesty in this "king of takeovers." He says: "I am very daring and ready to take a big risk."

Land and finance are the bedrock of Sura's empire. It takes finance to buy land, and land (as collateral) to get finance. That simple equation pervades his business history.

In 1964, when he was 23, Sura decided to buy 23 *rai* (3.7 hectares) of Soi Poonvithi 101, in Bangkok, allegedly to build a school.

The school was never built. A month after making the purchase he got a "very attractive" offer on the land. A real estate tycoon was born.

He has an instinctive knack for buying cheap and selling dear. In the early 1970s, Sura, and his brothers, began to buy swampland in Minburi. Its proximity to Bangkok turned their 650 hectares from a swamp into a goldmine.

He has also been building a complex web of finance-related companies under his Siam Vidhaya Group, largely through takeover bids. Details of exactly what, when and how much money was involved are almost impossible to come by—he is very secretive, something which he apparently uses to his advantage.

In 1984, Sura's Siam Vidhaya Group had a falling out with the management of Laem Thong Bank, in which it was a minor shareholder. The bank had refused to extend more credit for Sura's property deals. Further, the bank sued the group for failing to repay debts.

Quietly, by early 1987 Sura had amassed 57% of the bank's shares. In October he called an extraordinary general meeting and engineered a boardroom coup d'etat, ousting the old management team and replacing it with one more to his liking. One of the first orders of business was to drop the lawsuit against the Siam Vidhaya Group.

The financial empire almost dragged Sura down in the early 1980s, when Equity Development Finance & Securities, Ltd., one of the country's largest finance companies, collapsed. Many of Thailand's smaller finance and securities firms went under in a wave of panic.

Undaunted by the prospect of debt, Sura borrowed heavily. Property was, of course, the collateral. When the crisis had passed he was 8 billion *baht* (U.S.$312 million) in debt.

But again his instincts served him well. A real estate boom was in the making. Three years ago Sura said that in order to clear all his debts he would have to sell 50% of his assets. But by early this year, his assets had risen in value so much that he was able to pay off roughly half

(continued)

his debts by selling just a small portion of the assets. The remaining assets have gone on rising swiftly in value.

For Sura, whose collapse seemed imminent a few years ago, the real estate boom has been a godsend. After a profitable land sale last year, the secretive but not at all shy Sura told the press, "I'm ready to buy every piece of land which anyone wants to sell."

More recently he expressed his pleasure with the current state of things, "Now opportunity is on my side, something I have been waiting for for a long time. Once all the debts are cleared, nothing can stop our group."

The Best: 1984 to 1987—After a falling out with management, he spent three years quietly acquiring 57% of the shares of the Laem Thong Bank, which probably cost more than 1 billion *baht* (U.S.$40 million). At an EGM in October 1987, he threw out the board and installed his own. The bank then dropped a pending lawsuit against Sura's company.

The Worst? 1987 to 1989—Has had to sell off large amounts of assets to cover debts incurred while propping up his financial firms after the Thai financial crisis of 1984.

Reported by Lilian Ng in Singapore, Ranjit Gill in Malaysia, Peter Janssen in Thailand, Jose Marte Abueg in the Philippines, and John Keating in Hong Kong. © *Asian Business* magazine, Far East Trade Press, Ltd., 1989.

RICHEST TYCOONS OF SOUTHEAST ASIA

Most Westerners know from the popular television program, "Lifestyles of the Rich and Famous," and from *Forbes* magazine that the Sultan of Brunei, Sir Hassanal Bolkiah, is the richest man in the world, with a personal fortune estimated to be worth about $25 billion. But chances are that most Westerners are not as familiar with the region's other tycoons. After all, who has ever heard of Haji Bob Hassan, the tenth richest man in Indonesia (worth $150 million), or of Indonesian megabanker Mochtar Riady, who has personal assets in the neighborhood of $350 million?

A 1990 survey by Indonesian economics magazine *Warta Ekonomi* lifted the veil on the 25 richest men in Southeast Asia. Among the top ASEAN (Association of Southeast Asian Nations) tycoons are five Singaporeans, four Malaysians, four Filipinos, 10 Indonesians, and one each from Thailand and Brunei. Interestingly enough, 21 of those on the list are Chinese, although they prefer to do business in their adopted countries using native names.

Indonesia's richest mogul is Liem Sioe Long (alias Soedomo Salim, worth $2.4 billion), who owns 192 companies and who has close personal ties with President Suharto of Indonesia. He is followed on the list by William Soeryadyaya, who heads the Astra group, the nation's largest conglomerate. He's worth an estimated $700 million. His Chinese name is Tjia Kian Liong, and he is the sole distributor for Toyota cars in Indonesia. Third richest Indonesian is Eka Tjipa Widjaya (alias Oei Ek Tjong), owner of the Sinar Mas group of 150 companies, who is worth $700 million. The fourth and fifth richest Indonesians are in the business of manufacturing Indonesian "kretek" clove cigarettes.

They are Rachman Halim (alias Tjoa To Hing, worth $500 million) and the Oei brothers, who are jointly worth $400 million.

"If he succeeds, man praises himself; if he fails, he blames his ancestors."

Korean proverb

WORK ON THE RIM

WORK–LEISURE SURVEY

A 1988 survey by Taiwan's Directorate General of Budget, Accounting and Statistics revealed that the Japanese work 15 minutes a day longer than the Chinese. Motoyuki Miyano, the head of the Leisure Development Center, a publicly founded organization whose aim is to make the Japanese work less and take more recreation time, puts in as much as 50 hours a week trying to convince others to relax more. According to 1985 figures, Japanese workers worked an average of 2,168 hours, compared to 1,952 hours in Britain, 1,924 hours in the United States, 1,659 hours in West Germany, and 1,643 hours in France. Leading Japanese companies are frequently forced to demand that workers take days off because individuals are reluctant to take holidays.

THE HOUSE OF MITSUI

The House of Mitsui, which began as a small moneychanging firm 350 years before World War II, employed over three million workers by 1945—probably more employees than any firm in the history of mankind.

> SOURCE: *The House of Nomura* by Al Alletzhauser (Bloomsbury Publishing, Ltd., London, 1990).

THE ILLEGALS

TAIWAN'S TEMPS

Until its illegal alien worker crackdown in 1989, Taiwan was becoming the primary location in the Far East for jobseekers from poorer countries such as Malaysia and the Philippines (where the average daily wage was about $3.30 in 1988). In Taiwan, as many as 100,000 Filipinos, Thais, Malaysians, and Indonesians were earning up to $250 per month in a booming economy, where per capita income had soared to $6,100. But now, the illegal immigrants who have been doing the menial tasks spurned by newly affluent Taiwanese are undercover—fugitives from a government policy which says that cheap foreign labor is slowing the country's switch from labor-intensive to capital-intensive industry. Despite this, Taiwan's unemployment rate has dropped as low as 1.5% and many industries are suffering from a labor shortage.

Mainland Chinese seamen are available for hire in Taiwan through employment agencies in the port of Kaohsiung. Sales brochures advertise that wages for mainland sailors average only about NT$8,000 (about $285) plus NT$200 for pocket money monthly. Employers must also pay the seaman's air fare to and from Singapore, and an insurance pre-

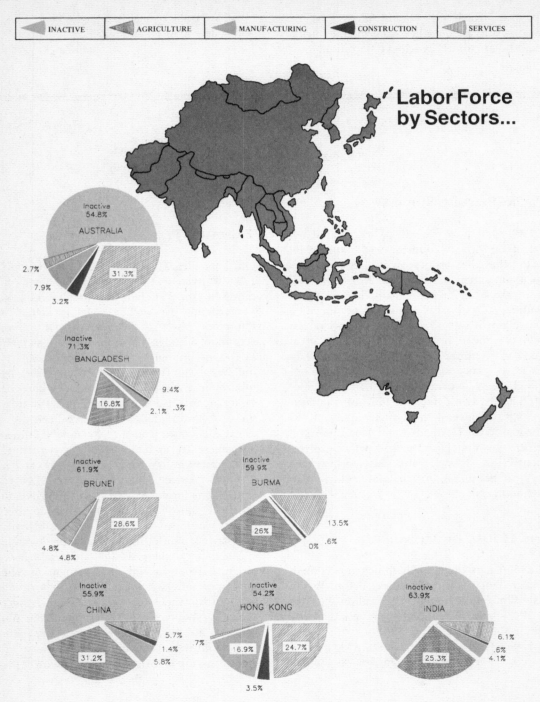

INACTIVE   AGRICULTURE   MANUFACTURING   CONSTRUCTION   SERVICES

Labor Force
by Sectors...

AUSTRALIA
Inactive 54.8%
31.3%
2.7%
7.9%
3.2%

BANGLADESH
Inactive 71.3%
9.4%
16.8%
2.1% .3%

BRUNEI
Inactive 61.9%
28.6%
4.8%
4.8%

BURMA
Inactive 59.9%
13.5%
26%
0% .6%

CHINA
Inactive 55.9%
5.7%
31.2%
1.4%
5.8%

HONG KONG
Inactive 54.2%
.7%
16.9%
24.7%
3.5%

INDIA
Inactive 63.9%
6.1%
25.3%
.6%
4.1%

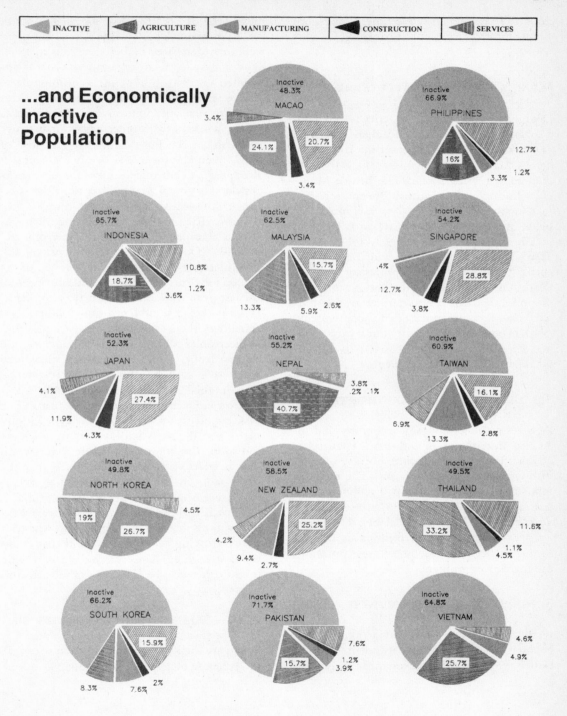

INACTIVE   AGRICULTURE   MANUFACTURING   CONSTRUCTION   SERVICES

...and Economically
Inactive
Population

MACAO
Inactive 48.3%
3.4%
24.1%
20.7%
3.4%

PHILIPPINES
Inactive 66.9%
16%
12.7%
3.3%
1.2%

INDONESIA
Inactive 65.7%
18.7%
10.8%
1.2%
3.6%

MALAYSIA
Inactive 62.5%
15.7%
13.3%
5.9%
2.6%

SINGAPORE
Inactive 54.2%
.4%
28.8%
12.7%
3.8%

JAPAN
Inactive 52.3%
4.1%
27.4%
11.9%
4.3%

NEPAL
Inactive 55.2%
3.8%
.2% .1%
40.7%

TAIWAN
Inactive 60.9%
16.1%
6.9%
13.3%
2.8%

NORTH KOREA
Inactive 49.8%
19%
4.5%
26.7%

NEW ZEALAND
Inactive 58.5%
25.2%
4.2%
9.4%
2.7%

THAILAND
Inactive 49.5%
33.2%
11.6%
1.1%
4.5%

SOUTH KOREA
Inactive 66.2%
15.9%
8.3%
7.6%
2%

PAKISTAN
Inactive 71.7%
15.7%
7.6%
1.2%
3.9%

VIETNAM
Inactive 64.8%
25.7%
4.6%
4.9%

mium. The Taiwan government does not allow direct hiring of mainland Chinese workers.

JAPAN'S UNDOCUMENTED ALIENS

Japan's ever-increasing prosperity is making it a magnet for undocumented aliens in search of work, most of whom enter the labor market by staying in the country illegally after their tourist visas expire. The Justice Ministry's Immigration Control Bureau reported that such violation of the law was increasing by as much as 30% per year, with Filipinos making up the largest category followed by Thai, Pakistani, Chinese, and Bangladeshi aliens. Sophia University professor Gregory Clark, the only foreign member of the Immigration Department's investigative committee, has recommended that such foreign laborers be brought into the country for a limited time on a contract basis to overcome what he sees as "social problems."

THAI'S SKILLED LABOR SHORTAGE

As a result of its booming economy and increased investment in industry, Thailand is now suffering from an acute shortage of qualified engineers and technicians. The industry ministry estimates that 7,000 engineers and technicians are needed in industrial sectors this year, but only 2,700 are available. Top priority needs: engineers and technicians in such sectors as electrical machinery, telecommunications, and computers.

SINGAPORE'S LABOR CRUNCH

Despite their determination to keep their country from becoming dependent on low-skilled foreign workers, Singapore authorities have been obliged to allow a certain amount of immigrant labor because the booming economy generated 66,000 new jobs in 1988. The newspapers are crammed with help-wanted ads and job-hopping is commonplace. There is fierce competition for the workers who are available, with newly opened stores luring workers from older department stores with higher starting salaries. At the close of 1987, unemployment was below 3% and still dropping. A controlled pool of foreign workers on short-term permits has been the solution to the job situation so far, and Finance Minister Richard Hu, announcing that this would continue for the next few years, explained: "Demand for foreign workers has been increasing rapidly. More than half of the 48,000 jobs created in the manufacturing sector last year were filled this way, and manufacturers are currently recruiting about 2,500 foreign workers each month."

Electronics companies in Singapore are finding labor in such short supply that there have been such benefits as cash payments, disco nights, and even training stints in Europe as inducements to join their firms. The cash payments are spread out over a lengthy period, so the new employees will not leave too soon. But some personal managers warn that is exactly what is happening—that the extra perks encourage job-hopping as well as increasing wage bills and, therefore, prices.

What is making the competition for workers even keener is that neighboring Malaysia is also thriving economically, and that country is absorbing many of the workers who might otherwise be looking for jobs in Singapore.

AAS—ASIAN-AMERICAN ACHIEVERS

"Who are the achievers in American society?" the Japanese magazine *Shukan Bunshun* asked.

"AAs, the Asian-Americans," the publication concluded. "They obey the laws. They aren't violent. They study and work hard."

In an analysis of the AAs, *The Economist* of London discovered that they have above-average family incomes. Why? Because they want their children to get a good education.

America's immigration law was revised in 1965 to allow family members and people with specific skills to immigrate. Since then, 40% of the annual 600,000 quota are Asians.

"They probably were able to immigrate to the U.S. because they were well-educated in their home countries," *Shukan Bunshun* observed. "In business, however, few AAs get past general manager. Hardly ever are they among the ranks of top management. Somewhere there seems to be an invisible ceiling. Bluntly put, society hates an achiever."

ASIAN IMMIGRANTS DOWN UNDER

An Australian study revealed that Asian migrants to Australia are better educated, more socially adaptable, and more likely to land good jobs than most immigrant groups. The 1988 study conducted by Laksiri Jayasuriya, a sociology professor at the University of Western Australia, showed that Asians earned an average of $12,830, more than all immigrant groups except expatriate New Zealanders and North Americans.

THE PHILIPPINES

CHILD LABOR IN PHILIPPINES

Almost one quarter of the country's 22 million children under 15 worked as hired hands on farms and in factories in the Philippines, with another nine million or so laboring without pay on family farms, according to a study by the nation's Department of Labor. Poverty is so endemic in the country that all the government can do is try to minimize exploitation and provide some opportunities for education.

In fact, it was not until former dictator Marcos was replaced by President Corazon Aquino that the problem was even studied seriously. "Very early in the game," says Aura Ancheta Sabilano, director of the Bureau of Women and Young Workers, "we had a hard time looking for the children because their employers would hide them."

Young girls mostly find employment wrapping sweets in candy factories or stitching and sewing buttons in cramped, unregistered sweat shops; boys hawk newspapers, spray pesticides on rice and vegetable farms, or work in some maritime activity which forces them to dive undersea without protective gear. "If children as little as these feel bitterness [about their role] at such an early age, psychologically that does not help at all," says Sabilano. "Years from now what kind of citizens will we have in this country?"

CHILD SLAVERY IN MINDANAO

Slavery is a growth industry in the Moslem-dominated Lanao del Sur province on Mindanao island in the southern Philippines. Wealthy Moslem families seeking household or farm help can buy kidnapped children in an underground market. Depending on physical condition, the price of a slave varies from 3,000 pesos ($150) to 5,000 pesos ($250), according to Lt. Col. Carlos Pena, the military commander of the province.

ROADS TO RICHES LEAD OVERSEAS
by Jose Marte Abueg

Amid all the economic chaos, the Philippines still has one world-beating export—people.

Pretty enough to be a model or a movie star-let, Crystal Quesada was 16 when she left the beer house in a dark sidestreet in central Manila where she had worked as a hostess in between nude shows. Two years on, she is earning far more as an "entertainer" in Japan.

Lourdes Guevara was an accountant in Manila before she went to Copenhagen. There, she earns more as a chambermaid at the SAS Hotel than she did in her profession in the Philippines.

Carmona Manuel now works in Saudi Arabia as a house maid. Before she left, she attended a mandatory pre-departure seminar at the Philippine Overseas Employment administration. At the seminar, neither she nor the two dozen other women showed any noticeable reaction when they were lectured on what to do after being raped—so the rape would not be repeated.

These jobs may not sound like everyone's dream, but for 2.5 million unemployed members of the Philippine labor force, they would be only too welcome. Not much better off are 7.6 million who are employed for less than 40 hours a week, in a country where the legal minimum wage for an eight-hour day is about U.S.\$3.30.

And little better off than the unemployed are the many thousands of young women from the countryside who eke out a living in Manila as domestic helpers, getting free board and lodging, but earning as little as U.S.\$4 a month.

The Philippine economy achieved an impressive growth rate of 6.8% for the final quarter of 1988, in bright contrast to the 10% contraction of 1984 to 1985. But unemployment remains high at around 12%, and the work force, which currently stands at around 21.2 million, increases by 700,000 every year.

The two million or so Filipinos who have found work abroad, and who made 1987 a banner year for labor exports, can therefore count themselves lucky.

The overseas contract workers run the gamut of occupational categories. Going abroad in 1988 were 105,538 professional, technical, and related workers—of whom 62,800 were women, including 31,579 entertainers bound mainly for Asia, especially Japan.

Managerial, executive and administrative workers number 1,503, of whom 131 were women; clerks totaled 13,694, 3806 of them women; and sales workers totaled 3,722, including 1,949 women.

But the biggest category was production and process workers, transport operators, and laborers—121,911 men and 4,942 women—94% of whom went to the Middle East.

Women dominated the service sector, with 106,800 going abroad compared with 21,904 men. Of the women, 82,338 left to work as domestic helpers, including 30,152 who went to Hong Kong and 16,638 to Singapore.

As overseas employment tends to require a good knowledge of English, those working as domestics abroad tend not to have been domestics in the Philippines. Some have left jobs as teachers or as clerks. Others were unemployed but carried college diplomas.

Viewed in this Roman Catholic country as less fortunate than the overseas domestics, although they earn more money, are the likes of Crystal—"entertainers" who work as bar girls or prostitutes abroad.

Promotion of foreign employment has become a necessity to the Philippines since the economy has a greater work force than it can employ, notes Tomas Achacoso, head of the Philippine Overseas Employment Administration (POEA), which licenses recruitment agencies and is the government's link with foreign markets.

The overseas contract workers bring in vast amounts of foreign currency. They are one of the country's largest dollar-earning sectors, contributing more than most commodity exports. According to official figures they remitted U.S.$680.44 million to the Philippines in 1986, U.S.$791.9 million in 1987, and U.S.$419.3 million in the first half of last year.

Unofficially, a great deal more money has been sent home by those overseas, with the government's Philippine National Bank estimating that at least U.S.$600 million a year slides in through various back doors.

This hemorrhaging of the official system prompted a crack-down by the central bank on money traders to flush out illegal operators —reportedly on the instigation of the International Monetary Fund—to put the dollars in and use them to augment the central bank's swiftly dwindling foreign-exchange reserves.

Recruitment has climbed steadily since president Corazon Aquino came to power nearly in 1986, despite various restrictions, says Achacoso.

One of those came into force in 1988 when the government banned the overseas employment of Filipinos as domestics, following numerous reports of abuse by employers. The prohibition has been lifted in certain countries that have formidable regulations, beginning with Hong Kong. It remains in force for a number of other destinations.

Overall, the Middle East is still the top market for Filipino contract workers overseas. As their oil revenues dwindle, the economies of the Gulf in particular are looking for productivity and efficiency in the work force, and in this regard Filipinos are favored over other imported workers, such as those from India, Burma, Pakistan, and Bangladesh. Another factor working in favor of Filipino workers, Achacoso adds, is their knowledge of English.

One effect this migration has had on local industries is to change the attitudes of some employers toward their personnel, Achacoso notes. Some companies have set up training programs to replace the people they lose to overseas employment, and these employers now "value their workers more," says Achacoso, although in most cases not enough, he notes, to prompt them to improve wages.

There are a couple of sectors which are now feeling the pinch. Foreign competition for highly skilled labor has been notably fierce in the airline industry, and Philippine Airlines has stepped up training and raised salaries and benefits of key technical personnel, Achacoso says.

Hospitals, too, have lost many nurses to foreign countries, to the point where secretary of health Alfred Bengzon has voiced alarm over unfilled vacancies in rural health centers. The low pay of nurses has been driving them to the U.S. for years and, in the past decade, to the Middle East.

But these two sectors are exceptional. In other fields, the push to export labor continues. POEA and labor department officials have been invited by corporations in Hong

Kong, Japan, Taiwan, and the Middle East—particularly Iran and Iraq—to discuss overseas employment policies.

In Hong Kong, Achacoso says, prospective employers have been seeking to ease the entry of Filipino construction and garment-industry workers, although so far the Hong Kong government has refused to allow them in.

In Japan, thousands of Filipinos have found jobs in construction. They work illegally but the authorities have so far left them alone, and they are thriving in Japan's underground economy, the POEA administrator says. Now with Japan facing an increasing aging population, corporations there are asking for more construction workers, computer operators, and health workers.

Philippine labor missions have been sent to Iran and Iraq to explore job opportunities, mostly in construction, as the two countries embark on massive reconstruction after the Iran-Iraq War. Achacoso says that, unlike many other countries, the Philippines never stopped sending workers to Iran and Iraq during the war, so Filipinos had a head start.

The effects of these foreign employment efforts will be felt (throughout the 1990s), Achacoso says. (Editorial note: The post-Persian Gulf War reconstruction of Kuwait, and possibly Iraq, is likely to offer another major opportunity.)

A labor surplus still exists in just about every industry in the Philippines, and is certain to continue until the upturn in the economy filters down to the lower levels, and that could take many years.

In the meantime, president Aquino has instructed officials to "eat employment, drink employment, sleep employment." But until they come up with some solutions, millions of Filipinos can do little more than dream employment.

COOLIE CHILD LABOR

Only about 17% of China's married couples have been obeying the country's one-child-only injunction according to the Xinhau News Agency, and the mainland's population is growing by 40 babies each minute or 20 million per year. Most children quit school aged 10, vast numbers working up to 15 hours each day for coolie wages of about $7 monthly, and rarely getting enough to eat or a bed of their own.

NO GOALS, LITTLE SATISFACTION

Japan's National Institute of Employment and Vocational Research announced an international study of work adjustment among young employees. The report compared about 1,000 workers between 25 and 30 years of age in Japan, England, and the United States. Some 85% of young workers in both the United States and England are satisfied with their jobs. In Japan, the satisfaction rate is only 57.8%. Furthermore, when asked if each day they got any closer to the realization of their life's goals, many young Japanese answered that they "have no goal" but that the day represented progress along "my way."

Young Japanese have a very good environment compared to either the United States or England, *Asahi Shimbun* noted. In Japan, there is little unemployment and little chance of being laid off, yet they have little sense of satisfaction. Why?

The report's analysis says that Japan's young workers are beginning to look for ways to capitalize on their individuality, that their values are broadening, but that they have a vague sense of discontent and no sense of where they want to go in life or work.

GOLDEN KANGAROO POUCH

It's the opposite of the golden parachute. And it's designed to keep senior Aussie management loyal and hopping. Former Australian mega-tycoon Alan Bond awarded about a dozen of his top ten executives bonuses worth more than $27.5 million. One of the biggest beneficiaries of the Bond Corp. chairman's largesse was managing director Peter Beckwith, who netted about $6.7 million. Part of the deal was that Beckwith had to agree not to join a rival corporation for a period of four years should he decide to turn his pouch into a parachute. Other senior Bond executives averaged loyalty payments of about $1.75 million each.

NEW ZEALAND

HARD-WORKING MIGRANTS SOUGHT
by Bevis England

Asian migrants, especially the Chinese, have played—and continue to play—a vital role in New Zealand's development.

When the first Chinese goldminers arrived at the southernmost tip of New Zealand's South Island in the 1860s, they began a long tradition of Chinese and Asian migration. They were among the hardest workers then, providing much of the infrastructure required by the 60,000 population of the gold-field areas.

A few generations later, hard-working Asian migrants moved into another crucial industry—market gardening for the Auckland metropolis. Although only a few have remained on the land, many of the city's Chinese population owe their present position to the dedication and hard work put into these gardens.

One fine example is Colin Chan, who arrived in 1952. He began his working life in New Zealand washing soy sauce bottles for a few shillings a day. For 20 years, he says, he worked "10 hours a day, seven days a week" for a variety of employers.

He and his wife raised seven children and cultivated a market garden, often working by torchlight. Drawing on experience he had gained during 10 years as an electrician with giant conglomerate Fisher and Paykel, he also built up an electrical contracting business.

Using subcontracted labor, that business has won some major contracts, including the Glenbrook Steel Mill, Auckland International Airport, and the Mangere Bridge. All of them, Chan says, were gained by word of mouth.

Chan and his family are also poised to take advantage of the expected Asian investment boom with a string of allied businesses: Orient World-Wide Travel, Orient World-Wide Finance and Investments, and Orient International Agencies, all designed to extend close business links with Hong Kong and Chinese companies.

All the time Chan had a dream: To own a piece of real estate and build a Chinese restaurant. That dream has now been realized in the recently opened 12-story Orient Towers development, complete with Chinese restaurant.

Chan even has architectural models for his next project, a hotel. "There's a wealth of opportunity here," he says, "but New Zealand lacks motivation."

The country is now trying hard to attract more such migrants, specifically for their entrepreneurial flair and business acumen. In a number of areas this drive is proving successful, and migration to New Zealand from Asian countries is going through a boom period.

A Hong Kong-based immigration consultant says that according to figures for June 1989, New Zealand had about 30,000 Chinese, most of them living in Auckland. He believes the figure could rise to nearly 100,000 by the year 2000, equating to almost 10% of the city's population.

Quality as well as quantity appears to be on the rise. Approvals for entry to New Zealand on business grounds accounted for 15% to 18% of all approvals for resident in 1987 to 1988, compared with just 1% the previous year. Furthermore, approvals of overseas takeovers of New Zealand companies, together with overseas companies starting business in New Zealand, have risen rapidly, from 988 in 1984 to 1,979 in 1988.

Such increases are to a great extent a reflection of the liberalization of New Zealand policies on immigration and investment from overseas.

© *Asian Business* magazine, Far East Trade Press, Ltd., 1989.

BIRTH OF A SALESMAN

On a lower corporate rung, yet just as gung-ho as his superiors, is the Japanese salesman. *Nikkei Venture* magazine polled 120 major Japanese corporations to construct a profile of their top salesperson. Here's what they found: He's 38.4 years old, has been working in sales for 11.3 years, earns about $71,000 per year, and makes 22.1 sales calls a day—12.3 of them to established accounts and 9.8 of them to prospective customers. He makes 9.9 phone calls a day, spends 30 minutes a day at his desk, and 36 minutes eating lunch. How much are these marathon sellers worth each year to their respective industries? On an individual basis they sold: $4.8 million in real estate; $4.4 million in food and beverage; $56 million in life insurance; and earned $3.3 million in handling fees for securities.

JAPANESE FOREIGN LEGION?

In a recent Japanese poll of how Japanese feel about hiring foreigners to do certain jobs in Japan, one category which did not fare well in the hands of foreigners was *"sushi* chef." A majority of those polled declared that the *sushi* counter was where they would draw the line in *"gaijin"* (foreigner) employment.

Now a controversial study by a Japan Defense Agency task force is proposing military recruitment of Asian laborers who have flocked to Japan in search of jobs. "Hiring mercenaries [into Japan's Self-Defense Force] from Asia would reduce personal costs and aid the economies of those nations," the report proposed. Other incentives being considered to entice dwindling Japanese recruits: relaxing curfews, off-base housing, and more attractive uniforms.

THE DESKLESS OFFICE

First there was the "paperless office," and now there is the "deskless office." Giant Japanese trading house C. Itoh, which had estimated revenues of about $117 billion in 1987, has been experimenting with some innovative cost-cutting measures. They've come up with the concept of the "deskless office" at their corporate headquarters in Tokyo. Salesmen should be on the road anyway, goes the thinking, so a communal work area should suffice for paperwork. The company expects to save about $54 million a year by renting out all the extra space.

ROBOTS ON THE RISE IN SEOUL

Since South Korea's period of labor unrest began in 1989, Korean industries have quietly begun to increase their research and development investment in robotics. They are also stepping up the development of industrial robot manufacturing plants around the country.

When Hyundai Group chairman Chung Ju-yung visited the southeast coastal city of Ulsan to dedicate a new Hyundai Heavy Industries robot manufacturing facility, he surprised his executives by announcing that Hyundai would build another robotics plant, thus doubling Hyundai's robot-manufacturing capacity. Hyundai currently has the largest robot production plant in Korea, turning out 300 "Hyunbots" a year.

The number-one customer for the Hyunbots, of course, is Hyundai Motor Co., the nation's largest automobile manufacturer. With increased U.S. protectionist pressure on South Korea—and with trade competition heating up among the Pacific Rim's NICs (newly industrialized countries, including South Korea, Taiwan, Hong Kong, and Singapore), the Koreans are looking at robots to cut costs and to boost profit margins.

Not only are the big Korean conglomerates planning to use robots for their own production purposes, they are also actively gearing up to export them as well. South Korea is the only NIC nation that manufactures and exports industrial robots today. (Korean robot industry leader Daewoo Heavy Industries won an order to supply U.S. firm Automaker, Inc. with 50 of its NOVA-10 robots at a price 30% cheaper than a comparable Japanese model.)

Robostats: South Korea's 13 robot-makers spent an estimated U.S.$13.5 million on R&D last year. The domestic Korean market for robots is still small, but it's growing. In 1985, it was a modest $750,000. In 1989, it was valued at about $6.4 million. According to a recent report issued by the Korean Advanced Institute of Science and Technology, the Korean robotics industry is projected to grow to about $35.7 million by 1990.

DAMNED IF YOU DO, DAMNED IF YOU DON'T

In every Japanese company, there are those relegated to a window seat," noted the *Mainichi Shimbun* in an op-ed piece. "Out of the main stream, they slowly divide themselves into two basic groups—the *Madogiwa Zoku* (The Windowseat Tribe) and the *Madogiwa Kizoku* (The Windowseat Nobility). The average Windowseat Tribe worker comes to the office at 9:00 A.M., reads the paper thoroughly, then goes to lunch. After lunch, a few cups of tea until the afternoon papers arrive. Read the papers thoroughly, leave for home at 5:00 P.M. Stop on the way for a little drink, watch the news on TV, go to bed.

The Windowseat Nobility worker leads the same life as their lesser brethren during the day. But after 5:00 P.M., all resemblance stops. Monday, hit the exhibitions; Tuesday, chamber music; Wednesday, take in a stage show; Thursday, have dinner with the family for a change. Then there's the guy who runs home, gobbles his food, kisses the family, and disappears into the other room to work on his personal computer. His is writing a book about his hobby.

Problem: Suddenly, everyone is interested in the Windowseat Nobility. In this day and age of corporate diversification, someone is bound to remember that o'l Sato, over by the window is a whiz at computer software, or he knows a lot about growing orchids, or he goes scuba diving every weekend . . . But is that situation appreciated by the Windowseat Nobility? Their outside interests are now contributing to the company. That's nice. Except that it means your private life can no longer be separated from the office. While you're enjoying yourself, you're sure to suddenly think, "I'll bet this could be used at work." Then suddenly, the Windowseat Nobility would be an endangered species.

Translated from *Mainichi Shimbun* by *Japan Free Press.*

"GOLDEN HANDCUFFS" FOR HONG KONG EXECS

Business people in the West are familiar with the notion of "golden parachutes" for top executives who have overstayed their welcome in a company. In Hong Kong, where professionals are fleeing abroad in record numbers before China takes over the territory in 1997, the brain drain crisis has created an opposite syndrome. There, the challenge is how to get qualified workers to remain in their jobs.

Multinational corporations with Hong Kong offices need to take drastic steps to secure their local operations, warned John Wilson, managing director of Russell Reynolds Associates/Hong Kong, a leading international executive recruitment agency. He suggested that multinationals should use "golden handcuff" programs, offering all sorts of lavish incentives to tie local executives to Hong Kong for the new few years. Although costly, this policy will prove to be ultimately more economical than facing high turnover and retraining cycles from now until 1997.

Other steps multinationals are taking to deal with the brain-and-talent drain: Companies like Apple Computer and General Electric are paying greater attention to setting up internal training programs for young local executives, putting them on the fast track with speedy promotions.

LADIES FIRST?

An innovative franchise idea in Australia is a funeral parlor operated entirely by women named White Lady Funerals. Women do all the work from clerical to embalming to final rites. Launched in Adelaide by Vanessa Hume, ex-wife of a local mortuary director, White Lady has been so busy, that franchises are being planned for Sydney, Melbourne, Perth, and Brisbane. The company's feminist-sounding motto is "The Caring Alternative" —and, as the firm's name suggests, the predominant color theme is white, from staff uniforms to curtains to hearse to coffin.

LADIES LAST?

A new ladies' monthly magazine in Hong Kong targets Chinese women, aged 18 to 38, who are either senior executives or who aspire to be. The magazine, called *New Female,* seeks to distance itself from other publications aimed at the woman of leisure. One of NF's mottos, as stated in its first issue, says it all: "Dress like a woman, act like a man and work like a dog."

A Hong Kong study reveals that women in the territory are paid an average of 38 percent less than men in various industries. According to a 3-year survey conducted by Edward Wong Yu-ti, lecturer in human resources management at Hong Kong's Baptist College, real wages for men are about $16.50 per day compared to women's daily wage of about $12.

NEW "OFFICE LADIES" (OL) GO TO WORK

Tobu Department Store queried 200 Tokyo metropolitan area women graduates about preparations for starting their new jobs. How much did you spend for clothes? Average: Y108,000 (about $830).

What did you buy?

1.	Suit	69.5%
2.	Shoes	45.5%
3.	Skirt and blouse	45.0%
4.	Dress	42.5%

What kind of OL do you want to be?

1.	The cute, lively, life-of-the-office type	38.0%
2.	The hard-working can-do type	16.5%
3.	The steady career woman type	13.5%

From *Yomiuri Shimbun,* translated by *Japan Free Press.*

FORCED SABBATICALS

Every 43-year-old *kacho* (section head) at Japan's TDK Corp. is given about $1,115 and three weeks off each year to "broaden his horizons." The giant magnet tape-maker calls it "research on the art of living." After the three-week sabbatical, the *kacho* must write a report of his experiences and present it to the Board of Directors. Here is what some of them did with their time, according a report in *Asahi Shimbun* newspaper.

One man spent the time throwing pots and discovered that there was something else in life besides work.

Another took a trip around Japan on local trains and spent an evening in a country pub discussing the meaning of life with an elderly couple.

A trip with the wife to Spain and Portugal showed one man that he had been running so fast through his life that he was now out of breath.

"Then there was the *kacho* who went to the outer islands of Okinawa, but couldn't get work off his mind. He averaged a telephone call to the office every three days.

"It's good to have the chance to reflect on the meaning of life," *Asahi Shimbun* noted. "But that opportunity can be a two-edged sword as far as a company is concerned. If an employee suddenly gets engrossed in his or her own life, suddenly there's a corporate soldier AWOL. Power drops. And productivity falters."

Says TDK training chief, Kondo Kunio, "Most companies have yet to make up the collective mind on just what the best method of employee training is. There are lots of ideas, while we Japanese are accused of being workaholics, while trade friction worsens, and while society ages. One thing is for certain. The methods of the past are no longer apropos."

SUBSIDIZED VACATIONS

The renowned paternalism of Japanese companies toward their employees has extended to subsidized vacations, with automobile manufacturers leading the way. Toyota signed up 450 people for a four-day cruise aboard a luxury liner, paying all costs except for about $90. Honda's labor union took 600 workers on an eight-day tour of China, charging them about $700 apiece. And 1,500 employees and family of Isuzu each contributed $120 for a three-day company jamboree with food, drink, and entertainment.

CLUB MED-STYLE HOUSING FOR NEW JAPANESE COMPANY RECRUITS

Japanese corporations have a new recruitment tool to lure university graduates to work for them—resort-like company housing. It used to be that new employees would be housed in drab and depressing company dorms. But increasing competition for qualified workers is now forcing recruiters to offer fancy incentives.

According to a spokesman from Recruit Co., a leading Japanese headhunting firm, every single male university student graduating next March is already being sought by a record average of 3.1 companies.

In addition, graduating students face a new corporate environment in which job hopping, once considered taboo in Japan, is now acceptable. So along with requirements for higher pay and longer vacations, comfortable housing is becoming a major factor in a graduate's decision to take a job.

Fujita Corp, is promoting a housing concept called "High Corp System," which features such amenities as condominium-type quarters, along with baby-sitting, massage, shopping and housecleaning services, as well as library, pool, gym, sauna, aerobics studio, golf practice room, barbecue garden, and other facilities.

One medium-sized company, Kanematsu-Gosho, recently spent about U.S.$10 million to refurbish company dorms after its competition did the same. The new look includes rooms which have doubled in size, all-weather tennis courts, and a large steamy art-deco Roman-style communal bath.

With skyrocketing real estate prices in Japan, some companies are even looking to provide affordable housing or their retired employees. Fanuc, a major robot manufacturer, is building about 100 homes for retired workers and their families, and plans to charge only about $75 a month in rent.

EXECUTIVE LAYOFFS, JAPANESE-STYLE

The scariest word these days for Japanese *buchos* (section chiefs who command a staff of about 40 workers) is *kata-takaki*. it means "tapping on the shoulder"—and the phenomenon is becoming endemic in Japan as the high yen and impending recession threaten seemingly secure "lifetime" jobs.

This is how *kata-takaki* works. Old *bucho* Suzuki is slaving away at his desk on Japan, Inc. business when—*pon!* (that's the official sound that's ascribed to the action), he feels a hand on his shoulder. He turns around—and, horrors, he sees the smiling face of a job broker who's been retained by the giant *sogo shosha* (trading company) to "relocate" top management. The problem, of course, is that the *bucho's* salary (average 12 million yen a year or about $80,000) is a bit steep for these belt-tightening times.

The *bucho* is "persuaded" that his services are urgently needed by one of the firm's struggling subsidiaries. He's got to take a salary cut in the process—personal sacrifice is necessary!—down from about $80,000 to about $50,000. The new firm that the *bucho* transfers to is generally undercapitalized, and destined for the Void.

A favorite *kata-takaki* technique of one of Japan's biggest banks, Sumitomo Ginko, for example, is to foist off unwanted executives onto one of the financially strapped small-to-midsize companies which owes the bank money. Rather than foreclose on the debts (which have little hope of ever being repaid), Sumitomo will retain a 10% to 15% ownership of those firms—and use them in effect as human wastebaskets for their *kata-takaki* victims before emptying those wastebaskets out.

For his services—and for saving the corporation "face" as well as a great deal of money—the *kata-takaki* broker earns a fee of about 20% of the *bucho's* original salary, or about $15,000.

One of the most successful *kata-takaki* agencies in Tokyo goes by the ominous name of "Human Refreshment Agency."

LATEST IN OFFICES

It's common knowledge that Tokyo has the most expensive office space in the world, with an average cost of $85 a square foot and rising. So what happens when you reach the prize ozone? The innovative Japanese have the answer: office compartments. For only about $200 a moth, you can now move into an approximately 29 square-foot space that comes equipped with a telephone, FAX machine, kanji word processor, air conditioning, television, bed, and closet. (Sorry, the toilet and bath are down the hall.)

TIAOCAO BELL

In China, where traditionally jobs are government-assigned and people are required to stick with them for life, the new fad is *tiaocao* or "jumping to a new workplace," a choice that most youths who were interviewed in Guangzhou said was justified if one disliked his or her job. A Ministry of Labor and Personnel spokesman concedes that although official policy has not changed, *tiaocao* could be useful in better matching jobs and talent.

"LOAN WORDS" AS JOB SPECS

Help-wanted magazines aimed at Japanese young people are filled with jobs parents would never recognize. Here's a representative sample of the so-called "loan words" (along with a translation of what they mean).

Sometimer	No one wanted to work as a part-timer so they changed the name.
Floor Lady	They use to call them hostesses.
Vegetable Staff	Hired hands on farms.
Seater	The person who leads you to your seat in the restaurant.
Close Staff	The people who clean up after everyone else has gone.
Hall Staff	Waiters and waitresses.
Goods Proposer	Sales person.
Stand Girl	Someone who works at a filling station.
Game Instructor	A person who works in a video game center.

From *Asahi Shimbun*, translated by *Japan Free Press*.

SINGAPORE'S SOCIAL SECURITY

CPF—the Central Provident Fund—is Singapore's unique national social security savings scheme. Every working Singaporean or permanent resident is automatically a member. Membership has grown from 180,000 in 1955, when the fund was launched, to 2.08 million in 1990. Employees chip in 24% of their pay and employers put in another 12%. These tax exempt-contributions grow with interest earned, which is compounded annually according to the current market rate.

Each member actually holds three accounts with the CPF: Ordinary, Special, and Medisave. The first two accounts are for old age and contingencies. However, the Ordinary account can be used at any time to buy residential properties under various CPF housing schemes and for home protection and dependents' protection. It can also be used to invest in approved shares, gold, and nonresidential properties to enhance the value of the CPF savings.

The Medisave Account picks up the tab for a member's hospital bills and, when necessary, those incurred by his or her immediate relations. Although CPF is somewhat comparable to social security schemes in the West, the concept and administration of the fund is different. In the Western welfare scheme, funds are usually collected from the working population through taxes, and then used to provide pensions and payments to retirees and other non-income earning persons. Here, whatever is put into the CPF by the member is guaranteed returnable to him with interest.

WOMEN'S DISCRIMINATION IN CHINA

Women are the first to be fired when a company seeks to reduce its labor force and the last to be hired, *China Women's News* reported. The paper charged that more women suffered from job discrimination as employers cut corners in pursuit of profit, and that many firms were reluctant to hire women in the first place because they were entitled to maternity leave and time off to care for sick children.

Taking up the cause of the nude model, China's leading daily for intellectuals, *Guangming,* said that many are subject to social scorn and often have difficulty finding boyfriends or husbands. Although they earned about twice as much as a factory worker (the equivalent of $54 monthly), they had no medical benefits and often couldn't afford to consult a doctor when they caught colds—a frequent occupational hazard.

UNLICENSED VENDORS

Underground economic activities, such as unlicensed street vendors and unlicensed factories, generate about $3.4 billion, according to a Taiwan survey conducted in 1987. The report revealed there were about 160,000 unlicensed vendors operating on the island, more than double the number five years earlier. A vendor starting out earns between $650 and $1,000 per month, but can easily pocket $3,500 monthly once they have learned the trade, according to police. The most successful vendors drive Mercedes-Benzes—even to the police station to pay their fines.

BLUE-WHITE COLLAR WAGE GAP

China's cost of living rose a massive 29.1% between 1988 and 1989, according to the *Economic Daily,* and the gap between blue and white collar income groups is growing, with many teachers earning less than they did 30 years ago. The paper attributes this to the fact that blue collar wages are linked to productivity while those of teachers, doctors, and civil servants are not.

JAPAN'S STREET PEOPLE

Although the one million homeless on America's streets are a frequent subject seen on Japanese television, that country has at least 100,000 homeless of its own—and for roughly the same reasons of unemployment, mental illness, and alcoholism. The country's two largest skid rows, in Tokyo and Osaka, account for perhaps half of the vagrants who are periodically scooped up by police but are usually left alone to be given occasional supplies and meals by Christian missions. Each winter sees the death of a handful from exposure, others from suicide, and their bodies are rarely claimed.

ASIAN MANAGERS

Asian managers tend to both start and finish their careers sooner than their American colleagues, according to a recent study at the University of Michigan, which added that they also smoke and eat less, and thus were as far underweight (from a statistical norm) as Americans were overweight. The study also found that the average salary for an Asian male manager was $27,722 (for women, $19,983) compared to $46,501 (women, $31,702) for an American counterpart, but part of this disparity may be due to age differences, with the Asian usually being up to six years younger.

GRAFT IN CHINA

Despite the almost constant announcement of new campaigns against graft in China, the difficulty of eradicating official corruption was emphasized in a story in the country's *Economic Daily,* which pointed out that it had been endemic in the country at least since the Tang Dynasty in the seventh century. The only difference today, the paper explained, was that officials were even more greedy. It listed examples of officials in one province ordering 10,000 businessmen to buy books the officials had written; a factory manager in Tianjin who said that he and his colleagues were obliged to pay for advertisements celebrating anniversaries; and a manager in Taiyuan who said he and his staff were charged for "training classes" they didn't attend. *The People's Daily* reported the case of officials who went to inspect a forest in the remote northeast devastated by fire and who stopped off first to buy 121 new cars so they could travel the bumpy roads in comfort.

MAID IN CHINA

One profession in which it's still easy to get a job in China is domestic service, especially in the city of Guangzhou, where rising incomes have made it possible for increasing numbers of successful business people to hire maids to look after their homes and children. The evening paper *Yangcheng Wanbao* reported that the city's Women's Federation had 1,200 people on the waiting list for maids and that when 40 women from China's poorest province, Guangxi, arrived in the city they found employers competing for their services as soon as they stepped off the bus. The Federation suggested that the shortage could be alleviated by bringing retired people back into the workforce.

WHEN FAN HITS THE EFFLUENT

When Fan Zhengyu, a peasant employed in Shandong province cleaning out public toilets, noticed that the excrement was going to waste, he invested in a mechanical digger to start a business selling the effluent as a fertilizer to melon growers. He has increased his meager income 20-fold.

FARMING FADING IN TAIWAN

Farming is a fading industry in Taiwan, where increasingly rural youths are taking up jobs in industry in urban areas according to a demographic survey by a professor at National Taiwan University. This emigration of the labor force has caused serious labor shortages in the countryside, reports Professor Chen Hsihuang, and in the long run will harm the country's agricultural development.

SINGAPORE'S PAWNBROKERS

Singapore pawnbrokers' registered income rose 12.4% from a year earlier to $207 million in the four months to April 1988, according to Singapore's Department of Statistics. Loans totaled $106.8 million and redemptions came to $104.7 million. Interest rates on such loans are restricted to 1.5%.

THE PERFECT STEREOTYPES

Japanese between 40 and 45 years old are perfect stereotypes, according to a 1989 survey by the Japanese Prime Minister's office. They work hard with no thought of promotion and hope to work on after retiring. The survey was conducted among 2,186 people born between 1945 and 1949, or just after World War II. Over 80% of them said they were happy, but more than 50% said they were stressed and 60% were worried about growing old. Of the respondents, 36% of the men said they worked more than 55 hours a week and more than 75% said they worked more than 45 hours a week.

INDONESIA'S UNEMPLOYMENT TIME BOMB

Unemployment in Indonesia, the largest country in Southeast Asia, could become a social time-bomb by the mid-1990s unless the government takes drastic steps, noted Bohmer Pasaribu, chairman of the Indonesian Workers Federation. He said the work force of almost 73 million was expected to grow to 86 million by 1995; and while the government officially estimated unemployment at 2.2% in 1987, what he called "disguised unemployment' stood much higher at 111 million. He made his remarks after the World Bank's an-nual report on Indonesia, which warned that unemployment in the cities could reach threatening proportions if job creation does not keep pace with population growth.

A tragic incident in 1988 when half a dozen people were trampled to death and 35 injured as 50,000 job applicants broke down a fence in East Java's Surabaya pointed up the unemployment problem. The crowd, some of whose members had camped out all night for the chance to hand in applications for 1,200 government jobs, demonstrated that the job situation in Indonesia "has reached a critical point," said the former chairman of the country's Labor Federation Agus Sudono.

KEEP ON TRUCKIN'

Starting salaries for truck drivers in Japan is about $3,800. That's because trucking companies are in dire straights, according to the *Nihon Keizai Shimbun*. "Unlike manufacturers, they can't use robots or illegal aliens." After three months of training, a driver at Tokyo trucking company Sagawa Express can bring home as much as $5,400 a month.

MADONNAS AT THE WHEEL

Tokyo taxis carry upward to 1.6 million passengers a day. Most of them are men. According to the Ministry of Transportation, there were 2,064 women drivers in all of Japan in 1987, but only 23 worked in Tokyo. The Tokyo Taxi Cab Association has launched a "Madonna Campaign" to recruit more women drivers, and projects as many as 10,000 women taxi drivers in Tokyo by the year 2000. The push for women drivers is on because taxi companies are hard pressed to fill their vacancies with men. As an inducement, women are being allowed to drive part-time.

4

❖

LIFE ON THE RIM

ASIA'S WORLD ORIGINS

THE EXTENDED ASIAN FAMILY

Some 400 years ago, the English explorer Martin Frobisher led an expedition to Greenland and Baffin Island in search of the theoretical Northwest Passage around Canada to the Pacific. One of Frobisher's captains, Christopher Hall, found the Eskimos near enough to Asians as to make no difference. He wrote: "They be like Tartars, with long blacke haire, broad faces and flatte noses, and tawnie in colour, wearing Seale skinnes."

The Eskimos, of course, not only look like but *are* Asians, the ancestors of these original, true Americans having migrated from Siberia across the Bering Strait land-bridge some 15,000 years ago. That epic advancement of the human frontier in prehistory says quite a bit in itself about Asia as a seedbed for important geographical contacts and cultural cross-fertilizations. Right up to the launch of European colonialism 500 years ago—an explosion propelled, in large part, by Chinese-invented gunpowder—Asia was the authentic middle of the world: a vast heartland where people of all races met and mingled, developed and traded the arts of civilization, and fanned out to the ends of the earth.

More important than what geographers came to define as the continent of Asia, however, is what the word "Asian" has meant historically and means today. Until comparatively recently, few people in Asia thought of themselves as "Asian," The word was of European manufacture, a convenient label for the grab-bag of lands and societies beyond early Europe's horizons. An English explorer in the 1570s could confidently see Greenlanders as Asians not only because of the ethnic connection with "Tartars" but because, in a practical sense, Europe was prepared to see everything and everyone outside its home turf as "Asia." The irony is that today, a generation after the close of the European imperial adventure, history in terms of this perspective is coming full circle.

Not only is the continent of Asia reemerging as the full-blooded engine of the world that it once was; not only are other non-European peoples turning to this center for new ideas and inspiration; in the fullest sense, this restoration of an older pattern of human com-

merce and identity turned the European view of the outside world on its head. A Hong Kong filmgoer can react with a glimmer of recognition of American Indians because Asians are aware of what being ethnic Asian means. Beyond a new consciousness of physical kinships, a true definition of "Asia" today might just as well be what the word originally implied. It's everything outside the European tradition, which burst on a shocked world for a few centuries and tried to shape it in an artificial mould. Asia, in short, extends not just from the Urals and Suez to the Pacific. It means most of the world.

It's probably a safe bet that Africans and Latin Americans won't begin referring to themselves and one another as "Asians" anytime soon. But the appeal of the many eco-

The Asia-Pacific Region:

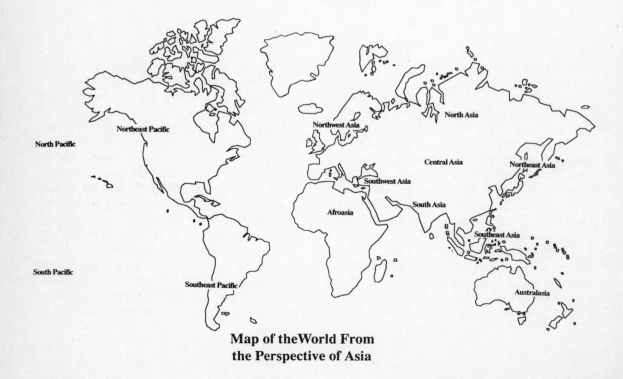

Map of the World From the Perspective of Asia

11-6 Housing Conditions in Japan[a)]
(1973—1988)

	1973	1978	1983	1988
No. of dwellings (1,000)	31,059	35,451	38,607	42,036
No. of households (1,000)	29,651	32,835	35,197	37,851
No. of dwellings per household	1.05	1.08	1.10	1.11
Ownership ratio (%)	59.2	60.4	62.4	61.4
Floor space per dwelling (m²)	77.14	80.28	85.92	89.90
No. of rooms per dwelling	4.15	4.52	4.73	4.87
No. of tatamis per dwelling[b)]	23.98	26.96	28.60	30.70
No. of persons per room	0.87	0.77	0.71	0.66

a) All Japan. b) One *tatami* mat ≒ 1.62m² (1.8m × 0.9m).
Source: Prime Minister's Office, Japan.

nomic success stories in Asia proper is verifiably reorienting their sights nowadays away from the Western cultural stamp that was impressed upon them in recent history. Not only is Japanese investment pouring into countries like Mexico and Brazil, for example, but the receivers are looking in turn to the Japanese miracle as a possible model of political and economic development to emulate.

The president of Mexico, Carlos Salinas de Gortari, is a technocrat who is positively bullish on everything Japanese—to the extent of sending his three children to the Mexican-Japanese School in Mexico City. African countries looking for more workable technologies than what the West can provide are turning toward such newly industrialized Asian economies as Taiwan and South Korea for help in development. Even the Soviets, beyond all their new diplomatic overtures to Asia as a way of building bridges more profitable to the Soviet economy, are studying ways of revamping their entire Leninist system along more Asian lines.

And the United States, for all its white ma-

jority and cultural inheritances from Europe, is now in the curious—not to say, paradoxical —position of being post-war capital of Western power and, at the same time, a more Asian-oriented society itself. No less an embodiment of American might than the retired U.S. Pacific Fleet commander, Admiral James A. Lyons Jr., says, "The compass needle of history has swung away from the Mediterranean and Atlantic civilizations and is pointing toward Asia. By 1990, 62% of the world's population will live around the Pacific Rim. The Pacific region already accounts for 60% of the world's GNP (gross national product, the value of all goods and services). Our trade with Asia is nearly 40% greater than that with Europe. The next 100 years will be the century of the Pacific."

It may be arbitrary to call the United States more inherently "Asian." But the more mixed the U.S. becomes ethnically, in terms of blacks, Latin Americans, and new trans-Pacific settlers, the greater it conforms to the pattern of human traffic more characteristic of what the word "Asia" originally meant than anything in the European experience. What America is becoming today, in fact, is more and more the vindication of Christopher Columbus's "mistake" in his calling the New World "the Indies." What the great navigator implied by that word, of course—and what it more precisely meant in getting attached to the "Dutch East Indies," today Indonesia—is the broader sense of "Asia." He may have been technically incorrect in terming aboriginal Americans "Indians," but the fact that they were just one other people off the European map arguably justified the name after all.

In the Soviet Union, the elevation of Mikhail Gorbachev to the Kremlin leadership in 1985 brought to power a crowd that saw virtue in learning from the Asian experience. Gorbachev's outreach to Asia in 1986, along with his renewed calls in 1988, while traveling through Siberia, marked a psychological turning point. "The Soviet Union," he said with more pride than Russians have been accustomed to show, "is also an Asian and Pacific country."

The Soviets have a lot of territory to prove that remark. Like Marxism, however, the very notion of "Asia," not to mention "Asianness," is a Western product, the brainchild of a European outlook on the world. The word itself came from the ancient Semitic civilizations of Mesopotamia and the eastern Mediterranean. In the Akkadian empire, *asu* meant "to go out—to rise," and had special reference to the suns. In Hebrew, a linguistic cousin, the word was *yatzah* and had the same application. It is likely that Greek merchants of 3,000 years ago first picked up this useful term when a Phoenician counterpart voiced it while jerking a thumb toward lands in the direction of the rising sun. Early on, in any case, at the time of the Hittite empire in Anatolia (now Turkey) a land of Assuwa is mentioned on what is the present-day Turkish coast directly east of Greece. Much later this became the Roman province of Asia.

The Greeks had a word for it, and they used it with a vengeance, for the early Hellenes were acutely conscious of their own values in contrast to those of outsiders. The Trojan war had to be fought against those Asians across the water. Later, in the classical age of Athens, the great dramatist Aeschylus stressed in his play *The Persians* that the warriors from the east constituted an Asian challenge to Europe. It became known as "the quarrel of the continents." "Asian" was applied indiscriminately, and the spiritual heirs of Greece and Rome eventually extended the term as far as it could go.

Europeans saw Asia as somehow embodying an organic whole, the precise counterpart of everything they felt to be their own special attributes, the *yin* to their *yang*. Europeans were scarcely unique in a tendency to lump outsiders together, of course. But they were the first to enforce such attitudes in an overpowering way *on* outsiders with the aid of ships fitted with cannon and shot. By the time the British Empire was rolling in high gear in 1821, the author Thomas De Quincey could describe, in his *Confessions of an English Opium-Eater*, everything that the myth of Asia represented to the Western fancy. His doped-out nightmares of "oriental imagery and mythological tortures" inspired, he wrote, "unimaginable horror."

In "the Asiatic scenery" of his opium dreams, he "brought together all creatures, birds, beasts, reptiles, all trees and plants, usages and appearances, that are found in all tropical regions, and assembled them together in China and Hindoostan. From kindred feelings, I soon brought Egypt and her gods under the same law. I was stared at, hooted at, grinned at, chattered at, by monkeys, by paroquets, by cockatoos. I ran into pagodas, and was fixed for centuries at the summit, or in secret rooms; I was the idol—I was the priest; I was worshipped, I was sacrificed, I fled from the wrath of Brama through all the forests of Asia: Vishnu hated me; Seeva lay in wait for me. I came suddenly under Isis and Orisis . . . I was kissed, with cancerous kisses, by crocodiles, and was laid, confounded with all unutterable abortions, amongst reeds and Nilotic mud."

DeQuincey explained where all these "awful images and associations" came from: "The very antiquity of Asiatic things, of their institutions, histories—above all, of their mythologies &c.—is so impressive that to me the vast age of the race and name overpowers the sense of youth in the individual."

And that explains a lot, for what the term Asia encompassed in the European mind did in fact include very nearly all of the world's oldest civilizations from Sumer and Egypt to the Indus Valley and Yellow River, from Babylon and Phoenicia to the Medes and Persians, the Mauryan and Gupta dynasties of India and the Han of China. Had he known about them, De Quincey would have thrown in the Olmecs and Maya of Mexico and Incas of Peru. This catch-all category of races and cultures also in fact included the birthplaces of all the world's great religions: Judaism, Hinduism, Taoism, Buddhism, Christianity, and Islam. While never thinking of themselves as "Asian"—indeed, never thinking of themselves as anything but Chinese, Khmers, Bengalis, Arabs, Malays or Ethiopians—these cultures did, however, share an early jump in reaching out to one another in contacts across vast land routes and oceans.

Aside from the Ice Age migrants from Asia who peopled the Americas, was there any later contact across this immense ocean, too? It can remain only speculation. But the original Asians who embarked on daunting voyages to populate Oceania in prehistory have some curious inheritances. The sweet potato, cultivated originally in Peru at least 1,900 years ago, was in Hawaii by the year 1250. The Incas of Peru called it *cumar*. The Polynesian name is *kumara*. The seed of a species of cotton cultivated in the Indus Valley some 4,000 years ago seems to have traveled the other way, getting hybridized with a native American strain. Birds are unlikely to have carried them halfway round the globe, especially since they don't eat cotton seeds.

Some distinctive architectural decor of ancient Peru also appeared in China and nowhere else about a century earlier. Temples in the form of stepped pyramids appeared in Cambodia and Mexico's Yucatan Peninsula at roughly the same time. Two twelfth-century structures, Cambodia's Angkor Wat and Mexico's Chichen Itza, both feature lotus motifs, vaulted galleries, and half-columns at doorways. As two scholars of the subject reasoned: "There is no psychological law which could have caused the peoples on both sides of the Pacific to stylize the lotus plant in the same manner and to make it surge from the mouth of a jawless demon's head, to invent the parasol and use it as a sign of rank, and to invent the same complicated game. There is no explanation other than the assumption of cultural relationship."

Some grounds exist, then, to assume a very extensive system of cultural cross-currents indeed. The peoples who developed it would not have called it Asia. They would have called it, if anything, simply "the world." But the challenge from the West, drawing sharp distinctions in its self-defined "quarrel of the continents," made societies in the strictly defined landmass of Asia aware, in their own acute way, of the term's significance. It provided a very broad, ethnically ill-defined but nonetheless concrete identity to a world struggling to rediscover its many particular destinies after a staggering punch.

"Asian" is only what the ancient Greeks meant when they used such interchangeable names as "barbarians" and "Scythians" to define every people from beyond the Black Sea. The Russia that came to adopt a Western heresy in self-defense framed its choices in less abstract terms a century ago. Russians then were fierce with debate over whether they in fact belonged to the Western tradition. Though the Slavic languages are among the many closely related European tongues, the debate began resurfacing as recently as 1972, when the anthropologist V. P. Alekseyev emphasized "the importance of the role of the *inozemtsy,* or non-Slavs, in the ethnic origin of the Russian people."

He was referring to Ural-Altaic peoples, in particular the Finns, who have at least some ethnic kinship with the Mongoloid peoples. Alekseyev concluded that the Russians were "slavic Finns," accent on the second term.

"Who are we?" he asked. "We are Scythians, that is to say Asiatics," The line deliberately echoed a famous verse, "The Scythians," by the Russian poet Alexander Blok (1880 to 1921): "You have your millions. We are numberless, Numberless, numberless. Try doing/ Battle with us! Yes, we are Scythians! Yes,/ Asiatics with greedy eyes slanting!"

And yet today that undertone of self-contempt is turning into a banner of pride. Distinctive to the region, says Yoshida Tamochi, adviser to the Industrial Bank of Japan, is a "highly educated workforce," an asset that "doubtless will be able to offer more value-added products in the maturing division of labor in future." More value-added trade orientations and political solutions as well, perhaps. Says Tsuzuki Kensuke of the Japanese Foreign Ministry's Asian Bureau, "In spite of, or perhaps because of, the diversity of Asia, we feel compelled to look at Asia as an entity or a bloc, a view we have preferred to avoid until now." That change has been triggered by what Tsuzuki recognizes as a shift by many Asian countries into a new stage of development. "We have been making policies as an individual nation. From now on, we have to keep a concept of the region in view."

Yusuf Wanandi, director of the Center for Strategic and International Studies in Jakarta, sees "the pragmatism of Asian leaderships" as crucial. "It helped Asian nations open up and make realistic compromises. It would be counterproductive if we closed to the other parts of the world. Asia's economic growth will be the engine of global growth." This view extends to the United States. In a book advocating American strategies for the 1990s, Roger Brooks of Washington's conservative Heritage Foundation urged the incoming president, George Bush, to switch the focus of foreign policy. He called on Bush to "formally tilt the primary U.S. focus away from the Atlantic and toward the Pacific" to lay the groundwork for the next century.

Americans have seen the signs. When Japan's Sony Corp. bought CBS Records in 1987 for $2 billion, it managed to get involved in a major institution of U.S. pop culture, a coup that in effect made Akio Morita, Sony's

---

JOURNEYS: A FILCHED FIRST

Quick now, who was the first man to sail around the world? Wrong! Not Magellan, who only got as far as Cebu before running fatally afoul of the local authorities. And not Basque navigator Juan Sebastian de Elcano, who guided the *Vittoria* back to Spain, arriving in 1522 to an ecstatic reception and, from the Emperor Charles V, a new coat of arms featuring the globe and the words, "You were the first to encircle me."

No, the first to go the distance was one Henrique of the East Indies, who had been taken to Lisbon via Africa some years earlier. In 1519 he shipped out with Magellan, who rounded South America. So when the little fleet called at Henrique's home, he had come full circle. But beyond a quite explicit mention in contemporary chronicles, nothing is known about him. He performed no feats of navigation—for which Elcano fairly earned his escutcheon, if not the motto. Since Henrique was only an Asian, he couldn't expect a place in Eurocentric history books. Still, he made the journey, and it is time to set the record straight.

Reprinted from *Asiaweek,* December 16, 1988.

longtime chairman, the paymaster of no less a rock superstar than Michael Jackson, the very emblem of American dynamism in much of the world. Of course, Jackson lives in California, which is becoming more Asianized by the year anyway. Scythians? Barbarians? "Greedy eyes"? No, just pragmatic and successful. Asians are merely restoring the dispensation of their forefathers—when that outlandish term "Asia" meant, in effect, the world.

Excerpted from *Asiaweek*, December 16, 1988.

ARCHEOLOGY

STONE AGE TOOLSHED

Australian archaeologists have reported finding a huge Stone Age "factory" in the Outback, where some 2,000 years ago aborigines crafted stone blades and cutting tools for barter. The site at Tiboobura, 850 kms northwest of Sydney, is so large that archaeologists believe its output may have formed the basis for a local export industry. According to Dan Witte, archeologist for the Government's National Parks and Wildlife Service of New South Wales, the Stone Age toolmakers most likely traded for the mildly hallucinogenic pituri, a drug reportedly used by nomadic aborigines to counteract hunger pains during their long treks between hunting grounds. The find followed the discovery of a fragment of a human bone in central Australia that has been dated at 60,000 years old, pushing back the date of human occupation of Australia by 20,000 years. Today, aborigines number about 160,000, almost one percent of Australia's 16.5 million population.

RAIN THREATENS EXCAVATED SITE

The famous excavation site of the Peking Man has become endangered because of rain erosion and cave-ins, according to a report by the United Nations Educational, Scientific and Cultural Organization (UNESCO). The Peking Man lived about 600,000 years ago on some hills in Zhoukoudouidian about 50 kms southwest of Beijing. Most of the early excavations were carried out in the 1920s, but scientists believe that only half of the site has been fully excavated. UNESCO has recommended placing polyethylene sheets covered with earth on the walls of some caves to keep them from crumbling.

"A dead leopard leaves its skin, a dead man his name."

—*Chinese proverb*

MONGOL FRESCOES STOLEN

One of China's biggest art heists—part of a recent wave of thefts—occurred at the Magao Grottos at Dunhuang, when valuable frescos were stolen in 1989. According to the *People's Daily,* the frescos, measuring about one sq. meter, were cut into five pieces by robbers who broke into a closed cave dating from the Yuan Dynasty (1279–1368), when the Mongols ruled China. One of the pieces was broken on the spot. Only 492 grottos with frescos remain intact in China today, although most of them are closed to the public. Most of the treasures they once contained—including ancient Buddhist texts—were removed by European, Japanese and American explorers in the 1900s. Relics smuggling has become rampant in China.

"STUPID" DINOSAUR FOUND

Chinese and Canadian scientists unearthed the remains of Asia's largest known dinosaur in the Gobi desert in 1987. The animal was approximately 30 meters long, strictly vegetarian and "as stupid as a modern chicken," scientists reported in a press conference. The team unearthed a dinosaur's graveyard in an area of desert said to be haunted by ghosts of an imperial Chinese army annihilated in battle more than 2,000 years ago, according to Canadian scientist Dale Russell. He added that growing evidence suggested that the Gobi reptiles, like other dinosaurs, were wiped out after a huge asteroid collided with the earth causing climactic changes that the animals could not survive.

THE SEX CULT

Recent discoveries by Chinese archeologists in Inner Mongolia reveal that 3,000 years ago people in the region elevated sex to cult status. Hundreds of ancient frescoes show nude figures and sexual acts, many with more than two participants.

GRAVES ATTRACT THIEVES

Tomb-robbing is still in style around China's ancient capital city of Luoyang where for thousands of years dynasties buried their dead. *China Daily* reported that 1,400 tombs have been desecrated and that, in a two-month period, 500 people were arrested for smuggling relics.

ELECTRONIC EXPLORERS

In a novel twist on archeology, Japanese archeologists performed a fiberscopic probe on the inside of a 2.35-meter-long stone coffin at an ancient tumulus in Nara, the country's eighth-century capital (710–784). They discovered a gold crown, a sword with a large ornamental ring on the handle, and other artifacts. An 8-mm-diameter fiberscope was moved at 5-cm increments and rotated 360 degrees at each point so pictures could be taken.

VILLAGE UNDER THE SEA

Chinese fishermen have discovered a sunken village at the bottom of the ocean about 425 miles south of Hong Kong, near the Paracel Islands, which are administered by China, but also claimed by Vietnam. First spotting two Buddhist statues whose heads stuck out from coral reefs in about 60 feet of clear water, divers subsequently found a temple with a pair of stone lions outside its entrance and pottery strewn on the floor. The village, which covers several thousand square feet, dates back to the late Ming Dynasty (1368–1644) or early Ching Dynasty (1644–1911), according to Hong Kong archeologists.

OBSOLETE CHINESE ALPHABET

China is famous for its 5,000-year-old unique writing system which evolved from pictographs. But now the Chinese have unearthed evidence that the ancient Chinese may also have invented an alphabetic script. Qian Yuzhi, an archeologist in Sichuan province, believes that mysterious graphs and signs often found on bronze vessels are a system of alphabetic letters which fell into disuse in ancient China. Sichuan was one of the first areas in China where silkworms were raised and the use of silk was developed. "As these symbols look very much like spiraling silk threads, I call them silk letters," Qian noted in the *Sichuan Cultural Relics* periodical.

FROM DJAKARTA TO JAKARTA

A group of Southeast Asian linguists are succeeding in standardizing Malay, spoken by more than 200 million people. Despite it being among the world's more widely spoken languages, a Malaysian and an Indonesian speaking Malay may not completely understand each other. Malay is spoken also in Brunei and Singapore (where it is called "Bahasa Melayu") and the southern Philippines, while pockets of ethnic Malays in Sri Lanka and Madagascar speak a pidgin version. The new system provides for words to be spelled as they sound. For example, Indonesia's capital "Djakarta" is now spelled "Jakarta."

DICTIONARY COVERS 36 CENTURIES

China's most comprehensive dictionary, listing 51,000 characters, compiled by noted scholar Wan Zhuxi was published in 1988. It lists simplified Chinese characters along with their original complex forms and those taken from inscriptions on bones and tortoise shells dating back to the Shang period (1600 to 1100 B.C.).

RECORDING CHINESE LITERATURE

All Chinese books since the beginning of Chinese history are being recorded on microfilm by the nation's library system, according to *China Daily*. Meanwhile Shenzhen University in South China has put nearly 50,000 Tang dynasty poems on floppy computer diskettes in a project designed to revolutionize the study of Chinese poetry. Now 48,900 poems by 2,200 poets are stored on 95 diskettes that can provide a wealth of information within seconds.

AGRICULTURE

SINGAPORE PIONEERS AGROTECH

Singapore is a pioneer in "agrotech" farming in Asia. Since growing urbanization has, over the last 15 years, steadily encroached on Singapore's farmland, it is estimated that by 1995 only 2,000 hectares of such land will be left for cultivation. Hence, agrotechnology (the application of technology to achieve higher production than conventional farming) is being urgently developed by the government.

As of 1989, there were 49 such high-tech farms cultivating such products as vegetables, orchids, shrimp, aquatic plants, and aquarium fish. The total production value is estimated to reach S$650 million (about U.S.$325 million) by the mid-1990s, when all these parks are in full production. According to Singapore's Primary Production Department, the plan is to establish Singapore as a regional service center for agrotech products.

Farming in Singapore is a highly lucrative

Climate

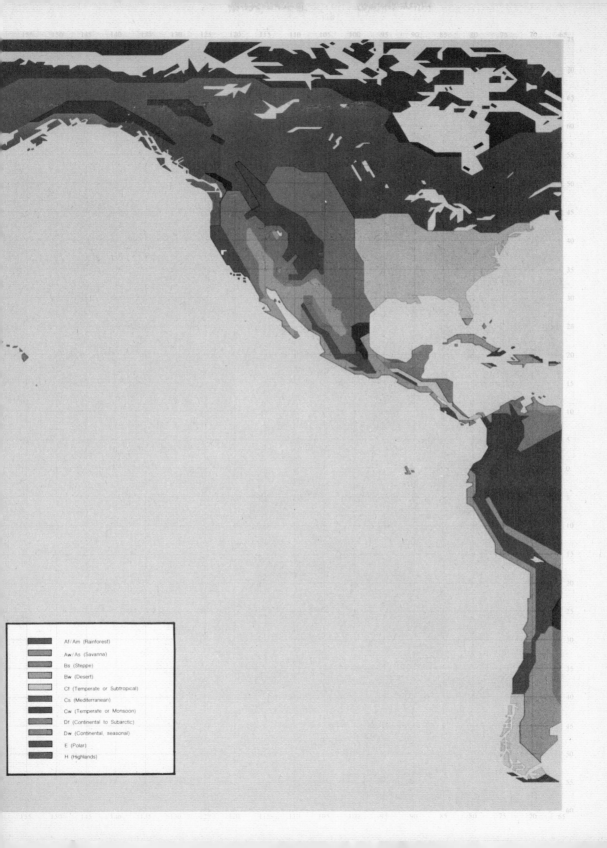

	Af / Am (Rainforest)
	Aw / As (Savanna)
	Bs (Steppe)
	Bw (Desert)
	Cf (Temperate or Subtropical)
	Cs (Mediterranean)
	Cw (Temperate or Monsoon)
	Df (Continental to Subarctic)
	Dw (Continental, seasonal)
	E (Polar)
	H (Highlands)

Agriculture and Fishing

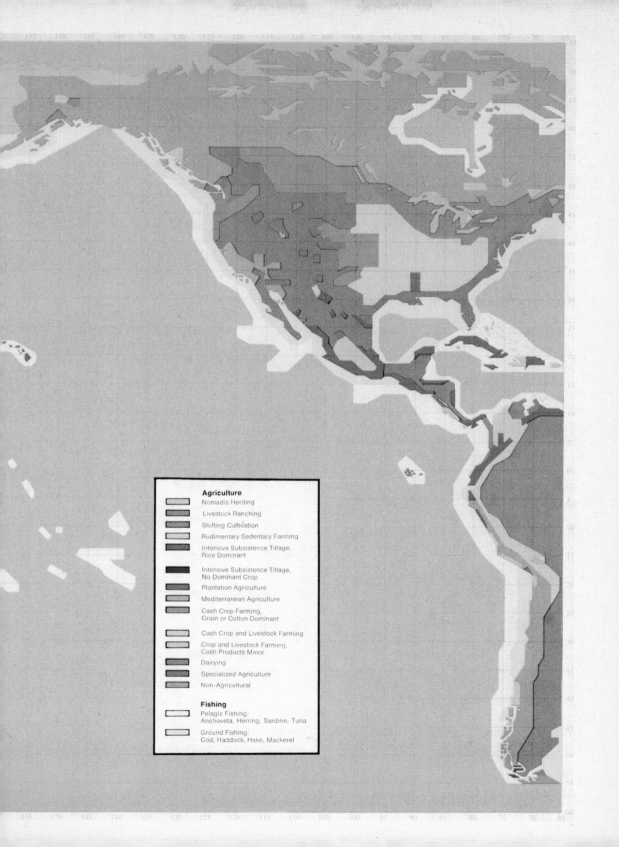

Agriculture

Nomadic Herding

Livestock Ranching

Shifting Cultivation

Rudimentary Sedentary Farming

Intensive Subsistence Tillage,
Rice Dominant

Intensive Subsistence Tillage,
No Dominant Crop

Plantation Agriculture

Mediterranean Agriculture

Cash Crop Farming,
Grain or Cotton Dominant

Cash Crop and Livestock Farming

Crop and Livestock Farming,
Cash Products Minor

Dairying

Specialized Agriculture

Non-Agricultural

Fishing

Pelagic Fishing:
Anchoveta, Herring, Sardine, Tuna

Ground Fishing:
Cod, Haddock, Hake, Mackerel

business. Over the last five years, the sector's output has been about $450 million a year. Singapore's 2.6 million consumers consumed over 107,614 tons of fish, 540 million eggs, 189,120 tons of fresh chilled and frozen meat, and 185,604 tons of fresh vegetables. At the same time, Singapore exports $60 million worth of aquarium fish, $8.5 million of aquatic plants, and $18.4 million of flowers, including cut orchids, ornamentals, and plants.

FLOWER BUSINESS BIG IN JAPAN

Leading Japanese corporations are getting into the business of growing and selling flowers. Nippon Steel sells flowers in a can ("Lucky Cantory") at Y800 (about $6.15). Slag left over from steel production is reduced to something like rock wool and used instead of plant soil. This is put in a ceramic brick with seeds to various flowers. You just water it and watch it grow. It's part of Nippon Steel's "make more use of materials" campaign.

NKK uses biotechnology to create a special planting soil that needs watering only every two or three months. The venture is part of NKK's diversification and personnel reassignment program.

Kurabo Industries set up orchid greenhouses on the site of their defunct plant in Okayama prefecture. Now they have started mail-order sales of quality gifts (Y20,000 to Y50,000, or $153 to $385) plants.

Others have their eyes on orchids as well—including Japan Tobacco, Osaka Gas, Kagome, Onoda Cement, and a number of other large companies.

According to the Ministry of Agriculture, Forestry and Fisheries, "The domestic flower industry totaled but Y138 billion (about $1.06 billion) in 1975, but had burgeoned to Y415 billion (about $3.1 billion) by 1985, a 300% growth rate. At retail prices, the flower industry must be at least a trillion yen (about $7.7 billion) by now."

"In this age of an overabundance of material wealth, more and more people seem to be opting for a slower pace and greater enjoyment of life," the *Yomiuri Shimbun* newspaper concluded. "Flowers are part of that movement, which means that more and more big businesses are going to get in the act because they go where the money is."

AVERAGE RICE YIELDS IN ASIA

(Metric tons per hectare; 1 hectare = 2.47 acres)

Philippines:	2.5
China (PRC):	5.2
Taiwan (ROC):	3.7
Japan:	6.4
North Korea:	6.5
South Korea:	6.4
Vietnam:	2.7

SOURCE: *Fire on the Rim* (A Food First Book, The Institute for Food and Development Policy, San Francisco, 1988).

DOWN-UNDER AGRIBUSINESS

Australia needs to break into the growing Southeast Asian agribusiness sector if it wants to maintain its share of agricultural exports, according to an Australian Foreign Affairs and Trade Department study. The report warned that Australian dairy, fruit, vegetable, live animal, and meat exports to the Association of Southeast Asian Nations (ASEAN) would be coming under increased pressure from Thailand, Malaysia, Indonesia, the Philippines, Singapore, and Brunei. The study urged Australian firms to go into selling "agrotechnology"—agricultural machinery and services in the region.

JAPANESE THINK TANK'S PHILIPPINE SOLUTION

The dire economic situation in the Philippines closely parallels the impoverished conditions in Japan's rural areas during the 1930s just prior to the Pacific War, according to Jiro Tokuyama, senior adviser to the Mitsui Research Institute, a prominent Japanese think tank.

"Japan also was a country of haves and have-nots just 50 years ago," noted Tokuyama in a recent article in the *Yomiuri Shimbun,* a leading Japanese newspaper. In his piece, Tokuyama cited the land reforms which the U.S. Occupation Forces carried out in Japan after World War II as being a model for the Philippines to follow today.

"In combination with other U.S. changes —dissolution of the *zaibatsu* (like the huge monopolies which existed in the Philippines under the Marcos regime, and which still exist in a less evident form today), a graduated income tax system, and heavy taxes on property, the land reform became the foundation of Japanese democracy and equitable income distribution . . . Thanks to these policies, Japan steered clear of socialism and communism and created an affluent, egalitarian society."

Tokuyama also noted that it was the disaffected young Japanese officer corps who— outraged by the lot of impoverished Japanese farmers—turned to radical solutions such as assassinations and coups to push their social reforms. The senior military leaders exploited this youthful extremism to gain control of the civilian government—a danger which also exists strongly in the Philippines today.

Tokuyama remains skeptical of the Philippine government's recently announced blueprint for land reform. "[President Aquino] and many of her Cabinet members hail from the landed gentry," he notes. "To stabilize the dangerous political situation, Mrs. Aquino must carry out the same sweeping transfer of land that occurred in Japan. A commitment to land reform would have to start with relinquishing her own huge holdings. Is she willing to go that far?"

NOMADS PAY RENT

For the first time in history, nomadic tribesmen in Inner Mongolia's Ar Horqin county are being introduced to the alien custom of paying rent for the use of land on which their livestock graze. Overuse of the shrinking grasslands by nearly one million additional sheep and goats plus devastating sand erosion have transformed what were once lush pastures into a near-desert. The new measures should make it uneconomical to overgraze the pastures beyond a set quota.

RIM REVIEW

FIRE ON THE RIM

Agrarian reform is so long overdue in the Philippines that, in addition to being a root cause of the country's extreme poverty and a continual spur to the armed movements which still persist after half a century, it is holding back the entire economy. That is the premise of *Fire on the Rim* (Institute of Food & Development Policy, 1989) by Joseph Collins, a leading expert on world hunger and third-world development. Dr. Collins is co-founder of the San Francisco-based institute which is dedicated to investigating and exposing the root causes of hunger in a world of plenty. His latest book includes 50 interviews with planters, military officers, rebels, priests, and others in a country where 70% of the schoolchildren are malnourished and the average rice yield per acre is half that of China's.

In his analysis of the situation, Collins points out that the cause of hunger in the Philippines—a country whose population is doubling every 25 years and where almost half the citizens are under 16—is not lack of food, but rather its inequitable distribution; that enormous quantities of food are shipped out of the country to make absentee landlords rich rather than being consumed by the very people who produce it. In a country where more than 70% of the population is rural, seven out of every 10 Filipinos who depend on farming for their livelihood do not own the land they till. The proportion of rural families living in poverty rose from 48% in 1971 to 64% in 1985, and in fertile Negros—the country's fourth largest province, where 98% of the people were totally deprived of land ownership—those at the "extreme poverty" level comprised an astonishing 82%. In these facts lies the solution to the problem: land reform, without any political stability and peace, is impossible.

But land reform—"the essential springboard for economic development"—is a subject that has been honored only in the breach for most of this century. It was first brought up by the U.S., which took possession of the archipelago in 1898 from the Spanish occupiers who, in turn, had expropriated what had basically been public land through their merchants, military officials, and religious orders.

At the turn of this century the U.S. Congress purchased large agricultural estates ostensibly to sell to small holders, at the same time giving U.S. citizens and corporations the right to buy land. Predictably, very few peasants could afford to buy, notwithstanding their mystification about why they had to pay the U.S. government for land that had been stolen from their ancestors.

"These and other land reform laws under American rule in fact worsened the land problem for the majority of Filipinos," explains Collins, pointing out that the so-called independence that the U.S. granted to the country in 1946 "was certainly not economic independence," merely consolidating the stranglehold of well-financed American corporations. Simultaneously it robbed the Philippine government of the power to regulate imports and currency exchange, "essential tools for any government that might seek to develop the country's economic plans beyond exporting low-value unprocessed agricultural goods and poorly paid labor."

The arrival of President Corazon Aquino presaged hopes that after 10 ineffectual land reform measures and 43 grandiose presidential decrees "that litter Philippine history," genuine land reform might take place. But, writes Collins, this has not been so because "the 19-page, fine-print land reform law is so full of limitations, exemptions, loopholes, and escape clauses for landowners that it is toothless." (Mrs. Aquino and her family are owners themselves of a 15,000-acre sugarcane plantation with its own mill on Luzon Island.)

One of the new law's exemptions, for example, is the provision that allows each landowner to keep at least 12.5 acres, to distribute an additional 7.5 acres to each child over 15 and to have a three-month grace period to transfer land titles—a period, Collins suggests, when it would be a simple matter to parcel out their land to proxy owners.

Successful land reform measures in Japan, Taiwan, and South Korea have restricted ownership to at most 7.5 acres (3 hectares) which is about the size of a typical plot in the Philippines. The obvious result of this "reform," Collins explains, is that there will be far too little land available for redistribution to benefit any more than a tiny portion of the 8.5 million landless Filipinos. CRAR, a 2.5 million-member coalition of farmworker organizations, joined in denouncing the law as "not even a step forward."

ARTS

EAST–WEST ARTS FUSION

There is a growing fusion of creative forces emerging on the Pacific Rim as a result of growing East–West contacts, notes Max Wyman, arts columnist at The Province *newspaper in Vancouver, B.C.*

"The two cultures of East and West have existed in parallel for centuries, always influencing and fascinating one another," says the Polish composer Zygmunt Krause, president of the International Society for Contemporary Music. "I hope we can all find beauty within both systems: the older one from Asia, representing tradition and amazing vitality, and the younger one from the West, exploring new ideas and in search of inspiration."

When we think, for instance, of the Peking Opera, we tend to think of an arcane and remote art form that has little to communicate to the West. By the 1970s, in fact, it had become so hidebound by tradition that it was even losing Chinese audiences.

But in Taiwan, Kuo Hsiao-chuang has worked with her 10-year-old Ya-Yin Ensemble to make the artform relevant to modern audiences by eliminating much redundant repetition, tightening narrative, making acting more realistic, and introducing such theatrical effects as subtitles (lines from the text projected by slides onto the theater's proscenium arch, a North American invention, first introduced by the Canadian Opera Company in Toronto) and sophisticated lighting and staging. The result: entertainment that both Chinese and Western audiences can appreciate.

The once-sacred Japanese tradition of Noh and Kabuki theater production is also considered fair game these days for revisionists. And experimental theater directors are experimenting with artistic cross-breeding on a massive scale; productions of Western classics like "Medea" or "Macbeth" come complete with Western-style scores and operatic acting.

The contemporary Western idiom is noticeably affecting the music of the Orient. The influence of jazz techniques on traditional music in Thailand dates back to the 1950s, when clarinetist Benny Goodman was the first Westerner to introduce jazz to the Thais, teaching jazz stylings to the Thai king.

In recent decades, Californian Bruce Gaston has worked with the traditional Fong Nam Siamese wind and percussion ensemble to explore the interaction between Thai music and Western styles, both jazz and classical.

Chinese composers are also beginning to use Western contemporary compositional techniques as tools to express their ideas about traditional Oriental concerns. In his work, "Taiji," for example, Shanghai composer Zhao Xiao-Sheng has used Western 12-tone compositional technique to explore the structure of the ancient Chinese book of divination, the *I Ching,* allocating note-values to the sounds made by 12 sacred Chinese bells and using those values to express the *I Ching* pictograms.

The effect of all these modifications has been a marked increase in accessibility to the traditional artforms of Asia. There has also been a corresponding increase in the ability of Western audiences to understand not only the music, but also the cultural sources from which these artforms derive, along with their role in the societies in which they continue to exist.

But it is by no means a one-directional trend. Southern Crossings, an Australian trio of musicians trained in the Western classical style, explore the musical links between East and West.

Playing a mix of three dozen instruments from around the world—including the Jingle Johnny—an instrument consisting of a long pole with beer-bottle caps attached to it, also known as a lagerphone—they produce an entrancing kind of world—music: not a pastiche, not a gluing-together of separate elements, but a fresh synthesis of influences that speaks in a totally cross-cultural way about the human reasons for making music.

The work of composer Alexina Louie, a third-generation Chinese-Canadian, represents another aspect of the Western approach to this synthesis. Her orchestral work, "Music for a Thousand Autumns," attempts to address the question of East–West musical cross-fusion in direct terms. She wrote it at the end of a period when she was exploring Oriental philosophy and musical concepts, and it uses as its *cantus firmus* a traditional Chinese melody she learned as a child.

She calls the work "a meditation on the ancient melody, but in twentieth-century musical language: myself, speaking about my heritage."

But as more and more composers find themselves drawn to take part in that search for a new beginning, Alexina Louie emphasizes that it is not enough simply to glue elements from one culture onto elements of another to create a superficial Chinoiserie effect.

What is important for Western composers, she says, is to explore not just the prettiness and delicacy that we traditionally associate with the Orient, but the depths of contrast and tension in Oriental art: to consider the *yin* as well as the *yang,* and "to use the synthesis to best advantage to speak what is in your soul."

Michael Atherton, of the music group Southern Crossings, believes that more and more Western-culture countries are examining who they are, in terms of cultural influence—and recognizing that they are, after all, different from Europe, and that Asian influences are part of that difference.

"But the most important part of this," says his colleague John Napier, "is the unconscious aspect of this cross-over, the process of gradual absorption that goes on."

"It's important that we don't simply borrow the sounds," emphasizes Atherton. "We listen and learn and make the music our own. And while we have to be mindful as artists that we stay clear of cultural homogeneity, it is also evident that, these days, the musicians of the world are closer than they have ever been."

Composer Chou Wen-chung, born in China but now a U.S. citizen, says he believes the world is in a period of musical stagnation and must look for a new beginning.

The old orders of East and West, he said, will not survive long; there has to be a new order, the beginning of a new cycle, that grows from a genuine international coming together.

John Thompson, artistic coordinator of Hong Kong's biennial Festival of Asian Arts, worries about the potential within this process for the destruction of traditional arts of the Orient—but he also believes the Western influence in Asia is going to be unstoppable.

"It's going to be there," he says, "and turning a blind eye isn't going to help. But what's important is that scholars document the music that exists. Because I do think that as people become more developed—as material circumstances improve—they become more aware of their own traditions, and this will lead to brilliant new artforms."

But Zygmunt Krause sounds a note of caution. He believes we are only at the beginning of the potential for this kind of cultural cross-fusion, and is guarded about the benefits that might have accrued. One of the basic problems, he says, is that Western-style contemporary composition is being introduced to countries whose composers are unused to contemporary music—countries that are not musically developed in the European sense. So that to build a musical culture comparable to that of the West, they are going to have to start from simple things and, essentially, compositional standards are going to have to be lowered.

On the other hand, not many Western composers have approached Oriental music from the other direction—and those few have usually only picked up the surface elements.

What he dreams of is an academy at which Western composers can study Eastern musical influences at the highest level. As a first step, he has organized an international seminar for young composers in Yugoslavia, dealing specifically with the East–West theme.

But ultimately, he says, "East or West notwithstanding, the beautiful object can only be created by the great artist—and these we can never fit into patterns."

Max Wyman is the author of The Royal Winnipeg Ballet: The First Forty Years *(Doubleday, 1978); the first full-length history of dancing in Canada,* Dance Canada: An Illustrated History *(Douglas & McIntyre, 1989); and the biography of ballerina Evelyn Hart (McClelland & Stewart, 1991). He continues to monitor the fusion of Pacific Rim artforms.*

JAPAN'S "NOBELS"

First winners of the "Praemium Imperiale" awards, financed by Japan's Fujisankei Communications International, Inc. as that country's equivalent of the Nobel Prizes, were painters Willem De Kooning and David Hockney; architect I. M. Pei; composer and conductor Pierre Boulez; director Michael Carne; and sculptor Umberto Mastroianni. Winners receive $100,000. For the first few years of the awards Japanese artists are not eligible.

HONG KONG CULTURE SEEKS TAX RELIEF

In relatively culture-starved Hong Kong, where world-class performers are few and far between, companies which sponsor arts events can earn considerable public gratitude if what they choose to support gives them sufficient exposure. But unlike in the United States, where companies donating up to 5% of their earnings can claim tax relief, there are no comparable tax breaks and potential corporate sponsors say this must change if the community ever expects to benefit from large-scale largesse. At present, the Hong Kong government spends about $20 million per year supporting local arts groups and presenting visiting performers, with the shortfall being made up by corporate sponsors, usually multinationals. But there is never enough to go around.

THE JAPANESE ART OF SELLING ART

After the spate of stock-market scandals and insider-trading incidents in Japan in recent years, attention is now being focused on Japan's "inside" way of conducting business in other areas as well. Apparently, insiders' influence-peddling extends not just to the world of high finance, but also to Japan's estimated $200 million art market.

Behind-the-scenes deal-making and manipulation of the art market in Japan is even more blatant than in the West, according to recent revelations. It is not uncommon for artists or galleries to make expensive gifts or to pay money to influential reviewers in exchange for reviews, which can make or break an art exhibit.

"Five years ago, it cost $500 here for a favorable review in a reputable magazine, $2,500 for the full treatment," according to author Donald Richie, the foremost Western authority on Japanese film and a longtime Tokyo resident. Richie spoke in Tokyo during a forum on Japan's art scene which was sponsored by *Nihon Keizai Shimbun,* Japan's leading financial newspaper. His observations were reported in *Nikkei,* the newspaper's bimonthly English newsletter.

Other eye-openers: Japanese department stores and galleries habitually show the works of some 300 "select" Japanese artists, who represent only 1% of the nation's visual artists. Together, these favored artists account for an estimated $5.8 million in annual sales of art in Japan.

Foreign artists can show their work in practically any leading Japanese gallery, but they have to pay all the show expenses and promotion costs. Only the space is provided free.

HOW JAPANESE BUYERS HAVE CHANGED THE WORLD ART SCENE

Multimillionaire Japanese investors, the source of whose money is sometimes questionable, are changing the face of the world art scene, escalating prices phenomenally and channeling scores of famous works from West to East. One of the largest buyers, Yasumichi Morishita, a Tokyo financier that the racier Japanese magazines have dubbed "the King of Shady Money," has spent $900 million on his collection—it includes Renoirs and paintings by van Gogh, Monet, Gauguin, Degas and Toulouse-Lautrec—and he keeps buying.

"This is purely business," the Tokyo financier and part-owner of Christie's auction house says. "I'm buying as an investment. It's just like buying stock—you have to think in the long term." Stocks are something Morishita, 57, knows about. Once owner of a finance company, he was found guilty of securities fraud in 1988, receiving a two-year suspended sentence for issuing fake stock certificates; a decade earlier he had received a two-year suspended sentence for extortion; and 10 years before that a 10-month suspended sentence for violating a money-lending law. He declines to comment on these matters.

Japanese industrialist Ryoei Saito, owner and honorary chairman of Daishowa Paper Manufacturing Co., bought the two most expensive paintings ever sold to date at an auction. In a $160 million acquisitions binge in May 1990, he bought the Renoir painting "Au Moulin de la Galette" for $78.1 million, only three days after spending a record-breaking $82.5 million for the 1898 "Portrait of Dr. Gachet" by Vincent van Gogh.

Saito reportedly borrowed from banks against his vast real estate holdings. As Japanese real estate and stockprices have skyrocketed in recent years, these assets have been used as collateral to purchase famous paintings.

Another big collector, former used-car dealer Shigeki Kameyama, paid $20.6 million for a Willem de Kooning canvas, "Interchange"—the current record price for a painting by a living artist—and owns works by Cy Twombly, Mark Rothko, and Egon Schiele among others. The source of his bankroll is unknown. Says Sotheby's David Nash, "Sometimes I'll ask him, 'What business are you in?' and he'll reply: 'Many businesses.' Then I'll say, 'Like what?' and he'll reply, 'Girls.' " Nash comments that if Japanese buyers disappeared tomorrow "the market would slow down considerably."

It is no longer unusual for Japanese collectors, speculators and dealers to spend $250 million or more within a single month at the art auctions; and although vast profits are often made with quick resales, the motives are sometimes deeper. "For us Western art has always been an aspiration, a dream" explains Kazuko Shiomi, president of Sotheby's Japan. "It was a status symbol. The fact that you understood Western things meant you were smart, that you were more international."

PUPPET GHOSTBUSTERS IN TAIWAN

The Chinese tradition of puppet theater goes back thousands of years, existing as an art form as well as a system of exorcism. Chinese believe that puppets have the power to dissipate calamity and dispel evil spirits—and puppet theaters, such as Taiwan's Hsieh Fu Hsuen troupe, are still recruited for ghostbusting assignments. For example, a busy street in the city of Chung Ho near Taipei was the scene of frequent car accidents. Believing these accidents were caused by wandering ghosts, the city invited the troupe to perform a puppet show to scare away the evil spirits.

BOWLED OVER

Hong Kong is emerging as a world center for the sale of Asian antiquities. At a 1989 auction of Chinese art works by international auctioneers Christie's, a single piece of jade realized a world record price of about $7 million. The piece, a light green Qing dynasty jadeite bowl, more than doubled its estimated sale price.

SALE OF INDIAN ART

A painting of Mother Teresa, the Nobel Prize winner who gives shelter to the poor and homeless, brought the top bid at the first auction ever conducted in India by London's venerable Christie's firm. More than 500 members of Bombay's high society turned out for a gala evening at the Taj Mahal Hotel as 34 pieces of contemporary Indian art fetched a total of 1.924 million rupees (about $148,000). "Mother Teresa" by leading Indian contemporary painter Maqbool Fida Husain sold for about $38,462 to Minoo Modi, a director of India's giant Tata industrial group.

CHINESE DISCOURAGE ART SMUGGLERS

Unsurprisingly, Hong Kong is the world's major center for Chinese art and most of it is smuggled across what one observer calls "a totally porous border." Dealers used to go out and meet the boats with their illegal cargoes and such trade "only slowed down when the Chinese put bullets in a couple of heads," the informant commented. Among the most commonly available items used to be 5,000-year-old Kansu pottery which, even at prices ranging up to $7000, was only one third of the price demanded elsewhere.

SOUNDS

SATELLITE CONCERTS

Satellite live concerts are aired live by broadcast satellite to as many as 10 other concert arenas across Japan. It's far cheaper to rent satellite time and do nationwide live concerts simultaneously than to go through all the staging costs to do concerts individually. Satellite concert promoter EPIC Sony sees this as a big chance for new business.

MUSIC BOXES FOR MIDDLE-AGED MEN

Miniature music box mechanisms have found an audience in middle-aged Japanese men. It used to be that grammar school students used to give them as birthday presents and young girls collected them. As recently as 1985, production was about 3,000 units a month. Suddenly in 1988 production reached about 300,000 units a month. Sankyo Seiki Manufacturing Co., Japan's largest maker of these music-box mechanisms, did some research. They found that businessmen in their forties were behind the buying surge.

> "The drum gets the beating, the drummer gets the money."
>
> *Chinese proverb*

PHILIPPINE GOVERNMENT'S SERENADE

Philippine radio stations were ordered by the National Telecommunications Commission in 1988 to play four local songs for every hour of music broadcast or face closure. Stations were warned that they would be fined 100 pesos ($4.77) for every violation. The government imposed the requirement on all radio musical programs to promote Filipino compositions which have failed to flourish due to the popularity of foreign pop music in the Philippines.

RAPPIN' IN TAIPEI

One of Taipei's hottest late night disc jockeys is an Afro-American k'ung fu master named Patrick Steel who hails from Chicago. He moved to Taiwan in 1981, and was "discovered" while breakdancing at a Hilton Hotel party and rapping in fluent Chinese.

JAPANESE BOOTLEGGERS EXPLOIT COPYRIGHT LAWS

Yoko Ono, widow of former Beatle John Lennon, blasted Japan's short copyright protection for singers and musicians which grants recording artists only 20 years protection compared to 75 years in the U.S. and 50 years in most of Western Europe. She was particu-larly incensed by a small Tokyo music company that has released more than 100 pre-1967 Beatles songs on CD without paying a single yen in royalties. It's a hot issue these days, especially since many early Beatles songs are being used as soundtracks for TV commercials. Furthermore, with the advent of Digital Audio Tapes (DATs), a whole new market of musical recordings has taken off in Japan.

Although the copyright for composers and lyricists extends to 50 years after the death of the artist, actual recordings are protected only for a period of 20 years. This flagrant loophole in Japan's copyright law is encouraging even major companies in Japan to make a quick killing by reissuing American pop songs and jazz classics. Among these firms, The Seibu Saison group, a giant marketing conglomerate, and Marubeni Corp., a leading Japanese trading house, have brought out CDs of hit records whose copyright protection in Japan has run out.

POP SONGS REDEEMED

Some 128 old songs, including "When Will You Come Back?", a song sung by a Chinese bar girl to Japanese soldiers back in the 1930s, were removed from Taiwan's official banned list of songs in 1988. Only pro-communist or immoral songs remained on the list after the government lifted the Emergency Decree which had banned 898 songs. Songs that are still not allowed include "Dark Paradise," a song exposing the gap between the rich and the poor in old-time Shanghai and "Homeland," a Russian folk song.

FANS WITH FANGS

Hong Kong's top pop singer Anita Mui, considered to be Hong Kong's Madonna, was banned by the local authorities from singing some of her more provocative songs in her concerts in Guangzhou (Canton) in South China. On the hit list: "Bad Little Girl," "Enchanting Lady," and "Red Lips Burning Flames." The measure was adopted after some other Hong Kong singers complained they were literally bitten by overzealous fans on stage when giving concerts in Guangzhou.

CHINA'S GREATEST HITS

Over 400,000 people throughout China voted for the best 15 pop songs composed over the past 15 years. Number 1 was "Full Moon," a song which expresses the yearning of separated soldiers and their wives. The vote was sponsored by the All-China Federation of Trade Unions, the Central People's Broadcasting Station, and the Chinese Musicians Association.

PAGES

SOUTH KOREA'S DURABLE BEST-SELLERS

Best-selling books in South Korea have staying power with popular titles remaining on best-seller lists for up to five years, according to a report issued by the Kyobo Book Center in Seoul, one of the country's leading book dealers. The firm released its best-seller list for the period from June 1981 to December 23, 1987. A novel on the life of ancient Chinese philosopher Hsun-tzu topped the list for 31 months after it was published in August 1984. Another novel, *The Human Market,* remained on the best-seller list for five years. Two Western novels appeared on the center's list of best-selling fiction, with *Lord of the Flies* by William Golding and *1984* by George Orwell, ranking fourth and fifth, respectively.

PSYCHOANALYSIS BY HAIKU

Professor Imori Makio of Tokyo Medical College's Psychology Department is using *haiku* (Japanese poems featuring three lines of 5-7-5 syllables) to help people with mental problems. He says that he can get them to open up by holding *haiku* sessions, either one on one or as group therapy, where patients read a *haiku* they wrote and it is discussed by the group or with the doctor. Imori claims a patient's move towards normalcy can be detected in their poems.

RENT A READING ROOM

The Mamae Book House, a private library in Kobe, Japan, offers patrons private reading areas. Thirty-one cubicles with translucent glass are available for about $2.30 for two hours.

IN JAPAN EVERYBODY IS A *MANGA* FAN

Japan's *manga* (comicbook) boom started in the mid-1960's. And it now accounts for 30% of all publications. The breakdown:

Copies published per year

Weeklies for boys	424.55 million
Weeklies for girls	25.83 million
General weeklies	277.85 million
Monthlies for children	215.34 million
General monthlies	328.93 million
Total	1.27 billion

Besides these magazines, there are the "comics," pocketbook *manga* as it were. Seven hundred million of these minimarvels are published annually, raising the yearly *manga* total to some 1.9 billion copies. Thus, of the 5,500 million copies of magazines and books published in Japan in 1987, for example, fully 34.5% were *manga.*

The reader's penchant for *manga* has led to the publishing of *manga* versions of politics, economics, literature, and other subjects traditionally treated only with the written word. Thus, the natural outcome of this trend has been a decline in sales of hardcover books of literature, history, and other subjects. It is also noteworthy that university students, the people who should be most engrossed in books, are divorcing themselves from the written word. A survey among university students asked, "What magazines do you read regularly?" Of the 10 most mentioned, seven were *manga;* the remaining three were information magazines. The traditional general weeklies did not make the list.

The comic market now extends through people in their thirties. But the day will come when it goes right through the sixties, according to *Yomiuri Shimbun.* So the big publishers are stepping in, usurping the *manga* market from those who started and developed it.

"Along with TV and radio, it's an audio-visual era," notes *Yomiuri Shimbun.* "And the values of the written-word generation are slowly losing their validity."

American readers have taken so wholeheartedly to English translation of these Japanese comics that within months of initially issuing 30,000 copies of "Lone Wolf and Cubs," Chicago's First Comics found back issues were changing hands for up to $30. "I thought it would sell," says the company's president Rick Obadiah, "but it's been much better than my expectations." A rival company, California's Eclipse Comics, is also publishing translations, and industry sources think interest will continue to grow—although not for the sexually explicit *manga,* so

popular in Japan because in the U.S. "comics are still considered kid stuff."

UNDERPAID TAIWANESE TRANSLATORS

Inadequate recompense for experienced work translates into a raw deal for Taiwan's prolific translators, whose skills make publishers rich according to Shin Ch-ching, one of the best of them. With an output of up to 40,000 words per day (at a meagre $10 per 1,000 words), Shih's best-known work, a translation of Lee Iaccoca's autobiography, sold 150,000 copies. "If I could ask for royalties, I could have received 20 times as much," she says, pointing out that a good translator usually represents a decade or more of experience. She herself has translated about 60 books from English into Chinese. "Faithful, smooth, and elegant" are the principles she observes, following a definition of the art by master translator Lin Yutang.

SHAKESPEARE IN CHINA

The complete works of Shakespeare are the most popular books in China's Jilin Province. "They are the latest gift to send to a newly married couple," according to Meng Xiangqiang, secretary of the Jilin Provincial Shakespeare Association. Every Sunday, the Jilin provincial radio station broadcasts one of its most popular programs, "Stories from Shakespeare."

. . . BUT NOT IN NEPAL

Nepalese authorities banned performances of Shakespeare's *Hamlet,* apparently because the brooding drama of the Prince of Denmark offends royalist sensibilities in the Himalayan kingdom. *Macbeth* is also unwelcome there.

KOREAN WRITERS UNBANNED

South Korea has lifted its ban on the works of about 100 writers who chose to live in Communist North Korea after World War II.

THE TYCOON CHRONICLES

Is he China's Lee Iacocca? A record high advance for a book—only $8,000 but still a record in the PRC—was paid by a Nanjing entrepreneur to a team of Chinese ghostwriters in 1988. Fei Zhiyuan, a Wuxi tycoon who operates seven factories, retained the services of the Philosophical Social Science Institute to write a book chronicling his firm's successes during the early stages of China's economic modernization reforms.

EMERGENCE OF THE TEN-PERCENTERS

Literary agents, a hitherto unknown breed in China, have appeared on the book publishing scene. Reportedly, these so-called "publication brokers" are upsetting some Chinese publishing firms with their aggressive demands for bigger advances for their clients. According to *Youth News* magazine, these budding Swifty Lazars are making big profits representing authors and translators. Where do they come from? They're mostly former book editors, bookstore staff, and book salesmen. Allegedly, they are also chiefly responsible for the wave of pornography inundating China today.

CHINESE BUY MORE BOOKS . . .

The Chinese spent over four times as much money buying books in 1988 as they did in 1978, the year before China's economic reforms were launched, according to the *People's Daily*. In 1988, they spent about $1.27 per capita buying books compared to about one quarter of that in 1978. There are some 64,800 bookstores in China and some 4,000 collectively run bookstores and 7,000 privately owned bookstores. Novels by Irving Wallace *(The Fan Club)* and Jackie Collins *(The Gamble)* were ordered destroyed by Chinese censors on the grounds that they were obscene and in the latter case had corrupted young people. Two senior officials of the Yanbian People's Publishing House, which distributed the Wallace novel, were sacked from their jobs.

SCREEN

. . . BUT WATCH FEWER MOVIES

China released 158 feature films in 1988, with *kung fu* movies reeling in the most profits at the box office for the third straight year. Fifteen kung fu productions earned about $2.7 million each in profits, followed by police dramas and comedies. Serious films, which have drawn international attention to China's film industry in recent years, fared worst. One art film managed to bring in only Rmb. 10,000 (about $2,300)

Movie audiences have been dropping steadily in China in recent years and analysts attribute this not only to the inroads of television and videos but perhaps more significantly to the heavy hand of government control. In 1987, 108 out of 142 movies failed to recover the cost of production according to a report in *Guangming Daily,* which said that audiences were dropping at the rate of 30 million each month. Film experts suggest that ways to correct this decline include allowing film studios to make independent decisions about everything from production to export of films, and tax reductions for the making of children's films. The government is also considering introducing a rating system for movies because of the increasing sex and violence that is showing up.

SHADES OF BRUCE LEE

Hong Kong, film capital of *kung fu* movies, appears to be losing its nerve as the 1997 takeover of the territory by China draws near. Now Hong Kong producers are setting their sights on relocating to Singapore, and at least two major producers are said to be negotiating with the Singapore government to shift their film production to the Southeast Asian city state.

Cinema City Group, one of the territory's largest producers of Cantonese movies, negotiated a deal to obtain Singapore passports for its employees. According to sources, the package includes a commitment to produce five films with a total budget of $5 million.

The company also will conduct training classes in scriptwriting, directing, and other technical areas in a bid to develop Singapore's nonexistent film industry.

HK Industry Review: Hong Kong is the world leader in making violent movies says a report compiled by a Friends of the Earth committee; and in a recent year, 1987, only one out of the 25 movies made in the colony was considered to have a beneficial effect on viewers. The group surveyed 1,500 films from 61 countries as a result of which they pinpointed Hong Kong and Mexico as producers of the highest proportion of graphically brutal and sadistic films.

TARGETING BOLD FILMS IN THE PHILIPPINES

Since the appointment of a devout Roman Catholic, Manuel Morato, as head of the Philippines' movie and TV censorship board, the production of sex movies has come to a halt and confiscatory raids have been made on more than 100 theaters. Producers who used to submit movies for censorship and then splice in sex scenes afterward have taken to showing 20 minutes of sex scenes after the main feature so that if the theatre is raided they can "just run away with one short reel."

SOCIETY

LOVE AND MARRIAGE

THE LOVE SURVEY

Almost half (47%) of the 3,800 wives aged between 20 and 50, who were queried in a survey by the Daihyaku Life Insurance Co.,

couldn't remember the last time their husbands said, "I love you." One fifth of the women admitted quarreling with their husbands weekly, almost one third (32%) once a month.

Fewer than 50% of Japanese women would marry the same man over again, according to a 1988 survey of 1,575 women by the Japanese Green Cross Society, a private research institute.

WHAT INTERESTS JAPANESE WOMEN?

*an*an* magazine asked 1,215 women between the ages of 20 and 25, "Right now, what interests you most?" The answers:

1. Fashion   97%
2. Love affairs   95%
3. Overseas vacations   91%
4. Makeup and hair styles   89%
5. Diets   87%
6. Money   82%
7. Getting out on my own   78%
8. Marriage   72%
9. Divination   70%
10. Changing jobs   67%

WIFE-FEARING HUSBANDS

Late-night carousing is not the only reason why 80% of Japanese men suffer from chronic fatigue, claims a Tokyo newspaper columnist, but also because men are staying away from home to avoid "aggressive, unappreciative women." The writer, Yoshihiko Inagaki, charges that an aversion syndrome is reaching epidemic proportions among downtrodden husbands, and quotes a survey by the Hakuhodo Institute, which found that in families where the wife's income is more than half her husband's she tends to dominate her spouse and makes financial decisions without stopping to consult him. The prospect of a five-day week is not one that pleases most wives, Inagaki writes. Of wives with husbands over 40, only one in five wishes her husband had more leisure time. "His being around just means extra work and less time to myself," said one.

DEPRESSED TAIWANESE HOUSEWIVES

Housewives depressed over marriage top the list of people who commit suicide in Taiwan, a police report said. Marital unhappiness was the common reason for suicide in 1985, the last year for which detailed figures are available, when 2,281 people took their own lives. Businessmen were second on the list. The report said the suicide rate in Taiwan, the world's 13th largest trading nation, was closely linked to swings in the island's economic fortunes. The number of people who killed themselves in 1985 jumped as the local New Taiwan dollar started appreciating against the U.S. dollar.

SEXUAL HARASSMENT: THE SEAMY SIDE OF JAPAN'S MACHO ECONOMY

In case you're one of those who believes that Japan is "sticking it" to the West, you're not the only one. Japanese women feel they're getting a bad deal, too.

These days Japanese women are asking, Whatever happened to women's power in Japan? Was it just media hype?

In August 1989, a 32-year-old woman editor in Fukuoka filed Japan's first-ever sexual harassment suit against her boss. Allegedly, her employer spread false rumors in the office about her promiscuity in an effort to get her to submit to his sexual advances.

That complaint opened up a can of worms. The Tokyo Bar Association set up a hot line just to cope with the flood of women's phone calls about incidents of *seku hara* (*sekusu harasumento,* or sexual harassment) on the job. A best-selling book by Japanese feminist author Mikiko Taga, entitled *Single Mind,* further raised public consciousness on the issue.

Now the women's rights crusade seems to have gone into the deep freeze. The dumping of the nation's only female Cabinet minister by Japanese Prime Minister Kaifu after his Liberal Democratic Party's landslide election victory in 1990 further dampened the cause of women's rights in Japan.

JAPAN'S "PANTY" PSYCHOLOGY

The problem of sexual harassment has not only faded from the front pages of Japanese newspapers, but in what can only be described as a cynical and kinky twist, the term *seku hara* itself has become the name of several Tokyo nightclubs where hostesses in miniskirts sit at desks in an office setting and let the male customers fondle them.

One of the biggest-selling gift items during "White Day" on March 14 (a month after Valentine's Day, when men are supposed to give gifts to ladies) is—panties. The Isetan department store in Tokyo's Shinjuku ward even has a panty vending machine dispensing cigarette-pack size containers (priced at about $7) with messages reading, "Please remember me, a shy man" and "I cannot stop my love for you."

Sales of lingerie in the weeks before White Day account for an estimated 12% of all panties sold during the year, according to Osamu

Kimura, executive director of the Nihon Body Fashion Association. And Wacoal Corp., Japan's leading lingerie maker, projects sales of about 360,000 pairs of panties around White Day alone, a company spokesperson said.

MACHO BELLES

Unlike their Western sisters who are still struggling for professional acceptance at home, women in the Philippines have long been accepted in top positions in government and in private industry. Now not only are they equal to their macho peers, but they can have an equalizer to prove it. In the leading Manila Bulletin, gunmaker Smith & Wesson is advertising its "Lady Smith" pistol in "convenient carrying case." Presumably no one would mistake the rod the ladies are packing for a compact.

ROTARY RELATIONS

Rotary clubs in Singapore voted to open their doors to women in 1989, ending an 84-year tradition of male-only membership.

CHINA'S FIRST TRANSSEXUAL

China's first transsexual operation, which took place some years ago, was revealed by a report in a U.S. magazine, *The Journal of Sex Research.* The patient was said to be the 20-year-old son of a prominent army official who was brought up as a girl by his parents "who wanted to maintain control over him." When he was later sent into the army he threatened to commit suicide unless he could resume his feminine identity and wrote to Beijing Medical University's Dr. Fang-Ru Ruan, who was the author of a column dealing with sexual matters. In 1983, Dr. Ruan arranged for the patient to have his sex-change operation following more or less standard Western practices.

SPLITTING UP IN SHANGHAI

The use of contracts to terminate marriages rather than quarrels or divorces is growing in Shanghai, where almost three quarters of the splitting couples, about 3,300, ended their relationships this way last year.

FIREFLY HUSBANDS

First, the Japanese husband was dubbed "oversized trash" because he just lay around the house not helping in household chores. Then they coined a new phrase, "industrial waste." Finally he became a "wet leaf"—no matter how hard you try to sweep it out of the house, it just sticks to the floor. Most recently, they've been calling their husbands "firefly people." That describes men who stand under the kitchen exhaust fan to smoke because their wives and daughters objected to their smoking anywhere else. After that, he was exiled to the veranda. The evening glow of lighted cigarettes gave birth to the term, "firefly people."

HOLLOW WIVES

Hollow wives are Japanese housewives who spend most of their time away from home engaged in recreational activities because modern conveniences have freed them from their housework. They make it home just in time to put on an apron and greet their hubby as he trudges in after a hard day's work. What do they like to do the most? Lunch with friends from the Culture Center at a French restaurant, shopping at the department store (really, they're there to "see" the art exhibit). "Often as not, hubby is told by his company to "keep abreast of the times," comments the *Nihon Keizai Shimbun*. "Chances are, however, that he is ignoring one of the best sources of trendy information—his own Hollow Wife."

CARTOON COURTSHIP

Esprit, a Tokyo-based creative planning company, makes animated cartoon versions of your courtship and marriage. The finished product is five minutes long and costs about $2,000. It takes three months to complete.

TEA FOR THREE

The Singapore government put more than 3,500 people in the mood to marry by 1988 since it took to match-making in 1984. Most of the new couples were college and university graduates who were considered to have a difficult time finding mates because of their higher expectations. (Former) Prime Minister Lee Kuan Yew voiced alarm in 1983 about what he called a declining talent pool, and other ministers said the falling birth rate would affect the manpower needs of Singapore's economy and defense. The family planning slogan of "Stop at Two," firmly enforced since 1972, has been abandoned for all except the less-educated.

LOVE AT FIRST SITE

Until the crushing of the pro-democracy movement in 1989, more than 10,000 Chinese married foreigners each year, often in haste to obtain a passport to the West, according to the *People's Daily*. Mixed marriages were rare 10 years ago, but they became more common thanks to simplified administrative formalities.

PRC PERSONALS

Educated Chinese women have taken to advertising themselves internationally in hopes of catching husbands with foreign citizenship, according to the *Shanghai Liberation Daily*. Chinese professional women, aged 30 to 45 and mostly from cosmopolitan areas such as Beijing and Shanghai, have taken out ads in American newspapers. The ads appear on "love hotline" and "love train" pages in Chinese newspapers abroad, and have reportedly brought together more than 10,000 couples since 1988. Still influenced by a traditionally patriarchal society, Chinese men are wary of marrying women with more education than themselves.

THE 100-YEAR HOME LOAN

Nippon Housing Loan Co., Ltd. introduced the world's first "100-Year Home Loan," which can be spread over three generations. Parents and children can choose to either pay the loan off in equal parts, or else hand it down to the grandchildren. This could only happen in Japan, where the price of real estate is so high that it's no wonder it might take three generations to pay for it.

WHAT HOUSEWORK DOES YOUR HUSBAND DO?

Lion Corporation interviewed 120 Japanese working women who have been married less than four years. Question: What jobs in the house does your husband do?

1. Fold up the *futon* (bedding)	25.8%
2. Clean the bath tub	21.7%
3. Take out the garbage	19.2%
4. Clean the vent fan	14.2%
5. Rearrange the furniture	10.8%
6. Clean the room	8.3%
7. Pay the bills	6.7%
8. Cooking	4.2%
8. Laundry	4.2%
8. Ironing	4.2%
Nothing	44.2%

OFFSPRING

MY EIGHT SONS

China's one-child-per-family policy is often contravened secretly, but a Communist party *secret* of Zhongqu village in Shaanxi province held a huge banquet and posted banners to celebrate his wife giving birth to their eighth child. In addition to expulsion from the party, Yang Jingchun, 38, was slapped with fines of $45 each year for every one of his unauthorized children until they reach 14.

ABANDONED BABIES IN CHINA

One effect of China's one-child-per-family policy has been the increasing number of abandoned babies found in the streets, railway stations, and hospitals of Beijing, a figure that has almost doubled in recent years due to the preference by Chinese parents for boys over relatively unproductive girls.

REGISTERING ARTIFICIAL INSEMINATORS

A young Shanghai woman filed for divorce after giving birth to a boy through artificial insemination because her husband refused to recognize the child as his own. As a result of the case, judicial authorities in Beijing took steps to introduce a law requiring the registration of all cases of artificial insemination. According to the court decision in the divorce, the man will have to give regular financial support to the baby. Several hundred Chinese women have given birth by artificial insemination since the technique was introduced to the country in 1982.

SEX SCAM IN CHINA

The Chinese tradition of "son worship" has resulted in some unusual rackets, according to the Xinhua News Agency which reported the case of the farming couple in northern Hebei province who, after giving birth to three girls, paid an unscrupulous dealer $540 for a supposed son and heir only to have his false genitals drop off one week later.

YOUNG BRIDES AND GROOMS

Families in some rural areas of China are finding marriage partners for children as young as seven and eight, the *People's Daily* reported. Surveys found that in rural areas around Wenzhou, a city noted for its prosperous private entrepreneurs, 86% of children 14 years old or younger were already engaged.

BABY SMUGGLING IN MALAYSIA

Barren Malaysian couples, often stigmatized for their inability to bear a child, have been paying up to $4000 for babies illegally brought in from Thailand. As many as 6,000 babies may have been smuggled across the border in recent years. One doctor pointed out that because a Malaysian husband can

marry again and again, until he finds a wife who can produce a baby, that illegally acquired infants may actually enable barren women to keep their husbands.

TAIWANESE MOMS

Seven out of ten of Taiwanese women who get married at 26, the national average, give birth to their first child five months later according to a government report.

> "Can the crab teach his children how to walk in a straight line?"
>
> *Malaysian proverb*

NEWSLETTER FOR ADOPTIVE PARENTS

Bridges is a publication intended to be of interest and help to non-Filipino adoptive parents of Filipino children, as well as to parents of Filipino-American children. For more information, write to Diverse Designs, 2262 Windsor Avenue, SW, Roanoke, Virginia 24015.

PRE-NATAL TESTS NIXED IN INDIA

Pre-natal tests to determine sex have been banned in India's western state of Maharashtra because too many families have been using them so that female fetuses could be aborted. Although dowries are illegal in India, they are still prevalent and many families cannot afford the high cost of marrying off a daughter.

DISCOURAGING RETARDED PARENTS

The Chinese province of Gansu in northwestern China has passed a law barring mentally retarded people from having children.

According to the *People's Daily,* more than 270,000 people in Gansu, or about 1.3% of the province's population, are retarded.

INADMISSIBLE NAMES FOR KIDS

Parents who might want to call their child Narul (Hell), Burok (Bad), or Wati (Intercourse) will not be allowed to register them in Malaysia whose National Registration Department has distributed a guidebook of names to its offices throughout the country. The blacklist of banned names also includes animals, trees, fruit, vegetables and professional titles.

CHINA'S UNTOUCHABLE KIDS

There are more than one million children in China who face tough lives because, as far as the state is concerned, they don't exist, according to the *People's Daily.* The children, whose births violated China's one-child-per family policy, either weren't registered with authorities at birth because their parents feared penalties or they weren't registered by officials who wanted to meet population-control targets. Because they aren't registered, they are ineligible for food rations, schooling, and jobs.

JAPANESE KIDS SPOILED

Japanese children are so busy playing computer games and watching television that they don't help with the household chores or play outdoors, according to a Japanese government report released in 1987. The *White Paper* reported that about one third of Japanese chil-

dren surveyed by the Health and Welfare Ministry said they have family computers for games, and 7.2% said they have their own personal computers. Computer games reportedly are more stimulating than watching television, which is a passive activity.

DOWN UNDER BOOB-TUBING

Australian children watch an average of three to five hours of television a day, according to a report by Australia's National Health and Medical Research Council. The report warned that television-viewing habits of Australian children may be encouraging the development of violent behavior and precocious sexuality. By the time the average child leaves school at 18, he or she will have spent more time in front of the television than in the classroom, it was disclosed.

LIFTING FACE

More and more Japanese high school kids are going in for facelifts. Citing the report of a well-known Tokyo plastic surgery clinic, 30% of their female patients in the first months of 1989 were high school students, *Shukan Shincho* magazine reported. Typically they seek, and get their parents' permission for the operations before studying for college entrance exams or looking for jobs. Most go in for nose and eye jobs, but some also want altered jaw lines and liposuction.

BANDAID FETISHES

Young teenage girls in Japan are wearing band-aids, not because they've cut themselves but because of a fad. Ever since a teenage girls' magazine called *My Birthday* ran an article about it, young girls have been writing the name of boys they'd like to have relationships with on the bandaids, then sticking them on the inside of their left arms. Supposedly, after three days their romantic wishes will come true.

CHILD ABUSE IN JAPAN

More than 1,000 child abuse cases were reported to child guidance centers in Japan between April and September 1989, according to a report by the National Juvenile Guidance Center. The report's statistics showed that 6.6 of every 100,000 children were abused.

CHILD PROSTITUTION IN THE PHILIPPINES

Child prostitution is a scourge in the Philippines—with pedophiles from all around the world continuing to gravitate toward the impoverished nation where they can find easy prey in the form of young boys and girls. The following are excerpts from a 1987 study published by the Health Action Information Network (P.O. Box 10340, Broadway, Quezon City, Philippines), entitled *Pom Pom: Child and Youth Prostitution in the Philippines:*

The cities of Bacolod and lloilo used to be the queen cities of the south, with a bustling economy built on the sugar industry. Iloilo's decline began in the early part of the century, while the disaster in Bacolod (and the entire province of Negros Occidental) is more recent. The crisis in Negros has been well publicized, with several thousands of sugar farm workers affected. Aid agencies are now trying to reach some 100,000 undernourished children on the island, but poverty and hunger continue.

Adult prostitution has long been in existence in the two cities, dating back to those prosperous years when the word *hacendero* still meant wealth. In the late 1970s and in this decade, child prostitution has emerged.

In Bacolod's plaza, there are child prostitutes who go freelance or are managed by pimps. The children sometimes pimp for each other. These are the *batang plaza* or *batang yagits,* many virtually living in the plaza. Aside from selling their bodies, they also shine shoes or sell cigarettes to make ends meet.

lloilo City, with its more conservative facade, has *casas,* while others operate in restaurants. Off Paney island is Boracay, a popular tourist resort, where the prostitutes are "imported" from other parts of the country, usually acting as "tourist guides."

THE SILVER GENERATION

THE AGING OF ASIA

Asian society is getting older. Twenty-five years ago, 45% of the region's population were over 60 years old. That figure has been rising for various reasons. First of all, families are having fewer children, so young children are forming a smaller segment of the total population. Second, Asians are living much longer.

Over 25 years ago, those who are over 60 years old comprised 45% of the region's population. By the early 1980s, that figure climbed significantly—by 5% in Singapore and 10.2% in Hong Kong. By the year 2010, it is estimated that one fifth of all Japanese will be over 60, while China will reach that level by 2025. By the turn of the century, 13.7% of Hong Kong's citizens and 10.8% of Taiwan's will be in that category. Other Asian nations expect the numbers of their elderly to double in the coming decade.

Today the Japanese have the longest life expectancy in the world: 84 years for women now aged 40 and 76 for men. Though Asians elsewhere have fewer years ahead—in Hong Kong, people can expect to live to 74; in Malaysia 72 (women) or 67 (men); in China 69 (women) or 66 (men); in Taiwan 74 (women) or 69 (men); in the Philippines 64 (women) or 62 (men); in Indonesia (56)—the figures are constantly rising. Prospects are that others will catch up with the region's sole developed nation.

Source: Asiaweek.

INTERNATIONAL COMPARISON: BEDRIDDEN ELDERLY

There are now 600,000 bedridden elderly in Japan, and experts estimate more than a million by the end of the century. A Welfare Ministry report on nursing homes shows some interesting discrepancies between Japan and Western nations.

	Bedridden	Can get out of bed or move about in wheel chairs
Japan	33.8%	25.4%
U.S.	6.5%	40.8%
Sweden	4.2%	61.8%

In Japan, the policy is "leave them in bed, don't burden the family," Asahi Shimbun noted. In the West, the policy is "help them back on their feet, help them be at least a little self-sufficient."

"If we were to care for our elderly as the Westerners do, the 600,000 bedridden elderly in nursing homes in our country could be reduced 20,000 to 30,000," Asahi Shimbun concluded.

FOUR KINDS OF SILVER SOCIETY

The Japan Food Industry Center has analyzed Japan's "Silver Society" of senior citizens. In an analysis, the Nihon Keizai Shimbun notes that the elderly fall into four categories:

1. *The Nervous Silvers:* People who act out a youngish life-style but are quite concerned about keeping traditions.
2. *The Active Silvers:* High-income people with a wide range of interests.
3. *The Local Silvers:* People who make the neighborhood their life.
4. *The Lonely Silvers:* People who spend their later years with no specific goal and without the energy to add zest to their lives.

From the Food Industry's point of view, the Active Silvers tend to eat out more, and the Lonely Silvers tend to depend on instant food products. Local Silvers tend to eat fish and rice, while the Nervous Silvers are into eating vegetables.

EAGER ELDERS

Surveys taken among the 1.6 million Shanghai residents over 60 years old revealed that a substantial percentage were bored with staying home, playing cards or chess, and wanted to make some contribution to society. Now many of them have been organized into volunteer patrols who supplement the city's harassed police force by watching for pickpockets in stores, settling minor disputes between shop assistants and customers, reproving spitters, and helping to guide cyclists through busy intersections. "When I retired I thought I was a useless person," one of this 30,000-member brigade remarked. "Now I have become a person respected by those around me."

RIM CENTENARIANS

Vietnam boasts 2,432 people aged over 100, more than two thirds of them women, the oldest being a 142-year-old lady, Ngan Thi Quang, a member of an ethnic Thai minority group, reports the Vietnam News Agency.

As of 1989, China had 3,851 people who had reached the age of 100. Seventy percent of the centenarians are women, and most live in rural areas of northwest and southwest China.

DEATH

BURIALS IN CHINA

If China's current burial practices continue to use scarce timber and encroach upon much-needed productive farmland, there will soon be a battle for the resources between the living and the dead declared the *People's Daily* in a diatribe against the country's rural burial practices. Although more than 1,000 crematoriums have been built since 1949 to dispose of most of the big cities' corpses, more than 90%—4.5 million people—of the rural dead are buried in wooden coffins in the traditional way. The paper estimated that 2.2 square meters of wood and 24,000 acres are needed for this purpose.

In most of Asia, it is commonly believed that prosperity is dependent on how well one looks after one's ancestors. The cost of a decent funeral in Shanghai is about $700—six times what it was a decade ago—and in rural areas about half that, or roughly one month's entire earnings for a peasant family. Newly introduced to Guangdong province is the practice of maritime burials, where relatives accompany their deceased on a boat leaving the Pearl River, throwing flowers overboard as the bodies are slipped into the South China Sea.

GRAVESTONE FASHION SHOW

Designer gravestones are the latest manifestation of tombstone fever which has been sweeping Japan in recent years. Taisho University's Masao Fuji says the trend away from the old-style family tomb to individual graves has created a demand for all kinds of different styles. A gravestone fashion show at a Tokyo hotel attracted in a single day more than 1,000 people who were able to admire sculptured tombstones at up to $25,000 each, designed by four of Japan's leading artists. This macabre fascination, however, is coming at an inopportune time, just when Tokyo, at least, is running out of burial plots. The city needs an estimated 40,000 plots per year, yet not only are the cemeteries full, but land is far too expensive to be devoted to new ones. By recycling graves every three years the city government had been able to meet a tiny fraction of the demand, but more commonplace is the new custom of depositing urns in stacked-up boxes in rows of lockers.

WHITE MUMS

White chrysanthemums are the flower of mourning at Japanese funerals. About 8,000 white chrysanthemum blooms are harvested each day in central Taiwan, which is the major supplier of chrysanthemums to the Japanese market. In anticipation of heightened demand of white mums for Emperor Hirohito's death in January 1989, Taiwanese flower growers tried to plant more chrysanthemums in late 1988 but were only able to supply the Japanese with 30% of the orders because of cooler than expected weather. The soaring demand had caused prices to jump about 60% from a year earlier to about 21 cents a blossom.

PERMANENT UNDERGROUND PARKING

Japanese who die in Tokyo, a city of astronomical land prices, will have to be laid to rest in multistory buildings like apartment blocks or stacked underground in parking-lot-type structures. Tokyo's metropolitan panel on graveyards recommended that permanent leases on graves should be abandoned in favor of time-limited ones, saving space for future needs.

CONDO URNS

A lavish Tang Dynasty-style complex, destined to be the final resting place for the urns of 40,000 people, became the largest Chinese columbarium to be built in Hong Kong. It cost $14 million to build and is called *Bo Fu,* or "Precious Luck."

CUSTOMS

HIGH BALINESE

A conversation between two strangers in Bali usually begins in the highest level of Balinese. Later on, the level of Balinese used in conversation may be adjusted according to the rank and caste of the people speaking. According to locals, if you start your conversation in "low" Balinese and later find out that the person you are talking to is of a higher caste, you will feel embarrassed.

ASIAN BODY LANGUAGE

The Indian "head wag" that looks somewhat like a western "no," actually means "yes" in Indian body language. The western side-to-side hand wave for "hello" is frequently interpreted by Indians as "no" or "go away." To the westerner, the hand wave that is done at chest or waist level with the palm down while opening and closing fingers looks like "go away." To Asians, it means "come here." Obviously, if you do something resembling a head wag to a rickshaw driver, or a hand wave (with palm facing downward) to a beggar, they will continue to follow you. How to discourage hustlers: Put on a New York-style, closed faced look as if you know where you are going, and ignore what you don't want. Stopping to argue will just intensify the situation, according to the Lonely Planet "Update" travel guide.

WHAT'S YOUR IQ (IRRITATION QUOTIENT)

How long before the average Japanese starts to get irritated? According to an informal survey by *Japan Free Press:*

Waiting for a train	10 minutes
Waiting for an order (at a coffee shop)	10 minutes
At a fast-food outlet	32 seconds
For the elevator	30 seconds
For the light to change	30 seconds
When making a call	10 rings

GAMES PEOPLE PREY

Mainichi Shimbun reports an alarming trend of socially deviant games which are becoming extremely popular among Japanese youth. Among the nihilistic best-sellers is "Whose child is this?" The object of the game is for an unwed mother to try to pin paternal responsibility on the wrong man. If the guy wriggles out of the trap, he wins. Comes with instant blood-typing kit (price about $10). "Digestion is a board game which starts at the mouth and works its way down. First player to reach the colon wins (priced about $13). Reflecting Japan's spiraling land prices, the game of "Real Estate Clout" is about pushing people off their property, forcing them to sell at rock-bottom prices, and other shenanigans. May the most rotten speculator win (costs about $20).

SINGAPORE CUSTOMS

Surveying the colony's Chinese residents, Singapore's *Straits Times* discovered that the vast majority of them still observed age-old Chinese customs from giving *hongbao* (red packets of money) at the Lunar New Year to observing such celebrations as All Souls' Day, Mooncake, Dragon Boat, and Hungry Ghosts. About 87% of Chinese families still held *man yue* celebrations for their firstborn, giving the traditional red eggs (96%) or cakes (84%) to friends and relatives. Eighty-eight percent observed the one-month isolation period after delivery and at least three quarters avoided funerals and weddings for a specific period. More than nine out of 10 Chinese families observed the tea ceremony and the custom of the bride returning to her mother's home as part of the wedding rituals but almost half were in favor of simplifying or dropping the ritualistic gift of such symbolic items as a pig or sugar cane. Four out of five of those surveyed have a religion, with 46% naming Shenism or the worship of Chinese deities, Buddhism (39%), and ancestor worship (37%) being the next most popular. Among the death rituals observed, *baijin* or donations to the bereaved family; watching the dead; wearing mourning garments; and burning joss were all observed by at least nine out of 10 Chinese.

PUBLIC BATHS DRYING UP

The centuries-old custom of communal bathing is dying out in Japan, brought about by a changing public morality and the increasing number of homes with their own bathtubs. A handful of public baths where the sexes are allowed to mix remain—mostly in resort areas—but even the bathing houses where they are segregated survive only for residents of relatively inexpensive apartments; the number of bathhouses in Tokyo has dropped more than 30% in the past two decades. Some bath house owners are resorting to ingenious ways to retain or increase their customers. "I put in a golf driving range on the roof," says one. "People come here to play golf and then take a bath or vice versa. It produces a multiplier effect."

BRIGHT LIGHTS, DULL CITY

A growing campaign to enforce communist morality and counter "bourgeois liberalism" has resulted in the closing of dozens of Shanghai bars accused of such sins as dim lighting, showing videos with "unhealthy contents," overcharging, and encouraging gambling. Such unlicensed bars, reports Shanghai's *Liberation Daily* have "seriously polluted the general mood of society by attracting customers

---

RIM VOICES

A DATE WITH FATE

I had to pay some taxes on a special regulation that no one seemed to know about (but) which in fact was absolutely legal (I learned later). At the same time many people I know who were in the same situation *exactly* had passed through and paid nothing. As my thoughts were that I'd been cheated, which is a very common thing especially when you have a white complexion and are without "good connections," I decided to ask a Thai friend to go with me and ask the reason why I had to pay and others didn't. I got may answers after just two questions:

"Why did I have to pay?"

"Tong sia (You had to pay)."

"But why didn't the others pay?"

"Pen boon korng khao (They were just lucky; it's just fate)."

But if we want to look deeper into the word *boon* (fate, luck, merit, destiny), we see that it can be related to past good or bad deeds, or even with the good or bad you did in your previous life. And so I just discovered that in Thailand everything is related to that word. It's just the answer to the meaning of life.

From Jean-Claude Neveu of Bangkok in *Bangkok Post*.

---

with pretty and coquettish-looking young women." The women were paid high salaries and handed over to their bosses a portion of payments from customers who accompanied them outside, the paper added.

BHUTAN: BALANCING THE OLD AND NEW

The Land of the Thunder Dragon, as the Himalayan kingdom of Bhutan styles itself, is trying to conduct a difficult balancing act: modernizing while simultaneously reinforcing its ancient way of life. Shocked by the ease with which its young students sent abroad to study adopted Western ways and casual clothing, Bhutan's government has made the traditional knee-length *kho* compulsory for its male civil servants, the ankle-length *kira* for women. Both must undergo examinations emphasizing cultural traditions, which in-

cludes the study of *driglam namzha* or traditional etiquette. Bhutan, a beautiful country of pine-covered mountains reaching to the clouds, with a population of 1.3 million spread over a mere 46,500 square kilometers, is sandwiched between India—which provides most of its aid—and China and Tibet. "As a small country surrounded by giant neighbors, Bhutan's culture can be easily swallowed up if we are not careful," says one official. There are no opposition parties in Bhutan, whose sole authority is King Jigme Singye Wangchuk, who is rumored to have four wives, all sisters.

SINGAPORE TO THE CORE

While Singapore should be open to other views and constructive criticism, such ideas should not be allowed to undermine national security or social cohesiveness in the view of

President Wee Kim Wee, who has sounded the alarm about the Asian city-state becoming too Westernized. Sustained and guided by the traditional Asian ideas of morality, duty, and society which had served so well in the past, Singapore should preserve its cultural heritage, Wee told parliament, retaining the "core values [which placed] society above self, upholding the family as the basic building block of society, resolving major issues through consensus instead of contention, and stressing racial and religious tolerance and harmony." Roughly three quarters of Singapore's 2.6 million inhabitants are Chinese, with 15% Malays, 6% Indian, and the remainder Eurasians and Europeans.

MONARCHY

LADIES FOR THE CHRYSANTHEMUM THRONE

Takako Doi, the first woman in Japan to head the Socialist Party, is in favor of a Japanese woman becoming emperor one day. "The emperor is the symbol of state and the unity of the people, so I think there is absolutely no reason to bar women from becoming emperor," she said in an interview with Kyodo, the Japanese news agency. She wants a revision on the Japanese law on imperial succession. When Emperor Hirohito died in 1989, his eldest son, Akihito, then 55, automatically succeeded him. Hirohito had two sons and five daughters, but none of the daughters— three of whom are still living—was in line for Japan's Chrysanthemum Throne.

EMPEROR'S ESTATE TAXES

Japan's late Emperor Hirohito left $13 million in taxable property, his estate being split by his wife, Nagako, now the empress dowager, and his eldest son, Akihito, whose share of the inheritance taxes was almost $3 million.

THE COST OF MAINTAINING JAPAN'S IMPERIAL FAMILY

The branches of Japan's Imperial Family appear to be growing again. Before World War II, there were 14 families in the Imperial Household. After the war, that was cut to three. Now there are six. But the economic strain on the taxpayer is increasing, according to *Shukan Gendai* magazine. How much does a branch of the Imperial Family cost? About $363,000 as an initial payment when it is first authorized. Then $181,000 per year to the head of the family; $90,000 per year to the wife; $11,115 for each minor child, three times that after they reach majority. As there is no tax paid on that income, the branch family gets the equivalent of a $615,000 annual salary. There's more. The new family gets a free place to live that would cost $7.6 million on the open market. Nor do they have to pay for utilities. Furthermore, by acting as honorary chairmen of schools, corporations, organizations, and the like, a further $77,000 per year comes in.

DEATH OF AN INDONESIAN MONARCH

The funeral of Javanese King Hamengku Buwono IX, who died in the United States of a heart attack in October 1988, was attended by about two million people in Yogyakarta. He was succeeded by his son, Mangkubumi, who assumed the title of King Hamengku Buwono X. The tiny sultanate of Yogyakarta in central Java is only one of two remaining kingdoms recognized by the Republic of Indonesia.

GREAT-GRANDSON OF LAST SHOGUN

The great-grandson of the last *shogun,* or military leader, who is a descendant from the Tokugawa clan that ruled Japan for more than 250 years during its feudal period of isolation from the world, is today an ordinary Japanese businessman. Tsuenari Tokugawa is a middle-manager of an insurance company in a Tokyo skyscraper that looks down upon the Imperial Palace in the center of the Japanese capital. Had history turned out differently, he would be living in the palace instead of Emperor Akihito. "It has been thought that there was a clean break between modern Japan and the dark period of the *shoguns,* when the country was closed," he told Clayton Jones of the *Christian Science Monitor* in an interview.

"But very recently, many books have suggested there was really a continuity—with no break. Certain cultural practices have persisted, such as loyalty, hierarchy, shame, and face. Perhaps these have strong roots in the Tokugawa time," he speculated.

ACCESSORIES

DESIGNER DOGS

Designer dogs have become fashion accessories for trendy Tokyoites, who often rent a pet for the day (fees begin at about $46 plus a refundable deposit of $385) so they can display on a Sunday promenade in Harajuku or along the Ginza. Because living space is scarce in Japan, pets—even temporary pets—are a sign of affluence and, according to writer Cassi Zarzyka, it's being seen with a pet that's important. For actual owners, even the death of a pet offers an opportunity for ostentatious display: elaborate funerals with a Buddhist monk or Shinto priest in attendance are commonplace. Accommodation for (live) dogs is big business, with doghouse sales amounting to an annual $40 million. One glorified "kennel" is equipped with air-conditioning, a light to repel insects, and a combination radio and TV set to keep its canine occupant amused.

HOME-DELIVERY TOILET PAPER

According to a survey among Japanese housewives, the three items they don't want to be seen carrying home are:

1. Detergent
2. Tissues (Kleenex)
3. Toilet paper

So Sumitomo Corp. latched on to the toilet paper-phobia and turned it into a profitable business. They have coreless rolls produced, eliminating waste and lowering prices, and have set up 450 home-delivery toilet paper shops around the nation. Twelve rolls to a pack cost about Y1,800 (about $14).

YENIMONY HITS JAPAN

Palimony lawyer Marvin Mitchelson is now plying his trade across the Pacific in high-yen Japan. He represented an obscure American singer named Joan Shepard in her divorce case against international Japanese financier Masao Sen. Shepard was asking for $276 million, but reportedly received only $38.5 million in the settlement. According to the Japanese weekly magazine *Focus,* Shepard got the family home, valued at $23 million, which was formerly the residence of the Ugandan ambassador in Tokyo's exclusive Hiroo district. She lives there with a menagerie of 14 cats, two dogs, and two turtles, and has resumed her nightclub career in Tokyo.

JAPAN'S CUPID AGENCY

It's called the Attack Agency, and it will propose for you if you are too shy or find your long-lost if you can't do it for yourself. Costs about $153 to approach her, or about $230 to locate a lost love.

ELEVATOR HEELS GET SHORT SHRIFT

Short men are given short shrift in Beijing's marriage market, and wearing high heels doesn't help, according to the Xinhua News Agency. Many Beijing women now set their sights on a 1.75 meter tall spouse, above average for a Chinese—and consider anyone shorter to be handicapped, according to the report. "Nowadays, girls put height first and academic level second when they look for a husband," an official at a match-making agency was quoted as saying. Seven to 10-centimeter heels are popular among many Chinese young men.

SILK UNDIES

Retailers in Japan and Taiwan have reported escalating sales in silk underpants—as much as four or five times the price of cotton or nylon—because of a belief that they increase virility.

WINDOW SNORKELING

Seibu Department Store teamed up with Mitsui Shipbuilding to build a steel and fiberglass tank suitable for scuba diving instruction. Seibu built one of the pools into their new store in Tokyo's Shibuya district and started scuba classes. "Bet Japan's the only place in the world where you can do your shopping and go diving at the same place," commented the *Yomiuri Shimbun*.

GOING WHOLE HOG

Gratitude comes expensive in Taiwan where a Hsinchu resident who wanted to sacrifice "the largest hog at the Ghost Festival celebrations" to thank the spirits for a profitable real estate deal found that the 600-kilo animal cost him U.S.$77,500.

BLIND DATE DISPENSER

A Japanese software company, All-Way, has developed a "Love-Seek" vending machine that dispenses "blind dates." You stick a thousand yen note (about $8) in the slot, and pictures of Japanese girls come up on the screen with their age, interests, vital statistics, and preferences in men. If you see something that looks interesting, you give the All-Way vendor a call for a date. The company has 10 date-vending machines on location in Osaka and Kyushu discotheques.

"The strongest perfumes attract the ugliest flies."

Chinese proverb

BEAUTY AND THE BIZ

HARROWING HAIRPIECES

Five Japanese men sued a leading Japanese wig-maker for allegedly selling them more toupees than they needed. Apparently, the company's salesmen pressured them into buying "new and improved" versions as well as "seasonal models" of their wigs. The underlying threat was that if they didn't buy the wigs, the company might scrimp on their customer service. One bereft man bought 33 toupees over an eight-year period at the cost of about $80,000.

PERMANENT FACIALS

Beauty parlors are doing booming business in China but hair-styling and facials are not all that are offered. One shop in Beijing's eastern district, for example, performs half a dozen cosmetic surgery operations on eyelids each week; another uses lasers to remove freckles, moles, and warts. The operations are inexpensive and often performed by moonlighting doctors from nearby hospitals who are sometimes also called upon to raise the bridges of noses, make double-fold eyelids, and remove wrinkles. Cosmetics are also in great demand and are increasing in price as quality improves. "Many people nowadays spend lots of money to make themselves look younger and more impressive," says Nie Baoxun, manager of the Monita Hair and Beauty Parlor, which also operates a popular training school offering four-month courses. "It is fashionable nowadays to be a beautician," explains Miss Baoxun.

HAIR PLAY

Hiru-sham, or "noon-time shampoos," are extremely popular with Tokyo office workers with 30-minute shampoo and blow-dry specials offered for only $7—about one quarter of the usual price. And a current big-seller is the Shampoo Dresser, an outsized sink low to the ground (to allow sitting) with mirror, cabinet, and hand-held shower nozzle. "Young women have recently become very concerned about their hair," says Yutaka Nakamura, spokesman for Toto, Ltd., a major maker of bathroom fixtures. "Students in Japan are very confined by school uniforms and dress codes. There is at least some freedom in washing and styling their hair as they wish."

TRADITIONS IN FLUX

NEO-KIMONOS

Traditionalists may deplore it but nothing has deterred Tokyo designer Akemi Sone's experiments to adapt the *kimono* to modern life, creating a parallel line of what she calls "very wearable clothing." Such variations as off-the-shoulder styles, sleeves worn as hood or shawl and kimonos hiked up as mini dresses to accompany high heels and jeans are Sone hallmarks. Terming these *kirumonos* ("wearable kimonos") the adventurous designer gained her insights into modernizing the traditional dress when she left her job as teacher at her parents' *kimono* school to become a music reviewer and came into contact with many entertainers who welcomed her advice on how to restyle Japan's basic garment. "I felt sad to see the number of women wearing kimono becoming ever smaller," she said, "Each era had their own unique style and I wanted [this one] to have one too."

JAPANESE FARMHOUSES ON THE MOVE

Centuries-old Japanese farmhouses, *minkas,* regarded as white elephants a few years ago because of their size and expensive-to-repair thatched roofs, are now selling for millions of dollars and being re-erected in such distant places as Honolulu and Buenos Aires, according to the *Japan Times.* Antique dealer Yoshihiro Takishita who lives in one himself on a mountainous Kamakura road has shipped a score of *minkas* to various parts of the world. Originally built without nails and boasting gracefully arched ceiling beams, the ancient houses can be modernized with central heating and efficient kitchens without spoiling their traditional look, although their reassembly by skilled carpenters takes months.

DEPARTMENT STORES SELL CLOSET SPACE

With a single phone call you can reserve "closet space" in Japan. Yokohama Takashimaya, for example, offers a "Trunk Room" service for Y30,000 (about $230) a year, including insurance against losses of up to Y1,000,000 (about U.S.$7,692). They plan to expand to carpets, furs, books, and clothing in the future, complete with appropriate cleaning services. "Yes. A closet away from home is convenient," notes *Shukan Shincho* magazine. "And kind of sad."

RENTAL WEDDING GUESTS

You can't say your wedding was a success unless high muckitymucks from your company and important friends of the family were in attendance.

Neko-no Te ("Cat's Paw"), a company in Tokyo provides these people if you are having trouble getting them to come to the wedding. In other words, if too few important acquaintances or company bigwigs are coming you can call *Neko-no-te* and get actors to take the parts. They've provided as many as 60 guests of a party of 80, for example. They can get away with this charade because of Japan's rigid seating system and the fact that little mixing is done at wedding receptions.

The people are not the only mock items at a wedding reception. The cake isn't real. And the dress doesn't belong to the bride . . . *Neko-no-te*'s business is growing, the *Wall Street Journal* reported.

NEW YEAR'S GRIEF

New Year's Eve is a dangerous time in the Philippines, where scores of people are wounded by firecrackers and a few killed by stray bullets annually in the frenzied celebrations that cap the holidays. Among the best-selling explosives are the Judas Belt, with 100 or more firecrackers strung on a bandolier, their fuses tied in a row to create a machine gun-like effect when they are set off. Also popular are the Baby Dynamite and the Super Grandfather, firecrackers which can cause temporary deafness with their blasts.

EDUCATION

ENGLISH CLASSES ON RAILS

Twice-a-week English classes are held on Japan Rail's Shonan Shinjuku Liner, which runs nonstop between Hiratsuka and Shinjuku every day. Three months of classes cost Y30,000 (about $230) in addition to the rail fare.

SWITCHING FROM ENGLISH TO TAGALOG

In an attempt to supplant English and hasten the development of its own national language,

President Corazon Aquino has mandated that government offices throughout the Philippines must communicate with each other in Filipino, a Malayo-Polynesian language based mainly on Tagalog, which has long been widely spoken in Manila and its neighboring provinces.

STUDENTS WED SOVIETS

Bangladesh students intending to study in the Soviet Union are made to sign a bond before they leave Bangladesh that they will not marry Soviet girls. The Bangladesh government took the step in 1989 because it was not happy with the behavior of the students who went to study in the Soviet Union, because most of them married Russian girls and brought them back to Bangladesh. According to a report in the *Bengali Daily,* there are over 700 Bangladesh students in the Soviet Union, with about 300 students married to Soviet girls.

CORPORATIONS FUND CHAIRS

Japan's Ministry of Education now allows universities to use funds received from corporations to create endowed chairs instead of putting those donations into the ordinary university treasury.

Endowed chairs are supposed to help alleviate two problems: One, corporate donations to institutions of higher learning outside Japan are twice as much as those to domestic universities; two, Japan's brightest and best are leaving the country to do research at overseas universities and few non-Japanese are coming to Japan for their advanced studies.

The University of Tokyo, Research Center for Advanced Science and Technology, plans to staff with all non-Japanese professors and assistant professors. The problem is, asks *Shukan AERA,* How many good non-Japanese researchers are going to be willing to leave the excellent facilities of their home country to work in Japan?

Endowed Chairs

University	Chair	Sponsor	Endowment
University of Tokyo	Future materials	Nippon Steel	Y30 million
Research Center for Advanced Science and Technology	Computing and communications	NEC	Y30 million
	Electronic communications	NTT	Y30 million
	Information sciences	CSK	Y35 million
School of Law	Securities exchange law	Nomura Securities	Y20 million
Tokyo Institute of Technology Research Laboratory of Engineering Materials	Ceramics	TDK	Y30 million
University of Tsukuba Graduate School	Finance	Yamaichi Securities	Y25 million
Kyushu University	Insurance studies	Yasuda Fire & Marine Insurance	Y20 million

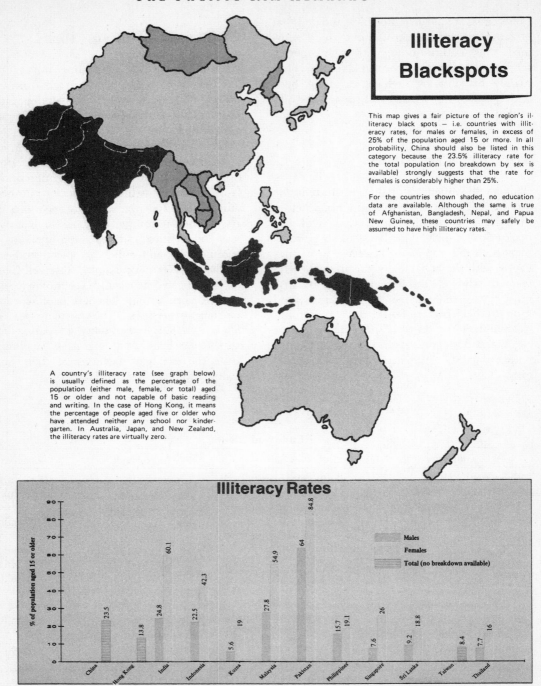

Illiteracy Blackspots

This map gives a fair picture of the region's illiteracy black spots — i.e. countries with illiteracy rates, for males or females, in excess of 25% of the population aged 15 or more. In all probability, China should also be listed in this category because the 23.5% illiteracy rate for the total population (no breakdown by sex is available) strongly suggests that the rate for females is considerably higher than 25%.

For the countries shown shaded, no education data are available. Although the same is true of Afghanistan, Bangladesh, Nepal, and Papua New Guinea, these countries may safely be assumed to have high illiteracy rates.

A country's illiteracy rate (see graph below) is usually defined as the percentage of the population (either male, female, or total) aged 15 or older and not capable of basic reading and writing. In the case of Hong Kong, it means the percentage of people aged five or older who have attended neither any school nor kindergarten. In Australia, Japan, and New Zealand, the illiteracy rates are virtually zero.

Illiteracy Rates

% of population aged 15 or older

Legend: Males / Females / Total (no breakdown available)

Country	Value 1	Value 2
China	23.5	
Hong Kong	13.8	
India	24.8	60.1
Indonesia	22.5	42.3
Korea	5.6	19
Malaysia	27.8	54.9
Pakistan	64	84.8
Philippines	15.7	19.1
Singapore	7.6	26
Sri Lanka	9.2	18.8
Taiwan	8.4	18.8
Thailand	7.7	16

Students per Teacher

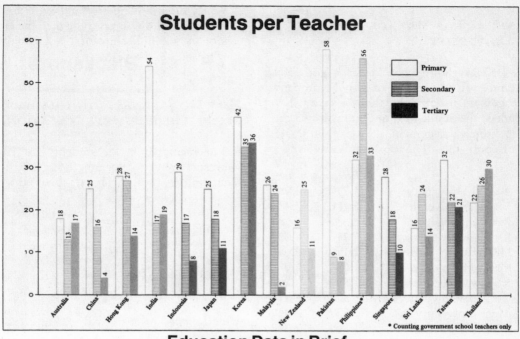

- Primary
- Secondary
- Tertiary

* Counting government school teachers only

Education Data in Brief

Schooling statistics refer in most cases to 1982. Exceptions are India (1980), Korea (1983), Malaysia (1984), Pakistan (1985), the Philippines (1984), Sri Lanka (1983), Taiwan (1985), and Thailand (1981). Definitions may also vary among countries.

AUSTRALIA
Primary schools
Enrollment 1,659,734
Teachers 91,306
Secondary schools
Enrollment 1,139,820
Teachers 86,364
Tertiary institutions
Enrollment 337,953
Instructors 19,377

CHINA
Primary schools
Enrollment 139,720,400
Teachers 5,504,600
Secondary schools
Enrollment 47,027,900
Teachers 2,870,500
Tertiary institutions
Enrollment 1,175,238
Instructors 286,908

HONG KONG
Primary schools
Enrollment 538,450
Teachers 19,388
Secondary schools
Enrollment 459,611
Teachers 16,871
Tertiary institutions
Enrollment 71,382
Instructors 4,992

INDIA
Primary schools
Enrollment 72,687,840
Teachers 1,345,376
Secondary schools
Enrollment 29,337,454
Teachers 1,731,987
Tertiary institutions
Enrollment 5,345,580
Instructors 277,500

INDONESIA
Primary schools
Enrollment 27,990,275
Teachers 971,893
Secondary schools
Enrollment 5,697,231
Teachers 336,336
Tertiary institutions
Enrollment 616,117
Instructors 74,470

JAPAN
Primary schools
Enrollment 11,901,000
Teachers 475,000
Secondary schools
Enrollment 10,011,340
Teachers 553,684
Tertiary institutions
Enrollment 2,391,915
Instructors 225,507

KOREA
Primary schools
Enrollment 5,257,164
Teachers 126,163
Secondary schools
Enrollment 4,571,459
Teachers 128,967
Tertiary institutions
Enrollment 1,075,969
Instructors 30,049

MALAYSIA
Primary schools
Enrollment 2,145,000
Teachers 83,700
Secondary schools
Enrollment 1,265,000
Teachers 53,859
Tertiary institutions
Enrollment 33,986
Instructors 16,508

NEW ZEALAND
Primary schools
Enrollment 359,011
Teachers 22,277
Secondary schools
Enrollment 351,034
Teachers 13,883
Tertiary institutions
Enrollment 82,666
Instructors 7,753

PAKISTAN
Primary schools
Enrollment 9,239,000
Teachers 159,062
Secondary schools
Enrollment 1,192,000
Teachers 128,467
Tertiary institutions
Enrollment 56,600
Instructors 7,042

PHILIPPINES
Primary schools
Enrollment 8,793,773
Teachers 273,699
Secondary schools
Enrollment 3,323,063
Teachers 59,263
Tertiary institutions
Enrollment 1,127,960
Instructors 33,935

SINGAPORE
Primary schools
Enrollment 289,092
Teachers 10,286
Secondary schools
Enrollment 187,148
Teachers 10,231
Tertiary institutions
Enrollment 30,966
Instructors 3,052

SRI LANKA
Primary schools
Enrollment 2,153,595
Teachers 133,650
Secondary schools
Enrollment 1,367,754
Teachers 57,854
Tertiary institutions
Enrollment 57,352
Instructors 4,120

TAIWAN
Primary schools
Enrollment 2,313,240
Teachers 71,853
Secondary schools
Enrollment 1,671,052
Teachers 76,129
Tertiary institutions
Enrollment 428,576
Instructors 20,848

THAILAND
Primary schools
Enrollment 7,449,219
Teachers 333,351
Secondary schools
Enrollment 1,990,866
Teachers 76,339
Tertiary institutions
Enrollment 1,056,809
Instructors 35,731

RANKING TOP MANAGEMENT BY UNIVERSITY

Toyo Keizai Shimposha research company announced the ranking of listed company management in Japan by the university they attended, the result of a questionnaire to the 36,886 top management personnel in 2,017 major companies. The top 10 universities:

School	Persons	Share
1. Tokyo University	4,770	12.9%
2. Waseda University	2,716	7.4%
3. Keio University	2,530	6.9%
4. Kyoto University	2,213	6.0%
5. Hitotsubashi University	1,118	3.0%
6. Chuo University	1,055	2.9%
7. Kobe University	882	2.4%
8. Tohoku University	874	2.4%
9. Meiji University	837	2.3%
10. Nihon University	800	2.2%

HERE'S A LOOK AT EDUCATION-RELATED COSTS IN JAPAN

A 39-year-old man who works for Japan's giant Mitsui & Co. heads a family of five. Here are his monthly education-related costs (for 1988), according to *Shukan Gendai*:

Yearly total: Y922,800 (about $7,098). And that's not all. It doesn't include the nine cram-school and violin lessons for a 9-year-old boy starting later in the year.

HOW DO JAPANESE 6TH GRADERS SPEND THEIR SUMMER VACATION?

600 elementary school students in Tokyo were surveyed to determine how they spent their summer vacation. Here's what 6th graders said.

I went to *juku* (cram school)	75% (24% of whom went every day)
Studied at home	
1 hour/day	52%
2 hours/day	13%
Went to *juku*	
2 hours/day	35%
3 to 4 hours	39%
Over 4 hours	35%

CHINA BY DEGREES

Since China began awarding academic degrees in 1981, the nation has granted over one

	Boy 10	Boy 9	Girl 5	Total
School	Y 4,500	Y 4,500		Y 9 000
Cram school	17,000			17,000
Abacus	5,000			5,000
Calligraphy		3,500		3,500
Piano	6,600		6,600	13,200
Ice-skating			6,400	6,400
Boy Scouts	4,000			4,000
Baseball	1,000	1,000		2,000
Swimming	4,500	4,500		9,000
Home Economics			7,800	7,800
Total	Y42,600	Y13,500	Y20,800	Y76,900

million bachelor's degrees, 53,300 Master's degrees, and 664 Ph.D. degrees, according to the State Council's academic degree committee.

CHINESE KIDS' ALLOWANCE

Middle-school students in Beijing receive pocket money of about Rmb 11 ($3) a month, a sum that is turning them into spendthrifts, the *Beijing Daily* reported. A survey of 259 students, aged 15 to 17, showed they carried around 10% of a worker's monthly salary of about Rmb 100 (about U.S.$27). They spent their money drinking, smoking, and eating in expensive restaurants while girls gave gifts to other classmates.

CHINESE STUDENTS GO OVERSEAS, FAIL TO RETURN

About half of the 40,000 Chinese students sent abroad to study have not returned and the Chinese government is now starting to take action by demanding compensation from their families. Before leaving, students usually must sign an agreement agreeing to compensate his work unit to the equivalent of about $5,000, but until recently this was rarely invoked. Now with so many students using overseas study as an illegal route to emigration, authorities are starting to crack down. In a Shanghai case where the court found that an absent student's wife did not have the ability to repay the guarantee, it was ruled that his parents were liable.

CHINA'S ILLITERATE TEENS

Blaming greedy parents and lazy teachers, the *Guangming Daily* reported that an increasing number of illiterate children under 15 were dropping out of school to work. In one impoverished town in southeast China's Jiangxi province, children comprised nearly a quarter of those working on building projects, readers told the paper; and in Hebei province, one third of the street peddlers were children. The trend was undermining the government's aim of nine years' compulsory education, the paper added. "The whole of society should pay attention. Send these dear children back to school."

THAILAND SHORT ON ENGINEERING STUDENTS

Because Thailand's universities and vocational schools have not adapted themselves to new economic trends, critics have charged they are still turning out a disproportionate number of civil-service aspirants and social-science graduates instead of the engineers, managers, foremen, and craftsmen the country more urgently needs. The engineering industry alone needs 7,000 new recruits each year but less than one third of this number is expected to graduate. Chira Hongladarom, director of Thammasat University's Human Resources Institute, said that more than half of Thailand's unemployed students who graduated each year were unqualified to work in industry and financial jobs. The computer, construction, electronics and tourism industries are all in need of more entrants. "If the current situation persists," says Chira, "it will take Thailand 10 years to become a newly industrialized country (NIC) instead of five."

SPICING UP JAPANESE TEXTBOOKS

Japan's textbook publishers are trying to counter their readers' diminishing attention span by spicing up the duller chapters with *manga* comics and references to such contemporary figures as athletes and singers. Environmental problems such as acid rain and desertification are also showing up in schoolbooks for the first time.

BANGLADESHI STUDENTS FEEL CHEATED

Nearly 100 people were injured when Bangladeshi students demanding the right to cheat during college final exams fought teachers and police. The students ransacked examination centers in northern Bogra district. Police also fought running battles with students in western Chuadanga district, where about 1,000 examinees walked out protesting against "too tight" monitoring.

CHINESE LEARNING MORE ENGLISH

English is now being taught in 76% of all urban Beijing elementary schools because foreign languages are becoming an integral part of China's opening to the outside world.

ASIAN MIGRANTS BETTER EDUCATED

An Australian study revealed that Asian migrants to Australia are better educated, more socially adaptable, and more likely to land good jobs than most immigrant groups. The 1988 study conducted by Laksiri Jayasuriya, a sociology professor at the University of Western Australia, showed that Asians earned an average of $12,830, more than all immigrant groups except expatriate New Zealanders and North Americans.

SAMURAI MATH

Along with the "Suzuki method" of teaching youngsters to play violin, there is another Japanese adjunct to education—the "Kumon" method of teaching math. Self-instruction, speed, and accuracy are the bases of the program, which was created 30 years ago in Japan by math teacher Toru Kumon in order to help his own son. Today, nearly 1.4 million students in Japan study Kumon in after-school centers in addition to their regular school instruction. There are now a number of Kumon centers in the United States. For more information, contact the Kumon Educational Institute at (415) 347-8818

HEALTH

EAST–WEST MEDICINE

China is the world's pioneer in the field of combining traditional holistic Chinese medicine with modern medicine and futuristic biotechnology techniques. Among recent Chinese medical breakthroughs are the following.

NEW METHOD OF CONTRACEPTION

Doctors in South China are training microwaves on acupressure points on men's genitals as a contraceptive method. Patients sit in a chair during the treatment, which lasts for 30 minutes each month, and raises the temperature of the scrotum to 40 or 42 degrees Celsius to slow the growth of sperm. Six months after stopping microwave sessions, a man recovers his fertility, according to doctors who are successfully employing this technique in Hengyang, Hunan province.

NEW ARTIFICIAL SKIN

Chinese doctors at a marine institute in the northeast Chinese city of Qingdao developed a new artificial skin which is composed mainly of shrimp and green turtle shells. The new skin substance was successfully tested on 124 patients, and was proven to adhere to scar tissue. It promotes new skin growth and is effective in preventing fungus infections. The artificial skin contains no toxins or proteins. It resembles the texture of real skin and will not be rejected by the body. It also allows air and moisture to pass through.

CEREBRAL PALSY CURE

China's doctors have found a new way to cure patients who suffer from atrophy of the cerebellum due to cerebral palsy. By employing a method which calls for the implantation of embryo tissue taken from the cerebellum in the brain, Shandong Medical University doctors have been successfully treating cerebral palsy victims since they began the program in 1987. Clinical symptoms of the disease include walking unsteadily, rigid movements, unclear speech, and dizziness.

LASERS STOP YOUR SMOKING

Dr. Wei Xiu-bing, a Chinese-American scientist who has been involved in researching the medical applications of lasers at the Massachusetts Institute of Technology, opened a stop-smoking center in Hong Kong based on laser-beam therapy. The use of laser beams on specific nerve centers induces the body to produce beta-endorphin which has a similar effect as nicotine, according to Wei. This helps relieve the effects of the sudden drop in nicotine in the body and reduces the craving for a cigarette. She prescribes 30 minutes of laser therapy every other day at her "Smoke-cut Center."

TRADITIONAL CHINESE MEDICINE IN SPACE

China has claimed initial success in treating space ailments with traditional Chinese medical theories and practices, according to the China Space Medicine Research Institute. Traditional Chinese medicine, breathing technique therapy, acupuncture, and moxibustion have been applied to the prevention of disturbances resulting from bone calcium shortage, noise, and radiation in space activities.

ALL EARS

Beijing doctor Long Xialing has introduced a new twist to traditional acupuncture methods by pressing hard seeds on specific points instead of injecting needles. Operating out of the General Hospital for the Armed Forces in the Chinese capital, Dr. Xialing claims to have cured more than 2,000 patients of a variety of ailments including hypertension, migraine, heart disease, obesity, and impotence. His favored method is to place seeds in the ears—which, according to classic Chinese works on the subject, house 360 acupuncture points—applying pressure with tiny pieces of rubberized fabric.

INFRARED ACUPUNCTURE

Demand is growing for an infrared ray lamp producing an electromagnetic wave which is said to improve circulation and make the body more resistant to diseases. Manufac-

Birth and Death Rates

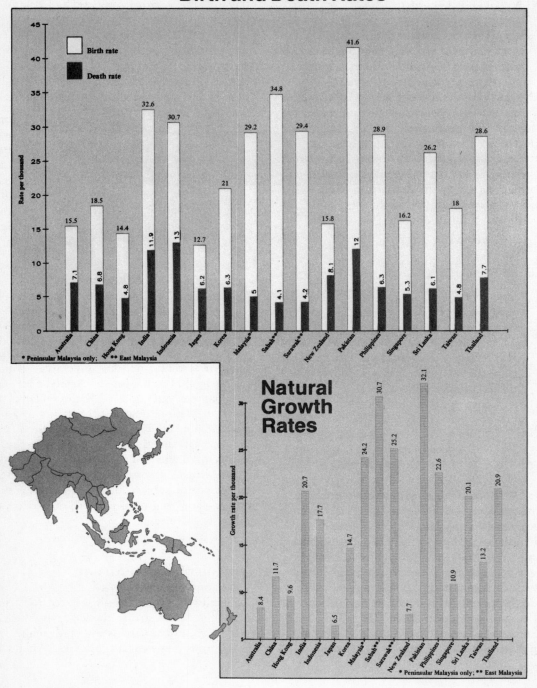

* Peninsular Malaysia only; ** East Malaysia

Natural Growth Rates

* Peninsular Malaysia only; ** East Malaysia

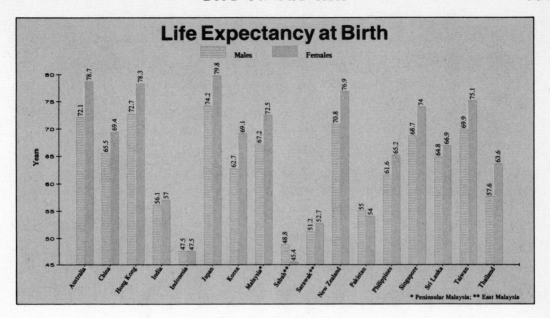

Life Expectancy at Birth

Males   Females

Differences in the life expectancy of females and males (above) are important indicators of not only a country's level of development, but also its social progress. In modern societies, women invariably tend to live considerably longer than men. Note that in Pakistan and the East Malaysian state of Sabah, men outlive women. In Indonesia, males and females still have the same life expectancy. In India, women have overtaken men in life expectancy only very recently, which is a sign of social and economic progress.

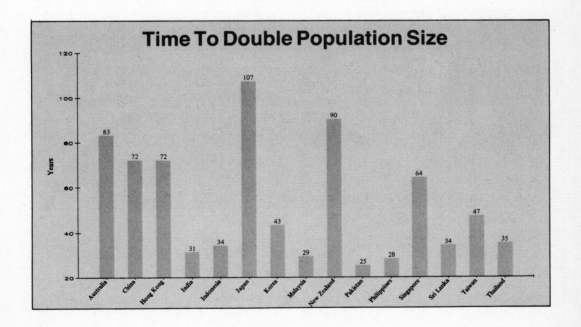

Time To Double Population Size

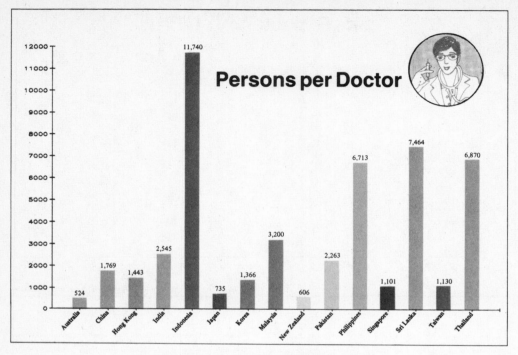

Persons per Doctor

Health Care Data in Brief

AUSTRALIA	
Hospitals:	1,142
Beds:	94,931
Doctors:	28,500
Dentists:	6,200
Pharmacists:	9,800
Nurses/midwives:	112,500

CHINA	
Hospitals:	66,662
Beds:	2,109,571
Doctors/Dentists:	587,564
Pharmacists:	33,541
Nurses/midwives:	925,444

HONG KONG	
Hospitals:	71
Beds:	22,110
Doctors:	3,626
Dentists:	779
Pharmacists:	436
Nurses/midwives:	17,401

INDIA	
Hospitals:	25,452
Beds:	1,066,164
Doctors:	268,712
Dentists:	8,648
Pharmacists:	155,621
Nurses/midwives:	368,320

INDONESIA	
Hospitals:	998
Beds:	83,101
Doctors:	12,400
Dentists:	2,500
Pharmacists:	1,800
Nurses/midwives:	139,099

JAPAN	
Hospitals:	9,403
Beds:	1,401,999
Doctors:	161,260
Dentists:	55,680
Pharmacists:	99,326
Nurses/midwives:	585,524

KOREA	
Hospitals:	n.a.
Beds:	63,804
Doctors:	28,365
Dentists:	4,266
Pharmacists:	26,307
Nurses/midwives:	22,054

MALAYSIA	
Hospitals:	182
Beds:	47,128
Doctors:	4,753
Dentists:	1,000
Pharmacists:	642
Nurses/midwives:	43,554

NEW ZEALAND	
Hospitals:	318
Beds:	23,052
Doctors:	5,210
Dentists:	1,160
Pharmacists:	2,300
Nurses/midwives:	22,000

PAKISTAN	
Hospitals:	652
Beds:	55,886
Doctors:	42,501
Dentists:	1,398
Pharmacists:	1,791
Nurses/midwives:	17,241

PHILIPPINES	
Hospitals:	1,635
Beds:	79,703
Doctors:	7,373
Dentists:	1,090
Pharmacists:	539
Nurses/midwives:	19,114

SINGAPORE	
Hospitals:	25
Beds:	9,899
Doctors:	2,219
Dentists:	501
Pharmacists:	374
Nurses/midwives:	8,006

SRI LANKA	
Hospitals:	493
Beds:	43,389
Doctors:	2,035
Dentists:	275
Pharmacists:	441
Nurses/midwives:	10,981

TAIWAN	
Hospitals:	1,000
Beds:	71,326
Doctors:	15,039
Dentists:	3,433
Pharmacists:	16,300
Nurses/midwives:	26,656

THAILAND	
Hospitals:	714
Beds:	71,718
Doctors:	6,867
Dentists:	1,224
Pharmacists:	2,650
Nurses/midwives:	42,713

tured by the Beijing Lock Factory, the Le Qun lamp is about the size and shape of a table lamp and works on a similar principle to that of moxibustion, an ancient form of Chinese medicine which is directed at acupoints without the need for acupuncture needles. It is already said to be in use in 100 Chinese hospitals.

	1965		1985	
	Men	Women	Men	Women
Average height (cm)	162.1	150.9	169.4	156.7
Average weight (kg)	55.8	48.5	61.0	49.9

DIAGNOSING FACIAL EXPRESSIONS

Facial expressions drawn by a computer are being used by doctors at Nagasaki University to convey checkup results to patients in an easy-to-understand manner, according to the *Japan Times*. Doctors show patients printed cards which depict their conditions—the cards range from bright-eyed to anemic-looking to stressed-out expressions, indicating high blood pressure. In 1986, the A-Bomb Victims Center developed a computer system that enabled conversions of data pertaining to some 100,000 patients into facial graphics.

JAPAN'S NEW BREED

Japan is breeding a new kind of Japanese. They call them the "New Breed" or the "New Species." They are aged between 20 and 25 and they really do have a new physical appearance:

Face: Rounded but less flat; smaller jaws; more prominent nose.
Legs: Longer, thinner with less flesh on the instep.
Body: Men's waists are larger; women's abdomens protrude.

Looking at the figures:

They spent their infancy in the late 1970s and early 1980s during Japan's high-growth era. Food was good and nutritious, but instant food products also gained a great deal of popularity. Because parents were busy, the children began to go to bed later. Instead of exercising at play in the daytime, they spent their time studying. So the new species appears to have lost their physical tone, and it shows in their physical attributes. They are tall, and their legs are long, but they lack muscle tone, according to *21* magazine.

MORE ROCKS, LESS POTATOES

Singapore proclaimed itself a "rugged society" in the 1960s after it withdrew from the Malaysian Federation. But now government leaders are worried that the incredible economic gains forged by this Asian Tiger are being jeopardized by a younger generation which is growing up too soft. Singapore's Advisory Council on Sports and Recreation is now promoting rugby, rock climbing, and sea sports in schools. "We do not want to develop a population of 'couch potatoes' whose gymnastics and activities are confined to the mind and whose fingers are only nimble at pressing buttons," declared Supiah Dhanabalan, cabinet minister for national development in a speech in Singapore.

SUPER-COLD TREATMENTS

While receiving super-cold treatments for rheumatism, Kajima Yukinari (40) noticed marked improvement on his skin where the treatments were done. He has now set up VLT Salon where liquid nitrogen-cooled air at −150°C is used to improve epidermal circulation, which improves the condition of your skin. It costs about $92 per session, and it takes several sessions to show results.

Freeze-Dried Follicles: The hottest new hair restoration treatment being offered by Tokyo beauty salons is called "Frozen Hair Restoring Method." According to the weekly *Shukan Post,* here's how it works: The scalp is stimulated with air that's cooled up 180 degrees below zero centigrade. The stress on the roots of the hair supposedly makes them active again. Three to six months treatment (for ladies only) costs about $3,850.

ACUPUNCTURE SUIT

The Japanese have developed a *shiatsu* (acupuncture points) suit which comes with all the points clearly marked on it so that even a beginner can provide a terrific Japanese *shiatsu* massage. From the Tokyo firm Field Sangyo, priced at about $150.

THE $6 MILLION DOLLAR MAN DOWN UNDER

In the future, football players with knee injuries may be down but not under, thanks to a radical new microsurgery technique developed by Australian surgeons at the Royal Adelaide Hospital.

The technique involves transplanting cartilage to injured joints by making a small incision in the knee with a specially designed instrument.

In a landmark operation, Australian surgeons transplanted cartilage from a dead automobile accident victim to a patient. Four days after the operation, the patient left the hospital without even a limp, ready to kick a fieldgoal.

Implications of this new surgery are wide-ranging, especially for those who suffer from degenerative diseases affecting the joints. Those crippled by arthritis, for example, may now seek the ultimate relief.

Australian medicine and biotechnology has long been on the cutting edge. In 1985, researchers at the University of Melbourne developed a bionic ear that uses a silicon chip to replace the snail-shaped cochlea in the inner ear.

They are now working on a "super-chip" that combines thousands of transistors onto a single silicon chip the size of the nail on the little finger. When that project is completed, deaf people should be able to hear normal conversations—and maybe even eavesdrop on conversations held a hundred miles away.

PLASTIC SURGERY IN THE PRC

Famous Taiwanese plastic surgeon Li Wenlong moved to the Shenzhen special economic zone in South China after performing cosmetic operations for more than 2,000 patients in Beijing. Li came to the mainland in 1986 and opened the first cosmetic surgery center in China. His operations include nose heightening, wrinkle removing, breast implants, and constructive surgery. The People's Republic of China has 700,000 patients who need plastic surgery but less than 500 specialists in this branch of medicine.

AIDS IN ASIA

Some Singapore tourist agencies specializing in arranging "sex tours" to Thailand are reporting business is down by as much as 40% since the AIDS scare took hold. And the proportion of single males between 30 and 50 who used to visit Bangkok and the resort of Haadyai is also down; a higher percentage of today's visitors are young married couples.

One 55-year-old administration officer told a Singapore newspaper that on his visits to Thailand, his custom was to hire a woman for about $50 a day in return for which she would provide him with massages, sex, and sometimes cooking and laundry as well. He had stopped doing this he said because it was too dangerous now. Another visitor said he had switched his activity to gambling because sleeping with prostitutes—there are an estimated 5,000 of them in Haadyai—was "like playing Russian roulette."

The Thai Health Ministry said about 8,000 people in Thailand were known to have the HIV virus which causes AIDS but some of the country's health experts say the estimate is too low and accuse the government of withholding information to protect the tourist industry. A report in Hong Kong's *Sing Tao Weekly* estimated the number of Thailand's HIV carriers as 13,000 but said that most of them were intravenous drug users, although up to 44% of prostitutes in northern tourist areas and 31% in the south were affected. As of early 1990, 22 of the 34 people reported to having come down with the disease had died.

Neighboring Malaysia, with eight out of 11 patients dead and 84 others identified as having the HIV virus, has tightened its borders. The situation in the Philippines, with 21 AIDS deaths, is comparable to Thailand because of the large numbers of prostitutes (61 of whom have been found to be HIV-positive) working near U.S. military bases. Certain visitors to the country—foreign sailors, U.S. servicemen, and women posted to American bases, as well as anyone seeking a visa to the country for more than six months—must now show AIDS-free certificates to enter. India requires arriving foreign students to take an AIDS test, and says this will also apply to all foreigners coming to stay for more than one year.

In China, foreigners applying for residence permits must present a local health certificate which includes an AIDS test. Taiwan (128 known carriers, 12 deaths) has distributed warning pamphlets to every household in the country, and Singapore (41 carriers, 9 deaths) has lifted a ban on condom advertising. A World Health Organization report at the close of 1989 counter 2,122 AIDS cases—less than 3% of the world total—in the Asia-Pacific region but Hong Kong Aids specialist Dr. Patrick Li Chung-ki has warned countries not to be complacent. "We need to act now. If we don't there is a real chance Asia will catch up to the rest of the world," he says.

The South Korean pharmaceutical firm Samchully Pharmaceutical Co. is producing AZT, the drug which brings hope to AIDS victims, and exporting it at half the current market price of $155 a milligram.

MEDICS SEARCH TIBETAN SCRIPTURES

Tibetan doctors in the remote Himalayan foothills have been seeking a cure for the killer disease AIDS in ancient Buddhist scriptures. Dr. Choedak, the Dalai Lama's personal physician, told the Harvard Medical School and the University of California, San Francisco, that AIDS is one of the 18 diseases which Tibetan scriptures prophesied would emerge during an era of degeneration, "[when] sentient beings indulge in various types of nonvirtues in thought and deed." He pointed out that AIDS destroys *Dhang* or the vital essence of life—a clear fluid found in the center of the heart. The doctor has developed a prescription based on *tsothe,* a potion which contains some 17 metals and minerals.

STRESS

CORPORATE STRESS IN JAPAN CLAIMS TOP MANAGEMENT

Corporate stress in Japan is rising—and it's increasingly claiming the lives of top Japanese management, according to a chilling report by the *Asahi Shimbun,* one of Japan's leading newspapers.

To blame are pressures stemming from Western protectionism, the high *yen*'s devastating impact on Japanese exports, the specter of rising unemployment, as well as an extremely painful period of industrial restructuring for the nation, not to mention a slew of political and corporate scandals like the Toshiba affair, which cost Toshiba Corp. about $3 billion in lost revenues since the U.S. Senate banned the company's imports for a period of up to five years.

During one particularly alarming period in 1987, when the syndrome was first detected, there was an average of one death each month of a president of a major Japanese corporation.

Among the leading industrialists who died then in quick consecutive order: Kondo Takeo (64) of Mitsubishi Corp., Sakabe Takeo (66) of Asahi Glass, Nakabe Tojiro (60) of Taiyo Fisheries, Shimizu Teruhisa (61) of Fuji Electric Co., Asano Kohosuke (63) of Nihon Light Metal, Ogawa Kohei (66) of Tombow Pencil, and Ichiro Hattori (52) president of Seiko-Epson, the leading Japanese computer-maker.

In its post-obituary analysis, the *Asahi Shimbun* entertained an eerie thought about what it was that made these executives ignore their health and drive themselves so relentlessly: "These men survived World War II, so they lived as if their lives were bonuses, not taking care of their health."

JAPAN'S STRESS CODE

As society's stress level rises so do sales of books, systems, and music designed to relieve it. CBS Sony has sold almost half a million of its "biomusic" tapes, after lengthy experiments to discover what sounds were most effective in relieving tension; and a Tokyo bookstore was besieged with mid-30s business types during its month-long campaign to push books devoted to meditation techniques. (See "Tranquility Stone," p. 406.)

Computer-filled offices have raised the pressure stakes, suggests Gakugei University's Takashi Asakura, "People working there are facing a situation in which mistakes, even the slightest ones, can cause devastating damage to their company." In Tokyo, the 16 armchairs—equipped with headphones and

---

THE ONE-MINUTE ZEN MANAGER

Stressed-out Japanese executives who are too busy to relax have now found the way. They practice instant Zen meditation in a chair. The new seated version is proving popular even with the young Japanese Sony Walkman generation who, spoiled by soft living, are unable to sit cross-legged on a tatami mat in the traditional full-lotus position.

"Chair *zazen*" is simple. Here is how you can practice it yourself:

Sit slightly forward in your seat—it is important not to lean against the back of the chair. Keep your spine straight and relax your shoulders. Nose and navel should be aligned.

Next, place the back of your left hand on the palm of your right and press the tips of your thumbs together lightly. Eyes should be half-closed. Lower your line of sight to a point in front of you one yard from the bridge of your nose. Close your mouth so that upper and lower teeth touch, and place the tip of the tongue against your teeth.

Once in position, sway gently to the left and right in a wide arc, gradually narrowing it until, like a pendulum, you come to a stop. Your upper body should now be erect and stable.

Take a long, deep breath through your mouth, then exhale slowly and quietly through your nose. Do not try to shut out random thoughts. Concentrate instead on maintaining the correct position and breathing properly. When posture and breathing feel comfortable, you will begin to experience a sense of mental serenity.

Meditation sessions can last from one minute to 10 minutes depending on how much time you can spare. Chances are you will feel completely refreshed even after you've had an exhausting, strenuous day at the office.

More and more Japanese are turning to Zen for answers to the problems of modern life. "To reduce stress, you must first learn how to control it," explains Zen master Tsugen Narasaki, a leader of the Soto sect of Zen, which introduced the concept. "Chair *zazen* is a good way to do that. You can practice while commuting, on a business trip, or even at the office."

---

special goggles—of the Brain Mind Gym are kept fully occupied. Members take turns to sit back and relax, geometrical patterns passing before their eyes, as they listen to a blend of pure sound and classical rock. "We figure that the stress caused by machines can be cured by other machines," explains gym manager Hiromitsu Hoshi.

Dai-Ichi Kangyo Bank's survey of 500 married salaried workers in Tokyo, aged between 20 and 59, found more than nine out of 10 with physical complaints (31% attributed to stress and 18% to overwork).

OXYGEN EASY CHAIR

The secret ingredient in the Nippon Sanso company's "chair of ultimate comfort" is oxygen, dispensed to the sitter together with a blend of music and vibrations. It's just the latest gimmick in the Japanese fad for inhaling oxygen as an antidote to polluted air. One Tokyo pub has a pure oxygen room where, for the equivalent of a dime, semi-inebriated customers can recuperate; and an Osaka cafe offers a 10-minute loan of an oxygen mask for about $6. (See index for other oxygen applications and services.)

INFRARED SHIRT COLLAR

Poppy Shirts markets a product that gives off far-infrared rays. It's a plain white shirt on the outside, but has a special fine ceramics powder on the inside of the collar and along the shoulders. The powder is supposed to give off the far-infrared rays. Supposedly, far-infrared rays cause blood vessels to expand, increasing circulation. So wearing a Poppy "Mount" shirt (60% cotton, 40% polyester, perma press), you're not supposed to suffer from stiff shoulders and other disorders due to fatigue.

VILE VIALS

NO SPEED LIMIT

One of Japan's biggest businesses is pharmaceutical—the sale of legalized "uppers" or *kusuri* (euphemistally translated as "medicine"). In 1985, sales of upper drinks reached 140 billion yen (about $915 million). You can spend a *sarariman's* (salaryman's) modest 130 yen (about 85 cents) for a 100 ml vial of the popular Lipovitan D tonic, which will give you a working buzz. Or if you're a *shacho* (company president), you can afford to pay 3,000 yen (about $20) for a hit of elite speed befitting your rank.

Streetcorner pharmacies base as much as 50% of their profits on sales of uppers, which are displayed in sturdy glass cases provided by leading companies. There are even specially formulated mixtures for Japan's school kids to help them get through cram schools and entrance exams. Taisho Pharmaceutical Co., the speed-drink market leader, had sales

of about $503 million in 1985—60% of which came from the 100 ml bottles of Lipovitan D. The company's total profits topped $196 million.

What's in these little brown glass tonic vials with their break-off tops? Sato Pharmaceuticals' best-selling "Yunkeru" tonic contains: Viper tincture, 100 mg, followed by Civet (cat) and Bezoar (goat) tinctures, plant extract, Royal (bee) Jelly, a collection of B vitamins, and 50 mg of anyhydrous caffeine. It's priced at 1,200 yen or about $7.80 for a 100 ml vial (See "Tokyo's Energy Pool," p. 367.)

TONICS

POWDERED ANTS, CHINA'S ANCIENT ELIXIR

For a bracing elixir once prized by the emperors of China, try powdered ants, Chinese experts say. According to the *China Daily,* powdered ants contain as much protein as similar quantities of soybeans or shrimp, and four times the calories of beef. Reportedly, ants were a delicacy on the menu of China's Imperial court for 3,000 years. Experts said homemade ant powder and medicinal drinks made from ants have cured diseases such as rheumatoid arthritis.

HERBS

POACHED HERBS

The Chinese government is attempting to stop the uncontrolled harvesting of traditional Chinese medicinal herbs in an attempt to protect the valuable plants from depletion, according to the *China Daily*. The State Administration Bureau of Traditional Chinese Medicines reported that severe damage has been inflicted on China's herbal resources because of indiscriminate harvesting.

Licorice root is rapidly disappearing from Gansu province, traditionally one of the herb's biggest producers. From 1985 to 1987, about 6 million kg of licorice root were dug up in Gansu, up to four times as a many as in the year before.

Ginseng Capital of the World: Eighty percent of China's ginseng and one fifth of the world's total is produced in Tonghua city in northwest China's Jilin province, which has been cultivating the roots of this herbal tonic for 400 years. The city's annual ginseng festival promotes more than 250 ginseng products available as medicine, tonics, drinks, and cosmetics.

Shanghai is China's top producer of traditional Chinese medicine, according to a government survey. The city produces 1,023 kinds of traditional Chinese medicine ingredients, of which 829 kinds are medicinal herbs and the remainder are ingredients taken from animals.

India's Legal Opium Exports

Despite stricter checks on narcotics trafficking, India continues to export more than 600 tons of opium (worth about $20 million) each year, the "mainly for medicinal use" crop being a substantial source of foreign exchange earnings.

Medicinal Rip-Offs

Peasants in the East China province of Zhenjiang made more than Rmb 100,000 (about $27,000) for selling fake tiger penises, feet, and extract. The peasants used the heart, feet, penis, skin, and kidney of cows and pigs to produce the fakes, which they sold to more than 200,000 people in 20 provinces and cities to treat rheumatism, stomach ache, dizziness, and other ailments.

Cancer Enhancer: The Public Health Bureau of Beijing's Haidian district closed down a clinic offering a "cancer cure" made from peanut shells and potato roots that clinical tests showed actually speeded up the disease's progress.

Philippine Health Index

Percentage of children who die before first birthday: 5.7%.

Percentage of school-aged children who are malnourished: 70%.

The leading causes of death of children: pneumonia, premature birth, diarrhea, measles.

Percentage of Filipinos without access to safe drinking water: 34%; lacking minimum sanitary disposal facilities: 70%; infected with tuberculosis: 32%.

Percentage of GNP for health services recommended by World Health Organization for third-world countries: 5%.

Percentage of Philippines GNP allocated for health services: 0.7%.

Percentage of Filipino doctors working abroad: 45%; nurses working abroad: 60%.

Number of persons in Negros Occidental Province per government doctor: 108,000; per government soldier: 900.

SOURCE: *Fire on the Rim* (A Food First Book, The Institute for Food and Development Policy, San Francisco, 1989).

Do Japanese Like to Be Sick?

A survey of 8,955 hospitals and dental clinics by Japan's Ministry of Health and Welfare showed:

- 8.07 million Japanese a day are treated in the nation's hospitals—one in every 15.2 persons.
- 1.436 million are inpatients.
- 6.6335 million are outpatients.
- 43% of all patients are over 65 years of age, of whom 41.9% have been hospitalized for more than six months.

CHECKING-IN FOR CHECK-UPS

In line with Singapore's campaign to offer "total services," more first-class hotels are now offering "medical packages" for foreign visitors, according to Singapore's *Business Times*. A survey revealed that overseas visitors (especially those from neighboring southeast Asian countries) spent about $17.85 million on medical and dental treatment in Singapore in 1986. Now as part of a travel package, you can have a hernia operation or inexpensive root canal work done.

DATING SERVICE FOR DOCTORS

So many "workaholic" doctors and nurses in Singapore General Hospital are unmarried that the private company which operates the hospital has set up a social development office to end their perceived loneliness.

SOUTH KOREAN AND TAIWANESE COUNTRY DOCTORS—IN JAPAN

Despite graduating about 8,200 doctors per year—more than are needed—Japan's rural areas lack medical help because most doctors won't leave the cities. Thus, doctors are being recruited from Taiwan and South Korea who will be required to pass a standard medical test written in Japanese and then restricted to work in rural hospitals. At present about 20% of such jobs are filled by Koreans and Taiwanese.

LUXURY RR IN HONG KONG

Because of a series of snafus involving its operating license, Hong Kong's first luxury "rest and recuperation" hospital, The Retreat, which opened its doors in 1989, had only one patient admitted during its first five months of operation. The patient, a top Hong Kong executive, underwent a stress reduction program tended to by a staff of about 30.

Built by Australian group Paul Ramsey Hospitals, Ltd., this $10 million facility for rich invalids and stressed-out executives features 70 plush suites on a 9,000 square meter hilltop site overlooking Hong Kong's scenic Port Shelter Harbor. It also boasts a gym, tennis courts, and a gourmet restaurant. Suites start at about $315 per night.

NOISE POLLUTION IN INCUBATORS

Dr. Hiroshi Tamura, an assistant professor at the Osaka University in Japan, studies the problems that occur at the man/machine interface. One of his special areas of interest is incubators with their environmental maintenance equipment and medical monitoring gadgets. He found that during ordinary operation, the sound level inside an incubator is about 58 decibels. (Daytime in the suburbs is between 40 and 45 decibels.) If a baby starts crying, the decibel level climbs to 1021. That's equivalent to standing beneath the railway bridge as the train goes by. Of course, the good doctor now wants someone to make a quiet incubator.

MUSIC TO OPERATE BY

Since 1986, Takigawa Hospital in Hokkaido, Japan's northernmost island, has been allowing surgery patients to pick their favorite music as BGM (Background Music) for the operating room. The program is popular because the music apparently soothes the patient's worries away, whether the choice is Japanese *enka* (traditional ballads), hard rock, pop, or classical music. As soon as the patient is put under anesthesia, the music is changed to something the surgeon prefers. Before the patient wakes up, their own selection is put on again. In a survey of 130 patients, nearly 80% said the BGM was "pleasant."

JET LAG PILL FROM DOWN UNDER

An Australian pharmaceutical firm has reportedly developed a pill for jet lag, which, it claims, will be the "revolutionary new drug for the 1990s." The pill contains melatonin, a hormone secreted by the brain that supposedly reduces the effects of fatigue caused by long-distance travel.

GENETIC ENGINEERING BREAKTHROUGH

Australian scientists have claimed a breakthrough in genetic engineering that could lead to the elimination of many viruses in plants and animals. Dr. Jim Peacock of the Commonwealth Scientific and Industrial Research Organization told a 1988 science conference in Sydney that the new technique allowed scientists to switch off the functions of individual genes. "This is going to be of great significance in warding off virus disease or in stopping the production of proteins and other products in the plant that give unwanted flavors or other undesirable characteristics," he said.

ABORIGINES IN POOR HEALTH

Aborigines in many parts of Australia are unhealthier than they have been for years, according to a study by the Australian Institute of Health. Research has shown that the death rate of young and middle-aged adult aborigines appeared to have worsened in recent decades. Aboriginal men in rural areas of New South Wales lived to an average of only 51, the study showed. They were therefore dying 21 years younger than other Australians. Infant mortality rates were three times higher than for white Australians. Western Australia, where many aborigines live, is the country's biggest and most arid state, where aborigines still roam in tribes.

CHINA'S FIRST SUICIDE PREVENTION CENTER

Suicides and unnatural deaths have jumped by 50% in China since 1980, according to Xinhua News Agency. A survey of 10 million people in 25 localities found that the death rate from unnatural causes increased from 31 per 100,000 people in 1981 to 47 out of 100,000 in 1987. Four fifths of the deaths were due to suicide, drowning, poisoning, and traffic accidents. A group in Guangzhou in South China, set up the nation's first nongovernmental suicide-prevention center in 1988.

MALARIA VOLUNTEERS

Thanks to the courage of Malaysian volunteers who were willing to lie in huts with lighted doorways which enticed mosquitoes inside, Kuala Lumpur researchers have been able to mount a major attack on the disease-bearing insects by identifying their "distribution and density." One of the volunteers, designated as "Bare Leg Catchers," said that when he started manning the trap huts he didn't enjoy it, "but now I am experienced and the bites don't bother me at all." Head researcher Anuar Sunn paid tribute to the vol-

unteers' "immense" contributions which, he said, had virtually wiped out malaria in the region.

THRIVING BLACK MARKET FOR ORGAN TRANSPLANTS

A thriving illegal and dangerous industry in India is the sale of organ transplants. Children

---

RIM OF FIRE

SMOKE ALERT IN CHINA

China's 300 million smokers, whose heart disease rate is one-and-a-half times the rate of nonsmokers, are dropping dead in Beijing from cardiovascular disease at the rate of one per hour reports the Xinhua News Agency. Official figures show that 70% of Chinese men but only 7% of Chinese women smoke, and the tobacco industry provides around 8% of state revenue.

CHAINSMOKING "LONG LIFE" CIGARETTES

Ten anti-smoking organizations in Taiwan have petitioned the Ministry of Economic Affairs to change the name of the locally made "Long Life" cigarettes—incompatible, they say, with medical reports about the effects of tobacco smoking.

WOMEN SMOKERS INCREASING IN JAPAN

The number of male smokers in Japan declined steadily in 1987, but the number of women smokers increased, according to a report by a Japanese tobacco firm. In May 1987, male smokers totaled almost 26 million, down 140,000 from the year before, but the number of female smokers was more than six million, up 410,000 from the year before. The report noted that most female smokers were in their 20s and 30s.

SNUFFING SNUFF

Australia banned the manufacture and import of smokeless tobacco, including chewing tobacco and snuff in 1988 because the products are a cancer risk.

and men in India are being sold for organ transplants, according to the *Bengali Daily* in Dhaka.

SINGAPORE ORGAN TRANSPLANTS

Singapore became the first country in Asia to allow doctors to remove the kidneys of fatal accident victims without prior consent. The Human Organs Transplant Act was passed by Singapore's Parliament in 1988.

WIPING OUT CANCER'S "SHADOW"

In Australia, two doctors from the University of Sydney's Queen Elizabeth II Research Institute claim to have discovered an energy force that can revolutionize cancer treatment. Supposedly, the monitoring of this force will enable doctors to detect cancer within 24 hours of the first carcinogen appearing in the body. Cancerous cells can be made to destroy themselves by reversing the energy field— thus wiping out the "shadow" of cancer.

HEART ATTACKS HIT INDIAN YOUTH

Heart attacks among India's younger generation are four times higher than that of the most advanced Western nations, according to a 10-year study carried out by Grant Medical College in New Delhi. The 1988 survey of 5,000 patients in Bombay revealed that the incidence of heart attacks in young patients is 15% in India compared to 4% in Western countries. About 60% of the patients were smokers.

ROBOTS DETECT TUMORS

A Japanese university research group from Waseda University have developed the world's first robot capable of locating breast tumors as precisely as a doctor. In the robot examination, the sensor-equipped rods move along the breast of a patient, taking about six minutes to examine an entire breast. Data from the examination is displayed on a color monitoring screen through computer graphic processing. But while the $40,430 robot can locate tumorous areas, a doctor is still needed to determine if the tumors are cancerous or not.

CHINA'S FIRST CENSUS ON THE DISABLED

China's first national census on the disabled found that slightly less than 5% of the population is handicapped. The 1987 study concluded that 51.6 million out of a population of 1.07 billion suffer some kind of handicap. The survey found that 17.7 million Chinese are deaf or suffer speaking defects, while 1.9 million are mentally ill. Another 10.2 million are mentally retarded, seven million suffer from bad eyesight, and seven million had other physical disabilities. About 6.7 million are disabled in more than one way.

One in every 100 Chinese children is mentally retarded, according to the Xinhua News Agency, which says that the incidence is slightly higher in rural areas.

ABORTION IN INDONESIA

Indonesia is alone among the world's most populous nations in outlawing abortion under any circumstances, even to save a woman's life. Yet most public hospitals and maternity clinics in Jakarta offer what they euphemistically call "menstrual regulation services," which is abortion by another name. The cost of a private operation can run as high as $570 or as little as $17 in one of the many crowded clinics. Traditional healers also offer their services, combining massage and mild poison with uterine interference and magic spells. The Indonesian government's birth control program has been phenomenally successful as more and more of the sprawling nation's 180 million adopt the use of contraceptives, thus helping the nation move to its target of zero-population growth.

CHINESE EUTHANASIA

Euthanasia is secretly being practiced in some Chinese hospitals to relieve the suffering of terminal cancer patients. According to a Shanghai newspaper *Jie-fang Ribao,* some hospitals in the city comply with patients' wishes to end their suffering. In one case, a young cancer victim was given a fatal injection after her parents convinced the hospital's chief physician they would not prosecute him. In another case, friends and relatives of a liver cancer patient signed a petition for a doctor to administer a lethal dose of morphine, which he did, the newspaper claimed. China has no law permitting euthanasia.

WEIGHT-LOSS GARRISON

China opened its first obesity research and treatment center in Beijing in 1987. Attached to the People's Liberation Army Beijing Garrison Hospital, the clinic used both traditional and Western medicines as well as special diets and massage to treat patients. A survey of 34,000 Beijing residents showed that 18% of children between seven and 13 and 30% of adults have a problem with obesity.

DIAGNOSTIC JOHNS

Japanese firms have developed a high-tech toilet which analyzes urine, takes the user's temperature, and reads their heart rate and stress levels. The information is then automatically transferred by phone on-line to a hospital for analysis, with the results coming back almost immediately. The toilets, named *Asa Ichiban* ("First Thing in the Morning"), were developed by sanitary ware manufacturer Toto along with communications giant Nippon Telegraph and Telephone and Tate-ishi Electric, which provided the measuring apparatus.

JAPAN'S BAD BREATH MACHINE

The Japanese have also developed a machine that detects bad breath. The *Iki-iki* sensor, a breath checker developed by the Grelan pharmaceutical company, measures mouth gas to determine whether breath smells "good, fair, poor, or bad." "If the sensor says your breath is poor, you'd better clean your teeth or wash your mouth with oral deodorant. If it says bad, you'd better see your dentist," a company spokesman said. The machine retails for about $130.

BAD TEETH IN CHINA

Half of China's one billion people have rotten teeth and many have never used a toothbrush, according to the *China Consumer News.* Even in the more well to do cities, only half of all households have a toothbrush and in some areas they are used only as a decoration.

"Diseases enter by the mouth'; misfortune issues from it."

Chinese proverb

ASIAN FOOD STYLES
By Cynthia Maslanik and Angela Brown

In China, the custom of seating the guest of honor facing the door is to reassure them that they will not be murdered from behind during the banquet (a standard way of disposing of a rival in ancient times).

Japan, the most modern nation in the world, has nevertheless retained many of its ancient recipes. In many cases, only the style of consumption has changed. Instead of the porcelain chawan (bowl), rice is served up in styrofoam.

One can actually trace the line of Chinese penetration in some Vietnamese highland villages, for example, by noting where chopsticks disappear and finger eating begins. The excellence of Vietnamese cooking owes a great deal to the example of China—and, in more recent generations, to that of France, which ruled the country for most of the past century.

The Vietnamese like and use vegetable oil instead of lard for frying. Their dislike of fat is one reason Vietnamese boil so many of their foods. A famous national dish of Vietnam owes its heritage to Emperor Hung Vuong V, the second emperor of the first dynasty. The father of Hung Vuong challenged each of his three sons to present him with a gift, the most meaningful of which would earn its bearer the throne.

The first son presented his father with a gift of rare jewels gathered from around the world. The second son gave a collection of exotic spices and fine silks. Hung Vuong gave his father a simple gift in comparison—banh chung, a rice cake steamed in banana leaves, a dish eaten during New Year's. Hung Vuong inherited the position of emperor, since his gift symbolized the simple riches of Vietnam, and its flat square shape symbolized the land ruled by his father. Made from sweet rice, mung beans, and pork, banh chung represents the main staple of the Vietnamese diet.

Singapore's position on the sea-air routes between East and West over the past 150 years has enabled its chefs to take wisely a little of this and a pinch of that to add to the collection of dishes that today constitute great Singapore eating. Singapore food is that of a simple mixture of many styles, even the various Chinese dishes originating from different provinces cannot escape the phenomenon of mutual borrowing. (The Chinese represent 77% of the island's population.)

In some of Taiwan's poshest restaurants, sipping soup straight from the soup bowl, spitting bones onto the tablecloth, and belching loudly at random intervals are not uncommon. On the other hand, afterdinner toothpick maneuvers must be discreetly shielded from view by the free hand. Taiwanese will put their chopsticks directly in serving bowls.

Wherever you eat in South Korea, do it heartily. It is a sign that you appreciate the quality of the food if you make slurping sounds. When drinking, a drinker doesn't pour his own glass, but humbly waits until his companion fills it for him, often cupping it with both hands as he does so. One drinker will give his cup to the other; whoever has received a cup has an obligation to empty it and pass it on without inordinate delay. A more extravagant version of the tradition involves a stemmed glass. The drinkers snap the foot from the glass at the outset so nobody can set it down. They pass it back and forth rapidly, usually filling it with straight whiskey. Drunkenness carries no social stigma; when most Koreans drink, they do so until they are drunk.

In Malaysia, the finger's of the diner's right hand are used to knead rice and spices before tucking them into the mouth. Forks and spoons are common, though it is generally agreed that manual eating brings out the food's fullest flavor.

FOOD HORROR STORIES AND SCARY FOOD

Since ancient times, from Emperor to common man, all Chinese sages emphasized success as a function of a strong body, and a strong body is a function of what is eaten. Many strange tonics and recipes for health and vigor are a result. One example is "Stewed Green Turtle With Brown Sauce" (to nourish the blood, strengthen energy, and nourish stamina). Here is one original recipe as written in "Chinglish" from an extraordinary cook book entitled "Chinese Food For Vigorous & Beautiful," published in Taiwan. The following is a literal excerpt:

"To use hot water spray on alive green turtle, made them excreted stool and urine etc., then clean them, grip their tail, adooman up, make head fallen on plate, cut off head, drop green turtle's blood in rice wine one small cup fast. Open hard shell pick out gall and drink it wine and blood blending together, it may nourish blood, strengthen stamina. (Gall in green turtles belly should not be broken) gall broken will make turtle's meat to bitter & off-ensive smell taste)"

From the Ramada Renaissance (Hong Kong) hotel's restaurant menu under "Winter Seasonal Specialties": Stewed Palm Civet with Bamboo Shoot and Black Mushrooms; Shredded Snake Sauteed with Fresh Milk; Braised Snake Soup with Bamboo Pith; Stewed Turtle Casserole.

Chinese rare food aficionados fancy snake soup, dog meat, baby seal, salamander, turtle, camel hump, yak, unborn baby jaguar, shark's fin, carp, sea slugs, snake bile (squeezed from the sac and served mixed with fiery *mao tai* liquor in a small glass), cockroach, monkey, elephant trunk, among other delicacies.

"100-year-old" eggs were originally made by soaking in horse urine, now they're made by soaking in lime juice, which gourmands consider to be a poor substitute.

Peking duck consists almost entirely of the different parts of the force-fed duck, such as the liver, webs, etc., culminating in the crisp outer skin with its underlying fat and meat. This is dipped in a dark-brown sauce (made from fermented dough), garnished with fresh spring onions and wrapped in thin, unleavened wheat pancakes. At the end of the meal, the tastiest parts of the duck are served—the halved head, containing the tiny brain, strips of flesh from along the spine and the fatty triangle from near the tail, followed by a delicious soup.

Bird's nest soup is made from the mucus from the salivary glands of the small salangane swallow. Nests are found on the walls of bat-inhabited sea caves and are retrieved at

A QUICK LESSON IN CHOPSTICK ETIQUETTE

1. *Don't* even out the ends of your chopsticks with your finger—a common practice of new-to-chopsticks users. This is tantamount to picking up a fork by its tines. *Do* even the ends by gently standing them on end on your plate.
2. *Do* put your chopsticks down if it is necessary to use the same hand to reach for something else, such as a serving bowl. *Don't* ever hold chopsticks in your fist to pick up something else.
3. *Don't* pass food chopstick-to-chopstick. This is probably the single most offensive chopstick breach possible. The reason: At Buddhist funerals all remains after cremation are passed by the priests chopstick-to-chopstick before being placed in an urn.
4. *Do* rest chopsticks on a chopstick rest. If none is provided, place them on your plate as you would a knife.
5. *Don't* place chopsticks sticking out vertically from, say, a bowl of rice. This has the same appearance as incense sticks in a bowl of ashes, a clear death symbol.
6. *Do* turn your chopsticks around to use the unused ends to pick up foods from a common serving dish. Although more commonly practiced by Japanese, it is common courtesy of all chopstick users.

great risk to life and limb. Typically, bamboo and rattan ladders are used by nest gatherers to reach the nests, normally built high above the ground away from predators. Perhaps the most horrific experience of gathering nests, however, lies on the bat guano-coated floors of the caves. There, a live, glistening carpet of cockroaches and other crawly cave dwellers thrive on bat guano.

Once the nests are picked off the cave wall, they are meticulously cleaned of feathers and other debris. The soup is made by boiling the nest and serving it in a sweet stock. Gelatinous in appearance, the strands of the nest resemble cooked rice noodles. It is said the dish is very good for the complexion.

The ultimate in fresh seafood: Live fish are laid out on display for discerning shoppers, skillfully, surgically scaled, skinned and filleted, with their hearts still beating to prove that as far as fresh goes, there's nothing

fresher. Some Hong Kong restaurants will serve a whole fish whose body is cooked, but whose head is still alive as evidenced by the fish's moving lips.

Fifth-generation baby mice: Yet another Chinese treat, this dish is the result of feeding four generations of mice on a diet of honey. The fifth generation is born translucent and said to be tender and tasty. To serve: Each guest should be presented with a lidded box containing half a dozen or so live mice. A glass of warm water should accompany the box. To eat: pick up a mouse by its tail and dip into the glass of water, swirling it in the glass until the mouse had drowned. Eat in one bite. For variety, the mice may be fed chocolate, or milk beforehand for added flavor.

Drunken Prawns: Huge prawns are brought to the table live and twitching in a lidded glass bowl. A bottle of Chinese dark rice wine is poured in through a hole in the lid. The prawns thrash about in the wine until they lose consciousness. They are then lifted out one by one and dropped into boiling soup stock. End result: Juicy, delicious marinated —from-the-inside-out taste treat.

On the South Korean Menu: Bear paw, braised deer tail, sauteed deer sinew, ginko tree nuts (they taste like a wad of cotton candy). Korea is also known for its tonic wines. Ginseng wine contains a whole ginseng root and is the most popular tonic wine. Snake wine contains a whole pickled snake in the bottle, and is also reputed to have tonic qualities. Like the ginseng root, the snake may be eaten after the wine has been consumed.

Filipino vino: *Balut* is unhatched duck embryo eaten straight from the shell and is considered a delicacy. Crack the end open, drink the juice, peel and eat.

Taiwanese diners favor pig stomach, duck blood, and braised toad.

Thais prefer "rice birds." These tiny sparrow-like creatures are soaked in special juices until the skull, beak and claws have softened and then quickly deep-fried and eaten whole.

Vietnamese eat *Nuoc mam*. This is a salty fish sauce condiment used extensively in Vietnamese cooking. It is the liquid that is drained off from wooden casks in which alternating layers of fresh fish and salt have been tightly packed and allowed to ferment.

Tiet canh is duck's blood mixed with duck broth and chilled until it is gelatinous. It is commonly served with boiled, sliced duck broth and chilled until gelatinous. It is commonly served with boiled, sliced duck liver and garnished with basil leaves, chopped peanuts, and lemon juice.

Crunchy grasshopper kebabs are the snack of choice on trains in Burma—and are as popular in Burma as popcorn is in the West.

DURIAN FRUIT

Sign seen in Manila hotel: "No Firearms or Durian Fruit Allowed in Rooms." A more common sign seen in Southeast Asia consists of a drawing of the offensive-smelling fruit with a broad red "X" drawn through it. Philippine Airlines only allows durian on its planes if it is packed in an innertube knotted at each end. It is said that durians emanate a stench redolent of open sewers. It is also said that durian and alcohol can be a fatal combination if taken together.

FEW VAMPIRES IN KOREA

Garlic-eating has been heartily appreciated by Koreans since the race's first breath, but little is it known—even in Korea—that the chili pepper did not even exist in Korea until the sixteenth or seventeenth century, when it was introduced by Portuguese traders.

HIGH ON SOUP

Furr is a Laotian breakfast soup containing noodles, pork, garlic, and marijuana.

BREAKFAST IN CAMBODIA

In Cambodia, breakfast rice for guests is placed in cold water to stand all night and is served with flowers as the only condiment.

"A real chili, seven fathoms under water, will still taste hot."

Burmese proverb

INDONESIAN TREAT

In Indonesia, *gudeg* is the specialty of Yod-gyakarta and consists of young jackfruit boiled in coconut cream and spices, served with buffalo hide boiled in chili sauce, chicken pieces, egg, and gravy. Other dishes reflect Dutch influence. (The Dutch East India Company, founded in 1602, established their base in West Java in 1619 on what is now present-day Jakarta and ruled Indonesia until the nation won its independence in 1949). In Sumatra, the food can be hot enough to burn your fingers —spicy hot, that is.

Another Indonesian treat is the "Sweetmeat of Salak Bali." Here is how one Indon-English label on a package describes this delicacy (sic): *"Salak Bali is a famous and unique product of Indonesia. It's pulp is very delicious, clear and crisp. But it's time of product is shortly and it's fresh fruit can not store too long. It is a pity that the foreigners have not the enjoyment of the palate. In view of this, we carefully choose the better to process by new equipment and method Salak Bali which are processed, it not only has the original sweet-smelling but also more sweet and delicious. It's package is very noble, elegant, and composed and very convenient to carry. it is the best gifts to give your friends and relatives."*

ASIA'S MOST POPULAR BEERS

Thailand: Payak, Amarit, Singha, Siam Ale
Singapore: Tiger, Anchor
China: Tsing Tao, Chung Hua, Double Lightness
Taiwan: Gold Medal
South Korea: OB
Philippines: San Miguel
Hong Kong: Sun Lik, San Miguel
Japan: Kirin, Sapporo, Asahi, Suntory
Vietnam: 33, Chau Tien

SNACKING IN SINGAPORE
by Cynthia Maslanik

It is 5:30 p.m. on a weekday. It could be any day of the week. We are seated at one of a string of Singapore's outdoor seafood restaurants overlooking the Strait of Malacca. A few twinkling lights over the causeway in Malaysia can be seen. The air is thick, moist, and greenhouse-warm.

Every plastic molded red chair in the restaurant is taken. Many other people, tourists and natives alike, are milling about, deciding which open-air restaurant to choose.

Our choice is a good one. We have ordered Singapore's famous chili crabs. Whole crab is steamed and served smothered in a chili-garlic-tomato-soy sauce made from red chili peppers. Hot!

To eat, one must crack the crab shell and remove the sweet crab meat. Messy! But it is so tasty, and accompanied by steamed rice and frosty beer, it is worth sticky fingers and a few orange spots on one's shirt. Besides, after the meal, steamed towels are provided. Just don't wear your fine Egyptian cotton dress shirt.

Eating out-of-doors (for dinner, that is, when the sun goes down), is a big business in Singapore. And there is absolutely no better way to experience the varied cuisine that Singapore is famous for than by having dinner at one of Singapore's outdoor hawker stalls. One of the most famous is Newton's Circus, a colorful carnival-like square of dozens of food stalls and long picnic-style tables, all dressed up with strings of bright lights.

What is there to eat? Satay, grilled chicken, beef, or pork served on bamboo skewers with a spicy peanut sauce. Curried vegetables. Grilled fish served in banana leaves. Chili prawns (the same idea as chili crabs, only huge whole prawns). Chicken rice. Fried noodles (mee goreng).

For sweets? Ice *kacang,* shaved ice with fruit syrup. *Chendol,* an Indonesian drink of sweet beans, gelatin, shaved ice, and coconut milk. *Bubor cha cha,* another Southeast Asian specialty of cubed sweet yams and coconut milk.

As an added enticement, a dinner at Newton's Circus can turn into more than dinner. It is not uncommon for well-mannered, fortune-tellers to offer their services to diners in exchange for a few coins.

It should be also noted that Singapore's outdoor stalls are visited daily by the health inspector and are subject to strict regulations.

For those who prefer the more traditional indoor setting but who would nevertheless like to try the local fare, Banana Leaf Apolo is an excellent choice. Each place setting in this spotless restaurant has a large banana leaf which, as it turns out, serves as a plate. A big scoopful of steamed rice is piled on the leaf, to which mixed vegetables and curried dishes (chicken or fish head) are heaped on. Tasty! And economical, too. With a glass of cold beer, the total tab may be $5.

Cynthia Maslanik is a Rim-hopping gourmand, and is president of Hemisphere Marketing Inc., a San Francisco-based marketing and media agency.

DANGEROUS FOOD COMBINATIONS
By Cynthia Maslanik

Can food play a role in determining a child's sex? The Chinese think so. According to Chinese folk wisdom, women who want a girl should eat chicken (dark meat only), fish, tomatoes, apples, pineapples, and oranges two to three weeks before conceiving. Men should eat seaweed, red grapes, asparagus, potatoes, cucumber, eggplant, lettuce, and mushrooms.

Children's gender aside, the Chinese also believe there are specific food combinations to avoid, such as: octopus and flour, shrimp and pumpkin, corn and snails, tomatoes and crab, eggplant and crab. And never, never, never, eat dog meat with garlic.

FOOD-POISONING INSURANCE

Shanghai restaurants, which were badly hit by a wave of hepatitis-related food poisoning in 1988, offer anxious diners insurance against death or illness with every dish they order. Under a new policy issued by the People's Insurance Company of China, customers can now claim up to $2,700 if they are stricken by food poisoning. The insurance scheme was devised to deal with incidents such as the mass food poisoning of 700 diners at Shanghai's East Wind Hotel.

ALL SOUPED UP

The Tokiya restaurant in Tokyo's Shibuya district serves only *miso* (soybean) soup, with abalone, bream, blowfish, shrimp, and matsutake mushrooms, at prices ranging from $6.15 to $61.

OF CABBAGES AND CONDOMS

The Cabbages & Condoms Restaurant is on Sukumit Road, Soi 12, right next door to the Thai Family Planning & Population Control Center in Bangkok. They sell T-shirts depicting condoms, buttons promoting birth control, key chains attached to condoms sealed in plastic displaying the words "Love carefully."

JAPAN'S GOURMET WATER

Gourmet water has proved to be as popular in Japan as in the rest of world, with 1989 sales of imported water up more than 250% over the previous year. Antarctic ice, at about $6 a kilo, is also selling well.

NOUVELLE NOODLES

The Kentucky Fried Chicken restaurant which opened in 1988 in Beijing may be the fast-food success story in China. But for sheer chutzpah in breaking into China's fast-food biz, you have to hand the Golden Bowl award to Chinese-American businessman Lee Peichi. This Los Angeles entrepreneur opened the first—and only—"Californian" restaurant in China. His "Beef Noodle King" in Beijing serves "California-style" noodles for 75 cents a bowl. The dish is really nothing more than a bowl of hot Chinese noodles with a piece of beef on top, but the California mystique obviously adds to the flavor. Every day more than 800 customers line up outside Peichi's centrally located restaurant in the busy Dongsi district for a taste of his New Age noodles.

LOW CHOLESTEROL CREDIT CARD

Now you can slip your lunch or dinner into your wallet. Just make sure you don't eat your American Express or Diner's Club card by mistake. Japan's Caugasha Inc. has introduced a line of credit-card-sized, ultraprocessed dried food called "Papier." Fifteen varieties of gourmet cards include beef, salmon, shrimp, rice, bean jam, honey, apple, banana, cocoa, and coffee flavors. Each card contains two 15 to 20 g, 1.5 cm thick sheets, priced at about $1.30. Papier was first developed as a portable food for mountain climbers before it caught the fancy of Japanese consumers on the run. As with real credit cards, the only danger is when you exceed your limit.

FOOD FOR THOUGHT

How many kernels of rice are there in a single bowl? Sudo Chiharu, a Japanese junior high school student in Chiba, spent an hour counting them. She found 3,583 kernels. She won a prize from the Food Agency for her ideas about rice and the use of rice. A stalk of rice usually has about 25 heads. They hold some 2,344 kernels. There are 18,626 stalks in a 10-acre (1,000 m²) paddy, so that means 12,185 bowls of rice are produced from it. Or, as Sudo puts it, "At three bowls of rice a day, one 10-acre paddy produces 11 years and 47 days worth of rice per year."

WHAT'S NEW IN JAPANESE FOOD PACKAGING?

"Pyu-pyu" from Ajinomoto squirts one gram of oil at a time. (*Pyu-pyu* is the sound it makes.) "Miso 21" from Hanamaruki is miso paste in a squeeze tube. Kewpie sells jam in a squeeze tube. Says the package design chief at Yamamuro Glass, "Food packaging is getting more individualized and portions are getting smaller. Function plays a big part, too."

Food fashion: Now fashion is riding on the shirttails of the new food style. Tokyo Blouse has introduced the "Phillip Shirt," a blouse of material that will not accept liquid of any sort —sauce, soy sauce, soup, any kind of liquid. It merely forms into droplets and rolls off the fabric. It costs $92 for a shirt, but you can save on cleaning bills over the long run.

A VERY GOOD YEAR FOR CHOPIN

The latest buzz in nouveau riche circles in Tokyo is what wine to drink during intermissions at classical music concerts. The million yen question is which wine "goes best" with a musical program: i.e., Chardonnay with Tchaikovsky, Gewurtzraminer with Chopin, or Bordeaux with Beethoven?

TOKYO'S TAKE-OUT NOUVELLE CUISINE—FROM FRANCE

Bonappetit, a French restaurant in Nakano, Tokyo offers the ultimate in take-out food— all the way from France. Fifteen top French chefs prepare the food, it's shipped from France to Japan in vacuum packs, and voila! There are 20 items on the menu, with full-course dinners ranging from about $20 to $50.

CAFE SOCIETY IN TOKYO

The famed Parisian literary cafe, Aux Deux Magots, which served as a meeting place for some of France's greatest thinkers for more than a century, opened a branch in Tokyo in 1989. The Japanese version of the historic French cafe—which was frequented by notables including nineteenth-century French poets Verlaine, Rimbaud, and Malarme and twentieth-century writers Jean-Paul Sartre, Simone de Beauvoir, and André Gide—is a joint venture between Japan's Tokyu Group and the French Deux-Magots company. The cafe also distributes various products, including coffees and wines, under the Deux Magots label, whose name refers to a type of grotesque Chinese porcelain figure.

USING THEIR NOODLES

In 1975, Nissin Food Products, now a $1.1 billion instant-noodles giant, ushered in a new era of instant soups in the United States when it introduced its revolutionary instant Cup O' Noodles in a styrofoam cup package. Oriental instant noodle soups now represent 68% of America's estimated $500 million dry-soup category market, according to U.S. grocery industry figures. Nissin's share of that appetizing market amounted to about $100 million in 1988.

WELCOME TO THE FOODIUM

Nissin has developed a 14 story (11 above ground, three basement) complex in Tokyo. They're using half of it for office space and the other half for restaurants. It's called the Foodium. And every restaurant is a noodle shop—*ramen, udon,* Chinese noodles, spaghetti . . . you name it. Nissin says these outlets will help them monitor what the public likes in the way of new instant foods. "In other words, if you eat at the Foodium, you're an instant guinea pig," notes the *Shukan Shincho.*

RAREST STEAK IN THE WORLD

The most expensive steak house in the world opened in Tokyo in 1989. It's the "Steak of Holytan" restaurant—where a steak dinner costs about $715. For the lunch crowd, there's a luncheon "special"—a T-bone which sells for a mere $150.

TAILOR-COOKED FOOD

Affluent Japanese with sophisticated palates can now order customized hams, sausages, even rice. At the Takashimaya Department Store in Tamagawa, customers can specify precise levels of salt, smoke flavor, spices, and fat in their hams. Allow for a two-week turnaround. At Rice Land in Nagoya, you can select from a wide variety of rice grains grown all over Japan—then have the rice blended and ground to your taste just as you would grind coffee beans. At Sogo Department Store in Yokohama, you can even order designer sausage links—with exactly the texture, spices, and flavor you like. The minimum order has gone down from about 10 pounds to 100 grams. Don't be surprised if monogrammed pancakes are next.

JAPAN'S NEW TASTES

Japanese chewing gum addresses a wide variety of tastes—and needs, according to Japan's giant gum-maker, Lotte. There's gum with caffeine in it to keep you awake. There's gum to clean your teeth, with an anti-tartar element. There's gum to relieve tension, with a smell like a clean forest and with an elixir of reindeer horn and lavender. The latest brand to help you maintain healthy gums is called "Dentist."

The Japanese were the first to introduce "dry beer" to the world, of course. Now they've developed "no-melt" chocolate: "DD" from Meiji, "NuBo" from Morinaga, and "Four Seasons" from Lotte are all big hits. Now a Japanese food company has also introduced the first "Dry Hamburger." A bevy of spices gives the burger its dry taste.

VEGETARIAN BRATWURST

Takano Fruit Parlor in Tokyo has developed vegetarian sausages made from 12 kinds of vegetables, including carrots, onions, spinach, bell peppers, and squash. They sell about $2,500 worth of veggie sausages every day, according to *Shukan Yomiuri.*

EFFETE EGGPLANTS

Fashionable vegetables at fancy prices are offered by Yoshihisa Tsuchiake's Kanesho store in a classy section of Kyoto. The produce, all from local farms, is confined to the 40 or so different types that have been grown around the ancient capital for centuries and were originally developed locally to satisfy the aristocratic tastes of noblemen who rarely saw seafood in this inland region. Tsuchiake's store, decked out with marble showcases, bamboo walls, and indigo blue curtains, opened up with a special gift promotion for wealthy customers looking for something new: a stylish package of five local eggplants (*Kamo nasu*) selling for about $27.

GOURMET VIDEO LIBRARY

For a Y2000 (about $15) annual charge, a Japanese supermarket chain allows customers to borrow videotapes that give instructions in gourmet cooking.

More than 100 programs weekly about food can be seen on television in the Tokyo area alone as a result of Japan's current gourmet-eating fad, a reflection of increasingly affluent lifestyles.

Anthropologist Ishige Naomichi of the National Museum of Ethnology attributes this to "everyone thinking alike; everyone wanting to eat the next most delicious thing," and says that European and American audiences are much more diverse in their tastes.

Other observers are worried more about the effect that Japanese eating habits are having on children. A study by the Wayo Joshi University College of Nutrition concludes that too many sweets and soft drinks and not enough vegetables and milk were turning even 5-year-olds into candidates for such adult diseases as obesity, high cholesterol, and high blood pressure. Another nutritionist points out that lack of exercise is also contributing to the situation, with many children preferring to stay indoors playing TV games.

TIME-SHARE DAIRY COW

Every Japanese investor with about Y500,000 (about $3,850) to spare can become a part-time dairy farmer with 8% of a milk cow's annual production—160 liters of milk delivered at the rate of three liters per week on the day of his/her choice. Investors can pay by installment, but those paying it off in one lump sum get a free trip to the farm to meet their very own bovine.

THE RICE BOWL GAZETTE

It's obligatory to have a license to sell rice in Japan but the government is so alarmed about declining consumption that it has issued hundreds of new licenses—to outlets such as kiosks, cleaning shops, and service stations. Soon, comments *Shukan Shincho,* "you'll be able to pick up a package of rice along with the evening paper."

DECLINING RATE OF CHEWS

Students at Kanagawa Dental University ate historical foods to compare how many bites and how long it took to masticate. The figures dropped progressively over the centuries: almost 4,000 chews and 51 minutes for the chow of 2,000 years ago; less than half that for seventeenth-century grub, and 620 mastications and 11 minutes for today's fast food. Jaws have gotten smaller, teeth more crooked, and if this continues (says Tokyo University's Dr. Inoue Naohiko) soon everyone will lose their teeth to pyorrhea and won't be able to chew at all.

VEGETARIANS IN MANILA

The Cosmic Plate in Makati near Makati Cinema Square is a health-food store which sells herbal teas and tasty vegetarian meals. A buffet-style meal costs $2 to $5, depending on your appetite. Divisoria is a good market for fruits and vegetables. Cashew nuts cost $3.75 per kg, according to the Lonely Planet *Update*.

JAPANESE MEAT PACKERS IN AUSTRALIA

Japan is viewed by the Australian meat industry as taking over investment in the meat industry. When Nippon Meat Packers Australia

Proprietary, Ltd. paid $26 million for an abattoir and a feedlot on Queensland's Darling Downs, alarms began to sound in the Australian beef industry. The concern is that such moves are predominantly meant to serve the Japanese market following the liberalization in Japan of meat imports.

JAPAN'S WHALE SMUGGLERS

Japan is the world's biggest consumer of whale meat. Although it officially ended its commercial whaling in Antarctica in 1987, when it caught 1,941 whales, the Japanese still try to circumvent the whale ban whenever possible—either by declaring they are hunting whales for "scientific purposes"—or else, by engaging in "whale smuggling." In one such incident, three bigtime whale smugglers were apprehended after smuggling 130 tons of whale meat valued at about $4.2 million from Singapore. Japan bans imports of whale meat except from member countries of the International Whaling Commission.

INDIGESTIBLE THEORY

Duck meat can be dangerous to your health, according to Dr. Lai Chin-the, a doctor in Taiwan who studied the subject for over 20 years. "There is an absolute connection between consumption of duck meat and the incidence of nose and throat cancers," he claimed. As a result of his pronouncement

about 400,000 duck eggs, some already incubated with ducklings, had to be destroyed because consumers stopped buying duck meat. Duck farmers protested against Dr. Lai, who apologized for his statement, but the damage had already been done.

FAKE SHARK FINS

Restaurateurs in Hong Kong do a roaring trade in fake shark fins soup, according to Hong Kong's Customs and Excise department which monitors imports. Diners, believing they are sampling the high-price delicacy, are instead paying for an inexpensive gelatin imitation imported from Singapore and Japan. The gelatin is packaged and clearly labeled "imitation shark fins." In a survey, the C&E department discovered that the equivalent of one million bowls, or 34 tons, of imitation shark fins was imported during the first nine months of 1988.

74.4% OF ALL TOKYO FAMILIES EAT OUT

The Bureau of Citizens and Culture Affairs of the Metropolitan Government surveyed 1,000 Tokyo families about their eating habits in October 1987. Of those answering the questionnaire, 74.4% said that they ate out at least once during the previous month in October. Here are some interesting facts about those who ate out, as reported by the *Mainichi Shimbun:*

How many times a month do you eat out?	Average: 2.4 times
How much did you spend eating out last month?	Average: Y12,069 (about $93) (Y1,569 or about $12 per person per outing)
Where did you eat?	
Western-style restaurant	56.7%
Chinese restaurant	46.6%
Sushi bar	38.0%

JAPAN'S CANNED COFFEE INDUSTRY

The market for canned coffee drinks in Japan topped $3.4 billion in 1988—and it's still perking. The first companies to market canned coffee were UCC and POKKA in 1971. Then Coca-Cola Japan entered in 1976, and the three companies dominated the market until recently. Now, almost every major beer brewer and every major food-maker have brands of canned coffee. No longer is canned coffee an insipid, sickeningly sweet, brown liquid. Some feature far infrared-roasted beans, some offer drip brewed coffee, some call it "power siphoned," ad infinitum. Canned coffee has moved from the situation where the number of vending machines you owned determined your share of the market to a situation where the brand name and quality of your preferred brand says a lot.

EXEC FOOD SURVEY

The *Sunday Mainichi* surveyed the presidents of 100 of Japan's top corporations to see what they eat at lunch:

> *The top three luncheon menus:*
>
> | | |
> |---|---|
> | Noodles *(soba* or *udon)* | 36% |
> | Set lunch | 30% |
> | Curry rice | 8.0% |
>
> *Where do you eat lunch?*
>
> | | |
> |---|---|
> | In the president's office | 28.0% |
> | In the executive dining room | 27.0% |
> | In the company dining room | 12.0% |

NOUVELLE NEPALESE CUISINE

What do South Asian heads of state eat at a royal banquet in Nepal? The five-course banquet hosted by Nepal's Kin Birendra in 1987 for government leaders attending a summit of the South Asian Association for Regional Co-operation were treated to "Nepalese nouvelle cuisine," according to the head chef at Kathmandu's Oberoi Soaltee hotel. "We served *halal* meat (slaughtered according to Moslem customs) and we did not serve beef or pork at all," the chef said. "You have to be careful when you have Hindus, Moslems, and Buddhists as your guests." Naturally, there was a foodtaster who sampled the food before dishes were served to make sure none of the dishes were poisoned.

BROKEN CROCKERY

Only nine Hong Kong restaurateurs were prosecuted in 1986 for serving food on broken crockery, according to Urbco's Food Hygiene Select Committee. Fines ranged from $38 to $79. The use of cracked or chipped utensils in either food service or preparation are forbidden by law in Hong Kong.

WORLD'S BIGGEST RESTAURANT

Tum Nak Thai, at 131 Ratchadapisek Road, in Bangkok is described in the Guiness Book of Records as being the biggest restaurant in the world. It has over 3,000 seats, 1,000 waiters (many of whom operate on roller skates), 14 computerized kitchens, and a menu with more than 350 dishes. Most of the food is Thai and Chinese, but there are some Japanese and European dishes on the menu as well. Prices are reasonable. It's open seven days a week, and there is Thai dancing every night between 8:00 and 9:30 p.m.

FINING SINGAPORE'S DINERS

Singapore lunchers have such a bad reputation for heaping more food on their plates from the buffet than they can eat, that some restaurants are trying to enforce posted rules that "fine" customers for excessive amounts of wasted food. "It's a matter of educating people," says one manager, "If people cannot be taught when they are young they will have to learn some other way." The bad habit has even attracted the attention of politicians one of whom, Lau Ping Sum, noted that a cruise line had canceled buffet meals on its Singapore route because locals wasted too much food. "Singaporeans tend to pile food on their plates because they are lazier about going back for second helpings," explains Rita Tham, manager of the Okoh restaurant, which fines two or three people each month for leaving over-heaped plates.

SINGAPORE'S MOST EXPENSIVE DISH

The most expensive dish in Singapore, a portion of "three heads" abalone, is so valuable that the manager of the Happy Valley Seafood and Sharkfin's restaurant, where it is served, keeps the dried shellfish under lock and key in his apartment. Nevertheless, affluent customers give the requisite advance notice about once a month during the year and sit down four days later to enjoy their repast—at about $350 per portion.

PAPA'S GOT A BRAND NEW BAGUETTE

Thick-sliced loaves of tasteless white bread, once the only kind available in rice-happy Japan, are giving way to the dazzling array of baked goods which have long been familiar to the rest of the world. Tokyo's Andersen Bakery on fashionable Aoyama-dori Avenue not only offers scores of different loaves, but has opened 40 branches to cope with the growing demand for Scottish baps, German brot, French croissants, and other national and regional specialty breads. "About 90% of Japanese people now eat toast for breakfast instead

of rice," explains Daisuke Hayashi, one of scores of Tokyo bakers who learned their craft from a German master baker who was brought over to show how to do things the right way. The Andersen chain, named after Danish storyteller Hans Christian Andersen, spends several million dollars each year sending 60 employees to Europe to keep up with bakery techniques. All this, of course, has its price: a loaf of specialty bread averages about $3.

SHRINKING BANQUETS

As part of its campaign against public waste and extravagance, Chinese ministries have been cutting back their traditional lavish banquets to a mere four courses and substituting wines for the familiar *mou tai* liquor which brought a tear to the eye of many a visiting dignitary.

China's Massive Slops: Investigations by the Beijing Economic Information estimate that customers to the city's 10,000 restaurants and dining halls leave 90 million kg of grain to be made into pig swill a year. The slops include staple foods such as rice, steamed bread, and steamed twisted rolls, and nonstaple food such as chicken, duck, fish, and different meats.

HOW GOOD ARE YOUR HERBAL MANNERS?

A fad for healthy food has been filling the restaurants of Singapore that offer dishes cooked with herbs, all part of a growing interest in nutritional practices that billions of Chinese have followed for centuries. "Food is medicine," declares Zheng Guangyou, an herbalist who dispenses the mix for dishes at the popular Imperial restaurant, which is part-owned by a pharmaceutical company. "You have to eat everything for a balanced diet so as to prevent an excess of either *yin* or *yang qi* (life force) in the body." And in a book on sale locally, *Chinese Herbal Medicine*, Daniel Reid writes, "Chinese physicians try to follow Sun Simiao's ancient dictum: 'First try food; resort to medication only when food fails to effect a cure.' Food is the first line of defense in traditional Chinese medicine." Sun was a Tang dynasty (618 to 907 A.D.) physician.

Common Chinese herbs, such as ginger, spring onions, dried longan, lotus leaves, garlic, wolfberry, and black soyabean, feature in a number of dishes in Singapore's restaurants and are proving increasingly popular with health-conscious diners. Such is their growing reputation for promoting health that the U.S. pharmaceutical giant, the Upjohn Co., has signed an agreement with China to test the efficacy of Chinese herbs. Traditional Chinese medicine is winning increasing influence in the world, and China has trained 1,200 acupuncturists for 102 counties.

SOYBEAN BOYS LOSE SHOWDOWN
by Ooi Guat Tin

After two years of campaigning against Malaysian palm oil, principally by labeling it a health threat, the American Soybean Association (ASA) decided to call it quits in 1989. It is said that it was ASA's realization that its campaign was in danger of backfiring that prompted the association to change its strategy, although some observers say intervention by Washington on behalf of Malaysia also helped—a market that currently accounts only for 4% of that country's total exports.

ASA's campaign used a fictional character called "Tropical Fats," who was allegedly clogging America's hearts with saturated fats that increased cholesterol levels.

Malaysia, which produces more palm oil than any other commodity exporter, threatened to play "tit for tat" by smearing soybean oil's image, using scientific data that show that processed soybean oil also contains highly saturated fats, and is therefore no less likely to cause coronaries.

What particularly enraged the Malaysians and provoked the threat of retaliation was ASA's attempt to get Congress to enact a bill requiring products using tropical oils to carry a health warning.

The bitter Malaysians maintain that ASA's campaign is not just dirty. By concentrating on bad-mouthing palm oil, while neglecting to promote soybean oils' supposed health attributes, ASA has actually damaged the whole vegetable oils market, which in the U.S. has dropped by 7%.

Henceforth, ASA will promote the merits of soybean oil rather than portraying palm oil and other tropical oils as the bogeymen.

But the damage to palm oil has been done. Major American food processors have stopped using it.

A top Malaysian official concedes that while it will take some time before U.S. food processors return to using palm oil, the consoling factor is that there won't be any more damage. "It was the food processors who had been most vocal in asking both palm oil producers and the ASA to cease campaigning against each other," he notes.

"I believe the food processors prefer to have the flexibility to choose which oil to use," says Wong Kum Choon, secretary general of the primary industries ministry.

Health conscious Americans, too, want the flexibility to choose, even though consumer loyalty doesn't always change overnight.

FAST-FOOD BOOM IN HONG KONG

Western-style fast food is enjoying record growth in Hong Kong, with a 13% annual growth rate recorded in 1988, according to Hong Kong's Census and Statistics department. The 452-seat Telford Gardens branch of Pizza Hut is the biggest of its kind in the world. McDonald's, the international hamburger chain, which pioneered fast food in Hong Kong in 1975, says more people pass through its outlets in the territory than anywhere else in the world. Each month Hong Kongites eat their way through 4,000 kg of pepperoni, two million hamburger buns, 108,000 whole chickens, and 66,666 kg of hamburger meat.

JAPAN'S BULLET EXPRESS NOODLES

The Japanese fast-food industry brought in $161.5 billion in sales in 1988, according to *Shukan Shincho* magazine.

FAT-FREE BEEF FORMULA

An Australian butcher-inventor has developed virtually fat-free, reduced cholesterol meat, which he hopes to pit against chicken and fish in the health-food industry. Dallas Chapman, an Australian butcher who left school at 15, likens the process which removes 96% of the fat and at least 30% of the cholesterol from meat, to butter being centrifugally separated from milk. His company

Chapman Meats (Australia) has applied for world-wide patents. He expects that his product costs 15% more than red meat bought at butcher shops. Journalists who tasted the process at Tokyo's Foodex Gourmet Exposition said the process made mutton taste like beef.

ASEAN RESTAURANTS ON THE HORIZON

The countries of the Association of South East Asian Nations (Thailand, Malaysia, the Philippines, Singapore, Brunei, and Indonesia) plan to establish restaurants in the world's major cities to popularize their cuisines, according to Malaysian Agricultural Minister Sanusi Junid. Besides making money, the restaurants could bring ASEAN and the rest of the world closer together, he explained. The restaurants would be owned and managed by private businessmen from ASEAN countries. Apart from trying traditional Southeast Asian cuisines, patrons would also see shows given by cultural troupes from the various ASEAN countries.

FISHY ICE CREAM

The Japanese coffee shop Fugestudo in Ishimaki, Miyagi prefecture offers mackerel ice cream. It's really made of fish. The recipe is: mackerel pike boiled in brandy and butter with white wine and vanilla added, along with cocoa, nuts, and cinnamon. Mackerel ice cream is full of protein and calcium, so it has to be good for you, the makers say.

IT'S A SOY!

Japan's ubiquitous soy sauce, normally dark in color, is now being marketed in red, blue, orange, green, purple, and clear colors.

HIGH-FIBER PRODUCTS

Not only are there high-fiber content drinks, now there are high-fiber ramen noodles that come in soy sauce, seafood, and curry flavors from Sanyo Foods.

EXCLUSIVE CAMPUS EATERIES

Gone are the days when the only eatery on a Japanese campus was in a dingy basement with the menu written on a piece of cardboard. These days, if the cafeteria isn't a touch gourmet, it's not in. At Showa Women's University, for example, the restaurant offers full-course French cuisine: about $20 for lunch. Shukutoku Junior College cafeteria features semiprivate booths.

SPECIAL DELIVERY CHEESE CAKES

Japan's Posts and Telecommunications Ministry launched a plan to enable Japanese consumers to import American food by post as part of an effort to ease trade frictions with the United States. The plan calls for delivering items such as oranges, papayas, tuna, lobsters, crabs, steaks, cheese cakes, and smoked salmon through 23,000 post offices across Japan. By paying about $215 a year, a consumer would be able to receive four packages a year from America, each containing about $54 worth of goods.

. . . AND DRINK

CHINA'S DRINKING PROBLEMS

The sometimes lethally strong liquor *Mou Tai* has become such universally accepted currency throughout China that more than 90% of it is bought for purposes of bribery, used as gifts to curry favor for unlawful, secret transactions with Communist officials. This was the conclusion of an investigation by *China News,* which added that empty *Mou Tai* bottles were also used by bootleggers to disguise bogus, home-made rotgut which had poisoned many people. The newspaper also disclosed these shocking statistics about alcoholism in China: (1) mainland China's 160 million alcoholics is the world's largest number; (2) their annual expenditure of $3.2 billion on Chinese spirits, $4.5 million on imported alcoholic beverages, and average consumption of 1.3 pounds of wine and spirits per head is also the world's largest; (3) more than 28,000 people were killed in car accidents due to excessive drinking and another 10,000 died of alcohol poisoning in 1988; and (4) well over half of the arrests on criminal charges are connected with excessive drinking.

About half of the 160 million children between the ages of six and twelve in China are wine drinkers, with almost 30% of them capable of downing a bottle of beer or champagne at one time according to a report in Beijing's *China Commercial News.*

China's liquor production in 1988 reached 50 billion liters, exceeding the output of the Soviet Union, and probably making it the biggest distiller of liquor in the world, according to the *People's Daily*. There are more than 40,000 distilleries in China, 70% of which are small rural businesses. According to the China Consumers Association, every year people spend about $3.51 billion on liquor.

ALCOCHECK

Japanese drinkers can test their level of inebriation with Alcocheck, a packet of 10 chemically treated strips (about $20) which change color according to the alcohol content of saliva.

TOKYO'S ENERGY POOL

Faddist drinks have always been popular among Tokyo commuters and the latest version—following "sports" drinks and tonics containing ginseng—is Fibe-mine, whose popularity is said to be based on its salmon-pink color, sweet taste, and fiber content. It has been selling 20 million bottles per month at around 50 cents U.S. per bottle. Another new favorite, Acelora Drink, tasting like plum juice and said to contain as much vitamin C as three lemons, is also selling well. A typical outlet for these and more than 180 similar "health drinks" is a counter bar called Energy Pool on the first floor of Tokyo station, where some drinks cost the equivalent of several dollars. "[Customers] drink a bottle of health drink just like a cup of coffee at a coffee shop," commented Hisae Kajiwara, spokesman for the Energy Pool's owners.

In a land where six-day weeks are still common, it's probably no surprise that there's a ready market for "energy-replenishing" drinks of the sort that in Japan has created an $880 million market. Most of that money is spent on tiny bottles of tonic with such exotic ingredients as cobra extract or essence of seal, which are gulped down by commuters at kiosks or drugstores. "Can you fight for 24 hours?" asks a commercial for a drink called Regain, a typical vitamin-enriched product. In a recent poll of 400 Tokyo businessmen, more than 80% were found to suffer work-related fatigue and one quarter of them said they fought it with tonic drinks. (See "No Speed Limit," p. 344.)

TAOIST HEALTH DRINK

China's best-known brewer, Tsingtao, is to start bottling a health drink whose recipe has until recently been a secret kept by Taoist monks on nearby Mount Lao for 1,000 years. The ingredients have not been revealed.

FROM TEA TO TSINGTAO

China, traditionally a nation of tea-drinkers, is brewing too much beer. The country leaped into sixth place among world beer producers by brewing over five million tons in 1987, an increase of more than a quarter over 1986. Zhejiang province in eastern China was in danger of failing to produce enough grain to eat because farmers were growing more and more barley for beer. Fast-growing demand for beer has caused unchecked expansion of production and poorer quality in some areas.

ROBOT WINE TASTER

Japanese scientists have developed the world's first robot that can distinguish between different whiskies and wines by their scents. "The robot can tell 11 different whiskies, wines, and Japanese rice wines from their smells," said Professor Toyosaka Moriizumi of the Tokyo Institute of Technology. His research team programmed graph-form analyses of different smells into the robot, which is equipped with 10 sensors. The robot distinguishes a smell by checking through its memory for a matching pattern. Once perfected, the process could have a wide range of uses including quality control in the food and cosmetics industries.

POPULATION

CHINA'S POPULATION PROBLEM

Between now and 1994, China is all-too-aware that 100 million Chinese women are in their peak child-bearing years (20 to 29) and therefore family-planning policies should continue to have a high priority. The country's population is expected to exceed 1.2 billion by the end of this century. Over the past decade, the policy has cut the previous 35 per-thousand-birth rate by almost two thirds, saving the state $270 because of the 100 million babies that weren't born.

China's economic problems are obviously cause for concern, but what is probably a bigger potential headache for the country to deal with is its escalating population which has been increasing each year by more than 15 million—equivalent to the entire population of Australia. Not only has the government's "one-child-per-family" been widely ignored but according to the *China Times* as many as 10 million "illegal" babies per year were not being reported. Beijing and other cities are flooded with transients, severely overtaxing transport and other facilities, at least three million are unemployed, and as many as 300 million are illiterate. China's arable land is about one seventh that of the entire world and yet its population is 22% of the world's four or five billion. Starvation is not an abstract concept, but something that is faced by millions every day.

JAPAN'S POST-WAR BABYBOOMERS

Of Japan's population of about 123 million, 76 million—or 62%—were born after World War II.

SINGAPORE'S MULTI-ETHNIC MIX

Of Singapore's 2.6 million people, 76% are Chinese, 15% are Malays, 6% Indians, and the rest Eurasian and Europeans. Religions include Buddhism, Taoism, Christianity, Islam, Hinduism, and Sikhism. Although the government stresses racial and religious tolerance, it has expressed a need for vigilance against increasing Western influences from books, magazines, television, and visitors. "The speed and extent of the changes to Singapore society are worrying," declared President Wee Kim Wee. "We cannot tell what dangers lie ahead as we rapidly grow more Westernized.

POPULATION IN THE PHILIPPINES

The Philippine population reached nearly 59 million in 1988, according to the National Statistical Coordination Board. The government has been encouraging family planning despite objections by the influential Roman Catholic hierarchy.

CHINESE IN MALAYSIA

The Chinese population in Malaysia is dwindling and may make up only 13% of the total population when it reaches an expected 70 million in 2070, according to Malaysian government projections. Currently, the Chinese represent 31% of Malaysia's 16.5 million, Malays make up 57%, and Indians 12%. According to Deputy Education Minister Woon See Chin, when Chinese people migrate to the cities, they prefer not to have too many children as they want a quality living standard.

HONG KONG'S BRAIN-DRAINERS

Nearly two thirds of Hong Kong executives, professionals, and entrepreneurs plan to leave the territory before it is handed over to China in 1997, according to a 1989 survey by the *South China Morning Post*.

"If you drop Hong Kong people down, not just in the north, but right in the middle of an Australian desert, they can turn it into a land flowing with milk and honey in about three months. What I'd really love to see is 150,000 Hong Kong citizens, chosen at random, dropped by parachutes into the city of Liverpool and turn it into a garden city," commented British newspaper columnist Bernard Levin, speaking at a seminar in Hong Kong. One of the most successful magazines in the territory, aimed at the brain-drainers, is *The Emigrant*.

In one literally far-fetched idea, the London-based Adam Smith Institute, a free-market think tank, suggested that the 5.6 million people of Hong Kong should be moved lock, stock, and barrel to a sparsely populated area of 150 to 220 square miles in western Scotland.

CULTURAL SURVIVAL

THE COLONIZATION OF ASIA'S TRIBAL PEOPLES

Colonialism may be on the wane in some parts of the world, but many of its worst features—racial discrimination, religious persecution, economic marginalization, and political oppression—are still a commonplace in Asia, where most of the world's indigenous and tribal peoples live. In country after country, ethnic minorities are under continuing threat as governments seek to displace them and turn their land over to commercial exploiters.

"It would not be an exaggeration to say that most tribal peoples in Asia are in conflict with their governments merely because they seek to remain a distinct people with some political and economic independence," writes Julian Burger in his pioneer study, *Report from the Frontier* (Cultural Survival, Inc., Cambridge, Massachusetts 1987), which is a comprehensive assessment of how for most of these groups the fight for self-determination continues to this day.

BURMA

In Burma, for example, as many as 300,000 people have already died in the war conducted by the Burmese army against the Karen and 10 other hill tribes who compose about one third of the country's 34 million population. The hill people, regarded as inferior and often drafted as unpaid porters, are frequently arrested, beaten, and killed according to an independent report to the Anti-Slavery Society. Thousands have fled from their native villages into the jungle or taken refuge in neighboring Thailand.

INDIA

A similar situation exists in northeast India where the hill peoples of Nagaland, Manipur, and Mizoram have been fighting a war against the government since the 1950s. They have sworn never to live under Indian rule and, as the leading magazine *India Today* expressed it, "India represents only a brown colonialism that replaces the white colonialism of the British." Scattered throughout India are more than 200 tribes speaking at least 100 main languages. About 85% of them live in the central states, but the fact that in none of these states

ASIAN PERSPECTIVES

Asia/Pacific is anything but a homogenous region. The list of differences among its many countries is nearly endless.

Political systems run the whole range from communism via socialism and various forms of true or suspect democracy   to constitutional or even absolute monarchy (Brunei) plus Hong Kong's colonial regime. Similarly, every conceivable form of economic management can be found, from the nearly totally free play of market forces in Hong Kong to the government-influenced way of business in Japan, the planning of India, and the economic state monopolies of Burma and the region's communist countries.

While the infrastructures of Australia, Hong Kong, Japan, New Zealand, or Singapore are among the world's best, those of many other countries rank among the worst. Some places count among the most densely populated, while others are nearly empty of people. In terms of total population, China is the world's largest, while Brunei and Macao are among the smallest. Some nations are plagued by high illiteracy rates and others benefit from highly educated populations — or you find both in the same country (e.g. in India). In some nations, the people can expect only a short life in poor conditions, while those next door have a long life expectancy.

A few countries are basically factories (e.g. Hong Kong, Japan, Korea, Singapore, or Taiwan), while others are mainly farms and/or quarries (Australia, Indonesia, Malaysia, the Philippines, or Thailand). Some run chronic trade deficits, while others accumulate huge foreign exchange reserves.

Standards of living may be among the highest anywhere (e.g. Australia, Japan, and New Zealand), fairly good (e.g. Hong Kong, Korea, Singapore, or Taiwan), or generally very poor (such as in virtually all countries of the Indian subcontinent).

Glaring differences may separate the rich from the poor (like in India), or incomes may be fairly evenly distributed (like in China). Rampant unemployment in many places contrasts with scarcity of labor in Hong Kong and Singapore. And while some countries possess a wealth of natural resources (e.g. Australia, China, Indonesia, Malaysia, Thailand, and less so the Philippines), others benefit from only a few minor ones (Japan, Korea, Pakistan, or Taiwan) or none at all (e.g. Hong Kong and Singapore).

Language, ethnic extraction, and religion are unifying forces in some parts of the region and highly divisive in others. While India is a mosaic of different people, dozens of languages, and various religions, Japan or Korea are practically homogenous. While different races live harmoniously together in Singapore, ethnic considerations play an important role in Malaysia and Indonesia. The Moslem minority in the Philippines has been on the war path for decades — and so have various tribes in Burma and the Tamils of Sri Lanka.

In brief, Asia is characterized by endless variety. The following section looks at all the differences among the region's various countries by comparing various factors that affect the economy and the business climate.

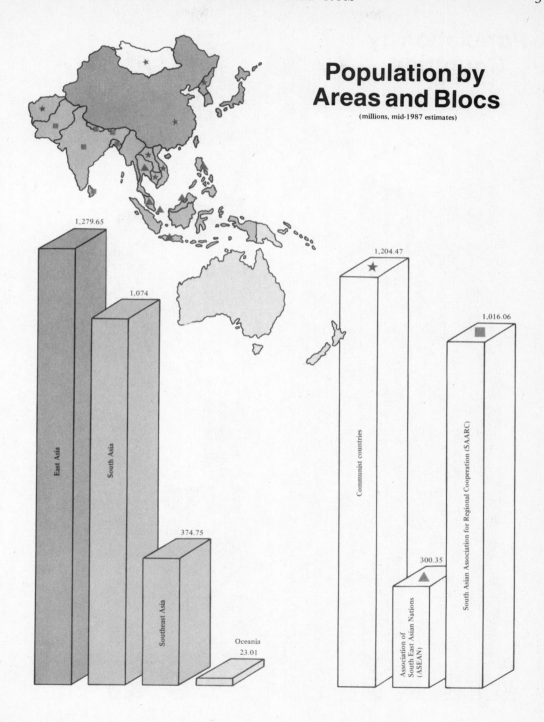

Population by Areas and Blocs

(millions, mid-1987 estimates)

East Asia 1,279.65

South Asia 1,074

Southeast Asia 374.75

Oceania 23.01

Communist countries 1,204.47

Association of South East Asian Nations (ASEAN) 300.35

South Asian Association for Regional Cooperation (SAARC) 1,016.06

Population by Countries

(millions, mid-1987 estimates)

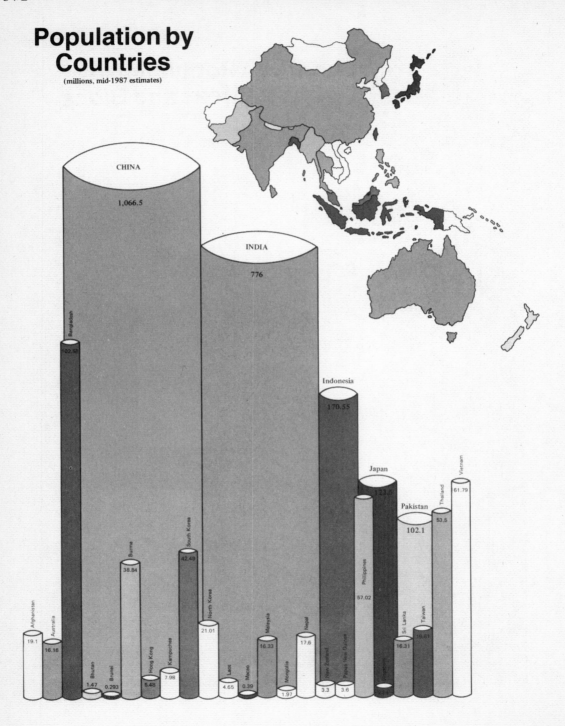

CHINA
1,066.5

INDIA
776

Indonesia
170.55

Japan
123.6

Pakistan
102.1

Thailand
53.5

Vietnam
61.79

Philippines
57.02

Bangladesh
102.56

South Korea
42.49

Burma
38.84

North Korea
21.01

Afghanistan
19.1

Australia
16.16

Taiwan
19.61

Sri Lanka
16.31

Nepal
17.6

Malaysia
16.33

Kampuchea
7.98

Hong Kong
5.48

Laos
4.65

Papua New Guinea
3.6

New Zealand
3.3

Mongolia
1.97

Bhutan
1.47

Macao
0.39

Brunei
0.293

Singapore
2.61

Land Area by Countries

(sq. km. '000)

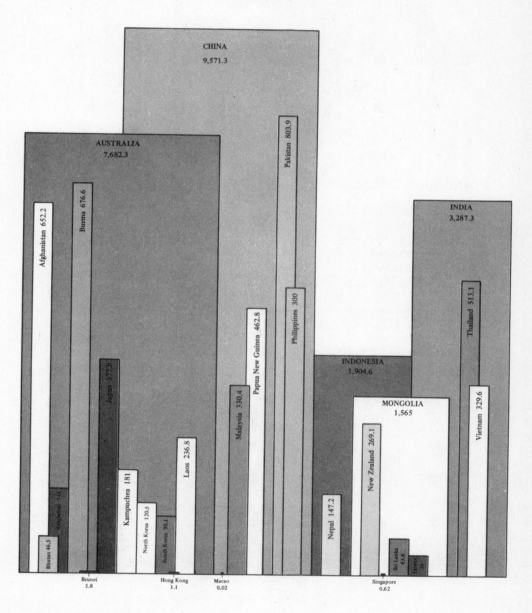

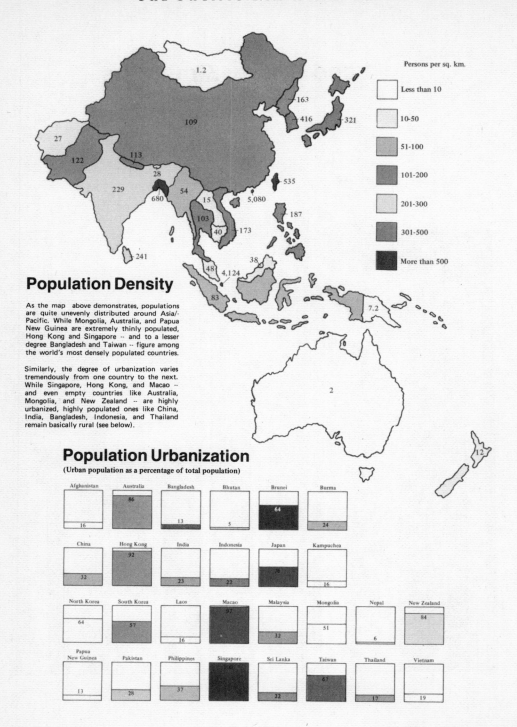

Persons per sq. km.

- Less than 10
- 10-50
- 51-100
- 101-200
- 201-300
- 301-500
- More than 500

Population Density

As the map above demonstrates, populations are quite unevenly distributed around Asia/-Pacific. While Mongolia, Australia, and Papua New Guinea are extremely thinly populated, Hong Kong and Singapore -- and to a lesser degree Bangladesh and Taiwan -- figure among the world's most densely populated countries.

Similarly, the degree of urbanization varies tremendously from one country to the next. While Singapore, Hong Kong, and Macao -- and even empty countries like Australia, Mongolia, and New Zealand -- are highly urbanized, highly populated ones like China, India, Bangladesh, Indonesia, and Thailand remain basically rural (see below).

Population Urbanization

(Urban population as a percentage of total population)

Afghanistan	Australia	Bangladesh	Bhutan	Brunei	Burma
16	86	13	5	64	24

China	Hong Kong	India	Indonesia	Japan	Kampuchea
32	92	23	22	76	16

North Korea	South Korea	Laos	Macao	Malaysia	Mongolia	Nepal	New Zealand
64	57	16	97	32	51	6	84

Papua New Guinea	Pakistan	Philippines	Singapore	Sri Lanka	Taiwan	Thailand	Vietnam
13	28	37	100	22	67	17	19

Dominant Ethnic Groups

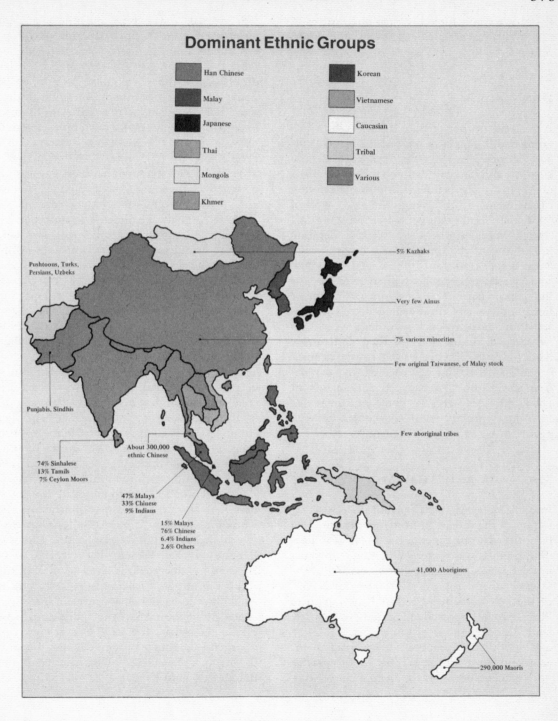

Han Chinese

Malay

Japanese

Thai

Mongols

Khmer

Korean

Vietnamese

Caucasian

Tribal

Various

Pushtoons, Turks,
Persians, Uzbeks

5% Kazhaks

Very few Ainus

7% various minorities

Few original Taiwanese, of Malay stock

Punjabis, Sindhis

Few aboriginal tribes

About 300,000
ethnic Chinese

74% Sinhalese
13% Tamils
7% Ceylon Moors

47% Malays
33% Chinese
9% Indians

15% Malays
76% Chinese
6.4% Indians
2.6% Others

41,000 Aborigines

290,000 Maoris

do they account for more than one quarter of the population attests to their lack of political power.

BANGLADESH

Across the border in Bangladesh in the Chittagong Hill Tracts, a region of forested hills and ravines, are 600,000 tribespeople whose customs and language differ totally from their neighbors in the plains. But with the creation of Bangladesh, following the civil war of 1971, the Chittagong people began to be colonized. Thousands of Bangladeshi families have been moved in, allocated "unoccupied" land, which traditionally belonged to the hill society as a whole, and will soon reduce the indigenous natives to a minority. They have been additionally disadvantaged by the construction of a hydroelectric dam which has submerged almost 40% of their cultivatable land. Since 1972, when a tribal resistance force called Shanti Bahini was formed, the Bangladesh government has rejected all demands for tribal autonomy and has constantly increased its military presence with consequent violence against tribespeople and their property.

MALAYSIA AND THAILAND

In both Malaysia and Thailand, it is the opening up of the forests to timber companies that has proved to be the biggest threat to indigenous populations. Over 40 logging companies in the 8,000-square mile Baram district of Sarawak, where tropical rainforests cover 75% of the land area, have reduced the region to "bare patches of eroded, barren, and useless land," according to a recent report.

The 50,000 tribespeople who lived in the area and once depended on the forests as "their main source of food, medicine, build-

ing material, and income are now facing an uncertain future." Tribal communities seeking concessions themselves are refused because they lack political power and can offer no bribes. "Timber is politics," says one, "if you support the right man, you get a timber area." Here, again, a massive dam is also under construction, and when completed will displace about 5,000 Kenyah and Kayan tribal people.

Thailand's government has been even more persistent in pursuing a forestry policy, opening up the hilly regions with a network of roads to facilitate the region's exploitation by mining and logging companies and, not incidentally, to make it easier to deal with insurgency. The consequent deterioration of the ecosystem has caused pollution of rivers, soil erosion, and increasing poverty among the native Karen in the region, most of whom (since they practise a policy of shifting cultivation) have no legal rights to the land they use.

More able to resist cultural and economic deterioration are the country's second-largest tribe, the Hmong, converted to Christianity late in the last century and retaining a stronger cultural identity than the Karen. They are also supported by a major cash crop, opium, whose virtually insatiable worldwide market causes enormous profits not only to Thai officials, who are bribed to allow its continuation, but to warlords and remnants of the Kuomintang, the Chinese National Army, which fled after the success of the Chinese Revolution. The Western-backed Thai government has tolerated the latter because of the counter-insurgency role it fills, and thus turns a blind eye to its principal source of income.

But of all the menaces to indigenous peoples in the world, few can be as poignant or as urgent—suggests Burger—as that which is threatening the million Melanesian people of Indonesia's West Papua.

INDONESIA

Transmigration is central to the political program of the Indonesian government, *Report from the Frontier* declares, and this policy has not allowed President Suharto's government to accept even modest claims of self-determination: the distinct peoples of Kalimantan, South Moluccas, East Timor, or West Papua must either conform to the Javanese notion of the state or disappear. Hundreds of thousands of tribal peoples have been forcibly relocated under the guise of "uplifting" their level of civilization, and up to one million landless Javanese peasants are being moved into West Papua, thus making the Papuans—who were not consulted—a minority in their own territory.

Ethnically distinct from their Javanese "occupiers," the Papuans share neither language nor religion with the Indonesians, who regard them as virtual savages and employ them in conditions of near slavery. The uninhibited exploitation of West Papuan oil and mineral resources has created very few jobs for the Papuans themselves, who number only 20% of the low-level labor force.

THE PHILIPPINES

Finally, there is the situation in the Philippines where, in a familiar pattern, communal land in use for centuries by tribal minorities was deemed to be public land at the advent of U.S. rule, and thus available for private or corporate acquisition and exploitation.

Traditional owners were driven away by force or deceit to allow the creation of vast estates growing sugar cane, pineapple, or bananas. More than half of the Philippines, deemed forest land and in the public domain, has traditionally been the home of most of the country's six million indigenous minority groups, who regard it as their ancestral land.

But a succession of Filipino governments, regarding the forests as unexploited and unclaimed, has awarded logging concessions at a rate virtually unparalleled elsewhere—espe-

Tribal Peoples in Asia

Country	Numbers	Total Population (%)
Afghanistan	6.7 million Pathan	35
	300,000 Baluchis	2
	3 million Koochis	16
Bangladesh	600,000 (official figures)	1
	1.5 million (estimates)	8
Burma	11 million (11 main groups)	30
India	51 million, over 200 groups	7
Indonesia	1.5 million (300 ethnic groups) (government figure)	1
Laos	800,000	23
Malaysia	Peninsula 71,000	Peninsula 4
	E. Malaysia 500,000	E. Malaysia 50
Pakistan	2.5 million federally administered	8
	5.2 million provisionally administered	5
Philippines	6.5 million	16
Sri Lanka	2,000	—
Taiwan	310,000 (10 main groups)	2
Thailand	500,000 (6 main groups)	1
Vietnam	800,000	2
Total	85 million	

Source: *Report from the Frontier.*

cially in northern Luzon; more than one third of the forests have been felled, mostly for the benefit of U.S. and Japanese corporations, which have thus threatened the livelihoods of at least five ethnic minorities. The situation has been exacerbated by the building of 31 dams, almost all on lands occupied by minorities, almost 1.5 million of whom will lose their homes if the program is completed.

The advent of President Aquino would seem to have presented an opportunity to change things for the better because of her "publicly expressed concern for social justice for the poor." But in the author's opinion, "vested political and economic interests continue to retain a grip on many key administrative posts so change, if it takes place at all, is likely to be slow."

"A fallen tree can be stepped over, but a fallen man cannot."

Thai proverb

SPORTS

CHINA'S FIRST PRIVATE SOCCER TEAM

Wan Jiachun, a businessman in the western Chinese town of Chengdu, has forked out $2,700 to start a soccer team named after himself and is seeking official approval to compete with foreign clubs and state-run teams in China. His 18 football trainees are all in colleges, factories, or government offices.

WHAT JAPANESE BASEBALL PLAYERS EARN

The players union of Japanese professional baseball put together the salary figures for the 678 Japanese players of the 12 pro clubs' major and farm teams.

	Team	Average	over Y50 million		under Y10 million	
1.	Lions	Y16.21 million	4 players	6.9%	32 players	55.2%
2.	Giants	Y15.48 million	8 players	14.8%	37 players	58.5%
3.	Dragons	Y13.84 million	2 players	3.7%	34 players	63.0%
4.	Carps	Y12.64 million	2 players	3.5%	35 players	61.5%
5.	Tigers	Y12.58 million	2 players	3.8%	35 players	66.0%
	12-team average	Y12.46 million	27 players	4.0%	444 players	65.6%

In other words, these pro players average about what a manager in a medium-sized company makes, *Shukan Yomiuri* noted.

(In U.S. dollars, the salaries ranged from about an average of $95,846 to a high of about $384,615.)

TAIWAN: WORLD'S LEADING SPORTS GOODS MAKER

Most, if not all sporting goods equipment in the world, is now made in Taiwan. Forty percent of the world's tennis rackets are produced in Taiwan, as are 80% of the world's golf club heads. Taiwan's sporting goods exports reached $1.14 billion in 1986, with another $1.5 billion in sportswear, and $1.1 billion in athletic shoes. Seventy-five percent of all these goods are "OEM"—original equipment manufacturing, in which local manufacturers produce foreign brands for exports.

BLACK BELT IN AEROBICS

"Karatebics" is not a new type of fast food but a style of exercise, combining karate and aerobics, devised by Japanese fitness specialist Eiko Hasegawa who claims it allows participants "to shape up while they practice self-defense and enhance spiritual well-being."

UNWILLING CAMEL JOCKIES

Pakistan is attempting to stop the smuggling of children who are sent to the Gulf states as camel jockeys, according to a minister in Islamabad. The children are tied, screaming, to camels. This is because camel racing is popular in the Gulf states and camel owners say the shrieks of the frightened boys strapped to the animal's back makes the camels race faster.

HIGH-RISE SLALOM

The world's first indoor ski slopes were constructed in Tokyo by leading Japanese builder Kajima Construction Company at a cost of about $57 million. The course features three spiral slopes, three ski lifts and nine artificial snow machines. The entire complex is housed in a six-story refrigerated building whose temperatures are maintained at between zero and five degrees centigrade.

Japan's second indoor ski slope, under construction in Chiba Prefecture, half an hour's drive from Tokyo, will be open 24 hours per day and is expected to cater to half a million skiers each year. Only 2,000 will be allowed in the domed, air-conditioned center at any one time to prevent overcrowding. The 1,640-foot ski slope, with a maximum elevation of 20 degrees, will be kept covered with artificial snow at just below freezing point. The Lalaport Ski Dome is a project of the Mitsui Real Estate Development Co., which will spend about $2 million on its construction.

THAI COURSES

Japanese businessmen's obsession with golf has spilled over into Thailand in the past few years with the country already boasting more than 50 golf courses, almost half of them in Bangkok's steamy suburbs on what were until recently rice paddy fields. One Thai developer, Thatree Boondicharoen, estimates that the number of golfers had tripled to 60,000, and that the typical player was now a young executive in his 30s who tended to use the links to lure reluctant clients. Foreign investors, particularly the Japanese, are heavily represented in club ownership, and with membership fees ranging from about $2000 to as much as $20,000 at Navatanee, Thailand's most exclusive course, profits are substantial. At the more modest courses, green fees start at about $8—almost three times the minimum daily wage.

CRIME

ON THE DARK SIDE OF THE RIM

HONG KONG TRIADS TRY OUT MAINLAND

After their apparent eradication 30 years ago, Hong Kong's notorious Triad gangs, with such names as "Green Dragon gang" and

"Black Tiger gang," have been setting up operations in China's four special economic zones (SEZs), operating underground gambling rackets, prostitution rings, and smuggling antiques out from the mainland, according to Chinese police sources. Reportedly, they have been bribing senior government officials in the Public Security Bureau and the Customs Departments in Shenzhen Xiamen, Shekou, and Zhuai. Among other things, the triads are said to be monopolizing the sale of seafood and pigeons, selling the produce direct to restaurants.

. . . WHILE MAINLAND GANGS TRY OUT HONG KONG

Mainland Chinese crime syndicates have been moving into Hong Kong, according to the Hong Kong Commissioner of Police. Reportedly, the worst of the Chinese criminals move in gangs and commit violent robberies before returning to safe territory on the mainland.

THE NEW YAKUZA

The Roppongi district in Tokyo is a land of discos and poolroom bars. It's a suave part of town, and the local *yakuza* present a much different image than their counterparts in Shinjuku and Ikebukuro. The Roppongi *yakuza* don't run around with punch perms and dark glasses. Instead, they're decked out in "DC"-brand suits and fashionable togs. In fact, they don't stand out from the crowd at all.

The *yakuza* in Roppongi are not into the protection racket. Instead, they work as bill-collectors, getting the money for overdue bar bills. (In some expensive clubs, customers will run up bills as much as Y1,000,000 or about $7,692 a month, notes the *Sunday Main-*

ichi). Mostly they collect from top management of big companies and owners of small companies. Of course, they could be taken to court for their failure to pay their bills, but that's a lot of trouble. What's more, these collectors don't even have to put on the muscle. Among the Roppongi *yakuza,* muscle men are even looked down upon.

The Metropolitan Police say there are some 30 *yakuza* offices in the Roppongi area. It looks like a move by the major *yakuza* gangs toward more legitimate means of funding their organizations.

THE MALTESE RIM

Manila has become the fake passport capital of the world, with over 80 international syndicates churning out fake visas and passports. In one sensational police bust, over 600 fake Polynesian passports were confiscated. Among those arrested was a phony Malaysian sheikh (he also represented himself as a Knight of Malta), who had in his possession a number of documents on "million-dollar transactions in the world's financial capitals." One such document was a $20 million stand-by letter of credit from an unnamed U.S. bank to guarantee a domestic loan for construction of a new building at Manila's domestic airport.

FILIPINO SMUGGLERS FLEECE ECONOMY

The Philippine economy has been losing $67 million annually to smugglers according to a report by the country's Economic Intelligence and Investigation Bureau, which says that a score of Filipino-Chinese syndicates are under observation for smuggling "high tariff goods that are either banned, controlled, regulated, or prohibited."

PAGING JOHN LE CARRÉ

You think monitoring illegal technology transfers from the West to East bloc nations is dull work? Try to untangle this plot: CIA agents monitoring North Korean agents monitoring North Korean trade representatives in Singapore discovered that 500 Japanese NEC 9800 series computers purchased by a Jakarta trading company were to have been diverted to North Korea. They notified the Japanese government, which promptly halted the shipment, according to a report in the *Korea Times*.

THE VIETNAM CONNECTION— SOUTHEAST ASIA'S NEW DRUG AXIS

The Socialist Republic of Vietnam appears to be fast developing into a major new transshipment center for marijuana in Southeast Asia. With the U.S. Drug Enforcement Agency stepping up its joint efforts with the government of Thailand to stem the flow of drugs from the notorious Golden Triangle (located in northeastern Burma, northern Thailand, and northern Laos), Vietnam is said to be assuming the leadership role as the new regional hub for North America-bound marijuana. Vietnamese ports on the Gulf of Thailand are apparently being used to load Laotian grass onto drug-smuggling freighters sailing to the West Coast of North America.

   "We have made a number of seizures, totaling more than 90 tons (of Laotian marijuana from Vietnam), at various West Coast ports of entry," says Con Dougherty, a DEA spokesman in Washington, D.C.

   "I don't believe it's Panama down there," said Donald Stader, the State Department's Vietnam analyst. "But widespread corruption exists in that country at the national level."

One well-known American private investigator, who prefers to remain anonymous, slipped into Vietnam to negotiate the release of an ill-fated American dealer being held for ransom by a syndicate operating in a town on the Gulf of Thailand. The American detective reported that he was quite free to move about the city without being challenged by Vietnamese authorities to produce his (nonexistent) travel documents because "they knew I was protected."

He believes that top Vietnamese officials are in collusion with Southeast Asian drug dealers who have set up a major pot-shipping operation centered on the Vietnamese side of the Gulf of Thailand. "They badly need the foreign exchange," he observed. "Vietnam's economy is a total wreck."

THE CHINA CONNECTION

Asian drug smugglers have developed southern China routes to transport heroin bound for the international market from the Golden Triangle of Burma, Laos, and Thailand to Hong Kong.

HANOI OPIUM DENS

Opium has become a plague in Hanoi, according to Vietnamese media. The newspaper *Hanoi Moi* reported there are 109 opium dens listed in the capital, most of them concealed in back rooms of some of the many small coffee shops that litter the capital. Opium smoking was widespread during the French colonial period, but was banned when the communists came to power in the north.

REACTIONARY LEFTISTS

Left-handed people are more likely to break the law than their right-handed counterparts, according to a survey of 756 juvenile delinquents in China by researchers at Xian Medical University. Some 7.4% of the young offenders surveyed were "totally or partially left-handed," China's *Health News* reported.

A TAXING MOBSTER

A convicted Japanese gangster who was taxed on his profits for illegal drug sales filed a complaint that the tax was too high, Japanese police and tax officials reported. The gangster claimed the tax office overestimated his income from the sales, and paid only $280,000 tax on the proceeds of his illegal drug deals.

COUNTERFEITING IACOCCA

Statistics show that $10 million worth of counterfeit goods from South Korea were confiscated by U.S. Customs officials in 1988, up from $6 million in the previous year. In Seoul, you can buy fake Louis Vuitton bags, Lacoste shirts, Gucci pants, and Reebok sneakers in a densely packed bazaar strip called Itaewon. When Chrysler Corp. chief Lee Iacocca visited Seoul a few years ago, his aides hastily stopped him from autographing a copy of his best-selling autobiography, after advising him it was a pirated version. With the U.S. government putting pressure on South Korea by threatening trade sanctions against countries that fail to respect U.S. intellectual property rights, the South Korean government has been making an effort to curb piracy.

INDONESIAN DEATH SQUADS

In his autobiography, which was published in 1989, Indonesian President Suharto revealed that bodies of criminals summarily executed by security forces were left in public places as "shock therapy" to stem a crime wave in 1984. In his book, entitled *Suharto: My Thoughts, Sayings and Deeds,* the Indonesian president explained that about 5,000 hardcore criminals, who were arrested and executed by security forces, were dumped into rivers, their hands and feet bound by nylon ropes, in order to "crush all the violent criminals that had passed beyond the bounds of humanity." The retired army general took power after an aborted leftist coup in 1965. He will be 72 years old when his current fifth term as president ends in 1993.

HAUNTED HOUSE CURE FOR DRUG ADDICTS

Malaysia, whose tough antidrug trafficking laws have sent over 53 people to the gallows since 1975, launched a novel cure for its 130,000 registered drug addicts in 1987. The battle plan called for moving junkies into vermin-infested, abandoned, and reputedly haunted houses. The program aimed to raise the success rate of its rehabilitation program for addicts from 25% to 40%. "We don't want to pamper them anymore—they must be tough and rugged," said Deputy Home Minister Megat Junid Megat Ayob, who headed Pemadan, a government-sponsored agency fighting drug abuse.

"Running from a tiger to fall in with a crocodile."

Malaysian proverb

DRUG ADDICTS OF SINGAPORE

Almost half of the drug addicts in Singapore are Malays, according to Harun Ghani, the Political Secretary for Home Affairs. In 1988, the 2,849 Malay addicts arrested made up 52.2 percent of all drug-abusers arrested in Singapore.

INTERNATIONAL CRIMINALS TARGET JAPAN

Tokyo police have set up a special investigative section to deal with the growing internationalization of crime and the increasingly serious international crimes committed in Japan. The International Investigation Division was established in 1987 with about 40 investigators, most of whom have had experience working abroad and an ability in foreign languages. In one sensational foreign crime committed in Japan, a group of Frenchmen carried out Japan's largest cash robbery of 300 million yen (about $2.4 million) and also were suspected of transporting stolen French paintings to Japan. Police also occasionally arrest foreign pickpockets and drug smugglers.

Estimating that there are about 50,000 illegal workers in Japan, the National Police Agency says that the number of crimes they commit has been increasing proportionately and has set up an office specially to deal with them. More than 2,000 crimes each year are being committed by foreign workers, the largest proportion by illegal Chinese immigrants. There are also about 400 arrests for prostitution by foreigners, about half of them being Thai women or Filipinos.

CENSORING VIDEOS IN SINGAPORE

Even the innocent pastime of watching some television program from abroad might constitute law-breaking is the warning that has been given to Singapore viewers by the head of the Board of Film Censors. "Under the law all tapes meant for viewing in Singapore must be passed by the Censorship Board," warns chairman Rama Mayyappan, who adds that censorship of tapes for private or domestic use takes about one week and costs about $3.

China's Crime Wave

Incidents of crime rose sharply in China in 1988, with serious offenses such as murder and robbery increasing 65.7% in a one-year period, according to the Vice-Minister of Public Security, Yu Lei. He blamed the crime wave on China's economic modernization, which has made more goods and money available to some people, and on the transient population—peddlers, construction workers, and drifters, estimated at about 50 million. There were 827,000 incidents of crime reported. Allegedly, police solved three out of every four crimes committed.

TRAIN ROBBERIES

Depressed economic conditions in China are contributing to a wave of train robberies. In the first 10 months of 1988, more than 3,000 train robberies occurred on lines connecting the provinces of Yunnan, Kweiochow, Sichuan, Kwangsi, Hunan, and Kwantung. Police reported more than 30,000 suspects were arrested. Most train robbers are said to be farmers. Instead of carrying guns, they wield swords and knives to relieve passengers of their valuables and steal cargo from trains. More than 500,000 farmers descended on Guangzhou in a single month in 1988. They were so desperate to find work, they were reportedly willing to work 16 hours a day for only $40 a month.

Lacking sufficient vehicles and walkie-talkies to do their job properly, railway police have been powerless to prevent widescale theft from goods shipped in open cars along many rural stretches of China's railway system. Color televisions and refrigerators are a popular target, but peasant plunderers also steal copper, aluminum, and other materials, reported Radio Beijing.

RUBBER-TREE CAPERS

Theft and looting of state rubber plantations in the South China province of Hainan to feed illegal factories skyrocketed, with 100 robberies a day reported between April and September in 1988, according to a report in the *Economic Daily*. The biggest rubber heist involved 1,000 people and resulted in the destruction of nearly 200,000 rubber trees and losses totaling about $10.8 million.

PARTYING IS SUCH SWEET SORROW

Wang Rulin, director of a North China pharmaceutical company, was severely disciplined for squandering $98,550 to entertain 240 guests during the three-day celebrations of his factory's 30th anniversary celebrations. The public money was spent on wine, fruit, gifts, and accommodations, reported the *People's Daily*.

CORRUPT CADRES

"These are only the flies. Who dares touch the tiger's bottom?" remarked Su Shaozhi, former head of the Institute of Marxism-Leninism-Mao Zedong Thought at the China Academy of Social Sciences in Beijing, in a reference to the government's ineffectual attempts to stop official corruption by attacking petty officials while ignoring the high officials.

More than 24,000 Chinese Communist Party and government officials, including 17 officials at ministerial and provincial levels, were reported by citizens to have committed crimes in the first half of 1988 alone.

China's Ministry of Public Security has charged that police officers who use their jobs for helping friends and relatives get ahead, embezzling money, and taking bribes have seriously damaged the reputation of the public security forces. Police officers had no excuse, it added, for watching or possessing pornographic videos and publications.

COMPUTER CRIMES IN CHINA

Computer fraud is booming in China with theft of confidential information as well as money, and security systems are unable to keep pace with the growing skill of the criminals, according to the People's Daily. The first case of computer fraud was discovered in 1986 at an office of the People's Bank of China in Shenzhen. The biggest of 15 major cases since then was the theft of about U.S.$218,000 from a bank in Chengdu in 1988.

CHINESE SECURITY FIRMS

By 1988, China had 99 private security companies protecting banks, hotels, factories and markets, according to the China Legal News. Commercial security companies, which first appeared in China only in 1985, employed 13,331 people and had contracts with more than 8,500 clients. Security companies in the southern city of Guangzhou helped police arrest about 3,000 criminals in 1987, the report said. Security companies in China provide escort and consulting services and install and repair burglar alarms.

Increased wealth is bringing increased crime to wealthy communities such as Daji township in South China's Fujian province, where affluent traders have hired the services of a private security firm paying up to $2.25 per month according to the value of their property.

Some affluent parents in Shanghai are hiring bodyguards to escort their teenage daughters to class in response to the soaring crime rate, according to Women's Daily.

WOMEN CRIMINALS OF JAPAN

Alone among industrialized counties, Japan reports two separate peaks for crimes committed by women—the first by women in their late teens and early 20s, and the second for women in their 40s and 50s. Sociologists explain that because Japanese women learn to act subserviently toward men and suppress their individuality, their lack of personal identity makes it hard for them to deal with mid-life crisis, thus many act out their anger through crime.

Housewives whose children are growing up and with absent, divorced (or dead) husbands are particularly vulnerable to what a writer for *Sankei Shimbun* terms "the siren call of personal freedom." Such women yearn to live for themselves but, not knowing how, experiment with drugs, prostitution, or shoplifting. Conversely, there are the women who chose a career over marriage, subsequently become obsessed with having a husband, and fall for married men, often some kind of con man or gangster. Other women, overly ambitious, resort to fraud in an effort to save failing businesses. Despite the rising female crime rate, however, it is men who still commit three quarters of the known crimes and women's presumed subordinate status often induces police to admonish rather than arrest and judges to offer fines or suspended sentences rather than incarceration.

PERFECT SECURITIES SCAM

A fraud ring swindled an estimated $115 million from some 10 Taiwanese securities houses. The ring lured cash-short securities firms with low-interest loans in exchange for stock certificates pledged as collateral, and then sold the stocks in other cities. It is against Taiwanese law to use stock certificates to secure a loan, so the brokerages involved were not forthcoming in reporting the fraud to the police.

NO EXIT FOR CROOKED HIGHWAY OFFICIAL

A Philippine anticorruption court sentenced a former government official to a maximum of 3,576 years in jail for graft. Public highways regional director Rolando Mangubat was also ordered to pay the government 43 million pesos ($2 million) in fines. He pleaded guilty, in 392 cases, to falsifying purchase orders and other documents to collect funds for nonexistent projects. Under Philippine law, a convicted person may not serve more than 30 years of the maximum sentence.

SHAME CULTURE PENALTY

In a bid to crack down on official corruption in Indonesia, the government approved a plan to publicize the identities of government figures wanted by authorities in connection with corruption. A spokesman for the Attorney-General said the move was aimed at creating a "shame culture" among Indonesians.

ILLEGAL LYRICS

For the mere possession of a copy of the lyrics of Paul Simon and Art Garfunkel's "Sparrow" song, a waiter was arrested by Philippine police on charges that he was a hitman for the New People's Army Sparrow Unit. Police said the song, which opens with the lines, "I'd rather be a sparrow than a snail, yes, I would," is the anthem of the NPA Sparrow members. The man denied the charges, saying he just wanted to learn the song on the guitar.

MANILA VICE

In a surprising report, the Philippine government declared that Manila's streets are safer than Tokyo, Hong Kong, and major American cities, and blamed the foreign press for allegedly distorting the crime rate in the Philippines. President Cory Aquino's office released a report revealing that metropolitan Manila's crime rate in 1986 was 16.30 per

---

RIM VOICES

ON SOLVING THE PIRACY PROBLEM

Police seem to be [in a no-win situation] in the never-ending campaign against pirates off Sabah's east coast. Whatever measures police take, there is always an escape route for pirates, who seem to be able to do pretty much as they like . . . In among myriad islands there will always be a bolt-hole for pirates to disappear, even if police saturate the area. And Philippine waters are only a few miles away—another beckoning refuge. Perhaps the only way to beat the terror is a vigilante radio network.

From "Not So Jolly Roger" of Sandakan, Sabah in *The Borneo Bulletin,* Brunei.

100,000 people, compared with 132 in Tokyo, 122.81 in Hong Kong, and 145 in Kuala Lumpur. The crime rate in Bangkok that year was 15.41 per 100,000. The crime rate in Los Angeles during 1985 was 783.90, compared with 776.09 in Chicago.

SINO-VIETNAMESE SMUGGLING

Vietnam, saying border trade with China is getting out of hand, announced it is cracking down on smuggling, cattle-rustling, slavery, holdups, and armed clashes between bandits and customs officials. "Cross-border traffic at the Sino-Vietnamese border has now exceeded the extent allowed," said army newspaper *Quan Doi Nhan Dan.* "These cross-border trading activities have given rise to numerous complicated problems of political security, social order, and safety."

SLAVERY AND PROSTITUTION

PROSTITUTION IN THE PRC

Prostitution is rampant in Shenzhen, on Hong Kong's border with China, where call girls are as much a part of room service as tea and

towels, according to *The Free China Journal,* a Taiwanese newspaper. These prostitutes are allegedly connected with such underworld gangs as the "14K" and "IQ." There are an estimated 14 gangland societies engaged in prostitution, robbery, kidnapping, smuggling, and narcotics in Shenzhen. And gambling has become rampant in Guangzhou (Canton), where police raided and closed down 690 casinos in the last quarter of 1988 alone.

HAINAN'S "GODMOTHERS"

Sex is a big money-maker for the "godmothers" of Hainan Island, the Chinese province off the South China coast, about 250 miles east of Hong Kong. At least 100 massage parlors and bath houses line the main street of Haikou, the island's capital, and the shady lady entrepreneurs who run these establishments are reported to pay their talented employees as much as U.S.$1,000 per month for keeping customers happy. Haikou police get paid by the hour to act as bodyguards for the girls and the local Communist administrators get a cut of the flesh peddlers' take, not least by authorizing the health department to charge about U.S.$83 for VD treatments.

Reporting this, Hong Kong's *Ta Kung Pao* says that these days it is women, mostly middle-aged, who benefit most from operating the sex slave trade as well as committing most of the major crimes, such as kidnapping and murder. They have a well-deserved reputation for being more brutal than men. About half of the numerous VD clinics that operate on Shanghai and Beijing back streets are staffed by female doctors and most of them are under the control of elderly "godmothers." The paper adds that VD victims routinely pay bribes to receive professional treatment in hospitals.

THE SWINGING SWALLOWS

Here's the seamy side of a high-yen Japanese vacationer: The murder of a Japanese woman tourist by a native male "escort" on the Micronesian island of Saipan has blown the lid open on organized sex tours for Japanese women. Earlier, the Korean weekly, *Sunday Seoul,* reported that record numbers of well-heeled Japanese ladies were traveling to south Korea to hunt for "swallows" (the Japanese euphemism for gigolo). A well-known Japanese travel agent admitted booking middle-aged women on four-day, three-night sex packages priced at about $1,200. "Korea was once considered Mecca for Japanese men looking for a good time, but times have changed," the Korean magazine noted. "Now Japanese women come looking for 'swallows.' "

POLYGAMOUS POLICE

Twenty-seven police officers faced disciplinary action in Kuala Lumpur for failing to inform superiors that they had more than one wife. According to police standing orders, police personnel have to inform their superiors of their marital status—and officers are to be sacked if they are found to be more interested in their many wives rather than in their jobs. Malaysian Moslems are allowed four wives, but the country outlaws polygamy for other races.

PROTESTING THAILAND'S SEX INDUSTRY

A provincial appeals court on the southern Thai tourist island of Phuket upheld a sentence of life imprisonment for the owner of a brothel where five imprisoned prostitutes died in a January 1984 fire, according to the *Bangkok Post.* The deaths of the five girls in what were apparently locked rooms drew loud protest from human rights activists and focused national attention on the dark side of the country's massive sex industry.

RED LIGHTS OF JAKARTA

The sex industry is growing rapidly in predominantly Muslim Indonesia and efforts should be made to control it before Jakarta becomes a sex capital like Manila or Bangkok, according to Sukarna Wiranata, an economist with the Indonesian Institute of Sciences. He proposed setting up special sex zones in the city.

In 1988, Indonesia had about 50,000 registered prostitutes and more than 6,300 pimps, according to Indonesia's Department of Social Rehabilitation.

MANILA'S SEX TRADE

In more of their periodic raids on Manila's gaudy Ermita district, police rounded up

2,000 "hospitality girls" employed by the scores of bars, restaurants, discos, nightclubs, and brothels that line the 10-block strip. The nightlife area, much of it owned by foreigners, pours millions of dollars into the economy, with even the smaller establishments earning about $720 per day, but the resulting tag of "Sin City of Asia" has proved to be an increasing embarrassment to the government. Commenting on the crackdown, police chief Alfredo Lim remarked, "When we hear of this reference all of us feel a furious sense of outrage for we all know that we don't deserve such notoriety." The police raids reduced business by 70% in some places, and one club manager charges that it is hypocritical to pretend that tourists come to the Philippines "just to see the sights."

TOKYO'S S&M CLUBS

Because of a loophole in the law that makes prostitution illegal but not sexual perversions, Tokyo has seen the emergence of hundreds of S&M clubs, typically offering 90 minutes of "gentle" pain for about $200 or "violent" suffering for around $300. The evening tabloids are rife with such ads and police say that as long as sexual intercourse is not offered the actions are not illegal. This had led to hookers carrying attaches cases filled with ropes, whips, and similar paraphernalia in case they are stopped and questioned by police.

BLACKMAIL IN THE PARK

Afraid of being reported for having premarital contact in a society which frowns upon such acts, young Chinese couples fall ready victim to con men posing as park officials who levy 15 yuan ($4) fines on them. The average take of such crooks is said to be at least $13 a night, according to *People's Daily*. Extramarital sex is illegal in China, and that law is rigorously enforced in cases involving foreigners and Chinese in a bid to prevent the spread of AIDS into the country.

MEAN STREETS OF HO CHI MINH CITY

Prostitution and drug addiction have reached alarming levels in southern Vietnam's Ho Chi Minh City (formerly Saigon), according to the Dai Doan Ket (Great Unity) weekly. There are some 10,000 prostitutes and 26,000 drug addicts in the city along with tens of thousands of street people.

JAPANESE PHONE SEX

An underground sex industry which has grown in Japan recently is "adult telephone clubs." Men will pay about $25 per hour to sit in a private booth with a telephone whose number has been listed in an "adult" telephone directory. A whole slew of adult telephone magazines have sprung up around this craze. It's sort of an obscene Russian roulette/blind dating service conducted over the telephone line. Young Japanese women, generally college students, will dial these listed numbers at random and engage in spontaneous conversations. "The aim is to set up dates as fast as possible," one telephone club aficionado explained. "The longer you talk, the less successful you are," he noted.

Some telephone addicts will try to set up several dates a day. Frequently, the women will place their phone calls from phone booths which are strategically located just outside the phone clubs. They'll ask a man who interests them to step outside for a moment so they can check him out in person from a safe distance. If they like him, they will make arrangements to go and visit a nearby "love hotel" and engage in quick sex.

The larger adult telephone clubs feature about 30 private booths with phones; the smaller ones have about 10 booths. The club switchboard operator charges clients about $6 for each phone call they receive. Some clubs are considered to be "hot" with good batting averages. Some are so "slow" that they close down almost immediately and get their lines disconnected.

RELIGION

RELIGIONS OF THE PACIFIC RIM

The major religions of Asia, each of which has millions of adherents, are *Islam, Hinduism, Buddhism,* and *Christianity,* and these are supplemented by a host of small religions. The issue is not clear-cut because in some countries, notably Japan, adherents sometimes have attachments to more than one faith.

Buddhism began in India prior to the fifth century B.C. with the birth into a warrior caste in Nepal of Siddartha (his family name was Guatama), who spent years seeking the enlightenment that eventually came to him as he sat under a Bodhi tree near the Ganges.

Following his death, after years of preaching in northern India, his doctrine was spread by missionaries throughout southeast Asia and to Japan and China, in both countries mingling with native beliefs. Seeking the *Middle Way* between the extremes of sensuality and asceticism, Buddhism seeks to inspire its followers through meditation and good deeds to acquire the necessary *karma* to achieve the state of *nirvana* enroute to a higher status in the life that follows. Southern Buddhists,

concentrated in Burma, Sri Lanka, and other regions, call themselves *Therevada;* northern Buddhists, chiefly in Tibet, where it is the state religion, follow the doctrine of *Mahayana.* Today, in America, there is a very strong Tibetan Buddhist following which adheres to various esoteric and tantric teachings.

The basic teachings of the Buddha are espoused in his *Four Noble Truths* as a solution to the cessation of human suffering. They are: the recognition of the universal fact of human suffering; the cause of suffering which is craving or desire; the cessation of suffering by ending craving; and the method of cessation by the Noble Eightfold Path. The *Noble Eightfold Path* is a system of discipline which is enforced by Right View and Resolve, Right Speech, Action and Livelihood, and Right Effort, Concentration, and Contemplation.

Japanese Buddhism (Buddhism came to Japan in the sixth century A.D. from Korea via China) adopted the Chinese Pure Land (Jodo) and Dian-Dai (Tendai) schools. Buddhism came to terms with the ancient Japanese Shinto religion by declaring that the ancient Shinto gods were incarnations of the Buddhist originals.

The animist philosophy of *Shinto* is the indigenous religion of the Japanese people, whose communal rites and symbolic expressions are expressed in a reverence for natural forces and departed heroes. As the Japanese official state religion until Japan's defeat in World War II, it assumed a doctrinaire, propagandistic theology which proclaimed the racial purity and superiority of the Japanese and held the Emperor to be the direct descendant of Amaterasu, the Sun Goddess. It was this fanaticism that justified Japan's ill-fated militaristic adventures abroad.

Today, there is still a controversial fine-line drawn between the present Imperial Family's personal Shinto rituals and government-sanctioned state ceremonies as evidenced by var-

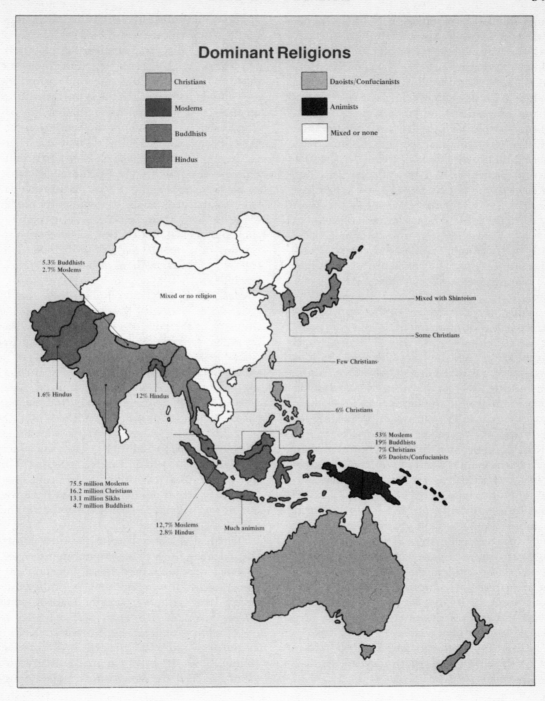

Dominant Religions

- Christians
- Moslems
- Buddhists
- Hindus
- Daoists/Confucianists
- Animists
- Mixed or none

5.3% Buddhists
2.7% Moslems

Mixed or no religion

Mixed with Shintoism

Some Christians

Few Christians

6% Christians

1.6% Hindus

12% Hindus

53% Moslems
19% Buddhists
7% Christians
6% Daoists/Confucianists

75.5 million Moslems
16.2 million Christians
13.1 million Sikhs
4.7 million Buddhists

12.7% Moslems
2.8% Hindus

Much animism

ious "double" ceremonies surrounding the funeral of the late Emperor Hirohito in 1989, and the subsequent ascension of Emperor Akihito to the throne.

Chinese *Chan* Buddhism—which stressed the quest for enlightenment in daily activities —was adopted by the Japanese as *Zen* Buddhism, becoming popular with the samurai military as well as artists and artisans who thrived on the discipline of living "in the moment." From Japan, Zen missions were dispatched to the Pacific islands during this past century, especially to Hawaii and the West Coast of the United States, where it has found a ready following first among intellectuals, and then among sixties-conscious young Americans, who have begun absorbing it into the mainstream American "Pacific Rim" culture.

Today, the immediacy of Zen can be discerned in various nonsectarian *New Age* holistic philosophies and schools of transpersonal psychology, which have blended various East–West traditions in to a cultural dynamic.

Hinduism owes its origins to the flourishing civilization around the Indus river in northern India as early as 25 centuries ago. Existing for centuries only in the form of oral texts, the *Vedas,* compiled by the regal Brahmin class, the system is united in the worship of certain deities such as Shiva, Vishnu, and the Mother, splitting otherwise into a bewildering array of sometimes contradictory offshoots and sects including the *Jains* (whose ascetic, nonviolent practices stem from their allegiance to the 24 Jinas who have renewed their religion since the world began) and the Sikhs. Dominant in the Punjab region of northwest India, *Sikhism* owes some of its origins to the influence of Islam and reveres the fifteenth-century guru Nanak and his nine successors. The *Parsis,* a relatively small minority, migrated to India in the ninth century and still conduct their rituals and hymns in ancient Persian.

Today, Hinduism is a vital part of the new Pacific Rim culture on the West Coast of America as yoga, transcendental meditation, and other yogic disciplines, including the practice of *kundalini* yoga (the vital cosmic energy rooted in the base of the spine that shoots up the seven main *chakras* or bioenergy circuits through the crown of the head, connecting with the cosmic source of "The All-That-Is," embodied by *Brahman*). In the past half-century, celebrated yogis, including Paramahansa Yogananda and Swami Muktananda, have established major followings in North America with their Self-Realization Fellowship and SYDA Foundation. There are numerous other yogic masters with their own followings, some of them of dubious mystical lineage.

Islam claims some 820 million followers in Asia and Africa, with Muslims providing the majority of the population of Indonesia, Malaysia (where it is the state religion), Afghanistan, Pakistan, and Bangladesh, and a minority in Thailand, the Philippines, Burma, Sri Lanka, China, and Soviet Central Asia. The monotheistic religion was founded at Medina on the Arabian peninsula in 622 A.D. by Muhammad, who passed on the divine wisdom revealed to him in the Koran, which is regarded as sacred and above criticism. The five duties of each Muslim are to profess the faith, pray five times daily, donate to charity, fast during Ramadan (the ninth month), and to visit Mecca.

Confucianism derives from the fifth century B.C. deliberations of a self-educated teacher, its creed a compound of moral precepts, state ritual, ancestral worship, and the indigenous beliefs that form the basis of Daoism with which it is akin. Kongfuzi or Master Kong (latinized as Confucius) lived in the state of Lu in north China (551 to 478 B.C.). He is credited with the authorship of a small book called the *Analects,* which stressed the importance of propriety in personal and social conduct. Filial piety and the correct observance of ancestral cults were promoted, along with the synergestic responsibility between rulers and subjects as well as servants and their masters.

By the second century B.C., Confucianism became enshrined as the state cult of China—and his teachings became the foundation for Chinese as well as other Chinese-influenced Asian societies, such as Japan and South Korea through modern times. Indeed, the Confucian model is attributed as a major reason for the success of the modern Pacific Rim trading dynamos, including Japan and the so-called Four Dragons (Taiwan, Singapore, Hong Kong, and South Korea).

Taoism, China's indigenous nature and mystical religion, is based on the "Tao," or "The Way." There is a Tao of heaven, a Tao of earth, and a Tao of man, which is in harmony with these two. Lao Zi (also known as Lao Tse) is a legendary figure who reputedly lived just before Confucius and who was said to have rebuked Confucius, although this is a subject of controversy. He is the alleged author of the Tao Te Jing (The Way and the Power), supposedly written in the third century B.C., which expressed the ineffable nature of the Tao.

The Tao is described as being "ineffable and external, it cannot be grasped, but by its quietness its influence extends over 10,000 material things."

Like Zen, Taoism has its appeal with the new Pacific Rim culture on the "New Age" West Coast, with contemporary offshoots of Taoist longevity and personal alchemy practices being promoted by such teachers as the Thai-Chinese master Mantak Chia, who teaches esoteric Taoist sexual techniques in the West.

Christianity, which began as an Asian religion, has millions of adherents throughout the Pacific Rim, although it remains in minorities in the Near East. The Syrian Orthodox Church in India claims to have been founded by the Apostle Thomas, and there is evidence of its existence since at least the fifth century. Burma and Sri Lanka have over one million Christians each, mainly Roman Catholic. There are an estimated 17 million Christians, mostly Protestant, in Indonesia, and about 3 million in South Korea and 1 million in Vietnam. There are numerous Christian sects in Japan, with more than 3 million members. The Philippines has the largest Christian population in Asia, totaling more than 44 million Roman Catholics and Protestants.

In Oceania and the South Pacific, especially in Australia and New Zealand, Christianity is the dominant religion. The influx of missionaries throughout the South Pacific in the nineteenth century was responsible for converting Maoris, Fijians, Samoans, and Tongans, at the cost of native cultures and their own animistic and shamanistic religions. There are an estimated 12 million Protestants and 6 million Roman Catholics in Oceania, including Australia and New Zealand, with smaller numbers of Christians in Papua New Guinea.

SOURCES: Background article, "The Religions of Asia," by Geoffrey Parrinder, "The Far East and Australasia, 1989" (Europa Publication, Ltd., London, 1989).

For a cross-section of East–West traditions fused in a California "New Age" context, please refer to *Common Ground: Resources for Personal Transformation,* a free quarterly catalog published by Common Ground, 305 San Anselmo Avenue, Suite 217, San Anselmo, California 94960.

ON THE NEW AGE RIM

Hard-driving, yet mellow California executives are discovering a new Pac-Rim productivity tool for the office—the *didjeridu.* A young San Francisco entrepreneur, Fred Gray Tietjen, has developed—and is now marketing—the first American high-tech version of this aboriginal Australian woodwind instrument whose origins date back some 40,000 years. "What American businessmen are seeking is power," explains Tietjen, who also runs a "shamanic counseling" practice in San Francisco. "By triggering the sound of the *didjeridu,* they can learn to alter their state of consciousness and become extremely empowered." Some New-Age-oriented execs are reportedly keeping *didjeridus* handy beside their laptop computers in their offices. It takes only about 10 minutes to learn how to get a good drone going, and its costs $85.

CHANGING CHANNELS IN TOKYO

With the once seemingly invincible Tokyo Stock Exchange going into crazy slides (the TSE has lost an estimated 22% of its yen value in the early months of 1990), many stunned Japanese investors and brokers are turning to unorthodox sources for an explanation of what is happening to the market. In one case, a self-styled British psychic who claims to be channeling the spirit of the Maitreya Buddha (the reputed "coming Buddha," according to Buddhist scriptures) has been speaking to full houses in Tokyo.

The channeler, Scottish-born Benjamin Creme, claims that "Maitreya" has descended from his retreat in the Himalayas and has taken up residence in the Asian community of East London. At one New Age seminar in Tokyo—complete with chants by Japanese Buddhist monks and the performance of religious *Noh* drama dances to get everyone in the mood—Creme explained to a rapt Japanese audience that Maitreya had caused the last big shock on the Tokyo Stock Exchange as a prelude to the collapse of stock exchanges all around the world. Why? Because the world is moving away from a monetary system. Creme even played a tape of the "chan-

neled" Maitreya (whose Japanese name is "Miroku Bosatsu"), speaking with a distinctly English accent.

PR MAN FOR THE SPIRIT WORLD

We're in an age of technology. Yet people seem to be turning more and more to the spiritual. Business, of course, takes advantage of these trends with games and movies and even tours of the Spirit World. Don't confuse these businesses with those who bilk people, notes *Shukan Sankei,* a Japanese magazine. These companies provide fun and entertainment. Take Tamba Tetsuro, for example. The well-known Japanese actor has appointed himself PR Man for the Spirit World. He's organized the "Afterlife Research Association," which now has 1,700 members, mostly in their 30s. Tamba says more and more young people are joining, too. The Association sells ouija boards and books on the Spirit World, and offers "tours of the Afterlife" (complete with a guarantee of no physical harm). "The tour is supposed to be a fun trip for adults and children alike," reports *Shukan Sankei.*

FARMERS WITH FAITH

About one in 10 of China's 100 million population subscribes to a religious faith and most of them are farmers, reports *China Daily,* adding that in order of popularity the main faiths are Buddhism, Islam, Catholicism, Protestantism, and Taoism.

MONK TYCOONS

Some Japanese priests and monks have taken out real estate licenses, while others have built restaurants on the temple premises and cater to groups and tours, sometimes "forgetting" to report the taxable income, according to *Shukan Shincho*. Some wheeler-dealers use the income from grave upkeep and funeral ceremonies to invest in apartment houses and condominiums. The Buddhist temple of Gion in Kyoto is said to be the top-selling area for a nationally distributed brand of hairpieces and the monks often wear wigs and suits when they go out to buy property. "There are 183,000 registered religious organizations in Japan," the magazine adds, "and most, it seems, are looking for new ways to get out of paying taxes."

THE RAMADAN TASK-FORCE

Just about the only officials who do any meaningful work during Ramadam, the fasting month (usually May) in the lunar-based Islamic calendar are those employed by the Religious Affairs Department, who are kept busy raiding massage parlors and other perceived "vice dens" arresting any Muslims found on the premises. In Malaysia and other Islamic communities throughout Asia and elsewhere, Ramadan is the time when most public activities grind to a halt, with fasting from food, drink, and tobacco between dawn and dusk being mandatory. Most restaurants put up signs warning their Muslim patrons they are liable to be prosecuted for not fasting, and even those who might be willing to risk it often can't get a waiter to serve them.

MOSLEM CONSUMER GROUPS

An Indonesian Moslem organization formed a consumer group, The Moslem Consumer Foundation, to ensure that products carrying government-issued labels declaring them *halal* met the requirement that they be free of pork fat. Some 85% of Indonesia's 176 million population are Moslems who are forbidden consumption or use of pork and its derivatives. In 1988, there was a nationwide consumer boycott of many best-selling brands—including instant noodles, milk powder, and toothpaste—after allegations in local newspapers that these products contained lard. The allegations were subsequently deemed unfounded.

"Even a Buddha must start out as a novice."

Japanese proverb

DIVINATION BOOM IN JAPAN

Divination is a $7.6 billion industry in Japan, according to the *Yomiuri* weekly magazine. The publication conducted a survey in Japan, which revealed that an estimated 30 million Japanese consult soothsayers, each spending about $230 a year to find out what the future holds for them. There are 78 known forms of divination practiced in Japan—from aeromancy to zoomancy. But the most widely used forms are those that trace their origins to China, where clairvoyance was practiced as far back as the second millennium B.C. In those days, bones or tortoise shells were heated and the cracks that resulted after cooking were used to make predictions.

In Tokyo, a computer software firm D.I.I. Company offers corporate fortune-telling software and also provides advice about how to deal with workers. On a more popular level, the Tariki is a fortune-telling emporium in the capital's trendy Harajuku district. Twelve booths with about 60 professional soothsayers cater to the public. The fee ranges from $23. With proper I.D., university students can get fortunes told for only $19, while high school students pay only $15.

THE STORE WITH MORE

In the Jiyugaoka area of Tokyo, there's a popular store named Infidel, which sells religious talismans, ranging from Buddhist items from Thailand to Catholic items from Italy. All are imported direct. The store's motto is "We don't ask your religion." According to *Shukan Sankei* magazine, the best customers are young girls.

ON THE (MEDITATION) BALL

Alpha-Q is a ball, 15 centimeters in diameter, with a special lens. There are two sensors to attach to your fingers. Ordinarily, when the sensors are attached, a series of eight LEDs light up on the globe. The lights get fewer and fewer as you relax and approach the proper state of meditation. Once that level is reached, the lenses light up and project an image of the Buddha. Costs about $385, from the Tokyo firm of Itoh Chotanpa.

CLOSE THAIS

The Thai government launched its "New Hope" project in 1989 to economically develop Thailand's five southernmost provinces as part of a project to pacify its Muslim separatists. While Muslim separatists represent 95% of the population in the provinces of Songkhla, Pattani, Yala, Narathiwat, and Satun, they amount to only 2% of Thailand's total population of 52 million which is predominantly Buddhist.

MERRY CHRISTMAS, MR. LI PENG

Christmas cards are gaining popularity in China as freedom of religion has eased in this nation. During the Christmas season of 1987, the Christmas card counter at the Kidan foreign language bookstores featured some 300 kinds of cards and sold 400,000 cards.

PRINTING GIDEONS IN CHINA

Amity Press, a social service organization founded in 1985 by Christians in China, launched a $7.3 million bible-printing plant in the city of Nanjing, the first in China devoted to printing the Christian scriptures. The plant has the capacity to print half a million bibles a year. The first order, for 100,000 copies, was placed by the China Christian Council, representing China's three million protestants. Christian organizations throughout the world donated $6 million through the United Bible Societies to purchase sophisticated printing equipment from West Germany, Italy, and Japan. Since 1981, 2.9 million bibles have been printed in China.

BORN-AGAIN YWCA

The Young Women's Christian Association of China resumed its activities in Shanghai, Beijing, Tianjin, Guangzhou, Nanjing, Hangzhou, and Xian in 1987.

UNIVERSAL ENERGY

QIGONG—REVOLUTIONARY BIONERGY

Chinese scientists have discovered that an ancient breathing art called *qigong* (pronounced "chee-goong"), used to treat various diseases including cancer, alters the molecular structure of liquids, according to Beijing's *China Daily* newspaper. It said researchers using laser technology found that *qi*—the "life energy" transmitted from a *qigong* master altered the molecular structure of water and three other liquids. China has more than 20 million practioners of *qigong,* which is used to treat hypertension, gastric ulcers, and cancer. *Qigong* has also been used as an anesthetic during surgery, the newspaper said.

SAY QI

It's the little things you rarely think about that may affect the way you do your job, says a Chinese professor, like the position a mirror hangs in a room or the route you take to your office. "You may enter one office and feel your breath coming freely and your spirits lifted," Professor Lin Yun told a Taiwan symposium. "Then you go to another and you are overcome with a feeling of oppression and become distracted . . . so an architect should pay attention not only to mundane principles of material and construction, but also to the often-ignored factors that influence a person's neural system."

Lacking understanding of such principles, he added, could contribute to mental pressures that defeated both talent and hard work. The professor, a folklorist who is well known for his promotion of "Esoteric Buddhism," believes that man is moved by the vital energy of *qi* in his body, and has toured widely in the United States conducting classes on this subject.

QIGONG MACHINE

A Chinese physician Dr. Lu Yan Fang has developed a *qigong* machine which generates certain low-level sound emissions—,"out of auditory range and in the infrared portion of the light spectrum," according to a *Meditation* magazine review of the product—that are healing to the body. He worked with over 20 Chinese *qigong* masters (those proficient in disciplined *qigong* techniques) in over 100 repeated lab experiments to create the electroacoustic technology that simulates the *qigong* energy emissions.

The resulting "Qi Gong Machine" has been awarded recognition by the Chinese Ministry of Health, the China Central Technology Committee, and the National Committee for Traditional Chinese Medicine, and is widely used in Chinese hospitals and by practitioners of Chinese traditional medicine. Reputedly, lab tests have shown it to stimulate the immune system and to have a therapeutic effect on various diseases and ailments. There is "also, an overall calmness, as if derived from an emotional energy massage," according to *Meditation.* A San Clemente, California based distribution company, Energetix, markets the product in America for $495.

GEOMANCY

FENGSHUI THE ART OF EARTH, WIND, AND WATER

The Chinese believe there are energy lines—*qi*—in the earth as well as in the body. The perfect balance of the positive and negative aspects of this energy produces a vibrant *qi.* That's why Chinese *fengshui* men (geomancers) are in such big demand by Chinese businesses, as well as individuals, all over Asia. Financially troubled Australian tycoon Alan Bond's fate was sealed, according to *fengshui* experts, when the Bond Centre building he owns in Hong Kong's Exchange Square was affected by the negative *fengshui* emanating from the sharp edges of the neighboring Bank of China tower designed by Chinese-American architect I. M. Pei. The Bond group is now staggering under the weight of debts totaling about U.S.$4.2 billion.

According to a report in the Singapore *Straits Times,* today's *fengshui* men, who consult on everything from placement of office furnishings to the orientation of doors on buildings—carry on a thriving trade, using fax machines to transmit altered floor plans to corporate clients. Last year, in Singapore, there were 80 businesses registered as geomancy consultancies.

Fengshui men in Singapore, Hong Kong, and Taiwan are not required by law to prove their credentials. As long as their clients are confident that they produce results, their business is assured. One of Singapore's top *fengshui* consultants, Lim Koon Hian, boasts a list of blue-ribboned clients, including First National Bank of Boston, Singapore Finance, Polygram Records, and ManuLife, a subsidiary of one of Canada's largest insurance companies.

Following his instructions, ManuLife Singapore's president Donald Ronahan had a spiral staircase built, ordered more partitioning screens so that all work stations faced the same direction, and slanted the entrance as well as several office doors, cabinets, and desks. The total cost—not including the geomancer's fees—came to about U.S.$15,000. He considers it money well spent.

Saatchi & Saatchi Integrated, a Singapore-based direct-marketing subsidiary of the world's biggest ad agency, also hired Lim, and they were suitably impressed. "I am very pleased to say that he arrived in a Mercedes and I thought, 'It probably works,' " remarked Saatchi's managing director Paul Lyzba.

5

❖

RIM ECOLOGY AND ENVIRONMENT

CASHING IN ON ASIA'S POLLUTION BOOM
by Brian Caplen

As Asia tackles pollution, specialist firms could make big money.

A pall of smoke over Asia has put a sparkle into foreign eyes. In the clouds of smog engulfing the continent, they see the glint of gold.

Rivers, too, coursing with a thick treacle of effluent and sewage, offer up hidden seams of opportunity. And hazardous waste, the fall-out from three decades of explosive growth, could be the icing on the cake.

In the push to clean up Asia, the message is strikingly clear. The West has the technology. Asia doesn't. Sales must follow—an exhilarating prospect for the American, European, and Australian companies which specialize in doing other peoples' dirty work.

Pollution experts are moving into the region. Tailor-made marketing strategies are being unveiled, and a host of conferences and exhibitions set in motion. Pollution control is the talk of the day, and a business bonanza in everything from building new sewers to supplying smoke detectors is expected.

"American businessmen are getting lathered up about this one because they realize what a powerful position they are in," says a top executive at a U.S. bank in Hong Kong.

"At last here is something that Asia can't do faster and cheaper than they can. There are no short cuts to pollution control. You just have to invest heavily in the right expertise and equipment. American companies have both."

The place where they could make some of their best sales is Taiwan. There, antipollution fervor is gathering pace and the government's Environmental Protection Agency (EPA) had its budget beefed up to U.S.$175 million in fiscal 1988.

Spending by state enterprises in Taiwan is also escalating. Investment in environmental projects by Chinese Petroleum Corp., Taiwan Power Co., China Steel Corp., and nine other state concerns (hit about) U.S.$600 million in 1989—more than three times the 1987 outlay.

The EPA's director general, Eugene Chien, estimates that by the year 2000, public and private sectors combined will need to invest a colossal U.S.$35 billion if Taiwan wants to match the level of environmental control in place in Japan, Europe, and the United States.

Given the mess that Taiwan is currently in —particularly smog-laden Taipei—this goal may seem ambitious. A generation of haphazard dumping of industrial waste has taken its toll on the landscape.

By the end of 1987, factories were dumping 82,000 tons of solid waste and 1.81 million liters of water a day, of which 10% were contaminated by cyanide, heavy metals, radioactive chemicals, and solvents.

Add to this the impact of growing populations of people, pigs, and cars—19.7 million, 6 million, and 7.7 million, respectively—and it's easy to see why Taiwan has a problem.

If piles of garbage were elephants, Hong Kong would spawn 3,000 of the beasts every day.

Not surprisingly, the country's new middle class is beginning to complain about the situation. They didn't struggle to get where they are today just to live in a polluted wasteland. They didn't graduate from the production line to the computer room so that they could be surrounded by factory filth. As part of their new consumer life-style, they demand a better environment.

The government is busy trying to deliver. But for the job to be done with any speed, foreign help will be needed.

EPA adviser Joseph Yang comments, "Much of [the EPA budget] will be spent on importing technology from abroad. We welcome foreign suppliers coming to Taiwan."

Indeed, the government has singled out the import of pollution control equipment as a way of reducing the island's embarrassingly high trade surplus with the United States.

The formula is working. American companies have dominated recent planning contracts for pollution-control projects. Bechtel, for instance, picked up a U.S.$700,000 deal while architects URS picked up three, worth a total of U.S.$2 million. All are water-pollution related.

Taiwan does possess its own engineering firms capable, in theory at least, of tackling pollution projects. But they are too thin on the ground to meet all the requirements.

"Local pollution control firms can supply less than 30% of our domestic needs," says Bob Hsiao, a market-development specialist for the China External Trade Development Council (CETRA). "Roughly 20 companies here can manufacture simple equipment, mainly devices used for water treatment. The rest of the engineering firms only distribute and install foreign equipment."

Another view is that Taiwanese firms have the expertise but not the experience in using it in this field.

"The critical gap is not expertise because Taiwan's engineers have that. The problem is lack of expertise in *environmental* applications," says Satish Almaula, an engineer with America's Harding Lawson Associates, which is hoping to pick up contracts in Taiwan. The company specializes in the disposal of hazardous waste and restoring contaminated sites.

Taiwan is not the only obvious target for such firms. Dynamic growth in other Asian countries has generated mountains of waste and a host of ecological disasters.

"There's a direct correlation between the gross domestic product of a country and the amount of garbage it produces," says Dr. Robert Keen, head of the Centre of Environmental Studies at Hong Kong Polytechnic. "You can't tell what stage of development a place has reached by the things it throws away."

In Hong Kong, Keen is well-placed to observe the practice of his theory. If piles of garbage were elephants, Hong Kong would spawn nearly 3,000 of the beasts every day. With a land area of only 1,000 km^2, and with urban dumps rapidly filling, disposing of such a huge volume of trash is a major challenge.

POLLUTED AIR AND WATER

Air and water are also trouble spots. At any one moment, the air in the first 100 meters over Hong Kong contains at least one ton of dust, including ash, plastic, dirt, and metals, such as lead. Each day, well over 1 million cubic meters of sewage, enough to fill 435 Olympic-size swimming pools, is dumped into Victoria Harbor—most of it untreated.

Relief may be at hand. Hong Kong's colonial governor Sir David Wilson has pledged himself to improving the territory's environment, and the government has committed U.S.$1.9 billion over the next 10 years to solving the problems. The largest part of this will be devoted to waste disposal, with a substantial sum going to sewage disposal.

Governments certainly have their work cut out. Even in cash-rich north Asia, the task of getting polluters both to stop polluting and to pay for the damage is difficult. In developing Southeast Asia, where over-stringent environmental controls might throw a marginal or nascent industry off the rails, the challenge is even greater.

Asia's green mission is made tougher by the region's industrial structure, consisting in the main of many small factories with insufficient resources to invest in antipollution equipment.

"In Hong Kong, most of the factories have less than 20 workers and are located, one above the other, in multistory flats. How can they squeeze a waste-treatment plant into the toilet, even if they had the money?" asks Stanley Fong, manager of Portals Water Treatment (Hong Kong).

He adds, "You must have a centralized system and the government has to pay for it. Yet some governments have stated quite clearly that they do not intend to foot the bill."

"Our policy is 'polluters pay,'" says Joseph Yang, adviser to Taiwan's EPA. "Industries that generate waste will pay to protect the environment."

Taiwan's approach is to enforce legislative controls by fining offenders." The EPA will gradually raise its standards. Taiwan is in a transition period. Eventually, polluting industries with low profit margins—those that cannot absorb the cost of pollution control—will have to close shop or move off the island," explains Yang.

But take an industry like electronics in Malaysia. Realizing that it is the country's biggest export earner, it's easy to see why the issue may be less than clear-cut.

"Basically, environmentalism does not rank high with the government, although it is becoming more accepted," observes Gurmit Singh, president of the independent watchdog Environmental Protection Society of Malaysia (EPSM).

With electronics, the dilemma is quite serious because of the highly toxic nature of the waste. In warehouses in the Bayan Lepas free-trade zone in Penang are stacked drum upon drum of hazardous waste, too dangerous to transport and with no dump site available.

Minister of Science, Technology, and Environment, Stephen Yong, has admitted the "urgent need for a treatment facility of international standard," and a site is said to have been selected. But in this case, the stalling may not be due to cost.

CATCHING FLAK IN PERAK

The government is still facing flak from residents in Perak about the siting of a radioactive waste dump for the Japanese-Malaysian joint venture company, Asian Rare Earth. Residents are demanding that the company be closed down and the matter is currently before the courts.

The story of the Asian Rare Earth dump clearly demonstrates the different stages in environmental control that north and south Asian governments have reached.

Originally, joint venture partner Mitsubishi Chemicals had been importing monazite—a by-product from Malaysia's tin industry—for processing in Japan to obtain xenotine and rare earth chlorides. But because the process has a dangerous radioactive by-product, de-

clared hazardous in Japan, the work was switched to Malaysia.

The problem with governments of the poorer countries accepting such business is that they lack the expertise to regulate it.

In Malaysia, the Department of Environment has only one high-volume air sampler for each state, not enough for continuous air monitoring. In Sabah, the DOE branch had the equipment but lacked the budget to do tests and calibrations.

An inadequate DOE can hardly expect to take on industrial polluters. "If [the enforcement officers] have no factory background, they can be taken for a ride by factory managers," comments the EPSM's Gurmit. "Furthermore, they rarely do surprise raids."

The same struggle to implement legislation is going on in Indonesia. Under a 1986 law, companies there are supposed to do an environmental impact analysis to get an operating license for new projects and expansions.

But an official for the State Ministry for Population and the Environment (KLH) says, "Even if all the companies did hand in environmental assessments, there's no way we could process them all."

To ease the pressure on KLH resources, a new set of standards has been introduced by the Industry Ministry, yet these too may not be rigorously enforced. Uneven application of the law is the biggest complaint that business has about environmental control.

In Indonesia, the conflict between business and the environment is brought sharply into focus. America's Scott Paper Co., for example, has permission from the country's investment board to set up a U.S.$653 million tree plantation and pulp mill in Irian Jaya.

Protests from environmentalists are threatening the project, and Scott says it's not going ahead unless all the conditions are right.

The controversy comes hot on the heels of another row about a pulp mill, this time in

North Sumatra. Problems began when a badly constructed waste disposal lagoon burst and contaminated the nearby Asahan River.

THE MUCKRAKERS

As a result, environmental groups are now suing the company, Inti Indorayon Utama, for violating environmental law and the government for failing to enforce it. The industry is watching with considerable interest to see how the government handles the affair.

In the Philippines, the battle over forests has heated up to the point of bloodshed. Two priests who were campaigning against logging in Mindanao have been killed, while a journalist and a leading conservationist have received death threats.

But while business and the environment may collide on short-term issues, in the longer term their interests converge. Apart from the public stigma of being a polluter, companies that chuck out waste indiscriminately may find themselves flushing valuable materials down the drain. On top of this, if resources are not conserved, companies that live by exploiting them eventually go out of business.

Even countries as far back in the development process as the Philippines and Indonesia are starting to realize this. The violence in the Philippines follows the Philippine House of Representatives' approval of a bill banning tree-cutting in all but nine of the country's 73 provinces. With the land area covered by rain forest down to 8% of what it was a quarter of a century ago, action cannot be put off.

Indonesia is in a similar position. The country owns the richest commercial forests in the world, but almost unchecked logging is ploughing through the 114 million hectare stock at an annual 900,000 hectare gallop.

Since Indonesia depends on its primary sector—agriculture, forestry, fishing, and mining—to produce 45% of gross domestic product, 85% of export earnings, and 55% of employment, it can't afford to kiss those trees goodbye quite that quickly.

So conservation and environmental protection are the way ahead for Asian governments. Business will have to fit into this mould by curbing polluting activities and helping to pay for the clean-up.

Meanwhile, those companies which make and sell pollution-control equipment are in for a bonanza. Never has there been such an opportunity to prove that where there's muck, there's brass.

By Brian Caplen, reported by Glenn Smith in Taiwan, Simon Tan in Malaysia, Adam Schwarz in Indonesia, John Keating and Brian Caplen in Hong Kong. © *Asian Business* magazine, Far East Trade Press, Ltd., 1989.

PAR FOR POLLUTION

Those vast stretches of healthy-looking greensward that have been taking over more and more of the Japanese countryside are taking a hidden toll on the environment, according to a recent book, *Golf Courses Will Be the Death of Japan,* many photos of which, showing drainage pipes spewing red water into nearby paddies, are more explicit than any words can be. "The problem," says Osaka University's Yamada Kunihiro, "is agricul-

GRASSROOTS PRESSURE

by Jung Nam Chi

Among the Asian NICs (newly industrializing countries), only South Korea is lagging behind in grasping the environmental nettle with both hands. While other governments are increasing their spending, Korea's Economic Planning Board (EPB) has cut the environmental bureau's budget by 27% to U.S.$56.5 million.

Critics suggest that pollution was only something that mattered to the government during the 1988 Seoul Olympics. During the games, smoky chimneys were regulated, civil engineering work was stopped, and Seoul became untypically clean.

Now, with the eyes of the international press corps diverted, no one seems to be bothering.

As in other countries, there is a noticeable gap between the rhetoric and the reality of government edicts. Factories that have been pressed to install antipollution equipment only use it when there is an inspection and, claims a labor organization official, they are tipped off in advance about inspections.

But not all observers think that Korea is a lost cause. Says A. W. Nem, editor of *Asian Water and Sewage,* "Even after its major clean up of the Han River for the Olympics, Korea has some schemes in hand.

"Two of the latest cover relatively small cities, Suweon and Jinju in Kyonggi province. They will cost U.S.$133 million, of which the Asian Development Bank has agreed to lend U.S.$20 million."

Another sign that the Korean market has potential for pollution specialists was the decision to stage a major exhibition of pollution-control equipment in Seoul in 1989. The organizers decided that even if the government is taking a cautious approach, private individuals may be willing to spend.

They may be right. Many households, for example, having lost faith in the country's drinking water, are buying purifiers. These were once considered a joke item that only soft American expatriates would buy. Now there are more than 50 firms supplying them and one dealer, S. C. Choi, claims to have installed more than 2,000 units.

Grassroots sentiments such as this will eventually persuade the Korean government to treat pollution as seriously as its NIC counterparts. A clean environment, is, after all, just another part of the democratic package.

© *Asian Business* magazine, Far East Trade Press, Ltd., 1989.

tural chemicals. Golf courses use weedkillers to protect the grass; insecticides, fungicides, and lots of other chemicals. What's more, they don't use ordinary chemicals, they use much stronger ones—in much larger doses." The result is twofold: chemicals seep into the groundwater supply via wells, lakes, and rivers, and undissolved chemicals collect on the skin of golfers and caddies causing nausea, sore eyes, and stomach problems as well as other maladies.

ON TOP OF OLD SMOKEY

Manila's largest garbage pile, where hundreds of scavengers live—and work—earning as much as $3 per day selling plastic, metal, and cardboard for recycling, is being phased out and its residents are on the verge of losing both their homes and their incomes. The dumping ground that once received 3,000 tons of trash each day now sees only one tenth of that amount, and Smokey Mountain, so-named because some part of it is always burning, will soon become the site for a new housing project. For some of the scavengers, however, there is hope for a new future. The U.S. Agency for International Development has allocated $50,000 to pay for new job training.

OZONE-HELPER

This may develop into one of the most lucrative new market areas to emerge since the world's scientists identified chlorofluorcarbons (CFCs) as destroyers of the earth's protective ozone layer. Japanese chemical firms are racing to discover commercially viable substitutes for CFCS, which are widely used as industrial cleaning agents, especially in the semiconductor industry. However, it could take about five years before acceptable substitutes are developed, according to a recent report by the Japan CFC Association. Currently, more than 33,000 Japanese manufacturing companies are reportedly using CFCs—and the use of the chemicals has been growing at an annual rate of more than 10%. The nation produces about 15% of the world's total CFC output.

AVERTING ACID RAIN

An "ultra-clean" coal that contains negligible amounts of ash-forming mineral matter, and could thus virtually eliminate acid rain, has been developed by Australian researchers. Produced by a patented cleaning technology, the coal could be delivered in liquid or powdered form and thus used as an alternative to bulky fuel.

TAIWAN'S POLLUTION PLIGHT

Taiwan's Environmental Protection Administration estimates that by the year 2000 expenditures on environmental protection could cost every individual in Taiwan about $175. In 1988, the EPA projected that $2.17 billion will be spent on short-term environmental protection projects. But to clean the major Tamsui River alone would cost an estimated $3.5 billion.

AIR CONDITIONER SHORTAGE

Taiwan's scorching summer heat has led to a booming business in air conditioner rentals. Because of extremely high demand for air conditioners, it has become difficult for consumers to purchase the machines. Now they can lease them for a monthly fee of about $52, with an installation fee of $289.

TOKYO TRASH COUNT

Trash collected per capita in Tokyo is 1.5 kilos per day. The city's garbage reflects its affluence. In 1988, oversize trash was at the top of the list of throwaways—430,000 tables, desks, and chairs were junked. Number 2 on the list were *futon* bedding and mattresses, 330,000 junked. Number 3: Bicycles, 170,000 thrown away, according to *Yomiuri Shimbun*.

RECYCLING INDUSTRIAL WASTE

China is expected to earn up to $675 million from extracting useful materials from industrial waste by the year 2000, according to the State Planning Commission. The program stipulates that the utilization ratio will be 75% for minerals, 50% to 80% for industrial liquids, and 100% for fuel gas by the turn of the century.

DOWN UNDER SEWAGE TREATMENT

Australian scientists developed a new sewage-treatment technique to halve the cost of building a sewerage plant and cut land use to a fifth of existing standard. The system has huge export potential to heavily populated regions, such as Japan, Britain, and Taiwan, and could save hectares of land on Sydney's north heads from being turned into sewerage ponds. By using magnetically charged iron oxide particles called magnetite, the scientists can clarify raw sewage in about 20 minutes, 20 times faster than conventional techniques. Furthermore, nitrogen and phosphorous can be more easily removed from sewage, making it more useful in the recycling process.

CHINA'S FESTERING WASTE

China's major cities are being clogged with garbage, while rats, mosquitoes, flies, and cockroaches are breeding at an alarming rate, according to the official Xinhua News Agency. Air pollution causes an estimated 14.5 million tons of carbon dust being released into the atmosphere, while 450,000 tons of human waste are said to flow directly into Shanghai's Huangpo River. Chinese authorities believe the worst problem is the failure to recycle domestic waste which is left to fester around cities. Beijing alone provided 7,000 tons of garbage a day. A census showed there were two billion rats in China.

HONG KONG LEADS NEW YORK IN PLASTIC WASTE

Nearly 1,000 tons of plastic waste is produced daily in Hong Kong, twice the amount produced by New York and three times that of London, according to a 1988 report by the Center of Environmental Studies at Hong Kong Polytechnic.

PAPER CANS FOR THE PRC

China announced a plan to use paper to replace tinplate as the major material in producing cans so as to reduce the imports of galvanized iron.

PRC POLLUTION PROFILE

Beijing has become one of the world's most polluted capitals, with air 35 times dirtier than London's and 16 times more contaminated than crowded Tokyo's, according to the *China Youth News,* which cited the results of China's first survey of industrial pollution conducted in 1988. The country has 165,000 polluting factories despite an environmental protection law. China was the only third-world country with a serious problem from acid rain, blamed for destroying large areas of forest near the city of Chongqing.

TRANQUILITY STONE

A hidden sensor turns the electronic *"Seijak-useki"* ("Tranquility Stone") on. After four or five seconds of silence, an endless tape comes on and plays the sound of the Japan's last natural stream which hasn't been disturbed by civilization, the Shimanto river on the island of Shikoku. It costs about $30.

FISHING TACKLE THAT ROTS

Fishing line and nets are major contributors to destruction of ocean environments. Now, the Japan Fisheries Agency has announced success in finding a bioplastic that allegedly disintegrates in sea water after a certain amount of time.

NIGHT OF THE *IWANA*

Atlas, the Japanese mineral water-maker, has been searching for the "finest water under the sun" for the past 15 years and they think they found the source for their "MIMI" brand water. They used the *iwana,* a native Japanese fish which is extremely difficult to breed in captivity, to test the purity of the water. The *iwana* passed MIMI with flying colors. Now the company says that the National Space Development Agency is considering using MIMI for their CELSS water system for a colony on the moon.

TROPICAL DOSSIER:

RAINFORESTS OF SOUTHEAST ASIA

The tropical rainforests of South East Asia cover approximately 1,000 miles from the peninsula of Burma, Thailand, Laos, Vietnam, Kampuchea, and mainland Malaysia to the scattered islands of the Philippines, Indonesia, and the island of Borneo. Due to a speciation process that took place during the Ice Age, the region's wide variety of plants and animals are recognized to be unique to this area. Southeast Asian rainforests provide the world with an array of ecological resources, such as medicines, fresh water, and air. However, as is the case with the plight of tropical rainforests elsewhere in the world, there is a grave danger of losing these irreplaceable resources because of ongoing irreversible rainforest destruction.

REASONS FOR DEFORESTATION

Many factors contribute to rainforest destruction from the logging industry and multinational corporations to landless people using slash-and-burn methods in order to clear land. Demand for high-status rare and exotic tropical timber, such as teak and mahogany, is the main contributor to rainforest depletion as loggers fell trees in order to meet the demand for furniture, veneers, and specialty items. Inexpensive types of wood, such as luan, used for chopsticks are a notorious end product. Multinational corporations, such as the Scott Paper Company and Mitsubishi Corporation, foster rainforest depletion. In recent years, Scott entered into a joint venture with a Malaysian company to establish a pulp mill. Mitsubishi has been one of the primary importers of Southeast Asian timber and timber products.

THE WORLD BANK

The World Bank is responsible for spending $600 million to find many projects in developing countries that encourage deforestation. One quarter of World Bank funding comes from U.S. tax dollars. An example is the Transmigration Program in Indonesia, aimed to resettle peasant farmers from Java and Bali to the more remote outer islands that contain dense rainforests. Initiated to alleviate the problems of overpopulation, the program expanded so that by 1984 over 3.6 million people had been resettled. Further acceleration is now planned. (See "The Colonization of Asia's Tribal People's," p. 369)

Transmigrants have suffered deeply from this program, finding themselves living in unfamiliar, badly managed lands, faced with fatal diseases, and exposed to toxic chemicals sprayed on vegetable crops in Irian Jaya. Furthermore, the indigenous peoples' land rights are being ignored by the Indonesian government. They have also lost traditional sources of protein and game as a result of Transmigration's elimination of wildlife habitats. Unless the program is redesigned, Transmigration will increasingly undermine the achievement of its own goals by destroying the local resource base—the primary forests.

THE CONSEQUENCES

Deforestation, and especially the timber trade, has caused serious environmental and psychological damage to the people, plants, and animals of Southeast Asia. Malaises, such as soil erosion, sedimentation, and flooding, not to mention the destruction of lives of the indigenous people, are common occurrences in the region. Land is the most important economic resource and it also has both spiritual and social significance to the native people of Sarawak, who depend on the trees for their survival. The island of Sarawak has already been 76% denuded and is well on its way to complete depletion if loggers and multinationals are allowed to continue. Their rights have been ignored, as the forests in which they live are under the "official" jurisdiction of the government. These areas are scheduled for logging.

Sarawak State Minister of the Environment and Tourism, James Wong, who pioneered upland logging in Sarawak and who has a personal stake in a 300,000 acre logging conces-

sion, has demonstrated a complete lack of concern for the forest and its people. He has been quoted by *Asian Business* magazine as saying, "We get too much rain in Sarawak. It stops me from playing golf." The Penans have attempted to protect the areas to be deforested by setting up blockades, but many have been arrested and await up to two years in prison and fines they cannot pay.

Illegal logging is blamed as the root cause of the flood that resulted in November 1988 in the loss of hundreds of lives and widespread destruction of homes and agriculture to a province in Thailand. As a result of the disaster, the Prime Minister of Thailand was pressured into establishing a new law to ban all logging in Thailand as of January 1989.

RAINFOREST MEDICINE

• There are many medicinal sources found in the Southeast Asian rainforests. Among them, the shrub *rauwolfia serpentina* has been an important tranquilizer in India and Southeast Asia for thousands of years. Twenty years ago, Western scientists recognized its value, and its derivative, reserpine, is now widely used to treat hypertension.

Seven thousand medical compounds in the modern Western pharmacopei are derived from plants. One quarter of all prescription drugs in the United States contain one or more of those compounds. Norman Farnsworth, a researcher at the University of Illinois, estimates that the value of plant-derived prescription drugs in the United States alone was $8 billion in 1980. The figure for nonprescription drugs is much higher; Americans bought $165 million worth of plant-derived laxatives alone in 1980. If drugs derived from animals and microbes are included, the

Southeast Asian Stats

- The tropical rainforest of Southeast Asia has been evolving, without catastrophic interruption, for more than 100 million years.
- In Sumatra, Borneo, Southern Thailand, and Peninsular Malaysia, roughly half of the land area has been cleared of forest. Where forest still stands, large areas have already been exploited for timber. The lowland rainforest is the tallest, and also the richest in plant and animal species. This is the most severely threatened forest zone; for it is the lowland areas that offer a wealth of timber for harvesting, and offer terrain most suitable for agricultural development.
- Due to a different speciation process that took place during the ice ages, the plants and animals that exist in the Southeast Asian rainforests are particularly rare and exotic. An area of Southeast Asia one quarter the size of Western Europe has 297 species of land mammals, more than twice as many as does Europe.
- A high proportion of animals and plants in tropical rainforests are endemic to one area—they live no- where else. This is especially true of Southeast Asia and Oceana, with its 20,000 species.
- The richest rainforests are in Southeast Asia, where the climate has remained stable and favorable to life— tropical and moist for many tens of millions of years. There animals such as the wormlike Peripatus (a link between two major groups of invertebrates, worms and caterpillars) and such plants as the ginkgo tree have survived almost unchanged since ancient times, living fossils.

United States spent $20 billion on medicines with a natural component in 1980. For the industrialized world as a whole, the value of such medicines, according to Farnsworth, was at least $40 billion.

The traditional Thai pharmacy uses 500 medicinal plants. At least 150 of these have never been scientifically identified or analyzed. In the Malay Peninsula, 2,432 species of plant, one third of all the species there, are used by the local people.

- Original area of Asian tropical rainforests in square miles: 1.4 million. Current area of tropical rainforest: 800,000. Projected area of tropical rainforest in the year 2000: 330,000. Estimated number of species extinct by the year 2000: 150,000 to 500,000. Leading causes of deforestation: Logging and subsistence farming.
- Thailand's once-abundant forests covered about 53% of the total land area in 1961 but by 1985 they had been reduced to 29% of land area. This represents a cut of 45% in forest cover during the 24-year period—a destruction rate of about 3.2 million *rai* a year (about 1.26 million acres). By contrast, the Royal Forestry Department has managed to replant about one third of a million *rai* (about 126,400 acres) in the past 80 years.

In the last 50 years Thailand has destroyed 80% of its forests, leaving only 16% of the country forested. As a result, Thailand, once a major timber exporter, is now a net importer of wood.

Thailand has less than 20% of its natural forest cover remaining and yet it holds some of the most important wildlife area in all of Southeast Asia. The adjoining Thung Yai and Huay Kha Khareng sanctuaries northwest of Bangkok together constitute the largest protected complex in mainland Southeast Asia.

- The Philippines lost 55% of its rainforests between 1960 and 1985.
- Indonesia has 10% of the world's tropical rainforests. The range of forest destruction rate in Indonesia is 600,000 to 1.5 million hectares per year. In the last 15 years, reforestation was conducted in 3.3 million hectares and regreening in 1.6 million hectares. This naturally does not compensate for the 9 to 22.5 million hectares of degraded forest in the last 15 years.
- After the Myanmar government (formerly Burma) suppressed the nation's prodemocracy movement in 1988, killing thousands of people, many countries condemned the action and foreign aid effectively ceased. The Burmese military, out of desperation for sources of income, negotiated with Thai logging companies to sell Burmese logging concessions. Since the Thai government has banned logging in their own country, the forests of Burma are now disappearing at an accelerating rate. United Nations estimates indicate that Burma has only a 40% forest cover, compared to 48% in 1980, as a 57% cover in the 1950s. Burma accounts for 80% of the world's remaining teak trees.

Furthermore, the right to log in Burma has encouraged the Thai government to ignore the rights of Burmese dissident students who took refuge in Thailand. In December 1988, after Thailand's Army Commander, General Chaovalit, visited Burma and arranged for the repatriation of Burmese students from Thailand, several Thai timber firms with military connections obtained timber concessions. In 1989, the teak trade expanded further into the frontier forests of Burma, which are inhabited by indigenous tribes including the Karen and the Karenni. As logging deals between Thailand and Burma accelerated in 1989 and 1990, human rights atrocities have also risen. (See "On the Indochina Rim, p. 168.)

BRIDGE OVER THE RIVER MOEI

In another related development, a proposed 339-yard long bridge linking Thailand to Burma is being planned, spanning the Moei river from Mae Sot in Thailand to Myawaddy, Burma. The project is to be financed by the Economic and Social Commission for Asia and the Pacific (ESCAP). Japan has agreed to finance the design and a feasibility study of the bridge. The bridge is purported to be part of the Asian Highway Project linking Asia with Europe through the Indian mainland. However, there are no roads that even link Myawaddy to Rangoon. Travel is limited to a combination of river transportation and dirt tracks. The bridge is thought to have no other purpose than to facilitate the transport of logs from the border areas across the Moei river into Thailand.

THE LOGGING DEBACLE

The logging industry is a major cause of rainforest destruction, particularly in Southeast Asia.

Most internationally traded timber comes from Southeast Asia, mainly from Indonesia and Malaysia. Commercial logging of tropical timber is responsible for the loss of at least 19,000 square miles of rainforest each year. Tropical hardwoods, such as mahogany, teak, and ebony, are widely used in construction, furniture manufacturing, and specialty products. Logging roads open the forest up to further exploitation by agriculture, mining, or cattle ranching. The logging itself violates the territories of the tribal peoples and threatens their survival. It is exactly this logging which is behind the destruction of the Penan tribe's homelands on the island of Borneo.

The average Southeast Asian logging concession wastes over one and a quarter cubic meters of wood for every cubic meter of useful timber removed from the forest.

Palawan, the Philippines' biggest province, shelters the country's largest remaining area of endangered tropical forest and its most fertile fishing grounds. Palawan, a long slender island southwest of Luzon, is the last frontier, the last national treasure of exotic flora and fauna. The island has been losing about 19,000 hectares of forest every year since 1979. In 20 years, it could lose more than 60% of its forest cover of 780,000 hectares, according to the *Far Eastern Economic Review*.

Malaysia is one of the largest exporters of tropical timber. It is estimated that within the next 10 years the peninsular Malaysian rainforests will have been destroyed. Already the national parks are being encroached upon by development projects. An example of this is the Kenyir Dam on the edge of Taman Negara National Park in Terengganu, which flooded 2,600 square kilometers of tropical rainforest.

While peninsular Malaysia has already lost over 85% of its primary forest after four decades of intensive development, the states of Sabah and Sarawak on the island of Borneo, with a land area exceeding that of peninsular Malaysia, is still largely covered with rainforest; Sabah is 50% primary forest, Sarawak is 76% forested (one third of which is primary forest). These forests are among the world's oldest and most diverse.

The state governments have limited sources of revenue so each forest-rich state guards timbered areas jealously as a lucrative revenue-generator. Numerous individuals involved in state politics have an interest in, or directly receive large profits from, forest resource exploitation. For example, Sarawak's Minister of the Environment Wong is the owner of Limbong Trading, a logging company with 100,000 hectares of timber concessions, according to the environmental organization Friends of the Earth. Virtually all the states' forests are held in concessions scheduled for eventual logging. The Malaysian logging industry has greatly expanded logging.

Japan buys around four fifths of all the timber exported from Malaysia and contributes to the forests' destruction through over-seas aid. Disposable chopsticks are a notorious end product. Less well known, but particularly wasteful, are the plywood panels used as forms for pouring concrete on building sites. These panels account for some 20% of imported timber, and produce 10% of all industrial waste. Almost all of the products made out of tropical timber can be replaced with other timber or nontimber materials. Tropical timber is chosen solely because of its cheap price.

The tropical storm which began on November 19, 1988 brought the worst flooding in decades to southern Thailand, resulting in the loss of hundreds of lives and widespread destruction of homes and agriculture. The root cause of the devastation has been blamed on illegal logging. Storms sent mud, logs, and trees cascading down denuded hills, slamming into houses and burying villages. The disaster affected 12 southern provinces and has resulted in 367 deaths and 2,000 injured overall. Estimates of the damage included 700,000 acres of orchards and rice patties inundated, 1,000 shrimp farms destroyed, and nearly 300 bridges damaged. The cost of the damage is thought to have exceeded $400 million, according to *The New York Times*.

As a result of public outcry following the storm, the Thai government announced an indefinite suspension of all logging in the southern region—and promised this would be just the first step which would lead to a revocation of all logging concessions in 12 of the region's 14 provinces.

DAMAGING METHODS OF LOGGING

There are two main ways of taking trees out of a forest, clear-cutting and selective logging. Under the latter system, only a proportion of the total number of trees is removed, the theory being that the forest is so little disturbed that it will regenerate naturally and in time to be ready for another cut. It is a sustainable system. In the Philippines, although they use the phrase selective logging, there is only one harvest, a big one. After that there is no more. The reason for this is that if a company takes out only 10% of the trees in an area, most of those remaining are often severely damaged by the way the loggers operate, especially in the construction of roads and tracks.

One study found that 14% of a logging area is cleared for roads, and another 27% for skidder tracks (on which logs are dragged out to feeder roads). Damage that is made on the soil by machinery can be reduced by using chain saws to do some initial cutting up while the logs are still in the forest, and by pulling them to the main rods with buffaloes or elephants instead of machines. A Filipino company that

tried this system found it economically sound. It also provides more jobs, since it uses four to five times as much labor as the more damaging mechanized method.

Researchers have also found that in dipterocarp forests, with an average of 58 trees per acre, for every 10 that are deliberately felled, 13 more are broken or damaged. Other studies have reached the same conclusion: Selective loggers damage more trees than they harvest. In one Malaysian dipterocarp forest, although only 10% of the trees were harvested, 55% were destroyed or severely damaged. Only 33% were unharmed. The logging manager of the Georgia-Pacific concession in Indonesia reported that they damage or destroy more than three times as many trees as they deliberately harvest. The others are butted by bulldozers, lose their branches to falling trees, or are brought down by the pull of tangled vines. The problem is made worse by the ease with which a broken limb or ripped bark can become infected in the tropics.

SLASH-AND-BURN AGRICULTURE

A distorted kind of shifting cultivation is called slash-and-burn agriculture. Most of the 200 million or so people farming in or on the fringes of the rainforest are slash-and-burners, who are used to conventional agriculture and don't have the skills and knowledge of the indigenous forest farmer. About one half of the primary rainforest that is destroyed each year is ruined by slash-and-burn farming. The worst loss is Southeast Asia, where slash-and-burn farmers now clear 33 thousand square miles each year, although much of it has been logged or cleared before. Almost two thirds of the 12 million square miles of land thus farmed is in the hills, where forest cover is most crucial.

PLIGHT OF THE PENANS

The Penans live in Sarawak on the island of Borneo, Malaysia, and are nomadic hunters and gatherers of its rainforests. A tribe of approximately 7000, it is one of the last remaining truly nomadic rainforest tribes in the world, and depends solely on the forests for its livelihood. The Penans hunt wild game with their wooden blow-pipes and poisonous darts, and obtain sago, their staple food, from wild palms, and herbs for medicine; damar, gaharu, and plant dyes are other substances which they gather.

Both the settled and the indigenous peoples' survival is threatened by the Malaysian logging industry, and these peoples have little effective recourse in stopping the destruction. The forests of Sabah and Sarawak are under the "official" jurisdiction of each state's governments, in which natives have virtually no representation. Furthermore, native customary tenure is not legally respected in the state's land code, which was written by nonnatives who settled on the island.

For the hunting and gathering Penans, even customary tenure is difficult to establish, because a claim to ownership requires that land show evidence of cultivation. Essentially, the land code denies that natives have any right to their land.

In the region of Sarawak where the Penans live, seven square kilometers of rainforest are cleared per day, the fastest rate of deforestation in the world. Eighty percent of the timber from this region is sold to Japan, and the remaining 20% goes to Europe, the United States, Singapore, and South Korea.

The logging is turning the natives' land into a virtual wasteland. Logging activities are causing massive erosion, flooding, pollution of watersheds, and destruction of species. The Penan and other tribal people are now facing starvation and disease since fishing waters are polluted, and food and medicinal sources are increasingly scarce. Say the Penan, "If we are lucky, we may come upon food after walking and searching for two to three days." Supplies of rattan can no longer be found, and even the Penans' ancestral burial mounds have been destroyed.

After months of protests, in 1990 Thailand shelved plans for the Nam Choan Dam, which would have destroyed its last virgin forests and flooded its fabled Tung Yai Wildlife preserve in an effort to increase the nation's electrical output by 2%. Prince Bernhard of The Netherlands, a former President of the World Wildlife Fund, came to Thailand and spoke against the dam. Britain's Prince Philip, the Sierra Club, and the International Union for Conservation of Natural Resources joined the newly powerful Thai environmental movement in demanding the wildlife preserves be saved.

Source: Rainforest Action Network. Based in San Francisco, RAN works with environmental and human rights groups in 60 countries, sharing information and coordinating the American sector's role in worldwide campaigns to protect the rainforests and their inhabitants. For more information, write RAN, 301 Broadway, Suite A, San Francisco, California 94133.

BIBLIOGRAPHY: *Lessons of the Rainforest,* edited by Suzanne Head and Robert Heinzman (Sierra Club Books, San Francisco, 1990).

CONSERVATION WATCH: THE PHILIPPINES

The emerging Philippine conservation movement composed largely of farmers, fishermen, and tribal minorities, faces an uphill battle against the combined forces of commercial fishing, enormous timber companies, and the politicians they buy with their vast resources. Conservationists charge that their opponents are plundering the country's natural resources, replacing the rain forests with eroded hills and the rice-fields with barren dustbowls.

Already, they charge, Manila appears to be the world's most polluted city in a country where 20% of the population owns 80% of the cultivated land. A leading environmentalist, Maximo "Junie" Kalaw, is calling for natural resources to be transferred to the people and all logging concessions to be canceled. "Our new constitution provides that natural resources belong to the state but in our case state equals politicians, state does not equal people," he says.

Kalaw, president of the Philippine Institute of Alternative Futures, claims that under President Aquino's regime, "there has been a lot of mouthing of environmental concern" but in effect the old system has been retained. And the Berkeley-based Philippine *Resource Center Monitor* charges that "government is the art of providing the facade of legitimacy behind which the traditional oligarchy can engage in the unrestrained pursuit of special interests."

The newsletter points to the way the Aquino government has trumpeted the "coup" of acquiring a $300 million petrochemical complex, which had been turned down by the Taiwanese themselves, who realized that although Taiwan "may be an economic success . . . it is also one of the world's worst environmental disasters," with rivers industrially contaminated and at least 30% of the rice crop polluted.

Commenting on the destructively excessive practices of commercial fishing operations; the chemical contamination of lakes, streams, and coastal waters; the silt deposits from logging operations; and the denuded slopes that had resulted in entire villages being washed away during typhoons, the newsletter said: "The Philippines is treading a suicidal path of environmental degradation that will plunge the majority of Filipinos into deeper poverty, hunger, and discontent."

JAPAN: AN ENVIRONMENTAL PACMAN?

Japan's high consumption of natural resources threatens to destroy the world's environment, the nation's Environment Agency warned in a report in 1988. It noted that Japan was the single largest importer of tropical wood in 1985, accounting for 52% of imports of tropical logs. The report also attributed the destruction of mangrove forests in Bangladesh, Thailand, and other Southeast Asian countries to increased Japanese imports of shrimps, which also accounted for one third of the world's shrimp imports in 1986. Japan is the largest importer of woods from Malaysia, which experts say will have exhausted its forest resources by the mid-1990s. Japan was also the largest single importer of cotton, coal, roundwood, and crude oil in 1985.

PESTICIDE LEADER OF THE WORLD

Japan uses more pesticides per acre than any other country in the world, in fact about five times the figure in America, and thus the health of Japanese consumers "is being attacked from the inside," charges the magazine *Shukan Gendai*. Although Japan's Ministry of Health and Welfare has "set residual levels" for pesticides, this applies to only a small fraction of the 300 used in the country, and lack of crop rotation and the increasing percentage of products grown in hot houses has compounded this "pollution" problem.

BEIJING'S ANCIENT TREES

Beijing has 23,527 trees which are over 100 years old, and three over 1,000 years old, according to the first detailed study of ancient trees by Beijing's Bureau of Parks and Woods.

GORGEOUS TAROKO

Taiwan's Taroko Gorge National Park in eastern Taiwan became listed as a world-class national park by the International Union for the Conservation of Nature and Natural Resources, the Fountainebleau, France-headquartered international organization which coordinates conservation efforts of government agencies and scientific and conservation organizations.

GREEN LUNGS OF SINGAPORE

More "green lungs" will become available in Singapore when 11 new parks, covering a total area of more than 150 hectares, sprout all over the city-state by 1994, as part of the government's 50-year development plan to provide people with areas for meaningful and healthy pursuits.

CHINA'S TREE PROBLEM

Half of China's 131 forestry administrations will have no trees left by 1997 if the nation doesn't overcome problems of overcutting and poor management, according to Forestry Minister Gao Sezhan. About 1,000 square kilometers of Chinese land turns into desert every year. Despite major tree-planting campaigns over the past three decades, only 33 million hectares of tree plantations, one third of the area planted, have survived because of poor management. About $3 billion will be invested in planting six million hectares of fast-growing trees by the year 2001.

BORN-AGAIN TREES

Famous trees at Japanese temples and shrines are dying at an alarming rate. There's a new company in Osaka named Ikilun Corp. that promises, "We'll bring your dying trees back to life." They have developed a new elixir for plants. Injected at the roots, it takes effect in as little as a month, and greenery begins to sprout from previously dead branches. The cost of treatment ranges from about $769 to about $7,690. The elixir is reportedly effective for trees suffering from acid rain, too.

CHEAPSHOTS AT CHOPSTICKS?

Targeting wooden chopsticks as a threat to the rain forests is begging the question according to The Institute of Life Folklore's Soichiro Honda, who says that the 25 billion pairs he estimates are used and thrown away each year account for less than half of 1% of the country's annual wood consumption. Nevertheless, he writes, Japan voraciously devours trees, importing 16 million cubic meters each year from tropical rain forests, which take at least a century to recover from the cutting, whereas timberland in Japan could be restored in less than half the time.

ASEAN'S FOREST MANAGEMENT AT A LOSS

The forest products sector of the Association of Southeast Asian Nations has contributed to the region's prosperity, but lacks positive direction, according to the ASEAN Institute of Forest Management director, Mok Sian Tuan, who addressed the first ASEAN Forest Products Conference in Kuala Lumpur in 1989. He said there appeared to be little interest in conserving the region's forest resources, according to Malaysia's national news agency Bernama.

> "When a tree falls, even the woodpeckers share in its death."
>
> *Malaysian proverb*

GREENHOUSE SCENARIO FOR THE SOUTHERN HEMISPHERE

The spectacle of millions of people fleeing their inundated islands in search of refuge elsewhere may be one of the results of the greenhouse effect according to the ominous scenario of two Australian scientists, Peter Roy and John Connell. The devastating climatic effects of a rise in the earth's temperature, with its consequent changed tidal patterns and raised sea levels, is likely to be the worst in Australia and surrounding regions, the scientists predict, with cyclones, storms, and floods battering coastal communities and tiny Pacific and Indian Ocean islands being submerged if sea levels rise by one meter by 2030.

ANIMALS

POACHING RARE SPECIES IN CHINA

Illegal hunters in China are said to be supplying "wild taste" restaurants in Kwantung province and other coastal areas with animal species that are almost extinct. Others are killing animals for parts used in Asian medicines. Altogether more than 100 animal species are faced with elimination including sand badgers, snow leopards, giant pandas and various breeds of tigers. The official *China Daily* reports that fewer than 100 gibbons are surviving in the wild and only 200 river dolphins. Also threatened are one million musk deer which are being slaughtered for the illegal smuggling of musk.

ELEPHANTS GO TO SCHOOL

Northern Thailand has two major elephant-training schools where elephants go from elementary familiarization with a mahout, or handler, through intermediate dragging and pushing to advanced carrying and piling. After graduation, they are sent to work in the fast-dwindling forests of Thailand, using their huge strength to clear valuable teak and eucalyptus logs. Thai elephants have a reputation for calmness. Many are sent to neighboring Malaysia where their peaceful spirit helps to relax their more excitable and less-schooled cousins.

RACEHORSES WITH ULCERS

Those sleek thoroughbred racing horses that make the pulse race to watch in action may have as many internal problems as do their spectators, judging by the report from a veterinarian for the Japan Racing Association who found that 51 of the 71 race horses he recently euthanized had stomach ulcers. The vet, Dr. Yoshihara Toyohiko, said that instead of frisking about in the pasture the creatures were "penned up in stalls, trained mercilessly with only racing in mind, fed 7,000 or more calories a day so they have enough energy to take the training and then pressured to get them up for the start. No wonder they get ulcers."

ON THE REPTILE RIM

HIMALAYAN CROCODILES RESURRECTED

Nepalese scientists over the past decade have hatched 1,126 young gharials, a near extinct species of crocodiles in the world, according to the Nepalese news agency RSS.

BRUTUS GOES WEST

Australia's oldest-known crocodile was allowed to spend his last days in the wilds of Western Australia rather than being forced to become the star attraction in a suburban park. Brutus, a 21-foot-long crocodile, estimated to have been around for between 60 and 140 years, now lives in the remote saltwater reaches of the Ord River in Western Australia's Kimberly region. The state government issued a license allowing the crocodile to be captured, but a tidal wave of public opinion forced the government to rescind the order.

TIGERS MAKE A COMEBACK

Indian forest reserves are nearly choked with tigers, a species which faced extinction only two decades ago. The tiger population will reach its peak of 5,000 in a few years, according to Indian wildlife expert, R. L. Singh, director of Project Tiger. India only had 1,827 tigers left in 1972.

Human dummies rigged up to automobile batteries that give a 230-volt shock are the state-of-the-art attempt by villagers at Arampur, India, to deter tigers who have killed 579 people in the vicinity since 1973.

ELUSIVE TASMANIAN TIGER

The Tasmanian Tiger is a unique marsupial that for 50 years has eluded sighting by people. Unphotographed since 1936, the Tiger has attained the mystique of America's mythical Bigfoot. *Cable News Network*'s Ted Turner has reportedly offered a $100,000 reward for proof of its existence. Meanwhile, Australia's Cascade Brewery is using the Tiger as its logo on its lager beer.

KOALAS UNDER THREAT

Launching a drive to raise $3.9 million for koala research, Steve Brown said that the lack of attention Australia gave to the furry marsupial was "a national disgrace." Now numbering less than 400,000 (half of which are infected), the cuddly creature has already disappeared in many parts of the country and faces extinction unless the remaining 20% of its habitat is protected. Since the fur trade was outlawed in 1927 (after 50 years of indiscriminate slaughter) more than three-quarters of the areas in which koalas used to live have been cleared for farmland.

Dr. Brown, a director of the World Koala Research Corp., maintaining that more koala research was coming from Japan and the United States than Australia added, "The koala's survival is threatened by disease and habitat destruction but the government does not seem to be accepting any responsibility." The prevalent disease among koalas is chlamydia, which causes blindness, lung disease, and infertility, but it was discovered that the antibiotics able to cure it also destroyed the koala's ability to digest its food, usually limited to eucalyptus leaves. Now a U.S. firm, the Upjohn Co., has developed an effective antibiotic without these harmful side effects.

K-Rations: Australian koalas in zoos around the world are now enjoying a fast-food concoction—"eucalyptus leaf biscuits"—thanks to joint work by biologists from the University of Sydney and New England University. The biscuits solve the major problem that koalas will eat leaves from only 25 of the 500 species of eucalyptus in Australia, which previously has meant air-freighting tons of leaves from Australia or building local greenhouses in which to grow eucalyptus in the United States, Canada, Britain, and Japan.

PANDAS STAY HOME

China's policy of loaning out about four pairs of pandas each year to foreign zoos has been cut back despite the almost $2 million it brings the country in fees. Conservation concerns are believed to have influenced the Forest Ministry, whose spokesman Zhang Yushan explained, "It's not that pandas absolutely can't go, just that such exhibits should be controlled. We believe the fewer the better, and no exhibits at all would be best."

Pandas from the Lab: Chinese scientists announced they have made a breakthrough that could lead to the world's first test-tube giant panda, according to the *People's Daily*. The development raises the possibility that the endangered animal, now said to be only 1,000 left in the wooded mountain areas of southwest China, could be conceived in a laboratory. Wild pandas are threatened by a shrinking habitat.

Beijing zoologists are now able to determine if a giant panda is pregnant as early as 96 hours after artificial insemination. Previously, it took about 50 days to determine whether a giant panda was pregnant after breeding.

FUNERALS FOR PETS

A Japanese company, Pet Angel Service in Osaka, offers a full-fledged funeral service for pets. Not only do they pick up the body, hold a funeral, cremate the pet, and dispose of the ashes, but the $385 fee brings a tape of the pet's voice "telling" the owner, "Thank you for caring for me for so long."

RAISING FRESH-WATER WHALES

Professor Isawa Hisao of Hokkaido University's School of Veterinary Medicine has a plan for a whale ranch. His first experiment was with a dolphin, which is first cousin to a whale. He put a 1.5-meter dolphin in a large plastic container filled with sea water. The plan is to gradually reduce the salt content of the water until it is completely fresh. By 1994, he plans to start the process with Minke whales, which grow to about eight meters in length and which Japanese consumers consider to be "as delicious as prime beef," according to the *Shukan Asahi* weekly magazine. The international conservation organization Greenpeace says the plan is ridiculous. But the professor is dead serious. "Whales are survivors," he says. "Proved by

ON THE CANINE RIM:

TEMPLE DOGS

Bangkok has launched a plan to sterilize thousands of dogs living at Buddhist temples in the city to reduce what Thai health authorities said is the highest rabies death rate in the world. Monks at 400 temples care for the strays. The city destroys some 50,000 stray dogs each year. The dogs reportedly caused more than 300 deaths from rabies in 1986, the highest number of rabies deaths per capita in any country.

A shelter has been built in Lhasa, capital of Tibet, to cope with the city's 17,000 dogs, 90% of them strays, who keep residents awake at night and cause a nuisance in parks and monasteries. The Tibetan religion prohibits the dogs from being destroyed despite the problems they cause. Authorities plan either to sterilize the dogs or to start a business breeding dogs for sale.

CHEWING ON CHOWS

Hong Kong's Royal Society for the Prevention of Cruelty to Animals is conducting an undercover operation to expose an illegal trade in breeding dogs for dinner. Gourmets have been paying around $1 per ounce for dog meat—the hosting of which is said to command great status.

DOG GETS APOLOGY

A Chinese woman accused of killing a neighbor's dog with a curse was forced to apologize to the animal and carry it, dressed in her clothes, through her village, the *Farmers Daily* reported. The incident took place in Yunnan, in southwest China.

A DOG'S LIFE

In the last few years, Singapore dogs have gone from being dinner delicacies to pampered pooches apt to wear stylish frilly panties and ride around in air-conditioned taxis. Increasingly, affluent Singaporeans spare no expense on their pets, eagerly forking out $40 for the trim, shampoo, and manicure charged by a midtown doggy salon in a busy shopping center. Meanwhile, David Oh's doggy shop across town offers slick, black raincoats for $25 and elegant $10 panties. And the cosseted canines can travel to and from their appointments in the taxi operated by former flight steward Raymond Wee, who says, "Most taxi drivers are reluctant to take on fares with pets and some people don't want their luxury cars dirtied by dogs, so I provide an essential service."

Dogs Run Up Fines: Singapore, fed up with dogs snapping at joggers and upsetting garbage cans, has instituted fines of up to $100 to owners who let their mutts run free.

the fact that they only need to bear one calf per year to keep the species alive. They will be great sources of food, and they're gentle and would make wonderful pets."

UNDER THE WAVES

Kobe's Suma Beach Aquarium installed a tank that, in addition to housing 10,000 fish, can also produce artificial waves. Meanwhile, a new aquarium in Osaka, Japan with a unique environmental message opened in 1990. Designed by the American firm Cambridge Seven Associates, which also designed the New England Aquarium in Boston and the National Aquarium in Baltimore, the Osaka Aquarium features more than 300 different species of fish, marine mammals, birds, reptiles, amphibians, and invertebrates that inhabit the Pacific Ocean and its volcanic perimeter known as the "Ring of Fire."

THE BEAR ON THE BUS

A would-be smuggler in eastern China was arrested for trying to transport an illegally obtained live wild bear aboard a passenger bus. The *Shanghai Evening News* said a man later identified by police bought the live brown bear, a protected species, for the "high price" of $540 and then loaded it "into a wooden box" and checked it aboard a passenger bus headed to Xuzhou City, 640 kms south of Beijing.

BUTTERFLY RUSTLERS, BEWARE

An avid Japanese butterfly collector was banned from China in 1988 for a period of five years for catching and collecting rare species of butterflies. The Tokyo University re-search fellow was caught in the act. Chinese police reportedly found 4,410 samples of insects and plants in his possession, including a pair of valuable Qinghai white thin-wing butterflies. Foreigners in China are not allowed to "collect, hunt or purchase living things."

MALAYSIANS BREED RABBITS

Malaysia aims to become the world's biggest producer of rabbit meat and skin, according to the Agriculture Minister Datuk Seri Sanusi Junid, who launched an "Eat Rabbit Meat" campaign in Kuala Lumpur. He said that Malaysia plans to export rabbit skin products including handbags and overcoats.

BIRDS

INDONESIA'S BIRD-DRAIN

Demand by foreign collectors for Indonesia's beautiful birds is threatening to wipe out many species even in the sanctuaries that have been set up to protect them. Prices as high as $5,000 for a pair of black palm cockatoos are a powerful lure to poachers who find it easy to evade bans on exporting without permits. At least 300 of the country's 1,500 bird species are considered endangered, and not infrequently they are found among those on sale in the ubiquitous bird markets in many Indonesian towns. Sometimes the traders are unaware the species is protected, others simply ignore the regulations. Buyers in Singapore, Taiwan, Hong Kong, and Malaysia eagerly snap up birds of paradise, cockatoos, and others of exotic plumage from eastern Indonesia. Among the country's string of 150 state-supervised game parks and nature reserves, one in western Bali is home to the last 100 Bali starlings in existence, but because of a shortage of funds and manpower they are inadequately protected.

COCKFIGHT RECIPE

In cockfighting in Bali, it is with great pride that the owner of the winning rooster takes home the loser's dead rooster and eats it.

BIRD SMUGGLING CURBED

Australia's State Environment Ministry has called for increased penalties for illegal trapping and trading of endangered fauna, a business which they allege has links with drug-smuggling and the Mafia. The difficulty of breeding rare Australian birds in captivity and their scarcity on world markets has brought prices as high as $7500 for Major Mitchell cockatoos, $200 for galahs, and up to $15,000 for a pair of rare Green Leek parrots.

OWLS CHANGE DIET

Lord Howe Island, a rat-infested region off Australia's east coast, is under threat not only from the rats but from Tasmanian masked owls that were introduced to kill them and which instead developed a taste for the island's rare birds. Chief ranger Cameron Leary says that more than 2,000 poisoning stations have been set up to eradicate the predators.

FOWL LANGUAGE

Owners of mynah birds entered for a speaking contest in Perak, Malaysia, were required to appear before a "censorship board" to ensure that their charges were not guilty of foul language.

OCEAN

THE PACIFIC OCEAN
By Gary A. Klee

The Pacific Ocean, the world's largest water body, occupies a third of the Earth's surface. Extending approximately 15,500 kilometers (9,600 miles) from the Bering Sea in the Arctic north to the icy margins of Antarctica's Ross Sea in the south, the Pacific reaches its greatest width at about 5 degrees north latitude, where it stretches approximately 19,800 kilometers (12,300 miles) from Indonesia to the coast of Columbia. The western limit of the ocean is often placed at the Strait of Malacca. The Pacific contains about 25,000 islands (more than the total number in the rest of the world's oceans combined), almost all of which are found south of the equator. The Pacific covers an area of 179.7 million square kilometers (69.4 million square miles). The lowest known point on Earth, in the Marianas Trench, lies within the Pacific.

Along the Pacific Ocean's irregular margins

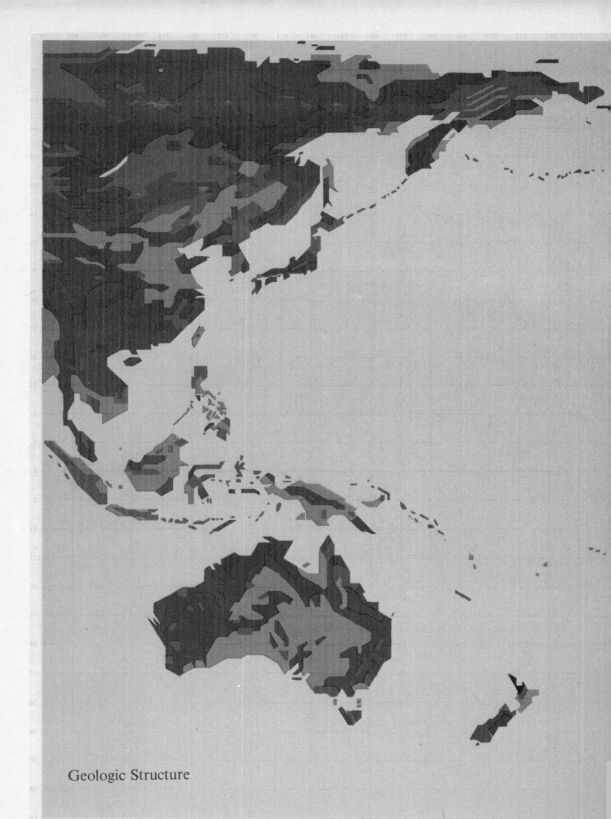

Geologic Structure

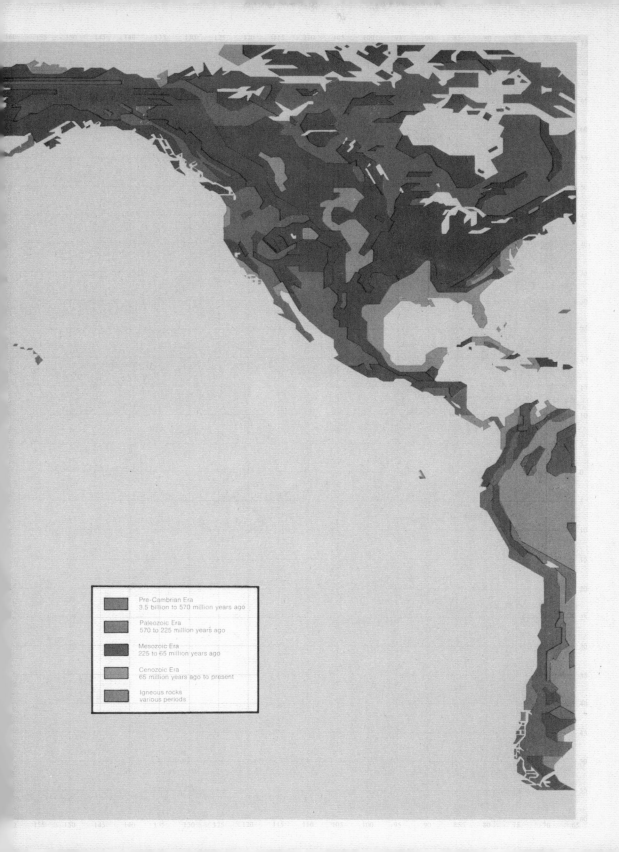

Pre-Cambrian Era
3.5 billion to 570 million years ago

Paleozoic Era
570 to 225 million years ago

Mesozoic Era
225 to 65 million years ago

Cenozoic Era
65 million years ago to present

Igneous rocks
various periods

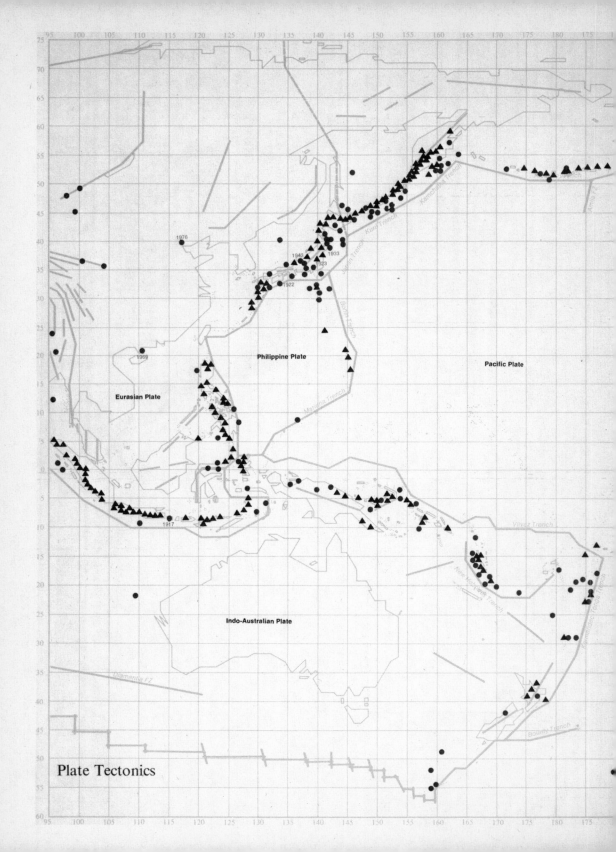

Plate Tectonics

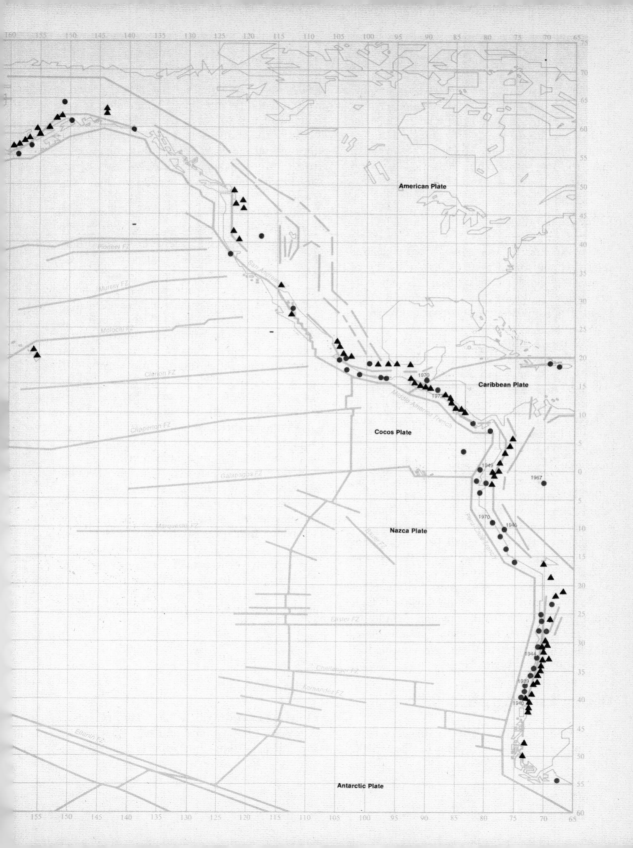

lie many seas, the largest of which are the Celebes Sea, Coral Sea, East China Sea, Sea of Japan, Sulu Sea, and Yellow Sea. The Strait of Malacca joins the Pacific and the Indian oceans on the west, and the Strait of Magellan links the Pacific with the Atlantic Ocean on the east.

OCEAN BOTTOM

The ocean floor of the central Pacific basin is relatively uniform, with a mean depth of about 4.270 miles (14,000 ft). The major irregularities in the area are the extremely steep-sided, flat-topped submarine peaks known as Seamounts. The western part of the floor consists of mountain arcs that rise above the sea as island groups, such as the Solomon Islands and New Zealand, and deep trenches, such as the Marianas trench, the Philippine Trench, and the Tonga Trench. Most deep trenches lie adjacent to the outer margins of the wide western Pacific continental shelf.

Along the eastern margin of the Pacific basin is the East Pacific Rise, which is a part of the world-wide mid-oceanic ridge. About 3,000 kilometers (1,800 miles) across, the rise stands about 3 kilometers (2 miles) above the adjacent ocean floor.

Because a relatively small land area drains into the Pacific, and because of the ocean's immense size, most sediments are authigenic or pelagic in origin. Authigenic sediments include montmorillonite and phillipsite. Pelagic sediments derived from seawater include pelagic red clays and the skeletal remains of sea life. Terrigenous sediments are confined to narrow marginal bands close to land.

WATER CHARACTERISTICS

Water temperatures in the Pacific vary from freezing in the poleward areas to about 29°C (84°F) near the equator. Salinity also varies latitudinally. Water near the equator is less salty than that found in the mid-latitudes because of the abundant equatorial precipitation throughout the year. Poleward of the temperature latitudes salinity is also low, because little evaporation of seawater takes place in these areas.

The surface circulation of Pacific waters is generally clockwise in the Northern Hemisphere and counterclockwise in the Southern Hemisphere. The Northern Equatorial Current, driven westward along latitude 15 degrees north by the trade winds, turns north near the Philippines to become the warm Kuroshio, or Japan, Current. Turning eastward at about 45 degrees north, the Kuroshio forks and some waters move northward as the Aleutian Current, while the rest turn southward to rejoin the North Equatorial Current. The Aleutian Current branches as it approaches North America and forms the base of a counterclockwise circulation in the Bering Sea. Its southern arm becomes the slow, south-flowing California Current.

The South Equatorial Current, flowing west along the equator, swings southward east of New Guinea, turns east at about 50 degrees south latitude, and joins the main westerly circulation of the Southern Pacific, which includes the Earth-circling Antarctic Circumpolar Current. As it approaches the Chilean coast, the South Equatorial Current divides; one branch flows around Cape Horn, and the other turns north to form the Peru, or Humboldt, Current.

CLIMATE

Only the interiors of the large land masses of Australia, New Guinea, and New Zealand escape the pervasive climatic influence of the Pacific. Within the area of the Pacific, five distinctive climatic regions exist: the mid-latitude westerlies, the trades, the monsoon region, the typhoon region, and the doldrums. Mid-latitude westerly air streams occur in both northerly and southerly latitudes, bringing marked seasonal differences in temperature. Closer to the equator, where most of the islands lie, steadily blowing trade winds allow for relatively constant temperatures throughout the year of 21 to 27°C (70 to 81°F).

The monsoon region lies in the far western Pacific between Japan and Australia. Characteristic of this climatic region are winds that blow from the continental interior to the ocean in winter and in the opposite direction in summer. Consequently, a marked seasonality of cloudiness and rainfall occurs. Typhoons often cause extensive damage in the west and southwest Pacific. The greatest typhoon frequency exists within the triangle from southern Japan to the central Philippines to eastern Micronesia. Although more poorly defined than the other climatic regions, two major doldrum areas lie within the ocean, one located off the western shores of central America and the other within the equatorial waters of the western Pacific. Both areas are noted for their high humidity, considerable cloudiness, light fluctuating winds, and frequent calms.

GEOLOGY

The Andesite Line is the most significant regional distinction in the Pacific. It separates the deeper, basic igneous rock of the Central Pacific Basin from the partially submerged continental areas of acidic igneous rock on its margins. The Andesite Line follows the western edge of the islands off California and passes south of the Aleutian arc, along the eastern edge of the Kamchatka Peninsula, the Kuril Islands, Japan, the Mariana Islands, the Solomon Islands, and New Zealand. The dissimilarity continues northeastward along the western edge of the Albatross Cordillera along South America to Mexico, returning then to the islands off California. Indonesia, the Philippines, Japan, New Guinea, and New Zealand—all eastward extensions of the continental blocks of Australia and Asia—lie outside the Andesite Line.

Within the closed loop of the Andesite Line are most of the deep troughs, submerged volcanic mountains, and oceanic volcanic islands that characterize the Central Pacific Basin. It is here that basaltic lavas gently flow out of rifts to build huge dome-shaped volcanic mountains whose eroded summits form island arcs, chains, and clusters. Outside the Andesite Line, volcanism is of the explosive type, and the so-called Pacific rim of fire is the world's foremost belt of explosive volcanism.

LANDMASSES

The largest landmass in the Pacific is the continent of Australia, which is approximately equal in size to the 48 contiguous U.S. states. About 3,200 kilometers (2,000 miles) southeast of Australia is the large island group of New Zealand. Almost all of the smaller islands of the Pacific lie between 30 degrees north and 30 degrees south latitude, extending form Southeast Asia to Easter Island; the rest of the Pacific Basin is almost devoid of land. The great triangle of Polynesia connecting Hawaii, Easter Island, and New Zealand encompasses the island arcs and clusters of the Cook, Marquesas, Samoa, Society, Tokelau, Tonga, and Tuamotu islands. North of the equator and west of the international date line are the numerous small islands of Micronesia, including the Caroline Islands, the Marshall Islands, and the Mariana Islands. In the southwestern corner of the Pacific lie the islands of Melanesia, dominated by New Guinea. Other important island groups of Melanesia include the Bismarck Archipelago, Fiji, New Caledonia, the Solomon Islands, and Vanuatu.

Islands in the Pacific Ocean are of four basic types: continental islands, high islands, coral reefs, and uplifted coral platforms. Continental islands lie outside the Andesite Line and include New Guinea, the islands of New Zealand, and the Philippines. These islands are structurally associated with the nearby continents. High islands are of volcanic origin, and many contain active volcanoes. Among these are Bougainville, Hawaii, and the Solomon Islands. The third and fourth types of islands are both the result of coralline island building. Coral reefs are low-lying structures that have built up on basaltic lava flows under the ocean's surface. One of the most dramatic is the Great Barrier Reef off northeastern Australia. A second island type formed of coral is the uplifted coral platform, which is usually slightly larger than the low coral islands. Examples include Banaba (formerly Ocean Island) and Makatea in the Tuamotu group of French Polynesia.

HISTORY AND ECONOMY

Important human migrations occurred in the Pacific in prehistoric times, most notably those of Polynesians from Tahiti to Hawaii and New Zealand. The ocean was sighted by Europeans early in the sixteenth century, first by Vasco Nunez de Balboa (1513) and then by Ferdinand Magellan, who crossed the Pacific during his circumnavigation (1519 to 1522).

For the remainder of the sixteenth century, Spanish influence was paramount, with ships sailing from Spain to the Philippines, New Guinea, and the Solomons. During the seventeenth century, the Dutch, sailing around southern Africa, dominated discovery and trade; Abdel Janszoon Tasman discovered (1642) Tasmania and New Zealand. The eighteenth century marked a burst of exploration by the Russians in Alaska and the Aleutian Islands, the French in Polynesia, and the British in the three voyages of James Cook—to the South Pacific and Australia, Hawaii, and the North American Pacific Northwest. Growing imperialism during the nineteenth century resulted in the occupation of much of the Pacific by the Western powers. Significant contributions to oceanographic knowledge were made by the voyages of the H.M.S. Beagle in the 1830s, with Charles Darwin aboard; the H.M.S. Challenger during the 1870s; the U.S.S. Tuscarora (1873 to 1876); and the German Gazelle (1874 to 1876). Although the United States took the Philippines in 1898, Japan controlled the western Pacific by 1914. By the end of World War II, the U.S. Pacific Fleet was the virtual master of the ocean.

Fourteen independent nations are located in the Pacific: Kiribati, Nauru, Papua New Guinea, Taiwan, Tuvalu, Western Samoa, Australia, Fiji, Japan, New Zealand, the Philippines, the Solomon Islands, Tonga, and Vanuatu. Also within the Pacific are the U.S. state of Hawaii and several island territories and possessions of Australia, Chile, France, Japan, New Zealand, the United Kingdom, and the United States.

Within the Pacific Ocean are some of the world's newest nations. Since 1960 eight islands or island groups have achieved independence as colonial nations have relinquished claims to their Pacific dependencies.

The exploitation of the Pacific's mineral wealth is hampered by the ocean's great depths. In shallow waters off the coast of Australia, petroleum and natural gas are extracted, and pearls are harvested along the coasts of Australia, Japan, Papua New Guinea, Nicaragua, Panama, and the Philippines, although in sharply declining volume. The Pacific's greatest asset is its fish. The shoreline waters of the continents and the more temperate islands yield herring, salmon, sardines, snapper, swordfish, and tuna, as well as shellfish. Tropical fish are rarely taken commercially. Whaling, once a major industry in the Pacific, has been halted by most nations in order to prevent extinction of the giant mammals.

SOURCE: Reprinted by permission of Grolier Academic Encyclopedia. © 1986 by Grolier International, Inc.

BIBLIOGRAPHY: Burdick, Eugene, *The Blue of Capricorn* (1961); Friis, H. R., ed., *The Pacific Basin* (1967); Gilbert, John, *Charting the Vast Pacific* (1971); Kennedy, T.F., *A Descriptive Atlas of the Pacific Islands* (1974); Lower, J. Arthur, *Ocean of Destiny: A Concise History of the North Pacific, 1500–1978* (1978); Shepard, F. P., *The Earth Beneath the Sea,* rev. ed. (1967); Soule, Gardner, *The Greatest Depths* (1970); Sverdrup, H. U., et al., *The Oceans* (1942).

PACIFIC DOSSIER

Among the critical environmental issues facing the region are increasing pollution of the ocean and a regional movement to make the Pacific Ocean a nuclear-free zone. The preservation of endangered coral reefs and conservation of wildlife species and fish are also major concerns.

The Pacific Ocean covers nearly one third of the world and is home to some 8 million indigenous people. Emerging from a history of colonialism, nuclear testing and increasing military pressures, many Pacific Island people are challenging years of exploitation and domination by large and powerful nations. Other countries in the Pacific region, such as South Korea, the Philippines, Japan, Australia, and New Zealand, have growing opposition to foreign military bases and nuclear weapons within their countries.

The debate over nuclear-free zones is growing constantly stronger in all regions of the world. Opposition to nuclear warship visits is gaining momentum day by day. It is certain that debates over future nuclear-free zones will revolve around the minimal protections guaranteed in the Treaty of Rarotonga (South Pacific Nuclear-Free Zone Treaty) and Treaty of Tlatelolco (Latin American Nuclear-Free Zone Treaty). Additionally, it will be incumbent on policy leaders involved in future nuclear-free zone debates to go beyond the minimal guarantees established in Rarotonga and Tlatelolco by analyzing their prohibitive provisions in comparison with other treaties.

China and the Soviet Union are the only nuclear powers that have signed the 1985 Treaty of Rarotonga, which bans the use or threatened use of nuclear weapons, and bans nuclear testing in a nuclear weapons-free zone in the South Pacific. Pacific nation signatories include Australia, Cook Islands, Fiji, Kiribati, New Zealand, Niue, Tuvalu, Western Samoa, Nauru, Papua New Guinea, and the Solomon Islands.

Among the Pacific island nations, New

Zealand risked its relations with the United States by declaring its ports nuclear-free. That 1984 policy decision, which was enshrined in legislation in 1986, led to the collapse of the 1951 military alliance known as ANZUS, which takes its name from participating countries Australia, New Zealand, and the United States (and which now does not include New Zealand).

REGIONAL INDEPENDENCE MOVEMENTS

Among notable expressions of self-determination by people of the Pacific Islands states are:

The Republic of Belau, the sole remaining component of the U.S. Trust Territory of the Pacific, has rejected U.S. nuclear weapons and efforts of the U.S. military to maintain access to Belauan lands—but still Belau is not a nuclear-free and sovereign nation.

Kanaks, the indigenous people of New Caledonia (of Kanaky, as they refer to it) are putting increasing pressure on the French for independence.

American Samoa, the Micronesian states, and Guam have not gained full self-determination in their relationship with the United States.

The peoples of East Timor and West Papua face genocide as they resist domination by Indonesia.

Indigenous people, now in the minority in Australia, New Zealand (or Aotearoa, according to its Maori name), Hawaii, and elsewhere, struggle for land rights and self-determination.

The drive for independence from colonial powers remains strong. The last two decades have witnessed the beginning of political independence for Papua New Guinea, Western Samoa, Tuvalu, Kiribati, Nauru, Fiji, and Vanuatu.

A MILITARIZED PACIFIC

The United States, Britain, and France have exploded over 215 nuclear bombs in the South Pacific.

France continues underground nuclear tests in French Polynesia (Tahiti) on the Mururoa Atoll.

The United States tests missiles at Kwajalein missile base in the Marshall Island. This base has dislocated local islanders. The Soviet Union and China have also tested missiles in the Pacific.

The United States has over 150 military bases and installations in the Pacific itself. France has 15. The Soviet Union has none.

The United States has another 350 bases on the Pacific Rim. Britain has 13, the Soviet Union has 10, and Australia and New Zealand have three each.

Japan proposes to dump nuclear waste in Pacific ocean trenches.

Despite progress to eliminate Intermediate Range Nuclear Forces, the United States is deploying hundreds of sea-launched cruise missiles in the Pacific, and the Soviet Union is following suit.

INCINERATING THE PACIFIC OCEAN

Ocean incineration is a method used to dispose of industrial, toxic waste by burning it in ships equipped with high-temperature incinerators. Approximately 100,000 tons of these wastes are burned each year, and the chemical gases released during the process contain some of the most harmful substances on earth. Once released into the environment, they threaten life in the oceans.

Although the practice of ocean incineration only occurs in Europe's North Sea, companies like the U.S. waste disposal giant, Waste Management Inc. (WMI), will soon be forced to stop using it there, according to the Greenpeace Pacific Campaign. The international treaty organization which regulates dumping at sea, the London Dumping Convention (LDC), has ordered that the practice be stopped by the end of 1994. In an unprecedented move, the LDC recognizes that ocean incineration is considered to represent "risks of marine and atmospheric pollution" and has the potential to interfere with other, legitimate uses of the sea.

Although 63 countries throughout the world are members of the London Dumping Convention, the many nonmembers are not bound by its rules. Few countries located in and around the Pacific are members and any one of these nonmember countries could easily import the technology to the Pacific. For ocean incineration operations to be profitable, a steady flow of large quantities of toxic waste is necessary. If a Pacific nation invited a waste disposal company to operate off its coast, it would not be long before other, more industrialized nations would begin exporting their waste to the region for incineration at sea, warns Greenpeace.

THE PACIFIC—NEW BURNSITE FOR TOXIC CHEMICAL WASTE?

The owners of the burnships have already begun maneuvering in the Pacific, notes the environmental protection organization Greenpeace. Two shiploads of Agent Orange from the U.S. stockpile were burned off Johnston Atoll near Hawaii in 1977, and Aus-

tralian chemical waste was burned in the Tasman Sea in 1982. Since then, WMI, which owns the burnships *Vulcanus I* and *II,* has gained controlling shares in waste companies in Australia and New Zealand. In 1987 the company sent the managing director of its Dutch subsidiary, Clean Combustion Services (OCS), to the Pacific to drum up support for a visit by one of its burnships. Soon after, Australia announced plans to investigate the possibility of building an ocean incineration vessel. While no action has been taken on the matter since, Australia still openly expresses its desire not to rule the option out, Greenpeace cautions.

POSSIBLE EFFECTS OF OCEAN INCINERATION ON THE PACIFIC

People living in the Pacific are particularly dependent on the oceans, with fish and shellfish being important for commercial and subsistence purposes. Contamination of these resources as a result of ocean incineration could extend far beyond the immediate vicinity of a burnsite. Currents and migratory fish could help spread toxic chemicals and their effects throughout the region.

Environmental damage to particularly sensitive areas in the Pacific could also be extensive and long-lasting, according to Greenpeace. Indigenous coral reefs, for example, are not only unique ecosystems, but are also highly productive and responsible for a substantial percentage of world annual fish/shellfish catch. Some of the most endangered species in the Pacific—dugongs, giant clams, and sea turtles—could be adversely affected, as could many other unique species which are found in small, vulnerable ecosystems throughout the region.

DRIFTNETS IN THE PACIFIC

High-seas driftnets are large-scale monofilament plastic gillnets deployed in the open ocean. A standard gillnet is a panel of strong plastic webbing suspended vertically in the water by floats attached at the top of the panel and weights attached at the bottom. The nets —used to catch salmon, squid, marlin, and other species—are so sheer that they cannot be seen by diving birds or detected by dolphin sonar. Marine creatures in search of food and lured by fish already caught in the nets, swim or dive into the plastic web, where they become entangled and drown.

High-seas driftnet fisheries are taking a dangerous toll on marine resources in the North Pacific. The large driftnet fleets of Japan, Taiwan, and the Republic of Korea are slaughtering tens of thousands of porpoises and dolphins, other marine mammals, and hundreds of thousands of marine birds during fishing operations annually. Driftnets are also dangerously depleting fisheries resources— including salmon species of North American origin. If ocean wildlife is to be preserved and fish stocks kept at sustainable yield levels, this practice of strip-mining the seas must be phased-out.

THE "GHOST NET"

Lost and abandoned driftnets, combined with discarded trawl nets, other fishing gear, plastics and other debris floating in the sea, entangle and kill thousands of seals, cetaceans, seabirds, marine turtles, and fish every year. Entanglement is one factor causing the population decline of the Northern fur seal. Still hopelessly entangled in shredded mesh, some seals manage to escape floating "ghost nets." They may then suffer for two to four months before dying from injury, starvation, or both.

Annually, the driftnet fleets leave approximately 500 to 600 miles of net floating in the North Pacific. At present rates of fishing, in the year 2000, there will be enough ghost nets to stretch one third the way around the world.

ASIAN DRIFTNET FISHING

In the Pacific Ocean, the nations of Japan, Taiwan, and the Republic of Korea have over 1500 ships that use driftnets. In the north, Japan operates over 200 salmon-fishing vessels, setting nine-mile-long nets. In the central North Pacific, Japan and Taiwan operate at least 600 driftnet vessels for fishing on billfish, primarily marlin and sailfish. In the North Pacific, the 700 squid driftnet boats of Japan, Taiwan, and the Republic of North Korea use nets up to 30 miles long. The use of driftnets makes sound, ecological management of fisheries resources impossible, according to the Greenpeace Pacific Campaign. During the fishing season, vessels set more than 20,000 miles of net each day—more than one million miles each year. And unlike the salmon fishery, the squid and billfish fisheries are not even regulated by an international fisheries convention.

DEATH TRAP FOR SEABIRDS

When seabirds dive into driftnets for fish, their feet or wings become entangled and they often drown. The driftnet fisheries are estimated to kill 800,000 or more seabirds each year. This figure does not include dead birds which drop out of the nets before retrieval by the fishing vessel. Because many of the nets of the Japanese mothership salmon fishery have been set near the Aleutian Islands' puffin, murre, and auklet nesting colonies, the birds' populations may well be declining. This driftnet fishery also kills a large number of short-tailed shearwaters which originate in the Southern Hemisphere.

MARINE MAMMAL KILLER

Thousands of Dall's porpoises die each year in the driftnets of the Japanese salmon fisheries. U.S. National Marine Fisheries Service (NMFS) scientists report that 80% of the dead female Dall's porpoise samples that have been collected in the mothership fishery are pregnant or lactating. Apparently, the driftnet fishery has operated in a breeding and calving ground for this species. Scientists are concerned that the viability of the western North Pacific populations of the Dall's porpoise could be jeopardized.

There is no NMFS observer program to monitor the squid fisheries. It is estimated that tens of thousands of marine mammals, including Dall's porpoises, Northern fur seals, common dolphins, and other species die in the hundreds of huge squid nets. Little information is available to determine the population levels of these species in the North Pacific. Driftnet killings could result in severe depletion of these species if it is not curtailed.

In the United States, the Department of Commerce issued a permit to the Japanese salmon driftnet fleet for an incidental take of up to 6,039 Dall's porpoise over a three-year period. The new permit requires increased monitoring on the salmon fleets, and requires observer access to the unregulated squid driftnet fleets and provides no quota for the take of Northern fur seals (a species declared depleted and protected by the Marine Mammal Protection Act).

Greenpeace, other environmental organizations and Alaskan fishing groups challenged the permit on the grounds that it is impossible for the fleet to operate in U.S. waters without killing Northern fur seals.

In June 1987, the fleet was enjoined from operating by a court order. Since then, the U.S. Department of Justice and the Japanese Salmon Federation have appealed the injunction all the way to the U.S. Supreme Court.

In June 1988, the full panel of the high court, however, refused a request for an emergency stay to the injunction, with the result that the Japanese are now not able to use driftnets in U.S. waters. Thousands of marine mammals and tens of thousands of seabirds have been saved already because two mothership fleets were not able to operate in 1988. In January 1989, the Supreme Court declined the petition for review of the case and upheld the prohibition of high seas driftnet fishing in U.S. waters.

LOSS OF SALMON

Driftnet fleets are hastening the decline of North American salmon. Scientists have shown that Japan's salmon driftnet vessels are catching salmon on the high seas that would normally return to North American waters and either be taken by U.S. or Canadian fisheries or return to their streams of origin to spawn. The squid driftnet fleets of Japan, Taiwan, and the Republic of Korea operate in areas inhabited by North American salmon and steelhead. NMFS enforcement officers have seized hundreds of thousands of pounds of salmon caught with driftnets for illegal shipments to Japan. European fish buyers have been offered "pirated" salmon from suppliers in Taiwan, Singapore, and Thailand.

Concerned about the loss of salmon, the fishing industries of Canada and the U.S. are demanding a phase-out of the driftnet fleets. The Soviet Union has formally notified Japan that it intends to curtail, and eventually to phase out, all Japanese allocations of Soviet-origin salmon.

The Australian government acted to prohibit large-scale driftnet fishing within their 200 mile limit by the Taiwanese fleet, and Canada called off their deep-sea driftnet research fishery.

SOURCES: Greenpeace National Office, Greenpeace Pacific Campaign, 1436 U Street, NW, Washington, D.C. 20009.

BIBLIOGRAPHY: *Political Handbook of the World 1988,* edited by Arthur S. Banks, CSA Publications, State University of New York at Binghamton, New York, 1988.

American Lake: Nuclear Peril in the Pacific, by Peter Hayes, Lyuba Zarsky, and Walden Bello, Penguin Books, Australia, 1986.

6

❖

ON THE SOUTH
PACIFIC RIM

THE TIDE OF THE NEW PACIFIC

The days of American hegemony in the South Pacific—as exemplified by the popular World War II song, "To be specific, it's our Pacific!"—are decidedly over. Today, American influence is limited only to a few territories, north of the equator. Most of the island groups have shed their colonial masters. As former New Zealand Prime Minister David Lange declared, "The myth of the Pacific as a quiet backwater has gone."

Today, there is a growing sense of self-mastery in the region, as evidenced by the decision of Kiribati (once called the Gilbert Islands) to lease fishing rights to the Soviet Union in 1985, despite vehement reaction by the United States, Australia, and New Zealand. In 1988, Papua New Guinea, Vanuatu, and the Solomon Islands formed the Melanesian Spearhead Group in order to pressure France to grant independence to its troubled protectorate, New Caledonia. In a similar expression of self-determination, the South Pacific Forum (consisting of 13 mini-states, including Australia and New Zealand) called for a South Pacific Nuclear-Free Zone.

Today, although many of the island groups still rely on foreign aid from former colonizers, there is a new influx of investment from Asian countries led by Japan. In 1987, the Japanese government invested $68 million into the region, a 24% increase from the year before. In August 1989, 10 South Pacific island-nation leaders descended on Tokyo for a conference on Japan's role in their regional economic development.

By far, the biggest Japanese investor in the South Pacific is a huge company called Electronic and Industrial Enterprises, with an estimated $6 billion worth of investments in Australia, Hawaii, Fiji, Tahiti, and New Caledonia. Most recently, the group has invested about $260 million to transform Fiji's Denarau Island into a total resort complex. Of course, one of Japan's largest construction companies, Kumagai Gumi, has been hired to do the project.

There has also been a rush of investment from the Four Tigers (Singapore, South Korea, Hong Kong, and Taiwan) to build factories in the larger South Pacific islands. Even China has sought to develop trade and other ties, establishing a National Committee for Pacific Economic Cooperation in 1987. Although Indonesia and Malaysia are understandably short on capital to invest, they, too, are talking in terms of extending technical help in agriculture and fishing in order to cultivate ties in the region.

But while the South Pacific islanders welcome the economic attention, they don't have any doubts about the real motivations of these cousins from the North Rim. As David Hegarty of the Research School of Pacific Studies at the Australian National University put it: "The region's vast ocean, extensive exclusive economic zones, important lines of communication, potential seabed mineral resources and possibly even the space above it are being increasingly regarded as strategically important."

Sources: Asiaweek, Islands Business, and Political Handbook of the World 1988 (CSA Publications, State University of New York at Binghamton)

PACIFIC ISLANDS OVERVIEW

SOCIAL AND CULTURAL

The Pacific Ocean is the earth's largest geographical feature, covering one-third of the globe's surface (see map on p. 437). The islands and peoples of the contemporary Pacific are divided into 21 political entities (see Map on p. 438). Of these, nine are independent nations, four are self-governing in free association with their former colonial rulers, and eight continue as dependencies of metropolitan powers—primarily France and the United States (see Table on p. 443).

Diversity

The Pacific is marked by an incredible diversity. The islands themselves range from the large continental forms that dominate the southwestern Pacific to the high volcanic peaks and low coral atolls that are found throughout the entire region. The continental island nations, particularly the two giants of Fiji and Papua New Guinea, are relatively well-endowed with natural resources. At the other end of the continuum are countries such as Kiribati and Tuvalu comprising coral atolls and having meager terrestrial resource bases. Most island countries fall somewhere between the two extremes. Marine resources are found in (and are abundant in a few of) the recently established 200-mile Exclusive Economic Zones (EEZs) that surround the island nations (see map on p. 437). The countries range in size from Niue, with a population of 2,500 living on one coral atoll, to Papua New Guinea, with a population of about 4,000,000.

The region's diversity is compounded by geographic isolation. Vast distances separate many of the small islands; in some cases, the populations of individual countries are spread across thousands of miles of ocean. In the large countries, particularly Papua New Guinea, rugged terrain and dense forest long left neighboring communities almost completely cut off from each other. Even today, communication between and within the island countries is often extremely difficult.

Traditionally, the societies and peoples of the Pacific have been divided into three major culture areas: Melanesia, Micronesia, and Po-

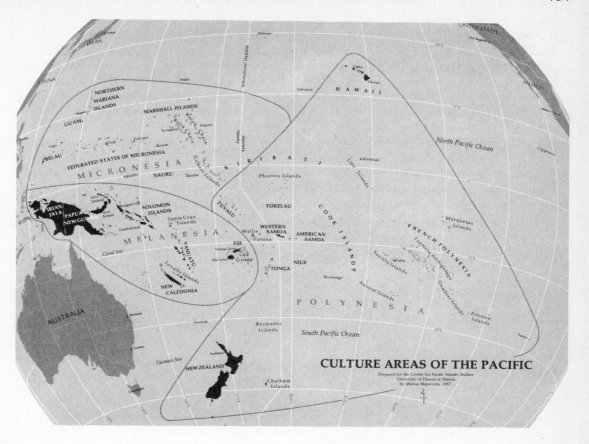

CULTURE AREAS OF THE PACIFIC
Prepared for the Center for Pacific Islands Studies
University of Hawaii at Manoa
by Manoa Mapworks, 1987

lynesia (see map, p. 438). Linguistic diversity reflects the region's vast cultural heterogeneity. Melanesia alone has approximately 1,200 languages, and another 100 or so are found in the other two culture areas. For some states, particularly those of Melanesia, such cultural and linguistic diversity poses immense problems for nation building and the forging of national identities. Importantly, three of the Melanesian states share a lingua franca (varieties of Pidgin) linking them in a common bond unique in the region. Throughout the area, the language of government and commerce is either English or French along with one or more of the local vernaculars.

Further complicating the diversity of the island world, subregions had different colonial histories. At the end of World War II, the entire Pacific was divided among six colonial powers: Australia, France, New Zealand, the Netherlands, the United Kingdom, and the United States. Their respective legacies are apparent in contemporary systems of government, styles of administration, education, and to some extent, world views. (In earlier times, Spain, Germany, and Japan had also been colonial players in the region.) Today, commerce and trade, lines of communication, transportation, shipping, opportunities for tertiary education, and foreign assistance tend to flow along and reflect the former colonial connections.

Today, the majority of Pacific Islanders, about 75 percent, remain rural dwellers with economies based on subsistence agriculture and, in many instances, marine resources. Their primary allegiances and identities are rooted in local extended kin groupings, villages, and particular islands within the larger nation-states. For many, the modern nation-state has little meaning in their everyday lives.

Again, however, there is great diversity. In most of the Melanesian states, rural dwellers account for about 90 percent of the populations. In contrast, over half of some Micronesian peoples live in urban areas.

Rapid Change

The rural character of most of the region notwithstanding, rapid change has characterized the Pacific since World War II. In recent years, particularly the last two decades, problems that were common to other Third World areas have emerged in the islands. In a few instances, there have been threats to the stability of the existing political order. Everywhere, population growth is rapid, and the rate of movement to urban centers is increasing. Urban infrastructures are frequently inadequate and overburdened. Urban landscapes are commonly characterized by an increased secularization, breakdowns in social

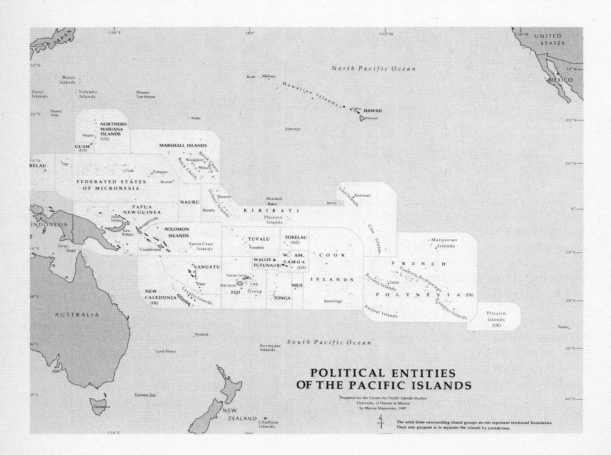

**POLITICAL ENTITIES
OF THE PACIFIC ISLANDS**

Prepared for the Center for Pacific Islands Studies
University of Hawaii at Manoa
by Manoa Mapworks, 1987

The solid lines surrounding island groups do not represent territorial boundaries.
Their sole purpose is to separate the islands by jurisdiction.

control, losses of traditional cultures and skills, personal and social maladjustments, health problems (including alcohol and other forms of substance abuse), and underemployment. At the same time, and as a consequence of increased worldwide communications (radio, movies, videos, and TV), the aspirations of island peoples are higher than at any previous time in history, and there are growing demands on the limited resources of the island countries.

While urbanization has brought greater secularization, the importance of Christianity is often underestimated. By the turn of the century, missionization reached even the remotest of the island groupings, and Christianity was reworked and thoroughly integrated as a part of island cultures. Indeed, Pacific Islanders are among the most deeply committed Christian peoples of the world. In rural areas, there is no separation of the sacred and the profane, and much of human activity is structured around church calendars. While appearances are often to the contrary, even in urban areas the influence of the religion remains strong, and many island government and political leaders owe much of their success to their positions as pillars of the church.

Pacific Identity

Lastly, and also crucial to an understanding of the contemporary Pacific, are regional phenomena. In the early post-war years, the colonial powers initiated and supported efforts at regional cooperation. The result has been a substantial proliferation of regional organizations, conferences, and other activities that have enjoyed considerable success. Among many of the educated and urban elites, there is now a strong regional identity of "Pacific Islander" that previously did not exist. There is a shared conviction that Pacific peoples have a common heritage and that there is a "Pacific Way" of conducting the affairs of the region. It is firmly linked to and very much a part of a sense of commitment to the health and welfare of the region, its peoples, and their future.

POLITICAL ISSUES

By comparison with most other world regions, the Pacific Islands are characterized by pervasive and democratic institutions and peaceful political processes and international relationships. Nevertheless, with independence and increasingly rapid economic and social change, the islands are beginning to face a variety of political challenges and issues, and these appear likely to grow more serious over the coming years.

Domestic

POLITICAL SYSTEMS

All the island countries face the challenge of adapting their political institutions to changing local conditions as well as to the demands of modernization. Prior to 1962, all 13 island countries had some form of colonial or protective relationship with external powers. Their government structures are based on the systems of the former colonial powers, except for Tonga and Western Samoa (and to an extent Fiji), whose political systems reflect local monarchical or aristocratic traditions.

Following two military coups in 1987, Fiji rewrote its original constitution. After ten years of independence, Vanuatu is now undertaking a year-long review of its constitution. In Western Samoa, a referendum will be held in late October on universal suffrage—its electoral system now allows only members of the aristocracy *(matai)* to vote. In Tonga, the constitutional monarchy faces increasing pressure to "democratize" the system by increasing the numbers and power of the commoner members in the parliament.

In many of the island states with parliamentary systems, political parties are not well established and political competition largely takes place among individual political leaders and their followers. This produces a tendency toward "revolving door" governments (such as in Papua New Guinea, Solomon Islands, and Nauru) as coalitions dissolve and are reconstituted. It also weakens the ability of governments to make difficult decisions or follow through on programs.

COMMUNAL AND SOCIAL CONFLICTS

The island societies are affected by many of the same ethnic, regional, and other cleavages as larger polities. In some of the islands, immigrant groups (often brought in by the colonial powers) compete with the indigenous groups for political power and economic position. There are also ethnic or regional divisions among the indigenous populations, sometimes exacerbated by the experience of the colonial period. Such social conflicts have been further magnified in many cases by population growth, urbanization, and generational divisions between better educated, impatient younger leaders and their more traditionally oriented seniors.

Papua New Guinea, the largest of the island countries, also has the greatest diversity with some 700 distinct language and ethnic groups and a long history of conflict among these groups. A major regional rebellion (1988–90) in the island province of Bougainville has seriously tested both the central government and fundamental national unity.

In Fiji, the military coups of 1987 were triggered by fears on the part of the indigenous Fijian population of domination by the immigrant Indian minority. In the French island territory of New Caledonia, a similar struggle for political power between the indigenous Kanak population and immigrant French and Southeast Asian groups led to a series of violent incidents over the period 1984–89.

In Vanuatu, local conflicts based on linguistic and religious preferences dating from that country's chaotic colonial period under a joint French-British "condominium" have been overlaid with personal competition among leaders and regional differences among the islands to create a volatile and unpredictable political scene. 1988–89 saw serious violence in the capital, an unsuccessful "constitutional coup," and a realignment of the major political parties.

LAND AND POWER

The single most important commodity and most potent political issue in any of the island societies is land. Control of land was the primary measure of power and economic standing in most of the traditional societies. Complex systems were developed governing the allocation and exploitation of land, often involving collective rights belonging to families or village units. The colonial era superimposed (or in some cases simply imposed) Western concepts of ownership, leaseholding or management, often creating incompatibilities with traditional patterns. The demands of modern economic development create further pressures on traditional land-tenure systems. When land issues are combined with political competition between individual leaders or groups, as has occurred in recent years in Vanuatu, Papua New Guinea, Fiji, and the Marshall Islands, the resulting conflicts can easily undermine political stability.

International

REGIONAL INSTITUTIONS

Today there are nine major regional bodies in the islands. The keystone of this network is the South Pacific Forum, set up by the island states in 1974 and currently comprising the 13 island countries plus Australia and New Zealand. Other regional institutions deal with a wide range of subjects, including education (the University of the South Pacific), resource management (the Forum Fisheries Agency), transportation (the Forum Line), and environmental protection (the South Pacific Regional Environmental Program). The activities of these institutions are loosely coordinated through the recently established South Pacific Organizations Coordinating Committee (SPOCC).

These regional institutions offer a number of benefits. They provide facilities and infrastructure that few of the island countries could afford. They provide a mechanism through which the states of the region can establish cooperation and avoid or mediate inter-state differences. Further, they provide a channel through which the many mini-states in the island region can conduct their relations and increase their bargaining leverage with the outside world. Since 1989, the Forum members have emulated the Southeast Asian ASEAN states in holding annual consultations (following their yearly summit meetings) with the major donor states, including the United States.

Nevertheless, the Pacific is not immune to the problems that have been encountered in cooperative undertakings in other regions. Competition among states over the location and allocation of benefits of programs, the development of regional subgroups (specifically the recent creation of the "Melanesian Spearhead," a caucus of the three Melanesian island states within the South Pacific Forum), conflicting interests of small and large member states, and the inevitable divisive tendencies resulting from personalities and leadership rivalries have all affected the island institutions.

SOVEREIGNTY

The island countries, through their five United Nations members, have pressed for the completion of the self-determination process in the Pacific Islands. In recent years this effort has focused on the French territory of New Caledonia, where the indigenous Kanak people have waged a long struggle to gain political recognition and control. A referendum on New Caledonia's status is now scheduled for 1998. The decolonization issue in the other French territories in the Pacific, French Polynesia and Wallis and Futuna, is receiving increasing attention. In early October, the Solomon Islands called for the reinscription of French Polynesia on the United Nations' listing of non-self-governing territories.

The island states have also united to seek international recognition of the independence and legitimacy of all the island countries. This has included lobbying for acceptance of the full sovereignty of the four island states (Cook Islands, Niue, the Marshalls, and the Federated States of Micronesia) that have entered into "free association" agreements with their former colonial powers (New Zealand for the first two, the United States for the others). Under these agreements, the larger partners are responsible for defense and, in some cases, foreign affairs functions, and also provide varying levels of continuing economic support—an innovative solution to the problem of ensuring the viability and security of mini-states. All four of the "Freely Associated States" have been granted full membership rights in the South Pacific Forum, and the Forum members have encouraged other states and international bodies to accord them the same status.

EXTERNAL POWERS AND INTERESTS

While the former colonial powers retain their interests and links with their former colonies, other external powers are seeking to develop ties with the island countries. The Soviet Union in the mid-1970s began making approaches to the newly independent island states. This Soviet foray evoked an immediate, concerned response from the Western powers (including the awakening of the United States from its previous posture of "benign neglect" of the island region), and corresponding increases in attention and assistance.

Other rivalries followed the East-West conflict into the region, such as Taiwan and the People's Republic of China, and Libya, the PLO and Israel. Other emerging regional powers, from Japan to the ASEAN states, have also become progressively more involved. Finally, a number of undesirable actors have been attracted to the region—criminal elements in search of financial havens, and drug traffickers looking for trans-shipment points.

With few exceptions, the island states retain very good relations with the former colonial powers. However, the new external interests have presented opportunities for the islands to expand their own international contacts and relationships, and in some cases have offered them the chance to profit from bidding wars among the external powers. To date the island states have proven rather more adept at these activities—and at safeguarding their own security interests—than some of the former colonial governments had feared. The waning of the Cold War has reduced some of these dangers, although ironically it also removes one of the earlier arguments for enhanced attention to the islands by the Western powers. Overall, however, the pattern of widening contacts between the islands and external parties will continue.

ISLAND-RIM RELATIONS

Efforts spanning three decades to establish a cooperative mechanism for the Asia-Pacific region bore fruit in November 1989 with the launching of the Asia-Pacific Economic Cooperation (APEC) process at a twelve-nation intergovernmental ministerial meeting in Canberra. A second meeting took place in Singapore in July this year, and further annual meetings are planned (first in Korea, then the United States).

For the Pacific Island countries, the establishment of such a regional forum presents both an opportunity and a dilemma. It is in their interest to be an integral part of the larger region and share in its dynamic growth as well as its consultative processes. However, with their limited resources it is difficult for the island states to fully participate in the APEC process. Although the islands were represented at the first APEC meetings through the secretary general of the South Pacific Forum Secretariat, he is not in a position to authoritatively represent the political interests and views of all the island states. Clearly some formula needs to be found which provides for appropriate island participation.

SECURITY COOPERATION

Although they face no immediate military threats, the islands do face the necessity of securing their sovereignty over their own territory and especially over the sometimes vast sea areas included in their Exclusive Economic Zones. The fisheries in these areas alone are a highly valuable resource, and only effective surveillance and enforcement capabilities will ensure that the island states receive their share of the revenues from exploitation of such resources.

Australia and New Zealand provide aerial surveillance of the region, and Australia is just completing a program to supply naval patrol boats to most of the independent island countries. Cost, however, poses a serious constraint to any such effort. The operation of the existing patrol boat fleet will constitute a major burden for the national budgets of many of the island states, yet even the present numbers will provide only very limited coverage. Except for the Freely Associated States, the problem of an adequate security capability has yet to be resolved.

In the past few years the islands have begun a tentative process of consultation on security issues. In 1990, a report commissioned by the New Zealand government proposed consideration of a broader framework arrangement to enable the island states to take a more comprehensive, coordinated approach to regional security concerns. This proposal has not been given formal consideration by the island governments, but the broad issue of security cooperation will almost certainly be a regular feature of future discussions among the island states.

ECONOMIC DEVELOPMENT

What are the important issues that Pacific Island nations face in trying to promote economic development? In common with most less developing countries these nations are constrained by inadequate infrastructure, limited entrepreneurial capacity, low savings for investment purposes, and limited human resources. But there are other formidable constraints which make the economic

Political Status of Pacific Island Nations

Current or Former Colonial Power	Independent Nation	Self-Governing in Free Association	Continued Dependent Status
New Zealand	West Samoa[1] (1962)[2]	Cook Is (1965)[2] Niue (1974)	Tokelau
United Kingdom	Fiji[1] (1970) Tonga (1970) Tuvalu (1978) Solomon Is[1] (1978) Kiribati (1979) Vanuatu[1] (1980)[3]		
Australia	Nauru (1968) Papua New Guinea[1] (1975)		
France	Vanuatu[1] (1980)[3]		Fr Polynesia New Caledonia Wallis & Futuna
United States		Marshall Is (1986)	American Samoa Guam
		Federated States of Micronesia (1986)	Commonwealth of N. Mariana Is Belau

[1] United Nations membership.

[2] Years in parentheses indicate dates independence or free association was achieved.

[3] Vanuatu appears twice in the list of independent nations as it was jointly ruled by the United Kingdom and France.

development efforts in the Pacific Islands especially challenging (see Table on p. 591).

Small Market, Narrow Economic Base

Most island countries have a weak economic foundation, with a limited quantity and variety of resources available. The Pacific Island regional market is relatively small, about 6 million people. Also, intra-Pacific Island trade is very small, accounting for 1.5 percent of total exports in 1988. Of this, Fiji accounted for 76 percent of the total. There is considerable variability in natural resource endowments. At one end of the spectrum is Papua New Guinea, which is rich in mineral and land resources. At the other extreme are the atoll countries with their severely limited arable land and fresh water resources. All the islands are dependent on imported goods and services. Most are subject to a high incidence of natural disasters, particularly tropical cyclones.

Earnings from traditional commodities (copra, sugar, coffee, cocoa, and palm oil) have stagnated in the face of exceptionally prolonged price deterioration and inadequate levels of capital investment. The rate of growth of export earnings fell by at least 75

Country	$ Millions Foreign Aid (1986)	$ Millions Trade Deficit (1986)
Papua New Guinea	263.6	− 105
Fiji	42.5	− 122
Solomon Islands	30.2	− 1
Western Samoa	23.3	− 32
Vanuatu	24.1	− 38
Tonga	15.1	− 26
Kiribati	13.4	− 11
Cook Islands	26.4	− 44.3

Donor	$ Millions
Australia (including aid to PNG)	302.8
Australia (excluding aid to PNG)	66.2
New Zealand	103.0
Japan	93.1
World Bank	40.3
United States	17.2

Source: Report of a Congressional Delegation to the South Pacific, August 5–16, 1989, p. 21.

percent in the 1980s. Thus, these economies have experienced slow export growth over the last decade, with some displaying a large and widening trade imbalance. This gap has been partly filled by foreign aid and the remittances of Pacific Islanders living abroad.

Foreign Aid Dependency

Although most Pacific Islands have identified self-reliance as a priority objective, they continue to have balance of payments difficulties and are dependent on foreign aid. For the smaller nations such as Tuvalu, Niue, Kiribati, and Cook Islands, infrastructure projects (roads, airport, power plant, telecommunication systems) are impossible without external financial assistance. In 1989, foreign aid to the South Pacific region from major donors was as follows:

Declining Terms of Trade, Need to Diversify

The price of traditional agricultural commodities relative to that of imported agricultural goods is expected to continue to fall. As a result, more and more exports are needed to pay for the same volume of imports. This has serious implication for the island economies which are heavily if not wholly dependent upon imports for the productivity of domestic resources. Thus there is an urgent need to di-

Vital statistics of selected Pacific Islands

	Cook Islands	Fiji	Kiribati	Papua New Guinea	Solomon Islands	Tonga	Tuvalu	Vanuatu	Western Samoa
GDP (millions US$)★	14	1,083	20	2,167	108	64	3	103	74
GDP per capita (US$)★	771	1,182	271	640	374	640	339	739	492
Land area (sq. mi.)	94	7,126	269	180,275	11,127	273	10	4,633	1,145
Arable land (sq. mi.)	23	920	140	1,459	207	211	n.a.	371	476
EEZ ('000 sq. mi.)	714	503	1,385	1,217	523	273	351	265	47
Total exports ('000 US$)★	3,403	162,113	3,946	889,553	68,056	4,195	248	18,141	15,660
Total imports ('000 US$)★	18,858	359,485	14,798	921,857	67,268	34,865	3,162	65,969	35,521
Food imports ('000 US$)★	6,535	71,011	4,061	148,521	10,243	7,682	734	13,406	12,880
Population ('000)	18	710	66	3,600	300	95	9	140	160
Population density (per sq. mi.)	192	100	245	20	27	348	888	30	140
Population growth (% per annum)	−0.3	2.1	1.9	2.6	3.5	0.6	2.8	3.2	0.3
Life expectancy (yrs. at birth)	69	68	53	52	58	64	59	63	65
Primary school enrollments (%)	95	100	100	65	73	77	58	61	91
Calories per day (per capita)	2,550	2,900	2,515	2,145	2,200	2,845	2,300	2,100	2,400

★ Economic data based on 1985 statistics

n.a. —not available

Sources: Browne (1989); SPC (1987); Commonwealth Secretariat (1987).

versify the economic base of these economies. But agricultural diversification is hampered by limited access to external markets and by the traditional communal land-tenure system. Tourism and manufacturing directed at specialized markets in industrialized countries offer growth opportunities for most countries. A few nations (such as Papua New Guinea) have resource development opportunities. However, most current efforts aim at expanding agricultural and marine activities, in which most of the population is already engaged. This will necessitate increasing exports, as domestic markets are small and offer limited growth prospects. Thus the Pacific Rim countries, by facilitating easy access to their markets, can make a major contribution to the economic diversification efforts of the islands.

Isolation from Markets

The vast distances of the islands from major markets poses problems for export and tourism development. These relate particularly to the availability and cost of transport. However, the locational factors are not necessarily all negative. The region's climate and relatively pest-free and unpolluted environment provide important, inherent advantages in the production of horticultural and other export commodities and in the development of tourism.

From Subsistence to Market Activity

The Pacific Island communities are predominantly rural societies, dependent on semi-subsistence agriculture and marine resource activities. They are also largely communal societies, where relations with the extended family, the village, and the clan are important. Land is held under varying systems of customary ownership, which are usually clan based. In Tonga, Solomon Islands, and Van-

uatu land cannot be purchased, while limited quantities of freehold land is available in Fiji, Papua New Guinea, and Western Samoa. Fiji has a well-developed institutional structure that enables the lease of a significant quantity of agricultural land on a medium-term basis. The land registration and leasing arrangements in the other countries are far less developed. These factors create particular challenges for the transition from traditional subsistence activity to commercial agriculture and mineral development.

Private Sector Gearing Up

Despite the constraints they face, there are grounds for cautious optimism regarding the future economic prospects for these island nations. In most cases they have enjoyed sound macro-economic management and their external debt levels are low by developing country standards. A dramatic shift is now occurring in the policy environment toward focusing on the private sector as the engine of economic development and on the expansion of exports. Indications are that the private sector is responding to this favorable investment environment. Market access to Pacific Rim countries, such as the United States, will also be crucial to the success of these initiatives.

PACIFIC ISLAND PROFILES AND MAPS

COOK ISLANDS

Geography

The Cook Islands are located between 156° and 167° W longitude and between 8° and 23° S latitude. Their nearest neighbors are French Polynesia to the east, Tonga and Niue to the west, and American Samoa to the northwest.

The Cook Islands comprise 15 islands with a total land area of 94 sq. miles in a sea area of 714,000 sq. miles. The main island is Rarotonga on which the capital of Avarua is located. The Cook Islands are a combination of volcanic islands and low-lying coral atolls.

Population

The population of the Cook Islands is about 18,000 with a population density of 190 per sq. mile. Most of the people live on the main island of Rarotonga. The people are mostly Polynesian. Cook Islands Maori and English are the main languages. Because of limited economic opportunity in the islands many Cook Islanders migrate to New Zealand in search of jobs.

Politics

The Cook Islands were administered by New Zealand until 1965. At that time they became self-governing in free association with New Zealand which takes care of defense and foreign affairs. The Cook Islands are a parliamentary democracy headed by a prime minister. The current prime minister is Geoffrey Henry.

Economy

The economy of the Cook Islands is mainly subsistence agriculture and fishing, with tourism also playing a major part. The primary exports are copra, fruit juices, and fruits and vegetables. The GNP of the Cook Islands is $20 million (1985) and the GNP per capita is $1,360.

FEDERATED STATES OF MICRONESIA (FSM)

Geography

The Federated States of Micronesia (FSM) is located between 0° to 14° N latitude and 136° to 166° E longitude. Its neighbors are Guam to the north, Palau to the west, and the Marshall Islands to the east. FSM is made up of hundreds of islands that range from lush high volcanic islands to low-lying coral atolls. These islands comprise a land area of 275 sq. miles scattered over thousands of sq. miles of ocean.

Population

The population of FSM is about 93,000. The people are mostly Micronesian with some Polynesians and Americans. The population density is about 340 per sq. mile. They speak mainly Micronesian dialects and English.

Politics

FSM is divided into the four states of Pohnpei, Chuuk (Truk), Yap, and Kosrae. The national government, based on the American system, is located on Pohnpei in the capital of Kolonia. FMS's colonial history includes rule by the Spanish, Germans, Japanese, and finally the United States when it became a United Nations Trust Territory at the end of World War II. FSM became self-governing in free association with the United States in 1986. The current president is John R. Haglelgam.

Economy

The GNP of FSM is US$ 106 million (1983). The economy of FSM is based mainly on traditional agriculture and fishing. There are very few exports from FSM. The main industries are copra, black pepper, and fisheries.

FIJI

Geography

The Republic of Fiji is located between 15° and 22° S longitude and 177° W to 175° E latitude. Its neighbors are Vanuatu to the West, Tonga to the Southeast, and Western Samoa to the Northeast. Fiji is made up of hundreds of islands comprising 7,100 sq. miles with a sea area of about 500,000 sq. miles. The largest and main islands are Vanua Levu and Viti Levu. There are large volcanic islands and many smaller coral atolls.

Population

The population of Fiji is about 732,000 with a density of 103 per sq. mile. The population is divided into 46 percent ethnic Fijians, 48 percent ethnic Indian, and 6 percent other. Most of the people live on the island of Viti Levu where the capital Suva is located. Languages widely spoken are Fijian, Hindustani, and English. Native Fijians are Melanesians.

Politics

Fiji was administered by the United Kingdom until independence in 1970. At that time a parliamentary democracy was established with a prime minister as the head of government. The parliament was suspended following two military coups in 1987. The government is currently headed by Prime Minister Ratu Sir Kamisese Mara. A new constitution has been written and elections under the new constitution are to be held soon.

Economy

The GNP of Fiji is about US$ 1,190 million (1989) with a GNP per capita of US$ 1,572. A large percentage of the population is subsistence farmers, with agriculture, tourism, and manufacturing being the major components of the economy. Major exports are sugar, textiles, gold, copra, fish, and timber.

KIRIBATI

Geography

Kiribati (pronounced 'Kiribas') is a country of 33 low-lying coral atolls in the middle of the Pacific Ocean. They comprise a total land area of 270 sq. miles in a sea area of 1.4 million sq. miles. They are scattered from 4° N to 11° S and 169° E to 150° W. Kiribati's neighbors are Nauru to the west, Tuvalu to the south, and Hawaii to the north.

Population

The population of Kiribati is 67,000 with a density of 248 per sq. mile. They are Micronesian and speak Gilbertese and English. They are called I-Kiribati. 33 percent of the people live on the main island of Tarawa. The capital is Bairiki on the island of Tarawa.

Politics

The islands of Kiribati were formerly administered as part of the British territory of the Gilbert and Ellice Islands. They became an independent state in 1979. The government is a democratic government with a president and a legislature. The current president is Ieremia Tabai.

Economy

Kiribati has an economy based on subsistence farming, copra, and fishing. Due to the nature of the low-lying coral atolls agricultural diversification opportunities are limited. The GNP of Kiribati is US$ 33 million (1989) with a GNP per capita of US$ 471. Main exports are copra and fish.

MARSHALL ISLANDS

Geography

The Marshall Islands are a series of 34 low-lying coral atolls compromising a land area of around 780,000 sq. miles. These islands are scattered between 5° and 15° N longitude and 162° to 173° E latitude. The Marshall Island's closest neighbors are FSM to the east, Nauru to the Southeast and Kiribati to the Southwest.

Population

The Marshallese people are of Micronesian descent and speak Marshallese and English. The population of the Marshall Islands is about 44,000 with a density of 657 per sq. mile. Most of the people live on the main island and capital of Majuro; 65 percent of the islanders live on Majuro and Eyebe in Kwajalein.

Politics

The Republic of the Marshall Islands became self-governing in free association with the United States in 1986. They were formerly part of the United States Trust Territory. They are governed by a legislature and president. The current president is Amata Kabua.

Economy

The mainstays of the economy are subsistence farming, fishing, copra production, and U.S. military spending at Kwajalein Atoll.

NAURU

Geography

Nauru is a single uplifted coral atoll with a land area of 8 sq. miles. Its EEZ is an area of 125,000 sq. miles. Nauru is situated a few miles south of the equator at 167° E longitude. Its closest neighbors are FSM and the Marshall Islands to the north, Kiribati to the east and Solomon Islands to the south.

Population

Nauruans are Micronesians. The island of Nauru has a population of about 8,000 with a population density of 1,000 per sq. mile. Of this 8,000, about 5,000 are native Nauruans. The others are imported laborers. The main languages are Nauruan and English.

Politics

Nauru was administered by Australia until independence in 1968. They have a democratic government headed by President Bernard Dowiyogo. The capital is Yaren.

Economy

The main economic activity of Nauru is phosphate mining that gives Nauru the highest GNP per capita, US$ 20,444, in the Pacific. The GNP of Nauru is US$ 186 million (1989) based almost entirely on phosphate mining. The phosphate will soon run out and Nauru invests its revenues to compensate for when that date arrives. A major issue is the reclamation of the mine area.

NIUE

Geography

Niue is a small uplifted coral atoll with an area of 100 sq. miles. Niue's EEZ is about 152,000 sq. miles. It is located at 19° S longitude and 169° W latitude. It's closest neighbors are

Tonga to the west, Cook Islands to the east, and American Samoa to the north. The capital is Alofi.

Population

There are about 2,500 Niueans on Niue with a population density of 25 per sq. mile. Niueans are Polynesian. Both Niuean and English are spoken. A large number of Niueans migrate to New Zealand. There are about three times as many Niueans in New Zealand as there are on Niue.

Politics

Niue was administered by New Zealand until it became self-governing in free association with New Zealand in 1974. Niue is a parliamentary democracy headed by a prime minister. The current prime minister is Sir Robert Rex.

Economy

The GNP of Niue US$ 3 million (1985) with a GNP per capita of US$ 1,080. Primary exports are fruit products (lime and passionfruit), root crops, coconut products, honey, and footballs.

PAPUA NEW GUINEA

Geography

Papua New Guinea is the largest of the Pacific Island states. It comprises a total land area of 180,000 sq. miles. Papua New Guinea is located between 0° to 12° S longitude and 141° to 160° E. This broad range encompasses an EEZ of 1.2 million sq. miles. The largest part of Papua New Guinea is situated on the eastern half of the island of New Guinea. Other major islands are New Britain, New Ireland, Bougainville, and Manus. These are large continental islands with rugged terrain. There are also many smaller islands. Papua New Guinea's nearest neighbors are Indonesia to the west, with which it shares a land border, and Australia to the south. Solomon Islands are to the Southeast and the Federated States of Micronesia and Papua are to the north.

Population

The population of Papua New Guinea is 3.5 million. With its large land mass there is a population density of only 19 per sq. mile. There are about 700 language and cultural groups in this Melanesian country. Many villages are isolated from each other. The capital of Port Moresby is on the southern part of the mainland and is separated from the populous central and northern parts of the country by rugged terrain. In addition to the 700 languages spoken, there are three languages spoken by many groups. These are Tok, Pisin, Hiri Motu, and English.

Politics

Papua New Guinea was totally under the administration of Australia from World War I until independence in 1975. The country is divided into 20 (including the National Capital District) administrative provinces. The national government is a parliamentary democracy headed by a prime minister. The current prime minister is Rabbie Namaliu.

Economy

Papua New Guinea has a GNP of US$ 2,823 million (1989) and a GNP per capita of US$ 820. The mainstays of the economy are subsistence and plantation agriculture, fisheries, and mining. Major exports are copper, gold, fish products, copra products, coffee, cocoa, timber, and tea.

SOLOMON ISLANDS

Geography

Solomon Islands are a chain of six large islands and many smaller islands located between 5° to 12° S longitude and 155° to 170° E latitude. They comprise a land area of 11,000 sq. miles with an EEZ of 525,000 sq. miles. Their closest neighbors are Papua New Guinea to the northwest and Vanuatu to the southeast.

Population

Solomon Islanders are Melanesians with about 90 different language and ethnic groups. There are a small number of Polynesians and Europeans. They number about 286,000 with a population density of 26 per sq. mile. The major urban center and capital is Honiara located on the island of Guadalcanal. The major lingua franca is Pidgin with English being the official language.

Politics

Solomon Islands were once the scene of major fighting during World War II when they were a British possession. They became independent in 1978. The government of Solomon Islands is a parliamentary democracy. The current prime minister is Solomon Mamaloni.

Economy

The GNP of Solomon Islands is US$ 133 million (1989) with a GNP per capita of US$ 410. Solomon Islands' society is based mainly on subsistence agriculture. The major exports are fish products, timber, palm oil and copra, cocoa, and some gold.

KINGDOM OF TONGA

Geography

The Kingdom of Tonga is located between 15° to 23° S longitude and 173° to 177° W latitude. Tonga's closest neighbors are Fiji to the northwest, American Samoa and Western Samoa to the north, and Niue and the Cook Islands to the east. Tonga comprises three main island groups (Tongatapu, Ha'apai, and Vava'u) that are mainly coral atolls with some volcanic islands. There are some 150 islands of which 36 are inhabited. These islands have a land area of 270 sq. miles with a sea area 270,000 sq. miles. The capital, Nuku'alofa is located on the southerly island of Tongatapu.

Population

Tongans are a Polynesian people with their own language group. They number about 96,000 located mostly on the island of Tongatapu. The population density of Tonga is 355 per sq. mile. Both Tongan and English are spoken. There are a large number of Tongans living in New Zealand and the United States.

Politics

Tonga is a constitutional monarchy dating back to its first constitution in 1875. Tonga was a protectorate of Great Britain until 1970 when it gained full control of its affairs. Tonga has a monarchy established by King Tupou I. The current king is King Taufa'ahau Tupou IV. The executive and legislative functions are invested in the king, the prime minister, and parliament. The current prime minister is Crown Prince Fatafehi Tu'ipelehake.

452 THE PACIFIC RIM ALMANAC

Economy

The GNP of Tonga is US$ 78 million (1989) with a GNP per capita of US$ 750. Most Tongans are involved in subsistence agriculture. The other main economic activities of Tonga are tourism, coconut products, bananas, vanilla, fish, squash, and some light manufacturing.

TUVALU

Geography

Tuvalu is a chain of 9 low-lying coral atolls located between 5° to 10° S longitude and 176° to 179° E latitude. These atolls rise only a few feet above the sea and comprise a land area of only 10 sq. miles in an ocean area of 350,000 sq. miles. The main island and capital is Funafuti. Tuvalu's closest neighbors are Kiribati to the north, Tokelau to the east, Fiji and Wallis and Futuna to the southwest and Western Samoa and American Samoa to the southeast.

Population

Tuvaluans are Polynesian. They speak Tuvaluan, which is closely related to Samoan, and also English. There are 9,000 inhabitants with a population density of 900 per sq. mile. Most live on the main island and capital of Funafuti.

Politics

Tuvalu was once a part of the British territory of Gilbert and Ellice Islands. The Gilbert Islands became a part of Kiribati and the Ellice Islands became the independent state of Tuvalu in 1978. Tuvalu is a parliamentary de-

mocracy. The current prime minister is Bikenibeu Paeniu.

Economy

Tuvaluans are engaged mainly in subsistence agriculture and fishing. The GNP is US$ 4 million (1989) with a per capita income of US$ 500. The only agriculture that the limited soil allows is copra production. There is also some export of fish.

VANUATU

Geography

Vanuatu is made up of about 80 islands located from 12° to 21° S longitude and 166° to 171° E latitude. They comprise a land area of 4,600 sq. miles with an EEZ of 265,000 sq. miles. Vanuatu's islands are a combination of large high islands and small coral atolls. Their nearest neighbors are Fiji to the east, the Solomon Islands to the north, and New Caledonia to the south. The capital is Port Vila on the island of Efate.

Population

Vanuatuans are a Melanesian people with 100 different ethnic and language groups. There are about 150,000 people in Vanuatu with a density of 32 per sq. mile. English, French, and Bislama are widely spoken. The people of Vanuatu are referred to as ni-Vanuatu.

Politics

Vanuatu was once administered jointly by Great Britain and France. Vanuatu gained independence in 1980. Vanuatu is a parliamentary democracy. The current head of government is Prime Minister Father Walter Lini.

Economy

The GNP of Vanuatu is US$ 87 million (1989) with a per capita income of US$ 568. The majority of the people live on subsistence agriculture. Major economic activities are tourism, copra production, cocoa, coffee, timber, fishing, and off-shore banking.

WESTERN SAMOA

Geography

Western Samoa is made up of 2 large and 2 small inhabited islands. They are located between 13° and 15° S latitude and 168° and 173° W longitude. The land area of Western Samoa is 1,150 sq. miles with an EEZ of 47,000 sq. miles. Western Samoa's neighbors are Fiji in the west, Tonga to the south, Tuvalu and Tokelau to the north, and American Samoa to the east. Western Samoa's main islands are large volcanic islands.

Population

The population of Western Samoa is 170,000. The population density is 147 per sq. mile. Western Samoans live mainly on the island of Upolu and around the capital and main city of Apia. Western Samoans are Polynesian and speak both the Samoan and English languages. While Western Samoa has a large population birth rate, the population growth rate is stable due to migration to New Zealand and the United States.

Politics

Western Samoa was once governed by Germany and became a League of Nations man-

dated and later UN trust territory administered by New Zealand. Western Samoa was the first country in the Pacific Islands to gain independence in 1962. Western Samoa has a parliamentary democracy based on the English model and traditional culture. The current prime minister is Tofilau Eti Alesana.

Economy

The GNP of Samoa is US$ 98 million (1989) with a per capita income of US$ 539. Most of the population is engaged in subsistence agriculture. There is some light manufacturing and tourism. Remittances from family members overseas contribute a large part to foreign exchange earnings. The primary exports are copra, timber, cocoa, bananas, and taro.

Source: This material has been excerpted from the published proceedings of "The Summit of the United States and the Pacific Island Nations, October 27, 1990." Reprinted by permission of the East-West Center, 1777 East-West Road, Honolulu, Hawaii 96848.

NETWORKING IN THE SOUTH SEAS

With the advent of high-tech communications and personal computer technology, once remote islands are becoming networked together. American Samoa (population 37,000) is in a computer boom, according to *Islands Business,* a Fiji-published business monthly. An estimated 150 offices now have fax machines—and there are 124 cellular phones in operation after a $1 million system was installed last year. With new cellular stations being planned, the range for users will expand to other islands, says American Samoa communications director Aleki Sene.

EXPLOSIVE TUNNELS

Secret Japanese tunnels filled with tons of ammunition left over from World War II were discovered above the volcanic Papua New Guinea capital of Port Moresby by children playing on New Year's Day in 1989. The tunnels contained thousands of rounds of high explosive artillery, anti-aircraft, and cannon shells, which were still in good condition, according to the Disasters Center, which arranged for Papuan troops to remove the explosives.

FIJI'S SUGAR INDUSTRY

While Hawaii's sugar industry has long been dying a slow death and the Australian sugar industry is in the doldrums, Fiji plans to develop a sugar market for itself. The Fiji Sugar Corporation has been buying and dismantling old Hawaiian sugar mills and shipping them to Fiji across 5,000 kilometers of ocean. FSC says it plans to invest $86 million in its facilities over the next five years. Gross revenues from sugar and molasses for 1989 are estimated at about $160 million.

COOK ISLANDS' HIGH-TECH GOLD MINE?

A seabed area off the Cook Islands in the South Pacific may hold the key to Japan's race to develop its lead in superconductivity technology, according to *Islands Business*. Japan's Mining Agency is now studying the feasibility of mining manganese nodules which have been detected on the seabed of Cook Islands' exclusive economic zone. The agency wants to know whether the nodules contain yttrium—a metallic element in great demand for superconductivity research.

NEW CALEDONIAN HOPES

Most of the luxury hotels along New Caledonia's east coast remain closed or occupied by the military six years after the civil disorder between the native liberation front (FLNKS) and the government of the South Pacific territory. But elsewhere in the region, authorities see encouraging signs of tourism returning, especially after the influx of $23 million of aid to revive the territory's economy. Authorities are pinning their hopes on cooperation with the Kanak Socialist Liberation Party which, though it shares FLNKS's dream of independence from France, has a more moderate agenda.

NEW ZEALAND: ENVIRONMENTAL DIPLOMAT

New Zealand took the lead in the worldwide "environment diplomacy" by approving a detailed policy which provides for an almost total phase-out of such ozone-depleting substances as chlorofluorocarbons (CFCs) and halons within the country by 1999.

NEW ZEALAND'S SUICIDE WAVE

The suicide rate for New Zealand men between 15 and 24 is nearly three times higher than their counterparts in England and is the second biggest killer of that age group according to the head of the country's Mental Health Foundation. Max Abbott said that studies of hospital admissions in 1987 showed one in 500 teenagers attempts suicide and that is probably a conservative figure because many attempts are not reported. The Rev. Charles Waldegrave, an Anglican social worker, said he believed there was a link between unemployment and suicide and that suicide was contagious; if one person in a group did it, others were apt to follow. New Zealand is undergoing financial problems at present due to economic restructuring, which has brought new levels of unemployment and poverty.

MAORIS RAISE CLAIMS

Echoes of an 1840 treaty between New Zealand's Maori tribesmen and British settlers are resonating with a recent court decision upholding the Muriwhenua tribe's claim to 5,000 square kilometers of fishing waters. Similar claims by representatives of the 300,000 Maoris—10% of the nation's total population—could affect much of New Zealand's coastline and three quarters of its land, and opposition leader Jim Bolger described it as an emerging crisis. "It is a legal fantasy . . . to hide behind an 1840s treaty and . . . not take account of developments [since]," he

said. New Zealand's fishing industry is estimated to earn $1.4 billion by the end of the century.

FIJI EXODUS

A mass exodus of ethnic Indian professionals from Fiji, in the wake of the May 1987 military takeover by military leader Major General Sitiveni Rabuka, has created a critical shortage of skilled professionals in the South Pacific island republic. Fiji has suffered shortages of doctors, lawyers, teachers, accountants, and civil servants in the wake of the military coup, which overthrew the elected government of Timoci Bavadra. Fiji's Information Ministry reported that 9,500 ethnic Indians, 1,800 Melanesians, and 1,000 members of other races had emigrated. The Fiji medical Association estimated that it lost 150 of the country's 280 doctors; the Fiji Law Society said it lost 110 of its 150 solicitors; and the Fiji Institute of Accountants reported losing 150 of its 400 members.

ASIA BY SEGMENTS

The following section divides Asia/Pacific into different, smaller segments — not just for convenience of graphic presentation, but also because many companies consider the countries in the various groups as alternatives when formulating marketing, investment, or licensing plans for the region. For greater ease of comparison, the region has therefore been split into the following segments:

The Giant: Japan

The economic size and weight of Japan in the region is so overwhelming that it cannot reasonably be measured by the same yardstick used for other countries in Asia. Many corporations have recognized Japan's uniqueness and treat it like a region of its own, rather than bringing it under the Asia/Pacific umbrella. Since Japan's GDP alone is larger than the economies of the whole rest of Asia, the country is treated as a segment of the region by itself — and therefore not compared with other countries of the region, but with the world's economic giants elsewhere, particularly the US.

The Whales: China and India

Characterized by huge land masses and enormous populations, China and India also share low per capita incomes and similar stages of economic development. Both also represent difficult markets, but with vast potential.

The Little Dragons: Hong Kong, Korea, Singapore, Taiwan

Aggressive manufacturers and exporters, these relatively small places have developed rapidly and now are — or are fast becoming — interesting markets in their own rights.

South Asia's Minnows: Bangladesh, Burma, Pakistan, Sri Lanka

Low on the ladder of economic development, the four have potential as investment sites, thanks to their sizeable populations and low labor costs. In due time, they are likely to become interesting markets (although Burma would have to abandon its closed economic stance before much progress can be achieved).

The Farms/Quarries: Indonesia, Malaysia, the Philippines, Thailand

Endowed with natural resources, these producers of farm and mining commodities have mixed and sometimes contradictory track records — but all are showing definite signs of progress, and their fortunes may change with rising commodity prices.

The Antipodes: Australia, New Zealand

Asia/Pacific's only countries with Western cultures are wealthy markets, with small populations enjoying high standards of living.

The Anchovies

The rest of the region — Bhutan, Brunei, Macao, Nepal, and Papua New Guinea — is often considered unimportant because these countries represent very small markets that are, moreover, often dominated by close neighbors (India in the case of Bhutan and Nepal, Singapore in the case of Brunei, China and Hong Kong in the case of Macao, and Australia/New Zealand in the case of Papua New Guinea). Yet, some firms have unearthed worthwhile opportunities in these more exotic places.

POPULATION BY SEX AND AGE

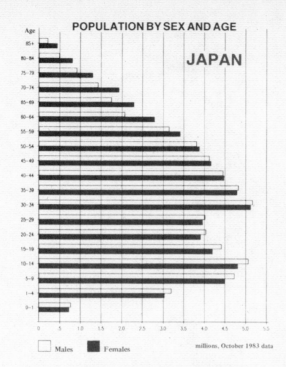

JAPAN

millions, October 1983 data

Males Females

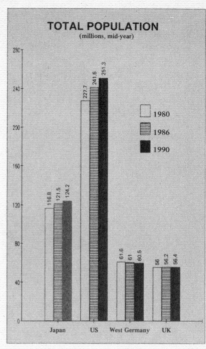

TOTAL POPULATION
(millions, mid-year)

1980
1986
1990

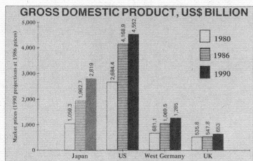

GROSS DOMESTIC PRODUCT, US$ BILLION

1980
1986
1990

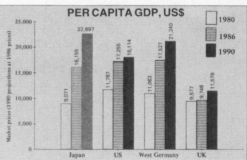

PER CAPITA GDP, US$

1980
1986
1990

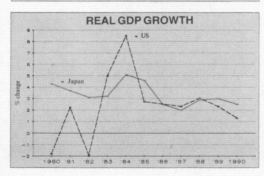

REAL GDP GROWTH

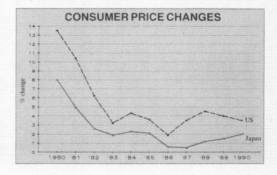

CONSUMER PRICE CHANGES

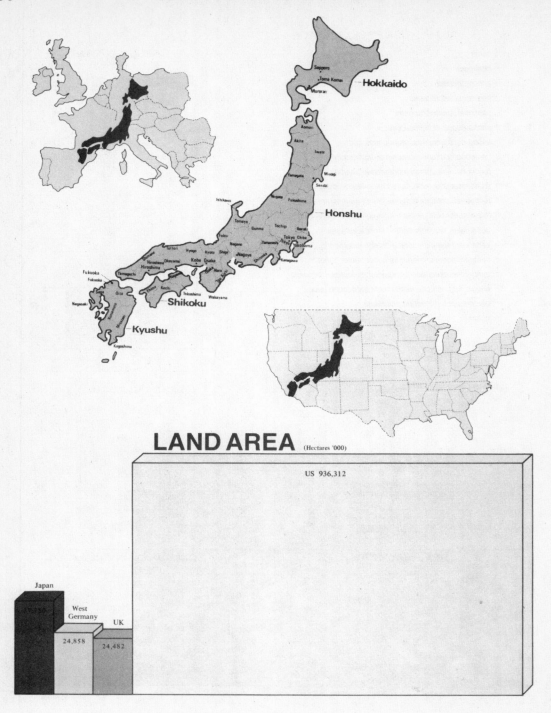

LAND AREA (Hectares '000)

US 936,312

Japan

West Germany
24,858

UK
24,482

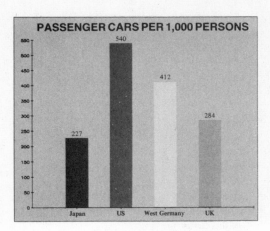

PASSENGER CARS PER 1,000 PERSONS

Japan: 227
US: 540
West Germany: 412
UK: 284

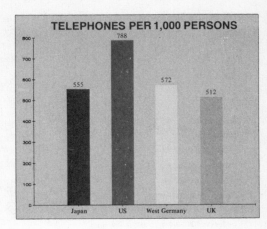

TELEPHONES PER 1,000 PERSONS

Japan: 555
US: 788
West Germany: 572
UK: 512

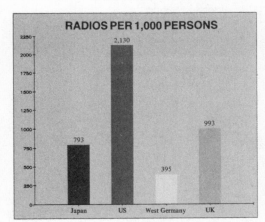

RADIOS PER 1,000 PERSONS

Japan: 793
US: 2,130
West Germany: 395
UK: 993

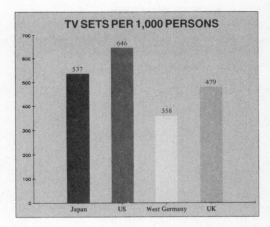

TV SETS PER 1,000 PERSONS

Japan: 537
US: 646
West Germany: 358
UK: 479

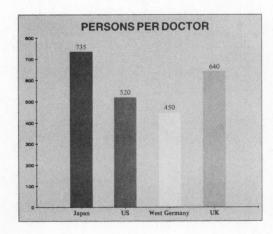

PERSONS PER DOCTOR

Japan: 735
US: 520
West Germany: 450
UK: 640

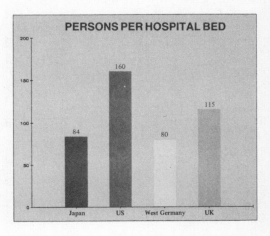

PERSONS PER HOSPITAL BED

Japan: 84
US: 160
West Germany: 80
UK: 115

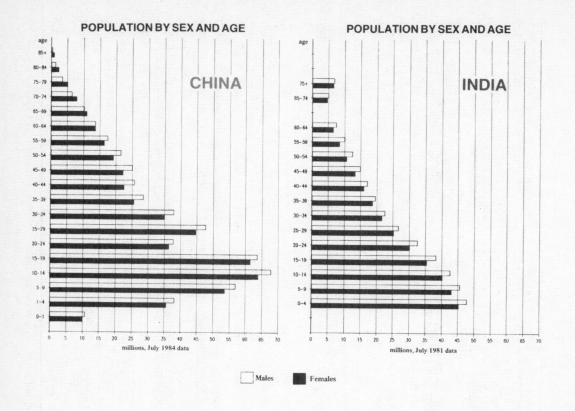

POPULATION BY SEX AND AGE

CHINA

millions, July 1984 data

POPULATION BY SEX AND AGE

INDIA

millions, July 1981 data

☐ Males   ■ Females

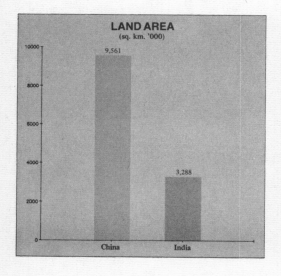

LAND AREA
(sq. km. '000)

9,561

3,288

China   India

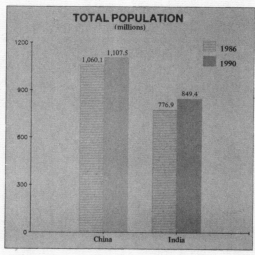

TOTAL POPULATION
(millions)

☐ 1986
■ 1990

1,060.1   1,107.5

776.9   849.4

China   India

THE PEOPLE'S REPUBLIC OF CHINA

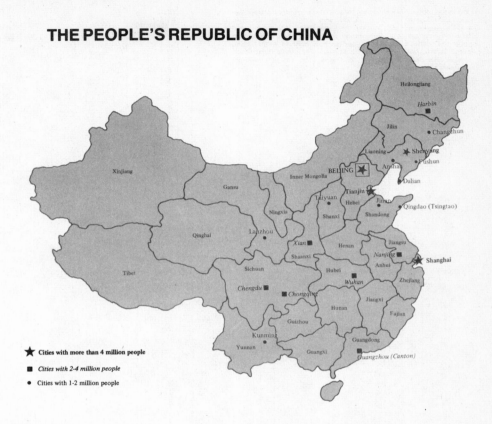

★ **Cities with more than 4 million people**

■ *Cities with 2-4 million people*

● Cities with 1-2 million people

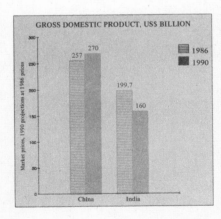

GROSS DOMESTIC PRODUCT, US$ BILLION

Market prices, 1990 projections at 1986 prices

	1986	1990
China	257	270
India	199.7	160

The People's Republic of China is subdivided into several administrative units. These are: 21 Provinces, 3 Municipalities, and 5 Autonomous Regions. The three municipalities — Beijing (or Peking), Tianjin (or Tientsin), and Shanghai — are under the direct control of the central government and treated, for all practical purposes, like provinces.

Officially, China has 22 provinces, not 21 as mentioned above. The one not covered is Taiwan, which is governed by a different government. The regime on Taiwan claims to represent all of China, including the entire mainland. The regime in Beijing claims the same and considers itself the legal government of Taiwan, too.

Autonomous regions are about the same as provinces, but enjoy a greater degree of self-government. China's many ethnic minorities (of which there are 55 different ones) live in greater concentration in these autonomous regions than in other parts of the country.

The five autonomous regions are Guangxi, Inner Mongolia, Ningxia, Tibet, and Xinjiang — all of which are along China's periphery.

THE UNION OF INDIA

All the Indian cities shown below are considered the country's prime urban markets, according to the Urban Market Index published by Hindustan Thompson Associates Ltd.   Among the Indian states, five are believed to have above-average per capita incomes, according to the Indo-American Chamber of Commerce in Bombay. They are, from north to south, Punjab, Haryana, Gujarat, Maharashtra, and Tamil Nadu. The capital Delhi, which is considered a Union Territory rather than a state, also is a relatively wealthy part of the country.

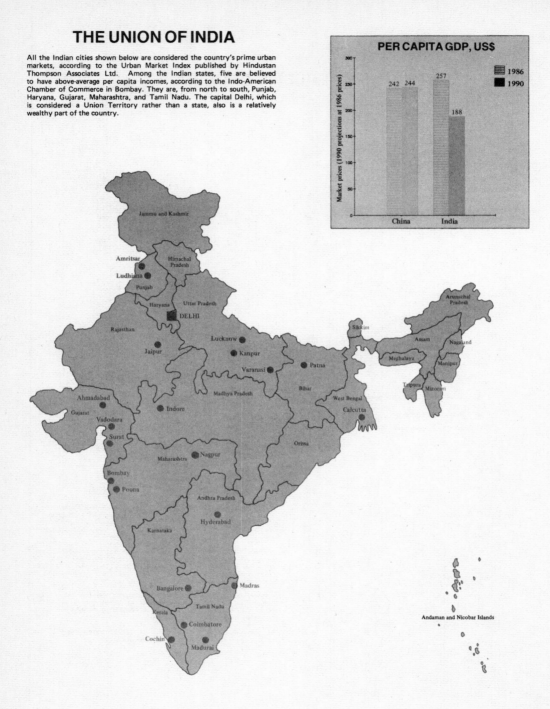

PER CAPITA GDP, US$

Market prices (1990 projections at 1986 prices)

1986
1990

242 244   257   188

China   India

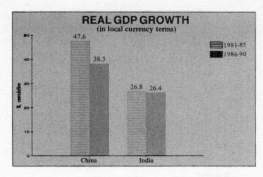

REAL GDP GROWTH
(in local currency terms)

CONSUMER PRICE CHANGES

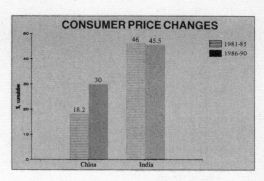

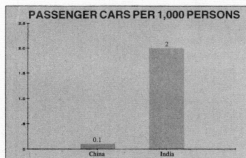

PASSENGER CARS PER 1,000 PERSONS

TELEPHONES PER 1,000 PERSONS

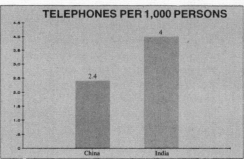

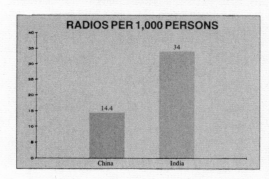

RADIOS PER 1,000 PERSONS

TV SETS PER 1,000 PERSONS

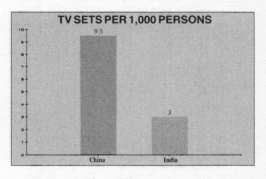

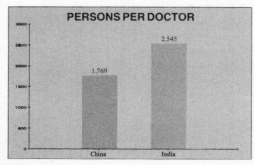

PERSONS PER DOCTOR

PERSONS PER HOSPITAL BED

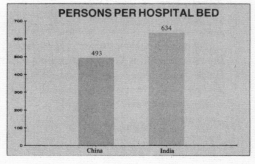

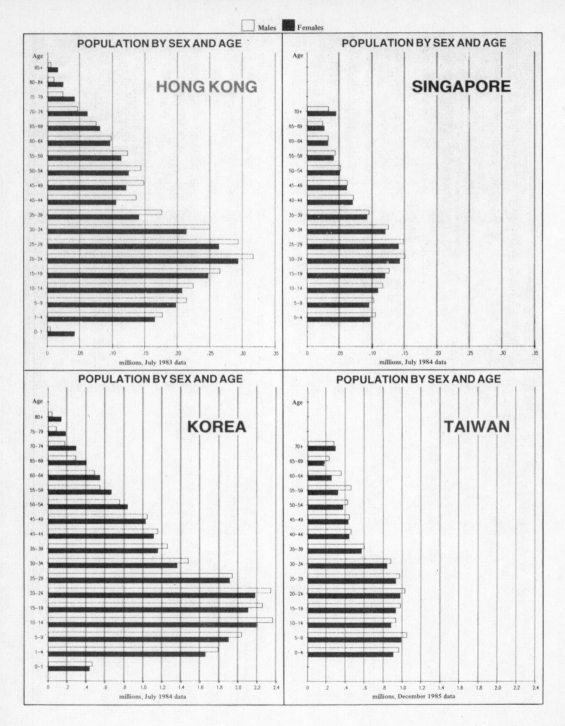

□ Males　■ Females

POPULATION BY SEX AND AGE

HONG KONG

millions, July 1983 data

POPULATION BY SEX AND AGE

SINGAPORE

millions, July 1984 data

POPULATION BY SEX AND AGE

KOREA

millions, July 1984 data

POPULATION BY SEX AND AGE

TAIWAN

millions, December 1985 data

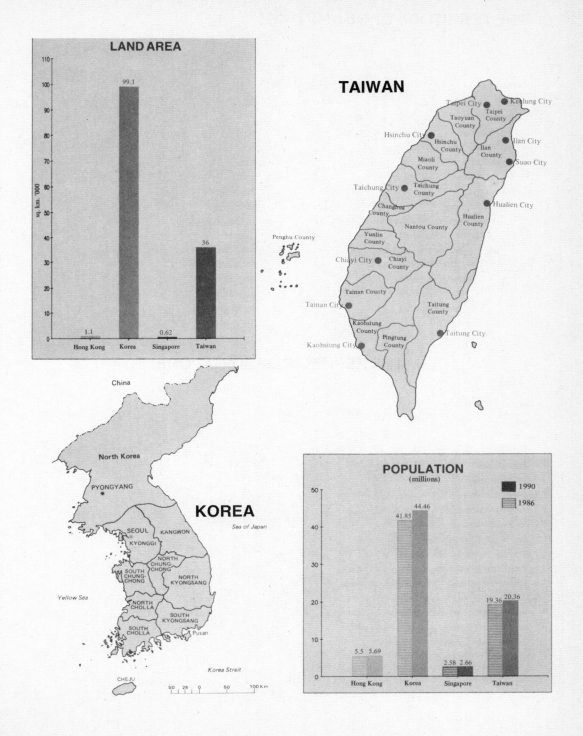

LAND AREA

sq. km. '000

- 99.1 (Korea)
- 36 (Taiwan)
- 1.1 (Hong Kong)
- 0.62 (Singapore)

Hong Kong | Korea | Singapore | Taiwan

TAIWAN

Taipei City · Keelung City · Taipei County · Taoyuan County · Hsinchu City · Hsinchu County · Ilan County · Ilan City · Suao City · Miaoli County · Taichung City · Taichung County · Changhua County · Nantou County · Hualien City · Hualien County · Yunlin County · Chiayi City · Chiayi County · Tainan County · Taitung County · Tainan City · Kaohsiung County · Taitung City · Kaohsiung City · Pingtung County · Penghu County

KOREA

China · North Korea · PYONGYANG · Sea of Japan · SEOUL · KANGWON · KYONGGI · NORTH CHUNG CHONG · SOUTH CHUNG CHONG · NORTH KYONGSANG · Yellow Sea · NORTH CHOLLA · SOUTH KYONGSANG · SOUTH CHOLLA · Pusan · CHEJU · Korea Strait

50 25 0 50 100 Km

POPULATION
(millions)

■ 1990
▦ 1986

- Hong Kong: 5.5 / 5.69
- Korea: 41.85 / 44.46
- Singapore: 2.58 / 2.66
- Taiwan: 19.36 / 20.36

THE TERRITORY OF HONG KONG

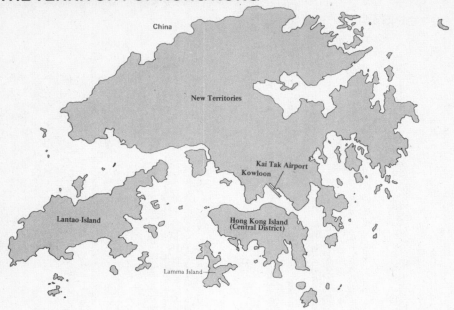

China

New Territories

Kai Tak Airport
Kowloon

Lantao Island

Hong Kong Island
(Central District)

Lamma Island

THE REPUBLIC OF SINGAPORE

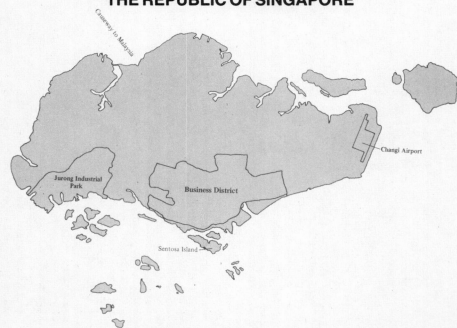

Causeway to Malaysia

Changi Airport

Jurong Industrial
Park

Business District

Sentosa Island

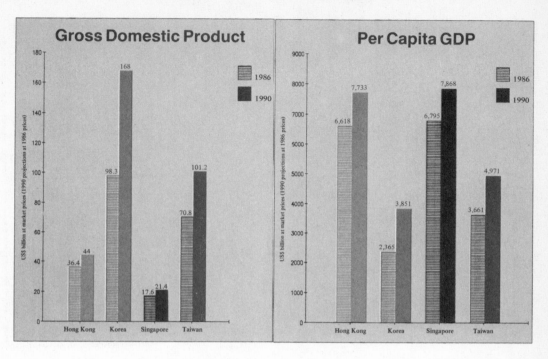

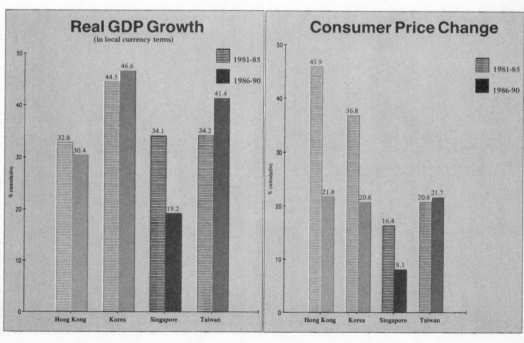

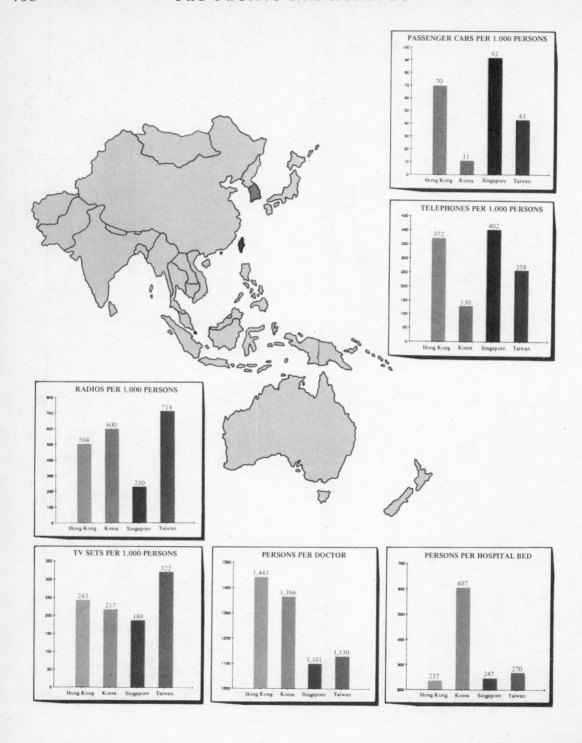

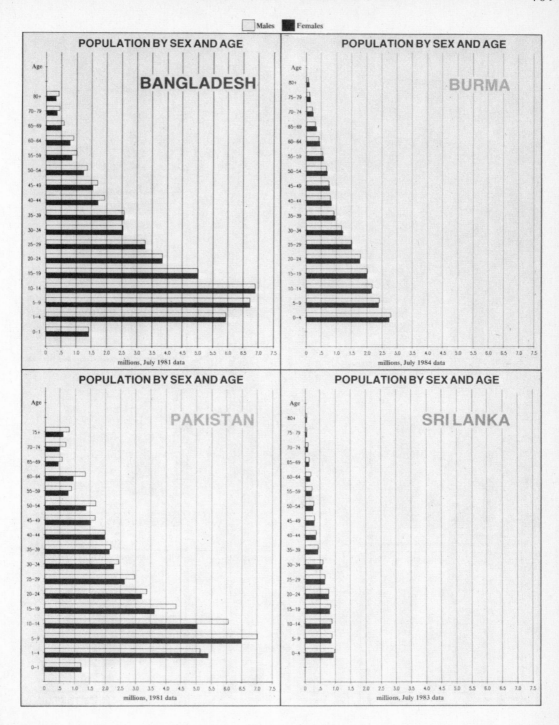

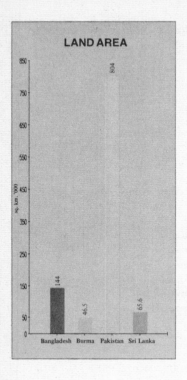

LAND AREA

sq. km. '000

- Bangladesh: 144
- Burma: 46.5
- Pakistan: 804
- Sri Lanka: 65.6

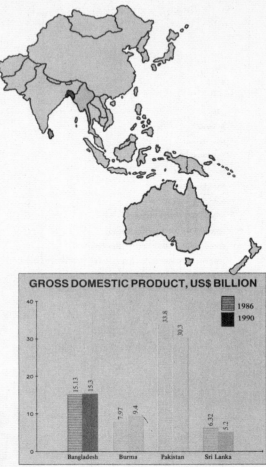

GROSS DOMESTIC PRODUCT, US$ BILLION

1986 / 1990

- Bangladesh: 15.13 / 15.3
- Burma: 7.97 / 9.4
- Pakistan: 33.8 / 30.3
- Sri Lanka: 6.32 / 5.2

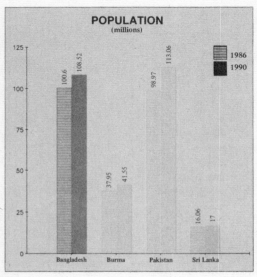

POPULATION
(millions)

1986 / 1990

- Bangladesh: 100.6 / 108.52
- Burma: 37.95 / 41.55
- Pakistan: 98.97 / 113.06
- Sri Lanka: 16.06 / 17

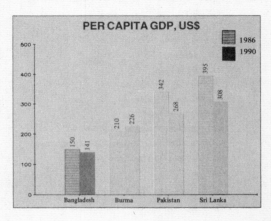

PER CAPITA GDP, US$

1986 / 1990

- Bangladesh: 150 / 141
- Burma: 210 / 226
- Pakistan: 342 / 268
- Sri Lanka: 395 / 308

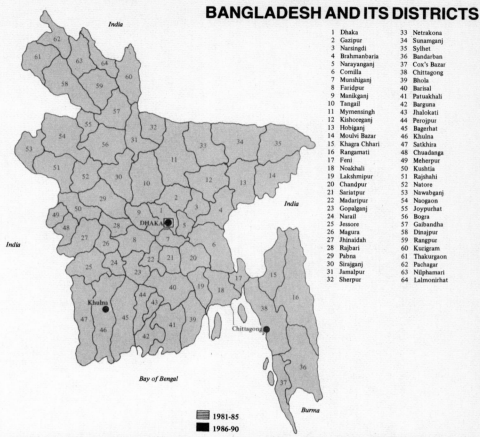

BANGLADESH AND ITS DISTRICTS

India

India

India

DHAKA

Khulna

Chittagong

Bay of Bengal

Burma

1	Dhaka	33	Netrakona
2	Gazipur	34	Sunamganj
3	Narsingdi	35	Sylhet
4	Brahmanbaria	36	Bandarban
5	Narayanganj	37	Cox's Bazar
6	Comilla	38	Chittagong
7	Munshiganj	39	Bhola
8	Faridpur	40	Barisal
9	Manikganj	41	Patuakhali
10	Tangail	42	Barguna
11	Mymensingh	43	Jhalokati
12	Kishoreganj	44	Perojpur
13	Hobiganj	45	Bagerhat
14	Moulvi Bazar	46	Khulna
15	Khagra Chhari	47	Satkhira
16	Rangamati	48	Chuadanga
17	Feni	49	Meherpur
18	Noakhali	50	Kushtia
19	Lakshmipur	51	Rajshahi
20	Chandpur	52	Natore
21	Sariatpur	53	Nawabganj
22	Madaripur	54	Naogaon
23	Gopalganj	55	Joypurhat
24	Narail	56	Bogra
25	Jessore	57	Gaibandha
26	Magura	58	Dinajpur
27	Jhinaidah	59	Rangpur
28	Rajbari	60	Kurigram
29	Pabna	61	Thakurgaon
30	Sirajganj	62	Pachagar
31	Jamalpur	63	Nilphamari
32	Sherpur	64	Lalmonirhat

1981-85
1986-90

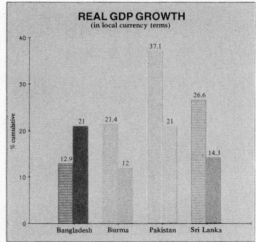

REAL GDP GROWTH
(in local currency terms)

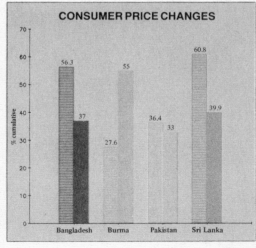

CONSUMER PRICE CHANGES

BURMA

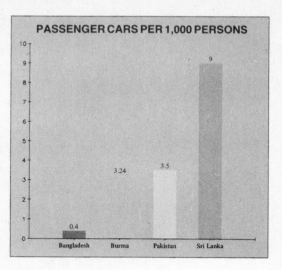

Note that the maps of Bangladesh (preceding page) and Burma (left) are not drawn to the same scale; Bangladesh is, in fact, more than three times Burma's size.

The smallest of the four countries covered in this section, Sri Lanka, is also the most advanced of the group — in terms of per capita GDP, passenger cars, telephones, radios, and TVs per 1,000 people. The poorest of the four, Bangladesh, is also likely to see the fastest real growth, along with Pakistan. The smallest in size, Burma, will probably also develop the slowest.

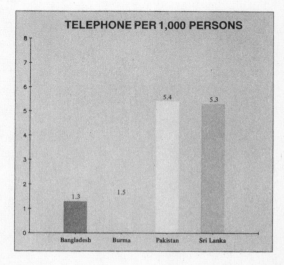

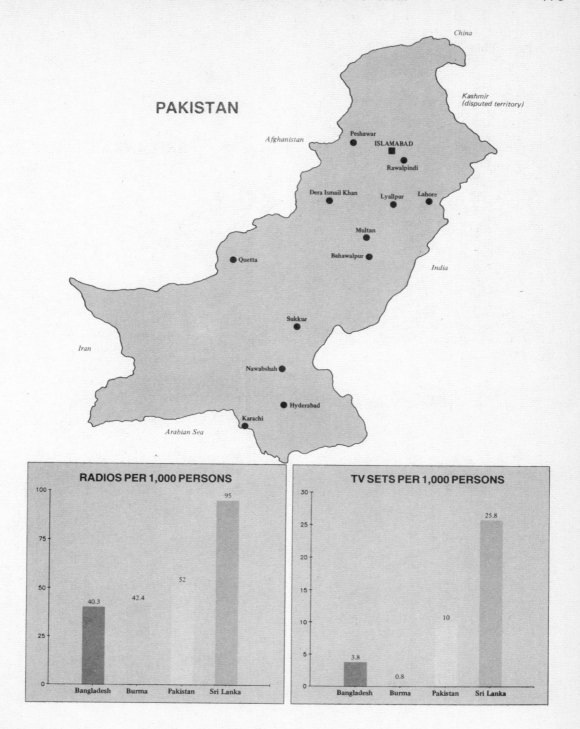

PAKISTAN

China

Kashmir
(disputed territory)

Afghanistan

Peshawar

ISLAMABAD

Rawalpindi

Dera Ismail Khan

Lyallpur

Lahore

Multan

Bahawalpur

India

Quetta

Sukkur

Iran

Nawabshah

Hyderabad

Karachi

Arabian Sea

RADIOS PER 1,000 PERSONS

100

75

50

25

0

40.3 Bangladesh

42.4 Burma

52 Pakistan

95 Sri Lanka

TV SETS PER 1,000 PERSONS

30

25

20

15

10

5

0

3.8 Bangladesh

0.8 Burma

10 Pakistan

25.8 Sri Lanka

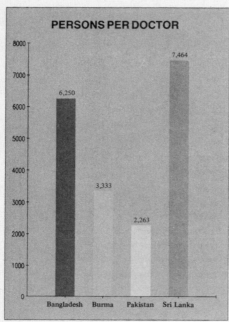

PERSONS PER DOCTOR

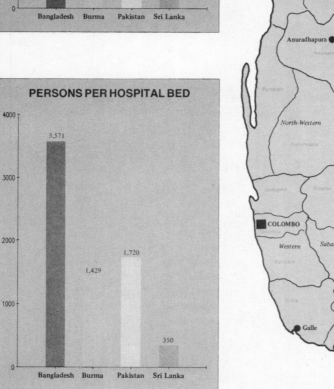

PERSONS PER HOSPITAL BED

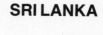

SRI LANKA

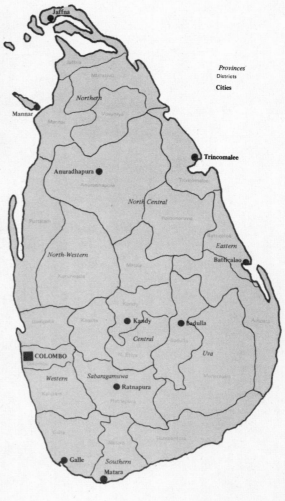

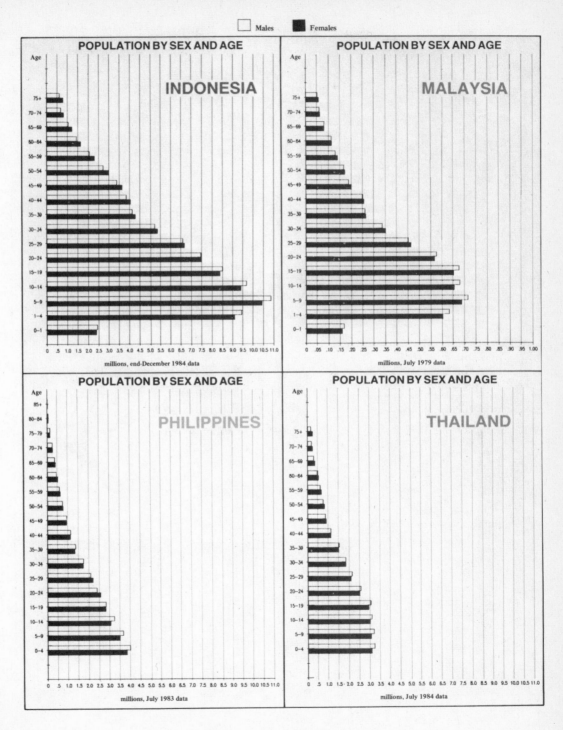

Males Females

POPULATION BY SEX AND AGE

INDONESIA

millions, end-December 1984 data

POPULATION BY SEX AND AGE

MALAYSIA

millions, July 1979 data

POPULATION BY SEX AND AGE

PHILIPPINES

millions, July 1983 data

POPULATION BY SEX AND AGE

THAILAND

millions, July 1984 data

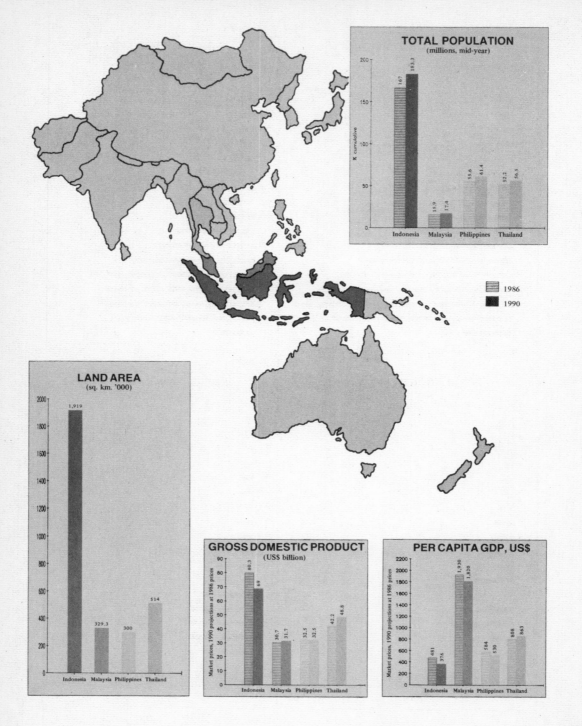

TOTAL POPULATION
(millions, mid-year)

% cumulative

- Indonesia: 167, 183.3
- Malaysia: 15.9, 17.4
- Philippines: 55.6, 61.4
- Thailand: 52.2, 56.5

1986
1990

LAND AREA
(sq. km. '000)

- Indonesia: 1,919
- Malaysia: 329.3
- Philippines: 300
- Thailand: 514

GROSS DOMESTIC PRODUCT
(US$ billion)

Market prices, 1990 projections at 1986 prices

- Indonesia: 80.3, 69
- Malaysia: 30.7, 31.7
- Philippines: 32.5, 32.5
- Thailand: 42.2, 48.8

PER CAPITA GDP, US$

Market prices, 1990 projections at 1986 prices

- Indonesia: 481, 376
- Malaysia: 1,930, 1,820
- Philippines: 584, 530
- Thailand: 808, 863

THE INDONESIAN ARCHIPELAGO

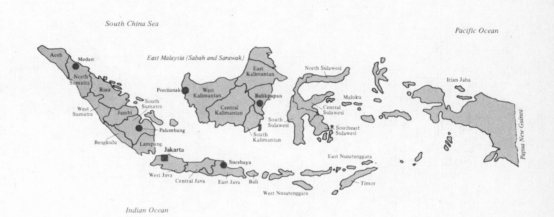

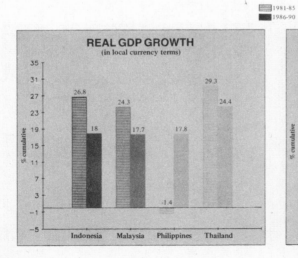

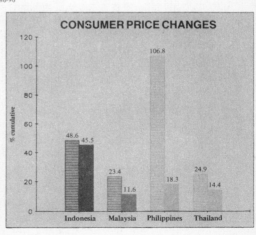

THE FEDERATION OF MALAYSIA

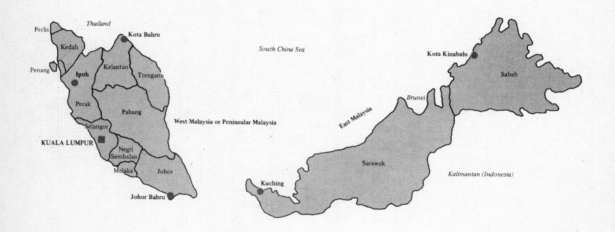

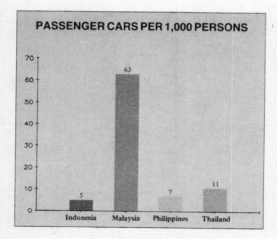

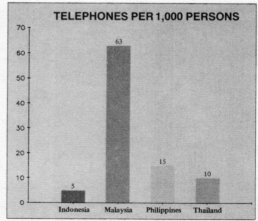

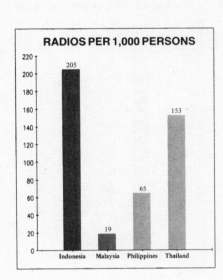

RADIOS PER 1,000 PERSONS

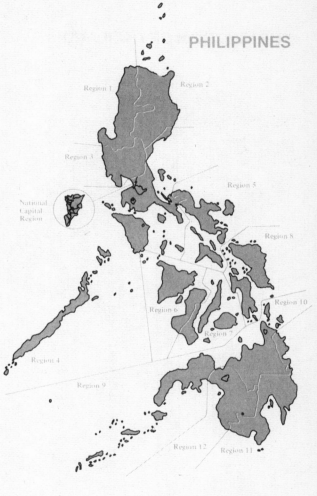

PHILIPPINES

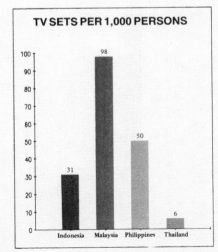

TV SETS PER 1,000 PERSONS

NATIONAL CAPITAL REGION: Metropolitan Manila
REGION 1: Ilocos (regional center, San Fernando, La Union)
REGION 2: Cagayan Valley (regional center, Tuguegarao, Cagayan)
REGION 3: Central Luzon (regional center, San Fernando, Pampanga)
REGION 4: Southern Tagalog (regional center, Metropolitan Manila)
REGION 5: Bicol (regional center, Legaspi City)
REGION 6: Western Visayas (regional center, Iloilo City)
REGION 7: Central Visayas (regional center, Cebu)
REGION 8: Eastern Visayas (regional center, Tacloban City)
REGION 9: Western Mindanao (regional center, Zamboanga)
REGION 10: Northern Mindanao (regional center, Cagayan de Oro)
REGION 11: Southern Mindanao (regional center, Davao City)
REGION 12: Central Mindanao (regional center, Cotabato City)

THE KINGDOM OF THAILAND

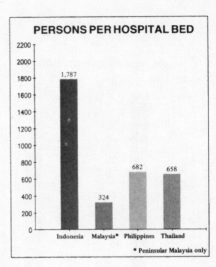

PERSONS PER HOSPITAL BED

* Peninsular Malaysia only

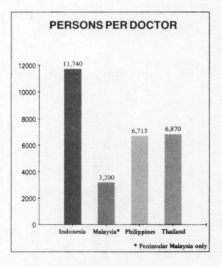

PERSONS PER DOCTOR

* Peninsular Malaysia only

POPULATION BY SEX AND AGE

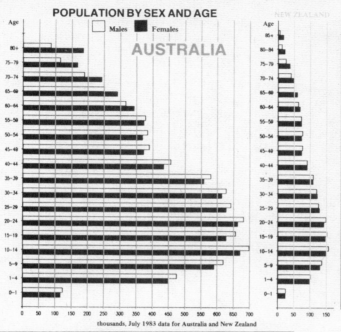

☐ Males ■ Females

AUSTRALIA

NEW ZEALAND

thousands, July 1983 data for Australia and New Zealand

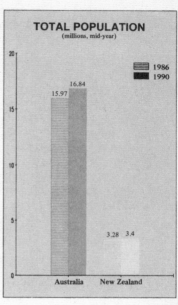

TOTAL POPULATION
(millions, mid-year)

▦ 1986
■ 1990

Australia: 15.97, 16.84
New Zealand: 3.28, 3.4

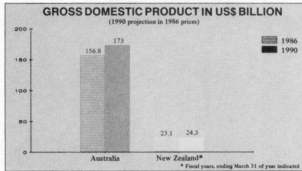

GROSS DOMESTIC PRODUCT IN US$ BILLION
(1990 projection in 1986 prices)

▦ 1986
■ 1990

Australia: 156.8, 173
New Zealand*: 23.1, 24.3

* Fiscal years, ending March 31 of year indicated

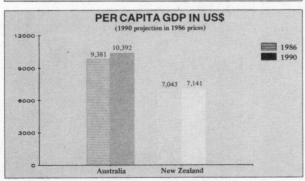

PER CAPITA GDP IN US$
(1990 projection in 1986 prices)

▦ 1986
■ 1990

Australia: 9,381, 10,392
New Zealand: 7,043, 7,141

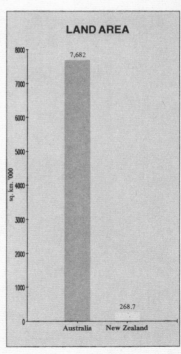

LAND AREA

sq. km. '000

Australia: 7,682
New Zealand: 268.7

THE COMMONWEALTH OF AUSTRALIA

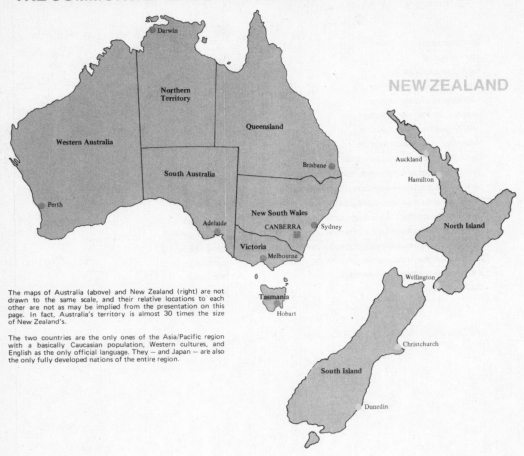

NEW ZEALAND

The maps of Australia (above) and New Zealand (right) are not drawn to the same scale, and their relative locations to each other are not as may be implied from the presentation on this page. In fact, Australia's territory is almost 30 times the size of New Zealand's.

The two countries are the only ones of the Asia/Pacific region with a basically Caucasian population, Western cultures, and English as the only official language. They — and Japan — are also the only fully developed nations of the entire region.

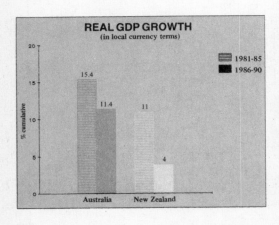

REAL GDP GROWTH
(in local currency terms)

1981-85
1986-90

% cumulative

Australia: 15.4, 11.4
New Zealand: 11, 4

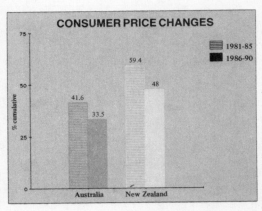

CONSUMER PRICE CHANGES

1981-85
1986-90

% cumulative

Australia: 41.6, 33.5
New Zealand: 59.4, 48

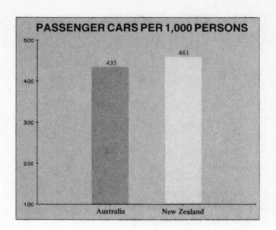

PASSENGER CARS PER 1,000 PERSONS

Australia: 435
New Zealand: 461

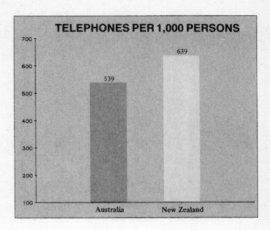

TELEPHONES PER 1,000 PERSONS

Australia: 539
New Zealand: 639

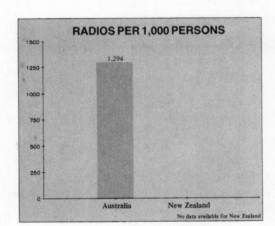

RADIOS PER 1,000 PERSONS

Australia: 1,294
New Zealand: No data available for New Zealand

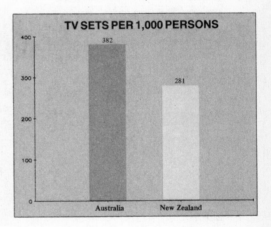

TV SETS PER 1,000 PERSONS

Australia: 382
New Zealand: 281

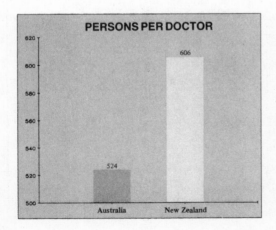

PERSONS PER DOCTOR

Australia: 524
New Zealand: 606

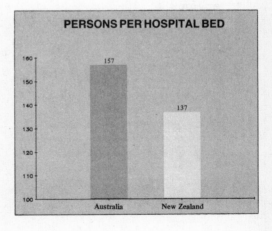

PERSONS PER HOSPITAL BED

Australia: 157
New Zealand: 137

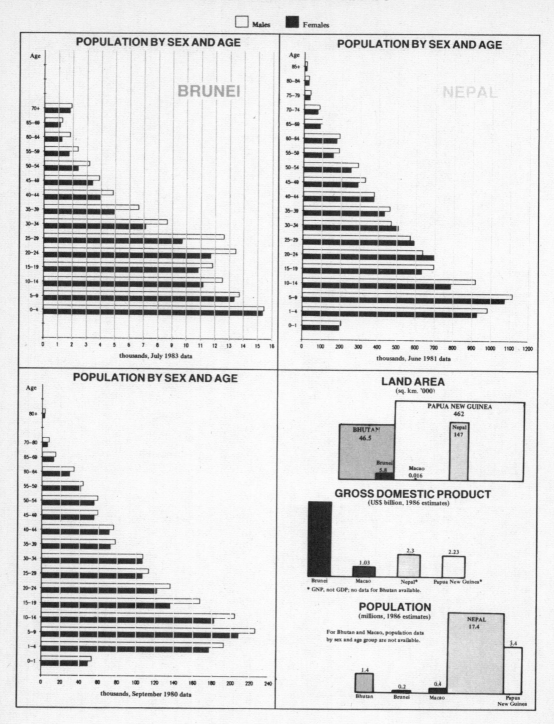

□ Males   ■ Females

POPULATION BY SEX AND AGE

BRUNEI

thousands, July 1983 data

POPULATION BY SEX AND AGE

NEPAL

thousands, June 1981 data

POPULATION BY SEX AND AGE

thousands, September 1980 data

LAND AREA
(sq. km. '000)

PAPUA NEW GUINEA
462

BHUTAN
46.5

Nepal
147

Brunei
5.8

Macao
0.016

GROSS DOMESTIC PRODUCT
(US$ billion, 1986 estimates)

Brunei   Macao 1.03   Nepal* 2.3   Papua New Guinea* 2.23

* GNP, not GDP; no data for Bhutan available.

POPULATION
(millions, 1986 estimates)

For Bhutan and Macao, population data
by sex and age group are not available.

NEPAL
17.4

Bhutan 1.4   Brunei 0.2   Macao 0.4   Papua New Guinea 3.4

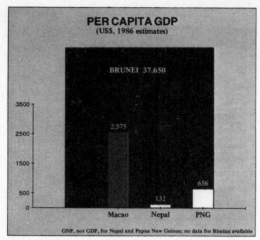

PER CAPITA GDP
(US$, 1986 estimates)

BRUNEI 37,650

2,575

132

656

Macao   Nepal   PNG

GNP, not GDP, for Nepal and Papua New Guinea; no data for Bhutan available

PNG = Papua New Guinea

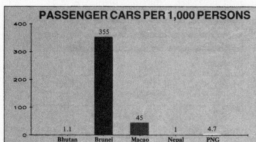

PASSENGER CARS PER 1,000 PERSONS

355

1.1   45   1   4.7

Bhutan Brunei Macao Nepal PNG

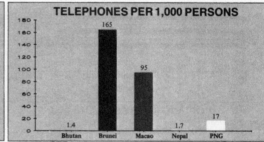

TELEPHONES PER 1,000 PERSONS

165

95

1.4   1.7   17

Bhutan Brunei Macao Nepal PNG

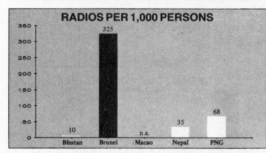

RADIOS PER 1,000 PERSONS

325

10   n.a.   35   68

Bhutan Brunei Macao Nepal PNG

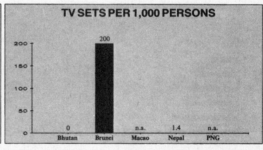

TV SETS PER 1,000 PERSONS

200

0   n.a.   1.4   n.a.

Bhutan Brunei Macao Nepal PNG

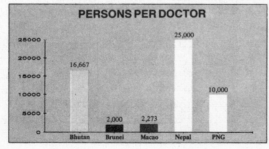

PERSONS PER DOCTOR

16,667

2,000   2,273   25,000   10,000

Bhutan Brunei Macao Nepal PNG

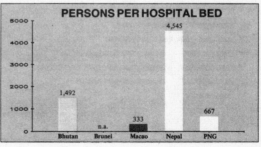

PERSONS PER HOSPITAL BED

1,492

n.a.   333   4,545   667

Bhutan Brunei Macao Nepal PNG

7

❖

INFORMATION

COMMUNICATIONS

STATE MONOLITHS BEGIN TO CRUMBLE

By Michael Selwyin

Telecoms are essential to economic growth, but state corporations cannot keep up with demands created by technology.

Just as sea, air, road, and rail routes supported Asia's economic development in the past, telecommunications will be vital to its growth in the future. More and more of the region's businesses demand—and expect—speedy and reliable service, and Asia's telecommunications industry is having to adapt.

In nearly all countries, telecom services are the preserve of government-owned post, telegraph, and telephone companies. Until re-

cently, their main responsibility was to provide basic services such as telephone and telex lines, and to provide connections with other countries.

No longer. Across Asia governments are realizing that state-of-the-art telecoms are an essential precondition of economic expansion and vital to attracting investment. They are turning to the private sector for help.

Recent events in Europe and North Amer-

486

ica give a hint of what's ahead. In 1984, American Telephone & Telegraph Corp. (AT&T), at that time the biggest corporation in the United States, with assets of U.S.$150 billion, was broken up.

Half of the United Kingdom's national telephone company is now privately owned, and its monopoly status is being dismantled. Throughout the European community (EC) telecoms are being deregulated in readiness for the 1992 single market.

While the quality of service in these regions is relatively uniform, in Asia it varies significantly. For example, in Hong King it takes a couple of minutes to place a call to New York. Yet the same call made from just 30 kilometers away, in China's Guangdong province, can take hours.

The role of the states also varies. In Singapore the government is making a conscious effort to invest in telecoms, through its wholly owned company Singapore Telecom. By contrast, Hong Kong's system is privately owned and unsubsidized. In Japan, the private sector is being encouraged to take a partial, but not exclusive, stake in the telecommunications system.

An example of the potential benefits of privatization and deregulation can be found in Britain. Under state ownership British Telecom (BT) lost the battle for state funds to other sectors such as health and education. It simply did not have the cash to expand and improve its services.

In 1984, 50.2% of BT's share capital was publicly floated. Since then, the number of telephone lines in the United Kingdom has risen from 20 million to 24 million, the proportion of BT's trunk network that has been digitized has gone from zero to 70%, and the subscriber waiting list, which for several years stood at more than 100,000, has been virtually eliminated. Meanwhile Mercury, a competing telephone service run by Cable & Wireless (C&W), is available to half the population.

Some kind of deregulation is on the agenda for just about every post, telegraph and telephone (PPT) company in Asia. The pace is being set by several factors.

The first is growing external political pres-

3-14 Data Bases Available in Japan (1988)

	Number on Record[a]			Real Number[b]		
	Foreign	Domestic	Total	Foreign	Domestic	Total
General	387	207	594	261	158	419
News	145	73	218	109	44	153
Technology	737	95	832	523	88	611
Medicine	171	26	197	101	22	123
Chemistry	105	9	114	83	8	91
Electronics	82	4	86	67	4	71
Society & Culture	110	10	120	68	9	77
Business	804	502	1,306	582	269	851
Business Information	183	135	318	135	65	200
Commodity Markets	89	40	129	63	30	93
World Economy	134	26	160	98	13	111
Finance	133	111	244	96	42	138
Other	2	4	6	2	4	6
Total	**2,040**	**818**	**2,858**	**1,436**	**528**	**1,964**

a) Statistics from distributors; some overlap included. b) Overlap excluded.
Source: MITI.

11-13 Communications Media

	Mail	Telephone	Television
	No. of letters sent in one year (per person)	No. of phones Per 100 people	No. of TV sets Per 100 people
Japan	**166**	**40.8**	**26.6**
U.S.A.	659	48.1	82.8
U.K.	245	42.4	34.3
Germany, F.R.	253	45.0	37.7
France	329	44.7	32.7
Canada	315	44.5	56.0
Sweden	447	65.6	39.1
Switzerland	712	52.9	35.8
Denmark	332	55.1	35.8

Source: Ministry of Posts and Telecommunications.

sure. In 1987 the British government forced Japan to allow C&W to make a major equity stake in one of Japan's two independent international phone operators. South Korea has been ordered to open up some of its telecom services to U.S. firms, or face trade sanctions under the "Super 301" provisions of the 1988 Omnibus Trade Act.

Second, Asia faces the challenge of keeping up with technology, which has made available a range of new services that were undreamed-of until recently, and for which PPTs weren't conceived. These include services such as facsimile, cordless phones, mobile communications system, high-speed data transmission, and electronic mail.

"Ten years ago you could say telecoms applications were awaiting the technology. Now the situation is reversed and the technology is awaiting the applications," says Hong Kong Telephone Co.'s general manager David Connolly.

This has caused chaos in some Asian cities. In Bangkok, for example, the two state telephone companies are battling for a share of the portable phone market, but the government has made little effort at coordination or

forward planning. Meanwhile the basic telephone network is still underdeveloped; Thailand has just 1.8 phones per 100 people, compared with the world average of 19.6.

Third, investment is proving too burdensome for many governments battling to balance their budgets and rein in foreign debt. While Singapore plans to spend U.S.$1 billion in the next five years to make its telephone network entirely digital, Thailand's PTTs are hamstrung by the Finance Ministry's U.S.$1.2 billion a year ceiling on foreign borrowings by state enterprises.

Fourth, the business sectors to which the PTTs cater have become a great deal more demanding.

"This is a direct result of the globalization of industries such as machinery, finance, petroleum, food, and entertainment," says Dwight Jasmann, president of AT&T Communications Pacific. Financial services, in particular, depend on first-rate telecommunications.

But the path toward liberalization isn't always a smooth one. In the Philippines the three large telephone operators and 40 local companies give the illusion of competition, but the system is woefully inefficient, a legacy of corruption during the Marcos years. Many parts of the country have no phone service at all, the overall penetration rate is only 1.32 lines per 100 people, and the waiting list stands at 400,000. Even in Hong Kong, where the level of sophistication in telecoms is second to none, the government's policy of fostering competition via a second telecommunications network has drawn accusations of ineptitude and mismanagement.

CHALLENGES OF PRIVATIZATION

Making public utilities (PUs) attractive to private investors isn't easy. In some cases they are still run as government departments—overmanned and self-serving—with staff unions rigidly opposed to commercialism. A lot of restructuring is needed before they can be floated.

Malaysia is a good example. Three years ago its PTT was taken away from the civil service and reestablished as a corporation, Syarikat Telekom Malaysia (STM), wholly owned by the Finance Ministry. The government is aiming to float STM on the Kuala Lumpur stock exchange in two years' time.

But first chairman Rashdan Baba wants to groom STM into a commercially oriented, market-driven entity. "Sometimes I wish the thinking of STM staff could be privatized," he was reported to saying recently. Two new divisions, marketing and customer services, have been created to win new subscribers.

STM's staffing ratio of 22 per 1,000 lines is being cut to around 145. Corporate debts, which stood at M$4.86 billion (U.S.$1.8 billion) at the end of 1987, are being paid off. And, in its advertising, STM now projects itself as, "Your business communications partner."

Because PTTs are such large organizations, their flotations test the mettle of Asia's emerging stock markets. STM is again a case in point. In 1987 its government-held share capital was already larger than that of any publicly listed Malaysian company.

Shareholders' funds amounted to M$2.16 billion (U.S.$801 million), surpassing some of Sime Darby (M$1.7 billion, U.S.$630 million) and Malaysian Airlines (M$724 million, U.S.$268 million). Even if only 10% of the government's stake were offered to the public, the offer would qualify as the country's biggest share issue.

The problem isn't confined to Asia's developing economies. At the other end of the scale, the Japanese government's sale of share in Nippon Telegraph & Telephone (NTT) has

run into problems. When the first block of shares was offered, in 1987, NTT was the hottest new issue on the Tokyo stock exchange. Within days the price of shares in the Japanese giant (it is capitalized at Y23.56 trillion, or U.S.$165 billion) has doubled to an extraordinary Y3 million (U.S.$21,000).

But NTT's stock price slumped in 1989, and was back to the 1987 starting price of Y1.6 million (U.S.$11,200). Fearing that a further issue would drain liquidity from a market that has already seen trading volume halved in the first eight months of this year, finance minister Ryutaro Hashimoto shelved a fourth sale of shares.

Whether publicly or privately owned, the market clout of PTTs can be a major factor in discouraging potential newcomers. In the United Kingdom, an independent regulatory agency, Oftel, seeks to ensure competition. It has barred British Telecom from certain markets, allowing rival networks like Mercury to gain a foothold. Says one observer, "Creating a competitive environment sometimes requires reregulation rather than deregulation."

But Jacqueline Ganim, who heads the Asia-Pacific operations of U.S. regional telephone operator Nynex, argues that, "Technology has made it easier for new companies to enter the market.

"Previously, the capital intensity of telecommunications kept many firms out. But now, with cellular telephone technology well-established, the cost of installing a mobile phone network isn't so prohibitive. A lot of companies you wouldn't have associated with telecoms a few years ago are trying to get in."

INVASION OF FOREIGN TELECOMS

This trend is particularly evident in Hong Kong, where investment company First Pacific brought 50% of the territory's third mo-

Asian Telephone Systems, 1988

| | Business lines | | International outgoing calls | | |
	Phones per 1,000 population	No. of lines	% of total lines	No. of calls (millions)	% change from 1987
Australia	555.0	1,800,000	26.9	47.8	+38.0
Burma	1.5	NAª	NA	NA	NA
China	6.0	NA	NA	NA	NA
Hong Kong	428.0	573,918	28.9	71.7	+63.0
Indonesia	5.0	NA	NA	6.8	+30.7
Japan	555.0	15,400,000	30.9	88.7	+40.0
Korea	183.0	1,700,000	19.4	23.0	+49.0
Malaysia	91.0	332,997	29.4	6.9	+50.0
New Zealand	670.0	342,608	24.9	15.6	+48.5
Philippines	15.0	187,482	42.2	7.8	+24.0
Singapore	420.0	249,034	28.4	30.8	+42.5
Sri Lanka	6.6	58,700	6.0	NA	NA
Taiwan	264.0	1,270,000	25.9	34.4	+62.3
Thailand	15.0	336,401	37.3	NA	NA

ª NA, Not available.
Source: AT&T, Business International.

bile telephone network, Cinatel, now called Pacific Link. Through another subsidiary, Asialink, it plans to set up cellular phone/paging networks in Malaysia, the Philippines, Thailand, Indonesia, and Australia.

Telecoms is also one of the fastest-growing areas of leading Hong Kong trading house Hutchison Whampoa. Within the territory, its affiliate Hutchison Telecom runs one of the world's most advanced mobile communications systems.

Overseas, it has bought a 55% stake in Australia's leading paper company, has entered the satellite communications business, and is setting up the United Kingdom's first mobile data network. "We're also actively looking at four or five other Asian markets," says Hutchison Telecom marketing director Fred Sum.

As competition for telecom services in Asia intensifies, Nynex's Ganim says, "The people with the greatest advantage will be companies that already offer an international service."

Nynex's target customers are telecom authorities, government agencies with large private network requirements, private companies with local and regional needs, and multinationals with global requirements.

Asia is already witnessing an invasion of foreign telecom companies. At least three "baby Bell" U.S. regional telephone companies have set up Asian regional offices in Hong Kong. The latest arrival, U.S. West, was part of the winning consortium for Hong Kong's cable TV network. Says vice-president for Asia, Alan Khoo, "The potential regional growth in telecommunications and related services is enormous."

Just how far deregulation will go is unclear. Some countries are considering using the state telephone company to provide basic switched voice communication, while hiving off value-added services such as data, video, and fax transmission to private companies.

But technology had already overtaken this concept; the introduction of digital networks, which enables both types of service to be carried on the same line, has blurred the distinction between the two types of communication.

Perceptions of the role of telecoms in Asia's economic and social fabric are therefore changing rapidly. Unregulated competition can mean chaos; however, if harnessed wisely, competition can deliver the right technology and the right kind of service.

MALAYSIAN VILLAGES ON-LINE

Every village in Malaysia will have at least one public telephone by the twenty-first century under a multimillion *ringgit* program drawn up by the Federal Government, according to Malaysia's newspaper, *The Star*.

SINGAPORE'S OPTIC-FIBER RIM

"Go for IT," is Singapore's rallying cry for the Information Age. IT stands for *information technology*. Singapore has a master plan calling for the transformation of this island republic of 2.6 million people into an "IT culture." Officials at the National Computer Board say Singapore had 1,200 computers installed per million people in 1986—second in Asia after Japan which had 1,500 computers installed per million people in 1985.

Singapore Telecom and France Telecom are jointly planning an optical fiber submarine cable which, when completed, will link Pacific Rim countries with Europe. Meanwhile similar cable linkup is under construction—to be completed by 1995—between Malaysia, Indonesia, Brunei, Thailand, and the Philippines, with the telecommunications administrations of these countries collaborating with Singapore Telecom. The cost is expected to reach $550 million.

As a result of an agreement signed with an American international paging company, Mobile Telecommunication Technologies Corp., Singapore became the first Asian country to introduce direct international paging in 1990. An overseas traveler can hear his pager beep within seconds of receiving an international call.

Singapore Telecoms and leading British telecom firm GEC-Marconi jointly developed a sophisticated telephone- and television-linked information system called Teleview. It reportedly offers significant technology advancements over France's pioneering Minitel videotex system. The new service was launched commercially in Singapore in 1990.

CELLULAR PHONES IN SINGAPORE SUBWAYS

Singapore's Telecommunications Authority introduced light portable cellular phones on the nation's underground railway system in 1989. This $15 million, first-ever mass transit cellular phone project is part of Singapore's bid to strengthen its "global position as a Total Business Center," according to Singapore Communications and Information Minister Yeo Ning Hong. He revealed that Singapore's telecommunication network would be entirely adapted to an Integrated Systems Digital Network (ISDN) system by the mid-1990s. (ISDN is the state-of-the-art telecommunications technology which enables high-quality transmission of voice, pictures, computer data, and text over optical fiber cables.)

HOW TELECOM SERVICES IN ASIA ARE OPENING UP

AUSTRALIA

At present domestic services are provided by Telecom Australia (TA), international services by OTC, and domestic satellite services by Aussat. Outright privatization is unlikely, but further deregulation is likely.

Some of TA's activities have already been liberalized, such as supply of terminal equipment and value-added services. Long-distance links may follow and TA's monopoly on first phone installation is up for review in 1991.

HONG KONG

The franchise for public domestic switched services is held by Hong Kong Telephone, and for international telecommunications by Cable & Wireless (HK). Both companies are part of the Hong Kong Telecom group, which is in turn owned 75% by Cable & Wireless of the United Kingdom.

The franchises expire in 1995 and 2006, respectively. The government has signaled greater competition in the future by awarding a license for the territory's first cable TV system, which will form the basis of a second telecoms network, to Hong Kong Cable Communication in open bidding.

Customer equipment, computer services, mobile radio networks, paging systems, and value-added services are not franchised.

JAPAN

In 1986 the government announced a partial sell-off of Nippon Telegraph & Telephone (NTT), the country's largest company, which would have placed 32% of NTT in private hands. Three blocks of 1.95 million shares have been sold so far, but a fourth offer of stock has been shelved.

Since 1987 NTT's monopoly on domestic longdistance calls has been challenged by Daini-Denden Inc. (DDI), Japan Telecom Co. (JTC), and Teleway Japan Corp. (TJC).

On international services, Kokusai Denshin Denwa (KDD) now faced competition from International Telecom Japan (ITJ), formed by a group including Mitsubishi and Mitsui, and International Data Communications (IDC), whose members include C Itoh, Toyota Motor, the United Kingdom's Cable & Wireless, and the United States' Pacific Telesis. Both are offering international calls at rates 23% below KDD's.

The government is expected to allow foreign companies to buy up to 20% of the public shares in both NTT and KDD.

SOUTH KOREA

The state-owned Telecommunications Authority (KTA) operates the domestic and international voice-switched networks, while value-added services are now run by Data Communication Corp. (Dacom), in which the government has a 51% stake, KTA 33%, and major private corporations 16%.

KTA disposed of its shareholding in Dacom in 1990 and both companies will be able to compete for each other's markets, thus creating two telecom companies.

The United States wants the value-added sector to be opened to foreign firms. The Communication Ministry says this will take two or three years to organize.

MALAYSIA

In 1986 the government reconstituted Jabatan Telekom, its telecommunications department, into a corporation, Syarikat Telekom Malaysia (STM), in an effort to increase efficiency. Last year STM's net profits soared 36-fold to M$180 million (U.S.$67 million). A stock market flotation is planned for 1991.

NEW ZEALAND

The Labor government says it is considering privatizing Telecom Corp. of New Zealand. If this goes ahead, it would add to a string of disposals of state assets that began two years ago. Telecom's net profit in the year (1989) to March 31 more than tripled to NZ$240 million (U.S.$144 million) from NZ$68.9 million (U.S.$41 million) in 1987/1988.

PHILIPPINES

Although private telephone companies are permitted, Philippine Long Distance & Telecommunications Co. (PLDT) holds a 94% share of long-distance traffic. The Aquino government says it wants to reduce this to 50%.

Digital Telecommunications Philippines (Digitel), 40%-owned by Cable & Wireless and 60% by local investors, is seeking to develop a new national telephone network and offer international services. But Digitel's license application has triggered strong opposition.

SINGAPORE

A study on possible privatization of Singapore Telecom (ST) is being conducted by management consultants Coopers & Lybrand. No decision has been taken on the timing of a sell-off.

TAIWAN

Partial deregulation of the telecom network took effect on July 1, 1989, when the government announced that private Taiwanese firms could offer value-added networks. These cover infor-

(continued)

mation storage and retrieval services; information-processing services; remote transaction services (such as home banking); voice-mail business services; and electronic mail.

The government will still control basic services, such as telephone, telegraph, telex, and packet switching. The existing telecommunications law, which is several decades old, prohibits foreign firms from promoting telecom services, but this is under review.

THAILAND

For the past 35 years the domestic network has been operated by Telephone Organization of Thailand (TOT). International services are handled by Communications Authority of Thailand (CAT). TOT, which is the country's third most profitable state enterprise, last year notching up gross profits of 2.7 billion *baht* (U.S.$105 million), is being considered for privatization.

Several options are being discussed, including flotation on the Securities Exchange of Thailand (SET), exemption from the Finance Ministry's U.S.$1.2 billion a year ceiling on borrowing by state enterprises, and the creation of a partly private, partly state-owned company to arrange equipment purchases.

Reported by Martin Barnett in Hong Kong, Michael Cross in Tokyo, and Peter Janssen in Thailand. © *Asian Business* magazine, Far East Trade Press, Ltd., 1989.

TRANSPAC TALK UP

According to AT&T, telephone traffic between Japan and America has been increasing at the rate of about 30% a year.

THANK YOU CALL—COMPLETE WITH TRANSLATOR

The wave of "internationalization" being what it is, each summer a myriad of Japanese youngsters travel abroad for "home stay" experience with foreign families. To serve that market, KDD's subsidiary, Teleserve, has initiated a new service called, "Thank You Call." It's only Y3,900 (about $30) for up to 10 minutes, complete with a translator to turn their Japanese into English—not counting the telephone charge from the telecommunications firm Nippon Telegraph & Telephone and KDD.

DIAL-A-DIALECT

Hong Kong businessmen are now able to communicate in seven languages over the phone with the help of a service providing instantaneous translation. Rates are about $39 for the first half-hour in addition to the regular conference call rates. "It is often quite difficult to do it by other means," says John Thody, project manager for Communication Services, Ltd. "With telex you can't have the on-going dialog." Languages available are English, Japanese, French, German, Italian, and two Chinese dialects.

HOLD THE SUBTITLES

Back in 1985, Koji Kobayashi, chairman of Japanese computer giant NEC, revealed his vision for a winning future product. His dream was that one day he would be able to pick up his phone, speak in Japanese and be heard at the other end in English. Today, NEC is on the verge of launching precisely this revolution in language translation. The company claims to have developed a voice recognition system that can translate Japanese speech—and even jargon—into English and vice versa.

NEC says this machine can be used to translate international phone calls because it is able to recognize any human voice rather than just a single individual's voice patterns. Potential uses include translation services for business negotiations, reservations and other applications which require abilities in different languages.

TALKING HEADS

NTT Regatt Co., a subsidiary of Nippon Telegraph & Telephone Corp., introduced a telephone with two receivers so that three people can chat at the same time (priced at about $117).

BUSY SIGNALS

The Republic of China on Taiwan is now the world's leading producer of telephones, supplying 20 million annually to the world market. Taiwan is outproducing Japanese, South Korean, and Hong Kong phone-makers, it was reported by Japan Industry and Technology Information Express, a Tokyo-based industry watchdog publication.

As part of its push to increase trade with the Eastern Bloc, Taiwan has launched direct-dialing telephone service to nine East European nations, including the Soviet Union and Albania.

Citing a survey by the Japan Economic and Industrial Research Institute, the report noted that the ROC, Hong Kong, South Korea, Singapore, Thailand, and Malaysia are stealing world markets from Western industrialized nations by producing low-cost quality telephone equipment. The survey further projects that export products from these newly industrialized nations will capture 30% of the world market by 1993.

U.S. CABLE TV COMPANY IN HONG KONG DEAL

The American cable television company U.S. West is a partner in a Hong Kong consortium, led by Hong Kong tycoon Sir Y.K. Pao, which was awarded what is being described as "the biggest cable TV franchise in the world" in 1989. The Hong Kong government accepted a $705 million bid from the Hong Kong Cable Communications consortium for a six-year exclusive franchise to operate cable TV in Hong Kong. U.S. West owns 25% of the shares in the company. Potentially, the cable TV consortium could have 1.6 million subscribers. But analysts say the real value of the franchise is the ability of the cable TV network to carry nonvoice telephone service. It also puts the franchise in a good position to bid against Hongkong Telecommunications when that company's monopoly of internal telephone services ends in the mid-1990s.

DUMB "BELL" AWARD?

Nittsuko, a communications equipment firm, has developed what is the world's first cordless pay phone (basic model priced at about $1,675). They're targeting coffee shops, beauty salons, and restaurants. The big marketing question is, how many phones will disappear at the end of the day as the result of conversations that find themselves "wandering," off the premises perhaps?

JAPANESE VOICE MAIL

Voice mail works on a system of code numbers. If you know the code number of a person's voice mail box, you can leave a message on the computer. The person then uses his or her code number to retrieve the message at their leisure.

Now Misawa VAN has added a new twist to the voice mail market. They sell prepaid cards, two to the packet, for about ($9.20). These cards allow the holders 130 calls. Misawa has centers in Tokyo, Nagoya, and Osaka. The cards can be used at any of the centers. Just call the center, enter the code number with the telephone dial pad, record your message in less than a minute, and hang up. The centers are on call 24 hours a day.

NTT (Nippon Telegraph & Telephone), on the other hand, lets you set your own code number. But the service is only available eight hours a day. The usage of voice mail in Japan in 1989 ran to about 20,000 messages a day, according to *Asahi Shimbun*.

TELEPHONE CARD VENDING MACHINES

Mituskoshi Department Store in Tokyo's Ginza district sells pre-paid telephone cards in their vending machine corner called "Hello Shop." More than 60 versions of cards selling up to Y250,000 (about $2,000) a day make the corner one of the most efficient in the whole store. One of the most popular cards during the summer of 1989 was the French Revolution Bicentennial Commemorative Card, selling about 1,600 a month from "Hello Shop."

During 1988, 257 million telephone cards were sold, up 12.4% from the year before. Some 49.8% are held by collectors and have never been used, according to *Nihon Keizai Shimbun*.

KOREA'S STATE-WRITTEN HOROSCOPE

Korea Telecommunication Authority (KTA) has introduced a new service to its telex subscribers: Dial-a-fortune-teller. KTA now provides a state-written horoscope and business advice for the coming year.

JAPAN'S FAX REVOLUTION: TAKING IT TO THE STREETS

Japan's fax culture is now spreading from the office environment—where an estimated 90% of all major companies are already fax-equipped—to the streets.

There are now 50,000 coin-operated "pay fax" machines—called *"gaito* fax" (or "street fax")—scattered throughout the nation in public places, such as railroad stations, convenience stores, stationery shops, and telephone companies.

In 1987, Japan's fax industry reached $21.4 billion, producing 2.8 million units, according to the Communications Industry Association of Japan. After saturating an estimated 90% of Japan's corporate market, home demand is now spurring the industry forward.

Japan's fax revolution is now spawning a slew of new service industries, according to a recent report by the *Japan Times*. Among them, the Japanese McDonald's has installed fax machines to receive take-out orders. Nippon Telegraph & Telephone is promoting "F-Net," a facsimile network which offers members information about new cars, health advice, and listing of winning lottery numbers. F-Net also offers a system for transmitting faxes to 100 destinations simultaneously.

Dial Service Co., Ltd., sponsored by NEC Corp., has launched *"Magokoro* (Heartfelt) Communication," a fax service for the handicapped. Private tutoring "cram schools" are using faxes to teach students at home. And Japan's Housing and Urban Development Corp. has built hundreds of apartments equipped with fax machines.

After running a successful pilot program in Osaka and Tokyo, Johnson & Johnson KK is setting up home fax machines for their salesmen all over Japan so they can fax their daily reports to the office instead of trudging in with the reports in person. With the extra time they now have, salesmen are now able to concentrate on developing new accounts.

TOWER BRIDGE CARD

Japan's telecommunications giant Nippon Telegraph & Telephone Corp. opened a subsidiary in England called NTT Europe (London). But its products and services are not aimed at the European market. The company sells souvenir telephone (pre-paid) cards to Japanese tourists. They can only be bought in London yet used only in Japan. There are four designs including the best-selling Tower Bridge Card.

INDIA'S UNDERGROUND FAX CULTURE

Fax machines became one of India's hottest smuggled items in 1988, causing the giant state-run telephone companies to retaliate with a price war, after legal measures proved ineffectual. The fax, which can transmit graphs, letters, pictures, and large documents in seconds, is a revolutionary concept in India, where queuing in a government telex office can take hours and private telephone connections are unpredictable and costly. An estimated 300 private fax owners are selling their services in small booths and offices in Bombay, the country's commercial heart.

CHINESE PHONES

Grappling with overburdened exchanges and corruption among workers, China is currently adding 1.25 million telephones to its system to bring a total of 13.5 million into operation throughout the country by 1990. Only Japan has more telephones than China among Asian countries, but on a per-capita basis China has only one phone per 90 people and user demand is increasing faster than telephone exchange capacity. Compounding the problem is the fact that many jump their places on the waiting list by bribing installers, a custom not unknown in the West.

POLES APART

The *Liberation Army Daily* announced the arrest of four people for cutting down telephone poles and using them to build houses. Military communications had also been interrupted, the paper added, by the theft in northeastern China of telephone cable which had been cut up and sold as scrap.

Almost one quarter (23%) of international telephone calls that showed up as official business of the Guangdong provincial radio and television department in a recent 10-month period were actually made from the private homes of the department's officials according to provincial authorities, announcing a crackdown as part of their drive to intensify public supervision.

INDIAN CAR PHONES

The Indian government plans to import millions of dollars worth of car telephones, and credit card-operated public telephones was decried as a needless luxury by New Delhi telecommunications planner Sam Pitroda. India, with a population of 750 million, has about 300 million people living below the official poverty line. As of 1987, India had only 18,000 coin-operated telephones, not all of which work. The 15,000 card-operated telephones and the proposed 5,000 car phones to be used by affluent private citizens, was estimated to cost about $100 million.

NTT CHALLENGES HACKERS

Japan's telecommunications giant Nippon Telegraph & Telephone Corp. challenged any hacker in Japan to break through its security code and enter the system. The one million yen ($7,000) offer was good till August 1991.

TECHNOLOGY/COMPUTING

HIGH-TECH SURPRISES IN THE 1990S: JAPAN'S NEW STRATEGY IN THE ASIA-PACIFIC MARKET

by Daniel Heyler

Japanese business strategies in the Asia-Pacific region are changing rapidly as a result of new perceptions of the threats and opportunities in Asia's newly industrialized economies (NIEs). In the early 1980s, most Japanese executives turned to the NIEs seeking lower land and labor costs outside of Japan for operating low-end semiconductor facilities or electronics factories.

Now it appears that high-level Japanese executives are adopting the view that the NIEs are an important market for semiconductors but that their drive for technological development will grow to threatening proportions by the end of the next decade.

Recent market research on Japanese business strategy in the Asia-Pacific region reveals that at least 70% of 500 high-level Japanese executives from publicly traded companies consider the rapid emergence of semiconductor and electronics industries in the NIEs, or the so-called Four Tigers (South Korea, Taiwan, Hong Kong, and Singapore), to be a direct threat to Japan's economic prowess. It seems very likely therefore that significant strategic surprises will emerge from the Asia-Pacific region in the 1990s.

THE TIGERS THREATEN JAPAN

Just as Japan's economic threats to certain key U.S. industries have resulted in critical attacks on corporate inefficiencies and the weak educational system in the United States, NIE economic threats to Japan are causing similar responses in that country. Nearly 25% of Japanese executives claim that their businesses have been seriously impeded by competition from the NIEs, and approximately 75% believe that the NIEs will hurt their businesses significantly before the year 2000.

The polled executives attribute the NIE strength in the 1990s to educational enthusiasm which, according to 80% of the executives, will be stronger in the NIEs than in Japan by the year 2000.

The second primary concern is that the NIE's price competitiveness and fast technological development definitely will affect their market share in Asia, Europe, and the United States—especially in the areas of consumer electronics and memories. The Japanese executives had the following strategic expectations of the NIEs:

• *South Korea:* More than three fourths of Japanese executives expect South Korea to be their greatest competitor among the four NIEs by the year 2000. South Korea's rapid technological progress and relentless work ethic continue to arouse Japanese concern

and fear that Japan's economic predominance will not last forever.

• *Taiwan:* Approximately 13% of the executives in Japan believe that Taiwan will be their major competitor within the NIE group. Taiwan's ability to adapt to international personal computer standards and its entrepreneurial zeal will contribute to the goal of creating a "Silicon Island." Already, the Taiwanese are moving into workstations and laptops to prepare for the next generation of personal computing.

• *Hong Kong:* Hong Kong's "port mentality" continues to make it a strong mercantile center in Asia, albeit technologically shortsighted. Less than 1% of Japanese business executives believe that Hong Kong will be a major business threat.

• *Singapore:* The third rising star in Asia is the city-state of Singapore, which is expected to outperform Hong Kong by the year 2000. Approximately 3.4% of the Japanese executives see Singapore as their major competitor among the newly industrialized economies.

In addition to the business impact of the NIEs, Japanese executives forsee threats com-

Greatest Threats to Japan—Rest of Asia (rank, country, and percentage)

Rank	Country	Percentage
1	China	37.8%
2	Thailand	35.4%
3	Malaysia	17.7%
4	Indonesia	11.3%
5	India	5.0%
6	Philippines	4.2%
7	Others	3.4%
8	No answer	20.9%

Source: Nihon Keizai, Dataquest.

ing from other Asia/Pacific nations as well. The table on p. 499 lists the other countries of Asia along with their ranks and the percentages of Japanese executives who consider them a threat to their own businesses.

Japan's strategy in the Asia-Pacific region for the 1990s already is showing a few noteworthy characteristics:

• Japan now views the Asia-Pacific as a market for its semiconductor products and equipment, and is likely to contract more and more of its technology out to NIE companies in order to gain market access, particularly in South Korea.
• Japanese executives want to continue to increase their long-term investment in China, because of the massive market prospects that country offers in the twenty-first century—more so than India or Indonesia.

• South Korea, Taiwan, and Singapore offer an almost no-risk environment for substantial long-term investment in electronics and semiconductor manufacturing.
• Newly emerging economic powers in Southeast Asia—such as Thailand and Malaysia—offer high prospects for growth and technology development, whereas the Philippines is still considered to be a high risk.
• Japanese corporations want to adjust managerial practices to facilitate the hiring, training, and cultural integration of non-Japanese Asian engineers into the rigid Japanese corporate culture. They believe that the Asia-Pacific region will be a source of hardworking, skilled technicians in the 1990s.

Daniel Heyler is the Asian technology analyst with the San Jose-based computer industry research firm Dataquest, Inc.

TWO ASIAN ARCHRIVALS FACE OFF: SOUTH KOREAN–JAPANESE COMPETITION IN THE 1990s

by Daniel Heyler

As the United States and Japan engage in perhaps their most important trade negotiations of the decade, South Korean semiconductor companies are concerned that patent law agreements enforcing U.S. patents in Japan could have an adverse effect on South Korea's competitiveness in the world semiconductor market.

Japan's ruling in 1989 that recognizes and enforces Texas Instruments' basic IC (integrated circuit) design patent indirectly pressures South Korean semiconductor companies to reform their patent laws according to internationally accepted standards. Furthermore, Japan has equipped itself with a powerful weapon—the choice to pursue more aggressive intellectual property litigation against its emerging Asian rival, South Korea.

Since 1985, South Korean semiconductor companies have made impressive gains into the restrictive Japanese distribution system at a faster rate than Europe, the United States, and any other country in Asia ever has. For a nation with a long history of national resentment toward Japan and vice versa, South Korea's achievement with respect to semiconductors seem even more remarkable.

THE BATTLE FOR MARKET SHARE IN JAPAN

In an ever-increasing battle for semiconductor market share in Japan, which is one of the least receptive regions to imports, South Korean companies continue to increase market share faster than European and U.S. companies. From 1982 to 1989, South Korean semiconductor companies increased market share at a compound annual growth rate (CAGR) of 82.1%, compared with Europe's 17.0%, and the United States' 18.3%.

Although rapid shipment growth is expected in this region in the 1990s, South Korea's penetration is astounding and alarming to Japanese semiconductor companies because of Korea's success in other regions of the world. South Korea's aggressive world strategy and accelerated technology development continues to weaken Japan's grip on the market.

Historical market share information and trends are meaningless unless one also considers the technological prowess involved in South Korea's rise to the world arena.

South Korean semiconductor companies began thinking about ICs in the late 1970s and began manufacturing memories in the early 1980s. Their ability to acquire and integrate foreign technology while continuously reinvesting in R&D has made IC companies that are capable of taking the same technological

leaps as Japan and the United States in much less time.

JAPAN'S KOREAN STRATEGY IN THE 1990s

Now that South Korea has entered the big leagues of semiconductor geopolitics, Japan views it not as a "little dragon" at all but as a full-grown dragon and a threat.

South Korean semiconductor companies began affecting the Japanese semiconductor industry in the late 1980s. Dataquest believes that South Korea's ambitious government–private sector strategy will negatively affect Japan's competition in the 1990s and possibly cause bitter relations for the following reasons:

- Japan no longer is the sole controller of DRAM (Dynamic Random Access Memory) chip prices.
- South Korea cut prices severely in mid-1989 when the chip market in Asia outside of Japan suddenly weakened.
- Samsung Electronics Co., Ltd., has plans for new major silicon wafer fabrication facility (fab) in Kiheung, which will produce 25,000 wafers per months and is likely to produce 5 million 4Mb (megabyte) chips per month, which could make Samsung the largest facility, at least temporarily.
- Toshiba no longer assumes that it will dominate the 4Mb market. Matsushita and NEC have counted on increasing production of 1Mb chips after Toshiba's success but froze 1Mb out because of price declines.

As South Korea and Japan enter a hostile international market environment in the new decade, coupled with a consumption downturn, world conditions could push Japan into playing tough with South Korean companies. The following market factors will intensify market competition between Japan and South Korea, possibly proving detrimental to South Korea's continued growth.

Several overwhelming market factors and industry trends might force Japanese trade policy or semiconductor strategic direction into an adversary mode. Dataquest believes that the relationship between the Japanese and South Korean semiconductor industries will be highly competitive in the consumer appli-

cations markets during the 1990s. South Korea's increased market share in Japan in the 1980s, its hurried technical advancement, and its global offensive will hurt Japanese companies in the 1990s. Japan is not likely to sit back and watch the rise of a new Asian power. Instead, the relationship between the two countries will turn toward litigation and negotiation rather than the cutthroat price wars of the past. The market conditions will dictate the extent and direction of their intense competition in the 1990s.

SOURCE: Dataquest, Inc.

AUSSIE COMPUTER FOR THE BLIND

Musician Stevie Wonder endorsed the Australian-made Eureka laptop braille computer. He's already bought three of them, including one for his pal Ray Charles.

Developed by Melbourne-raised Robotron P/L and The Royal Victorian Institute for the Blind, the new Eureka braille laptop offers a variety of integrated features currently not available on any other computers for the visually handicapped—including one feature about which Stevie Wonder is especially enthusiastic. The Eureka can be used to compose and score music.

"It's like an electronic braille secretary," explained Marc Maurer, president of the National Federation of the Blind, a Baltimore-headquartered organization which is also endorsing the machine.

This slim, 3-pound IBM PC compatible comes with a voice synthesizer chip which activates a personal appointments calendar as well as a notetaker. Even if the machine has

been turned off, the diary feature will switch on the Eureka to announce scheduled appointments. In addition, the laptop has a built-in word processor which can print out in braille or in regular type—and it can be easily networked with other PCs. For good measure, it also announces the time and temperature.

CHINA'S APPLE COMPUTER

Beijing-based Hope Computers hopes to become the Apple Computer of China. In 1988, this start-up Chinese computer firm earned about $520,000 from total sales of about $4.3 million, up from practically zero in 1986. Sales reached an estimated $13.4 million in 1989. Within a few years, the company expects to start shipping cheap PCs to the U.S. and other foreign markets as an alternative to high-end personal computer clones from Asia. "Apple started in a garage," noted Hope's general manager, Zhou Mingtao. "We also started in a very dirty, small building three years ago."

PROBLEMATIC PCS IN CHINA

Only 20% of the 280,000 computers in China are being fully utilized, largely because of a lack of software, China's Xinhua News Service reported in 1988.

BYPASSING COCOM

Despite the dramatic improvement of relations between East and West, the Paris-headquartered international Coordinating Committee for Multilateral Export Controls (COCOM), still vigilantly monitors the sale of high-technology military level equipment to East bloc nations.

A few years ago a division of Japan's Toshiba Corp. was caught selling technology to the Soviet Union, which the USSR used to develop silent submarine engines. As a result, Toshiba was ostracized from the American market and suffered hundreds of millions of dollars in damages and lost revenues.

Now some enterprising Hong Kong exporters have figured out a legitimate way to bypass COCOM'S restrictions and ship sensitive military-level technologies to China.

According to COCOM rules, electric devices which run on DC (direct current) don't require export licenses to be shipped to China, whereas AC-operating (alternating current) devices do. That's because years ago, AC devices were considered to be much more advanced than DC instruments.

Shrewd Hong Kong exporters have discovered an ingenious loophole in the rules. The very latest generation of silicon chips also run on DC power, although they are embedded in devices which plug into AC sources. So the exporters are pulling the DC silicon chips out of the AC devices and legally mailing them to China in plain envelopes. Export licenses are

the obtained from the "chip-less" nonsensitive equipment. Everything gets reassembled once it's on the mainland—and it's all completely legal, notes Nury Vittachi of the *South China Morning Post* in Hong Kong.

CLEANING UP WITH FUZZY LOGIC

Japan's latest consumer craze is "fuzzy logic." Fuzzy logic is an artificial intelligence-like technology which imitates human skills to sort out unclear information. In the United States, fuzzy logic is still mainly the domain of the military establishment and aerospace industry.

But in Japan, Sony has introduced its fuzzy logic handheld computer which recognizes handwriting; while fuzzy showers adjust water pressure and temperature; and consumers have a choice of fuzzy logic washing machines that save on water and spin cycles. Optical sensors in the machines determine just how dirty the water is and adjust the water level accordingly. Priced at about $580, they cost only a little more than old-fashioned washing machines.

But according to a Matsushita Electric Industrial spokesman, the company will have to sell about 500,000 machines just to break even on R&D. Still they're not worried. "If we can't get return on R&D costs from just one model, that is okay. We'll just introduce fuzzy theory into the next washing machine and in future ones."

FUZZY FLOWER ARRANGEMENT

Applying fuzzy logic to their traditional arts, the Japanese have developed a robot that will make *ikebana* flower arrangements, using fuzzy logic to decide just where which flowers and stems should go.

SOUTH KOREANS LOOK AROUND

Japanese companies have started to shy away from lending technology to South Korea, so Korean electronics firms have turned to small foreign companies abroad for technology transfers. "The Japanese are unwilling to assist in developing high technology because they fear a boomerang effect," said an official responsible for high-tech research at the Korean Institute for Economics and Technology, a government think-tank.

A CHAIR-SETTING-UP ROBOT

Where it would take 30 people five hours to set up 3,000 chairs in an auditorium, a robot developed by Kanto Auto Works, Ltd., and Kajima Corp. can do the job in just 10 minutes. Appropriately enough, the robot is named Chair Robot. A team of four robots complete with 360 chairs (they sell chairs, too) is only $384,615.

TAIWAN'S COMPUTER GIANT STILL AIMING HIGH

Acer, Inc., Taiwan's leading personal computer-maker, hit one million in sales in 1989, making it one of the 10 biggest personal computer manufacturers in the world. Acer Chairman Stan Shih said the company's next goal is to become one of the world's top five IBM-compatible computer-makers.

Taiwan's information-industry exports are projected to reach $10 billion by 1992, surpassing the other three leading NIEs (newly industrialized economies) in the region. According to a recent study by Taiwan's Institute of Information Industry, South Korea's output is expected to reach $6 billion by 1992; Singapore's info exports will amount to about $5.7 billion, while Hong Kong will lag behind at $1.7 billion. Meanwhile, Taiwan's exports of computers and related information-industry projects reached about $5.5 billion in 1990.

RIM REVIEW

CHINA'S SOFTWARE PRIDE—AND AMERICAN PREJUDICE

China, Inc.: How To Do Business with the Chinese by Roderick Macleod is probably one of the most insightful books you will ever read on the subject. Born out of practical, long-suffering experience, it is full of anecdotes—and antidotes.

Macleod was the first foreign accountant ever to be based in China, representing the Big 8 accounting firm, Coopers & Lybrand in Shanghai. Enthused by the experience of working successfully with the Chinese, he went on to become president and CEO of his own Sino-American joint venture, International Technology Development Corp.

The firm's subsidiary, Shanghai Software Consortium, had a unique marketing concept. It was to send cheap, qualified software engineers from China to the U.S. on contracts with American software firms to translate their software programs from one computer language to another.

These software migrant workers undertook months-long assignments, working long hours, eating home-cooked Chinese food and sleeping in shifts in the bunk beds provided for them at SSC's San Francisco headquarters-cum-dormitory.

Their wages, in much desired U.S. currency, were remitted directly to the Chinese partner in Shanghai. Apart from receiving basic spending money here, the Chinese programmers were paid in Chinese currency at home. Of course, the personal experience of working with American software firms was considered priceless instruction—and a boon to Shanghai's own budding software industry.

"It was basically an awfully good idea," Macleod said. "They were much cheaper and better workers than American software scientists."

But China expert Macleod never anticipated the pitfalls of mainland Chinese working in America, Inc. The software venture never really succeeded for reasons euphemistically summarized by Macleod in one word: "ethnocentricism." Racism by any other name, it was further compounded by cultural mistrust.

"American companies were reluctant to use software engineers from the PRC," he noted. "They've got no problem using Chinese computer scientists—as long as they're Chinese-American.

RIM BEEPERS

A U.S. high-tech firm, Millicom, introduced the world's first Chinese character electronic pager in Hong Kong. The new gizmo has a vocabulary of 500 Chinese characters.

JAPANESE WORDRUNNER

WordRunner is a super-compact word processor that converts handwritten input to printed Japanese. Memory holds up to 500 characters, 3,637 Japanese ideograms are held in ROM (Read Only Memory)—from PLU.S. for Y19,800 (about $152).

ELECTRONICS LIPS AT CLUB VOLVO

Hong Kong's Club Volvo became notorious when it almost went public on the Hong Kong Stock Exchange before the market crashed in October '87. Since then, the owners have installed the very latest in point-of-sale equipment in the 70,000 square foot nightclub which employs 1,000 hostesses and 600 support staff. Terminals on each dimly lit table now feature keys showing a pair of pink lips, a female escort with handbag, and other pictograms. Pressing the handbag button indicates that the hostess is leaving with the customer, so he gets charged accordingly.

MACWORLD ASIA

MacWorld Expo Asia, the region's Apple Macintosh computer show, was launched in Singapore in 1989. The current Macintosh-installed base on the Rim is 150,000, and is projected to grow up to 700,000 units by 1991, according to market analysts IDG/Hong Kong.

Desktop publishing is fast-making inroads

in Asia, especially in the print media. Major Asian newspapers using Macintosh systems for composition and layout include the *Singapore Straits-Times*, the *Manila Chronicle,* and the *Moo Deung Daily* in Seoul. A variety of language systems are available on the Macintosh with type fonts ranging from Japanese *kanji* and Chinese ideograms to Hangul (Korean), Bahasa (used in Indonesia and Malaysia), and Thai script, as well as about 14 dialects of Indian, including Sanskrit, Tamil, and Urdu.

THE GODDESS AND THE MAC

Thanks in large part to Macintosh technology, an explanation was found for the drastic failure of the Indonesian government's hydrological program to improve on the 2,000-year-old system of rice-growing on the island of Bali. California scientists from the University of Southern California were able to input a wide variety of data to create a dazzling graphics scenario explaining what had gone wrong with the government's program.

"With another button stroke, the screen displayed the system of temples scattered over the steep jungled hills. The graphs appeared, revealing the patterns of good and bad crops that come and go with the rains, with drought, with outbreaks of pests and with various planting intervals . . . Kremer then ran a simulation that mimicked official new government farming methods. And, on the computer just as had happened where government hydrologists were in charge, crippling outbreaks of pests ruined the crops," according to a report by *San Francisco Chronicle* science writer Charles Petit.

OPENING ICONS

In another "Mac-cultural" development, Sam Holland, director of the Los Gatos, California-based Foundation for Recovery of Ancient Wisdom, has become the Macintosh guru to the Dalai Lama's private office in Darmasala, India. The former Apple Computer engineer arranged for the donation of a complete Mac II system, including Tibetan fonts, to the Dalai Lama, and is instructing the spiritual leader and his staff on how to use the Macintosh in temporal affairs.

INDIA'S HIGH-TECH EXPATRIATES

India has been making a special pitch to Indian professionals who are living and working in the United States. There are an estimated 400,000 Indian expatriates living in the United States.

Most of them are highly trained professionals pursuing careers as doctors, lawyers, engineers, computer programmers, and businessmen. In the San Francisco Bay Area alone, about 10% of an estimated 50,000 Indian residents are millionaires, according to Rameshwar Singh, president of the California Society of Professional Engineers, a statewide organization based in San Jose.

Organizations such as the Silicon Valley Indian Professionals association are springing up to serve as communications links between Indian industry and Indian professionals living abroad.

The so-called "Non-Resident Indians" (NRIs) are increasingly becoming a hot commodity for cash-starved India. It is estimated that about $873 million a year flows to India in the form of NRI investments. Total NRI assets in India amount to about $4.4 billion, which is about 23% more than India's total foreign exchange reserves, or roughly the same size as India's 1985/1986 trade deficit.

Although Indians have generally maintained a low profile in this country, they are starting to become more visible. One very successful Indian professional couple, both of them doctors, achieved local notoriety when they constructed their home to resemble a scaled-down version of the Taj Mahal, building it on a 76-acre parcel of land in Fremont, California. In this case, however, it was reportedly the wife who urged the husband to build the monument for her.

HOLDING ON:

THE HAND-HELD RACETRACK

Forget about monitoring the stock market on your hand-held Quotrek system, this is much more fun. Hong Kong's Royal Jockey Club introduced a small hand-held personal computer terminal which bettors can use to place their bets. It works from anywhere in Hong Kong, even from overseas. The system is capable of handling all kinds of bets from simple wins to complex exotic play selections.

THE HAND-HELD TRANSLATOR

The Japanese electronic firm Casio introduced the world's first hand-held copying machine. Now Epson, another Japanese company, has introduced the world's first handy translation device. You run the 15.-cm long wand over imprinted English-language phrases, and get the Japanese version to appear on the display screen within seconds. The Epson English–Japanese translator can recognize more than 30,000 words, and sells for about $225.

LOTUS YI-ER-SAN/ICHI-NI-SAN

More and more American software is being customized for use in Asian markets. Lotus Corp.'s best-selling Lotus 1-2-3 spreadsheet has now been translated into Korean and Chinese. There are currently an estimated 50,000 legitimate users of the English-language version in Asia. Ashton-Tate has entered into its first joint venture with the People's Republic of China to translate its dBASE IV and Framework II software packages into simplified Chinese.

Mitch Kapor, founder of Lotus Development Corp., cited the case study of marketing the best-selling Lotus 1-2-3 spreadsheet in Japan at an Alliance Japan seminar in San Francisco. Contrary to Lotus' original projections, Kapor said it was not an easy sell even though Japan was tagged as being potentially the second largest software market in the world. The company thought it would take only nine months to adapt the Japanese version of 1-2-3. Instead, it took more than two years and cost about $5 million. The pay-off was worth it, however. In 1989, Lotus sales were an estimated $44 million in the Japanese market.

Kapor mentioned just a few of the "hundreds of minor changes" which Lotus had to incorporate into the new program, Lotus 1-2-3 J.

The Japanese record their dates according to the year of the emperor's reign. For example, the year 1985 (when Lotus 1-2-3 J was first introduced in Japan) was "Showa 65," or the 65th year of the late Emperor Showa's reign. Lotus thought "it would be clever" to include a provision for entering the new emperor's name in the software. "We were politely told not to even dream of marketing a product that questioned the emperor's mortality," Kapor recalled.

Another cultural taboo was the sound of the beep the program emits whenever a user makes a spreadsheet error. "Because the Japanese work so closely [together] in the office, it was not only distracting to broadcast the beep to co-workers, but embarrassing to advertise your mistakes," Kapor said, explaining why the beep was offered as an option instead of as a regular feature.

HARD DISKS TO SINGAPORE

Taiwan has become one of Singapore's main suppliers of computer terminals, hard disks, and other equipment, according to trade analysts' reports. Taiwan exported $624 million worth of computer peripheral equipment to Singapore in 1988, or 11% of Singapore's total computer peripheral imports.

DATA

JAPAN'S PAPER CHASE
by Kevin Sullivan

Despite the futuristic technical achievements of companies such as NEC and Fujitsu, the average Japanese company appears to be stuck in the last century when it comes to applying computers to day-to-day clerical work.

In Asia's most advanced economy, a visit to any government office is likely to present the quaintly Dickensian spectacle of rows and rows of bulging files, with teams of workers engaged in such archaic tasks as addressing envelopes by hand. The paperless office may have been brought closer by Japanese technology, but it is still a long way from downtown Tokyo.

There are several reasons for the delay in unclogging Japan's notoriously cumbersome office organization. Foremost among these is the fact that most major players in the office equipment market still tend to prefer old-fashioned instruments such as paper and pen, or at least photocopy and fax.

The main office furniture suppliers depend on sales of conventional low-grade desks and filing cabinets for the bulk of their sales, rather than the modular terminal units and sophisticated lighting systems beloved of interior designers.

In addition to this, the manufacturers of copiers and fax machines are, understandably, loath to see an end to the paper chase. A spokesman for Ricoh, one of Japan's largest suppliers of office equipment, and particularly strong in copiers, explains: "There are few people now who believe offices will become paperless. We are supplying machines which make use of paper so, of course, we would not benefit from the paperless office. Our main products still are—and will continue to be—copiers, facsimile machines, and laser printers."

One of the primary reasons Japanese companies seem determined not to take advantage of innovative office automation products is the peculiar nature of Japanese office organization. Two things are universal in offices from Hokkaido to Okinawa, from the largest bank to the meanest hole-in-the-wall outfit.

The first is the *hanko* or seal, without which a document carries little or no authority. Until a report has been chopped by the section head it goes no further than the section; the same applies to departmental and divisional bosses, all the way up to the board of directors. In addition to ensuring tight control over the flow of information inside companies, this system necessitates the use of hard copy.

A second peculiarity of Japanese corporate life is the emphasis on consensus, which results in the incessant presentation of reports. Decisions are not made until large numbers of personnel have been brought up to date on the issues at stake and given a chance to comment. This has led in the last 20 years to an alarming proliferation of photocopied memos and position papers.

The first Japanese-character word processors did not arrive on the market until the beginning of the 1980s, and since the Japanese have never used typewriters except when writing in non-Japanese languages, the general unfamiliarity with letter keyboards is often cited as another reason for the slow rate of computerization.

A spokesman for Fujitsu, the largest Japanese computer-maker, explains that the personal computer market is expanding rapidly but alludes to "keyboard allergy" from which many Japanese suffer as a result of the traditional writing system.

However, she adds that the growing availability of easy-to-use and much improved Japanese-language software is making this less of a problem. Japan is also pioneering the development of "keyboardless" computers utilizing speech or handwritten input.

© *Asian Business* magazine, Far East Trade Press, Ltd., 1988.

THE FAX THAT FUMBLED

Prior to the Tiananmen Square massacre of June 4, 1989, the new economic call in China was, "Let a thousand answering services bloom." At least, that was the message expounded at the Sino-U.S. Industry, Trade, and Economic Joint Session, a bilateral trade conference held in 1988 in Beijing's Great Hall of the People. About a thousand private agencies have sprung up offering foreign and Chinese firms 24-hour business services, including fax, telex, phone paging, direct mail, document translation, market research, business liaison, and even assistance in making travel arrangements and appointments.

In his address at the Sino-U.S. trade conference, S. H. Tu, owner of the Beijing-based Realinform Consultancy & Agency, noted that the business prospects for such privately owned, multifunction "super post offices" are very bright indeed. If just 10% of China's one million medium and small enterprises (including an estimated 225,000 private companies) were to install telex and fax machines, the basic installation cost would easily reach $1 billion, Tu observed.

That figure would be an equivalent percent of the PRC's total investment in domestic transport and telecommunications in 1983—a prohibitive investment in foreign exchange-starved China. The obvious answer lies in establishing centralized information services in China, Tu maintained. Foreign firms can benefit, too, by saving on the exorbitant cost of opening an office in China. "A modest Beijing office costs $100,000 per year at least," he pointed out, whereas a Chinese agency's costs are comparatively minimal to break into the China market, he asserted.

Following the aborted pro-democracy movement in China in 1989, the Beijing government ordered offices in China to intercept and hand over the "reactionary propaganda" being sent via fax machines from Chinese dissidents abroad. There are an estimated 5,000 fax machines in China.

CHINA'S NATIONAL DATA BANK

Since it was first launched in 1987, China's largest data bank stores about 2.5 million items of information in 20 categories including industry, agriculture, finance, energy, and transport for the central government, provinces, municipalities, and autonomous regions. The information all comes from the State Statistical Bureau, ministries, and other departments under the State Council, China's governing body.

CHINA ON-LINE

Boeing's on it, Bechtel's on it, CBS Broadcast International's on it, not to mention Dow Chemical, Champion Spark Plug, and other major American as well as international China players. They're all on-line subscribers to a thriving China business database called "China Express." The data service, which is maintained by London-based 21st Publishing, may be accessed by any personal computer via NEWSNET (call 212-527-8030 for details and free trial).

PORTABLE PAPER SHREDDER

Footwork, the parcel delivery people, has developed a portable, personal paper shredder.

It's 28 cm wide, 7 cm thick, and 16 cm wide, and weighs only 3.6 kg. Its arm can be adjusted so it will fit any wastebasket, and it cuts those secrets up into 0.4 mm strips. It sells for about $292.

DIALING FOR DATABASES

Information Library RUKIT in Tokyo offers access to databases via 15 personal computers of six different makes. For an initiation fee of Y10,000 (about $77) and monthly dues of Y1,000 (about $7.70), users have access to database information on business, science, medicine, pharmaceutics, biology, and patents. "From now on, the real test of a businessman will be whether or not he can use database information to advantage," comments *Bulldog* magazine.

TOUCHING RIM DATABASES

Japanese information service Hirata & Co, provide daily summaries of 60 Chinese newspapers, plus TV and radio news, to subscribers for about $53 a month. They plan to expand their service to cover other Pacific Rim countries as well.

(See Appendix G for a list of Pacific Rim Information Networks.)

MATCHING CASH AND IDEAS

Data Bank 02 Japan, founded in 1988, has developed a system for getting entrepreneurs with a viable idea but no cash together with financiers with no ideas but plenty of money. 02 says the idea man is the one who has to put his own idea to work. Otherwise, the idea will never fly. The company's monthly magazine, *02,* analyzes the successes and failures of start-up companies.

KEEPING IT SECRET

In an age of international investment, Japanese corporations' loathing for disclosure is a major problem. According to a 1986 survey by Keizai Koho Center, 81 % of all Tokyo Stock Exchange-listed companies had no international PR section. Most Japanese companies did not have domestic PR departments until pollution became a problem in the mid-1970s.

THE COST OF COMMUNICATING

The average charges for local translation services in 1988 were, according to *Asiaweek* magazine:

cies can be reported directly. The moment the door of the police box opens, the TV cameras and microphones come on, and the person on duty at the main station appears on the monitor screen. Or, if it's a life or death situation, one punch of the emergency button alerts the nearest patrol car which will be on the scene in minutes.

CORPORATE COMIC BOOKS

Japanese publishers are now publishing *mangas* (comic books) as backgrounders to major corporations. So far there are more than a dozen corporate manga on the stands, including Sumitomo Bank, Suntory, Honda, and

	Verbal interpreter (per hour)	Text Translator (per page)	Phrase books
Bangkok	$10.00	$ 8.00	$2.50–$4.00
Hong Kong	20.00	21.00	2.50 +
Jakarta	9.00	5.00	2.00–16.00
Kuala Lumpur	16.00	12.00	4.00–7.00
Manila	10.00	6.00	1.00–9.00
Seoul	67.50	7.00	3.00 +
Singapore	28.50	9.50	9.50–23.50
Taipei	12.00	5.00	2.00–4.00
Tokyo	33.00	18.50	5.00–6.50

INTELLIGENT POLICE BOXES

Some American cities—notably San Francisco—have adopted the Japanese neighborhood "police box" system, with friendly police officers available to help citizens. But now the Japanese police in Oita prefecture have come up with an "intelligent police box system" without police officers. Police boxes are hooked up with the main police station via TV camera and local area network service. So even if the local police officer is out, emergen-

Dentsu, published by Sekai Bunkasha publishing house. The companies say, "It would help if prospective employees would read them . . . and it may help our image, too." Some are even starting to use them for internal training. It beats reading a tome on company history, they claim.

WEATHER CARDS

Misawa Home Group's information company, Misawa Van, introduced telephone weather cards which will automatically dial up detailed weather reports from any card-accepting pay phone. Cards are valued at about $7 for 10 calls up to $70 for 100. Misawa has already produced 100,000 of them and expects to sell a million annually.

COMMUTER'S CARD

Citizen has put out a credit-card-sized product that will remember train, subway, bus and other transportation schedules. It even differentiates between express and super-express trains. What's more, when turned on, it immediately displays the departure time closest to the current time. The product sold more than 10,000 units in its first two months on the market at the cost of $76.

RATING THE RIM REPORTERS

How accurate are Japanese and U.S. business reporters when it comes to covering U.S.–Japan trade affairs? Rubenstein, Wolfson & Co., Inc., a New York-based financial public relations firm, in conjunction with the University of Georgia Center for International Mass Communications, recently conducted a survey of 138 leading Japanese and American business reporters and corporate executives on the subject.

Among the report's findings: Only 3% of American journalists said Japanese were objective; while 53% of the Japanese journalists credited the Americans with objectivity. Two thirds of U.S. executives found that the U.S. media's treatment of U.S.–Japanese economic issues was superficial or spotty. In turn, Japanese journalists complained that American journalists do not have the necessary foreign language skills, cross-cultural education, or experience to provide a historical context for reporting on economic events in Japan.

On corporate communications: 40% of U.S.-based Japanese executives who were surveyed said they never provide information to the American press; while 27% said they don't provide information to the Japanese press either. On the other side, only 9% of American businesses in Japan said they never talk to the Japanese media, while 18% do not communicate with U.S. reporters.

BABY-BOOMER COMMUNICATIONS

Japan's Dentsu Institute for Human Studies conducted a 1989 study about the differences in middle-aged people's values between Japan and the United States. They surveyed 700 adults each in Tokyo, New York, and Los Angeles.

	Tokyo	*N.Y.*	*L.A.*
Our society is affluent	52%	63%	70%
My life is comfortable	42%	78%	82%

Goals and objectives proved to be very much alike in the three cities, Fukuda Yuji, director of Dentsu's study, observed, "As the two countries' baby boomers become more central to their respective societies, their values move closer and closer together."

But Nagasaka Toshihisa, head of Japan External Trade Organization's international economics department, noted, "The problem is this. Baby boomers from Japan and the

United States never get the chance to meet. If we have a seminar, representatives from the States are in their forties; the Japanese attending are often in their sixties. How are we supposed to get this same-values, same-age group of people together?"

DATA ACTION PLAN

HOW THE JAPANESE KEEP UP

Here are tips for Japanese who want to keep up with the times, as compiled by *Shukan Gendai* weekly (and translated by *Japan Free Press*):

• Get the latest trends for Y3,000 a month from Tokyo's Fax Press.
• See Business News from 6:00 a.m. on Channel 12.
• Walk the center street in Shibuya to see what youngsters are wearing.
• Get short-term secretarial and answering services from Short Relief.
• Japan Management Association teaches you how to "lead your subordinates."
• The 1990s will be "younger years." The people with the greatest amount of indirect knowledge (gained from books, conversations, etc.) will come out on top.
• The cross-industry discussion group held by the Marunouchi Junior Chamber of Commerce is open to all.
• Electronic bulletin boards keep you abreast of what's happening, even if you don't live in Tokyo.
• Even individuals can utilize think tanks.
• Hotels double as offices, complete with FAX and modem services.
• CNN 24-hours-a-day by satellite keeps you one step ahead.
• Deep breathing helps get rid of fatigue, high blood pressure, and constipation.
• Read *EC togo* (Uniting the EC) for the latest on the scheduled 1992 EC unification.

JAPAN IN THE EYES OF THE WORLD

It's in vogue for non-Japanese to write about Japan. Each seems to have his or her pet theory about Japan and the Japanese. But now, at last, the National Diet Library has cataloged this kind of book *Sekai no mita Nippon* or "Japan in the eyes of the world."

There are some 3,000 books on Japan, written by non-Japanese, that have been translated. The major subjects:

History	580
Politics	298
Geography	264
Society	229
Economics	183
Sociology	171

RIM INSIGHT

DECIPHERING CHINESE MIND GAMES

It's more than 2,000 years since the Chinese organized the world's first government bureaucracy, a system that has become so woven into a cocoon of red tape that the Chinese themselves find it hard to penetrate. What chance, therefore, does an innocent American businessman stand of winning the games the Chinese play? In her classic study, *The Chinese Mind Game: The Best Kept Trade Secret of the East* (AMC Publishing, Beaverton, OR, 1989), Chin-Ning Chu makes it clear that when dealing with his Asian counterpart a foreign businessman not only doesn't understand the rules but all-too-often isn't even aware that a game is going on.

The Chinese concept of business, explains Chu, stems from the notion that the marketplace is a battlefield with deception, provocation, and misdirection perfectly acceptable weapons. The titles of her chapters are self-explanatory: *"One Should Arouse an Opponent's Anger Creating Disorder, Causing the Opponent to Make Foolish Moves and Creating Opportunities"; "You Must Express Humbleness, Sincerity and Weakness, Allowing Your Enemy to Grow Proud and Arrogant";* and *"Keep Plans as Dark and Impenetrable as Night, Move Like a Thunderbolt."*

"Friendship," she says is a tool, interpreted somewhat differently by Americans than by the Chinese who tend to regard it—at least in business—as a tool for exploitation. Outlining positions that Western firms can take to avoid being duped by these ancient business tactics, Chu, a Chinese-American who heads Asian Marketing Consultants, Inc., an Oregon-based East Asian trade consulting firm, also lists practical countermeasures.

To begin with, there are obvious precautions to be taken: Making sure that one's translator or interpreter conveys one's message accurately and without ambiguity; being genuinely informed about the history and culture of the country you are dealing with; and realizing that the most important person to deal with is sometimes *Ho-Tai* ("backstage") and not necessarily the one of highest rank. Chu's training in philosophy and psychology provided her with a powerful tool to explain and amplify the age-old *I Ching (Book of Changes)*-related 36 strategies, which historically have been used both offensively and defensively.

Briefly summarized, they elaborate on the ideas of misdirection, hiding something in plain sight, provoking a third party into fighting one's enemy, delaying combat until the enemy has lost his enthusiasm, inspiring trust so that one's opponent relaxes his guard, willingness to sacrifice part to benefit the whole, enticing a powerful person into an unfamiliar environment, and listening carefully for hints or indirect statements. China's greatest military strategists were well-versed in these and similar methods. Sun Tzu, for example, in his *Art of War,* stated that the best strategy to overcome an enemy was to stand as still as a forest on a windless day, to be as immobile as a mountain, to be as impenetrable as darkness.

In explaining Strategy no. 17—*Bait a Piece of Jade with Brick*—Chu imparts an important piece of wisdom for U.S. government officials in China seeking more favorable trade regulations and sometimes getting not the jade they want but camouflaged brick. "Because the West needs to justify the existence of its bureaucracy, it tends to do something, anything, to show that it is moving ahead. The Chinese bureaucracy," she explains "has the opposite philosophy: doing nothing is better than doing something if there is the least possibility of being in error."

DATA WITH A CONSCIENCE

PHILIPPINE DATABASE FEATURES
ON-LINE AID

Would you like to adopt a primitive tribe in the Philippines? The Ata tribe of Santo Tomas in Davao Del Norte can now be adopted—all 110 tribal families—for only $3,500. That sum is enough to provide a $2,000 community center, a water supply for $1,000, and the $500 in capital which is necessary for the tribespeople to launch a duck-raising project that will eventually feed them indefinitely. The Ata program is just one of many economic self-help packages listed in a database which has been compiled by the Manila-based Philippine Exchange Assistance Center Foun-

dation (PEACE). Unlike some other economic aid programs which expend considerable funds on administrative costs, the Peace Foundation channels money directly to projects which have been identified and evaluated as economically viable.

In case you don't wish to adopt a primitive tribe, the Peace database lists other options including adoption of rebel families from Bagong Sirang, Macabog, and Sorsogon, who are willing to come down from the hills to engage in black pepper production.

ASIA AND PACIFIC RESOURCES

"Where can I find documentation on child labor in Southeast Asia?" a TV producer asks. "Where can I find documentation on child labor in Southeast Asia?" a union organizer asks. *Asia and Pacific: A Directory of Resources* (Orbis Books, Maryknoll, New York, 1986),

like its sister volume *Third World Resources,* is the standard yellow pages for peace and justice in the Pacific Rim. It lists organizations, books, periodicals, pamphlets and articles, audiovisual materials, and other resources including clipping services, telephone hotlines, and university and research programs focusing on social issues in the Asia-Pacific region.

RIM REVIEW

INDIA'S INFORMATION REVOLUTION

The sacred cows that roam the streets of Bangalore, India's Silicon Valley in the southern state of Rarnataka, still outnumber the

Porsches being driven by the city's high-tech gurus and entrepreneurs.

But there can be no doubt that a third-world-style information revolution is sweeping the subcontinent. In their sweeping study, *India's Information Revolution* (Sage Publications Inc., P.O. Box 5084, Newbury Park, California 91359, cloth $28, paper $14), coauthors Arvind Singhal and Everett M. Rogers study the impact of communications technologies on the Indian subcontinent.

They chart the development of all types of media—press, radio, film, television, VCR, telecommunications, and computers. The book is peppered with colorful anecdotes and case studies, including a humorous account of how television was first introduced to the Himalayan kingdom of Nepal less than five years ago.

The mountain kingdom's very first satellite television transmission featured live coverage of King Birendra's state visit to Australia in September 1985. It was a miracle the program was even aired. The airline lost the Nepalese television crew's camera, so they had to rent a home video camera from a store in Canberra. Minutes before the king's arrival in the Australian capital, the crew was "frantically trying to decipher the camera's instruction manual." Today, there are over 40,000 TV sets for a population of 16 million in Nepal.

THE INDIA INTERFACE

How India develops into an information society—if it ever fully manages to do so—is one of the most crucial development issues facing the world today. Why? Because it is estimated that 950 out of 1,000 people born between now and the year 2000 will be in the third world countries of Latin America, Africa, and Asia. India is an important test case.

Yet India remains a mindboggling enigma, as Singhal and Rogers note. It is a nation of the information-rich versus the information-poor, of free market forces versus centralized state planning, and of the 650 million mass of people (mainly farmers) versus the 150 million middle-class elites and the one million super-elites (India's rich and famous). India not only has the largest number of university students in the world, it also has the largest number of illiterates—and both groups are growing rapidly. Amazingly, the 10% of the country's workforce that is employed in service and information jobs accounts for a whopping 42% of India's GNP. Even as these elites trigger a consumer boom for high-tech products—demanding credit-card operated public telephones and cellular fax machines for their cars—the Indian government faces the challenge of satisfying the needs of the 650 million have-nots.

But their demands seem much more modest by comparison: One public telephone per village, cheaper TV sets (color TVs cost more in India than in the U.S., about $500 to $700 for a set—practically several lifetimes' pay for some of these destitute villagers), and domestically produced television programs in a language they can understand and that deal with their problems. (Only 40% of India's 800 million population understand Hindi, the national language, while the rest speak scores of different dialects.)

Unlike other export-driven Asian economies, such as the Four Dragons (Singapore, Hong Kong, Taiwan, and South Korea), India therefore does not have to depend heavily on export sales. The size of the domestic market is potentially one of the biggest in the world. "Eventually, however, if India wants to be on the cutting edge of microelectronics, it must export," conclude the co-authors, who are both affiliated with the Annenberg School of Communications at the University of Southern California.

CUTTING THROUGH WHITE TAPE

Computerization is at least five years away in the Bangladesh government, which even its own officials admit is close to strangulation in the functioning of its paralyzed bureaucracy. More than 18,000 different forms are used in organizing the nation's operations, all unchanged from the time of British rule and passed from desk to desk and hand to hand among the 1.2 million government function-aries working for or directed by the nine-story Central Secretariat in Dhaka. "We move a file here to there but very little work is done," a senior official admitted. "arbitrariness, high-handedness, overcentralization, corruption of all kinds—these are rampant in the bureaucracy. The problem is that nothing can be decided by anybody." There has been one major change over the years: the red tape once used to bind shut millions of files has been supplanted by (cheaper) white tape.

WORLD VIEW

PAX JAPONICA IN THE ERA OF THE PACIFIC RIM: TOWARD QUALITY INTENSIVE WORLD MANAGEMENT

by Tosiyasu Kunii

It has been the speed in which information is processed and transmitted that historically has been responsible for world domination, according to Tosiyasi Kunii, professor and chairman of the department of information science at the University of Tokyo. Therefore, the world has nothing to fear from what might be termed the "Pax Japonica," or Japan's rise to global power in the 1990s and beyond.

"Pax Japonica in the era of the Pacific Rim means quality-intensive world management," he insists. "And not, as in the past, simple domination of the world." Here he presents his intriguing historical interpretation of the true nature of the global power shift in the world today.

Pax Romana was centered around the Mediterranean Sea and the neighboring areas of two million square kilometers which contained Rome, Athens, and Cairo. At that time, information was carried on foot by messengers, and the speed was on the order of 10 kilometers per hour. The power shift took place having one thousand years as a unit.

Pax Britannica took place when the world power structure encompassed the North Atlantic Ocean. Madrid, London, Paris, and New York were the participating power cities, with the area of 20 million square kilometers around them. Engine-driven surface vehicles enabled information to be carried at 10 times the speed, or at about 100 kilometers per hour with human beings being used to process the information. The power shift of Pax Britannica spanned a hundred years.

The replacement of surface vehicles by airplanes which can go at the speed of 1000 kilometers per hour further expanded the number of cities actively participating in the world power structure outside the Atlantic Ocean to cover the Pacific Ocean, including the Pacific Rim cities such as San Francisco, Tokyo, Beijing, Hong Kong, Singapore, and Sydney. Particularly after the World War II, the air force intensive military power of America and American dollar power has dominated the Free World. The power came to be known as the *Pax Americana.* The area connecting these cities was around 200 million square kilometers.

Since the whole surface of the globe is approximately 500 million square kilometers, this is the total area covered by today's new *Pax Japonica.* However, the major difference between today's global power structure and

in the past has been the shift from military-dominated power to economic power.

Furthermore, today, in the era of instant communication via computers, the rapid flow of information has to a large extent undercut the effectiveness of military power. Five minutes are too short for any power to move from one area to another. This means that no single power can exist to dominate the rest. And seeing that transmission "speed limits" have been reached, only quality remains to be improved.

Therefore, Pax Japonica, if it does exist at all, does not mean any dominating power position, but is rather a humble position to coordinate world activities of an economic and cultural nature rather than any military threat.

ASIA PACIFIC INFORMATION NETWORK (APIN)

This is a service of The Asia Foundation Center for Asian Pacific Affairs, headquartered in San Francisco. Established in 1987, the organization is designed to disseminate information on the conferences, research, publica-

tions, and other activities of nonprofit organizations that focus on contemporary Asia-Pacific economy, strategy, and foreign policy issues.

(For APIN's directory of Asia-Pacific electronic information services, please see Appendix G.)

INTELLECTUAL PROPERTIES

WELCOME TO DONGFANGLAND

Back in 1987, when an amusement park in the Southern Chinese city of Guangzhou announced plans to call itself the "Dongfang Disneyland," the Walt Disney Co. had no recourse. Such flagrant trademark infringement has been nipped in the bud ever since China signed the Paris Convention for the Protection of Industrial Property in March of 1985.

Today, the Disney Co. has registered more than 300 trademarks for Donald Duck and Mickey Mouse products in the PRC.

China's Patent Office has processed more than 10,000 patent applications from foreign companies. Although only 438 foreign patents have been approved so far, the tide of would-be trademarks from the West shows no sign of abating. According to the State Patent Office, applications from the U.S. are increasing faster than those from any other country, with more than 624 American applications submitted so far, followed closely by Japan with 540 patent applications.

"Filing for a Chinese patent can be time-consuming, taking as much as two years," notes Thomas F. Smegal Jr., managing partner of San Francisco-based Townsend and Townsend, a leading U.S. patent, copyright, and trademark law firm which represents Gerber Co., the babyfood manufacturer, and Tandem Computers, a high-tech company, in China.

One of the major reasons for the delay is that most foreign patent applications involve technology which requires at least two years of testing before the patent is finally approved by the Chinese government.

Because business and government in China are still virtually inseparable, obtaining a patent insures that Chinese private enterprise will not compete with a Western firm—at least for the time being. "If you are fortunate enough to receive a patent in China, you essentially have a monopoly until the day comes when another company comes in and infringes your patent," says Smegal.

China's Patent Office has established an office in New York, the China Patent Technology and Trade (U.S.A.), Ltd., to provide free consultation to American companies that are thinking of applying for Chinese patents and trademarks.

(For an overview of different Asian legal systems and traditions, as well as a checklist of important legal issues to consider before doing business in Asia, please refer to "The Traditions of Legal Systems in Pacific Rim Countries" on page 119.)

PIRATES VS. PIRATES

It's a sign that times are changing when pirates sue pirates. For years, Taiwan had a well-deserved reputation for pirating intellectual property in the form of books, records, and software. Then in a landmark case in 1988 a Taiwanese author battled Mainland Chinese pirates of his own book. Raymond Fu Chuang-han, author of a popular English language textbook, sued a large PRC state publishing house for ripping off his book, ironically titled "Two-Way Communication."

"Kick an attorney down the stairs, and he'll stick to you for life."

Indian proverb

INTELLECTUAL PROPERTY SUPERMARKET

Distribution and retailing are not known for their patents. But Nichii, a large supermarket chain, decided that intellectual properties will be one of their growth businesses. Says Nichii President Kobayashi Toshimine, "Traditionally, not only were we not interested in patents in the retail trade, but we also ignored designs and trademarks. Now, however, trademark character goods sell well. If we don't start paying attention to patents and trademarks, we may end up on the short end of the stick."

In August 1987, Nichii set up their Technomart Division. They recruited a retired Ministry of Trade and Industry man who knows all about patenting. And the division has been given control of all Nichii intellectual properties. "Now they have 50 patents, 399 trademarks, and 21 designs pending," reported the *Mainichi Shimbun* newspaper. "They will now look for profits in licensing these properties to others."

CARDIN CHALLENGES CLONES

If you can't fight 'em, outfit 'em. Designer Pierre Cardin has decided the most effective way to fight fashion pirates in Southeast Asia is to manufacture the original product locally. The French fashion magnate is reportedly negotiating with Malaysian companies for a joint venture to produce a wide range of Cardin products in Malaysia. He has also licensed a Thai manufacturer. In addition, about 80 companies in Japan and 30 companies in South Korea have also received licenses to produce the Cardin line of designer goods.

ALARMING MOVES

Seiko, the Japanese watchmaker, sued Hong Kong watch-movement manufacturers on the grounds that it owns the patent on quartz analog movements. More than 40 million QAMs are produced in the territory annually. Seiko wanted the firms to pay them about 15 cents per movement, which should net the company over $6 million each year.

OFF THE CUFF

The licensing of famous designs has become a booming business for Japan's so-called "design agencies." There are over 10,000 such agencies in Japan, which collect commissions from selling designs of world famous designers—up from 7,801 agencies in 1986, according to *Asahi Shimbun* newspaper.

STIFLING INVENTIVENESS IN CHINA

China's most prolific inventor, whose 300 ideas have brought him 10 patents, including those for a driverless car, a painless injection, and super-sensitive radar, says that because of China's stifling bureaucracy it is a waste of his time working in that country. "Even if you can think straight [in state research labs] and manage to invent something, the department chief takes all the credit," complains Ge Xiaofeng, 25. "After I became famous by working alone they asked me to join a state-run research center. I refused. I hate the way my country ignores talent." Ge was paid the equivalent of $55,000 by a medical factory for his "no-pain" injection device.

NEW ZEALAND

LACK OF CONFIDENCE KILLS BRIGHT IDEAS
by Bevis England

New Zealand's inventors are some of the most innovative, but lack of finance means many ideas are sold abroad or sink without a trace.

Interlock, a New Zealand company, started off with two bright men and a garage and now has a significant slice of the Japanese market for aluminium windows.

Another local company, Kent Heating, is leading the way with environmentally clean wood-fired stoves in the tight U.S. market, while Izard Engineering, which makes specialist saw blades, can only just fill the export orders that are pouring in.

There is no lack of technological innovation in New Zealand, but only a few such entrepreneurs have made any kind of impact on the global market. Many have just sold their copyrights or have simply given up because of the barriers to further research.

For instance, the Yale lock was invented by Wellington businessman William Bacon, but sold to a U.S. company. The designs for the carrier-scraper and loader-dozer, two earth-moving machines invented in New Zealand in the 1930s and used in the construction of the Mount Cook airport between 1931 and 1935, were subsequently bought (and claimed as its own) by International Harvester.

An innovative microchip-controlled baby incubator was bought by an American company, Airshields. But Airshields is a subsidiary of the Vickers Group, which has a global incubator market. As soon as the deal was signed, the incubator was buried. It was only bought to kill the potential competition. The inventor, Paul Martin, is now trying to get his manufacturing rights back.

More recently, electronic environment monitoring techniques and system control technology invented in New Zealand have been taken over by a British company, with its production and design operations being shifted to Australia, while the New Zealand operation has become nothing more than a marketing office.

Such stories are all too common in New Zealand. The problem, inventors and academics say, is lack of funds and state support.

With very few exceptions, the New Zealand government and investment circles have not been prepared to back the nation's researchers and inventors, says Dr. Ian Shearer, dean of the Auckland Institute of Technology's faculty of science and engineering, who was also minister for science and technology in the pre-1984 National Party government.

"We're the only country without this support—and we have the ideas," says Shearer. The result, he says, is that New Zealand's manufacturing industry will be unable to compete efficiently in the world markets.

The solution, in Shearer's opinion, is to offer a set of research bounties similar to those available in Australia, or to encourage venture capital companies to invest in New Zealand.

"We have always had the ideas. Where we fall down is the lack of capital for these ideas, and the ability to commercialize them."

Bevin Cornwall of the Department of Scientific and Industrial Research says, "To a certain extent we still have to prove to Kiwis that Kiwis can match the world's best, and that we should have confidence in our own ideas."

© *Asian Business* magazine, Far East Trade Press, Ltd., 1989.

SCIENCE AND SPACE

ASIA 2000

ASIA IN SPACE: THE JAPANESE HAVE THE RIGHT STUFF

by Michael Selwyn

Japan has the technology, the commitment, and above all the cash to become a leader in space by the year 2000.

At the time Neil Armstrong set foot on the moon, the notion of Asia becoming a major force in space technology was laughable.

But as memories of the first lunar landings have faded and the cost of space exploration has spiraled upward, the United States and USSR have had little choice but to scale back their ambitions. The next generation of space missions will require international cooperation, and Asia will play a major role.

Already China, Japan, and India are capable of putting rockets into space. Indonesia, Taiwan, and South Korea are developing satellites. But it is Japan that is likely to show the world the way to the leading-edge technologies of the early twenty-first century.

By 2000 the Japanese expect to build a space shuttle, launch rockets and satellites that are entirely Japanese-built, develop the basic technology for manned space activity, operate their own permanently manned space laboratory, and lay the groundwork for a Japanese moon base.

In public, officials are coy. "Our primary objective is to create our own technology, so that we can cooperate internationally," says Tsuneto Nakamura, director of space activities planning at the research and development bureau of Japan's Science & Technology Agency (STA).

In a similar vein, the government's Space Advisory Council (SAC) sees Japan's space effort as "elucidating scientific truths and broadening the scope of human endeavor."

Such uplifting but essentially vague sentiments should be taken with a pinch of salt. Japan's space program may be state-financed, but it is commercially driven. The hundred or so companies participating in it have their eyes firmly fixed on the first decade of the next century, when they intend to reap rich commercial rewards from manufacturing and processing in space.

Baring Securities' Tokyo office reckons that by 2000 Japan's space industry will be worth Y1 trillion (U.S.$7 billion), half the size of its defense and civil aerospace industries.

The main players—Mitsubishi Heavy Industries (MHI), Nissan, and Ishikawajima Harima Heavy Industries with rockets, and NEC, Mitsubishi Electric, and Toshiba with satellites—talk about cornering 20% of the world market for space applications by 2000. "Space will provide the technological experience to provide the next generation of cost-effective industrial goods in computers, automobiles, aerospace, and medicine," Baring says.

The size of this market is still unclear. Some analysts expect it to be as large as the current world market for consumer electronics.

The U.S. Center for Space Policy quotes a figure of U.S.$25 billion a year by 2000, with spaceborne drug-making offering the biggest share, while Japanese sources quote a figure of U.S.$35 billion.

Japan has some way to go to reach its targets. While it has carried out a lot of research into satellites—more than 40 have gone up since 1970—it still hasn't come up with its own launch vehicle, nor has it put people into space.

And that will change in the 1990s. By 1994, the H-2, the first rocket to be produced using entirely Japanese technology, expertise, and materials, will blast off from the Tanegashima space center, 1,000 kilometers southwest of Tokyo.

One of the H-2's first tasks will be to place in orbit a reusable unmanned vehicle, the space flyer unit (SFU). This will conduct scientific experiments in space by remote control and be brought back to earth by the U.S. space shuttle.

Meanwhile, in 1991, Japan's first astronaut will circle the earth aboard a laboratory inside the U.S. shuttle, and carry out the first of 34 scientific experiments in a microgravity environment.

These activities are a prelude to Japan's participation in Freedom, the world's first permanently manned orbiting space station. The U.S.$50 billion project, led by NASA, will be assembled in stages in the late 1990s, using American space shuttles to ferry men and materials.

Attached to the station will be the Japan Experimental Module (JEM). JEM will perform experiments in the manufacture, under weightless conditions, of products such as ultrahigh-purity pharmaceuticals, protein crystals, semiconductors, and new metals. JEM, which will go up in 1997, will cost Y600 billion (U.S.$4.2 billion).

Equipment will be ferried to and from the laboratory by the H-2 Orbiting Plane (HOPE), a Y300 billion (U.S.$2.1 billion) winged, unmanned space plane whose design is similar to the U.S. space shuttle. HOPE will be launched on the H-2 rocket and return to earth under its own power, landing automatically.

Beyond 2000, Japanese construction firms are studying their own projects in space. Shimizu recently announced plans for a space hotel to be constructed in orbit around the earth after 2020. Projected prices for a five-night stay would start at around U.S.$200,000!

Shimizu and Ohbayashi have looked at the possibilities of moon bases, initially unmanned, to be built after 2010. Ohbayashi has also done a comprehensive study for a "lunar city" complex on the moon, for completion in 2050, that would include factories, research facilities, hotels, and sports facilities. The company is looking at ways to create ecological support systems in space.

Some of the commercial spinoffs of Japan's space effort can already be seen. For example, a consortium of seven aluminium manufacturers is spending Y2 billion (U.S.$14 million) to develop an aluminium/lithium alloy for the HOPE spaceplane, with high levels of heat and rust resistance. It will have wide applications for other industrial sectors, such as nuclear power and industrial machinery.

Nissan hopes to incorporate some of its research on advanced composites for rockets into future car designs.

It's easy, however, to get carried away with fanciful notions about Japan's prospects in space. In reality, Japan has a lot of ground to make up before its technology rivals the West's. Japan's space program has the following five main obstacles to grapple with.

LOW LEVEL OF FUNDING

Japan's total space budget for the 1989 fiscal year was Y155 billion (U.S.$1 billion), one ninth of the amount NASA spent in 1988. Japan, unlike the United States, has no military rocket program it can lean on.

RELIANCE ON FOREIGN TECHNOLOGY

Japan's two space agencies, the National Space Development Agency and the Institute of Space and Astronautical Science, still depend on Western rocket technology. Japan's most powerful rocket, the H-1, is based on a 25-year-old American design. It can't be used to carry satellites for third countries without U.S. consent.

LACK OF POWER

The H-1 only has enough power to push 550 kilos of payload into geostationary orbit—one quarter the capacity of the European Ariane 4 rocket or the U.S. space shuttle.

The H-1's successor, the H-2, will have a payload capacity of 2,200 kilos. But this is significantly less than the 6,800 kilos of the Ariane 5, which enters service in the mid-1990s, the same time as H-2.

Meanwhile, problems with the fuel pump of the LE-7 engine, which will power the H-2, recently caused the rocket's debut launch to be postponed for 12 months until early 1993, pushed up the development cost by 10% to approximately 230 billion yen (U.S.$1.6 billion). A fire in October at the engine test site may cause further delays.

HIGH LAUNCH COST

The country's main launch pad is in Tanegashima island, at the southern end of Japan. The Ariane and NASA launch sites are much closer to the equator, enabling their rockets to get into geostationary or low earth orbit faster, and guzzle less fuel. Satellites can therefore be launched much more cheaply on European and U.S. rockets than on Japanese ones.

At present all satellites launched from Tanegashima are for government agencies. Japanese commercial satellite owners say they can't afford local launch fees, and have gone elsewhere. For example, the pan-European satellite launching company Arianespace has won four contracts in Japan, among them one for state broadcasting company NHK.

RESTRICTED LAUNCH DATES

Launches at Tanegashima are limited to two 45-day periods a year, in deference to complaints from local fishermen. This means a maximum of four satellite launches a year can take place. By contrast NASA's launch pads at Cape Canaveral are open 365 days a year.

In 2000, Japan will still depend on the U.S. shuttle to take its astronauts into space, and JEM's future hinges on the U.S. Congress voting sufficient funds to enable NASA to proceed with the Freedom space station.

This puts Japanese space officials in a dilemma. On the one hand, they are anxious to take the plunge into manned space travel. On the other, their hands are tied by political factors outside their control.

U.S. proposals to cut the budget of the Freedom space station and push back the launch schedule are making the Japanese visibly impatient. "We are concerned about the possibility of a general delay caused by the United States. We may need a contingency plan," says Hiroshi Saito, general manager of MHI's space systems department.

This could mean developing a manned version of HOPE before 2000, Saito adds, and bringing forward plans for an independent Japanese space station, originally due to go up 10 years after Freedom.

If NASA falls down on its commitment to the Freedom project, pressure will grow for Japan to make its way in space without U.S. help. But it would be extremely difficult for Japan to go it alone. The H-2, the main symbol of Japanese self-sufficiency, has already run into technical difficulties—which Japan can't blame on the United States, as it's done with earlier rockets.

Such a move would also be costly, and provoke strong opposition from fiscally conservative Japanese politicians. In May 1988, the government's Space Advisory Commission recommended a spending target of Y6 trillion (U.S.$42 billion) for 1986 to 2000. But as funding is approved on an annual basis, the space agencies have to fight a constant battle with politicians and bureaucrats.

Most observers, though, expect the government to put its money where its mouth is.

"It regards aerospace as a critical technology and will see to it that adequate funds are made available," says Stephen Marvin, a senior analyst with Jardine Fleming Securities in Tokyo. "The money given to space research is a drop in the bucket compared with the subsidies given to sectors such as shipbuilding."

Argument about the weakness of Japan's space technology are missing the point, he argues. "By 2000, Japan will have had a decade to cut its teeth on its own space technology, enough time to learn from its mistakes and close the gap on its competitors."

Already, Japan's foray into space is arousing the same mixture of suspicion and envy among its trading partners as its advances into other areas of high-tech.

In June, 1989, the United States cited Japan's satellite-buying policies as one of the factors that defined it as an unfair trading nation, under the "Super 301" provision of the 1988 Omnibus Trade Act. But just a few months later, U.S. vice-president Dan Quayle was in Tokyo urging Japan to join the U.S. space effort.

Three years ahead of its launch, the H-2 became a target of international controversy. The rocket will allow Japan to enter the lucrative commercial satellite-launching market, which is now split between Europe (60%) and the U.S. (40%). By 2000, MHI expects to be launching two satellites a year for commercial use, Saito says.

The Europeans are concerned that the H-2 will enjoy an unfair advantage. "Governments in Europe, the United States, and Japan all provide money for public-use satellites incorporating their own technology. That isn't a problem," says Dieter Brand of Arianespace's Tokyo office. "The problem is to what extent the Japanese government is subsidizing satellite launchers that will be put to commercial use."

At present about 15 or 20 commercial satellites a year are launched worldwide, Brand explains.

"You need about seven launches a year to be viable. This only leaves room for two or three launch contractors."

Senior officials in Tokyo aren't prepared to guess when the country's space industry will be exposed to market forces. "We have no plans to enter the commercial market with our rockets," says the STA's Nakamura.

Yet at some stage the government will expect companies to dig into their pockets and shoulder some of the development costs. A recent policy document makes this point clear: "Japan is to encourage private sector activities with proper role-sharing between the public and private sectors."

Space programs are too costly and too risky for any company, or indeed country, to manage alone. When the U.S. shuttle was conceived in the 1970s, NASA expected it to become commercially self-supporting. This hope had faded well before the Challenger explosion in 1986, and the shuttle program has cost the U.S. an estimated U.S.$30 billion.

CHINA AND INDIA ENTER SPACE RACE

Japan may be the first in Asia to develop a permanently manned space station, but it is by no means the only Asian country to have a space program.

China launched its first satellite in 1970. India followed suit in 1980. Almost all Asian countries use satellites for telecommunications, and to monitor weather patterns and the environment.

China's hopes of furthering its space technology were dealt a major blow when, following the bloodshed in Tiananmen Square, the United States banned the sale to Beijing of military-related technology. Although the sanctions are apparently being applied somewhat flexibly, they must have underlined the need for self-sufficiency in the minds of China's leaders, including Premier Li Peng.

Li's involvement in the space program virtually ensures that China will continue developing its Long March rockets and satellites, despite the lack of hard currency. Now rockets with higher carrying capacities are planned.

The Long March 3A rocket will be able to lift satellites of 2.5 tons into orbit 800 kilometers from earth. The Long March 2E will carry satellites of 8.8 tons into low orbit (about 400 kilometers up).

Longer term plans call for the development of a three-stage carrier, based on the 2E, capable or putting satellites weighing 4.5 tons into the higher orbit. The present Long March 1, designed to launch small low orbit satellites, will have its capacity upgraded.

China intends to have three of its own communications satellites in orbit by the end of this year. With West German help, China is also working on a satellite for voice and data communications, to be launched in 1992.

Beijing's renewed desire for self-sufficiency extends to all areas of high technology, from fiber-optic cable manufacture to the development of computer systems.

When President Bush affirmed U.S. intentions to revisit the moon and send a manned mission to Mars, he didn't give a timetable or cost estimate. Since the Challenger accident—which halted U.S. manned space flights for three years—officials have become wary of setting target dates, and these new programs aren't expected to get under way until 2000.

To achieve them, the United States will have little choice but to swallow its misgivings over technology transfer, and enlist Japanese help. The USSR is also casting around for foreign partners for its program, and Soviet space agency Glavkosmos has proposed joint development of spacecraft with Japan.

By the same token, Japan is unlikely to get a man into space by 2000 without a lot of help from its friends. But no other nation has so much of the right stuff—high technology, financial resources, long-term commitment—or is as well-prepared to translate its ambitions in space into bottom-line results on earth.

With foreign exchange revenues dropping, China wants to maximize its earnings from commercial satellite launches to fund the development of new space systems. In the case of the AsiaSat telecoms satellite, it was prepared to undercut foreign competitors by as much as 40% to clinch the launching contract.

India's aim of attaining self-sufficiency in rockets by 2000 has also run into problems. The Augmented Satellite Launch Vehicle (ASLV), the country's second generation rocket, was recently grounded for extensive redesign following two abortive test flights. India has developed several of its own satellites, mainly for rural communications.

In Taiwan tentative approval has been given for a U.S.$380 million program to develop and manufacture low-orbit scientific satellites, the first of which will be launched in 1994. South Korea is also carrying out satellite research. Like Japan, both countries will initially rely on foreign technology through licensing deals.

Tom Kelly, vice-president of Grumman Data Services of the United States, wants Asian companies to get involved in the multibillion dollar freedom space station. Grumman is working on the project with U.S., European, Canadian, and Japanese space agencies.

During a visit to Hong Kong to mark the twentieth anniversary of the first moon landing, Kelly said, "I very much hope government bodies and companies in Asia take part in the development of space technology and in scientific and technical experiments that will be carried out in future projects.

"By pooling our international talents and resources, large-scale projects will be possible and we will be able to realize the development of space far sooner."

© *Asian Business* magazine, Far East Trade Press, Ltd., 1990.

Commercial Spin-Offs of Space Technology

Field of technology	Space technology	Examples of earthbound application
Material and equipment technology		
Technology to make smaller or lighter items	Integrated circuits (ICs), honeycomb structure materials	ICs, small-sized medical equipment (i.e., pacemakers), aircraft parts
Environment technology	Heat insulators, heat pipes, composite materials, bearings	Heat insulators for housing, high-efficiency heat exchangers, aircraft and automobile bodies, mechanical parts
Sensor technology	Solar batteries, fuel cells, rocket engines	Fuel cells, solar batteries
	Acceleration sensors, proximity sensors, environmental sensors	Automobile-use crash prevention sensors, environmental supervision systems
System technology		
Control technology, communications technology	Inertial navigation methods and inertial guidance technology, telemetering systems	Inertial guidance systems for civil aircraft, emergency medical systems for remote places
Image-processing technology	Data transmission	Data communications, high-density transmission systems
Computer technology	Digital imaging	Heterochromosome detection processing systems
		Large-scale computer systems for banks and other institutions
Production technology		
Design technology	Structure analysis, simulation	Structure analysis for civil engineering
Processing and assembly technology	Clean rooms	Clean rooms for semiconductors or medical treatment
Testing and inspection technology	Measuring instruments, environmental test systems, defect detection systems	Industrial measuring instruments, medical ultrasound diagnosis equipment, rehabilitation equipment
Control technology	Production control	Production control systems for industries, particularly engineering

Source: Aerospace Industry Association of Japan.

JAPAN'S MOON CITY

A self-contained city on the moon with hotels, offices, farms, research labs, and a dome for sporting events in space is the ambitious plan being contemplated by the Japanese government, which will call on its usual big-business partners to make it all work. One of the first priorities will be the development of a space craft that can shuttle routinely between Earth and a ring of intermediate space stations in low orbit. And although the initiative is being taken by the Japanese, it is inevitable that other nations will be drawn into the project because the immense amount of money needed for financing.

"Development costs are so high that cooperative, international projects are the only realistic course," says Seishi Suzuki of the Shimizu Corp., one of Japan's largest construction firms. Shimizu has held discussions with such possible partners as Lockheed Corp. and the Bechtel Group and is already participating with four U.S. firms in such space-related businesses as launch-pad technology and space-vehicle construction.

Shimizu, along with Mitsubishi Corp. and other companies are also planning to invest about $10 million in the Spacelab project, which also has European, Canadian, and U.S. involvement, and the Japanese construction giant, Ohbayashi Corp., is helping to finance a lunar base technology research center near the Kennedy Space Center in Florida.

INDIA BUILDS WORLD'S LARGEST RADIO TELESCOPE

India is building the world's largest radio telescope in the western city of Pune, which would give astronomers a chance to see "the very edge of the universe," according to Dr. Niruopama Raghavan, director of the Nehru Planetarium. The $16 million telescope is being built with Indian know-how and is scheduled to be completed by 1992, designated the International Year of Space.

ON THE CYBER RIM

Prize-winning Hong Kong industrial designer Francis Wa Chu recently unveiled a personal computer with a display that's contained in a pair of glasses. Inspired by a NASA prototype of a helmet computer, Chu's cyberspecs resemble an optician's eye-testing device. The hand-held control unit—which is based on the "mouse" principle as opposed to a keyboard—is about the size of a small cassette player.

CASHEWS IN SPACE

Indian scientists believe that cashew nuts belong in orbit, according to Minister for Science and Technology K. R. Narayan. Heat-resistant resin, based on liquid extracted from cashew nut shells, can be used as a heat shield for spacecraft, he said. The resin was developed by the regional research laboratory in the southern state of Kerala, India's largest cashew nut producer.

FAR OUT:

AFTER SUPERCONDUCTIVITY, FAR INFRARED

There are 400 to 500 products on the market that use far infrared waves. And more than

1,000 companies are working at developing ultra-infrared products. Some say that far-infrared goods may eventually become a Y20 trillion (about U.S. $153 billion) annual market, *Shukan Bunshun* magazine noted.

Among infrared rays, far infrared waves are given off with relatively low heat. Their use of energy is efficient, as is their heat-transfer properties. When a source of heat is surrounded by fine ceramics, emissions of far infrared waves increase. Saunas, carpets, hot plates, and other cooking appliances—anything made to fry, roast, boil, or warm—use far infrared waves.

But the boom in far infrared wave products comes from something else. While it has not been scientifically proven, organic things grow better in the presence of ceramics that give off far infrared waves at room temperatures. In humans, the metabolism improves, as does the circulation. With plants, growth is stimulated, and the fruit lasts longer after harvest.

New products taking advantage of this room temperature far infrared property include sleep wear, clothing, health goods, preservation goods, etc. One example is now on the market, a sheet of plastic impregnated with a ceramic material that pulls in infrared rays and then emits far infrared waves. Put it in the refrigerator and place your fruits and vegetables on it; it supposedly makes them stay fresh for twice as long.

"Obviously the next rash of far infrared wave products will be aimed at the nemesis of modern man—health," concluded *Shukan Bunshun*.

JAPAN'S FANTASTIC VOYAGE

A tiny robot that can travel inside the human body and locate and treat diseased tissue is under development by Japanese scientists. The team, headed by Iwao Fujimasa of Tokyo University, said that their goal is a robot less than 1 mm in size whose presence in the body would still present problems that must be solved. "Researchers for many years have sent probes to study the oceans and outer space," said Fujimasa, an artificial heart specialist. "We hope to be able to study the inner world."

BACTERIA STRIKE OIL

Hungry bacteria living in oil wells produce a kind of detergent-like substance when fed which in turn frees more oil from hidden nooks and crannies in the rock. This is the basis of research into "microbiological enhanced oil recovery" which has progressed from pouring raw sewage appetizingly mixed with molasses or waste dairy products down oil wells into more sophisticated techniques. Australian researchers claim that they are far ahead of the rest of the world in such experiments and that their latest methods can raise "by many percent" the amount of oil recoverable at a cost of about 71 cents U.S. per barrel.

CHINESE LASER CRYSTALS

Despite lagging behind developed countries such as the United States and Japan in scientific research, in certain areas such as permanent magnets, superconductors, and biochemistry, China is well able to hold its own reports Chen Heneng of the Chinese Academy of Sciences. He cited the country's development of laser crystals, selling for $3000 each, in which it led the world.

LASER FUEL FOR NUCLEAR PLANTS

Indian nuclear scientists are actively engaged in laboratory-level action to develop processes to use lasers as fuel for nuclear power plants.

MINERAL TROVE DOWN UNDER

Scientists are uncovering an underground treasure trove of minerals in Australia, a nation which is already a major quarry for industrial nations. Arid and mostly uninhabitable, Australia holds all major minerals except sulphur. A modern "scratching" of the surface—by underground explosion—is being conducted in the Channing Basin, a 430,000 km² area of northwest Australia. Australia produces 66 percent of the world's zircon, 55% of rutile, 40% of bauxite, 15% of lead, and 10% of uranium. It trades internationally some 28% of the world's black coal and 22% of the iron ore. Mineral products in 1987/1988 earned about $13.6 billion, representing more than 40% of Australia's total merchandise exports.

THE 30 MILLION YEAR SWATCH

Physicists at the University of Western Australia in Canberra are developing a clock which they believe will keep time more accurately than any other in the world. It will be made from ultra-pure, artificial sapphire. When completed, the clock will lose or gain only one second every 30 million years. The oversized, handless time pieces could be produced for $100,000 each.

NEURAL NERDS

Fujitsu, Ltd., one of Japan's leading computer companies, has simulated the workings of a neural computer and plans to develop a prototype by the early 1990s, according to a company spokesman. Neural computers are based on the design principles of human nervous systems that evolve through time and experience. Their ability to learn makes them adept at pattern recondition and judgment applicable to industrial, financial, and educational fields. Fujitsu's simulator has a processing capacity of 100,000 neurons, processing data 10 to 100 times faster than the fastest simulators developed at American academic institutes.

JAPANESE GENIUS INVENTOR

The 60-year-old inventor of the floppy disc is spending time in his Tokyo laboratory trying to think of a way he can live until the year 2068. "My target is 140 years of life," says Dr. Yoshiro Nakamats [sic] who began his career while still a teenager by dreaming up the kerosene pump, now a heating fixture in most Japanese homes. Lifestyle, says Nakamats, means everything to the creative mind, which is why he sleeps only four hours a night and divides the time spent at his Akasaka home between a "calm room" and a "dynamic room" to enhance his thinking. All of his sleeping and many of his working hours are spent in Cerebrex, the "brain chair" he invented to stimulate brain activity by increasing blood flow and thus pumping more oxygen to the brain. "It's very good for new ideas," he explains.

BLACK HOLES ON THE BARBIE

The Australia Telescope, a complex $50 million device on which work began a decade ago, will give a first close look at southern skies and may unlock the secret of black holes. It comprises half a dozen 22-meter dishes, each weighing 400 tons and connected by fiber-optic cables, mounted on an east-to-west rail line (for easy repositioniing) near

Narrabri, about 300 km northwest of Sydney. "For the first time in the southern hemisphere," says astronomer John Whiteoak, "we have a facility to probe radio sources that can't be seen as clearly by northern astronomers."

Of special interest to the Australian observers will be the Magellanic Clouds, the two galaxies closest to our Milky Way, and about which aborigines have a legend that they are the camping places of an old man and woman for whom star people collect fish in the sky river, the Milky Way. The Small Cloud (200,000 light years away) and the Large Cloud (170,000 years) are both rich with new star formations, and Whiteoak says that radio examinations have already shown that something chaotic is happening at the latter's center which the new telescope may help to explain. "By definition you can't see a black hole so you have to prove that they are there by looking at the material around them, gathering evidence of gravitational forces, explosions or what have you."

8

❖

INFRASTRUCTURE

ASIA 2000

RIM METROPOLIS
by Eric Stone

Asian cities in the year 2000 will be a mix of new ideas and old problems.

By the year 2000, Hong Kong and Bangkok will be in decline, the former made anemic by the draining of too many brains and the latter viewing a future under water and a present stalled in traffic.

Singapore and Saigon (having readopted that name in 1996) will be in the ascendant, with Singapore having become the entrepot and service center for the increasing manufacturing power of Indonesia and Malaysia, and Saigon having attracted a lot of the foreign

investment that used to go to China before the hardliners consolidated their power.

Tokyo will be richer than any city in history and, despite a population of slightly over 20 million, no more crowded than it is today.

The future, as always, has a nasty habit of springing surprises. But based on current trends the above scenario has a better than even chance of coming true. On firmer ground are some predictions about Asia's cities 10 years from now which, barring

major, generally catastrophic, unforeseen circumstances, can confidently be made.

- The population of every major urban center
  in Asia will increase. At the moment the
  fastest growing is Kuala Lumpur.

One exception may be Hong Kong, where
a deteriorating political situation could lead to
a mass exodus of population just before or
shortly after the change of sovereignty in
1997. This is already beginning to happen.

- Growing populations, greater affluence, and
  further industrialization will generate more
  waste, noise, dirty air, and bigger crowds.
  It's as simple as that.

Take China, where most sewage is not
washed down drains and into sewers. If China
were to go on a massive sewer building binge
to bring itself up to modern standards by the
year 2000, the system would carry 364 million
tons (182,000 Olympic-sized swimming
pools) of raw sewage every day.

It is questionable whether any country
could afford such a scale of investment in
plumbing over the next 10 years, and it's certain that China won't be able to build the necessary waste treatment plants at the same
time.

Environmental engineer James Tam, Hong
Kong general manager of Danish engineering
firm I Kruger, thinks that Hong Kong and
Singapore, being smaller and richer, and
Japan, thanks to its wealth, could clean up
their acts.

But he believes that industrialization in
China's Pearl River delta is likely to dump
chemicals into the water that will flow down-
river to Hong Kong.

These chemicals, he says, "will make *E. coli*
(the common, dangerous bacteria generated
by sewage) seem relatively harmless by comparison."

- Standards of living and gross domestic
  products will rise. In most of Asia's developing countries new power plants and water
  projects will bring electricity and running
  water to the majority of the people who
  don't currently have them. Industrialization
  will mean more money in more pockets.
- Traffic pollution will get worse everywhere.

By 1997 Taiwan expects to have 175 vehicles for every 1,000 people, giving it one of
the highest vehicle densities in the world.

A combination of worsening traffic and
pollution will drive the people of Bangkok
out of that city and into new urban centers.
The opening of the Eastern Seaboard Development will accelerate the trend, and the sea-
side resort of Pattaya, because of its close
proximity, could possibly become Thailand's
second city.

Dr. Nimit Nontapunthawat, chief economist and manager of Bangkok Bank's research departments, says if Bangkok can't
solve its traffic woes, "It will be a dying city.
It will be so much trouble living in Bangkok
that people like myself will move out."

Nimit is not optimistic about Bangkok's
future. He believes that while the city will not
disappear, it will lose its center stage position.

- In the most developed areas, particularly
  Japan, Hong Kong, and Singapore, which
  will continue to move toward service-based
  economies, people are likely to need work
  space at home.

Due to advances in telecommunications, "we may be the last generation who need to go to the office," suggests Terry Curthoys, director of strategic planning for Communications Systems, Ltd., of Hong Kong.

In Japan, Hong Kong, and Singapore, offices will become smaller and homes larger and less dependent on locations near the business districts.

• In the developed countries, where savings rates are high and working hours are shrinking, more people will buy telephones, televisions, refrigerators, cars, and home computers, and will want more living space.

But cities seldom grow in only one direction. Rather, expansion takes place in disorderly pockets surrounding a city. In capitals, such as Bangkok, Jakarta, and Manila, the transport infrastructure will probably still be a good 10 to 20 years behind what is needed in the year 2000.

Kuala Lumpur's light rail and Taipei's subway are both scheduled to open in phases, starting from the mid-1990s. Both are likely to be overcrowded from the word go, and by the year 2000 will still be lagging behind the cities' expanding populations and areas.

Most of the infrastructure development in Asia that will be completed by 2000 will at best allow the increased populations to hold congestion and pollution down to their current—1990—levels.

• The oceans will rise. A growing number of environmental scientists have sounded the alarm about the "greenhouse" effect leading to worldwide warming and melting parts of the polar ice caps. This will result in a rise in the sea level.

An often cited figure is a rise of 1.0 to 1.5 meters by the middle of next century. "Bangkok is already sinking," says Peter Hills, assistant director of the Center for Urban Studies at Hong Kong University. "A rise in the sea level over the next 40 or 50 years will drown it."

Hills points out that many of Asia's major cities are on coasts or estuaries, and are therefore at risk from any significant rise in sea level.

"Planning and projects should start as soon as possible," he says. "Certainly by 2000 we should be ready to adapt to what is inevitable and have a plan to stabilize the situation at acceptable levels."

• Physically, much will change. There will be taller buildings. There will be longer bridges and tunnels, wider roads and more public transport. In some cities, most notably Hong Kong and Tokyo, there will be more land, thanks to reclamation.

Hong Kong, Pyongyang, Taipei, and Tokyo are all making plans to build what they hope will be the world's tallest building. Pyongyang's and Taipei's will be government-financed attempts to garner prestige, while Hong Kong's and Tokyo's will be towering monuments to private enterprise.

But if you fall asleep today and don't wake up until 2000, chances are good—if no one has moved your slumbering body—that after getting over your initial awe, you will recognize where you are.

To help you get your bearings, here are some specific predictions as to the shape of Asia's cities in the year 2000. Some are based on projects that are already underway, others are speculative. (*Population figures are United Nations projections for greater urban areas in 2000. Figures in brackets are estimates of population in 1989.*)

A QUICK TOUR OF ASIA'S CITIES IN THE YEAR 2000

THE HIGH AND MIGHTY

Tokyo—The greatest city of the world's greatest economic power.
Osaka-Kobe—The second city of the world's greatest economic power.
Singapore—Performing for Indonesia the role that Hong Kong used to play for China.
Jakarta—The capital of the Indonesian manufacturing boom.
Surabaya—The second city and port of the Indonesian manufacturing boom.
Saigon—Political and economic reform has allowed it to make use of its geography, resources, and population.
Thailand's Eastern Seaboard Development—Where the Bangkok action and money have moved to.

ON THE WAY DOWN

Bangkok—Sinking, congested, polluted, and too aggravating to attract overseas business or hold onto domestic companies.
Hong Kong—Too many brains down the drain.

VERY PROSPEROUS BUT SECOND STRING

Pusan—South Korea is hardly an international power, but it is a manufacturing power. Pusan is its port.
Seoul—Doing very well but too close to Japan for anyone to take much notice.
Taipei—Still a lot of cash on the books, mostly from high-tech manufacturing, but the island is too small.

HONG KONG

Population   6.4 million
               (5.8 million)

Planned

• The world's longest suspension bridge (approximately 1.4 km) will link the north end of Lantau island, near the new airport, to Tsing Yi island.

• The Western Cross Harbour Tunnel will run from Kennedy Town on Hong Kong Island to Yau Ma Tei in Kowloon.
• Jardine House, currently about 50 meters from the harbor's edge in Central, will be 300 meters in from the waterfront and will no longer have a harbor view.
• The "Tallest Building In The World" (160 stories) will be in Wanchai. It will be part hotel, part office block, and part residential flats.

LESS PROSPEROUS BUT STILL SECOND STRING

Chiang Mai—Thailand's city of the north but most of the interest is along the Eastern Seaboard.

Kuala Lumpur (or "KL," as aficionados call it)—A pretty, quiet place; up-to-date enough to do business from. Multinationals go there to hold meetings.

Penang—Malaysia's second city, prettier than KL and even nicer for meetings.

GOING NOWHERE FAST

Beijing, Guangzhou, Shanghai—The latest generation of hardliners is making everyone nervous.

Manila—So many islands, so little infrastructure, and so much politics.

ANYBODY'S GUESS (THE WORLD IS A FUNNY PLACE)

Cebu (the second biggest urban center in the Philippines after Manila)—Could make it with refugee Hong Kong money and if oil is discovered.

Phnom Penh—Possibilities if peace breaks out and a highway is built from Saigon to Thailand's Eastern Seaboard.

Pyongyang—Reunification with the south could have its benefits.

Rangoon (capital of Myanmar, formerly Burma)—A way-station between the growing clout of India and Southeast Asia, if the politics are ever sorted out.

Vientiane (capital of Laos)—High on the vice that Thailand has become too developed for.

Speculative

- The hottest property market will be the site of the old Kai Tak airport and the land undergoing reclamation between there and Hung Hom.

SINGAPORE

Population	3 million
	(2.7 million)

Planned

- Public utilities and telecommunications will have expanded to the point where Singapore has a "cashless society," relying on electronic funds transfer rather than money.
- Phase three of the Mass Rapid Transit System will have almost completely done away with traffic problems.
- Public housing will have been improved and expanded. The city will comfortably house its entire population, with room to spare.

Proposed

- The tallest building will be 78 stories.

Speculative

- As much as 35% of the population will work at home.

TOKYO

Population	Greater City	20.2 million
	Inner city	14.75 million
		(14 million)

Planned

- Transport will be so efficient that 45% of Japan's population will be able to make one-day round-trips to the city.
- About 100,000 commuters will travel daily between Tokyo and Osaka on high-speed "magnetic levitation' (maglev) trains.
- 10,000 hectares of new residential complexes will house more than 3 million people.

Proposed

- Three 50-story office buildings will "float" on Tokyo Bay, built on a foundation of giant caissons.
- "The World's Tallest Building" (2,001 meters, 500 stories) will be under construction on an artificial island in Tokyo Bay.

MANILA

Population	11.1 million
	(10 million)

Planned

- Major commercial and university development on 2,915 hectares reclaimed from Manila Bay during the Marcos era.

Proposed

- A canal system on Quezon City that will ease flooding.
- A centralized public transport system will be under construction.

Speculative

- Intramuros and Sam Miguel will be the booming property markets.
- There will be skyscrapers in Metro Manila. The tallest will be 70 stories.

KUALA LUMPUR

Population	2 million
	(1.2 million)

Planned

- The city will be more Islamic in architecture. It will be greener and more than half the population will be ethnic Malays.
- A private-sector light rail transit network will run from north to south and west toward Port Klang.
- The outer ring road system and North Klang Valley Expressway will divert heavy goods transport away from the vicinity of the city, thus easing traffic between the city and the port.

Speculative

- Suburbs around the city will have expanded to the point of merging with the surrounding towns of Petaling Jaya, Kepong, Shah Alam, Sungei Buluh, Rawang, and Bangi.
- Despite government planning to reduce the number of squatters in the city, the growth in population will keep the number at its present level of about 25% of the urban population.

BANGKOK

Population   10.7 million
              (7.4 million)

Planned

- The Skytrain mass rapid transit system will be operational. (A subway system to supplement it is likely to be rejected as too expensive.)
- Highway linkages with the Eastern Seaboard Development area will create a Bangkok to Chonburi megalopolis.
- U-Tapao, near Pattaya, will be the major Thai international airport and Bangkok's Don Muang airport will have greatly decreased in importance.
- Laem Chabang on the Eastern Seaboard will be Thailand's main port. Bangkok's Klong Toey will decline.

Speculative

- The Thai Parliament will have moved to Ayuthaya.

TAIPEI

Population   3 million
              (2.3 million)

Planned

- The Mass Rapid Transit System will be 70% completed. When fully completed it will be capable of carrying 105,000 passengers per hour. The four lines are expected to be full from the day they open.
- An urban renewal project will be completed in the area of the new central train station. The government hopes this will create a new commercial center in the western district.
- A tunnel will connect Taipei to Ilan on the east coast, cutting the travel time to 45 minutes and making it a satellite industrial city of Taipei.

Proposed

- A high-speed (300 kilometers per hour) bullet train linking Taipei, Taichung, and Kaohsiung.
- "The World's Tallest Building" (620 meters, or about 155 stories) on the east side of Taipei.

SEOUL

Population   13.8 million
              (10.2 million)

Planned

- The mass transit system will have expanded into all the suburbs and out to the recently expanded airport.
- The U.S. Army base near the center of town will have moved out and the land turned into a public park, although there is likely to be mounting pressure to open it for development.
- Housing estates averaging between 30,000 and 50,000 residents will have opened in the suburbs causing a big demand for large-scale retail development.
- Kwangiu and Taegu will have international airports which will take some of the pressure off Seoul.

Speculative

- The triangular region between Seoul Inchon and Suwon will be one huge city.

© *Asian Business* magazine, Far East Trade Press, Ltd., 1989.

Project	Estimated cost (US$ million)	Project period
TABLE 1: MAJOR INFRASTRUCTURE PROJECTS IN ASIA		
JAPAN		
New Kansai international airport	8,300	1986-93
Supporting road, rail and other facilities	18,300	mid-1990s
Trans-Tokyo Bay highway	8,900	1988-96
Haneda airport	6,200	1983-93
SOUTH KOREA		
Expansion of Kimpo international airport	3,100	1987-91
Third international airport at Chongju	6,700	1987-91
Pusan port development	2,900	1986-90
TAIWAN		
Taipei mass rapid transport system	14,800	1989-99
Fourth nuclear power plant	6,300	1990-98
Taichung coal-fired power plant	3,300	1990-95
Mingtan pumped-storage hydro project	1,850	1989-95
Fifth naphtha cracking plant	500	1989-93
Sixth naphtha cracking plant	1,000	1989-95
First section of second freeway	2,000	Early 1990s
Tunnel expressway	1,500	1988-96
HONG KONG		
Kai Tak airport expansion, new airport and related facilities	7,600	1988-96
Port development (Terminal 7)	960	1988-90
Major roads and rail extensions linking Kwun Tong and Junk Bay	2,170	mid-1990s
Eastern harbour crossing	500	1986-90
Tate's Cairn tunnel	300	1988-91
Land reclamation	2,300	mid-1990s
Urban redevelopment (first 7 projects)	1,600	1989-94
CHINA		
Guangzhou-Shenzhen-Zhuhai superhighway	1,500	1988-93
Shajiao C power station (2 x 660 MW)	1,000	1989-92
SINGAPORE		
10-year plan to expand ports, public utilities and telecommunications	5,140	1990-2000
Mass rapid transit system, phase III	1,130	1990-92
MALAYSIA		
North-south highway	1,260	1988-95
Peninsula gas project, phase II	500	1988-91
National rural water supply scheme	520	1986-91
THAILAND		
Bangkok mass rapid transit 'Skytrain'	1,680	1990-95
Bangkok expressway	1,120	1989-95
Don Muang airport tollway	380	1989-92
Laem Chabang port	800	1988-91
PHILIPPINES		
300 MW coal-fired power plant	280	1989-92
700 MW coal-fired power plant	540	1993-96
Intra-city highway system	700	1990-95
Telecommunications	530	1989-92
110 MW geothermal power plant	690	1991-93
INDONESIA		
Pan-island bridge (Java-Madura)	230	1989-91

Source: Asian Business

TABLE 2: MAJOR PARTICIPANTS	
Project	**Companies**
TAIWAN	
Taipei Mass Rapid Transit	American Transit Consultants (partnership of Parsons Brinckerhoff, Bechtel Engineering and Kaiser Engineering International)
Mass Rapid Transit	Matra Transport (France)
Gas supply	M W Kellog Co (US)
HONG KONG	
Port development, Terminal 7	Kumagai Gumi (Japan), Hollandesche Aanneming (Holland) and Mitsui (Japan)
Eastern Harbour Crossing	Kumagai Gumi/Marubeni (Japan)
Tait's Cairn tunnel	Jardine Matheson (HK), Trafalgar House (Gammon) (UK), C Itoh, Nishimatsu (Japan), New World Development (HK)
Route 5 tunnel	Dragages (France), Gammon and Skanska (Sweden)
Tuen Mun Light Rail Transit system	Leighton Contractors (Asia) Ltd (Australia)
CHINA	
Guangzhou superhighway	Hopewell Holdings (HK)
Shajiao B & C coal power stations	Hopewell Holdings
THAILAND	
Bangkok Expressway	Kumagai Gumi, Expressway and Rapid Transit Authority of Thailand
Bangkok 'Skytrain'	Lavalin International Group (Canada)
Laem Chabang port	Italian Thai Development Corp
Industrial estates	Marubeni Corp
MALAYSIA	
Peninsula gas project	Malaysian/Japanese consortium: Sinar Berlian, Mitsubishi Corp, Antah Oil Tools Services Corp, C Itoh, Pelita, Marubeni Corp, Laiman Corp and Sumitomo Corp
Peninsula gas project	Malaysian/Brazilian consortium: Sabandra-Hamison, Petrobras Commercio International-Interbras and Confab Industrial
North-south highway	Projek Lebuhraya Utara-Selatan (Malaysia)
PHILIPPINES	
Power barges	Mitsui and John Brown (UK)
90 MW gas turbine power station	Marubeni Corp
110 MW geothermal power plant	Gruppo Industrie Electro Meccaniche (Italy)
200 MW gas turbine power station	Hopewell Holdings
INDONESIA	
Java-Madura bridge	Mitsui and Mitsubishi with PT PAL, PT Boma Bisma Indra, and PT Barata (Indonesia)

Source: Asian Business

ASIAN CHRONICLES

A VIEW OF MANILA IN THE 19TH CENTURY

The 19th century French traveler and adventurer Paul de la Cironiere lived in the Philippines for a number of years, and recorded his experiences in a book entitled Adventures d'un Gentilhomme Breton Aux Iles Philippines, *which was later published in English as* Adventures of a Frenchman in the Philippines. *This is his description of the colorful and boisterous city of "Manilla" in the last century:*

Manilla and its suburbs contain a population of about one hundred and fifty thousand souls, of which Spaniards and Creoles hardly constitute the tenth part, the remainder is composed of Tagalogs, or Indians, Mestizos, and Chinese. The city is divided into two sections—the military and the mercantile—the latter of which is the suburb. The former, surrounded by lofty walls, is bounded by the sea on one side, and upon another by an extensive plain, where the troops are exercised, and where of an evening the indolent Creoles, lazily extended in their carriages, repair to exhibit their elegant dresses and to inhale the sea breezes.

This public promenade—where intrepid horsemen and horsewomen, and European vehicles, cross each other in every direction—may be styled after the Champs Elysees, or the Hyde Park, of the Indian Archipelago. On a third side, the military town is separated from the trading town by the river Pasig upon which are seen all the day boats laden with merchandise, and charming gondolas conveying idlers to different parts of the suburbs, or to visit the ships in the bay. The military town communicates by the bridge of Binonduc with the mercantile town . . . In general, the highways are macadamised, and kept in good condition. Such is the effeminacy of the people, they could not endure the noise of carriages upon pavement. The houses, large and spacious, (are) palaces in appearance.

WORLD'S LONGEST ESCALATOR

The Hong Kong government is building the biggest and most spectacular escalator in the world, connecting Central Hong Kong's financial district with the territory's residential Mid-Levels district. Comprising 21 escalators, three moving platforms, and several footbridges, the 800-meter covered link is due to become operational by mid-1992. Engineers say it will take 30 minutes to travel up its whole length and 19 minutes to go down to the bottom. Since the "travelator" will run only one-way at a time, direction will be regulated on a "tidal basis"—uphill between 10 a.m. and 10 p.m., and downhill between 6 a.m. and 10 am. The system (which is estimated to cost about $15 million) is designed to carry up to 27,000 people a day.

VANCOUVER'S PACIFIC PLACE

A gigantic commercial and residential project on the site of the old Vancouver Expo has been planned by a group of Hong Kong developers who estimate that it will take 15 years to complete and run to a total cost of $14 billion. Called Pacific Place it will include an international financial center, a 400-room hotel, entertainment complex, shops, offices, and homes, as well as 40 acres of parks and waterfront promenades. The company, Concord Pacific Developments, has paid more than $2 billion for the site, which was purchased only 10 years ago by the British Columbian government for $381 million.

ON THE NEW AMERICAN RIM

Welcome to Alhambra, the American Rim town of the future. While some small California cities have been forced to make painful cultural and economic adjustments in absorbing the growing wave of Asian immigrants and investment, other communities have seen the calligraphy on the wall. They've chosen to go with the flow rather than to fight it.

Alhambra, a small southern California town which borders Los Angeles to the west and Pasadena to the north, is a prime example of what might be called an "NDARC"—a "newly developing American Rim community." In a sense, it's becoming more of a suburb of Taipei than it is of Los Angeles—yet it is firmly planted on the West Coast.

Over the past few years, more than $100 million of Asian capital has been invested in Alhambra's local business and real estate market. Forty percent of its total population of 73,000 is now Asian, with Taiwanese comprising 85% of that number. By 1999, according to the Alhambra Chamber of Commerce, it is estimated that 75% of its residents will be Asian.

Most of the businesses located on Valley Boulevard, a 3.5 mile business strip, are Asian-owned. Twelve Asian banks have sprung up in town. Real estate prices have skyrocketed. Some $200,000 homes are now selling for $350,000. In certain parts of the city, local zoning laws permit multiple units to be built on the sites of formerly single family residences, further fueling the real estate boom.

Yet in spite of all this social and economical upheaval, Alhambra has managed to keep its ethnic tensions under control and has not allowed them to get in the way of business development.

"It's lucky that all the troubles (the much publicized racial strife between the local Anglos and Asian immigrants) happened in neighboring Monterey Park first," observed Richard Nichols, executive manager of Alhambra's chamber of commerce. "We were prepared for the tremendous influx of Asians buying property and business. Our city government formed a committee right away to deal with the issues," he said.

As a result of its foresight, for example, Alhambra is the only town in the area which does not have ordinances regulating foreign language signs, according to Nichols. He jokingly cites the case of one Chinese bookstore in Alhambra which does not have an English sign in front. "All I do is sell Chinese books. Why do I need a sign in English?" asked the store owner.

"So that people will know where to send the fire department in case of fire," we explained. He still has only the Chinese sign.

"We have no objection to that, most people in Alhambra don't.

"We've been able to avoid controversy by working with the Asians, not rebuffing them," Nichols says. "We have here a very good sense of controlled growth without having a lot of laws."

In a form of reverse ping-pong diplomacy, Alhambra has put itself on the Asian-Pacific map by hosting the Pacific Rim International Table Tennis tournament each year. That was where, in 1985, players from the Republic of China on Taiwan competed for the first time against players from the PRC.

SOUTH KOREAN SHIPBUILDERS

South Korea overtook Japan in 1987 to become the world's top shipbuilding nation, according to the Japan Shipbuilding Association. Citing data supplied by Lloyd's Register of Shipping, JSA said South Korea built 88 ships aggregating 2.33 million gross tons compared with 284 ships totaling 2.30 million gross tons for Japan.

CHINESE SHIP REPAIRERS

China is setting its sights on becoming one of the world's major ship repair sites. In the first 11 months of 1988, China State Shipbuilding Corp., the state-operated ship-repairing agency, repaired 781 ships, 287 of them foreign-owned, earning $100 million, $22 million of which was in foreign exchange. Client nations include the United States, Cuba, Iran, the Soviet Union, and even the Republic of China on Taiwan, although Taiwanese ships do not fly the ROC flag when they come into port.

STUPIDITY BLAMED FOR INDUSTRIAL WASTAGE

Mismanagement and stupidity are being blamed by China's *Economic Information* news-paper for immense industrial wastage which has resulted in millions of dollars worth of imported factory equipment lying around unused, rusting, and in some cases still unpacked. In one textile concern in the central province of Anhui, 531 machines still sat unopened in their shipping boxes. In another, the imported machines have been employed at only one seventh of their capacity. The paper reported that an investigation into nine factories built in 1979 at a cost of $27 million to make fiber board revealed that some of the equipment had rusted into scrap. "In one factory the machines stand in rows covered in dust like a giant animal in deep sleep," the paper added, blaming the waste on incompetent officials who knew that funds came from the state and did not have to be repaid.

CHINA'S UNPAVED ROADS

Less than 20% of China's roads are paved, according to the *China Daily*. A recent study by the Ministry of Communications revealed that of the country's 980,000 km of roads, more than 500,000 km are almost impassable during rainy weather because of the mud. Few highways have been designated limited access for vehicular traffic, which in most cases includes bicycles and animal-drawn carts. China acknowledged the urgent need to boost its road network if it hopes to cope with the economic modernization program.

KAOHSIUNG'S CONTAINER KINGDOM

The southern Taiwan port of Kaohsiung became the world's second largest container port in 1988, handling more than 3 million TEUs (20-ft equivalent units), a record in its container service history. Harbor Administration officials predict Kaohsiung will replace Hong Kong as the world's No. 1 container port by the year 2000. Rotterdam, the world's largest container port, fell to third place in 1988 after being surpassed by Hong Kong, which handled 3.3 million TEU containers.

MACAO

BETTING ON MACAO

Macao's racetrack is to get a $250 million upgrade to international standard and 67 flat race meetings a year if plans by a Taiwanese business syndicate go through. The group headed by Jenn Woei Investing Development Co., Inc. has already spent about the same amount to acquire the track and predicts that it can be making profits before 1999 when Macao is handed back to China. After that date it will retain control, assuming that both countries permit it. Flat racing has not been successful in Macao since before World War II, and the decade-old Macao Trotting Club has been a losing enterprise.

The government of Macao, optimistic about retaining a high level of autonomy after the Chinese takeover in 1999, is introducing new industrial projects, building a new airport, and introducing a bilingual system to ease the transfer. Under Portuguese rule since 1557, Macao will be a Special Administrative Region of China for 50 years after coming under Beijing's overall authority.

SECOND-HAND DEMAND

China imported more than $250 million worth of second-hand equipment since 1983 in order to save foreign exchange, according to the *China Daily*. The same equipment would have cost $1.2 billion, if it had been bought new.

THE CHINA COAST

China plans to develop its entire central east coast whose 14 cities account for 7.7% of the country's population and 25% of its industrial output as an export zone, according to Beijing University economist Prof. Fu Lyuan. He predicted that the country's extraordinary economic growth would have a massive impact on the Asia-Pacific region, and urged Japan to give greater help to China's modernization by allowing the transfer of high technology. Guangzhou, across the border from Hong Kong, is one town that has benefited enormously by processing materials and parts supplied by its capitalist neighbor. More than 40 factories and a dozen industrial areas have been created in recent years. But the professor's rosy scenario is being called into question, at least in Shanghai, which Hong Kong's *Sing Tao* described as on the verge of "social collapse." China's biggest city, the paper charged, is suffering from declining productivity, horrendous transit problems, inadequate telephone service which works "haphazardly," a housing shortage, a polluted water supply, and the highest food prices in the country.

THAILAND'S GREAT SOUTHERN LANDBRIDGE

The Thai government has announced an ambitious new scheme to link the Andaman Sea (on the Indian Ocean side) with the Gulf of Thailand—thus bypassing the Strait of Malacca and removing the nation's dependence on Singapore for the transshipment of Thai goods to Burma, Bangladesh, India, the Middle East, and Europe. Thais hope to have this

---

TOKYO BAY CITY—FUTURE MEGATROPOLIS

Not far from the heart of Tokyo is a different world. A place with lots of greenery, where apartment houses stand tall beside modern marinas; where you watch the windsurfers as you walk to work at a leading-edge intelligent building; where the evenings are spent at a nearby concert hall listening to Beethoven's 9th . . . This is the concept behind Tokyo Bay City, and it's starting to take shape.

Here are the 10 biggest projects as listed by *Nikkei Trendy* magazine [broken down by; (1) budget, (2) area, (3) completion date, (4) prime mover, (5) final working population, and (6) resident population]:

Tokyo Teleport Town—A new urban center that will rise on Tokyo Bay; (1) Y14 trillion, (2) 448 hectares, (3) 2000, (4) Tokyo government, (5) 110,000, (6) 60,000.

Minato Mirai 21—Yokohama's major urban redevelopment project; (1) Y2 trillion, (2) 186 hectares, (3) 2000, (4) Yokohama government and Minato Mirai 21 Corp., (5) 190,000, (6) 10,000.

Makuhari New Urban Center—A convention and exhibition center located between Tokyo and the Narita airport; (1) Y1 trillion, (2) 437.7 hectares, (3) 1990, (4) Chiba prefectural government, (5) 100,000, (6) 25,000.

Trans-Tokyo Bay Highway—A transportation link across the Bay of Tokyo between Kawasaki and Kisarazu on the Boso Peninsula; (1) Y1.15 trillion, (2) 15.1 km, (3) 1996, (4) Trans-Tokyo Bay Highway Corp.

Takeshiba, Hinode, Shibaura Pierfront Project—Renewal of three old pier areas and construction of modern office buildings; (1) Y110 billion, (2) 36.9 hectares, (3) 1989, (4) Tokyo government.

Civil Port Island Project—Kawasaki's land reclamation project, where distribution and warehousing centers will be located; (1) Y93.93 billion, (2) 443 hectares, (3) 1995, (4) Kawasaki city government.

Okawabata River City—One of Tokyo's first high-rise office/housing combinations; (1) unknown, (2) 15.2 hectares, (3) 1991, (4) Okawabata Riverside Development Association.

Urayasu Marina East 21—A major residential project that will help housing shortage in the Tokyo area—15 km from central Tokyo; (1) Y62.1 billion, (2) 232.6 hectares, (3) 1995, (4) Chiba prefectural government.

Haneda Reclamation Project—Will be used to double the area of the Haneda airport; (1) Y880 billion, (2) 1,100 hectares, (3) 1995, (4) Ministry of Transportation.

Tokyo Disneyland Expansion Project—A second theme park, hotel, and 24-hour leisure land; (1) unavailable, (2) 82.5 hectares, (3) not determined, (4) Oriental Land.

"Looks like Tokyo Bay City is going to be a combination of work, play, home life, and commerce," commented *Nikkei Trendy* magazine, which compiled the above list.

120 kilometer landbridge—consisting of a four-lane highway, and including an oil distribution center and two deep-sea ports for tankers—constructed by 1993. According to Thailand's National Economic and Social Development Board, American engineering firms will be given first crack at the project, but the Japanese won't be too far behind in the event the Americans don't make the best offer. Also on the drawing boards is a proposal to build a highway that would link Rangoon and Hong Kong with a road cutting through China, Vietnam, Laos, and Thailand.

PAN-ASIAN HIGHWAY

A proposed Pan-Asian highway stretching from Turkey and Iran all the way to Vietnam and Singapore is under consideration by the United Nations, which hopes it can be in place by the end of the century.

PEARL RIVER BRIDGE

A Hong Kong businessman has outlined plans for a 23-mile bridge across China's Pearl River estuary which would cut driving time between Hong Kong and Macao to under one hour. Gordon Wu, managing director of Hopewell Holdings, which has built highways and power stations in China as well as Guangzhou's luxurious China Hotel, says the proposed bridge could woo away many of the 12 million people who spend $100 million each year making the crossing by ferry, and it could also support water pipes bringing water to the colony from the West River. Wu, the son of a taxi driver, was studying engineering at Princeton University when he first decided to become a millionaire and figured out that Hong Kong was the place to do it, if only

because of his realization that the 25% tax rate demanded on his salary as a surveyor would be less than half that in the colony. Starting in business for himself in 1962, he claimed that work has never been hard to find.

HAINAN'S HANDICAP

Lack of roads and the basic infrastructure of electricity and telephones may abort China's attempt to "clone" Taiwan on the undeveloped, tropical island of Hainan off its southern coast. Although its six million people have been promised more freedom and autonomy than any other area of communist China with free movement of capital, foreigners, and goods to and from Hainan, its progress toward becoming a trading zone has been slow. "If Japanese firms want to invest in China," says one visitor, "they will choose already-developed areas with a better infrastructure and a skilled work force." Although the island, with just a short railroad and a handful of military roads, is still relatively primitive, it has attracted job applications from 150,000 people of which 26,000 have turned up in person and remain mostly unemployed.

TAIPEI TUNNEL

The Taiwanese government is building a $1.4 billion highway tunnel linking the eastern part of the capital Taipei with Ilan County in northeastern Taiwan. The estimated 45 km-long project is the biggest engineering project of its kind in Taiwan and is expected to be completed in 1998. The tunnel will cut travel time in half between the two points, and reduce the two-hour commuting time to less than one hour.

NEW JAPANESE CAPITAL

When it comes to land reclamation the Japanese tend to thing *big*. Partly as a result of pressure to boost the domestic economy and certainly because of soaring prices for the available space, authorities are mulling over a plan to spend $384 billion—more than the country's entire annual budget—to create four artificial islands in Tokyo Bay to house a government and business center. On this new landfill, totaling 100 square kilometers, would be a new parliament (Diet) and buildings for various ministries, highways, railways, an international airport, and apartments for one million people. An alternative project under consideration at an estimated cost of $980 billion envisages one man-made island housing five million people. Tokyo property prices increased almost 80% in 1988, bringing the cost of one square meter in the "downtown" Ginza district to $166,000, and there are already plans to start relocating government offices outside the city to reduce crowding. One plan under consideration is to build a completely new capital on the lines of Brasilia or Canberra.

JAPANESE TAX-FREE ZONE

Japan's first tax-free trade zone was inaugurated on Okinawa Island in the East China Sea in 1988. The 2.8 hectare duty-free complex is located near Naha airport.

CAM RANH, COME ALL

In order to bring in foreign currency to its beleaguered economy, Vietnam is prepared to open up Cam Ranh Bay to the West for ship fueling and repair, according to the *Manila Chronicle,* which quoted Vietnamese Deputy Foreign Minister Tran Quang Co. Currently, only Soviet warships are allowed to use the facilities.

THROWING IN THE TAWI

Their hopes raised by a visit from President Corazon Aquino and a UN-sponsored project for laying water pipes, the 250,000 residents of Tawi-Tawi have slumped back into apathy after nothing happened. The 10 islands at the southern tail of the 7,000-island Philippine archipelago could be a tropical paradise natives claim—if they could be provided with more electricity than the present four hours per night and if their supply of water from deep artesian wells could be supplemented. (The UN project was aborted when salt water seeped into the pipes). "This place is so small there is nothing to do," complains Sgt. Bong Judloman, a member of the marine battalion stationed to keep the peace after a rebellion by the Mindanao rebels had been put down.

OFFITEL

If you want to open an office in the center of Tokyo, they'll ask for 15 to 20 months' deposit, plus key money, monthly maintenance fees, and other costs. This problem gave birth to the concept of the "Offi-tel," a combination office and hotel. From 9:30 a.m. to 6:00 p.m., it's communal offices with five secretaries, telephones, word processors, and fax machines. From 8:00 p.m. to 8:30 a.m., it's a membership hotel. About $13,385 buys your business 365 nights of hotel use by anyone you designate.

HOME AUTOMATION 2001

by Jack Maisano

Guess who is likely to be out in front when the "home automation" race enters the home stretch? Japan.

Home automation is the introduction of computer-controlled coordination of household electronic appliances. The companies that will benefit most from the home automation boom are the ones that win the standardization battle that is now under way. These companies will supply the communications hardware that will allow users to telephone the rice cooker, central heating, or lighting system before coming home.

"It's not the smartest standard that's going to conquer the market," said technical information publisher Egis in a recent report. "It's the standard that is strongest."

What's the long-range market worth? "Hundreds of billions of dollars," in long-range economic expenditure, transfers and shifts in market shares of all residential products and services. Why will Japan be out in front in this competition? The market will be dominated by an alliance of two industries: construction and electronics. Japan is extremely strong (vis-à-vis the West) in both industries—and even better at forging alliances.

© *Asian Business* magazine, Far East Trade Press, Ltd., 1989.

SKY HIGH 'SCRAPERS

Japan's Takenaka Corp. plans to build 1,000-meter high skyscrapers in the middle of Tokyo. They estimate that 35,000 people would live in the mammoth project, with 130,000 people commuting to work there. The plan consists of only five buildings, but the whole of Tokyo's Minato-ku business section could be housed inside. Considering the high cost of land in Tokyo, the commuting problem, and the crowding of the inner city, this project has been meeting with widespread approval by planners. Takenaka expects the project will take 14 years to complete at the cost of about $362 million.

WORLD'S LONGEST UNDERWATER TUNNEL

Travel time between Tokyo and Sapporo has been reduced by 2.5 hours to 11 hours with the completion of the world's longest (53.85 km) underwater tunnel connecting Honshu with the northern island of Hokkaido. Almost half of the tunnel is actually under the sea. Initial digging began in 1964, and on completing last year the 80-year-old ferry service between Aomori and Hakodate was suspended to be replaced by 32 passenger trains operating each day.

JAPANESE CARS AND HOW THEY GOT THAT WAY: A CULTURAL HISTORY OF JAPAN'S CAR-MAKING INDUSTRY

by Joe Troise

In 1958, some funny-looking cars checked into the Los Angeles Import Car Show. They had names like Toyopet Crown and Nissan-Fuji-Go. Sturdy, ugly little machines, they were met by a few words of praise and a good deal of unbridled snickering. Built for the narrow, badly paved roads of Japan, and with little consideration for Western notions of style and beauty, they promptly fell on their little chrome faces.

Ten years later, these same companies returned to America in force. They had gone back to Japan to do their homework, and judging from the stylish, spirited, high-quality cars they now presented to their American teachers, they had learned their lessons diligently, and perhaps too well. Next to this new generation of cars called Corona, Corolla, 510 and 1200, other popular imports suddenly didn't look so salable. The VW bug seemed all too familiar, and technically rather long in the tooth; the popular Renault Dauphine could not match the Japanese cars in reliability, the vast majority of British sedans began to gather dust in their showrooms.

As for the American "import fighters," the Ford Pinto and the Chevrolet Vega, the comparison was painful to contemplate. The country that once mass-produced the finest cars in the world in unprecedented numbers and at breathtaking speed had met the Japanese challenge with hastily assembled junk on wheels. Far worse, we thought we were going to get away with it.

One could hardly construct a more unfortunate miscalculation. By 1981, the Japanese auto industry surpassed the United States in production. In 1986, 11 Japanese auto and truck plants were producing cars at 153 sites in 43 countries. Toyota, No. 1 in Japan, had by itself collected about 9% of the entire world's market.

How did this happen? Every little kid in post-World War II America had grown up with Ford and Chevrolet in his vocabulary—and even Jaguar, Ferrari, and Mercedes—but Honda? Weren't they just making noisy little trail bikes a few years ago?

Depending on whom you ask, the economic miracle now manifested in the Japanese auto industry of 1989 can be explained any number of ways. For Lee Iacocca, it was mostly luck laced with healthy doses of decidedly un-American, unsportsmanlike conduct; for Ralph Nader, it came from hard work and guts; for the U.S. congresspeople advocating protectionist legislation, it was most assuredly American generosity and/or stupidity that spurred our economic rivals. Any one of these answers taken alone is incorrect, but all three

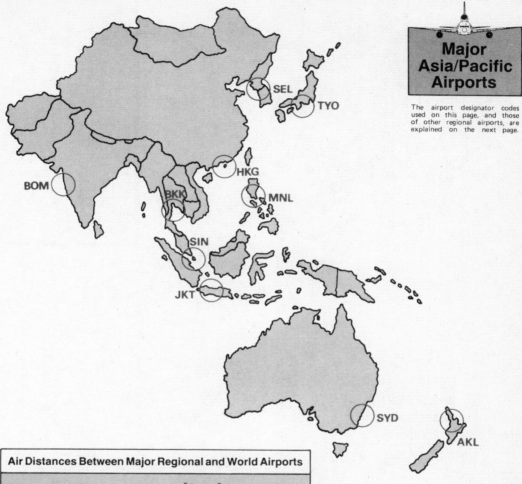

Major Asia/Pacific Airports

The airport designator codes used on this page, and those of other regional airports, are explained on the next page.

Air Distances Between Major Regional and World Airports

Kilometers	Frankfurt	London	New York	Paris	San Francisco	Sao Paulo	Stockholm	Zurich
Auckland	18,700	19,055	14,675	19,160	11,260	13,495	20,515	18,825
Bangkok	8,975	9,595	15,920	9,440	12,825	18,410	9,145	9,210
Bombay	6,570	7,210	12,620	7,010	15,155	15,750	7,785	6,545
Hong Kong	9,900	10,505	13,580	10,205	11,110	18,325	11,110	10,060
Jakarta	11,150	11,755	16,850	11,610	14,495	17,630	12,360	11,185
Manila	11,030	11,635	13,875	11,335	11,285	19,985	12,240	11,115
Seoul	11,400	13,950	11,495	13,615	9,435	19,780	12,590	11,115
Singapore	10,280	10,885	16,170	10,740	13,600	17,035	11,490	10,405
Sydney	16,520	17,140	16,030	16,985	12,035	19,770	17,735	16,710
Tokyo	9,550	10,045	10,860	10,005	8,265	18,585	10,765	12,310

Distances are not always the shortest or most direct ones, but those of the most likely routes.

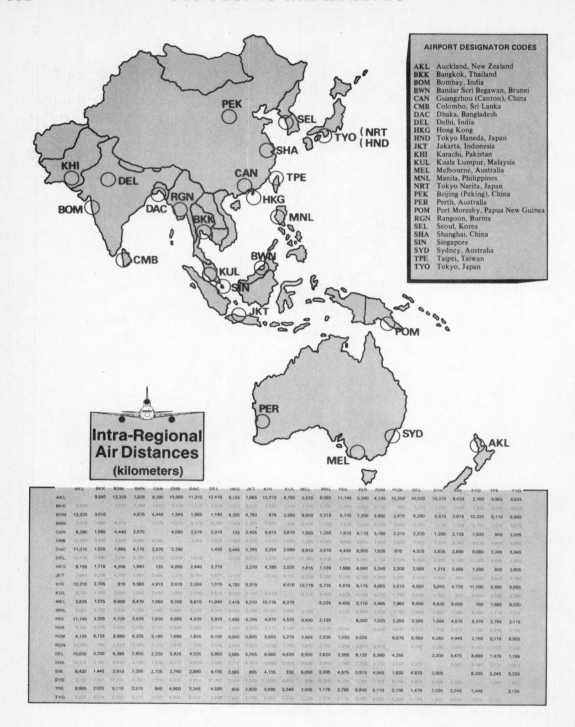

Intra-Regional Air Distances (kilometers)

	AKL	BKK	BOM	BWN	CAN	CMB	DAC	DEL	HKG	JKT	KHI	KUL	MEL	MNL	PEK	PER	POM	RGN	SEL	SHA	SIN	SYD	TPE	TYO
AKL		9,590	12,335	7,925	9,290	10,990	11,310	13,475	9,155	7,665	13,210	8,750	2,635	8,065	11,145	5,340	4,135	10,350	10,030	10,370	8,420	2,160	9,965	8,835
BKK	9,590		3,010	1,860	1,685	2,590	1,535	2,920	1,715	2,335	3,705	1,205	7,375	3,305	3,305		6,135	2,475	3,700	2,565	1,445	10,235	2,520	4,815
BOM	12,335	3,010		4,875	4,440	1,945	1,885	1,140	4,305	4,780	875	3,590	9,900	5,215	4,770	7,300	8,860	2,475	6,390	5,515	3,915	10,220	5,110	6,885
BWN	7,925	1,860	4,875		2,075							1,500	6,470	1,250	3,925		6,235		3,855	3,160	1,290		2,375	4,275
CAN	9,290	1,685	4,440	2,075		4,080	2,575	3,910	135	3,405	4,915	2,670	7,550	1,265	1,910	6,175	5,180	2,215	2,220	1,200	2,725	7,520	940	3,005
CMB	10,990	2,590	1,945		4,080		2,290		3,535		2,410	2,695	8,355	5,650	5,695	7,925	7,685		6,320	5,700	2,740	8,650	3,930	6,960
DAC	11,310	1,535	1,885	4,175	2,575	2,290		1,430	2,440	3,785	2,355	2,590	8,910	3,570	4,430	6,805	7,835	970	4,525	3,655	2,890	9,080	3,245	5,345
DEL	13,475	2,920	1,140		3,910		1,430		3,775		1,070	3,635	11,040	4,905	3,810		9,100	2,300	5,880	4,890	4,155	11,365	4,580	5,832
HKG	9,155	1,715	4,305	1,940	135	4,055	2,440	3,775		3,270	4,780	2,535	7,415	1,130	1,990	6,040	5,045	2,300	2,585	1,215	2,585	7,385	805	2,905
JKT	7,665	2,335	4,780	1,880	3,405	2,725	3,785	5,075	3,270		5,515	1,190	5,210	2,790	5,255	3,045	5,845	2,920	5,310	4,465	895	5,540	3,940	5,795
KHI	13,210	3,705	875	5,565	4,915	2,410	2,355	1,070	4,780	5,515		4,410	10,775	5,725	4,870	8,175	9,685	3,210	6,865	5,945	4,735	11,095	5,590	6,985
KUL	8,750	1,205	3,590	1,500	2,670	2,695	2,590	3,635	2,535	1,190	4,410		6,370	2,485	4,525	4,190	5,275	1,730	4,620	3,895	330	6,620	3,340	5,295
MEL	2,635	7,375	9,900	6,470	7,550	8,355	8,910	11,040	7,415	5,210	10,775	6,370		6,325	9,400	2,710	3,465	7,960	8,950	8,630	6,050	705	7,505	8,520
MNL	8,065	3,305	5,215	1,250	1,265	5,650	3,570	4,905	1,130	2,790	5,725	2,485	6,325		3,120	4,190	2,620	2,430	2,995	1,860	2,385	6,305	1,118	3,015
PEK	11,145	3,305	4,770	3,925	1,910	5,695	4,430	3,810	1,990	5,255	4,870	4,525	9,400	3,120		8,030	7,035	3,250	2,585	1,080	4,575	9,370	2,795	2,115
PER	5,340		7,300		6,175	7,925	6,805		6,040	3,045	8,175	4,190	2,710	4,190	8,030			5,340	7,795	7,910		3,280	6,110	5,180
POM	4,135	6,135	8,860	6,235	5,180	7,685	7,835	9,100	5,045	5,845	9,685	5,275	3,465	3,930	7,035	6,035		6,875	6,560	6,260	4,945	2,755	5,110	6,950
RGN	10,350	2,475	2,475	7,945	2,215		970	2,300	2,300	2,920	3,210	1,730	7,960	2,430	3,250	5,340	6,875		4,295	3,280	1,930	9,305	3,100	
SEL	10,030	3,700	6,390	3,855	2,220	6,325	4,525	5,880	2,585	5,310	6,865	4,620	8,950	2,625	2,585	8,125	6,560	4,295		2,200	4,670	8,890	1,475	1,195
SHA	10,370	2,565	5,515	3,160	1,200	5,700	3,655	4,890	1,215	4,465	5,945	3,895	8,630	1,860	1,080	7,910	6,260	3,280	2,200		3,845	8,105	1,303	1,805
SIN	8,420	1,445	3,915	1,290	2,725	2,740	2,890	4,155	2,585	895	4,735	330	6,050	2,385	4,575	3,915	4,945	1,930	4,670	3,800		6,305	3,245	5,330
SYD	2,160	10,235	10,220	7,589	7,520	8,650	9,080	11,365	7,385	5,540	11,095	6,620	705	6,305	9,370	3,280	2,755	9,305	8,890	8,105	6,305		7,445	7,820
TPE	9,965	2,520	5,110	2,375	940	3,930	3,245	4,580	805	3,940	5,590	3,340	7,505	1,175	2,795	6,845	6,110	3,100	1,475	2,020	3,245	7,445		2,125
TYO	8,835	4,815	6,885	4,275	3,005	6,960	5,345	5,832	2,905	5,795	6,985	5,295	8,520	3,015	2,115	5,180	6,950		1,195	1,805	5,330	7,820	2,125	

taken together offer a pretty fair view of the truth.

Nonetheless, reciting these rather abstract reasons doesn't make it easier for the average American to understand how this massive foreign engine of production got loose in our land. Perhaps a look at the humble beginnings of the Japanese auto industry, and its subsequent unorthodox development, might serve to explain how America failed to see the size of the challenge that was being set down before it.

THE EARLY YEARS

The title of "First Japanese Car" could legitimately be awarded to any one of a number of machines, depending on your criteria. The first gasoline-powerd car that actually seems to have worked was the Takuri, built in 1907 by the Automobile Trading Company. But only a few of these were ever manufactured and sold. Masujiro Hashimoto founded the Kwaishinsha Motor Car Company in 1911 and produced an experimental car called the DAT. Again, it was not at all ready for mass-production, although history would remember Hashimoto as the father of the Datsun (yes, it was named to mean "son of the DAT").

These marginal production figures thus leave the honors of "first car" to the 1917 Mitsubishi Model A, a design based on the Fiat Zero. Mitsubishi's venture was also the first move into automobile production by the powerful business groups (*zaibatsus,* or "financial cliques") that fueled Japan's industrialization in the period from the 1860s to the 1940s. The Model A was made until 1921, and although suitable for large-scale production, was never made in significant numbers. Some 20 years later, Mitsubishi would design and produce the famous Zero fighter plane used in the Pacific War.

The Japanese auto industry's inconsequential output remained the status quo well into the 1930s. Figures published just after the terrible Yokohama earthquake of 1923 show a total of only 12,000 vehicles in all of Japan, of which less than 1,000 were made at home, and most of those European makes assembled under foreign license. The earthquake did, however, spur the Japanese government to become more interested in the nation's auto and truck industry, primarily because most of Japan's railway network had been destroyed. But again, as in the past, the Japanese relied on foreign industry and capital to produce the cars it needed. The Japan Ford Motor Company appeared in Yokohama in 1925, and Japan General Motors followed in 1927 in Osaka. In 1929, 35,000 vehicles of all types were distributed throughout the country, and yet only 400 were designed and built by Japanese firms.

In the 1930s, all this began to change. Japan's military elite held a strong position in government, and their dreams of empire focused on the annexation of the Chinese province of Manchuria. To accomplish this, the government found it expedient to encourage investment in those companies that could ensure a steady supply of industrial and military vehicles. This buildup, which soon enough would bring Japan to the greatest tragedy of its history, encouraged a number of fledgling joint ventures that survive today as powerful and familiar automotive conglomerates. The first Mazda truck (1931), the first car called Datsun (1932), and Toyota's A-1—a copy of the 1935 Chrysler Airflow—were born in this energetic and dangerous era.

As you might surmise, foreign interference in Japan's automobile industry was by then deeply resented, and the passage of the Motorcar Manufacturing Enterprise Law of 1936

Major Asia/Pacific Ports

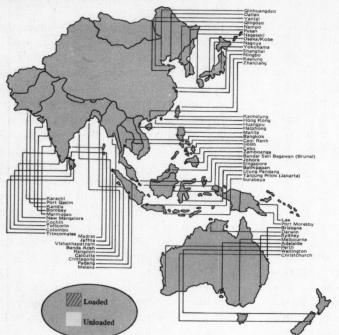

Qinhuangdao
Dalian
Yantai
Qingdao
Nampo
Pusan
Nagasaki
Osaka/Kobe
Nagoya
Yokohama
Shanghai
Ningbo
Kaelung
Zhanjiang

Kaohsiung
Hong Kong
Huangpu
Haiphong
Manila
Bangkok
Cam Ranh
Iloilo
Cebu
Zamboanga
Bandar Seri Begawan (Brunei)
Johore
Singapore
Balikpapan
Ujung Pandang
Tanjung Priok (Jakarta)
Surabaya

Karachi
Port Qasim
Kandla
Bombay
Marmugao
New Mangalore
Cochin
Tuticorin
Colombo
Trincomalee
Madras
Jaffna
Vishakhapatnam
Banda Aceh
Rangoon
Calcutta
Chittagong
Padang
Melaka

Lae
Port Moresby
Brisbane
Darwin
Sydney
Melbourne
Adelaide
Perth
Wellington
Christchurch

Loaded
Unloaded

Seaborne Freight

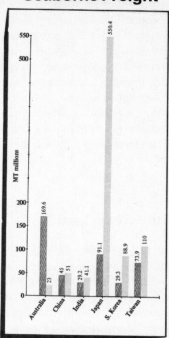

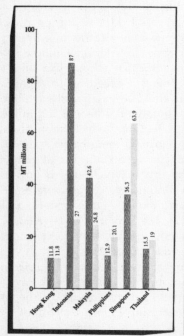

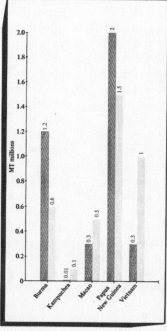

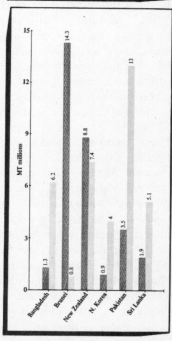

effectively gave the boot to both Ford and GM. In 1937, as Japan marched toward China, the American car-makers headed for home.

Private automobile production was still not ready to expand in Japan, however, despite strong government cooperation. Obviously, priority was given to military vehicles. In any case, the truly abysmal condition of the road system in Japan, coupled with the nation's lack of technical know-how in making automobiles, would have made a car boom impossible.

In 1941, on the eve of Pearl Harbor, total car production reached about 45,000 and the majority of those were for the military. Henceforth, all car companies would be pressed into military service. One of these was Mazda, a company so named a decade earlier as a reference to the Zoroastrian god of light. In that year, it had produced its first four-wheel car, a prototype that would be tested briefly on the streets of Hiroshima.

THE POSTWAR YEARS

At the end of 1945, Japan stood in ruins. The devastation was so complete that the occupying American forces did not have to guard against looters. There was nothing left for anyone to steal.

The industry of Japan—the buildings, the machinery, the men to run them—all were either destroyed or dispersed. In one air raid alone, on March 10, 1945, one third of Tokyo's factories and two thirds of its commercial buildings were annihilated. One lucky car-maker did not suffer total destruction, however, and received permission from the Allies in December 1945 to start building minitrucks. This was Mazda, which managed to survive the atomic blast in Hiroshima by virtue of its location 1.8 miles from ground zero.

No understanding of the remarkable recovery of postwar Japan would be possible without a look at the successes and failures of what might have been the last public recital of the Myth of the Conqueror that our century will ever see. The hero was no *shogun* but an American general; he strode, rather recklessly, some would say, unarmed and lightly escorted, onto the stage that was Japan in September 1945—a starving, humiliated, and totally unpredictable nation.

As supreme commander for the Allied Powers, General Douglas MacArthur wielded great power. Yet—conservative, stubborn, and dictatorial as he was—he did not see postwar Japan as a target for punishment, but rather as an opportunity to create a democracy from scratch. Many in Washington were quite content to let the Japanese starve. MacArthur cabled back defiantly to Congress, "Give me bread or give me bullets!"

They sent bread, and lots of it. Needless to say, the Japanese were ready to accept this generosity. They were less inclined, however, to embrace MacArthur's edicts of land reform, the creation of adversarial labor unions, the liberalization of customs governing women in the workforce, and the dismantling of the industrial cartels, or Japanese "old-boy networks," if you will. But as a conquered people, what choice did they have?

In fact, history would show that those changes the Japanese finally accepted, such as land reform, a fiscal conservatism, and removal of the military from political life, proved highly beneficial. Equally interesting is how well the Japanese were served by the American ideals they ultimately rejected when they regained self-rule in 1952.

Out the window went adversarial labor unions and the subversive notion of undermining the family unit by putting women in the workforce; and back in place, with plenty of new blood thanks to American purges, were the cozy alliances of businessmen, bankers, and bureaucrats that had been running things in Japan for a hundred years before the war.

If the MacArthur era in Japanese history seems schizophrenic, it's worth remembering that the Allied Powers did not initially view defeated Japan as they saw a defeated Germany. While Europe needed to be re-industrialized so it might serve as a bastion against Communism, no such threat was perceived in Asia. It was not until the victory of the Communists in China in 1949 that the United States began to see the need to re-industrialize Japan.

It would be interesting to know how aware the Japanese people might have been of the irony enveloping them in the closing months of the 1940s. One war had completely devastated them in 1945, but a mere five years later another was about to revitalize them. With the outbreak of hostilities in Korea, the United States and the United Nations poured more than $3 billion into the static Japanese economy. A former deadly enemy had now become the arsenal of democracy, and this enormous economic banquet of which the motor vehicle industry took some healthy bites—must be regarded as the historical point in the rebirth of the Japanese nation.

THE ROAD TO RECOVERY

Among the painful lessons the Japanese learned from World War II was that they were defeated not only by the skill and courage of Allied forces, but also by the Allies' superior technology. So the early 1950s were characterized by a search for Western technology and the appropriate consultants to help the Japanese put it in place.

One Westerner, an engineer and quality-control specialist, brought no machinery with him, but the contents of his briefcase would soon win him a degree of respect and admiration formerly reserved for only MacArthur himself. His name was W. Edwards Deming, and his specialty was applying statistical controls and mathematical models to the assembly line.

His ideas, once eagerly cultivated by the U.S. War Department through the Stanford University think-tank where Deming was employed, were then yawned at or rejected out of hand by American industry and the managers who ran it. At best, quality control in the booming American economy of the 1950s meant sticking a few slogans on a bulletin board in the employee cafeteria. Why should an auto manufacturer, for instance, worry about quality when the average car buyer was grabbing everything one made as fast as one could make it?

The Japanese had a different set of problems to overcome. They were totally frustrated by their quality-control problems, and Deming offered them a method of creating quality from the ground up.

Deming's theories operated on the principle that quality was based on total commitment. One could not, for instance, build a superior automobile by placing a few quality-control vigilantes near an assembly line or by applying pressure at the lowest levels of production. The president of the company, the managers on all levels, and the people who did the actual building must all be dedicated to a quality product. Group participation was essential on all levels as well. Slogans were forbidden. Quality was to be measured, discussed, actually lived by everyone involved.

To the Japanese, the high value Deming placed on meaningful work, on loyalty, on a committed group effort, and on personal pride was an evocation of their national character expressed in a technological world. Just as the eccentrically brilliant MacArthur had given a great gift by making war constitutionally illegal, the equally formidable Deming had effectively banned the production of shoddy products. To this day, a highly coveted medal is awarded each year in Deming's honor to the Japanese company that best embodies his principles in its products. Nissan Motors was the first auto-maker to take this prize, in 1960.

All this is not to imply that the Japanese let foreigners run with the ball for very long. As early as 1953, the government—under the auspices of the newly formed and all-powerful Ministry of International Trade and Industry—issued a "Draft Plan for Economic Recovery," the goals of which were to "tighten the economy and increase production on a modest scale." By 1955, a new "Five-Year Program for Economic Independence" was in place, the aim of which was to crank up production and employment.

It was at this time that the ministry announced its desire to see an all-Japanese car, one that was no longer the product of licensing and assembly agreements with foreign manufacturers, such as Austin, Hillman, and Willys (Jeep). Toyota was the first company to actually produce such a car, called the Crown. The 1950s also saw some fierce competition among Japanese motorcycle manufacturers trying to dominate the home market. The chief rivals were Tohatsu and Honda, and we needn't mention who won.

THE YEARS OF EXPANSION

Economic activity became so intense that the five-year plan was discarded in 1958, and a "Long-Term Economic Program" was put in place. By 1960, it became apparent that what

Deming and a handful of other American advisers had predicted for the Japanese economy was coming true—that when the substantial Japanese middle class reached the stage where it could afford to buy consumer goods on a grand scale, the growth would be explosive.

In 1961, Prime Minister Ikeda instituted the famous "Double Your Income" program, a 10-year strategy that helped bring Japan into the international export market. And for the first time, the Japanese were producing automobiles that could compete with cars made throughout the world.

This phenomenal record of achievement in the 1960s was the product of a system that appears to be the antithesis of both freewheeling capitalist theory and oppressive, totalitarian economic planning; yet, in many ways, the Japanese borrow the best parts of both philosophies. Japanese industry, labor unions, government bureaus, and the local branches of the national bank work together in a consortium so intimate and friendly that it sometimes appalls the Westerner.

With government at the controls—usually through the Ministry of International Trade and Industry—advice, subsidies, protective tariffs, and political pressure are at the ready for whatever industries need in order to prosper under the latest economic plan. To finance these plans, a branch bank located literally at each industrial group is poised to lend money generously. And labor unions, in spite of their reputation for vigorous demonstration and hard negotiation (they're not above hanging management in effigy), still end up rewarding their toughest leaders with a chance to work for management.

It's no wonder all this drives Lee Iacocca to apoplexy, as he points out in his autobiography. It's tough to play in the same league with a system that American executives snidely refer to as "Japan, Inc."

Japan's automobile industry grew in proportion to her newfound wealth and technical proficiency. In 1956, only 12,000 private cars were made—and most of those were tiny, unattractive, and technically backward. By 1960, however, more than 300,000 cars were produced, of which almost 50% were standardized models. In 1967, 1 million cars rolled out of the factories.

Although Japan started exporting cars in considerable numbers in the mid-1960s, it wasn't until 1968 that a serious assault was made on the enormous American market. This time the Japanese were in the right place at the right time with the right product. The Datsun 510 literally stunned the American automotive press. Here was a brilliant knock-off of the BMW at one third the price. Years of hard work, a brutally tough attitude toward acquiring market share, and an upcoming oil crisis were about to bring the Japanese auto industry to the threshold of a dream.

JAPAN SELLS TO THE WORLD

The oil crisis of 1973 cooled Japan's domestic automobile market, but it didn't slow down international sales. Japan exported about 30% of its cars in 1971, and more than 50% in 1976.

When the Western nations began to respond to this merciless assault on their domestic markets with protective tariffs of their own, the Japanese automakers moved deftly to refine their expansionist techniques. They accepted voluntary import quotas from the United States and Europe. They formed minority-held mergers with U.S. car companies. They even built factories abroad so as to train and employ foreign labor and, of course, circumvent the import quotas. Even in the 1990's, their flexibility serves them well. Since

the rise in the value of the yen makes their cars less competitive with American cars in price, they are now shipping U.S.-built Japanese cars back to Japan and selling them there.

INTO THE FUTURE

So where could the Japanese auto industry possibly go from here? After this incredible rate of expansion, which is pushing the limits of America's tolerance for trade deficits and Japan's tolerance for breathing space on its roads, the last thing either country needs is more Japanese cars. But there is still room at the top, in the luxury car markets—room, that is, once you knock off some expensive European merchandise. So it seems likely that the successful marketing of middle-range and high-end cars will be the final frontier for the Japanese automakers to conquer in the 1990s.

If the Acura Legend coupe is any indication, Americans and Europeans are willing to pay $20,000 plus for a car made in Japan. But will they pay $35,000 or more? Reactions to the Toyota and Nissan entries in the luxury car market (called Lexus and Infiniti, respectively) have been interesting.

Gunter Kramer, chairman of BMW of North America, sees no threat. "Japanese companies that build four million cars a year simply do not have the same prestige as a company like BMW, which builds 480,000 cars a year," he told the *Wall Street Journal*.

But Raymond Ketchledge, past president of Austin Rover of North America, was more cautious when interviewed by the same newspaper, "You see a lot of Nikon, Canon, and Minolta cameras these days, but when was the last time you saw somebody with a German-made Leica?" Maybe Ketchledge was also thinking back to Great Britain's experience with Japanese competition, when Honda, Suzuki, Yamaha, and Kawasaki rolled over the British motorcycle industry in less than 10 years.

But perhaps the most telling, and succinct, comments comes from *Automobile Magazine,* which carried the following subhead to its road test of the new Toyota Lexus, "All you guys from Munich, Stuttgart, Coventry—call your offices."

Joe Troise is an automotive historian and cartoonist living in Sausalito, CA. © 1989 by Joe Troise.

TAIWAN'S AUTO PRODUCTION PLAN

Taiwan's automotive industry will produce a million cars a year by 1995, with a minimum 70% domestic content rate, according to a five-year plan released by the Industrial Development Bureau.

SECOND-HAND EXPORTS

Japan has been exporting used cars to the Soviet Union since 1988. Most of the vehicles are no longer legal in Japan because they don't carry a *shaken* (safety inspected) sticker. Soviet sailors on cargo vessels have been buying them for about $385 each. Perestroika has loosened the restraints on private car ownership in the Soviet Union but lack of supply means a five- to six-year wait. Soviet-built cars run about $10,000 each, so even with the import duty and taxes, Japanese cars are cheaper. According to the *Nihon Keizai Shimbun,* 1.8 liter cars from the 1979 to 1981 model years are the most popular.

MINI-MOTORS BOOM

One Japanese family in three owns a mini-car, up 100% from the one-in-six of 1979, according to a 1989 survey by the Japan Mini-Motor Vehicles Association. The great increase in women drivers is a major reason for the mini-car boom, the study said, with many of the cars being the second in the family.

PRC TRAFFIC DEATHS

One Chinese was killed every 10 minutes in 1988 in PRC traffic accidents and one person was injured every three minutes, according to *China Times,* a Taiwanese newspaper. In Beijing alone there are more than 6 million bicycles. Reportedly, all public transportation is 40% to 80% overloaded with trains carrying 700,000 passengers a day, double the numbers the available cars are designed to hold. In Guangzhou (Canton), China's biggest southern city, there are 2,300 buses and trams to serve 3 million residents and an estimated 1.2 million transients. Each one of the buses is expected to carry 1,000 passengers a day.

TAIWAN'S TRAFFIC JAMS

The number of cars jamming Taiwan's roads reached an all-time high of 1.9 million in 1988, according to a Ministry of Communications study. Per capita ownership is equivalent to one car for every 10 people. In Taipei, 10,000 licenses were issued in the month of August 1988 compared to 2,000 a month in August 1986.

TOYOTA EUROPE

Toyota Motor Co., Japan's biggest car-maker, is planning to produce 200,000 cars a year in Britain to meet the challenge of the economic integration of Europe in 1992. The plant is expected to cost about $1.1 billion to build, and local components will account for 80% of production, which is targeted for 1992.

> *"The centipede doesn't stop just because of one bad leg."*
>
> *Burmese proverb*

SPARE PARTS

Taiwan is aiming to become a major supplier of car components and spare parts, according to the *Free China Journal,* a Taipei-based newspaper. Last year, Taiwan exported about $900 million worth of spare auto parts and components.

NINETEENTH CENTURY ENGINE IN TWENTY-FIRST CENTURY CAR

A Japanese automobile accessories firm, Aisin Seiki Co., a Toyota affiliate, has produced a car engine based upon a nineteenth century idea which will save fuel, make less noise, and create less pollution than conventional engines. The external combustion engine, named after the nineteenth century Scottish engineer Robert Sterling, can be powered by a variety of fuels such as natural gas, coal, and even solar heat.

FRESH CARS IN THE PRODUCE DEPARTMENT

A new Japanese car, the Lettuce, has gone on sale in the country's supermarkets, the only place it can be bought. Offered in red, white, or black (but not green) the Mitsubishi-made auto costs the equivalent of $4,700. The car could be called a three-door sedan. It's aimed at mothers of small children. With no rear door on the driver's side, a youngster cannot jump out into the stream of traffic.

CREDIT CARD FOR PARKING METERS

Hong Kong has been experimenting with a plastic credit card for use in parking meters, hoping to eventually replace the coin-oper-ated meters and save on costs of collection and servicing.

DEPARTMENT STORE CAR DEALERS

Traditional automobile distribution in Japan is in the throes of a revolution as department stores, supermarkets, and other large retailers have started selling cars. The Mitsukoshi De-partment Store's World Motors Komazawa outlet sold 220 cars in the first three months since it opened in 1989.

THERE'S A GOOD LADA

Low-cost Soviet-made cars are competing with South Korean Ponies for the lower end of Singapore's booming car market. Intraco, a government trading company, introduced the Soviet Lada to Singapore's roads in 1988. The 1.3 liter Lada costs about $15,000.

HALF-TANKED IN SINGAPORE

"Half-tanked" has taken on a new meaning in Singapore, where motorists driving across the border to buy cheaper gasoline in Malaysia—thereby costing the government $1 million in excise taxes—face fines of $258 if found with tanks less than half full.

LICENSED TO KILL

In India, a driver's license can reportedly be bought for life for as little as $2. As estimated 117 people die in traffic accidents each year per 10,000 vehicles, while the figure reaches about 140 deaths per 10,000 cars in Pakistan. But in the Himalayan Kingdom of Nepal, where the fatality rate is only about 100 people killed each year, drivers' tests are strenuous. Would-be drivers must answer detailed questions on how a car functions, its maintenance and traffic regulations, and then must face an oral exam and an intelligence test. Sri Lanka is one of the few countries to have instituted a helmet requirement for the safety of motorcyclists and then lifted it, after helmeted gunmen went on a killing spree.

HIGH-YEN CHOPPERS

As a result of the high-flying yen, more and more Japanese are importing helicopters for personal use. The Japanese Ministry of Transportation reported a 35% increase in helicopters registered in 1988—876 choppers in 1988 over the 650 registered in 1987. This has created a mini-industry for American helicopter-flying schools because it's much cheaper to get a license in the U.S. than it is in Japan. You can obtain an American pilot's license in as little as two months of intensive training for about $7,800. In Japan, it takes a year and costs as much as $39,000. In Japan, only about a dozen pilots get licensed each year. But in 1989, an estimated 250 pilots received their chopper licenses from abroad. Japan's Ministry of Transportation announced it would begin instituting "safety seminars" for overseas-licensed pilots.

MOVING ALONG
MOVING DAY 2001

A futuristic moving van loads the entire contents of an eight-person Japanese household—including the family members—into a plus $300,000 vehicle known as a "Dream Saloon." Once on board, they're served refreshments and enjoy various video entertainments as movers pack away their furnishings into specially constructed cargo-holds. Art Moving Center, a Tokyo moving company, plans to introduce this "Dream Saloon" moving concept to the United States in the future.

Why lug your skis or golf clubs around? They'll be waiting for you on the slopes or on the course when you arrive. Executives on business trips send their dirty laundry home to be washed and returned by messengers. Gifts of delicacies—fresh shrimp or crab straight from the sea—are delivered on ice to family, friends, and business associates. Taking a holiday? Send your luggage on ahead and travel unburdened and carefree.

Major Japanese corporations are also moving in unprecedented numbers—seeking larger headquarters with greater energy conservation and increased automation. One firm paid $1.25 million to move into new offices less than a mile away from its former premises.

BUY FIAT

What's the cheapest car in China, the one that's favored by private car owners? The Polish Fiat, which sells for about U.S.$2,700. There are 15,000 of them on Chinese streets today. In 1982, there were only 64 privately owned cars in Beijing, but the figure has been growing. Chinese auto-industry research figures project that privately owned cars will be commonplace in China by the year 2000, when the nation's per capita income will reach $800 to $1,000.

In fact, the number of privately owned cars in Beijing is expected to reach 10,000 by the end of the century, more than double the current figure predicts Traffic Administration Deputy Director, Zhao Jiaying, who told *China Daily* that they had not imposed serious enough problems for the state to impose controls. Cars imported from Eastern Europe are in the majority with their owners being mostly businessmen, actors, and sports figures.

DONGS OF WAR

The second-hand car market in Hanoi is heating up. Hanoi businessmen are paying top prices for foreign cars left over from the Vietnam War. The going rate: 10 million *dongs* (about $3,125) for a reconditioned '68 Ford Pinto, 35 million *dongs* (about $11,000) for a 1985 Toyota Corolla, with a lowball 3.6 million *dongs* ($1,140) for a Renault-8. Auto imports are currently not allowed into Vietnam.

WAKE UP, LITTLE SUZUKI

For drivers who tend to nod at the wheel during long trips, there is now a high-tech Japanese waker-upper. It's called "Doze Alert." It clips behind your ear—and if your head droops beyond the allowable limit of 20 degrees, the gizmo will buzz you awake. It costs $10. It's even said to be popular among Japanese students cramming for university entrance exams.

BEATING THE TRAFFIC COPS IN TAIPEI

Car dealers in Taipei compiled a list of locations of computerized speeding monitors on the Sun Yat-sen freeway, and distributed copies to customers as a sales gimmick. The speed limit on the freeway is 90 kms per hour.

TAIWAN'S ACCIDENT RATE

Taiwan suffered 5,014 traffic accidents, resulting in 3,763 deaths and 5,026 injuries in 1988, according to the Taiwan Provincial Department of Communications. The island's accident rate was 6.88 per 10,000 people. There were 7.27 million motorcycles and automobiles in Taiwan in 1988. Taipei and Kaohsiung accounted for 1.65 million of the total.

TICKET TO WRITE

There were 55.16 million cars in Japan in 1988, but only 1.34 million parking spaces, according to the White Paper on Traffic Safety of Heisei Year One (1989). In Tokyo, 190,000 cars are illegally parked at any one moment—1,400 a day get ticketed.

PRIVATIZING PARKING METERS

Hong Kong formed a task force to consider privatizing the territory's 17,000 parking meters. Kuala Lumpur, the Malaysian capital, already has privatized meters.

ORANGE CLOCKWORK

Japanese National Railways' "orange cards" are outpacing Nippon Telegraph & Telephone Corp.'s telephone cards. Hiro Yamazaki, JNR's Passenger Bureau marketing man, explains why, "It takes about 20 seconds to buy a ticket at the ticket-selling machine with coins, but you need only six or seven seconds to get a ticket if you use an orange card."

TAXI SERVICES

Kyoto-headquartered taxi firm MK Taxi is famous for the lengths they go to provide service for customers, including their refusal to raise cab fares. Even though Japanese cabs have automatic doors, the bow-tie clad MK drivers routinely jump out to open and close the door manually for each passenger. Now MK is going the extra mile to please. They've opened "Station MK"—a taxi cab station for passengers who want to travel the 50 miles or so from Osaka to Kyoto in the middle of the night. First floor is a bar. Second floor is a salon with hostesses. If you don't feel like drinking, the coffee is free.

"Home Net" is a company formed by a coalition of Japanese taxi firms. Customers subscribe to the "emergency service," which is in operation 24 hours a day. Each subscriber family is given an emergency button. Its signal is tied into the computers of all radio dispatch stations in the country. One punch of the button and the nearest radio cab is there in minutes.

More and more Japanese taxis have receipt printers. Printed on the receipt are the date, time, price, and taxi number. It's convenient not only for keeping track of job-related expenses but also if you happen to leave an expensive umbrella behind.

CHINA'S LEADING FOREIGN CAR JOINT VENTURES

In May 1983, the first joint venture to produce complete vehicles, known as the Beijing Jeep Corporation (BJC) was set up. Then came the establishment of Shanghai Volkswagen Corp. (SVC), and in 1986, Guangzhou Peugeot Corp. (GPC). The industrial output of BJC has grown at an average rate of 16.7% a year, with the company turning out about 4,000 vehicles in 1988.

IT'S A "VFT" (VERY FAST TRAIN)

Australia and Japan are planning to build the world's fastest train, linking Melbourne and Sydney, by 1995. Backed by some of Australia's largest companies—including resources giant The Broken Hill Proprietary, brewing and investment company Elder IXL, and worldwide transport company TNT—together with Japanese engineering firm Kumagai Gumi, the so-called "Very Fast Train" (VFT) would propel passengers the 550 miles in just three hours at 220 mph, with a stop at the capital Canberra. The service plans to have 35 trains running a day, carrying 6 million passengers per year when it begins operations. France's TGV high-speed train service holds the current speed record for a national rail system, with a peak of 170 mph, according to the Guinness Book of Records.

BEIJING'S CABBIES

Chinese cabbies earn about $95 a month, about three times the average urban income.

Beijing cabbies have been murdered by people wanting their cars.

A few years ago, the PRC's *People's Daily* warned visitors to beware of crooked taxi drivers in the capital. Nearly 200 taxi drivers have lost their licenses, and 18 taxi companies were shut down for fleecing passengers.

HOT CARS IN CHINA

Tighter controls on the import of cars by China have created a huge market for spare parts on the mainland and led to a huge increase in smuggling from Hong Kong, according to Hong Kong insurance company officials. Syndicates strip down cars, take them across the border, and sell them on the black market. In particular, there has been a strong demand for used Toyota Crown parts. A new Toyota Crown costs about about $53,846 in China.

TAIWAN'S AIRPLANE INDUSTRY

The Taiwanese government teamed up with private investors in 1989 to launch the first domestic airplane-manufacturing company. The airplane company—whose investors include Taichung Machinery Works, Yue Loong Motors Co., and Air Asia Co.—will manufacture airplane parts and components in cooperation with Boeing Co. and McDonnell Douglas Corp., according to Taiwan's Industrial Development Bureau.

SUPER-FAST OCEAN FREIGHTER

Japan launched a plan in 1989 to develop a high-speed ocean freighter that can sail 2.5 times as fast as container ships now in operation. According to the Transport Ministry, the $4.3 million super-vessel, which will be ready in 1993, will have a speed of more than 50 knots, or 93 km an hour, compared with an average speed of 20 knots. It will be about 330 feet long and will be capable of carrying more than 1,000 tons, and cover the distance between Japan and United States in about three days, or about half the time needed now for ocean crossings.

SINGAPORE'S MRT

Singapore's newly built 67 km Mass Rapid Transit system, completed in June 1990, features nine underground stations designed specially to double as bomb shelters during wartime. The cost of the MRT was estimated at about $2.3 billion.

TAIPEI'S MASS TRANSIT

A transport system capable of carrying 20,000 passengers per hour on a 12-kilometer route between a zoo in suburban Taipei and the domestic airport at Sungshan is expected to be operational by 1991. Equipment and services worth the equivalent of U.S.$271 million purchased from a French company make this the most expensive project undertaken by the Taipei city government.

BIKES ON THE RIM

Because of the rising cost of labor, Japan has virtually abandoned the production of bicycles, beginning a scramble among other Asian companies to dominate a market that accounts for almost eight million bicycles a year. Currently, Taiwan appears to be in the lead with about 50 companies manufacturing bicycles. Companies in South Korea, Thailand, Indonesia, and mainland China are also competing. It is China that is the biggest threat, says one Taiwanese exporter, because raw materials and labor are much cheaper there. But the quality of their product is still low, an important factor in selling to Japan, whose buyers usually demand first-rate products. Meanwhile, China's *Economic Daily* reported that a company in the northeast industrial city of Dalian, had developed a new kind of chainless bike which used gear transmission and was easy to assemble, repair, and ride.

TAIPEI'S CARS

The number of cars jamming Taiwan's roads reached an all-time high of 1.9 million in 1988, according to a Ministry of Communications study. Per capita ownership is equivalent to one car for every 10 people. 10,000 licenses were issued in Taipei in the month of August 1988, compared to 2,000 a month in August 1986.

KING'S RANSOM FOR TAIPEI PARKING SPACE

In Taipei City, where it's customary to buy a permanent parking space rather than rent it, the average price of such a spot is now $46,154, rising to as much as $76,923 in the central downtown Ta-an district. Land is now so valuable in that crowded city that real estate prices have soared to the fourth highest in the world behind Tokyo, Osaka, and Paris. The lowest residential property in the city, for example, costs about $4000 per ping (35 square feet), yet citizens of Taipei are near the bottom of the world list in purchasing power. The average annual family income is about $15,000, against the lowest price for a walk-up apartment of about $89,000.

TRANS-RIM TRAVEL

ASIA 2000

BOOKING TICKETS FOR THE BOOM
By Murray Bailey

By the year 2000, the global travel business will double in size.

There is no serious dispute about the size of the travel business in Asia in the year 2000. It will be double the size it is today. The implications of this growth may be hard to grasp. The industry will need, mathematically speaking, twice as many airports (or twice as many runways, thus increasing the area of existing airports by about 50%). It will need twice the number of hotels, twice the number of beach resorts, twice the number of souvenirs. And, surely, the return of the 24-hour suit for the traveler in a hurry.

But if there is little dispute over the future size of the travel industry, the structure it will take may not be so obvious. What follows may help would-be travel investors get a better idea of the way things are heading, particularly in Asia.

TRAVEL NUMBERS

There are now five countries in Asia that produce more than one million travelers each year. They are, in order, Japan, Taiwan, Hong Kong, Malaysia, and the Philippines. By 1990, they will probably be joined by Singapore and South Korea.

During 1990, Japan alone will provide 12 million travelers. The other six will boost the total to 20 million. A conservative estimate is that 10 years from now the total will be closer to 50 million, with Indonesia, Thailand, and China having joined the one million-plus club.

Most of these travelers, perhaps 60%, will stay within the region.

Not only will the travelers be more numerous, they will also spend more time on their holidays. As leisure time increases, so more of that will be spent in traveling. Each of the 50 million travelers in 2000 will therefore be much more "valuable" than today's traveler.

Perhaps the best illustration of how this works is Japan. The government there has decreed that the average working year in Japan, now 2,150 hours, should be cut to 1,800 hours by 1992. That represents about 30 extra days leisure time. Conservatively, again, it can be reckoned that the travel business will get 10%

of those 30 additional days, adding three days to current travel patterns.

These days travelers from Japan spend up to four days at a time in destinations, such as Hong Kong, Singapore, the Philippines, and Thailand. Add three days to that and hotels can expect as much as 75% more business from their Japanese guests, even if the number of Japanese arriving is no greater than it is this year.

Although not all market sectors are likely to see such a dramatic boost, more leisure time is a worldwide trend, and Asia has been lagging behind other parts of the world from the start.

NEW RIM AIRLINES

There will be a wave of new start-up airlines. In fact, the new generation is already emerging with as many as 10 new airlines being set up in Taiwan, and others already flying in the Philippines, in Korea, and Hong Kong. In addition, new international airlines are on the drawing board in Singapore, Taiwan, and even in tiny Macao.

Again, Japan has shown how rapidly things can change. All Nippon Airways, which was already larger than Japan Airlines on domestic routes, flew its first international route (to Guam) in 1986.

As an international airline, ANA still has a long way to go, but with the volume of traffic likely to come out of Japan and into it, ANA's international size could easily be 25% that of JAL in 10 years' time. It targets five million passengers by the mid-1990s, compared with JAL's six million at the start of the 1980s.

While the upstart new generation of airlines grabs for routes and passengers, the existing big carriers will by no means be sitting on their hands. ANA, Cathay Pacific, JAL, and

Airline Shareholding in Large Airlines[a]

Owning airline	Object airline	Share[b] (%)
All Nippon Airways	Austrian Airlines	3.5
	Nippon Cargo Airlines	10.0
Ansett Australia	American Air West	19.0
	Ansett New Zealand	100.0
American Airlines	Air New Zealand	8.0
British Airways	Sabena	20.0
Delta	Swissair	5.0
Garuda Airways	Merpati	100.0
Japan Airlines	Air New Zealand	8.0
	Hawaiian Airlines	19.0
KLM	Northwest	10.0
	Sabena	20.0
Qantas Airways	Air New Zealand	20.0
SAS	British Midland	25.0
	Texas Air[c]	10.0
Singapore Airlines	Tradewinds	100.0
Swissair	Austrian Airlines	8.0
	Delta	5.0

[a] Not all confirmed or ratified.
[b] Actual or approximation.
[c] Continental, Eastern.
Source: Travel Business Analyst.

Singapore Airlines each have about 20 B747-400s either in the air, on order, or on option, as well as other types of aircraft.

AVIATION POLICY

In which direction is commercial aviation heading? It is going in several different ways at once, but this does not necessarily mean there will be a collision.

In one direction there is deregulation. Started in the United States in 1978 and slowly exported, first to the Netherlands, then the United Kingdom, now espoused in the Asia-Pacific region by Singapore and domestically in Australia and Taiwan, it is a force that is going to be hard to resist.

But if deregulation promises more competition, the other trend would seem to move in the opposite way, toward more joint operations, more "code-sharing," more comprehensive marketing and operational alliances, and more cross-shareholding between airlines.

The process is already underway, as illustrated in the table above. International airlines that are particularly keen on cross-border activity are SAS, KLM, and British Airways. In the Asia-Pacific region, both Japan Airlines and All Nippon Airways have shown similar tendencies and Qantas is already a major shareholder in Air New Zealand.

A leading advocate of tie-ups is Singapore Airlines, and its marketing drive may see liaisons with such airlines as British Airways, Qantas, and Japan Airlines. In 1989, Singapore Airlines announced a joint marketing and equity swap with Delta Airlines, Inc. of the United States.

Likewise, SAS has long had strong links with Thai International. Look also for a colonial and historical link between liberal KLM and Garuda. There may also be a tie-up between KLM and its old commercial partner Philippine Airlines, and perhaps even with Air Lanka. (KLM was previously linked with Air Ceylon, Air Lanka's forerunner.)

With all this activity, will bilateral air rights get more cozy? It might be assumed that if All Nippon Airways has a share in Austrian Airlines, then bilateral negotiations between Japan and Austria will be more friendly and cooperative. But they will not, of course, because Japan Airlines and Lauda Air, the two rival airlines in those two countries, will ensure that competition continues.

COMPUTERIZED RESERVATION SYSTEMS (CRS)

Another matter that is intricately connected with all these developments is the development of the super-CRS. As with airlines, there is cross-marketing and cross-shareholding in the super-CRS sector of the travel business.

The question arises: If Singapore Airlines, Cathay Pacific, Malaysia Airline, and China Airlines all own a part of the same super-CRS —which they do—and if that CRS controls all booking activity in a neutral display— which it should—will competition between those cooperating airlines be reduced? The answer, despite the airlines' assertions to the contrary, is that it will.

Because of the selling power of the super-CRSs, developments with these companies are as important to the travel industry as developments with the airlines themselves.

It may not be possible to separate the inter-airline liaisons from super-CRS liaisons. Many such liaisons have already been formed. The table on p. 567 shows the airline links that would be formed if super-CRS links extended into airlines themselves.

But a factor in all this has to be what will happen to the super-CRSs. Most assume that there will be mergers, strengthened partly by the fact that three of the world's eight super-CRSs are derivatives of the big four.

Take the experience of Delta Airlines' Datas. It is the fifth largest super-CRS in the United States, after the big four—Sabre, Apollo/Covia, Pars, and System One—and is in the same technological league as the other four.

But Datas is vulnerable because it does not have the same marketing power (mainly because of its smaller distribution). So it has been looking around for partners. Punters say the most likely will be Pars, with which it has held talks, and which also needs some help to get it closer to the coverage that market leaders Sabre and Apollo have.

If Datas is having trouble because it is "small," the problems facing the Asian airlines' Abacus could be overwhelming.

Any shareholding change in super-CRS ownerships will most probably go further in the same direction as now. It would take only one move to divide the world clearly into three super-CRS alliances, which no other consortium could begin to match, certainly in the next decade. That move would be a link between Sabre and Pars.

Sabre is already linked to Air New Zealand and Qantas. A link-up with Pars would bring in Japan Airlines (which still wants to go it alone, but must know this is not possible).

System One would have to tighten its link with Europe's Amadeus, which would become the dominant partner. The third grouping already exists—Apollo/Covia with the European Galileo group.

In such a scenario, Asia's Abacus would have to decide which camp to jump into. As it is technically linked to Pars, the most likely would be Sabre/Pars.

AIR ROUTES

There are still many air routes that do not follow the Great Circle (the shortest route between two points on the globe). Even if more Great Circle routes are introduced, many of the conventional routes will remain.

The Great Circle routes of particular interest to Asia are those that could cross China and the Soviet Union. Assuming continuing improvement in terms of technical skills in those two countries, there will be many new air routes, more direct, over the next 10 years. Those middle-of-the-night stops in the Middle East and the Indian subcontinent will disappear.

Air routes and policies could also create new destinations. This might breathe life into one forgotten part of the region—Soviet Asia.

There are signs of recognition. Singapore included services to Khabarovsk in Soviet Asia when it recently negotiated a bilateral agreement with the USSR. The Soviets have also held talks with the United States for Aeroflot flights from Soviet Asia across to the United States. Last summer there were even charter flights from Alaska to four towns just across the Bering Straits.

ENTERTAINMENT

Inflight entertainment (IFE) now has to cover more than just entertainment. It also has to include the increasing demand for business facilities.

IFE will be highly sophisticated 10 years from now. The seat area will be an electronic station. You will order drinks from there (the first inseat drinks dispenser will be tested within the next 10 years); select your choice of movies from a list of hundreds, and watch them when you want on an individual mini-screen; see local TV at the destination point or the departure point; play computer games; write letters on the built-in word processing facility; and, if you wish, use the telephone or the fax.

Much of the leading edge of such consumer technology will be in your airline seat five years after it hits the shops.

TRAVEL AGENTS

With the advent and spread of the super-CRS, the role of travel agents will change radically. They will become travel sales outlets, in which the super-CRS is housed. They will still consolidate travel deals, although more of that will be done by unseen operators on the super-CRS.

It is to be hoped they will provide real experience and knowledge of the travel product. But to do that they will have to be smart— and to make the most of technology.

Computer services will not only show the customer pictures of his hotel, but will even show him the room he has booked, plus other aspects of the hotel, such as the squash courts or the gym or the coffee shop. By 2000, these pictures will probably be moving pictures. Customers will also be able to use their aircraft inseat videos to check what their room looks like and even change rooms and book extra services while in the air.

HOTELS

Rooms will reflect the contemporary technology, like checking in for a flight from the room, sending faxes from it, withdrawing money from the local bank, watching a TV program from your home country, seeing as many videos as you want, and, of course, linking up with your office PC. The possibilities are endless.

There will also be more hotels, most of them chain hotels. The big increase in the coming decade will be expansion by hotel management companies into a comprehensive range of hotels—city centers, resorts, secondary towns, conference hotels, all-suite hotels, grandluxe hotels, tourist hotels, group hotels.

Independent hotels will still exist, but they will find it harder to match the service and overall quality of the group hotels. They will also be less profitable than chain hotels.

NEO-DESTINATIONS

Currently, there is still a strong trend for beach holidays, even among Asian travelers, who most pundits hitherto assumed had enough sun during the year and did not want to go and sit in it on vacation.

What seems to have happened is that Asian travelers regard beach holidays also as leisure holidays; this is not the same for sightseeing or shopping holidays.

But by 2000 this desire will probably have begun to fade among the nouveau-travelers from Asia, and even among sun-starved northern Europeans. They will probably want open spaces, and hill resorts will be the places to go.

If the Philippines can keep on the same steady path as at present, it should be able to develop the beach business and also be ready for the hill business, when that comes. So should Indonesia, a country of many attractions but one which has only just begun to promote destinations other than Bali.

The country that should do best in Asia is Malaysia. It already has hill resorts, and if the shift is toward adventure holidays as well, Malaysia is well placed for that, too. Of the long-shots, Hainan island in China is the best bet. Another is Ho Chi Minh City, which not only has a lively Bangkok-type atmosphere, but also has beaches around Vungtau and the hill station at Dalat.

TECHNOLOGY

The influence of technology in the travel business is immense, although most of it is in the hands of the aviation part of the industry. And that in turn is related to technological advance in the economy at large.

Two extensions of existing technology that are becoming established now, and should be well-established by the end of the century, are the microwave landing system (MLS) and tilt-rotor aircraft.

The MLS is the updated equivalent of the ILS, or instrument landing system, the technology that guides aircraft into airports.

MLS is about 10 years behind schedule, but it is now being tested by the Federal Aviation Administration at some U.S. airports, and by the U.K. and Dutch authorities at London's Gatwick airport.

The system reduces the time needed for an aircraft to land and take off by reducing the amount of air space it requires for these movements. This therefore increases the number of flights that can be handled by an airport.

It also enables simultaneous landing on parallel runways. This can be important. For example, if a light aircraft follows a B747, it needs greater separation to avoid being blown about by the B747's exhaust. With MLS, the small aircraft would be able to land on a parallel runway at the same time as the B747, thus freeing the slot behind the jumbo for another B747, doubling the volume that the airport can handle.

If the trials are a success, MLS will improve airport capacity by around 40%. There will also be cost savings as less time is required to land—an amazing 32 minutes per flight in peak periods.

By January 2000, all International Civil Aviation Organization countries (basically all those that matter) should have switched over to MLS at their international airports.

Another extension of existing technology is the tilt-rotor aircraft, the first being the V22 Osprey. It takes off vertically, then the propeller blades, which are at the tips of the wings are tilted forward; the aircraft then moves forward at propeller-driven aircraft speeds.

This aircraft is the first step toward eliminating runways and airports as we now know them. The tilt-rotor will give way to bigger and faster aircraft that do the same thing—take off vertically, and fly forward fast enough to be of interest to those who want to save time by taking a flight from the city center airport.

For those still hankering after the supersonic life, it is likely that work will begin on a new generation of supersonic aircraft over the next 10 years, but it seems unlikely that any such aircraft will be in operation before 2005.

More likely are variations on current themes, such as double-deck aircraft, although both McDonnell Douglas and Boeing talk of the end of the 1990s before they do anything on this.

More likely in the short term will be stretched aircraft, the current favorite candidate being the new MDII. After a stretch, this aircraft would have capacity close to that of a B747, and is thus likely to be welcomed by many as an alternative to the B747. After 20 years, the B747 still has no competitor, despite its commercial success.

If we have learned anything since World War II, it is that the lead-time for technological improvements is forever decreasing. This is certain to continue, and many projects could materialize in advance of these predictions. The latest technology applied in a service-oriented business like the travel industry should prove an astounding success formula.

©*Asian Business* magazine, Far East Trade Press, Ltd., 1989.

TAIWANESE TOURISTS

The total number of Taiwanese traveling overseas in 1988 shot up by 51.4% to reach 1,601,992, mainly spurred by a steep rise in the number of people visiting the Chinese mainland. Over 1.37 million of 85% of Taiwan's outbound travelers visited Asian destinations.

JAPANESE DOWN UNDER

Spending an average of A$127 per day (about $112) during his week-long trip to Australia, the typical Japanese tourist is worth more in export dollars to his host country than 20 tons of wheat, according to a report in *Asian Advertising & Marketing*. "And there is still plenty of room for growth," says the magazine, because the 215,000 Japanese who visited their southern neighbor in 1987 accounted for a mere 7% of all Japanese going abroad.

But accustomed to exceptional levels of service and a wide variety of attractively packaged goods in their own country, the Japanese visitors are not always enchanted by "laid-back" or "downright lackadaisical" Australian attitudes, and a recent investigatory commission appointed by the tourist industry recommended that these complaints be addressed.

THE INDONESIAN MARKET

Indonesia announced plans in 1989 to build 91 hotels with a total capacity of 15,500 rooms by 1992 in an effort to boost tourism. At the time of the announcement, Indonesia had 410 rated hotels, with 31,210 rooms and 3,336 guest houses with 68,962 rooms. Tourist officials say the government plans to boost tourist arrivals from 1.29 million in 1988 to 3.5 million by 1994.

Taking advantage of easing foreign investment restrictions, Sheraton Corp. announced it will be entering the Indonesian market for the first time. The international hotel chain, which has 36 properties in Asia, plans to develop and operate 20 hotels, including 5-star luxury resorts in Bali and Jakarta, as well as less luxurious Sheraton Inn-type hotels in provincial cities.

TICKET TO THAILAND

Tourism has been Thailand's leading foreign exchange earner since 1982. But in 1987, all records were broken as a result of the Tourism Authority of Thailand's (TAT) hugely successful international promotion ("Visit Thailand" '87), which coincided with the nation's year-long celebration of King Bhumibol Adulyadej's 60th birthday. There were 3.48 million tourists and other visitors in 1987. They pumped an estimated $2 billion into the nation's economy. Leading the parade were 300,000 Japanese visitors, and 220,000 travelers from the United States. (Of these figures, an estimated 60% were tourists, while 40% were there on business.) There

were an estimated 4.25 million arrivals in 1988 (a 26.03% increase over the previous year), according to Sumonta Nakornthab, director of public relations for TAT.

BURMA

COUNTRY IN DECLINE

"It's like going back 20 years in a time tunnel," was the written comment of one guest after a stay at Rangoon's once-proud Strand Hotel which, like the rest of Burma, seems to be decaying away. A correspondent for *Sing Tao* reported the hotel infested with mice and advised visitors to ask for a room with a cat rather than one with a view, which in any case was now one of "squalor and abject poverty."

MICRONESIAN HOLIDAY

Noting that the aviation trend toward "advanced technology long-range aircraft" will make stop-overs on the North and Middle Pacific routes virtually obsolete by the end of the decade, Mitsunari Kawano, managing director and executive officer in charge of international passengers for Japan Air Lines, proposed the creation of "new tourist resources" in a central Pacific location, which would be equidistant from "all Western rim Pacific nations."

Speaking at Lloyd's of London Press Eighth Annual Civil Aviation Conference in San Francisco, Kawano suggested that the Micronesian islands might fit the bill. In a sort of time-share arrangement on a mass scale, these tourist resources would be developed so that "all people on the northern and southern sides of the Pacific could visit the Micronesian islands for summer vacations alternately every half year." In that event, perhaps the Micronesians will make like the Parisians and paddle away at the first sign of a tourist onslaught during high season.

HOCHIMEX

No, it's not Vietnamese-Mexican cuisine—but Vietnam's first foreign joint venture with the Hong Kong-based Hochimex Co. The $3 million joint venture is a transportation service shuttling tourists to and from Vung Tau, a seaside resort southeast of Ho Chi Minh City (formerly Saigon).

OCCIDENT EXPRESS

Venice Simplon Orient Express Co., the London-based firm which operates the fabled Orient Express railway service between London–Vienna–Venice, plans to launch its first direct railway link between Singapore and Bangkok via Kuala Lumpur by the early 1990s. The $15 million venture will feature luxury vintage railway cars.

REROUTING THE RIM

The New Zealand government suspected a racket was behind a 50% jump in the number of arrivals who are claiming "refugee" status. According to Article 33 of the United Nations convention (of which New Zealand is a signatory), no state "shall expel or return a refugee in any manner whatsoever to the frontiers of territories where his life or freedom could be threatened." But with 200 to 300 cases on the books since August 1988, New Zealand's Immigration Service began to suspect a travel scam, especially since most of these arrivals are connecting via Asian flights originating in Singapore—where visas to New Zealand are not checked. Among of-

fending airlines: Qantas, Australia's flag carrier, Indonesia's Garuda, Royal Thai Airlines, and Malaysian Airline Systems.

GOLDEN TRIANGLE PROPERTY

A Thai company has developed a luxury "paradise" resort in the "Golden Triangle," the notorious frontier area that produces most of the world's opium. The five-star 200-room hotel, complete with bungalows and golf course, is the first Thai investment project in Burma, according to Prasit Pothasuthon, chairman of the Bangkok-headquartered PP Group.

HOTEL BLUES

With Taiwan's booming economy attracting increasing numbers of visiting foreign businessmen, the ROC is suffering a major hotel room shortage. There are now 107 international hotels in Taiwan, with about 20,200 rooms. But demand rose to 24,900 rooms in 1987, according to the ROC's Tourism Bureau. The bureau is predicting that 2.1 million foreign travelers will visit Taiwan in 1991. Even with the expected addition of five major international hotels in Taipei over the next few years, there will still be a shortage of about 7,400 rooms in the ROC capital.

HIGH-YEN PILGRIMS

It's not just their Gucci bags that Japanese travelers are determined to uplift, but their souls as well. In the single biggest tourism development project ever to be launched in the subcontinent, Japan has loaned India $80 million to develop special facilities for high-yen pilgrims visiting the nation's sacred sites of Buddhist culture and tradition.

THE ASIAN TRAVEL BOOM

FROM HERE TO UNCERTAINTY

The Pacific Asia Travel Association's (PATA) 1989 conference in Singapore had an appropriate theme, "Creating and Sustaining Demand." By the turn of the twenty-first century, the Asia-Pacific will be the biggest tourist market in the world, leading travel industry experts agreed.

But along with the Rim's super-drawing power, there will be a critical shortage of hotel rooms and insufficient airline flights to cope with booming international traffic. Regional air capacity is already so tight that thousands of passengers are being turned away daily, observed Cheon Choon Kong, managing director of Singapore Airlines.

"The regulators and rule-makers refuse to heed the chorus of demand. Capacity remains tightly regulated, and market realities be damned!" he said, as he pleaded for governments to ease restrictions.

By 1992, more than 12 million, or 10% of Japan's population, will be traveling annually, predicted Isao Matsuhashi, managing director of Japan Travel Bureau (JTB), the island-nation's biggest travel agency. This year alone, the number is expected to exceed 10 million, two years ahead of the 1991 target.

"We are entering the age of the grand tour," Matsuhashi declared. He also noted a new travel trend emerging in Japan. Women in their twenties account for 40% of all women travelers—or 16% of all Japanese travelers. These so-called "office ladies" constitute the fastest growing segment of Japanese travelers.

Nikkei Resort magazine surveyed 1,600 single working women in major companies. The results showed that 60% go abroad once every two years. They spend the most money abroad in shopping (53.4%), and tend to stay at resort hotels (49.8%).

TIPS FOR DEALING WITH JAPANESE TOURISTS

At a Singapore seminar for tour guides and travel agents, Nobuaki Kuniya, a Japanese psychologist who works for JTB, had this advice on how to handle Japanese travelers. "Go for the ego," he said. "Tell the Japanese tourist he is the first intellectual Japanese to ask such and such question even if you have heard it umpteen times before."

Secrets of the Japanese psyche: Kuniya explained that Japanese tourists want to satisfy their intellectual curiosity, their sense of superiority, and their need to record achievements. This latter point explains why Japanese are so fond of taking photographs and collecting souvenirs, he revealed.

ROC RR

Tourists from the Republic of China on Taiwan have become the second largest group traveling to the PRC after the Japanese. About 450,000 Taiwanese went to China in 1988, compared with 590,000 Japanese.

BACK TO BUGIS

Singapore's notorious Bugis Street, the once sleazy haunt of pimps, prostitutes, and particularly transvestites until razed four years ago to make way for a new subway system, is to be recreated on a nearby vacant lot after the tourist board reviewed complaints that the city's nightlife had become too boring.

UNSAFE FERRIES OF THE PHILIPPINES

Ferries are one of the most common and cheapest means of transport around the 7,000 islands of the Philippines but the state of many of them and of the shipping business in general leaves a lot to be desired. According to industry officials more than 100 accidents each year are the result of storms, decrepit ships, and an indifference to maritime rules. In one two-month period about three quarters of the crew members tested by the coast guard failed basic competence tests, and the purchase of fraudulent licenses by unqualified crew members seeking jobs is said to be a common practice.

JAPANESE TOURISTS NOT YOBBOS

The Japanese have discovered Australia's Gold Coast, that 25-mile tropical stretch of sun and sand stretching south of Brisbane, and are voraciously buying up everything in sight, from cheap souvenirs to multimillion dollar hotels. Japanese tourism in Queensland, already nearing 100,000 visitors a year could increase fivefold by the close of the century, according to a recent report and they are big spenders, typically leaving as much as $5,000 behind them after a three-day stay.

"Since they'll spend the rest of their lives working, they're prepared to blow a vast amount of money in a limited time," observes Yukako Shimaburi, a sales executive at the Japanese-owned Ramada Hotel, which is popular with honeymooners. One hotel manager said that Japanese were popular guests because, "they are not mad drinkers, they don't fight in the streets, and they're not yobbos." And they have made some major real estate deals totaling hundreds of millions of dollars.

COME TO GUAM

Visitors to Guam have doubled in the past decade, with 90% of them Japanese, and especially on weekends the island's 3,400 hotel rooms are filled to capacity. Because of the lack of local capital, Japanese investors have been financing the new hotels. Guam sees almost 600,000 visitors each year—nearly three times the island's total population.

BIG ON BUSINESSMEN

The ratio of tourists to business visitors to Taiwan luxury hotels is dropping, which pleases the hoteliers because they make more money from the latter. "One commercial customer equals three tourists," explains Lin Min-shan, an executive at the Ambassador Hotel. Apart from paying a higher price for their rooms business visitors also spend more on such additional services as car rental, bar and laundry. Another change has been that whereas in previous years business visitors came to buy because of Taiwan's relatively cheap production costs, many of these same customers are now coming as sellers or investors.

PHILIPPINE TOURISM

The Philippines earned almost $1 billion from tourism in 1988, the best year for tourism since 1981, with more than one million foreigners visiting the archipelago, according to the Philippine Department of Tourism.

JAPAN'S CONCORDE—THE HST

Japan Air Lines is developing a supersonic transport (HST) plane, which will be capable of flying from Tokyo to New York in three hours. The superfast HST, said to be the next generation plane, will be capable of flying at Mach 5—or five times the speed of sound.

SLOW BLIMP TO CHINA

For future travelers who are not overly enthusiastic about the advent of the transPacific space shuttle, there is a more laid-back alternative. Why rush when you can enjoy a slow blimp to China? There will be an international airship service to China and Japan in operation by 1992, according to Wren Skyships, Ltd., an Isle of Man-based airship company. The 2,240 kilometer trip from Tokyo to Hong Kong, for example, will be a pleasant overnight haul in a comfy sleeper, complete with a mint on your pillow.

TAIWAN'S BEST-SELLING MAPS

Maps of China, train timetables, and airline schedules became best-selling items in Taiwan when the Taiwanese government ruled to allow its citizens to visit mainland China for humanitarian reasons so they could visit relatives. Almost two million people, including 600,000 soldiers belonging to Generalissimo Chiang Kai-shek's Kuomingtang (KMT) Army retreated to Taiwan. The Red Cross supervises travel to China by registering people. Taiwan hopes that the tens of thousands of Taiwanese roaming China will be effective advertisements for the island's capitalist system, scoring propaganda points for the KMT against the communists. The KMT still claims to rule China and wants reunification on its own terms.

THE MARCOS CRUISE ON MANILA BAY

A luxury yacht, used by former Philippine President Ferdinand Marcos to hold lavish parties for cronies, is now being used as a tourist boat around Manila Bay. Variously called *The President* and *777,* a Marcos lucky number, the former government ship can hold 200 people.

ROLLS AUCTIONS IN HONG KONG

Every seven years, the Peninsula Hotel, Hong Kong's grand old dame, periodically auctions off its fleet of nine Rolls Royce Silver Shadows, which are used to ferry guests between the hotel and airport. At the last auction in 1987, the cheapest Silver Shadow II went for about $25,000, while one bidder bought three of them for a total of $74,000.

RIM ROOM SERVICE

ASIA'S PREMIER HOTELS: THAT TOUCH OF SUPERIORITY

by Murray Bailey

Asian hotels are recognized around the world as being a cut above the rest. Part of the secret is in who owns or manages them.

Bangkok's Oriental hotel is regularly labeled as the best hotel in the world, whatever that means.

The Mandarin Oriental (originally just Mandarin) and the Regent in Hong Kong also frequently win similar (or even the same) accolades. And the Peninsula in Hong Kong has featured in enough films for its name to be synonymous with style in Asia.

These hotels, their achievements, and those of other hotels in the region have brought international recognition to Asian hotels.

These four hotels are part of Asian hotel chains, and their success appears to be greater than that for the traditional, almost exclusively American, chain hotels, which brought the concept of modern hotel management into the Asia-Pacific region.

A hotel management company (HMC), loosely defined, is one that has at least five hotels outside its base country—although for a number of reasons, this definition should not be rigid.

Asian HMCs are different from the big names, such as Hilton, Holiday Inn, Hyatt, Inter-Continental, and Sheraton. Most Asian HMCs are owners/operators—even if they are not majority shareholders, they tend to have some equity, which normally amounts to more than most international chains are prepared to put in.

There are four HMCs that can be considered the leaders, although they are not the largest. In alphabetical order, they are as follows.

MANDARIN ORIENTAL

Previously operated as the hotel arm of Hongkong Land, a real estate company, Mandarin Oriental was demerged in 1987, and is now publicly listed. Its best-known hotels are the Oriental in Bangkok and the Mandarin Oriental in Hong Kong.

MO's two Hong Kong hotels (the second is Excelsior, which it describes as an associate hotel) are very strong, accounting for more than 80% of the group's earnings.

The company has named New York, London, Frankfurt, Sydney, and Tokyo as some of the gateway cities it is interested in. And it now has a new managing director Robert Riley, who has a background in real estate and is thus expected to speed up the company's expansion.

Although growth over the past three years has not been as fast as many expected, MO has improved its image in the market (which was already good), as well as improving group profitability.

PENINSULA GROUP

This actually began in 1892 with the original Hongkong Hotel. It developed as Hong Kong and Shanghai Hotels until the name Peninsula Group was created in 1973 to facilitate international expansion.

Its Repulse Bay Hotel (now demolished) officially opened on New Year's Day 1920, followed, eight years later, by the Peninsula.

Recently, it has had some setbacks. In 1985 it lost four hotels that formed the Marco Polo group; and since then it has dropped what is now the Regent in Bangkok, and the Jianguo in Beijing. Thus, despite its long history, it had only five managed hotels open at the start of 1989. In 1988, prospects suddenly started to look much better, with announcements of prestige projects in New York, which is open, Los Angeles, and London.

REGENT INTERNATIONAL

This group was the realization of a dream of hotelier Robert Burns, who foresaw the future in catering to the top end of the market.

Burns incorporated Regent in Hong Kong in 1970, with partners Siegfried Beil (now running Beaufort), George Rafael (now owner of Rafael Hotels), and Adrian Zecha (now major owner of Southern Pacific Hotels Corp.). Today, Burns holds 65% of the company, with Japanese development company EIE holding 30%, and the Hongkong & Shanghai Bank the remaining 5%.

EIE has become an important part of growth at Regent, making it similar to the other owner/operators in Asia, in that it has equity in a number of existing Regent hotels and particularly in its projects. The most striking of these is the U.S.$300 million hotel planned for New York.

A pause followed the departure of Rafael and Zecha in 1986 (and one hotel, Okinawa, went out of the system, and another, Tokyo, changed HMCs), but there are now significant expansion plans.

Singapore was added at the end of 1988, quickly followed by switching hotels in Kuala Lumpur to one better suited to Regent's standards than the hotel that carried its name.

But the key hotel project is in New York, due to open in 1992. This may do for Regent in North America what its flagship hotel in Hong Kong did for Asia, and its hotel in Sydney did for Australasia.

SHANGRI LA

Another group synonymous with quality in the industry, but little-known internationally, is Shangri La International, which operates many hotels of deluxe standard. It is the largest owner/operator in the region, with majority shareholdings in all hotels in the group apart from the newly acquired Tanjung Aru Beach Resort.

Shangri La, the most aggressive of the Asian groups, is part of the Kuok group, headed by Robert Kuok, whose interests also include trading and shipping. Started as the hotel division of Penang-based Kuok Brothers, it became Shangri La International Hotels, in 1979, and moved to Singapore, and then later to Hong Kong.

Although it is not widely known, Shangri La is the largest of the big four HMCs, with 12 hotels in operation and another 12 to 15 opening in the next five years.

Its hotels are market leaders in Kuala Lumpur, on Penang beach, and arguably in Beijing and Singapore. In Bangkok, after only two years, it is in second place, equal with the Regent, and only behind the Oriental.

There was a breakthrough of sorts in 1988 when Shangri La took over the disputed management contract of Tanjung Aru in Kota Kinabalu, Malaysia, previously managed by Beaufort. This was the group's first management-only deal.

Its biggest project, the U.S.$440 million China World Trade Centre in Beijing, will be ready in 1990. This includes two hotels, one with 743 rooms and the other with 308, as well as a convention and exhibition center, two office blocks, and residential apartments. That will give Shangri La three hotels in Beijing.

It has also announced plans to build two hotels in Manila. These will be the first major hotels to be built in the city since the disastrous overbuilding of hotels that began in 1976.

In Hong Kong, the Island Shangri La is being built, and it is expected that within the next two years, the group will take over the Kowloon Shangri La. This is currently managed by Westin Hotels, but the majority shareholding is held by Kuok interests.

OTHER GROUPS

There are many other hotel groups in Asia that are growing into international status in different ways. They include three—Inter-Continental, Southern Pacific, and Westin—that have recently been sold to Asian companies.

- Westin Hotels and Hilton International were owned by Allegis, previously the parent company of United Airlines. Shareholder pressure forced Allegis to put both on the market.

  Hilton went to British gaming company Ladbroke's, and Westin went east. Texan investor Robert Bass teamed up with Japanese construction company Aoki in October 1987 to buy the Westin chain for U.S.$1.53 billion. Aoki took about 60%. The new owners then sold the Westin Maui in Hawaii for U.S.$325 million, and the Plaza in New York for U.S.$410 million.

  Westin has 62 hotels and 35,000 rooms, with equity in about 25 hotels. But growth has been slow, particularly in Asia. By 1991, Westin hopes to rectify this by opening in Shanghai and Tokyo.
- Inter-Continental Hotels was bought in 1988 by Japanese conglomerate Seibu Saison, which has substantial interests in railways and real estate.

  Seibu paid Grand Metropolitan U.S.$2.27 billion for Inter-Continental's 98 hotels and 37,391 rooms. Another 12 hotels with 4,194 rooms are under construction.

  Inter-Continental hotels have good regional coverage, although the company has had setbacks in Asia-Pacific, losing hotels over the past three years in Bangladesh, Japan, Pakistan, and Singapore.

  These losses have been offset by recent additions in Sydney and Seoul, which have actually enhanced the company's reputation as they are of a higher standard than others in the group.
- Southern Pacific Hotels Corp (SPHC) is better known by two of its four brand names, Parkroyal (five-star) and Travelodge (three-star). The other two were announced last year; they are four-star Centra, and the two-star TravelCourt.

  The company was bought by William Hunt Holdings, controlled by Adrian Zecha, with the help of the Pritzker family of Chicago (owners of Hyatt International). William Hunt paid U.S.$450 million for 6,800 rooms in 39 hotels, of which 34 were owned and managed, and five were management contracts.

SPHC plans to expand in Asia. Its first move was to acquire a 49.9% stake in what was previously the Regent in Kuala Lumpur. A U.S.$10 million conversion program is planned for that hotel, and a U.S.$10 million deal has been agreed for a 210-room Travelodge in Bangkok.

- ANA Hotels is a subsidiary of All Nippon Airways, and, like its airline parent, is expanding internationally. It currently has 29 hotels, with 23 in Japan. It also owns and manages the Century Park Sheratons (these are Sheraton franchise hotels) in Manila and Singapore. In 1990, it opened hotels in Beijing and Xian.

- Beaufort International Hotels is a promising Singapore-based company which has announced plans for new hotels in Sydney, Brisbane, Bali, Singapore, Bangkok, and two in Switzerland.

But so far it operates only two hotels, having lost the Tanjung Aru in Kota Kinabalu and the Malacca Village Resort in West Malaysia.

Beaufort is owned by Regent founder Siegfried Beil, although many of his expansion plans are projects sponsored by Adrian Zecha, another ex-Regent shareholder.

- Mandarin (Singapore) International Hotels was created when Mandarin Oriental Hotels was known as Mandarin International Hotels, causing much confusion as the two companies have no links.

A dormant HMC for many years, with only its own Mandarin in Singapore, MSIH has recently added the Marina Mandarin in Singapore, the Mutiara in Penang, and the Pelangi in Langkawi, and is to manage a hotel in Shanghai.

- Omni Hotels Asia started life in 1986 as Marco Polo Hotels, based in Hong Kong with four hotels. In 1988 its owners, the Wharf Group, bought U.S.-based Omni Hotels, which had 39 hotels, for U.S.$200 million. Marco Polo Hotels was therefore renamed Omni Hotels Asia Pacific.

- New Otani has 18 hotels in Japan, and one each in Singapore, Hawaii, and Los Angeles. Its flagship is the 2,056-room New Otani in Tokyo. This year it is adding one in Beijing.

- Nikko Hotels, the hotel management arm of Japan Air Lines, is, internationally, the best-known Japanese HMC.

Most hotels listed in Nikko's brochure have reservations links only, but the company also manages 27 hotels, including those in Beijing, Shanghai, Hong Kong, Manila, Taipei, Guam, Palau, Saipan, and Jakarta. In the Americas, it manages hotels in Chicago, New York, San Francisco, and Mexico, and in Europe it is present in London, Paris, and Dusseldorf.

- Pan Pacific Hotels & Resorts is the overseas hotel division of Tokyu Group. It is managing 18 hotels in which its parent company has some equity, with some in secondary centers such as Dhaka (Bangladesh), Palau and Pangkor (Malaysia), Wuxi (China), and Vanuatu.

Some of its hotels (such as the Sari Pan Pacific in Jakarta, the Sonargaon in Dhaka, and the Mauna Lani on the Big Island of Hawaii) are operated under their own names, but all other properties feature the Pan Pacific name. It opened hotels in Auckland, Australia's Gold Coast, San Diego, and plans to open a hotel in Johor Bahru, Malaysia in 1991. In 1990, it acquired the Portman Hotel in San Francisco, renaming it the Pan Pacific San Francisco.

- Park Lane Hotels International (PLHI), established in Hong Kong in 1987, first gained attention when it bought the Churchill

Hotel in London for U.S.$200 million, or U.S.$385,000 per room.

At the same time it signed up with Radisson (a U.S.-based group of 160 hotels) as master licensee for Asia-Pacific. But this has caused some confusion, as Radisson has also signed a similar deal in Europe with Movenpick, and Movenpick has opened a hotel in China and is hoping for more in Asia. These hotels have no connection with PLHI.

PLHI owns and operates the Park Lane Radisson in Hong Kong, the Churchill in London, and Coco Palms in Hawaii. It also owns two California hotels, the Ramada Renaissance in San Francisco and the Hyatt Regency in Oakland.

Since 1988, it has added the Fountains in Phoenix and the St. Anthony in San Antonio. Its license agreement with Australia's Argus group has brought Park Lane Radisson projects in Cairns, Port Douglas, and a resort near Sydney.

©*Asian Business* magazine, Far East Trade Press, Ltd.

Managed Hotels of Leading Asian Hotel Management Companies

City	Hotels managed	City	Hotels managed
Mandarin Oriental		Melbourne	Regent
Hong Kong	Mandarin Oriental	Milan	Regent
	Excelsior	New York	Mayfair Regent
Jakarta	Mandarin Oriental		Regent (opening 1992)
Macao	Mandarin Oriental	Singapore	Regent
Manila	Mandarin Oriental	Sydney	Regent
San Francisco	Mandarin Oriental	Taipei	Regent
Singapore	Oriental	*Shangri La*	
Peninsula		Bangkok	Shangri La
Guangzhou	Garden	Beijing	Shangri La
Hong Kong	Peninsula		China World Hotel
Kowloon			Traders Hotel
Los Angeles	Belvedere	Fiji	Fijian, Mocambo
Manila	Peninsula	Hong Kong	Kowloon Shangri La
New York	Peninsula		Island Shangri La
Shanghai	Portman	Kota Kinabalu	Tanjung Aru
Regent		Kuala Lumpur	Shangri La
Auckland	Regent	Manila	(Two hotels, estimated
Bangkok	Regent		opening 1991)
Chicago	Mayfair Regent	Penang	Golden Sands
Fiji	Regent		Palm Beach
Hong Kong	Regent		Rasa Sayang
Istanbul	Regent		Shangri La
Jakarta	Regent	Singapore	Shangri La
Kuala Lumpur	Regent	Vancouver	Pacific Palisades
Los Angeles	Beverly Wilshire		
	Regent		

Source: Travel Business Analyst.

Greedy Cousins

In the first year after Taiwan lifted the ban, 246,747 of its citizens visited mainland China —and almost 90% of them returned home. Most of the returnees attributed their frustration and disappointment to unbearable living conditions and the greed of their mainland relatives. The owner of a Taipei laundry told the *China Times* how he gave his children all the money he brought with him (about $10,000) but even then they searched him, asking for another handout. Mainland Chinese no longer understood the word love, he charged, and regarded any relative from Taiwan as "Santa Claus with a sack of money." A columnist in Taiwan's *Free China Journal* reported that tour guides on the mainland had become greedy beggars and that hotel employees were demanding exorbitant tips to provide routine items, such as toilet paper. "Mainland China is becoming a land of money-crazy people," he wrote. "The communists are giving new meaning to the term robber barons."

Nepalese Roulette

Originally aimed at affluent tourists as a diversion from their temple-visiting, the casino in Nepal's most luxurious hotel, Kathmandu's Soaltee Oberoi, has found a new clientele among India's teeming millions. Rubbing shoulders with the high-flying rich around the roulette and blackjack tables are pajama-clad peasants and women holding babies in one arm as they pull one-arm bandits with the other. "We have done away with the dress code here," says the Filipino manager, who estimated that Indians now comprised most of the 60,000 or 70,000 visitors to the casino each year. Most of those coming by bus and on package tours have been enticed with free playing coupons.

With 13 out of the world's 20 highest mountains and cheap hotels in some towns as low as $1 per night, the Himalayan kingdom of Nepal would seem to be well-placed to expand its tourist industry almost indefinitely. And indeed the government has announced plans to try and lure one million visitors a year by the end of the century. But tourist experts warn that the plan is unrealistically ambitious and that too much onus for providing the $1.4 billion required to implement it is being placed on the private sector. Tourism currently earns Nepal, a desperately poor country of 17 million people, about $60 million per year, and more than half the annual visitors come from Western Europe and North America, an incalculable proportion anxious to see the world's highest mountain, 27,000-foot Everest.

Malay Playtime

Since the prices for its major commodities— tin, palm oil, rubber, and oil—began to plummet in the past few years, Malaysia has begun to see tourism as a more important source of foreign earnings. Until now it has lagged behind its fellow-members of the Association of Southeast Asian Nations, Indonesia, Thailand, the Philippines, and Singapore, all of which have become big tourist lures. "Malaysia has everything but doesn't know how to sell itself," says Dario Regazzoni, vice president of the country's hotel association. But maybe it is learning: for the last three years visitors have exceeded three million, bringing around $800 million annually, and almost half of the tourist budget is now being devoted to foreign advertising extolling the superb beaches, the jungles, and rare wildlife. "A lot of countries have a lot of one thing but not many have a little of everything," boasts tourist minister Datuk Sabbaruddin Chik.

PRIMITIVE PANHANDLERS

Primitive tribesmen in the once-remote villages of northern Thailand are becoming "shameless beggars" because of the rapid, unplanned expansion of foreign trekkers into the hilly regions, say local officials, and the unspoiled cultures the visitors hoped to find are being undermined by their presence. "We have to control this. It has become a free for all," says the head of the Chiangmai Professional Guides Association, Supoj Kimpraneet. "The tribesmen are normally very honest, straight people. Now they're learning to be devious; they're thinking only about commission." Since 1987, which the government designated as "Visit Thailand Year," tourism has increased more than 40%, and the number of unregulated, fly-by-night trekking companies has vastly increased as has the incidence of violence against foreign visitors.

RAFFLES REDUX

The century-old Raffles Hotel, with its overhead fans, creaking floors, and wide verandas, is undergoing a $27.3 million restoration to the relief of worldwide fans who feared that the value of its real estate would lead to its demise. Opened in 1886 and named after Singapore's founder, Sir James Raffles, the 127-room hotel became a key outpost in the British Empire, widely patronized by colonial adventurers of all types who knocked back endless glasses of gin-based Singapore Slings, invented by bartender Ngian Tong in World War I. (Until it was closed for restoration, the hotel still prepared 1,000 of the cocktail every day.) "Raffles," wrote Somerset Maugham, "stands for all the fables of the exotic east," and legend records Joseph Conrad as having got the idea for his novel Lord Jim while sitting on the hotel's veranda.

BORING SINGAPORE?

The *Economist* magazine's annual report, "The World in 1988," dubbed Singapore as being the most "irredeemably boring" of the 48 countries surveyed—more boring than the Soviet Union, Iran, Iraq, or Libya. Singapore placed joint 36th with East Germany, ahead of neighboring Malaysia (38th) and Indonesia (42nd) but behind the Philippines (24th) and Hong Kong, a joint seventh with Britain. The *Economist* also moved its regional editorial office from Singapore to Hong Kong, but there was no indication that boredom had anything to do with the decision.

THE UGLY KOREAN
by Bruce Cheesman

The first hordes of tourists to invade Southeast Asia were the Japanese. They were closely followed by the Taiwanese. Now the South Koreans are coming.

Within a few short months of Seoul lifting all age restrictions on travel abroad in 1988, the South Koreans made their presence felt to such an extent that an "ugly Korean" image has emerged.

Previously, because of foreign exchange

controls and security limitations, Seoul managed to keep a lid on some of the rather curious mannerisms of the "hermit kingdom." Since the Korean War there has been a ban on pleasure trips abroad by Koreans under 50, which has restricted foreign travel to businessmen and the well-heeled upper crust with the necessary connections to secure a passport.

The businessmen, as they winged their way across the region with their aggressive personalities and somewhat cavalier attitude to contractual obligations, did little to endear themselves to most Asians, but they were fairly few and far between.

Now, as all age restrictions on travel have been lifted as part of the more liberal attitude of president Roh Tae-woo, Koreans from all walks of life are allowed to peregrinate.

Domestic tourism department chief Koo Yeon-seok blames the "ugly Korean" image on misunderstandings and inexperience. "It must be remembered that for so many years Koreans have had little experience of overseas cultures. Despite the Olympics, most Koreans still have little idea about other countries. It is also easy to get the wrong impression of Koreans as we are very open and lack the etiquette of other Asians and Europeans.

"We are very hot blooded and affectionate. It is difficult for Koreans to show restraint, but we hope that in the future our tourists will quickly adjust," he said.

© *Asian Business* magazine, Far East Trade Press, Ltd., 1989.

"If you love your son, let him travel."

Japanese proverb.

9

❖

THE FUTURE

DAWN OF THE ASIAN MILLENIUM
by Brian Caplen

What is the Pacific Rim going to be like in the twenty-first century? Certainly the conventional world order will be turned upside down. In an intriguing scenario, Brian Caplen, editor of Asian Business, *a Hong Kong-published regional business magazine, describes the state-of-the-Rim in a letter addressed to a mythical Asian CEO.*

And to think, Mr. Asian Chief Executive, that you ever worried about anything as trivial as trading blocs. By the year 2000, the blocs will exist in name only and your corporation can claim the credit for helping remove them from the map.

It was your corporation, after all, that marched into Europe's single market, geared up production with 100% local content, and still outdid the competition.

It was your corporation that began using technology in Europe that even head offices didn't have. It was your corporation that led the way for the rise of Asia's first true multi-nationals (MNCs).

Ask a London pedestrian in the year 2000 what the nationality of Sony or Nissan is, and he will either say "European" or "I don't know." By then the big Japanese and Korean MNCs will be as international as Ford or

585

IBM. They will operate in Europe and America totally independently of Tokyo or Seoul. They will blend in perfectly with their surroundings.

If protectionism is still in vogue it will not be applied to "them"; Sony and Nissan by that stage will be very much a part of the Western "U.S." South American companies, or maybe those from Asia's next wave—Thailand, Indonesia, and Malaysia—will be the new targets.

Even if Brussels or Washington did try to get heavy-handed with Asia's major corporations, (and the signs are that they will try once or twice in the 1990s), it will matter a whole lot less than now. By the year 2000 the Asian market will be as big as Europe's or North America's. By the next century it will be the largest of the three. This regional market will provide base support for Asian corporate growth and will insulate companies from periodic Western backlashes.

More than this, since the Asian market is going to be the world's largest, conquering it will be a major step toward global success. Asian companies will clearly have an advantage in their own regional market and this alone will put them in a world lead.

So Mr. Asian Chief Executive, you can look forward to a very profitable decade ahead. And not only will you make profits but you will feel very satisfied about your achievements. Unlike in the 1980s, when governments assisted your corporate effort with export subsidies and promotion, this time you will succeed entirely by yourself.

The 1990s will be the decade in which the strong alliance between government and business that has characterized the region's development—and so irritated Western competitors—will break down.

No longer will governments protect markets, subsidize exports, and clamp down on labor disputes to please their golden-egglay-

Shares in World GDP by region, 1988 and 2000

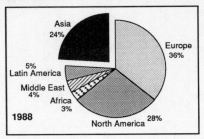

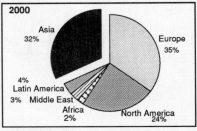

Source: Business International

ing prodigies. They will have to take account of other considerations, such as international opinion, the demands of a newly enfranchised electorate, and powerful labor unions.

These economic and political changes demand a radically different corporate strategy from that of the past.

CORPORATE STRATEGY

The rise of trading blocs, especially Europe 1992 and the North America Free Trade Arrangement, will be judged by history as the catalyst that finally created the Asian multinational.

Doubtless the Asian MNCs would have come anyway but the fear of protectionism will advance their birth. Without protectionism the attractions of the old strategy—low-cost production in Asia and mass marketing overseas—would be hard to resist. Just as labor shortages force companies to upgrade technologically, so protectionism encourages them to upgrade structurally. As they do, trading blocs lose their bite.

"Trading blocs will be declared null and void by companies which learn how to outmaneuver them," says top academic and former German minister of state for foreign affairs, Sir Ralf Dahrendorf. "In an increasingly protectionist world, it will be interesting to watch how dynamic companies continue to trade freely.

"Trade, remember, is conducted between companies, not countries, and MNCs are masters at operating successfully in restrictive environments.

"By becoming multicultural, MNCs don't have to impose their nationality on a place and this makes them much more acceptable," says Dahrendorf, who is himself a director of a multinational, the pharmaceutical company Glaxo.

"Take a company like Nissan. It moves into the EC. It abides by the rules. It never complains. It makes money."

Ranjan Pal, director of forecasting services at Hong Kong-based consultancy Business International, agrees that trading blocs are already losing their sting and will continue to do so. "As Asian MNCs become true MNCs and produce throughout the world, trading blocs will cease to matter to them. Japanese and Korean companies will become European just as Ford in Europe is a European firm not an American one. The same will be true of Sony.

"The Japanese are doing it cleverly," says Pal. "They are blending into the European landscape and diffusing some of the 'us against them' attitude."

Gross Domestic Product of Asian Countries in 1988 and 2000

Country	1988 GDP (U.S.$ billion)	2000 GDP (US$ billion)	Average real GDP growth (% per annum)
Australia	239	345	3.1
China[a]	315	720	7.1
Hong Kong	54	100	5.2
Indonesia	73	123	4.4
India	272	467	4.6
Japan[b]	2,841	4,198	3.3
South Korea	164	349	6.5
Malaysia	34	64	5.4
Pakistan	44	86	5.8
Philippines	39	67	4.6
Singapore	24	48	6.0
Sri Lanka	7	13	5.0
Taiwan	116	255	6.8
Thailand	55	103	5.4

[a] For China, net material product is used instead of GDP.
[b] For Japan, gross national product is used instead of GDP.
Source: Asian Business.

The fact that MNCs will be unaffected by the restrictions of the European and North American trading blocs makes it even more unlikely that an Asian trading bloc will be formed as a counterbalance, despite the growing following that this idea has gained over the past 12 months.

Says Pal, "It requires a political consensus that doesn't exist at present, and by the year 2000 the pattern of trade and investment flows will have made the idea redundant."

One big change in the pattern of trade will be the size of the Asian market and the strength that Asian corporations will have within it. Europe 1992 grew up partly because European firms were being beaten by foreigners at home, missing out on those famous (thanks to EC propaganda) 350 million consumers.

No such failing is predicted for Asia. "The single biggest thing that people are missing in global strategic understanding is that the Asian market will be as big as Europe's or North America's (in GDP terms) by the year 2000," says George Baeder, managing director of the Pacific Rim Consulting Group. "By the year 2050, it will be four or five times the size.

"Consider the role that the market base has played in the growth of European and U.S. companies, and it's obvious that Asian companies will become world leaders. Lucky Goldstar will be the largest chemical company in the world; Samsung the second or third largest consumer electronics firm."

Baeder comments that Western companies only have about 5 or 10 years to establish themselves in the Asian market. If they leave it much longer, the niches in which they currently have an advantage will be taken by Asian companies.

He cites the Asian tendency to invest today for projected future demand—against the Western tendency to wait for the demand to materialize and then invest—as a reason why the West could lose out.

Firm evidence of the speed at which Asian companies anticipate and react to changes is the move offshore by Japanese, Korean, and Taiwanese firms. Motivated by the need to offset rising costs and currencies at home, this trend will continue in the decade ahead and will increase in sophistication.

Instead of shifting production to a single country, companies will divide it between two or three. As technology is transferred, direct investment is less vital, and a network of subcontractors can be established. This allows the big companies of north Asia to get every part of their production process completed in the most cost-effective center without running into political objections.

"Everyone is becoming everyone else's subcontractor," says American management guru Tom Peters. "The reality of more sophisticated telecoms links is that it makes possible the siting and control of production all over the place. Companies are looking round the world to find out who is best at what. As to where production will end up, who knows?"

Peters, the author of best-selling business books *In Search of Excellence* and *Thriving on Chaos,* thinks the changes will help usurp the growing protectionism of the next decade and provide further ammunition against trading blocs.

But shifting offshore is not only about production; it is also about markets.

As the Japanese market opens up—as much in response to consumer pressure as to U.S. pressure—the clear strategy of Japanese corporations is that they, and not foreign firms, should supply the new imports. This they will do from their overseas production bases.

One result is that no matter how much the Japanese market liberalizes it will not shrink the trade surplus with the United States.

Western companies that want to crack the Japanese market are advised to get involved in these offshore ventures.

"The best way to do business with Japan is to set up a project with a Japanese company in somewhere like Indonesia," says Bob Broadfood, managing director of the Hong Kong-based Political and Economic Risk Consultancy.

Meanwhile, for those Asian companies that aren't moving offshore, the domestic market will continue to grow in importance. Korea car production, for example, is expected to reach three million by 1995, split evenly between domestic and export sales. This trend will be reflected in many other areas.

The export-or-die strategy that fired the hearts and minds of economic planners in the NICs for two decades is up for renewal.

FUTURE ECONOMY

Export strategy is not the only policy the technocrats will have to rethink. In the 1990s their whole mandate will come under scrutiny.

The growth of democracy in Asia means the technocrats can no longer run economies as business machines. They will have to pay attention to a whole array of issues that never cluttered up their lives before. These include:

- A see-sawing balance of trade. Under pressure from consumers, import barriers are being lifted to bring prices down. The see-saw effect on the balance of trade, as consumers buy 10 million oranges one month, then a 1,000 tons of beef the next, will be a new experience for Asian planners.
- The impact of social welfare benefits. There is pressure from the electorate to provide them; soon there will be a huge debate about who is going to pay for them.

- Liberalization of capital markets and exchange rates. A veritable can of worms if ever one existed. The old days, when interest rates were dictated by finance ministry technocrats and the national currency was pegged to the dollar, are almost gone.
- Foreign exchange outflows. As if buying foreign goods and investing in other countries wasn't bad enough, people actually want to visit these places, the elderly technocrats complain! Soaring overseas travel will be another factor in the balance of payments equation.
- Slower growth rates. Projections put average real GDP growth for Japan in the 1990s at 3.3% per annum; for the NICs (Hong Kong, Singapore, Taiwan, and Korea) between 5.2% and 6.8%; and for second wave Asia (Indonesia, the Philippines, Thailand, and Malaysia) between 4.4% and 5.4%. (See Table on p. 591.)
- These are healthy but not as dynamic as during the 1980s. With a major recession certain at some point in the 1990s, governments will need to temper their borrowing, and plan spending carefully to avoid indebtedness.
- The services boom. In north Asia particularly, the 1990s will require as much attention to the service sector as to manufacturing. This requires different ground rules, and bureaucrats will be compelled more than ever before to address issues such as copyright and tax evasion

"The well-oiled machine isn't going to perform as well as before," says Business International's Ranjan Pal. "There will be more consumer lobbies and environmental activists to take account of. Politicians rather than bureaucrats will run ministries. It could slow economies down a bit."

But while finance ministries will no longer be able to dictate economic policy, it is unlikely that Asia will go the way of rampant inflation and crippling indebtedness. The mandarins will only loosen their grip. They won't abdicate.

This is probably just as well because in addition to the more macroeconomic teasers, the mandarins will have to keep abreast of a pressing need for new infrastructure, the continual demand for up-to-date technology, and increasing labor strife. Small wonder that civil servants will be pushing these problems over to companies to solve.

Infrastructure is a case in point. Breakneck growth in the newly emerging countries—Thailand is the best example—is stretching ports, roads, sewerage systems, and power supplies to the absolute limit. The huge resources needed to solve these problems are simply not there.

The obvious answer is to hand things over to the private sector, in the form of build-operate-transfer (BOT) contracts. That way a building contractor takes care of the financing and runs the project for an agreed period. During that time, service fees repay the contractor's outlay and, if his figures are right, give him a profit. At the end of the contract, the project is handed over to the government. BOT contracts are very much in vogue in Asia, and will remain so throughout the 1990s.

Infrastructure bottlenecks will also be tackled through the vast Japanese foreign aid program that will reach its zenith in the region in the 1990s, and act to cement that country's position as a superpower. Japanese contractors will be favored in the projects that result, and Western companies' role will shrink.

Japan will also play a major role in transferring technology to the rest of Asia. Gone are the days when Japanese companies would keep technology to themselves for fear of helping the competition. Now they realize that competitors are rising up anyway and it is better for Japanese companies to work alongside them than against them.

One result will be a strong alliance between Japan and South Korea, which is closest behind Japan in the technology race and hungry to take the baton from Japan's faltering industries.

Another result will be that Asia, and possibly the rest of the world, will follow the Japanese model of technological development. This drives technology forward from a strictly commercial standpoint, as opposed to the military lead given in the West.

"Governments that focus on the commercial application of technology rather than military applications will be the ones tapping the new sources of national power," comments Pacific Rim's George Baeder.

This doesn't mean that Japan will stay out of the defense business. Quite the opposite. But the clamor to get into defense will come from Japanese electronics corporations, wanting new applications for their commercially derived technologies.

Companies will find themselves leading the way in the 1990s in contrast to the Japan Inc. and Korea Inc. approaches of the past. But with leadership come new responsibilities, such as handling labor problems without government assistance.

"Governments will be less willing to take the side of companies in labor disputes," says one observer. "In the past they said 'growth is the thing and all else be damned.' They did not hesitate to clamp down on strikes. Now they are saying, 'we represent *all* the people, not just businessmen.' "

It's easy to see why simple export-or-die strategies won't wash in the years ahead. Economies are vastly more complex. Pressures from all corners of society, and from overseas, are combining to make economic management more like the juggling act it already is in the West.

Per Capita GDP of Asian Countries in 1988 and 2000

Country	1988 GDP per capita (U.S. $)	2000 GDP per capita (U.S. $)
Australia	145,000	18,100
China[a]	289	654
Hong Kong	9,510	15,600
Indonesia	416	553
India	344	480
Japan[b]	23,132	32,679
South Korea	3,841	7,077
Malaysia	2,010	2,790
Pakistan	414	573
Philippines	662	866
Singapore	9,040	16,180
Sri Lanka	442	662
Taiwan	5,850	11,220
Thailand	1,000	1,535

[a] For China, per capita net material product is used instead of GDP.
[b] For Japan, gross national product is used instead of GDP.
Source: Asian Business.

Population of Asian Countries, 1988 and 2000

Country	1988 population (million)	2000 population (million)	Growth rate (% per annum)
Australia	16.5	19.1	1.2
China	1,090.0	1,258.0	1.2
Hong Kong	5.7	6.4	1.0
Indonesia	175.9	222.7	2.0
India	791.5	973.3	1.7
Japan	122.8	128.5	0.4
South Korea	42.6	49.3	1.2
Malaysia	17.0	22.9	2.5
Pakistan	105.4	150.4	3.0
Philippines	58.7	77.6	2.35
Singapore	2.64	2.98	1.0
Sri Lanka	16.6	19.8	1.46
Taiwan	20.0	22.8	1.1
Thailand	54.6	66.7	1.7

Source: Asian Business.

Even in those countries tipped as the new NICs—Thailand, Malaysia, sometimes the Philippines and Indonesia—the export-or-die policy will not apply.

These four countries are vastly different in population and resource base from the old NICs (South Korea, Taiwan, Singapore, and Hong Kong). The huge rural populations of

Indonesia, the Philippines, and Thailand can't be switched overnight into manufacturing. Agriculture must play a larger role, and it's unlikely that these economies will be as outward-looking.

It would be a great mistake to believe that Thailand or the Philippines will be the South Korea of the 1990s. They will develop for sure . . . but differently.

Hong Kong university professor Edward Chen uses the term Newly Agro-Industrializing Economy (NAIE) to describe what is happening. "The degree of openness has to be matched against factor endowment," he says. "If you are resource rich, it's unlikely that you will go in for full-scale export orientation."

So the coming era will throw up new models for both companies and economies. It will also demand new political structures.

FUTURE POLITICS

The authoritarian governments that launched the NICs, and are expected to do the same for the NAIEs, won't hold up indefinitely. At a certain stage of development, a new model is required.

The search for a political model that can provide "advanced Asian democracy" promises to be the most soul-wrenching and heart-stopping drama of the 1990s.

A key driving force for this is the need of the NICs to go high-tech. Authoritarianism is unsuitable for a high-tech society because it stifles innovation. Managers need to express new ideas. Authoritarian governments don't want people to voice new ideas.

Likewise, as production becomes more sophisticated, the cooperation of the work force, as opposed to blind subservience, is essential. Again, this can't be obtained through fear.

Finally, a freer environment and accounta-

ble government are part and parcel of a mature society. They cannot forever be offset by rising living standards. Eventually, mind becomes more important than matter.

South Korea, Taiwan, and Singapore (Hong Kong is rather a special case) are already in the throes of this transition, and it promises to occupy a great deal of their time in the decade ahead.

The main difficulty is in evolving something distinctively Asian, which allows greater openness and creativity, but at the same time preserves the cultural traits that have proved their worth in achieving economic success.

These include the ability to reach major decisions through consensus, the paternalistic structure of companies, the image and dignity of senior leaders.

Western multiparty democracy, with its confrontations and media hounding of public figures, is clearly not the answer. Instead, the NICs will probably settle on a system that apes the Japanese set-up, before its recent convulsions over the Recruit Cosmos scandal.

This means a one-party system that allows opposing factions to express themselves within it, but in the final analysis agrees on a common face.

While the NICs will adopt the Japanese model, Japan itself is in transition to a more advanced stage. Greater wealth demands even greater accountability. The behind-the-scenes deal-making that has characterized latterday Japanese politics is on the way out. But again, don't think it will be replaced by Western party democracy. Japan's Liberal Democratic Party will still be in power in the year 2000, though operating a machine that can cope with a more divergent spectrum of views and interests.

In the NAIEs, the tension between executive control and democracy is at its most acute. Different interest groups are so far apart in their requirements that it's impossible for all their conflicts to be settled democratically.

This dichotomy will continue throughout the 1990s, with governments in the Philippines, Thailand, Malaysia, and Indonesia switching back and forth between authoritarianism and democracy.

No such switching is forecast for China, where authoritarianism will remain in place throughout the 1990s. Regardless of who wins subsequent power struggles in Beijing, the Communist Party's grip will remain tight. Economic reforms that threaten to upset the status quo will be canceled.

The outlook is not all bad. Because of China's indebtedness and its dependence on export earnings, the open door will be kept open as far as possible. Business opportunities in export processing and infrastructural work should continue.

But what isn't going to emerge is an independent entrepreneurial establishment. That scenario once seemed in prospect during the halcyon days of early 1989, but is now out, and for a lot longer than the three or four years estimated by the overseas dissidents.

This means that China's consumer buying power will remain depressed. The one billion market will be as elusive in the year 2000 as it was in the 1980s. Foreign investors can exploit China for its cheap labor, but not for its market.

China's continued reliance on central planning combined with export effort has been dubbed by one academic as "the open Stalinist model." It's a telling description and one that bodes darkly for Hong Kong.

The Chinese government never has had—and still doesn't have—bad intentions toward Hong Kong. It means to keep its promise to preserve the British colony's capitalist system.

But its difficult to see how the central planners, schooled in the demands of a vast "cabbage and coal" economy (and not always successful at coping with those), will find the expertise to govern an open, entrepreneurial trading enclave.

What happens when the stock market crashes and needs overhauling? What happens when there's a bout of currency speculation?

Of course Beijing could defer to Hong Kong's own legislators in such matters and most often it will. But at some point the interests of China will clash. It's a clash that Hong Kong will lose.

Political dissent is the most obvious flashpoint. Like the other NICs, Hong Kong will need to make further advances in hi-tech to progress. As already explained, hi-tech and repression don't mix.

When China clamps down on dissent in Hong Kong, upscale manufacturing and finance operations will move out. Hong Kong's post-1997 role will be as a trade conduit only.

The search for a new finance center for Asia outside Tokyo promises to be an engaging spectator sport as the decade unfolds.

Labor Force in Asian Countries, 1988 and 2000

Country	1988 labor force (million)	2000 labor force (million)	Growth rate (% per annum)
Australia	7.7	9.2	1.4
China	612.5	735.1	1.5
Hong Kong	2.7	3.2	1.3
Indonesia	70.6	102.6	3.2
India	300.6	404.8	2.5
Japan	61.5	68.1	0.85
South Korea	16.9	20.0	1.4
Malaysia	6.6	9.0	2.7
Pakistan	31.6	46.3	3.2
Philippines	23.5	31.6	2.5
Singapore	1.28	1.52	1.5
Sri Lanka	6.6	8.5	2.1
Taiwan	8.3	10.0	1.6
Thailand	29.7	37.8	2.0

Source: Asian Business.

MEMO TO THE FUTURE

THE FUTURE AS HISTORY
by Hank Koehn

Date: *September 24, 2010*
Place: *That region of our planet known as the Pacific Rim*
Futurists and think-tank gurus frequently offer useful reference points to those who are interested in where trends are leading society. One of the most engaging and visionary Pacific Rim futurists was Los Angeles future consultant Hank Koehn, who died in 1987.
Following are some highlights from his far-reaching "PacRim 2010" report which he originally prepared for the Security Pacific National bank.

Fifty years ago, in the year 1960, a geologist described the Pacific Rim as a "halo of energy," referring to the volcanos which circle the Rim. It was a narrow, but perhaps appropriate description.

Today, in 2010, the energy that gives the Pacific Rim its cohesiveness and vibrancy flows not from molten rock and steam, but from the presence of a vast, powerful, and interconnected economic and cultural community containing 4.5 billion people—over half the global population and 60% of the world's consumers.

Technological advances in communication

and transportation—especially in the years between 1990 and 2005—have reduced the barriers of time and distance within the Pacific Rim region and have made possible the lively and profitable exchange of ideas and commodities that today so profoundly shape our lives.

THE PACIFIC MATRIX

There exists today a Pacific matrix, a vast and complex web of interdependence: a natural and complimentary mix of natural resources, skilled and unskilled labor, agricultural capabilities, an research/educational/training facilities. Nations of the region tend to have economic sectors in each of the first, second, and third "waves": Agriculture, industrial, and information/communication/service, all of which have become thoroughly infused with high technologies, from microbiology and genetic engineering to microelectronics and artificial intelligence to fiber optics and lasers.

The result is a regional synergy. The economic synergy of abundant markets, capital, human resources, and raw materials is enhanced by the cultural synergy of advanced communication, information entertainment, and transportation systems. Not surprisingly, citizens of the Pacific Rim today have multiple loyalties.

The California inhabitants of the eastern portion of the Rim think of themselves as citizens of the Pacific community and have strong ethnic, emotional, and economic ties to the region. The Pacific Ocean, once looked upon as a barrier or a theater of war, today has become an electronic, as well as physical, highway which touches and links the Rim countries.

The overall strength of the Pacific Rim can best be measured by its impact upon California. Today, the California lifestyles are transnational and the perspectives cross-cultural. California is part of the collective consciousness that exists throughout the Rim, open to a multiplicity of ideas and possibilities for continued growth. While enclaves of traditional culture remain protected, Rim inhabitants also embrace a regional consumerist culture, arising from the extensive movement of people, goods, and information about the region.

Today, at 2010, this region is the planet's focus of international trade. The Los Angeles Metroplex is the center of the Rim's financial community, functioning as an electronic nerve center for a multitude of transnational services—electronic funds transfer, trade finance, currency risk management, global funds management. L.A. Metroplex's 11-year-old offshore banking facility is now housed in the newly erected Eastasian Financial Center in Monterey Park.

The Mexican Pacific port of Salina Cruz, linked by rail to the Gulf of Mexico, has joined Vancouver, San Francisco, and Los Angeles as a major shipping port on the Pacific.

PACIFIC RIM PLAYERS

Back in the early 1980s it seemed almost impossible to visualize how dramatically the Pacific Rim would develop as an entity. But even then, all the players and elements were in place:

- The mineral resources of Australia, Canada, China, Antarctica, and Siberia.
- The petroleum resources of Alaska, Mexico, Indonesia, and the South China Sea.
- The industrial labor pools of Mexico and China.

- The agriculture, aerospace, electronics, and entertainment/training products of California.
- The forestry products of Canada, the United States, Siberia, and Indonesia.
- The global granaries of Canada, Australia, and the United States.
- The new manufacturing capabilities of Japan, Thailand, South Korea, and Taiwan.
- The Pacific Ocean itself as a vast source of protein, energy, minerals.
- The advancing communication technologies, especially direct satellite communications and fiber-optical transmission.
- And perhaps most important, the readiness of Eastern and Western cultures to embrace the best traits of each other's societies.

RIM SATELLITES

A key event in the development of the interrelationships of the Pacific Rim countries was the launching in 1995 by the Japan Space Transport Authority of the "PacRim II" satellite, whose capabilities included:

- multinational/multiterminal user transparency
- full transmission encryption protection services
- value-added services for small users
- wide-band digital services
- video teleconferencing
- high-speed data and facsimile transmission and electronic mail
- individuals-in-transit services
- circuit and packet-switched databased access
- store and forward services

The Pac Rim II satellite was launched six months after PacRim I was inadvertently destroyed by a laser beam from a Soviet space-defense weapon. The accident increased a sense of military hostility in the region for a full eight weeks. Military tension has been mounting since the mid-1980s, when the Soviets increased bomber overflights between Sakhalin Island and the Vietnamese port of Cam Ranh Bay, which by 1993 had become the headquarters of the Soviet Pacific fleet.

Executive conferences are routinely conducted via the PacRim satellite, whose facilities are based at the East-West Center in Honolulu. A recent article in the multilingual *Trans Pacific Times* stated, quite accurately, that the Center had become the Rim's philosophical and cultural home.

RIM'S HEART AND MIND

But if the Rim's heart is in Hawaii, one would have to say its mind resides in the vast data banks of the L.A. Metroplex. These computer software systems, which offer everything from crisis management and political risk analysis to currency forecasting and macroeconomic modeling, are instantly accessible to any and all of the Pac Rim governments.

Remote sensing, resource, and environmental monitoring for the region are performed by LANDSAT 7. Resulting data are processed and stored in the University of Hawaii's computer center.

RIM LABOR

The division of labor among the Pacific Rim countries in 2010 has become increasingly refined, and products and services are truly transnational in character, with each component manufactured and assembled where it is cheapest to do so. (The importance of production-sharing was first pointed out as early as 1980 by Peter Drucker in *Managing in Turbulent Times*.) The Pacific Production Sharing

Guild, established in 1995 with an eye toward the reduction and eventual elimination of all trade tariffs by 2025, is making considerable progress toward its goal.

OPEN ELECTRONIC BORDERS

The issue of Trans-border Data Flow regulations was resolved five years ago in 2005 with the decision to have unrestricted flow of all electronic business data across the region's national borders.

This electronic open-border has been extremely beneficial to all countries regarding commerce and business, but there is still a concern for protecting cultural integrity. In fact, the Philippine government, as early as 1991, restricted the direct transmission of Mexican, American, and Japanese television to a maximum of one hour each per day.

CULTURAL SYNERGY

By 1999, the mystique of the Australian Outback had replaced the American Old West as a favorite theme in Asian countries.

The region of Southern California—SoCal as it is now called—is not only a major Rim contributor of people, products, and basic research, it is also the gateway of East–West exchange. It is interesting to note that U.S. sea trade with Asia surpassed that with Europe in 1982 and has been growing ever since.

Major SoCal industries now include off-planet aerospace, optical data storage, fiber-optic distribution systems, speech-recognizing artificial intelligence computers, sensors, robots, and genetic engineering.

L.A. Metro is also the training capital of the Western World. What was once the movie entertainment industry is now the world's video training industry. This industry turns businesses' operational procedures into video

tape/disk training aids. Indeed, writing, directing, and acting in training videos employ more writers, actors, and directors than the entertainment segment of the industry. In the postindustrial society of 2010, almost 75% of all teaching is via video. Human learning instructors provide the 25% of education that is tutorial.

RIMFOMATION

Clearly, information is one of California's most exportable and in-demand commodities in whatever form it takes, whether as raw material, processed product, or finished goods. The wellness maintenance industry thrives on information we were aware of back in the 1990s. A product of this industry used by all traveling inhabitants of the Pacific Rim is the Health Background ID card. This card is an extension of the "chip card" technology developed by the French *telematique* program, comprising a microprocessor and an indelible memory.

AGRICULTURE 2010

California has remained a major agricultural exporter—cotton, sugar, beans, flowers and foliage, mushrooms, lettuce, tomatoes, grapes, melons, olives, turkeys, eggs. The irradiation storage technique, which was implemented by the second fruit fly scare of 1984, has vastly extended the shipping of agricultural items Rim-wide.

TRANSNATIONAL TOURISM

With the increased affluence in the region, especially in the Asian countries, transnational tourism is a major Pacific Rim industry. The hordes of Chinese factory workers are the foremost practitioners of "Rim-Hopping" tours arranged by the region's largest travel agency, Okinawa Sam's. The most popular tour is "Trade Routes of Ancient Polynesians."

RIM ART

Conceptual art is the dominant art form of the Rim. Boasting a tradition that found expression in the Japanese Shinto religions and Southwest American Indian art, it seems appropriate that conceptual art emerged as the favorite vehicle for transmitting the technologically inspired symbols of the Pacific Rim. Mickey Mouse, still ever popular, remains the dominant share image of the Rim, on view everywhere in training films, entertainment and novelty items, and the new Jakarta Disneyworld.

RIMVIRONMENT

Environmental protection is strongest in Fiji, Tonga, and Marshall Islands, Easter Island, and the Galapagos Islands.

RIM ISLAM

One of the more curious developments since the turn of the century has been the establishment of what people are calling the "Muslim Center of the Pacific." This city-state on Mindanao in the Philippines has become a world center of Islamic faith.

EARTHQUAKE STUDY

The Center for Earthquake Study in Tokyo is a transnational facility funded by Mexico, California, China, and Japan.

MINERAL RIGHTS

There's a continuing debate as to whether the depletion of strategic minerals in the Pacific Rim is critical, or whether synthetic substitutes, improved extraction techniques, and moon-mining can fill the gap. The mineral richness of Antarctica has created an ongoing political problem for the region. The first sign of today's current troubles, widely unrecognized at the time, was the Falkland Islands dispute between Great Britain and Argentina in 1982.

ECONOMIC SEA ZONES

The conflicting and overlapping claims to economic sea zones off Antarctica have since brought several countries to the brink of a shooting war. In 1994 the government of one of the Rim's South American members ordered its navy to sink an oil rig that had been built by one of its neighbors.

Two-hundred-mile economic sea zones began to overlap in the late 1970s. The United States alone had a 4-billion-acre exclusive economic zone in the Pacific, containing 35% of its recoverable oil, gas, cobalt, manganese, and nickle.

The privately-owned Pacific Minerals Consortium is responsible for seabed mining beyond territorial waters—and within territorial waters under contract to individual nations (Soviet Russia excepted).

Of course, affordable fresh water is the critical resource everywhere.

NEW RIM CONSCIOUSNESS

The citizens of the Pacific Rim possess a consciousness of community that has been shaped by technology, trade, and history. An openness to new ideas, coupled with the richness and diversity of the natural and human resources of the Rim, has given them, in the year 2010, a regional neighborhood second to none.

HEALTH 2010

CALIFORNIA HEALIN'
by Dael Walker

California, as the New Age Lourdes, is the region's frontrunner in blending Western technology with traditional Eastern spiritual and holistic health techniques. This article is a look at the future health-and-consciousness industry as it may develop on the West Coast in the 21st century:

The client enters the large domed room measuring forty feet in diameter. The dome was constructed in two days by inflating a balloon and spraying it with a fast drying cement and foam mixture. The inside of the shell was then sprayed with crushed quartz powder which glistened with the sparkle of a million stars.

There is a presence, a feeling about the inside of the room, a stillness which immediately begins to quiet the turmoil inside the client. The center of the top of the dome displays a large, polished clear crystal attached to a movable fixture. In the circular foundation of the dome other crystals have been implanted. They were connected together and activated by mind into a powerful geometric energy grid field. Ancient mantras and chants were placed in the energy field to create vibrational thoughtforms which affect all who come into contact with them.

The client removes all clothing and lies down on a softly upholstered couch. A technician places sensors on the major meridian points, processes that information through the computer and displays a diagram on the monitor. A rippling mosaic represents the energy pulses moving through the body. This pattern is automatically compared to thousands of patterns stores in the immense computer memory banks. A diagnostic readout spotlights the physical deficiencies. A small lock of hair is clipped from the client and inserted into a chamber in another machine. This radionics device uses the vibrations of the hair to tune to the etheric body of the client and analyzes the subtle energy flows. Comparison between the two systems leads to an agreement concerning the imbalance.

A team of four therapists enters and they position themselves around the client. At an unspoken signal, crystals are held against the feet, sides and head of the client. All four therapists repeat out loud a three-line phrase three times. The computer monitor readout of the energy flows through the meridians, jumps and swirls as powerful healing pulses balance all the energy systems of the body. The therapists continue to hold in place until their sensitivity tells them the process is completed. They pull away from the client. When the energy image on the monitor stabilizes, a check against the computer's stored data verifies their feeling. All systems are now in balance. Special television monitor goggles are placed over the eyes. Thousands of images are flashed at extremely high speeds, faster than can be normally comprehended. The sensors attached to the client's body monitor any negative emotional response, and store and automatically print out the results.

A button is pushed. Curved sides rise silently from the table and gently enclose the body of the client. Light, color and sound begin in an intricate, modulating sequence. A pleasing fragrance fills the air. Underneath the sound, subliminal messages—pitched at frequencies above and below human ears—are repeated at a rate of one million times an hour. Special affirmations neutralize the negative emotions triggered by the flashing images. Sensors constantly monitor the energy flows. A second high-speed scan shows no negative reactions. The emotional thoughtforms causing the disease have all been neutralized. A final energy scan by both computer sensors and radionics shows all systems are now in balance.

The side panels unfold from around the client and recess back under the table. The client is helped down from the treatment table, and taken to the radiant pool which is eight feet square and four feet deep. A simple webbing device, like a hammock, allows the body to rest submerged in the water, yet not sink. The water is purified and charged by geometric energy grid mandalas embedded in the walls and floor of the pool. As the client lies in the pool, radiant life force energy created by the energy grid floods every cell.

The entire procedure takes less than two hours. Each day the client is counseled and taught meditative and personal balancing techniques to counteract any recurrence of the same stress and disease pattern. A special program of yoga and simple exercise movements is designed for the individual.

Additional treatments are done every other day, allowing the body and mind time to stabilize after each change. Each time, the body and mind are monitored and treatments are adjusted accordingly. When all monitoring shows balance and stability at all body, mind and emotional levels, the client is released and encouraged to come to the continuous meditation, prayer and yoga programs.

Excerpted from *The Crystal Healing Book* by Dael Walker. © Copyright 1988 by Dael Walker. Walker's Crystal Awareness Institute is one of the few organizations in California licensed by the state Board of Registered Nursing to offer continuing education units for registered nurses in crystal healing. For more information, write CAI, 2119 Pacheco St., Concord, CA 94520.

JAPAN IN THE YEAR 1999

With pressures for democracy in China, *perestroika* in the Soviet Union, the United States now the world's largest debtor nation, and the twenty-first century less than a decade away, Japanese futurists took a look at their nation in the year 1999:

"Japan will achieve its peak in economic power by about 1995, and move into an era of prosperity."—Tokuda Kiromi, Nomura Research Institute

"The GNP will be on a par with the U.S. and will account for about one fourth of the world GNP. The per capita GNP will be the largest in the world."—Hirose Yoshio, economics commentator

"Services without serious world competitors will grow but cheap manufactured products coming from abroad will push manufacturing into a corner."—Makino Noboru, Mitsubishi Research Institute

"The current average per annum salary of the 35 to 39-year-old corporate warrior is Y5.5 million (about $42,300). Ten years from now it will be Y8.95 million (about $68,846)."—the Management & Coordination Agency

Ten years from now, the seniority system will have virtually broken down. It will be a "post-less" (i.e., title-less) era, and job-hopping will be the norm."—Esaka Akira, economics commentator

"Days off per year will jump from 100 to 140. Working hours per year will drop from 2,100 to 1,800. With free time on their hands, the Japanese will flock to resorts and overseas travel."—Kanamori Hisao, Japan Center for Economic Research

NORTH–SOUTH KOREAN REUNIFICATION?

North and South Korea will achieve reunification by the end of the century, according to a prediction by South Korean President Roh Tae Woo. The North and South, arch enemies since they fought a war from 1950 to 1953, have been moving cautiously toward a thaw since Roh declared an end to mutual animosity and proposed wide-ranging exchanges when he took office in 1988. Roh's mini-summit meeting with Soviet President Mikhail Gorbachev in San Francisco in 1990 was a major step in increasing pressure on North Korea to be more amenable to a North–South rapprochement.

South Korean business tycoon Chung Ju-Yung, founder and honorary chairman of the giant Hyundai Group, made the first business trip to North Korea since the Korean Peninsula was divided in 1945. The plan is to develop tourist facilities on North Korea's scenic Kumngang Mountains as an initial step toward warming trade relations with the north.

CHINA, ASIA—AND THE FUTURE

by Jack Maisano

Asia will not take its full place on the world economic scene until China approaches NIC (newly industrialized country) status. Japan could hardly be richer. Taiwan and more particularly South Korea are approaching fully developed (OECD) status. And prosperity appears to be everywhere. But it isn't. Successful Asian economies are "tiny prosperous islands giving on the edge of a sea of poverty." The sea is China. Its poverty is a problem for the islands. For that reason they will not leave it alone. Capitalism and prosperity will be thrust on China, however long it takes. And that will change the world and how we live.

© *Asian Business* magazine, Far East Trade Press, Ltd., 1989.

JAPAN'S QUEST FOR CALIFORNIA'S ORACLES

With their growing interest in biofeedback and other brain machines that enhance mental processes, the Japanese appear to be increasingly tuning into California's right-brain culture.

For a number of years, teams of information-gatherers from Japan have been regularly crossing the Pacific to consult with various West Coast oracles and channelers.

Their interest lies on in their personal "auras"—nor in their "chakras"—but is focused resolutely on the bottom-line.

In one case, Shiseido, a leading Japanese cosmetics firm, wanted to develop a line of organic cosmetic products. The scientist heading the project in Shiseido's lab in Tokyo contacted the Center for Applied Intuition, an "intuitive" think-tank based in Fairfax, Ca., to receive some channeled input that would help them select the right mix of ingredients for their organic soap.

The center's group of "intuitive consultants'—which includes celebrity channelers like Kevin Ryerson (who was made famous by actress Shirley MacLaine's best-selling book and subsequent TV mini-series, *Out on a Limb*)—went to work on the assignment with all the seriousness of chemists employed by Proctor & Gamble.

Not only did they arrive at a precise formula for the organic toileteries, but they provided additional insights such as their suggestion to "expose the ingredients to the sunlight" before packaging the product.

How do the channels work? By entering into a light or total trance in order to access a higher intelligence, Kautz says. Although

California-style channeling has become associated with spiritual and often kooky psychic pursuits, he notes that channels can be utilized to "identify business opportunities, make detailed medical prescriptions, supply scientific explanations of physical and other processes, and forecast future events and trends."

"They deal with that part of the mind (the superconscious) which is not accessed ordinarily," explained the institute's director, William Kautz, who founded the center in 1979, after thirty years of working as the staff scientist at SRI International, the distinguished Palo Alto think-tank.

According to Kautz, who received several graduate degrees from MIT and who has lectured at highly respected institutions around the world including Stanford University, the Technical University of Denmark, and the Tata Institute of Fundamental Research in Bombay, the Japanese are keen on tapping into altered states to gain an extra edge for their product development and marketing programs.

Although he would not identify Japanese clients who prefer to remain anonymous, he revealed that his client list includes the Matsuya department store (one of the biggest department stores in Japan), as well as leading insurance companies, a couple of green tea companies, a kimono firm, and "the largest computer software company in Japan."

Back in 1983, Kautz was commissioned by a private Japanese think-tank to undertake a pioneering study entitled "The Future of Japan." Employing a novel technique of inquiry which he has dubbed "intuitive consensus," Kautz led a team of his best intuitives, including Ryerson, to develop "a realistic scenario for the nation of Japan up to the year 2000."

The following is an excerpt from that study which was originally published in Japanese in 1984 by Tama Publishing Co. in Tokyo, and is reprinted here by permission from the publisher. This is the first time that any part of this study has ever appeared in English. The five intuitives included Kevin Ryerson, Richard Lavin, Lenora Huett, Sanya Roman, and Aron Abrahamsen.

OVERVIEW OF JAPAN'S FUTURE

We wish to inquire about the future of the country of Japan, principally between now and the year 2000, with regard to: major events, advances, and any catastrophes; religious, political, socioeconomic, educational, and geologic aspects; the significance of these impending changes in the context of human development; and how the people of Japan can best respond to them.

KEVIN RYERSON

We find in Japan the roots of the structure of an entirely new system for the developing nations, a focus of transformation that will make its imprint upon the whole world over the next 50 to 100 years. From within the roots of this culture there shall be the dispensing of conceptual information, appropriate technologies, and above all, the economic seed of transformation throughout the whole of the Pacific basin: California, Argentina, Chile, Brazil, New Zealand, Australia, Taiwan and Hong Kong.

Through the economic forces of insights of the Japanese, there shall be the beginnings of an entire new system of consciousness, an entirely new realignment and system of thought, and above all else, much cooperation among individuals in order to facilitate coming changes within the social order. Japan will study and demonstrate how a single nation of older values and traditions can meet the needs of a rapidly growing technological society. This has already begun.

There will also arise a new system of thought within California regarding concepts of information distribution, transcendental concepts and personal psychologies that will be immediately adaptable and assimilatable within Japan. A vast merger of East and West will ensure that Japan dispenses its rapidly evolving technologies in cooperation with technologies in California. Both parties will partake in this wave of transformative social consciousness, which has already been patterned out and has begun to take place.

. . . The key element of this social transformation will be an upgrading of the quality of lifestyle amongst all peoples, without a setting aside of the traditions of these peoples. It will generate an appropriate consciousness that will enable the traditions of each culture to contribute to a national identity, without necessarily binding the individual to the limitations of that national identity. This will give a whole new dimension and structure to these cultures, not to where the society is internally divided, but rather becomes more plasma-like and self-evolving . . . This change will also result in greater evolved freedom among the Chinese and the Korean peoples.

. . . The Japanese are a unique people who have suffered within the psyche, but have also experienced in the psyche the threshold of Armageddon. Never has there been a people so socially conditioned, wherein they stand upon the threshold of a complete new order of things with a complete abandonment of older military traditions. They will become a uniting and central factor behind the unaligned nations . . . not through military means or the control of resources, but through a developing, highly palatable, and easily distributed system of consciousness which will evolve out of the manner and needs of the people. This system of consciousness will take the form of a new concept of industriousness, through the seeking of information.

This will be one of the key points of this particular people as they try to bring forth a unique advantage within the context of the rapidly developing knowledge industry. Japan will become a testing ground for new concepts and ideas, which will be rapidly impressed upon society and then quickly rejected or quickly assimilated and distributed throughout the entire social order. And by this ability to rapidly assimilate changing technologies, this group of people will become the hub of the rapidly developing knowledge industry.

Unlike European quarters, where there are many fractionary elements, the homogeneous nature of the Japanese traditional society will reflect more accurately the input of rapidly evolving knowledge. Japan will remain upon the cutting edge of social change and technology and will be a leader among the nations.

RICHARD LAVIN

Japan is going through a tumultuous time. Japan is one of the earlier countries upon this planet where, once an idea or a belief has been ingrained, almost the entire population acknowledges and accepts this belief. Therefore, the mass consciousness of the islands of Japan is the most critical aspect in the development of Japan in the next 20 years and after. Her people are very, very connected with one another. This is why they have chosen to have such a large population on such a small piece of land. How can you not be connected when you are living on top of your neighbor?

But the people of Japan feel very threatened these days. They acknowledge the importance of their contribution in the world especially in the technological realms, but they feel vastly inferior in their ability to protect themselves from what they view as tremendously violent energies around them. Unfortunately, this mass consciousness could—if the consciousness does not change—create that which they most fear.

So it is very important for Japan to acknowledge that she can be a leader in the world *without* feeling she is going to be squashed by some superpower. This is part of the reason there is such a curiosity within the Japanese population and culture. They realize the dangers they are facing, but do not know how to deal with these dangers, and, because of their religious training, they are not realizing what the dangers are. The biggest physical danger to Japan comes from the Soviet Union. The greatest economic danger comes from the United States. So they are surrounded, to a certain degree, with potential adversaries.

Even though there is much danger, the future of Japan is bright, though filled with many, many vast changes. . . . Japanese dealings with the world are determined by their thought projection and mass consciousness projection. They cannot separate their thoughts and their projections from the way they are dealt with by the world. This is manifesting now as economic difficulties with the United States, and to a certain degree, some physical difficulties and sabre-rattling going on between them and the Soviet Union. They are scared. They do not quite know what to do. But actually, they are able to change and choose a pathway where they can have the brightest, most enjoyable future possible. This is not only as Japan by itself, but on a planetary level also. . . .

The political structures in Japan will remain constant until Japan realizes that these structures are not working any more. This is also happening in the United States, the Soviet Union, and other nations that have a dogmatic political structure. Whether or not the Japanese people choose to let this political structure die a pleasant death or choose to revolt has not yet been determined. It will be influenced by the desires of the population. If Japan did not change its consciousness at all, there would be much difficulty. But the consciousness of Japan will change, not without its drama, but it will change for the better.

The future of Japan can be bright, but it rests upon the consciousness of its people and the people who deal with Japan. That which Japan perceives outside of itself in its relation to its neighbors is merely a projection of its own insecurities, fears and desires. Japan is projecting what it is she needs most for her own growth, whether it be positive or negative. She is doing this in order to ensure the positive projection and the positive growth that is necessary for the consciousness of her people, so they will alter and become more in touch with the *global* considerations of their behavior and their actions.

LENORA HUETT

The future of Japan is one of a flowering nature, one in which the nation as a whole will become more productive, not merely in a ma-

terial way, such as in the electronics industry, nor even in the meditative field, as has been in the past, but in what they can do to help better the world as a whole. Those Japanese who are alert to the world around them are beginning to look into their own needs on the earth and their own contributions to the earth. They will be looking into the sciences and into research forms available to them, and they'll be discussing ways in which they can help to communicate with other nations and help them also to develop. There will be less of a selfish nature, less of a monetary emphasis, and more of a giving, a flowing-through.

The search will not be easy, as there will be strong opposition from those who are in the government, who will feel that this is not necessary to the growth of the nation. There will be attempts to stamp out such research. I see them with boots, stamping on little fires, like they try to overturn it with a strong, military-like authority.

This new wave will emerge from middle-class and upper-middle-class people, those who are in production and moneymaking things now, active business people, as opposed to students, teachers and librarians. Those with books are staying where they are. These individuals will have satisfied their acquisitive needs and will be reaching out. They'll be researching psychic development as a tuning from mind to mind, as opposed to traditional meditation.

For example, they'll be working with electrodes on flowers, to find the connection between man and plants. It's a scientific approach to many things, trying to find what the universe is besides just a place to live; it's not just the arts . . . California-style experiential training workshops are coming, though that's not the first step. Small groups are being formed at this time, but they are the forerunners for those who will later be the teachers.

SANAYA ROMAN

Economic changes stand out as being the overriding influence on both the thinking and the lifestyle of the people. The economy has a feeling of both acceleration and deacceleration. The de-acceleration is a segmenting, a specialization, with more and more economic subgroups. The acceleration is a state of higher and higher output, but increasing pressure along with that higher output. There's coming a time at which these two forces are going to be diametrically opposed.

One small group will be valuing free time and questioning more and more the ethics of hard work and productivity. There will be a lessening of productivity and some rebellion starting among the workers (in the nineties).

There will also be an appreciation of the fact that the health of the people—body and mind—is in direct conflict with the economy; the economy is the most important driving force behind business; and business is the driving force of the country. This will be a grassroots movement upwards, a flow of ideas directed against a lifestyle that is becoming increasingly stressful.

These diametrically opposed forces will be moving into the forefront. The old belief in social unity and the sacrificing of the individual to the group mind will be undergoing change, too. This is being influenced greatly by Western culture. The movement towards less productivity is going to manifest as inflation and declining productivity later in this century, with the people wanting to decentralize the big conglomerates.

Appendix A

The Pacific Rim: Current Trends and Future Concerns

Iraqi President Saddam Hussein's lightning invasion of Kuwait in August 1990 and the subsequent world response with the U.S.-led Coalition Forces' victory over Iraq in February 1991 should act as a telling reminder of the difficulties in making long-range forecasts in the realm of international affairs. Any predictions of economic, financial or political developments made on August 1st were made instantly obsolete on the morning of the 2nd. While the chaos and unpredictability of events in the last several years would seem to make planning for the future an exercise in futility, it is actually of increasing importance. As the ability to divine the future decreases, there is a corresponding increase in the value of thoughtful planning.

Events in 1989 and 1990—from Tiananmen Square to Wenceslas Square and from Panama to the Persian Gulf—underscore the uncertain times in which we find ourselves. While the pace and timing of events may be impossible to predict, the options available to world leaders depend in large part upon political, economic and demographic constraints that are easily tracked and analyzed. In the Pacific Rim, economic growth over the last two decades has given rise to four major trends which will challenge regional governments and which promise to shape the way we face the 1990's. These trends are:

- National rivalries increasing with reduced superpower tensions
- Political pluralism—the spread of people power
- Industrialization's growing energy demands
- Population stabilization and demographic transition

Bipolar Stability to Multipolar Instability

With the current reductions in U.S. military forces in Korea and Japan and the prospect of the closure of U.S. bases in the Philippines, America's ability to act as a "stabilizing" force in the Pacific is being steadily reduced. However, the Soviets, too, are decreasing regional military activity. Soviet President Mikhail Gorbachev is increasingly concerned with maintaining order within the Soviet Union, and is unwilling to present an aggressive posture to the part of the world which could provide the consumer goods and the foreign investment the Soviet Union desperately needs. While this is a welcome sign for the United States and its allies, it does not guarantee a reduction in regional tensions.

The draw-down of U.S. and Soviet forces will give greater emphasis to regional military balances in a region with a number of potential flashpoints. The Korean Peninsula, Indochina, the Taiwan Straits, the South China Sea are all areas where regional tension could boil over into armed conflict. Instability will undoubtedly increase as regional powers begin creating new security roles in an area without established security structures, like NATO and the Warsaw Pact. Pronouncements of the primacy of economic power and the diminution of the role of military power are not to be taken seriously; recent increases in military budgets and expanded procurement programs throughout the Pacific Rim give telling evidence of the continued value placed in military forces.

PEOPLE POWER

Although the rapid disintegration of the communist regimes of Eastern Europe have captured the imagination of Americans in the last few years, those efforts were certainly influenced by the attempts (both successful and otherwise) of Asian people to hold their governments accountable. Dramatically begun in the Philippines in 1986, a wave of political and economic reform swept through South Korea, Taiwan, and, with tragic results, China. Even in stable, democratic Japan, voters gave the complacent Liberal Democratic Party a defeat in the 1989 Upper House elections, in response to corruption and sex scandals and an unpopular tax increase.

Although the most notable example of "People Power"—Corazon Aquino's triumph in the Philippines—was due to economic stagnation and the loss of legitimacy by the Marcos regime, much of the democratic reform in the Pacific Rim has been fueled by economic growth and the resultant individual prosperity. Taiwan and South Korea showed how authoritarian regimes could peacefully make their way toward democracy, without succumbing to instability and economic chaos. In Singapore Prime Minister Lee Kwan Yew has stepped down; an office whose powers he has wielded ably, if less than meekly, since independence. Indonesia, too, is making strides toward representative government—preparing for the final term of President Suharto and shaping yet another version of Asian democracy. The new governments will have to deal with many problems resulting from the very economic growth that created them. Among the most important of these is the dramatic rise in energy consumption.

ENERGY DEMAND: FUELING THE ENGINE OF GROWTH

The economic successes of the Pacific Rim have fueled more than increases in wealth and standards of living. The rapid industrialization has led to massive increases in energy demand, oil and gas exploration, coal consumption in China, and—ominously—energy imports. In addition, the infrastructure of many industrializing economies is being strained to the breaking point. Growing electrical power generation and distribution requirements, huge increases in automobile traffic, as well as large-scale telecommunications system upgrading all must be solved quickly and simultaneously. By the turn of the century, it is predicted that regional demand will outstrip regional supplies by nearly 3 to 1, and that 90% of the region's oil imports will come from the Persian Gulf.

As the events of the last year make clear, such a dependence on a volatile part of the world is not in the region's long-term interests. However, with continued opposition to nuclear power, limited geothermal and hydroelectric potential, there will be little choice in the near term. The technological strength of the region will soon be harnessed (more out of necessity than conviction) to reduce the consumption of energy as a percentage of the Gross National Product. Efforts will most likely include increased energy efficiency in electric power generation, increased fuel efficiency requirements for automobiles and appliances, as well as more sophisticated construction techniques to reduce energy losses in commercial and residential buildings.

In all likelihood, however, these efforts will be unable to curb demand significantly. This would encourage direct government restrictions on the use of automobiles and other mandatory reductions in energy consumption. Efforts to reduce automobile traffic will likely be instituted, at least for the central districts, in many Pacific Rim capitals. Tokyo regulations already make car ownership difficult, and it would not be surprising if similar policies were undertaken in Taipei, Seoul, or Bangkok in the near future. Without any indigenous supplies of energy, the Pacific Rim will be forced to choose between three rather undesirable options: continued dependence of foreign energy supplies; expensive research and development programs to increase energy self-sufficiency and efficiency; or expanded use of unpopular nuclear power.

THE GRAYING OF ASIA

As with Europe before it, the Pacific Rim is now experiencing a slowing (and eventually, a halting) of population growth. It is a little appreciated, but well-documented, phenomenon that as average incomes rise, the number of children born to each woman falls. In fact, it falls below the natural replacement level (roughly 2.1 children per woman) as the Per Capita Gross National Product of a country rises above the $5,000 to $7,000 range. In 1990, it is estimated that in addition to Japan, Australia, and New Zealand, all of the "Four Tigers" had fertility rates at or below replacement level.

ASEAN, as well, will see its population growth significantly reduced in the coming decade as prosperity, increased female participation in the labor force, easier access to birth control, and increased education levels bring about similar declines in fertility. In the 1980s, both Indonesia and Malaysia had their fertility levels drop more than 25%. Thailand had its fertility drop over 30% in the same period. In fact, nearly all Pacific Rim countries have experienced reductions in fertility. One of the most successful programs at halting population growth has been in China, where a draconian "One Child Family" program has reduced fertility over 60% from its 1965 level.

The Pacific Rim thus faces rapidly aging populations, (especially in China, Japan, Singapore, and Taiwan) as birth rates continue to drop and life expectancies increase. For example, it is estimated that by the year 2025, nearly a quarter of Japan's population will be over 65 years old. This aging population will, in turn, cause a number of challenges which Pacific Rim governments are only now beginning to face. The resultant decline in the supply of new labor will spur efforts to increase capital investments, move production offshore or increase immigration—or all three. In addition, the aging population will begin to exhibit changing consumption patterns (fewer cars and appliances, more healthcare services) as well as a lower propensity to save (as retirees dip into bank accounts accumulated over a lifetime). Finally, a direct government response will be needed to deal with the rising costs of social security, pension and medical programs, and related government services.

Whether through tax increases, cuts in other programs, or debt, these demographic changes will force major shifts in the spending priorities of regional governments in the near future.

CONCLUSION

While all of the above trends are the result of a remarkable period of growth and prosperity, many challenges remain to be faced. As America struggles to redefine its role in a changing world, it is important to realize that Japan and the rest of Asia have struggles of their own. Continued prosperity is by no means assured, but the wealth created and institutions built over the past two decades will provide the necessary resources to meet the challenges facing the Pacific Rim, providing the increasingly democratic nations of the region have the political will and the skillful leadership necessary. In addition, political and business leaders on both sides of the Pacific must have easy access to timely, accurate information.

Without a firm statistical foundation upon which to base business or political decisions, actions are destined to be flawed. Yet there are few sources of information which provide a broad range of statistics on the nations of the Pacific. Too often, information is provided only for a single country, or only a single topic, or only for a single year. To overcome these limitations, and to provide context for the preceding chapters, key economic, political, military, and social statistics on 34 countries and territories in Asia have been compiled. This appendix is a special version of the *U.S. and Asia: Statistical Handbook,* which is published annually by the Asian Studies Center of The Heritage Foundation. Updated in 1990 for this almanac, it presents each country in a "snapshot" format, with information provided for the most recent year available, and with a time series for economic data.

SOURCES UTILIZED

The basic sources used include: the Agency for International Development's *Congressional Presentation,* the Far Eastern Economic Review's *Yearbook,* the International Institute of Strategic Studies' *The Military Balance,* the International Monetary Fund's *International Financial Statistics Yearbook* and *Direction of Trade Statistics Yearbook,* the Department of Commerce's *Survey of Current Business,* the Central Intelligence Agency's *World Factbook,* the World Bank's *World Development Report* and *World Bank Atlas,* the U.S. Department of State's *Country Reports on Economic Policy and Trade Practices,* and Comwell Systems' PCGLOBE+ computer program. In addition, newspaper and magazine articles, and foreign research organizations and foreign government reports were utilized to fill in the gaps in the information.

Thomas J. Timmons
Research Associate
Asian Studies Center
The Heritage Foundation

EXPLANATORY NOTES

Land

Total area and land use estimates in square miles.

Population

Mid-year 1989 estimate for total population, with 1988 estimates for the other pertinent variables.

Infant mortality: Number of deaths prior to one year of age per 1,000 live births.

Literacy: Percentage of adults with a functional reading ability in dominant native language.

Fertility: Average number of children born per woman in her life.

Life expectancy: Average number of years to be lived for a group born in 1987.

Workforce: Labor force size and distribution estimates for 1987.

Political

Voting with U.S. at the U.N.: Totals for 44th General Assembly session, from September to December 1989, indicating percentage agreement on votes on which both countries voted either yes or no (absences and abstentions are not included).

Freedom House: Index from *Freedom in the World 1989–1990.*

U.S. Foreign Economic Assistance: Includes Direct Assistance, Economic Support Funds, Food Aid, Anti-Narcotics Aid, and Peace Corps.

U.S. foreign military assistance: Includes International Military Education and Training, Military Assistance Program, and Foreign Military Sales.

Economy

GDP (gross domestic product): Measures total production of goods and services within a country.

GNP (gross national product): GDP adjusted for international transactions, such as trade.

Per Capita GNP: GNP divided by the population, an aggregate measurement of average personal income. Growth: Real GNP or GDP increase, adjusted for inflation.

CPI (Consumer Price Index): Increase in cost of living.

CurAccount (Current Account Balance): Overall balance in the trade of goods, services, investment income, tourist expenditures, and government grants and gifts.

Currency: Prevailing exchange rate for year-end 1989.

Numbers that are in **Bold Print** are estimates. Figures for GNP, Current Account, and Trade are all given in *Current Dollars;* no adjustment has been made for the varying value of the dollar due to inflation or currency revaluations.

Military

Military budget increase: Change in U.S. dollar value.

Regular forces and reserves: Does not include militias.

Foreign military personnel: Each country with forces present is indicated and broken down when known.

Armed opposition groups: Only included are active insurgent and/or terrorist groups.

Investment: Amount represents year-end Foreign Direct Investment position as found in the *Survey of Current Business.* Negative numbers represent net withdrawals of capital.

AUSTRALIA

Land

Area: 2,968,000 square miles
   Cultivated: 2.5%
   Forest: 14%
   Pasture: 58%
Resources: Bauxite, coal, copper, iron ore, tin, silver, uranium, nickel, mineral sands, lead, zinc, diamonds, natural gas, oil

Population

1989 estimate: 16,452,000
Annual growth: 1.2%
Life expectancy: 76 years
Literacy: 98.5%
Infant mortality: 8
Fertility: 1.9%
Ethnic divisions: Caucasian 95%, Asian 4%, Aboriginal 1%
Workforce: 8,050,000
   Unemployment: 7.0%
   Commerce and services: 65.8%
   Agriculture and fishing: 6.1%
   Government and public authorities: 4.8%
   Manufacturing: 16.2%
   Construction: 7.1%
Students:
   Primary and secondary: 3,000,000
   University: 1,800,000

Political

Official name: Commonwealth of Australia
Type of government: Federal Parliamentary State
Name of chief of state: Queen Elizabeth II
Name of head of government: Prime Minister Robert Hawke
Foreign minister: Gareth Evans
1989 Freedom House Index (1 is highest, 7 is lowest):
   Political freedom: 1
   Civil liberties: 1
1989 voting with U.S. at U.N.: 40.8%

FY 1989 U.S. foreign assistance (actual obligations):
   Economic: None
   Military: None

Economy

Currency: Australian dollar, 1 US$ = 1.263 A$
Major industries: Mining, iron and steel, industrial equipment, food-processing, textiles, aircraft, ships, chemicals.
Major agricultural products: Wheat, barley, oats, corn, hay, lamb, beef, sugarcane, dairy products, wine, fruit, vegetables
Major imports: Machinery, manufactures, transport equipment, chemicals, petroleum, metal goods, textiles and clothing

Major exports: Wheat, coal, wool, iron ore, metal manufactures, meat, dairy products, petroleum, machinery
Per capita GNP: US$12,350 (1989)

Military

1987/1988 military budget: US$5,030,000,000
Increase over 1986/1987: 5.2%
Outlays as a share of GNP: 2.6%
As a share of government spending: 14.6%
Total regular forces: 70,500
   Army: 32,00
   Navy: 15,800
   Combat aircraft: 95
   Reserves: 27,580
   Air Force: 22,600
   Naval vessels: 6 attack submarines, 3 destroyers, 9 frigates, 22 large patrol craft, 2 minehunters
Security alliance with U.S.: ANZUS (without New Zealand)
U.S. military installations: U.S. Navy has access to Cockburn Sound Naval facilities, joint Australian–U.S. communication/intelligence facilities at Northwest Cape, Nurrungar, and Pine Gap
U.S. military personnel: 250 Air Force, 600 Navy
Armed opposition groups: None

Australia: Economic Statistics (billions of US$, percentages where appropriate)[a]

	1982	1983	1984	1985	1986	1987	1988
GNP	163.13	159.29	173.23	153.17	159.63	198.53	201.9
Growth	3.1%	0.4%	6.7%	55%	1.8%	4.4%	1.7%
CPI rise	11.1%	10.1%	4.0%	6.7%	9.1%	8.5%	**4.3%**
Exports	22.077	20.651	23.875	22.611	22.541	26.510	**34.425**
to U.S.	2.552	2.442	2.899	3.067	2.873	3.287	3.5
Imports	24.073	19.420	23.423	23.499	23.916	27.007	**33.615**
from U.S.	4.534	3.954	4.793	5.440	5.551	5.495	7.0
CurAccount	−8.514	−5.969	−8.549	−8.717	−9.810	−7.975	**−9.7**

[a] Australia is the **16th** largest U.S. trading partner.

Investment

1989 U.S. direct investment:
US$14,495,000,000
**1989 Australian direct investment
in the U.S.:** US$6,236,000,000

BANGLADESH

Land

Area: 55,600 square miles
    Cultivated: 59.7%
    Forest: 16%
    Pasture: 4%
Resources: Natural gas, uranium,
offshore oil

Population

1989 estimate: 114,718,000
Annual growth: 2.8%
Life expectancy: 53 years
Literacy: 29%
Infant mortality: 138
Fertility: 5.8
Ethnic divisions: Bengali 98%,
tribal groups and others 2%
Workforce: 47,900,000
    Unemployment: 30%
    Commerce and services:
    16.2%
    Agriculture and fishing: 60.6%
    **Government and public
    authorities:** 10.1%
    Manufacturing: 10.2%
    Construction: 2.9%

Students:
    Primary and secondary:
    13,540,000
    University: 43,500

Political

Official name: People's Republic of
Bangladesh
Type of government: Multi-Party
Republic
Name of chief of state: Begum
Khaleda Zia, Head of State
Name of head of government:
Same
Foreign minister: Anisul Islam
Mahmud
**1989 Freedom House Index (1 is
highest, 7 is lowest):**
    Political freedom: 4
    Civil liberties: 4
1989 voting with U.S. at U.N.:
13.5%
**FY 1989 U.S. foreign assistance
(actual obligations):**
    Economic: US$174,383,000
    Military: US$300,000

Economy

Currency: Taka, 1 US$ = 32.10
Taka
Major industries: Jute manufactures,
food-processing, cotton textiles,
garments, sugar, tea, leather,
fertilizer
Major agricultural products: Jute,
rice, fish, tea, sugar, wheat

Major imports: Capital equipment,
foodgrains, petroleum, raw cotton,
fertilizer, manufactured products
Major exports: Raw and
manufactured jute, leather, tea,
textiles
Per capita GNP: US$180 (1989)

Military

1986/1987 military budget:
US$216,750,000
Increase over 1985/1986: 28.1%
Outlays as a share of GNP: 2.0%
**As a share of government
spending:** 18.3%
Total regular forces: 101,500
    Army: 90,000
    Navy: 7,500
    Reserves: 30,000
    Air Force: 4,000
    Combat aircraft: 55
    Naval vessels: 3 frigates, 4 fast-
    attack craft (missile), 16 fast-
    attack craft (patrol), 4 fast-
    attack craft (torpedo), 11
    coastal patrol craft, 5 river
    patrol boats
Security alliance with U.S.: None
U.S. military installations: None
U.S. military personnel: None
Armed opposition groups: Shanti
Bahini, 8,000

Investment

1989 U.S. direct investment:
US$13,000,000

Bangladesh: Economic Statistics (billions of US$, percentages where appropriate)[a]

	1982	1983	1984	1985	1986	1987	1988
GDP	11.98	11.72	13.80	14.89	15.13	16.58	16.6
Growth	0.8%	3.6%	4.2%	3.7%	4.4%	4.5%	**2.9%**
CPI rise	12.5%	9.4%	10.5%	10.7%	11.0%	9.5%	**11.0%**
Exports	0.768	0.724	0.931	0.999	0.889	1.077	**1.170**
to U.S.	0.088	0.109	0.159	0.227	0.264	0.370	0.368
Imports	2.419	2.291	2.693	2.526	2.550	2.730	**2.895**
from U.S.	0.227	0.190	0.303	0.219	0.165	0.193	0.258
CurAccount	−0.656	−0.060	−0.543	−0.540	−0.615	−0.338	**−0.500**

[a] Bangladesh is a minor U.S. trading partner.

1989 Bangladeshi direct investment in the U.S.: None

BHUTAN

Land

Area: 17,800 square miles
    Cultivated: 8.8%
    Forest: 68.7%
    Pasture: 1.9%
Resources: Timber, hydroelectric power, gypsum

Population

1989 estimate: 1,534,000
Annual growth: 2.0%
Life expectancy: 48 years
Literacy: 5%
Infant mortality: 139
Fertility: 5.1
Ethnic divisions: Bhote 60%, Nepalese 25%, Tribal groups 15%
Workforce: 650,000
    Unemployment: NA
    Commerce and services: 3.6%
    Agriculture and fishing: 93%
    Government and public authorities: 2%
    Manufacturing: 0.7%
    Construction: 0.7%
Students:
    Primary and secondary: 58,800
    University: 720

Political

Official name: Kingdom of Bhutan
Type of government: Monarchy
Name of chief of state: King Jigme Singye Wangchuck
Name of head of government: Same
Foreign minister: Lyonpo Dawa Tsering
1989 Freedom House Index (1 is highest, 7 is lowest):
    Political freedom: 6
    Civil liberties: 5
1989 Voting with U.S. at U.N.: 12%
FY 1989 U.S. foreign assistance (actual obligations):
    Economic: US$458,000
    Military: None

Economy

Currency: Ngultrum, 1 US$ = 16.6 Ngultrum
Major industries: Cement, wood products, chemical products, mining, distilling, food-processing, handicrafts
Major agricultural products: Maize, rice, oranges, potatoes, wheat
Major imports: Aircraft, fuel, rice, motor vehicles, textiles, machinery
Major exports: Cement, talc powder, agricultural products, sawn timber, potatoes
Per capita GNP: US$160 (1989)

Military

1987/1988 military budget: NA
Increase over 1986/1987: NA
Outlay as a share of GNP: 1.0%
As a share of government spending: NA
Total regular forces: 600
    Army: NA
    Navy: NA
    Reserves: NA
    Air Force: NA
    Combat aircraft: NA
    Naval vessels: 0
Security alliance with U.S.: None
U.S. military installations: None
U.S. military personnel: None
Indian military personnel: Small number of advisors
Armed opposition groups: None

Investment

1989 U.S. direct investment: NA
1989 Bhutanese direct investment in the U.S.: NA

BRUNEI

Land

Area: 2,226 square miles
    Cultivated: 1%
    Forest: 85%
    Pasture: 1%
Resources: Oil, natural gas, timber

Bhutan: Economic Statistics (billions of US$, percentages where appropriate)[a]

	1982	1983	1984	1985	1986	1987	1988
GDP	120.0	120.0	130.0	156.6	171.0	205.0	215.0
Growth	**6.4%**	**6.4%**	**6.4%**	**6.4%**	6.0%	6.5%	**2.6%**
CPI rise	NA	NA	8.4%	10.0%	10.1%	13.0%	**4.0%**
Exports	17.70	14.04	15.6	17.4	22.2	25.3	NA
to U.S.	NA	NA	NA	NA	NA	NA	NA
Imports	54.86	39.40	80.4	69.4	75.7	88.0	NA
from U.S.	NA	NA	NA	NA	NA	NA	NA
CurAccount	NA	NA	NA	−83.3	−77.04	**−93.2**	**−80.0**

[a] Bhutan is a minor U.S. trading partner.

Brunei: Economic Statistics (billions of US$, percentages where appropriate)[a]

	1982	1983	1984	1985	1986	1987	1988
GDP	4.09	4.16	3.89	3.97	3.571	3.5	3.7
Growth	11.7%	3.0%	2.0%	−10.0%	−10.0%	−10.0%	3.0%
CPI rise	6.4%	0.3%	3.1%	4.0%	2.3%	NA	**2.3%**
Exports	3.786	3.367	3.183	2.934	1.798	1.796	**2.3**
to U.S.	0.219	0.020	0.11	0.002	0.064	0.017	NA
Imports	0.732	0.724	0.622	0.606	1.653	1.297	NA
from U.S.	0.079	0.058	0.034	0.051	0.202	0.093	NA
CurAccount	NA	NA	NA	NA	NA	NA	NA

[a] Brunei is a minor U.S. trading partner.

Population

1989 estimate: 345,000
Annual growth: 8.0%
Life expectancy: 75 years
Literacy: 45%
Infant mortality: 12
Fertility: 3.1
Ethnic divisions: Malay 64%, Chinese 20%, Other 16%
Workforce: 90,000
  Unemployment: NA
  Commerce and services: 25%
  Agriculture and fishing: 5%
  Government and public authorities: 47%
  Manufacturing: 4%
  Construction: 19%
Students:
  Primary and secondary: 64,700
  University: 350

Political

Official name: State of Brunei Darussalam
Type of government: Sultanate
Name of chief of state: Sultan Sir Hassanal Bolkiah
Name of head of government: Same
Foreign minister: Prince Mohamed Bolkiah
1989 Freedom House Index (1 is highest, 7 is lowest):
  Political freedom: 6
  Civil liberties: 6

1989 voting with U.S. at U.N.: 12.4%
FY 1989 U.S. foreign assistance (actual obligations):
  Economic: none
  Military: none

Economy

Currency: Brunei dollar, 1 US$ = 1.904 B$
Major industries: Crude petroleum, liquefied natural gas, construction
Major agricultural products: Rice, pepper, timber
Major imports: Machinery and transport equipment, manufactured goods, foodstuffs, consumer goods, chemicals
Major exports: Crude petroleum, petroleum products, liquefied natural gas
Per capita GNP: US$11,000 (1989)

Military

1988 military budget: US$232,420,000
Increase over 1987: 13.2%
Outlays as a share of GNP: 6.3%
As a share of government spending: 13.9%
Total regular forces: 4,000
  Army: 3,200
  Navy: 500
  Reserves: 0
  Air Force: 300
  Combat aircraft: 2

Naval vessels: 3 fast-attack craft (missile), 3 patrol craft
Security alliance with U.S.: None
U.S. military installations: None
Foreign military personnel: British 900, Singaporean 500
Armed opposition groups: None

Investment

1989 U.S. direct investment: US$ − 18,000,000
1988 Bruneian direct investment in the U.S.: None

BURMA

Land

Area: 261,149 square miles
  Cultivated: 12.2%
  Forest: 47.6%
  Pasture: 3.3%
Resources: Oil, copper, asbestos, marble, limestone, teak, gems, timber, tin, tungsten, copper, lead, natural gas

Population

1989 estimate: 40,452,000
Annual growth: 2.0%
Life expectancy: 53 years
Literacy: 78%
Infant mortality: 99
Fertility: 4.2

Burma: Economic Statistics (billions of US$, percentages where appropriate)[a]

	1982	1983	1984	1985	1986	1987	1988
GDP	6.01	6.20	6.39	6.62	6.37	7.78	7.9
Growth	5.7%	4.3%	5.6%	4.3%	3.7%	1.0%	2.3%
CPI rise	5.3%	5.7%	4.8%	6.8%	9.2%	23.3%	**17.8%**
Exports	0.509	0.555	0.531	0.519	0.517	0.520	NA
to U.S.	0.018	0.012	0.015	0.015	0.015	0.013	NA
Imports	0.899	0.721	0.623	0.656	0.676	0.679	NA
from U.S.	0.034	0.015	0.016	0.010	0.016	0.008	NA
CurAccount	−0.499	−0.344	−0.218	−0.206	**−0.250**	**−0.360**	**−0.280**

[a] Burma is a minor U.S. trading partner.

Ethnic divisions: Burmese 68%, Shan 9%, Karen 7%, Raljiome 4%, Chinese 3%, Indian 2%, Other 7%
Workforce: 15,130,000
   Unemployment: NA
   Commerce and services: 13%
   Agriculture and fishing: 64.7%
   Government and public authorities: 6.1%
   Manufacturing: 8.5%
   Construction: 1.6%
Students:
   Primary and secondary: 6,420,000
   University: 211,000

Political

Official name: Union of Myanmar
Type of government: Military Dictatorship
Name of chief of state: General Saw Maung
Name of head of government: Same
Foreign minister: Same
1989 Freedom House Index (1 is highest, 7 is lowest):
   Political freedom: 7
   Civil liberties: 7
1989 voting with U.S. at U.N.: 12.6%
FY 1989 U.S. foreign assistance (actual obligations):
   Economic: US$120,000
   Military: US$260,000

Economy

Currency: Kyat, 1 US$ = 6.65 Kyat (official rate)
Major industries: Agricultural processing, textiles and footwear, wood and wood processing, petroleum refining, copper, tin
Major agricultural products: Rice, cotton, pulses, sugarcane, beans, peanuts, teak and hardwoods, maize, oilseeds
Major imports: Machinery and transportation equipment, building materials, oil equipment, consumer goods, capital goods
Major exports: Teak, rice, pulses, beans, base metals, ores, gems
Per capita GNP: US$200 (1989)

Military

1987/1988 military budget: US$291,600,000
Increase over 1986/1987: 15.5%
Outlay as a share of GNP: 3.1%
As a share of government spending: 20.7%
Total regular forces: 186,000
   Army: 170,000
   Navy: 7,000
   Reserves: 0
   Air Force: 9,000
   Combat aircraft: 27
   Naval vessels: 2 corvettes, 2 coastal patrol craft, 30 inshore patrol craft, 5 river patrol craft
Security alliance with U.S.: None

U.S. military installations: None
U.S. military personnel: None
Armed opposition groups:
   Communist Party of Burma, 10,000; National Democratic front, 20,000; private armies include— Mong Tai Army, 2,100; Kan Chit, 450; United Revolutionary Army, 1,000; Loi Maw Rebels/Army, 3,000

Investment

1989 U.S. direct investment: NA
1989 Burmese direct investment in the U.S.: NA

CAMBODIA

Land

Area: 69,900 square miles
   Cultivated 11%
   Forest: 74%
   Pasture: 3%
Resources: Timber, gemstones, iron ore, manganese, phosphates

Population

1989 estimate: 6,838,000
Annual growth: 2.2%
Life expectancy: 48 years
Literacy: 48%
Infant mortality: 131
Fertility: 4.6

Cambodia: Economic Statistics (millions of US$, percentages where appropriate)[a]

	1982	1983	1984	1985	1986	1987	1988
GDP	NA	NA	630.0	NA	NA	1100.0	1100.0
Growth	NA	NA	NA	NA	NA	NA	0.0%
CPI rise	NA	NA	NA	NA	NA	NA	**10.0%**
Exports	NA	2.55	4.4	3.21	NA	NA	NA
to U.S.	0.0	0.0	0.0	0.4	0.5	0.4	NA
Imports	NA	47.9	47.9	27.6	NA	NA	NA
from U.S.	2.0	1.0	1.0	0.0	0.2	0.1	NA
CurAccount	NA	NA	NA	NA	NA	NA	NA

[a] Cambodia is a very minor U.S. trading partner.

Ethnic divisions: Khmer 90%, Chinese 5%, Other 5%
Workforce: 2,740,000
    Unemployment: NA
    Commerce and services: NA
    Agriculture and fishing: 80%
    Government and public authorities: NA
    Manufacturing: NA
    Construction: NA
Students:
    Primary and secondary: 1,669,000
    University: NA

Political

Official name: State of Cambodia
Type of government: Communist state
Name of chief of state: President Heng Samrin
Name of head of government: Prime Minister Hun Sen
Foreign minister: Same
1989 Freedom House Index (1 is highest, 7 is lowest):
    Political freedom: 7
    Civil liberties: 7
1989 Voting with U.S. at U.N.: 12.0%
    [The U.N. recognizes the Coalition Government of Democratic Kampuchea (CGDK), led by Prince Norodom Sihanouk, Son Sann, and Khieu Samphan, as the legitimate government of Cambodia, not the Heng Samrin regime]
FY 1989 U.S. foreign assistance (actual obligations):
    Economic: US$6,255,000 (to the CGDK)
    Military: None

Economy

Currency: Riel, 1 US$ = 218.0 Riel
Major industries: Textiles, cement, fishing, wood and wood products, rubber, rice milling
Major agricultural products: Rice, rubber, corn, vegetables
Major imports: Fuel, consumer goods, raw materials, fertilizer, international food aid, military equipment
Major exports: Rubber, rice, pepper, timber, fish
Per capita GNP: US$150 (1989)

Military

1988 military budget: NA
Increase over 1987: NA
Outlay as a share of GNP: 6.0%
Percentage of government spending: NA
Total regular forces: 31,800
    Army: 30,000
    Navy: 1,000
    Reserves: 25,000 (provincial forces)
    Air Force: 800
    Combat aircraft: 12

Naval vessels: 2 torpedo patrol craft, 9 inshore patrol craft
Security alliance with U.S.: None
U.S. military installations: None
U.S. military personnel: None
Vietnamese military personnel: 3,000 troops (reducing)
Armed opposition groups: Khmer Rouge, 40,000; Khmer People's National Liberation Front, 15,000; Armee Nationale Sihanoukienne, 10,000

Investment

1989 U.S. direct investment: NA
1989 Cambodian direct investment in the U.S.: NA

CHINA, PEOPLE'S REPUBLIC OF

Land

Area: 3,691,521 square miles
    Cultivated 10.1%
    Forest: 12.5%
    Pasture: 33.3%
Resources: Coal, iron, petroleum, mercury, tin, tungsten, antimony, manganese, uranium, zinc, bauxite, lead

Population

1989 estimate: 1,112,300,000
Annual growth: 1.6%
Life expectancy: 69 years

PRC: Economic Statistics (billions of US$, percentages where appropriate)[a]

	1982	1983	1984	1985	1986	1987	1988
GDP	184.4	201.1	225.2	252.2	271.9	332.2	349.3
Growth	7.4%	9.1%	12.0%	12.3%	7.4%	9.4%	11.0%
CPI rise	2.0%	2.0%	2.7%	11.5%	6.0%	7.3%	18.5%
Exports	21.865	22.096	24.824	27.329	31.367	39.464	**47.54**
to U.S.	2.502	2.477	3.381	4.224	5.241	6.910	8.5
Imports	18.920	21.313	25.953	42.480	43.247	43.222	**55.25**
from U.S.	2.912	2.173	3.004	3.856	3.106	3.497	5.0
CurAccount	5.823	4.487	2.509	− 11.417	−7.034	**0.3**	**−4.0**

[a] The PRC is the **14th** largest U.S. trading partner.

Literacy: 75%
Infant mortality: 34
Fertility: 2.5
Ethnic divisions: Han Chinese, 93.3%; Zhuang, Uygur, Hui, Yi, Tibetan, Mioa, Manchu, Mongol, Korean, and Others, 6.7%
Workforce: 542,000,000
   Unemployment: 2.0%
   Commerce and services: 12.2%
   Agriculture and fishing: 62.5%
   Government and public authorities: 1.6%
   Manufacturing: 16.7%
   Construction: 4.2%
Students:
   Primary and secondary: 182,400,000
   University: 2,000,000

Political

Official name: People's Republic of China
Type of government: Communist state
Name of chief of state: President Yang Shangkun
Name of head of government: Premier Li Peng
Foreign minister: Qian Qichen
1989 Freedom House Index (1 is highest, 7 is lowest):
   Political freedom: 7
   Civil liberties: 7
1989 voting with U.S. at U.N.: 11.1%

FY 1989 U.S. foreign assistance (actual obligations):
   Economic: None
   Military: None

Economy

Currency: Renminbi Yuan, 1 US$ = 4.72 Yuan
Major industries: Iron, steel, coal, machine-building, armaments, textiles, light industrial products, petroleum
Major agricultural products: Rice, wheat, soybeans, cotton
Major imports: Grain, chemical fertilizer, steel, industrial raw materials, machinery, textiles, iron and steel
Major exports: Manufactured goods, agricultural products, oil, mineral fuels, textiles, metals
Per capita GNP: US$300 (1989)

Military

1988 military budget: US$5,780,000,000
Increase over 1987: 2.5%
Outlay as a share of GNP: 1.9%
As a share of government spending: 8.2%
Total regular forces: 3,160,000
   Army: 2,390,000
   Navy: 300,000
   Reserves: 1,200,000
   Air Force: 470,000
   Combat aircraft: 6,180

Naval vessels: 1 ballistic missile submarine, 3 cruise submarines, 110 attack submarines, 19 destroyers, 37 frigates, 10 corvettes, 91 coastal patrol craft, 380 inshore patrol craft, 50 river patrol craft, 235 fast-attack craft (missile), 185 fast-attack craft (torpedo), 128 minesweepers
Security alliance with U.S.: None
U.S. military installations: None
U.S. military personnel: None
Armed opposition groups: None

Investment

1989 U.S. direct investment: US$310,000,000
1989 PRC direct investment in the U.S.: US$83,000,000

CHINA, REPUBLIC OF (TAIWAN)

Land

Area: 13,814 square miles
   Cultivated 25%
   Forest: 64%
   Pasture: 5%
Resources: Small deposits of coal, natural gas, limestone marble, asbestos, timber

| ROC: Economic Statistics (billions of US$, percentages where appropriate)[a] | | | | | | |
	1982	1983	1984	1985	1986	1987	1988
GDP	51.0	54.1	57.7	60.08	73.25	97.57	119.51
Growth	3.8%	7.5%	10.9%	4.3%	10.8%	11.9%	7.1%
CPI rise	3.1%	1.4%	0.0%	−0.2%	0.7%	0.355	1.5%
Exports	22.09	25.09	30.42	30.69	39.78	53.54	60.59
to U.S.	9.586	12.110	16.088	17.761	21.252	26.407	24.8
Imports	18.81	20.31	21.99	20.12	24.16	34.96	49.65
from U.S.	4.367	4.667	5.003	4.669	5.524	7.413	12.1
CurAccount	2.248	4.412	6.976	9.195	16.217	18.172	**12.50**

[a] The Republic of China is the **5th** largest U.S. trading partner.

Population

1989 estimate: 20,233,000
Annual growth: 1.14%
Life expectancy: 73 years
Literacy: 94%
Infant mortality: 18
Fertility: 1.8
Ethnic divisions: Taiwanese, 84%;
Mainland Chinese, 14%,
Aboriginal, 2%
Workforce: 8,227,000
   Unemployment: 1.85%
   Commerce and services:
   35.3%
   Agriculture and fishing: 17%
   **Government and public
   authorities:** 7%
   Manufacturing: 33.8%
   Construction: 6.8%
Students:
   Primary and secondary:
   4,090,000
   University: 465,000

Political

Official name: Republic of China
Type of government: One-party
dominant republic
Name of chief of state: President
Lee Teng-hui
Name of head of government:
Prime Minister Hau Pei-Tsun
Foreign minister: Frederick
Chien
**1989 Freedom House Index (1 is
highest, 7 is lowest):**

Political freedom: 4
Civil liberties: 3
1989 voting with U.S. at U.N.:
Not a member of the U.N.
**FY 1989 U.S. foreign assistance
(actual obligations):**
   Economic: None
   Military: None

Economy

Currency: New Taiwan dollar,
1 US$ = 26.15 NT$
Major industries: Textiles, clothing,
petrochemicals, electronics,
plywood, consumer goods,
cement, shipbuilding
Major agricultural products: Rice,
sweet potatoes, sugarcane, bananas,
pineapples, citrus fruits, peanuts,
pears
Major imports: Machinery and
equipment, crude oil, chemicals,
chemical products, basic metals,
foodstuffs, machine tools
Major exports: Textiles, electronic
and general machinery,
telecommunications equipment,
basic metals, foodstuffs
Per capita GNP: US$7,520 (1989)

Military

1988/1989 military budget:
US$6,700,000,000
Increase over 1986/1987: 13.4%
Outlay as a share of GNP: 7.3%

**As a share of government
spending:** 34.2%
Total regular forces: 405,500
   Army: 270,000
   Navy: 65,500
   Reserves: 1,657,500
   Air Force: 70,000
   Combat aircraft: 500
   Naval vessels: 4 attack
   submarines, 26 destroyers, 10
   frigates, 54 fast-attack craft
   (missile), 3 offshore patrol
   craft, 12 inshore patrol craft, 8
   minesweepers
Security alliance with U.S.: 1954
Mutual Defense Treaty (abrogated
by President Carter in 1979),
security guarantees in the 1979
Taiwan Relations Act
U.S. military installations: None
U.S. military personnel: None
Singaporean military personnel:
Small number of trainers
Armed opposition groups: None

Investment

1989 U.S. direct investment:
US$1,949,000,000
**1989 ROC direct investment in the
U.S.:** US$620,000,000

FIJI

Land

Area: 7,056 square miles
   Cultivated 15%
   Forest: 65%
   Pasture: 3%
Resources: Timber, fish, gold, copper

Population

1989 estimate: 757,000
Annual growth: 2.1%
Life expectancy: 67 years
Literacy: 80%
Infant mortality: 19
Fertility: 3.1
Ethnic divisions: Indian 50%, Fijian 45%, Others 5%
Workforce: 81,000
   Unemployment: NA
   Commerce and services: 12.4%
   Agriculture and fishing: 50%
   Government and public authorities: 11.1%
   Manufacturing: 6.0%
   Construction: 2.6%
Students:
   Primary and secondary: 173,000
   University: 4,000

Political

Official name: Fiji
Type of government: Republic
Name of chief of state: President Ratu Sir Penaia Ganilau
Name of head of government: Prime Minister Ratu Sir Kamisese Mara
Foreign minister: Same
1989 Freedom House Index (1 is highest, 7 is lowest):
   Political freedom: 6
   Civil liberties: 4
1989 voting with U.S. at U.N.: 21.2%
FY 1989 U.S. foreign assistance (actual obligations):
   Economic: US$1,360,000
   Military: US$50,000

Economy

Currency: Fijian dollar, 1 US$ = 1.56 F$
Major industries: Sugar-refining, tourism, gold, lumber, light manufacturing, mining
Major agricultural products: Sugar, copra, ginger, rice, bananas
Major imports: Manufactured goods, machinery, foodstuffs, fuel, transport equipment, consumer goods
Major exports: Sugar, copra, gold, coconut oil, fish
Per capita GNP: US$1,500 (1989)

Military

1987 military budget: US$13,790,000
Increase over 1987: −4.6%
Outlays as a share of GNP: 1.0%
As a share of government spending: 4.0%
Total regular forces: 3,500
   Army: 3,200
   Navy: 300
   Reserves: 5,000
   Air Force: 0
   Combat aircraft: None
   Naval vessels: 3 coastal patrol craft, 2 inshore patrol craft
Security alliance with U.S.: None
U.S. military installations: None
U.S. military personnel: None
Armed opposition groups: None

Investment

1988 U.S. direct investment: US$500,000
1988 Fijian direct investment in the U.S.: US$500,000

HONG KONG

Land

Area: 404 square miles
   Cultivated: 8.8%
   Forest: 12%
   Pasture: 1%
   Resources: None

Fiji: Economic Statistics (billions of US$, percentages where appropriate)[a]

	1982	1983	1984	1985	1986	1987	1988
GDP	1.195	1.124	1.179	1.163	1.239	1.26	1.29
Growth	−1.1%	−4.0%	8.4%	−4.8%	9.0%	11.0%	2.7%
CPI rise	7.0%	6.7%	5.3%	4.4%	1.8%	5.7%	**10.5%**
Exports	0.284	0.240	0.256	0.230	0.239	0.280	**0.3**
to U.S.	0.027	0.020	0.025	0.011	**0.012**	**0.055**	NA
Imports	0.509	0.484	0.450	0.441	0.378	0.315	NA
from U.S.	0.019	0.019	0.018	0.018	**0.018**	**0.020**	NA
CurAccount	0.093	0.065	−0.027	−0.013	0.005	NA	**0.007**

[a] Fiji is a minor U.S. trading partner.

Hong Kong: Economic Statistics (billions of US$, percentages where appropriate)[a]

	1982	1983	1984	1985	1986	1987	1988
GDP	30.4	28.2	31.85	34.1	38.43	46.17	**53.0**
Growth	2.4%	5.2%	6.0%	0.6%	8.7%	14.6%	**7.5%**
CPI rise	10.6%	9.9%	8.5%	3.4%	3.2%	5.3%	**7.5%**
Exports	20.996	21.953	28.318	30.185	35.452	48.461	63.11
to U.S.	5.895	6.825	8.899	8.994	9.474	10.490	10.2
Imports	23.444	24.005	28.558	29.701	35.360	48.463	64.15
from U.S.	2.453	2.563	3.062	2.786	0.030	3.983	5.7
CurAccount	NA	NA	NA	NA	NA	NA	**2.48**

[a] Hong Kong is the **10th** largest U.S. trading partner.

Population

1989 estimate: 5,709,000
Annual growth: 1.0%
Life expectancy: 78 years
Literacy: 75%
Infant morality: 6
Fertility: 1.4
Ethnic divisions: Chinese 98%, Other 2%
Workforce: 2,750,000
    Unemployment: 1.4%
    Commerce and services: 37.3%
    Agriculture and fishing: 1.6%
    Government and publicauthorities: 18%
    Manufacturing: 33.8%
    Construction: 8.0%
Students:
    Primary and secondary: 1,021,000
    University: 32,975

Political

Official name of country: British Crown Colony of Hong Kong
Type of government: British Dependent Territory, scheduled to revert to Chinese control in 1997
Name of chief of state: Queen Elizabeth II
Name of head of government: Sir David Wilson
Foreign minister: Under the auspices of Britain

1989 Freedom House Index (1 is highest, 7 is lowest:
    Political freedom: 4
    Civil liberties: 3
    Voting with U.S. at U.N.: Not a member of the U.N.
FY 1989 U.S. foreign assistance (actual obligations):
    Economic: None
    Military: None

Economy

Currency: Hong Kong dollar, 1 US$ = 7,807
Major industries: Textiles and clothing, tourism, electronics, plastics, toys, watches and clocks
Major agriculture products: Small amounts of rice and vegetables
Major imports: raw materials and semimanufactured goods, fuel, consumer goods, capital goods, footstuffs, chemicals
Major exports: Clothing and textiles, electrical products, electronics, footwear, machinery, telecommunications, toys
Per capita GNP: US$10,940 (1989)

Military

1988 military budget: US$208,000,000
Increase over 1987: 9.9%
Outlay as a share of GNP: 0.7%
As a share of government spending: 3.8%

Total regular forces: 8,505 (combined British, Gurkha, and Chinese)
    Army: 7,540
    Reserves: NA
    Navy: 700
    Air Force: 265
    Combat aircraft: None
    Naval vessels: 3 patrol craft, 12 patrol boats
Security alliance with U.S.: None
U.S. military installations: None
U.S. military personnel: None
British military personnel: Army, 6,300 (including Gurkhas); Navy/ Marines, 300; RAF, 265
Armed opposition groups: None

Investment

1989 U.S. direct investment: US$5,853,000,000
1989 Hong Kong direct investment in the U.S.: US$1,198,000,000

INDIA

Land

Area: 1,269,420 square miles
    Cultivated: 50.3%
    Forest: 11.3%
    Pasture: 4.5%
Resources: Coal, iron ore, manganese, bauxite, chromite, natural gas, limestone, diamonds, oil, bauxite

India: Economic Statistics (billions of US$, percentages where appropriate)[a]

	1982	1983	1984	1985	1986	1987	1988
GDP	187.15	204.31	200.76	210.56	227.01	230.69	234.8
Growth	3.7%	7.8%	3.8%	6.3%	5.1%	2.5%	**10.0%**
CPI rise	7.9%	11.9%	8.3%	5.6%	8.7%	8.8%	**7.0%**
Exports	9.753	9.831	10.638	10.211	10.516	12.430	**14.6**
to U.S.	1.522	2.334	2.737	2.479	2.465	2.725	3.0
Imports	15.904	15.900	17.687	17.769	18.996	20.683	21.4
from U.S.	1.599	1.828	1.570	1.642	1.536	1.464	2.5
CurAccount	−2.524	−1.932	−2.343	−4.214	−4.627	**−4.4**	**−10.6**

[a] India is the **24th** largest U.S. trading partner.

Population

1989 estimate: 833,422,000
Annual growth: 2.0%
Life expectancy: 57 years
Literacy: 36%
Infant mortality: 91
Fertility: 3.9
Ethnic divisions: Indo-Aryan 72%, Dravidan 25%, Mongoloid and Other 3%
Workforce: 319,000,000
   Unemployment: NA
   Commerce and services: 10.5%
   Agriculture and fishing: 52.3%
   Government and public authorities: 6.5%
   Manufacturing: 6.5%
   Construction: 7.2%
Students:
   Primary and secondary: 149,300,000
   University: 3,800,000

Political

Official name: Republic of India
Type of government: Federal republic
Name of chief of state: President Rarnaswamy Venkataramanan
Name of head of government: Prime Minister Chandra Shekhar submitted his resignation on March 6, 1991; no replacement announced.

Foreign minister: V. C. Shukla (From Chandra Shekhar's cabinet; no replacement announced.)
1989 Freedom House Index (1 is highest, 7 is lowest):
   Political freedom: 2
   Civil liberties: 3
1989 voting with U.S. at U.N.: 5.4%
FY 1989 U.S. foreign assistance (actual obligations):
   Economic: US$162,502,000
   Military: US$300,000

Economy

Currency: Rupee, 1 US$ = 16.96 Rupees
Major industries: Textiles, food-processing, steel, machinery, transportation equipment, cement, jute manufactures
Major agricultural products: Rice, cereals, pulses, oilseeds, cotton, jute, sugarcane, tobacco, tea, coffee
Major imports: Machinery and transport equipment, petroleum, edible oils, fertilizer
Major exports: Textiles, clothing, tea, machinery, oil, gems
Per capita GNP: US$320 (1989)

Military

1988/1989 military budget: US$9,890,000,000
Increase over 1987/1988: 2.5%
Outlay as a share of GNP: 4.7%

As a share of government spending: 12.1%
Total regular forces: 1,367,000
   Army: 1,200,000
   Reserves: 240,000+
   Navy: 52,000
   Air Force: 115,000
   Combat aircraft: 723
   Naval vessels: 1 cruise missile submarine, 13 attack submarines, 2 aircraft carriers, 24 frigates, 5 corvette, 13 fast-attack craft (missile), 14 inshore patrol craft, 17 minesweepers
Security alliance with U.S.: None
U.S. military installations: None
U.S. military personnel: None
Soviet military personnel: 200 advisers and technicians
Armed opposition groups: Sikh separatists, number unknown

Investment

1989 U.S. direct investment: US$549,000,000
1989 Indian direct investment in the U.S.: US$25,000,000

INDONESIA

Land

Area: 741,101 square miles
   Cultivated: 14%
   Forest: 67%

Indonesia: Economic Statistics (billions of US$, percentages where appropriate)[a]

	1982	1983	1984	1985	1986	1987	1988
GDP	91.46	77.36	80.79	81.54	82.64	85.29	89.2
Growth	2.2%	4.2%	6.2%	1.9%	1.9%	3.0%	4.2%
CPI rise	9.5%	11.8%	10.5%	4.7%	5.8%	9.3%	6.2%
Exports	22.329	21.146	21.881	18.580	11.071	16.548	**19.0**
to U.S.	4.509	5.657	5.867	4.933	3.657	3.719	3.2
Imports	16.859	16.351	13.880	10.214	10.724	20.234	**13.3**
from U.S.	2.025	1.466	1.217	0.795	0.946	0.767	1.1
CurAccount	−5.324	−6.338	−1.856	−1.923	−3.911	1.678	**−1.7**

[a] Indonesia is the **27th** largest U.S. trading partner.

Pasture: 7%
Resources: Oil, tin, natural gas, nickel, timber, bauxite, copper

Population

1989 estimate: 187,651,000
Annual growth: 1.9%
Life expectancy: 59 years
Literacy: 62%
Infant morality: 80
Fertility: 3.4
Ethnic divisions: Javanese 45%, Sundanese 14%, Madurese 7.5%, Coastal Malay 7.5%, Other 26%
Workforce: 74,500,000
  Unemployment: 2.5%
  Commerce and services: 18.2%
  Agriculture and fishing: 53.5%
  Government and public authorities: 13.0%
  Manufacturing: 9.1%
  Construction: 3.3%
Students:
  Primary and secondary: 41,300,000
  University: 1,440,000

Political

Official name: Republic of Indonesia
Type of government: Republic
Chief of state: President Suharto
Head of government: Same
Foreign minister: Ali Alatas
1989 Freedom House Index (1 is highest, 7 is lowest:

Political freedom: 5
Civil liberties: 5
Voting with U.S. at U.N.: 11.5%
FY 1989 U.S. foreign assistance (actual obligations):
  Economic: US$69,379,000
  Military: US$2,800,000

Economy

Currency: Rupiah, 1 US$ = 1,801 Rupiah
Major industries: Petroleum, textiles, mining, cement, chemical fertilizer, timber, palm oil, light manufactures
Major agriculture products: Rice, rubber, copra, coffee, sugar
Major imports: Rice, wheat, flour, cereals, textiles, chemicals, iron and steel products, machinery, transport equipment
Major exports: Petroleum, liquefied natural gas, timber, rubber, coffee, tin, palm oil, tea, copper
Per capita GNP: US$430 (1989)

Military

1987/1988 military budget: US$1,320,000,000
Increase over 1986/1987: −19.5%
Outlays as a share of GNP: 1.5%
As a share of government spending: 12.0%
Total regular forces: 284,000
  Army: 215,000

Reserves: 800,000
Navy: 43,000
Air Force: 26,000
Combat aircraft: 85
Naval vessels: 2 attack submarines, 15 frigates, 4 fast-attack craft (missile), 2 fast-attack craft (torpedo), 1 coastal patrol craft, 22 inshore patrol craft, 2 minesweepers
Security alliance with U.S.: None
U.S. military installations: None
U.S. military personnel: None
Australian military personnel: small number of advisers
Armed opposition groups: Revolutionary Front for an Independent East Timor, 1,500; Free Papua Movement

Investment

1989 U.S. direct investment: US$3,696,000,000
1989 Indonesian direct investment in the U.S.: US$377,000,000

JAPAN

Land

Area: 147,470 square miles
  Cultivated: 15.5%
  Forest: 66.4%
  Pasture: 1.7%
  Resources: Negligible mineral resources, fish

Japan: Economic Statistics (billions of US$, percentages where appropriate) [a]

	1982	1983	1984	1985	1986	1987	1988
GDP	1082.8	1181.3	1256.5	1330.0	1966.2	2384.5	2568.6
Growth	3.1%	3.2%	5.1%	4.7%	2.5%	4.4%	6.3%
CPI rise	2.7%	1.9%	2.3%	2.0%	0.6%	1.6%	0.3%
Exports	138.443	146.982	169.748	177.189	211.735	231.332	**260.0**
to U.S.	39.931	43.559	60.371	72.380	85.457	88.074	89.8
Imports	131.566	126.520	136.142	130.516	127.660	150.926	**188.0**
from U.S.	20.966	21.894	23.575	22.631	26.882	28.249	37.7
CurAccount	6.85	20.80	25.00	49.17	85.83	86.96	94.0

[a] Japan is the **2nd** largest U.S. trading partner.

Population

1989 estimate: 123,220,000
Annual growth: 0.5%
Life expectancy: 79 years
Literacy: 99%
Infant morality: 5
Fertility: 1.7
Ethnic divisions: Japanese 99.4%, Other (mostly Korean) 0.6%
Workforce: 61,200,000
  Unemployment: 2.6%
  Commerce and services: 53.9%
  Agriculture and fishing: 8.5%
  Government and public authorities: 3.4%
  Manufacturing: 24.7%
  Construction: 9.1%
Students:
  Primary and secondary: 15,770,000
  University: 1,990,000

Political

Official name: Japan
Type of government: Constitutional monarchy
Chief of state: Emperor Akhito
Head of government: Prime Minister Toshiki Kaifu
Foreign minister: Hiroshi Mitsuzuka
1989 Freedom House Index (1 is highest, 7 is lowest):
  Political freedom: 1
  Civil liberties: 1

Voting with U.S. at U.N.: 61.0%
FY 1989 U.S. foreign assistance (actual obligations):
  Economic: None
  Military: None

Economy

Currency: Yen, US$ = 143.50 Yen
Major industries: Machinery, autos, metallurgy, engineering, electrical and electronics, textiles, chemicals, fishing
Major agriculture products: Rice, sugar, vegetables, fruit, fish
Major imports: Fuel, manufactures, foodstuffs, machinery, wood, coal, metal ore, raw
Major exports: Machinery and equipment, motor vehicles, metals, chemicals, textiles, electronics, semiconductors
Per capita GDP: US$22,800 (1989)

Military

1988 military budget: US$29,630,000,000
Increase over 1987: 16.6%
Outlay as a share of GNP: 1.01%
As a share of government spending: 6.5%
Total regular forces: 245,000
  Army: 156,000
  Reserves: 44,900
  Navy: 44,000
  Air Force: 45,000

Combat aircraft: 473
Naval vessels: 14 attack submarines, 36 destroyers, 25 frigates, 5 fast-attack craft (torpedo), 9 patrol craft, 2 minelayers, 42 minesweepers
Security alliance with U.S.: Mutual cooperation and security treaties 1951, 1960
U.S. military installations: Yokosuka Naval Base, Yokohama Naval Base, Atsugi Naval Air Facility, Sasebo Naval Base, Futenma (Marines), Iwakuni Marine Air Base, Misawa Base, Kadena Air Base, Yokota Air Base, Zukeran Marine Air Base, Makiminato (Army), Atsugi Naval Air Facility, Kamiseya (Navy)
U.S. military personnel: 2,400 Army, 8,100 Navy, 16, 200 Air Force, 38,150 Marines
U.S. military personnel: 2,400 Army, 8,100 Navy, 16,200 Air Force, 38,150 Marines
Armed opposition groups: None

Investment

1989 U.S. direct investment: US$19,341,000,000
1989 Japanese direct investment in the U.S.: US$69,699,000,000

KIRIBATI

Land

Area: 266 square miles
  Cultivated: 5%
  Forest: 3%
  Pasture: 0%
  Resources: Copra, fish

Population

1989 estimate: 68,800
Annual growth: 1.5%
Life expectancy: 55
Literacy: 90%
Infant mortality: 58
Fertility: 4.2
Ethnic divisions: Micronesian 100%
Workforce: 7,800 (1985)
  Unemployment: NA
  Commerce and services: NA
  Agriculture and fishing: NA
  **Government and public
    authorities:** NA
  Manufacturing: NA
  Construction: NA
Students: NA

Political

Official name: Republic of Kiribati
Type of government: Republic
Chief of state: President Ieremia T.
  Tabai
Head of government: Same
Foreign minister: Same

**1989 Freedom House Index (1 is
  highest, 7 is lowest):**
  Political freedom: 1
  Civil liberties: 2
1989 Voting with U.S. at U.N.:
  Not a member of the U.N.
**FY 1989 U.S. foreign assistance
  (actual obligations):**
  Economic: US$509,000
  Military: None

Economy

Currency: Australian dollar, 1 US$
  = 1.263 A$
Major industries: Fishing,
  handicrafts
Major agricultural products:
  Copra, subsistence vegetables,
  coconuts, melons, bananas, hogs,
  poultry
Major imports: Foodstuffs, fuel,
  transport equipment, manufactured
  goods, machinery
Major exports: Copra, fish,
  handicrafts
Per capita GNP: US$480 (1989)

Military

Kiribati has no military forces
Security alliance with U.S.: None
U.S. military installations: None
U.S. military personnel: None
Australian military personnel:
  Small number of advisers
Armed opposition groups: None

Investment

1989 U.S. direct investment: NA
**1989 Kiribati direct investment in
  the U.S.:** NA

KOREA, NORTH

Land

Area: 47,077 square miles
  Cultivated: 19%
  Forest: 74%
  Pasture: 1%
  Resources: Coal, lead, tungsten,
    zinc, graphite, magnesite, iron
    ore, copper, gold, phosphates,
    salt, fluorspar

Population

1989 estimate: 22,520,000
Annual growth: 2.4%
Life expectancy: 70
Literacy: 95%
Infant mortality: 32
Fertility: 3.5
Ethnic divisions: Korean 100%
Workforce: 8,100,000
  Unemployment: NA
  Commerce and services: NA
  Agriculture and fishing: 43%
  **Government and public
    authorities:** 18%
  Manufacturing: 39%
  Construction: NA

Kiribati: Economic Statistics (billions of US$, percentages where appropriate)[a]

	1982	1983	1984	1985	1986	1987	1988
GDP	NA	.NA	25.0	25.8	32.0	32.0	NA
Growth	NA	NA	NA	NA	NA	NA	NA
CPI rise	NA	NA	NA	NA	NA	NA	NA
Exports	2.0	4.0	11.0	4.0	4.1	NA	NA
to U.S.	NA	NA	NA	NA	NA	NA	NA
Imports	23.0	20.0	21.0	18.0	32.64	NA	NA
from U.S.	NA	NA	NA	NA	NA	NA	NA
CurAccount	NA	NA	NA	NA	NA	NA	NA

[a] Kiribati is a minor U.S. trading partner.

North Korea: Economic Statistics (billions of US$, percentages where appropriate)[a]

	1982	1983	1984	1985	1986	1987	1988
GDP	17.64	18.16	18.9	19.7	20.1	19.59	20.18
Growth	3.7%	0.9%	2.7%	4.0%	2.0%	2.0%	3.0%
CPI rise	NA	NA	NA	NA	NA	NA	NA
Exports	0.736	0.654	0.691	0.640	0.684	0.783	NA
to U.S.	0.0	0.0	0.0	0.0	0.0	0.0	0.0
Imports	1.019	0.980	0.822	0.835	0.827	1.094	NA
from U.S.	0.0	0.0	0.0	0.0	0.0	0.0	0.0
CurAccount	NA	NA	NA	NA	NA	NA	NA

[a] Trade with North Korea is illegal.

Students:
Primary and secondary: 5,000,000
University: 100,000

Political

Official name of country: Democratic People's Republic of Korea
Type of government: Communist state, one-man rule
Chief of state: President Kim Il-Sung
Head of government: Same
Foreign minister: Kim Yong Nam
1989 Freedom House Index (1 is highest, 7 is lowest):
Political freedom: 7
Civil liberties: 7
1989 voting with U.S. at U.N.: Not a voting member of the U.N.
FY 1989 U.S. foreign assistance (actual obligations):
Economic: None
Military: None

Economy

Currency: Won, 1 US$ = 2.18 Won (official rate)
Major industries: Machine-building, electric power, chemicals, mining, metallurgy, textiles, steel, cement
Major agricultural products: Corn, rice, vegetables, fruits
Major imports: Petroleum, machinery and equipment, coking coal, grain, chemicals, transport equipment
Major exports: Minerals, metallurgical products, agricultural products, manufactures, machinery, chemicals
Per capita GNP: US$930 (1989)

Military

1988 military budget: US$4,130,000,000
Increase over 1987: −2.1%
Outlay as a share of GNP: 20%
As a share of government spending: 30%
Total regular forces: 842,000
Army: 750,000
Reserves: 540,000+
Navy: 39,000
Air Force: 53,000
Combat aircraft: 800
Naval vessels: 21 attack submarines, 2 frigates, 4 corvettes, 30 fast-attack craft (missile), 173 fast-attack craft (torpedo), 6 coastal patrol craft, 152 inshore patrol craft, 40 minesweepers
Security alliance with U.S.: None
U.S. military installations: None
U.S. military personnel: None
Armed opposition groups: None

Investment

1989 U.S. direct investment: None
1989 North Korean direct investment in the U.S.: None

KOREA, SOUTH

Land

Area: 38,211 square miles
Cultivated: 21.6%
Forest: 65.8%
Pasture: 12.6%
Resources: Coal, tungsten, graphite, iron ore, limestone

Population

1989 estimate: 43,350,000
Annual growth: 1.3%
Life expectancy: 69
Literacy: 93%
Infant mortality: 24
Fertility: 2.2
Ethnic divisions: Korean 100%
Workforce: 17,200,000
Unemployment: 3.0%
Commerce and services: 22.4
Agriculture and fishing: 23.6%
Government and public authorities: 23.6%
Manufacturing: 24.7%
Construction: 5.7
Students:
Primary and secondary: 9,640,000
University: 1,100,000

South Korea: Economic Statistics (billions of US$, percentages where appropriate)[a]

	1982	1983	1984	1985	1986	1987	1988
GDP	69.4	76.0	82.4	83.7	95.3	118.6	142.3
Growth	5.7%	10.9%	8.6%	5.4%	11.7%	11.1%	12.1%
CPI rise	7.3%	3.4%	2.3%	2.5%	2.8%	3.0%	7.2%
Exports	21.827	24.460	29.259	30.289	34.732	47.301	59.66
to U.S.	6.011	7.657	10.027	10.713	13.497	17.991	20.2
Imports	24.250	26.196	30.628	31.058	31.580	41.019	48.11
from U.S.	5.529	5.925	5.983	5.956	6.355	8.099	11.3
CurAccount	−2.650	−1.606	−1.372	−0.887	4.617	9.854	14.27

[a] South Korea is the **7th** largest U.S. trading partner.

Political

Official name: Republic of Korea
Type of government: Multiparty republic
Chief of state: President Roh TaeWoo
Head of government: Same
Foreign minister: Choi Ho-Joang
1989 Freedom House Index (1 is highest, 7 is lowest):
   Political freedom: 2
   Civil liberties: 3
1989 voting with U.S. at U.N.:
   Not a voting member of the U.N.
FY 1989 U.S. foreign assistance (actual obligations):
   Economic: None
   Military: US$1,500,000

Economy

Currency: Won, 1 US$ = 679.6 Won
Major industries: Textiles and clothing, food-processing, chemicals, steel, electronics, shipbuilding, automobiles
Major agricultural products: Rice, barley, vegetables, legumes
Major imports: Machinery, oil, steel, transportation equipment, textiles, organic chemicals, grains
Major exports: Textiles and clothing, footwear, electrical machinery, steel, ships, automobiles, fish
Per capita GNP: US$4,830 (1989)

Military

1987 military budget:
   US$5,730,000,000
Increase over 1986: 12.1%
Outlays as a share of GNP: 4.0%
As a share of government spending: 30.4%
Total regular forces: 629,000
   Army: 542,000
   Reserves: 1,500,000
   Navy: 54,000
   Air Force: 33,000
   Combat aircraft: 490
   Naval vessels: 3 attack submarines, 18 frigates, 11 fast-attack craft (missile), 94 inshore patrol craft, 9 minesweepers
Security alliance with U.S.:
   Mutual Cooperation and Security, 1954
U.S. military installations: Kunsan Air Base, Uijong-Bu HQ, Tongduchon Army Base, Osan Air Base
U.S. military personnel: 29,100 Army, 11,200 Air Force
Armed opposition groups: None

Investment

1989 U.S. direct investment: US$1,889,000,000
1989 South Korean direct investment in the U.S.: US$216,000,000

LAOS

Land

Area: 91,428 square miles
   Cultivated: 4%
   Forest: 58%
   Pasture: 3%
   Resources: Tin, timber, gypsum, hydroelectric power

Population

1989 estimate: 3,936,000
Annual growth: 2.2%
Life expectancy: 49
Literacy: 85%
Infant mortality: 128
Fertility: 5.2
Ethnic divisions: Lao 48%, Kha 25%, Tribal Thai 14%, Other 13%
Workforce: 1,850,000
   Unemployment: NA
   Commerce and services: 19%
   Agriculture and fishing: 75%
   Government and public authorities: NA
   Manufacturing: 6%
   Construction: NA
Students:
   Primary and secondary: 565,000
   University: 20,093

Laos: Economic Statistics (millions of US$, percentages where appropriate)[a]

	1982	1983	1984	1985	1986	1987	1988
GDP	475.7	534.2	530.0	600.0	643.0	679.0	693.0
Growth	NA	NA	NA	NA	NA	NA	2.0%
CPI rise	NA	NA	20.0%	20.0%	20.0%	20.0%	65.0%
Exports	25.657	26.564	11.425	18.371	14.388	27.713	NA
to U.S.	1.456	2.546	2.001	0.455	0.273	0.910	NA
Imports	88.062	92.721	50.428	64.816	70.331	89.437	NA
from U.S.	0.440	0.110	0.110	0.220	0.1	0.220	NA
CurAccount	NA	NA	NA	NA	NA	NA	130.0

[a] Laos is a very minor U.S. trading partner.

Political

Official name of country: Lao People's Democratic Republic
Type of government: Communist state
Chief of state: President Phoumi Vongvichit
Head of government: General Secretary Kaysone Phomvihan
Foreign minister: Phoun Sipaseuth
1989 Freedom House Index (1 is highest, 7 is lowest):
    Political freedom: 7
    Civil liberties: 7
1989 Voting with U.S. at U.N.: 10.8%
FY 1989 U.S. foreign assistance (actual obligations):
    Economic: US$1,517,00
    Military: None

Economy

Currency: Kip, 1 US$ = 713.0 K
Major industries: Tin-mining, timber, coffee, electric power
Major agricultural products: Rice, corn, vegetables, tobacco, cotton, coffee
Major imports: Rice and other footstuffs, petroleum products, machinery, transport equipment
Major exports: electric power, forest products, tin, coffee
Per capita GNP: US$180 (1989)

Military

1988 military budget: NA
Increase over 1987: NA
Outlays as a share of GNP: NA
As a share of government spending: NA
Total regular forces: 55,150
    Army: 52,500
    Reserves: NA
    Navy: 650
    Air Force: 2,000
    Combat aircraft: 30
    Naval vessels: 40 river patrol craft
Security alliance with U.S.: None
U.S. military installations: None
U.S. military personnel: None
Soviet military personnel: 500 advisers
Vietnamese military personnel: 50,000 troops
Armed opposition groups: United Lao National Liberation Front, 2,000

Investment

1989 U.S. direct investment: NA
1989 Laotian direct investment in the U.S.: NA

MACAO

Land

Area: 6.17 square miles
    Cultivated: 2%
    Forest: 5%
    Pasture: 0%
Resources: None

Population

1989 estimate: 436,500
Annual growth: 1.3%
Life expectancy: 77 years
Literacy: 90%
Infant mortality: 8
Fertility: 2.2
Ethnic divisions: Chinese 98%, Portuguese 2%
Workforce: 190,000
    Unemployment: NA
    Commerce and services: 34%
    Agriculture and fishing: 6%
    Government and public authorities: 7%
    Manufacturing: 5%
    Construction: 8%
Students:
    Primary and secondary: 62,300
    University: 6,890

Macao: Economic Statistics (millions of US$, percentages where appropriate)[a]

	1982	1983	1984	1985	1986	1987	1988
GDP	NA	788.1	979.8	1030.0	1137.7	1992.0	2110.0
Growth	8.0%	8.0%	8.0%	2.5%	6.2%	12.4%	6.0%
CPI rise	NA	NA	11.1%	2.07%	1.7%	4.7%	NA
Exports	720.84	755.04	910.59	907.09	1033.55	NA	NA
to U.S.	217.7	246.4	339.0	370.1	444.5	568.7	NA
Imports	713.29	724.16	793.32	775.68	874.31	NA	NA
from U.S.	58.28	46.16	55.83	55.69	53.10	54.43	NA
CurAccount	NA	NA	NA	NA	NA	NA	NA

[a] Macao is a minor U.S. trading partner.

Political

Official name of country:
Macao
Type of government: Chinese
Territory under Portuguese
Administration
Chief of state: Governor Carlos
Melancia
Head of government: Same
Foreign minister: Portugal is
responsible for foreign affairs
**1989 Freedom House Index (1 is
highest, 7 is lowest):**
Political freedom: 3
Civil liberties: 3
1989 Voting with U.S. at U.N.:
Not a member of the U.N.
**FY 1989 U.S. foreign assistance
(actual obligations):**
Economic: None
Military: None

Economy

Currency: Pataca, 1 US$ = 8.05
Pataca
Major industries: Textiles, toys,
plastic products, gambling,
furniture, tourism, garments
Major agricultural products: Rice,
vegetables
Major imports: Foodstuffs, fabric,
machinery, oil
Major exports: Textiles and
clothing, toys, electronics, fish
Per capita GNP: US$5,000 (1989)

Military

Defense is the responsibility of
Portugal
1985 military expenditure:
US$24,900,000
Increase over 1984: 114%
Outlay as a share of GNP: 2.5%
**As a share of government
spending:** 11.1%
Total regular forces: NA
Army: NA
Reserves: NA
Navy: NA
Air Force: NA
Aircraft: NA
Naval vessels: NA
Security alliance with U.S.: None
U.S. military installations: None
U.S. military personnel: None
Armed opposition groups: None

Investment

1988 U.S. direct investment: less
than US$500,000
**1988 Macau direct investment in
the U.S.:** NA

MALAYSIA

Land

Area: 127,316 square miles
Cultivated: 14.3%
Forest: 70%
Pasture: 1%

Resources: Tin, petroleum, timber,
copper, iron, palm oil, rubber

Population

1989 estimate: 16,727,000
Annual growth: 2.0%
Life expectancy: 67 years
Literacy: 65%
Infant mortality: 31
Fertility: 2.9
Ethnic divisions: Malay 59%,
Chinese 32%, Indian 9%
Workforce: 6,662,000
Unemployment: 8.1%
Commerce and services:
22.9%
Agriculture and fishing: 35.1%
**Government and public
authorities:** 15.0%
Manufacturing: 14.5%
Construction: 6.6%
Students:
Primary and secondary:
3,610,000
University: 47,946

Political

Official name of country: Malaysia
Type of government: Federal
Constitutional Monarchy
Chief of state: Sultan Azlan
Muhibuddin Shah ibni al-Marhum,
Sultan Yussuf Izzuddin
Ghafarullahu-Iahu Shah

Malaysia: Economic Statistics (billions of US$, percentages where appropriate)[a]

	1982	1983	1984	1985	1986	1987	1988
GDP	25.56	28.07	31.65	28.92	29.48	29.90	31.46
Growth	5.9%	6.3%	7.8%	−1.0%	1.0%	4.7%	7.4%
CPI rise	5.8%	3.7%	3.9%	0.3%	0.7%	1.1%	2.7%
Exports	12.044	14.128	16.563	15.408	13.977	17.934	**20.80**
to U.S.	1.959	2.205	2.825	2.399	2.534	3.053	3.7
Imports	12.409	13.241	14.057	12.301	19.828	12.701	**15.40**
from U.S.	1.736	1.684	1.856	1.539	1.730	1.897	2.1
CurAccount	−3.601	−3.497	−1.671	−0.684	0.035	2.336	**1.21**

[a] Malaysia is the **23rd** largest U.S. trading partner.

Head of government: Prime Minister Dr. Mahathir bin Mohamad

Foreign minister: Datuk Abu Hassan

1989 Freedom House Index (1 is highest, 7 is lowest):
  Political freedom: 5
  Civil liberties: 4

1989 Voting with U.S. at U.N.: 10.6%

FY 1989 U.S. foreign assistance (actual obligations):
  Economic: None
  Military: US$950,000

Economy

Currency: Ringgit (Malaysian dollar), 1 US$ = 2.699 M$

Major industries: Rubber and palm oil processing, textiles, tin-mining, logging, petroleum production, electronics

Major agricultural products: Natural rubber, palm oil, rice, coconuts, pepper, pineapples

Major imports: Machinery and transport equipment, manufactured goods, crude petroleum, foodstuffs, mineral fuels, chemicals

Major exports: Natural rubber, palm oil, tin, timber, petroleum, light manufactures

Per capita GNP: US$2,000 (1989)

Military

1987 military budget: US$853,310,000

Increase over 1987: −14.8%

Outlay as a share of GNP: 2.9%

As a share of government spending: 14.6%

Total regular forces: 114,500
  Army: 90,000
  Reserves: 47,600
  Navy: 12,500
  Air Force: 12,000
  Combat aircraft: 61
  Naval vessels: 4 frigates, 8 fast-attack craft (missile), 2 offshore patrol craft, 27 inshore patrol craft, 4 minesweepers

Security alliance with U.S.: None

U.S. military installations: None

U.S. military personnel: None

Australian military personnel: Army and RAAF elements, plus a small number of advisers

Armed opposition groups: Communist Party of Malaya, 850; North Kalimantan Communist Party, 50

Investment

1989 U.S. direct investment: US$1,098,000,000

1989 Malaysian direct investment in the U.S.: US$50,000,000

MALDIVES

Land

Area: 115 square miles
  Cultivated: 5.7%
  Forest: 3.3%
  Pasture: 3%
Resources: Fish, coconuts, shells

Population

1989 estimate: 211,000
Annual growth: 3.7%
Life expectancy: 60 years
Literacy: 36%
Infant mortality: 80
Fertility: 7.0
Ethnic divisions: Sinhalese, Dravidan, Arab, and African
Workforce: 66,000
  Unemployment: NA
  Commerce and services: NA
  Agriculture and fishing: 30%
  Government and public authorities: 4.8%
  Manufacturing: 22.5%
  Construction: 4.98%
Students:
  Primary and secondary: 6,006
  University: NA

Political

Official name of country: Republic of Maldives
Type of government: Republic

Maldives: Economic Statistics (millions of US$, percentages where appropriate)[a]

	1982	1983	1984	1985	1986	1987	1988
GDP	60.22	66.1	76.17	83.97	87.0	94.0	101.0
Growth	9.1%	5.8%	4.0%	14.4%	7.0%	NA	7.0%
CPI rise	22.0%	NA	NA	NA	NA	NA	5.0%
Exports	13.00	13.10	13.80	24.00	29.10	23.7	40.0
to U.S.	NA	NA	NA	NA	NA	NA	NA
Imports	66.70	66.20	71.90	71.10	79.20	99.4	NA
from U.S.	NA	NA	NA	NA	NA	NA	NA
CurAccount	−19.1	−24.2	−16.5	−8.8	NA	NA	NA

[a] The Maldives are a minor U.S. trading partner.

Chief of state: President Maumoon Abdul Gayoom
Head of government: Same
Foreign minister: Fathulla Jameel
1989 Freedom House Index (1 is highest, 7 is lowest):
   Political freedom: 6
   Civil liberties: 5
1989 Voting with U.S. at U.N.: 13.9%
FY 1989 U.S. foreign assistance (actual obligations):
   Economic: None
   Military: US$30,000

Economy

Currency: Rufikaa, 1 US$ = 8.4 Rufikaa
Major industries: Fish-processing, tourism, garments, handicrafts
Major agricultural products: Fish, coconuts, fruit, millet

Major imports: Food, manufactured goods, petroleum products, capital goods, machinery, chemicals
Major exports: Fish, shells, apparel, minerals, fuels
Per capita GNP: US$470 (1989)

Military

1985 military budget: US$2,700,000
Increase over 1984: 50%
Outlay as a share of GNP: 2.9%
As a share of government spending: 11.3%
Total regular forces: NA
   Army: NA
   Reserves: NA
   Navy: NA
   Air Force: NA
   Combat aircraft: NA
   Naval vessels: NA
Security alliance with U.S.: None

U.S. military installations: None
U.S. military personnel: None
Armed opposition groups: None

Investment

1989 U.S. direct investment: NA
1989 Maldivian direct investment in the U.S.: NA

MONGOLIA

Land

Area: 604,247 square miles
   Cultivated: 0.7%
   Forest: 10.2%
   Pasture: 78.8%
Resources: Coal, tungsten, copper, molybdenum, gold, tin, nickel, zinc, wolfram, fluorspar, phosphates

Mongolia: Economic Statistics (millions of US$, percentages where appropriate)[a]

	1982	1983	1984	1985	1986	1987	1988
GDP	NA	NA	1900.0	NA	NA	1823.0	1889.0
Growth	NA	NA	NA	NA	NA	NA	3.6%
CPI rise	NA	NA	NA	NA	NA	NA	NA
Exports	523.0	568.0	625.0	618.0	NA	NA	NA
to U.S.	NA	1.0	2.0	4.0	1.0	1.5	NA
Imports	736.0	864.0	898.0	988.0	NA	NA	NA
from U.S.	NA	0.0	0.0	0.05	0.1	0.9	NA
CurAccount	NA	NA	NA	NA	NA	NA	NA

[a] Mongolia is a minor U.S. trading partner.

Population

1988 estimate: 2,068,000
Annual growth: 2.8%
Life expectancy: 64 years
Literacy: 80%
Infant mortality: 52
Ethnic divisions: Khalkaia Mongol 75%, Other Mongols 8%
Workforce: 390,000
    Unemployment: NA
    Commerce and services: 25%
    Agriculture and fishing: 11%
    Government and public authorities: 34%
    Manufacturing: 23%
    Construction: 7%
Students:
    Primary and secondary: 488,400
    University: 23,500

Political

Official name: Mongolian People's Republic
Type of government: Liberalizing Communist state
Chief of state: General Secretary Jambyn Batmonh
Head of government: Prime Minister Sharauyn Gunjaadorj
Foreign minister: Tserenpiliyn Gombosuren
1989 Freedom House Index (1 is highest, 7 is lowest):
    Political freedom: 7
    Civil liberties: 7
1989 voting with U.S. at U.N.: 10.1%
FY 1989 U.S. foreign assistance (actual obligations):
    Economic: None
    Military: None

Economy

Currency: Tugrick, 1 US$ = 2.8 Tugrick (official rate)
Major industries: Cement, knitwear, footwear, meat, coal, textiles, chemicals, building materials, mining

Major agricultural products: Livestock, wheat, oats, barley, feedgrains, potatoes, vegetables
Major imports: Petroleum, sheet metal, trucks, fertilizer, paper, sugar, tea, chemicals, machinery, garments
Major exports: Timber, wool, meat, copper, molybdenum, fluorspar, hides, phosphates
Per capita GNP: US$920 (1989)

Military

1987 military budget: US$249,440,000
Increase over 1986: 5.9%
Outlay as a share of GNP: 13.2%
As a share of government spending: 13.5%
Total regular forces: 24,500
    Army: 21,000
    Reserves: 200,000
    Navy: 0
    Air Force: 3,500
    Combat aircraft: 30
    Naval vessels: 0
Security alliance with U.S.: None
U.S. military installations: None
U.S. military personnel: None
Soviet military personnel: 55,000 troops
Armed opposition groups: None

Investment

1989 U.S. direct investment: NA
1989 Mongolian direct investment in the U.S.: NA

NEPAL

Land

Area: 56,136 square miles
    Cultivated: 18%
    Forest: 29%
    Pasture: 13.4%
Resources: Quartz, timber, hydroelectric potential, lignite, copper, cobalt, iron ore

Population

1989 estimate: 18,700,000
Annual growth: 2.4%
Life expectancy: 49 years
Literacy: 20%
Infant mortality: 101
Fertility: 5.7
Ethnic divisions: Newars, Indians, Tibetan, Gurungs, Magars
Workforce: 7,960,000
    Unemployment: NA
    Commerce and services: 0.2%
    Agriculture and fishing: 91.1%
    Government and public authorities: 0.1%
    Manufacturing: 1.3%
    Construction: 0.03%
Students:
    Primary and secondary: 3,350,000
    University: 64,900

Political

Official name: Kingdom of Nepal
Type of government: monarchy, pending elections
Chief of state: King Birendra Bir Bikram Shah Dev
Head of government: Prime Minister Krishna Prasad Bhattarai
Foreign minister: Shailendra Kumar Upadhaya
1989 Freedom House Index (1 is highest, 7 is lowest):
    Political freedom: 4
    Civil liberties: 5
1989 voting with U.S. at U.N.: 12.2%
FY 1989 U.S. foreign assistance (actual obligations):
    Economic: US$16,988,000
    Military: US$100,000

Economy

Currency: Rupee, 1 US$ = 24.0 Rupees
Major industries: Oilseed, sugar, jute and rice mills, match, cigarette and brick factories, cement, garments

Nepal: Economic Statistics (millions of US$, percentages where appropriate) [a]

	1982	1983	1984	1985	1986	1987	1988
GDP	2.34	2.32	2.32	2.29	2.36	2.59	2.65
Growth	3.8%	−3.0%	7.8%	3.0%	4.0%	2.3%	1.9%
CPI rise	11.7%	12.4%	2.8%	8.1%	19.0%	10.8%	**10.9%**
Exports	0.070	0.080	0.090	0.138	0.146	0.167	**0.2**
to U.S.	0.002	0.006	0.008	0.052	0.038	0.032	0.053
Imports	0.251	0.254	0.253	0.297	0.321	0.493	NA
from U.S.	0.006	0.008	0.004	0.007	0.008	0.056	0.064
CurAccount	−0.086	−0.146	−0.095	−0.122	−0.119	−0.123	**−0.12**

[a] Nepal is a minor U.S. trading partner.

Major agricultural products: Rice, jute, corn, wheat , oilseeds, sugarcane, potatoes, millet

Major imports: Manufactured consumer goods, fuel, construction materials, fertilizers, food products

Major exports: Rice and other food products, jute, timber, manufactured goods, sugar, hides and skins

Per capita GNP: US$170 (1989)

Military

1987/1988 military budget: US$37,100,000

Increase over 1986/1987: 13.2%

Outlay as a share of GNP: 1.4%

As a share of government spending: 5.3%

Total regular forces: 35,000

    Army: 30,000

    Reserves: 0

    Navy: 0

    Air Force: 0

    Combat aircraft: 1

    Naval vessels: 0

Security alliance with U.S.: None

U.S. military installations: None

U.S. military personnel: None

Armed opposition groups: None

Investment

1989 U.S. direct investment: NA

1989 Nepalese direct investment in the U.S: NA

NEW CALEDONIA

Land

Area: 8,548 square miles

    Cultivated: 0%

    Forest: 51%

    Pasture: 14%

Resources: Nickel, chrome, iron, cobalt, manganese, silver, gold, lead, copper

Population

1989 estimate: 152,000

Annual growth: 1.0%

Life expectancy: 70 years

Literacy: NA

Infant mortality: 35

Fertility: 3.0

Ethnic divisions: Melanesian 42.5%, European 37.1%, Wallisian 8.4%, Polynesian 3.8%, Indonesian 3.6%, Vietnamese 1.6%

Workforce: 50,469 (1980)

    Unemployment: NA

    Commerce and services: NA

    Agriculture and fishing: NA

    Government and public authorities: NA

    Manufacturing: NA

    Construction: NA

Students: NA

Political

Official name: Territory of New Caledonia and Dependencies

Type of government: French overseas territory

Chief of state: French President François Mitterand

Head of government: High Commissioner Clement Bouhin

Foreign minister: Under the auspices of France

1989 Freedom House Index (1 is highest, 7 is lowest):

    Political freedom: 2

    Civil liberties: 2

1989 voting with U.S. at U.N.: Not a member of the U.N.

FY 1989 U.S. foreign assistance (actual obligations):

    Economic: None

    Military: None

Economy

Currency: Comptoirs Français du Pacifique Franc, 1 US$ = 113.63 CFPF

Major industries: Nickel mining

Major agricultural products: Cattle, coffee, maize, wheat, cotton, manioc, tobacco, bananas, pineapples

Major imports: fuels, minerals, machines, and electrical equipment

Major exports: Nickel metal, nickel ore

Per capita GNP: US$8,030 (1983)

New Caledonia: Economic Statistics (billions of US$, percentages where appropriate)[a]

	1982	1983	1984	1985	1986	1987	1988
GDP	NA	1.21	NA	NA	NA	NA	NA
Growth	NA	NA	NA	NA	NA	NA	NA
CPI rise	NA	11.0%	NA	NA	NA	NA	NA
Exports	0.266	0.153	0.207	0.272	0.208	0.244	NA
to U.S.	0.015	0.011	0.012	0.014	0.013	0.017	NA
Imports	0.367	0.304	0.310	0.347	0.531	0.624	NA
from U.S.	0.052	0.031	0.020	0.029	0.025	0.024	NA
CurAccount	NA	NA	NA	NA	NA	NA	NA

[a] New Caledonia is a minor U.S. trading partner.

Military

France is responsible for military affairs.
Security alliance with U.S.: None
U.S. military installations: None
U.S. military personnel: None
French military personnel: 9,500 combined Army, Marine, and Air Force
Armed opposition groups: Kanak Socialist National Liberation Front

Investment

1989 U.S. direct investment: NA
1989 New Caledonian direct investment in the U.S: NA

NEW ZEALAND

Land

Area: 103,883 square miles
  Cultivated: 3%
  Forest: 26.4%
  Pasture: 52.7%
Resources: Natural gas, iron, sands, coal, timber, gold

Population

1989 estimate: 3,373,000
Annual growth: 0.9%
Life expectancy: 75 years
Literacy: 98%
Infant mortality: 10
Fertility: 1.9
Ethnic divisions: European 88%, Maori 8.9%, Pacific Islander 2.9%, Other 0.2%

Workforce: 1,657,000
  Unemployment: 5.0%
  Commerce and services: 34.9%
  Agriculture and fishing: 10.4%
  Government and public authorities: 20.6%
  Manufacturing: 22%
  Construction: 6.4%
Students:
  Primary and secondary: 665,300
  University: 194,900

Political

Official name: New Zealand
Type of government: Parliamentary Democracy within Commonwealth
Chief of state: Queen Elizabeth II
Head of government: Prime Minister Jim Bolger

New Zealand: Economic Statistics (billions of US$, percentages where appropriate)[a]

	1982	1983	1984	1985	1986	1987	1988
GDP	22.78	22.09	21.27	21.34	23.31	24.99	25.36
Growth	3.1%	0.1%	6.6%	1.5%	−1.0%	1.0%	1.5%
CPI rise	16.2%	7.4%	6.2%	15.4%	13.2%	12.3%	8.9%
Exports	5.644	5.403	5.518	5.714	5.921	7.158	**7.7**
to U.S.	0.8770	0.828	0.880	0.969	1.097	1.181	1.2
Imports	5.793	5.334	6.144	5.944	5.997	7.263	**7.2**
from U.S.	0.897	0.620	0.708	0.728	0.881	0.819	0.942
CurAccount	−1.612	−0.968	−1.748	−1.265	−1.294	−1.317	**−1.1**

[a] New Zealand is the **40th** largest U.S. trading partner.

Foreign minister: Doug McKinnon
1989 Freedom House Index (1 is highest, 7 is lowest):
    Political freedom: 1
    Civil liberties: 1
1989 voting with U.S. at U.N.: 40.2%
FY 1989 U.S. foreign assistance (actual obligations):
    Economic: None
    Military: None

Economy

Currency: New Zealand dollar, 1 US$ = 1.68 NZ$
Major industries: Food-processing, wood and paper products, textiles, machinery, transport equipment, banking, mining
Major agricultural products: Meat, wool, timber, wheat, dairy
Major imports: Oil and petroleum products, motor vehicles, iron and steel, machinery, electrical equipment
Major exports: Meat, wool, forest products, dairy products, fruits and vegetables, aluminum and alloys, manufactured equipment
Per capita GNP: US$10,000 (1989)

Military

1987/1988 military budget: US$807,000,000
Increase over 1986/1987: 43.8%
Outlay as a share of GNP: 3.2%

As a share of government spending: 5.4%
Total regular forces: 12,800
    Army: 6,000
    Reserves: 9,700
    Navy: 2,600
    Air Force: 4,200
    Combat aircraft: 43
    Naval vessels: 4 frigates, 8 patrol craft
Security alliance with U.S.: ANZUS treaty signatory. In 1985, New Zealand declared it would not allow nuclear-powered or nuclear-armed ships into its ports, effectively terminating the treaty. In 1986, the U.S. declared it would not honor security-obligations to New Zealand due to its anti-nuclear policies
U.S. military installations: None
U.S. military personnel: None
Armed opposition groups: None

Investment

1989 U.S. direct investment: US$1,167,000,000
1989 New Zealand direct investment in the U.S.: US$237,000,000

PAKISTAN

Land

Area: 310,524 square miles
    Cultivated: 20.7%
    Forest: 0.8%
    Pasture: 0.8%
Resources: Natural gas, petroleum, coal, iron ore, copper, salt

Population

1989 estimate: 110,407,000
Annual growth: 2.7%
Life expectancy: 54 years
Literacy: 26%
Infant mortality: 120
Fertility: 6.5
Ethnic divisions: Punjabi 66%, Sindhi 13%, Pushtun 8.5%, Urdu 7.6%
Workforce: 30,500,000
    Unemployment: 3.6%
    Commerce and services: 25.9%
    Agriculture and fishing: 55.4%
    Government and public authorities: 1%
    Manufacturing: 13%
    Construction: 4.7%
Students:
    Primary and secondary: 11,220,000
    University: 550,000

Pakistan: Economic Statistics (billions of US$, percentages where appropriate)[a]

	1982	1983	1984	1985	1986	1987	1988
GDP	29.31	30.61	32.59	32.41	34.89	35.55	38.4
Growth	6.2%	6.4%	5.3%	8.0%	7.5%	7.7%	2.4%
CPI rise	5.9%	6.4%	6.1%	5.6%	3.5%	4.7%	**7.0%**
Exports	2.402	3.075	2.559	2.738	3.383	4.168	**4.30**
to U.S.	0.181	0.183	0.268	0.299	0.353	0.438	0.461
Imports	5.460	5.326	5.852	5.889	5.363	5.819	**6.50**
from U.S.	0.700	0.812	1.093	1.042	0.830	0.733	1.093
CurAccount	−0.802	0.025	−1.195	−1.080	−0.645	−0.554	**−1.6**

[a] Pakistan is a minor U.S. trading partner.

Political

Official name: Islamic Republic of Pakistan
Type of government: Federal Republic
Name of chief of state: President Ghulam Ishaq Khan
Head of government: Prime Minister Nawaz Sharif
Foreign minister: Mian Mohammad Nawaz Sharif
1989 Freedom House Index (1 is highest, 7 is lowest):
  Political freedom: 3
  Civil liberties: 3
1989 voting with U.S. at U.N.: 8.94%
FY 1989 U.S. foreign assistance (actual obligations):
  Economic: US$352,126,000
  Military: US$230,915,000

Economy

Currency: Rupee, 1 US$ = 21.4 Rupees
Major industries: Cotton textiles, steel, food-processing, tobacco, chemicals, natural gas, mining, fertilizer
Major agricultural products: Rice, wheat, cotton, sugarcane
Major imports: Petroleum, cooking oil, defense equipment
Major exports: Sporting goods, rice, cotton, textiles, carpets
Per capita GNP: US$360 (1989)

Military

1988/1989 military budget: US$2,240,000,000
Increase over 1987/1988: 8.3%
Outlay as a share of GNP: 5.8%
As a share of government spending: 27.6%
Total regular forces: 483,600
  Army: 450,000
  Reserves: 513,000
  Navy: 16,000
  Air Force: 17,600
  Combat aircraft: 341
  Naval vessels: 6 attack submarines, 2 midget submarines, 8 destroyers, 8 fast-attack craft (missile), 4 fast-attack craft (torpedo), 4 coastal patrol craft, 13 inshore patrol craft, 3 minesweepers
Security alliance with U.S.: None
U.S. military installations: None
U.S. military personnel: None
Armed opposition groups: None

Investment

1989 U.S. direct investment: US$190,000,000
1989 Pakistani direct investment in the U.S: US$21,000,000

PAPUA NEW GUINEA

Land

Area: 178,704 square miles
  Cultivated: 3%
  Forest: 78%
  Pasture: 2%
Resources: Gold, copper, silver, gas, timber

Population

1989 estimate: 3,736,000
Annual growth: 2.3%
Life expectancy: 54 years
Literacy: 32%
Infant mortality: 97
Fertility: 5.1
Ethnic divisions: Papuan, Melanesian, Negrito, Micronesian, Polynesian
Workforce: 1,892,000
  Unemployment: NA
  Commerce and services: 10.5%
  Agriculture and fishing: 77%
  Government and public authorities: 7%
  Manufacturing: 2.5%
  Construction: 3%
Students:
  Primary and secondary: 437,400
  University: 5,000

Papua New Guinea: Economic Statistics (billions of US$, percentages where appropriate) [a]

	1982	1983	1984	1985	1986	1987	1988
GDP	2.27	2.22	2.35	2.19	2.43	2.46	2.47
Growth	0.4%	3.4%	0.5%	4.4%	3.3%	2.9%	0.5%
CPI rise	5.5%	7.9%	7.4%	5.7%	5.2%	3.0%	**4.9%**
Exports	0.773	0.822	0.894	0.918	1.048	1.172	**1.34**
to U.S.	0.019	0.027	0.029	0.036	0.048	0.024	**0.026**
Imports	1.018	0.975	0.845	0.788	0.844	1.055	**1.29**
from U.S.	0.066	0.084	0.053	0.041	0.051	0.051	**0.073**
CurAccount	−0.483	−0.383	−0.345	−0.164	−0.101	−0.325	**−0.47**

[a] Papua New Guinea is a minor U.S. trading partner.

Political

Official name: Papua New Guinea
Type of government: Parliamentary Democracy with Commonwealth
Chief of state: Queen Elizabeth II
Head of government: Prime Minister Rabbie Namaliu
Foreign minister: Michael Somare
1989 Freedom House Index (1 is highest, 7 is lowest):
  Political freedom: 2
  Civil liberties: 2
1989 voting with U.S. at U.N.: 15.9%
FY 1989 U.S. foreign assistance (actual obligations:)
  Economic: US$1,788,000
  Military: US$50,000

Economy

Currency: Kina, 1 US$ = 0.86 Kina
Major industries: Wood products, copper-mining, fish-canning, construction, food-processing, tourism
Major agricultural products: Coffee, cocoa, copra, palm oil, timber, tea, rubber
Major imports: Machinery, fuels, food, chemicals
Major exports: Gold, copper, coffee, palm oil, logs, cocoa
Per capita GNP: US$800 (1989)

Military

1986 military budget: US$34,450,000
Increase over 1985: 0.4%
Outlay as a share of GNP: 1.4%
As a share of government spending: 3.3%
Total regular forces: 3,200
  Army: 2,900
  Reserves: 0
  Navy: 200
  Air Force: 100
  Combat aircraft: None
  Naval vessels: 5 inshore patrol craft
Security alliance with U.S.: None
U.S. military installations: None
U.S. military personnel: None
Australian military personnel: 100 engineers and advisers
Armed opposition groups: None

Investment

1989 U.S. direct investment: US$181,000,000
1989 Papuan direct investment in the U.S.: NA

THE PHILIPPINES

Land

Area: 115,831 square miles
  Cultivated: 39.1%
  Forest: 37%
  Pasture: 4%

Resources: Timber, petroleum, nickel, iron, cobalt, silver, gold

Population

1989 estimate: 64,907,000
Annual growth: 2.7%
Life expectancy: 66 years
Literacy: 88%
Infant mortality: 48
Fertility: 4.6
Ethnic divisions: Christian Malay 91.5%, Muslim Malay 4%, Chinese 1.5%
Workforce: 23,690,000
  Unemployment: 10.6
  Commerce and services: 37.9%
  Agriculture and fishing: 49%
  Government and public authorities: 10%
  Manufacturing: 9.7%
  Construction: 3.4%
Students:
  Primary and secondary: 13,430,000
  University: 2,050,000

Political

Official name: Republic of the Philippines
Type of government: Republic
Chief of state: President Corazon Aquino
Head of government: Same
Foreign minister: Raul Manglapus

Philippines: Economic Statistics (billions of US$, percentages where appropriate)[a]

	1982	1983	1984	1985	1986	1987	1988
GDP	36.28	34.08	31.58	32.12	32.13	32.70	33.32
Growth	2.9%	0.9%	−6.0%	5.3%	−7.7%	5.1%	1.9%
CPI rise	10.2%	10.0%	50.3%	23.1%	0.77%	3.8%	**8.0%**
Exports	5.020	4.932	5.343	4.614	4.807	5.696	**6.67**
to U.S.	1.956	2.160	2.622	2.334	2.150	2.481	2.7
Imports	8.263	7.863	6.262	5.351	5.211	6.937	**7.80**
from U.S.	1.854	1.807	2.766	1.379	1.363	1.5999	1.9
CurAccount	−3.21	−2.751	−1.268	−0.018	0.996	−0.539	**−0.7**

[a] The Philippines are the **26th** largest U.S. trading partner.

**1989 Freedom House Index (1 is
highest, 7 is lowest):**
    Political freedom: 2
    Civil liberties: 3
1989 voting with U.S. at U.N.:
    13.7%
**FY 1989 U.S. foreign assistance
(actual obligations:)**
    Economic: US$366,518,000
    Military: US$127,600,000

Economy

Currency: Philippine Peso, 1 US$ =
22.44 Peaos
Major industries: Textiles,
pharmaceuticals, wood products,
food-processing, electronics,
chemicals, oil products
Major agricultural products: Rice,
coconut, sugarcane, corn, bananas,
abaca, tobacco, pineapples
Major imports: Petroleum,
industrial equipment, wheat
Major exports: Sugar, lumber,
bananas, garments, nickel,
electrical components
Per capita GNP: US$620 (1989)

Military

1988 military budget:
    US$532,120,000
Increase over 1987: −26.6%
Outlay as a share of GNP: 1.6%
**As a share of government
spending:** 9.1%

Total regular forces: 147,500
(including constabulary)
    Army: 65,000
    Reserves: 48,000
    Navy: 23,000
    Air Force: 16,000
    Combat aircraft: 62
    Naval vessels: 3 frigates, 10
    offshore patrol craft, 2 coastal
    patrol craft, 39 inshore patrol
    craft
Security alliance with U.S.: U.S.–
Philippine Mutual Defense
Treaties: 1957, 1983
U.S. military installations: Subic
Bay Naval and Airbase, Clark Field
Airbase
U.S. military personnel: 5,900
Navy, 1,200 Marines, 9,300 Air
Force
Australian military personnel:
Small number of advisers
Armed opposition groups: Moro
National Liberation Front, 15,000;
Moro Islamic Liberation Front
(breakaway from MNLF), 2,900;
New People's Army, 25,500

Investment

1989 U.S. direct investment:
    US$1,682,000,000
**1989 Philippine direct investment
in the U.S.:** US$158,000,000

Singapore

Land

Area: 239 square miles
    Cultivated: 9.5%
    Forest: 4.6%
    Pasture: 0%
Resources: None

Population

1989 estimate: 2,674,000
Annual growth: 1.1%
Life expectancy: 74 years
Literacy: 87%
Infant mortality: 9
Fertility: 1.6
Ethnic divisions: Chinese 76.4%,
Malay 14.9%, Indian 6.4%
Workforce: 1,277,000
    Unemployment: 3.3%
    Commerce and services: 60%
    Agriculture and fishing: 0.8%
    **Government and public
    authorities:** 15%
    Manufacturing: 20%
    Construction: 5%
Students:
    Primary and secondary:
    463,000
    University: 44,800

Singapore: Economic Statistics (billions of US$, percentages where appropriate)[a]							
	1982	*1983*	*1984*	*1985*	*1986*	*1987*	*1988*
GDP	14.85	17.30	19.13	18.33	19.26	20.72	23.31
Growth	6.9%	8.2%	8.3%	−1.6%	1.7%	8.8%	7.5%
CPI rise	3.9%	1.2%	2.6%	0.5%	−1.4%	0.5%	**1.4%**
Exports	10.787	21.832	24.070	22.812	22.497	28.596	**38.0**
to U.S.	2.274	2.969	4.121	4.412	4.884	6.395	8.0
Imports	28.176	25.158	28.667	26.237	25.513	34.498	**42.0**
from U.S.	3.214	3.759	3.675	3.476	3.380	4.053	5.8
CurAccount	−1.296	−0.610	−0.385	−0.004	0.542	0.539	**1.0**

[a] Singapore is the **12th** largest U.S. trading partner.

Political

Official name: Republic of
Singapore
Type of government: One-Party
Dominant Republic
Chief of state: President Wee
KimWee
Head of government: Prime
Minister Goh Chok Tong
Foreign minister: S. Dhanabalan
**1989 Freedom House Index (1 is
highest, 7 is lowest):**
    Political freedom: 4
    Civil liberties: 4
1989 voting with U.S. at U.N.:
14.6%
**FY 1989 U.S. foreign assistance
(actual obligations):**
    Economic: None
    Military: US$50,000

Economy

Currency: Singapore dollar, 1 US$
= 1.90 S$
Major industries: Petroleum-
refining, rubber-processing,
electronics, food-processing, ship
repair, garments
Major agricultural products: Hogs,
poultry, orchids, vegetables
Major imports: Capital equipment,
manufactured goods, crude oil,
transport equipment, consumer
goods
Major exports: Machinery,
manufactured goods, transport

equipment, petroleum, rubber,
electronics
Per capita GNP: US$9,000 (1989)

Military

1986 military budget:
    US$1,130,000,000
Increase over 1985: 9.7%
Outlay as a share of GNP: 5.4%
**As a share of government
spending:** 21%
Total regular forces: 55,500
    Army: 45,000
    Reserves: 212,0000
    Navy: 4,500
    Air Force: 6,000
    Combat aircraft: 187
    Naval vessels: 6 fast-attack craft
    (missile), 20 inshore patrol
    craft, 2 minesweepers
Security alliance with U.S.: None,
although U.S. and Singaporean
forces periodically exercise together
U.S. military installations: None
U.S. military personnel: None
Foreign military personnel:
Australia—50 Army, some RAAF,
small number of advisers; New
Zealand—730 Army
Armed opposition groups: None

Investment

1989 U.S. direct investment:
    US$2,213,000,000
1989 Singaporean direct

investment in the U.S.:
    US$1,216,000,000

SOLOMON ISLANDS

Land

Area: 10,640 square miles
    Cultivated: 2%
    Forest: 93%
    Pasture: 1%
Resources: Timber, marine shells,
phosphates, gold, bauxite

Population

1989 estimate: 324,000
Annual growth: 3.6%
Life expectancy: 68
Literacy: 60%
Infant mortality: 41
Fertility: 6.4
Ethnic divisions: Melanesian 93%,
Polynesian 4%, Micronesian 1.5%,
European 0.8%, Chinese 0.3%
Workforce: 23,448
    Unemployment: NA
    Commerce and services: NA
    Agriculture and fishing: 32.4%
    **Government and public
    authorities:**   NA
    Manufacturing: 3%
    Construction: 3%
Students: NA

Solomon Islands: Economic Statistics (millions of US$, percentages where appropriate)[a]

	1982	1983	1984	1985	1986	1987	1988
GDP	153.99	123.11	151.99	130.40	149.0	123.0	128.0
Growth	**6.4%**	**6.4%**	**6.4%**	**6.4%**	**6.4%**	**6.4%**	4.0%
CPI rise	13.0%	6.2%	11.0%	9.6%	13.6%	NA	NA
Exports	57.278	62.159	89.780	69.819	63.351	62.695	NA
to U.S.	0.540	6.981	1.052	1.676	0.043	0.005	NA
Imports	57.654	61.892	65.589	69.224	60.932	67.172	NA
from U.S.	3.180	2.480	2.188	1.442	2.328	0.336	NA
CurAccount	−10.5	−5.8	5.3	−18.9	NA	NA	NA

[a] The Solomon Islands are a minor U.S. trading partner.

Political

Official name: Solomon Islands
Type of government:
Parliamentary democracy
Chief of state: Queen Elizabeth II
Head of government: Prime
Minister Solomon Mamaloni
Foreign minister: Paul Tovua
**1989 Freedom House Index (1 is
highest, 7 is lowest):**
Political freedom: 1
Civil liberties: 1
**1989 voting with U.S. at
U.N.:** 14.9%
**FY 1989 U.S. foreign assistance
(actual obligations):**
Economic: US$1,269,000
Military: US$30,000

Economy

Currency: Solomon Island dollar, 1
US$ = 2.1 SI$
Major industries: Fish-canning,
palm products, rice-milling, wood
products, furniture, garments,
handicrafts, boatbuilding
Major agricultural products: Fish,
coconuts, timber, yams, taro
Major imports: Transport
equipment, foodstuffs, mineral
fuels, manufactured goods,
chemicals
Major exports: Fish, timber, copra,
palm oil, seashells
Per capita GNP: US$400 (1989)

Military

1987/1988 military budget: NA
Increase over 1986/1987: NA
Outlay as a share of GNP: NA
**As a share of government
spending:** NA
Total regular forces: NA
Army: NA
Reserves: NA
Navy: NA
Air Force: NA
Combat aircraft: NA
Naval vessels: NA
Security alliance with U.S.: None
U.S. military installations: None
U.S. military personnel: None
Australian military personnel:
Small number of advisers
Armed opposition groups: None

Investment

1989 U.S. direct investment: NA
**1989 Solomon Islands direct
investment in the U.S.:** NA

SRI LANKA

Land

Area: 25,332 square miles
Cultivated: 35.7%
Forest: 44.2%
Pasture: 6.5%
Resources: Limestone, graphite,
mineral sands, gems,
phosphates

Population

1989 estimate: 16,881,000
Annual growth: 1.5%
Life expectancy: 69 years
Literacy: 87%
Infant mortality: 31
Fertility: 2.4
Ethnic divisions: Sinhalese 74%,
Tamil 18%, Moor 7%, Burger,
Malay, Veddha 1%
Workforce: 7,000,000
Unemployment: 21%
Commerce and services:
26.3%
Agriculture and fishing: 45.9%
**Government and public
authorities:**   NA
Manufacturing: 13.3%
Construction: 5%
Students:
Primary and secondary:
3,950,000
University: 20,000

Political

Official name: Democratic Socialist
Republic of Sri Lanka
Type of government: Republic
Chief of state: President Ransinghe
Premadasa
Head of government: Same
Foreign minister: Rangan Wijeratne
**1989 Freedom House Index (1 is
highest, 7 is lowest):**
Political freedom: 4
Civil liberties: 5

Sri Lanka: Economic Statistics (billions of US$, percentages where appropriate)[a]

	1982	1983	1984	1985	1986	1987	1988
GDP	4.82	5.14	5.87	5.95	6.30	6.63	6.82
Growth	5.1%	5.0%	4.1%	5.3%	4.5%	1.5%	2.9%
CPI rise	10.8%	14.0%	16.6%	1.5%	8.0%	7.7%	**12.0%**
Exports	0.996	1.054	1.436	1.265	1.162	1.364	**1.5**
to U.S.	0.195	0.206	0.302	0.313	0.376	0.417	0.424
Imports	1.773	1.795	1.846	1.832	1.829	2.124	2.1
from U.S.	0.198	0.075	0.092	0.073	0.066	0.077	0.123
CurAccount	−0.549	−0.466	0.001	−0.419	−0.412	**−0.36**	**0.35**

[a] Sri Lanka is a minor U.S. trading partner.

1989 voting with U.S. at U.N.:
12.1%
**FY 1989 U.S. foreign assistance
(actual obligations):**
Economic: US$70,199,000
Military: US$160,000

Economy

Currency: Sri Lankan Rupee, 1 US$
= 39.88 Rupees
Major industries: Rubber, consumer
goods, textiles, garments, tea and
coconut processing, oil products
Major agricultural products: Tea,
rice, rubber, coconuts, spices
Major imports: Petroleum,
machinery, transport equipment,
sugar, textiles, rice, wheat,
electrical machinery
Major exports: Tea, rubber,
petroleum products, textiles,
coconuts, gems and jewelry,
marine products
Per capita GNP: US$415 (1989)

Military

1988 military budget:
US$583,290,000
Increase over 1987: 2.1%
Outlay as a share of GNP: 8.6%
**As a share of government
spending:** 12.8%
Total regular forces: 49,200
Army: 40,000
Reserves: 25,000
Navy: 5,500

Air Force: 3,700
Combat aircraft: 6
Naval vessels: 2 coastal patrol
craft, 34 inshore patrol craft
Security alliance with U.S.: None
U.S. military installations: None
U.S. military personnel: None
Indian military personnel: 53,000
Indian Peace-Keeping Force
Armed opposition groups:
Liberation Tigers of Tamil Eelam,
7,500 (prior to arrival of IPKF);
remnants of other Tamil groups
include—Tamil Eelam Liberation
Organization and Eelam
Revolutionary Organization of
Students (strength unknown);
Janatha Vimmukthi Peramura
(Sinhalese extremist group,
strength unknown)

Investment

1989 U.S. direct investment:
US$13,000,000
**1989 Sri Lankan direct investment
in the U.S.:** none

THAILAND

Land

Area: 198,500 square miles
Cultivated: 38%
Forest: 29%
Pasture: 1%

Resources: Tin, rubber, natural gas,
tungsten, tantalum, timber,

Population

1989 estimate: 55,524,000
Annual growth: 1.7%
Life expectancy: 65 years
Literacy: 82%
Infant mortality: 50
Fertility: 2.7
Ethnic divisions: Thai 75%,
Chinese 14%, Other 11%
Workforce: 29,553,000
Unemployment: 6.4%
Commerce and services:
19.3%
Agriculture and fishing: 61.1%
Government and public
authorities: 5.3%
Manufacturing: 8.3%
Construction: 2.0%
Students:
Primary and secondary:
9,100,000
University: 180,600

Political

Official name: Kingdom of Thailand
Type of government:
Constitutional monarchy
Chief of state: King Bhumibol
Adulyadej (Rama IX)
Head of government: Prime
Minister Anand Panyarachoon
Foreign minister: Arsa Sarasin

Thailand: Economic Statistics (billions of US$, percentages where appropriate)[a]

	1982	1983	1984	1985	1986	1987	1988
GDP	35.64	39.11	40.49	36.83	41.37	44.31	46.1
Growth	4.1%	5.9%	5.5%	3.2%	3.5%	6.3%	4.0%
CPI rise	5.3%	3.7%	0.9%	2.42%	1.85%	2.5%	9.0%
Exports	6.935	6.368	7.414	7.122	8.864	11.302	15.8
to U.S.	0.956	1.035	1.426	1.543	1.873	2.387	3.2
Imports	8.532	10.283	10.415	9.260	9.166	13.003	19.5
from U.S.	0.915	1.063	1.113	0.849	0.936	1.544	2.0
CurAccount	−1.003	−2.874	−2.109	−1.537	0.247	−0.530	−1.7

[a] Thailand is the **25th** largest U.S. trading partner.

1989 Freedom House Index (1 is highest, 7 is lowest):
  Political freedom: 2
  Civil liberties: 3
1989 voting with U.S. at U.N.: 14.1%
FY 1989 U.S. foreign assistance (actual obligations):
  Economic: US$28,082,000
  Military: US$24,200,000

Economy

Currency: Baht, 1 US$ = 25.69 Baht
Major industries: Agricultural processing, textiles and garments, wood, cement, mining, light manufactures, tourism, tobacco
Major agricultural products: Rice, sugarcane, corn, rubber, tobacco, cassava
Major imports: Machinery and transport equipment, fuels and lubricants, base metals, chemicals and fertilizers
Major exports: Rice, sugar, corn, rubber, tin, tapioca, textiles and garments, integrated circuits, canned seafood, fruits
Per capita GNP: US$1,800 (1989)

Military

1987/1988 military budget: US$1,740,000,000
Increase over 1986/1987: 10.8%
Outlay as a share of GNP: 4.5%

As a share of government spending: 15.5%
Total regular forces: 256,000
  Army: 166,000
  Reserves: 500,000
  Navy: 42,000
  Air Force: 48,000
  Combat aircraft: 165
  Naval vessels: 5 frigates, 2 corvettes, 6 fast-attack craft (missile), 1 offshore patrol craft, 14 coastal patrol craft, 30 inshore patrol craft, 7 minesweepers
Security alliance with U.S.: Informal Rusk–Thanat Communique of 1962, U.S. and Thai forces also participate in annual military exercises
U.S. military installations: None
U.S. military personnel: None
Australian military personnel: Small number of advisers
Armed opposition groups: Communist Party of Thailand: 600; Thai People's Revolutionary Movement: 1,500 (claimed); Patani United Liberation Organization and Barisan Revolusi Nasional (Islamic): 400

Investment

1989 U.S. direct investment: US$1,279,000,000
1989 Thai direct investment in the U.S.: US$71,000,000

VANUATU

Land

Area: 4,707 square miles
  Cultivated: 6%
  Forest: 1%
  Pasture: 2%
Resources: Manganese, hardwood, cattle, fish

Population

1989 estimate: 160,000
Annual growth: 3.2%
Life expectancy: 69
Literacy: 15%
Infant mortality: 39
Fertility: 5.6
Ethnic divisions: Melanesian 90%, French 8%, Other 2%
Workforce: NA
  Unemployment: NA
  Commerce and services: NA
  Agriculture and fishing: NA
  Government and public authorities: NA
  Manufacturing: NA
  Construction: NA
Students: NA

Political

Official name: Republic of Vanuatu
Type of government: Republic
Chief of state: President Fred Timakata

Vanuatu: Economic Statistics (millions of US$, percentages where appropriate)[a]

	1982	1983	1984	1985	1986	1987	1988
GDP	NA	NA	79.0	NA	NA	89.0	88.0
Growth	NA	NA	2.0%	5.0%	NA	NA	−1.0%
CPI rise	6.2%	1.7%	5.5%	1.0%	4.8%	NA	NA
Exports	22.87	29.60	43.30	36.06	30.38	31.70	NA
to U.S.	5.83	5.39	NA	NA	NA	0.09	NA
Imports	58.85	63.96	61.59	65.81	70.55	95.44	NA
from U.S.	0.60	0.52	NA	NA	NA	NA	NA
CurAccount	11.8	8.4	19.3	1.3	−2.8	NA	NA

[a] Vanuatu is a minor U.S. trading partner.

Head of government: Prime Minister Walter Lini
Foreign minister: Daniel Kalpokas
1989 Freedom House Index (1 is highest, 7 is lowest):
Political freedom: 2
Civil liberties: 3
1989 voting with U.S. at U.N.: 11.0%
FY 1989 U.S. foreign assistance (actual obligations):
Economic: None
Military: None

Economy

Currency: Australian dollar, 1 US$ = 1.263 A$
Major industries: Fish-freezing, canneries, tourism
Major agricultural products: Copra, cocoa, coffee, taro, yams, coconuts, fruits, vegetables
Major imports: Food, consumer goods, machinery, transport equipment, fuels
Major exports: Copra, frozen fish, meat
Per capita GNP: US$750 (1989)

Military

Vanuatu maintains no armed forces
Security alliance with U.S.: None
U.S. military installations: None
U.S. military personnel: None

Australian military personnel: Small number of advisers
Armed opposition groups: None

Investment

1989 U.S. direct investment: NA
1989 Vanuatan direct investment in the U.S.: less than US$ 500,000

VIETNAM

Land

Area: 127,207 square miles
Cultivated: 20%
Forest: 31.3%
Pasture: 14.8%
Resources: Phosphates, coal, manganese, bauxite, apatite, chromite

Population

1989 estimate: 66,820,000
Annual growth: 2.5%
Life expectancy: 64
Literacy: 78%
Infant mortality: 51
Fertility: 4.3
Ethnic divisions: Vietnamese 85%, Chinese 3%, Muong, Thai, Meo, Khmer, Man, Cham 10%
Workforce: 34,000,000
Unemployment: NA
Commerce and services: 5%
Agriculture and fishing: 73%

Government and public authorities: NA
Manufacturing: 14%
Construction: NA
Students: NA

Political

Official name: Socialist Republic of Vietnam
Type of government: Communist state
Name of chief of state: Secretary General Nguyen Van Linh
Head of government: Prime Minister Do Moui
Foreign minister: Nguyen Co Thach
1989 Freedom House Index (1 is highest, 7 is lowest):
Political freedom: 6
Civil liberties: 7
1989 voting with U.S. at U.N.: 9.9%
FY 1989 U.S. foreign assistance (actual obligations):
Economic: None
Military: None

Economy

Currency: Dong, 1 US$ = 4,500 Dong
Major industries: food-processing, textiles, machine-building, mining, cement, chemical fertilizer, glass, tires

Vietnam: Economic Statistics (billions of US$, percentages where appropriate)[a]

	1982	1983	1984	1985	1986	1987	1988
GDP	NA	NA	8900.0	NA	NA	1279.0	1292.0
Growth	NA	NA	NA	NA	NA	NA	1.0%
CPI rise	NA	NA	NA	NA	1000.0%	1000.0%	**800.0%**
Exports	209.8	235.1	269.2	331.9	324.2	403.2	**700.0**
to U.S.	0.0	0.0	0.1	0.0	0.2	0.0	NA
Imports	512.6	489.4	595.3	642.9	634.2	640.2	NA
from U.S.[b]	35.3	22.8	24.3	20.2	30.0	23.4	NA
CurAccount	NA	NA	NA	−1111.0	NA	NA	−800.0

[a] Vietnam is not a U.S. trading partner.
[b] "Imports" from U.S. are mostly remittances sent to relatives.

Major agricultural products: Rice, rubber, fruits and vegetables, corn, sugarcane, cassava, coffee

Major imports: Petroleum, steel, railroad equipment, chemicals, medicines, military equipment, wheat, corn, fertilizer

Major exports: Agricultural and handicraft products, coal, ores

Per capita GNP: US$200 (1989)

Military

1987/1988 military budget: NA

Increase over 1986/1987: NA

Outlay as a share of GNP: 20.0%

As a share of government spending: NA

Total regular forces: 1,245,000

    Army: 1,100,000

    Reserves: 3,000,000

    Navy: 33,000

    Air Force: 112,000

    Combat aircraft: 250

    Naval vessels: 7 frigates, 8 fast-attack craft (missile), 21 fast-attack craft (torpedo), 2 offshore patrol craft, 31 inshore patrol craft, 5 minesweepers

Security alliance with U.S.: None

U.S. military installations: None

Soviet military installations: Airbase at Da Nang, air and naval base at Cam Ranh Bay

Soviet military personnel: 2,500 advisers and troops

Armed opposition groups: United Front for the Liberation of the Oppressed Races, 2,500; another 22,500 including—National Salvation Movement and remnants of the Army of the Republic of Vietnam (Hoa Hao)

Investment

1988 U.S. direct investment: less than US$ 500,000

1989 Vietnamese direct investment in the U.S.: None

WESTERN SAMOA

Land

Area: 1,133 square miles

    Cultivated: 24%

    Forest: 47%

    Pasture: 0%

Resources: Hardwood, fish, copra, cocoa

Population

1989 estimate: 182,000

Annual growth: 2.2%

Life expectancy: 66 years

Literacy: 90%

Infant mortality: 48

Fertility: 4.8

Ethnic divisions: Samoan 88%, Euronesian 10%, Other 2%

Workforce: 37,000

Unemployment: NA

Commerce and services: NA

Agriculture and fishing: 59.4%

Government and public authorities: NA

Manufacturing: NA

Construction: NA

Students: NA

Political

Official name: Independent State of Western Samoa

Type of government: Constitutional monarchy under native chief

Name of chief of state: King Malietoa Tanumafili II

Head of government: Prime Minister Tofilau Eti

Foreign minister: Same

1989 Freedom House Index (1 is highest, 7 is lowest):

    Political freedom: 2

    Civil liberties: 2

1989 voting with U.S. at U.N.: 22.0%

FY 1989 U.S. foreign assistance (actual obligations):

    Economic: US$1,129,000

    Military: None

Economy

Currency: Western Samoan Tala, 1 US$ = 2.2 WS Tala

Major industries: Timber, tourism, light industry, fishing

Western Samoa: Economic Statistics (millions of US$, percentages where appropriate)[a]

	1982	1983	1984	1985	1986	1987	1988
GDP	NA	NA	NA	86.8	93.0	94.0	96.0
Growth	−1.0%	0.5%	NA	NA	NA	NA	2.0%
CPI rise	18.3%	16.5%	11.9%	9.1%	5.7%	4.6%	NA
Exports	13.33	16.78	22.02	27.26	10.49	11.08	NA
to U.S.	3.73	5.52	6.00	16.19	1.02	1.88	NA
Imports	49.77	48.37	68.07	54.15	48.50	67.94	NA
from U.S.	4.83	5.37	3.96	1.98	2.31	2.86	NA
CurAccount	−6.62	3.51	0.68	1.86	6.64	6.29	NA

[a] Western Samoa is a minor U.S. trading partner.

Major agricultural products:
Cocoa, bananas, copra, coconuts
Major imports: Food, manufactured
goods, machinery, fuel
Major exports: Cocoa, timber,
mineral fuel, bananas, cocoa
Per capita GNP: US$550
(1989)

Military

1987/1988 military budget: NA
Increase over 1986/1987: NA
Outlay as a share of GNP: 1.0%

**As a share of government
spending:** NA
Total regular forces: NA
 Army: NA
 Reserves: NA
 Navy: NA
 Air Force: NA
 Combat aircraft: NA
 Naval vessels: NA
Security alliance with U.S.: None
U.S. military installations: None
U.S. military personnel: None
Australian military personnel:
Small number of advisers
Armed opposition groups: None

Investment

1989 U.S. direct investment:
US$1,000,000
**1989 Western Samoan direct
investment in the U.S.:** NA
*Source: U.S. and Asia Statistical
Handbook,* 1989 Edition and 1990
Edition compiled and edited by
Thomas J. Timmons, The Heritage
Foundation, Asian Studies Center.

APPENDIX B

ASIAN INVESTMENT GUIDE 1991

Compiled by *Asian Business* Magazine, Far East Trade Press Ltd., Hong Kong

STOCKS

RULES AND REGULATIONS

Hong Kong

The Hong Kong Stock Exchange is probably the Asian market most open to foreigners. There are no restrictions on the amount or kind of stock foreign investors can own. Several of the major Hong Kong companies quoted are also listed on exchanges outside Hong Kong.

Taxation: Foreigners are not subject to tax on any Hong Kong dividends they receive. There is no tax on capital gains, nor is investment in Hong Kong securities subject to income tax.

Indonesia

The Jakarta Stock Exchange has taken off dramatically in the past year, with the index rocketing to unexpected highs, only to slump again after Saddam Hussein's invasion of Kuwait.

Foreigners may now own shares in all quoted stocks on the exchange except banking stocks, although foreign ownership of equity is limited to a maximum of 49% for most securities.

An over-the-counter market with simpler listing requirements began trading a year ago, but is almost inactive.

The government is working to tighten laws protecting investors against fraud, a major criticism in the past. It is also encouraging the establishment of stock exchanges in cities other than Jakarta.

Taxation: Under most circumstances, there is no capital gains tax or income tax liability stemming from the sale of Indonesian securities by foreign individuals or funds. But foreigners are subject to a 20% withholding tax on dividends, which is deducted by the Indonesian company.

Japan

Most of the legal restrictions and limitations on foreign ownership of Japanese stocks have been eased, so foreign access to the equity markets is relatively free.

Exceptions are a 20% ceiling on foreign ownership in broadcasting companies (limited to 20%) and a bar on nonresidents owning any shares in the two major telephone companies, Kokusai Denshin Denwa (KDD) and Nippon Telegraph & Telephone (NTT).

Taxation: The standard withholding tax rate on dividends and coupons for nonresidents is 20%. But that rate is reduced if Japan has a double-taxation agreement with the foreign national's country of domicile. Among the Asian countries which have signed such agreements with Japan are South Korea, Singapore, and Malaysia. Koreans pay Japanese withholding tax at a rate of 12%, and Singaporeans and Malaysians at 15%. Dividends can be repatriated in full.

Capital gains tax for individuals are either 1% withholding tax on the value of the sale of shares, or 20% of the realized profits.

A securities transfer tax, payable by the seller, is 0.3% of the value of the shares sold.

Malaysia

Generally, there are no restrictions on foreigners buying shares in the Malaysian stock market but certain quoted companies have a maximum limit (usually 30%) which may be held by non-Malaysians.

Malaysian International Shipping Corp	30%
Malaysia Airlines	30%
Public Bank	30%
Syarikat Telekom Malaysia Bhd	25%

In addition, regulations and procedures put into place by the government essentially deny foreign investors access to subscriptions for new listings.

Taxation: There is no tax on capital gains, but interest and dividend income are subject to tax. A non-resident shareholder will receive the full dividend less 36% in tax, with the exception of dividends paid by companies enjoying Ministry of Trade and Industry "pioneer" status. These are tax-exempt.

Malaysia has double taxation agreements on incomes such as dividends, profits and interest with a number of countries, including Japan, South Korea, the Philippines, Singapore and Thailand.

Approval from the Foreign Investment Committee is required under the following conditions: When any single foreign investor or group acquires 15% of the voting rights; when foreign interests acquire 30% in total in the takeover, acquisition or merger of a Malaysian company; and when foreign interests or assets in a company exceed 5 million ringgit (US$1.9 million) in value.

The Philippines

There are two types of common stock available in the Philippines: Class A, which is limited to Philippines citizens; and Class B, which both locals and foreigners can own. Both receive the same dividends and carry the same privileges.

By law, foreigners can buy up to 40% of a company's share capital, usually through B shares. The investment must be reported to the Board of Investments and the Central Bank of the Philippines to facilitate future capital repatriation and profit remittance. If the foreign investor wants to buy more than 40%, prior approval must be obtained from the Board of Investments.

Taxation: For nonresident investors, dividends from a Philippine company are taxed at a 30% withholding rate. Capital gains from the sale or exchange of stock in any domestic company are taxed at various rates.

If the gains are from shares not traded through a local stock exchange and amount to no more than 100,000 pesos (US$4,700), the tax rate is 10%. Above that sum, the rate is 20%. If the shares were listed and traded through a local stock exchange, the tax is 0.025% of the gross selling price.

Singapore

Stocks, bonds and warrants are traded on the Stock Exchange of Singapore (SES). Trading is fully computerized. Investors may buy or sell any shares quoted on the exchange through any broker or securities dealer except for the following shares, which have the foreign ownership limits below.

DBS Bank	40%
G K Goh Securities	49%
Hong Leong Finance	20%
Industrial & Commercial Bank	40%
Kay Hian James Capel	49%
Kim Eng Securities	49%
Neptune Orient Lines	49%
OCBC Bank	40%
Overseas Union Bank	40%
Overseas Union Trust	20%
RMCA Reinsurance	49%
Singapore Aerospace	15%
Singapore Airlines	27%
Singapore Bus Service	20%
Singapore Finance	20%
Singapore Investments and Finance	20%
Singapore Petroleum	49%
Singapore Press Holdings	49%
Singapore Reinsurance	49%
Singapore Shipbuilding & Engineering	15%
Tat Lee Bank	40%
Tat Lee Finance	20%
United Overseas Bank	40%
United Overseas Finance	20%
United Overseas Insurance	20%

There are three boards: The SES main board that trades most of the Singapore issues, the Clob International board that trades selected regional stocks, and SESDAQ, which trades in smaller Singapore companies. As of October of last year, there were 164 counters on the main board, 144 on Clob and 17 on SESDAQ.

Market performance is generally measured by the Straits Times Industrial (STI) Index and the SES Composite Index.

Taxation: There is no capital gains tax, nor are there any foreign exchange controls. Dividend income is subject to a 31% withholding tax.

South Korea

The interpretation of the timetable on direct foreign investment in the Korean securities market is disputed, and under current policy foreigners seem unlikely to be allowed to buy equities before at least 1993–94.

Three other avenues of investment exist for foreigners: Funds (see Unit Trusts section), convertible bonds, and warrants.

Convertible Bonds

	Premiums at 30/9/90
Samsung	29.8%
Daewoo Heavy	18.2%
Yukong	54.3%
Goldstar	90.2%
Saehan Media	127.4%
STC	356.0%
Dong Ah Construction	127.7%
Samick	156.2%
Miwon Co	121.2%
Sunkyong Ind	30.9%

Warrants

Sammi Steel	399.8%
Hyundai Motor	348.7%

Taxation: Sales of Korean securities by a non-resident of Korea to another non-resident are subject to a capital gains tax of either 10.75% of the sale price, or 26.875% of the capital gains, whichever is lower.

With some countries, Korea has tax treaties that void this capital gains liability but in any case payment has not been actively sought out in the past, and there does not appear to be a practical way for the government to enforce collection.

Dividends paid out in either cash or shares to a non-resident are also subject to a withholding tax of 26.875% unless they are reduced by an applicable tax treaty. Korea has tax treaties with many countries.

The seller is obliged to pay a securities transation tax of 0.2% on sales proceeds stemming from sales of shares in Korea. No tax is paid if the share price is below par.

Taiwan

The dramatic crash in the Stock Exchange of Taiwan (SET) index, which knocked 80% off the value of the index in the six months to October 1990, prompted the Taiwanese government to open the stock market to foreign institutional investment.

The sudden implementation of the new measures owes much to finance minister Wang Chienshien's personal initiative, designed to deflect criticism that the government was doing nothing to stem the stock exchange crash.

As the proposals currently stand, foreign fund managers, banks and insurance companies, if they have more than US$3 billion of assets and have been in operation for at least five years, may apply to invest between US$5 million and US$50 million in the Taiwan market. Once proof has been forwarded to the SEC in Taipei and the application has been approved, the investor must remit the money to Taiwan within three months.

What this means for individual investors is not clear. While the Ministry of Finance takes a distinctly positive attitude to the possibility of transactions, the Central Bank has been more negative. Therefore, at the present stage, it seems unlikely that foreign institutions would risk displeasing the authorities by accommodating individual foreign investors.

Another avenue for investment is the four mutual funds. These are listed in the Unit Trusts section of this guide (see p. 672).

Thailand

For foreigners, investing in the Thai Stock Exchange is complicated and frustrating, though by law many Thai companies may be up to 49% foreign-owned (percentages vary according to sector). But companies themselves often choose to limit foreign ownership further.

Taxation: Foreign individual investors face a 15% withholding tax on dividends. Foreigners are not subject to capital gains tax.

Asian Stock Markets

Country	Index	Index level (Oct 31, 1990)	1991 est price/ earnings ratio
Hong Kong	Hang Seng	3,012	7.5
Indonesia	Composite	469	19.0
Japan	Nikkei	25,242	40.0
Malaysia	Composite	498	17.0
Philippines	Composite	597	10.0
Singapore	ST	1,164	13.0
South Korea	Composite	711	25.0
Taiwan	Market	3,319	21.0
Thailand	SET	673	13.0

USEFUL CONTACTS

Hong Kong

Barings Securities (Hong Kong)., Ltd.
8th Floor
3 Exchange Square
8 Connaught Place
Central
Tel: 8488488
Tlx: 89271 BFES HX
Fax: 8685192

Citicorp Vickers (HK), Ltd.
42nd Floor
1 Exchange Square
8 Connaught Place
Central
Tel: 8435777
Tlx: 74562
Fax: 8459303

James Capel (Far East), Ltd.
39th Floor
2 Exchange Square
Central
Tel: 8439111
Tlx: 75100
Fax: 8107673

Jardine Fleming Securities, Ltd.
46th Floor
Jardine House
Central
Tel: 8438888
Tlx: 75608
Fax: 8105411

Merrill Lynch Int'l Inc.
12th Floor
St. George's Building
2 Ice House St., Central
Tel: 8445678
Tlx: 80120 MLIBK MX
Fax: 8450767

Peregrine Securities, Ltd.
16th Floor
New World Tower
18 Queen's Rd., Central
Tel: 8456111
Tlx: 69251
Fax: 8459411

Schroders Asia Securities (HK)
25th Floor
2 Exchange Square
Central
Tel: 5211636
Tlx: 62162
Fax: 8681023

S G Warburg Securities Far East, Ltd.
20th Floor
Alexandra House
Central
Tel: 5246113
Tlx: 83495
Fax: 8452075

Sun Kung Kai Securities, Ltd.
3rd Floor
Admiralty Centre
18 Harcourt Rd.
Wanchai
Tel: 8225678
Tlx: 74782
Fax: 8225664

WI Carr (Far East), Ltd.
21st Floor
St. George's Building
2 Ice House St., Central
Tel: 5255361
Tlx: 73036
Fax: 8681524

Indonesia

PT Aperdi
Gedung Bursa
3rd Floor
Jakarta
Tel: 353-054

PT Bersepindo Utama
Bldg. TIFA
5th Floor
J1 Kuningan Barat 26
Jakarta
Tel: 511-373

PT Binaartha Parama
7/F Chase Plaza Tower
Jl Jend Sudirman Ka, 21 Jakarta
Tel: 570-4335
Fax: 570-6381
Contact person: Natalia Soebagjo

PT Danatama Makmur
Jl Tanah Abang II No. 71
Jakarta Pusat
Tel: 380-1928/9, 362-173
Fax: 380-0356
Contact person: P. Taylor

PT Eferindo Agung
Gedung Bank Niaga
4th Floor
Jl Thamrin 55, Jakarta
Tel: 332-007
Fax: 333-923

PT Lumbung Persada Khatulistiwa
Gedung Bursa
3rd Floor
No. 14, Jl Merdeka Setatan
Jakarta
Tel: 365-509
Fax: 421-4545

PT Makindo
Gedung Bursa
3rd Floor
No. 14, Jl Merdeka Setatan
Jakarta
Tel: 359-707

PT Murni Segara Lestari
Gedung Bursa
3rd Floor
Jakarta
Tel: 377-149

PT Prima Securities
2001/2002 Landmark Centre I
Jl Sudirman No. 1, Jakarta 12910
Tel: 570-7000/578-0029/578-0035
Tlx: 46281/44895 BTREP IA
Fax: 578-0124
Contact person: Mia A. Djarkasih

Japan

Baring Securities (Japan) Ltd.
Shin-Kasumigaseki Building
3-2 Kasumigaseki 3-chome
Chiyoda-ku, Tokyo 100
Tel: 595-8811
Tlx: 25791
Fax: 593-2634

Citicorp Scrimgeour Vickers International, Ltd.
24th Floor
ARK Mori Building
12-32, Akasaki I-chome, Minato-ku
Tokyo 107
Tel: 2798-5411
Tlx: 28304 CITIJ
Fax: 246-0561

Daiwa Securities
6-4, Ohtemachi 2-chome
Chiyoda-ku, Tokyo 100
Tel: 243-211 1
Tlx: 22411
Fax: 245-0363

DB Capital Markets Asia, Ltd.
22nd Floor
ARK Mori Building
12-3 Akasaka 1-chome
Minato-ku, Tokyo 107
Tel: 589-1986
Tlx: 34943 DBCMP J
Fax: 589-4810

Jardine Fleming Securities, Ltd.
1-7, Uchisaiwaicho 1-chome
Chiyoda-ku, Tokyo 100
Tel: 508-0261
Tlx: 28173 JFTKY J
Fax: 595-1924

Merrill Lynch Japan, Inc.
2, Otemachi,
Chiyoda-ku, Tokyo 100
Tel: 213-7000
Fax: 22952

Nikko Securities
3-1, Marunouchi 3-chome
Chiyoda-ku, Tokyo 100
Tel: 283-2211
Tlx: 22410
Fax: 660-2142

Nippon Kangyo Kakumaru
6-1, Marunouchi I-chome
Chiyoda-ku, Tokyo 100
Tel: 286-7111
Tlx: 24930
Fax: 216-4965

Nomura Securities
9-1, Nihombashi 1-chome
Chuo-ku, Tokyo 103
Tel: 211-1811
Tlx: 22392
Fax: 278-0420

Yamaichi Securities
4-1, Yaesu 2-chome
Chuo-ku, Tokyo 103
Tel: 276-3181
Tlx: 73747
Fax: 529-3667

Arab-Malaysia Securities Sdn Bhd.
ISth Floor
Bangunan Arab-Malaysian
55 Jln Raja Chulan
50200 Kuala Lumpur
Tel: 238-2788
Fax: 238-3162

BBMB Securities Sdn Bhd.
Suite 21, 2nd Floor
Jln Raja Ismail
50250 Kuala Lumpur
Tel: 261-9900
Tlx: 21335
Fax: 261-3087

K&N Kenanga Sdn Bhd.
8th Floor
Pernas International Building
No. 801, Jln Sultan Ismail
50250 Kuala Lumpur
Tel: 261-3066
Tlx: 31070 KEN MA
Fax: 261-4990

Maybank Securities Sdn Bhd.
30th Floor
Menara Maybank
100 Jln Tun Perak
50050 Kuala Lumpur
Tel: 232-3822
Tlx: 20294 MAYSEC MA
Fax: 232-3807

Rashid Hussain Securities Sdn Bhd.
10th Floor
Menara Tun Razak
Jln Raja Laut, 50786
Kuala Lumpur
Tel: 293-4166

Seagroatt & Campbell Sdn Bhd.
Wisma Hamzak-Kwong
Hing
7th Floor
No. I Leboh
Ampang
50100 Kuala Lumpur
Tel: 232-7122
Tlx: MA 32816
SEAGRO
Fax: 232-7420

TA Securities Sdn Bhd.
19th & 20th Floors
UBN Tower
Jln P Ramlee
50250 Kuala Lumpur
Tel: 232-1277
Tlx: 30848 TASEC MA
Fax: 232-2369

UMBC Securities Sdn Bhd.
21st Floor
Bangunan UMBC
Jln Sultan Sulaiman
50000 Kuala Lumpur
Tel: 274-9288
Fax: 274-9907

The following foreign representative offices do substantial research and marketing of Malaysian Stocks:

Antah Jardine Fleming
19th Floor
Pernas International Building
Jln Sultan Ismail
50250 Kuala Lumpur
Tel: 261-8255
Fax: 261-2220

Barings Securities
8th Floor, UBN tower
Jln P Ramlee, 50250
Kuala Lumpur
Tel: 230-4660

Crosby Securities
1208 Pernas International Building
Jln Sultan Ismail
50250 Kuala Lumpur
Tel: 261-0955
Tlx: 21224 CROSMA MA
Fax: 261-9073

GK Goh Securities
9th Floor, UBN Tower
Jln P Ramlee
50250 Kuala Lumpur
Tel: 230-1511
Fax: 230-4939

Morgan Grenfell Asia Securities
10th Floor
UBN Tower
Jln P Ramlee
50250 Kuala Lumpur
Tel: 232-6929
Fax: 232-7026

The Philippines

AEA Development Corp.
151 Legaspi St.
Makati, Metro Manila
Tel: 817-4864

Anscor Capital and Investment Corp.
Asian Plaza 1
Makati, Metro Manila
Tel: 819-3151

Citicorp Investment Philippines
379 Sen Gil J Puyat Ave.
Makati, Metro Manila
Tel: 815-7391

First Metro Investment Corp.
Metrobank Plaza Building
Makati, Metro Manila
Tel: 810-3311/85-99-11

First Pacific Capital Corp.
349 Sen Gil J Puyat Ave.
Makati, Metro Manila
Tel: 818-4084/9111

Manila Equities Corp.
6772 Ayala Ave.
Makati, Metro Manila
Tel: 810-1063

Multinational Investment Bank Corp.
Ayala Ave.
Makati, Metro Manila
Tel: 817-9609/1511

PCI Capital Corp.
Makati Ave.

Makati, Metro Manila
Tel: 817-4527/818-4287/4186/3965

Philippine Pacific Capital Corp.
RCBC Building
Sen Gil J Puyat Ave.
Makati, Metro Manila
Tel: 818-4321

Private Development Corp. of The Philippines
PDCP Building
Ayala Ave.
Makati, Metro Manila
Tel: 810-0231

Singapore

BT Brokerage & Associates Pte Ltd.
20 Collyer Quay
No. 19-QO Tung Centre
Tel: 224-9233

DBS Securities Singapore Pte Ltd.
10 Collyer Quay
No. 27-01 Ocean Building
Tel: 535-9455

Fraser, Roach & Co. Pte Ltd.
10 Collyer Quay
No. 27-01 Ocean Building
Tel: 535-9455

JM Sassoon & Co. Pte Ltd.
I RaMes Place
No. 44-00 OUB Centre
Tel: 535-2888

Keppel Securities Pte Ltd.
15 McCallum St.
No. 03-01/03 NatWest Centre
Tel: 221-5688

Morgan Grenfell Asia & Partners
Securities Pte Ltd.
65 Chulia St.
No. 26-01 OCBC Centre
Tel: 533-1818

OCBC Securities Pte Ltd.
18 Church St., No. 06-00
OCBC Centre South
Tel: 535-2882
Fax: 530-2768

OUB Securities Pte Ltd.
50 Collyer Quay
No. 01-01 Overseas Union House
Tel: 225-1166

Paul Morgan & Associates (Securities) Pte Ltd.
11 Collyer Quay
No. 18-01 The Arcade
Tel: 221-9991

Sun Hung Kai Securities Pte Ltd.
20 Collyer Quay
No. 18-01 Tung Centre
Tel: 224-1688

South Korea

Coryo Securities Corp.
25-5, I-ka, Chungmu-ro
Choong-ku, Seoul 100-011
Tel: 771-36
Tlx: 21817 COSCO K
Fax: 752-7221

Daewoo Securities
34-3 Yoido-dong
Youngdeungpo-ku
Seoul 150-010
Tel: 784-8851/3311
Tlx: 26332 DWSEC K
Fax: 784-0826

Daishin Securities
34-8 Yoido-dong
Youngdeungpo-ku
Seoul 150-010
Tel: 784-1711/8

Dongsuh Securities
34-1 Yoidi-dong
Youngdeunngpo-ku
Seoul 150-010
Tel: 784-1211

Jardine Fleming
1, I-ka Chongro
Chongro-ku
Seoul 110-121
Tel: 737-7712

Lucky Securities
34-6, Yoido-dong
Youngdeungpo-ku
Seoul 150-010
Tel: 784-7111

Merrill Lynch International Inc.
Suite 1311
Kyobo Building
1, I-ka, Chongro
Chongro-ku, Seoul
Tel: 735-7651
Tlx: 32135 MLCMSO K
Fax: 730-7898

Nikko Securities
25th Floor
I Sokong-dong
Choong-ku, Seoul 100-721
Tel: 778-1456/7
Tlx: 28148 NIKKOSL K
Fax: 752-7690

Ssangyong Securities
198, 2-ka, Ulchiro
Choong-ku
Seoul 100-192
Tel: 771-12

WI Carr (Overseas) Ltd.
21st Floor
I Sokong-dong
Choong-ku, Seoul
Tel: 734-1250

Taiwan

Asia Securities Inc.
3rd Floor
225 Nanking E Rd., Sec. 3
Taipei
Tel: 718-3456

BT Yuen Foong Securities Co.
51 Chungking S Rd.
Sec. 2
Taipei
Tel: 322-7777

Foremost Securities Co.
237 Chienkuo S Rd.
Sec. 1
Taipei
Tel: 754-2866

Grand Cathay Securities Corp.
4th floor
46 Kuanchien Rd.
Taipei
Tel: 383-1111

Jih Sun Securities Co.
4th floor
111 Nanking E Rd. Sec. 2
Taipei
Tel: 507-2722
Fax: 508-1103

Master Link Securities Co.
209 Fuhsing S Rd.
Sec. 1
Taipei
Tel: 731-3888

Pacific Securities Co.
13th Floor
200 Chunghsiao E Rd.
Sec. 4
Taipei
Tel: 75 1-7655

Taiwan International Securities Co.
5th Floor
248 Nanking E Rd., Sec. 3
Taipei
Tel: 775-4567

Yuen Ta Securities Co.
12th Floor
225 Nanking E Rd., Sec. 3
Taipei
Tel: 717-7777

Yung Li Securities Co.
2nd Floor
77 Yenping S Rd.
Taipei
Tel: 311-1540

Thailand

Asia Credit, Ltd.
320 Rama IV Rd.
Bangkok 10500
Tel: 235-1477
Tlx: 84641 ACREDIT TH
Fax: 236-1556

Bangkok First Investment and Trust Ltd.
300 Silom Rd.
Bangruk, Bangkok 10500

Tel: 237-6097/237-6797
Tlx: 84297
Fax: 237-6736

CMIC Finance and Securities Co., Ltd.
209 Soi Asoke
Sukhumvit Rd.
Klong Toey, Bangkok 10110
Tel: 258-0351-9
Tlx: 72278 CMIC TH
Fax: 258-3418

First Pacific Asia Securities Ltd.
7th Floor
Bank of Asia Building
191 Sathorn Tai Rd.
Bangkok 10120
Tel: 213-2680
Fax: 213-2677

Multi-Credit Corp. of Thailand, Ltd.
Kian Gwan Bldg.
140 Wireless Rd.
Patumanwan, Bangkok 10500
Tel: 252-9830-49
Tlx: 21047 MRC TH
Fax: 253-5594

National Finance and Securities Co., Ltd.
Maboonkrong Tower
444 Phyathai Rd.
Patumwan, Bangkok 10500
Tel: 217-9595/217-9622
Tlx: 20971 NFS BKK
Fax: 217-9642

Phatra Thanakit Co., Ltd.
183 Soi 13-15
Sukhumvit Rd.
Bangkok 10110
Tel: 253-0121
Tlx: 72513 PHATRA TH
Fax: 254-1240

Securities One Ltd.
Maneeya Bldg.
Ploenchit Rd.
Bangkok 10500
Tel: 255-1380/8
Fax: 254-8354

Thai Investment and Securities Co., Ltd.
138 Boonmitr Bldg.
Silom Rd.
Bangkok 10500
Tel: 237-7788

Tlx: 82554 TISCO TH
Fax: 236-2769

Union Asia Finance, Ltd.
Roamsermkij Bldg.
132 Silom Rd.

Bangruk, Bangkok 10500
Tel: 236-7511
Tlx: 84689 UAFL TH
Fax: 236-7518

BONDS

by Gregory P. Miller
Director, Wardley Investment Services (HK), Ltd.

Fixed-interest securities are one of the safest investments available, and usually yield considerably higher returns than fixed-interest accounts at the bank. There are six major decisions an investor must make.

How much risk should I take? There are two grades of bonds: investment grade and noninvestment grade bonds. The latter are commonly called junk bonds and will not be considered here.

Investment grade bonds are so named because a rating agency has assigned them a credit rating. This measures how likely the bond issuers are to default and, where appropriate, how likely they are to continue making interest payments.

The two most commonly used rating agencies are Moody's, and Standard and Poor's. They continually re-rate all types of bonds: those issued by countries, governments, government agencies, supranationals, and corporations.

What currency should choose? Foreign exchange movements can quickly alter the performance of a portfolio. An investor must decide whether or not to play it safe.

For example, if your liabilities are in Hong Kong dollars, the safest thing may be to keep your portfolio denominated in that currency. That way you eliminate all foreign exchange risk and can concentrate just on the yield curve.

But if you believe that the Hong Kong dollar and the U.S. dollar, to which it is linked, are going to depreciate against other currencies, you may want to put some of the portfolio in other currencies.

How long should I hold? If you have to make a number of payments at certain specific dates in the future, bonds can be chosen which mature on those dates or close to them. Alternatively, you can choose a portfolio to produce a lump sum on retirement.

How can I save tax? The different domestic markets have different tax treatments, depending on whether investors are resident or nonresident. Eurobond markets are tax-free.

You may also need to consider, for tax purposes, whether to generate income or capital gains.

The Japanese Government Bond Market is taxable for all nonresidents, except central banks or approved government agencies, at different rates for different countries of domicile (i.e., 10% for the U.K., 15% for Singapore, 20% for Hong Kong).

Japanese resident investors are taxed according to their own particular status.

The United Kingdom Government Bond (gilt-edged) Market is taxable for residents.

But some issues are specified as being nontaxable for nonresident investors.

The United States Government Bond (Treasury) Market is tax-free for both resident and non-resident investors.

The Eurobond markets are tax-free. Created in the 1950s to meet a demand for tax-free investments, they have since boomed. Eurobonds offer slightly more favorable terms to borrowers. They cater mainly to government borrowers, and supranationals, as well as corporations.

On the Euromarkets, you can lend to almost any company, although some governments prevent their corporations from borrowing their own currency in the Eurobond markets.

Income or capital gains? For tax purposes, some investors wish to generate income, while others prefer capital gains. You can choose.

If you buy bonds close to their final redemption price and hold to maturity, the portfolio will generate interest income only and no capital gains.

If you buy a zero coupon bond, it will be priced at a discount. At maturity, you will realize a large capital gain.

Alternatively, you can buy a combination of both: a bond with an interest rate lower than the prevailing rate, which will consequently be priced at a discount.

Bonds or unit trusts? To all intents and purposes, direct investment by individuals in the bond markets is off-limits to all but the wealthiest people.

It is difficult for an individual to run his or her own portfolio without a minimum of US$1 million available for investment.

The alternative is to invest in a bond fund run by a professional manager, your private banker, investment advisor, or through a unit trust.

This manager can then put all smaller clients with similar requirements together and operate them as one big portfolio, achieving the same result.

WHERE TO BUY BONDS

Many banks and securities companies run bond operations. They can advise and offer free custodian services, since it is not recommended to take physical delivery of bonds.

Except in Japan, the corporate bond market in Asia is not very liquid, with trading volumes generally quite low.

The bond market in Japan is one of the largest in the world. Two of the more widely held instruments in recent years have been onshore convertible bonds and Eurobonds with warrant issues.

The Eurodollar convertible bond market has been faltering since it is usually possible to finance at a lower interest rate using bonds and warrant issues.

The Yen bond and warrant issues that were developed a few years ago are now in limbo, after Japan's Finance Ministry decision to bar the splitting of bond and warrant issues into separately traded vehicles.

Tax on interest on bonds, debentures, and bond investments trusts for nonresidents is 20%, except for residents of certain countries that have double-taxation agreements with Japan.

Among the Asian countries with such agreements are: Korea, 12% (withholding tax rate); the Philippines, 15%; Singapore, 15%; and Thailand, 10%.

RULES AND REGULATIONS

Korea

Permission from the Korean Government is needed for a Korean company to offer and issue bonds outside Korea and for the payment of principal, premium, and interest to nonresidents.

Regarding convertible bonds, no bondholder can exercise the conversion right if that would result in a nonresident holding more than 3% of the shares of the company which were outstanding when the bonds were issued.

Malaysia

The secondary market for private commercial paper, notes, and bonds is not liquid, with investors holding onto top-rated private corporate issues for redemption.

The inactivity is mainly due to the fact that interest on corporate bonds is taxed at corporate or individual rates, while government securities are taxed less.

The market is active in government mortgage bonds and treasury bills, which are dominated by banks and other institutions.

For individuals, there is a unit trust fund called Arab-Malaysia Gilts, which invests 90% of its funds in government securities and the remainder in commercial paper, such as bankers' acceptances, negotiable certificates of deposit, and trade bills.

Only the income received by individuals residing in Malaysia is tax-exempt. But companies and institutions are taxable.

USEFUL CONTACTS

Hong Kong

Bankers Trust
30th Floor
Admiralty Center, Tower 1
18 Harcourt Rd., Central
Tel: 8618000
Tlx: 73046
Fax: 8663029

Baring Brothers Co., Ltd.
703 Three Exchange Square Central
Tel: 8489600
Tlx: 75148
Fax: 5296317

Crédit Suisse First Boston
1/F I Exchange Square, Central
Tel: 847-0388
Tlx: 66652
Fax: 868-4394
Contact person: Shao Liu

Goldman Sachs Asia, Ltd.
35th Floor
Edinburgh Tower
Landmark, Central
Tel: 8682600
Tlx: 64114
Fax: 8684631

Jardine Fleming Investment Management, Ltd.
47th Floor
Jardine House
1 Connaught Place Central
Tel: 8438888
Tlx: 75608
Fax: 8101694

Merrill Lynch Int'l Inc.
12/F, St. George's Building
2 Ice House St., Central
Tel: 844-5678
Tlx: 80120 MLIBK HX
Fax: 845-0767

Morgan Guaranty Trust Co. of New York
23rd Floor
Edinburgh Tower
Landmark, Central
Tel: 8411311
Tlx: 73061
Fax: 8681473

Nomura International (HKG), Ltd.
46th Floor
Far East Finance Centre
16 Harcourt Rd., Central

Tel: 5201811
Tlx: 73299
Fax: 8610218

Salomon Brothers (HKG), Ltd.
21st Floor
3 Exchange Square
Central
Tel: 8418000
Tlx: 69145
Fax: 8418092

Schroders Asia Ltd.
25th Floor
2 Exchange Square
8 Connaught Place
Central
Tel: 521 1633
Tlx: 62162
Fax: 8681023

Wardley Investment Services (HKG) Ltd.
12th Floor
Bank of America Tower
12 Harcourt Rd., Central
Tel: 8479600
Tlx: 73934
Fax: 8450226

Indonesia

ASEAM Indonesia
16th Floor
Bank Bumi Daya Plaza
Jl Imam Bonjol 61
Jakarta
Tel: 321-932
Tlx: 61483
Fax: 336861

**Bank Pembangunan Indonesia
(Bapindo)**
Jl/RP Soeroso 2-4
Jakarta Pusat
Tel: 321-908
Tlx: 61335/61394
Fax: 324794/333633/333644

PT Finconesia
5th Floor
Summitmas Tower, LT6
Jl Sudirman Kav 61-62
Jakarta
Tel: 520-1500
Tlx: 62799 FINCO IA
Fax: 5200790

**First Indonesian Finance and
Investment Corp. (Ficorinvest)**
Jl Rasuna Said Kav C-18
Jakarta
Tel: 520-4048

**Indonesian Finance and
Investment Co. (IFI)**
15th Floor
Chase Plaza
Jl Sudirman Kav 21
Jakarta
Tel: 570-0170

**Indonesian Investments
International (Indovest)**
24th Floor
Menara BDN
Jl Kebon Sinh 83
Jakarta Pusat
Tel: 380-1985
Fax: 380-1890

**Inter Pacific Financial Corp.
(Interpacific)**
9th Floor
Wisma Metropolitan 11
Jl Sudirman Kav 31

Jakarta
Tel: 578-1095

**Merchant Investment Corp.
(Merincorp)**
21st Floor
Summitmas Tower
Jl Sudirman Kav 61-62
Jakarta
Tel: 520-0808

**Multinational Finance Corp.
(Multicor),**
12th Floor
Wisma BCA
Jl Sudirman Kav 22-23
Jakarta
Tel: 578-1450
Tlx: 56278

**Usaha Pembiayaan Pembangunan
Indonesia (Uppindo)**
Jl Abdul Muis 28
Jakarta
Tel: 354-621

Japan

Bank of Tokyo
3-2 Nihonbashi
Hongokucho 1-chome
Chuo-ku, Tokyo 103
Tel: 245-1111
Tlx: 22220
Fax: 2461708

Dai-Ichi Kangyo Bank, Ltd.
1-5, Uchisaiwai-cho 1-chome
Chiyoda-ku, Tokyo 100
Tel: 596-2193
Tlx: 22315/79
Fax: 8504437

Daiwa Bank, Ltd.
1-8, Bingomachi 2-chome
Higashi-ku, Osaka 541
Tel: 271-1221 (Osaka)
Tlx: 63284/63457
DAIBANK J
Fax: 222-1880

Fuji Bank
1-5-5, Otemachi 1-chome
Chiyoda-ku, Tokyo 100
Tel: 216-2211
Tlx: 24311/22722

FUJIBANK J
Fax: 2870905

Industrial Bank of Japan
3-3, Marunouchi 1-chome
Chiyoda-ku, Tokyo
Tel: 214-1501
Tlx: J33716
Fax: 2143675

Kyowa Bank, Ltd.
1-2, Otemachi 1-chome
Chiyoda-ku, Tokyo 100
Tel: 287-2111
Tlx: 24275
KYOWABK J
Fax: 287-0953

Mitsui Bank
1-2, Yurakucho 1-chome
Chiyoda-ku, Tokyo 100
Tel: 501-1111
Tlx: 22378/643
MITSUIBK J
Fax: 508-2478

New Japan Securities Co., Ltd.
11, Kanda Surugadai 3-chome
Chiyoda-ku, Tokyo 100
Tel: 219-1111
Tlx: 22666/26216
SHINNIHON J
Fax: 292-6937

Nippon Credit Bank, Ltd.
13-10, Kudankita 1-chome
Chiyoda-ku, Tokyo
Tel: 263-1111
Tlx: 26921/28788
NCBTOK J
Fax: 265-7024/230-3548

Yamaichi Securities
4-1, Yaesu 2-chome
Chuo-ku, Tokyo
Tel: 276-3181
Tlx: 22505/959
YAMAYORKJ
Fax: 276-2947

Malaysia

Arab-Malaysian Gilts
21st Floor
Bangunan Arab-Malaysian
Jln Raja Chulan

50200 Kuala Lumpur
Tel: 238-2633/2644
Fax: 238-2842

Singapore

CS First Boston
50 Raffles Place
#36-05 Shell Tower
Tel: 225-3088
Tlx: 25410
Fax: 224-0586
Contact person: Tan Kok Wee

Nomura Singapore
6 Battery Road
#39-01 Standard Chartered Bank
Bldg.
Tel: 220-8766
Tlx: 21198
Fax: 224-0966
Contact person: Peter Hu

NDC Merchant Bank
6 Shenton Way
#24-00 DBS Bldg.
Tel: 220-8133
Tlx: 22553
Fax: 224-4532
Contact person: Carina Lee

United Overseas Bank
1 Bonham Street
Raffles Place
Tel: 533-9898
Tlx: 21539
Fax: 534-3028
Contact person: Joseph Chen Seow
Chan

DBS Bank
6 Shenton Way
DBS Building
Tel: 220-1111
Tlx: 24455
Fax: 221-1306
Contact person: Frank Koh

Overseas Union Bank
1 Raffles Place
OUB Centre
Tel: 530-2351
Tlx: 22375
Fax: 5332360
Contact person: Ng Kuan Chow

Daiwa Singapore
6 Shenton Way
#38-00 DBS Building
Tel: 224-2022
Tlx: 21126
Fax: 225-3797
Contact person: Bernard Ong

OCBC Bank
65 Chulia Street
#11-00 OCBC Centre
Tel: 532-6177
Tlx: 21209
Fax: 533-7891
Contact person: Sio Tat Hiang

South Korea

Coryo Securities Corp.
25.5 1-ka Chungmu-ro
Choong-ku, Seoul
Tel: 77136
Tlx: 23817 COSCOK
Fax: 752-7221
Contact person: Park Young-jun

Dae Woo Securities
34-3 Yoido-dong, Youngdeungpo-ku
Seoul
Tel: 784-8851/3311
Tlx: 26332 DWSEC K
Fax: 784-0826
Contact person: Kang Chang-Hee

Daishin Securities
34-8 Yoido-dong, Youngdeungpo-ku
Seoul
Tel: 784-1711/8
Tlx: 29471 DAISHINK
Fax: 784-7195/4909
Contact person: Mun Byung-Hyun

Dangshu Securities
34-1 Yoido-dong, Youngdeungpo-ku
Seoul
Tel: 784-1211
Tlx: 24493 DONG SUH K
Fax: 784-2946
Contact person: Song Kyung-Hyun

First Securities Co. Ltd.
44-11 Yoido-dong, Youngdeungpo-
ku
Seoul
Tel: 784-7233

Tlx: 23110 KOFIRSE K
Fax: 783-5159
Contact person: Kang-wook Choi/
Cho Kyu-ha

Hanil Securities Co. Ltd.
34-10 Yoido-dong, Youngdeungpo-
ku
Seoul
Tel: 785-6611
Fax: 785-2396
Contact person: Yim Hee-kyu

Hyundai Securities
77 Mukyo-dong, Chung-gu
Seoul
Tel: 783-6611
Fax: 782-0009
Tlx: 33876 HKSCLK
Contact person: Lee Jim-yong

Lucky Securities Co. Ltd.
34-6 Yoido-dong, Youngdeungpo-ku
Seoul
Tel: 784-7111
Tlx: 29771 LUSCO K
Fax: 784-8621
Contact person: Shin Dong-Hoo

**Ssangyong Investment &
Securities Co. Ltd.**
198 2-ka Ulchi-ro, Chung-ku
Seoul
Tel: 771-12
Tlx: 29179 SISCO K
Fax: 756-4870
Contact person: Lee Chung-chul

Yuhwa Securities Co. Ltd.
36/F 63 Building, 60 Yoido-dong,
Youngdeungpo-ku
Seoul
Tel: 785-7951
Tlx: 29571 Yuscok
Fax: 785-4793
Contact person: Lee Jae-Duk

Taiwan

Asia Securities Inc.
3rd Floor, 225 Nankins E. Rd. Sec 3,
Taipei
Tel: 718-3456
Tlx: 17347
Fax: 718-2366
Contact person: Steven Kwiakowski

Asia Trust & Investment Corp.
116 Nanking E Road, Sec 2, Taipei
Tel: 531-5678
Tlx: 25329 Asiagrp
Fax: 521-5504
Contact person: Rita Sun

BT Yuen Foong Securities Co.
51 Chung Ching S Rd., Sec 2, Taipei
Tel: 322-7777
Fax: 322-4976
Contact person: Peter Kwok

Cathay Investment & Trust Co.
1 Nanyang St., Taipei
Tel: 311-4881
Tlx: 28027 CATHAYIT
Fax: 331-3271
Contact person: Wu-Tien Chiang/
Albert Chen

China Bills Finance Co.
6/F, 64 Tunhua N. Road, Taipei
Tel: 731-4944
Fax: 771-9551
Contact person: Jean Cheng

China Trust Co.
122 Tunhua N. Rd., Taipei
Tel: 715-5040
Fax: 716-3116
Contact person: Alex Chen

China United Trust & Investment Corp.
136 Sungchiang Rd., Taipei
Tel: 551-0168
Tlx: 17923 Cutico
Fax: 564-2575
Contact person: W. H. Chen

Chung Hsing Bills Finance Co.
4/F, 125 Nanking E. Rd., Sec 2, Taipei
Tel: 506-9141
Fax: 507-3727
Contact person: Nora Liang

International Bills Finance Co.
13/F, 62 Tunhua N Rd., Taipei
Tel: 772-5335
Fax: 741-8411
Contact person: Harvey Liu

Jardine Fleming Securities Co.
2/F, 547 Kuangfu S Rd., Taipei
Tel: 723-0001
Tlx: 14592 Jarflem
Fax: 723-0002
Contact person: Paul Tsai

Master Link Securities Co.
LST SL 209, Fuhsing S Rd., Sec 1, Taipei

Tel: 731-3888
Fax: 731-3350
Contact person: T. C. Yau

National Securities Co.
9/F, 2 Kuanchien Rd., Taipei
Tel: 312-3322
Fax: 371-9516
Contact person: Vincent Huang

Overseas Trust Corp.
236 Tunhua N Rd., Taipei
Tel: 713-9911
Fax: 713-8350
Contact person: May Wang/Mary Sun

Taiwan First Investment & Trust Co.
85 Jenai Rd., Sec 4, Taipei
Tel: 752-5353
Fax: 777-8539
Contact person: J. H. Chen

Taiwan International Securities Co.
4th Floor, 248 Nanking E Rd., Sec 3, Taipei
Tel: 775-4567
Tlx: 17599
Fax: 775-4109

REAL ESTATE

RULES AND REGULATIONS

by Michael Wood
PR/Marketing Manager, First Pacific Davies

Hong Kong

This is probably the least restrictive property market in Asia, but also the most volatile sector of Hong Kong's economy. The longterm outlook is uncertain, with the British colony reverting to Chinese sovereignty in 1997.

All land in the territory is owned by the Crown, and land leases are sold by the gov-

ernment, usually by public auction, but occasionally by tender.

Since the Sino-British Joint Declaration on Hong Kong's future was signed in 1984, government land disposal is limited to only 50 hectares a year.

Land grants have been made for terms expiring no later than June 30, 2047. These grants are made at a premium and nominal rental until June 30, 1997, after which time an annual event equivalent to 3% of the property's rateable value will apply.

While there are no subsidies or other incentives to attract foreign investors, Hong Kong's tax structure is attractive.

Tax on profits arising in or derived from Hong Kong are payable at the company rate of 16.5%, but gains from the realization of capital assets are not taxed.

Indonesia

The Indonesian government stipulates that all foreign investment must be in the form of joint ventures with an Indonesian partner, be it a corporation or an individual.

The government usually requires that at least 20% of the equity in a foreign investment be owned by the local partner, with this being raised to no less than 51% within 15 years.

Indonesian land legislation does not recognize the concept of freehold land rights. Instead, the various rights attached to land are divided into separate elements and are subject to separate titles.

For the foreign investor, the following three main rights are significant:

- The right of exploitation *(hak guna usaha)*. This is the right to use state-owned land of not less than 25 hectares for agricultural use, including fishing and cattle raising.
- The right of building *(hak guna Bangunan)*.
- The right of use *(hak pakai)*.

These rights differ in the duration of validity, the nature of use, the opportunity to mortgage, and the proof of title.

A number of foreign governments provide investment guarantees to their nationals who make investments in other countries, providing compensation in case of nationalization or expatriation, war, revolution, or insurrection. Indonesia has concluded agreements of this general type with South Korea, the United States, Canada, and the United Kingdom, among others.

The maximum tax rate on both personal income and corporate profit is 35% on any amount above Rp50 million (US$30,000).

Japan

The rapid rise of Japanese domestic property values over the past three years has leveled off, but prices are likely to stay high, with people reluctant to sell.

When it is possible to make a buy, the returns are extremely low, often dipping below 1%. Taxes are also high. Ownership restrictions make it difficult for foreigners to penetrate. Foreigners acquiring real estate must report the purchase in advance to the Ministry of Finance.

Malaysia

Foreign investment in Malaysia has suffered for some years as a result of government policy, lack of confidence in political stability, and from economic recession.

But recently, significant changes have been made in policies and incentives, including the easing of rules on the proportion of equity which new foreign investors may hold.

The Malaysian government imposes no legal restriction on the acquisition of land by foreigners but neither are there incentives or special benefits for property investors.

To curb speculation, any foreign buyer of property can source a maximum of 50% of financing for the deal from the local market. Any foreign buyer who borrows from Malaysian banks for property deals must repay in full within three years.

The amending of the Real Property Gains

Tax Act of 1987 means that profits on the sale of properties by both local and foreign sellers goes to a flat 20%, if sold within two years of purchase, and 5% if sold after five years. Before, foreigners had to pay a flat 40% rate no matter how long they held ownership.

Rent or other payments made to a nonresident under an agreement or arrangement for the use of any movable property are subject only to withholding tax.

The launching of property trusts has stirred some foreign interest, especially now that the corporate tax on gains made by property unit trusts on property transactions has been lifted. Under Malaysian law, only local financial institutions are given licenses to manage these trusts. Foreigners can hold only minority interests.

The Philippines

A politically uncertain climate is giving some foreigners pause over investing in the Philippines. They also face a number of restrictions regarding property ownership.

The government reserves the right to limit private land ownership to Philippines citizens only. Foreigners may only own buildings on leased land or condominium units, provided they do not acquire direct interest in the land on which the condominium is built and that they have less than a 40% interest in the developer.

Although there are no specific property-related investment incentives, the government does encourage foreign investments through business incentives. These are chiefly reserved for "pioneering" and export-oriented ventures, business in less-developed regions, and those registered as export processing zone activities in one of the nation's four export-processing zones.

Tax concessions include an income tax holiday, deductions from taxable income for labor expenses, and deductions equal to the construction costs of major public infrastructure facilities.

The government gives no tax incentives to foreign investors in real estate holding companies, trust operations, or finance companies.

Property tax consists of real property taxes as well as residence taxes. Nonresident aliens not engaged in trade or business in the Philippines are taxed at the rate of 30% on their capital gains. If they are involved in trade or business in the country, they are subject to normal taxes ranging from 1% to a maximum of 35%. A 5% tax is levied on the sale of property.

Singapore

Foreigners face restrictions on owning residential properties. They cannot invest in landed properties or in apartments which are lower than six stories, except in approved condominiums, unless they receive permission from the Land Dealings (Approval) Unit.

To reach its decision, the unit weighs heavily the economic contribution the foreigner is likely to make. They are also barred from owning Housing Development Board apartments. Otherwise, foreign investors can freely buy properties in Singapore.

Property transactions are subject to stamp duties, which may add up to 3% of the total cost. Property agents also charge between 1% and 2% of the purchase price. Legal fees range from S$5,000 to S$15,000 (US$2,500 to US$7,500), depending on the complexity of the purchase deal. Most banks in Singapore offer attractive financing schemes for home purchases.

Prices for quality private residential properties have soared recently, spurred by increased investment by Hong Kong residents after the upheavals in Beijing.

There is no capital gains tax, but property tax amounts to 25% of the annual value of the property.

South Korea

The right of foreigners to own property in South Korea is mainly governed by the Alien Land Acquisition Act, which contains several restrictions.

But the government has promised to be flexible in enforcing the restrictive rules and to simplify the procedures by which foreigners can buy land.

Recently, the government has followed an "open door" policy toward foreign investment and has actively encouraged investment which helps to develop the national economy, improves South Korea's balance of payments position and brings in advanced technology.

But corporate income tax incentives tend to favor high-technology manufacturing industries rather than real estate investment.

Taiwan

Foreign individuals may own property, but only if their government permits Taiwan citizens to buy real estate in their country. In addition, the property must be for the foreigner's own use. High taxes, low yields, and an overheated real estate market make Taiwan a difficult place to crack for foreign investors.

Thailand

Under the Thai Land Code, aliens are normally not allowed to own land or condominiums in Thailand. "Alien" in this context includes a person who is not of Thai nationality and a partnership or company in which more than 49% of the interest or shareholding is owned by aliens.

It is possible to "own" land through a minority interest in a Thai company. If certain proposed laws are passed, foreigners may be permitted to own up to 40% of a condominium project.

Leases, which foreigners may hold, are limited to 30 years. Renewal is possible, but not certain.

An alternative is "usufruct," which gives the right to use, occupy, and enjoy a property for a maximum of 30 years. Under civil law, a usufruct agreement is not easily terminated. This right could offer alien investors added security in their real property activity.

Since foreigners are not allowed to own land in Thailand, there are no incentives to encourage their investment in real property. However, the Board of Investment will grant permission to own land as a special incentive for certain business investments. There are several taxes applicable to land ownership, leases, and usufruct, and on the gains from the sale of such interests. In the latter case, these include a 1% "recording fee" on the transaction, a 25% transfer of rights tax and, for Thai vendors, including corporations conducting business in Thailand, a 35% tax due on the net gain from a sale. Rental income is taxed at 35%, if accruing to a Thai resident or company deemed to be carrying on a trade or business in Thailand, or at 25% in the case of a foreign company.

Useful Contacts

Hong Kong

Chesterton Petty, Ltd.
28th Floor
Jardine House
Connaught Rd., Central
Tel: 8401177
Tlx: 63334
Fax: 8400600

Cheung Kong (Holdings), Ltd.
18th–22nd Floors
China Building
29 Queen's Rd., Central
Tel: 5266911
Tlx: 86209
Fax: 8452940

First Pacific Davies (Hong Kong), Ltd.
2 Exchange Square
Central
Tel: 5254418
Tlx: 61851
Fax: 8684386

Hongkong Land Co., Ltd.
8th Floor
1 Exchange Square
Central
Tel: 8428428
Tlx: 75102
Fax: 8459226

Jones Lang Wootton, Ltd.
25th Floor
1 Exchange Square
Central
Tel: 8465000
Tlx: 74247
Fax: 8459117

New World Development Co., Ltd.
30th Floor
New World Tower
16-18 Queen's Rd.
Central
Tel: 5231056
Tlx: 81053
Fax: 8104673

Indonesia

S Widjojo Centre
3rd Floor
Jl Sudirman 71
Jakarta
Tel: 584-481

Five Pillars Indonesia
Jl Mt. Haryono
58-60
Jakarta
Tel: 799-2608
Fax: 7992244

Lintas Gapura Mas
Jl Hayam Wuruk 1-RXY
Jakarta Pusat
Tel: 347-965/383-821

Megapolitan Development Corp.
Jl Gajah Mada 3-5, Block B 28-29
Duta Merlin, Jakarta
Tel: 355-991/355-992/365-389
Fax: 358-285

Multi Alam Garden
Jl Sudirman 1
Panin Centre, Jakarta
Tel: 713-430

Procon Indah
Suite 803
Lippo Life Building 1
Jl Rasuna Said Kav B-10
Jakarta
Tel: 520-0727/510899
Tlx: 62211 JLWORLD 1A
Fax: 5200594

Pudjadi & Sons Estates
Jl Hayam Wuruk 126
Jayakarta Tower Hotel
Jakarta
Tel: 629-2500
Tlx: 47411
Fax: 711347

Ratu Sayang International
Jl Sudirman 9
Jakarta
Tel: 739-4499
Tlx: 47411
Fax: 711347

Ujatek Baru
Jl Yusuf Adiwinata 41
Jakarta
Tel: 336-61 1

Japan

Daiwa Danchi Co., Ltd.
4-12 Itachibori, 1-chome
Nishi-ku, Osaka 550
Tel: 532-6251

Heiwa Real Estate Co., Ltd.
10 Nihonbashi
Kabutocho, 1-chome
Chuo-ku, Tokyo 103
Tel: 666-0181

Kakuei Construction Co., Ltd.
8-1 Shinjuku, 1-chome
Shinjuku-ku, Tokyo 160
Tel: 350-4111
Fax: 350-8880

Mitsubishi Estate Co., Ltd.
4-1 Marunouchi, 2-chome
Chiyoda-ku, Tokyo 100
Tel: 287-5100
Tlx: 22174 MECDIA J
Fax: 214-7036

Mitsui Real Estate Development Co., Ltd.
1-1 Nihonbashi
Muromachi, 2-chome
Chuo-ku, Tokyo 103
Tel: 246-3155
Tlx: 222-5474 MEDJ
Fax: 246-3543

Sumitomo Realty and Development Co., Ltd.
4-1 Nishishinjuku, 2-chome
Shinjuku-ku, Tokyo
Tel: 346-1011

Taiheiyo Kouhatsu, Inc.
Toranomon Mitsui
Building 8-1
Kasumigaseki, 3-chome
Chiyoda-ku Tokyo
Tel: 591-1271

Tokyu Land Corp.
21-2 Dogenzaka, 1-chome
Shibuya-ku, Tokyo 150
Tel: 463-661 1
Tlx: 242-4448 TOKYU F
Fax: 780-4358

Tokyo Tatemono Co., Ltd.
9-9 Yaesu, 1-chome
Chuo-ku, Tokyo 103
Tel: 274-0113
Fax: 274-0013

Toyo Trust and Banking Co., Ltd.
4-3 Marunouchi, 1-chome
Chiyoda-ku, Tokyo 100
Tel: 287-2211
Tlx: 22141 TYTBKI J
Fax: 201-1448

Malaysia

Jones Lang Wootton,
8th Floor
Wisma Getah Asli
148 Jln Ampang
50450 Kuala Lumpur
Tel: 261-2522
Tlx: MA 30926
Fax: 261-8060

CH Williams Talhar & Wong
Plaza MBF
Jln Ampang
50450 Kuala Lumpur
Tel: 261-5622

Rahim & Co.
Wisma Jayanita
64 Jln Raja Muda
50738 Kuala Lumpur
Tel: 291-9922
Tlx: 32195 RAHIM MA

Collings Hui
7th Floor
Menara Boustead
Jln Raja Chulan
50200 Kuala Lumpur
Tel: 241-3244/242-6211

Philippines

Active Real Estate Marketing Corp.
Pilipinas-ACT Tower Building
135 Sen Gil J Puyat Ave.
Makati
Tel: 817-7876/864-801-848/6412

Ayala Land, Inc.
Makati Stock Exchange Building,
Ayala Avenue
Makati, Metro Manila
Tel: 810-1031
Tlx: RCA 22066 AYCPH
Fax: 815-0764

BF Homes, Inc.
Tropical Ave.
Metro Manila
Tel: 828-5788/802-1594/1493

Cityland Development Corp.
USIPHIL Building
Makati, Metro Manila
Tel: 817-2462
Fax: 793-577

Filinvest Development Corp.
Filinvest Development Building
San Juan, Metro Manila
Tel: 70-06-11

Household Development Corp.
CLMC Building
Mandaluyong
Metro Manila
Tel: 783597

Ortigas and Co., Ltd., Partnership
Greenhills Shopping Center
San Juan, Metro Manila
Tel: 721-0572/631-1231/38

Philippine Realty Corp.
12 1 Arzobispo
Manila
Tel: 475970

Sta Lucia Realty and Development Inc.
State Financing Center Building
Mandaluyong
Metro Manila
Tel: 773086/7214776
Fax: 722-5022

Urdec Holdings Group (Rufino Group)
Glass Tower Building, 115C Palanca Jr St.
Makati, Metro Manila
Tel: 816-3842
Tlx: 66123 WOLMNL PN
Fax: 815-8376

Singapore

Allied Appraisal Consultants Pte, Ltd.
400 Orchard Rd.
No. 06-26 Orchard Towers
Tel: 235-1077

Allsworth Properties
135 Middle Rd.
No. 04-04 Bylands Building
Tel: 339-8303
Fax: 339-6536

Asian Appraisal
51 Thomson Road
195B Goldhill Centre
Tel: 252-5866
Fax: 255-4009

Colliers Goh & Tan Pte, Ltd.
No. 18-03 Ocean Building
Tel: 535-9622

Debenham Tewson & City Valuers Pte, Ltd.
11 Collyer Quay
No. 13-01 The Arcade
Tel: 225-5884
Tlx: 22990
Fax: 224-2531

ERA Real Estate
95 South Bridge Road, #0621
Pidemco Centre
Tel: 226-2000
Fax: 534-1198

Jones Lang Wootton
50 Raffles Place
No. 45-00 Shell Tower
Tel: 220-3888
Tlx: 23108 JLW
Fax: 221-5775

Knight, Frank, Cheong, Hock, Chye & Baillieu
16 Raffles Quay
No. 29-01 Hong Leong Building
Tel: 222-1333
Tlx: 34722
Fax: 224-5843

OCBC Property Services
65 Chulia St.
No. 28-08 OCBC Centre
Tel: 533-3196
Tlx: 40130 OPSPL
Fax: 533-5244

Chong Hwa Real Estate Agency
1st Floor
Chong Hwa Apt. Shopping Center
22-2 Itaewon-dong
Yongsan-ku, Seoul
Tel: 793-2156

Ko Sung Development Co., Ltd.
730 Hannam-dong
Yongsan-ku, Seoul
Tel: 797-9901/2
Tlx: 27170 KOSUNG K
Fax: 797-2477

Rana Realty Services
Baejae Annex Building
A-dong, 409 Ho
34-5, Chung-dong
Chung-ku, Seoul
Tel: 755-6510/6520
Tlx: 23231 MOCNDM K
Fax: 755-3969

Shin Seong Realty
124-6 Itaewon-dong
Yongsan-ku, Seoul
Tel: 797-1110

South Korea

A&A Co. Realty Info Svce.
135-35 Itaewon-dong, Yongsan-ku, Seoul
Tel: 794-1133/794-5032/794-1153
Fax: 798-0201

Chung Hwa Real Estate Agency
1/F, Chong Hwa Apt. Shopping Centre,
22-2 Itaewon-dong, Yongsan-ku, Seoul
Tel: 793-2156
Fax: 792-5377

Joy Realty Service
5-1 Itaewon-dong Yongsan-ku, Seoul
Tel: 794-7434
Fax: 792-1975

Ko Sung Development Co. Ltd.
730 Hannam-dong, Yongsan-ku, Seoul
Tel: 797-9901/2
Tlx: 27170 KOSUNG K
Fax: 797-2477

Pacific Brokerage
1510 Changkang Bldg.
22 Dowha-dong, Mapo-ku
Tel: 701-745
Fax: 701-7450

Rana Realty Services
Baejae Annex Bldg., A-dong, 409 Ho
34-5, Chung-dong, Chung-ku, Seoul
Tel: 755-6510/6520
Tlx: 23231 MOCNDM K
Fax: 755-3969

Shin Seong Realty
124-6 Itaewon-dong
Yongsan-ku, Seoul

Tel: 797-1110
Fax: 798-7333

Taiwan

CITC Real Estate Co.
9th Floor
36 Nanking E Rd., Sec. 3
Taipei
Tel: 507-8266
Fax: 507-3628

Investec (Taiwan), Ltd.
14th Floor
147 Chien Kuo N Rd.
Sec. 2
Taipei
Tel: 501-1908
Tlx: 28514 INVESTEC
Fax: 501-4753

Pacific Rehouse
102 Kuangfu S Rd.
Taipei
Tel: 741-3457
Fax: 731-6039/755-1064

Thailand

First Pacific Davies (Thailand) Co., Ltd.
144 Sukhumvit
Bangkok 101 10
Tel: 254-5050/59
Fax: 254-9956/254-9909

Richard Ellis (Thailand) Co., Ltd.
26th Floor, CP Tower
313 Silom Rd.
Bangkok 10500
Tel: 231-0123
Tlx: 21071 KENGKOK TH
Fax: 231-0134

GOLD

by Robert Y. K. Cheung
Director—Financial Engineering, Wardley Thomson Ltd.

GOLD. Its allure as a desirable and reliable form of money has endured for thousands of years. Prized as a portable, "liquid" asset, it is held as a form of insurance against future uncertainties. As the world's "fear thermometer," its value rises when political or economic turmoil heats up.

Today, investors view gold both as a hedge against inflation and as a solid, long-term investment. Generally, financial advisors say investors should hold between 5 percent and 15 percent of their wealth in gold to diversify and stabilize their portfolios.

The main complaint against gold used to be that it was a non-interest bearing asset. No more. Even locked away in a vault, physical gold—such as bullion, bars and wafers—can earn interest when its owners write gold loans with it.

But physical gold, be it bars, coins, or even jewelry, is only one way to invest in the precious metal. A thriving market has developed in "paper gold" including gold futures and gold mine stocks, which are often risky but offer the lure of high returns.

International gold dealers look to London —considered the world's gold capital—for their reference price. Twice a day, the top five bullion firms there meet to set an equilibrium price, based on supply and demand, for all buying and selling orders.

Prices are usually quoted for spot delivery. But since investors may want to hedge their future commitments when the market is volatile, forward prices for specific maturity dates are also quoted. Margin requirements are negotiated on an individual basis.

The basic unit of trading in the London market is a bar weighing about 400 troy ounces (12.44 kilos). Buying and selling prices are usually expressed in US dollars per troy ounce, with delivery to vaults in London. Each of the big five firms has high security vaults for keeping gold bars and coins, and can also arrange to transport gold throughout the world. A shipping and insurance fee is charged.

For the many customers who do not want to take physical possession of gold, member firms open allocated or unallocated gold accounts. Allocated accounts have specific amounts of gold physically segregated with detailed lists of weights and assays (measurements of purity). With unallocated accounts, customers have a general entitlement to gold. This is the most convenient, least expensive and most popular way of holding gold.

In Asia, the hub of gold trading activity is unquestionably Hong Kong. It provides a link to gold trading around the clock with its activities helping to bridge the time gap between the close of New York's COMEX and the opening of the London market.

Only a small part of Hong Kong's trading is in physical gold. Most trading is in paper transactions, in which gold is treated as a financial vehicle, rather than as a commodity for investment, hedging or speculation.

For example, the market is used to arbitrage against positions in derived products such as bull and bear bonds. It is also used to capture momentary differentials arising from the mispricing of the Hong Kong dollar exchange rate and short-term interest rates.

There are two basic markets in Hong Kong: the local one, called the Chinese Gold and Silver Exchange Society; and the Location ("Loco" for short) London market, an extension of the London gold market.

Spot prices in Loco London are quoted in US dollars per troy ounce, with transactions in bars of 400 troy ounces and 99.5% purity usually geared to delivery in the London vaults of the major bullion houses. The Chinese Gold and Silver Exchange quotes prices in Hong Kong dollars per tael (equivalent to 1.20337 troy ounces) with transactions in 100-tael lots and 99% purity.

Arbitrage between the Loco London market and the Chinese Exchange has often been quite active because of the differences in the size of the contract traded, the quality of the gold and the currency. Since the Hong Kong dollar became pegged to the US dollar in 1983, however, arbitrage possibilities have been less attractive.

Price variations between the two markets also stem from differences in the location of gold delivery, the supply and demand characteristics, and the methods of financing and carrying the forward positions.

Delayed settlement has given the Loco London market a futures element that has helped it surpass the volume of the Hong Kong market.

How gold rates as an investment vehicle depends on the time frame. Since 1980, gold has been a laggard. It has dropped about 30% in US dollar terms. In the early 1980s the price moved between US$270 and slightly above US$500 as various political crises came and went.

But in recent years the gold price has been more stable, despite crises of greater severity. For instance, an upward movement in oil prices no longer produces a corresponding rise in gold prices.

In the future, I believe gold will be most affected by the development of reforms in the Soviet Union and in China. People in those countries have faith in the US dollar and in gold. The less confidence they have in their economic system, the greater will be the flight to gold.

Although gold is a good inflation hedge when a particular currency depreciates sharply, it will not actually protect against a downturn in the economy. In fact, the worst time to buy is when a recession causes consumer spending to weaken. As spending slumps, the price of gold inevitably falls.

Before investing in gold, it is best to consult the services of the various brokerage houses and banks in Asia where experts can advise one on international prices and possible investment strategies.

RULES AND REGULATIONS

Hong Kong

Hong Kong is the center of gold trading in Asia, and is thus a free market for gold.

Indonesia

Gold may be exported, but only under government license. There is no export duty.

Japan

A free market for gold, but banks cannot buy or sell gold on the free market.

Malaysia

Gold wafers are available in 5 gram to 50 gram pieces from certain foreign banks. The buyer receives a certificate guaranteeing its purity. Prices are posted daily.

Philippines

All buying and selling of gold is regulated and controlled by the central bank. Its gold refinery buys raw bullion from primary gold mines, gold panners and traders and the Philippine Associated Smelting and Refining Corporation (PASAR).

The refined gold bars make up a substantial portion of the central bank's reserves. Some of the gold is sold to foreign traders through the central bank treasury.

There are no restrictions on gold trading, and no duties or taxes, but private transactions involving individuals or companies are small by comparison with the trade with foreign traders. Pawnshops, jewelers, and dentists make up the bulk of these sidewalk transactions.

Singapore

Most banks buy and sell gold wafers varying from 5 grams to 1 kilogram as well as 1-ounce gold coins. For higher denominations, investors may either open gold accounts or obtain gold certificates. There are no restrictions in trading gold.

South Korea

Though difficult, it is possible for an individual to own gold for investment. There are plans to make it easier for the private sector to import gold. Import tariffs and excise taxes are being introduced.

Taiwan

Taiwan's Central Trust of China, the government financial institution which oversees gold transactions, places no restrictions on trading by foreigners. Customs regulations, however, prohibit the export of gold bullion or bars. In 1988, gold and gold products were exempted from the 5% sales tax.

Thailand

The gold trade is strictly controlled by the government. There is no legal market for investments is gold, but the government is trying to take positive steps to encourage jewelry-making. There is a sales tax on gold.

USEFUL CONTACTS

Hong Kong

Cheerful (Int.) Securities & Investment Co.
Rm 2105, World-Wide House
19 Des Voeux Rd., Central
Tel: 523-6131
Tlx: 61695 CFFLL HX
Fax: 868-0146
Contact person: Kenny Lee

Chow Tai Fook Jewellery Co. Ltd.
31st Floor, New World Tower
16 Queen's Rd., Central
Tel: 524-3166
Tlx: 73064 CTFHK HX
Fax: 810-4297

Citibank
46th Floor, 1 Exchange Square
8 Connaught Place, Central
Tel: 843-5333
Tlx: 63220
Fax: 845-0732

Hongkong and Shanghai Banking Corp.
1 Queen's Rd.
Central
Tel: 822-1111
Tlx: 73201 HKBC HX
Fax: 810-1112

King Fook Gold & Jewellery Co. Ltd.
30-32 Des Voeux Rd.
Central
Tel: 523-5111
Tlx: 61570 KFJLY HX
Fax: 845-1820
Contact person: Paul Cheung

Lee Cheong Gold Dealers Ltd.
Rm 705, 71 Des Voeux Rd.
Central
Tel: 521-3106
Tlx: 83005
Fax: 845-2649

Shun Loong Co.
Rm 2502 Admiralty Centre, Tower 1
18 Harcourt Rd.
Tel: 520-0111
Fax: 865-7017

Standard Chartered Bank
18/F, Standard Chartered Bank
Building
4-4A Des Voeux Road C
Tel: 820-3360
Fax: 877-0645
Contact person: Mary Shek

Sun Hung Kai Bullian Co. Ltd.
3rd Floor, Admiralty Centre, Tower 2
Harcourt Road
Tel: 527-7898
Tlx: 89545 SHKBD
Fax: 529-1641
Contact person: Gary Cheung

Thomson Bullion Co.
5th Floor, Hutchison House
10 Harcourt Rd.
Tel: 521-1661
Tlx: 63473
Fax: 810-0145

Indonesia

Bank Indonesia
Jl Thamrin 2
Jakarta
Tel: 372-408

Malaysia

Ban Hin Lee Bank Bhd.
43 Lebuh Pantai
10300 Penang
Tel: 230-5511
Tlx: 31260
Fax: 238-4937
Contact person: Benny Tan

Chung Khiaw Bank Ltd.
Chung Khiaw Bank Bldg.
Jln Raja Laut, Kuala Lumpur
Tel: 292-4511
Tlx: 30350
Fax: 291-0281
Contact person: Lawrence Teoh

Dexin Bullion & Futures Sdn Bhd.
1704-7, 17/F, Wisma Lim Foo Yong
86, Jln Raja Chulan, Kuala Lumpur
Tel: 242-9133
Tlx: 30149
Fax: 338-0886
Contact person: Ng Chee Leong

K M Oli Mohamed (M) Sdn Bhd.
Plaza Yow Chuan, Jln Tun Razak
Kuala Lumpur
Tel: 241-8259
Fax: 241-9932
Contact person: Cik Mariam

Kwong Yik Bank Bhd.
75 Jln Bandar
Kuala Lumpur
Tel: 232-5633
Tlx: 32733
Fax: 238-7227
Contact person: Mohd Yusof Hj
Nasir

Lee Wah Bank Ltd.
Chung Khiaw Bank Building
Jln Raja Laut, Kuala Lumpur
Tel: 292-7722
Tlx: 31877
Fax: 291-0281
Contact person: Tan Siak Tee

Standard Chartered Bank
Jln Ampang
Kuala Lumpur
Tel: 232-6555

Tlx: 31384
Fax: 238-3295
Contact person: John James

The Bank of Nova Scotia
Menara Boustead
Jln Raja Chulan, Kuala Lumpur
Tel: 241-0766
Tlx: 21123
Fax: 241-2160
Contact person: Aziz Haque

The Pacific Bank Ltd.
Wisma Genting
JlN Sultan Ismail, Kuala Lumpur
Tel: 261-4822
Tlx: 21133
Fax: 261-8253
Contact person: Ong Meng Teck

Philippines

**Central Bank Mint & Gold
Refinery Dept.**
East Avenue, Quezon City
Tel: 977071
Contact person: Guillermo Flores Jr.

Singapore

Credit Suisse
6 Battery Rd.
#37-01, Standard Chartered Bank
Building
Singapore 0104
Tel: 225-2055
Tlx: 24680
Fax: 229-1256
Contact person: Kelvin Kum

DBS Bank
6 Shenton Way
DBS Building
Tel: 220-1111
Tlx: 24455
Fax: 221-1306
Contact person: Jarrod Ong

First Interstate Bank of California
5 Shenton Way
#23-00 UIC Building
Tel: 225-2619
Tlx: 21798
Fax: 225-2850
Contact person: Daniel Goh

N M Rothschild & Sons (Singapore) Ltd.
9 Battery Road
#01-02 Straits Trading Building
Tel: 535-8311
Tlx: 21884
Fax: 535-8713
Contact person: William Woo

OCBC Bank
65 Chulia St.
OCBC Centre
Tel: 535-7222
Tlx: 21209
Fax: 533-7891
Contact person: Richard Lim

OUB Bullion and Futures Ltd.
1 Raffles Place
OUB Centre #15-00
Singapore 0104
Tel: 533-7000
Tlx: 22373/4
Fax: 533-2360
Contact person: Victor Liew/John Liau

Republic National Bank of New York (S) Ltd.
143 Cecil Street
#01-00 GB Building
Tel: 224-0077
Tlx: 20237
Fax: 225-5769
Contact person: Richard Tan

The Royal Bank of Canada
140 Cecil St.
#01-00 PIL Building
Tel: 224-7311
Tlx: 23411
Fax: 224-5635
Contact person: Tham Ming Soong

United Overseas Bank Ltd.
1 Bonham St.
Raffles Place
Tel: 533-9898

Tlx: 21539
Fax: 534-3028
Contact person: Teo Lye Hock

South Korea

Korea Exchange Bank 181 2-ka Ulji-ro
Chung-ku, Seoul
Tel: 77146
Tlx: 23141
Fax: 729-8874
Contact person: Yu Jong-sup

Korea First Bank
100 Kongpyong-dong
Chongro-ku, Seoul
Tel: 733-0070
Tlx: 24249
Fax: 774-7013
Contact person: Park Yong-Yi

Taiwan

Central Trust of China, Trading Dept.
49 Wuchang St.
Taipei
Tel: 331-3695
Tlx: 26254 TRUSTTRADE
Fax: 382-1047
Contact person: Lu Chin-chiao

Central United Development Corp.
2/F, 158 Anho Rd.
Taipei
Tel: 700-1262
Fax: 700-1265
Contact person: Daniel Peng

China Trust Precious Metals Co. Ltd.
3/F, 122 Tunhua N Rd.
Taipei 10590
Tel: 718-1811
Tlx: 16229 CTPM
Fax: 718-1773
Contact person: Charles Yang

Confederated Precious Metals Co.
11/F, Nanking E Rd., Sec 4,
Taipei
Tel: 717-6469
Fax: 718-8112
Contact person: Eugene Chen

Crédit Suisse, Representative Office
9/F, 685 Minsheng E Rd., Taipei
Tel: 717-0174
Tlx: 17704 CSTPE
Fax: 712-6509
Contact person: Michel Piquerez

Sky Shine International Corp.
12/F, Nanking E Rd., Sec 3, Taipei
Tel: 712-2500
Fax: 715-3000
Contact person: Elia Chang

Swiss Bank Corp., Representative Office
8/F, 687 Minsheng E Rd., Taipei
Tel: 719-4406
Tlx: 10060 SBCTPE
Fax: 719-4407
Contact person: B. Kriech

Taiwan Gold & Silver Corp.
9th Floor, 52 Nanking E Rd., C1
Taipei
Tel: 511-7511

Union Bank of Switzerland, Representative Office
11/F, 87 Chunghsiao E Rd., Sec 4,
Taipei
Tel: 772-3161
Tlx: 17296 UBSTPE
Fax: 752-4665
Contact person: Ernst Quiring

Wang Ding Precious Metal Co. Ltd.
64-2 Tayung Rd., Kaohsiung
Tel: 531-6126
Fax: 531-5033
Contact person:. Lin Chin-chang

UNIT TRUSTS

by John Snelgrove
General Manager (Marketing), National Mutual Investment Services, Ltd.

It's a safe bet that with rising affluence and a burgeoning middle class in Asia, demand for unit trusts will grow along with the region.

These investment vehicles allow investors to buy stakes in a professionally managed fund that is invested in a widely diversified portfolio, which investors might not be able to assemble on their own.

For small investors, the appeal is twofold.

First, even with limited funds, they can buy a share in a fund designed to minimize risks and maximize chances for profit, largely through diversification.

A general rule of thumb is that a carefully chosen portfolio of 15 international shares will reduce 90% of specific risk. To eliminate the other 10%, you will need between 500 and 1,000 shares.

Second, they gain entry to the specialist and overseas markets, where direct investment often demands an investment of time and knowledge that all but the most sophisticated investors lack.

Like investment trusts, unit trusts are a type of mutual fund. But while investment trusts are closed-ended (with a subscription limit), unit trusts are open-ended (no limit).

A unit trust is divided into equal portions called *units*. These are priced regularly, usually daily. Two prices are quoted for the units: the higher (offer) price, which is the price the investor pays for the units; and the lower (bid) price, which is the amount he or she will receive for the units.

Unit trusts rode a wave of growth during the 1980s that seemed to have crested when the stock market crashed in 1987. Fund sizes shrank as unit holders rushed to cash in their holdings when share prices plunged.

Many fund managers, in search of above-average performance, had taken above-average risks, investing in second or third line stocks, warrants, and special situations. Their clients paid the price.

Since then, administrative procedures have been tightened in most countries, and the industry has tracked a slow recovery. Most funds have recouped their losses.

Several funds managed to outperform market indices, mainly thanks to the robust performance of Asian-Pacific economies.

Regional funds invested in a wide range of smaller stock markets registered the highest-mid-range returns last year. These included: Singapore-Malaysia funds, Hong Kong funds, and Australian and Far Eastern funds, which have Japanese stocks in their portfolio. Japanese funds also did well.

Although the volatility of Far Eastern equity markets remains a cause for concern for many foreign investors, the region's long-term prospects for growth continue to attract investors.

Hong Kong, Singapore, and Malaysia are

the more traditional markets for investment. Other markets, such as Thailand, Korea, and Taiwan, remain less accessible.

Thailand, for example, restricts foreign holdings in equities, while Taiwan and Korea remain essentially closed to direct foreign investment, which is only possible through a number of closed-end unit trusts.

Regional fund managers still treat these countries as a bit of spice to be added to a core of Japanese stocks, which provide the element of stability in a portfolio. Fund managers have been creating an increasing number of new products tailored to almost every possible investment taste.

There are now funds invested by economic sector, in specific countries or regions, special situations, emerging economies and fledgling industries, currencies and bonds, and commodities and natural resources.

Faced with this stunning array of choice, investors should keep the basics in mind. They should identify their requirements: Whether they want a steady income stream or capital appreciation, and buy funds targeted at those objectives.

The risk factor attached to funds varies considerably. Since most funds invest globally, currency risks loom large. The risk can be lessened by a wider geographical spread and a balanced portfolio of several trusts with different objectives.

But to benefit fully from unit trusts, investors should recognize that the instruments are designed as long-term investments, and so should allocate only surplus funds not needed in the near future.

The advent of "umbrella" funds allows investors to obtain not only an effective spread but also the flexibility to be able to switch emphasis in changing market conditions.

Many of these umbrella funds have subfunds, which invest in currencies and fixed interest securities, as well as specialist and blue-chip equity funds.

Many advisors now offer Unit Trust Portfolio Management Services, whereby they will manage a client's funds, sometimes for a small fee. Given the client's preferences, the advisor will select a portfolio, make switching decisions, and remove most of the paperwork from the client.

Some fund managers are also beginning to introduce packages that offer some type of guaranteed investment return.

Trusts locking in a highest unit price or guaranteeing a rate of return or a return of original capital have stirred a great deal of interest among investors.

RULES AND REGULATIONS

Hong Kong

Following the October 1987 global stock market crash, Hong Kong moved to regulate the orderly growth and development of unit trusts.

A local Code of Unit Trusts and Mutual Funds already exists. The Unit Trust Association is studying the possibility of creating a self-regulatory organization.

One of the key tasks would be to examine how to set up risk-ranking of all funds authorized in the territory, so that investors can be better informed when they invest in a unit trust.

The following unit trusts are registered with the Hong Kong Securities Commission:

Baring Hong Kong Fund
Barclays ASF Hong Kong Fund
CEF Hong Kong Trust
Citicorp CI Hong Kong Equity
Colonial Securities Hong Kong Fund
Dao Heng Hong Kong Fund
G T Hong Kong Fund

GAM Hong Kong Inc.
Indosuez Hong Kong Fund
JF Hong Kong Trust
Mansion House HK Trust
NM Hong Kong Fund
Old Court Hong Kong Fund
Schroders Asia Hong Kong Fund
SHK Hong Kong Equity Fund
Thornton Hong Kong & China Gateway Fund
Wardley Global Selection HK Equity

Indonesia

A resource-rich country on the brink of industrialization, Indonesia has recently lured a number of fund management houses anxious to establish a foothold there to invest in its fledgling stock market.

Many believe Indonesia's market is poised for substantial development and want a piece of the action. Jardine Fleming's US$25 million Indonesia fund was floated in April and was fully subscribed.

There is one unit trust available to foreigners—the Indonesia Growth Trust—managed by Royal Trust Asia Ltd. Two other funds which foreigners can invest in are closed-end. They are the Malacca Fund, managed by Indosuez Asia Investment, and the Jakarta Fund, managed by Thornton Management Asia.

There is only one domestic institution which is currently permitted to sell unit trusts: Pr Danarek, at Jl Merdeka Selatan 13, Jakarta. Tel: 360-408. However, deregulation of the domestic unit trust industry is expected in 1991.

Japan

Recently, there has been a surge in unit trust investment by the Japanese. There are currently 14 investment trust management companies, all controlled by major stockbrokers.

Malaysia

The domestic mutual fund industry is relatively undeveloped.

Authorities have imposed a ceiling on the amount of funds that unit trusts can raise, except for ASN, a large equity trust only for ethnic Malays.

Most equity trusts in Malaysia have done poorly recently, and have underperformed the KLSE composite index for the past few years.

There are currently 26 mutual funds and unit trusts listed in Malaysia.

Here is a selection of international funds invested in Malaysian and Singaporean equities, managed from Hong Kong and available to foreign investors:

Barclays ASF Malaysia Fund
Baring Malaysia and Singapore Fund
Bridge Singapore and Malaysia Trust
GAM Singapore Malaysia Int.
Gartmore Singapore and Malaysia Trust
NM Singapore and Malaysian Fund
Wardley Global Selection

There are also some, closed-end country funds catering strongly to foreign institutions. They include:

- Malaysia Fund, Inc., a US$84 million fund listed on the New York Stock Exchange, managed by Morgan Stanley Asset Management, Inc. and administered at Vanguard Financial Center, Valley Forge, Pennsylvania 19482, USA. Tel: (215) 6486000.
- Malaysia Growth Fund, managed by Arab-Malaysian Unit Trusts Bhd, 22nd Floor, Bangunan Arab-Malaysian, Jalan Raja Chulan, 50200 Kuala Lumpur. Tel: 2382633, Fax: 2382842 This closed-end US$50 million equity trust fund is aimed at Japanese investors, but is open to all foreigners.

Philippines

There are five mutual funds that allow investment by foreigners in the Philippines stock market. They are: The Jardine Fleming Philippines Trust, Thornton Philippines Redevelopment Fund, IndoSuez Manila Fund, Jardine Fleming Philippines Investment Trust, First Philippines Investment Trust (Thornton).

The third is the Manila Fund, a closed-end fund managed by Indosuez Asia Investment Services and listed on the London Stock Exchange.

Singapore

The following funds are listed on the Stock Exchange of Singapore:

Investment trusts:
General Securities Investments, Harimau Investments, Overseas Union Securities, United International Securities.

Unit trusts:
AGF Growth Equity Fund, Asean Fund, Asian Development Equity Funds A & B, Indonesia Development Fund, Nomura Gulf Fund, Nomura Rosenberg Alpha Funds A & B, The Java Fund (Cayman), The Thai Prime Fund, Yamaichi Fund.

Investors should contact their stockbrokers to buy or sell the above.

South Korea

The Korean unit trust industry is the largest in Asia outside Japan. There are more than 150 unit trusts, investing both in bonds and equities, owned by more than 10% of the population, and managed by just three investment trust companies: Citizens Investment Trust Management Co., Daehan Investment Trust Co. and Korea Investment Trust Co.

These three companies also provide open-end and closed-end investment trust funds for

Korean Funds available—with direct access to market			
Name	*Type*	*Manager*	*Premium at 30/9/90*
Korean International Trust	open	Korea Inv	0.33%
The Korea Fund	cl NYSE	Scudder Stevens	9.79%
Korea Smaller Comps Trust	open	Korea Inv	NA
The Korea Trust	open	Daehan Inv	0.20%
Seoul International Trust	open	Korea Inv	0.33%
Seoul Trust	open	Daehan Inv	0.51%
Korea Growth Trust	open	Citizens Inv	19.95%
Korea Emerging Comps Trust	open	Citizens Inv	NA
Korea Europe Fund	cl LSE	Schroder Fund Man	0.49%
Korea Liberalisation Fund	cl LSE	Lucky/Tyndal	NA
Daehan Korea Trust	open	Daehan Inv	3.82%
Korea Pacific Trust	open	Korea Inv/Kleinwort	8.74%
Seoul Asia Index Trust	open	Citizens Inv/Bankers Trust	22.99%
Korean Funds available—without direct market access			
Barings Korea Fund	open	Baring Asset Mmt	
GT Korea Fund	open	GT Asia Ltd	
Barclays Korea Fund	open	Barclays ASF Ltd	

foreigners. One year ago, these funds were characterized by sizable premiums to net asset values based on scarcity value. The premiums have shrunk dramatically as the market has fallen, and since it has also become clear that the authorities intend to allow more foreign funds. Most of these funds are available through retail brokers. Those without direct market access either buy into direct funds or buy convertible bonds.

Taiwan

In the space of three years, Taiwan has seen the expansion and bursting of one of the biggest speculative bubbles in the recent history of finance.

Between February and October last year, the Stock Exchange of Taiwan (SET) index lost over 10,000 points, falling 80% to 2,560. Market capitalization fell from over US$290 billion, or 200% of GNP, to US$62 billion—just 40%.

As the index hurtled downwards through 3,000, the government's mounting anxiety resulted in the rushing through of three market liberalization measures with important long-term consequences: Government pension funds, or approx. NT$8 billion (US$290 million), in stocks; the Kuomintang-owned Fu Hwa was deprived of its monopoly on margin financing; and selected institutional investors were allowed to invest directly in the Taiwanese market.

The aim of all this is to stabilize the market by attracting local and foreign institutional interest. Institutions accounted for only 4.7% of the market when last tabulated by the TSE in 1988. The high level of involvement by unsophisticated retail investors has meant that trading is done on a momentum, rather than a countercyclical basis, resulting in extraordinary volatility.

The Taiwan market has also been notorious for its vulnerability to price manipulation by so-called "big hands"—large-scale price-manipulators. The government is believed to hold about 25% of the total shares outstanding in the market. Various family and corporate groups hold another 45% on a long-term basis. That means that the "free float" is small, and the trading velocity is extremely high.

From mid-1988 to March 1989, all tradeable shares were on average changing hands once a month. The market is not helped by the daily stock price movement limit of plus or minus 5%, a speculators' dream, which results in the market moving up or down by 5% most days. The system, which is designed to dampen speculative price movements, creates a "grey market" in shares, actually resulting in increased speculation.

For all this, the recent declines in the index mean that investment has arguably become, for the first time in three years, reasonable. Current index levels are likely to remain volatile, but at levels of around 3,500, the market stands on a historical P/E of 22 and prospective multiple of 29, with a yield of just under 1%.

Industrial blue chips trade at a much lower level: Taiwan's 40 largest companies trade at an average P/E of 19 and a yield of 1.6, the reason being that the larger share floats of the blue chips have made them poorer targets for speculators. In fact a reassessment of the valuation of the blue chips can be expected, as Taiwanese investors anticipate foreign interest in these larger companies.

Though foreign institutional investors can buy stocks (see Stocks section of this guide), individual foreign investors may not yet do so. But there are good opportunities to be had by buying into one of the existing country funds, which are typically long on blue-chips, short on financials. There are two open-ended funds, the *Formosa Fund* and the *Taipei Fund*, which have units to re-issue at NAV plus 1.4% sales charge, and can always be redeemed. There are two closed-end funds, the low-turnover *ROC Fund,* and the smaller *Taiwan Fund.* Ask your broker to check the discounts/premiums on these funds before buying.

Thailand

There are over 20 country funds investing in Thai equities. The majority are offshore, while five funds are listed and actively trade at SET.

Those listed at the SET tend to offer excellent value as they trade at near 20% discounts to their net asset values.

DEGREE OF RISK

High Risk

Equity funds invested in the more volatile markets or in specialist markets, where the base currency differs from that of the investor (i.e., gold, Singapore, Philippines, Thailand).

Medium to High Risk

Equity funds invested mainly in blue-chip stocks in major world markets (i.e., Japan, Europe, United States).

Medium Risk

Equity investments in either the investor's own base currency or with a wide geographical spread (i.e., international funds).

Low to Medium Risk

Fixed interest investments involving a currency risk (i.e., bonds, gilts).

Low Risk

Fixed interest investments in the investor's base currency or in currency funds (i.e., managed currency).

No Risk

Currency fund in the investor's base currency.

Note: Buying a unit trust means buying the underlying securities plus the base currency. The gain (or loss) is the sum of the change in value of the securities and the difference in the exchange rate (unless the fund manager has hedged the currency risk).

USEFUL CONTACTS

Hong Kong

CEF Investment Management, Ltd.
16th Floor
China Building
29 Queen Rd., Central
Tel: 8463688
Tlx: 82516
Fax: 8452920

Fidelity International, Ltd.
19th Floor
Jardine House
1 Connaught Place
Central
Tel: 848 1700
Tlx: 62739
Fax: 8459051

Gartmore Fund Managers (Far East), Ltd.
3608 2 Exchange Square
8 Connaught Place
Central
Tel: 5220160
Tlx: 65149
Fax: 8452141

GT Management (Asia), Ltd.
17th Floor
3 Exchange Square
8 Connaught Place
Central
Tel: 8427200
Tlx: 74579
Fax: 8685863

Jardine Fleming Unit Trusts, Ltd.
47th Floor
Jardine House
1 Connaught Place
Central
Tel: 8438888
Tlx: 85608
Fax: 810541 1

National Mutual Life Association of Asia, Ltd.
20th Floor
National Mutual Centre
151 Gloucester Rd.
Wanchai
Tel: 5757282
Tlx: 83497
Fax: 8345736

Schroder Asia, Ltd.
25th Floor
2 Exchange Square
8 Connaught Place
Central
Tel: 521 1633
Tlx: 75862/62162
Fax: 8681023/8681066

Sun Hung Kai Unit Trust Managers, Ltd.
9th Floor
Far East Finance Centre
16 Harcourt Rd., Central
Tel: 8662366
Tlx: 69330
Fax: 8612721

Thornton Management, Ltd.
10th Floor
United Centre
95 Queensway
Tel: 5283141
Tlx: 72009
Fax: 8656443

Wardley Investment Services (Hong Kong), Ltd.
12th Floor
Bank of America Tower
12 Harcourt Rd.
Tel: 8479600
Tlx: 73934
Fax: 8450226

Japan

Daiwa Banks, Ltd.
56 Bingomachi 2-chome
Higashi-ku, Osaka 541
Tel: 271-1221
Tlx: 63284/63457 DAIBANK J
Fax: 203-3414/246-2706

Mitsubishi Bank Ltd.
7-1, Marunouchi 2-chome
Chiyoda-ku, Tokyo 100
Tel: 240-1111
Tlx: 22358/22960

New Japan Securities Co., Ltd.
11, Kanda Surugadai chome
Chiyoda-ku, Tokyo 100
Tel: 219-111 1
Tlx: 22666/26216 SHINNIHON J

Malaysia

Kuala Lumpur Mutual Funds Bhd
IGB Plaza
Jalan Pekeliling
50400 Kuala Lumpur
Tel: 441-8344

Arab-Malaysian Equity Trust
21st Floor
Bangunan Arab-Malaysian
Jalan Raja Chulan,
50200 Kuala Lumpur
Tel: 238-2633
Fax: 238-2842

The Philippines

Anscor Capital and Investment Corp.
Asian Plaza 1
Legaspi Village
Makati, Metro Manila
Tel: 819-3151

Asian Oceanic Holdings (Philippines), Inc.
Makati Stock Exchange Building
Makati, Metro Manila
Tel: 815-9416

Ayala Investment Management, Inc.
Makati Stock Exchange Building
Makati, Metro Manila
Tel: 810-0961/2165

Citicorp Investment Philippines
379 Sen Gil J Puyat Ave.
Makati, Metro Manila
Tel: 815-739 1

First Metro Investment Corp.
7th Floor
Metrobank Plaza
Sen Gil J Puyat Ave.
Makati, Metro Manila
Tel: 810-3311

Multinational Investment Bancorporation
Prudential Bank Building
Ayala Ave., Makati
Metro Manila
Tel: 817-151 1/9609

PAIC Securities Corp.
PAIC Building
Paseo de Roxas
Makati, Metro Manila
Tel: 85-70-06

Philippine Veterans Investment Development Corp.
DAO 1, Salcedo St.
Legaspi Village
Makati, Metro Manila
Tel: 818-1338

Private Development Corporation of the Philippines
PDCP Building
6758 Ayala Ave.
Makati, Metro Manila
Tel: 810-0231

State Investment House Incorp.
State Centre Building
233 Juan Luna St.
Binondo, Manila
Tel: 49-22-19/29/30

DBS Bank
6 Shenton Way,
DBS Building
Tel: 220-111 1

Nomura Capital Management (S), Ltd.
6 Battery Rd.
No. 39-00 Standard Chartered Bank Building
Tel: 220-8766

OCBC-SIMBL Investment
65 Chulia St.
OCBC Centre
Tel: 535-7222

OUB Investment Management
50 Collyer Quay
No. 02-03 Overseas Union House
Tel: 222-3753

Royal Trust Asset Management
50 RaMes Place
No. 19-01 Shell Tower
Tel: 220-6233

Singapore Unit Trust
No. 13-03 Straits Trading Building
Battery Rd.
Tel: 532-3761

United Overseas Bank
UOB Building
1 Bonham St.
Raffles Place
Tel: 533-9898
Fax: 223-4300

Wardley Investment Services
21 Collyer Quay
No. 17-01 Hongkong Bank Building
Tel: 530-2828

South Korea

Baring Brothers & Co., Ltd.
1212 Kyobo Building
1, I-ka Chongro,
Chongro-ku, Seoul 110
Tel: 736-0692/4
Tlx: 33 166
Fax: 736-0695

Citizens Investment Trust Management Co., Ltd.
Dong Won Building
112-1 Ineui-dong,
Chongro-gu, Seoul
Tel: 743-7310/7450

Daehan Investment Trust Co.
44-31, Youido-dong
Yongdungpo-gu, Seoul
150-010
Tel: 785-166

Jardine Fleming (Securities), Ltd.
1, I-ka Chongro,
Chongro-ku, Seoul
110-121
Tel: 737-7712

Korean Investment Trust Co., Ltd.
24-4, Youido-dong
Yongdungpo-ku, Seoul
Tel: 789-41 14/785-1212
Tlx: 22216 KOINT K
Fax: 784-3178

Merrill Lynch Intl., Inc.
Suite 1311
Kyobo Building
1, I-ka Chongro,
Chongro-ku, Seoul
Tel: 735-7651/7357/5441/5442
Tlx: 32135 MLCMSO K
Fax: 730-7898

Prudential-Bache Securities Intl.
1, I-ka Chongro
Chongro-ku, Seoul
Tel: 739-3696

Vickers Da Costa, Ltd.
1, I-ka Chongro
Chongro-ku, Seoul
Tel: 738-1644

Taiwan

China Securities Investment Trust Co.
12th Floor
125 Nanking E Rd., Sec. 5
Taipei
Tel: 760-6123

Citibank
742 Minsheng E Rd.
Taipei
Tel: 537-8100

Fidelity Securities Investment Consultant Corp.
1 2th Floor
125 Nanking E Rd., Sec. 5
Taipei
Tel: 784-8935

International Investment Trust
17th Floor
167 Fuhsing N Rd.
Talpei
Tel: 7 13-7702

Jardine Fleming Taiwan, Ltd.
10th Floor
209 Sec. 1, Fuhsing S Rd., Taipei
Tel: 775-411 1

Kwang Hua Securities Investment & Trust Co.
11th Floor
658 Tunhua S Rd.
Taipei
Tel: 705-2690

National Investment Trust Co.
17th Floor
30 Chungking S Rd., Sec. 1
Taipei
Tel: 361-1561

Thailand

Asia Securities Trading Co., Ltd.
13th Floor
Bangkok Bank Building
333 Silom Rd.
Bangkok 10500
Tel: 224-7567
Fax: 236-3863

Bangkok First Investment and Trust, Ltd.
300 Silom Rd. Bangruk
Bangkok 10500
Tel: 237-6097/6797
Tlx: 84297 TH
Fax: 237-6736

**The Book Club Finance &
Securities Co., Ltd.**
500 Ploenchit Rd.
Bangkok
Tel: 256-9113
Fax: 253-9622

Cathay Trust Co., Ltd.
Finance & Security
Room 455

46-9 Rama V1 Rd.
Bangkok
Tel: 215-3850-2

The Mutual Fund Co., Ltd.
1770 New Petchburi Rd.
Bangkok 10310
Tel: 252-0570/9, 254-8000/20
Tlx: 82163 IFCTHAI TH
Fax: 253-1742/3992

Phatra Thanakit Co., Ltd.
183 Soi 13-15
Sukhumvit Rd.
Bangkok 10110
Tel: 253-0121
Tlx: 72513 PHATRA TH
Fax: 254-1240

WARRANTS

One of Asia's fastest-growing investment vehicles is not stocks or even money market instruments. It is warrants.

Warrants are the cheapest way for an investor to take a position and profit from any rising trend on the stock market, which is why they are so popular in Hong Kong, Singapore, and Tokyo, and why they will probably spread soon to other regional centers.

A warrant is similar to an option. The main difference is that options expire in six months, while warrants usually last two or three years.

Like options, the chief attraction of warrants is that they gear up your exposure to a company, costing you only a fraction of the share price.

For example, if you decide to buy a 1992 warrant for 10¢ in Share X with a conversion price of $1.00, you are buying the right to convert that warrant into stock for $1.00 any time before the warrant expires in 1992.

If the price of Share X rises from 80¢ to $1.60, the increase is 100%. But the value of the warrant could leap from 10¢ cents to 60¢ (the profit on the value of the share, which can still be bought at $1.00), a 500% jump.

Of course, any plunge in the share price will also cause the warrant price to fall. But when that happens, two factors come into play that cushion losses for warrant holders.

A warrant builds up a premium when a share price falls because there are always some market players who believe that the shares are bound to rise above the conversion price at some time in the future. Also, by holding warrants instead of stock, investors have in effect removed some of their cash from the stock market and can invest it in instruments bearing interest.

RULES AND REGULATIONS

Hong Kong, Singapore, Thailand and Malaysia

Warrants can be bought and sold in the same way as any other stock. Simply place an order with your broker. Hong Kong's and Singapore's markets are well established. New warrant markets emerged in 1990 in Thailand, Malaysia and Korea.

Japan

The Japanese warrant market is a different story. For one thing, there is no trading floor. It is an international market conducted by large market-making companies.

Another problem is that few Japanese market-makers can be bothered with retail investors. The major players are mutual funds and banks.

Two brokers that *will* deal for individual investors are Nomura Securities and James Capel. Their research is top notch and they have many retail outlets throughout Asia.

Like other Japanese market-makers, they make their money on the price difference between the buying and selling price, or the "spread." There is no other commission payable.

Though the center of market-making activity remains in London, Tokyo is where the greatest demand is. As Japanese trade in warrants increases, it seems likely that the current inefficient method of pricing will improve.

USEFUL CONTACTS

Hong Kong

Barings Securities (Hong Kong), Ltd.
8th Floor
3 Exchange Square
8 Connaught Place
Central
Tel: 8488488
Tlx: 89271 BFES HX
Fax: 8685192

Citicorp Scrimgeour Vickers (HK), Ltd.
42nd Floor
I Exchange Square
8 Connaught Place
Central
Tel: 8435777
Tlx: 74562
Fax: 8459303

James Capel (Far East), Ltd.
39th Floor
2 Exchange Square
Central
Tel: 8439111
Tlx: 75100
Fax: 5202945

Jardine Fleming Securities, Ltd.
46th Floor
Jardine House
Central
Tel: 84398888
Tlx: 75608
Fax: 8105411

Merrill Lynch Asia Pacific, Ltd.
15th–16th Floors
St. George's Building
2 Ice House St., Central

Tel: 8445678
Tlx: 73250
Fax: 8104160

Peregrine Securities, Ltd.
16th Floor
New World Tower
18 Queen's Rd., Central
Tel: 8456111
Tlx: 69251
Fax: 8459411

Schroder Asia Securities (HK)
25th Floor
2 Exchange Square
Central
Tel: 521 1636
Tlx: 62162
Fax: 8681023

SG Warburg Securities Far East, Ltd.
20th Floor
Alexandria House
Central
Tel: 5246113
Tlx: 83495
Fax: 8452075

Sun Hung Kai Securities, Ltd.
3rd Floor
Admiralty Centre
18 Harcourt Rd.
Wanchai
Tel: 8225621
Tlx: 74782
Fax: 8225664

WI Carr (Far East), Ltd.
21st Floor
St. George's Building
2 Ice House St., Central

Tel: 5255361
Tlx: 73036
Fax: 8681524

Japan

James Capel Pacific, Ltd.
I-I Marunouchi 3-chome,
Chiyoda-ku, Tokyo 100
Tel: 282-0111
Tlx: 23489
Fax: 282-0123

Nomura Securities
9-1, Nihombashi 1-chome
Chuo-ku, Tokyo 103
Tel: 211-1811

Singapore

BT Brokerage & Associates Pte, Ltd.
20 Collyer Quay
No. 19-00 Tung Centre
Tel: 224-9233

DBS Securities Singapore Pte, Ltd.
DBS Securities Building
22 Malacca St.
Tel: 533-9688

Fraser, Roach & Co. Pte, Ltd.
10 Collyer Quay
No. 27-01 Ocean Building
Tel: 535-9455

JM Sassoon & Co. Pte, Ltd.
I RaMes Place
No. 44-00 OUB Centre
Tel: 535-2888

Keppel Securities Pte, Ltd.
15 McCallum St.
No. 03-01/03 NatWest Centre
Tel: 221-5688

Morgan Grenfell Asia & Partners Securities Pte, Ltd.
65 Chulia St., No. 26-01
OCBC Centre
Tel: 533-1818

OCBC Securities Pte, Ltd.
18 Church St., No. 06-00
OCBC Centre South
Tel: 535-2882
Fax: 530-2768

OUB Securities Pte, Ltd.
50 Collyer Quay
No. 01-01 Overseas Union House
Tel: 225-1166

Paul Morgan & Associates (Securities) Pte, Ltd.
11 Collyer Quay
No. 18-01 The Arcade
Tel: 221-9991

Sun Hung Kai Securities Pte, Ltd.
20 Collyer Quay
No. 18-01 Tung Centre
Tel: 224-1688

South Korea

Coryo Securities Corp.
25-5 I-ka Chungmu-ro,
Choong-ku, Seoul 100-011
Tel: 771-36
Tlx: 23817 COSCO K
Fax: 752-7221

Daewoo Securities
34-3 Yoido-dong
Youngdeungpo-ku
Seoul 150-010
Tel: 784-8851/331 1
Tlx: 26332 DWSEC K
Fax: 784-0826

Daishin Securities
34-8 Yoido-dong
Youngdeungpo-ku
Seoul 150-010
Tel: 784-1711/8

Dongsuh Securities
34-1 Yoido-dong
Youngdeungpo-ku
Seoul 150-01
Tel: 784-1211

Jardine Fleming
I, I-ka Chongro
Chongro-ku, Seoul 110-121
Tel: 737-7712

Lucky Securities
34-6 Yoido-dong
Youngdeungpo-ku
Seoul 150-010
Tel: 784-7111

Merrill Lynch International, Inc.
Suite 1311, Kyobo Building
1, I-ka, Chongro
Chongro-ku Seoul
Tel: 735-7651
Tlx: 32135 MLCMSO K
Fax: 730-7898

Nikko Securities
25th Floor, I Sokong-dong,
Choong-ku, Seoul 100-721
Tel: 778-1456/7
Tlx: 28148 NIKKOSL K
Fax: 752-7690

Ssangyong Securities
198 2-ka Ulchiro
Choong-ku, Seoul 100-192
Tel: 771-12

WI Carr (Overseas), Ltd.
21st Floor, I Sokong-dong
Choong-ku, Seoul
Tel: 734-1250

FUTURES

by Peter Tryde
Director, Anderson Man (Investment Services), Ltd.

Futures markets have burst onto the global scene with such force that they now far exceed the world's stock markets in volume turn-over. Futures are actively traded in Asia, especially in Japan, Hong Kong, and Singapore.

A futures contract is an agreement to buy or sell a commodity or financial instrument at a set price on a specified date. It was originally designed to help shield commodity producers from price fluctuations. Futures contracts now cover precious metals such as gold, silver, and platinum, and energy sources like crude oil.

One of the major growth areas has been in

financial futures. Investors can buy contracts covering stock index futures, which provide a barometer of trends on the world's stock markets. Interest rate futures offer an attractive way of investing in government fixed interest securities, such as U.S. Treasury bonds, U.K. gilts, or Eurodollars. Currency futures provide access to the world's foreign exchange markets.

Futures offer a number of real advantages over equities and bonds. Their flexibility makes it possible to reap profits from futures in both rising and falling markets, in times of recession and inflation.

Since there is evidence that price changes on the futures market (other than the stock indices) are not closely tied to stock market price changes, futures are a good way to diversify a portfolio.

Also, they are highly geared investments, meaning that the margin payment is capable of securing a contract 10 times or more its value. The markets are very liquid and now strictly regulated.

Many investors have been wary of futures, regarding them as high-risk instruments best left to wealthy speculators. But investors with limited funds can do well in the market, if they don't allow the relatively low cost of entering the market to blind them to the potentially large downside risk, should prices fall.

The key to successful trading is tight money-management control, a disciplined strategy and a consistent approach to the various commodity markets.

To buy or sell a futures contract, the investor must first make a cash deposit, called the margin, which is usually 10% of the face value of the contract. This is really a security deposit to protect against price changes and not an equity payment or down payment on the asset.

The price of the contract is established through open bid and offer between buyers and sellers on the exchange floor until a transaction is made.

If the market moves against investors, they will be subject to a margin call. That means they will be required to provide more money to cover the loss and maintain the deposit at the original level. Here is where the potential for trouble lies. Before the stock market crash in 1987, the low margin required for trading futures attracted many small investors, who did not realize that their risk was virtually unlimited when prices plunged.

Daily profits or losses on futures positions are determined by the difference between the contract price when the position was opened and the current futures settlement price. Such gains and losses are adjusted, or marked to the market, at the end of each business day.

Few contracts result in the physical delivery of a commodity. Most futures positions are liquidated with offsetting trades before the contracts mature. The usually high liquidity of the market makes it easy for the trader to enter or leave the market.

For the small investor ready to enter the futures market, it is best to contact a broker to help implement a trading strategy. Based on sophisticated chart analysis, a broker can help determine the best entry point and employ what is known as stop-loss orders. These are price levels at which the positions are automatically liquidated because the market has gone against the investor.

A word of caution: Stop-loss orders cannot fully protect the investor. When the market is moving quickly and the volume is thin, a broker may be unable to liquidate his customer's position at the specified price. So the investor may incur losses beyond those he was willing to risk when entering the futures market.

In Asia, Japan and Hong Kong are the major centers of futures activity. New Japanese bond, stock index, currency, and interest rate contracts are being launched.

RULES AND REGULATIONS

Hong Kong

The Hong Kong Futures Exchange is trying to recover from the hard knock it took when the stock market crashed in 1987, causing defaults of US$1.8 million on stock index futures contracts.

The Securities and Futures Commission, a government watchdog agency set up after the crash to reform Hong Kong's markets, has postponed approval of a new interest rate futures contract until early this year. The contract will be based on the three-month Hong Kong interbank offered rate, or Hibor. The main snag appears to be how much to increase the margin level.

The main contract offered on the Hong Kong Futures Exchange is the Hang Seng Index. It is a weighted aggregate made up of 33 major stocks representing 75% of the total market capitalization. The minimum price fluctuation is one index point or HK$50. The initial margin is HK$30,000.

Indonesia

Futures are not traded in Indonesia.

Japan

Osaka is the region's pioneering futures market. Its Stock Futures 50 contract is the world's second largest, lagging just behind the Standard & Poor's 500 contract in Chicago in value terms.

Recently, the Tokyo Financial Futures Market debuted, with trading in U.S. Treasury bonds, Euroyen, and Eurodollar interest rates as well as foreign exchange.

Index futures have been available in Japan since September 1988, when two contracts were launched: the Tokyo First Section (TOPIX Index), which trades on the Tokyo Stock Exchange, and the Nikkei Stock Index, which trades in Osaka.

Malaysia

Although the idea of having stock index futures based on the Kuala Lumpur Stock Exchange Composite Index has been much discussed, there has been little progress. The futures market is concentrated in primary commodities.

Formed in 1980, the Kuala Lumpur Commodity Exchange (KLCE) launched its first futures contract in crude palm oil. After a stormy period of defaulting contracts and finally a temporary shutdown, the exchange was restructured in 1985. The new rules are similar to, if not more stringent than, those in the United States. There are rubber, tin, and cocoa futures, the last two contracts quoted in U.S. dollars.

Membership in the exchange is open to any company incorporated in Malaysia.

Alternatively, traders can become trade affiliates. Trade affiliates have no voting rights but can trade on their own accounts or for the accounts of overseas clients at reduced brokerage.

To open an account, any player who is not a member must deal through a broker registered with the Commodities Trading Commission in Malaysia and also through a member of the KLCE.

Singapore

The Singapore International Monetary Exchange (SIMEX) trades in currency futures and options, interest rate futures, Nikkei, gold, and fuel oil futures. Currencies traded are the Deutschmark, Japanese yen, and pound sterling.

The two interest rate futures contracts are the three-month Eurodollar and Euroyen contracts. Trading is done through SIMEX members. Margin requirements vary according to contracts and the volatility of market conditions.

Taiwan

Futures are not yet legally available, although they are offered illegally by underground investment houses. Legislation is currently under consideration.

Thailand

Futures, along with warrants and options, are undeveloped instruments on the local capital market. Although a few local banks, foreign banks and certain finance companies are trying to pioneer these more sophisticated products, the lack of a clear government policy has inhibited their growth, as has general market interest. The organization of a commodities futures market is being considered.

USEFUL CONTACTS

Hong Kong

Barings Securities (Hong Kong), Ltd.
8th Floor
3 Exchange Square
8 Connaught Place
Central
Tel: 8488488
Tlx: 89271 BFES HX
Fax: 8685192

Citicorp Scrimgeour Vickers (HK), Ltd.
42nd Floor
1 Exchange Square
8 Connaught Place
Central
Tel: 8435777
Tlx: 74562
Fax: 8459303

Elders Hong Kong
7th Floor
Hong Kong Club Building
38 Chater Rd.
Tel: 8488100
Tlx: 62699
Fax: 8450949

James Capel (Far east), Ltd.
39th Floor
2 Exchange Square
Central
Tel: 8439111
Tlx: 75100
Fax: 5202945

Jardine Fleming Securities, Ltd.
46th Floor
Jardine House
Central
Tel: 8438888
Tlx: 75608
Fax: 81054411

Schroder Asia Securities (HK)
25th Floor
2 Exchange Square
Central
Tel: 521 1636
Tlx: 62162
Fax: 8681023

Sun Hung Kai Securities, Ltd.
3rd Floor
Admiralty Centre
18 Harcourt Rd.
Wanchai
Tel: 8225621
Tlx: 74782
Fax: 8225664

Union Bank of Switzerland (HK)
13th Floor
Gloucester Tower
11 Pedder St., Central
Tel: 8461111
Tlx: 73629
Fax: 8461123

Wardley Thomson, Ltd.
7th Floor
Hutchinson House
Harcourt Rd.
Tel: 8418888
Tlx: 75440 WRDLY HX
Fax: 8459047

Japan

Baring Securities, Ltd.
10th Floor
3-2 Kasumigaseki 3-chome
Chiyoda-ku Tokyo 100
Tel: 595-8811
Tlx: 25791
Fax: 593-2634

Citicorp Scrimgeour Vickers International, Ltd.
24th Floor
12-32 Akasaka 1-chome
Minato-ku, Tokyo 107
Tel: 589-7400
Tlx: 28304
Fax: 581-4196

Daiwa Securities
6-4, Ohtemachi 2-chome
Chiyoda-ku, Tokyo 100
Tel: 243-2111
Tlx: 22411
Fax: 245-0363

DB Capital Markets Asia, Ltd.
22nd Floor
1-12-32, Akasaka 1-chome
Minato-ku, Tokyo 107
Tel: 589-1986
Tlx: 34943
Fax: 589-4810

Jardine Fleming Securities, Ltd.
1-7, Uchisaiwai-cho 1-chome
Chiyoda-ku, Tokyo 100
Tel: 508-0261
Tlx: 28173
Fax: 595-1924

Merrill Lynch Japan, Inc.
3, Otemachi
Chiyoda-ku, Tokyo 100
Tel: 213-7000
Tlx: 22952
Fax: 213-7005

Nikko Securities
3-1, Marunouchi 3-chome
Chiyoda-ku, Tokyo 100
Tel: 283-2211
Tlx: 22410
Fax: 283-3090

Nomura Securities
9-1, Nihonbashi 1-chome
Chuo-ku, Tokyo 103
Tel: 211-1811
Tlx: 22393
Fax: 278-0420

Yamaichi Securities
4-1, Yaesu 2-chome
Chou-ku, Tokyo 103
Tel: 276-3181
Tlx: 22959
Fax: 660-5697

Malaysia

The Kuala Lumpur Commodity Exchange Baring Securities, Ltd.
4th floor, Citypoint
Jln Sultan
Hishamuddin
50740 Kuala Lumpur

Tel: 293-6822
Tlx: 31472
Fax: 274-2215

The Philippines

Agrotex Commodities, Inc.
Allied Bank Center
Makati, Metro Manila
Tel: 815-8801

Golden Commodities Corp.
Athenaeum Building
Makati, Metro Manila
Tel: 819-2668/2698/2701

Goldwell Commodities Traders, Inc.
Vernida I Building
Makati, Metro Manila
Tel: 808-1221

Imperial Commodities, Inc.
Producers Bank Building
Makati, Metro Manila
Tel: 819-3351

Madura Merchandise Futures, Inc.
ARCO Building
Makati, Metro Manila
Tel: 8 15-2743

Masters Commodities Futures, Inc.
Montepino Building
Makati, Metro Manila
Tel: 818-3128/3286

Onapal Philippines Commodities, Inc.
Dolmar Gold Tower
Makati, Metro Manila
Tel: 818-83 11/8325
Fax: 817-9540

Singapore

Citicorp Futures, Ltd.
5 Shenton Way
No.26-02 UIC Building
Tel: 225-9422

Credit Lyonnais Rouse (Pte), Ltd.
50 RaMes Place

No.13-03 Shell Tower
Tel: 221-3380

DBS Trading Pte, Ltd.
6 Shenton Way
DBS Building
Tel: 220-1111

Drexel Burnham Lambert (S) Pte, Ltd.
No.22-08 UIC Building
5 Shenton Way
Tel: 225-1388

Merrill Lynch Futures (S) Pte, Ltd.
50 Raffles Place
No.27-01 Shell Tower
Tel: 221-0555

Nomura Futures (S) Pte, Ltd.
6 Battery Rd.
No.39-01 Standard Chartered Bank Building
Tel: 220-8766

Prudential-Bache Securities Asia Pacific, Ltd.
5 Shenton Way
26th Floor
UIC Building
Tel: 224-6122

Wardley-Thomson Futures (S) Pte, Ltd.
21 Collyer Quay
No.20-02 HK Bank Building
Tel: 225-4007

South Korea

Cargill Investor Service Korea
80 Chuksun-dong, Chongno-ku, Seoul
Tel: 739-2163
Fax: 739-0581
Contact person: Whang Ku-bong

CL-Rouse
541, 5-ka Namdaemun-ro, Chung-ku, Seoul
Tel: 754-5161
Fax: 755-5379
Contact person: Lee Kang-heok

FOREIGN EXCHANGE

RULES AND REGULATIONS

Hong Kong

Hong Kong has no central bank. There are no exchange control regulations, so investors can freely move capital and repatriate profits. Dividends and interest are fully remittable.

Indonesia

The Indonesian rupiah is freely convertible. It is linked to a basket of currencies of Indonesia's trading partners. However, the government has allowed the currency to depreciate against the U.S. dollar.

Japan

The Ministry of Finance, the Ministry of International Trade and Industry, and the Bank of Japan operate the foreign exchange control system. But most of the authority for verifying normal payments rests with authorized foreign exchange banks.

There are no taxes or subsidies on the buying or selling of foreign exchange.

Malaysia

A nonresident does not need the permission of the controller of foreign exchange to undertake direct or portfolio investment in Malaysia. Payments to countries outside Malaysia can be made in any foreign currency other than the currencies of South Africa and Israel.

Foreign investors can freely repatriate realized capital gains, dividends, interest, and principal. But they must notify the central bank of Malaysia, Bank Negara, when making remittances above M$5,000 (US$1,860).

Foreign investors must also seek Bank Negara's approval when making remittances for more than M$2 million (US$742,000) in a single transaction. Borrowing Malaysian dollars locally to finance investments abroad is usually not allowed.

The Philippines

The Central Bank must authorize all incoming and outgoing capital. If an authorized securities dealer handles the transactions, approval is automatic. The dealer/broker is responsible for registering securities transactions by foreigners. The process can be slow, but full repatriation of capital is guaranteed.

Singapore

There are no restrictions in the trading of foreign exchange. Investors may contact any of the major banks for rates and quotes.

South Korea

Foreign exchange control is extremely complex, with incoming and outgoing currency flows closely watched by the Korean government. That said, rules are slowly being loosened.

Taiwan

Resident foreigners may sell up to US$1 million per year in foreign exchange. They may buy up to US$5 million per year. Foreign visitors may bring in or sell up to US$5,000 in foreign exchange, but may not buy any unless they can show receipts of previous sales transactions.

Thailand

Foreign exchange is strictly controlled by the government and organized speculation violates local laws. But there is no limitation on the amount of foreign exchange that can be remitted to Thailand for portfolio investment. Such transactions must be registered with the central bank, the Bank of Thailand, in order for profits to be repatriated.

USEFUL CONTACTS—FOREIGN EXCHANGE

Hong Kong

Bank of America NT & SA
22nd Floor, Bank of America Tower
12 Harcourt Rd., Central
Tel: 8476382/8100821
Tlx: 73373
Fax: 8475410

The Chase Manhattan Bank, NA
40th Floor, 1 Exchange Square
8 Connaught Rd., Central
Tel: 8414295
Tlx: 7 1 958
Fax: 843 1240

Citibank NA
45th Floor, 1 Exchange Square
8 Connaught Place, Central
Tel: 8100177/0900/1861
Tlx: 73000
Fax: 8101861

Dresdner Bank AG
4th Floor, World Wide House
19 Des Voeux Rd., Central
Tel: 5210104/5286346
Tlx: 65545
Fax: 8459071

The Hongkong and Shanghai Banking Corp.
1 Queen's Rd.
Central
Tel: 822211 1
Tlx: 75 130
Fax: 8681646

Jardine Fleming & Co., Ltd.
45th Floor, Jardine House
1 Connaught Place, Central
Tel: 8438463/8438467/8452009
Tlx: 89088
Fax: 8452009

Manufacturers Hanover Trust Co.
43rd Floor, Edinburgh Tower
The Landmark, Central
Tel: 8416888
Tlx: 73951
Fax: 8459062

The Mitsubishi Bank, Ltd.
14th Floor, Tower 1, Admiralty Centre
18 Harcourt Rd.
Tel: 8236666
Tlx: 74357
Fax: 8610794

Union Bank of Switzerland
13th Floor, Gloucester Tower
11 Pedder St., Central
Tel: 5223036/8461 123
Tlx: 60210
Fax: 8461 123

Wardley, Ltd.
6th Floor, Hutchison House
10 Harcourt Rd.
Tel: 8418888
Tlx: 73934
Fax: 8450226

Indonesia

American Express Bank
Gedung Arthaloka
Jl Sudirman 2, Jakarta
Tel: 587-401

Bank Bumi Daya
Jl Imam Bonjol 61
Jakarta
Tel: 333-721

Bank Dagang Negara
Menara BDN
Jl Kebon Sirih 83, Jakarta
Tel: 380-0800

Bank Expor Impor Indonesia
Jl Lapangan Stasiun 1
Jakarta
Tel: 673-122

Bank Indonesia
Jl Thamrin 2
Jakarta
Tel: 372-408

Bank Negara Indonesia
Jl Sudirman Kav I
Jakarta
Tel: 570-0706. Fax: 570-0980

Bank of America
Wisma Antara
Jl Merdeka Selatan 17, Jakarta
Tel: 347-031

Bank Rakyat Gedung BRI
Jl Sudirman Kav 42-43
Jakarta
Tel: 587-621

Hongkong & Shanghai Banking Corp.
Jl Hayam Wuruk 8
Jakarta
Tel: 380-3306

Standard Chartered Bank
Wisma Kosgoro
Jl Thamrin 53, Jakarta
Tel: 325-008

Japan

Bank of Tokyo
3-2, Nihonbashi Hongokucho 1-chome
Chuo-ku, Tokyo 103
Tel: 245-111 1
Tlx: 2220

Dai-Ichi Kangyo Bank
1-5, Uchisaiwai-cho 1-chome
Chiyoda-ku, Tokyo 100

Tel: 596-2533
Tlx: 22379/223 15
Fax: 596-5349

Daiwa Bank
2-1 1 Otemachi
Chiyoda-ku, Tokyo 100-91
Tel: 231-1231

Fuji Bank
5-5, Otemachi 1-chome
Chiyoda-ku, Tokyo 100
Tel: 216-2211
Tlx: 24311
Fax: FUJIBANK J

Industrial Bank of Japan
3-3 Marunouchi 1-chome
Chiyoda-ku, Tokyo 100
Tel: 214-111
Tlx: 22325

Mitsubishi Bank
7-1, Marunouchi 2-chome
Chiyoda-ku, Tokyo 100
Tel: 240-1111
Tlx: 22358

Mitsui Bank
1-2 Yurakucho 1-chome
Chiyoda-ku, Tokyo 100
Tel: 501-1111
Tlx: 22378 MITSUIBK J
Fax: 50-2478

Sanwa Bank
10, Fushimimachi 4-chome
Higashi-ku, Osaka 541
Tel: 202-2281
Tlx: 63234
Fax: 229-1064

Sumitomo Bank
1-3-2 Marunouchi
Chiyodda-ku, Tokyo 100
Tel: 282-5111. Fax: 292-5706

Malaysia

Bangkok Bank, Ltd.
105 Jln Bandar
50000 Kuala Lumpur
Tel: 232-8677/8793
Tlx: 30359

Bank Bumiputra Malaysia Bhd
Menara Bumiputra
Jln Melaka, 50913 Kuala Lumpur
Tel: 298-8011/1011
Tlx: 30911/31673

Chung Khaiw Bank, Ltd.
Jln Raja Laut,
50944 Kuala Lumpur
Tel: 292-5293/291-0281
Tlx: 30232

Citibank NA
28 Medan Pasar
50050 Kuala Lumpur
Tel: 230-5058/232-8763
Tlx: 31046/30628

Deutsche Bank
15 Jln Raja Chulan
50200 Kuala Lumpur
Tel: 230-1081
Tel: 31071

Malayan Banking Berhad
100 Jln Tun Perak
50050 Kuala Lumpur
Tel: 230-8833
Tlx: 30964

Oriental Bank
111 Jln Bukit Bintang
55100 Kuala Lumpur
Tel: 242-0111/243-0935
Tlx: 21323/32580

Pacific Bank Berhad
Wisma Genting
Jln Sultan Ismail, 50250 Kuala
Lumpur
Tel: 230-5033/232-1549
Tlx: 30075

Standard Chartered Bank
2 Jln Ampang
50450 Kuala Lumpur
Tel: 232-7766/230-0867
Tlx: 32947

**United Malayan Banking Corp.
Bhd**
Jln Sultan Sulaiman
50935 Kuala Lumpur
Tel: 230-9866/232-2627
Tlx: 30309

The Philippines

American Express Bank, Ltd.
3rd Floor, 121 Paseo de Roxas
Makati, Metro Manila
Tel: 817-2611/2589
Tlx: 25474

The Bank of Tokyo
3rd Floor, 121 Paseo de Roxas
Makati, Metro Manila
Tel: 88-19-76
Tlx: 22182

Banque Nationale de Paris
G/f, Makati Ave and H V De La
Costa St.
Makati, Metro Manila
Tel: 85-85-12/817-9237
Tlx: 45489/64408

Central Bank of the Philippines
A Mabini and Vito Cruz
Metro Manila 2801
Tel: 50-70-51/93, S2-23-98
Tlx: 7232/66140

Metropolitan Bank & Trust Co.
Sen Gil J Puyat Ave.
Makati, Metro Manila
Tel: 810-3311/50, 817-6248
Tlx: 63555

**Philippine Commercial
International Bank**
19th Floor, PCIB Tower I
Makati Ave., Makati, Metro Manila
Tel: 817-1041/818-3946
Tlx: 63156

Philippine National Bank
PNB Building
Escolta, Manila
Tel: 48-41-11
Tlx: 63 186

Pilipinas Bank
135 Puyat Ave., Salcado Village
Makati, Metro Manila
Tel: 819-1931

Piso Bank
853 Pasay Rd.
Makati, Metro Manila
Tel: 88-86-91/5, 86-70-81/5
Tlx: 63237

Rizal Commercial Banking Corp.
333 Sen Gil J Puyat Ave.
Makati, Metro Manila
Tel: 819-3061/0458
Tlx: 22454/22701

Singapore

Algemene Bank Nederland NV
18 Church St.
Tel: 535-5511

Citicorp
UIC Building
5 Shenton Way
Tel: 224-2611

Deutsche Bank AG
No. 01-01 Treasury Building
8 Shenton Way
Tel: 224-4766

Malayan Banking Berhad
No. 01-00 Malayan Bank Chambers
2 Battery Rd.
Tel: 535-2266

Morgan Guaranty Trust Co of New York
No. 30-01 DBS Building
6 Shenton Way
Tel: 220-8144

NM Rothschild & Sons (S), Ltd.
No. 01-02 Straits Trading Building
9 Battery Rd.
Tel: 535-8311

National Australia Bank, Ltd.
No. 26-02/07 Ocean Building
10 Collyer Quay
Tel: 535-7655
Fax: 534-4264

The National Bank of Kuwait
No. 20-00 Tung Centre
20 Collyer Quay
Tel: 222-5348

Swiss Volksbank
No. 08-00 Hong Kong Bank Building
21 Collyer Quay
Tel: 220-8188

The Sumitomo Bank, Ltd.
No. 01-09 DBS Building
6 Shenton Way
Tel: 220-1611

South Korea

American Express Bank, Ltd.
20th Floor, No. 541 S-ka
Namdaemoon-ro
Chung-ku, Seoul
Tel: 253-2646/8, 755-5186
Tlx: 32287

ANZ Bank
18th Floor, Kyobo Building 1-Ka
Chongro-Ku, Seoul
Tel: 730-3151/60, 737-6325
Tlx: 24604

Asian Banking Corp.
Hanyang Investment Finance Corp Bldg. 9-10
2-ga Ulchiro, Chung-gu, Seoul
Tel: 778-0521/9, 756-4408
Tlx: 23447

Banque Indosuez
22/F Kyobo Building
1-1 Chongro, Chongro-ku, Seoul
Tel: 723-6241/2, 738-0325
Tlx: 28124

The Chase Manhattan Bank NA
50-1 -ka Ulchiro
Chung-ku, Seoul
Tel: 777-5781/758-5114
Tlx: 22858/2551

Citibank NA
89-29-Ka Shinmoon-Ro
Chongro-gu, Seoul 110
Tel: 739-6649/738-0095
Tlx: 25707

Korea Development Bank
I 0-2 Kwanchol-dong
Chongnoku, Seoul 100
Tel: 732-9941/733-4768
Tlx: 22261/2

Korea Exchange Bank
181 2-ka Ulchiro
Chung-ku, Seoul
Tel: 752-2851/757-2276
Tlx: 27774/5

The Korea Housing Bank
36-3 Yoido-dong
Youngdeungpo-ku, Seoul
Tel: 784-7711/3403
Tlx: 27879

Standard Chartered Bank
13th Floor, 2-ka Ulchi-ro
Chung-ku, Seoul
Tel: 752-8185/757-7444
Tlx: 33101

Taiwan

Bank of Taiwan
120 Chungking S Rd., Sec. I
Taipei
Tel: 314-7377. Fax: 381-2284

Chase Manhattan Bank
72 Nanking E Rd., Sec. 2
Taipei
Tel: 537-8100

Chemical Bank
7th Floor, 685-Minsheng E Rd.
Taipei
Tel: 712-1181

Citibank
742 Minsheng E Rd.
Taipei
Tel: 715-593i

The Export-Import Bank of the Republic of China
7th Floor, 3 Nanhai Rd., Taipei 10728
Tel: 321-05 11/394-0630
Tlx: 26044

First Commercial Bank
30 Chungking S Rd., Sec. I
Taipei
Tel: 311-1111

Hollandsche Bank-Unie
483 Minsheng E Rd.
Taipei
Tel: 503-7888

Hongkong & Shanghai Banking Corp.
14th Floor, 333 Keelung Rd., Sec. I
Taipei
Tel: 738-0088
Fax: 757-6333

International Commercial Bank of China
100 Chilin Rd.
Taipei
Tel: 563-3156

Standard Chartered Bank
337 Fuhsing N Rd.
Taipei
Tel: 716-6261

Thailand

Bangkok Bank, Ltd.
333 Silom Rd.
Bangruk, Bangkok 10500
Tel: 234-3333
Tlx: 82638 BKBANK TH

Bangkok Metropolitan Bank, Ltd.
2 Chalermkhetr 4 Rd.
Pomrab, Bangkok 10100
Tel: 223-0561
Tlx: 72047 METROBK TH

Bank of Ayudhya, Ltd.
550 Ploenchit Rd.
Lumpini, Bangkok 10500
Tel: 253-8601
Tlx: 82334

Banque Indosuez
142 Wireless Rd.
Bangkok 10500
Tel: 250-1917
Tlx: 81156

Citibank NA
127 South Sathorn Rd.
Bangkok 10120
Tel: 286-3392/4
Tlx: 82429 CITIBK TH

The International Commercial Bank of China
95 Suapa Rd.
Bangkok 10110
Tel: 221-8121/4
Tlx: 87369

Krung Thai Bank, Ltd.
35 Sukhumvit Rd.
Bangkok 10110
Tel: 251-2111
Tlx: 81179

Siam Commercial Bank, Ltd.
1060 Phetchaburi Rd.
Bangkok 10400
Tel: 251-31 14
Tlx: 82995

Standard Chartered Bank
G/F Dusit Thani Office Building
946 Rama IV Rd., Bangkok 10500
Tel: 234-0821
Tlx: 81163

The Thai Military Bank, Ltd.
34 Phyathai Rd.
Phayathai, Bangkok 10400
Tel: 246-0020
Tlx: 87900

BANKS

Hong Kong

Bank of America
23rd Floor, Bank of America Tower
12 Harcourt Rd.
Tel: 8476031
Tlx: 63762
Fax: 8476660

Bank of Tokyo
1st Floor, Far East Finance Center
16 Harcourt Rd.
Tel: 8627888
Tlx: 73252
Fax: 5293821

Citibank NA
Citicorp Centre, 18 Whitfield Rd.
North Point
Tel: 8078211
Tlx: 73243
Fax: 8078322

Commercial Bank of Hong Kong, Ltd.
The Commercial Bank of Hong Kong Building
120 Des Voeux Rd., Central
Tel: 5419222
Tlx: 73085
Fax: 5410009

Dai-Ichi Kangyo Bank, Ltd.
31st Floor, Gloucester Tower
11 Pedder St., Central

Tel: 5266591
Tlx: 60489
Fax: 8101326

Hang Seng Bank, Ltd.
77 Des Voeux Rd.
Central
Tel: 8255111
Tlx: 733 11
Fax: 8684047

Hongkong and Shanghai Banking Corp.
1 Queen's Rd.
Central
Tel: 8221111
Tlx: 73205
Fax: 868 1646

Overseas Trust Bank, Ltd.
OTB Building
160 Gloucester Rd.
Tel: 5756657
Tlx: 74545
Fax: 868 1646

Standard Chartered Bank
14th Floor, Edinburgh Tower
15 Queens Rd., Central
Tel: 8422333
Tlx: 73230/74750
Fax: 8100651

Union Bank of Hong Kong, Ltd.
Union Bank Building
59-65 Queen's Rd., Central
Tel: 5251041
Tlx: 73264
Fax: 8680051

Indonesia

Bank Bali
Jl Hayam Wuruk 84-85
Jakarta
Tel: 649-8006

Bank Central Asia
Wisma BCA, Jl Sudirman Kav 22-23
Jakarta
Tel: 578-0022

Bank Danamon
Jl Kebon Sirih 15
Jakarta
Tel: 380-4800

Bank Duta
Jl Kebon Sirih 11-12
Jakarta
Tel: 380-0900

Bank Internasional Indonesia
Jl Juanda 37-38
Jakarta
Tel: 377-688

Bank Niaga
Jl Thamrin 55
Jakarta
Tel: 373-651

Bank Surya Indonesia
Jl Coklat 29,
Surabaya
Tel: 20-611

Bank Umum Nasional
Jl Prapatan 50
Jakarta
Tel: 365-563

Lippo Bank
Lippo Life Building
Jl Rasuna Said Kav B-10, Jakarta
Tel: 511-561

Pan Indonesia Bank
Panin Bank Centre
Jl Sudirman, Jakarta
Tel: 739-4545

Japan

Bank of Tokyo
1-3-2 Nihonbashi-Hongoku-cho
Chuo-ku, Tokyo 103
Tel: 245-1111

Dai-Ichi Kangyo Bank
5 Uchisaiwai-cho
Chiyoda-ku, Tokyo 100
Tel: 596-1111

Daiwa Bank
2-1-1 Otemachi
Chiyoda-ku, Tokyo 100
Tel: 231-1231

Fuji Bank
1-5-5 Otemachi
Chiyoda-ku, Tokyo 100
Tel: 216-2211

Mitsubishi Bank
2-7-1 Marunouchi
Chiyoda-ku, Tokyo 100
Tel: 240-1111

Mitsui Bank
2 Yurakucho
Chiyoda-ku, Tokyo
Tel: 501-1111

Sanwa Bank
I Otemachi
Chiyoda-ku, Tokyo 100
Tel: 216-3111

Sumitomo Bank
1-3-2 Marunouchi
Chiyoda-ku, Tokyo 100
Tel: 282-5111

Taiyo Kobe Bank
1-3-1 Kudan-Minami
Chiyoda-ku, Tokyo 100-91
Tel: 230-3111

Tokai Bank
2-6-1 Otemachi
Chiyoda-ku, Tokyo 100
Tel: 242-2111

Malaysia

Amanah Merchant Bank
19th Floor
Bangunan Komplek Kewangan
82 Jln Raja Chulan, 50200 Kuala
Lumpur
Tel: 261-0155
Fax: 261-5770

**Arab-Malaysia Merchant Bank
Bhd**
Bangunan Arab-Malaysian
55 Jln Raja Chulan, 50200 Kuala
Lumpur
Tel: 238-2633
Tlx: 31 167
Fax: 238-2842

Aseambankers Malaysia Bhd
33rd Floor, Menara Maybank
100 Jln Tun Perak, 50050 Kuala
Lumpur
Tel: 238-4211
Fax: 238-4194

**D&C Mitsui Merchant Bankers
Bhd**
22nd Floor, Wisma On-Tai
161 B Jln Ampang, 50450 Kuala
Lumpur
Tel: 261-2444
Tlx: 30913 DCNOMU MA
Fax: 261-9241

The Philippines

Allied Banking Corp.
Allied Bank Center, 6754 Ayala Ave.
Makati, Metro Manila
Tel: 816-3311/31

Bank of the Philippine Islands
BPI Building, Ayala Ave Corner
Paseo de Roxas
Makati, Metro Manila
Tel: 810-2791/818-5541

Citibank NA
Citibank Center, 8741 Paseo de
Roxas
Makati, Metro Manila
Tel: 815-7000/818-9161

Citytrust Banking Corp.
379 Sen Gil J Puyat Ave.
Makati, Metro Manila
Tel: 818-0411

Far East Bank and Trust Co.
Far East Bank Complex, Muralla St.
Intramuros, Manila
Tel: 40-10-21/30

Metrobank
Metrobank Plaza Building
Sen Gil J Puyat Ave.
Makati, Metro Manila
Tel: 810-3311

**Philippine Commercial
International Bank**
I PCI Bank Towers 1, Makati Ave.
(corner)
HV de la Costa
Makati, Metro Manila
Tel: 817-1021/9794

Philippine National Bank
Escolta
Manila
Tel: 40-20-51/60-41

Rizal Commercial Banking Corp.
333 Sen Gil J Puyat Ave. Extension
Makati, Metro Manila
Tel: 819-3061

Solidbank Corp.
Solidbank Building, Dasmarinas corner
Juan
Luna St.
Binondo, Manila
Tel: 49-43-11/21

Singapore

Bangkok Bank Ltd.
180 Cecil St.
Singapore 0106
Tel: 221-9400

Bank of Tokyo
16 RaMes Quay, No. 01-06 Hong Leong Building
Singapore 0104
Tel: 220-8111

Citibank NA
5 Shenton Way, UIC Building
Singapore 0106
Tel: 224-2611

DBS Bank
6 Shenton Way, DBS Building
Singapore 0106
Tel: 220-1111

Hongkong & Shanghai Banking Corp.
10 Collyer Quay, No. 01-01 Ocean Building
Singapore 0104
Tel: 530-5000

Indian Overseas Bank
64 Cecil St., IOB Building
Singapore 0104
Tel: 225-1100

OCBC Bank
65 Chulia St.
No. 11-00 OCBC Centre
Singapore 0104
Tel: 535-7222

Overseas Union Bank, Ltd.
1 Raffles Place, OUB Centre
Singapore 0104
Tel: 533-8686

Standard Chartered Bank
6 Battery Rd.
Singapore 0104
Tel: 225-8888

South Korea

Bank of 110, Namdaemun-ro Ka
Chung-ku, Seoul
Tel: 771-07
Tlx: 24711 KOREABK K

Bank of Seoul
10-1, 2-ka, Namdaemun-ro
Chung-ku, Seoul
Tel: 771-60

Cho Hung Bank
14, 1-ka Namdaemun-ro
Chung-ku, Seoul
Tel: 733-2000
Tlx: 23321

The Citizens National Bank
9-1, 2-ka, Namdaemun-ro
Chung-ku, Seoul
Tel: 771-40

Commercial Bank of Korea
111- I, 2-kq Namdaemun-ro
Chung-ku, Seoul
Tel: 771-30
Tlx: 24611

Hanil Bank
130, 2-ka, Namdaemun-ro
Chung-ku, Seoul
Tel: 771-20
Tlx: 23824

The Korea Development Bank
10-2, Kwanchul-dong
Chongro-ku, Seoul
Tel: 733-2121

Korea Exchange Bank
181, 2-ka, Ulji-ro
Chung-ku, Seoul
Tel: 771-46
Tlx: 23141

Korea First Bank
100 Kongpyong-dong
Chongro-ku, Seoul
Tel: 733-0070
Tlx: 24249

Shinhan Bank
120, 2-ga, Taepyung-ro
Chung-ku, Seoul
Tel: 765-0505

Taiwan

Bank of Communications
91 Hengyang Rd.
Taipei
Tel: 361-3000

Bank of Taiwan
120 Chungking S Rd., Sec. 2
Taipei
Tel: 314-7377

Chang Hwa Commercial Bank
38 Tsuyu Rd., Sec. 2
Taichung
Tel: 222-2001

Citibank
742 Minsheng E Rd.
Taipei
Tel: 715-5931

Cooperative Bank of Taiwan
77 Kuanchien Rd.
Taipei
Tel: 311-8811

First Commercial Bank
30 Chungking S Rd., Sec. 1
Taipei
Tel: 311-1111

Hollandische Bank-Unie
483 Minsheng E Rd.
Taipei
Tel: 503-7888
Fax: 502-3017

Hua Nan Commercial Bank
38 Chungking S Rd., Sec. 1
Taipei
Tel: 361-9666

International Commercial Bank of China
100 Chilin Rd.
Taipei
Tel: 563-3156

Shanghai Commercial & Savings Bank
16 Jenai Rd., Sec. 2
Taipei
Tel: 393-3111

Thailand

Bangkok Bank, Ltd.
333 Silom Rd.
Bangruk, Bangkok 10500
Tel: 234-3333
Tlx: 82638 BKBANK TH

Bangkok Metropolitan Bank, Ltd.
2 Chalermkhetr 4 Rd.
Pomrab, Bangkok 10100
Tel: 223-0561
Tlx: 72047 METROBK BK

Bank of Ayudhya, Ltd.
550 Pleonchit Rd.
Bangkok 10330
Tel: 253-8601/8632
Fax: 253-8589
Tlx: 82334

First Bangkok City Bank, Ltd.
20 Yukhon 2 Rd.
Pomprab, Bangkok 10100
Tel: 223-0500/19

The Industrial Finance Corp. of Thailand (IFCT)
1770 New Petchburi Rd.
Bangkapi, Bangkok 10310
Tel: 253-6520/9
Tlx: 82163 IFCTHAI TH
Fax: 253-9677

Krung Thai Bank, Ltd.
35 Sukhumvit Rd.
Bangkok 101 10
Tel: 255-2222
Tlx: 81179/82331 KTBANK TH

The Siam Commercial Bank
1060 New Petchburi Rd., Magasun
Phyathai, Bangkok 10400

Tel: 251-31-14
Tlx: 82876 SIAMCOM TH

The Thai Farmers Bank, Ltd.
400 Phaholyothin Rd.
Phyathai, Bangkok 10400
Tel: 270-1122/270-1133
Tlx: 72083-8

The Thai Military Bank, Ltd.
34 Phyathai Rd.
Phyathai, Bangkok 10400
Tel: 246-0020
Tlx: 82324 MILITBK TH
Fax: 246-1576

Thai Thai Danu Bank, Ltd.
393 Silom Rd.
Bangkok 10500
Tel: 233-9160/9
Tlx: 82959 DANUBAN TH

ACCOUNTANCY FIRMS

Hong Kong

Arthur Andersen & Co.
25th Floor, Wing On Centre
111 Connaught Rd., Central
Tel: 8520222
Tlx: 74096
Fax: 8150548

Coopers & Lybrand
23rd Floor, Sunning Plaza
10 Hysan Ave.
Tel: 8394321
Tlx: 74378
Fax: 5761507

Deloitte Haskins & Sells
26th Floor, Wing On Centre
111 Connaught Rd., Central
Tel: 5450303
Tlx: 73175
Fax: 5411911

Ernst & Young
15th Floor, Hutchison House
10 Harcourt Rd., Central
Tel: 8469888
Tlx: 76449
Fax: 8459208

Ivan Tse & Co.
Rm 504, Kai Wong Commercial Building
222-226 Queen's Rd., Central
Tel: 54 13502
Fax: 8541087

Peat Marwick
8th Floor, Prince's Building
Chater Rd.
Tel: 5226022
Tlx: 74391
Fax: 8452588

Price Waterhouse/LowBingham & Matthews
22nd Floor, Prince's Building
Chater Rd.
Tel: 5222111
Tlx: 73751
Fax: 8109888

Thomas Le C Kuen & Co.
Rm 2207, Wing On Centre
111 Connaught Rd., Central
Tel: 5434144
Tlx: 83932
Fax: 5417268

Touche Ross & Co.
31st Floor, 1 Exchange Square
8 Connaught Place
Tel: 8100776
Tlx: 74590
Fax: 8105323

Indonesia

Bernardi Drs. & Co.
Jl Cokroaminoto 117
Jakarta
Tel: 342-894

Drs. Hadi Sutanto
4th Floor, Ficorinvest Building
Jl Rasuna Said Kav C-18, Jakarta
Tel: 513-516

Drs. Hans Kartikahadi & Co.
Jl Kaji 33M
Jakarta
Tel: 355-076

Drs. Paul Hadiwinata & Co.
Jl Panglima Polim Ivl 1

Jakarta
Tel: 770–883

Drs. S. Reksoatmodjo
Jl Wahid Haysim 2
Jakarta
Tel: 327–860

Drs. S. Sudomo
Jl Percetakan II/S I
Jakarta
Tel: 773–478

Drs. Siddharta & Siddharta
3rd Floor, Bina Mulia Building
Jl H R Rasuna Said, Kav 10, Jakarta
Tel: 512–151

Drs. Utomo & Co.
8th Floor, Chase Plaza
Jl Sudiman Kav 21, Jakarta
Tel: 570–3691

Hanadi Sudjendro & Co.
12th Floor, Wisma Dharmala Sakti
Jl Sudiman 32, Jakarta
Tel: 578–1718

Konsultan Subhan Basuki
3rd Floor, Bina Mulia Building
Jl Rasuna Said Kav 10, Jakarta
Tel: 520–7370

Japan

Arthur Andersen & Co.
Nihonseimei Akasaka Building
I-19 Akasaka
8-chome, Minato-ku, Tokyo
Tel: 403–4211

Arthur Young
Nissei Building 1-18 Ageba-cho
Shinjuku-ku, Tokyo 162
Tel: 235–8551
Tlx: 33920 ASCINTL J
Fax: 235–8555

Coopers & Lybrand
29th Floor, Kasumigaseki Building
2-5 Kasumigaseki
3-chome, Chiyoda-ku, Tokyo 100
Tel: 581–7535
Tlx: 24971 COLYBRAND J
Fax: 593–2410

Deloitte Haskins & Sells
Mita Kokusai Building, 4–28, Mita 1-chome
Minato-ku, Tokyo 108
Tel: 454–1251
Tlx: 26252 DHSTOK
Fax: 455–8775

Ernst & Whinney
c/o Showa Ota & Co.
Hibiya Kokusai Building
2-2-3 Uchisaiwai-cho, Chiyoda-ku
Tokyo 100
Tel: 503–1191
Tlx: 27625 ANK BK OTA
Fax: 503–1196

Peat Marwick Minato
3 M Building, 1-21 Akasaka, 7-chome
Minato-ku, Tokyo 107
Tel: 403–2551
Tlx: 28609 PMMTYO
Fax: 423–1826

Malaysia

Arthur Andersen
24th Floor, Menara Tun Razak
Jln Raja Laut, 50786 Kuala Lumpur
Tel: 293–5133
Fax: 293–5360

Arthur Young
3 Jln Kampung Attap
50460 Kuala Lumpur
Tel: 274 3722
Tlx: 31517 LIMALI MA
Fax: 274–8227

Coopers & Lybrand
IGB Plaza 22/23 Floor
Jalan Kampar, Kuala Lumpur
Tel: 441–1188
Tlx: 31156 COLYB MA
Fax: 441–0880

401 Kompleks Antarabangsa
JIN Sultan Ismail, 50250 Kuala
Lumpur
Tel: 242–2533
Tlx: 30418 ERNST MA
Fax: 241–0676

HRM Sdn Bhd
Level 5-Block C (South), Pusat
Bandar
Damansara
Damansara Heights, 50734 Kuala
Lumpur
Tel: 255–7000
Tlx: 31182 HARUM MA
Fax: 255–5332

Peat Marwick
Wisma Perdana
50490 Kuala Lumpur
Tel: 254–3833
Tlx: 30974
Fax: 255–0971

Price Waterhouse
10th–11th Floors, Wisma Sime Darby
Jln Raja Laut
50350 Kuala Lumpur
Tel: 293–1077
Fax: 293–0992

Philippines

Berris and Co.
Metrobank Plaza Building
Makati, Metro Manila
Tel: 818-8526/9081

Carlos J. Valdes and Co.
108 Aguirre St.
Makati, Metro Manila
Tel: 85-77-06/99-61

Garcia Matienzo Alon and Co.
Ferros Building
Makati, Metro Manila
Tel: 818-5046/5055

Guzman Bocaling and Co.
Regina Building
Manila
Tel: 47-38-45/40-24-67

JP Tolentino and Co.
Filipinas Life Building
Makati, Metro Manila
Tel: 815-0957/810-0702

Joaquin Cunanan and Co.
B A Lepanto Building
Makati, Metro Manila
Tel: 818-7622

LC Diaz and Co.
Zeta Building
Makati, Metro Manila
Tel: 86-43-25

Punongbayan and Araullo
Vrnida IV Building
Makati, Metro Manila
Tel: 810-9741/815-2630

Roraldo Gatdula Rosales and Co.
Legaspi Towers 200
Makati, Metro Manila
Tel: 817-9214/7090

Sycip, Gorres, Velayo and Co.
6760 Ayala Ave.
Makati, Metro Manila
Tel: 819-3011

Arthur Andersen & Co.
No. 21-00 UIC Building
5 Shenton Way
Tel: 220-4377

Boon Suan Lee & Co.
220 Orchard Rd.
No. 05-01 Midpoint Orchard
Tel: 235-3388

Coopers & Lybrand
No. 12-00 Supreme House
9 Penang Rd.
Tel: 336-2344

Deloitte Haskins & Sells
No. 27-01 Standard Chartered Bank
Building
6 Battery Rd.
Tel: 224-8288
Fax: 224-7520

Ee Peng Liang & Co.
No. 21-01 Ocean Building
10 Collyer Quay
Tel: 535-7777

Ernst & Young
10 Collyer Quay
No. 21-01 Ocean Building
Tel: 535-7777

Foo Kon & Tan
No. 05-04 Chinese Chamber of
Commerce & Industry Building
47 Hill St.
Tel: 336-3355

Peat, Marwick
No. 22-00 Hong Leong Building
16 RaMes Quay
Tel: 220-741 1

Touche Ross & Co.
1 RaMes Place
No. 40-00 OUB Centre
Tel: 532-4177

South Korea

Ahnjin & Co.
5th Floor Samwhan Camus Building
17-3 Yoido-dong
Youngdeungpo-ku, Seoul 150-010
Tel: 784-8906
Tlx: 29720 ERNST
Fax: 785-4753

Ahn Kwon Co.
9-10th Floor, International Insurance
Building
120, 5-ka, Namdaemun-ro
Choong-ku, Seoul
Tel: 753-0215/9
Tlx: 4350
Fax: 753-3486

**Arthur Andersen Management
Information Consultants**
Suite 1600, Kyobo Building 1, I-ka
Chongno, Chongno-ku, Seoul
Tel: 739-9000
Tlx: 29194
Fax: 739-6999

Ernst & Young
11-14th Floor, Dae Yu Bldg, 25-15
Yeoidodong, Yungdeungpo-ku,
Seoul
Tel: 785-0981/0985
Tlx: 24263
Fax: 785-6991

Samil Accounting Corp.
Suite 2100, Kukje Center Building
191, 2-ka, Hankang-ro, Yongsan-ku
Seoul
Tel: 796-7000
Tlx: 27549 LYBRAND K
Fax: 796-7027

San Tong & Co.
7th Floor, Koreana Building, 61-ka
Taipyung-ro

Chung-ku, Seoul
Tel: 733-2345
Tlx: 26432 PEATCO K
Fax: 733-5317

Seihwa Accounting Corp.
9th floor, Sam Whan Building
98-5, Uni-dong, Chongro-ku, Seoul
Tel: 745-8500
Tlx: 24908 PRICEHS K
Fax: 738-0447

Young Wha Accounting Corp.
11th-14th Floor, Dae Yu Building
25-15, Yeoido-dong
Youngdeungpo-ku, Seoul
Tel: 784-5261
Tlx: 24263 ATYOUNG K
Fax: 785-6991

Taiwan

Price Waterhouse
27th Floor, 333 Keelung Rd.
Sec. I, Taipei
Tel: 738-6000
Fax: 757-6371/2

**Chiang, Lai, Lin & Co
(Touche Ross International)**
13th Floor, 102 Kuangfu S Rd.,
Taipei
Tel: 711-3927

**Der Ching & Co.
(Deloitte Haskins & Sells)**
6th Floor, 18 Chang-an E Rd. Sec. 1
Taipei
Tel: 523-8686

Diwan Ernst & Young
333 Keelung Rd.
Sec. 1, Taipei
Tel: 736-4000

Peat, Marwick, Mitchell & Co.
12th Floor, 367 Fuhsing N Rd.
Taipei
Tel: 713-8001

Prosperity United Firm
10th Floor, Pan-Asia Building
130 Chung Hsiao E Rd.
Sec. 2, Taipei
Tel: 351-7201

TN Soong & Co.
7th Floor, 53 Nanking E. Rd., Sec. 2
Taipei
Tel: 551-7272
Fax: 521-5755

Thailand

Cooper & Lybrand
8th Floor, Sathorn Thani Building
90/14-16 North Sathom Rd.
Bangkok 10500
Tel: 236-5227
Tlx: 82840 COLYB TH
Fax: 236-5226

Ernst & Young
9th Floor, Sinthon Bldg.
132 Wireless Rd., Bangkok
Tel: 255-5240
Tlx: 87661 ERNST TH
Fax: 254-7418

Solomon & Chang CPAs
4th Floor, 9 Tsingtao E Rd.
Taipei
Tel: 341-5151

LAW FIRMS

Hong Kong

Baker & McKenzie
Rm 1401, Hutchison House
Harcourt Rd., Central
Tel: 8461888
Tlx: 76416
Fax: 8450476

Coudert Brothers
Rm 3105, Alexandra House
16-20 Chater Rd., Central
Tel: 8104111
Tlx: 74073 AMLAW HX
Fax: 8459021

Clifford Chance
30th Floor, Jardine House
1 Connaught Place, Central
Tel: 8100229
Tlx: 61770
Fax: 8104708

Deacons
3rd-8th Floor, Alexandra House
16-20 Chater Rd., Central
Tel: 8259211
Tlx: 73475
Fax: 8100431

Kao Lee & Yip Solicitors
Rm 630, Swire House
Chater Rd., Central
Tel: 8444888
Tlx: 65902
Fax: 8100620

Kaye, Scholer, Fierman, Hays & Handler
32nd Floor, Admiralty Centre, Tower 1
18 Harcourt Rd., Central
Tel: 8657676
Tlx: 62816
Fax: 8661062/8661259

Paul, Weiss, Rifkind, Wharton & Garrison
Rm 2008, 2 Exchange Square
8 Connaught Place, Central
Tel: 5220041
Tlx: 66208
Fax: 8680124

Robert WH Wang & Co.
4th Floor, Edinburgh Tower
15 Queens Rd., Central
Tel: 8437333
Tlx: 64003
Fax: 8459125/8452504

Slaughter & May
27th Floor, 2 Exchange Square
8 Connaught Place, Central
Tel: 5210551
Tlx: 86230
Fax: 8459079

Stevenson Wong & Co.
Rm 1438, Swire House
Chater Rd., Central
Tel: 5266311
Tlx: 65868
Fax: 8459184

Indonesia

Ali Budiardjo, Nugroho, Reksodiputro
10th Floor, Wisma Argo Manunggal
J1 Gatot Subroto 22, Jakarta
Tel: 516-744

Gani Djemat & Associates
J1 Imam Bonjol 76-78
Jakarta
Tel: 321-816

JP Rooney & Associates, Ltd.
4th Floor, Panunee Building
518/3 Ploenchit Rd., Bangkok 10500
Tel: 251-2323/252-0177
Tlx: 87238

Price Waterhouse
4th Floor, Chongkolnee Building
56 Surawong Rd., Bangkok 10500
Tel: 233-1470/5
Tlx: 82329 PWCOBKK TH
Fax: 236-0264

SGV-Na Thalang & Co., Ltd.
Na Thalang Building
514/1 Larnluang Rd, Dusit
Bangkok 10300
Tel: 280-0900
Tlx: 82805 CERTBKK TH

Kusnandar & Associates
1 6th Floor, Central Plaza
J1 Sudirman 48, Jakarta
Tel: 516-840

Lubis, Hadiputranto, Ganie, and Surowidjojo
27th Floor, Bank Bumi Daya Plaza
J1 Imam Bonjol 61, Jakarta
Tel: 334-441

Makarim & Taira
17th Floor, Summit Mas Building
J1 Sudirman 61-62, Jakarta
Tel: 586-726

Mochtar, Karuwin & Komar
14th Floor, Wisma Metropoltan 11
J1 Sudirman Kav 31, Jakarta
Tel: 578-1130

Oei That Hway
CS J1 Kali Besar Barat 5
Jakarta
Tel: 677-226

Padmo Sumasto & Associates
J1 Cinajur 9
Jakarta
Tel: 340-094

Ratna Wulan & Partner
20th Floor, Wisma Kosgoro
J1 Thamrin 53, Jakarta
Tel: 321-631

Japan

Asahina & Co.
7th Floor, NS Building, No. 2-22
Tanimachi 2-chome, Chuo-ku,
Osaka 540
Tel: 943-8922
Tlx: J63752 BREVAT

Nagashima & Ohno
Toraya Building, Akasaka 4-chome
Minato-ku, Tokyo 107
Tel: 404-9171

Nakagawa Godo
11-3 Akasaka, 3-chome
Minato-ku, Tokyo 107
Tel: 589-2921

Tomotsune, Kimora & Mitomi
14-2 Nagatacho, 2-chome
Chiyoda-ku, Tokyo 100
Tel: 580-0800

Malaysia

Chooi & Co.
Bangunan Ming, Jln Bukit Nanas
505250 Kuala Lumpur
Tel: 2327344

Shearn Delamore & Co.
Bangunan Standard Chartered Bank
2 Benteng, 50050 Kuala Lumpur
Tel: 2300644

Shook Lin & Bok
25th Floor, Wisma HLA, Jln Raja
Chulan
50200 Kuala Lumpur
Tel: 2480088
Fax: 243-8067

Skrine & Co.
Bangunan Straits Trading
4 Lebuh Pasar Besar

50050 Kuala Lumpur
Tel: 2985111

Zain & Co.
Bangunan Dato Zainal, Jln Ampang
50450 Kuala Lumpur
Tel: 2986255

The Philippines

**Angara, Abello, Concepcion,
Regala and Cruz Associates**
ACCRA Building
Makati, Metro Manila
Tel: 817-0966

Carpio, Villaraza and Cruz
5th Floor, 118 Perea, Legaspi Village
Makati, Metro Manila
Tel: 818-9836

**Castillo, Laman, Tan and
Pantaleon**
138 HV de la Costa
Salcedo Village, Makati, Metro
Manila
Tel: 817-6791/8lo-4371n3

**Herrera-Laurel, de los Reyes,
Roxas and Teehankee**
5th Floor, NCR Center, Alfaro St.
Salcedo Village, Makati, Metro
Manila
Tel: 815-8846

**Ponce-Enrile, Cayetano, Reyes
and Manalastas**
Vemida IV Building
Makati, Metro Manila
Tel: 815-9571

**Quasha, Aspirilla, Ancheta, Pena
and Nolasco**
Don Pablo Building
Makati, Metro Manila
Tel: 86-30-11/87-57-36

**Quisumbing, Torres and
Evangelista**
10th Floor, 156 Valero St.
Salcedo Village, Makati, Metro
Manila
Tel: 817-3016/0940

**Romulo, Mabanta, Buenaventura,
Sayoc & de los Angeles**
King's Coun

Makati, Metro Manila
Tel: 86-50-61

**Siguion-Reyna, Montecillo and
Ongsiako**
A Soriano Building
Makati, Metro Manila
Tel: 810-0281

**Sycip, Salazar, Hernandez and
Gatmaitan**
105 Paseo de Roxas
Makati, Metro Manila
Tel: 817-9811/2001

Singapore

Allen & Gledhill
No. 18-01 City House
36 Robinson Rd.
Tel: 225-1611

Donaldson & Burkingshaw
No. 15-00 Clifford Centre
24 Raffles Place
Tel: 533-9422
Fax: 534-3905

Drew & Napier
No. 27-01 Clifford Centre
24 Raffles Place
Tel: 535-0733

Godwin & Co.
No. 13-01 Raffles City Tower
North Bridge Rd.
Tel: 339-9983

Haridass Ho & Partners
No. 28-05
Shell Towers
Tel: 225-5656

Laycock & Ong
No. 09-01 Sinsov Building
55 Market St.
Tel: 533-9115

Lee Boon Leong & Co.
No. 11-00 HMC Building
2 Mistri Rd.
Tel: 222-3122

Shook Lin & Bok
No. 06-00 Malayan Bank Chambers
2 Battery Rd.
Tel: 535-1944

Sinclair Roche & Temperley
No. 52-02 OUB Centre
I Raffles Place
Tel: 534–1444
Fax: 532 5454

Wee Swee Teow & Co.
Jo. 27-01 OCBC Centre
65 Chulia St.
Tel: 532-2966

South Korea

Central International
5th Floor, Korean Re-Insurance
Building
No. 80, Soosong-dong, Chongro-ku,
Seoul
Tel: 735–562
Tlx: 23250 CENTPAT K
Fax: 744–520

Kim & Song
Suite 2206, Kukdong Building
60-1, 3-ka, Chungmu-ro, Chung-ku
Seoul
Tel: 274–6788
Tlx: 28677 KSLAW K
Fax: 274–6392

Lee & Ko
Suite 1607, 118, 2-ka Nandaemun-ro
Chung-ku, Seoul
Tel: 753–2151
Tlx: 22887 LAWLEE K
Fax: 753-0375

Lim, Chung & Suh
Suite 1709, 541, S-ka, Namdaemun-
ro
Choong-ku, Seoul
Tel: 755–8288
Tlx: 29887 NAMSAN K
Fax: 754-0077

Shin & Kim
1-122, 2-ka, Shinmun-ro
Chongro-ku, Seoul 110
Tel: 732–6336
Tlx: 22375 JUSTICE K
Fax: 739-492

Taiwan

Baker & McKenzie
4th Floor, 685 Minsheng E Rd.
Taipei
Tel: 712-6151

Century International
12th Floor, 65 Sungkiang Rd.
Taipei
Tel: 506-7197

McCutchen, Doyle, Brown & Enerson
10th Floor, 333 Keelung Rd., Sec. 1
Taipei
Tel: 738-5000

Ding & Ding
4th Floor, 205 Tunhwa N Rd.
Taipei
Tel: 713-6300

Formosa Transnational
15th Floor, 136 Jen Ai Rd., Sec. 3
Taipei
Tel: 741-7366

Huang & Partners
10th Floor, 683 Minsheng E Rd.
Taipei
Tel: 713-5428

Kaplan, Russin & Vecchi
9th Floor, 205 Tunhwa N Rd.
Taipei
Tel: 713-6110
Fax: 713-4711

Lee & Li
7th Floor, Formosa Plastics Building
201 Tunhwa N. Rd., Taipei
Tel: 715-3300

Taiwan International Patent & Law Office
7th Floor, 125 Nanking E Rd., Sec. 2
Taipei
Tel: 507-2811

Tsar & Tsai
9th Floor, 477 Tunhwa S Rd.
Taipei
Tel: 781-4111

Thailand

Baker & McKenzie
19th Floor, North Sathorn Rd.
Bangrak, Bangkok 10500
Tel: 234-8620/9
Tlx: 82129 ABOGADO TH
Fax: 236-6072

Chandler & Thong-Ek
10th Floor, Southeast Insurance
Building
315 Silom Rd., Bangkok 10500
Tel: 234-8475/3738
Tlx: 82154 CHANDLR TH
Fax: 236-4191

International Legal Counsellors Thailand, Ltd.
18th floor, Bangkok Bank Building
333 Silom Rd., Bangkok 10330
Tel: 236-0151/235-0780
Tlx: 81166 LAWYERS TH
Fax: 236-7185

Tilleke & Gibbons ROP
64/1 Soi Tonson
Ploenchit Rd., Bangkok 10500
Tel: 254-2640/59
Tlx: 82978 LYMAN TH
Fax: 254-4304

Vickery, Prapone, Pramuan & Worachai, Ltd.
9th Floor, Central Plaza Office
Building
1693 Phaholyothin Rd., Bangkok
10900
Tel: 541-1235/44
Tlx: 20182 VPPWLAW TH
Fax: 541-1245

GOVERNMENT, REGULATORY AND PRIVATE SECTOR OFFICIALS

Hong Kong

Banking, Securities, Insurance & Companies Division
24th Floor, Admiralty Centre, Tower
II
Central
Tel: 5278337
Tlx: 75776
Fax: 8656146

Exchange Fund Division
24th Floor, Admiralty Centre, Tower
II
Central
Tel: 5290024
Tlx: 75776
Fax: 8656146

**Finance Branch, Government
Secretariat**
Central Government Offices
Lower Albert Rd., Central
Tel: 8102540
Fax: 8101530

**Hong Kong General Chamber of
Commerce**
22nd Floor, United Centre
95 Queensway, Central
Tel: 5299229
Tlx: 83535
Fax: 8662035

**Commissioner for Securities &
Commodities Trading**
32nd Floor, Alexandra House
16-20 Chater Rd., Central
Tel: 8427666
Tlx: 69429
Fax: 5265304

Indonesia

Bank Indonesia
J1 Thamrin 2
Jakarta
Tel: 372-408

Dept. of Justice
J1 Rasuna Said, Blok X-6
Kuningan
Jakarta
Tel: 513-006

**Dept. of Tourism, Post and
Telecommunications**
J1 Kebon Sirih 36
Jakarta
Tel: 366-705

Finance Ministry
J1 Lapangan Banteng Timur 24
Jakarta
Tel: 365-364

Industry Ministry
J1 Gatot Subroto Kav 52-53
Jakarta
Tel: 511-738
Fax: 512-720

Information Ministry
J1 Medan Merdeka Barat 9
Jakarta
Tel: 374-392

Investment Coordinating Board
J1 Gatot Subroto 44
Jakarta
Tel: 510-023

**National Development Planning
Board**
J1 Suropati 2
Jakarta
Tel: 334-371

**National Development
Information Office**
12th Floor, Wisma Antara
J1 Merdeka Selatan 17, Jakarta
Tel: 347-412

Trade Ministry
J1 Moh Ikhwan Ridwan Rais 5
Jakarta
Tel: 366-318

Japan

Economic Planning Agency
1-1, Kasumigaseki 3-chome
Chiyoda-ku, Tokyo 100
Tel: 581-0261

**Japan Chamber of Commerce and
Industry**
2-2, Marunouchi 3-chome
Chiyoda-ku, Tokyo 100
Tel: 211-4411

**Japan Federation of Economic
Organisations (Keidanren)**
9-4, Otemachi 1-chome, Chiyoda-ku
Tokyo 100
Tel: 279-1411

Ministry of Finance
1-1, Kasumigaseki 3-chome
Chiyoda-ku, Tokyo 100
Tel: 581-4111

**Ministry of International Trade
and Industry**
3-1, Kasumigaseki 1-chome
Chiyoda-ku, Tokyo 100
Tel: 501-1511

Ministry of Justice
1-1, Kasumigaseki 1 chome
Chiyoda-ku, Tokyo 100
Tel: 580-4111

**Securities Dealers Association of
Japan**
5-8, Nihombashi Kayabacho 1-chome
Chuo-ku, Tokyo 103
Tel: 666-8009

Tokyo Stock Exchange
6, Nihombashi Kabutocho 1-chome
Chuo-ku, Tokyo 103
Tel: 666-8009

Malaysia

**Bank Negara Malaysia (Central
Bank of Malaysia)**
Jln Dato' Onn
50480 Kuala Lumpur
Tel: 298-8044
Tlx: MA 30201
Fax: 291-2990

Capital Issues Committee
Kementarian Kewangan, 11th Floor
Block 9
Jln Duta, 50592 Kuala Lumpur
Tel: 254-6066
Tlx: MA 30242 FEDTRY

**Foreign Investment Committee
Secretariat**
Economic Planning Unit
Jln Dato' Onn
50502 Kuala Lumpur
Tel: 230-0133

Kuala Lumpur Stock Exchange
3rd & 4th Floor, Block A, Komplek
Bukit Naga
Damansara Heights, 50490 Kuala
Lumpur
Tel: 254-6433/6513
Tlx: MA 30241, 28009 KLSE

Malaysian International Chamber of Commerce & Industry
10th Floor, Wisma Damansara
Jln Semantan, 50490 Kuala Lumpur
Tel: 254-1690/2117
Tlx: MA 32120 COMER
Fax: 255-4946

Ministry of Finance
Blok 9, Kompleks Pejabat-Pejabat
Kerajaan
Jln Duta, 50592 Kuala Lumpur
Tel: 254-6066/0011
Tlx: MA 30242, 32369 FEDTRY

Panel on Takeovers and Mergers Malaysia
Economic Planning Unit
Jln Dato' Onn
50502 Kuala Lumpur
Tel: 230-0133

Philippines

Central Bank of the Philippines
A Mabini St.
Manila
Tel: 59-89-88/50-70-51

Dept. of Agriculture
Elliptical Rd.
Quezon City
Tel: 99-87-51

Exponet, Ministry of Trade and Industry
361 Sen Gil J Puyat Ave.
Makati, Metro Manila
Tel: 818-5701

Export Processing Zone Authority
Legaspi Towers 300
Roxas Blvd., Manila
Tel: 521-8659

International Economic Affairs and Development Division
Philippine International Convention
Center
Roxas Blvd., Manila
Tel: 831-8988

National Economic and Development Authority
NEDA Building, Amber Ave., Pasig

Metro Manila
Tel: 673-6313

Board of Investments
377 Sen Gil J Puyat Ave. Extension
Makati, Metro Manila
Tel: 86-36-38

Undersecretary for Industry and Investments
377 Sen Gil J Puyat Ave. Extension
Makati, Metro Manila
Tel: 86-84-85/818-1835/39

Secretary of Finance
Finance Building, Agrifina Circle
Manila
Tel: 58-67-19/59-69-13

Securities and Exchange Commission
SEC Building, EDSA
San Juan, Metro Manila
Tel: 78-09-31

Singapore

Economic Development Board
No. 24-00 Rames City Tower
Tel: 336-2288

Ministry of Finance
Treasury Building
8 Shenton Way
Tel: 225-9911

Ministry of Trade & Industry
Treasury Building
8 Shenton Way
Tel: 225-9911

The Monetary Authority of Singapore
10 Shenton Way
MAS Building
Tel: 225-5577

Singapore Chinese Chamber of Commerce
47 Hill St.
Tel: 337-8381

Singapore International Chamber of Commerce
No. 05-00 Denmark House
Tel: 224-1255
Fax: 339-0605

Singapore Manufacturers' Association
20 Orchard Rd.
SMA House
Tel: 338-8787

Singapore Tourist Promotion Board
No. 36-04
Rames City Tower
Tel: 339-6622

Telecommunications Authority of Singapore
Comcentre
31 Exeter Rd.
Tel: 734-3344

Trade Development Board
1 Maritime Square
No. 10-40 World Trade Centre
Tel: 271-9388

South Korea

The Bank of Korea
110, ka Namdaemun-ro
Chung-ku, Seoul
Tel: 771-07

Foreign Investment Promotion Division
Rm 203, Complex No. 3, 1
Chungang-dong
Kwacheon City, Kyongki-do
Tel: 503-9276/7

Korean Chamber of Commerce and Industry
45, 4-ka Namdaemun-ro
Chung-ku, Seoul
Tel: 757-0757

Ministry of Justice
1 Chungang-dong
Kwacheon City, Kyongki-do
Tel: 503-7011

Taiwan

Industrial Development and Investment Center (IDIC)
Ministry of Economic Affairs
10th Floor, 7 Roosevelt Rd., Sec. 1,
Taipei
Tel: 394-7213

Ministry of Finance (MOF)
2 Aikuo W Rd.
Taipei
Tel: 351–1611

**Securities and Exchange
Commission**
MOF
12th Floor, Yangteh Building
Nanhai Rd., Taipei
Tel: 392–8572

**Dept. of Export Promotion
(DEP)**
22/7 Rachadapisek Rd.
Bangkhen, Bangkok 10900
Tel: S11–SO66N7

**The Industrial Estate Authority of
Thailand (IEAT)**
618 Nikhom Makkasan Rd.
Phayathai, Bangkok 10400
Tel: 253–0561

**Office of the Board of Investment
(BOI)**
555 Viphavadee Rangsit Rd.
Bangkhen, Bangkok 10900
Tel: 270–1400/270–1410
Tlx: 72435 BINVEST TH
Fax: 271–0777

**Securities Exchange of Thailand
(SET)**
Sinthorn Building
132 Wireless Rd., Bangkok 10500
Tel: 250–0001/8

APPENDIX C

THE PACRIM TOP 500 COMPANIES

Asian Finance, a Hong Kong–published business magazine, publishes an annual list of the region's top 500 corporations. In 1989, their list featured 671 companies.

Countrywise their breakdown is:

Hong Kong	100
Indonesia	2
Japan	150
Korea	100
Malaysia	80
Philippines	80
Singapore	50
Taiwan	30
Thailand	60

In each country, all companies included in this listing have been ranked by assets in 1987, with comparable ranks in 1986 wherever available. In addition to total assets, the accompanying tables provide stockholders' equity, turnover/sales, net income, return on assets, return on equity, and net profit margin (actually net income as a proportion of turnover/sales).

Hong Kong: Year to December 31 (HK$'000)

Rank 1987/ 1986	Company	Total assets	Shareholders' equity	Turnover/ sales	Net income	Return on assets	Return on equity	Net profit margin
1/1	Swire Pacific	36,142,200	14,933,300	20,166,400	3,570,500	9.88	23.91	17.70
2/5	Hutchison Whampoa	28,731,000	14,374,000	10,524,000	2,153,000	7.49	14.98	20.46
3/2	Hongkong Land	27,952,000	23,819,000	1,784,000	1,113,000	3.98	4.67	—
4/8	Wharf (Holdings)	27,572,600	18,817,500	2,391,200	1,112,100	4.03	5.91	46.51
5/3	Cathay Pacific	19,482,100	4,266,300	11,708,700	2,130,600	10.94	49.94	18.20
6/4	Jardine Matheson Holdings	16,340,000	6,246,000	12,720,000	895,000	5.48	14.33	7.04
7/7	Sun Hung Kai Properties (June 1988)	14,280,510	8,023,604	5,781,297	2,022,470	14.16	25.21	34.98
8/10	Cheung Kong (Holdings)	13,866,300	11,056,100	2,323,100	1,607,500	11.59	14.54	69.20

703

Hong Kong: Year to December 31 (HK$'000) (Continued)

Rank 1987/ 1986	Company	Total assets	Shareholders' equity	Turnover/ sales	Net income	Return on assets	Return on equity	Net profit margin
9/9	China Light & Power (Sept. 1988)	13,177,000	7,861,000	8,873,000	2,360,000	17.91	30.02	26.60
10/15	World Int'l Holdings	12,624,000	10,133,400	2,168,100	720,200	5.70	7.11	33.22
11/23	Cavendish Int'l	10,834,800	9,037,300	593,300	667,900	6.16	7.39	112.57
12/—	HK Telecom (March 1988)	10,605,300	7,282,800	6,792,000	3,039,400	28.66	41.73	44.75
13/6	HK Electric	10,011,600	6,055,100	3,018,600	1,405,000	14.03	23.20	46.54
14/13	Henderson Land (June 1988)	8,475,044	5,178,179	2,281,326	1,002,183	11.82	19.35	43.93
15/28	Amoy Properties (June 1988)	8,425,649	6,870,442	473,566	352,035	4.18	5.12	74.34
16/21	Sino Realty (June 1988)	7,502,768	2,728,073	2,075,952	890,432	11.87	32.64	42.89
17/16	Hysan Development	7,283,264	5,443,030	524,438	282,560	3.88	5.19	53.88
18/14	Hang Lung Development (June 1987)	6,721,898	4,539,211	2,920,782	922,856	13.73	20.33	31.60
19/18	Liu Chong Hing Investment	6,536,512	612,003	124,375	108,538	1.66	17.73	87.27
20/12	New World Development	6,280,882	4,886,921	5,296,855	1,392,505	22.17	28.49	26.29
21/22	Dairy Farm Int'l	6,039,000	3,711,000	12,780,000	457,000	7.57	12.31	3.58
22/19	HK Realty & Trust (March 1988)	5,944,825	3,584,932	445,553	390,843	6.57	10.90	87.72
23/25	Sino Land (June 1988)	5,701,036	4,366,029	690,539	325,228	5.70	7.45	47.10
24/47	Bond Corp Int'l	4,697,488	2,800,651	101,553	350,667	7.46	12.52	345.30
25/37	Harbour Centre Development (March 1988)	4,450,628	2,761,907	770,662	177,090	3.98	6.41	22.98
26/—	Mandarin Oriental	4,170,200	3,451,000	753,300	244,800	5.87	7.09	32.50
27/45	Lai Sun Garment (July 1988)	4,145,000	1,903,333	3,014,627	533,490	12.87	28.03	17.70
28/20	Hopewell Holdings (June 1988)	3,898,000	2,376,000	1,349,000	461,000	11.83	19.40	34.17
29/24	New Town (NT) Properties (June 1988)	3,783,000	3,037,000	552,908	468,318	12.38	15.42	84.70
30/31	Miramar Hotel (March 1988)	3,761,000	3,093,000	625,787	104,398	2.78	3.37	16.68
31/29	Regal Hotels (Holdings)	3,627,420	2,839,255	543,123	172,342	4.75	6.07	31.73
32/26	First Pacific Int'l	3,569,054	477,282	7,118,732	175,828	4.93	36.84	2.47
33/35	Realty Development Corp. (March 1988)	2,927,415	2,274,991	205,318	151,056	5.16	6.64	73.57
34/30	Shui On Group (March 1988)	2,877,000	1,278,000	3,048,925	58,460	2.03	4.57	1.92
35/40	Lane Crawford (March 1988)	2,466,042	1,503,638	748,477	145,688	5.91	9.69	19.46
36/27	Wing On (Holdings)	2,416,608	880,007	1,205,132	83,031	3.44	9.47	6.89
37/51	Century City Holdings	2,311,926	1,222,751	414,790	134,926	5.84	11.03	32.53
38/34	HK & China Gas	21,267,800	1,428,400	1,309,000	320,700	14.14	22.45	24.50
39/38	New World Hotels (June 1988)	2,259,563	1,127,316	904,269	308,516	13.65	27.37	34.12
40/41	Kowloon Motor Bus	2,006,517	715,885	1,732,050	254,857	12.70	35.60	14.71
41/56	Paliburg Investments	1,990,397	1,682,420	176,544	137,245	6.89	8.16	77.74
42/43	Nan Fung Textiles (March 1988)	1,943,000	1,369,000	1,815,000	523,000	26.92	38.20	28.81
43/44	Tiam Teck Land (March 1988)	1,936,761	696,260	279,825	44,812	2.31	6.44	16.01
44/46	Associated Int'l Hotels (March 1988)	1,868,630	1,355,950	275,809	47,861	2.56	3.53	17.35
45/39	Winsor Industrial (March 1987)	1,841,215	1,168,852	2,185,146	323,173	17.55	27.65	14.79
46/32	Evergo Industrial (April 1988)	1,652,000	1,506,000	2,783,228	(296,609)	(17.95)	(19.69)	(1.66)
47/42	Wing On Co	1,612,164	1,116,932	1,025,678	90,793	5.63	8.13	8.85
48/49	HK & Shanghai Hotels	1,535,630	776,042	875,057	242,914	15.82	31.30	27.76

Hong Kong: Year to December 31 (HK$'000) (Continued)

Rank 1987/ 1986	Company	Total assets	Shareholders' equity	Turnover/ sales	Net income	Return on assets	Return on equity	Net profit margin
49/11	Orient Overseas (Holdings)	1,498,090	58,397	—	18,919	1.26	32.40	—
50/67	Great Eagle (Sept. 1987)	1,470,997	739,758	693,770	182,901	12.43	24.72	26.36
51/62	Allied Properties (June 1988)	1,445,773	938,648	1,669,854	263,666	18.24	28.09	15.79
52/48	Wing Tai Development (June 1987)	1,428,850	900,401	509,062	201,898	14.13	22.42	39.66
53/54	Wormald Pacific	1,396,019	869,714	444,357	128,687	9.22	14.80	28.96
54/50	Conic Investment Co.	1,356,899	173,263	881,514	(58,730)	(4.33)	(33.90)	(6.66)
55/73	Green Island Cement	1,269,579	829,689	553,906	80,500	6.34	9.70	14.53
56/76	Chevalier (HK) March 1988)	1,245,066	470,302	959,102	48,073	3.86	10.22	5.01
57/85	Laws Fashion (March 1988)	1,242,976	775,635	1,463,764	245,983	19.79	32.55	16.80
58/61	Tak Wing Investment	1,209,474	114,270	392,623	7,053	0.58	6.17	1.80
59/60	HK-TVB	1,183,631	515,671	1,325,850	408,901	34.55	79.29	30.84
60/53	Tai Cheung Properties (March 1988)	1,180,690	1,025,340	714,160	259,070	21.94	25.27	36.28
61/57	Stelux Holdings (March 1988)	1,175,000	704,000	610,000	220,000	18.72	31.25	36.07
62/52	Hsin Chong Holdings (March 1988)	1,158,000	830,335	1,153,311	161,988	13.99	19.51	14.04
63/—	Kumagai-Gumi HK (Sept. 1987)	1,156,000	511,006	1,753,530	76,076	6.58	14.89	4.34
64/33	Impala Pacific (June 1988)	1,125,153	268,917	27,695	(444,869)	(39.54)	(165.43)	(1,606.31)
65/58	Furama Hotel (March 1988)	1,089,020	951,033	271,430	91,361	8.39	9.61	33.66
66/77	IHD Holdings (14 mos. to Feb. 1988)	1,059,498	310,308	278,330	11,775	1.11	3.79	4.23
67/55	Novel Enterprises	1,056,398	761,509	1,629,720	164,692	15.59	21.63	10.10
68/72	HK & Yaumati Ferry	1,047,696	810,305	636,302	84,978	8.11	10.49	13.35
69/78	Tai Shing Development Holdings	1,043,522	751,046	1,126,382	62,063	5.95	8.26	5.51
70/69	Far East Consortium (March 1988)	1,027,000	644,000	409,444	19,590	1.91	3.04	4.78
71/68	Sime Darby HK (June 1988)	973,000	580,000	2,188,000	150,000	15.42	25.86	6.86
72/66	Shaw Brothers (March 1988)	956,000	838,000	190,145	162,198	16.97	19.35	85.30
73/59	Wah Kwonq Properties (June 1987)	949,976	510,595	114,442	42,923	4.52	8.41	37.51
74/64	Tai Sang Land Development	927,207	400,938	112,493	27,384	2.95	6.83	22.36
75/99	Chung Wah Shipbuilding (March 1988)	859,000	145,000	684,542	21,920	2.55	15.12	3.20
76/63	South Sea Textile	858,294	265,210	887,822	140,590	16.38	53.01	15.83
77/70	China Entertainment	843,904	784,893	4,340,893	(368,091)	(43.62)	(46.90)	8.48)
78/90	Johnson Electric (March 1988)	810,217	712,901	802,049	162,935	20.11	22.85	20.31
79/74	Kwong Sang Hong	760,598	687,683	162,944	70,805	9.31	10.30	43.45
80/71	Sing Tao (March 1988)	755,138	593,298	701,390	78,556	10.40	13.24	11.20
81/65	Paul Y Construction (March 1988)	733,514	626,906	343,687	45,874	6.25	7.32	13.35
82/—	Shun Ho Investments (March 1988)	692,681	547,105	203,813	94,500	13.64	17.27	46.37
83/83	HK Aircraft	638,972	446,844	1,011,679	175,773	27.51	39.34	17.37
84/—	Ocean Land Development (March 1988)	632,702	383,177	108,771	229,664	36.30	59.94	211.14

Hong Kong: Year to December 31 (HK$'000)

Rank 1987/ 1986	Company	Total assets	Shareholders' equity	Turnover/ sales	Net income	Return on assets	Return on equity	Net profit margin
85/75	Far East Hotels	619,720	528,910	134,119	16,152	2.61	3.05	12.04
86/94	Zung Fu Co	594,935	359,303	764,947	124,715	20.96	34.71	16.30
87/—	Oriental Press (March 1988)	588,290	466,870	440,290	142,480	24.22	30.52	32.36
88/96	Shun Tak Enterprises	551,989	263,732	535,689	139,616	25.29	52.94	26.06
89/93	San Miguel Brewery	531,363	410,729	691,265	87,014	16.38	21.18	12.59
90/79	Wong's Industrial	519,219	512,605	1,145,737	83,819	16.14	16.35	7.32
91/89	Unisouth (March 1988)	518,000	351,000	264,310	64,629	12.48	18.41	24.45
92/95	China Motor Bus (June 1988)	517,585	243,364	564,647	70,753	13.67	29.07	12.53
93/87	Kader Industrial	509,914	423,898	768,470	(151,893)	(29.79)	(35.83)	(19.77)
94/86	Allied Investors Corp. (March 1988)	505,236	412,958	69,389	37,477	7.42	9.07	54.01
95/81	Rainbow Orient Corp. (July 1988)	505,107	586,120	333,372	(8,944)	(1.77)	(1.53)	(2.68)
96/88	Hong Kong Resort (April 1987)	500,457	(117,143)	342,824	178,359	35.64	(152.26)	52.03
97/97	Chow Sang Sang Holdings	471,467	261,571	2,240,032	22,972	4.87	8.78	1.02
98/—	Paladin Int'l (March 1987)	468,393	443,102	440,381	46,642	9.96	10.53	10.59
99/100	Gold Peak Industries (March 1988)	462,265	205,880	690,342	45,343	9.81	22.02	6.57
100/92	Lap Heng Co. (March 1988)	450,000	390,000	471,690	72,920	16.20	18.70	15.46

Indonesia: Year to December 31 (Rp million)

Rank 1987/ 1986	Company	Total assets	Shareholders' equity	Turnover/ sales	Net income (loss)	Return on assets	Return on equity	Net profit margin
1/2	Teijin Indonesia Fibre	207,046	137,758	67,934	8,549	4.13	6.21	12.58
2/1	Unilever Indonesia	188,506	104,603	331,032	31,518	16.72	30.13	9.52
3/3	Semen Cibinong (Oct. 31, 1987)	95,246	45,122	75,049	6,398	6.72	14.18	8.52
4/7	Jakarta Int'l Hotel	83,817	57,171	23,637	7,472	8.91	13.07	31.61
5/9	Supreme Cable Manufacturing	78,125	30,274	71,608	5,139	6.58	16.97	7.18
6/6	Bayer Indonesia	74,234	19,609	77,838	2,127	2.86	10.85	2.73
7/4	Goodyear Indonesia	73,746	36,490	79,804	5,202	7.05	14.26	6.52
8/5	BAT Indonesia	69,337	50,183	51,771	4,630	6.68	9.23	8.94
9/8	Multi Bintang Indonesia	60,663	38,719	50,646	8,864	14.61	22.89	17.50
10/13	Hotel Prapatan	53,315	10,720	8,188	1,536	2.88	14.33	18.76
11/11	Sepatu Bata	33,349	23,474	45,292	3,513	10.53	14.96	7.76
12/12	Delta Djakarta	28,350	7,959	26,726	1,168	4.12	14.67	4.37
13/10	Century Textile Industry (March 31, 1986)	28,341	9,554	17,736	(117)	(0.41)	(1.22)	(0.66)
14/14	UnHex	24,886	15,532	23,232	1,740	6.99	11.20	7.49
15/15	Sari Husada	16,957	13,017	19,377	1,521	8.97	11.68	7.85
16/16	Merck Indonesia	14,644	10,332	11,431	2,974	20.31	28.78	26.02
17/17	Pfizor Indonesia (Nov. 30, 1987)	10,482	4,255	12,583	775	7.39	18.21	6.16
18/19	Richardson Vicks Indonesia	8,952	5,603	16,860	2,391	26.71	42.67	14.18

Indonesia: Year to December 31 (Rp million) (Continued)

Rank 1987/ 1986	Company	Total assets	Shareholders' equity	Turnover/ sales	Net income (loss)	Return on assets	Return on equity	Net profit margin
19/18	Squibb Indonesia (Nov. 30, 1987)	8,486	6,593	12,997	1,170	13.79	17.75	9.00
20/—	Singer Industries Indonesia	7,836	(3,869)	4,659	(596)	(7.61)	(15.40)	(12.79)
21/20	Regnis Indonesia (Dec. 31, 1986)	6,379	(3,707)	2,811	(2,351)	(36.85)	(63.42)	(83.64)

Japan: Year to March 31 (Y million)

Rank 1988/ 1987	Company	Total assets	Shareholders' equity	Turnover/ sales	Net income (loss)	Return on assets	Return on equity	Net profit margin
1/—	Nippon Telegraph & Telephone	10,927,689	3,662,622	5,662,001	243,236	2.23	6.64	4.30
2/1	Tokyo Electric Power	9,895,328	1,332,844	3,940,298	138,326	1.40	10.38	3.51
3/2	Mitsubishi Corp.	6,212,301	436,825	12,281,698	26,135	0.42	5.98	0.21
4/3	Kansai Electric Power	5,127,037	977,647	2,012,294	118,233	2.31	12.09	5.88
5/4	Orient Finance Co.	4,971,866	179,942	326,238	12,588	0.25	6.98	3.85
6/6	Toyota Motor Corp.	4,553,593	2,797,127	6,691,299	238,006	5.23	8.51	3.56
7/11	Nomura Securities Co. (Sept. 1988)	4,293,744	1,126,098	846,434	189,389	4.41	16.82	22.38
8/7	Mitsui & Co.	4,150,755	268,658	14,131,236	12,836	0.31	4.78	0.09
9/8	Marubeni Corp.	3,770,158	155,766	13,209,400	9,842	0.26	6.32	0.07
10/—	Chubu Electric Power	3,767,163	823,912	1,633,748	69,363	1.84	8.42	4.25
11/16	Daiwa Securities Co. (Sept. 1988)	3,595,999	698,114	526,776	115,239	3.21	16.51	21.88
12/10	C. Itoh & Co.	3,390,235	192,992	14,921,991	10,822	0.32	5.61	0.07
13/9	Nippon Steel Corp.	3,145,732	600,368	2,147,038	31,883	1.01	5.31	1.48
14/15	Tokio Marine & Fire Insurance	2,984,658	425,062	758,136	35,980	1.21	8.47	4.75
15/13	Nissan Motor Co.	2,907,113	1,338,881	3,418,671	38,584	1.33	2.88	1.13
16/12	Hitachi, Ltd.	2,838,109	975,556	2,919,539	65,138	2.29	6.68	2.23
17/23	Nikko Securities Co. (Sept. 1988)	2,781,903	630,097	454,918	80,381	2.89	12.76	17.67
18/27	Yamaichi Securities Co. (Sept. 1988)	2,739,835	555,727	431,216	76,525	2.79	13.77	17.75
19/14	Mitsubishi Heavy Industries	2,611,722	530,829	1,708,256	21,152	0.81	3.98	1.24
20/21	Sumitomo Corp.	2,552,031	285,598	13,693,087	25,334	0.99	8.87	0.19
21/25	Orient Leasing Co.	2,544,999	73,651	493,468	4,158	0.16	5.65	0.84
22/19	Matsushita Electric Industrial Co.	2,538,978	1,439,666	3,277,613	85,343	3.36	5.93	2.60
23/18	Toshiba Corp.	2,419,325	700,385	2,682,781	37,040	1.53	5.29	1.38
24/17	NKK Corp.	2,300,510	266,723	1,050,325	12,665	0.55	4.75	1.21
25/24	Yasuda Fire & Marine Insurance	2,256,339	157,613	565,267	14,358	0.64	9.11	2.54
26/22	NEC Corp.	2,064,157	608,113	2,304,392	37,477	1.82	6.16	1.63
27/20	Sumitomo Metal Industries	1,899,047	318,922	909,271	1,317	0.07	0.41	0.14
28/29	Fujitsu, Ltd.	1,789,854	666,131	1,714,425	32,066	1.79	4.81	1.87

Japan: Year to March 31 (Y million) (Continued)

Rank 1988/ 1987	Company	Total assets	Shareholders' equity	Turnover/ sales	Net income (loss)	Return on assets	Return on equity	Net profit margin
29/26	Kawasaki Steel Corp.	1,692,143	331,853	936,372	6,916	0.41	2.08	0.74
30/—	Kobe Steel	1,671,860	217,679	975,932	7,640	0.46	3.51	0.78
31/28	Mitsubishi Electric Corp.	1,668,849	473,665	1,954,187	19,819	1.19	4.18	1.01
32/30	Taisho Marine & Fire Insurance	1,543,327	146,029	371,148	14,021	0.91	9.61	3.78
33/31	Kajima Corp.	1,420,835	227,351	440,623	5,605	0.39	2.47	1.27
34/37	Kumagai Gumi Co. (Sept. 1988)	1,387,434	242,259	859,281	11,628	0.84	4.80	1.35
35/—	Sumitomo Marine & Fire Insurance	1,361,594	127,374	309,364	12,251	0.90	9.62	3.96
36/35	Mitsui Real Estate Development	1,309,998	278,117	394,869	18,663	1.43	6.71	4.73
37/33	Honda Motor Co.	1,231,521	542,823	1,249,737	24,135	1.96	4.45	1.93
38/34	Taisei Corp.	1,228,220	215,047	1,033,557	11,352	0.92	5.28	1.10
39/38	Nippon Oil Co.	1,186,272	309,433	1,725,814	16,739	1.41	5.41	0.97
40/36	Shimizu Corp.	1,176,982	163,828	1,101,712	10,576	0.90	6.46	0.96
41/43	Sony Corp.	1,140,906	515,811	1,029,891	30,681	2.69	5.95	2.98
42/41	Sharp Corp.	1,131,426	453,334	872,707	18,857	1.67	4.16	2.16
43/—	Nippon Fire & Marine Insurance	1,111,859	91,347	262,425	9,322	0.84	10.21	3.55
44/—	Daikyo Inc. (Sept. 1988)	1,086,102	115,543	410,288	11,334	1.04	9.81	2.76
45/39	Ohbayashi Corp.	1,085,012	166,873	820,288	9,305	0.86	5.58	1.13
46/55	Sanyo Electric Co.	1,070,361	559,261	909,393	14,128	1.32	2.53	1.55
47/50	Fujita Corp.	974,100	77,524	181,348	1,706	0.18	2.20	0.94
48/44	Mitsubishi Estate Co.	973,165	341,928	236,355	29,892	3.07	8.74	12.65
49/—	Cosmos Oil Co.	966,383	51,901	1,297,594	6,944	0.72	13.38	0.54
50/42	Japan Air Lines	963,732	150,662	848,992	16,739	1.74	11.11	1.97
51/32	Ishiwakajima-Harima Heavy Industries	954,355	106,883	714,714	1,514	0.16	1.42	0.21
52/—	Kawasaki Heavy Industries	878,437	79,287	579,731	1,016	0.12	1.28	0.18
53/45	Mazda Motor Corp. (Oct. 1987)	870,863	289,457	1,602,293	4,438	0.51	1.53	0.28
54/48	Mitsubishi Chemical Industries (Jan. 1988)	858,424	165,557	623,010	12,911	1.50	7.80	2.07
55/60	Sekisui House (Jan. 1988)	858,411	250,145	605,597	15,025	1.75	6.01	2.48
56/46	Nippondenso Co. (Dec. 1987)	835,084	444,071	994,007	27,889	3.34	6.28	6.06
57/56	Kirin Brewery Co. (Jan. 1988)	813,499	323,039	1,266,349	34,059	4.19	10.54	2.69
58/51	Tokyo Corp.	805,308	137,016	222,183	5,575	0.69	4.07	2.51
59/72	Haseko Corp. (formerly Hasegawa Komuten)	785,674	175,112	267,875	7,516	0.96	4.29	2.81
60/47	Komatsu, Ltd.	782,940	374,184	123,861	2,271	0.29	0.61	1.83
61/53	Daiei, Inc. (Feb. 1988)	775,021	159,987	1,550,314	6,909	0.89	4.32	0.45
62/57	Fuji Photo Film (Oct. 1987)	768,945	491,023	680,052	61,838	8.04	12.59	9.09
63/52	Asahi Chemical Industry	768,679	240,912	765,483	20,146	2.62	8.36	2.64
64—	All Nippon Airways	750,463	184,248	527,540	6,005	0.80	3.26	1.14
65/71	Showa Shell Seklyu (Dec. 1987)	750,353	54,719	1,265,623	7,373	0.98	13.47	0.58

Japan: Year to March 31 (Y million) (Continued)

Rank 1988/ 1987	Company	Total assets	Shareholders' equity	Turnover/ sales	Net income (loss)	Return on assets	Return on equity	Net profit margin
66/—	Kinki Nippon Railway	749,440	125,605	193,622	8,508	1.14	6.77	4.39
67/61	Asahi Glass Co. (Dec. 1987)	744,152	373,081	721,234	32,518	4.37	8.72	4.51
68/59	Toray Industries	718,785	287,137	541,511	16,223	2.26	5.65	3.00
69/79	Sumitomo Realty & Development	687,618	191,927	124,852	10,657	1.55	5.55	8.54
70/69	Dai Nippon Printing Co.	684,291	354,933	680,850	23,569	3.44	6.64	3.46
71/68	Canon Inc. (Dec. 1987)	683,957	309,439	578,644	8,853	1.29	2.86	1.53
72/64	Takeda Chemical Industries	675,909	313,728	539,754	31,387	4.64	10.01	5.82
73/—	Isuzu Motors	675,840	152,304	909,916	9,386	1.39	1.03	1.03
74/62	Nippon Yusen KK	663,459	174,489	413,778	2,434	0.37	1.39	0.59
75/63	Sumitomo Chemical Co. (Dec. 1987)	659,434	124,764	515,762	11,236	1.71	9.01	2.18
76/67	Kubota, Ltd.	672,497	302,672	557,979	14,068	2.22	4.65	2.52
77/66	Tobu Railway Co.	616,580	96,542	172,401	4,091	0.66	4.24	2.37
78/77	Bridgestone Corp.	609,396	309,637	557,243	29,277	4.80	9.46	5.25
79/76	Fuji Heavy Machinery	597,227	172,625	686,239	10,431	1.75	6.04	1.52
80/83	Toppan Printing Co.	561,465	265,194	557,027	17,074	3.04	6.44	3.07
81/54	Hitachi Zosen Corp.	559,077	59,344	256,318	8,386	1.50	14.13	3.27
82/—	Mitsui OSK Lines	555,352	121,502	345,716	(2,775)	(0.50)	(2.28)	(0.80)
83/71	Showa Denko KK (Dec. 1987)	554,642	68,684	415,609	5,550	1.00	8.08	1.34
84/84	Matsushita Electric Works	553,188	249,386	662,710	17,216	3.11	6.90	2.60
85/88	Daiwa House Industry	540,713	172,978	462,289	14,380	2.66	8.31	3.11
86/—	Tobishima Corp.	539,729	36,324	344,512	2,650	0.49	7.30	0.77
87/73	Hitachi Credit Corp.	524,235	95,717	288,363	4,104	0.78	4.29	1.42
88/80	Nippon Express Co.	514,037	108,709	924,546	8,827	1.72	8.12	0.95
89/81	Honshu Paper Co.	513,213	42,308	366,975	3,979	0.78	9.40	1.08
90/86	Mitsubishi Metal Corp.	513,070	77,396	656,441	5,345	1.04	6.91	0.81
91/89	Ricoh Co.	505,910	263,986	560,017	13,054	2.58	4.95	2.33
92/—	Fuji Electric Co.	503,444	104,657	402,301	5,020	1.00	4.80	1.25
93/75	Nisshin Steel Co.	496,733	116,641	363,555	12,267	2.47	10.52	3.37
94/82	Ajinomoto Co.	495,680	267,812	432,524	14,079	2.84	5.26	3.26
95/98	Hazama-Gumi, Ltd. (Sept. 1988)	492,579	77,524	455,349	3,871	0.79	4.99	0.85
96/85	Tijin Ud	492,034	190,328	309,666	15,621	3.18	8.21	5.04
97/—	Hankyu Corp.	486,631	80,525	129,818	5,076	1.04	6.30	3.91
98/87	Sumitomo Electric Industries	482,201	196,876	550,115	12,517	2.60	6.36	2.28
99/103	Dainippon Ink & Chemicals	480,406	124,804	417,697	6,243	1.30	5.00	1.49
100/92	Oki Electric Industries	473,332	112,638	416,204	4,108	0.87	3.65	0.99
101/—	Kokusai Denshin Denwa Co.	466,944	249,704	248,460	15,318	3.28	6.13	6.17
102/112	Tokyu Construction Co. (Sept. 1988)	461,485	44,352	370,682	2,039	0.44	4.60	0.55
103/90	Marui Co. (Jan. 1988)	460,559	221,504	444,098	18,328	3.98	8.27	4.13
104/96	Ito-Yokado Co. (Feb. 1988)	453,690	254,282	1,055,006	30,808	6.79	12.12	2.92
105/—	Nagoya Railroad Co.	452,537	65,275	122,579	3,368	0.74	5.16	2.75
106/99	Oji Paper Co.	451,681	175,194	387,759	15,738	3.48	8.98	4.06
107/91	Mitsubishi Oil Co.	436,968	37,809	671,719	5,196	1.19	13.74	0.77
108/—	Odakyu Electric Railway	434,731	70,461	110,418	3,595	0.83	5.10	3.26
109/—	Suzuki Motor Co.	432,946	99,945	759,550	5,872	1.36	5.88	0.77

Japan: Year to March 31 (Y million) (Continued)

Rank 1988/ 1987	Company	Total assets	Shareholders' equity	Turnover/ sales	Net income (loss)	Return on assets	Return on equity	Net profit margin
110/101	Tokyu Land Corp. (Sept. 1988)	429,998	88,365	151,697	1,956	0.46	2.21	1.29
111/97	Maeda Corp.	428,985	111,371	126,346	1,288	0.30	1.16	1.02
112/100	Jujo Paper Co.	428,535	95,731	342,620	9,392	2.19	9.81	2.74
113/—	Mitsui Engineering and Shipbuilding	427,623	88,190	182,354	856	0.20	0.97	0.47
114/94	Nishimatsu Construction	426,972	76,401	404,725	3,420	0.80	4.48	0.85
115/108	Kao Corp.	420,224	193,976	490,019	13,247	3.15	6.83	2.70
116/102	Kyocera Corp.	415,773	310,369	271,166	19,882	4.78	6.41	7.33
117/—	Keio Teito Electric Railway	410,913	55,511	88,414	2,827	0.69	5.09	3.20
118/109	TDK Corp.	402,610	238,946	352,210	15,709	3.90	6.57	4.46
119/105	Okumura Corp.	395,851	87,620	250,633	5,058	1.28	5.77	2.02
120/—	Keihin Electric Express Railway	386,809	53,933	111,447	2,693	0.70	4.99	2.42
121/—	Sato Kogyo Co. (Sept. 1988)	385,431	36,735	327,341	2.469	0.64	6.72	0.75
122/107	Victor Co. of Japan	380,675	181,006	578,904	5,596	1.47	3.09	0.97
123/—	Nichii Co. (Feb. 1988)	377,795	129,033	568,509	9,509	2.52	7.37	1.67
124/119	Minebea Co.	370,691	191,129	156,521	7,109	1.92	3.72	4.54
125/111	Nippon Seiko KK (Oct. 1987)	367,561	149,900	265,225	6,101	1.66	4.07	2.30
126/132	Sapporo Breweries (Dec. 1987)	365,830	108,557	467,046	5,250	1.44	4.84	1.12
127/110	Shiseido Co. (Nov. 1987)	361,176	198,792	320,228	9,622	2.66	4.84	3.00
128/—	Sumitomo Heauy Industries	330,487	63,053	200,026	306	0.09	0.49	0.15
129/118	Fujisawa Pharmaceutical	330,143	171,446	190,293	8,364	2.53	4.88	4.40
130/—	Sagami Railway Co.	326,005	33,531	97,774	2,368	0.73	7.06	2.42
131/—	Kinki Electrical Construction	325,737	107,364	310,994	8,527	2.62	7.94	2.74
132/114	Sanyo Kokusaku Pulp Co.	318,269	77,671	279,701	7,835	2.46	10.09	2.80
133/120	Taiyo Fishery Co. (Jan. 1988)	306,879	29,437	550,445	363	0.12	1.23	0.07
134/121	Sumitomo Metal Mining	306,666	63,727	429,239	2,287	0.75	3.59	0.53
135/117	Alps Electric Co.	301,299	118,938	304,060	6,417	2.13	5.40	2.11
136/126	Penta-Ocean Construction Co.	294,889	37,957	333,138	2,565	0.87	6.76	0.77
137/130	Fanuc, Ltd.	292,603	241,052	116,741	16,654	5.69	6.91	14.27
138/125	Sankyo Co.	288,127	146,136	291,724	10,473	3.64	7.17	3.59
139/140	Kyowa Hakko Kogyo (Dec. 1987)	276,280	105,161	231,496	7,035	2.55	6.69	3.04
140/—	Sumitomo Construction Co.	273,175	28,341	248,337	1,452	0.53	5.12	0.58
141/—	Nippon Ligm Metal Co.	272,762	31,964	248,023	10,016	3.67	31.34	4.04
142/131	Nihon Cement Co.	271,865	73,571	155,138	4,292	1.58	5.83	2.77
143/146	Mitsukoshi, Ltd.	271,479	109,172	643,356	4,220	1.55	3.87	0.66
144/133	Murata Manufacturing Co.	268,134	166,601	189,856	11,318	4.22	6.79	5.96
145/—	Asahi Breweries (Dec. 1987)	266,235	79,851	345,112	2,509	0.94	3.14	0.73
146/—	Yamanouchi Pharmaceutical Co. (Dec. 1987)	265,712	138,854	164,054	16,745	6.30	12.06	10.21
147/136	Mitsubishi Rayon Co.	263,718	83,442	193,973	3,683	1.40	4.41	1.90
148/142	Kandenko Co.	259,037	78,497	360,984	7,632	2.95	9.72	2.11
149/—	Uny Co. (Feb. 1988)	256,004	112,539	451,123	8,032	3.14	7.14	1.78
150/—	Nippon Sheet Glass Co.	254,980	96,015	203,918	6,393	2.51	6.66	3.14

Korea: Year to December 31 (Won million)

Rank 1987/ 1986	Company	Total assets	Shareholders' equity	Turnover/ sales	Net income (loss)	Return on assets	Return on equity	Net profit margin (%)
1/—	Pohang Iron & Steel Co.	5,139,175	1,641,330	2,919,369	92,844	1.81	5.66	3.18
2/5	Daewoo Securities (March 31, 1988)	2,695,986	192,750	144,374	51,831	1.92	26.89	35.90
3/1	Daewoo Corp.	2,393,065	381,761	4,453,250	44,806	1.87	11.74	1.01
4/3	Korea Air Lines	2,011,066	187,499	1,422,351	37,049	1.84	19.76	2.60
5/2	Hyundai Engineering & Construction	1,876,407	274,765	1,521,724	36,856	1.96	13.41	2.42
6/4	Hyundai Motor Co.	1,858,589	310,686	2,840,211	91,738	4.94	29.53	3.23
7/6	Gold Star Co.	1,684,503	324,369	2,029,563	31,450	1.87	9.70	1.55
8/7	Yu Kong, Ltd.	1,172,986	327,016	2,573,168	67,889	5.79	20.76	2.64
9/9	Sam Sung Electronics Co.	1,137,468	222,044	2,381,312	45,765	4.02	20.61	1.92
10/13	Daelim Industrial Co.	1,095,205	244,170	524,026	11,113	1.01	4.55	2.12
11/—	Kia Motors Corp.	1,082,691	304,085	1,052,996	27,307	2.52	8.98	2.59
12/19	Daewoo Electronics Co.	996,425	136,269	867,864	15,219	1.53	11.17	1.75
13/14	Samsung Semiconductor	973,379	105,259	564,301	18,239	1.87	17.33	3.23
14/10	Ssang Yong Cement	966,530	270,485	543,452	18,408	1.90	6.80	3.39
15/8	Dong Ah Construction	958,226	155,660	656,689	7,570	0.79	4.86	1.15
16/11	Keung Nam Enterprises	907,305	26,539	173,322	221	0.02	0.83	0.13
17/16	Lucky Co.	835,458	203,829	928,352	45,257	5.42	22.2	4.87
18/17	Daewoo Heavy Industries, Ltd.	759,655	185,956	492,009	12,175	1.60	6.55	2.47
19/21	Korea Shipping Corp.	682,483	(227,284)	217,613	(94,242)	(13.81)	(41.46)	(43.31)
20/20	Hanil Synthetic Fiber (March 31, 1988)	675,465	259,911	463,073	39,478	5.84	15.19	8.52
21/15	Ham Yang Corp.	668,390	42,025	275,880	25	0.004	0.06	0.009
22/18	Kukje Corp.	623,527	(51,389)	344,098	(38,948)	(6.25)	(75.79)	(11.32)
23/22	Sun Kyung, Ltd.	529,843	90,667	1,734,150	18,159	3.43	20.03	1.05
24/36	Tong Yang Nylon Co.	495,103	216,860	400,456	11,029	2.23	5.09	2.75
25/34	Kolon Industries	481,144	168,920	407,614	13,964	2.90	8.27	3.43
26/33	Hang Yang Chemical Corp.	477,291	270,803	337,820	9,097	1.91	3.36	2.69
27/—	Ssangyong Oil Refining Co.	469,179	149,836	706,611	47,370	10.10	31.61	6.70
28/35	Gold Star Cable Co.	439,213	89,120	431,388	3,057	6.96	3.43	0.71
29/—	Kyung In Energy Co.	432,908	137,127	498,690	7,621	1.76	5.56	1.53
30/28	Cheil Sugar Co.	428,509	66,908	602,159	8,011	1.87	11.97	1.33
31/24	Samsung Co.	424,851	91,845	5,669,803	12,067	2.84	13.14	0.21
32/—	Sam Sung Construction Co.	413,240	52,192	319,822	2,674	0.65	5.12	0.84
33/29	Kohap, Ltd.	379,427	61,754	302,801	10,142	10.58	16.42	3.35
34/—	Sammi Steel Co.	374,991	81,467	401,530	24,138	6.44	29.63	6.01
35/—	Poongsan Metal Co.	372,210	46,043	375,341	19,210	5.16	41.72	5.12
36/32	Lucky Goldstar Int'l	370,930	55,552	2,201,962	8,633	2.33	15.54	0.39
37/30	Sam Mi Corp.	370,076	68,548	471,243	5,575	1.51	8.13	1.18
38/23	Samho Int'l Co.	365,702	20,299	98,335	201	0.05	0.99	0.20
39/26	Nam Kwang Engineering	358,603	24,381	32,853	171	0.05	0.70	0.52
40/43	Kum Ho & Co.	344,338	70,811	400,548	15,414	4.48	21.77	3.85
41/39	Han 11 Development Co.	340,173	122,539	307,674	11,468	3.37	9.36	3.73
42/27	Life Housing & Construction Co.	327,528	(28,195)	114,653	(34,111)	(10.41)	(120.98)	(29.75)

APPENDIX C

Korea: Year to December 31 (Won million) (Continued)

Rank 1987/1986	Company	Total assets	Shareholders' equity	Turnover/ sales	Net income (loss)	Return on assets	Return on equity	Net profit margin (%)
43/44	Sam Yang Co.	316,473	102,721	411,617	17,378	5.49	16.92	4.22
44/40	Kang Won Industrial Co.	310,308	66,335	362,694	4,101	1.32	6.18	1.13
45/66	Samsung Electron Devices	309,886	81,066	406,532	13,973	4.51	17.24	3.44
46/56	Korea Mining & Smelting Co.	306,003	38,923	406,273	17,896	5.85	45.98	4.40
47/31	Kukdong Construction Co.	305,745	78,220	173,863	1,459	0.48	1.86	0.84
48/46	Choong Nam Spinning Co.	305,736	60,918	316,048	21,272	6.96	34.92	6.73
49/—	Inchon Iron & Steel Co.	304,023	73,936	374,468	19,592	6.44	26.50	5.23
50/75	Korea Explosives Co.	297,351	123,021	126,200	8,363	2.81	6.80	6.63
51/57	Oriental Brewery Co.	284,357	50,494	546,945	5,742	2.02	11.37	1.05
52/48	Taiham Electric Wire Co.	280,745	78,011	281,094	6,408	2.28	8.21	2.28
53/42	Han Shin Construction Co.	278,623	41,945	182,855	1,493	0.54	3.56	0.82
54/50	Kwang Ju Highway Lines, Inc.	273,095	37,428	135,960	1,599	0.58	4	1.18
55/—	Dongkuk Steel Mill Co.	271,662	65,943	358,825	17,821	6.56	27.02	4.97
56/41	Sam Whan Corp.	269,177	115,206	217,294	3,153	1.17	2.74	1.45
57/49	Dong Bu Steel Co.	268,696	61,869	400,520	16,474	6.13	26.63	4.11
58/62	Tae Kwang Industrial Co.	267,525	114,018	319,262	50,132	18.74	43.97	15.70
59/52	Korea Express Co.	262,638	58,860	213,973	7,035	2.68	11.95	3.29
60/55	Cheil Synthetic Textile Co.	258,959	53,933	307,502	6,511	2.51	12.07	2.12
61/80	Hyundai Motor Service Co.	258,947	50,867	322,119	12,908	4.98	25.38	4.01
62/70	Tong Il Co.	257,814	124,773	141,336	6,478	2.51	5.19	4.58
63/—	Saehan Media Co.	249,789	93,615	148,794	15,033	6.02	16.06	10.10
64/38	Samick Corp.	249,674	(52,837)	78,430	(37,601)	(15.06)	(71.16)	(47.94)
65/61	Sun Kyung Industry	248,241	65,231	211,807	9,485	3.82	14.54	4.48
66/54	Tong Yang Cement Corp.	246,575	77,069	210,771	15,772	6.40	20.46	7.48
67/53	Sam Wha Co.	245,805	4,952	152,743	(880)	(.36)	(17.77)	0.58
68/—	Sam Sung Electro-Mechanics Co. (March 31)	243,395	57,946	335,418	11,078	4.55	19.12	3.30
69/76	Ankuk Fire & Marine Insurance	236,702	17,527	138,279	2,240	0.95	12.78	1.62
70/68	Cheil Woo/Textile Co.	231,510	42,197	185,662	5,585	2.41	13.23	3.01
71/65	Pacific Chemical Co.	229,694	63,329	252,265	13,286	5.78	20.98	5.27
72/45	Hyo Sung Co.	226,238	42,385	870,129	1,582	0.70	3.73	0.18
73/64	Han Kook Tire Manufacturing Co.	225,381	70,036	288,505	10,695	4.74	15.27	3.71
74/51	Lucky Development Co.	223,617	41,987	285,351	3,403	1.52	8.10	1.19
75/69	Han Kuk Glass Industry Co.	222,147	71,006	171,083	13,611	6.13	19.17	7.96
76/67	Haitai Confectionery Co.	219,051	28,799	206,087	4,334	1.98	15.05	2.10
77/71	Anam Industrial Co.	207,126	50,478	180,335	5,871	2.83	11.63	3.26
78/58	Union Steel Manufacturing Co.	205,330	89,973	442,677	32,856	16.00	36.52	7.42
79/77	Oriental Chemical Industrial Co.	203,181	51,568	159,251	8,255	406	16.01	5.18
80/60	Tong Kook Corp.	198,806	24,114	299,129	3,368	1.69	13.97	1.13
81/—	Samsung Aerospace Industrial	198,396	30,884	128,890	2,864	1.44	9.27	2.22
82/63	Hyundai Corp.	195,026	46,995	5,253,780	5,031	2.58	10.70	0.10
83/—	Ssangyong Motor Co.	194,880	39,829	100,759	290	0.15	0.73	0.29
84/—	Mando Machinery Co.	194,241	33,051	188,486	10,178	5.24	30.79	5.40
85/72	Cho Sun Brewery Co.	191,729	36,989	303,919	3,318	1.73	8.97	1.09

Korea: Year to December 31 (Won million) (Continued)

Rank 1987/ 1986	Company	Total assets	Shareholders' equity	Turnover/ sales	Net income (loss)	Return on assets	Return on equity	Net profit margin (%)
86/73	Sung Shin Cement Industrial Co.	187,794	72,198	121,175	9,627	5.13	13.33	7.94
87/74	Mi Won Co.	187,780	44,936	127,315	3,497	1.86	7.78	2.75
88/—	Shinsegae Department Store	183,284	37,254	231,959	13,062	7.13	35.06	5.63
89/—	Han Jin Transportation	182,138	46,689	116,776	4,403	2.42	9.43	3.77
90/47	Pacific Construction	178,035	68,352	144,263	(8,368)	(4.70)	(12.24)	(5.80)
91/—	Keam Kang Co.	162,658	57,554	138,774	13,449	8.27	23.37	9.69
92/—	Goldstar Tele-Electric	161,717	54,883	157,377	5,466	3.38	9.96	3.47
93/—	Sam Yang Foods Co.	157,726	40,374	242,746	4,037	2.56	10.00	1.66
94/—	STC Corp.	152,153	39,694	149,889	5,338	3.51	13.45	3.56
95/—	Lotte Confectionery Co.	151,182	34,831	236,051	5,337	3.53	15.32	2.26
96/—	Taihan Textile Co.	149,459	27,665	109,158	12,822	8.58	46.35	11.75
97/—	Dong San Construction	146,179	43,408	150,090	5,769	3.95	13.29	3.84
98/—	Chonju Paper Manufacturing	142,601	31,608	145,935	6,350	4.45	20.09	4.35
99/—	Sambu Construction	142,584	69,264	99,137	816	0.57	1.18	0.82
100—	Hanil Cement Manufacturing	142,504	63,546	124,380	10,535	7.39	16.58	8.47

Malaysia: Year to December 31 (M$'000)

Rank 1987/ 1986	Company	Total assets	Shareholders' equity	Turnover/ sales (loss)	Net income assets	Return on equity	Return on margin	Net profit
1/2	Sime Darby Bhd (June 30, 1988)	4,167,000	2,054,200	3,367,200	206,100	4.95	10.03	6.12
2/1	Malayan United Industries	4,159,787	702,526	312,756	(3,419)	(0.08)	(0.49)	(1.09)
3/—	Malaysian Int'l Shipping Corp.	3,506,739	946,812	1,383,809	286,495	8.17	30.26	20.70
4/—	Malaysian Airline System (March 31, 1988)	2,688,808	831,488	1,577,506	151,600	5.64	18.23	9.61
5/3	Multi-Purpose Holdings	2,138,227	569,369	467,143	(47,898)	(1.53)	(8.41)	(10.25)
6/4	Harrisons Malaysian Plantations (March 31, 1988)	1,904,715	1,705,276	523,109	85,744	4.50	5.03	16.39
7/6	Supreme Corp. (June 30, 1986)	1,148,714	219,819	158,997	(35,506)	(3.09)	(16.15)	(22.33)
8/7	Kuala Lumpur Kepong (Sept. 30, 1987)	1,109,937	932,972	277,722	60,429	5.45	6.48	21.76
9/8	Consolidated Plantations (June 30, 1988)	1,109,635	804,796	619,997	58,677	5.29	7.29	9.46
10/10	Genting Bhd	1,090,166	788,269	402,660	85,396	7.83	10.83	21.21
11/9	Hong Leong Credit (June 30, 1987)	1,027,147	218,207	136,690	8,419	0.82	3.86	6.16
12/11	Malaysia Mining Corp. (Jan. 31, 1988)	970,192	713,238	524,664	35,828	3.69	5.02	6.83
13/17	IGB Corp.	806,101	276,468	224,081	12,668	1.57	4.58	5.65
14/13	Selangor Properties (Oct. 31, 1987)	768,281	528,178	—	2,808	0.36	0.53	—
15/14	Bousted Holdings (June 30, 1987)	765,419	307,399	307,337	(1,552)	(0.20)	(0.50)	(0.50)
16/16	Tan Chong Motor Holdings	707,845	403,332	521,412	(17,905)	(2.53)	(4.44)	(3.43)
17/12	Faber Merlin Malaysia	659,357	234,747	94,599	(67,534)	(10.24)	(28.77)	(71.39)

Malaysia: Year to December 31 (M$'000) (Continued)

Rank 1987/ 1986	Company	Total assets	Shareholders' equity	Turnover/ sales (loss)	Net income assets	Return on equity	Return on margin	Net profit
18/18	United Estate Project	640,100	517,910	140,300	18,090	2.83	(3.49)	(12.89)
19/15	Promet Bhd	610,311	254,900	40,941	(13,845)	(2.27)	(5.43)	(33.82)
20/21	Arab-Malaysian Development (March 31, 1987)	600,249	352,666	115,881	6,269	1.04	1.78	5.41
21/26	Shell Refining Co.	580,325	343,294	1,130,725	45,750	7.88	13.33	4.05
22/22	Highlands and Lowlands	543,782	483,654	127,275	19,118	3.52	3.95	15.02
23/24	Hong Leong Industries (June 30, 1988)	536,113	278,784	246,103	13,639	2.54	4.89	5.54
24/73	Berjaya Corp. (M)	528,289	277,911	168,473	14,874	2.81	5.35	8.83
25/27	Island & Peninsular Development (Jan. 31, 1988)	511,186	316,150	86,385	12,373	2.42	3.91	14.32
26/42	Innovest Bhd	491,835	185,046	308,501	10,847	2.20	5.86	3.52
27/20	Esso Mabysia	483,630	229,784	937,949	39,706	8.21	17.28	4.23
28/34	Rothmans of Pall Mall (M) (June 30, 1988)	469,087	256,599	706,546	70,636	15.06	27.53	10.00
29/28	Batu Rawan (Aug. 31, 1987)	460,137	425,640	80,538	19,772	4.30	4.64	24.55
30/31	Kuab Sidim Rubber Co. (June 30, 1988)	447,136	203,469	135,089	17,414	3.89	8.56	12.89
31/32	Perlis Plantations (Sept. 30, 1987)	425,078	337,166	415,323	38,934	9.16	11.55	9.37
32/25	General Corp.	410,924	161,341	137,452	(5,771)	(1.40)	(3.58)	4.20
33/33	Malaysian Tobacco Co. (15 mos. to Dec. 31, 1987)	410,919	274,443	777,105	44,806	10.90	16.33	5.77
34/19	UMW Holdings (formerly known as UMW Corp.)	397,678	41,144	297,733	(24,412)	(6.14)	(59.33)	(8.20)
35/35	Oriental Holdings	393,120	294,195	—	15,873	4.04	5.39	—
36/41	Tractors Malaysia (June 30, 1988)	386,103	295,862	406,573	36,354	9.42	12.29	8.94
37/30	Malaysian Resources Corp.	379,965	85,936	15,091	(52,196)	(13.74)	(60.74)	(345.87)
38/36	East Asiatic Co. (Malaysia)	371,936	305,989	186,567	18,003	4.84	5.88	9.65
39.29	Hume Industries (Malaysia) (June 30, 1988)	371,727	191,033	182,651	8,498	2.29	4.45	4.65
40/55	New Straits Times Press (Aug. 31, 1987)	361,826	169,229	165,738	11,916	3.29	7.04	7.19
41/38	Grand United Holdings (Dec. 31, 1986)	361,128	181,322	52,247	(19,265)	(5.33)	(10.62)	(36.87)
42/54	Malaysian Mosaics Bhd (March 31, 1988)	355,444	184,196	239,369	10,758	3.03	5.84	4.49
43/37	Bandar Raya Development	354,287	276,665	26,162	420	0.12	0.15	1.60
44/44	Federal Flour Mills	353,239	206,606	628,122	34,022	9.63	16.47	5.42
45/47	Lion Corp.	318,646	145,303	81,684	12,387	3.89	8.52	15.16
46/23	Magnum Corp.	317,871	92,806	599,240	(12,495)	(3.93)	(13.46)	(2.08)
47/46	Poxy Electric Industries (M)	317,159	165,802	19,603	(59,258)	(18.68)	(35.74)	(302.29)
48/39	Palmco Holdings (June 30, 1987)	316,995	149,412	—	(21,881)	(6.90)	(14.64)	—
49/43	Guthrie Ropel	316,619	272,744	76,733	7,593	2.40	2.78	9.89
50/—	Chemical Co. of Malaysia (15 mos. to Dec. 31, 1987)	312,882	146,419	521,311	20,493	6.55	14.00	3.93

Malaysia: Year to December 31 (M$'000) (Continued)

Rank 1987/ 1986	Company	Total assets	Shareholders' equity	Turnover/ sales (loss)	Net income assets	Return on equity	Return on margin	Net profit
51/40	Cement Industries of Malaysia (June 30, 1988)	309,461	75,428	62,077	(4,014)	(1.30)	(5.32)	(6.47)
52/49	United Plantations	287,016	230,629	80,653	4,533	1.58	1.96	5.62
53/53	Malayan Cement (Nov. 30, 1987)	281,854	274,071	178,985	10,930	3.88	3.99	6.11
54/52	Keck Seng (Malaysia)	276,859	224,475	247,732	13,948	5.04	6.21	(5.63)
55/60	DMIB Bhd (June 30, 1988)	260,830	194,379	221,799	13,855	5.31	7.13	6.25
56/56	Metroplex (13 mos. to Jan. 31, 1988)	258,217	131,963	40,487	5,954	2.31	4.51	14.71
57/51	Tasek Cement (June 30, 1987)	254,602	174,445	126,778	6,305	2.48	3.61	4.97
58/67	Antah Holdings (March 31, 1988)	252,122	127,881	154,883	5,510	2.18	4.31	3.56
59/57	Mabyawata Steel (March 31, 1988)	248,100	5,919	157,736	(5,293)	(2.13)	(89.42)	(3.36)
60/48	Pan Malaysia Cement Works (March 31, 1988)	244,993	224,765	—	4,724	1.93	2.10	—
61/45	Landmarks Holdings	233,998	119,024	32,681	(9,415)	(4.02)	(7.91)	(28.81)
62/62	Petaling Garden	222,647	134,562	14,293	(293)	(0.13)	(0.22)	(2.05)
63/61	Cold Storage (Malaysia)	219,469	171,409	154,325	3,362	1.53	1.96	2.18
64/69	Uniphone Telecommunications (formerly Malayan Cables) (Jan. 31, 1988)	218,145	111,246	113,546	3,329	1.71	3.35	3.28
65/63	Guiness Malaysia	214,210	161,845	255,225	28,896	13.49	17.85	11.32
66/64	Malayan United Manufacturing	194,231	145,633	13,163	(1,881)	(0.97)	(1.29)	(14.29)
67/72	Austral Enterprises (Jan. 31, 1988)	187,560	123,910	32,974	8,449	4.50	6.82	25.62
68/66	Malayan Flour Mills	179,276	110,563	173,181	8,847	4.93	8.00	5.11
69/68	Mount Pleasure Holdings	178,825	94,687	9,766	(6,932)	(3.88)	(7.32)	(70.98)
70/71	Selangor Coconuts	178,288	144,154	51,947	5,388	3.02	3.74	10.37
71/70	Pegi Malaysia (March 31, 1987)	175,965	145,696	5,829	(3,920)	(2.23)	(2.69)	(67.25)
72/74	Federal Auto Holdings (Dec. 31, 1985)	161,477	59,735	139,546	4,188	2.59	7.01	3.00
73/75	CI Holdings (June 30, 1988)	155,668	61,543	71,613	1,921	1.23	3.12	2.68
74/5	Killinghall (Malaysia)	153,057	106,296	—	5,863	3.83	5.52	—
75/78	Kemayan Oil Palm (May 31, 1988)	149,150	136,874	18,515	3,524	2.36	2.57	19.03
76/76	Kulim (Malaysia)	148,549	129,447	64,311	7,702	5.18	5.95	11.98
77/—	Kumpulan Emas (July 31, 1987)	146,352	76,127	77,234	3,101	2.12	4.07	4.01
78/—	South Malaysia Industries (Dec. 31, 1986)	145,019	50,893	24,630	(4,750)	(3.27)	(9.33)	(19.28)
79/79	Batu Lintang Rubber Co. (Sept. 30, 1987)	144,928	43,169	6,536	(4,444)	(3.07)	(10.29)	(67.99)
80/—	Matsushita Electric Co. (March 31, 1988)	140,097	90,491	201,413	10,207	7.29	11.28	5.07

APPENDIX C

Philippines: Year to December 31 (P'000)

Rank 1987/ 1986	Company	Total assets	Shareholders' equity	Turnover/ sales (loss)	Net income assets	Return on equity	Return on margin	Net profit
1/—	Phil. National Oil Co.	27,966,630	7,785,392	18,311,514	749,203	2.68	9.62	4.09
2/1	Phil. Long Distance Telephone	21,264,200	6,261,100	6,590,800	1,362,100	6.41	21.75	20.67
3/4	Sam Miguel Corp.	15,189,861	7,183,159	16,014,621	1,757,533	11.57	24.47	10.97
4/2	Manila Electric Co.	13,716,246	5,548,651	14,843,157	500,124	3.65	9.01	3.37
5/3	Phil. National Const. Corp. (Dec. 1985)	12,524,572	2,732,125	1,295,356	(791,426)	(6.32)	(28.97)	(61.10)
6/5	Phil. Air Lines (March 1987)	11,675,754	(3,525,839)	10,040,584	318,128	2.72	(9.02)	3.17
7/7	Philipinas Shell Petroleum	11,365,617	3,295,795	13,697,019	301,854	2.66	9.16	2.20
8/6	National Steel Corp. (Dec. 1986)	10,333,972	4,824,135	5,061,157	503,590	4.87	10.44	9.95
9/9	Caltex (Phils)	9,500,945	1,140,117	15,779,543	(116,261)	(1.22)	(10.20)	(0.74)
10/8	Atlas Consolidated Mining	8,039,643	47,713	3,718,445	(175,339)	(2.18)	(367.49)	(4.71)
11/11	Paper Industries Corp.	4,841,578	295,901	2,245,956	(219,721)	(4.54)	(74.25)	(9.78)
12/10	Benguet Corp.	4,591,100	1,315,200	3,457,900	207,900	4.53	15.81	6.01
13/13	Coca–Cola Bottlers Phils.	4,171,417	1,488,196	5,042,385	241,142	5.78	16.20	4.78
14/12	Petrophil Corp. (Dec. 1986)	3,843,215	1,146,084	14,213,269	403,632	10.50	35.22	2.84
15/17	Ayala Corp.	3,399,831	2,684,630	974,506	515,602	15.16	19.21	52.91
16/15	Phil. Petroleum Corp.	3,343,027	1,861,580	2,301,104	379,915	11.36	20.41	16.51
17/19	Philex Mining Corp.	2,645,999	2,105,657	2,120,849	655,322	24.77	31.12	30.90
18/26	Shoemart Inc. (March 1987)	2,333,671	536,100	3,059,522	118,865	5.09	22.17	3.88
19/18	Shell Gas Phils.	2,182,546	159,992	680,767	27,990	1.28	17.49	4.11
20/32	Del Monte Phils. (formerly Phil. Packing Corp.) (Nov. 1987)	2,004,488	1,174,795	2,235,644	414,291	20.67	35.26	18.53
21/22	Nestle Phils.	1,941,020	777,861	5,120,170	248,498	12.80	31.95	4.85
22/21	Universal Robina Corp. (Dec. 1985)	1,923,862	555,566	1,692,638	—	—	—	—
23/36	United Laboratories	1,839,901	1,278,904	2,152,217	143,909	7.82	11.25	6.69
24/20	Atlantic Gulf & Pacific Co.	1,746,305	744,773	1,245,776	(35,420)	(2.03)	(4.76)	(2.84)
25/30	Ferrochrome Phils.	1,619,516	(498,225)	504,854	(324,544)	(20.04)	(65.14)	(64.28)
26/34	Lepanto Consolidated	1,575,656	1,123,752	1,328,827	290,883	18.46	25.88	21.89
27/16	Phil. Geothermal	1,574,086	—	1,293,365	618,553	39.30	—	47.82
28/23	CFC Corp. (Sept. 1985)	1,566,511	582,483	1,000,740	72,645	4.64	12.47	7.26
29/24	Filipinas Synthetic Fiber (Dec. 1986)	1,560,438	487,798	1,268,086	41,427	2.65	8.49	3.27
30/35	Phil. Refining Co.	1,484,759	755,882	2,871,237	78,069	5.26	10.33	2.72
31/25	Planters Products (Dec. 1985)	1,472,949	22,543	711,803	(299,916)	(20.36)	(1,330.42)	(42.13)
32/31	Texas Instruments (Phils.) (Dec. 1986)	1,385,720	—	2,560,693	100,222	7.23	—	3.91
33/38	Eastern Telecommunications	1,333,594	535,377	495,961	159,119	11.93	29.72	32.08
34/33	Marcopper Mining Corp. (Dec. 1986)	1,266,927	(184,297)	785,300	(341,960)	(26.99)	(185.55)	(43.54)
35/40	Mercury Drag Corp.	1,219,716	252,090	3,652,825	64,143	5.26	25.44	1.76
36/43	Rubber World (Phils.)	1,171,475	331,235	924,620	24,908	2.13	7.52	2.69
37/28	First Phil. Holdings (June 1987)	1,139,888	521,011	78,399	(108,668)	(9.53)	(20.86)	(138.61)
38/44	Colgate Palmolive Phils.	1,139,242	538,905	1,595,889	56	—	0.01	—

Philippines: Year to December 31 (P'000) (Continued)

Rank 1987/1986	Company	Total assets	Shareholders' equity	Turnover/ sales (loss)	Net income assets	Return on equity	Return on margin	Net profit
39/55	Progressive Development Corp. (Sept. 1987)	1,138,798	847,153	209,105	22,630	1.99	2.67	10.82
40/41	RFM Corp. (June 1987)	1,211,201	376,025	2,181,053	48,796	4.03	12.98	2.24
41/45	Phil. Communications Satellite (March 1988)	1,115,997	827,170	—	—	—	—	—
42/58	Metro Drug Corp. (Nov. 1987)	1,064,141	179,031	2,498,612	52,691	4.95	29.43	2.11
43/50	La Tondena Distillers	1,010,968	201,653	438,557	1,653	0.16	0.82	0.38
44/42	Phil. Sinter Corp.	992,603	553,808	713,742	156,534	15.77	28.26	21.93
45/52	Procter & Gamble Phils. (June 1987)	973,241	477,528	2,179,871	76,347	7.84	15.99	3.50
46/48	Victorias Milling Co. (Aug. 1987)	967,731	608,741	1,513,801	150,083	15.51	24.65	9.91
47/46	Phil. Overseas Telecommunications (March 1988)	928,849	896,526	32,380	219,096	23.59	24.44	676.64
48/49	La Suerte Cigar (Dec. 1985)	922,942	525,531	4,520,688	139,823	15.15	26.61	3.09
49/39	Engineering Equipment, Inc.	912,984	40,990	2,162,282	(368,832)	(40.40)	(899.81)	(17.06)
50/59	San Pablo Manufacturing (June 1987)	879,838	292,800	679,923	18,061	2.05	6.17	2.66
50/51	Pacific Cement Co. (Dec. 1986)	863,990	(193,970)	104,977	(147,427)	(17.06)	(76.00)	(140.44)
52/53	Phil. Global Communications (Dec. 1986)	851,054	399,739	542,858	254,848	29.94	63.75	46.95
53/62	Dole Phils.	833,594	329,884	1,845,199	51,266	6.15	15.54	2.78
54/54	Floro Cement Corp. (Dec. 1985)	832,971	—	252,090	(111,338)	(13.37)	—	(44.16)
55/56	Solid Mills, Inc. (Dec. 1985)	810,867	161,877	479,661	(18,648)	(2.30)	(11.52)	(3.89)
56/61	Manila Papers Mills	764,609	360,485	387,938	2,744	0.36	0.76	0.71
57/63	Phil. Telegraph & Telephone (June 1987)	751,608	318,551	235,176	16,280	2.17	5.11	6.92
58/—	Resins, Inc.	654,802	590,917	519,484	135,196	20.65	22.88	26.02
59/65	Republic Cement Corp.	649,672	424,791	418,049	42,142	6.49	9.92	10.09
60/66	Tagum Agricultural Development (Dec. 1986)	637,251	243,413	917,635	63,809	10.01	26.21	6.95
61/71	Phimco Industries (Dec. 1986)	614,338	383,191	663,215	77,839	12.67	20.31	11.74
62/77	Hydro Resources Contractors	586,054	431,181	134,209	(67,070)	(11.44)	(15.55)	(49.97)
63/—	Pilipinas Kao	584,237	369,981	661,403	60,154	10.30	16.26	9.09
64/—	Precision Electronics Corp. (March 1988)	579,502	398,000	1,079,383	85,256	14.71	21.42	7.90
65/64	Bacnotan Consolidated (June 1985)	576,436	—	340,287	23,583	4.09	—	6.93
66/73	Vitarich Corp. (Dec. 1985)	556,668	289,821	707,175	14,407	2.59	4.97	2.04
67/75	Kimberly-Clark Phils. (Dec. 1985)	547,794	275,495	549,845	58,687	10.71	21.30	10.67
68/76	Pantranco North Express (Dec. 1986)	532,508	(85,908)	1,680	916	0.17	(1.07)	54.52
69/78	Phil. Steel Coating Corp. (Dec. 1986)	519,535	334,305	499,531	4,485	0.86	1.34	0.90

Philippines: Year to December 31 (P'000) (Continued)

Rank 1987/ 1986	Company	Total assets	Shareholders' equity	Turnover/ sales (loss)	Net income assets	Return on equity	Return on margin	Net profit
70/—	Globe-Mackay Cable & Radio	511,743	263,398	342,275	107,882	21.08	40.96	31.52
71/80	Pillsbury-Mindanao Flour Milling (Dec. 1986)	507,076	266,675	603,301	86,916	17.14	32.59	14.41
72/—	Coca-Cola Export Corp.	500,680	—	791,277	288,979	57.72	—	36.52
73/60	F. F. Cruz & Co.	498,056	84,306	9,120	1,038	0.21	1.23	11.38
74/—	Abbott Laboratories (Nov. 1987)	492,168	383,096	657,295	113,390	23.04	29.60	17.25
75/—	Reynolds Phil Corp. (Sept. 1986)	487,561	(261,303)	318,914	(70,451)	(14.45)	(26.96)	(22.09)
76/—	Calfornic Manufacturing Co.	485,251	236,068	1,005,439	121,791	25.10	51.59	12.11
77/—	PNOC Shipping & Transport Corp.	484,061	196,306	371,266	39,440	8.15	20.09	10.62
78/79	Oriental Petroleum & Minerals	483,071	464,856	193,490	68,960	14.27	14.83	35.64
79/—	Shell Chemical Co. (Phils.)	482,603	158,525	675,115	70,070	14.52	44.20	10.38
80/—	Steniel Manufacturing Corp.	478,705	187,661	314,565	17,693	3.70	9.43	5.62

Singapore: Year to December 31 (S$'000)

Rank 1987/ 1986	Company	Total assets	Shareholders' equity	Turnover/ sales (loss)	Net income assets	Return on equity	Return on margin	Net profit
1/1	Singapore Airlines (March 1988)	6,364,000	3,207,200	4,010,900	602,600	9.47	18.79	15.02
2/2	Neptune Orient Lines	2,159,074	440,641	1,096,405	23,599	1.09	5.36	2.15
3/3	Keppel Corp.	1,764,894	491,757	670,726	23,891	1.35	4.86	3.56
4/5	Singapore Land (Aug. 31, 1987)	1,181,644	749,876	—	17,177	1.45	2.29	—
5/6	City Development	1,034,535	542,900	164,645	23,849	2.30	4.39	14.48
6/4	Singapore Press Holdings (Aug. 31, 1987)	983,870	672,491	790,768	91,167	9.27	13.56	11.53
7/15	Fraser & Neave, Ltd. (Sept. 30, 1987)	955,477	442,930	811,901	401,845	4.27	9.22	5.03
8/14	United Industrial Corp.	758,604	448,889	364,339	31,411	4.14	7.00	8.62
9/11	United Overseas Land	748,609	309,100	61,554	(8,443)	(1.13)	(2.73)	(13.72)
10/7	Straits Steamship	720,009	503,917	131,294	9,068	1.26	1.80	6.91
11/8	Overseas Union Enterprise	677,443	416,427	96,599	6,900	1.02	1.66	7.14
12/12	Parkway Holdings	622,132	272,130	84,291	17,168	2.76	6.31	20.37
13/9	Straits Trading Co.	587,114	516,731	210,078	25,343	4.32	4.90	12.06
14/17	Malaysia Breweries, Ltd. (Sept. 30, 1987)	526,710	375,271	559,978	55,465	10.53	14.78	9.90
15/10	Inchcape Bhd	524,634	351,553	438,049	53,219	10.14	15.15	12.15
16/13	Cold Storage Holdings (Jan. 31, 1988)	514,715	353,195	332,358	18,146	3.52	5.14	5.46
17/23	Singapore Bus Service	464,847	251,487	355,548	36,930	7.94	14.68	10.39
18/22	Sembawang Shipyard	447,113	239,141	184,800	18,517	4.14	7.74	10.02
19/24	Wearne Brothers (Sept. 30, 1987)	426,311	285,933	193,761	9,610	2.25	3.36	4.96
20/19	National Iron & Steel Mills	426,299	318,259	408,686	30,496	7.15	9.58	7.46

Singapore: Year to December 31 (S$'000) (Continued)

Rank 1987/ 1986	Company	Total assets	Shareholders' equity	Turnover/ sales (loss)	Net income assets	Return on equity	Return on margin	Net profit
21/16	Sim Lim Investments (March 31, 1988)	375,966	32,415	101,833	35,841	9.53	110.57	35.20
22/20	Hong Fok Corp.	373,404	144,935	46,910	(17,096)	(4.58)	(11.80)	(36.44)
23/27	Haw Par Brothers Int'l	361,644	295,388	303,293	24,972	6.90	8.45	8.23
24/25	Gaodwood Park Hotel (Sept. 30, 1987)	344,816	187,766	136,827	9,765	2.83	5.20	7.14
25/26	Hwa Hong Corp.	329,263	166,086	144,710	5,558	1.69	3.35	3.84
26/29	Cycle & Carriage Ud (Sept. 30, 1987)	315,729	275,525	229,813	14,765	4.68	5.36	6.42
27/30	Shangri-La Hotel	313,304	274,908	93,670	14,351	4.58	5.22	15.32
28/28	Far East Levingston Shipbuilding	290,396	228,578	—	9,939	3.42	4.35	—
29/31	Prima, Ltd.	284,638	197,562	58,276	22,392	7.87	11.33	38.42
30/32	Yeo Hiap Seng	263,580	156,802	185,068	9,107	3.45	5.81	4.92
31/35	Hotel Properties	255,100	157,195	36,558	1,173	0.46	0.75	3.21
32/34	Metro Holdings (March 31, 1988)	234,824	96,076	366,669	12,582	5.36	13.10	3.43
33/21	Jock Chia-MPH (March 31, 1988)	230,301	147,130	77,482	6,100	2.65	4.15	7.87
34/37	Metal Box (Singapore) (March 31, 1988)	226,629	121,022	259,672	13,124	5.79	10.84	5.05
35/36	Gold Coin, Ltd.	209,832	67,471	460,272	5,694	2.71	8.44	1.24
36/33	Intraco, Ltd.	205,538	156,944	407,685	6,722	3.27	4.28	1.65
37/42	Rothmans Industries, Ltd. (June 30, 1988)	199,293	161,417	152,514	24,979	12.53	15.47	16.38
38/41	Cerebos Pacific, Ltd. (July 31, 1987)	194,679	196,818	277,189	19,226	9.88	9.77	6.94
39/40	King's Hotels, Ltd.	181,589	135,466	26,753	(168)	(0.09)	(0.12)	(0.63)
40/39	Bonvests Holdings	177,715	139,133	72,997	(9,136)	(5.14)	(6.57)	(12.52)
41/43	Hotel Marco Polo	164,353	154,770	27,722	(2,021)	(1.23)	(1.31)	(7.29)
42/44	Isetan (S), Ltd. (Nov. 30, 1987)	150,143	73,863	158,508	5,353	3.56	7.24	3.38
43/—	First Capital Corp. (formerly Sealion Hotels)	144,409	135,217	2,854	1,132	0.78	0.84	39.66
44/46	Hotel Malaysia (Sept. 30, 1987)	138,374	36,440	24,810	(4,152)	(3.00)	(11.39)	(16.73)
45/—	OAF, Ltd. (March 31, 1988)	136,109	24,479	234,686	(14,060)	(10.33)	(57.44)	(5.99)
46/—	Metal Containers, Ltd. (June 30, 1987)	131,328	64,235	72,868	4,245	3.23	6.61	5.83
47/45	Central Properties, Ltd.	123,562	114,722	10,774	9,669	7.82	8.43	89.74
48/49	Apollo Enterprises	112,499	19,801	10,925	(3,514)	(3.12)	(17.75)	(32.16)
49/—	Robinson & Co. (June 30, 1988)	105,838	94,682	86,447	6,506	6.15	6.87	7.53
50/—	Hind Hotel Int'l	100,894	57,119	10,946	(6,619)	(6.56)	(11.59)	(60.47)

Taiwan: Year to December 31 (NT$'000)

Rank 1987/ 1986	Company	Total assets	Shareholders' equity	Turnover/ sales (loss)	Net income assets	Return on equity	Return on margin	Net profit
1/1	China Steel Corp.	137,517,821	102,516,399	41,175,752	7,794,852	5.67	7.60	18.93
2/3	Nan Ya Plastics Corp.	37,740,202	11,685,201	50,736,056	4,462,798	11.82	38.19	8.80
3/2	Ta Tung Co.	34,063,810	8,168,585	26,739,187	1,109,529	3.26	13.58	4.15
4/4	Evergreen Marine Corp.	31,443,244	12,674,501	22,048,903	2,072,140	6.59	16.35	9.40
5/5	Formosa Plastics	28,395,720	17,329,643	24,111,886	3,920,158	13.80	22.62	15.61
6/6	Far Eastern Textiles, Ltd.	26,675,092	12,069,464	18,534,978	3,954,444	14.82	32.76	21.33
7/7	Chung Shing Textile Co.	21,042,253	7,099,582	12,741,485	800,146	3.80	11.27	6.28
8/9	Yue Loong Motor Co.	16,528,344	10,576,273	21,953,294	2,886,623	17.46	27.29	13.15
9/10	Asia Cement Corp.	16,390,218	9,130,820	7,361,235	2,712,307	16.55	29.70	36.85
10/8	Hualon Corp.	16,313,120	8,483,126	11,107,186	1,802,386	11.05	21.25	16.23
11/11	Taiwan Cement Corp.	11,250,093	8,665,373	10,675,496	1,870,899	16.63	21.59	17.52
12/18	Walsin Lihwa Electric Wire & Cable Corp.	8,771,882	4,830,164	6,821,171	1,891,601	21.56	39.16	27.73
13/12	China Rebar Co.	8,661,328	2,974,316	4,862,601	32,505	0.37	1.09	0.67
14/14	Taiwan Glass Industrial Corp.	8,648,439	5,469,294	4,121,711	1,062,750	12.29	19.43	25.78
15/16	Teco Electric & Machinery Co.	7,460,554	3,141,309	9,035,619	922,318	12.36	29.36	10.21
16/13	Yuen Foong Yu Paper Mtg. Co.	7,454,382	4,142,583	7,034,724	715,126	9.59	17.26	10.17
17/17	Pacific Electric Wire & Cable Co.	7,422,821	3,975,965	6,841,449	803,354	10.82	20.20	11.74
18/20	Cheng Loong Co.	7,325,250	3,430,026	7,919,622	984,107	13.43	28.69	12.43
19/15	Sampo Corp.	7,205,834	3,185,116	10,401,089	511,?59	7.09	16.05	4.91
20/23	Chung Hwa Pulp Corp.	5,485,892	4,080,600	4,688,710	1,215,807	22.16	29.79	25.93
21/21	Chia Hsin Flour Mill	5,184,852	2,149,006	4,685,754	333,576	6.43	15.52	7.12
22/19	Chia Hsin Cement Corp.	5,156,763	3,554,617	2,727,241	727,035	14.10	20.45	26.66
23/22	Wei Chuan Foods Corp.	5,114,461	2,548,858	6,705,460	378,398	7.40	14.85	5.64
24/25	General Plastics	4,474,060	2,439,001	6,569,233	510,583	11.41	20.93	7.77
25/24	USI Far East Corp.	4,321,407	3,415,914	5,462,755	1,016,593	23.52	29.76	18.61
26/—	Kuo Chan Development & Construction Co.	4,011,262	1,872,236	2,129,371	310,400	7.74	16.58	14.58
27/26	Ruentex Industries, Ltd.	3,594,683	2,002,193	2,600,024	56,477	1.57	2.82	2.17
28/27	Lien Hwa Industrial Corp.	3,323,551	2,396,541	1,040,478	488,896	14.71	20.40	46.99
29/29	Ve Wong Corp.	3,228,956	1,747,242	4,646,610	298,825	9.25	17.10	6.43
30/—	Taiwan Kolin Co.	3,194,032	1,651,995	3,623,265	306,177	9.59	18.53	8.45

Thailand: Year to December 31 (Baht'000)

Rank 1987/ 1986	Company	Total assets	Shareholders' equity	Turnover/ sales (loss)	Net income assets	Return on equity	Return on margin	Net profit
1/1	Siam Cement Co.	11,322,909	4,279,451	13,618,574	1,232,780	10.89	28.81	9.05
2/2	Siam Motors Co. (Dec. 31, 1986)	6,113,027	589,673	1,184,617	(500,468)	(8.19)	(84.87)	(42.45)
3/3	Siam City Cement Co.	5,423,092	3,100,534	3,495,450	728,227	13.43	23.49	20.83
4/4	Esso Standard Thailand	4,950,499	322,411	24,841,867	107,922	2.18	33.47	0.43
5/5	United Flour Mill	4,557,553	491,870	747,503	7,196	0.16	1.46	0.96

Thailand: Year to December 31 (Baht'000) (Continued)

Rank 1987/ 1986	Company	Total assets	Shareholders' equity	Turnover/ sales (loss)	Net income assets	Return on equity	Return on margin	Net profit
6/6	Mah Boonkrong Drying & Silo Co. (Dec. 31, 1986)	4,000,588	890,779	165,684	27,892	0.70	3.13	16.83
7/7	Thai Central Chemicals	3,440,304	359,565	2,455,163	25,553	0.74	7.11	1.04
8/—	Padaeng Industry Co.	3,219,908	1,161,303	1,529,441	278,257	8.64	23.96	18.19
9/11	Toyota Motors (Thailand)	2,984,991	686,898	8,543,535	181,427	6.08	26.41	2.12
10/8	Saha Union Corp.	2,956,463	1,212,665	6,135,796	226,466	7.66	18.67	3.69
11/9	Italian Thai Development Corp.	2,520,178	268,702	2,173,946	17,068	0.68	6.35	0.78
12/12	Boonward Brewery Co.	2,127,521	1,663,716	5,083,422	164,217	7.72	9.87	3.23
13/10	Singer Thailand	2,116,372	401,386	1,873,280	74,691	3.53	18.61	3.99
14/13	Union Textile Industries	1,846,532	758,438	2,451,759	319,805	17.32	42.17	13.04
15/15	Thai Plastic & Chemical	1,693,324	426,268	2,467,436	151,452	8.94	35.53	6.14
16/16	Thai Tinplate Manufacturing	1,597,496	494,966	2,817,156	143,378	8.97	28.97	5.09
17/14	Lucky Tex (Thailand) (Dec. 31, 1986)	1,580,061	20,253	1,962,160	(170)	(0.01)	(0.84)	(0.01)
18/17	Berli Jucker Co.	1,480,705	509,933	2,686,882	67,085	4.53	13.16	2.50
19/18	Lever Brothers (Thailand)	1,428,055	732,386	2,672,120	199,415	13.96	27.23	7.46
20/19	East Asiatic Co. (Thailand)	1,408,607	1,079,411	2,003,741	168,032	11.93	15.57	8.39
21/21	Serm Suk Co.	1,244,239	520,823	3,182,427	120,423	9.68	22.69	3.78
22/22	Jalaprathan Cement Co.	1,221,668	705,681	1,605,730	120,557	9.87	17.08	7.51
23/20	Sittipol Motors Co. (Dec. 31, 1986)	1,198,861	6,146	1,755,994	3,128	0.26	50.89	0.18
24/25	Int'l Cosmetics Co.	1,182,494	485,211	2,044,750	101,602	8.59	20.94	4.97
25/26	Thai Asahi Caustic Soda	1,154,185	75,816	598,295	15,879	1.38	20.94	2.65
26/48	Bangkok Agro Industrial Products	1,098,457	695,360	1,233,776	57,011	5.19	8.20	4.62
27/—	Bangkok Produce Merchandising Co.	1,074,608	733,775	5,486,599	80,791	7.52	11.01	1.47
28/37	Dusit Thani Corp.	1,040,838	758,035	524,481	105,507	10.14	13.92	20.12
29/—	Thai Textile Industry	1,024,214	323,509	1,392,108	50,453	4.93	15.59	3.62
30/—	Siam Pulp & Paper Co.	958,158	837,320	869,916	180,318	18.82	21.53	20.73
31/23	Thai Union Paper Co.	951,375	277,404	1,188,934	15,793	1.66	5.69	1.33
32/24	Kamol Sukosol Co.	848,181	214,107	175,531	59,944	7.07	28.00	34.15
33/32	Borneo Co. (Thailand)	817,230	276,997	1,610,154	31,774	3.89	11.47	1.97
34/27	Thai-Wah Co.	803,187	355,540	801,309	20,603	2.56	5.79	2.57
35/29	Saha Pathanapibul Co.	783,582	287,233	2,004,688	44,647	5.70	15.54	2.23
36/31	Siam Tyres Co.	745,538	342,145	1,214,804	74,137	9.94	21.67	6.10
37/28	Colgate-Palmolive (Thailand)	735,077	291,261	1,464,590	61,800	8.41	21.22	4.22
38/30	Union Thread Industries	651,475	284,769	674,525	41,542	6.38	14.59	6.16
39/35	Thai Glass Industries	648,116	391,960	836,617	59,973	9.25	15.30	7.17
40/40	Saha Pathana Inter-Holding	645,545	267,197	356,620	35,114	5.44	13.14	9.85
41/33	Thai Seri Cold Storage Co. (Dec. 31, 1986)	637,690	331,097	113,985	(427)	(0.07)	(0.13)	(0.37)
42/34	Siam Ford Products	636,017	230,521	638,096	67,497	10.61	29.28	10.58
43/45	Thai Rayon Co.	601,096	327,729	1,005,146	118,136	19.65	36.05	11.75
44/38	Datamat, Ltd.	588,637	102,604	329,226	9,580	1.63	9.34	2.91
45/—	Charoen Pokphand Fredmill Co.	584,791	415,104	735,623	89,602	15.32	21.58	12.18

Thailand: Year to December 31 (Baht'000) (Continued)

Rank 1987/ 1986	Company	Total assets	Shareholders' equity	Turnover/ sales (loss)	Net income assets	Return on equity	Return on margin	Net profit
46/39	Goodyear (Thailand)	569,954	239,879	837,021	26,120	4.58	10.89	3.12
47/47	Bangkok Rubber Co.	563,119	376,480	529,124	25,805	4.58	6.85	4.88
48/41	Foremost Friesland (Thailand)	525,629	239,498	941,161	62,147	11.82	25.95	6.60
49/36	Italthai Holding	521,786	283,236	62,210	15,340	2.94	5.42	24.66
50/—	Pan Asia Footwear Co.	519,115	82,520	565,388	15,767	3.04	19.11	2.79
51/42	Thai–German Ceramic Industry	502,429	205,829	648,077	37,002	7.36	17.98	5.71
52/52	Thai Wacoal Co.	473,467	238,235	595,031	28,156	5.95	11.82	4.73
53/46	Asia Fiber Co.	456,324	264,764	725,902	90,284	19.78	34.10	12.44
54/—	Metal Box Thailand	432,240	228,583	812,171	51,890	12.00	22.70	6.39
55/44	Thailand Carpet Manufacturing	425,096	174,341	290,187	22,211	5.22	12.74	7.65
56/49	Thai Toray Textile Mills	402,583	291,328	765,198	64,114	15.93	22.01	8.38
57/56	Thai Iryo Co.	394,446	135,981	662,016	11,394	2.89	8.38	1.72
58/54	Thai President Foods Co.	392,341	197,096	792,454	49,307	12.57	25.02	6.22
59/50	Vorachak Yontr Co. (Dec. 31, 1986)	386,579	10,286	715,714	(3,105)	(0.80)	(30.19)	(0.43)
60/43	G.S. Steel Co.	383,104	39,294	631,371	(58,968)	(15.39)	(150.07)	(9.34)

APPENDIX D

PACIFIC RIM TRADE ORGANIZATIONS

THE ASIA-PACIFIC COUNCIL OF AMERICAN CHAMBERS OF COMMERCE (APCAC)

APCAC was formed in 1968. It currently represents the interests of about 35,000 businessmen and 6,500 business entities participating in 18 American Chambers of Commerce (Amcham) throughout the Asia-Pacific region. The APCAC membership manages trade volumes in excess of US$180 billion and investments of over US$40 billion. For more information, contact:

APCAC Chairman c/o Honeywell Inc.
Nagai International Bldg., 2-12-19 Shibuya
Shibuya-ku, Tokyo 150, Japan

ASIA-PACIFIC AMCHAM DIRECTORY

Australia

American Chamber of Commerce in Australia
50 Pitt St., 3rd Floor
Sydney NSW 2000
Australia
Tel: 241-1907
Tlx: 72729 ATTIAU
Cable: AMCHAM SYDNEY
Fax: 001-61-2-251-5220

Guam

Guam Chamber of Commerce
102 Ada Plaza Center Agana
Guam 96910
Tel: 472-6311/472-8001
Tlx: 6160 BOOTH GM
Cable: CHAMAGANA
Fax: 472-6202

Hong Kong

American Chamber of Commerce in Hong Kong
Room 1030, 10/F Swire House
Central, Hong Kong
Tel: 260-165
Tlx: 83664 AMCC HX
Cable: AMCHAM HONG KONG
Fax: 810-1289

Indonesia

American Chamber of Commerce in Indonesia
The Landmark Center
22nd Floor
Suite 2204 Jln Jendral
Sudirman Kav 70A
Jakarta 10002
Indonesia
Tel: 578-0656
Tlx: 48116 CIBSEM IA
Fax: 819-8362

Japan

American Chamber of Commerce in Japan
Fukide Bldg., No 2 4-1-21
Toranomon
Minato-ku, Tokyo 105, Japan
Tel: 433-5381
Tlx: J 2425104
Cable: AMCHAM TOKYO
Fax: 436-1446

South Korea

American Chamber of Commerce in Korea
Room 307, Chosun Hotel 87
Sokong-Dong, Chung-Gu
Seoul 100, Korea
Tel: 753-6471/753-6516/752-3061
Tlx: K28432 CHOSUN
Cable: AMCHAMBER SEOUL
ATTN AMCHAM-K
Fax: 755-6577

Malaysia

American Business Council Malaysia
15.01, 15th Floor
AMODA
22 Jalan Imbi
Kuala Lumpur 55100
Malaysia
Tel: 248-2407/248-2540
Tel: MA 32956 FCSKL
Fax: 243-7682

New Zealand

American Chamber of Commerce in New Zealand
5th Floor, Agriculture House (Cnr Featherston & Johnston Streets)
P.O. Box 3408
Wellington, New Zealand
Tel: 727-549
Tlx: 3514 INBUSMAC NZ
Cable: AMCHAM NEW ZEALAND
Fax: 712-153

Okinawa

American Chamber of Commerce in Okinawa
Room 125, Sheraton Okinawa Hotel
1520 Kishaba
23 Kitanakagusuku-son
Okinawa City 904
Okinawa, Japan
Tel: (098) 935-2684
Tlx: J79828 SHEROKA
Cable: AMCHAM OKINAWA
Fax: (098) 935-3546

Pakistan

American Business Council of Pakistan
3rd Floor, Shaheen Complex
M R Kayani Rd.
G.P.O. Box 1322
Karachi 0111, Pakistan
Tel: 526-436
Tlx: 25620 CHASE PK

The Philippines

American Chamber of Commerce of the Philippines
2nd Floor, Corinthian Plaza
Paseo de Roxas
P.O. Box 1578
MCC, Makati
Metro Manila 3117 Philippines
Tel: 818-7911
Tlx: (ITT) 45181, 22748
AMCHAM PH
Cable: AMCHAMCOM MANILA
Fax: 817-6582

Republic of China

American Chamber of Commerce in Republic of China
N-1012 Chia Shin Bldg.
1196 Chung Shan No Rd., Sec. 2
P.O. Box 17-277
Taipei, Taiwan, Republic of China

Tel: 551-2515
Tlx: 27841 AMCHAM TPF
Cable: AMCHAM TAIPEI
Fax: 542-3376

Saipan

Saipan Chamber of Commerce
P.O. Box 806
Saipan, CM 96950
USA
Tel: 234-6132
Tlx: 657 JMC SPN
Fax: 234-7151

Singapore

American Business Council Singapore
1 Scotts Road, No. 16-07
Shaw Centre
Singapore 0922
Tel: 235-0077
Tlx: 50296 ABCSIN
Fax: 732-5917

Thailand

American Chamber of Commerce in Thailand
7th Floor, Shell House
140 Wireless Rd.
P.O. Box 11-1095
Bangkok, Thailand
Tel: 251-9266/7-251-1605
Tlx: 82778 KGCOM TH
Cable: AMERCHAM BANGKOK
Fax: 253-7388

APAC ASSOCIATE MEMBERS

Alaska

Anchorage Chamber of Commerce
415 F St.
Anchorage, Alaska 99501-2254
USA

Washington

Greater Seattle Chamber of Commerce
1200 One Union Sq.
Sixth and University St.
Seattle, Washington 98101, USA
Tel: (206) 461-7200
Fax: (206) 461-7221

India

Indo-American Chamber of Commerce
1C Vulcan Insurance Building
Veer Nanman Rd.
P.O. 11057
Bombay 400 020, India
Tel: 221-4131221–485
Tlx: 011-3891

CHAMBER OF COMMERCE OF THE UNITED STATES OF AMERICA (COCUSA)

Asia/Pacific Affairs
Intl. Div.
1615 H St. NW
Washington, D.C. 20062, USA
Tel: (202) 463-5486
Tlx: 248302 CCUS UR
Fax: 463-3114

UNITED STATES DEPARTMENT OF AGRICULTURE FOREIGN AGRICULTURAL SERVICE (ASIA-PACIFIC SECTIONS)

The Foreign Agricultural Service (FAS) is the worldwide agency of the U.S. Department of Agriculture. The agency's principal mission is the promotion of U.S.-produced food and agricultural commodities in export markets. FAS has a global network of personnel in more than 70 posts, covering over 100 countries. Through the FAS agricultural officers, USDA gathers and assesses information and publishes reports on world agricultural production and trade.

A key function of FAS officers in foreign countries is advising American exporters about local markets and business practices and arranging appointments with prospective customers. FAS officers also develop promotion activities such as food shows, menu promotions, and retail events to publicize American products among the food trade and consumers. FAS officers work closely with U.S. agricultural market promotion boards known as "cooperators." These include over 50 commodity specific boards.

FAS also offers the Agricultural Information and Marketing Service known as AIMS, which is a trade leads service of USDA. The service provides a computerized, high-speed link between prospective buyers and sellers of U.S. food and agricultural items.

Australia

Canberra
American Embassy
James V. Parker,
Counselor
Tel: (011-61-62) 705-000
Tlx: 62104 USAEMB
Street Address: Moonah Place
Canberra, ACT 2600
Mailing Address:
APO San Francisco CA 96404

China, People's Republic of

Beijing American Embassy
David M. Schoonover, Counselor
Tel: (011-86-1) 532-3831/Direct Line: 532-2962
Tlx: 22701 AMEMB CN
Street Address:
Xiushu Dongjie 2
Mailing Address:
FPO San Francisco CA 96655-0001

Agricultural Trade Office
Jonathan P. Gressel,
Agricultural Trade Officer
Tel: (011-86-1) 523-831, Ext. 274
Fax: (011-86-1) 532-2962

Guangzhou
Agricultural Trade Office
Phillip A. Shull,
Agricultural Trade Officer
Tel: (011-86-20) 66-33-88, Ext. 1259, 1260, 1261

Tlx: 662775
Fax: 660703
Street Address: Room 1261, Liu Hua
Lu
China Hotel Office Tower
Guangzhou
Mailing Address:
ATO Consulate General
China Hotel Office Tower
Box 30 FPO
San Francisco, CA 96655

Hong Kong

Hong Kong
American Consultate General
(also cover Macao)
Phillip C. Holloway,
Agricultural Officer
Tel: (011–852–5) 239–011
Tlx: 63141 USDOC HX
Fax: (011–852–5) 845–0943
Street Address: 18/F St. John's
Building
33 Garden Rd.
Mailing Address:
Box 30
FPO San Francisco, CA 96659-0002

India

New Delhi
American Embassy
(also cover Sri Lanka and Bangladesh)
Lyle J. Sebranek, Counselor
Tel: (011–91–11) 600–651, Ext. 267,
367
Tlx: 031-65-269 USEM-IN
Street Address: Shanti Path
Chanakyapuri 21
Mailing Address:
New Delhi
Department of State
Washington, D.C. 20520-9000

Indonesia

Jakarta
American Embassy
Kenneth L. Murray, Attache
Tel: (011–62–21) 360-360, Ext 2161

Tlx: 44218 AMEMB JKT
Fax: (011–62–21) 360-644
Street Address: Medan Merdeka
Selatan 5
Mailing Address:
APO San Francisco, CA 96356-0001

Japan

Tokyo
American Embassy
James V. Parker, Counselor
Tel: (011–81–3) 224–5000
Tlx: 2422118
Fax: (011–81–3) 589–0793
Street Address: 1 0-5 Akasaka
1-Chome, Minato-ku
Tokyo 107
Mailing Address:
Box 226
APO San Francisco, CA 96503

Korea

Seoul
American Embassy
George J. Pope, Counselor
Tel: (011–82–2) 732-2601, Ext. 4297
Tlx: AMEMB 23108
Street Address: 82 Sejong-Re
Chongro-Ku
Mailing Address:
APO San Francisco, CA 96301

Agricultural Trade Office
Howard R. Wetzel, Agricultural
Trade Officer
Tel: (011–82–2) 732-2601, Ext. 4188
Tlx: K 25823 SOLATO
Fax: (011–82–2) 752-5626
Street Address: 63 1-KA Eulchi-Ro
Chongro-Ku Seoul 100
Mailing Address:
APO San Francisco, CA 96301

Malaysia

Kuala Lumpur
American Embassy
Jeffrey A. Hesse, Attache
Tel: (011–60–3) 248-9011
Tlx: FCSKLMA 32956

Fax: (011–60-3) 243-2450
Street Address: 376 Jalan Tun Razak
P.O. Box 10035
50700 Kuala Lumpur
Malaysia
Mailing Address:
Kuala Lumpur
Department of State
Washington, D.C. 20520-4210

New Zealand

Wellington
American Embassy
Evans "Duffy" Browne, Attache
Tel: (011–64–4) 722-068
Tel: NZ 3305
Street Address: 29 Fitzherbert Ter.
Thorndon Wellington
Mailing Address:
FPO San Francisco, CA 96690-0001

Philippines

Manila American Embassy
Robert M. McConnell, Counselor
Tel: (011–63–2) 521-71-16
Tlx: 722-27366 AME PH
Fax: 522-4361
Street Address:
1201 Roxas Boulevard
Mailing Address:
APO San Francisco, CA 96528

Singapore

Singapore American Embassy
(also cover Brunei)
Geoffrey W. Wiggin, Agricultural
Trade Officer
Tel: (011–65) 737-12331734–1802
Tlx: RS55318 USDA
Fax: (011–65) 732-8307
Street Address: 541 Orchard Road 08-
04
Liat Towers
Singapore 0923
Mailing Address:
FPO San Francisco, CA
96699-0001

Thailand

Bangkok American Embassy
Weyland M. Beeghly, Attache
Tel: (011-66-2) 252-5040, Ext. 2468
Tlx: 20966 FCS BKK TH
Fax: (011-66-2) 254-2543
Street Address: 95 Wireless Rd.
Mailing Address:

Box 41
APO
San Francisco, CA 96346-0001

Taiwan

Taipei American Institute in
Taiwan
Kenneth E. Howland, Agricultural

Officer
Tel: (011-886-2) 709-2000
Tlx: 23890 USTRADE
Street Address: 7/9 Lane 134
Hsin Yi Road Section 3
Mailing Address:
American Institute in Taiwan
P.O. Box 1612
Washington, D.C. 20013

UNITED STATES DEPARTMENT OF COMMERCE FOREIGN COMMERCIAL SERVICE (ASIA-PACIFIC SECTIONS)

The Foreign Commercial Service (FCS), the overseas arm of the U.S. Department of Commerce represents American commercial interests overseas. The primary mission of FCS is to promote U.S. exports of products and services. As part of this promotional effort, the FCS counsels American businessmen on business opportunities, locates agents and distributors for American firms, assists local businessmen in finding U.S. suppliers, conducts credit checks on local firms on behalf of American firms, assists with trade disputes between local and U.S. firms, provides regional trade opportunities to the offices of American companies based overseas, provides guidance for the licensing of items under export controls, and reports on commercial activities.

Australia

Sydney American Consulate
General Robert Taft,
Senior Commercial Officer
Tel: 011-61-2-264-7044
Tlx: 74223 FCSSYD
Street Address: Hyde Park Tower
36th Floor
Park and Elizabeth Streets
Sydney, NSW
2000, Australia
Mailing Address:
APO San Francisco, CA 96209

Brisbane American Consulate
Keith Sloggett, Commercial/
Assistant
Tel: 011-61-7-839-8955
Street Address:
383 Wickham Terrace
Brisbane, Queensland 4000
Mailing Address:
APO San Francisco, CA 96209

Melbourne American Consulate
General Donald Schilke,
Commercial Officer
Tel: 011-61-3-697-7900
Tlx: 30982 AMERCON
Street Address: 24 Albert Rd.
South Melbourne, Victoria 3205
Mailing Address:
APO San Francisco, CA 96405

Perth American Consulate
General Charles Reese, Commercial
Officer
Tel: 011-61-9-322-4466
Tlx: 93848 AMCON
Street Address:
246 St. George's Terrace
Perth, Western Australia 6000
Mailing Address:
APO San Francisco, CA 96211-00065

China

Beijing American Embassy
Lyn Edinger, Senior Commercial
Officer
Tel: 52-3831
Tlx: 22701 AMEMB CN
Street Address:
Xiu Shui Bei Jie 3
Mailing Address:
FPO San Francisco, CA 96655

Guangzhou American Consulate
General Todd Thurwatcher,
Commercial Officer
Tel: 69900, ext. 1000
Tlx: 44439 G2DSHCN
Street Address: China Hotel
Liu Hua Lu
Mailing Address:
Box 100
FPO San Francisco, CA 96659

Shanghai American Consulate General
Nora Sun, Commercial Officer
Tel: 379-880
Street Address:
1469 Huai Hai Middle
Mailing Address:
Box 200
FPO San Francisco, CA 96659

Shenyang American Consulate General
Will Center, Commercial Officer
Tel: 290038
Tlx: 80011 AMCS CN
Street Address:
40 Lane 4, Section 5 Sanjing St.
Heping District
Mailing Address:
Box 45
FPO San Francisco, CA 96559-0002

Hong Kong

Hong Kong American Consulate General
Ying Price, Chief Commercial Officer
Tel: 011-852-5-23901 1
Tlx: 63141 USDOC HX
Street Address: 26 Garden Rd.
Mailing Address:
Box 30
FPO San Francisco, CA 96659

India

New Delhia American Embassy
Mel Searls, Senior Commercial Officer
Tel: 011-91-600651
Tlx: 031-65269 USEM IN
Street Address:
Shanti Path
Chanakyapuri 110021
Mailing Address:
U.S. Department of State
(New Delhi)
Washington, D.C. 20520-9000

Bombay American Consulate General
Commercial Officer
Tel: 822-3611 to 828-0571

Tlx: 011-6525 ACON I N
Street Address:
Lincoln House
78 Bhulabhai Desai Rd.
Mailing Address:
U.S. Department of State
(Bombay)
Washington, D.C. 20520-6240

Calcutta American Consulate General
Sanjit Gupta, Commercial Specialist
Tel: 44-3611 to 44-3616
Tel: 021-2483
Street Address:
5/1 Ho Chi Minh Sarani
Calcutta 700071
Mailing Address:
U.S. Department of State
(Calcutta)
Washington, D.C. 20520-6250

Madras American Consulate General
A.V. Subramanian, Commercial Specialist
Tel: 473-040
Street Address:
Mount Rd. 600006
Mailing Address:
U.S. Department of State
(Madras)
Washington, D.C. 20520

Indonesia

Jakarta American Embassy
Paul Walters, Senior Commercial Officer
Tel: 011-62-21-360360
Tlx: 44218 AMEMB JKT
Street Address:
Medan Merdeka Selatan 5
Mailing Address:
APO San Francisco, CA 96356

Japan

Tokyo American Embassy
Keith Bovetti, Senior Commercial Officer
Tel: 011-81-3-583-7141

Tlx: 2422118
Street Address: 10-1 Akasaka 1-chome
Minato-ku (107)
Mailing Address:
APO San Francisco, CA 96503

Fukuoka American Consulate
Yoshihiro Yamamoto, Commercial Assistant
Tel: 011-81-92-751-9331
Tlx: 725679
Street Address: 5-26 Ohori 2-chome
Chuo-ku Fukuoka-810
Mailing Address:
Box 10
FPO Seattle, WA 98766

Osaka-Kobe American Consulate General
Michael Benefiel, Commercial Officer
Tel: 011-81-06-361-9600
Tlx: 5623023 AMCON J
Street Address: 9th Fl Sankei Bldg.
4-9 Umeda 2-chome
Kita-ku Osaka (530)
Mailing Address:
APO San Francisco, CA 96503

Sapporo American Consulate
Kenji Itaya, Commercial Specialist
Tel: 011-81-641-1115
Tlx: 935338 AMCONS J
Street Address: Kita 1-Jyo Nishi 28-chome
Chuoku Sapporo 064
Mailing Address:
APO San Francisco, CA 96503

Korea

Seoul American Embassy
George Mu, Senior Commercial Officer
Tel: 011-82-2-732-2601
Tlx: 23108 AMEMB
Street Address:
82 Sejong-Ro Chongro-Ku
Mailing Address:
APO San Francisco, CA 96301

Malaysia

Kuala Lumpur American Embassy
Jonathan Bensky, Senior Commercial Officer
Tel: 011-60-3-248-9011
Tlx: 32956 FCSKL MA
Street Address:
376 Jalan Tun Razak
Mailing Address:
U.S. Department of State
(Kuala Lumpur)
Washington, D.C. 20520-4210

Philippines

Manila American Embassy
Theodore Villinski, Senior Commercial Officer
Tel: 011-63-2-818-6674
Tlx: 22708 COSEC PH via RCA
Street Address:
395 Buendia Ave.
Extension Makati
Mailing Address:
APO San Francisco, CA 96528

Singapore

Singapore American Embassy
Beaumount Lower, Senior Commercial Officer
Tel: 011-65-338-0251
Street Address:
30 Hill Street
Singapore 0617
Mailing Address:
APO San Francisco, CA 96699-55

Thailand

Bangkok American Embassy
Robert C. Bodden, Senior Commercial Officer
Tel: 011-66-2-251-9260
Tlx: 20966 FCSBKK
Street Address:
R Floor Shell Building
140 Wireless Rd.
Mailing Address:
APO San Francisco, CA 96346

The American Institute in Taiwan
Important Non-US & FCS Commercial Office
Craig Allen, Head, Commercial Unit
Tel: 011-886-2-709-2000
Tlx: 23890 USTRADE

AMERICAN BUSINESS CONTACTS IN CHINA

Beijing

United States Embassy
American Ambassador
Xiu Shui Bei Jie 3
100600, Beijing
Tel: 86-1-532-3831
Tlx: AMEMB CN 22701
Fax: 86-1-532-3297

AmCham in Beijing
Lucille Barale
Coudert Brothers
802 Noble Tower
22 Jian Guo Men Wai Ave.
Beijing

Chengdu

American Consulate
General Jan De Wilde, Consulate General
Jinjiang Hotel
180 Renmin Rd.
Chengdu, Sichuan
Tel: 86-1-24481, Ext. 131
Tlx: 60128 ACGCH CN
Fax: 86-24-55-4521
Street Address:
7 Lane 134
Hsin Yi Road Section 3
Mailing Address:
American Institute in Taiwan
Commercial Unit, PO

Gua Ngzhou

American Consulate General
Mark S. Pratt, Consulate General
Dong Fang Hotel
Liu Hua Rd.
Guangzhou

Tel: 86-20-669900, Ext. 1000
Tlx: GZDFHCN 44439
Fax: 86-20-66-6409

AmCham in Guangzhou
Mr. Hector Veloso, General Manager
Guangmei Foods Co., Ltd.
Beatrice Food Co., Inc.
(Joint Venture)
Yuancun Fourth
Sideroad
Tianhe District
East Suburb of Guangzhou 510655
Guangdong Province
Box 1612
Washington, D.C. 20013
Mailing Address:
(packages):
American Institute in Taiwan
Commercial Unit
Department of State (Taipei)
Washington, D.C. 20520

Shanghai

American Consulate General
Charles T. Sylvester, Consulate General
1469 Huai Hai Middle Rd.
Shanghai
Tel: 86-21-336-880
Tlx: 33383 USCG CN
Fax: 86-21-33-157

AmCham in Shanghai
George C. Hsu
John McCoy
Co-Presidents
GPO Box 246
Shanghai

Shenyang

American Consulate General
C. Eugene Dorris, Consulate General
40 Lane 4
Section 5, Sanjing St.
Heping District
Shenyang
Tel: 86-24-290000
Tlx: 80011 AMCS CN
Fax: 86-24-29-0074

USA CONTACTS: UNITED STATES DISTRICT OFFICES OF INTERNATIONAL TRADE ADMINISTRATION

The district offices of the U.S. and Foreign Commercial Service are headquartered in principal cities of the United States. The principal functions of the district offices are to:

• Counsel U.S. firms on overseas marketing, technical export information, and provide guidance on marketing opportunities and strategies;

• Conduct seminars, workshops, and conferences;
• Obtain commercial information from U.S. firms for use in planning and evaluating trade programs; and
• Disseminate to the business community information on trade developments, trade policy issues, and technological developments.

District Directors in the 10 Uniform Federal Regional Council Cities act as Regional Emergency Coordinators in accordance with guidance of the Office of Industrial Resource Administration.

U.S. DEPARTMENT OF COMMERCE INTERNATIONAL TRADE ADMINISTRATION

Lew W. Cramer, Director General
U.S. and Foreign Commercial Service
Rm 3802, HCH Bldg.
14th & Constitution Ave., N.W.
Washington, D.C. 20230
Tel: (202) 377-5777
Fax: (202) 377-5777

Genevieve McSweeney Ryan,
Deputy Assistant Secretary
U.S. and Foreign Commercial Service
Rm 3804, HCH Bldg.
14th & Constitution Ave., NW
Washington, D.C. 20230
Tel: (202) 377-0725
Fax: (202) 377-0725

T. Fleetwood Mafford, Deputy Assistant
Secretary for Domestic Operations
Rm 3810, HCH Bldg.
14th & Constitution Ave., NW
Washington, D.C. 20230
Tel: (202) 377-4767
Fax: (202) 377-4767

Alabama

Birmingham*
Gayle C. Shelton, Jr., Director
Rm 302, Berry Bldg.
2015 2nd Ave. N
AL 35203
Tel: (205) 731-1331
Fax: (205) 229-1331

Alaska

Anchorage
(Vacant)
701 C St.
P.O. Box 32
AK 99513
Tel: (907) 271-5041
Fax: (907) 271-5041

Arizona

Phoenix
Donald W. Fry, Director
Federal Bldg.
Rm 3412
230 North 1st Ave.
AZ 85025
Tel: (602) 261-3285
Fax: (602) 261-3285

Arkansas

Little Rock
Lon J. Hardin, Director
Suite 811, Savers
Federal Bldg.
320 W. Capital Ave.
AR 72201
Tel: (501) 378-5794
Fax: (501) 740-5794

California

Los Angeles
Daniel J. Young, Director
Rm 800
11777 San Vicente Blvd.
CA 90049
Tel: (213) 209-6707
Fax: (213) 793-6707

Santa Ana**
Suite #1
116 West 4th St.
CA 92701
Tel: (714) 836-2461
Fax: (714) 799-2461

San Diego
Richard Powell, Director
Suite 250
6363 Greenwich Dr.
Tel: (619) 557-5395
Fax: (619) 895-5395

San Francisco★
Betty D. Neuhart, Director
450 Golden Gate
Box 36013
CA 94102
Tel: (415) 556-5860
Fax: (415) 556-5860

Colorado

Denver
Jim Manis, Deputy Director
Suite 600
1625 Broadway
CO 80202
Tel: (303) 844-3246

Connecticut

Hartford★
Eric B. Outwater, Director
Rm 610B, Federal Office Bldg.
450 Main St.
CT 06109
Tel: (203) 240-3530
Fax: (203) 244-3530

Delaware

Serviced by the Philadelphia District
Office

District of Columbia

Washington, D.C.
(Baltimore, MD District)★★
Department of Commerce
Rm 1066, HCH Bldg.
14th & Constitution Ave., NW
D.C. 20230
Tel: (202) 377-3181
Fax: (202) 3181

Florida

Miami
Ivan A. Cosimi, Director
Suite 224, Federal Bldg.
51 SW 1st Ave.
FL 33130
Tel: (305) 536-5267
Fax: (305) 350-5267

Clearwater★★
128 North Osceola Ave.
FL 34615
Tel: (813) 461-0011
Fax: (813) 826-3738

Jacksonville★★
Suite 200A
3100 University Blvd., S
Fl 32216
Tel: (904) 791-2796
Fax: (904) 946-2796

Orlando★★
Suite 1439
111 North Orange Ave.
FL 32802
Tel: (407) 648-1608
Fax: (407) 820-6235

Tallahassee★★
Rm 401, Collins Bldg.
107 W Gaines St.
FL 32304
Tel: (904) 488-6469
Fax: (904) 965-7194

Georgia

Atlanta
George T. Norton, Director
Suite 504
1365 Peachtree St., NE
GA 30309
Tel: (404) 347-7000
Fax: (404) 257-4872

Savannah
James W. McIntire, Director
120 Barnard St. A107
GA 31401
Tel: (912) 944-4204
Fax: (912) 248-4204

Hawaii

Honolulu
George B. Dolan, Director
P.O. Box 50026
300 Ala Moana Blvd.
HI 96850
Tel: (808) 541-1782
Fax: (808) 551-1782

Idaho

Boise
(Portland OR District)★
2nd Floor, Hall of Mirrors
700 W State St.
ID 83720
Tel: (208) 334-3857
Fax: (208) 554-9254

Illinois

Chicago
Michael V. Simon, Acting Director
Rm 1406, Mid-Continental Plaza
Bldg.
55 E Monroe St.
IL 60603
Tel: (312) 353-4450
Fax: (312) 353-4450

Palatine★★
W.R. Harper College
Roselle & Algonquin Rd.
IL 60067
Tel: (312) 397-3000, Ext 2532

Rockford ★★
515 North Court St.
P.O. Box 1747
IL 61110-0247
Tel: (815) 987-8123
Fax: (815) 363-4347

Indiana

Indianapolis★
Mel R. Sherar, Director
Suite 520
One North Capitol
IN 46205
Tel: (317) 226-6214
Fax: (317) 331-6214

Iowa

Des Moines
John H. Steuber, Jr., Acting Director
817 Federal Bldg.
210 Walnut St.
IA 50309
Tel: (515) 284-4222
Fax: (515) 862-4222

Kansas

Wichita
(Kansas City, MO District)
Suite 580
River Park Place
720 North Waco
KS 67203
Tel: (316) 269-6160
Fax: (316) 752-6160

Kentucky

Louisville
Donald R. Henderson, Director
Rm 636B, Gene Snyder Courthouse
and Customhouse Bldg.
601 W Broadway
KY 40202
Tel: (502) 582-5066
Fax: (502) 352-5066

Louisiana

New Orleans
Paul L. Guldry, Director
432 World Trade Ctr.
No 2 Canal St.
LA 70130
Tel: (504) 589-6546
Fax: (504) 682-6546

Maine

Augusta
(Boston, MA District)
77 Sewall St.
ME 04330
Tel: (207) 622-8249
Fax: (207) 833-6249

Maryland

Baltimore
LoRee P. Silloway, Director
413 US Customhouse
40 South Gay St.
MD 21202
Tel: (301) 962-3560
Fax: (301) 922-3560

Massachusetts

Boston
Francis J. O'Connor, Director
Suite 307, World Trade Ctr.
Commonwealth Pier Area
MA 02210
Tel: (617) 565-8563
Fax: (617) 835-8563

Michigan

Detroit
Donald L. Schilke, Director
1140 McNamara Bldg.
477 Michigan Ave.
MI 48226
Tel: (313) 226-3650
Fax: (313) 226-3650

Grand Rapids**
Rm 409
300 Monroe NW
MI 49503
Tel: (616) 456-2411
Fax: (616) 372-2411

Minnesota

Minneapolis
Ronald E. Kramer, Director
108 Fed Bldg.
110 S. 4th St.
MN 55401
Tel: (612) 348-1638
Fax: (612) 777-1638

Mississippi

Jackson
Mark E. Spinney, Director
328 Jackson Mall Office Ctr.
300 Woodrow Wilson Blvd.
MS 39213
Tel: (601) 965-4388
Fax: (601) 490-4388

Missouri

St. Louis*
Donald R. Loso, Director
Suite 610

7911 Forsyth Blvd.
MO 63105
Tel: (314) 425-3302
Fax: (314) 279-3302

Kansas City
John R. Kupfer, Director
Rm 635
601 E 12st St.
MO 64106
Tel: (816) 426-3141
Fax: (816) 867-3141

Montana

Serviced by the Denver District
Office

Nebraska

Omaha
George H. Payne, Director
11133 O St.
NE 68137
Tel: (402) 221-3664
Fax: (402) 864-3664

Nevada

Reno***
Joseph J. Jeremy, Director
1755 E Plumb Lane, No. 152
NV 89502
Tel: (702) 784-5203
Fax: (702) 470-5203

New Hampshire

Serviced by the Boston District
Office

New Jersey

Trenton*
Thomas J. Murray, Director
Suite 100
3131 Princeton Pike
Bldg. 6
NJ 08648
Tel: (609) 989-2100
Fax: (609) 483-2100

New Mexico

Santa Fe
(Dallas TX District)★★
c/o Economic Dev. and Tourism
Dept.
1100 St.
Francis Drive
NM 87503
Tel: (505) 827-0264

Albuquerque
(Dallas, TX District)★★
517 Gold SW, Suite 4303
NM 87102
Tel: (505) 766-2386
Fax: (505) 474-2386

New York

Buffalo
Robert F. Magee, Director
1312 Federal Bldg.
111 W Huron St.
NY 14202
Tel: (716) 846-4191
Fax: (716) 437-4191

Rochester★★
121 E Ave.
NY 14604
Tel: (716) 263-6480
Fax: (716) 963-6840

New York
Joel W. Barkan, Director
Rm 3718, 26 Federal Plaza
NY 10278
Tel: (212) 264-0634
Fax: (212) 264-0634

North Carolina

Greensboro★
Samuel P. Troy, Director
324 West Market St.
P.O. Box 1950
NC 27402
Tel: (919) 333-6345
Fax: (919) 699-5345

North Dakota

Serviced by the Omaha District
Office

Ohio

Cincinnati★
Gordon B. Thomas, Director
9504 Federal Bldg.
550 Main St.
OH 45202
Tel: (513) 684-2944
Fax: (513) 684-2944

Cleveland
Toby T. Zettler, Director
Rm 600
668 Euclid Ave.
OH 44114
Tel: (216) 522-4750
Fax: (216) 942-4750

Oklahoma

Oklahoma City
Ronald L. Wilson, Director
Suite 200
5 Broadway Executive Park
6601 Broadway Extension
OK 73116
Tel: (405) 231-5302
Fax: (405) 736-5302

Tulsa★★
440 South Houston St.
OK 74127
Tel: (918) 581-7650
Fax: (918) 745-7650

Oregon

Portland
Richard Lenahan, Director
Rm 618
1220 SW Third Ave.
OR 97204
Tel: (503) 221-3001
Fax: (503) 423-3001

Pennsylvania

Philadelphia
Robert E. Kistler, Director
Suite 202
475 Allendale Rd.
King of Prussia
PA 19406

Tel: (215) 962-4980
Fax: (215) 486-7954

Pittsburgh
John A. McCartney, Director
2002 Federal Bldg.
1000 Liberty Ave.
PA 15222
Tel: (412) 644-2850
Fax: (412) 722-2850

Puerto Rico

San Juan (Hato Ray)
J. Enrique Vilella, Director
Rm G-55, Federal Bldg.
PR 00918
Tel: (809) 766-5555
Fax: (809) 498-5555

Rhode Island

Providence
(Boston, MA District)★
7 Jackson Walkway
RI 02903
Tel: (401) 528-5104
Fax: (401) 838-5104

South Carolina

Columbia
Edgar L. Rojas, Director
Suite 172, Strom Thurmond Federal
Bldg.
1835 Assembly St.
SC 29201
Tel: (803) 765-5345
Fax: (803) 677-5345

Charleston ★★
Rm 128, JC Long Bldg.
9 Liberty St.
SC 29424
Tel: (803) 724-4361
Fax: (803) 677-4361

South Dakota

Serviced by the Omaha District
Office

Tennessee

Nashville
Jim Charlet, Director
Suite 1114, Parkway Towers
404 James Robertson Parkway
TN 37219-1505
Tel: (615) 736-5161
Fax: (615) 852-5161

Memphis★★
Suite 200, Falls Bldg.
22 North Front St.
TN 38103
Tel: (901) 521-4137
Fax: (901) 222-4137

Texas

Dallas★
C. Carmon Stiles, Director
Rm 7A5
1100 Commerce St.
TX 75242-0787
Tel: (214) 767-0542
Fax: (214) 729-0542

Austin★
Suite 1200
816 Congress Ave.
P.O. Box 12728
TX 78711
Tel: (512) 482-5939
Fax: (512) 770-5939

Houston
James D. Cook, Director
Rm 2625
515 Rusk St.
TX 77002
Tel: (713) 229-2578
Fax: (713) 526-4578

Utah

Salt Lake City★★★
Stephen P. Smoot, Director
Rm 340, US Courthouse
350 South Main St.
UT 84101
Tel: (801) 524-5116
Fax: (801) 588-5116

Vermont

Serviced by the Boston District
Office

Virginia

Richmond
Philip A. Ouzts, Director
8010 Federal Bldg.
400 N 8th St.
VA 23240
Tel: (804) 771-2246
Fax: (804) 925-2246

Washington

Seattle
C. Franklin Foster, Director
Suite 290
3131 Elliott Ave.
WA 98121
Tel: (206) 442-5616
Fax: (206) 399-5615

Spokane★★
Rm 623, West 808
Spokane Falls Bldg.
WA 99201
Tel: (509) 456-4557
Fax: (509) 439-4557

West Virginia

Charleston
Roger L. Fortner, Director
3402 Federal Bldg.
500 Quarrier St.
WV 25301
Tel: (304) 347-5123
Fax: (304) 930-5123

Wisconsin

Milwaukee
Patrick A. Willis, Director
Rm 606
517 East Wisconsin Ave.
WI 53202
Tel: (414) 291-3473
Fax: (304) 362-3473

Wyoming

Serviced by the Denver District
Office

★ Denotes regional office with
supervisory regional responsibilities.

★★ Denotes trade specialist at a
branch office.

★★★ Denotes office which may be
relocating, contact Domestic
Operations for current address
information, (202) 377-2683

NB: Letters in brackets indicate U.S.
Postal Service abbreviations for state
names.

U.S. STATE OFFICES OF INVESTMENT
AND ECONOMIC DEVELOPMENT

State investment and economic offices dealing
with international investors go by various
names, but virtually all U.S. states maintain
one. They maintain libraries, answer queries,
and generally work to promote their state's
products for export, reverse investment into
their state, and tourism.

Alabama

Montgomery
Fred F. Denton, Jr., Director
Int'l Development and Trade
Division Dept. of Economic and
Community Affairs
P.O. Box 2939
AL 36105-0939
Fax: (205) 284-8700

Alaska

Anchorage
Daniel Dickson, Director
Int'l Trade Dept. of Commerce and
Economic Development
3601 C St.
Suite 722
AK 99503
Tel: (907) 465-2500

Arizona

Phoenix
Sharon S. R. Chou, Trade Specialist
—Asia Dept. of Commerce
1700 West Washington St.
Rm 505
AZ 85007
Tel: (602) 255-5374

Arkansas

Little Rock
Maria Haley, Director
Int'l Marketing Dept. of Economic
Development
One Capitol Mall
AR 72201
Tel: (502) 371-7678

California

Sacramento
Gregory Mignano, Executive
Director
California State World Trade
Commission
1121 L Street
Suite 310
CA 95814
Tel: (916) 324-5511

Colorado

Denver
Vance Baugham, Director
Int'l Trade Office
1625 Broadway
Suite 1710
CO 80202
Tel: (303) 892-3840

Connecticut

Hartford
Gary H. Miller, Director
Int'l Division
Dept. of Economic Development
210 Washington St.
CT 06106
Tel: (203) 566-3842

Delaware

Dover
Larry Windley
Delaware Development Office
Division of Economic Development
99 Kings Highway
P.O. Box 1401
DE 19903
Tel: (302) 736-4271

Florida

Tallahassee
Tom Slattery, Development
Representative Supervisor
Florida Dept. of Commerce
107 West Gaines St.
FL 32301
Tel: (904) 488-6124

Georgia

Atlanta
Johnny Whitworth, Director
Division of Trade
Dept. of Industry and Trade
P.O. Box 1776
GA 30301
Tel: (404) 656-3538

Hawaii

Honolulu
Kenneth Kwak, Chief, Int'l Services
Branch
Dept. of Planning and Economic
Development
P.O. Box 2359
HI 96804
Tel: (808) 548-3048 or 4621

Idaho

Boise
Jay Engstrom, Manager of Economic
Development
Division of Economic & Community
Affairs
State Capital
Room 108
ID 83720
Tel: (208) 334-2470

Illinois

Chicago
Hendrik Woods, Manager
Int'l Business Division
Dept. of Commerce & Community
Affairs
100 W. Randolph St.
Suite C-400
IL 60601
Tel: (312) 782-7164

Indiana

Indianapolis
Phillip M. Grebe, Director
Int'l Trade Division
Dept. of Commerce
One North Capitol
IN 46204-2248
Tel: (317) 232-8864

Iowa

Des Moines
Max L. Olsen, Marketing Manager
Int'l Trade
Iowa Dept. of Economic
Development
200 East Grand Ave.
IA 50309
Tel: (515) 281-3138

Kentucky

Frankfort
Theodore M. Sauer, Jr., Executive
Director
Office of Int'l Mktg.
Kentucky Commerce Cabinet
Capitol Plaza Tower, 241F
KY 40601
Tel: (502) 564-2170

Louisiana

Baton Rouge
Jerry Medicus, Assistant Secretary
Office of Int'l Trade Finance &
Development
P.O. Box 44185
LA 70804
Tel: (504) 342-5359

Maine

Augusta
Michael Davis, Director
Int'l Trade State Development Office
Statehouse, Station 59
ME 04333
Tel: (207) 289-5700

Maryland

Baltimore
Harold R. Zassenhaus, Executive
Director
Office of Int'l Trade
World Trade Center
401 E. Pratt St.
MD 21202
Tel: (301) 333-4295

Massachusetts

Boston
Mary Ellen Sutherland, Program
Director
Office of Int'l Trade
100 Cambridge St.
Suite 902
MA
Tel: (617) 367-1830

Michigan

Lansing
Trygve Vigmostad, Director
U.S. Int'l Division
Manufacturing Development Group
Dept. of Commerce
P.O. Box 30225
MI 48909
Tel: (517) 373-6390

Mississippi

Jackson
William A. McGinnis, Director
Marketing Division
Dept. of Economic Development
P.O. Box 849
MS 38205
Tel: (601) 359-3444

Missouri

Jefferson City
Glenn Boos, Manager
Int'l Business Development
Dept. of Commerce & Economic
Development
P.O. Box 118
MO 65102
Tel: (314) 751-4855

Montana

Helena
John Maloney
Int'l Trade Office
Montana Dept. of Commerce
State Capitol
MT 59620
Tel: (406) 444-3923

Nebraska

Lincoln
Susan Rouch, Director
Development Division
Dept. of Economic Development
301 Centennial Mall South
NE 68509
Tel: (402) 471-3111

Nevada

Carson City
Andrew Grose, Director
Dept. of Economic Development
Capital Complex
NV 89710
Tel: (702) 885-4325

New Hampshire

Concord
James N. Parks, Supervisor
Foreign Trade & Comm.
Development
Dept. of Resources & Economic
Development
105 Loudon Rd.
Bldg. 2
NH 03301
Tel: (603) 271-2591

New Jersey

Newark
Ming Hsu, Governor's Special Trade
Rep. & Director
Int'l Trade Dept. of Commerce
Energy & Economic Development
744 Board St.
Suite 1709
NJ 07102
Tel: (201) 648-3518

New Mexico

Santa Fe
David S. Hinkel, Jr., Director
Economic Development Division
Economic Development & Tourism
Dept.
Jos M. Montoya Bldg.
1100 St. Francis
NM 87503
Tel: (505) 827-0272

New York

New York
Alan S. Parter, Deputy
Commissioner
Int'l Division

Dept. of Commerce
230 Park Ave.
NY 10169
Tel: (212) 309-0502

North Carolina

Raleigh
James Hinkly, Director
Int'l Division
Dept. of Commerce
430 North Salisbury St.
NC 27611
Tel: (919) 733-7193

North Dakota

Bismarck
Jack Minton, International Trade
Consultant
Economic Development Commission
Liberty Memorial Building
ND 58501
Tel: (701) 224-2810

Ohio

Columbus
Philip Code, Director
International Trade
Ohio Dept. of Development
Int'l Trade Division
30 East Broad St.
251FI
OH 43266
Tel: (614) 466-5017

Oklahoma

Oklahoma City
Bill Maus, Director
Int'l Trade Division
Dept. of Economic Development
4024 North Lincoln Blvd.
OK 73152
Tel: (405) 521-3501

Oregon

Portland
Douglas Frengle, Director
Int'l Trade Division

Dept. of Economic Development
1500 SW First Ave.
Suite 620
OR 97201
Tel: (503) 229-5625

Pennsylvania

Harrisburg
Alberta Norton, Int'l Projects
Manager
Bureau of Int'l Commerce
408 S Office Blvd.
PA 17120
Tel: (717) 787-7190

Rhode Island

Providence
Christine M. B. Smith, Int'l Trade
Director
Dept. of Economic Development
7 Jackson Walkway
RI 02903
Tel: (401) 277-1601
Fax: (401) 277-2102

South Carolina

Columbia
James A. Kuhlman, Associate
Director
Int'l Business Development
South Carolina State Development
Board
P.O. Box 927
SC 29202
Tel: (803) 734-1400

South Dakota

Vermillion
John Huminski, Director
South Dakota Int'l Trade Center
USD-School of Business
414 E Clark St.
SD 57069-2390
Tel: (605) 677-5536

Tennessee

Nashville
Thomas Turner, Acting Director
Export Promotion Office
Dept. of Economic & Community
Development
71FI, 320 Sixth Ave., N
TN 37219
Tel: (615) 741-5870

Texas

Austin
Laurel Anderson, Manager
Int'l Business Development Dept.
Texas Economic Development
Commission
P.O. Box 13561
TX 78711
Tel: (512) 472-5059

Utah

Salt Lake City
Osamu Hoshimo, Director
Int'l Business Development
Economic and Industrial
Development Division
6150 State Office Bldg.
UT 84114
Tel: (801) 533-5325

Vermont

Montpelier
Gramme Freeman, Director
Industrial Business
Dept. of Economic Development
Pavilion Office Bldg.
VT 05602
Tel: (802) 828-3221

Virginia

Richmond
Roger McCauley, Director
Int'l Marketing
1010 Washington Bldg.
VA 23219
Tel: (804) 786-3791

Washington

Seattle
Don Lorentz, Manager
Int'l Trade & Investment Division
312 First Ave., North
WA 98109
Tel: (206) 464-6282

Bryson Bailey, Director
Domestic & Int'l Investment
Washington State Dept. of Trade &
Economic Development
312 First Ave., North
WA 98109
Tel: (206) 464-6282

West Virginia

Charleston
Steve Spence, Industrial Development
Representative
Governor's Office of Economic &
Community Development
State Capitol, Room B-517
WV 25305
Tel: (304) 348-2234

Wisconsin

Madison
Steve Lotharius, Director
Bureau of Int'l Business Development
Department of Development
123 West Washington Ave.
WI 53702
Tel: (608) 296-1716

Wyoming

Cheyenne
Cynthia Ogburn, Director
Int'l Business Office
Hershlier Bldg, 2/F East
WY 82002
Tel: (307) 777-7574

PACIFIC RIM CHAMBERS OF COMMERCE IN THE UNITED STATES

China

New York
Chinese Chamber of Commerce
Confucius Plaza
33 Bowery, Rm C203
New York, NY 10002
Tel: (212) 226-2795

San Francisco
730 Sacramento St.
San Francisco, CA 94108
Tel: (415) 982-3000

India

New York
India Chamber of Commerce of
America
445 Park Ave.
18th Floor
New York, NY 10022
Tel: (212) 755-7181

Indonesia

New York
American–Indonesian Chamber of
Commerce, Inc.
711 3rd Ave.,
17th Floor,
New York, NY 10017
Tel: (212) 687-4505

Japan

Honolulu
Honolulu–Japanese Chamber of
Commerce
74-4 South Beretania St.
Honolulu, HI 96826
Tel: (808) 949-5531

Chicago
Japanese Chamber of Commerce and
Industry of Chicago
401 North Michigan Ave.
Room 602
Chicago, IL 60611
Tel: (312) 332-6199

New York
Japanese Chamber of Commerce of
New York, Inc.
1451 West 57th St.
New York, NY 10019
Tel: (212) 246-9774

San Francisco
Japanese Chamber of Commerce of
Northern California
World Affairs Center
312 Sutter St.
Room 408
San Francisco, CA 94108
Tel: (415) 986-6140

Los Angeles
Japanese Chamber of Commerce of
Southern California
244 South San Pedro St.
Room 504
Los Angeles, CA 90012
Tel: (213) 626-3067

Japanese Business Association of
Southern California
45 South Figueroa St.
Suite 206
Los Angeles, CA 90071
Tel: (213) 485-0160

Korea

Los Angeles
Korean Chamber of Commerce
981 South Western Ave.
Suite 201
Los Angeles, CA 90006
Tel: (213) 733-4410

New York
U.S.–Korea Society
725 Park Ave. 7th Floor
New York, NY 10021
Tel: (212) 517-7730

Mexico

Phoenix
Mexican Chamber of Commerce of
Arizona
P.O. Box 626
Phoenix, AZ 85001
Tel: (602) 252-6448

Los Angeles
Mexican Chamber of Commerce of
the County of Los Angeles
125 Paseo de la Plaza
Room 404
Los Angeles, CA 90012
Tel: (213) 688-7330

New York
Mexican Chamber of Commerce of
the U.S., Inc.
15 Park Row
Suite 1700
New York, NY 10038
Tel: (212) 227-9171

Mexican Trade Commission
655 Madison Ave.
16th Floor
New York, NY 10021
Tel: (212) 759-9505

U.S.–Mexico Quadripartite
Commission
Center for Inter-American Relations
680 Park Ave.
New York, NY 10021
Tel: (212) 249-8950

Washington, D.C.
U.S.–Mexico Chamber of
Commerce
1900 L St., NW
Suite 602
Washington, D.C.
Tel: (212) 296-5198

Pakistan

New York
U.S.–Pakistan Economic Council
c/o Morton Zuckerman
17 Battery Pl.
Rm. 1128
New York, NY 10004
Tel: (212) 943-5828

Philippines

New York
Philippine–American Chamber of
Commerce, Inc.
711 3rd Ave.
17th Floor

New York, NY 10017
Tel: (212) 972-9326

San Francisco
c/o Philippine Consulate
447 Sutter St.
San Francisco, CA 9410X
Tel: (415) 433-6666

REGIONAL ORGANIZATIONS

Asia

New York
ASEAN–U.S. Trade Council
40 East 49th St.
Suite 501
New York, NY 10017
Tel: (212) 688-2755

Asian Society
725 Park Ave.
New York, NY 10021
Tel: (212) 288-6400

Washington, D.C.
Asia Society
1785 Massachusetts Ave., NW
Washington, D.C. 20036
Tel: (202) 387-6500

Latin America

New York
Chamber of Commerce of Latin
America in the U.S., Inc.
Suite 2343
One World Trade Center
New York, NY 10048
Tel: (212) 432-9313

Council of the Americas
680 Park Ave.
New York, NY 10021
Tel: (212) 628-3200

Pan American Society of the U.S.,
Inc.
680 Park Ave.
New York, NY 10021
Tel: (212) 744-68681

Central America

New Orleans
Chamber of Commerce/New
Orleans & The River Region
P.O. Box 30240
New Orleans, LA 70190
Tel: (504) 527-6971

SOURCE OF EXPORT INFORMATION

Export Licensing Control Agencies in
the U.S. Government

U.S. Department of Commerce
*The following offices are located at 14th
Street and Constitution Avenue, NW,
Washington, D.C. 20230:*

Export Administration (EA):
(202) 377-2000
**International Trade
Administration (ITA):**
(202) 377-2000

**Office of Anti-Boycott
Compliance:**
(202) 377-2381
Office of Export Enforcement:
(202) 377-4255
**Office of National Security
Programs:**
(202) 377-3634

U.S. Customs Service
1301 Constitution Ave., NW
Washington, D.C. 20229
Tel: (202) 566-8195

U.S. Department of the Interior
C Street between Eighteenth and
Nineteenth Sts., NW
Washington, D.C. 20240
Tel: (202) 343-3171

U.S. Department of Justice
Constitution Ave. and Tenth St.,
NW
Washington, D.C. 20530
Tel: (202) 633-2000

U.S. Department of State
Office of Munitions Control
2201 C St., NW
Washington, DC 20520
Tel: (202) 647-4000

U.S. Nuclear Regulatory Commission
1717 H St., NW
Washington, D.C. 20555
Tel: (301) 492-7000

FOREIGN CREDIT INSURANCE ASSOCIATION (FCIA)

The FCIA is an agent of the Export–Import (EXIM) Bank of the United States.

New York
40 Rector St.
11th Floor
New York, NY 10006
Tel: (212) 227-7020
States Served:
New York, New England, New Jersey, Pennsylvania, Delaware, Maryland, Virginia, and District of Columbia

Chicago
20 North Clark St.
Suite 910
Chicago, IL 60602
Tel: (312) 641-1915
States Served:
Ohio, Indiana, Michigan, Illinois, Wisconsin, Minnesota, North Dakota, South Dakota, Iowa, Missouri, Nebraska, Kansas, Kentucky, and West Virginia

American Association of Exporters and Importers
11 West 42nd St.
New York, NY 10036
Tel: (212) 944-2230

Note: The AAEI is a nongovernmental, nonprofit organization that serves as a consulting agency to U.S. firms on export licensing regulations before the Executive Branch, Congress, the U.S. Trade Representative, the U.S. Customs Service and government regulatory agencies. It has regional representation in Chicago, Los Angeles, San Francisco and Portland.

Houston
Texas Commerce Tower
600 Travis
Suite 2860
Houston, TX 77002
Tel: (713) 227-0987
States Served:
Louisiana, Oklahoma, Arkansas, New Mexico, North Carolina, South Carolina, Texas, Mississippi, and Tennessee.

Los Angeles
Wells Fargo Center
Suite 2580
333 South Grand Ave.
Los Angeles, CA 90071
Tel: (213) 687-3890
States Served:
Alaska, Washington, Oregon, California, Hawaii, Nevada, Arizona, Montana, Wyoming, Colorado, and Utah

Miami
World Trade Center
80 Southwest 8th St.
Miami, FL 33130
Tel: (305) 372-8540
States Served:
Florida, Alabama, Georgia, Puerto Rico, and the U.S. Virgin Islands

U.S. DEPARTMENT OF COMMERCE COUNTRY DESK OFFICES (IN WASHINGTON, D.C.)

The following offices can be contacted by telephone to obtain information on current events and traveling conditions in specific Pacific Rim countries:

Countries *Dial (202) 377 plus extension*

Afghanistan	2954
ASEAN	3875
Australia	3647
Bangladesh	2954
Bhutan	2954

Brunei	3647
Burma (Myanmar)	5334
Cambodia (Kampuchea)	2462
Canada	3101
Chile	1495
Hong Kong	2462
India	2954
Indonesia	3875
Japan	4527
Kampuchea (see Cambodia)	
Korea (North)	3583
Korea (South)	4958

Countries *Dial (202) 377 plus extension*

Laos	2462
Macao	2462
Malaysia	3875
Mexico	2527
Mongolia	3583
Nepal	2954

Pacific Islands:
(All islands ext. 3647)
Fiji
Wallis & Futana
Tuvalu
Kiribati
Tonga
New Caledonia
French Polynesia
Papua New Guinea
Vanuatu
Western Samoa

Tokelau
Niue
Cook Islands
Nauru
Republic of
the Marshall Islands
Federated States of
Micronesia
Republic of Palau

Pakistan	2954
Panama	2527
People's Republic of China	3583
Philippines	3875
Singapore	3875
Sri Lanka	2954
Taiwan	4957
Thailand	3875
USSR	4655
Vietnam	2462

PACIFIC RIM WORLD TRADE CENTERS

Headquarters:
World Trade Centers Association (WTCA)
One World Trade Center
Suite 7701

New York, NY 10048
Tel: (212) 313-4610
Tlx: 285 472 WTNY UR,

NETWORK
Mailcode: PENNY
Fax: (212) 488-0064

The WTCA coordinates a global network of World Trade Centers including the following organizations located in the Pacific Rim:

Australia

Melbourne
World Trade Centre, Melbourne
Corners Flinders and Spencer Streets
P.O. Box 4721
Melbourne, Victoria
Australia 3001
Tlx: AA342 11
Cable: HARBOR
Fax: (03) 611-1905
WTC Network: WTCME
Tel: (03) 611-1666

Canada

Vancouver
World Trade Centre, Vancouver
The Vancouver Board of Trade
999 Canada Place
Suite 400
Vancouver, B.C.
Canada V6C 3C1
WTC Network: WTCVN
Tel: (604) 681-2111

Hong Kong

Causeway Bay
World Trade Centre, Club Hong Kong
2M/F & 3/F World Trade Centre
Causeway Bay
Hong Kong
Tlx: 71729 WTCEN HX
Cable: WTCENTRE HONG KONG
FAX: 5-725 127
WTC Network: WTCHK
Tel: 5-779528

India

Bombay
World Trade Center, Bombay
Visvesvaraya Industrial Research &
Development Centre
Cuffe Parade
Colaba, Bombay-S
India
Tlx: 011-6846 WTCB IN
Cable: VIRDCOM
Tel: 21-44-34/21-73

Indonesia

Jakarta
World Trade Center, Jakarta
Wisma Metropolitan
11, Lt. 16
Jalan, Sudirman Kav. 31
P.O. Box S/KBY.MP
Jakarta 12920
Indonesia
Tlx: 62838 WTCJKT IA
Cable: WORLDTRADE JAKARTA
Fax: 61-021-578-1673
WTC Network: WTCJK
Tel: 62-021-5781945/578-1302

Japan

Tokyo
The World Trade Center of Japan,
Inc.
P.O. Box 57
World Trade Center Building
4-1, 2-chome, Hamamatsu-cho
Minato-ku, Tokyo
105 Japan
Tlx: 2422661 WORLDT J
Cable: WORLDTRADE TOKYO
Fax: (03) 4364368
WTC Network: WTCTO
Tel: (03) 435-5651

Korea

Seoul
World Trade Center, Korea
Korean Traders Association
10-1, 2-Ka Hoehyon-Dong, Chung-
Gu
Seoul

Korea
Tlx: KOTRASO K24265
Cable: KOTRASO SEOUL
Fax: 02-754 1337
WTC NETWORK: WTCSL
Tel: (02) 77141

Malaysia

Kuala Lumpur
Putra World Trade Centre
P.O. Box 11619
50752 Kuala Lumpur
Malaysia
Tlx: PUTRA MA 28100
Fax: 03-2930494
Tel: 03-2933888

People's Republic of China

Macau
World Trade Center, Macau
Centro Commercial de Prai Grande
Room 160 1
Macau, PRC
Tlx: 88831 WTCOM
Fax: 563398 WTCM
WTC Network: WTCMC
Tel: 565225, 562151

Xiamen
World Trade Center, Xiamen
Exhibition City
Shuang Han
Xiamen, PRC
Tlx: 93040 XBIEA CN
Cable: 0261
Fax: 26098
Tel: 26188 or 26005

Singapore

Singapore
World Trade Centre, Singapore
I Maritime Square, No. 09-72
World Trade Center
Singapore 0409
Republic of Singapore
Tlx: RS 34975 WTCS
Cable: "TANJONG" SINGAPORE
WTC Network: WTCSI
Tel: 3212791 or 3212187

Taiwan

Taipei
Taipei World Trade Center Co., Ltd.
201 Tun Hwa North Rd., IOF
Taipei
Taiwan
Tlx: 21676 CETRA
Cable: CETRA TAIPEI
Fax: (02) 716-8783
WTC Network: WTCTP
Tel: (02) 715-1515

USSR

Moscow
World Trade Center, Moscow
v/o SOVINCENTR 12
Krasnopresnenskaya nab
123610 Moscow
USSR
Tlx: 411486 SOVIN SU
Tel: 256 63 03

In Progress:

Thailand

Bangkok
World Trade Center, Bangkok
8th Floor, Sinthon Building
132 Wireless Rd.
Bangkok, 10500
Thailand
Tlx: 21369 WTCB TH
Cable: METROBANK-CODES:
PETERSON
4TH EDITION: PRIVATE
Fax: (02) 2534488
WTC Network: WTCBK
Tel: 250 1801

Affiliates:

India

New Delhi
Trade Development Authority
Bank of Baroda Bldg.
16 Sansad Marg
P.O. Box 767
New Delhi, I 10001
India

Cable: ADEPT
Tel: 312819, 310519

People's Republic of China

Beijing

World Trade Club
Beijing c/o 28/F.
Citic Building
Jianguomenwai
Beijing
PRC
Tlx: 22996 FUHUA CN
Tel: 5002255, Ext. 2828

Beijing

World Trade Centre
Club Beijing
Room 311
Qilin Hotel
Chaoyang District
Beijing
PRC
Tlx: 210333 BCPIT
CN
Cable: BJCCPIT
Tel: 482431-311

Chengdu

World Trade Center
Club Chengdu
Sichuan Jin Jiang Hotel
No. 36, Section 2
Ren Min N'an Rd.
Sichuan
PRC
Tlx: 60216 WTCCD
CN
Cable: 44X ICH
ENGDU
Fax: 244X1-683
Tel: 24481-681/682

Guangzhou

Guanzghou Consultants Company
for Foreign Economic Relations and
Trade
Garden Tower Hotel
Suites 834–837
Guangzhou
PRC
Tlx: 44341 WTCG
CN

Cable: 4735
Tel: 338999, Ext.
7834/7837

Hefei

Hefei World Trade Centre Club
Anhui Provincial Foreign Economic
Relations and Trade Consultants
Corporation Import & Export Bldg.
Jinzhai Road Hefei
Anhui Province
PRC
Tlx: 90011 AHFTB CN
Cable: AHFETCC
Tel: 61210, 61397

Nanjing

World Trade Centre
Club Nanjing
c/o Jinling Hotel Xin Jie
Kuo Nanjing
PRC
Tlx: 34110 JLHNJ CN
Cable: 6855 NANJING CN
Fax: 02543396
Tel: 44141, 41121, Ext. 4123, 4125

Shanghai

World Trade Centre, Shanghai
33 Zhong Shan Dong
Yi Lu
Shanghai
PRC
Tlx: 33290 SCPIT CN
Cable: "COMTRADE"
SHANGHAI
Tel: 219213

Shenzhen

Shenzhen Convention Center
(Silver Lake Resort Hotel)
Parker Hill
Shenzhen
PRC 20036
Tel: (202) 785-1400
Tlx: 42280 SSLRH CN
Cable: 0450
Tel: 22827

Xian

World Trade Center
Club Xi'An China
Council for the Promotion of

International Trade
Shaanxi Sub-Council
Xinchengnei Xi'an
PRC
Tlx: 70126 ADBFI CN
Cable: 6345
Tel: 22206, 716345

PACIFIC RIM EMBASSIES IN THE UNITED STATES

Australia

1601 Massachusetts Ave., NW
Washington, D.C. 20036
Tel: (202) 797-3000

Bangladesh

2201 Wisconsin Ave., NW
Suite 300
Washington, D.C. 20007
Tel: (202) 342-8372

Burma (Myanmar)

2300 S St., NW
Washington, D.C. 20008
Tel: (202) 332-9044

Canada

1746 Massachusetts Ave., NW
Washington, D.C. 20036

Chile

1732 Massachusetts Ave., NW
Washington, D.C. 20036
Tel: (202) 785-1746

China (People's Republic of)

2300 Connecticut Ave., NW
Washington, D.C. 20008
Tel: (202) 328-2500

Fiji

I U.N. Plaza, 26th Floor
New York, NY 10017
Tel: (212) 355-7316

India

2107 Massachusetts Ave., NW
Washington, D.C. 20008
Tel: (202) 939-7000

Indonesia

2020 Massachusetts Ave., NW
Washington, D.C. 20036
Tel: (202) 775-5200

Japan

2520 Massachusetts Ave., NW
Washington, D.C. 20008
Tel: (202) 234-2266

Korea (South)

2370 Massachusetts Ave., NW
Washington, D.C. 20008
Tel: (202) 939-5600

Laos

2222 S St., NW
Washington, D.C. 20008
Tel: (202) 332-6416

Malaysia

2401 Massachusetts Ave., NW
Washington, D.C. 20008
Tel: (202) 328-2700

Mexico

2829 16th St., NW
Washington, D.C. 20009
Tel: (202) 234-6000

Nepal

2131 LeRoy Place, NW
Washington, D.C. 20008
Tel: (202) 667-4550

New Zealand

37 Observatory Circle, NW
Washington, D.C. 20008
Tel: (202) 328-4800

Pakistan

2315 Massachusetts Ave., NW
Washington, D.C. 20008
Tel: (202) 939-6200

Panama

2862 McGill Terrace, NW
Washington, D.C. 20008
Tel: (202) 483-1407

Papua New Guinea

1330 Connecticut Ave., NW
Suite 350
Washington, D.C. 20008
Tel: (202) 659-0857

Philippines

1617 Massachusetts Ave., NW
Washington, D.C. 20036
Tel: (202) 483-1414

Singapore

1824 R St., NW
Washington, D.C. 20009
Tel: (202) 667-7555

Thailand

2300 Kalorama Rd., NW
Washington, D.C. 20008
Tel: (202) 483-7200

Union of Soviet Socialist Republics

1125 16th St., NW
Washington, D.C. 20036
Tel: (202) 628-8548

Western Samoa

820 2nd Ave.
Suite 800
New York, NY 10017
Tel: (212) 599-6196

U.S. EMBASSIES IN PACIFIC RIM COUNTRIES

Australia

Canberra
A.C.T. 2600
Moonah Place, APO
San Francisco, CA 96404
Tlx: 62104 USAEMB
Tel: (61) (62) 705000

Bangladesh

Dhaka
Adamjee Coult Bldg., 5th Floor
Motijheel Commercial Arca
G.P.O. Box 323
Ramna
Tlx: 642319 AEDKA BJ
Tel: (880) (2) 237161–63
235093–99, or 235081–89

Brunei

Bandar Seri Begawan
P.O. Box 2991
Tlx: BU 2609 AMEMB
Tel: (673) (2) 29670

Burma (Myanmar)

Rangoon
581 Merchant St.
G.P.O. Box 521
APO San Francisco, CA 96346
Tlx: 21230 AIDRCN BM

Canada

Ottawa, Ontario
100 Wellington St.
K1P ST1
P.O. Box 5000
Ogdensburg, NY 13669
Tlx: 0533582
Tel: (613) 238-5335

Chile

Santiago
Codina Bldg., 1343
Agustinas
APO Miami, FL 34033

Tlx: 2400062-USA-CL
Tel: (56) (2) 710133/90 or 710326/75

China, (People's Republic of)

Beijing
Xiu Shui Bei Jie 3, 100600
PRC Box 50
FPO San Francisco, CA 96655
Tlx: AMEMB CN 22701
Tel: (86) (1) 532-3831

Fiji

Suva
31 Loftus St.
P.O. Box 218
Tlx: 2755 AMEMBASY FJ
Tel: (679) 314-466
314069

Hong Kong

Hong Kong
26 Garden Rd.
Box 3
FPO San Francisco, CA 96659-0002
Tlx: 63141 USDOC HX
Tel: (852) (5) 239011

India

New Delhi
Chanakyapuri 110021
Tel: 031-6269 USEM IN
Tel: (91) (11) 600651

Indonesia

Jakarta
Medan Merdeli
Selatan 5
APO San Francisco, CA 96356
Tlx: 44218 AMEMB JKT
Tel: (62) (21) 360-360

Japan

Tokyo
1-1, Akasaki 1-chome
Minato-ku (107)
APO San Francisco, CA 96503

Tlx: 2422118 AMEMB J
Tel: (81) (3) 224-5000

Korea

Seoul
82 Sejong-Ro
Chongro-ku
APO San Francisco, 96301
Tlx: AMEMB 23108
Tel: (82) (2) 732-260-1-18

Laos

Vientiane
Rue Bartholonie
B.P. 114, Box V
APO San Francisco, CA 96346
Tel: 2220, 2357, 2384

Malaysia

Kuala Lumpur
376 Jalan Tun Razak
50400 Kuala Lumpur
P.O. Box 10035
50700 Kuala Lumpur
Tlx: FCSKL MA 32956 (6) (03) 248-9011

Marshall Islands

Majuro
P.O. Box 680
Rep. of the Marshall Islands 96960
Tel: 692-4011

Mexico

Mexico, D.F.
Paseo de la Reforma
305 Mexico 5, D.F.
P.O. Box 3087
Laredo, Texas 78044
Tlx: 017-73-091, 017-75-685

Micronesia

Kolonia
P.O. Box 12X6
Pohnpei, Fcd. States of Micronesia
96941
Tel: 691-320-2187

Mongolia (People's Republic of)

Ulaanbaatar
c/o U.S. Embassy
Beijing PRC
Tlx: 253 TLX UB 29095

Nepal

Kathmandu
Pani Pokhiu
Tlx: NP 2381 AEKTM
Tel: (977) 411179, 412718, 411601

New Zealand

Wellington
29 Fitzherbert Ter.
Thorndon, P.O. Box 1190
FPO San Francisco, CA 96690-0001
Tlx: NZ 3305
Tel: (64) (4) 722-068

Pakistan

Islamabad
Diplomatic Enclave
Ramni 5 P.O. Box 1048
APO New York, NY 09614
Tlx: 82-5-864
Tel: (92) (51) 8261-61/79

Palau, Republic of

Koror (USLA)
P.O. Box 602
Republic of Pillau
96940
Tel: 160-680-920/990

Panama

Panama
Apartado 6959
Panama 5 Rep. of Panama
Box E
APO Miami 34002
Tel: (507) 27-1777

Papau, New Guinea

Port Moresby
Armit Street
P.O. 1308 1492
Tlx: 221X9 USAEM
Tel: (675) 211-455/594/654

Philippines

Manila
Roxas Boulevard
APO San Francisco, CA 96528
Tlx: 722-27366 AME PH
Tel: (63) (2) 521-7116 1201

Singapore

Singapore
30 Hill St.
FPO San Francisco, CA 96699
Tlx: RS 42289 AMEM13
Tel: (65) 338-0251

Solomon Islands

Honiara
Mud Alley
P.O. Box 561
Tel: (677) 23890

Sri Lanka

Columbo
210 Galle Rd.
P.O. Box 106
Tlx: 21305 AMEMBCE
Tel: (34) (1) 276-3400/3600

Union of Soviet Socialist Republics

Moscow
Ulitsa Chaykovskogo 19/21/23
APO NY 09862
Tlx: 413160 USGSOSU

U.S. Commercial Office
Ulitsa Chaykovskogo 15
Tlx: 413-205-USCOSU
Tel: (7) (096) 255-48-48,
and 255-46-60

Taiwan

Taipei
American Institute in Taiwan
7 Lane 134
Hsin Yi Rd., Sec. 3
Tlx: 23890 USTRADE
Tel: (886) (2) 709-2000

Koahsiung
3rd Floor, No. 2
Chung Cheng, 3rd Rd.
Tel: (07) 251-2444/7

Thailand

Bangkok
95 Wireless Rd.
APO San Francisco, CA 96346
Tlx: 20966 FCSBKK
Tel: (66) (2) 252-5040

Western Samoa

Apia
P.O. Box 3430
Tlx: (779) 275 AMEMBSX
Tel: (685) 21631

*Sources: The American Chamber of
Commerce in Hong Kong 1989/1990
Members Directory* (Publications
manager and general editor, Fred S
Armentrout); *Export Sales and
Marketing Manual* (John R. Jagoe,
Editor, Export USA Publications,
Minneapolis, Minnesota, 1989).

APPENDIX E

RIM RESEARCH ORGANIZATIONS AND UNIVERSITIES

Research organizations, or "think tanks," conduct research on topics that interest their supporters, who may be individuals, foundations, corporations, or political groups. The research organizations listed in this section are interested in Asia for a variety of reasons, including national security, foreign policy, and trade policy.

These organizations conduct studies, organize conferences, issue reports, and make policy recommendations. They also provide a place for Asian experts to develop and refine their knowledge. Because of their expertise, some of these organizations offer political and economic risk-analysis services to business.

American Enterprise Institute for Public Policy Research (AEI)
1150 17th St. NW
Washington, D.C. 20036
Tel: 202-862-5800, 800-424-2873
Publications: 202-862-5869, 800-424-2873

International Policy Studies
1150 17th St. NW
Washington, D.C. 20036
Tel: 202-862-6402

Conducts research on national and international policy; offers free publications catalog.

Aspen Institute for Humanistic Studies
Wye Plantation
P.O. Box 222
Queenstown, MD 21658
Tel: 301-827-7168

Organizes seminars and conferences on social and economic policy for business leaders

Berkeley Roundtable on the International Economy (Brie)
2234 Piedmont Ave.
University of California
Berkeley, CA 94720
Tel: 415-642-3067

Conducts research on international competition in high technology; interested in Pacific Rim trade issues; has conducted studies on international competition in microelectronics, elecommunications, and robotics; with the University of Nebraska, has studied international trade in agriculture; offers free list of working papers.

Brookings Institution (BI)
1775 Massachusetts Ave., NW
Washington, D.C. 20036
Tel: 202-797-6000

The Brookings Institution conducts research on economic, defense, and foreign policy.

Carnegie Endowment for International Peace (CEIP)
11 Dupont Circle, NW
Washington, D.C. 20036
Tel: 202-797-6400

Conducts research on U.S. foreign policy; makes policy recommendations.

Cato Institute
224 Second St. SE
Washington, D.C. 20003
Tel: 202-546-0200

Conducts research on domestic and foreign policy; dedicated to limited government, individual liberty, and peace, encourages U.S. allies, such as Korea, to assume more of the burden of their own defense; free publications catalog available.

Center for Strategic and International Studies (CSIS)
1800 K St., NW
Suite 400
Washington, D.C. 20006
Tel: 202-887-0200

International Business and Economics Program
1800 K St., NW
Washington, D.C. 20006
Tel: 202-775-3227

Conducts research on defense and foreign policy; offers country assessment and political risk analysis to corporate supporters.

Council on Foreign Relations (CFR)
58 East 68th St.
New York, NY 10021
Tel: 212-734-400

Council on Foreign Relations
11 Dupont Circle, NW
Suite 900
Washington, D.C. 20036
Tel: 202-79760

Individuals are invited to join based on their expertise in international affairs; examines international aspects of economic, political, and strategic problems; bimonthly journal, *Foreign Affairs,* provides frequent coverage on the Pacific Basin.

East-West Center (EWC)
1777 East-West Rd.
Honolulu, HI 96848
Tel: 808-944-7111

Resource Systems Institute
1777 East-West Rd.
Honolulu, HI 96848
Tel: 808-944-7111

Conducts research on the environment, energy, minerals, forests, and natural resources issues in the Pacific Basin.

East-West Population Institute
1777 East-West Rd.
Honolulu, HI 96848
Tel: 808-944-7111

Conducts demographic research.

Ethics and Public Policy Center (EPPC)
1030 15th St., NW
Washington, D.C. 20005
Tel: 202-682-1200

Conducts research on the ethical implications of domestic and foreign policy decisions.

Foreign Policy Association (FPA)
729 Seventh Ave.
New York, NY 10019
Tel: 212-764-050

Washington Office
1800 K St., NW
Washington, D.C. 20006
Tel: 202-293-1051

Sponsors educational programs designed to create a climate of informed public opinion on U.S. foreign policy; operates "Great Decisions" and "Great Decisions in Business" citizen education programs; cooperates with World Affairs Councils around the country, offers free publications catalog.

Harvard-Yenching Institute (HYI)
2 Divinity Ave.
Cambridge, MA 02138
Tel: 617-495-3369

The Harvard-Yenching Institute is an independent foundation concerned with education in Asia.

Harvard-Yenching Library
2 Divinity Ave.
Cambridge, MA 02138
Tel: 617-495-2756

Collection of materials in East Asian languages; has extensive holdings on contemporary East Asia.

Heritage Foundation
214 Massachusetts Ave., NE
Washington, D.C. 20002
Tel: 202-546-4400

Conducts research and makes recommendations in the areas of economic, defense, and foreign policy; committed to free enterprise, limited government, individual liberty, and a strong national defense; free annual report lists publications.

Asian Studies Center
214 Massachusetts Ave., NE
Washington, D.C. 20002
Tel: 202-546-4400

Hoover Institution on War, Revolution, and Peace
Stanford University
Stanford, CA 94305
Tel: 415-723-1754

Conducts research on domestic and international affairs; library has large East Asia collection. Offers free publications catalog.

Hudson Institute
Herman Kahn Center
5395 Emerson Way
P.O. Box 26-919
Indianapolis, IN 46226
Tel: 317-545-1000

Washington Office
4401 Ford Ave.
Suite 200
Alexandria, VA 22302
Tel: 703-824-2048

Founded by the late Herman Kahn, renowned futurist; studies public policy issues, including national security and foreign policy.

Institute for International Economics (IIE)
11 Dupont Circle, NW
Washington, D.C. 20036
Tel: 202-328-0583

Studies international trade and economic policy; makes policy recommendations; offers free publications catalog.

Investor Responsibility Research Center (IRRC)
1755 Massachusetts Ave., NW
Suite 600
Washington, D.C. 20004
Tel: 202-939-6500

Information service for institutional shareholders concerned about the policies of their portfolio companies; offers free publications catalog; monthly newsletter *News for Investors*.

National Center for Export-Import Studies (NCEIS)
1242 35th St., NW
Suite 501
Washington, D.C. 20057
Tel: 202-625-4797

Conducts studies of international trade policy; develops practical solutions to assist U.S. exporters; works to strengthen communication among the business, policy, and academic sectors of the international trade community; supports free trade; runs Georgetown Export Trading, Inc., a prototype export trading company; offers free publications catalog; publishes bimonthly *NCEIS Trade Analyst*.

The Pacific Basin Institute
7 East Mission St., Suite C
Santa Barbara, CA 93101
Tel: 805-687-2378
Fax: 805-687-8618

Los Angeles Office
1680 N. Vine, Suite 811
Los Angeles, CA 90028
Tel: 213-469-2453
Fax: 213-469-1501

Engages in a far-reaching program of academic research, journalist exchanges, conferences and films. Although originally dealing mainly with Japan–U.S. relations, PBI quickly expanded its focus to include a study of other Pacific Rim countries, particularly as they relate to the United States. A major project is a 10-hour television series titled *The Pacific Century* which will air on PBS stations early in 1992. Also underway is the Library of Japan, encompassing some fifty volumes of mostly modern Japanese fiction and non-fiction works for American readers.

Population Reference Bureau (PRB)
P.O. Box 96152
Washington, D.C. 20090
Tel: 202-639-8040

Conducts research and provides information service on population around the world; members receive monthly publications and personal responses to inquiries by reference librarians and demographic analysts; offers free publications catalog; publishes annual *World Population*

Data Sheet, quarterly *Population Bulletin,* and monthly *Population Today*.

Potomac Associates
1740 Massachusetts Ave., NW
Washington, D.C. 20036
Tel: 202-663-5880, 202-686-9695

Conducts studies of domestic and international public policy issues; analyses are based on public opinion surveys, both in the United States and abroad; offers free publications list.

Rand Corporation
1700 Main St.
P.O. Box 2138
Santa Monica, CA 90406-2138
Tel: 213-393-0411

Conducts research on national security and public welfare issues; most research done under contract to federal, state, and local governments; publishes much of its unclassified government research; free special bibliographies available.

Washington Institute for Values in Public Policy (WI)
1667 K St., NW
Suite 200
Washington, D.C. 20006
Tel: 202-293-7440

Conducts research on the ethical implications of domestic and foreign policy decisions; offers free publications catalog; published *Human Rights in East Asia: A Cultural Perspective,* edited by James C. Hsiung.

World Environment Center (WEC)
419 Park Ave.,
Suite 1403
New York, NY 10016
212-683-700
President, Whitman Bassow
Technical Assistance Programs, Anthony Marcil

Provides environmental information and technical assistance worldwide through conferences, meetings, publications, and the services of experts from U.S. industry; supported by contributions and grants from industry, governments, and foundations; offers free publications catalog.

Universities

There are over 35 American universities that provide information about Asian business, culture, economics, and politics.

American Graduate School of International Management
Thunderbird Campus
Glendale, AZ 85306
Tel: 602-987-7244

Specializes in preparing students for careers in international business management.

Boston University
Economics Depart.
212 Bay State Rd.
Boston, MA 02215

Asian Management Center
685 Commonwealth Ave.
Room 129
Boston, MA 02215
Tel: 617-353-2670

Bradley University
Institute of International Studies
Bradley Hall 303
Peoria, IL 61625
Tel: 309-676-7611

Brandeis University
415 South St.
Sachar Building
Waltham, MA 02254
Tel: 617-736-2240

Brigham Young University David M. Kennedy Center for International Studies
237 HRCB
Provo, UT 84602
Tel: 801-378-3378
Publications Office, Tel: 801-378-6528

The Center for International Studies publishes an extensive series of reports to help Americans understand foreign cultures (and to help foreigners understand Americans). Their four-page *CultureGram* on

Asian nations covers customs, business etiquette, the people, their lifestyle, and other useful information for the traveler.

California Institute of Integral Studies
765 Ashbury St.
San Francisco, CA 94117
Tel: 415-53-6100

Founded in 1968, the California Institute of Integral Studies is an accredited, nonprofit, nonsectarian graduate school dedicated to the integration of Eastern and Western traditions of knowledge.

Columbia University East Asian Institute
420 West 118th Street
New York, NY 10027
Tel: 212-280-2591

Department of East Asian Languages and Cultures
407 Kent Hall
Columbia University
New York, NY 10027
Tel: 212-280-2574

Starr East Asian Library
300 Kent Hall
Columbia University
New York, NY 10027
Tel: 212-280-4318
Director, Marsha Wagner

Cornell University
Department of Asian Studies
Rockefeller Hall
Ithaca, NY 14853
Tel: 607-255-4144

Olin Research Library
Wason Collection
Cornell University
Ithaca, NY 14853
Tel: 607-255-4144

Dominican College
Pacific Basic Studies Program
1520 Grand Ave.
San Rafael, CA 94901
Tel: 415-457-4440, Ext. 330
Director: Fran LePage

George Washington University
2025 F St., NW
Washington, D.C. 20052
Tel: 202-994-1000

Institute for Sino-Soviet Studies
601 Melvin Gelman Library
2130 H St., NW
Washington, D.C. 20052
Tel: 202-994-6340

Their *Journal of Northeast Asia Studies* covers China, Japan, and Korea.

Political Science Department
George Washington University
Washington, D.C. 20052
Tel: 202-994-6290

Georgetown University
School for Foreign Service
Asian Studies Program
Intercultural Center, Room 506A
Washington, D.C. 20057
Tel: 202-625-4216

Harvard Business School
Soldiers Field Rd.
Boston, MA 02163
Tel: 617-495-6000

Harvard University
Cambridge, MA 02138
Tel: 617-495-1000

John K. Fairbank Council on East Asian Studies
1737 Cambridge St.
Cambridge, MA 02138
Tel: 617-495-4657

Established in 1972 to coordinate all teaching and research in East Asian studies at Harvard; publishes the *Harvard East Asian Monograph Series*.

Harvard Institute for International Development
1737 Cambridge St.
Cambridge, MA 02138
Tel: 617-495-2161

Offers course on *Banking and Monetary Policy in Developing Countries*.

Korea Institute
1737 Cambridge St.
Cambridge, MA 02138
Tel: 617-495-9602

Sociology Dept.
Cambridge, MA 02138
Professor, Ezra Vogel
Tel: 617-495-4014

Illinois Institute of Technology
3300 South Federal St.
Chicago, IL 60616
Tel: 312-567-5122

Indiana University
Bloomington, IN 47405
Tel: 812-332-0211

Dept. of East Asian Languages
Goodbody Hall
Bloomington, IN 47405
Tel: 812-335-1992

Dept. of Economics
901 Ballatine Hall
Bloomington, IN 47405
Tel: 812-335-1021

Massachusetts Institute of Technology (MIT)
77 Massachusetts Ave.
Cambridge, MA 02139
Tel: 617-253-1000

Political Science Dept.
30 Wadsworth St.
Cambridge, MA 02139
Professor, Lucian Pye
Tel: 617-253-5262

Dr. Pye is an expert on Asian culture, business etiquette, and negotiation styles. He is the author of *Asian Power and Politics: The Cultural Dimensions*.

East Asian Studies Program
77 Massachusetts Ave.
Room 4209
Cambridge, MA 02139
Tel: 617-253-1354

Princeton University
Asian Studies Dept.
211 Jones Hall
Princeton, NJ 08544
Tel: 609-452-4729
Professor of History and East Asian Studies, Marius B. Jansen

Dr. Jansen is the author of a chapter on Japan and Korea in the *Encyclopedia of Asian History*, published in 1987 by The Asia Society.

Gest Oriental Library and East Asian Collections
317 Palmer Hall
Princeton, NJ 08544
Tel: 609-452-3182

Provides information services on China, Japan, and Korea.

Woodrow Wilson School of Public and International Affairs
Princeton University
Princeton, NJ 08544
Tel: 609-452-4804
Asia Specialists: Kent Calder, Lynn White,
John Lewis

Rutgers University
(The State University of New Jersey)
East Asian Library
Alexander Library
College Ave.
New Brunswick, NJ 08903
Tel: 201-93-7161

Trinity University
History Dept.
715 Stadium Dr.
San Antonio, TX 78284
Tel: 512-736-7621

University of California at Berkeley
Institute of East Asian Studies (IEAS)

2223 Fulton St.
Sixth Floor
Berkeley, CA 94720
Tel: 415-642-2809

Activities of IEAS include sponsoring sabbaticals for Asian dignitaries, lecture series, publications, and a series of conferences on North Korea. If you'd like to receive notices of activities and new publications, request a free subscription to the bimonthly *IEAS Bulletin*.

Center for Korean Studies
2223 Fulton Street, Room 512
UC-Berkeley
Berkeley, CA 94720
Tel: 415-642-5674

In addition to its work on South Korea's economy and society, the IEAS Center for Korean Studies has conducted extensive research on North Korea. Mr. Jo is conducting research on U.S.–Korea military relations.

East Asiatic Library
208 Durant Hall
UC-Berkeley
Berkeley, CA 97420
Tel: 415-642-2556

University of California at Los Angeles
Center for Pacific Rim Studies
1250 Bunche Hall
Los Angeles, CA 90024
Tel: 213-206-0223

University of California at San Diego
Graduate School of International Relations and Pacific Studies
Q-062
La Jolla, CA 92093
Tel: 619-534-6074
Professor of International Relations, Lawrence Krause.

Dr. Krause is an expert on Pacific Rim economic relations. Before coming to UC-San Diego, he was the Korea specialist at the Brookings Institution.

University of Chicago
Dept. of History
1126 East 59th St.
Chicago, IL 60637
Tel: 312-702-8398

University of Cincinnati
Political Science Dept.
Crosley Tower, Room 1013
Cincinnati, OH 45221
Tel: 513-475-3211

University of Detroit
Finance Dept.
4001 West McNichols Rd.
Detroit, MI 48221
Tel: 313-927-1160

University of Hawaii at Manoa
1881 East-West Rd.
Honolulu, HI 96822
Tel: 808-948-7041

Hamilton Library
East Asia Collection
2550 The Mall
Honolulu, HI 96822
Tel: 808-948-8042

Williarn S. Richardson School of Law
2515 Dole St.
Honolulu, HI 96822
Tel: 808-948-6363

University of Illinois at Chicago
Political Science Dept.
1102 Behavioral Science Building
Box 4348 Chicago, IL 60680
Tel: 312-996-3108

University of Maryland
Dept. of East Asian Languages and Literature
University of Maryland
College Park, MD 20742
Tel: 301-454-5152

East Asia Collection
McKeldin Library
College Park, MD 20742
Tel: 301454-5459

University of Pennsylvania
Dept. of International Relations
246 Stiteler Hall
Philadelphia, PA 19104
Tel: 215-898-7657

University of Pittsburgh
East Asian Library
201 Hillman Library
Pittsburgh, PA 15260
Tel: 412-648-7573

University of San Francisco Center for the Pacific Rim and The Institute for Chinese-Western Cultural History
Lone Mountain, RM 282
San Francisco, CA 94117-1080
Tel: 415-666-6357
Fax: 415-666-2291
Director: Barbara Bundy

University of Southern California
Los Angeles, CA 90089
Tel: 213-743-2311

History Dept.
University of Southern California
Los Angeles, CA 90089-0034
Tel: 213-743-7522

International Business Education and Research Program (IBEAR)
Graduate School of Business
Administration
University of Southern California
Los Angeles, CA 90089-1421
Tel: 213-743-2272
Director, Richard Drobnick

IBEAR offers a graduate program in international business management; a substantial proportion of the students are from Asia, and many IBEAR alumni hold top management positions in industry, banking, and government.

In 1985, IBEAR developed the *Pacific Rim Management Programs,* a series of one-week courses for executives on *Doing Business with Japan, Korea, and Taiwan*. Courses are held each year in May or June.

Von Kleinsmid Library
East Asia Collection
University Park, MC0182
Los Angeles, CA 90089-0182
Tel: 213-743-7347

University of Texas at Dallas Dept. of International Management Studies

P.O. Box 830688
Richardson, TX 75083-0688
Tel: 214-543-2033

University of Washington
Seattle, WA 98195
Tel: 206-543-2100

Asian Library
322 Gowen Hall, DO-27
University of Washington
Seattle, WA 98195
Tel: 206-543-4490

Henry M. Jackson School of International Studies
411 Thompson Hall
University of Washington
Seattle, WA 98195
Tel: 206-5434370

East Asia Resource Center
University of Washington
Seattle, WA 98195
Tel: 206-543-1921

Provides multimedia information resources.

University of Washington School of Law
JB-20
Seattle, WA 98195
Tel: 206-543-4550

Western Michigan University
Kalamazoo, MI 49008
Tel: 616-383-1600

International Education and Programs
2090 Friedman Hall
Western Michigan University
Kalamazoo, MI 49008
Tel: 616-383-0483

Political Science Dept.
3028 Friedman Hall, NN
Western Michigan University
Kalamazoo, MI 49008
Tel: 616-383-0483

Yale University
New Haven, CT 06520
Tel: 203-4324771

Council on East Asian Studies
85 Trumbull Street
Box 13A, Yale Station

New Haven, CT 06520
Tel: 203-624-3426
Director, Conrad Totman

Political Science Dept.
Yale University

New Haven, CT 06520
Tel: 203-432-5283

Sterling Memorial Library
East Asian Collection
Yale University

New Haven, CT 06520
Tel: 203-432-1790

Specializes in Chinese, Japanese, and
Korean politics, government,
economics, and law.

U.S.–ASIAN CONSULTING FIRMS

This section lists American consulting firms that provide a wide variety of services, including market research, economic forecasting, lobbying, political risk analysis, credit checks, and cross-cultural training.

Richard V. Allen Company
905 16th Street, NW
Washington, D.C. 20006
Tel: 202-737-2824

Among the firm's clients are U.S. and European companies involved in international trade. Allen was Assistant to the President for National Security Affairs in 1981. He is Chairman of the Advisory Board, Asian Studies Center, Heritage Foundation, and Senior Counselor for Foreign Policy and National Security Affairs, Republican National Committee.

American Demographics, Inc.
P.O. Box 68
Ithaca, NY 14851
Tel: 607-273-6343
Toll free: 800-828-1133 nationwide,
800-62-8686 in NY state

Wholly owned subsidiary of Dow Jones & Company; issues publications in the demographics field, sponsors conferences, and provides other services to businesses that need consumer market information; publications of interest are described below. Publishes *Consumer Markets Abroad* and *International Marketing Primer,* which provides guidance for evaluating a country's market potential.

Apco Associates
1200 New Hampshire Ave., NW
Suite 320
Washington, D.C. 20036
Tel: 202-778-1000

Consulting arm of Arnold & Porter, a major Washington, D.C. law firm; assists clients who want to invest, transfer technology, or establish joint ventures in Asia.

Armstrong, Byrd & Associates
1875 Connecticut Ave., NW
Suite 1110
Washington, D.C. 20009
Tel: 202-234-5900

Assists clients with Asian business ventures.

Business Environment Risk Information (BERI)
1355 Redondo Ave.
Long Beach, CA 90804
Tel: 213-597-8879

Collects information on business and financial risks worldwide; offers reports, seminars, and consulting services.

Business International Corp. (BI)
1 Dag Hammarskjold Plaza
New York, NY 10027
Tel: 212-750-6300
President, James Whitcomb

Business International Asia/ Pacific, Ltd.
Asia/Pacific Headquarters
1111-1119 Mount Parker House
City Plaza, Taikoo Shing
Quarry Bay, Hong Kong
Tel: (852-5) 670-4918
Tlx: 74364

Business International is a private firm dedicated to helping international companies manage their worldwide operations for maximum growth. With a network of consultants and researchers in 75 countries, BI distributes newsletters, reports, and analyses on markets, companies, and business conditions worldwide. BI offers consulting services, custom research, political risk assessments, and educational programs. It has offices in Chicago, San Francisco, Washington, D.C., as well as eight offices in the Asia/ Pacific Region. The company has expanded its global network by merging with the Economist Intelligence Unit.

Cahners Exposition Group
7315 Wisconsin Ave., NW
P.O. Box 70007
Washington, D.C. 20088
Tel: 301-657-3090

Manages trade shows in Asia including the *International Electronic Production and Semiconductor Exhibition* held each year in Seoul in March.

Chase Econometrics
150 Monument Rd.
Bala Cynwyd, PA 19004
Tel: 215-667-6000, 800-367-3266

Provides econometric analysis forecasting and consulting services; produces nearly 100 databases, some available through DIALOG; a few databases with information about Asia include:

Far East Forecast provides macroeconomic data and forecasts for 12 countries
Monthly Far East provides financial and economic data for 13 countries
World Debt Tables provides data on external debt for 105 developing countries

Data Resources, Inc. (DRI)
1750 K St., NW
Ninth Floor
Washington, D.C. 20006
Tel: 202-663-7600

DRI provides economic information, analyses, and consulting services. The company offers the *Asian Economic Service,* a comprehensive package of economic models, forecasts, and historical data for 11 Asian countries.

Dataquest, Inc.
1290 Ridder Park Dr.
San Jose, CA 95131-2398
Tel: 408-971-9000

Market research firm for high technology and industrial products; offers publications, databases, and consulting services.

Asian Semiconductor and Electronic Industry Service
1290 Ridder Park Dr.
San Jose, CA 95131-2398
Tel: 408-971-9000

Provides information on the Asian market and competition from Asia in electronics and semiconductors.

Dun and Bradstreet International (D&B)
1 Diamond Hill Rd.
Murray Hill, NJ 07974-0027
Toll-free credit check orders: 800-932-0024

D&B provides credit information on companies worldwide. It offers a wide range of financial reporting services on foreign companies. For a complete description, request *The Dun & Bradstreet International Product/ Service Guide,* available free.

Dun's Marketing Services
49 Old Bloomfield Ave.
Mountain Lakes, NJ 07046
Tel: 01-299-8228, 800-526-0651

Dun's Marketing Services sells numerous publications with detailed information about companies. Among its Asian-related publications are *Asia's 7500 Largest Companies,* annual (providing rankings for the 7500 largest companies in Asia), and *Who Owns Whom: Australasia and the Far East,* annual, showing corporate ownership relationships for companies in Asia and the Pacific.

The Economist Intelligence Unit
40 Duke St.
London WIA IDW
United Kingdom
Tel: (44-1) 493-6711
Tlx: 266353
Fax: (44-1) 499-9767

U.S. Office
10 Rockefeller Plaza
New York, NY 10020
Tel: 212-541-5730

Founded by the publishers of *The Economist* business news magazine, EIU draws on the magazine's worldwide network of special correspondents and information sources to provide international

economic analysis and forecasting. Among its offerings to business is a credit risk reporting service and hundreds of country and industry studies. EIU has expanded its global network by merging with Business International.

Elm International, Inc.
P.O. Box 1740
East Lansing, MI 48826
Tel: 517-482-3543
Fax: 517-351-3032

Provides information about the Japanese, Korean, and U.S. automotive industries; serves as matchmaker for U.S. auto parts companies that want to sell to Korean auto manufacturers; has published a directory of U.S. OEM Auto Parts Companies.

ETL Testing Laboratories
Industrial Park
Cortland, NY 13045
Tel: 607-753-6711

ETL (Electrical Testing Laboratory) tests and certifies products for exporters.

Financial Times, LTD.
Business Information Service (BIS)
Bracken House
10 Cannon St.
London EC4P 4BY
United Kingdom
Tel: (44-1) 248-8000
Tlx: 895-4871

U.S. Office
14 East 60th St.
New York, NY 10022
Tel: 212-752-4500

Founded by the publishers of the *Financial Times* business newspaper, BIS draws on the paper's worldwide network of special correspondents and information sources to provide international economic analysis and forecasting. It offers consulting services, conferences, specialized newsletters, and other business information products. A descriptive brochure and publications catalog are available free.

FIND/SVP
The Information Clearing House, Inc.
625 Avenue of the Americas
New York, NY 10011
Tel: 212-645-4500

FIND/SVP provides a wide range of information and research services.

The company also publishes and distributes hundreds of studies about companies, markets, industries. A descriptive brochure and publications catalog are available free.

SVP Korea
Joongang Daily News
7, Sunhwa-dong, Jung-gu
58-9 Seosomun-dong
Joong-gu, Seoul
Tel: (82-2) 752-7741

Information clearinghouse offering market research and information services; uses the resources of the *Joongang Daily News* and the SVP Network worldwide.

Frost & Sullivan, Inc. (F & S)
106 Fulton St.
New York, NY 10038
Tel: 212-233-1080

F&S produces market research reports, seminars, and conferences for the health, electronics, defense, chemicals, transportation, and machinery industries. It also offers a political risk-assessment service that includes consulting, seminars, newsletters, and reports.

Country Facts, quarterly, provides concise political and economic information about 120 countries, including North Korea—$125 one issue, $285 a year.

William Gleysteen
435 Riverside Dr.
Apartment 1A

New York, NY 10025
Tel: 212-865-7565

Gleysteein was U.S. Ambassador to Korea from 1978 to 1981.

Global Information Services, Inc.
7730 Carondelet
Suite 407
St. Louis, MO 63105
Tel: 314-726-2731
President, Mary Koemer

Provides annual and quarterly reports in English, for 50 Korean companies; fee is $1 per page.

Global Quest, Inc.
2101 Crystal Plaza Arcade
Suite 238
Arlington, VA 22202
Tel: 703-683-4485

Publishes international business handbooks; conducts market research for clients.

Global USA, Inc.
1823 Jefferson Place, NW
Washington, D.C. 20036
Tel: 02-296-2400

Assists clients with Asian business ventures.

Hill and Knowlton Public Affairs Worldwide
901 31st St., NW
Washington, D.C. 20007
Tel: 202-333-7400

Develops public relations campaigns for American companies in Asia and Asian companies in the United States.

Hudson Analytical Services, Inc.
Herman Kahn Center
5395 Emerson Way
P.O. Box 26-919
Indianapolis, IN 46226
Tel: 317-545-1000

Subsidiary of the Hudson Institute; established to conduct proprietary research for private sector clients; has expertise in Asian trade policy;

conducts political and economic risk analysis.

International Business and Economic Research Corp. (IBERC)
2121 K St., NW
Suite 700
Washington, D.C. 20037
Tel: 202-955-6155

International Business-Government Counsellors, Inc. (IBC)
1625 I St. NW
Suite 708
Washington, D.C. 20007
Tel: 02-872-8181

Provides a wide variety of information services for multinational corporations, including political risk analysis, monitoring of international organizations, and research on foreign trade and investment policy; publishes a bimonthly newsletter, *Washington International Business Report,* and two monthlies, *Washington International Organizational Guide* and *Who's Who in International Washington.*

Korea Strategy Associates, Inc. (KSA)
124 Mount Aubum St.
Suite 200
Cambridge, MA 02138
Tel: 617-576-5773

Korea Strategy Associates was established in 1984 to help American firms do business in Korea; staff members are fluent in Korean.

Mead Ventures, Inc.
P.O. Box 44952
Phoenix, AZ 85064
Tel: 602-840-8277

Publishes newsletters on the automotive and high-technology industries in developing countries; among them *Korea Automotive Review* and *Korea High Tech Review* provide information about Korean companies, market opportunities, and joint ventures with U.S. and Japanese companies; each is published monthly and costs $295 a year.

Malgrem, Inc.
2001 L St., NW
Suite 760
Washington, D.C. 20036
Tel: 202-466-8740

Assists clients with Asian business ventures.

Moran, Stahl and Boyer, Inc.
355 Lexington Ave.
New York, NY 10017
Tel: 212-661-4875

International Division
900 28th St.
Boulder, CO 80303
Tel: 303-449-8440

Conducts cross-cultural training for Americans going to Asia and Asians coming to the United States; publishes monthly magazine, *Corporate Expatriate.*

The Pacific Rim Consulting Group
Room 904
Tower II, South Seas Centre
75 Mody Rd.
T.S.T. Kowloon
Tel: 723-2166
Fax: 724-0477
Director, George Baeder

An international consulting group assisting U.S. and European firms to compete in Asia and Latin America.

Pacific Strategies
141 Laurel Ave.
Atherton, CA 94027
Tel: 415-326-7559
Fax: 415-724-0477
Director, William Grindley

A member of the Pacific Rim Consulting Group based on the West Coast.

Rayfield Associates
767 Fifth Ave.
New York, NY 10153
Tel: 212-418-6436
President, Gordon Rayfield

Mr. Rayfield is a political risk analyst with expertise in Korea.

Search Associates, Inc.
International Research
3422 Q St. NW
Washington, D.C. 20007
Tel: 202-337-3656

An international research firm focusing on trade and politics; specializes in on-demand, hard-to-get business information in Asia and Europe; compiles biographies of foreign officials.

SRI International
333 Ravenswood Ave.
Menlo Park, CA 94025
Tel: 415-326-6200

Provides consulting and research services for clients worldwide; specializes in technology assessment and high-technology markets; publishes reports and newsletters; has offices in Japan, Singapore, and Taiwan.

World Business Division
333 Ravenswood Ave.
Menlo Park, CA 94025
Tel: 415-859-5164

Supported by 400 corporate subscribers; monitors technological, industrial, economic, and political trends; provides strategic information to corporate managers worldwide; produces reports, newsletters, and databases.

STEWART TRADE DATA SERVICES CORP. (STDSC)
1000 Connecticut Ave., NW
Washington, D.C. 20036
Tel: 202-785-4194

Provides international and domestic trade information; has created several

databases, including one with trade statistics for Pacific Rim countries.

Underwriters Laboratories
333 Pfingsten Rd.
Northbrook, IL 60062
Tel: 312-272-8800

Washington Office
81818th St., NW
Suite 400
Washington, D.C. 20006
Tel: 292-296-7840

Conducts testing and certification service for electrical and electronic products.

Technical Assistance to Exporters
Underwriters Laboratories
1285 Walt Whitman Rd.
Melville, Long Island, NY 11747
Tel: 516-271-6200

Provides assistance to companies to insure that their electrical products will meet foreign standards.

Washington Information Group, Ltd.
P.O. Box 19352
20th Street Station
Washington, D.C. 20036
Tel: 204-463-7323

Conducts research for clients on companies and markets; conducts document retrieval from U.S. government and international organizations in Washington, D.C.; has special expertise in telecommunications.

Washington Researchers, Ltd.
2612 P St., NW
Washington, D.C. 20007
Tel: 202-333-3499

Conducts research for clients on companies and markets; offers seminars on "Researching Foreign Markets" and "Researching Foreign Companies"; publishes a monthly newsletter, the *International Information Report,* filled with information sources and tips on researching foreign markets and companies; $120 a year.

Weatherly and Associates
1330 Connecticut Avenue, NW
Suite 340

Washington, D.C. 20036
Tel: 202-775-8130

Assists clients with Asian business ventures.

Wharton Econometric Forecasting Associates, Inc.
150 Monument Rd.
Bala Cynwyd, PA 19004
Tel: 215-667-6000

Produces databases with industry and economic forecasts; gathers data on industries and countries; produces World Model and Pacific Basin databases; has offices in Chicago,

Houston, New York, and San Francisco.

WHK Industries, Inc.
1250 Oakmead Parkway, Suite 210
Sunnyvale, CA 94088-3599
Tel: 408-739-3723
Fax: 408-746-3630

Promotes technology transfer, foreign investment, and joint ventures in Korea, especially in

electronics and related industries. Publishers of the *Dr. Kim Report On Korea* newsletter.

Worden & Company
1331 Pennsylvania Ave.
Suite 507 North
Washington, D.C. 20004
Tel: 202-783-8440
Vice President, Holly Pollinger

Develops public-relations campaigns for companies or trade associations that have filed petitions for relief from unfair trade practices before the U.S. International Trade Commission or the U.S. Trade Representative; also does public-relations work for foreign clients.

Source: Updated from *International Business Handbook: Republic of Korea,* edited by Lorraine A. Underwood, Shirley G. Sullivan and Dennis L. Albrecht (Global Quest, Inc., Arlington, Virginia © 1988, reprinted by permission).

APPENDIX F

DIRECTORY OF PACIFIC BASIN INSTITUTIONS

ADB (ASIAN DEVELOPMENT BANK)

2330 Roxas Blvd., P.O. Box 789
Metro Manila, Philippines 2800

Membership

Afghanistan
Australia
Austria
Bangladesh
Belgium
Burma
Canada
Ceylon
China
Cook Islands
Denmark
Fiji
Finland
France
Germany
Hong Kong
India
Indonesia
Italy
Japan
Kampuchea
Kiribati
Korea
Laos
Malaysia
Maldives
Nepal
Netherlands
New Zealand
Norway
Pakistan
Papua New Guinea
Philippines
Singapore
Solomon Islands
Spain
Sri Lanka
Sweden
Switzerland
Taipei, China
Thailand
Tonga
United Kingdom
United States
Vietnam
Western Samoa

Purpose

The Bank's purpose is to promote and finance investment in the ESCAP region for development purposes.

Background

ADB is a regional development bank to loan funds provided by the developed industrial nation members to Asian LDC members. Organized in 1965 partly out of the interest and needs voiced by ESCAP (Economic and Social Commission for Asia and The Pacific of the United Nations) members, membership is open to all ESCAP members (and non-ESCAP developed nations). Interest rates are flexible and set separately for each loan. It coordinates its lending program to some degree with World Bank lending activities in the region. Operation is overseen by a board of governors with voting strength proportional to the capital contribution to the bank. Japan and the United States are the major capital contributors. Customarily, the president is a Japanese.

Effectiveness

The ADB has been effective in channeling development loans into Asia, which extends beyond the Pacific Area considered here. Its focus does not extend beyond this function of development loans, although it did coordinate a major study of Southeast Asia's Economy in the 1970s, which had an important effect on the region's approach to foreign economic policies.

ASEAN (ASSOCIATION OF SOUTH-EAST ASIAN NATIONS)

The ASEAN Secretariat, Jalan Sisingamangaraja
P.O. Box 2072, Jakarta, Indonesia

Membership

Brunei
Indonesia
Malaysia
Philippines
Singapore
Thailand

Purpose

ASEAN's goals are the acceleration of economic growth and cultural progress among its members, cooperation on agriculture and industry, expansion of trade, and development of a common negotiating front toward major trading nations.

Background

ASEAN was established in 1967 at Bangkok, succeeding ASA (Association of Southeast Asia), which consisted of Malaysia, the Philippines, and Thailand. Its original purpose was to reduce regional tensions and promote cooperative economic development. Unity was intended to give the region a stronger voice in the direction of outside development and aid toward regional priorities; it also grew out of some dissatisfaction with ESCAP. ASEAN operates with annual meetings, including ministerial level representatives from member nations, plus permanent (standing) groups on specific topics under the standing committees.

Effectiveness

In the early 1970s, ASEAN was considered to be in a transformation period and not yet a fully effective organization. With the American withdrawal from Vietnam, ASEAN rapidly emerged as an important regional grouping and has made advances in developing a common frame in bargaining with other

countries. It has a permanent secretariat based in Indonesia. The United States makes ASEAN a central reference point in forming its Southeast Asia policies.

ESCAP (ECONOMIC AND SOCIAL COMMISSION FOR ASIA AND THE PACIFIC OF THE UNITED NATIONS)

United Nations Building, Bangkok, Thailand

Membership

Afghanistan
Australia
Bangladesh
Bhutan
Brunei
Burma
China
Cook Islands
Democratic Kampuchea
Fiji
France
Gilbert Islands
Hong Kong
India
Indonesia
Iran
Japan
Korea
Laos
Malaysia
Maldives
Mongolia
Nauru
Nepal
The Netherlands
New Zealand
Pacific Islands
Pakistan
Papua New Guinea
Philippines
Samoa
Singapore
Socialist Republic of Vietnam
Solomon Islands
Sri Lanka
Taiwan
Thailand

Tonga
United Kingdom
United States
USSR
Western Samoa

Purpose

The Commission was established to initiate and participate in measures for facilitating economic and social development in Asia and the Pacific and for strengthening relations among those nations, and between them and the rest of the world.

Background

Formerly this commission was titled ECAFE (Economic Commission for Asia and the Far East), which was established in 1947. It was an original contact point in the move to establish ADB. In its deliberations, the commission covers a wide range of issues and projects. ECAFE was virtually the only semi-regional organization (along with the Colombo Plan) until the 1960s. ESCAP has established a number of subsidiary bodies, including the Asian Center for Development Administration, Asian Highway Coordinating Committee, Asian Institute for Economic Development and Planning, Asian Statistical Institute, the Committee for Coordination of Joint Prospecting for Mineral Resources in the Asian Offshore Area, and the Typhoon Committee.

Effectiveness

ESCAP has been criticized somewhat for failure to coordinate with other regional organizations, although it is currently revising its approach. Among its achievements in the past have been setting up the Asian Development Bank, and the development of the Mekong Basin and the Asian highway.

PAFTAD (PACIFIC TRADE AND DEVELOPMENT CONFERENCE)

Australia-Japan Research Centre, Research School of Pacific Studies Australian National University, P.O. Box 4, Canberra ACT 2601 Australia

Membership

PAFTAD is guided by a steering committee of members from Australia, Japan, Canada, Southeast Asia, and the United States. Participants from other Pacific countries have been involved in its meetings.

Purpose

PAFTAD promotes policy-oriented academic study and discussion of Pacific Area economic issues. It serves as the major intellectual resource for those in the Pacific area interested in the analysis of regional economic prospects.

Background

This is an informal private academic conference series originally begun in 1968 with Japanese Foreign Ministry support to consider a proposal for a Pacific Free Trade Area. Seventeen conferences have been held since that time in different Pacific countries, involving a wide group of policy-interested economists, to discuss regional foreign economic policy issues mainly among the Pacific Five and Western Pacific developing economies. Some conferences have, however, included Latin America and Soviet participation.

Effectiveness

The conference series has brought together area economists and stimulated academic research on the Pacific Area. It does not have direct policy impact, but provides indirect input into policymaking through its published work, the policy activities of participants, and the information and perspectives gained by officials of the various governments in attendance at the Conference as observers.

PBEC (PACIFIC BASIN ECONOMIC COUNCIL)

222 Kearny Street, Suite 604 San Francisco, CA 94118, (415) 788-6992

Membership

Member Committees, comprising major business firms, exist in the following countries:

Australia
Canada
Japan
Korea
New Zealand
Taiwan
United States

Purpose

PBEC exists to strengthen economic and business relations among its approximately 850 members. It is dedicated to the expansion of trade and investment through free markets and open investment policies.

Background

PBEC was organized in 1967, holding its first meeting in 1968. Approximately 300 PBEC members attended the most recent General Meeting in May 1988. A private group, PBEC holds annual meetings with a permanent secretariat located in San Francisco.

Effectiveness

PBEC has increased business interest and understanding of Pacific Basin needs and problems. It has increased communications between government leaders and business leaders and it serves as a mechanism for senior business leaders in the Pacific countries to come to know each other personally.

PECC (PACIFIC ECONOMIC COOPERATION CONFERENCE)

1988–1989 Secretariat: New Zealand National Committee for Pacific Economic Cooperation c/o Ministry of Foreign Affairs Private Bag, Wellington New Zealand

Membership

PECC has member committees and institutions located in:

Australia
Brunei
Canada
China
Indonesia
Japan
Korea
Malaysia
New Zealand
Pacific Islands
Philippines
Singapore
Taipei (Chinese)
Thailand
United States

(PBEC and PAFTAD are represented in Standing Committee and Coordinating Group meetings.)

Purpose

The PECC exists to bring senior government, business, and private institutional leaders together to examine key problems and issues influencing regional economic growth. It identifies regional interests in global issues, as well, and generally acts to facilitate regional cooperation in specific economic sectors.

Background

The PECC began in Canberra in September 1980 at the suggestion of the Prime Ministers of Japan and Australia. Since Canberra, PECC General Meetings have been held approximately every 18 months in various Pacific Rim locations, the most recent being PECC VI in Osaka, Japan.

Effectiveness

The PECC is increasingly viewed as the nucleus of a Pacific economic organization. With the establishment of a Central Fund to support stronger participation by developing countries, the organization appears poised for further institutionalization, including perhaps a permanent rather than rotating secretariat. It has been especially active in formulating Pacific positions to produce substantive progress in the Uruguay Round of GATT trade negotiations.

PECC MEMBERS

Australia

National Pacific Co-operation Committee of Australia
c/o Australia-Japan Research Centre
Research School of Pacific Studies
Australian National University
GPO Box 4, Canberra ACT
2601, Australia
Tel: (61) -062-47-3877, 49-4387
Fax: (61) -062-47-9078

Brunei

(No National Committee has yet been established. To be contacted through the local Embassy of Brunei, Darussalam.)

Canada

Canadian National Committee on Pacific Economic Cooperation
c/o The Canadian Chamber of Commerce
55 Metcalfe Street, Suite 1160
Ottawa, Ontario K1P BN4
Canada
Tel: 613-238-4000
Fax: 613-238-7643

China

China National Committee for Pacific Economic Cooperation
c/o China Institute of International Studies
Toutiao, Taijichang, Beijing, China 100005
Tel: (86) -1-54-9483
Fax: (86) 5123744

Indonesia

Indonesian National Committee for Pacific Economic Cooperation
c/o Centre for Strategic and International Studies
Jalan Tanah Abang III/23-27
Jakarta 10160, Indonesia
Tel: (62)-021-356S32/5,3809637/9
Fax: (62)-021-375317

Japan

Japan National Committee for Pacific Economic Cooperation
c/o Japan Institute of International Affairs
1-2-20, Toranomon, Minato-ku
Tokyo 105, Japan
Tel: (81) -03-501-3277
Fax: (81)-03-501-3270

Korea

Korea National Committee for Pacific Economic Cooperation
c/o Korea Development Institute
P.O. Box 113, Cheong Ryang
Seoul 131, Korea
Tel:(82)-02-960-5164, 967-8811
Fax:(82)-02-961-5092

Malaysia

Malaysian National Committee for Pacific Economic Cooperation
c/o Institute of Strategic and International Studies
No. 1, Jalan Sultan Salahuddin
P.O. Box 12424
50778 Kuala Lumpur, Malaysia
Tel:(60) -03-2 93-9439, 9366
Fax: (60)-03-243-6971

New Zealand

New Zealand Committee for Pacific Economic Cooperation
c/o Ministry of Foreign Affairs
Private Bag, Wellington
New Zealand
Tel: (64) -04-728-877
Fax: (64)-04-729-596

Pacific Island Nations

South Pacific Bureau for Economic Co-operation
G.P.O. Box 856, Suva, Fiji
Tel: (679)-312600, (direct)302375
Fax: (679)-302204

The Philippines

Philippine Pacific Economic Cooperation Committee
P.O. Box 10196
Makati Commercial Center
Metro Manila, Philippines
Tel: (63)-2-816-2664/5
Fax: (63) 2-819-2508

Singapore

Singapore National Committee for Pacific Economic Cooperation
c/o Dept. of Economics and Statistics
National University of Singapore
Kent Ridge, Singapore 0511
Tel: (65)-7723941, 7723961
Fax: (65)-7770751

Chinese Taipei

Chinese Taipei Pacific Economic Cooperation Committee
c/o Taiwan Institute of Economic Research
11 Fl., 178, Nanking East Rd. Sec. 2
Taipei, Taiwan
Tel: (886)-02-507-3980
Fax: (886) -02-506-1945

Thailand

Thailand National Committee for Pacific Economic Cooperation
c/o International Center
Ministry of Foreign Affairs
Saranrom Place
Bangkok 10200, Thailand
Tel: (66)-2-221-2883, 9171, ext. 230
Fax: (66) -2-224-7095

USA

United States National Committee for Pacific Economic Cooperation
1755 Massachusetts Ave., N.W.
Suite 420-421
Washington, D.C. 20036
Tel: 202-745-7444
Fax: 202-4S2-8149

PAFTAD

Pacific Trade and Development Conference Secretariat
c/o Australia-Japan Research Centre
Research School of Pacific Studies
Australian National University
G.P.O. Box 4

Canberra ACT
2601, Australia
Tel: (61) -062-47-3877, 49-4387
Fax: (61) -062-47-9078

PBEC

Pacific Basin Economic Council
World Affairs Center
312 Sutter Street
Suite 610,
San Francisco, CA 94108, U.S.A.
Tel: 415-788-6992
Fax: 415-788-0147

SPC (SOUTH PACIFIC COMMISSION)

P.O. Box D5, Noumea, New Caledonia

Membership

Australia
Fiji
France
Nauru
New Zealand
Papua New Guinea
Solomon Islands
Tuvalu
United Kingdom
United States
Western Samoa

Purpose

The Commission's purpose is to promote the economic and social welfare and advancement of the peoples of the South Pacific region.

Background

The Commission was established by an agreement signed in Canberra, Australia in 1947. It holds annual conferences attended by representatives of the Commission with equal voting powers.

Effectiveness

Although the Commission has contributed much to the South Pacific in terms of research on development problems and providing development assistance, it remains somewhat stigmatized by its establishment in the immediate post-World War II era when some islands had yet to achieve their independence from their colonial overseers. The Commission's reluctance to tackle some of the more sensitive political issues in the region, such as fishing rights of the distant metropolitan nations, was a significant factor in the movement to create the South Pacific Forum.

SPF (SOUTH PACIFIC FORUM)

G.P.O. Box 856, Suva, Fiji

Membership

Australia
Cook Islands
Federated States of Micronesia
Fiji
Gilbert Islands
Marshall Islands
Nauru
New Zealand
Niue
Papua New Guinea
Tuvalu
Tonga
Western Samoa

Purpose

The Forum facilitates cooperation and consultation between its members on trade, economic development, transportation, tourism, and other related matters.

Background

The South Pacific Forum is the gathering of heads of government of the independent and self-governing states of the South Pacific. Its first meeting was held in August 1971. It has a Secretariat and a committee formed of one member from each participating country. Australia and New Zealand each contribute one third the budget and the island countries the rest. Until September 1988, the Secretariat of the Forum was known as the South Pacific Bureau for Economic Cooperation, or SPEC.

Effectiveness

The Forum provides the major intergovernmental consultative mechanism within the South West Pacific and has been partially successful in more effective representation of the interests of the small states and dependencies toward the larger Pacific nations.

SOURCE: Pacific Economic Cooperation Conference. For more information, contact: U.S. National Committee for Pacific Economic Cooperation, c/o The Asia Foundation, P.O. Box 3223, San Francisco, CA 941119.

APPENDIX G

PACIFIC RIM INFORMATION NETWORKS

ACCESS: A SECURITY INFORMATION SERVICE

1730 M St., NW, Suite 605
Washington, D.C. 20036 USA
Tel: 202-785-6630

ACCESS (established 1985) is a nonprofit, nonadvocacy clearinghouse on international peace and security issues. Its special attribute is its intent to provide a comprehensive view of opinions and analyses on these issues, and not to endorse any position. ACCESS is an inquiry service, available to any individual or organization which chooses to use it. Information is available only through personal contact with ACCESS (by telephone or letter) not via computer. ACCESS maintains an internal database of 1400 organizations in 70 countries to provide responses to questions concerning security issues. The following is a sampling of the information contained in the database: regional conflicts, arms control and disarmament, East–West and North–South relations, economic dimensions of security, and alternative security concepts.

Individual rates are set at $30/year. ($45 non-U.S.); small nonprofit organizations, $75/year. ($90 non-U.S.); and large nonprofit organizations, $150/year. ($175 non-U.S.).

NETWORK (WORLD TRADE CENTER OF SAN FRANCISCO)

110 Sutter St., Suite 408
San Francisco, California 94104 USA
Telephone: 415-392-2705

This service is oriented toward commercial users. It allows users affiliated with World Trade Centers to exchange messages, locate services and products offered by other members, and post information related to global sales opportunities. Access to the system is via private computer, with modem, over ordinary telephone lines. The system is offered in four languages, and reaches 800 cities in 64 countries. Calls to the system are usually free because they are local, but users pay the cost of other transactions (i.e., sending electronic messages, and posting messages and reading full-text advertisements on the bulletin board). Network charges range from $25 for posting a one-screen advertisement, to $1.25 per 1000 characters to exchange messages, to $0.25 to read the full text of advertisements run by other members.

OLIADS

Intellibanc Corp.
2214 Torrance Blvd.
Torrance, California 90501
Telephone: 213-618-6900

This is a commercial service that screens thousands of international export and project opportunities, locates foreign companies for direct sales or joint ventures, determines the best source of financing for exporters, and helps users locate the largest and fastest growing foreign markets for their products.

PACIFIC CONNECTIONS

Pacific Rim Commercial Exchange Program (PRCEP)
Management Development Institute
School of Business Administration
California State University, Sacramento
6000 J Street
Sacramento, California 95819 USA
Tel: 916-278-7141, 6346

The purpose of PRCEP (established in 1987) is to improve the quality and quantity of Pacific Rim commerce in California. *Pacific Connections,* an electronic journal, is one part of the PRCEP program. It has three goals: to provide easy access to Pacific Rim commercial information; to serve as a single source of information for groups monitoring others active in promoting Asia-Pacific commerce; and to act as a forum for discussion among those active in or interested in Pacific Rim commerce. Although the basic orientation is toward the business community, PRCEP will also contain information useful to the noncommercial user.

Users can access the system with a Macintosh computer. There is a one-time $300 sign-on charge and a $50/hour user fee. The system utilizes the VAX mainframe, and a database written with *Oracle*. U.S. users can access this system via Telenet, and overseas users via Tymnet.

PACIFIC INFORMATION EXCHANGE

Asia Pacific Foundation of Canada
666-999 Canada Place
Vancouver, British Columbia
Canada V6C 3E1
Tel: 604-684-5986

The Asia Pacific Foundation of Canada established the Pacific Information Exchange (PIE) to provide information to assist the Canadian economic sector in pursuing Pacific Rim trade opportunities. PIE is a network of people, institutions, associations, and organizations, and is a national reference and referral service for the Canadian public. The main components of PIEs Asia-Pacific Information Bank are the following: organizations which provide funding, services, and information about the region (currently 400, including associations, government agencies, universities, and international organizations); specialists in Asia-Pacific studies (over 1400 in Canadian universities); education courses offered by Canadian universities on Pacific Rim topics; and international databases (over 300), including analysis of Asia-Pacific content and effectiveness for Canadian firms.

Users may utilize the Asia-Pacific Information Bank either by direct request to foundation staff via telephone or letter, or by subscription. The latter method allows the user to have a copy of the databank software for use onsite with a personal computer. As of fall 1989, dialup access is available through arrangement with InfoGlobe, one of the largest Canadian database vendors.

The Asia-Pacific Information Bank maintains its databanks through the assistance of Resource Centers across Canada. These centers include the Atlantic Provinces Economic Council (Halifax, Nova Scotia), The Banff Centre School of Management (Banff, Alberta), Centre d'Etudes de L'Asie de L'Est (Montreal, Quebec), Institute of Asian Research (University of British Columbia, Vancouver), and Joint Centre for Asia Pacific Studies (University of Toronto—York University, Toronto, Ontario). Users of the system include businesses, government officials, educators, trade association administrators, and librarians.

PACIFIC RIM DATA BANK INTERNATIONAL PROGRAM

Pacific Rim Relations
University of Utah
252 Orson Spencer Hall
Salt Lake City, Utah 84112 USA
Tel: 801-581-6267

Established in 1988, this system focuses on development of international trade relations. It provides information about U.S. relations with the Pacific region, and contains economic and demographic statistics for Asian-Pacific and other nations. The system also maintains information on export firms for the state of Utah; it expects to add statistical information from the United Nations, World Bank, Government of Singapore, and the European Community. The system utilizes a UNIX minicomputer, and has a custom-designed database written in C language. The database is presently structured for access at no charge through academic Internet network accounts; business community subscription use is being considered.

RESOURCES AND INFORMATION PROGRAM

Research Institute for Asia and the Pacific
University of Sydney
Sydney 2006 NSW
Australia
Tel: 02-692-2805

The Research Institute is a newly established university unit. The focus is on Asia-Pacific research, and serves as a contact point for the business community and the community at large. The "Resources and Information Program" is one of five institute programs. The staff plan to develop Asia-Pacific databases, and other bibliographic and information services, to provide more resources to the business, government, and academic communities than are currently available from Australian libraries and research centers.

SOVSET

Soviet Studies Program
Center for Strategic and International Studies
1800 K St., NW, Washington, D.C. 20006 USA
Tel: 202-887-0200

Established in 1984, SOVSET is a computer network serving the Soviet and East European affairs community. It currently links over 500 members worldwide, chiefly in Europe and the United States. SOVSET services include: (1) electronic mail (private, one-to-one electronic mail system allows members to send messages, drafts, or research papers to individual SOVSET members or to a number of members simultaneously); (2) computer conferencing on 32 topics (e.g., arms control, foreign affairs, nationalities, domestic priorities, etc.); and (3) data library—full-text articles from daily and weekly sources on Soviet and East European political and economic news, including sources such as Radio Free Europe, Radio Liberty (Soviet media); reports from the Kennan Institute for Advanced Russian Studies in Washington, D.C.; and various periodical sources such as the *PlanEcon Report*.

SOVSET charges a flat $40/hour connection fee, discounted to $25 for students and academics. Overseas users may have to pay additional communications charges (about $10/hour). The service is accessible with virtually any mainframe or personal computer through Compuserve, Tymnet, BITNET, and Telenet. Soviet nationals are excluded from access to SOVSET. This service is offered in collaboration with the University of Arizona. SOVSET utilizes the university mainframe computer.

SOURCE: Asia Foundation Center for Asian Pacific Affairs.

ASIA PACIFIC INFORMATION NETWORK (APIN)

The Asia Foundation Center for Asian Pacific Affairs
P.O. Box 3223, San Francisco, California 94119
Tel: 415-982-4640; Fax: 415-391-8863

The San Francisco-headquartered Asia Foundation Center for Asian Pacific Affairs is proceeding with plans for the Asia Pacific Information Network (APIN). APIN strives to build broader-based linkages among nonprofit organizations focused on contemporary Pacific Rim economic, foreign affairs, and strategic policy issues. The aim of the network is to encourage more regularized communication among key institutions and individuals in the Asia-Pacific public-policy field.

SOURCE: APIN.

Appendix H

ASIAN ADVERTISING, MARKETING, AND PUBLIC RELATIONS FIRMS

THE MULTINATIONAL AD AGENCIES

Asatsu Inc.

Wholly owned by Asatsu Inc., Japan. Offices in Hong Kong, Singapore, Bangkok, Taiwan, and Japan (Tokyo, Osaka, Nagoya, Fukuoka, Sapporo Sendai, Hiroshima, Okayama and Takamatsu).

Major regional accounts include: Hitachi, Universal Cars, Nissin Foods, Maxell Jusco Stores, Konica, Four Seas Mercantile, and JCB.

Address:
Asatsu International (HK), Ltd.
1 9/F 11 I Leighton Rd.
Causeway Bay
Hong Kong.
Tel: 895-2806
Fax: 576-4762

N.W. Ayer

Partners associates in Hong Kong (Lee Davis Ayer), Indonesia (Matari Advertising), Japan (Chuo Senko Advertising), Malaysia (Francis Lim, Zukifli & Ayer), the Philippines (Advertising & Marketing Associates), Taiwan (DIK-Ocean), and Thailand (Synergie Communications Co., Ltd.).

Major regional accounts include: Bristol Myers, Iberia Airlines, and Nordica.

Address:
Worldwide Plaza
825 Eighth Avenue
New York, NY 100 19-7498, USA
Tel: (212) 474-5000
Tlx: (023) 177307
Fax: (212) 474-5400

Backer Spielvogel Bates

Wholly owned subsidiaries in Hong Kong, Singapore and Taiwan. Majority holdings in Malaysia (48.9%), Thailand, and Japan. Minority holding in Korea (Diamond Advertising). Affiliates in the Philippines (Ace-Compton) and Indonesia (Bates Mulia).

Major regional accounts include: BAT, De Beers, DHL Effem Foods (Mars), Ericsson, Everyready Battery Company, Hongkong Bank, Mandarin Oriental Hotel Group, Pfizer, Selleys, Shakeys, Tambrands, and Thomas Cook.

Address:
Backer Spielvogel Bates
IO/F Malaysia Building
50 Gloucester Road
Hong Kong

Tel: 823-011 1
Tlx: 65321 BATES HX
Fax: 861-3935

The Ball Partnership

A member of the Eurocom WCRS Della Femina Ball (EWDB) Group plc. Offices in Hong Kong, Singapore, Bangkok, Taiwan, Sydney, Melbourne, and Auckland.

Major regional accounts include: British American Tobacco, City Chain, Hewlett-Packard, Puma, BMW, and World Gold Council.

Address:
The Ball Partnership
3/F 153 Walker St.
North Sydney
NSW 2060, Australia
Tel: (2) 963-7711
Tlx: 74443 BALL AA
Fax: (2)957-5766

Address:
The Ball Partnership
12 F Vicwood Plaza
199 Des Voeux Rd.
Central, Hong Kong
Tel: 544-3800
Tlx: 62517 Ball HX
Fax: 845-54 11

Batey Ads

Offices in Singapore, Hong Kong, Kuala Lumpur, and Los Angeles.

Major regional accounts include: BP, Chase Manhattan Bank (Corporate), Malayan Breweries, Omni Hotels Asia-Pacific, Singapore Airlines, Singapore Tourist Promotion Board, UOB Group, Dragonair Hongkong, R.J. Reynolds, Hong Kong Parkview, Ovaltine, Tangs.

Address:
Batey Ads
61 B New Bridge Road
Singapore O 105
Tel: 532 2288
Tlx: RS 28565 BATEY
Fax: 532-6773

BBDO Asia Pacific

Majority holdings in Hong Kong (BBDO Hong Kong, Ltd.), Singapore (BBDO Advertising Pte., Ltd.) Taiwan (Stentor/BBDO Advertising Ltd.), and Malaysia (Wings/BBDO Worldwide Sdn Bhd). Minority holdings in Japan (Asatsu, Inc.), the Philippines (PAC BBDO Worldwide, Inc.), India (R.K. Swamy/BBDO Advertising Pvt., Ltd.), Australia and New Zealand (Clemenger BBDO, Ltd.). Associated network agencies in Korea (L.G. Ad, Inc.), Pakistan (Manhattan International Pvt., Ltd.), and Indonesia (P.T. Sulisto, Inc.)

Major regional accounts include: Apple Computer, Hyatt Hotels, Philips Polaroid, Pepsi, CPC International, Cartier, Caltex Alfred Dunhill, Visa, and Delta Airlines

Address:
BBDO Asia Pacific, Ltd.
30/F Bank of China Tower
1 Garden Rd.
Central, Hong Kong
Tel: 820- 1888
Tlx: 66806 BBDO HX
Fax: 877-2 164

Bozell

Offices in Hong Kong, Japan, Korea, Taiwan, Australia, Singapore, Malaysia, and Sri Lanka. Affiliations in Thailand (Synergie), the Philippines (Atlas Bozell), and Indonesia (Matari).

Major regional accounts include: Merrill Lynch, Jacobs Suchard, Seiko, Samsung Malaysia Tourist Development, and Sunkist.

Address:
Bozell
Thongsia Building
30 Bideford Rd.
02-00 Singapore 0922
Tel: 732-2555
Tlx: 23382 BJKE RS
Fax: 733-8950

Bozell
1101 Citicorp Centre
18 Whitheld Rd.
Causeway Bay
Hong Kong
Tel: 807-5678
Tlx: 74383 BJKE HX
Fax: 807 3503,806-3846

Chiat Day/Mojo

Wholly owned subsidiaries in Hong Kong (regional office) and Singapore. Affiliations in Japan (Standard Advertising), Taiwan (Brain Advertising), Thailand (Spaulding & Associates), Malaysia (Union 45), Fiji (Wilson Addison), South Korea (Seoul Advertising), and Hong Kong (Lee Davis Ayer).

Major regional accounts include: Oberoi Hotel, Qantas Airways, Australian Tourist Commission, Koala Springs, Goodman Fielder Foods (Meadow Lea).

Address:
Chiat Day/Mojo
339 Military Rd.
Cremorne, NSW 2090
Australia

Tel: (2) 908-6666
Tlx: AA22342
Fax: (2) 953-5203

Chuo Senko Advertising

Offices in Japan (Osaka, Nagoya, Sapporo, Hiroshima, Fukuoka, Sendai, Takaoka, and Tokyo), Hong Kong (Chou Senko Advertising HK, Ltd.), Indonesia (PT Hikmad & Chusen), Thailand (Chou Senko Thailand Co., Ltd.), Singapore (Chou Senko Advertising (S) Pte., Ltd.), and Malaysia (Fortecomm Malaysia).

Major regional accounts include: Ajinomoto, Hitachi, TDK, and Wacoal.

Regional headquarters:
Chuo Senko Advertising Co., Ltd.
Chuo-ku Ginza Building
2-6-1 Ginza, Chuo-ku
Tokyo 104, Japan
Tel: (03) 562-0151
Tlx: CHUSENAD J282 10
Fax: (03) 535-3576

Chuo Senko Advertising (HK), Ltd.
Room 503
Silvercord
Tower 1, 30 Canton Rd.
Kowloon, Hong Kong
Tel: 721-1194
Tlx: 45615 CSAD HX
Fax: 72 1-0574

Daiko Advertising, Inc.

Offices in Osaka, Tokyo, Nagoya, Kyoto, Kobe, Fukuoka, Hiroshima, and a further 20 cities in Japan, Beijing, and New York (subsidiary). Subsidiary in Hong Kong (Daiko Communications Asia Co., Ltd.). Joint ventures in Tokyo with Grey USA (Grey-Daiko) and FCB USA (Daiko-FCB Impact). Affiliations in Seoul (Union Advertising) and the U.S. (Grey Advertising and Foote, Cone & Belding).

Major regional accounts include: Amada, Hitachi, Kogome, Suntory, Takeda Chemical, Kintetsu Group, Kao, Sekisui House, Cecile, Nihon Bunka Center, Japan Tobacco, Matsushita Electric.

Address:
Daiko Advertising, Inc.
3-39 Miyahara 4-chome
Yodogawa-ku
Osaka 532, Japan
Tel: (06) 392-8011
Fax: (06) 392-8230

Shuwa Shiba Park Building
2-4-1 Shiba Koen
Minato-ku
Tokyo 105, Japan
Tel: (03) 433-3121
Fax: (03) 433-5367

Daiko Communications Asia Co., Ltd.
Rooms 513–516
Sun Hung Kai Centre
30 Harbour Rd.
Hong Kong
Tel: 891-9688
Fax: 838-4896

D'Arcy Masius Benton & Bowles

Partnership in Hong Kong (50% in DMB&B Modern); majority holding in Singapore and Thailand; minority holding in South Korea (20% in Seoul Advertising Co., Ltd.); partnerships in Indonesia (Perwana VDMB&B), Malaysia (Spencer Azizul Advertising), the Philippines (Asia-West), and Taiwan (Tokyu Eastern International).

Major regional accounts include: American Tobacco, Anheuser-Busch (Budweiser Beer), Bonia, Bristol Myers, Burger King, East Asiatic Company, Effem Foods (Dolmio), Northwest Airlines, Philips, Procter & Gamble, and Richardson-Vicks.

Address:
DMB&B
10/F East Wing
Hennessy Centre

500 Hennessy Rd.
Causeway Bay
Hong Kong
Tel: 890-5340
Tlx: 65160 DMBB HX
Fax: 576-6480

DDB Needham Worldwide

Majority holdings in Hong Kong (75% in DDB Needham DIK) and Singapore (51% in DDa Needham DIK): minority holding in Malaysia (20% in Naga DDB Needham DIK): partnership in Taiwan (51% in DDB Needham, Taiwan); 51% in DDB Needham Thailand, minority holding in Thailand (10% in Far East Advertising); 60% of DDB Needham Japan, minority holding in Dai-ichi Kikaku (2%): affiliates in Korea (Daehong), India (Mudra No. 3), and the Philippines (PAC).

Major regional accounts include: Boots, China Airlines, Fuji, Martell, McDonald's, Michelin, Mobil, and Sara Lee. Goins in HK/region: Rothmans Far East, Sheraton Asia Pacific, Chase Manhattan Bank (HK only), and American Airlines.

Address:
DDB Needham Worldwide, Inc.
437 Madison Ave.
New York, NY 10022, USA
Tel: (212)415-2000
Tlx: 62794
Fax: (212)415355j3562/3282

Dentsu, Inc.

Wholly owned by Dentsu Inc., Japan. Offices in Japan (Tokyo and all major towns and cities), Hong Kong, Taiwan (Taipei), and China (Beijing and Shanghai). Subsidiaries in Thailand (Dentsu Thailand, Ltd.) and Australia (Dentsu Australia Pty, Ltd.).

List of major regional accounts not available.

Address:
Dentsu, Inc.
I-II Tsukiji
Chuo-ku
Tokyo 104, Japan
Tel: (813) S44-5599
Fax: (813) 546-2967

FCB International

Offices in Hong Kong (Foote, Cone & Belding), Japan (Daiko/FCB Impact and AccariiFCB), Indonesia (Focus/FCB), Malaysia (AP:Foote, Cone & Belding Sdn Bhd), the Philippines (Basic/Foote, Cone & Belding), and Thailand (Prakit & FCB). Exclusive affiliates in Singapore (Advertising Associates), South Korea (Geoson Advertising), and Taiwan.

Major international accounts handled in the Asia-Pacific region include: California Raisins, Campbell's Soup, Colgate Palmolive, Garuda Indonesian Airlines, Hawley & Hazel, Kimberly Clark, Mazda (Trucks), Nestle, 7-Eleven, Warner Lambert, and Wilkinson Sword.

Address:
FCB International
605 Mount Parker House
1111 Kings Rd.
Quarry Bay
Hong Kong
Tel: 886-0933
Tlx: 68375 FCBI HX
Fax: 568-5080

Grey Pacific

Offices in Australia (Canberra—Grey Canberra, Melbourne—Grey Melbourne, Sydney—Grey Advertising NSW), Hong Kong (People & Grey), India (Bombay, Calcutta, New Delhi, Madras, and Ahmedabad—Trikaya Grey), Japan (Tokyo—Grey Daiko), Malaysia (Kuala Lumpur—Grey Malaysia), New Zealand (Auckland, Wellington

—Grey New Zealand), the Philippines (Manila—Aspac & Grey), Singapore (Adcom & Grey and C.R. & Grey), Taiwan (Taipei—Hwa Wei & Grey), and Thailand (Bangkok—Amex & Grey). Affiliations in Indonesia (Jakarta—Binamark Indonesia), South Korea (Seoul—Union Advertising, Inc.), and Pakistan (Karachi—Blazon Advertising).

Major regional accounts include: Bayer, Beecham, Block, Bristol-Myers, Canon, Corning, General Foods, Mars, Procter & Gamble, Remington, Rothmans, U.S. Mint, and Wrigley.

Regional headquarters:
Grey Pacific
2013-1 B Shui On Centre
6-B Harbour Rd.
Hong Kong
Tel: 529-068S/865-5009
Tlx: 63930 PEOAD HX
Fax: 86 1-2827

Hakuhodo, Inc.

Wholly owned by Hakuhodo Inc. Japan. Offices in Hong Kong (Hakuhodo Hong Kong, Ltd.), Taiwan (Taipei—H&Y Communications, Inc.), Malaysia (Kuala Lumpur—Hakuhodo Malaysia Sdn Bhd), Singapore (Hakuhodo Singapore Pte, Ltd.), and Thailand (Bangkok—Hakuhodo Bangkok Co., Ltd., and Thai Hakuhodo Co., Ltd.).
List of major regional accounts not available.

Regional headquarters:
Thai Hakuhodo Co., Ltd.
11th Floor
Central Chidlom Tower
22 Soi Somkid
Ploenchit Rd.
Bangkok lOSOO, Thailand
Tel: 254-7031/2-8
Tlx: 82533 THAIHAK TH
Fax: 254-7042

HDM Worldwide

Wholly owned subsidiaries in Hong Kong, Singapore, Taiwan, and Thailand; majority holding in Malaysia (70% in DYR Sdn); minority holding in the Philippines (30% in Alcantara/DYR, Inc.); affiliates in India (India Rediffusion), Indonesia (Metro), and Pakistan (Spectrum).

Major regional accounts include: Adidas, Air Canada, Colgate Daimler Benz, Du Pont, Hitachi, Hong Kong Tourist Association, Jacobs Suchard, Japan Airlines, Kao, Kirin Beer, Minolta, Royal Canadian Mint, Swire, Unisys.

Address:
HDM, Ltd.
418 Mount Parker House
1111 King's Rd.
Hong Kong
Tel: 884-6668
Telex: 86012 DYRHK HX
Fax: 996 0999

Area headquarters:
HDM Worldwide
Tokyo, 10 Tsukiji
Chuo-ku
Tokyo 104, Japan
Tel: (3) 544-7137
Tlx: 26223 DENTSU J
Fax: (3) 545-5656

Leo Burnett

Wholly owned offices in Hong Kong, Taiwan, Singapore, and Thailand; majority holding in Japan (Leo Burnett Kyodo); minority holdings in Malaysia and the Philippines (Hemisphere Leo Burnett); affiliate office in India (Chaitra) and Korea (Dong Bang).

Major regional accounts include Cathay Pacific Airways, Philip Morris, Procter & Gamble, Regent International Hotels, United Airlines, Kellogg, United Distillers Group.

Address:
Leo Burnett, Ltd.
9/F Mount Parker House
1111 King's Rd.
Hong Kong
Tel: 567-4333
Telex: 75468 LEO HK HX
Fax: 885-3209

Lintas: Worldwide

Wholly owned subsidiaries in Hong Kong, Singapore, Malaysia, and Taiwan; majority holdings in Thailand (80%); 50/50 joint venture in Japan (Hakuhodo: Lintas); minority holding in the Philippines (30%); affiliations in Indonesia (P.T. Citra:Lintas) and Korea (Samhee Communications).

Major regional accounts include: Aliblia, Canon, Citibank, Diners Club, ICI, Inter-Continental Hotels, Johnson & Johnson, Lipton, Nabisco, NEC, Philips, Philippine Airlines, Rowntree Mackintosh, Sterling Drug, Tree Top, Unilever, Volvo, and Wander.

Address:
Lintas: Worldwide
6/F Sathorn Thani Building
North Sathorn Rd.
Bangkok 10500, Thailand
Tel: (2) 236-0266
Telex: 21587 LINTBKK TH
Fax: (2) 236-3298

Lintas: Worldwide
One Dag Hammarskjold Plaza
New York, NY 10017, USA
Tel: 605-8000
Telex: 422773
Fax: 838-2331

McCann-Erickson Worldwide

Wholly owned subsidiaries in Australia, Hong Kong, Malaysia, New Zealand, the Philippines, Singapore, and Thailand; majority holdings in Japan (McCann-Erickson Hakuhodo, Inc.) and Taiwan

(McCann-Erickson Taiwan); minority holdings in India (Tara Sinha Associates) and Malaysia (Multiara-McCann); affiliations in Indonesia (Graf k Advertising) and Pakistan (Paragon Advertising).

Major regional accounts include: Casio, Coca-Cola, Del Monte, Exxon/Esso, Gillette, Goodyear, General Motors, Levi Strauss, L'Oreal, Lufthansa, Nestle, Nabisco, R.J. Reynolds, and UPS.

Address:
McCann-Erickson Worldwide
Asia Pacific
Shin Aoyama Building East
1-1 Minami-Aoyama
1-chome
Minato-ku
Tokyo 107, Japan
Tel: (03) 746-8030
Telex: 2426611 MACADCJ
Fax: (03) 746-8017

Ogilvy & Mather Worldwide

Majority holdings in Thailand, Singapore, Malaysia, Hong Kong, and Taiwan; minority holdings in the Philippines (30% in Olbes, Ogilvy & Mather), India (40% in Ogilvy & Mather), and Korea (30% in Korad, Ogilvy & Mather); affiliations in Indonesia (PT Indo-Ad) and Pakistan (Interflow). Representative offices in Beijing and Shanghai, China.

Major regional accounts include: American Express, Philips, Seagram. Unilever, Guinness, Beecham, Kimberly-Clark, PepsiCo, Shell, BMW, Nestle, Chesebrough-Ponds, Kraft General Foods, Korean Air, Watsons, and Warner Lambert.

Address:
Ogilvy & Mather Worldwide
B/F Mount Parker House
Taikoo Shing
Hong Kong
Tel: S68-0161
Tlx: 86617 OMHK HX
Fax: 885-3510

Saatchi & Saatchi Advertising

Wholly owned subsidiaries in Singapore, Hong Kong, and Taiwan; majority holdings in Thailand, Korea, Malaysia, and Japan. Associates in the Philippines, Indonesia, and India.

Major regional accounts include: British Airways, The Peninsula Group, Procter & Gamble, Berger Paints, Jacobs Suchard, Sarah Lee, Toyota, and Courvoisier,

Address:
Saatchi & Saatchi Advertising
22/F Shui On Centre
6-8 Harbour Rd.
Wanchai, Hong Kong
Tel: 864-3333
Telex: 60625 COMAD HX
Fax: 865-1213/865-2602

J. Walter Thompson

Wholly owned subsidiaries in Japan, Hong Kong, the Philippines, Singapore, Taiwan, Thailand, Sydney, and Melbourne; majority holdings in New Zealand (Auckland and Wellington) and Malaysia (PTM Thompson): minority holdings in India (Contract Advertising), Sri Lanka (Thompson Lanka), Brisbane and Perth (Kestall McManis & Thompson); affiliates in Indonesia (Ad Force), India (Hindustan Thompson Associates), Pakistan (Asiatic Advertising Group), and Korea (Business World Services).

Major regional accounts include: Lever, Kodak, Nestle. R.J. Reynolds, IBM, Warner Lambert, Camus, Scott, Kelloggs, Kraft, General Foods, McDonnell Douglas, and Rolex.

Address:
J. Walter Thompson Co., Ltd.
10/F International Trade Building
Taipei World Trade Centre
333 Keelung Rd.
Sec. 1, Taipei
Taiwan
Tel: (2) 757-6228

Telex: 17062 JWT TPE
Fax: (2) 757-6096

Transphere International

Wholly owned subsidiaries in Berlin, Hong Kong, and Taiwan; associates in Japan and Singapore.

Major regional accounts include: California Pistachio Commission, Conner Peripherals, Data Preference, Fujitsu APD, Genstar, Netronix, and Tops.

Address:
608 Folsom St.
San Francisco, CA 94107, USA
Tel: (415) 243-8080
Fax: (415) 546-5252

PUBLIC RELATIONS: THE ASIAN NETWORKS

Ernest Beyl Public Relations, Inc.

Headquartered in San Francisco.
Major accounts include: Qantas Airways, Cathay Pacific Airways, Air Pacific, Seabourn Cruise Lines, Camtpon Place Hotel (San Francisco).

Contact:
Ernest Beyl, President
560 Pine St.
San Francisco, CA 94108
Tel: (415) 986-8255
Tlx: 297336 EBPR US
Fax: (415) 986-0429

Burson-Marsteller

Offices in Hong Kong, Malaysia, Singapore, South Korea, and Thailand; joint venture in Japan (51% in Dentsu Burson-Marsteller Co., Ltd.); partnership in China (China Global Public Relations Co.); affiliations in India (Roger Pereira Public Relations), Taiwan (United Pacific International), and the Philippines (Zorrilla & Partners).

Major regional accounts include: American Express, Du Pont, General

Motors, Industrial Development Board of Northern Ireland, Coca-Cola, Saudi Basic Industries Corp. (SABIC).

Regional office:
Burson-Marsteller Asia, Ltd.
23/F United Centre
95 Queensway, Hong Kong
Tel: 527-6725
Telex: 73995 BUMAR HX
Fax: 527-5360

GCI Group

Wholly owned by Grey Advertising, Inc. GCI Group partners in Hong Kong (GCI Hong Kong), Australia (Professional Public Relations Pty, Ltd.), Indonesia (Indo-PR), India (GCI Prof le), and Taiwan (GCI Hwa Wei); group associates in Malaysia/ Singapore (Bostock Mohammad Communication Strategies), Japan (Sun Creative Publicity), and Korea (Communications Korea).

List of major regional accounts not available.

Contact:
Joseph Spitzer, managing director
GCI Hong Kong
(Tel: 520-1268)

Richard Lazar, managing director
Professional Public Relations (Pty), Ltd.
Sydney
Tel: 8 18-4044

Head office:
GCI
777 Third Ave.
New York, NY 10017
USA
Tel: (212) 546-2200
Tlx: 15307 GREY UT
Fax: (212) 546-2381

Gibson Public Relations

Gibson Public Relations has companies in Singapore and Hong Kong, both of which are wholly

owned subsidiaries of London-based Shandwick plc, the world's largest independent (non-advertising agency owned) public relations consultancy group. Its Asian network includes Shandwick-owned consultancies in Japan (IPR Japan), Australia (IPR Australia), New Zealand (IPR New Zealand), Thailand (Presko), and Brunei. (Shandwick, Ltd., Brunei). Associate operations in South Korea, PRC, Taiwan, Malaysia, Indonesia, and the Philippines.

Major regional accounts include: Mars, Garuda Indonesia, Hayes Microcomputers, Australian Meat and Live-Stock Corp., Waddingtons International, Standard Chartered International Trustee, Ltd., Scimitar Asset Management Ltd., Egon Zehnder International, Telerate, Inc.

Address:
Gibson Public Relations (HK), Ltd.
12/F Printing House
6 Duddell St.
Central, Hong Kong
Tel: 524-1 106
Tlx: 66608 GPRHK HX
Fax: 868-0224

Gibson Public Relations (S) Pte, Ltd.
250 North Bridge Rd.
No. 12-04 Rames City Tower
Singapore 06 17
Tel: 339- 1333
Tlx: RS 28986 GIBSPR
Fax: 339-0559

Hill and Knowlton Asia, Ltd.

Wholly owned by Hill and Knowlton, Inc., headquartered in New York with 60 offices in 22 countries. The Asia Pacific operations have offices in Hong Kong, Beijing, Hawaii, Kuala Lumpur, Penang, Singapore, Taiwan, Tokyo, Australia (Sydney, Adelaide, Brisbane, Canberra, Melbourne, Perth), and New Zealand (Auckland Wellington).

Major regional accounts include: PepsiCo, Hannover Messe, Texas Instruments, Kodak, Patek Philippe,

Exchange, Unilever, Kellogg, Nestle, Heinz, Selleys Chemicals, Hutchison Whampoa, Ltd., Hutchison Telecommunications, Ltd.

Contact:
Charles Crawford, president and CEO
Asia Region
Tel: HK 894-6200

Anne Forrest, managing director
Hong Kong and China
Tel: HK 894-6240

Robert McNulty, general manager
Singapore
Tel: 338-5344

Keith Sargeant, managing director
Kuala Lumpur
Tel: 261-3788

David Chard, general manager
Taiwan
Tel: 736-9820

Joseph Grimes, president
Tokyo
Tel: 288-3671

Richard Tan, manager
Penang
Tel: 622-428

Clifton Kagawa, chairman and CEO
Hawaii
Tel: 521-5391

John Connolly, general manager
Australia and New Zealand
Tel: 231-3300

Regional office:
Hill and Knowlton
Asia Pacific
28/F Windsor House
311 Gloucester Rd.
Causeway Bay, Hong Kong
Tel: 894-6201
Tlx: 73904EWAHK HX
Fax: 576-3551

MA Public Relations

Wholly owned subsidiary of The Ketson Group plc. Offices in Hong Kong, Singapore, Manila, and Taipei.

Major regional accounts include: Philip Morris. Cathay Pacific, Upjohn Pharmaceuticals, The Royal Mint, Remy Martin, CMI.

Contact:
Bella Kwok/Paul Wood, group directors
Hong Kong
Tel: 566-4711

Eric Chan, general manager
Singapore
Tel: 225-7172

Evelyn Tatlonghari, general manager
Manila
Tel: 819-2624

Groline Sapnel, general manager
Taipei

Regional headquarters:
The JMA Group
19/F Sing Pao Building
101 Kings Rd.
Hong Kong
Tel: 566-47 11
Telex: 62483 PRJMA HX
Fax: 887- 1576

Ogilvy & Mather Public Relations

O&MPR operations in Hong Kong, China, India, Indonesia, Malaysia, the Philippines, Singapore, Taiwan and Thailand. Full service capabilities in Japan and Korea through associate relationships.

List of major regional accounts not available.

Regional office:
Ogilvy & Mather Public Relations
8/F Mount Parker House
Taikoo Shing, Hong Kong
Tel: 567-4461
Tlx: HX 86205 OMHK
Fax: 885-3227/567-3545

Rowland Worldwide Asia/Pacific

Rowland Worldwide, an independent subsidiary or Saatchi & Saatchi plc, is the fifth-largest public relations firm in the world. Offices in Australia (Rowland Neilson McCarthy)—Sydney, Melbourne, Canberra, Darwin, Brisbane, Perth, and Adelaide—Hong Kong (TurnerSpurrier/Rowl and Limited), Taipei, Taiwan (Rowland Gaynor Public Relations), Tokyo, Japan (The Rowland Company). Affiliate offices in Singapore (Hickson Public Relations) and Korea (KPR).

List of major regional accounts are not available.

Address:
Rowland Neilson McCarthy
18 Argyle St.
Sydney, NSW 2000
Australia
Tel: 241-3131
Fax: 22 1-2676

TurnerSpurrier/Rowland Limited,
4/F, 2-10 Lyndhurst Terrace
Hong Kong
Tel: 543-8882
Tlx: 82840 TSPUR
Fax: 543-3030

Rowland Gaynor Public Relations
17-1 127 Flushing South Rd.
Sec. 1, Taipei
Taiwan, ROC
Tel: 721-0286
Fax: 772-8534

The Rowland Company
6/F Izumikan Sanbancho Building
3-8 Sanbancho
Chiyoda-ku
Tokyo 102 Japan
Tel: 221-8511
Fax: 221-8510

SOURCE: *Asian Advertising & Marketing Magazine,* Hong Kong.

APPENDIX I

PACIFIC RIM REGIONAL PUBLICATIONS

Architects & Designers Catalogue
Commercial and domestic
architecture and design.
Far East Trade Press, Ltd.
2/F Kai Tak Commercial Bldg.
317 Des Voeux Rd.
Central, Hong Kong
Tel: 453026
Fax: 446979
Annual, English

Asia Computer Weekly
News about Asia's computer
industry.
Asian Business Press Pte, Ltd.
100 Beach Rd.
No. 26–00 Shaw Towers
Singapore 0718
Tel: 2943366
Fax: 2985534
Fortnightly, English

Asia Magazine
Regional feature stories.
South China Morning Post (HK)
6/F Morning Post Bldg.
Tong Chong St.
Quarry Bay, Hong Kong
Tel: 652332
Fax: 659441
Fortnightly, English

Asia Pacific Aerospace
Features and news about the region's
aerospace industry in Pacific Rim.
Asian Business Press Pte, Ltd.
100 Beach Rd.

No. 26–00 Shaw Towers
Singapore 0718
Tel: 2943366
Fax: 2985534
Monthly, English

Asia Pacific Forest Industries
Covers logging, processing, and
furniture industries in Asia.
Safan Publishing Sdn Bhd
Suite 2403, 24/F Plaza See Hoy Chan
Jalan Raja Chulan
50200 Kuala Lumpur
Malaysia
Fax: 2384064
Monthly, English

Asia Pacific Leather Directory
Lists 6,000 leather-related companies.
Asia Pacific Directories, Ltd.
6/F Wah Hen Commercial Centre
381 Hennessy Rd.
Hong Kong
Tel: 8936377
Fax: 8935752
Annual, English

Asia Pacific Leather Yearbook
Covers leather trade in 15 Asian
countries.
Asia Pacific Directories, Ltd.
6/F Wah Hen Commercial Centre
381 Hennessy Rd.
Hong Kong
Tel: 8936377
Fax: 8935752
Annual, English

Asia Technology
News about the latest technology
with a focus on Asia.
Review Publishing Company, Ltd.
4/F Centre Point
181 Gloucester Rd.
Wanchai, Hong Kong
or GPO Box 160
Hong Kong
Tel: 8328300
Fax: 8653440
Monthly, English

Asia Travel Trade
Covers travel industry news in 14
Asian countries along with
destination reports.
Interasia Publications, Ltd.
190 Middle Rd.
No. 14–08 Fortune Centre
Singapore 0718
Tel: 3397300
Fax: 3398521
Monthly, English

*Asia Pacific Broadcasting &
Telecommunications*
Covers radio, television and
telecommunications industry.
Asian Business Press Pte, Ltd.
100 Beach Rd.
No. 26–00 Shaw Towers
Singapore 0718
Tel: 2943366
Fax: 2985534
Monthly, English

Asia-Pacific Dental News
Reports on dental industry.
Adrienne Yo Publishing, Ltd.
4/F Vogue Bldg.
67 Wyndham St.
Central, Hong Kong
Tel: 253133
Fax: 8106512
Quarterly, English and Chinese

Asian Advertising & Marketing
Covers advertising, marketing, and
media industry in Asia.
Travel & Trade Publishing (Asia),
Ltd.
16/F, Capitol Centre
5-19 Jardines Bazaar
Causeway Bay, Hong Kong
Tel: 89903067
Fax: 8952378
Monthly, English

Asian Aviation
Covers aviation, aerospace, and
defense industries.
Asian Aviation Publications
Maritime House, Cantonment Rd.
Singapore 0208
Tel: 2255444
Fax: 2258390
Monthly, English

Asian Business
Regional business magazine covering
investing, banking, finance, corporate
profiles, industries, travel business,
and marketing.
Far East Trade Press, Ltd.
3/F Kai Ta Commercial Bldg.
317 Des Voeux Rd.
Central, Hong Kong
Tel: 457200
Fax: 446979
Monthly, English

Asian Computer Directory
Lists computer companies and
installations in 14 Asian countries.
Computer Publications, Ltd.
3/F Wilson House
19 Wyndham St.
Central, Hong Kong
Tel: 223185
Fax: 8684511
Monthly, English

Asian Computer Monthly
Covers region's computer industry.
Computer Publications, Ltd.
3/F Wilson House
19 Wyndham St.
Central, Hong Kong
Tel: 223185
Fax: 8684511
Monthly, English

Asian Defence Journal
Covers region's defense industry,
military technology, and strategy.
Syed Hussain Publications Sdn Bhd
61 A & B Jelan Dato Haji Eusoff
Damai Complex
P.O. Box 10836
50726 Kuala Lumpur
Malaysia
Tel: 4420852, 4428585
Fax: 4427840
Monthly, English

Asian Electricity
Covers electrical industry in region,
with focus on distributors, agents,
and electrical engineers.
Reed Business Publishing, Ltd.
5001 Beach Rd.
No. 06-12 Golden Mile Complex
Singapore 0719
Tel: 2913188
Fax: 2913180
11 issues a year, English

Asian Electronics Engineer
Covers global electronics industry
from an Asian perspective.
Trade Media, Ltd.
11/F Amber Comm Bldg.
70-74 Morrison Hill Rd.
Hong Kong
Tel: 727253
Fax: 729818
Monthly, English/Chinese, English/
Korean

Asian Exporters Electronics Directory
Covers region's electronics industry.
Asian Exporters Publication, Ltd.
10/F Sing Ho Finance Bldg.
166-168 Gloucester Rd.
Wanchai, Hong Kong

Tel: 8912799
Fax: 831699
Bi-annual, English

*Asian Exporters Gifts & Houseware
Directory*
Targets international importers and
exporters.
Asian Exporters Publication, Ltd.
10/F Sing Ho Finance Bldg.
166-168 Gloucester Rd.
Wanchai, Hong Kong
Tel: 8912799
Fax: 831699
Annual, English

*Asian Exporters Jewellery & Watch
Directory*
Editorial geared to overseas
importers.
Asian Exporters Publication, Ltd.
10/F Sing Ho Finance Bldg.
166-168 Gloucester Rd.
Wanchai, Hong Kong
Tel: 8912799
Fax: 831699
Quarterly, English

Asian Exporters Magazine
Targets international merchandisers.
Asian Exporters Publication, Ltd.
10/F Sing Ho Finance Bldg.
166-168 Gloucester Rd.
Wanchai, Hong Kong
Tel: 8912799
Fax: 831699
Bimonthly, English

Asian Furniture
Covers furniture manufacturing
industry.
Asian Business Press/Benn
Publications Plc
100 Beach Rd.
No. 26-00 Shaw Towers
Singapore 0718
Tel: 2943366
Fax: 2985534
Quarterly, English

Asian Hospital
Report news about Asian hospitals.
Techni-Press Asia, Ltd.
P.O. Box 20494
Hennessy Rd.

Hong Kong
Tel: 278399, 278682
Quarterly, English

Asian Hotel & Catering Times
Covers Asian food & beverage
industry.
Thomson Press (HK), Ltd.
19/F Tai Sang Commercial Bldg.
23-34 Hennessy Rd.
Hong Kong
Tel: 283351
Fax: 8650825
Bimonthly, English

Asian Jewelry
Covers regional jewelry trade.
Bliss Press, Ltd.
18/F Flat B
Loyong Court
212-220 Lockhart Rd.
Wanchai, Hong Kong
Tel: 8910155
Fax: 83355477
Bimonthly, English with Japanese
supplement

Asian Meetings & Incentives
Reports on meetings and incentive
travel industry in Asia.
Travel & Trade Publishing (Asia),
Ltd.
16/F, Capitol Centre
5-19 Jardines Bazaar
Causeway Bay, Hong Kong
Tel: 89903067
Fax: 8952378
Monthly, English

Asian Printing
Reports on graphic arts and printing
industry in Asia.
Travel & Trade Publishing (Asia),
Ltd.
16/F, Capitol Centre
5-19 Jardines Bazaar
Causeway Bay, Hong Kong
Tel: 89903067
Fax: 8952378
Monthly, English

Asian Property
Covers Asian and international
property markets.

Travel & Trade Publishing (Asia),
Ltd.
16/F, Capitol Centre
5-19 Jardines Bazaar
Causeway Bay, Hong Kong
Tel: 89903067
Fax: 8952378

Asian Wall Street Journal
Asian business and financial news.
Dow Jones Publishing Co. (Asia),
Inc.
2/F AIA Bldg.
1 Stubbs Rd.
GFD Box 9B25
Hong Kong
Tel: 737121
Fax: 8910794
Daily, English

Asian Media Buyers Guide
Lists publications with advertising
specs.
Asian Business Ltress (HK), Ltd.
1302 East Point Centre
555 Hennessy Rd.
Causeway Bay, Hong Kong
Tel: 8335022
Fax: 8345132
Annual, English

Asian Medical News
Covers Asian medical industry.
Medical News-Tribune Ltd.
9/F Citicorp Centre
18 Whitfield Rd.
Causeway Bay, Hong Kong
Tel: 700707
Fax: 788060
Biweekly, English

Asian Oil & Gas
Covers Asia's oil and gas industry.
Asian Oil & Gas Publications, Ltd.
13/F Tung Sun Comm Bldg.
200 Lockhart Rd.
Hong Kong
Tel: 8921301
Fax: 726846
Monthly, English

Asian Plastics News
Covers Asian plastics industry.
Reed Business Publishing, Ltd.

Reed Asian Publishing Pte Ltd.
5001 Beach Rd.
No. 06-12 Golden Mile Complex
Singapore 0719
Tel: 2913188
Fax: 2913180
Quarterly, English

Asian Security & Safety Journal
Covers Asia's security and safety
industry.
Elgin Consultants, Ltd.
Tungnam Bldg.
Suite 5D, 475 Hennessy Rd.
Causeway Bay, Hong Kong
Tel: 724427
Fax: 725731
Bimonthly, English

Asian Timber
Targets senior and top executives in
lumber and processing industry.
Asian Business Press/Benn
Publications Plc
100 Beach Rd.
No. 26-00 Shaw Towers
Singapore 0718
Tel: 2943366
Fax: 2985534
Bimonthly, English

Asian Water & Sewage
Covers Asian water industry
treatment.
Techni-Press Asia, Ltd.
P.O. Box 20494, Hennessy Rd.
Hong Kong
Tel: 278399, 278682
Quarterly, English

Asiaweek
Asian affairs newsweekly.
Asiaweek, Ltd.
16/F Caxton Housxe
1 Duddell St.
Central, Hong Kong
Tel: 214555
Fax: 8106078
Weekly, English

Britain Trades
Covers British trade and industry in
Asia.
Elgin consultants, Ltd., for British
Trade Commission

Tungnam Bldg.
Suite 5D, 475 Hennessy Rd.
Causeway Bay, Hong Kong
Tel: 724427
Fax: 725731
Monthly, English/Chinese

Building & Construction News
Covers building and construction
industry in Asia.
Al Hilal Publishing (FE) Lte, Ltd.
50 Jalan Sultan, No. 20-06, Jalan
Sultan Centre
Singapore 0719
Tel: 2939233
Fax: 2970862
Weekly, English

Business PRC
Covers trade and economy in China.
Enterprise Intl.
1604 Eastern Commercial Centre
393-407 Hennessy Rd.
Hong Kong
Tel: 734161
Fax: 8383469
Bimonthly, English

Business Traveller Asia-Pacific
Covers frequent flying industry in
Asia.
Interasia Publications, Ltd.
200 Lockhart Rd., 13/F
Wanchai, Hong Kong
Tel: 749317
Fax: 726846
Monthly, English

Business Week Asia Edition
Business publication targets top
executives in Asia.
McGraw Hill, Inc.
Seavex, Ltd., 503 Wilson House
19 Wyndham St.
Central, Hong Kong
Tel: 8682010
Fax: 8101283
Weekly, English

CAAC
Inflight magazine for national airline
of The People's Republic of China.
Bi-No Bi Art Publishing Co., Ltd.

103-28 Tanakamonzencho, Sakyo-ku
Kyoto 606, Japan
Bimonthly, English, Japanese,
Chinese

Cardiology in Practice
Targets doctors and surgeons in
Southeast Asia.
Medical News-Tribune
9/F Citicorp Centre
19 Whitehead Rd.
Causeway Bay, Hong Kong
Tel: 700708
Fax: 788060
Bimonthly, English

Cargo Clan
Covers cargo news.
Emphasis (HK), Ltd. for Cathay
Pacific
Airways, Ltd.
10/F Wilson House
19-27 Wyndham St.
Central, Hong Kong
Tel: 215392
Fax: 8106738
Quarterly, English

Cargonews Asia
Covers shipping and transport
industry in Asia.
Far East Trade Press, Ltd.
2/F Kai Tak Commercial Bldg.
317 Des Voeux Rd.
Central, Hong Kong
Tel: 453026
Fax: 446979
Monthly, English

Cargonews Yearbook
Far East Trade Press, Ltd.
2/F Kai Tak Commercial Bldg.
317 Des Voeux Rd.
Central, Hong Kong
Tel: 453026
Fax: 446979
Annual, English

Catering & Hotel News
Covers Asian hotel, food and
beverage industry.
Al Hilal Publishing (FE) Lte, Ltd.
50 Jalan Sultan
No. 20-06, Jalan Sultan Centre
Singapore 0719

Tel: 2939233
Fax: 2970862
Biweekly, English

Catering & Hotel News, International
Covers hotel, food and beverage
industry in Asia, Pacific, and Middle
East.
Al Hilal Publishing (FE) Lte, Ltd.
50 Jalan Sultan
No. 20-06, Jalan Sultan Centre
Singapore 0719
Tel: 2939233
Fax: 2970862
Biweekly, English

Cathay Pacific's Jetshop Leaflet
Duty free/direct mail booklet.
Emphasis (HK), Ltd. for Cathay
Pacific Airways, Ltd.
10/F Wilson House
19-27 Wyndham St.
Central, Hong Kong
Tel: 215392
Fax: 8106738
Monthly, English

China Aviation News
Covers China's aerospace industry for
export market.
Conmilit Press, Ltd.
22/F Sing Pao Bldg.
101 King's Rd.
North Point, Hong Kong
Tel: 716039
Fax: 8070219
Monthly, English

Computerworld Asia
Regional industry trade magazine.
Asia Computerworld
Communications, Ltd.
701-4 Kam Chung Bldg.
54 Jaffe Rd.
Wanchai, Hong Kong
Tel: 8613238
Fax: 8610953
Weekly, English

*Contractors Plant & Equipment
Catalogue*
Covers building and civil engineering
industry.
Far East Trade Press, Ltd.
2/F Kai Tak Commercial Bldg.

317 Des Voeux Rd.
Central, Hong Kong
Tel: 453026
Fax: 446979
Annual, English

Discovery
Cathay Pacific Airways' inflight
magazine.
Emphasis (HK), Ltd. for Cathay
Pacific Airways, Ltd.
10/F Wilson House
19-27 Wyndham St.
Central, Hong Kong
Tel: 215392
Fax: 8106738
Monthly, English

Dynasty Magazine
China Airlines' inflight magazine.
China Airlines, Ltd.
ProCom International Ltd.
7/F, 180 Chunghsiao E Rd.
Sec. 4, Taipei, Taiwan
Fax: 7764831
Monthly, English, Chinese, and
Japanese

Far East Construction
Covers Asian building and
construction industry.
Al Hilal Publishing (HK), Ltd.
21/F Washington Plaza
230 Wanchai Rd.
Hong Kong
Tel: 8335676
Fax: 8335326
Quarterly, English and Chinese

The Economist
Asian edition of English newsweekly.
The Economist Newspaper, Ltd.
1329 Prince's Bldg.
10 Charter Rd.
Hong Kong
Fax: 8681425
Weekly, English

Far East Health
Covers medical and health industry in
Asia and worldwide.
Update-Siebert Publications, Ltd.
Reed Asian Publishing Pte, Ltd.
5001 Beach Rd.

No. 06-12 Golden Mile Complex
Singapore 0719
Tel: 2913188
Fax: 2913180
9 issues a year, English

Far East Traveler
Lifestyle, travel magazine aimed at
guests of 57 leading regional hotels.
Far East Reporters, Inc.
1-4-28 Moto-Azabu
Minto-ku
Tokyo 106, Japan
Tel: 4520705, 4524971
Fax: 4520474
Monthly, English, Bilingual
Japanese-English

Far Eastern Economic Review
Newsweekly covering Asia's political
economic, and financial affairs.
Review Publishing Company, Ltd.
4/FCentre Point
181 Glouocster Rd.
Wanchai, Hong Kong
or G.P.O. Box 160
Hong Kong
Tel: 8328300
Fax: 8653440
Weekly, English

Golden Dragon
Dragonair's inflight magazine.
Al Hilal Publishing (HK), Ltd.
21/F Washington Plaza
230 Wanchai Rd.
Hong Kong
Tel: 8335676
Fax: 8335326
Bimonthly, English, Chinese, and
Japanese

Hilton Horizon
Covers Asia-Pacific region for hotel
guests.
Hilton of Hong Kong, Ltd.
1/F, Nos 2-4 Hongkong Hilton
2 Queen's Rd.
Central, Hong Kong
Tel: 233111, Ext. 511
Fax: 8452590
Quarterly, English

Humsafar
Pakistan International Airlines inflight
magazine.
Media Transasia Thailand, Ltd.
14/F Orakam Bldg.
26 Chidlom Rd.
Ploenchit, Bangkok 10500
Thailand
Tel: 2519905
Fax: 2535335
Bimonthly, English

Innasia
Covers Asia-Pacific region for
Holiday Inn Hotels guests.
Far East Trade Press, Ltd.
2/F Kai Tak Commercial Bldg.
317 Des Voeux Rd.
Central, Hong Kong
Tel: 453026
Fax: 446979
Quarterly, English

International Construction
Covers worldwide building and
construction industry.
Reed Business Publishing, Ltd.
Reed Asian Publishing Pte, Ltd.
5001 Beach Rd.
No. 06-12 Golden Mile Complex
Singapore 0719
Tel: 2913188
Fax: 2913180
Monthly, English

International Herald Tribune
Asian editor of the international
newspaper.
International Herald Tribune
7/F Malaysia Bldg.
50 Gloucester Rd.
Wanchai, Hong Kong
Tel: 8610616
Fax: 8613073
Daily (Mon–Sat), English

International Journal of Clinical Practice
Aimed at doctors in Southeast Asia.
Medical News-Tribune Ltd.
9/F Citicorp Centre
18 Whitfield Rd.
Causeway Bay, Hong Kong
Tel: 700707
Fax: 788060
Quarterly, English

International Tax and Duty Free Buyers Index
Aimed at duty-free shop managers and concessionaires worldwide.
Pearl & Dean Publishing, Ltd.
9/F Chung Nam Bldg.
1 Lockhart Rd.
Hong Kong
Tel: 8660395
Fax: 2999810
Annual, English

Kaleidoscene
Korean Air's inflight magazine.
Korean Air
CPO Box 864
Seoul, Korea
Tel: 7517449
Fax: 7555220
Monthly, Korean, English, Japanese

Lloyd's Maritime Asia
Covers shipping industry in Asia backed by Lloyd's database services.
Lloyd's of London Press (FE), Ltd.
903 Chung Nam Bldg.
1 Lockhart Rd.
Hong Kong
Tel: 202356
Fax: 291545
Monthly, English

Lui Yau Yip
Covers travel industry for Chinese execs.
Far East Trade Press, Ltd.
2/F Kai Tak Commercial Bldg.
317 Des Voeux Rd.
Central, Hong Kong
Tel: 453026
Fax: 446979
Monthly, Chinese

Mabuhay Magazine
Philippine Air Lines' inflight magazine.
Eastgate Publishing Corp.
Penthouse Suite
Emerald Bldg.
Emerald Ave.
Pasig 1600, Philippines
Tel: 6735728, 6737772
Fax: 6730828
Monthly, English

Mandarin Oriental Magazine
For hotel guests of all Mandarin Oriental Group Hotels.
Emphasis (HK), Ltd. for Mandarin Oriental Group Hotels
10/F Wilson House
19-27 Wyndham St.
Central, Hong Kong
Tel: 215392
Fax: 8106738
Quarterly, English

Marco Polo News
Club magazine for Marco Polo Club members.
Emphasis (HK), Ltd. for Cathay Pacific Airways
10/F Wilson House
19-27 Wyndham St.
Central, Hong Kong
Tel: 215392
Fax: 8106738
Bimonthly, English

MD-Asia
Aimed at doctors in Hong Kong, Singapore, Malaysia.
Medical News-Tribune Ltd.
9/F Citicorp Centre
18 Whitfield Rd.
Causeway Bay, Hong Kong
Tel: 700708
Fax: 788060
Bimonthly, English

Media
Covers region's advertising and marketing industry.
Asian Business Press (HK), Ltd.
1302 East Point Centre
555 Hennessy Rd.
Causeway Bay, Hong Kong
Tel: 8335022
Fax: 8345132
Weekly, English

Media Yearbook
Listings on print media, TV, and radio.
Asian Business Press (HK), Ltd.
1302 East Point Centre
555 Hennessy Rd.
Causeway Bay, Hong Kong
Tel: 8335022

Fax: 8345132
Annual, English

Medicine Digest Asia
Covers medical and health care industry in Asia.
Medicine Digest Asia
Rm 1903, Tung Sun Commercial Centre
194-200 Lockhart Rd.
Wanchai, Hong Kong
Tel: 8939303
Fax: 8912591
Monthly, English

Newsweek International
Asian edition of international newsweekly.
Newsweek, Inc.
Rm 2007, Wing On House
71 Des Voeux Rd.
Central, Hong Kong
Tel: 810455
Fax: 201867
Weekly, English

Off-Duty
Leisuretime stories for U.S. military in Asia-Pacific.
Off Duty Publications, Ltd.
14/F Commercial Centre
8 Shelter St.
Causeway Bay, Hong Kong
Tel: 777215
Fax: 8901761
Monthly, English

Oil & Gas News
Covers oil and refining industry.
Al Hilal Publishing (FE) Lte, Ltd.
50 Jalan Sultan
No. 20-06, Jalan Sultan Centre
Singapore 0719
Tel: 2939233
Fax: 2970862
Weekly, English

Pata Travel News Asia/Pacific
Covers travel industry for Pacific Area Travel Association members.
Asian Business Press (HK), Ltd.
1302 East Point Centre
555 Hennessy Rd.
Causeway Bay, Hong Kong
Tel: 8335022

Fax: 8345132
Monthly, English

Petroleum News, Asia's Energy Journal
Covers oil and related industries in
Asia.
Petroleum News Southeast Asia, Ltd.
6/F, 146 Prince Edward Rd. West
Kowloon, Hong Kong
Tel: 805294
Fax: 970959
Monthly, English

Petromin
Covers energy and mining industries
in Asia-Pacific region.
Safan Publishing Pte, Ltd.
510 Thomson Rd.
Block A No. 08-01 SLG Bldg.
Singapore 1129
Fax: 2589945
Monthly, English

The Recent Magazine
Upscale magazine for guests of
Regent Intl. Hotels worldwide.
Cheney Communications, Ltd.
17/F Century Square
1-13 D'Aguilar St.
Central, Hong Kong
Tel: 213671
Fax: 8453509
Quarterly, English

Sawasdee
The in-flight magazine of Thai Airways.
Travel & Trade Publishing (Asia),
Ltd.
16/F Capitol Centre
5-19 Jardines Bazaar
Causeway Bay, Hong Kong
Tel: 89903067
Fax: 8952378
Monthly, English

Scientific American (Asia)
The American magazine edited for
the Asian market.
Scientific American, Inc.
Cheney Communications, Ltd.
17/F Century Square
1-13 D'Aguilar St.
Central, Hong Kong
Tel: 213671

Fax: 8453509
Quarterly, English

Shipping & Transport News
Covers shipping and transport
industries in Asia and Middle East.
Al Hilal Publishing (FE) Lte, Ltd.
50 Jalan Sultan, No. 20-06 Jalan
Sultan Centre
Singapore 0719
Tel: 2939233
Fax: 2970862
Biweekly, English

Signature
Asian edition of Diners Club
magazine for basic cardholder.
Diners Publishing (S) Pte, Ltd.
420 North Bridge Rd.
No. 05-40 North Bridge Centre
Singapore 0718
Tel: 3366638
Fax: 3361703
Monthly, English

South East Asia Traveller
Travel magazine covering Southeast
Asia.
Compass Publishing Pte, Ltd.
1090 Lower Delta Rd.
No. 01-16
Singapore 0316
Tel: 2749111
Fax: 2733855
9 times a year, English

South Magazine
Covers politics, business, finance, and
technology relating to third-world.
South Publications UK, Ltd.
12/F Union Commercial Bldg.
12-16 Lyndhurst Terrace
Central, Hong Kong
Tel: 454808
Fax: 449577
Monthly, English

Southeast Asia Building
Covers construction, architecture,
interior design industries.
Safan Publishing Pte, Ltd.
510 Thomson Rd.
Block A, No. 08-01 SLG Bldg.
Singapore 1129
Fax: 2589945
Monthly, English

*Southeast Asia Manufacturing Equipment
News*
Aimed at equipment purchasers and
production engineers in Southeast
Asia.
Safan Publishing Pte, Ltd.
510 Thomson Rd.
Block A, No. 08-01 SLG Bldg.
Singapore 1129
Fax: 2589945
Monthly, English

Southeast Asian Journal of Social Science
Targets social scientists and sociology
students doing research on Southeast
Asia.
Chopmen Publishers
865 Mountbatten Rd.
No.05-28, Katong Shopping Centre
Singapore 1543
Tel: 3441495
Fax: 3440180
Twice a year, English

Time
Asian edition of international
newsweekly.
Time, Inc.
31/F East Tower
Bond Centre, 89
Queensway, Hong Kong
Tel: 8446611
Fax: 8104116
Weekly, English

Tourism Asia
Covers Asian travel trade.
Venture Publishing Pte, Ltd.
400 Orchard Rd.
No. 19-06 Orchard Towers
Singapore 0923
Tel: 2356511
Fax: 7330075
Bimonthly, English

Travel & Tourism News International
Covers transportation and travel
industries in Asia and Middle East.
Al Hilal Publishing (FE) Lte, Ltd.
50 Jalan Sultan
No. 20-06, Jalan Sultan Centre
Singapore 0719
Tel: 2939233
Fax: 2970862
Biweekly, English

Travel Business Analyst
Covers travel industry for senior
management.
Travel Business Analyst, Ltd.
14/F, 200 Lockhart Rd.
Hong Kong
Tel: 749317
Fax: 726846
Monthly, English

Travel Trade Gazette Asia
Covers Asian travel industry.
Asian Business Press Pte, Ltd.
100 Beach Rd.
No. 26-00 Shaw Towers
Singapore 0718
Tel: 2943366
Fax: 2985534
Weekly, English

Travelnews Asia
Covers travel industry in Asia.
Far East Trade Press, Ltd.
2/F Kai Tak Commercial Bldg.
317 Des Voeux Rd.
Central, Hong Kong
Tel: 453026
Fax: 446979
Biweekly, English

Triple A
(Incorporating *Asiabanking*)
Covers banking and corporate finance
in region.
BRW Publications
Rm 1101, Tai Yau Bldg.
181 Johnston Rd.
Hong Kong
Tel: 8336667
Fax: 8930904
Monthly, English

TTG Asia Hotel Guide
Guide to more than 600 leading hotels
in Asia.
Asian Business Press Pte, Ltd.
100 Beach Rd.
No. 26-00 Shaw Towers
Singapore 0718
Tel: 2943366
Fax: 2985534
Twice a year, English

USA Today Asia Edition
Asian edition of the international
American newspaper.
Gannett Co.
Seavex, Ltd.
503 Wilson House
19 Wyndham St.
Central, Hong Kong
Tel: 8682019
Fax: 8101283
Daily, English

Voyages
Consumer's guide to tour packages in
Southeast Asia, Pacific, USA, and
Europe.
Pacom Publiocations Pte, Ltd.
190 Middle Rd.
No. 15-07, Fortune Centre
Singapore 0718
Tel: 3370255
Fax: 3398521
Twice a year, English
Circ: 18,000

What's New in Computing
Information about new products in
computing aimed at end users and
business professionals.
Asian Business Press Pte, Ltd.
100 Beach Rd.
No. 26-00 Shaw Towers
Singapore 0718
Tel: 2943366
Fax: 2985534
Monthly, English

Wings of Gold
Malaysian Airlines System's inflight
magazine.
PR Dept. MAS
32/F Jalan Sultan Ismail
50250 Kuala Lumpur
Malaysia
Fax: 2613472
Monthly, English and Bahasa
Malaysia

World Executives Digest
Magazine with management articles,
condensations aimed at Asia's leading
exec.

World Executive's Digest, Inc.
3/F Garden Square Bldg.
Greenbelt Drive
Legaspi Village
Makati, Metro Manila, Philippines
Tel: 8183289
Fax: 8185177
Monthly, English

World Jewelogue
International jewelry industry trade
annual.
Headway International Publications
Co.
9/F Sing-Ho Finance Bldg.
168 Gloucester Rd.
Fax: 745356
Annual, English

World Leatherlogue
International leather industry annual.
Headway International Publications
Co.
9/F Sing-Ho Finance Bldg.
168 Gloucester Rd.
Hong Kong
Fax: 745356
Annual, English

World Money Analyst
Global business analysis for wealthy
investors.
WMA Publishing Co., Ltd.
45 Lyndhurst Terrace, 5/F
Central, Hong Kong
Tel: 416110
Fax: 8541695
10 issues a year, English

World Naval Almanac
Reports on world's navies for
Chinese shipping industry and
People's Liberation Army naval
force's top brass and researchers.
Conmilit Press, Ltd.
22/F Sing Pao Bldg.
101 King's Rd.
North Point, Hong Kong
Tel: 716039
Fax: 8070219
Every two years, Chinese

Yazhou Zhoukan
Regional newsweekly for Chinese-speaking business elite in the region.
Asiaweek, Ltd.
16/F Caxton House
1 Duddell St.

Central, Hong Kong
Tel: 214555
Fax: 8106078
Weekly, Chinese

SOURCES: *Media '89 Year Book,* Asian Business Press

(Hong Kong), Ltd.;
International Media Guide 1988/ 89, Business/Professional, Asia/Pacific South Norwalk, Connecticut.

APPENDIX J

DIRECT MARKETING TO THE PACIFIC RIM

Most of the preceding publications make their mailing lists available for direct mail promotions through list brokers. Apart from major international list brokers, there are literally only a couple of brokers in the United States who specialize exclusively in Asian direct marketing. They include:

Hemisphere Marketing Inc.
Cynthia Maslanik, President
100 Spear St., Suite 220
San Francisco, CA 94105
Tel: (415) 771-1171
Fax: (415) 777-2371

Times Direct Marketing
Chris Peterson, President
330 Rita St.
San Francisco, CA 94107
Tel: (415) 896-0861
Fax: (415) 856-0879

DIRECT MARKETING TO THE PACIFIC RIM
by Alfred M. Goodloe

Direct marketing allows any business, large or small, to take a giant step toward developing its potential market in the Pacific Rim. These countries are growing faster than anywhere else. The collective Gross National Product is almost as large as that of the United States or Europe.

WHAT CAN YOU SELL?

Information products and services are easiest to sell because there are no customs duties and few restrictions. Publishers of newspapers, magazines, books, newsletters, and research services successfully sell their products on a worldwide basis. But the Asian market is especially responsive because, with the exception of Japan, most of the countries are small, and they do not have indigenous publishing industries covering a variety of market niches.

Merchandise represents more of a problem. You would have to arrange to stock your products with a distributor or a joint-venture partner. Some products could be shipped directly to customers in Asia, but the cost might be prohibitive. Bulk shipments and local distribution is far more cost effective.

RIM RESPONSES

Your responses in the Asia–Pacific region will vary considerably by country. Your best responses will probably come from Hong Kong, Malaysia, Singapore, Australia, New Zealand, and the Philippines. This has been the experience of most direct marketers.

Why? It's a matter of psychology. These countries were part of the British colonial system or the American system, in the case of the Philippines. Their thinking is decidedly Western. English facility is high. As a result, direct mail that works in the United States will in most cases work in these areas—but with some modification.

What about Japan, South Korea, and Taiwan? Aren't these supposed to be the hottest markets in the region, according to popular opinion? Yes, but here's a fact you must face. These nations have never been for any length of time under American or British influence. Their thought patterns are distinctly Asian. English-language fluency is less.

Direct marketing is based on the premise that a prospect will be emotionally aroused by your sales message, and that he (another fact of life, most of the target audience are men in Asia) is in a position to make a decision. If a recipient has a problem with the language, he has to translate and, therefore, the message becomes disembodied.

In these markets, local language mailings are essential for strong penetration. But this still may not be enough. In China, for example, direct marketing is practically unknown. And what direct marketing is done would be through officially sanctioned government offices.

In Japan, the consensus environment holds. When a Japanese receives an offer (even in the Japanese language), he won't respond like an American—even if the benefits are mouthwatering. Instead, the Japanese will want to know who you are. Are you part of the system? So you will have to do some extra things. For example, you will need to spend

---

"There is more recognition of Tom Peters [author of *Thriving on Chaos* and coauthor of *In Search of Excellence*] in the general business community in Asia than you would find in the American business community today . . . They love the notion of American management in Asia. After all, there's hardly any place to get an MBA in the region . . . Americans are the ones who created business as an academic discipline."

Cynthia Maslanik is president of Hemisphere Marketing, Inc., a San Francisco-headquartered, Pacific Rim direct marketing specialist.

money to arrange suitable introductions into the market. A lack of introduction doesn't mean Japanese won't respond to direct mail. It just means the response will be much lower than in other areas.

Interestingly enough, it's easier to sell small businessmen, professionals, and consumers in Japan. They aren't a part of a group. And they don't have to check with their colleagues. But even here, the consensus syndrome prevails to some extent. Japanese want to know who you are, what is the quality of product or service, and who else uses your product?

How to Reach the Pacific Rim— the Low Cost Way

The U.S. Postal Service can help with its ISAL (International Surface Air Lift) program. The price is US$0.22 for a promotion piece weighing up to 2 ounces.

Another alternative is to print and mail from Singapore. You don't have to go to Singapore to do it. You can handle all of the necessary communications by mail, fax, and telephone. Simply send photo negatives of your promotion to a Singapore printer. Once printed, he will turn the material over to a lettershop where the various pieces will be inserted and mailed throughout the area.

Singapore Surface Air Lift rates within the Asian Rim would cost you less than for doing the same mailing from the United States. The printing costs may be a little lower, too, so the combined advantages encourage many U.S. firms to go "off shore." Furthermore, there is even a bigger bargain around and that's the *Malaysian surface rate*. To mail from Malaysia would cost you just 6 cents (U.S.) for a 1 ounce letter and would cost 5 cents for a .7 ounce letter.

While postage and printing costs can be below equivalent U.S. prices, there is always a catch. And that catch is the cost of list rental fees.

There are two kinds of lists—multinational and national. An example of the multinational list is that of *Business Week* magazine. *Business Week* has subscribers in all of the countries of the Pacific Rim. The people on the *Business Week* list are English-reading, and have responded to offers from the United States. There are a number of multinational business and consumer lists in the United States and the United Kingdom that have readers throughout the Rim. In addition, there are many more national lists in almost any interest area. But you should know that national lists, in general, don't respond as well as the multinational ones.

These are the basics of direct marketing to the Pacific Rim. Learning the international direct marketing game takes time and will have its frustrations. But keep at it and through the use of direct marketing methods, you will get a jump on your competitors. You will speed up your penetration of Rim markets, perhaps beyond your most reasonable expectations.

Al Goodloe is president of Publisher's Multinational Direct, an international direct marketing consultancy. For more information, write PMD, *150 East 74th Street, New York, NY 10021-03528; Tel: (212) 861-4188; Fax: (212) 988-1632.*

INDEX

PERMISSIONS

Material in the "Asian Marketing in Review" section of Chapter 1 is reprinted by permission of *Asian Advertising and Marketing,* copyright © 1991, published by Travel & Trade Publishing (Asia), Hong Kong.

Material from Chapter 2 is reprinted from *Export Today's* Special Supplement—"The Pacific Rim: Export Outlook for the 1990s," October 1989, by permission of the publisher, SIRCO International 733 15th St. NW, Suite 1100, Washington, D.C. 20005, (202) 737-1060.

The artwork on pages 80–82, 208–209, 268–269, 328–329, 334–336, 369–373, 390, 456–485, 551–552 and 554 is reprinted by permission of *The New Asian Market Atlas,* copyright © 1988, published by Business International.

The artwork on pages 84–88, 287, 486 and 488 is reprinted by permission of *Japan 1991: An International Comparison,* Japan Institute for Social and Economic Affairs.

The chart on p. 141 is reprinted by permission of *Japan Free Press,* C. T. Whipple Company.

The map on p. 286 is reprinted by permission of the Asian Studies Center, The Heritage Foundation, Washington, D.C.

The artwork on pages 294–297 and 422–425 is reprinted by permission of *Whole Pacific Catalog,* Pacific Basin Institute.

The maps on pages 437–438 are reprinted by permission of the Public Education Office, East–West Center, Honolulu, Hawaii.

Material in the "Asian Investment Guide 1991" in Appendix B and the tables on pages 204 and 232 are reprinted by permission of *Asian Business Magazine,* copyright © 1989, 1990 and 1991, published by Far East Trade Press, Ltd.

Please refer to individual articles for specific credits.